Brazil

THIS EDITION WRITTEN AND RESEARCHED BY

Regis St Louis,

Gary Chandler, Gregor Clark, Bridget Gleeson,

Anna Kaminski, Kevin Raub

CALGARY PUBLIC LIBRARY

JUN 2016

PLAN YOUR TRIP

LARISSA CARVALHO/GETTY IMAGES ©

PARATY P128

JIMODENNEY/GETTY IMAGES ©

THE AMAZON P569

ON THE ROAD

Contents

ON THE ROAD

T PHOTOGRAPHY/SHUTTERSTOCK ©

PARINTINS P615

JANE SWEENEY/GETTY IMAGES ©

IPANEMA BEACH P51

Contents

SALVADOR P399

Welcome to Brazil

Tropical islands, lush rainforests, marvelous cities and picture-perfect beaches set the scene for the great Brazilian adventure.

Landscapes & Biodiversity

One of the world's most captivating places, Brazil is a country of powdery white-sand beaches, verdant rainforests and wild, rhythm-filled metropolises. Brazil's attractions extend from frozen-in-time colonial towns to otherworldly landscapes of red-rock canyons, thundering waterfalls and coral-fringed tropical islands. Add to that, Brazil's biodiversity: legendary in scope, its diverse ecosystems boast the greatest collection of plant and animal species found anywhere on earth. There are countless places where you can spot iconic species in Brazil, including toucans, scarlet macaws, howler monkeys, capybaras, pink dolphins, sea turtles and thousands of other living species.

The Rhythms of Brazil

Wherever there's music, that carefree Brazilian lust for life tends to appear – whether dancing with *cariocas* (residents of Rio) at Rio's atmospheric samba clubs or following powerful drumbeats through the streets of Salvador. There's the dance-hall *forró* music of the Northeast, twirling *carimbó* music of the Amazon, scratch-skilled DJs of São Paulo and an endless variety of regional sounds that extend from the twangy country music of the sunbaked Sertanejo, to the hard-edged reggae of Maranhão.

Joie de Vivre

Brazil's most famous celebration, Carnaval, storms through the country's cities and towns with hip-shaking samba and *frevo* (music and dance style), dazzling costumes and parties that last until sunup, but Brazilians hardly limit their revelry to a few weeks of the year. *Festas* (festivals) happen throughout the year, and provide a window into Brazil's incredible diversity. The streets are carpeted with flowers during Ouro Preto's Semana Santa (Holy Week), while in the north, Bumba Meu Boi blends indigenous, African and Portuguese folklore. For a taste of the Old World, hit Blumenau's beer- and schnitzel-loving Oktoberfest, the largest outside of Germany. Several cities, such as Recife, Fortaleza and Natal, even host Carnaval at other times of year.

Days of Adventure

Brazil offers big adventures for travelers with budgets large and small. There's horseback riding and wildlife watching in the Pantanal, kayaking flooded forests in the Amazon, ascending rocky clifftops to panoramic views, whale watching off the coast, surfing stellar breaks off palm-fringed beaches and snorkeling crystal-clear rivers or coastal reefs – all are part of the great Brazilian experience.

Why I Love Brazil

By Regis St Louis, Writer

The music, the beaches, the wildlife, and most importantly the people: it's hard not to fall for Brazil. Rio de Janeiro is one of my favorite cities: I never tire of watching the sunset from Arpoador, chasing the samba scene in Lapa or wandering the village-like streets of Santa Teresa. But Rio is just the beginning, and in Brazil there really is no end. I have fond memories spotting wildlife (especially in the Pantanal and the Amazon), making friends in small towns and finding incredible musicians in unlikely places. There's really no other country that offers so much.

For more about our writers, see page 736

Above: Festival, Salvador (p399)

Brazil

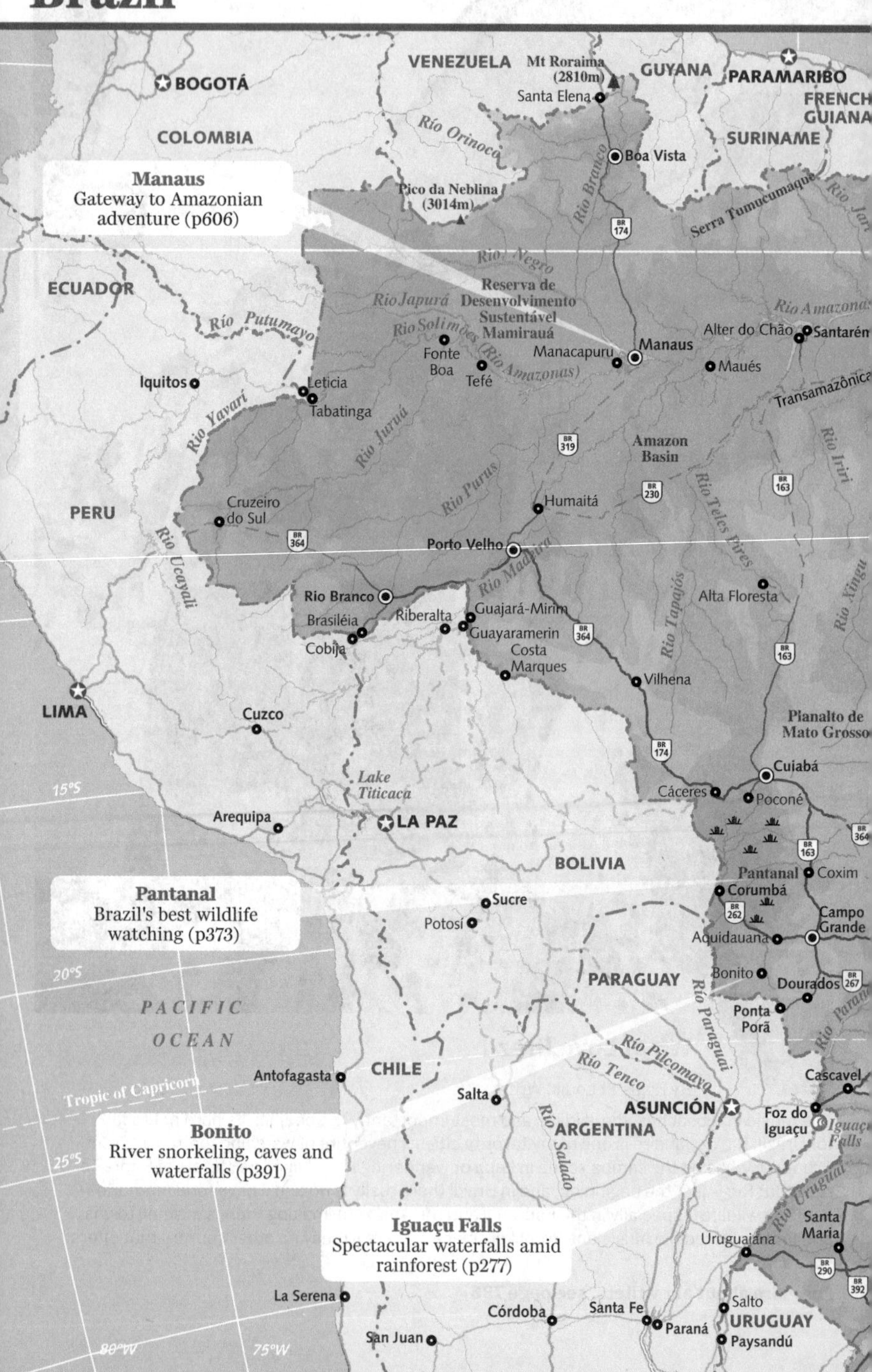
Manaus
Gateway to Amazonian adventure (p606)
Pantanal
Brazil's best wildlife watching (p373)
Bonito
River snorkeling, caves and waterfalls (p391)
Iguaçu Falls
Spectacular waterfalls amid rainforest (p277)
BOGOTÁ
COLOMBIA
VENEZUELA
Mt Roraima (2810m)
GUYANA
PARAMARIBO
FRENCH GUIANA
SURINAME
Santa Elena
Río Orinoco
Boa Vista
Pico da Neblina (3014m)
Rio Branco
Serra Tumucumaque
Rio Negro
ECUADOR
Reserva de Desenvolvimento Sustentável Mamirauá
Río Putumayo
Rio Japurá
Rio Solimões (Rio Amazonas)
Rio Amazonas
Alter do Chão
Santarém
Fonte Boa
Tefé
Manacapuru
Manaus
Maués
Iquitos
Leticia
Tabatinga
Transamazônica
Río Yavarí
Rio Juruá
Amazon Basin
Rio Iriri
Rio Purus
Rio Teles Pires
PERU
Cruzeiro do Sul
Humaitá
Porto Velho
Rio Madeira
Río Ucayali
Rio Tapajós
Rio Xingu
Alta Floresta
Rio Branco
Brasiléia
Cobija
Riberalta
Guajará-Mirim
Guayaramerin
Costa Marques
Vilhena
LIMA
Cuzco
Planalto de Mato Grosso
Cuiabá
Lake Titicaca
Cáceres
Poconé
15°S
Arequipa
LA PAZ
BOLIVIA
Pantanal
Coxim
Corumbá
Sucre
Potosí
Campo Grande
Aquidauana
20°S
PARAGUAY
Bonito
Dourados
Río Paraguai
PACIFIC OCEAN
Ponta Porã
Rio Paraná
Río Pilcomayo
Río Tenco
Antofagasta
CHILE
Cascavel
Tropic of Capricorn
Salta
ASUNCIÓN
Foz do Iguaçu
Iguaçu Falls
Río Salado
ARGENTINA
25°S
Rio Uruguai
Santa Maria
Uruguaiana
La Serena
Salto
Córdoba
Santa Fe
Paraná
URUGUAY
San Juan
Paysandú
80°W
75°W

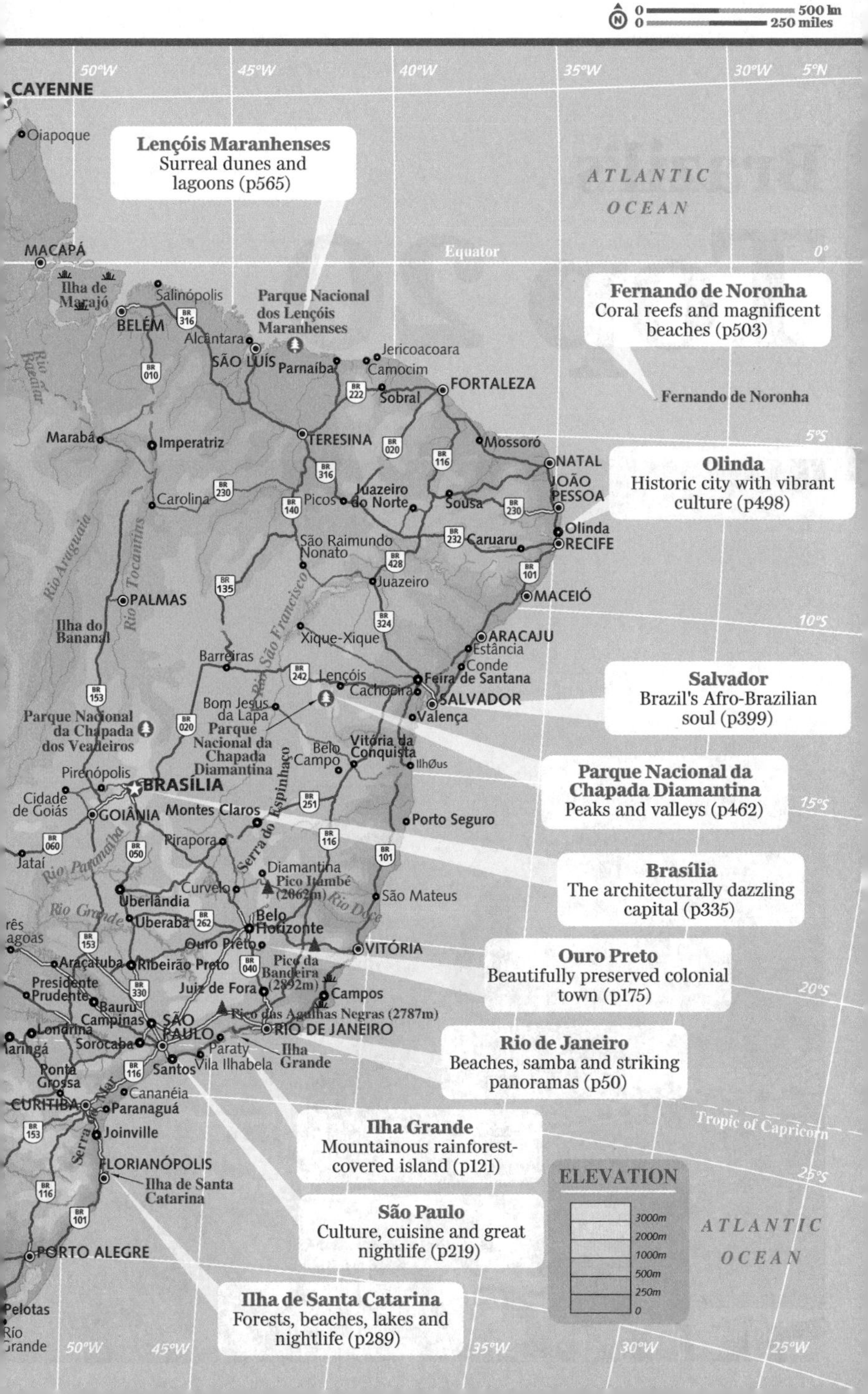

0 — 500 km
0 — 250 miles

Lençóis Maranhenses
Surreal dunes and lagoons (p565)

Fernando de Noronha
Coral reefs and magnificent beaches (p503)

Olinda
Historic city with vibrant culture (p498)

Salvador
Brazil's Afro-Brazilian soul (p399)

Parque Nacional da Chapada Diamantina
Peaks and valleys (p462)

Brasília
The architecturally dazzling capital (p335)

Ouro Preto
Beautifully preserved colonial town (p175)

Rio de Janeiro
Beaches, samba and striking panoramas (p50)

Ilha Grande
Mountainous rainforest-covered island (p121)

São Paulo
Culture, cuisine and great nightlife (p219)

Ilha de Santa Catarina
Forests, beaches, lakes and nightlife (p289)

ATLANTIC OCEAN
Equator
Tropic of Capricorn

CAYENNE
Oiapoque
MACAPÁ
Ilha de Marajó
Salinópolis
BELÉM
Alcântara
SÃO LUÍS
Parque Nacional dos Lençóis Maranhenses
Parnaíba
Jericoacoara
Camocim
Sobral
FORTALEZA
Fernando de Noronha
Marabá
Imperatriz
TERESINA
Mossoró
NATAL
JOÃO PESSOA
Carolina
Picos
Juazeiro do Norte
Sousa
Olinda
RECIFE
Caruaru
São Raimundo Nonato
Juazeiro
MACEIÓ
PALMAS
Ilha do Bananal
Xique-Xique
ARACAJU
Estância
Conde
Barreiras
Lençóis
Cachoeira
Feira de Santana
SALVADOR
Valença
Bom Jesus da Lapa
Parque Nacional da Chapada Diamantina
Parque Nacional da Chapada dos Veadeiros
Belo Campo
Vitória da Conquista
Ilhéus
Pirenópolis
BRASÍLIA
Cidade de Goiás
GOIÂNIA
Montes Claros
Porto Seguro
Jataí
Pirapora
Diamantina
Pico Itambé (2062m)
Curvelo
Uberlândia
São Mateus
Uberaba
Belo Horizonte
Três Lagoas
Ouro Preto
VITÓRIA
Araçatuba
Ribeirão Preto
Pico da Bandeira (2892m)
Presidente Prudente
Juiz de Fora
Campos
Bauru
Campinas
Pico das Agulhas Negras (2787m)
SÃO PAULO
RIO DE JANEIRO
Londrina
Sorocaba
Maringá
Paraty
Ilha Grande
Ponta Grossa
Santos
Vila Ilhabela
Cananéia
CURITIBA
Paranaguá
Joinville
FLORIANÓPOLIS
Ilha de Santa Catarina
PORTO ALEGRE
Pelotas
Rio Grande

Rio Araguaia
Rio Tocantins
Rio São Francisco
Rio Paranaíba
Rio Grande
Rio Doce
Serra do Espinhaço
Serra do Mar

ELEVATION
3000m
2000m
1000m
500m
250m
0

Brazil's Top 20

1

Pão de Açúcar, Rio de Janeiro

1 Some say to come around sunset for the best views from this absurd confection of a mountain (p61). But in truth, it doesn't matter when you come; you're unlikely to look at Rio (or your own comparatively lackluster city) in the same way. From here the landscape is pure undulating green hills and golden beaches lapped by blue sea, with rows of skyscrapers sprouting along the shore. The ride up is good fun: all-glass aerial trams that whisk you up to the top. The adventurous can rock climb their way to the summit.

Below: View over dome-shaped Pão de Açúcar, seen from above Corcovado

Iguaçu Falls

2 No matter the number of waterfalls you've checked off your bucket list, no matter how many times you have thought to yourself you'd be just fine never seeing another waterfall again, Iguaçu Falls (p278) will stomp all over your idea of water trickling over the edge of a cliff. The thunderous roar of 275 falls crashing across the Brazil and Argentina border floors even the most jaded traveler. Loud, angry, unstoppable and impossibly gorgeous, Iguaçu will leave you stunned and slack-jawed at the absolute power of Mother Nature.

JEREMY WALKER / GETTY IMAGES ©

2

JOAN GAMEL/ 500PX ©

Fernando de Noronha

3 This archipelago (p503) of one 10km-long island and 20 smaller ones, 350km out into the Atlantic from Natal, has everything a tropical getaway should have – jaw-dropping scenery and seascapes, fine beaches, the best diving and snorkeling in the country, good surfing, memorable hikes, plentiful visible wildlife, good accommodations and restaurants – and no crowds, for visitor numbers are restricted by the limited number of plane seats available each day. Visiting Noronha is expensive, but it's worth every centavo if your budget will stretch far enough. Below: Baia dos Porcos (p505)

Salvador

4 The world capital of Afro-Brazil, Salvador (p399) is famous for capoeira, Candomblé, Olodum, colonial Portuguese architecture, African street food and one of the oldest lighthouses in the Americas. The city's past, marked by gritty stories of Portuguese seafaring and the heartbreaking history of the African slave trade, is characterized by hardship. But today's lively Bahian capital offers a unique fusion of two vibrant cultures. The festive music and nightlife scene culminates every February when Salvador hosts one of the best Carnavals in Brazil.

3

4

RICARDO RIBAS / ALAMY ©

ANORAMIC IMAGES / GETTY IMAGES ©

Ouro Preto

5 With more ups and downs than a roller coaster, the 18th-century streets of Ouro Preto (p175) veer precipitously between one baroque masterpiece and the next. You can admire the sculpted masterpieces of Aleijadinho, discover the 18th-century African tribal king turned folk hero Chico-Rei, and gaze upon opulent gilded churches. The elaborate Holy Week processions are among the country's most spectacular. From gold town to state capital, revolutionary hotbed to Unesco World Heritage site, this colonial gem has been at the center of the action for more than 300 years. Above: Igreja de São Francisco de Assis (p178)

Beers of Blumenau

6 Ubiquitous lagers such as Brahma and Skol certainly suffice as beat-the-heat treats throughout the country, but Brazil's best brews come from greater Blumenau (p303). Along with *lederhosen* and *leberkäse* (a meat dish), German immigration in the 1800s brought Reinheitsgebot, Germany's beer purity law, and these German-Brazilians aren't too fond of sharing. That means with the exception of the once-micro Eisenbahn, seriously good artisanal suds such as Schornstein Kneipe, Bierland and Das Bier don't fall too far from the tree. You'll need to venture into Santa Catarina's Vale Europeu to quench your thirst.

Pantanal

7 Few places on earth can match the wildlife-watching experience provided by the Pantanal (p373), a wondrously remote wetland in the heart of Mato Grosso. From cute capybaras to stately storks, the animal life simply abounds and is remarkably easy to see in the open marshy surroundings. There are a million reasons not to miss out on this particular eco-experience, and not least among them is that there is no better place in South America to see the elusive jaguar. Above: Toucan

Brasília Architecture

8 What the city of the future (p335) really needed to back up its claim to be the harbinger of Brazil's 'new dawn' was an architect capable of designing buildings that looked the part. In Oscar Niemeyer, Brasília found the right man for the job. The 'crown of thorns' Catedral Metropolitana is a religious masterwork and the interplanetary Teatro Nacional is out of this world! Brasília is a city overloaded with architectural gems, designed by a genius inspired by the concept of a better future. Below: Catedral Metropolitana (p338)

Carnaval in Rio

9 Get plenty of sleep before you board the plane, because once you land, it's nonstop revelry (p35) until Ash Wednesday (sort of) brings it all to a close. With nearly 500 street parties happening all over town, you will not lack for options. For the full experience, join a samba school and parade amid pounding drum corps and mechanized smoke-breathing dragons before thousands of roaring fans in the Sambódromo. Or assemble a costume and hit one of the Carnaval balls around town. The build-up starts weeks in advance.

8

JANE SWEENEY / GETTY IMAGES ©

9

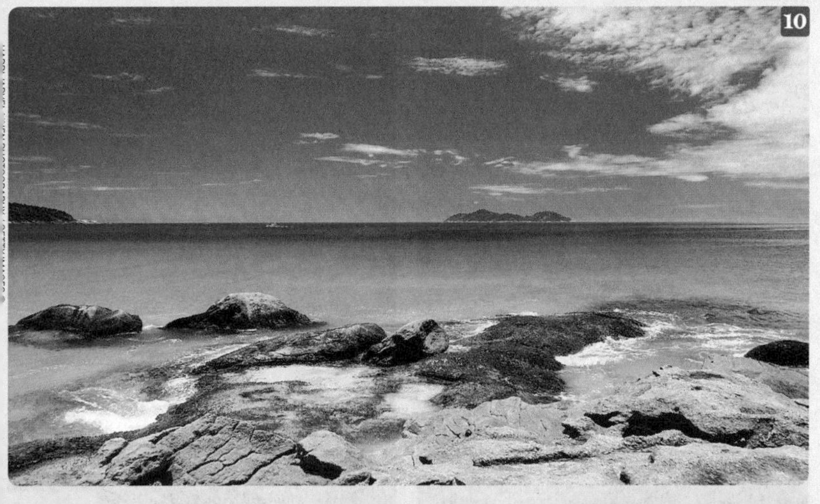

Ilha Grande

10 Thanks to its isolation, Ilha Grande (p121) served for decades as a prison and leper colony. Spared from development by this unusual history, its jungle-clad slopes and dozens of beaches are some of the best preserved in all of Brazil. Days are spent hiking through lush Atlantic rainforest, snorkeling amid aquamarine seas and basking in crisp waterfalls. With no motor vehicles to spoil the party, this is one clean, green island – a true nature lover's paradise. It's also an easy day's journey from Rio.

Jungle Trips

11 Needless to say, the best reason to visit the Amazon (p569) is to get out into the jungle: to ply the winding waterways in a canoe, hike lush leafy trails, and scan the canopy for monkeys, sloths and other creatures. The world's biggest and best-known rainforest has outdoor excursions of all sorts, and for all types of travelers: from easy nature hikes to scaling 50m trees, from luxury lodges to makeshift camps in the forest. Whatever your interest, experience, ability or budget, there's a jungle trip in the Amazon waiting to blow your mind.

ALEXANDRE CAPPI / GETTY IMAGES ©

Parque Nacional da Chapada Diamantina

12 A pristine outdoor wonderland of rushing waterfalls, crystal-blue pools, rugged hiking trails and natural waterslides, Chapada Diamantina (p462) is a deliciously unspoiled national park well off the beaten path – it's one of the only inland attractions in the beach-happy state of Bahia. Those who make the effort to explore the park, either on day excursions from Lençóis or on the Grand Circuit with a local guide, often count the Chapada Diamantina as one of their top outdoor travel experiences in Brazil.

São Paulo Nights

13 Rivaling the frenetic pace of New York, the modernism of Tokyo and the prices of Moscow but swamping all of them in options, São Paulo city (p219) is home to a pool of 20 million potential foodies, clubbers and cocktail connoisseurs and nearly 30,000 restaurants, bars and clubs to satiate them. From the contemporary gourmet haunts of Itaim Bibi and Jardins, to the edgy offerings of Baixo Augusta, to bohemian bars in Vila Madalena, it's a gluttonous avalanche of *bolinhos* (appetizers), booze and beats that outruns the sunrise on most nights. *Saúde!*

Tiradentes

14 The colonial town of Tiradentes (p190) is so well preserved, and its natural setting so appealing, you could be excused for feeling like you've wandered onto a movie set. Cobbled lanes, flower-draped walls and some stunning colonial architecture make every step a delight – even more if you like to hike. The surrounding mountains are threaded with trails, Tiradentes' hyperactive restaurant scene serves up delicious traditional meals, and its charming guesthouses make a relaxing spot to recharge.

Lençóis Maranhenses

15 Of all Brazil's landscape spectacles, the most unexpected has to be the Lençóis Maranhenses (p565) in Maranhão – a 70km-long, 25km-wide expanse of high dunes resembling *lençóis* (bed sheets) spread across the landscape. From around March to September (best in July and August), the dunes are partnered by thousands of crystal-clear, freshwater lagoons from rainwater filling the hollows between them. Visit by 4WD tour, by boat down the jungle-lined Rio Preguiças or, for the adventurous, on a three- or four-day trek right across the Lençóis.

Bonito

16 Bonito (p391) is beautiful! Book yourself on a smorgasbord of aquatic adventures in the jaw-dropping surroundings of the Serra da Bodoquena and prepare for a wild wet-suited adventure like you've never experienced before. Whether you are taking your first foray into flotation on the Rio da Prata or journeying to the center of the earth at the Abismo de Añhumas, Bonito is packed with unique experiences that will rank among your most cherished memories of any trip to Brazil.

Bottom: Gruta do Lago Azul (p393)

15

16

17

18

Recife & Olinda

17 These two contrasting Northeastern neighbors with an intertwined history and shared culture make a heady double act. Recife (p487) is the big-city big sister with the skyscrapers and traffic, but also a fascinating historic center becoming ever more appealing through renovations and new museums, restaurants and cultural centers. Cute, tree-covered Olinda (p498) has tranquil winding lanes, colonial churches and artists' galleries. Their vibrant shared heritage comes together at Carnaval with some of Brazil's most riotous street festivities. Top: Carnaval (p499), Olinda

Alter do Chão

18 Alter do Chão (p597) truly has it all: a slice of Jericoacoara in the heart of the rainforest. Alter do Chão is best known for its beach: an island made entirely of fine white sand lapped by cool tea-colored water. But Alter do Chão also is a gateway to a major national forest, with massive *samaúma* trees and a chance to live with local rubber-tapper families. With so much to do, hotels for all budgets, and a great laid-back vibe, it's a place you'll want to linger for a while – and many travelers do just that.

Beaches of Santa Catarina

19 Santa Catarina (p288) is synonymous with the good life and that has a whole lot to do with its sun-toasted shores. Whether you hang out in Florianópolis, where an easy path to paradise boasts 42 idyllic beaches sitting within an hour's drive; or head south of the capital to Guarda do Embaú, one of Brazil's best surfing spots, or Praia do Rosa, the state's most sophisticated beach resort, a powerful punch of wow will greet you the first time you dig your toes into the state's unspoiled sands. Top: Praia da Joaquina (p296)

Paraty

20 No place in Brazil offers such an enticing blend of colonial architecture and natural beauty as Paraty (p128). Located a few hours southwest of Rio in the picturesque Costa Verde, it has long been a favorite *carioca* getaway. Drop-dead gorgeous beaches and a stunning mountain backdrop jostle for attention with the multihued, cobblestoned charms of the 18th-century town center. If you get bored with sunbathing and sightseeing, cool off with a caipirinha, go hurtling down a natural waterslide nearby, or whip up a gourmet Brazilian meal at the local cooking school.

Need to Know

For more information, see Survival Guide (p701)

Currency
Real (R$)

Language
Portuguese

Visas
Required for some nationalities, including holders of passports from the US, Canada and Australia.

Money
ATMs widely available. Credit cards accepted in most hotels and restaurants.

Cell Phones
Local SIM cards can be used in unlocked European and Australian phones, and in US phones on the GSM network.

Time
Brazil has four time zones. Rio and São Paulo are on Brasília time (GMT/UTC minus 3 hours).

When to Go

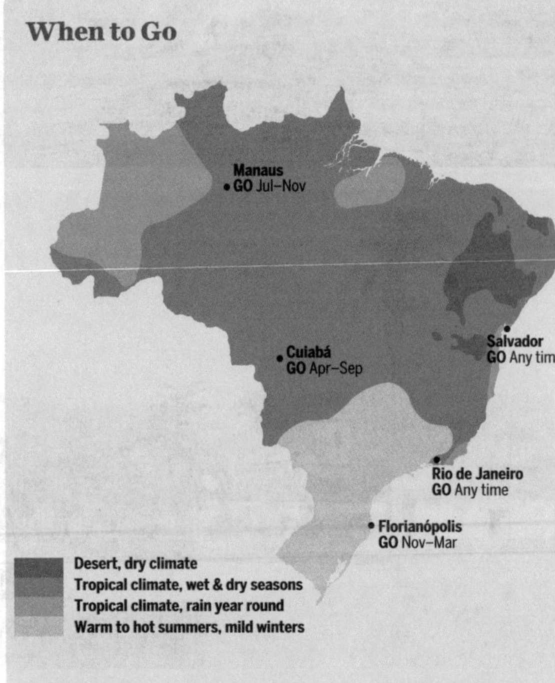

High Season
(Dec–Mar)

➡ Brazil's high season coincides with the northern-hemisphere winter.

➡ It's a hot, festive time – expect higher prices and minimum stays (typically four nights) during Carnaval.

Shoulder
(Apr & Oct)

➡ The weather is warm and dry along the coast, though it can be chilly in the south.

➡ Prices and crowds are average, though Easter week draws crowds and high prices.

Low Season
(May–Sep)

➡ Aside from July, which is a school-holiday month, you'll find lower prices and mild temperatures in the south.

➡ July to September are good months to visit the Amazon or Pantanal.

Useful Websites

Embratur (www.visitbrasil.com) Official site of Brazil's Ministry of Tourism.

Insider's Guide to Rio (www.ipanema.com) Tips and planning info, with special sections on Carnaval and gay Rio.

Lonely Planet (www.lonelyplanet.com) Summaries on Brazil travel, the popular Thorn Tree bulletin board and other resources.

Rio Times (www.riotimesonline.com) English-language news and resources on Rio and beyond.

Cultural Brazil (www.culturalbrazil.org) Articles on literature, art and film.

Gringoes (www.gringoes.com) Articles written by Anglophones living in Brazil.

Important Numbers

Brazil country code	✆55
Ambulance	✆192
Fire	✆193
Police	✆190
International collect call	✆0800-703-2111

Exchange Rates

Argentina	AR$1	R$0.42
Australia	A$1	R$2.83
Bolivia	B$1	R$0.56
Canada	C$1	R$2.98
Euro zone	€1	R$4.45
Japan	¥100	R$3.28
New Zealand	NZ$1	R$2.52
UK	UK£1	R$6.11
USA	US$1	R$3.94

Daily Costs

Budget: less than R$200

➡ dorm bed: R$40–60

➡ sandwich and drink in a juice bar: R$14–20

➡ long-distance buses: R$15 per hour of travel

Midrange: R$200–400

➡ Standard double room in a hotel: R$160–300

➡ Dinner for two in a mid-range restaurant: R$80–160

➡ Jungle trip: R$250 per day

➡ Admission to nightclubs and live-music venues: R$20–50

➡ One-way flight from Rio to Salvador/Iguaçu/Manaus: from R$450/500/510

Top end: more than R$400

➡ Boutique hotel room: R$500–800

➡ Upscale jungle lodge outside Manaus: per night R$500–1000

➡ Dinner for two at top restaurants: R$200–400

Opening Hours

Banks 9am–3pm Monday to Friday

Restaurants noon–2.30pm and 6–10:30pm

Cafes 8am–10pm

Bars 6pm–2am

Nightclubs 10pm–4am Thursday to Saturday

Shops 9am–6pm Monday to Friday and 9am–1pm Saturday

Arriving in Brazil

Aeroporto Galeão (GIG; Rio de Janeiro) Premium Auto Ônibus (www.premiumautoonibus.com.br; R$15) operates buses approximately every 30 minutes to Flamengo, Copacabana, Ipanema, Leblon and other neighborhoods. It takes 75 minutes to two hours. Taxis cost about R$65 to R$90 for Copacabana and Ipanema (45 minutes to two hours).

Aeroporto GRU (GRU; São Paulo) The Airport Bus Service (www.airportbusservice.com.br; R$42) is the most efficient way to/from GRU Airport, making stops at Aeroporto Congonhas, Barra Funda, Tiête, Praça da República and various hotels around Av Paulista and Rua Augusta. Guarucoop (www.guarucoop.com.br) is the only taxi service allowed to operate at the airport (R$136 to Av Paulista, R$161 to Vila Madalena).

Getting Around

Plane Useful for crossing Brazil's immense distances; can save days of travel; prices are generally high, but airfare promotions are frequent.

Bus Extensive services from *comun* (conventional) to *leito* (overnight sleepers) throughout the country, except for the Amazon. For timetables and bus operators, check out Busca Ônibus (www.buscaonibus.com.br).

Boat Slow, uncomfortable, but brag-worthy transport between towns in the Amazon, with trips measured in days rather than hours. You'll need a hammock, snacks, drinking water and a high tolerance for boredom.

For much more on **getting around**, see p713

If You Like...

Beaches

Brazil has some of the finest beaches on earth: you'll find idyllic island getaways, vibrant big-city beaches and rainforest-backed sands all along the coastline.

Baia do Sancho On Fernando de Noronha, this is easily one of Brazil's most gorgeous beaches. (p505)

Ilha Grande Enchanting island with gorgeous beaches, a welcome lack of cars and a laid-back island vibe. (p121)

Trancoso Cliff-backed beaches are a short stroll from this pretty Bahian village. (p451)

Jericoacoara Hip international beach scene with good activities, pousadas (guesthouses), restaurants and nightlife. (p547)

Ilhabela Dense jungle, waterfalls and picturesque beaches a few hours from São Paulo. (p259)

Ilha de Santa Catarina Protected dunes, and cliff- and forest-lined beaches, plus stunning lagoons in the interior. (p289)

Scenery

Blessed with verdant rainforests, thundering waterfalls, craggy mountains and tropical islands, it's easy to see why Brazilians say '*Deus e Brasileiro*' (God is Brazilian).

Rio de Janeiro The Cidade Maravilhosa (Marvelous City) lives up to its name with forested mountains and lovely beaches. (p50)

Fernando de Noronha Cliffs, rock pinnacles, beautiful bays and beaches all packed into one 10km-long island. (p503)

Iguaçu Falls Spread between Argentina and Brazil, these are some of the most spectacular waterfalls on earth. (p278)

Parque Nacional da Chapada Diamantina In the Bahian interior, you can hike across dramatic plateaus and swim in waterfalls. (p462)

Lençóis Maranhenses An otherworldly landscape of windswept dunes and sparkling blue lagoons. (p565)

Alter do Chão Startling white-sand beaches surrounded by jungle deep in the Amazon. (p597)

IF YOU LIKE... TRAIN RIDES

Hop aboard the Serra Verde Express for stunning views of mountain canyons and tropical lowlands en route between Curitiba and Morretes. (p270)

Wildlife

Brazil is home to a staggering array of plant and animal species, with memorable wildlife watching in the rainforests, wetlands and along the coast.

The Amazon Manaus is still one of the top gateways for a journey into the mother of all rainforests. (p569)

The Pantanal You're likely to see a great many animal species in these wildlife-rich wetlands. (p373)

Fernando de Noronha World-class diving and snorkeling amid abundant marine life. (p503)

Praia do Rosa Watch southern right whales off the coast between June and October. (p312)

Parque Nacional de Monte Pascoal Part of the bio-rich Atlantic rainforest, this park lies just south of Salvador. (p455)

Food & Drink

Specialties in Brazil range from African-influenced stews to delectable Amazonian fish. Grilled meats, tropical fruits and abundant international

VICTOR ANDRADE / GETTY IMAGES ©

Top: Parque Nacional da Chapada Diamantina (p462)

Bottom: Macaws, the Pantanal (p373)

influences are all part of Brazilian gastronomy.

Ipanema & Leblon These twin beachfront neighborhoods have some of the best restaurants in Rio. (p89)

São Paulo With great pizzerias, sushi bars, and restaurants serving first-rate Brazilian and international fare, you won't go hungry in Sampa. (p238)

Vale dos Vinhedos This scenic valley in the south is the heart of Brazil's wine-growing region, and has top restaurants as well. (p326)

SENAC Take a cooking class or simply come for the buffet, which spreads all the great Bahian dishes. (p407)

Belém Sample lip-numbing *tacacá* (a soup) and many delicious Amazonian fish such as the prized *tucanaré* (peacock bass). (p579)

Tiradentes Great place to feast on *mineira* cooking, particularly during its 10-day gastronomic festival. (p190)

Getting Off the Beaten Path

Pre-Colombian rock art, deserted beaches, end-of-the-earth fishing villages: these are just a few of the sights you can see by heading off the tourist path.

Parque Nacional da Serra da Capivara This dramatic rocky landscape contains thousands of prehistoric rock paintings. (p555)

Peninsula de Maraú Peaceful and remote, the Bahian peninsula's quiet beaches feel far removed from the tourist crowds. (p436)

Itaúnas Charming beach town in the little-visited state of Espírito Santo, with a wildlife-filled state park nearby. (p211)

Algodoal Isolated little village on the edge of wild beaches near the mouth of the Amazon. (p586)

Reserva Xixuaú-Xiparinâ Magnificent rainforest reserve 500km north of Manaus. (p622)

São Miguel das Missões Gateway to the mystical 17th-century ruins left behind by Jesuit missionaries. (p319)

Adventure

Brazil offers some memorable ways to experience its stunningly diverse landscapes, from multiday treks across dunes to snorkeling in crystalclear rivers.

Trekking Take the three- to four-day journey across the spectacular Lençóis Maranhenses and see the dunes by moonlight. (p565)

Hang Gliding Soar over Rio's stunning tropical landscape on a tandem glide off a mountain. (p79)

Ecotourism Bonito is a great spot for adventure, with river snorkeling, cave crawls, hiking and rappelling (abseiling). (p391)

Climbing The scenic high-country Parque Nacional do Itatiaia is a must for hikers and rock climbers. (p136)

Slow-Boating String up your hammock and travel the old-school way on a riverboat trip between towns in the Amazon. (p584)

Tree Climbing Get an intimate view of the rainforest canopy on an ascent inside the Amazon. (p615)

Kitesurfari Go on a long-distance kitesurfing adventure near Jericoacoara. (p548)

Festivals

Whether you prefer the colorful pageantry of Semana Santa (Holy Week) or the unbridled revelry of Carnaval, Brazil has you covered. Here are a few events worth planning a trip around.

Carnaval Many cities throw a wild bash, but Rio, Salvador, Olinda and Corumba are among the most festive. (p34)

Gay Pride São Paulo hosts the world's biggest gay pride parade. (p247)

Oktoberfest Experience Brazil's European roots at this beer- and bratwurst-loving bash in Blumenau. (p304)

Bumba Meu Boi São Luís erupts with color, music and dance in this fascinating June festival. (p557)

Semana Santa Colorful designs carpet the streets of Ouro Preto during this elaborate four-day fest. (p180)

Festas Juninas Huge celebrations in Salvador and elsewhere in Bahia. (p409)

History

You can delve into the past on a stroll through Brazil's colonial centers, some of which are Unesco World Heritage sites.

Salvador Bahia's star attraction is packed with historic churches and Afro-Brazilian culture. (p399)

Ouro Preto One of Brazil's most alluring colonial towns, hilly Ouro Preto is packed with 18th-century treasures. (p175)

Olinda Remnants of lovely architecture left by the Portuguese as well as the Dutch. (p498)

Alcântara Fascinating town in Maranhão full of restored and abandoned mansions and churches. (p563)

Paraty Picturesque cobblestone village with beautifully preserved 18th-century buildings. (p128)

Museu Histórico Nacional One of the best places to learn about the presence of the Portuguese royals in Rio. (p69)

Nightlife

Nightlife here is electric, fueled by the nation's incredible music scene. Samba, Afro-Brazilian drumming, rock and hip hop are all essential parts of the Brazilian soundtrack.

Lapa The epicenter of Rio's nightlife is packed with bars and samba clubs, and transforms into a street party on weekends. (p108)

Baixo Augusta Bars and clubs at this Paulista neighborhood attract a wildly eclectic crowd. (p248)

Pelourinho Salvador's historic center is the place to hear drum corps like Olodum laying down the heavy rhythms. (p417)

Lagoa da Conceição Live music, lake views and top-notch DJs are the big draw of this town on Ilha de Santa Catarina. (p296)

Belo Horizonte Take in the lively arts scene and buzzing nightlife of the Minas Gerais capital. (p163)

Búzios Bask on the beach by day and hit the clubs by night at this stylish resort town. (p156)

Month by Month

TOP EVENTS

Carnaval, February or March

Semana Santa, April or May

Bumba Meu Boi, June

Oktoberfest, October

Reveillon, December

January

Following the excitement of New Year's Eve, Brazil starts off the year in high gear, with steamy beach days and the buzz of pre-Carnaval revelry.

Lavagem do Bonfim

In Salvador, on the second Thursday in January, this equal-parts Catholic and Candomblé fest features a ritual washing of the church steps followed by all-night music and dancing. (p409)

Sommerfest

Blumenau's German-themed Oktoberfest is so popular that the city also throws another version of it mid-summer. Expect cheery crowds fueled by micro-brews and hearty servings of bratwurst. (p304)

February

High season is in full swing, with people-packed beaches, sold-out hotel rooms and the unbridled revelry of Carnaval. It's a festive and pricey time to travel, and advance planning is essential.

Festa de Iemanjá

On Praia Rio Vermelho in Salvador, Candomblé groups pay homage to the *orixá* Iemanjá, goddess of the sea and fertility, on 2 February, followed by a lively street party. (p409)

Carnaval

In February or March, for the five days preceding Ash Wednesday, the famous bacchanalian event happens nationwide, and is liveliest in Rio, Salvador, Olinda and Corumbá, with parades, costumes and round-the-clock merrymaking.

April

After Carnaval, prices dip, the intense heat subsides and the crowds dissipate, particularly in the north and northeast (when heavy rains continue through June). In Minas Gerais, however, Holy Week festivals keep things lively.

São Paulo Restaurant Week

South America's culinary powerhouse is well worth visiting during São Paulo Restaurant Week, when more than 100 top restaurants offer special menus and promotions (www.restaurantweek.com.br). Dates vary, though it's held twice a year (usually April or late March, then again in late September or October).

Semana Santa

In Ouro Preto, Holy Week (the week before Easter) is a colorful event of processions and streets 'painted' with flowers. São João del Rei's Holy Week features parades accompanied by fabulous traditional orchestras. Other well-known Holy Weeks happen in Congonhas and Cidade de Goiás. (p180)

May

May is a quiet time for tourism with cooler temperatures beginning to arrive (particularly in the south) and heavy rains still falling in the Amazon.

Festa do Divino Espírito Santo

Popularly known as Cavalhadas, this old-fashioned folk festival in Pirenópolis comprises medieval tournaments, dances and festivities. It takes place over three weeks around Pentecost, 50 days after Easter (May or June).

Festival Internacional de Balonismo

The far southern beach town of Torres springs to life for five days in early May or late April when it hosts a colorful hot-air balloon festival. Concerts, extreme sports, films and a country-style fair are among the attractions. (p331)

June

In the south, winter arrives (with cold weather the norm through August). Tourism-related activities remain curtailed (also through winter) in the north, south and northeast, though it's a good time to visit the Pantanal.

Festas Juninas

Spanning the month of June, the feast days of various saints mark some of the most important folkloric festivals in Brazil. Expect concerts, food stands, fireworks and bonfires. Bahia is one of the best places to be.

São Paulo Pride

It's official, São Paulo throws the largest gay pride parade on earth in early June, attracting more than three million people to this massive event.

ANDREA DAMATO / GETTY IMAGES ©

T PHOTOGRAPHY / SHUTTERSTOCK ©

Top: Semana Santa, Ouro Preto (p180)

Bottom: Boi-Bumbá, Parintins (p615)

Bumba Meu Boi

Maranhão's magnificent mythic bull festival has African, Indian and Portuguese roots and features singing, dancing, poetry and countless ox costumes. Held from 13 to 30 June.

Boi-Bumbá

In Parintins, this popular traditional folk festival on the last weekend of June recounts the death and resurrection of an ox, with music and dancing. (p615)

July

After months of rain, the dry season arrives in the Amazon, making it a good time to visit. The weather is mild (cold in the far south), but Brazilians travel during July, which is a school-holiday month.

Festival Nacional de Forró

Music lovers wanting to get off the beaten track should make their way up to the pretty beach town of Itaúnas, which hosts 10 days of concerts and dancing (to *forró* music). (p212)

August

The tail end of winter is a quiet time, with fewer tourists (and limited services) in the south and north. Temperatures are pleasant in the tropics and cold in the south.

Festa Literária Internacional de Paraty

This important literary festival in early August brings together celebrated authors from around the world, and also includes film screenings, exhibitions and musical performances. (p133)

Festival de Gramado

The European-style town of Gramado hosts an important film festival each year, running for nine days in August. This long-running fest (around since 1973) is a showcase for Brazilian and other Latin American films. (p323)

September

It's a good time for wildlife watching with dry skies in both the Amazon and the Pantanal. The weather is mild from Rio north, but remains cool in the south.

Rio International Film Festival

Rio's international film festival – Latin America's biggest – features more than 200 films from all over the world, shown at some 35 theaters from late September through early October. (p83)

Bienal de São Paulo

This major art event occurs in even-numbered years (next in 2016 and 2018) between October and December and showcases the work of over 120 artists from around the globe. (p233)

October

The tourist masses and high-season prices haven't yet arrived, though the weather is beginning to warm, and Rio is already livening up for next year's Carnaval.

Círio de Nazaré

Belém's enormous annual event on the second Sunday in October brings one million to the streets to take part in the procession of one of Brazil's most important icons. (p578)

Oktoberfest

This beer-drinking extravaganza in Blumenau is the best place to connect to southern Brazil's German roots. Held in mid-October. (p304)

December

Summer marks the beginning of Brazil's most festive season (through February), with hot temperatures and ideal beach days. The crowds are growing and prices are rising (but typically rise even more in January and February).

Carnatal

The country's biggest 'off-season Carnaval' is this Salvador-style festival held in Natal in the first week of December. It features raucous street parties and pumping *trios elétricos* (bands playing atop mobile speaker-trucks). (p520)

Reveillon

Some two million revelers, dressed in white, pack the sands of Copacabana Beach in Rio on 31 December, where music concerts and fireworks ring in the New Year. (p83)

Itineraries

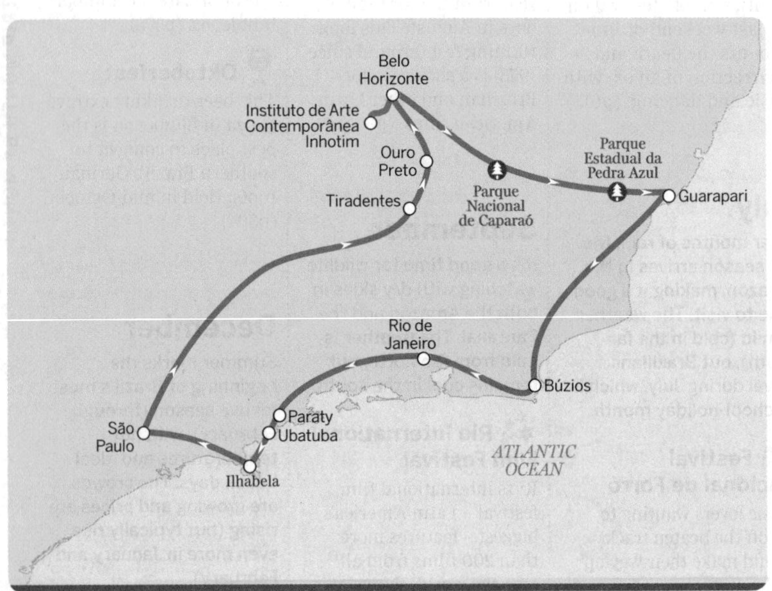

Rio & the Southeast

Gorgeous beaches, rainforest-covered islands and colonial towns are just some of the things you'll experience on this loop around the Southeast.

Spend a few days discovering **Rio** and its beaches, restaurants and music scene before heading to **Paraty**, a beautifully preserved colonial town with rainforest hikes and stunning beaches nearby. Next, stop in **Ubatuba** with its jungle-clad mountains and spectacular coastal scenery. **Ilhabela** is a car-free island of beaches, forests and waterfalls. Stop in **São Paulo** for high culture, including the nation's best museums and restaurants.

Head next to exquisite **Tiradentes** and **Ouro Preto**, some of Brazil's finest colonial gems. Afterwards, take in a bit of friendly *mineira* hospitality, good restaurants and buzzing nightlife in **Belo Horizonte**. Make a day trip to the outstanding galleries and gardens at the **Instituto de Arte Contemporânea Inhotim**, 50km southwest of Belo Horizonte.

Visit the hiker's paradise of **Parque Nacional de Caparaó**; further east, relish the dramatic beauty of **Parque Estadual da Pedra Azul**. Continue to the coast, for beach action and seafood in **Guarapari**. Further south you'll find the stunning beaches and high-end dining and nightlife of **Búzios**, which makes a great final stop before heading back to Rio.

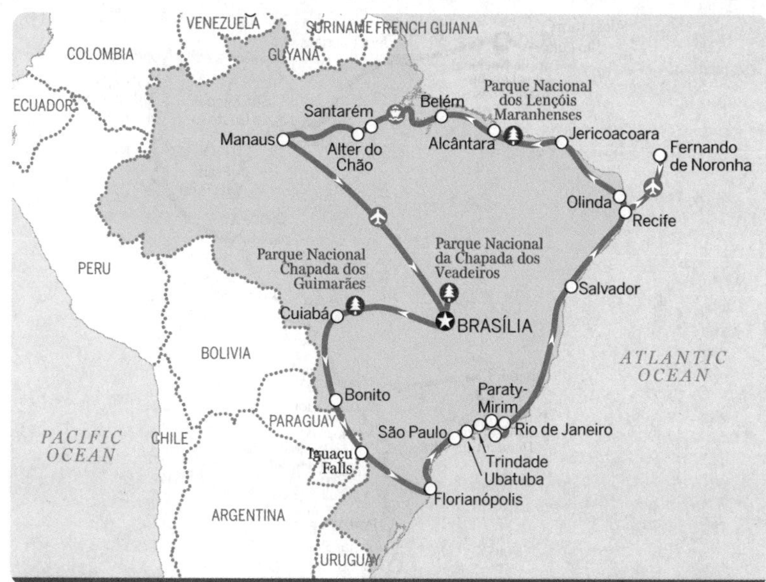

Best of Brazil

On this epic trip you'll experience the rhythm-infused towns of the Northeast, the jungles of the Amazon and the biodiversity of the Pantanal, with beaches, tropical islands and historic towns thrown into the mix.

From **São Paulo**, head east towards Rio, stopping at glorious beaches such as **Ubatuba**, **Trindade** and **Paraty-Mirim**. Leave a couple of days for hiking the rainforest paths and basking on the beaches of **Ilha Grande**. Continue northeast to **Rio**, for a hearty dose of nightlife, beach culture and panoramic views.

From there head north, via bus or plane, to **Salvador**, the country's Afro-Brazilian gem that's known for its colorful colonial center, drumming in the streets, and lively (and numerous) festivals. Further up the coast visit historic and arts-loving **Olinda**, then catch a flight from neighboring **Recife** to the spectacular archipelago of **Fernando de Noronha**, where you find pretty beaches, snorkeling, diving and a paradise-like setting.

Back on the mainland, travel north, stopping in the backpackers' paradise of **Jericoacoara** en route to the surreal dunes in the **Parque Nacional dos Lençóis Maranhenses**, a stark contrast to the colonial beauty of **Alcântara**. To the west lies **Belém**, a culturally rich city near the lush island of Ilha de Marajó. Catch a boat up the Amazon to **Santarém** and on to **Alter do Chão** for a trip into the jungle, and continue on to the burgeoning city of **Manaus**.

From Manaus, fly to **Brasília** to take in its stunning architecture, then visit **Parque Nacional da Chapada dos Veadeiros**, for waterfalls, canyons and dips in natural swimming pools. Next head to **Cuiabá**, gateway to the breathtaking canyons of **Chapada dos Guimarães**. Spend a few days horseback riding and boating in the Pantanal, one of Brazil's best destinations for wildlife watching. Head south via Campo Grande to **Bonito** for crystal-clear rivers, lush forests and caves. Continue south to the awe-inspiring **Iguaçu Falls**. Before completing the circle, explore the secluded beaches and charming Germanic towns around **Florianópolis**.

6 WEEKS Bahia & the Northeast

Those looking for the soul of Brazil would do well to focus on the Northeast. A confluence of music, history and culture amid spectacular natural scenery makes for an unforgettable journey.

Catch a flight to **Porto Seguro**, then quickly make your way to the pretty towns of **Arraial d'Ajuda** and **Trancoso**, both blessed with great guesthouses and restaurants, festive nightlife and access to walks on a seemingly endless cliff-backed beach. Continue north to **Itacaré**, a lively town with great surf and cove beaches reached via trails through hilly rainforest. Then head on to rhythm-filled **Salvador**, Bahia's most vibrant and colorful city. From there, catch a boat to **Morro de São Paulo**, an island with enchanting beaches and a laid-back vibe. Don't miss boat rides around the island – taking in mangroves, reefs, oysters and the quiet village of Boipeba.

Detour west to the tranquil diamond-mining town of **Lençóis**, which has pretty outdoor cafes, cobblestone streets, and caves, rivers and waterfalls nearby. From here, head into the **Parque Nacional da Chapada Diamantina** for crisp mountain streams, panoramic views and an endless network of trails. Back on the coast, go north to **Maceió**, a vibrant, youthful city with gorgeous beaches nearby. Keep going north to reach **Olinda**, one of Brazil's best-preserved colonial cities and a Unesco World Heritage site. From Olinda's buzzing neighbor **Recife**, fly out to **Fernando de Noronha**, an exquisite archipelago of rich marine life and splendid beaches.

Returning to the mainland, visit **Praia da Pipa**, then hit the coastline stretching from **Natal** to Jericoacoara, including the coastal spots of **São Miguel do Gostoso** and **Galinhos**. In the sandy-street village of **Jericoacoara**, try your hand at sandboarding, kitesurfing and beachfront capoeira, and watch memorable sunsets. West of Jericoacoara, **Parque Nacional dos Lençóis Maranhenses** is a striking landscape of dunes, lagoons and beaches. Continue west to the reggae-charged **São Luís**, home to 18th-century buildings, seafood restaurants and buzzing nightlife. It's worth planning a trip around one of the town's many folkloric fests. The last stop is the untouristy colonial gem of **Alcântara**.

Top: Praia da Pipa (p525)

Bottom: Street scene, Salvador (p399)

MAREMAGNUM / GETTY IMAGES ©

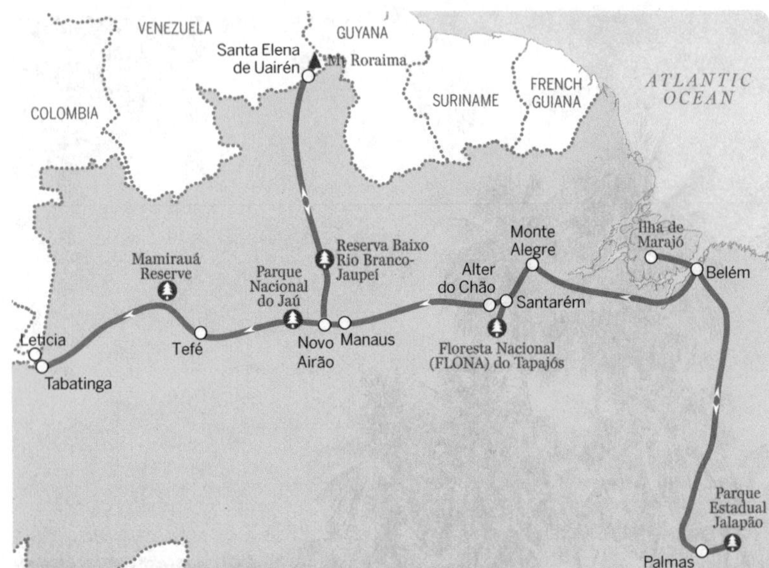

Waterways of the Amazon

Few places ignite the imagination like the Amazon. The largest forest on the planet has an incredible array of plant and animal life. Surprising to many visitors, these wetlands also contain vibrant cities, architectural treasures and beautiful river beaches.

Begin in **Belém**, a culturally rich city at the mouth of the great river. Explore the revitalized riverfront docks, visit the waterfront market, sample Amazonian dishes and catch a performance at the lavish Teatro da Paz. From here, explore the forest-covered island of **Ilha de Marajó**, which has bird-filled forests, friendly locals and itinerant water buffalo roaming the streets. Back in Belém, dip south to **Palmas**, another ultra-planned city like Brasília, and jumping-off point for 4WD tours of rugged **Parque Estadual Jalapão**.

Get a hammock and prepare yourself for a few hardy days of boat travel up the Amazon River. Stop in **Monte Alegre** to see ancient rock paintings, the oldest-known human creations in the Amazon, which are sprinkled among sandstone hills beyond town. Upstream is **Santarém**, a pleasant city with many nearby attractions. Also reachable is the rainforest of the **Floresta Nacional (FLONA) do Tapajós**, where you can lodge in simple pousadas and hike through pristine forest in search of massive *samaúma* trees. It's also worth stopping in **Alter do Chão** for its picturesque lagoon with startling white-sand beaches.

Continue upriver to **Manaus**, Amazonia's largest city. Visit the city's opera house, market, indigenous museums and nature parks, and the Encontro das Águas. From here, go west of Manaus to the small town of **Novo Airão**, the jumping-off point to **Reserva Baixo Rio Branco-Jauperí**, a remote and pristine rainforest reserve where you can see a stunning array of plant and animal life. You can also travel to **Santa Elena de Uairén**, Venezuela, for six-day treks up **Mt Roraima**. West of Manaus lies the fairly unexplored **Parque Nacional do Jaú**.

Outside of **Tefé**, visit the **Mamirauá Reserve**, a vast rainforest reserve where you can see dolphins, sloths, macaws, various monkey species (including the rare uakari) and other wildlife. From there, continue by river to **Tabatinga**, and into **Leticia** in Colombia for stays at jungle lodges along the Rio Javari.

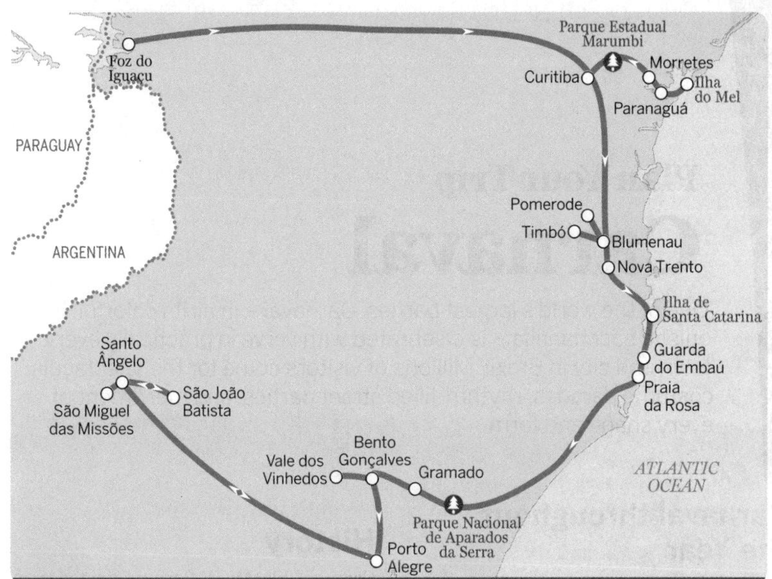

Southward Bound

This trip through Brazil's southernmost states takes in forested islands and scenic beaches, mountainous national parks, historic missions and Bavarian-style towns with largely European roots.

Start in **Foz do Iguaçu** to gaze at the most impressive waterfalls on the planet. Take short day trips to Argentina and Paraguay to get a taste of lush rainforests before heading east (by overnight bus or quick flight) to **Curitiba**, a city with an intriguing environmentally friendly design, plus pretty botanic gardens and an Oscar Niemeyer museum. Next, take the scenic train ride to the sleepy waterfront town of **Morretes**. From there you can visit the **Parque Estadual Marumbi**, a lush reserve that offers memorable walks amid the highlands. Continue on to **Paranaguá** to car-free **Ilha do Mel**. The forest-covered island has lovely beaches and low-key guesthouses, and is skirted by some pretty trails.

Next head to **Blumenau** and nearby **Vale Europeu**, where **Pomerode**, **Timbó** and **Nova Trento** boast Teutonic architecture and a local brew more Bavarian than Brazilian. Head back east to the coast and continue south to **Ilha de Santa Catarina**, a forested gem of sand dunes, sparkling beaches, pretty lagoons and sleepy fishing villages. Keep going south to **Guarda do Embaú**, a seaside bohemian town with excellent surf. A short jaunt south is **Praia da Rosa**, which has pretty beaches and whale watching.

On into Rio Grande do Sul, explore the dramatic canyon and waterfalls of **Parque Nacional de Aparados da Serra**. It's worth heading further inland to **Gramado**, a charming mountain resort where gourmet chocolates, fondue and excellent infrastructure might make you feel like you've stepped into a Swiss portal. Continue west to **Bento Gonçalves**, gateway to the award-winning vineyards of the **Vale dos Vinhedos**, set amid the rolling hills of the Serra Gaucho.

Head south to **Porto Alegre** for transport to **Santo Ângelo**, which leads on to the Jesuit missions. From there you can visit **São Miguel das Missões**, **São João Batista** and numerous other holy sites; true grail-seekers can even cross into Paraguay or Argentina for a look at even more Jesuit missions. At trip's end, return to Porto Alegre for an onward flight.

Plan Your Trip
Carnaval

One of the world's largest parties, Carnaval – in all its colorful, hedonistic bacchanalia – is celebrated with verve in practically every town and city in Brazil. Millions of visitors come for the spectacular costume parades, rhythm-filled street parties, and merriment of every shape and form.

Carnaval throughout the Year

If you can't make it to Brazil during Carnaval, you can still join the party by hitting one of the so-called out-of-season Carnavals.

Carnatal

Natal's huge out-of-season Carnatal (www.carnatal.com.br) is the country's biggest and kicks off in the first week of December, with extensive street parties and Salvador-style *trios elétricos* (electrically amplified bands playing atop trucks).

Recifolia

Recife throws not one but two Carnavals (www.carnavalrecife.com). The first happens February/March, the second late October or November.

Fortal

Half a million revelers celebrate Carnaval street-party style at Fortaleza's big bash (www.fortal.com.br) in the last week of July.

Marafolia

The massive Salvador-style party (www.marafolia.com) in São Luís takes place in mid-October.

History

Carnaval, like Mardi Gras, originated from various pagan spring festivals. During the Middle Ages, these tended to be wild parties until tamed, in Europe, by both the Reformation and the Counter-Reformation. But not even the heavy hand of the Inquisition could squelch Carnaval in the Portuguese colony, where it came to acquire *índio* (indigenous) costumes and African rhythms.

Some speculate that the word *carnaval* derives from the Latin *carne vale*, meaning 'goodbye meat,' owing to the 40 days of abstinence (from meat and other worldly pleasures) that Lent entails. To compensate for the deprivation ahead, sins are racked up in advance with wild parties in honor of King Momo, the king of Carnaval.

Carnaval Dates

The following are the Carnaval dates (Friday to Shrove Tuesday) in coming years:

2017 February 24 to 28

2018 February 9 to 13

2019 March 1 to 5

2020 February 21 to 25

Carnaval in Rio de Janeiro

If you haven't heard by now, Rio throws an exceptional party, with music and dancing filling the streets for days on end. The culmination of the big fest is the brilliantly colorful parade through the Sambódromo, with giant mechanized floats, pounding drummers and whirling dancers – but there's lots of action in Rio's many neighborhoods for those seeking more than just the stadium experience.

Out-of-towners add to the mayhem, joining *cariocas* (residents of Rio) in the street parties and costumed balls erupting throughout town. There are free live concerts throughout the city (near the Arcos do Lapa, on Largo da Machado and on Praça Floriano, among other places), while those seeking a bit of decadence can head to the various balls about town. Whatever you do, prepare yourself for sleepless nights, an ample dose of caipirinhas and samba, and mingling with joyful crowds spilling out of the city.

To get more information on events during Carnaval, check *Veja* magazine's *Veja Rio* insert (sold on Sunday at newsstands) or visit Riotur (p117), the tourist organization in charge of Carnaval.

Carnaval on the Streets

Joining the *bandas* and *blocos* (street parties) is one of the best ways to have the *carioca* experience. These marching parades consist of a procession of brass bands (in the case of *bandas*) or drummers and vocalists (in the case of *blocos*) followed by anyone who wants to dance through the streets. Currently there are more than 400 street parties, filling every neighborhood in town with the sound of pounding drums and old-fashioned Carnaval songs – not to mention thousands of merrymakers. For many *cariocas*, this is the highlight of Carnaval. You can don a costume (or not), learn a few songs and join in; all you have to do is show up. For Zona Sul fests, don't forget to bring your swimsuit for a dip in the ocean afterwards.

For complete listings, pick up a free *Carnaval de Rua* guide from Riotur. It's wise to confirm dates and times before heading out.

AfroReggae (Av Atlântica, near Rainha Elizabeth; ⌚10am Carnaval Sun) A massive and hugely popular *bloco*, with a heavy rhythm section, that celebrates along the beachfront in Ipanema.

Banda de Ipanema (Praça General Osório, Ipanema; ⌚4pm 2nd Sat before Carnaval, Carnaval Sat & Carnaval Tue) This long-standing *banda* attracts a wild crowd, complete with drag queens and others in costume. Don't miss it.

Banda de Sá Ferreira (cnr Av Atlântica & Rua Sá Ferreira, Copacabana; ⌚5:30pm Carnaval Sat) This popular Copacabana *banda* marches along the ocean from *posto* 1 to *posto* 6.

Banda Simpatia é Quase Amor (Praça General Osório, Ipanema; ⌚4pm Sat before Carnaval & Carnaval Sun) A favorite Ipanema *banda*, with a 50-piece percussion band.

Barbas (cnr Rua Assis Bueno & Rua Arnoldo Quintela, Botafogo; ⌚4pm Carnaval Sat) One of the oldest *bandas* of the Zona Sul parades through the streets with a 60-piece percussion band.

Carmelitas (cnr Rua Dias de Barros & Ladeira de Santa Teresa, Santa Teresa; ⌚1pm Carnaval Fri & 10am Carnaval Tue) Crazy mixed crowd (some dressed as Carmelite nuns) parades through Santa Teresa's streets.

Céu na Terra (Curvelo, Santa Teresa; ⌚8am Carnaval Sat) Follows along the *bonde* (streetcar line) on a memorable celebration through Santa Teresa en route to Largo das Neves.

Cordão do Bola Preta (Primeiro de Março, near Rua Rosário, Centro; ⌚9am Carnaval Sat) The oldest and biggest *banda* still in action. Costumes are always welcome, especially those with black-and-white spots.

Dois Pra Lá, Dois Pra Cá (Rua da Passagem 145, Carlinho de Jesus Dance School, Botafogo; ⌚10am Carnaval Sat) This fairly long march begins at the Carlinho de Jesus Dance School and ends at the Copacabana Palace.

Monobloco (Av Rio Branco, near Pres Vargas, Centro; ⌚7am 1st Sun after Carnaval) Rise and shine! This huge *bloco* attracts upwards of 500,000 revelers who, nursing hangovers (or perhaps still inebriated) gather in Centro for a final farewell to Carnaval.

Que Merda É Essa? (Garcia d'Ávila, near Nascimento Silva, Ipanema; ⌚2:30pm Carnaval Sun) This playful gathering (its name means 'What the shit is this?') is a big draw in Ipanema – and eventually makes its way along the beach.

Suvaco de Cristo (Rua Jardim Botânico, near Rua Faro, Jardim Botânico; ⌚10am Sun before Carnaval) Very popular *bloco* (whose name means 'Christ's armpit', in reference to the open-armed Redeemer looming overhead). It also meets on Carnaval Saturday, but doesn't announce the time (to avoid overcrowding), so ask around.

Samba-School Parades

The highlight of any Carnaval experience is attending (or participating in) a parade at the Sambódromo. There before a crowd of some 90,000 (with millions more watching on TV), each of the 12 samba schools has its 80 minutes to dance and sing through the open Oscar Niemeyer–designed stadium. The pageantry is not simply eye candy for the masses. Schools are competing for top honors in the parade, with winners announced (and a winner's parade held) on the Saturday following Carnaval.

Here's what to expect: each school enters the Sambódromo with amped energy levels, and dancers take things up a notch as they dance through the stadium. Announcers introduce the school, then the lone voice of the *puxador* (interpreter) starts the samba. Thousands more voices join him (each school has 3000 to 5000 members), and then the drummers kick in, 200 to 400 per school, driving the parade. Next come the main wings of the school, the big allegorical floats, the children's wing, the celebrities and the bell-shaped *baianas* (women dressed as Bahian aunts) twirling in elegant hoopskirts.

Costumes are fabulously lavish, with 1.5m feathered headdresses; long, flowing capes that sparkle with sequins; and rhinestone-studded G-strings.

The whole procession is also an elaborate competition. A handpicked set of judges chooses the best school on the basis of many components, including percussion, the *samba do enredo* (theme song), harmony between percussion, song and dance, choreography, costumes, story line, floats and decorations. The dance championship is hotly contested, with the winner becoming not just the pride of Rio but all of Brazil.

The Sambódromo parades start with the *mirins* (young samba-school members) on the evening of Carnaval Friday, and continue on through Saturday night when the Group A samba schools strut their stuff. Sunday and Monday are the big nights, when the Grupo Especial – the 12 best samba schools in Rio – parade: six on Sunday night, and six more on Monday night. The following Saturday, the six top schools do it again in the Parade of Champions, which generally has more affordable tickets than on the big nights. Each event starts at 9pm and runs until 4am.

Most visitors stay for three or four schools, and come to see their favorite in action (every self-respecting *carioca* has a school they support, just as they have a favorite football team). If you're really gung-ho, wear your school's colors and learn the theme song (the words are found on each of the school's websites) so you can sing along when it marches through the Sambódromo.

Tickets

Getting tickets at legitimate prices can be tough. Liesa (http://liesa.globo.com), the official samba-school league, begins selling tickets in December or January, most of which get immediately snatched up by travel agencies then later re-sold at

JOINING A SAMBA SCHOOL

Those who have done it say no other part of Carnaval quite compares to donning a costume and dancing through the Sambódromo before roaring crowds. Anyone with the desire and a little extra money to spare can march in the parade. Most samba schools are happy to have foreigners join one of the wings. To get the ball rolling, you'll need to contact your chosen school in advance; they'll tell you the rehearsal times and when you need to be in the city (usually a week or so before Carnaval). Ideally, you should memorize the theme song as well.

The biggest investment, aside from the airfare to Rio, is buying a *fantasia* (costume), which will cost upwards of R$1000.

If you speak Portuguese, you can contact a school directly; some Rio travel agencies can also arrange this.

KEREN SU / GETTY IMAGES ©

Top: Carnaval, Rio de Janeiro

Bottom: Carnaval (p490), Recife

higher prices. Check with Riotur about where you can get them, as the official outlet can vary from year to year. At face value, tickets run from R$140 to R$500, though you'll probably have to pay about twice that (or more) if you buy just before Carnaval. The best sectors, in order of preference, are sectors 9, 7, 11, 5 and 3. The first two (9 and 7) have great views and are in the center, which is the liveliest place to be.

By Carnaval weekend, most tickets are sold out, but there are lots of scalpers. If you buy a ticket from a scalper (no need to worry about looking for them – they'll find you!), make sure you get both the plastic ticket with the magnetic strip and the ticket showing the seat number. The tickets for different days are color-coded, so double-check the date as well.

If you haven't purchased a ticket but still want to go, during Carnaval you can show up at the Sambódromo at around midnight. This is when you can get grandstand tickets for about R$50 from scalpers outside the gate. Make sure you check which sector your ticket is for. Most ticket sellers will try to pawn off their worst seats.

And if you can't make it during Carnaval proper, there's always the cheaper Parade of Champions the following Saturday.

Open-Air Concerts

Lapa becomes a major focal point during Carnaval. In front of the Arcos da Lapa, the Praça Cardeal Câmara transforms into an open-air stage, with concerts running through Carnaval. About half a dozen different bands play each night (samba, of course) during this event, which is called Rio Folia. The music starts at 10pm and runs past 2am, though revelers pack Lapa until well past sunrise.

Samba-School Rehearsals

Around September, rehearsals start at the *escolas de samba* (samba schools or clubs). Rehearsals usually take place in the favelas (slums, informal communities) and are open to visitors. Salgueiro (p110) and Mangueira (p110) are among the easiest schools to get to.

Carnaval in Salvador

Although Rio's Carnaval hogs all the attention, Salvador hosts its own magnificent bash. In fact, this is one of the largest Carnavals in Brazil, attracting over two million revelers at last count.

Carnaval in Salvador usually kicks off Thursday night, with the mayor handing King Momo the keys to the city at Campo Grande (though in recent years it's happened at Praça Castro Alves). It all comes to an end on Ash Wednesday, with a handful of street parades giving a final afternoon send-off.

As elsewhere in Brazil, music plays a key role in the celebration, and in Salvador that means *axé,* an Afro-Bahian musical genre that incorporates a wide range of sounds, from samba-reggae and *forró* (a Northeastern two-step) to calypso and fast-passed *frevo* (a fast, syncopated, brass-band beat). It's the undisputed pop anthem during Carnaval in Salvador, and in many other parts of the Northeast.

Trios Elétricos & Blocos

The other integral element for the Salvadoran party is the *trio elétrico* – a long, colorfully decorated truck that's covered with oversized speakers. Small stages perch up top, with a band pumping out the rhythms as the *trio* slooowly winds through town. Hundreds of thousands line the streets of the parade route, packing in tightly – indeed, moving freely becomes a Sisyphean task.

Each *trio* is the centerpiece of a *bloco,* the gathering of revelers that surrounds the trucks. Those who want to be a part of the *bloco* pay anywhere from R$100 to upwards of R$700 (depending on the popularity of the *bloco*); this gives access to the *cordão,* the safer, roped-off area guarded by security personnel that surrounds the *trio. Bloco* members receive an *abadá,* an outfit (usually T-shirt and shorts) that identifies them as part of the group.

Those who don't want to pay to join a *bloco* can always choose to *fazer pipoca* (be popcorn) in the street. Once you get over the initial crush of the surrounding crowds, you can enjoy a wide variety of music and be spared the hassle involved with picking up the *abadá.*

You can also escape some of the madness by buying a day in a *camarote*, the walled-off, roadside bleachers with their own facilities. Head to the tourist office for information on *camarote* tickets.

Afoxés & Blocos Afros

Sprinkled between each of the *blocos* – and densely concentrated in the Pelourinho, where there are no *trio elétricos* – are *afoxés,* groups that parade to the rhythms, songs and dances found in Candomblé (the polytheistic Afro-Brazilian religion). Years ago, *afoxé* groups would perform a ritual in the *terreiro* (house of worship) before hitting the streets. Today, this is not mandatory, and in fact many *afoxé* members don't worship the *orixás* (the gods that the groups celebrate).

One of the most famous *afoxé* groups around today is the **Filhos de Gandhy** (www.filhosdegandhy.com.br), founded in 1949. Although Gandhi was not born in Brazil, the *bloco*'s founding members felt he was an important symbol of peace; their nonviolent approach earned the *bloco* respect in the eyes of the authorities, which took a largely repressive stance toward Afro-Brazilian culture in the early 20th century. The *bloco* also helped pave the way for numerous other *afoxés*. Today, the Filhos are now the largest *afoxé,* with more than 10,000 members. They wear blue-and-white outfits with white turbans, shimmering sashes and blue-and-white beaded necklaces. Like some other *afoxés,* the group plays the serene rhythms of *ijexá* (a style of African-influenced music), and sprays the crowd with perfume.

The assortment of *blocos afros* also plays an intrinsic role in the Carnaval festivities in Salvador. These are groups that celebrate African or Afro-Brazilian heritage in both costumes and themes. The most famous *bloco afro* performing today is **Olodum** (http://olodum.uol.com.br), a group widely credited for creating samba-reggae during Carnaval in 1986. Today the powerful drum corps parades with some 200 drummers, a handful of singers and thousands of costumed members.

Carnaval in Other Cities

Most foreign travelers tend to join the party in Rio or Salvador, but there are scores of other places to rack up a few sins Brazilian-style before Ash Wednesday (or perhaps the week after) brings the revelry to a close.

Corumbá This small town near the Bolivian border goes wild during Carnaval, with massive, Rio-style parades, complete with samba schools. (p389)

Florianópolis One of Brazil's most gay-friendly Carnavals (after Rio); the biggest and best bash in the South. (p291)

Olinda Spontaneous, inclusive and playful; lasts 11 days and begins with a parade of more than 400 'Virgins' – men in drag. (p499)

Porto Seguro Similar to Salvador's Carnaval; lasts a full week, ending the Saturday after Ash Wednesday. (p447)

Recife Costumed re-enactments, diverse music, ample audience participation (bring a costume) and huge street parties, including the Galo da Madrugada, which gathers over two million celebrants on the official Saturday-morning Carnaval opening. (p490)

São Paulo While less riotous than most, São Paulo's Carnaval celebrations include a spectacular parade in its own Sambódromo; fewer crowds and lower prices are appealing. (p219)

Plan Your Trip
Outdoors

Brazil's coastline, its forests and mountainous interior set the stage for fresh-air adventures. Wildlife watching is world-class in the Pantanal and the Amazon. There are hundreds of great surf spots all along the Atlantic, while the chapadas (tablelands) are good destinations for hikes and treks. Other big draws include rock climbing, canyoning, paragliding and diving.

Top Activities

Watching

See monkeys, macaws, capybaras, caimans, toucans and dozens of other species on a wildlife-watching trip in the Amazon or the Pantanal.

Hang Gliding

Take to the skies off Pedra Bonita in Rio de Janeiro.

Surfing

Ride the excellent breaks off Itacaré in Bahia.

Diving

Dive amid abundant coral and marine life off Fernando de Noronha.

Rock Climbing

Take on challenging routes surrounded by craggy peaks in the Serra dos Órgãos in Rio state.

Hiking

Take the five- to eight-day Grand Circuit trek in the beautiful mountainous setting of Parque Nacional da Chapada Diamantina. Or hike to waterfalls set in a picturesque valley of the Parque Nacional da Chapada dos Veadeiros.

Snorkeling

Explore the crisp rivers around Bonito.

Climbing

Climbing in Brazil is best in the cooler, drier months, from April to October. Brazil has lots of fantastic climbs, ranging from beginner level to routes yet to be conquered. Rio de Janeiro is the hub of Brazilian climbing, with some 350 documented climbs within an hour's drive of the city. You can even climb inside the city limits. The ascent up Pão de Açúcar has dozens of routes, from easy to quite challenging. Rio is also the best place to set up a climb if you're heading further afield.

Other places famous for rock climbing:

Parque Nacional da Serra dos Órgãos (p145), Rio de Janeiro state

Parque Nacional do Itatiaia (p136), Rio de Janeiro state

Parque Nacional de Caparaó (p207), Minas Gerais

Diving & Snorkeling

The *mergulho* (diving) here doesn't match the Caribbean, but is worthwhile if you're keen. By far the best diving in the country is in the **Fernando de Noronha archipelago** (p503). Here you'll find excellent visibility (up to 40m), warm seas and abundant marine life, including 15 coral species and more than 200 fish species. There are several reputable dive operators.

Other good places for diving include:

Arraial do Cabo (p152), Rio de Janeiro state

Ponta do Seixas (p514), near João Pessoa in Paraíba

Lagoa Misteriosa (p393), freshwater cave-diving near Bonito

The snorkeling is also quite good on Fernando de Noronha, including places where you can swim with sea turtles at high tide. Snorkel-by-boat excursions are available. For something completely different, nothing compares to the experience of snorkeling in the crystal-clear rivers around Bonito and Bom Jardim and seeing some of the Pantanal's most famous (and tastiest!) fish: pintados, pacus and dourados.

You can also go snorkeling on boat excursions from the following places:

Morro de São Paulo (p431), Bahia

Parque Nacional Marinho de Abrolhos (p456), Bahia

Maceió (p472), Alagoas

Maragogi (p482), Alagoas

Wildlife Encounters

Home to an astounding variety of creatures great and small, Brazil is one of the world's best places for seeing wildlife. A few top experiences for nature lovers:

Mamirauá Reserve (p632) Spot five species of monkey, toucans, sloths, river dolphins and caimans deep in the Amazon jungle.

Cristalino Jungle Lodge (p371) Take a day trip or overnight at this lodge, home to an awe-inspiring collection of wildlife.

Fernando de Noronha archipelago (p503) Swim with sea turtles.

Pantanal (p373) Look for wildlife (including jaguars) while boating near Porto Jofre.

Praia da Rosa (p699) Watch southern right whales – mothers and calves – from the beach.

Parque Nacional do Superagüi (p276) Spy an amazing variety of birds on a boat trip around the mangroves and Atlantic rainforest.

Reserva Baixo Rio Branco-Jauaperí (p618) Immerse yourself in Amazonian animal life.

Alter do Chão (p597) Paddle across the Lago Verde to the squawks of tropical birds.

Estação Biológica de Caratinga (p205) Encounter the largest primate in the Americas, the endangered *muriqui* monkey.

Hang Gliding & Paragliding

Probably one of the world's most scenic places to go hang gliding, **Rio de Janeiro** (p79) offers memorable tandem flights over tropical rainforest with views of the beach and island-filled ocean in the distance.

Paragliding (parapente) can also be arranged. Another place you can do a tandem hang-gliding flight is Rio da Barra, near Trancoso in Bahia.

Hiking

Hiking in Brazil is highly popular. It's best done during the cooler months of April to October. During the summer, the tropical sun heats the rock to oven temperatures and turns the jungles into steamy saunas. If you plan to hike in the Amazon, aim to come when the water levels are low (roughly August to December); at other times the forest is flooded and virtually all your activities will be by canoe.

There are lots of great places to hike in Brazil, both in the national and state parks and along the coastline, and especially in the Southeast and South. Outstanding areas include:

Floresta da Tijuca, Rio de Janeiro (p79) Atlantic rainforest, peaks and ocean views inside the city limits.

Ilha Grande, Rio de Janeiro state (p121) Atlantic rainforest hikes to gorgeous beaches and tiny villages.

Manaus (p606) Best for a multiday 'survival tour' with rainforest hiking, fishing for dinner, building shelters and sleeping in hammocks.

Parque Estadual Marumbi, Paraná (p270) Well-signposted network of old pioneer trails.

Parque Nacional da Chapada Diamantina, Bahia (p462) Spectacular day hikes and multiday treks; Lençóis is a good base.

Parque Nacional da Serra dos Órgãos, Rio de Janeiro state (p145) Hiking amid peaks and forest; several hours north of Rio.

Parque Nacional da Chapada dos Veadeiros, Goiás (p358) Vast, 650-sq-km park in high-altitude cerrado with scenic day hikes taking in waterfalls, swimming holes and lunar landscapes.

Parque Nacional de Caparaó, Minas Gerais (p207) Summit hikes to the highest mountains in the south, including Pico da Bandeira (2892m).

Parque Nacional de Aparados da Serra, Rio Grande do Sul (p328) Stunning canyons, waterfalls and panoramas in the Serra Gaúcha.

Parque Nacional do Itatiaia, Rio de Janeiro state (p136) Climbing, trekking, wildlife watching amid mountains and rainforest.

Parque Nacional da Serra do Cipó, Minas Gerais (p204) Huge mountain park with river valleys, adventure activities, and short and multiday hikes.

Serra de São José, Minas Gerais (p190) Short hikes through protected Atlantic rainforest in the mountains near Tiradentes.

Kayaking & Canoeing

There are some great places to get out on the water, paddle in hand, and take in the great Brazilian landscape. Foremost among them is the Amazon, where you can go canoeing through the flooded forest and winding *igarapés* (creeks or small rivers). You can also go kayaking off Ilha Grande, Paraty, on the Lagoa da Conceição on Ilha de Santa Catarina, on excursions in the Pantanal, and from Itacaré and other beach destinations in the Northeast.

For a different aquatic experience, grab an inner tube and launch down the Rio Nhundiaquara.

Surfing & Stand-Up Paddleboards

On many beaches, surfing is a way of life, and several Brazilian professionals are usually to be found in the top 20 of the world rankings. Boogie boarding is popular too.

There's surf virtually all along the coast, with particularly good waves in the South. The best surf beaches are in Santa Catarina state; the Brazilian championships are held here at Praia da Joaquina, on Ilha de Santa Catarina. São Francisco do Sul, Ilha do Mel, Ubatuba, Ilhabela, Maresias and the Boiçucanga area all serve up good waves.

There's also excellent surf just outside of Rio and within a day's travel of the city in Saquarema, Búzios and Ilha Grande. The waves are best in the Brazilian winter (from June to August).

Renting boards can be difficult outside of popular tourist areas, though. If you plan to do a lot of surfing in less-traveled places, you'll need to bring your own board.

SURFING VOCABULARY

Despite their reputation for aggressiveness in the water, once on land Brazilian surfers are fairly keen on meeting foreign surfers and hearing about their travels. Some are even willing to lend you a board if you ask politely.

body board – boogie board

onda – wave

Pode me emprestar sua prancha por favor? – Could I borrow your board please?

prancha – surfboard

quebrar – to break

surfista – surfer

Tem ondas? – Are there any waves?

Vamos pegar ondas – Let's go surfing

vento – wind

Further to the north, Itacaré, Sítio, Porto de Galinhas and Fernando de Noronha are among the better spots.

A curious event is the national *pororoca* (tidal bore) surf championship held at São Domingos do Capim at the time of the full moon nearest the March equinox. Waves can reach a few meters in height, and the rides are legendary (the record is a 12.5km, 37-minute ride).

Stand-up paddleboards are becoming increasingly popular in Brazil. You can rent them and go for a paddle in Rio (off Copacabana Beach) and in Bahia – Itacaré and Arraial d'Ajuda – among other places.

Windsurfing

Windsurfing has caught on in Brazil. In Rio you can rent equipment at Barra da Tijuca, but there are better conditions, and equipment to rent, northeast of Rio at Búzios. In São Paulo state there's good windsurfing at Ilhabela and around Boiçucanga. But Brazil's hardcore windsurfing mecca can be found much further north, along the Ceará coast, northwest of Fortaleza, where constant, regular, strong trade winds blow from July to December. Jericoacoara is one of the best spots in the country for windsurfing. Near Fortaleza, the beaches of Praia do Futuro and Praia de Iracema are also popular spots.

Plan Your Trip

Travel with Children

Long distances in Brazil can make family travel challenging, but the rewards are considerable: endless fun on sun-kissed beaches, walks in rainforests, boat and train rides, and abundant wildlife-watching opportunities. Best of all is the warm reception from Brazilians themselves, who go out of their way to make kids feel welcome.

Best Regions for Kids

Rio de Janeiro state

Funicular rides and scenic views in Rio city, island-exploring on vehicle-free Ilha Grande, wandering cobblestone streets and taking schooner cruises off Paraty. You can even get a taste of mountain scenery in Parque Nacional do Itatiaia, and visit imperial sites in Petrópolis.

Minas Gerais

Time-travel to the 18th century in the colonial mountain town of Ouro Preto, which is near an old gold mine you can visit. You can also ride an old steam train from São João del Rei to Tiradentes. Don't miss the Santuário do Caraça to take swims in waterfalls and see the maned wolf come in at night.

Bahia

Lots of great food, music and street entertainment in Salvador. Catch the hydrofoil to car-free Morro de São Paulo for pretty beaches, a zipline and panoramic views from a hilltop lighthouse. Head inland for the canyons, waterfalls and swimming holes of Parque Nacional da Chapada Diamantina.

Brazil for Kids

Brazil is a family-friendly country that has a wide range of attractions for kids. Travel here with kids does require some advance planning, but most Brazilians will do their best to make sure children are well looked after.

Eating Out

Dining out isn't usually a problem, even for fussy eaters. Ubiquitous per-kilo places are a good place for a meal: children will have a huge range of options, and you can get in and out without a lot of fuss. Familiar food – pizza, burgers, ice cream – is widely available, and sometimes takes fun new forms (pizza with chocolate, or with bananas and cinnamon). Food courts in shopping malls are excellent spots for quick meals.

Juice bars are handy for snack breaks. At these ubiquitous spots, you can order dozens of tangy juices, as well as grilled burgers, sandwiches, *pão de queijo* (cheese bread) and other bites.

Most sit-down restaurants will have a *cadeira alta* (high chair), though few have menus for kids. Portions are huge, however, so kids can share what their parents order. Bring crayons, paper or other

JUNGLE LODGES

Many jungle lodges near Manaus offer fairly low-impact excursions, making them good for families with kids. High-water season may be best, as you do more canoeing than hiking. Black-water areas have far fewer mosquitoes and much lower risk of malaria.

amusement, as Brazilian restaurants don't provide these things.

Transportation

Given the great size of Brazil, transport presents challenges. You'll either spend long hours on buses or have to rely on pricier flights. Sticking to one or two regions is the best way to keep your holiday hassle-free. Renting a car can save you cash and help you move about more efficiently.

Children typically fly free or pay half-fare for flights if aged under two, and pay 10% to 25% of the fare if age two to 12. On buses, it's all or nothing: they ride free if sitting on a lap and full fare if they take up a seat.

Children's Highlights

Coastal Highlights

Ilha Grande (west of Rio de Janeiro; p121) A tropical rainforest-covered island, an old abandoned prison, boat trips, snorkeling, lovely beaches, howler monkeys – and all of it completely free from traffic.

Balneário Camboriú (Santa Catarina; p308) This resort town has many attractions for kids, including an aerial tram, beaches and a roller coaster, all with proximity to the Beto Carrero World (p308) amusement park.

Porto Belo (Santa Catarina; p298) Another laid-back resort spot in the South, Porto Belo has lovely snorkeling, plus a scenic nature reserve and eco-museum at an island just offshore.

Arraial d'Ajuda (Bahia; p449) This low-key beach-lovers' town has the usual coastal attractions, plus you can rent a buggy for exploring sandy coastal paths around the area.

Jungle Highlights

Foz do Iguaçu & Around (Paraná; p277) The thundering waterfalls are quite family-friendly, with discount entry for kids, and kids stay and eat free all over town; there are also various wildlife adventures and boating activities.

Serra Verde Express (Paraná; p270) This memorable train ride traverses lush forests with sweeping views down to the coast.

Bonito (Mato Grosso do Sul; p391) Bonito has caves, lush rainforests, tree-top canopy walks and crystal-clear rivers that you snorkel down.

Planning

For general advice on traveling with young ones, see Lonely Planet's *Travel with Children*. Don't forget to arrange visas (if needed) before you depart.

What to Bring

If you plan on renting a car, bring your own car seats with you as availability is unreliable with most rental agencies.

Diapers (nappies) are widely available in Brazil. You may not easily find creams, baby foods or familiar medicines if you are outside larger cities. Bring insect repellent, sunscreen and other essentials, as prices for these things are much higher here.

Baby food is available in most supermarkets.

Health & Safety

If you are planning a trip outside of the main coastal cities, you'll need to enquire about vaccines and anti-malarial medications (particularly for the Amazon).

When to Go

To beat the worst of the crowds, but still enjoy warm beach weather, plan on coming from November through January or late March and April.

Accommodations

Children under five typically stay free. Under-12s often pay half-price. Cribs (cots) are not always available, so have an alternative plan before arriving.

Babysitters are readily available in most hotels.

Regions at a Glance

The great challenge of Brazil, with its vast size and incredible diversity, is deciding where to go. Rio figures high on most itineraries, with nightlife, beaches and scenery. Tropical islands and the historic colonial towns of Minas Gerais lie nearby. The Northeast offers a mix of picturesque towns, beaches and outdoor adventures, and its vibrant cities (Salvador, Olinda) offer a window into rich Afro-Brazilian culture. The South, meanwhile, has notable European influence (Oktoberfests, vineyards, mountain towns) and stellar highlights such as Iguaçu Falls and the Ilha de Santa Catarina. For outstanding wildlife watching, visit the Pantanal (Cuiabá in Mato Grosso is a major gateway) and the Amazon. Other Brazilian hits include modernist architecture in Brasília, otherworldly dune landscapes in Maranhão, and the jaw-dropping island beauty of Fernando de Noronha.

Rio de Janeiro City

Scenery
Nightlife
Culture

Mountains & Beaches

Rainforest-covered peaks, sparkling beaches and a coastline dotted with islands – Rio's setting is breathtaking, especially when viewed from panoramic heights atop Corcovado or Pão de Açúcar.

Sounds of Samba

Rio's dizzying nightlife includes open-air bars, stylish nightclubs and old-school dance halls dominated by the addictive rhythms of samba.

Historic Treasures

At first glance, Rio's downtown is a bustling hive of business and commerce. Look deeper, and you'll discover surprising landmarks, including 18th-century baroque churches, a former royal palace and an extravagant opera house.

p50

Rio de Janeiro State

Beaches
Outdoor Adventure
History

Sun, Surf & Sand

For easy access to dreamy beaches, Rio state is as good as it gets, from gleaming white dunes to island-studded bays backed by jungle-clad mountains.

Hiking & Climbing Paradise

The crags of Itatiaia and the peaks of the Serra dos Órgãos are the twin capitals of Brazilian rock climbing; hikers also thrill to the wild trails of Serra da Bocaina and Ilha Grande.

The Golden Road & Imperial Past

Near Paraty, the 18th-century Caminho do Ouro once brought gold from Minas Gerais, while Dom Pedro II's Petrópolis palace was the 19th-century seat of Brazilian imperial power.

p120

Minas Gerais & Espírito Santo

History
Food
Outdoors

Baroque Grandeur

With an incredible density of historical monuments, Minas' *cidades históricas* (historic colonial towns) are showcases for Brazil's baroque style.

Bountiful Feast

From Espírito Santo's delectable seafood stews to Minas' hearty wood-fired ranch fare, this is foodie paradise. Don't forget the obligatory shot of smooth *Minas cachaça* (Brazil's best).

Wildlife & Waterfalls

With natural pools and waterfalls, Minas' cerrado ecosystem is a hiker's dream. To the east, awe-inspiring mountains rear their heads and patches of rainforest shelter the endangered *muriqui* (woolly spider monkey).

p162

São Paulo State

Food & Drink
Beaches
Landscapes

Culinary Powerhouse

São Paulo city holds its own with any gastronomic capital in the southern hemisphere. Cutting-edge Brazilian chefs such as Alex Atala (D.O.M.) and Helena Rizzo (Maní) have received worldwide acclaim. And then there's the nightlife, baby!

The Green Coast

From the rainforest-lined coast of Ubatuba to the sophisticated getaway of Ilhabela, São Paulo's coastline is part of Brazil's Costa Verde (Green Coast), a world-class stretch of postcard-perfect beaches and islands.

Scenic Setting

Wide swaths of Mata Atlântica rainforest, modest but wonderful Serra de Mantiqueira peaks and sun-kissed sands: São Paulo is easy on the eyes.

p218

Paraná

Scenery
Nature
Architecture

Photogenic Panoramas

Besides the spectacular Iguaçu Falls, splendid scenery awaits elsewhere, most notably on the car-free island retreat of Ilha do Mel, and the superb Serra Verde Express train, which snakes past lushly covered mountains from Curitiba to the tranquil town of Morretes.

Waterfalls, Islands & Rainforest

Iguaçu Falls offers impressive hiking and adventure excursions amid subtropical rainforest, while isolated Parque Nacional do Superagüi and Parque Estadual Marumbi boast abundant bird and plant life.

A Glorious Past

Morretes, Paranaguá and Curitiba's Largo da Ordem are cobblestoned glimpses into Brazil's colonial past.

p263

Santa Catarina

Beaches
Culture
Microbreweries

Seductive Shorelines

Whether you seek solitude, surf or socializing, Santa Catarina has the sands for you. The state has outstanding surfing, laid-back fishing villages, rainforest-backed beaches and sophisticated resort towns.

European Past

Nowhere is Brazil's rich melting pot more evident than throughout Santa Catarina's interior, where German architecture, Italian and German food, and distinctly European faces will leave you wondering if you've received a new passport stamp upon arrival.

Brew Culture

Brazil's best microbrews hail from Blumenau and its environs, offering the chance to sample beers unavailable in most other parts of the country.

p288

Rio Grande do Sul

Landscapes
Wine Tasting
Culture

Canyonlands

Parque Nacional de Aparados da Serra and Parque Nacional da Serra Geral offer Southern Brazil's most striking landscape. Magnificent canyons have earned the region the nickname of the 'Brazilian Grand Canyon.'

Venerable Vineyards

Around 90% of Brazilian wine comes from the Vale dos Vinhedos, a little touch of Tuscany in the heart of Cowboy Country that defies notions of typical Brazil.

Gaúcho Traditions

With its *chimarrão* (*maté* tea), *churrasco* (grilled meat) and traditional Farroupilha dress, Rio Grande do Sul's *gaúcho* (cowboy) culture lives on in this unique region.

p314

Brasília & Goiás

Architecture
Scenery
Culture

A Capital Idea

Niemeyer's genius proved that a few bags of concrete and a creative mind were all that was needed to make Brasília a must-see for building buffs.

Striking Panoramas

The breathakingly beautiful cerrado is the perfect frame for heavenly sunsets on the planalto, especially at the otherworldly Vale da Lua in the Chapada dos Veadeiros.

Medieval Mischief

Pirenópolis converts itself from a kooky artists' enclave into a centre of historical re-creation, as the town goes medieval during the Festa do Divino Espírito Santo (Cavalhadas).

p333

Mato Grosso & Mato Grosso do Sul

Aquatic Adventure
Wildlife Watching
Fishing

Surreal Snorkeling

Squeeze into your wetsuit and let the current take you on a fish-watching adventure in the aquatic playgrounds of Bonito and Nobres.

Animal Encounters

The Pantanal has incredible wildlife watching, with capybaras, anacondas, macaws, capuchins and giant river otters just a few of many species you're likely to see.

Catch Your Dinner

Sling your hook for some of the world's best fishing in the waterways of Mato Grosso and maybe pick up a pacu!

p361

Bahia

Beaches
Outdoor Adventure
Culture

Bahian Beauty

Featuring more than 900km of coastline, the state of Bahia is rightfully renowned for its gorgeous beaches, from idyllic island getaways and surfers' hot spots to quiet fishing villages.

Hiking & Trekking

Head inland to see one of Brazil's finest national parks, Chapada Diamantina, which has great hiking and trekking, plus waterfalls, natural swimming holes and other idyllic spots to cool off.

Afro-Brazilian Star

Salvador is the center of Afro-Brazilian culture: capoeira and Candomblé, glittering churches, and pounding drums on the cobblestoned streets of the Pelourinho. Nearby Cachoeira is renowned for its woodcarving traditions.

p397

Sergipe & Alagoas

Scenery
History
Seafood

Coastal Allure

Alagoas' star attraction is its coastline, with its white-sand beaches and aquamarine waters. Top picks include Praia do Francês, Praia do Gunga and buzzing Maceió. The Galés marine reserve off the coast of Maragogi is a favorite for snorkelers.

Colonial Remnants

These neighboring states have a number of colonial highlights, including the grand churches of historic Penedo, cobblestone Laranjeiras and hilltop São Cristóvão.

Dining & Dancing

Seafood lovers won't want to miss the open-air restaurants of Aracaju, which specialize in fresh crabs; many also serve up live *forró* music, which makes a great ending to a crab feast.

p465

Pernambuco, Paraíba & Rio Grande do Norte

Beaches
Festivals
Outdoors

Endless Sands

The 1000km coast curving round Brazil's northeast corner is a succession of sandy beaches fronted by enticing tropical waters; bask on the beach, sip coconuts and enjoy great meals in laid-back beach bars.

Carnaval, Northeastern Style

During Carnaval, head to the contrasting neighboring cities Recife and Olinda for their unbelievably euphoric explosions of color, music and fun.

Shoreline Adventures

This is the place for swimming, snorkeling, surfing, kitesurfing or buggy-riding. Fernando de Noronha, an archipelago getaway 350km offshore, has Brazil's best diving and snorkeling.

p483

Ceará, Piauí & Maranhão

Scenery
Outdoors
Cities & Towns

Dunes & Bays

The setting is spectacular: a sequence of long, dune-backed sweeps and small, palm-lined bays all along the tropical shoreline. There's also the unique dune-and-lagoon mosaic of the Lençóis Maranhenses.

Sun-Drenched Adventures

You can do most things you've dreamed of in, on and beside the water, with steady winds providing some of the world's best conditions for kitesurfing.

Coastal Enclaves

Hang out at legendary Jericoacoara, enjoy the urban vibes of Fortaleza or head to end-of-road beach villages like Atins or Icaraí de Amontada for a tropical escape.

p531

The Amazon

Wildlife Watching
Adventure
Culture

Biodiversity Hotspot

The Amazon is a fabled setting for wildlife watching. You can stay in rainforest resorts or community-run ecotourism outfits, both great bases for seeing wildlife.

Rainforest Experiences

The world's greatest rainforest offers memorable adventures, from tree-climbs through dense canopy, to silent canoe paddles across flooded forest. You can also take multiday boat trips between towns.

Amazonian Riches

Culturally rich cities such as Belém and Manaus are the best places to sample Amazonian cuisine, hear unique musical styles and browse colorful markets. There are beach towns in the interior and on the coast.

p569

On the Road

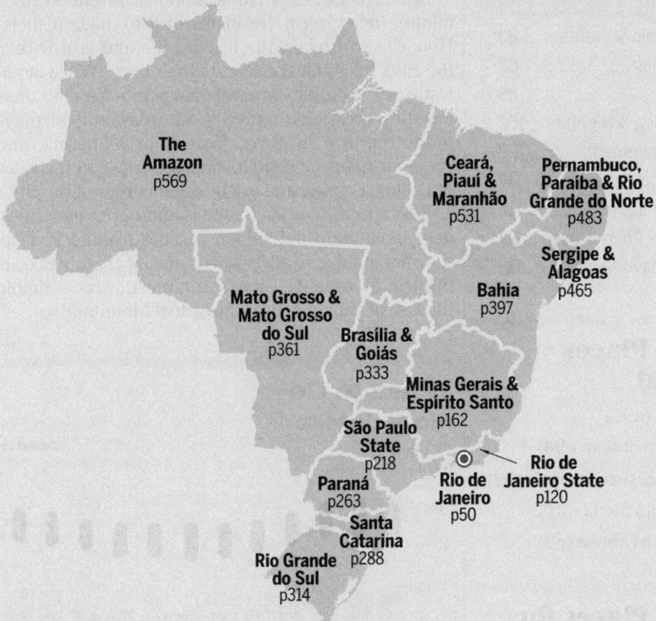

The Amazon
p569

Ceará, Piauí & Maranhão
p531

Pernambuco, Paraíba & Rio Grande do Norte
p483

Sergipe & Alagoas
p465

Bahia
p397

Mato Grosso & Mato Grosso do Sul
p361

Brasília & Goiás
p333

Minas Gerais & Espírito Santo
p162

São Paulo State
p218

Rio de Janeiro State
p120

Rio de Janeiro
p50

Paraná
p263

Santa Catarina
p288

Rio Grande do Sul
p314

Rio de Janeiro City

☎0XX21 / POP 6.35 MILLION

Includes ➡

Best Places to Eat

- ➡ Lasai (p99)
- ➡ CT Boucherie (p94)
- ➡ Zazá Bistrô Tropical (p93)
- ➡ Espírito Santa (p102)
- ➡ Ferro e Farinha (p99)

Best Places for Nightlife

- ➡ Cabaret Lounge (p106)
- ➡ Estrelas da Babilônia (p103)
- ➡ Palaphita Kitch (p104)
- ➡ Comuna (p106)
- ➡ Rio Scenarium (p109)

Why Go?

Planted between lush, forest-covered mountains and breathtaking beaches, the Cidade Maravilhosa (Marvelous City) has many charms at its disposal.

Although joie de vivre is a French invention (as is the bikini), the *cariocas* (residents of Rio) made it their own. How else to explain the lust for life and zeal with which the city's inhabitants celebrate their days? While large-scale festivities such as Carnaval make Rio famous, there are countless occasions for revelry: Saturdays at Ipanema Beach, *festas* (parties) in Lapa, football at Maracanã, and impromptu *rodas de samba* (samba circles) on the sidewalks of Leblon, Copacabana or any other corner of the city.

Rio's spectacular landscape is another of its virtues. Verdant mountains and golden beaches fronting a deep blue sea offer a range of adventures: surfing great breaks, hiking through Floresta da Tijuca's rainforest or rock climbing up the face of Pão de Açúcar (Sugarloaf Mountain).

When to Go

Rio de Janeiro

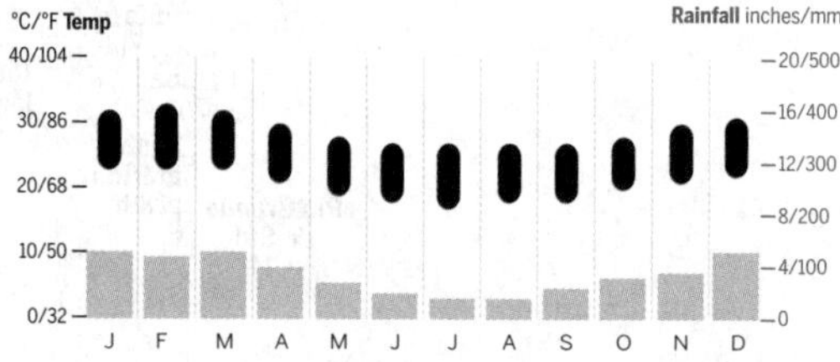

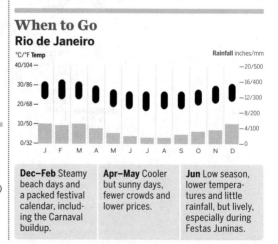

Dec–Feb Steamy beach days and a packed festival calendar, including the Carnaval buildup.

Apr–May Cooler but sunny days, fewer crowds and lower prices.

Jun Low season, lower temperatures and little rainfall, but lively, especially during Festas Juninas.

History

Portuguese explorer Gonçalo Coelho was the first European to land in Rio. In January 1502 he entered a huge bay, which he allegedly mistook for a river, thus bequeathing the future city its lasting moniker. Portuguese settlement proceeded in fits and starts, but by the 17th century Rio was Brazil's third-most important settlement (after Salvador da Bahia and Recife-Olinda). African slaves streamed in and the sugar plantations thrived. Even more slaves arrived to work in the gold mines of Minas Gerais during the 18th century.

In 1807 the Portuguese prince regent (later known as Dom João VI) and his entire court of 15,000 set sail for Brazil to escape the impending invasion of Napoleon Bonaparte.

Dom João fell in love with Brazil. He declared Rio the capital of the United Kingdom of Portugal, Brazil and the Algarve. He became the only European monarch to rule from a New World colony.

At the end of the 19th century the city's population exploded as a result of European immigration and internal migration (mostly of ex-slaves from the declining coffee and sugar regions).

The early 1920s to the late 1950s were Rio's golden age. With the inauguration of the grand hotels, Rio became a romantic, exotic destination for Hollywood celebrities and high society.

During the 1960s, modern skyscrapers rose in the city, and some of Rio's most beautiful buildings were lost. During the same period, the favelas (slums, informal communities) of Rio grew to critical mass, with immigrants from poverty-stricken areas of the Northeast swelling the number of Rio's urban poor. The Cidade Maravilhosa began to lose its gloss as crime and violence increased.

As Rio entered the new millennium, social problems continued to plague the city, with violence claiming thousands of lives – particularly in the favelas. Rio's middle and upper classes seemed mostly resigned to life behind gated and guarded condos, while poverty and violence surged in the slums nearby.

While violence and poverty still remain worrying problems in Rio, things have improved in the past decade. Favela pacification (a program that removed drug lords and installed a permanent police presence in some favelas) has brought down the level of violence, while sanitation and transport have also improved in some favelas. In the build-up to the 2014 World Cup and 2016 Summer Olympics, large investments have been used to revitalize Rio's waterfront port, vastly expand its metro system and create new museums and cultural spaces around town.

⊙ Sights

The once mighty 'capital of the Brazilian empire' (as one Portuguese king called it), Rio has much more than just pretty beaches. From the bohemian lanes of old Santa Teresa to the village charm of Urca, Rio's colonial streets, magnificent churches and leafy plazas provide urban wanderers with days of exploration.

Rio's historic center, its lake (Lagoa Rodrigo de Freitas), the lush Jardim Botânico (Botanical Gardens) and the Atlantic rainforest that trims many parts of the city make for some fascinating discovery. There are also fantastic overlooks from Pão de Açúcar and Cristo Redentor, tranquil islands in the bay, wildly beautiful beaches to the west, and vibrant markets, with vendors peddling everything from vintage samba recordings to tangy *jabuticaba* (a native fruit).

⊙ Ipanema & Leblon

Truly among the world's most enchanting addresses, Ipanema and Leblon are blessed with a magnificent beach, and open-air cafes, bars and restaurants scattered along tree-lined streets. Here you'll find a mix of wealthy *cariocas*, young and old, gay and straight.

★Ipanema Beach BEACH

(Map p54; Av Vieira Souto) One long stretch of sun-drenched sand, Ipanema Beach is demarcated by *postos* (posts), which mark off subcultures as diverse as the city itself. *Posto* 9, right off Rua Vinícius de Moraes, is where Rio's most lithe and tanned bodies migrate. The area is also known as Cemetério dos Elefantes because of the handful of old leftists, hippies and artists who sometimes hang out there. In front of Rua Farme de Amoedo is Praia Farme, the stomping ground for gay society.

Praia de Leblon BEACH

(Map p54) Separated from Ipanema by the gardens and canal of Jardim de Alah, Leblon Beach attracts families and has a slightly more sedate vibe than its eastern counterpart. Parents with little ones may want to

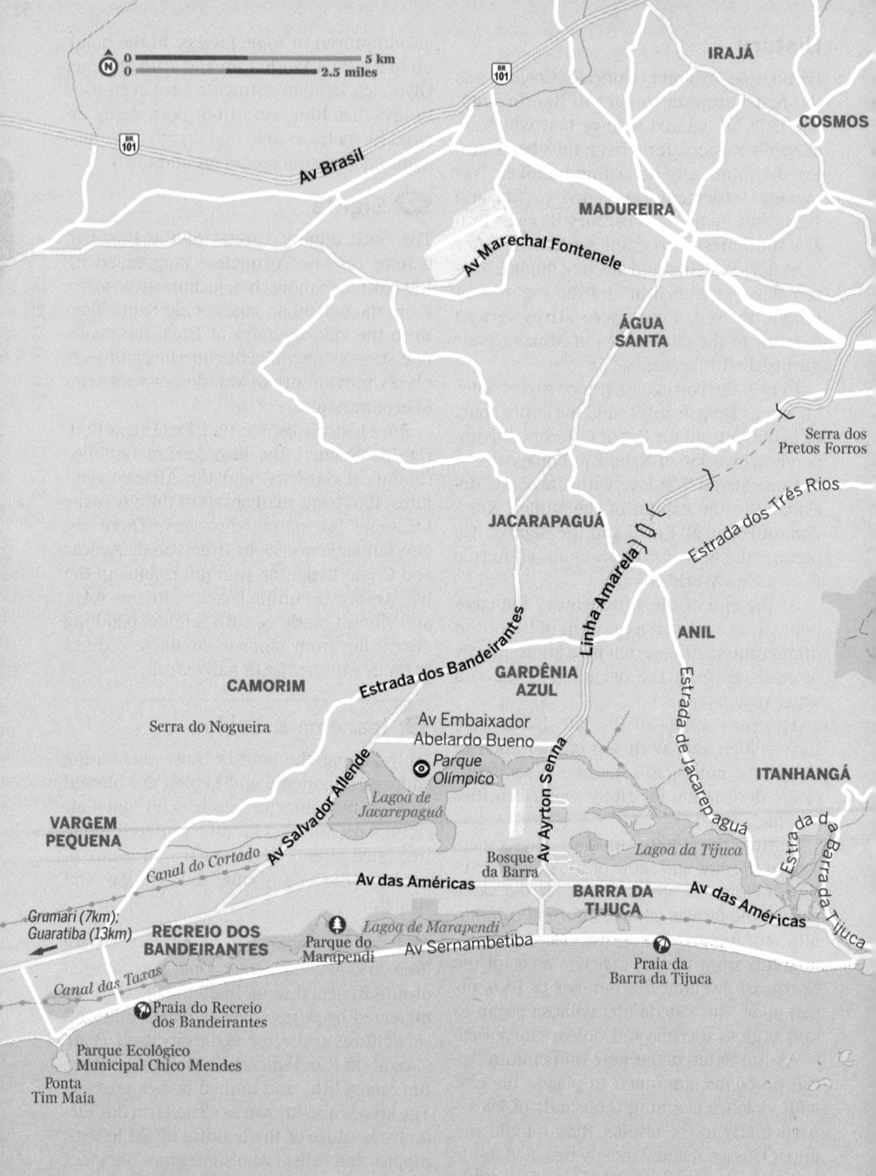

Rio de Janeiro City Highlights

1. Frolicking in the waves, while watching the parade of passing people on lovely **Ipanema Beach** (p51).
2. Basking in the sunshine on **Copacabana Beach** (p60), followed by drinks at an oceanfront kiosk.
3. Taking the cog train up Corcovado for stunning views beneath the open-armed **Cristo Redentor** (p65).
4. Finding the perfect beat at a samba club in **Lapa** (p108), Brazil's most musically charged neighborhood.

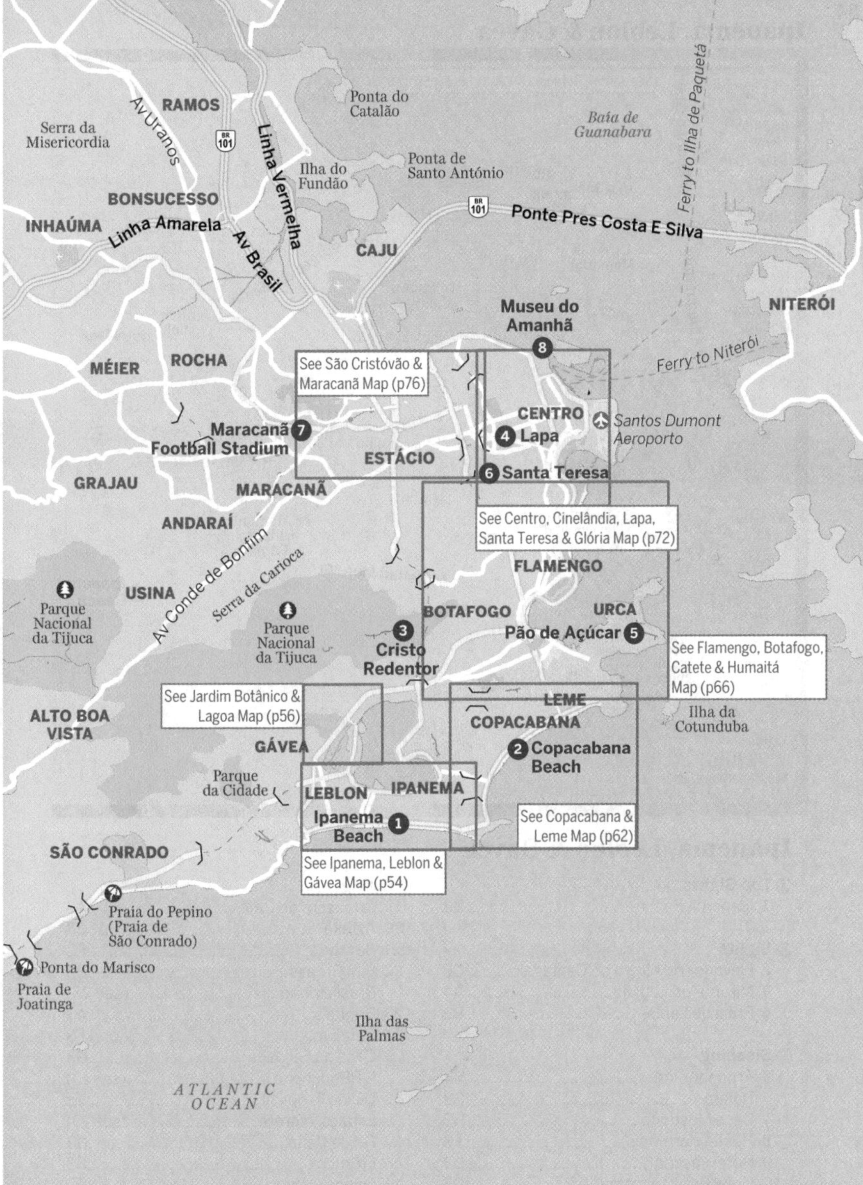

❺ Admiring the Cidade Maravilhosa from the craggy heights of **Pão de Açúcar** (p61).

❻ Catching the *bonde* (cable car) up to **Santa Teresa** and take a scenic stroll through this village-like neighborhood.

❼ Feeling the roar of the crowds inside hallowed **Maracanã Football Stadium** (p112).

❽ Contemplating the future in the new **Museu do Amanhã** (p68) on revitalized Praça Mauá.

Ipanema, Leblon & Gávea

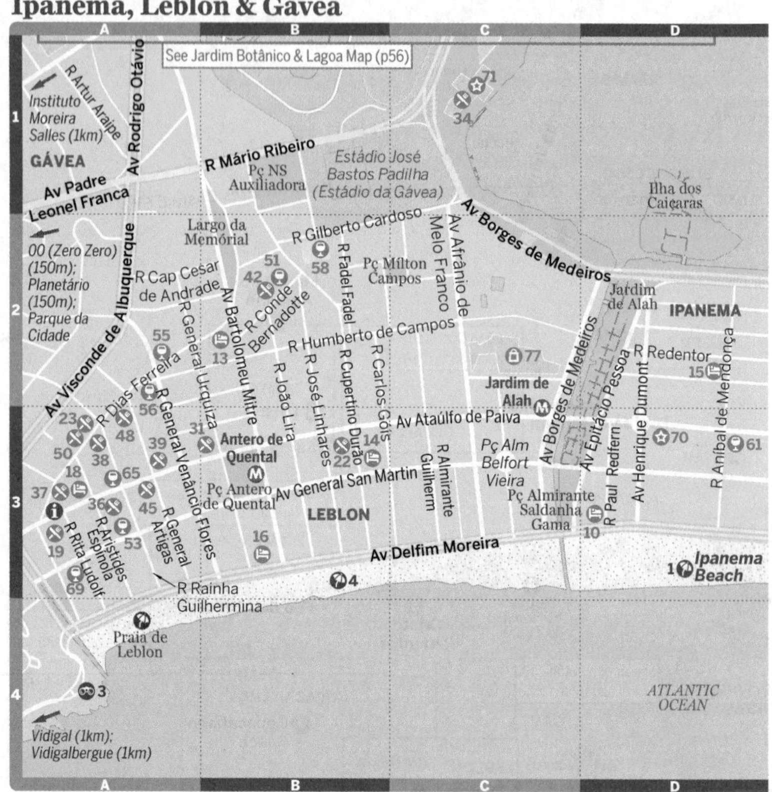

Ipanema, Leblon & Gávea

Top Sights

1 Ipanema Beach D3

Sights

2 Elevador do Morro do Cantagalo G2
3 Mirante do Leblon A4
4 Praia de Leblon B3

Sleeping

5 Arpoador Inn H4
6 Bonita G3
7 Casa Mosquito H3
8 Hostel Harmonia F3
9 Hotel Fasano G3
10 Hotel Praia Ipanema D3
11 Ipanema For Rent F3
12 Ipanema Hotel Residência F2
13 Leblon Spot Design Hostel B2
14 Lemon Spirit Hostel B3
15 Margarida's Pousada D2
16 Marina All Suites B3
17 Rio Hostel – Ipanema H3
18 Ritz Plaza Hotel A3

Eating

19 Armazém do Café A3
20 Azteka G3
21 Bazzar E2
22 Bibi Crepes B3
Brasileirinho .... (see 25)
23 Brigite's A3
24 Cafeína F3
25 Casa da Feijoada G3
CT Boucherie .... (see 13)
26 Delírio Tropical E3
Espaço 7zero6 .... (see 10)
27 Felice Caffè G3
28 Frontera G3
29 Gringo Cafe F2
30 Koni Store E3
31 Kurt B3
32 La Carioca Cevicheria E2
33 Laffa G3
34 Lagoon C1
35 New Natural F3
36 Prima Bruschetteria A3
37 Stuzzi A3
38 Sushi Leblon A3
39 Talho Capixaba A3

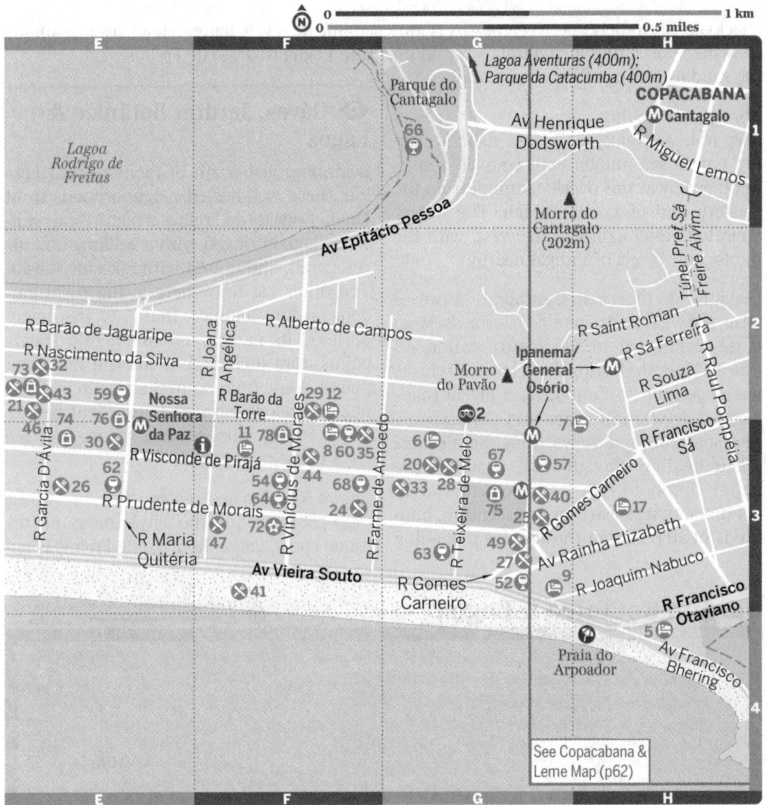

40 Terzetto Cafe G3
41 Uruguai F3
42 Vegetariano Social Club B2
43 Venga! E2
44 Vero F3
45 Vezpa A3
46 Via Sete E2
47 Zazá Bistrô Tropical F3
48 Zona Sul Supermarket A3
49 Zona Sul Supermarket G3
50 Zuka A3

Drinking & Nightlife

51 Academia Da Cachaça B2
52 Bar Astor G3
53 Bar Veloso A3
Baretto-Londra .... (see 9)
54 Barzin F3
55 Belmonte A2
56 Brewteco A2
57 Canastra G3
58 Cobal do Leblon B2
59 Complex Esquina 111 .... E2
60 Delirium Cafe F3
61 Devassa D3
62 Empório E3
63 Galeria Café G3
64 Garota de Ipanema F3
65 Jobi A3
66 Palaphita Kitch G1
67 Shenanigan's G3
68 Tô Nem Aí F3
69 Usina A3

Entertainment

70 Estação Net Ipanema D3
71 Miranda C1
72 Vinícius Show Bar F3

Shopping

73 10Aquim E2
74 Gilson Martins E3
75 Hippie Fair G3
Maria Oiticica .... (see 77)
76 Osklen E2
77 Shopping Leblon C2
78 Toca do Vinícius F3

check out Baixo Bebê, between *postos* 11 and 12, where you'll find a small playground on the sand as well as other young families.

Mirante do Leblon LOOKOUT
(Map p54; Av Niemeyer) A few fishers casting out to sea mingle with couples admiring the view at this overlook uphill from the western end of Leblon Beach. The luxury Sheraton Hotel looms to the west, with the photogenic favela of Vidigal nearby.

Elevador do Morro do Cantagalo VIEWPOINT
(Map p54; Barão da Torre & Teixeira de Melo) FREE Connected to the metro station off Praça General Osório, this elevator whisks passengers up to Cantagalo, a favela that's wedged between Ipanema and Copacabana. The sparkling sea views from the elevator are quite fine, though local residents are happy simply to have a convenient way to get home that doesn't mean ascending hundreds of steps. From the top, keep heading uphill for even better views over Ipanema and Lagoa Rodrigo de Freitas.

Gávea, Jardim Botânico & Lagoa

Beginning just north of Ipanema and Leblon, these well-heeled neighborhoods front Lagoa Rodrigo de Freitas, a picturesque saltwater lagoon ringed with a walking and cycling trail, and dotted with lakeside kiosks. The other big draw here is the royal garden, Jardim Botânico, that gave the neighborhood its name. Here you'll find stately palms, rare orchids and colorful flowering plants. Aside from natural attractions, these neighborhoods have some excellent restaurants, trendy bars, a planetarium and the city's horse-racing track.

Lagoa Rodrigo de Freitas LAKE
(Map p56) One of the city's most picturesque spots, Lagoa Rodrigo de Freitas is en-

Jardim Botânico & Lagoa

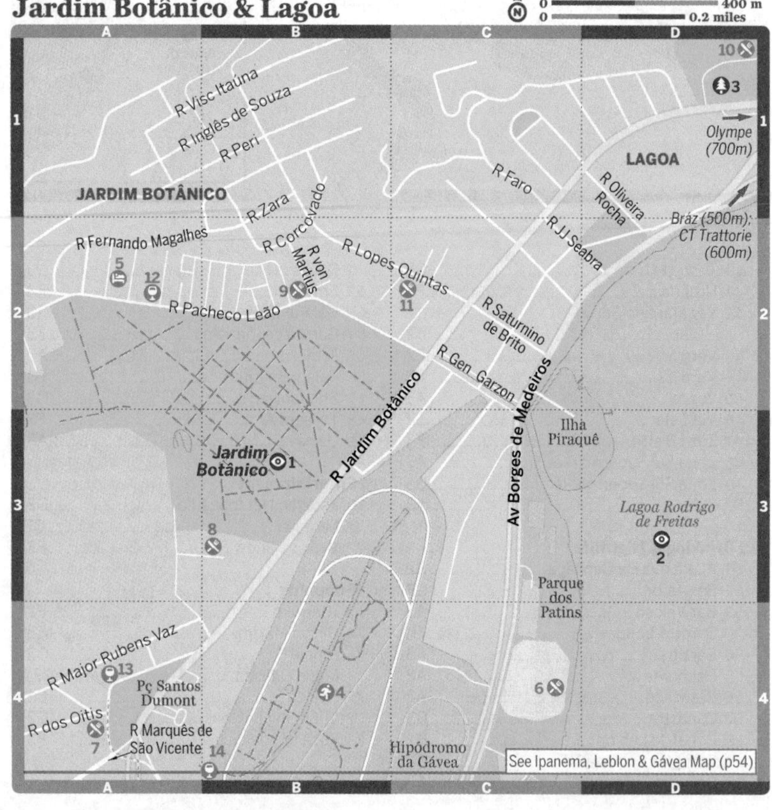

circled by a 7.2km walking and cycling path. Bikes are available for hire from stands along the east side of the lake, as are paddle boats. For those who prefer caipirinhas (cocktails) to plastic swan boats, the **lakeside kiosks** on either side of the lake offer alfresco food and drinks, sometimes accompanied by live music on warm nights.

Jardim Botânico GARDENS

(Map p56; ☎3874-1808; www.jbrj.gov.br; Jardim Botânico 920; admission R$9; 9am-5pm) This exotic 137-hectare garden, with more than 8000 plant species, was designed by order of the Prince Regent Dom João (later to become Dom João VI) in 1808. The garden is quiet and serene on weekdays and blossoms with families on weekends. Highlights of a visit here include the row of palms (planted when the garden first opened), the Amazonas section, the lake containing the huge Vitória Régia water lilies, and the enclosed **orquidário**, home to 600 species of orchids.

Planetário PLANETARIUM

(☎2274-0046; www.planetariodorio.com.br; Av Padre Leonel Franca 240; adult/child R$12/6, incl cúpula session R$24/12; 9am-noon & 2-5pm Mon-Fri, 2:30-5pm Sat & Sun) Gávea's stellar attraction, the Planetário features a museum, a *praça dos telescópios* (telescopes' square) and a couple of state-of-the-art operating *cúpulas* (domes), each capable of projecting more than 6000 stars onto its walls. Forty-minute sessions in the domes take place on weekends and holidays. Visitors can also take a peek at the night sky through the telescopes on Wednesdays from 7:30pm to 8:30pm (6:30pm to 7:30pm from June to August).

Parque Lage PARK

(Map p56; ☎3257-1800, guided visits 3257-18721; www.eavparquelage.rj.gov.br; Jardim Botânico 414; 9am-7pm) This beautiful park lies at the base of Floresta da Tijuca, about 1km from Jardim Botânico. It has English-style gardens, little lakes, and a mansion that houses the **Escola de Artes Visuais** (School of Visual Arts), which hosts free art exhibitions and occasional performances. The park is a tranquil place and the cafe here offers a fine setting for a coffee or a meal.

Parque da Catacumba PARK

(☎2247-9949; www.parquedacatacumba.com.br; Av Epitácio Pessoa; 8am-5pm Tue-Sun) On the edge of the Lagoa Rodrigo de Freitas, across a busy road, this park and sculptural garden has a short but steep trail to the Mirante do Sacopã lookout, which offers memorable views from a height of 130m above Lagoa. It's a 15-minute walk along a 600m forest-lined path. For a bit more excitement, you can scale a rock-climbing wall, go rappelling (abseiling) or take a treetop walk offered by **Lagoa Aventuras** (☎4105-0079; www.lagoaaventuras.com.br; Av Epitácio Pessoa 3000; zipline R$20, climbing wall R$25, treetop walk R$35, rappelling R$130; 9:30am-4:30pm Tue-Sun;).

Instituto Moreira Salles CULTURAL CENTER

(IMS; ☎3284-7400; www.ims.com.br; Marquês de São Vicente 476; 11am-8pm Tue-Sun) FREE This beautiful cultural center hosts impressive exhibitions, often showcasing the works of some of Brazil's best photographers and artists. The gardens, complete with artificial lake and flowing river, were designed by Brazilian landscape architect Roberto Burle Marx. There's also a craft shop and a quaint cafe that serves lunch and afternoon tea.

Parque da Cidade PARK

(☎2512-2353; www.rio.rj.gov.br/cultura; Estrada de Santa Marinha 505; 8am-5pm Tue-Sun) On the outer reaches of Gávea, this lush park of native Mata Atlântica rainforest and replanted

Jardim Botânico & Lagoa

LONELY PLANET IMAGES / GETTY IMAGES ©

1. Carioca da Gema (p109)
Samba music and dancing in this warmly lit club.

2. Ipanema Beach (p51)
This long stretch of sand is very popular.

3. Bonde (p75)
The *bonde* that travels up to Santa Teresa from Centro is the last of the historic streetcars that once crisscrossed the city.

4. Cristo Redentor (p65)
Christ the Redeemer gazes over Rio with a placid expression on his face.

LPHILIPPE COHAT / GETTY IMAGES ©

ANDY CAULFIELD / GETTY IMAGES ©

3

JOHN W BANAGAN / GETTY IMAGES ©

secondary forest provides a refreshing escape from the heavy traffic on nearby Rua Marques de São Vicente. Local residents come to jog here, to go for long walks with their dogs, and to let their kids run about at the large playground.

Copacabana & Leme

Framed by mountains and deep blue sea, Rio's most beautiful beach curves 4.5km from end to end. No longer a symbol of Rio's glamour, Copacabana is a fascinating but chaotic place, its art deco buildings, aging beachfront hotels and tree-lined side streets forming the backdrop to a wildly democratic mix of tourists, elderly middle-class *cariocas*, and favela dwellers (who live in the hillsides surrounding the neighborhood). Despite its faults, the neighborhood has its charms: old-school *botecos* (small open-air bars), eclectic restaurants, vibrant street life and the handsome beach still entrance many visitors.

★Copacabana Beach BEACH

(Map p62; Av Atlântica) A magnificent confluence of land and sea, the long, scalloped beach of Copacabana extends for some 4.5km, with a flurry of activity along its length: over-amped soccer players singing their team's anthem; *cariocas* and tourists lining up for caipirinhas at kiosks; favela kids showing off their soccer skills; and beach vendors shouting out their wares among the tanned beach bodies.

Museu do Imagem e Som MUSEUM

(Map p62; www.mis.rj.gov.br; Av Atlântica, near Miguel Lemos) Copacabana finally has an outstanding rainy-day attraction, thanks to the stunning Museum of Image and Sound, which opens in 2016. The building, designed by celebrated New York firm Diller Scofidio + Renfro (who also designed NYC's High Line), will feature high-tech interactive galleries devoted to the great Brazilian music and film that has played such a pivotal role in the nation's culture. Performance halls and an open-air rooftop amphitheater (for outdoor films) are other highlights.

Forte de Copacabana FORT

(Map p62; ☎2521-1032; Av Atlântica & Rua Francisco Otaviano; adult/child R$6/free; ⏲10am-7:30pm Tue-Sun) Built in 1914 on the promontory of the old Our Lady of Copacabana chapel, the fort of Copacabana was one of Rio's premier defenses against attack. You can still see its original features, including walls that are up to 12m thick, defended by Krupp cannons. Inside is a museum with several floors of exhibits tracing the early days of the Portuguese colony through to the mid-19th century. The views out across the full length of Copacabana are striking.

There are several cafes with fine vantage points, including Cafe Colombo (p97).

Forte Duque de Caxias FORT

(Forte do Leme; Map p62; ☎3223-5076; Praça Almirante Júlio de Noronha; adult/child R$4/free; ⏲9:30am-4:30pm Tue-Sun) More commonly known as Forte do Leme, this military base is open to the public. Visitors can walk to the top of Morro do Leme (Leme Mountain) along a steep 800m trail that passes through Atlantic rainforest. At the top stands an 18th-century fort affording magnificent views of Pão de Açúcar and the Cagarras Islands.

Botafogo

A largely middle-class residential area, Botafogo boasts some fine, small museums, several cinemas and some lively bars and restaurants.

Museu do Índio MUSEUM

(Map p66; ☎3214-8700; www.museudoindio.org.br; Rua das Palmeiras 55; ⏲9am-5:30pm Tue-Fri, 1-5pm Sat & Sun) FREE Featuring multimedia exhibitions on Brazil's northern tribes, the small Museu do Índio provides an excellent introduction to the economic, religious and social life of Brazil's indigenous people. Next to native food and medicinal plants, the four life-size dwellings in the courtyard were actually built by four different tribes.

GaleRio GALLERY

(Map p66; São Clemente 117; ⏲10am-6pm Mon-Fri) FREE Set in a grand 19th-century mansion on busy São Clemente, GaleRio is a showcase of cutting-edge urban street art. You'll find a changing array of paintings, installations, sculptures and repurposed objects (like stop signs turned into panoramic backdrops or payphone booths transformed into furniture).

Urca

The tranquil, shady streets of Urca offer a pleasant escape from the urban bustle of other parts of the city. An eclectic mix of

HISTORICAL SITES

Paço Imperial (p71) The former imperial palace was home to the royal family when they arrived from Portugal.

Praça XV (Quinze) de Novembro (p71) Named after the date Brazil declared itself a republic (November 15, 1822), this plaza has witnessed a lot of historical action, including the crowning of two emperors and the abolition of slavery.

Travessa do Comércio (p71) This narrow alley is a window into colonial Rio, with 18th-century buildings converted into bars and restaurants.

Museu Histórico Nacional (p69) Set in the 18th-century royal arsenal, this museum houses Rio's best assortment of historical artifacts.

Jardim Botânico (p57) Prince Regent Dom João VI ensured the city would have no shortage of green spaces, and ordered this verdant garden planted in 1808.

Museu da República (p65) Formerly known as the Palácio do Catete, this mansion was Brazil's presidential home from 1896 to 1954. Getúlio Vargas was the last president to live here; he committed suicide in one of the upstairs rooms.

Praça Floriano (p71) Centro's picturesque main square has long been the meeting ground for popular demonstrations, including uprisings against the military dictatorship in the 1960s and more recent protests against government corruption.

Garota de Ipanema (Map p54; ☎2522-0340; Vinícius de Moraes 49; ⊙noon-2am) Famed drinking spot where Tom Jobim and Vinícius de Moraes penned the song 'The Girl from Ipanema', whose international success introduced the world to bossa nova.

building styles and manicured gardens lines its streets, where local residents like to stroll. Along the sea wall, which forms the northwestern perimeter of Pão de Açúcar, fishers cast for dinner as couples lounge beneath palm trees, taking in views of Baía de Guanabara and Cristo Redentor off in the distance. Tiny Praia Vermelha, in the south, has one of Rio's finest beach views. A short but scenic walking trail begins from here.

★Pão de Açúcar MOUNTAIN
(Sugarloaf Mountain; Map p66; ☎2546-8400; www.bondinho.com.br; Av Pasteur 520, Urca; adult/child R$62/31; ⊙8am-7:50pm) Seen from the peak of Pão de Açúcar, Rio is undoubtedly a Cidade Maravilhosa (Marvelous City). There are many good times to make the ascent, but sunset on a clear day is the most rewarding. Two cable cars connect to the summit, 396m above Rio. At the top, the city unfolds beneath you, with Corcovado mountain and Cristo Redentor (Christ the Redeemer) off to the west, and Copacabana Beach to the south.

Praia Vermelha BEACH
(Map p66; Praça General Tibúrcio) Beneath Morro da Urca, narrow Praia Vermelha has superb views of the rocky coastline from the shore. Its coarse sand gives the beach the name *vermelha* (red). Because the beach is protected by the headland, the water is usually calm.

Pista Cláudio Coutinho WALKING TRAIL
(Map p66; ⊙6am-sunset) Everyone loves this paved 2km trail winding along the southern contour of Morro da Urca. It's a lush treed area, with the waves crashing on the rocks below. Look out for families of marmosets with their gray fur, striped tails and tiny faces. To get there, walk 100m north along the edge of Praia Vermelha (with your back to the cable-car station) and you'll see the entrance to the path straight ahead, just past the beach.

About 300m along the path, there's a small trail leading off to Morro da Urca. From there you can have a fine view over the city that won't cost a thing (except plenty of sweat – the path up is steep!). Pão de Açúcar can also be climbed – but it's not recommended without an experienced guide and climbing gear.

⊙ Flamengo

Flamengo was once Rio's finest residential district, but it lost its glitter after the tunnel to Copacabana opened in 1904. Along tree-shaded sidewalks, old-school

Copacabana & Leme

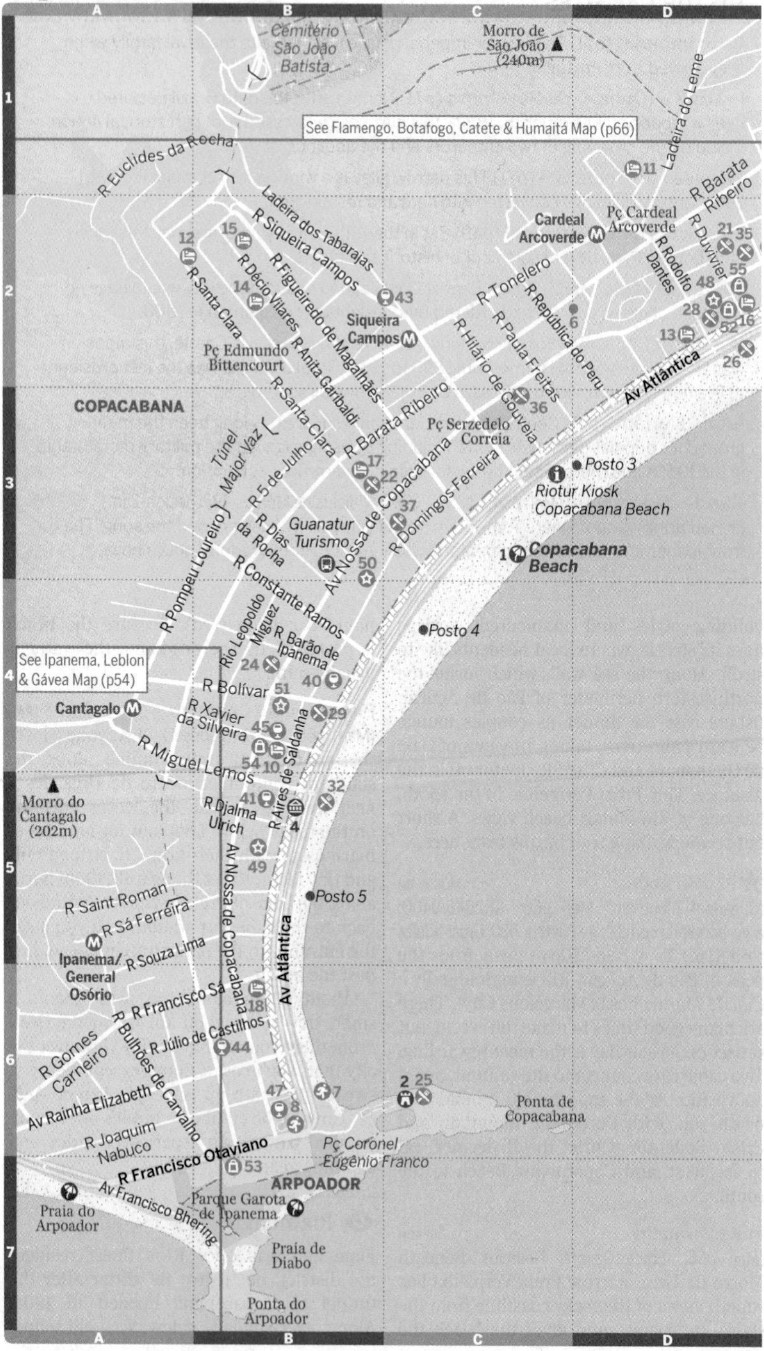
Cemitério São João Batista
Morro de São João (240m)
See Flamengo, Botafogo, Catete & Humaitá Map (p66)
Ladeira do Leme
R Euclides da Rocha
Ladeira dos Tabarajas
R Siqueira Campos
R Décio Vilares
R Figueiredo de Magalhães
R Santa Clara
Pç Edmundo Bittencourt
R Anita Garibaldi
Siqueira Campos
Cardeal Arcoverde
Pç Cardeal Arcoverde
R Barata Ribeiro
R Duvivier
R Rodolfo Dantes
R Tonelero
R República do Peru
R Paula Freitas
R Hilário de Gouveia
Av Atlântica
COPACABANA
Túnel Major Vaz
R 5 de Julho
R Barata Ribeiro
Pç Serzedelo Correia
Av Nossa de Copacabana
R Domingos Ferreira
Posto 3
Riotur Kiosk Copacabana Beach
Copacabana Beach
Guanatur Turismo
R Dias da Rocha
R Pompeu Loureiro
R Constante Ramos
Posto 4
Rio Leopoldo Miguez
R Barão de Ipanema
See Ipanema, Leblon & Gávea Map (p54)
R Bolívar
Cantagalo
R Xavier da Silveira
R Aires de Saldanha
R Miguel Lemos
Morro do Cantagalo (202m)
R Djalma Ulrich
Av Nossa de Copacabana
Posto 5
R Saint Roman
R Sá Ferreira
Ipanema/ General Osório
R Souza Lima
R Francisco Sá
Av Atlântica
R Bulhões de Carvalho
R Júlio de Castilhos
R Gomes Carneiro
Av Rainha Elizabeth
Ponta de Copacabana
R Joaquim Nabuco
R Francisco Otaviano
Pç Coronel Eugênio Franco
ARPOADOR
Av Francisco Bhering
Praia do Arpoador
Parque Garota de Ipanema
Praia de Diabo
Ponta do Arpoador

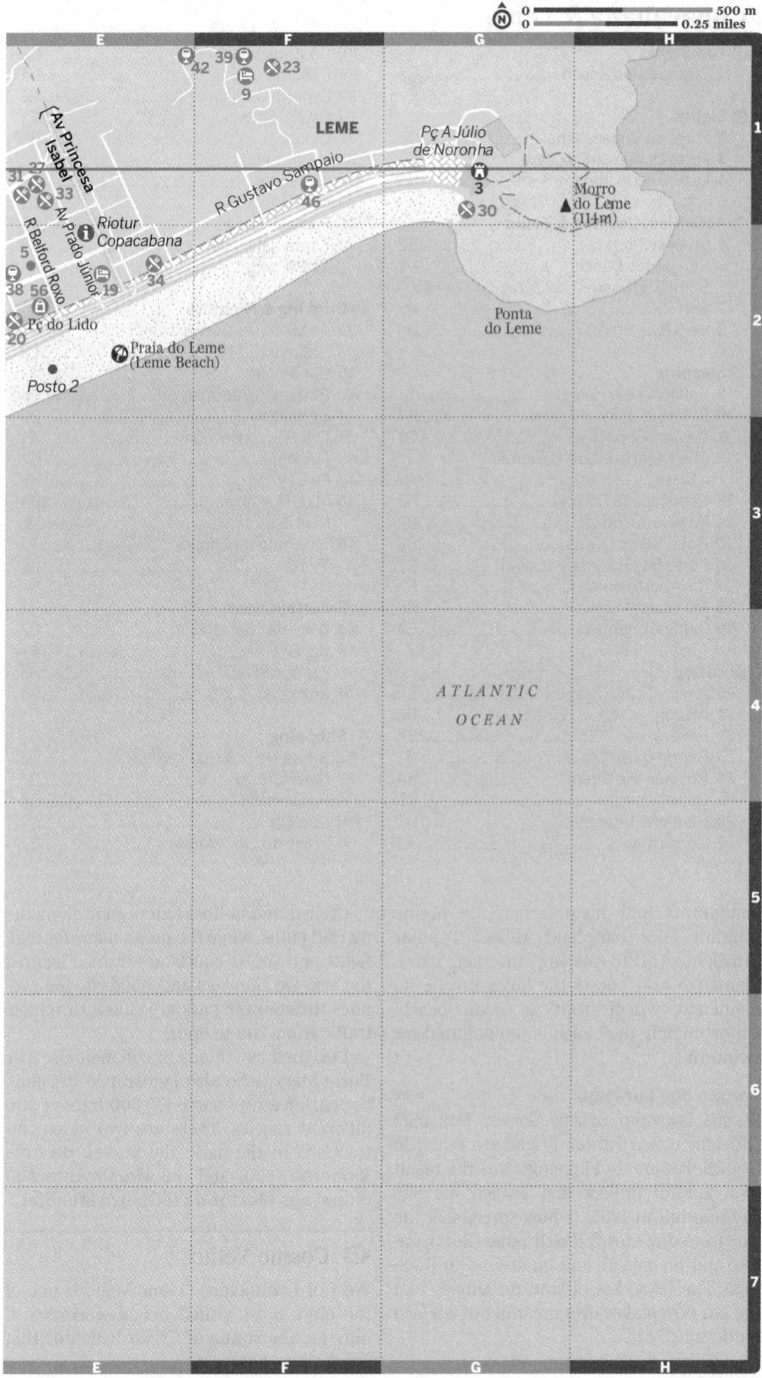
0 500 m
0 0.25 miles
E
F
G
H
42
39
23
9
LEME
Pç A Júlio de Noronha
Av Princesa Isabel
31
27
33
R Gustavo Sampaio
3
46
Morro do Leme (114m)
30
R Belford Roxo
Av Prado Júnior
Riotur Copacabana
5
38
56
19
34
Pç do Lido
20
Ponta do Leme
Praia do Leme (Leme Beach)
Posto 2
ATLANTIC OCEAN
1
2
3
4
5
6
7

Copacabana & Leme

Top Sights
1 Copacabana Beach.....C3

Sights
2 Forte de Copacabana.....C6
3 Forte Duque de Caxias.....G1
4 Museu do Imagem e Som.....B5

Activities, Courses & Tours
5 Cook in Rio.....E2
6 Rio Samba Dancer.....D2
Spirit Surfboards.....(see 53)
7 Surf Rio.....B6
8 Velô Bike Store.....B6

Sleeping
9 Babilônia Rio Hostel.....F1
10 Blame It on Rio 4 Travel.....B4
11 Cabana Copa.....D1
12 Che Lagarto – Suites Santa Clara.....A2
13 Copacabana Palace.....D2
14 Edifício Jucati.....B2
15 Hotel Santa Clara.....B2
16 Porto Bay Rio Internacional.....D2
17 Rio Apartments.....B3
18 Rio Guesthouse.....B6
19 Rio Spot Homes.....E2

Eating
20 Amir.....E2
21 Azumi.....D2
22 Bakers.....B3
23 Bar do David.....F1
24 Boulangerie Guerin.....B4
25 Cafe Colombo.....C6
26 Cantinho Cearense.....D2
27 Cervantes.....E1
28 Churrascaria Palace.....D2
29 El Born.....B4
30 Espetto Carioca.....G1
31 Galeto Sat's.....E1
32 Globo.....B5
33 HortiFruti.....E1
34 Joaquina.....E2
35 Nonna Ridolfi.....D2
36 Pão de Açúcar.....C3
37 Santa Satisfação.....C3
TT Burger.....(see 53)

Drinking & Nightlife
38 As Melhores Cervejas do Mundo.....E2
39 Bar do Alto.....F1
40 Botequim Informal.....B4
41 Escondido.....B5
42 Estrelas da Babilônia.....E1
43 Fosfobox.....C2
44 Le Boy.....B6
45 Mais Que Nada.....B4
Mud Bug.....(see 28)
46 Sindicato do Chopp.....F1
47 TV Bar.....B6

Entertainment
48 Beco das Garrafas.....D2
49 Bip Bip.....B5
50 Espaço SESC.....B3
51 Roxy.....B4

Shopping
52 Bossa Nova & Companhia.....D2
53 Galeria River.....B7
54 Havaianas.....B4
55 Loja Fla.....D2
56 Praça do Lido Market.....E2

restaurants and historic bars lie beside fragrant juice bars and Música Popular Brasileira (MPB)–playing internet cafes. Flamengo also boasts the large Parque do Flamengo, which fronts a scenic beach. Unfortunately the beach is too polluted for swimming.

Parque do Flamengo PARK
(Parque Brigadeiro Eduardo Gomes; Map p66)
Officially called Parque Brigadeiro Eduardo Gomes, Parque do Flamengo was the result of a landfill project that leveled the São Antônio hill in 1965. It now spreads all the way from downtown Rio through Glória, Catete and Flamengo, and on around to Botafogo. The 1.2 sq km of land reclaimed from the sea now stages every manner of *carioca* outdoor activity.

Cyclists and in-line skaters glide along the myriad paths, while the park's many football fields and sports courts are framed against the sea. On Sundays and holidays, the avenues through the park are closed to vehicle traffic from 7am to 6pm.

Designed by famous Brazilian landscaper Burle Marx (who also landscaped Brasília), the park features some 170,000 trees of 300 different species. There are two indoor attractions in the park: the **Museu de Arte Moderna** (p70) and the **Monumento Nacional aos Mortos da II Guerra Mundial**.

Cosme Velho

West of Laranjeiras, Cosme Velho is one of the city's most visited neighborhoods – if only for the statue of Cristo Redentor that soars above its streets.

★Cristo Redentor MONUMENT

(Christ the Redeemer; ☎2558-1329; www.corcovado.com.br; cog station, Cosme Velho 513; adult/child R$62/40; ⏰8am-7pm) Standing atop Corcovado (which means 'hunchback'), Cristo Redentor gazes out over Rio, a placid expression on his well-crafted face. The mountain rises straight up from the city to 710m, and at night the brightly lit, 38m-high open-armed statue – all 1145 tons of him – is visible from nearly every part of the city.

Corcovado lies within the Parque Nacional da Tijuca. The most popular way to reach the statue is to take the red narrow-gauge train that departs every 30 minutes, and takes approximately 20 minutes to reach the top. To reach the cog station, take any 'Cosme Velho' bus: you can take bus 583 from Copacabana, Ipanema or Leblon.

You can also go by Parque da Tijuca–authorized van to visit the monument. These depart from three locations around town: Copacabana (in front of Praça do Lido from 8am to 4pm; adult/child R$62/40), Largo do Machado (8am to 5pm; adult/child R$62/40) and Paineiras, a few kilometres north of the statue (from 8am to 6pm; adult/child R$35/free).

Museu Internacional de Arte Naïf do Brasil MUSEUM

(Map p66; ☎2205-8612; www.museunaif.com; Cosme Velho 561; adult/child R$12/6; ⏰10am-6pm Tue-Fri, to 5pm Sat & Sun; 🚌180, 184, 583, 584) A short walk west from the Corcovado cog station, this small museum has a fascinating collection of colorful paintings made by artists often working well outside of the establishment. Also known as primitivist, *arte naïf* paintings often deal with marginalized peoples – Roma, sharecroppers, ghetto dwellers – and although small, the collection has pieces from 100 countries, giving a truly global reach to the exhibition.

Largo do Boticário HISTORIC SITE

(Map p66; Cosme Velho 822) The brightly painted but sadly dilapidated houses on this picturesque plaza date from the early 19th century. Largo do Boticário was named in honor of the Portuguese gentleman – Joaquim Luiz da Silva Souto – who once ran a *boticário* (apothecary) utilized by the royal family. The sound of a brook coming from the nearby forest adds to the plaza's charm. Occasional art and cultural events are hosted here.

Catete & Glória

Like the nearby neighborhood of Flamengo, these twin districts flourished in the mid-19th century, when their location at the outskirts of the city made them desirable places to live. The area's star attraction is the Palácio do Catete (now the Museu da República), which was the republic's seat of power before the capital was transferred to Brasília.

Igreja de Nossa Senhora da Glória do Outeiro CHURCH

(Map p72; ☎2557-4600; www.outeirodagloria.org.br; Praça NS da Glória 135; ⏰9am-noon & 1-4pm Mon-Fri, 9am-noon Sat & Sun) This tiny church atop Ladeira da Glória commands lovely views out over Parque do Flamengo and the bay. Considered one of the finest examples of religious colonial architecture in Brazil, the church dates from 1739 and became the favorite of the royal family upon their arrival in 1808.

Museu da República MUSEUM

(Map p66; ☎2127-0324; museudarepublica.museus.gov.br; Rua do Catete 153; admission R$6, Wed & Sun free; ⏰10am-5pm Tue-Fri, 2-6pm Sat & Sun) The Museu da República, located in the **Palácio do Catete**, has been wonderfully restored. Built between 1858 and 1866 and easily distinguished by the bronze condors on its eaves, the palace was home to the president of Brazil from 1896 until 1954, when President Getúlio Vargas committed suicide here. The museum has a good collection of art and artifacts from the Republican period, and also houses a good lunch restaurant, an art-house cinema and a bookstore.

Museu de Folclore Edison Carneiro MUSEUM

(Map p66; ☎3826-4434; www.cnfcp.gov.br; Rua do Catete 179; ⏰11am-6pm Tue-Fri, 3-6pm Sat & Sun) FREE Created in 1968, this museum is an excellent introduction to Brazilian folk art, particularly that from the Northeast. Its permanent collection comprises 1400 pieces, and includes Candomblé costumes, ceramic figurines and religious costumes used in festivals. The museum also features a folklore library and a small shop that sells handicrafts, books and folk music. The museum is located next door to the Palácio do Catete.

Centro Cultural Oi Futuro ARTS CENTER

(Map p66; ☎3131-3060; www.oifuturo.org.br; Dois de Dezembro 63; ⏰11am-8pm Tue-Sun) FREE

Flamengo, Botafogo, Catete & Humaitá

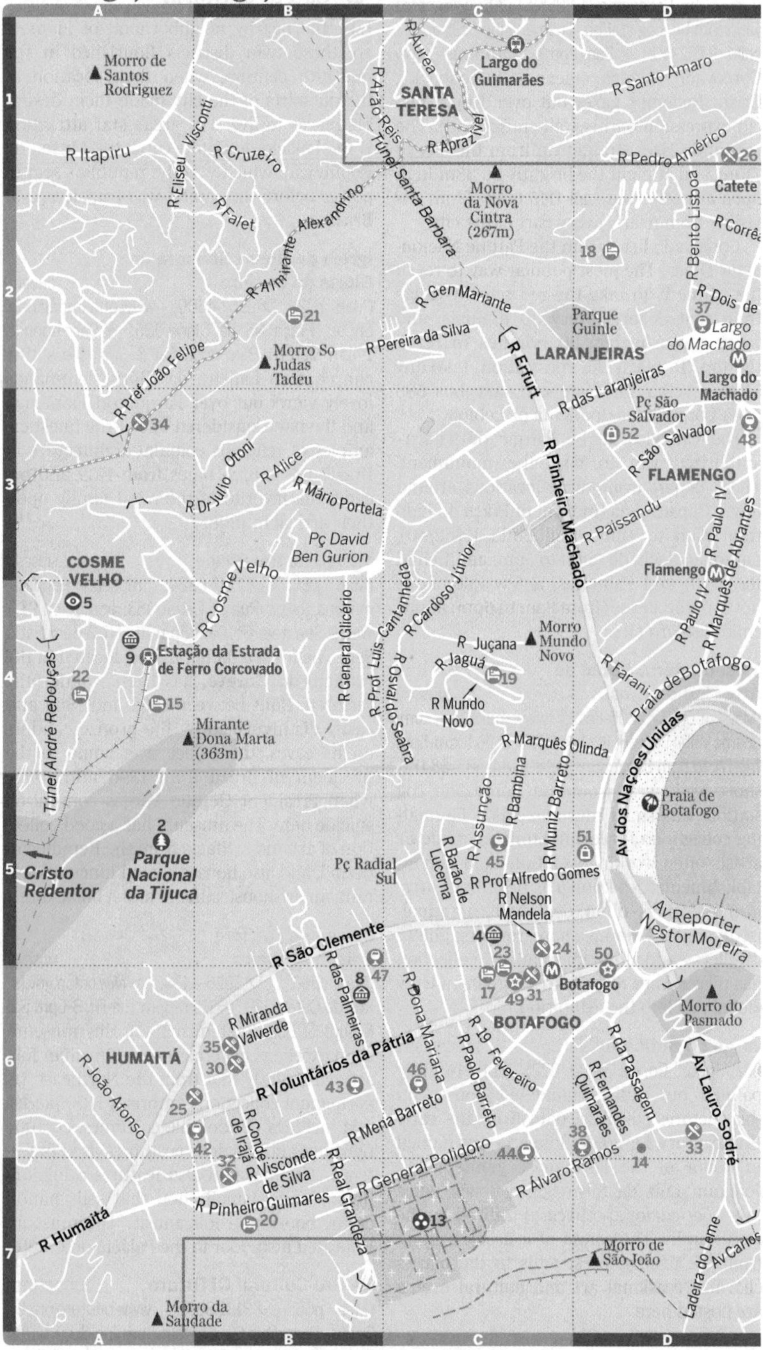

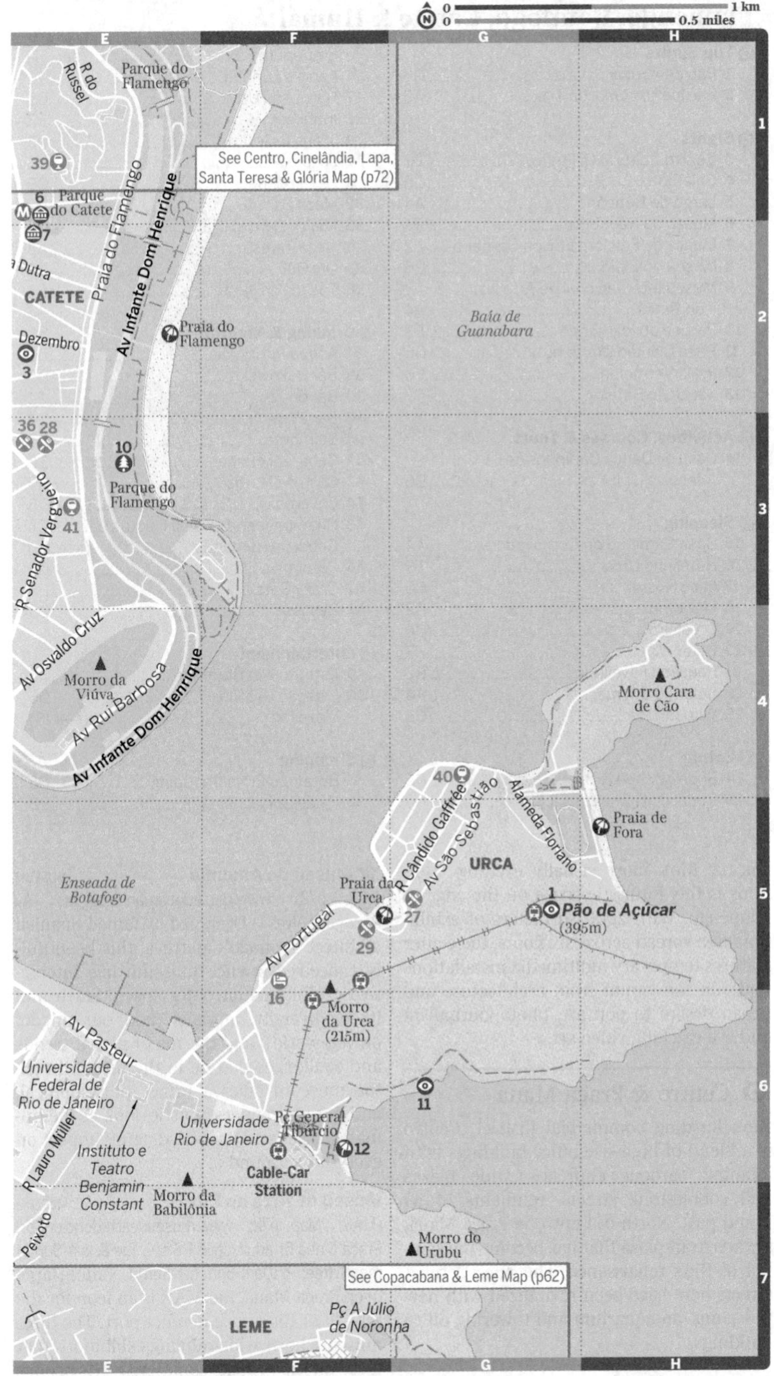
0 1 km
0 0.5 miles
Parque do Flamengo
R do Russel
39
6 Parque do Catete
7
See Centro, Cinelândia, Lapa, Santa Teresa & Glória Map (p72)
Praia do Flamengo
Av Infante Dom Henrique
Dutra
CATETE
Praia do Flamengo
Dezembro
3
Baía de Guanabara
36 28
10
Parque do Flamengo
R Senador Vergueiro
41
Av Osvaldo Cruz
Morro da Viúva
Av Rui Barbosa
Av Infante Dom Henrique
Morro Cara de Cão
40
R Cândido Gaffrée
Av São Sebastião
Alameda Floriano
Praia de Fora
URCA
Enseada de Botafogo
Praia da Urca
27
29
1
Pão de Açúcar
(395m)
Av Portugal
16
Morro da Urca
(215m)
Av Pasteur
Universidade Federal de Rio de Janeiro
11
Universidade Rio de Janeiro
Pç General Tibúrcio
12
R Lauro Müller
Instituto e Teatro Benjamin Constant
Cable-Car Station
Morro da Babilônia
Peixoto
Morro do Urubu
See Copacabana & Leme Map (p62)
LEME
Pç A Júlio de Noronha

Flamengo, Botafogo, Catete & Humaitá

Top Sights
1 Pão de Açúcar ... G5
2 Parque Nacional da Tijuca ... A5

Sights
3 Centro Cultural Oi Futuro ... E2
4 GaleRio ... C5
5 Largo do Boticário ... A4
6 Museu da República ... E1
7 Museu de Folclore Edison Carneiro ... E2
8 Museu do Índio ... B6
9 Museu Internacional de Arte Naïf do Brasil ... A4
10 Parque do Flamengo ... E3
11 Pista Cláudio Coutinho ... G6
12 Praia Vermelha ... F6
13 São João Batista ... C7

Activities, Courses & Tours
14 Casa de Dança Carlinhos de Jesus ... D6

Sleeping
15 Casa Caminho do Corcovado ... A4
16 Hotelinho Urca ... F5
17 Injoy Hostel ... C6
18 Maze Inn ... D2
19 O Veleiro ... C4
20 Oztel ... B7
21 Pousada Favelinha ... B2
22 Solar do Cosme ... A4
23 Vila Carioca ... C6

Eating
24 Boua Kitchen & Bar ... C5
25 Cobal do Humaitá ... B6
Emporium Pax ... (see 51)
26 Ferro e Farinha ... D1
27 Garota da Urca ... G5
28 Intihuasi ... E3
29 Julius Brasserie ... F5
30 Lasai ... B6
31 Le Depanneur ... C6
32 Meza Bar ... B7
33 Miam Miam ... D6
34 Nega Teresa ... A3
35 Oui Oui ... B6
36 Tacacá do Norte ... E3

Drinking & Nightlife
37 Adega Portugália ... D2
38 Bar Bukowski ... D6
39 Bar do Zé ... E1
40 Bar Urca ... G4
41 Belmonte ... E3
42 Cabaret Lounge ... B6
43 Casa da Matriz ... B6
44 Caverna ... C6
45 Champanharia Ovelha Negra ... C5
Cobal do Humaitá ... (see 25)
46 Comuna ... C6
47 Crazy Cats ... B5
48 Devassa ... D3

Entertainment
49 Estação Net Botafogo ... C6
50 Estação Net Rio ... D6
Maze Inn ... (see 18)

Shopping
51 Botafogo Praia Shopping ... D5
52 Pé de Boi ... D3

One of Rio's most visually exciting additions is this futuristic space on the edge of Flamengo. With 2000 sq meters of exhibition area spread across six floors, the center features temporary multimedia installations that run the gamut from architecture and urban design to pop art, photo-journalism and eye-catching video art.

Centro & Praça Mauá

Rio's bustling commercial district, Centro is a blend of high-rise office buildings with looming baroque churches, wide plazas and cobblestone streets, remnants of its grand past. North of Centro is Praça Mauá, a waterfront plaza that has become the symbol of Rio's renaissance. The once derelict streets here have been revitalized with new museums, an aquarium and towering office buildings.

★ **Museu do Amanhã** MUSEUM

(Map p72; www.museudoamanha.org.br; Av Rodrigues Alves 1) Designed by famed Spanish architect Santiago Calatrava, this beautifully conceived science museum has interactive exhibitions on outer space, Earth and its biodiversity, humans (and our impact on the world), and the major global trends and challenges that lie in the future. In all, the museum takes a rather philosophical, and not entirely pessimistic, look at the human species and its long-ranging impact on everything around it.

Museu de Arte do Rio MUSEUM

(MAR; Map p72; www.museudeartedorio.org.br; Praça Mauá 5; adult/child R$8/4, Tue & last Sun of month free; 10am-6pm Tue-Sun) Looming large over Praça Mauá, the MAR is an icon for the rebirth of Rio's once derelict port. The huge museum hosts wide-ranging exhibitions that focus on Rio in all its complexity – its people, landscapes, beauty, challenges and conflicts. Start off by taking the elevator to the top (6th) floor, and absorbing the view over the bay. There's also an excellent restaurant here. Then work your way down through the galleries, taking in a mix of international and only-in-Rio exhibitions.

AquaRio AQUARIUM
(2558-3735; www.aquariomarinhodorio.com.br; Av Rodrigues Alves 379; admission R$40; 9am-6pm) The largest aquarium in South America is Rio's newest major downtown attraction. You can get an up-close look at some 350 different species (there are more than 8000 animals in all), spread among two dozen different tanks. The highlight is a 3.3-million-liter aquarium with a tunnel through the middle that gives the impression of walking right through the depths of a rich aquatic zone.

Morro da Conceição HISTORIC SITE
(Map p72) One of Rio's oldest neighborhoods, this pretty area feels like a tiny slice of Portugal, with its old shuttered houses, quiet cobblestone streets and twittering birds. While there isn't a lot to do here (it's really just one long winding street), there are a few galleries open to visitors (look for 'atelier' signs) and a good local restaurant. There's also a hostel if you want to stay overnight. Saturday is the liveliest time to visit.

To get here on foot, take the narrow uphill lane Ladeira João Homem, reachable just off Praça Mauá.

Mosteiro de São Bento CHURCH
(Map p72; 2206-8100; Dom Gerardo 68; 7am-5:30pm) This is one of the finest colonial churches in Brazil. Built between 1617 and 1641 on Morro de São Bento, the monastery has an excellent view over the city. The simple facade hides a baroque interior richly decorated in gold. Among its historical treasures are wood carvings designed by Frei Domingos da Conceição and made by Alexandre Machado, and paintings by José de Oliveira Rosa.

Centro Cultural Banco do Brasil CULTURAL CENTER
(CCBB; Map p72; 3808-2020; culturabancodobrasil.com.br; Primeiro de Março 66; 9am-9pm Wed-Mon) FREE Housed in a beautifully restored 1906 building, the Centro Cultural Banco do Brasil (CCBB) hosts some of Brazil's best exhibitions. Facilities include a cinema, two theaters and a permanent display of the evolution of currency in Brazil. There is always something going on, from exhibitions, and lunchtime and evening concerts, to film screenings, so look at *O Globo*'s entertainment listings or the *Veja Rio* insert in *Veja* magazine before you go.

Museu Histórico Nacional MUSEUM
(Map p72; 3299-0311; www.museuhistoriconacional.com.br; off General Justo, near Praça Marechal Âncora; admission R$8, Sun free; 10am-5:30pm Tue-Fri, 2-6pm Sat & Sun) Housed in the colonial arsenal, which dates from 1764, the impressive Museu Histórico Nacional contains relics relating to the history of Brazil from its founding to its early days as a republic. Highlights include gilded imperial coaches, the throne of Dom Pedro II, massive oil paintings depicting the horrific war with Paraguay, and a full-sized model of a colonial pharmacy.

Centro de Arte Hélio Oiticica MUSEUM
(Map p72; 2242-1012; Luis de Camões 68; noon-8pm Mon, Wed & Fri, 10am-6pm Tue, Thu & Sat) FREE This avant-garde museum is set in a 19th-century neoclassical building that originally housed the Conservatory of Music and Dramatic Arts. Today the center displays permanent works by the artist, theoretician and poet Hélio Oiticica, as well as bold contemporary art exhibitions, well-tuned to Oiticica's forward-leaning aesthetics.

Ilha Fiscal HISTORIC BUILDING
(Map p72; 2233-9165; tours R$25; tours 12:30pm, 2pm & 3:30pm Thu-Sun) This eye-catching lime-green neo-Gothic palace sitting in the Baía de Guanabara looks like something out of a child's fairy-tale book. It was designed by engineer Adolfo del Vecchio and completed in 1889. Originally used to supervise port operations, the palace is famous as the location of the last Imperial Ball on November 9, 1889. Today it's open for guided tours, which leave from the dock near Praça XV (Quinze) de Novembro. Purchase tickets from the **Museu Naval** (Map p72; 2104-5506; Dom Manuel 15; noon-5pm Tue-Sun) FREE.

Igreja de Nossa Senhora do Carmo da Antiga Sé CHURCH
(Map p72; Sete de Setembro 14; 8:30am-3:30pm Mon-Fri, 9:30am-noon Sat) This beautifully restored church and former cathedral dates back to the 1770s, and it played an important role in the imperial days of Rio. The elaborately gilded rococo-style interior

WORTH A TRIP

EXPLORING THE BAY

To the east of Centro lies Rio's scenic bay. Unfortunately, it's too polluted for swimming, but it makes a fine backdrop for a boat ride to Ilha de Paquetá or Niterói.

Ilha de Paquetá

This car-free **island** (☎ferry 0800-721-1012; www.grupoccr.com.br/barcas) provides a pleasant escape from the city's bustle. Transport is by foot, bicycle (there are hundreds for rent) or horse-drawn carts. There's a certain decadent charm to the colonial buildings, unassuming beaches and businesses catering to local tourism. The place gets crowded on weekends. Boats leave from near Praça XV (Quinze) de Novembro in Centro. The ferry takes 70 minutes and will cost you R$10 for a return trip. There are 12 departures daily, roughly every 90 minutes from about 7am.

Niterói

East of Rio, the city of Niterói's principal attraction is the photogenic **Museu do Arte Contemporânea** (MAC; ☎2620-2400; www.macniteroi.com.br; Mirante da Boa Viagem, Niterói; admission R$10; ⏲10am-6pm Tue-Sun). The cruise across the bay, however, is perhaps just as valid a reason for leaving Rio. The ferry costs about R$10 return and leaves near Praça XV (Quinze) de Novembro in Centro; it's usually full of commuters. Once you reach the dock, the immediate area is a busy commercial district, full of pedestrians and crisscrossing intersections. From here catch bus 47B to the MAC, 2.1km south, or simply return on the next ferry.

witnessed royal baptisms, weddings and funereal rites. Several kings were crowned here – including Pedro I in 1822 and his son Pedro II in 1841; it is the only place in the New World where this occurred. The royal family used to sit in the balcony boxes overlooking the altar.

Igreja São Francisco da Penitência & Convento de Santo Antônio CHURCH

(Map p72; ☎2262-0129; Largo da Carioca 5; ⏲church 8am-6pm Mon-Fri, 8-11am Sat) Overlooking the Largo da Carioca is the baroque Igreja São Francisco da Penitência, dating from 1726. Restored to its former glory, the church's sacristy, which dates from 1745, has blue Portuguese tiles and an elaborately carved altar made out of jacaranda wood. It also has a roof panel by José Oliveira Rosa depicting St Francis receiving the stigmata.

Igreja de Nossa Senhora de Candelária CHURCH

(Map p72; ☎2233-2324; Praça Pio X; ⏲8am-4pm Mon-Fri, 9am-noon Sat, to 1pm Sun) Built between 1775 and 1894, NS de Candelária was the largest and wealthiest church of imperial Brazil. The interior is a combination of baroque and Renaissance styles. The ceiling above the nave reveals the origin of the church. The cupola, fabricated entirely from limestone shipped from Lisbon, is one of its most striking features. Mass is said at 7am daily except Monday and Saturday, and at 9am and 11am on Sunday. But be sure to watch out for traffic as you cross to the church.

Museu de Arte Moderna MUSEUM

(MAM; Map p72; ☎3883-5600; www.mamrio.org.br; Av Infante Dom Henrique 85, Parque do Flamengo; adult/child R$14/free; ⏲noon-6pm Tue-Fri, 11am-6pm Sat & Sun) At the northern end of Parque do Flamengo, the Museu de Arte Moderna (MAM) is immediately recognizable by its striking postmodern edifice designed by Alfonso Eduardo Reidy. The landscaping of Burle Marx is no less impressive. Inside, the design feels a bit dated, but it's still worth a visit for the superb collection of Brazilian artists, which includes works by Bruno Giorgi, Di Cavalcanti and Maria Martins.

Curators often bring excellent photography and design exhibits to the museum, and the cinema hosts regular film festivals throughout the year. After a devastating fire in 1978 that consumed 90% of its collection, the MAM is finally back on its feet, and it now houses 11,000 permanent works.

Museu Nacional de Belas Artes MUSEUM

(Map p72; ☎3299-0600; www.mnba.gov.br; Rio Branco 199; adult/student R$8/4, Sun free; ⏲10am-6pm Tue-Fri, noon-5pm Sat & Sun) Rio's fine-arts museum houses more than 18,000 original paintings and sculptures, some of which date back to works brought over from Portugal by Dom João VI in 1808. One of its most important galleries is the **Galeria de Arte Brasileira**, which includes 20th-century classics such as Cândido Portinari's *Café*. Other galleries display Brazilian folk art, African art and furniture, as well as contemporary exhibits. Audio guides are available (R$8).

Paço Imperial HISTORIC BUILDING

(Map p72; ☎2215-2622; Praça XV (Quinze) de Novembro 48; ⏰noon-6pm Tue-Sun) FREE The former imperial palace was originally built in 1743 as a governor's residence. Later it became the home of Dom João and his family when the Portuguese throne transferred the royal seat of power to the colony. In 1888 Princesa Isabel proclaimed the Freedom from Slavery Act from the palace's steps. The building was neglected for many years but has been restored and today it hosts excellent changing exhibitions and concerts. There's also a good cafe and several restaurants here.

Praça XV (Quinze) de Novembro HISTORIC SITE

(Map p72; near Primeiro de Março) The first residents on this historic site were Carmelite fathers who built a convent here in 1590. It later came under the property of the Portuguese crown and became Largo do Paço, which surrounded Paço Imperial, the royal palace. The square was later renamed Praça XV (Quinze) de Novembro after Brazil declared itself a republic on November 15, 1822.

Travessa do Comércio STREET

(Map p72; near Praça XV (Quinze) de Novembro) Beautiful two-story colonial town houses line this narrow cobblestone street leading off Praça XV (Quinze) de Novembro. The archway, called **Arco de Teles**, leading into the area was once part of an old viaduct running between two buildings. Today, Travessa do Comércio contains half-a-dozen restaurants and drinking spots that open onto the streets. It's a favorite spot for *cariocas* after work.

Praça Floriano PLAZA

(Map p72; Av Rio Branco) The heart of modern Rio, the Praça Floriano (known to *cariocas* simply as Cinelândia) comes to life at lunchtime and after work when the outdoor cafes are filled with a beer-swilling office crowd. The square is also Rio's political marketplace and is a major meeting point for protestors.

Real Gabinete Português de Leitura HISTORIC BUILDING

(Map p72; ☎2221-3138; Luís de Camões 30; ⏰9am-6pm Mon-Fri) FREE Built in the Portuguese Manueline style in 1837, the gorgeous Portuguese Reading Room houses more than 350,000 works, many dating from the 16th, 17th and 18th centuries. It also has a small collection of paintings, sculptures and ancient coins.

Theatro Municipal THEATER

(Map p72; ☎2332-9220; www.theatromunicipal.rj.gov.br; Av 13 de Maio, Praça Floriano; guided tours R$10) Built in 1905 in the style of the Paris Opera, the magnificent Municipal Theater is the home of Rio's opera, orchestra and ballet. Its lavish interior contains many beautiful details – including the stage curtain painted by Italian artist Eliseu Visconti, which contains portraits of 75 major figures from the arts, including Carlos Gomes, Wagner and Rembrandt.

Lapa

This former red-light district is the center of a vibrant bohemian scene in Rio, with dozens of music clubs, bars and old-fashioned restaurants scattered along its avenues.

On weekend nights revelers pack the neighborhood's samba clubs, its streets and the wide plaza in front of the Arcos da Lapa, the neighborhood's prominent landmark.

★**Escadaria Selarón** LANDMARK

(Map p72; stairway btwn Joaquim Silva in Lapa & Pinto Martins in Santa Teresa) One of Rio's best loved attractions, the steps leading up from Rua Joaquim Silva became a work of art when Chilean-born artist Jorge Selarón decided to cover the steps with colorful mosaics. A dedication to the Brazilian people, the 215 steps are a vivid riot of color.

Catedral Metropolitana CHURCH

(Map p72; ☎2240-2669; www.catedral.com.br; Av República do Chile 245; ⏰7am-5pm, museum 9am-noon & 1-4pm Wed, 9am-noon Sat & Sun) This enormous cone-shaped cathedral was inaugurated in 1976 after 12 years of construction. Among its sculptures, murals and other works of art, the four vivid stained-glass windows, which stretch 60m to the ceiling, are breathtaking.

Centro, Cinelândia, Lapa, Santa Teresa & Glória

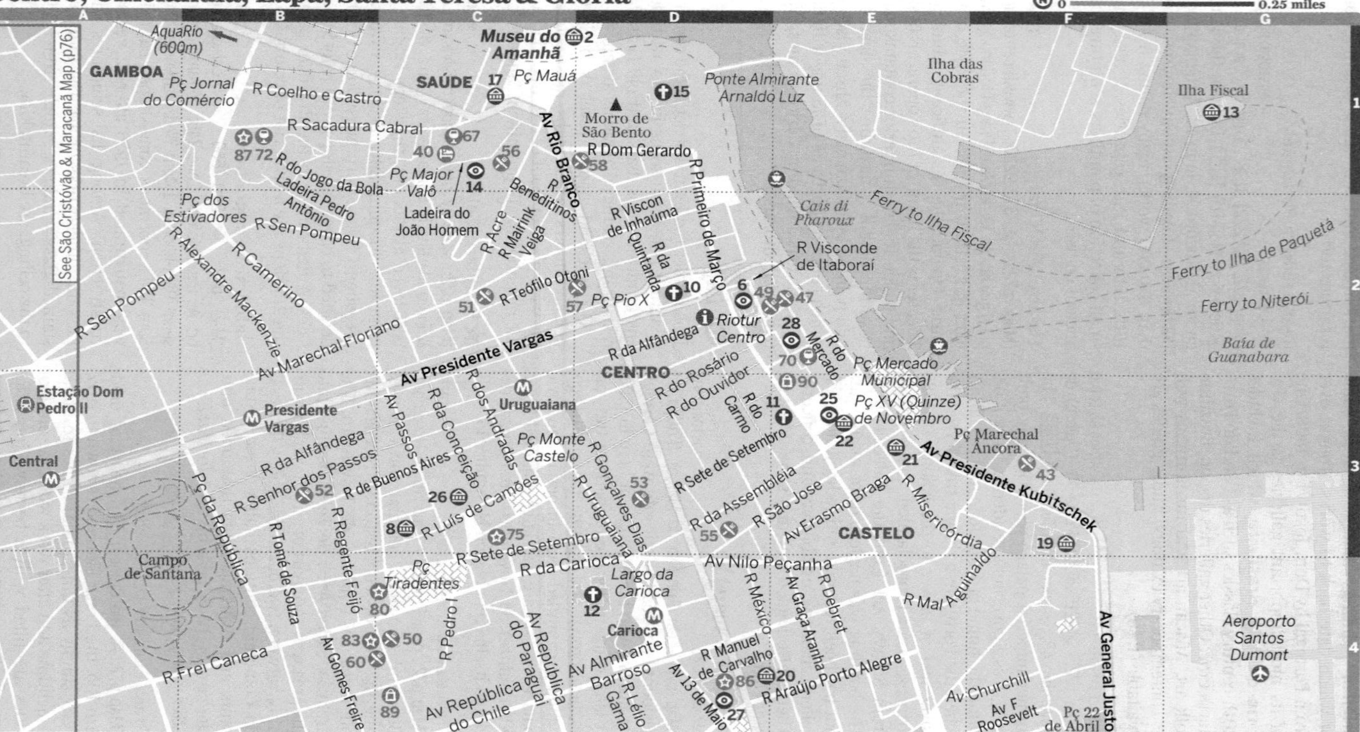

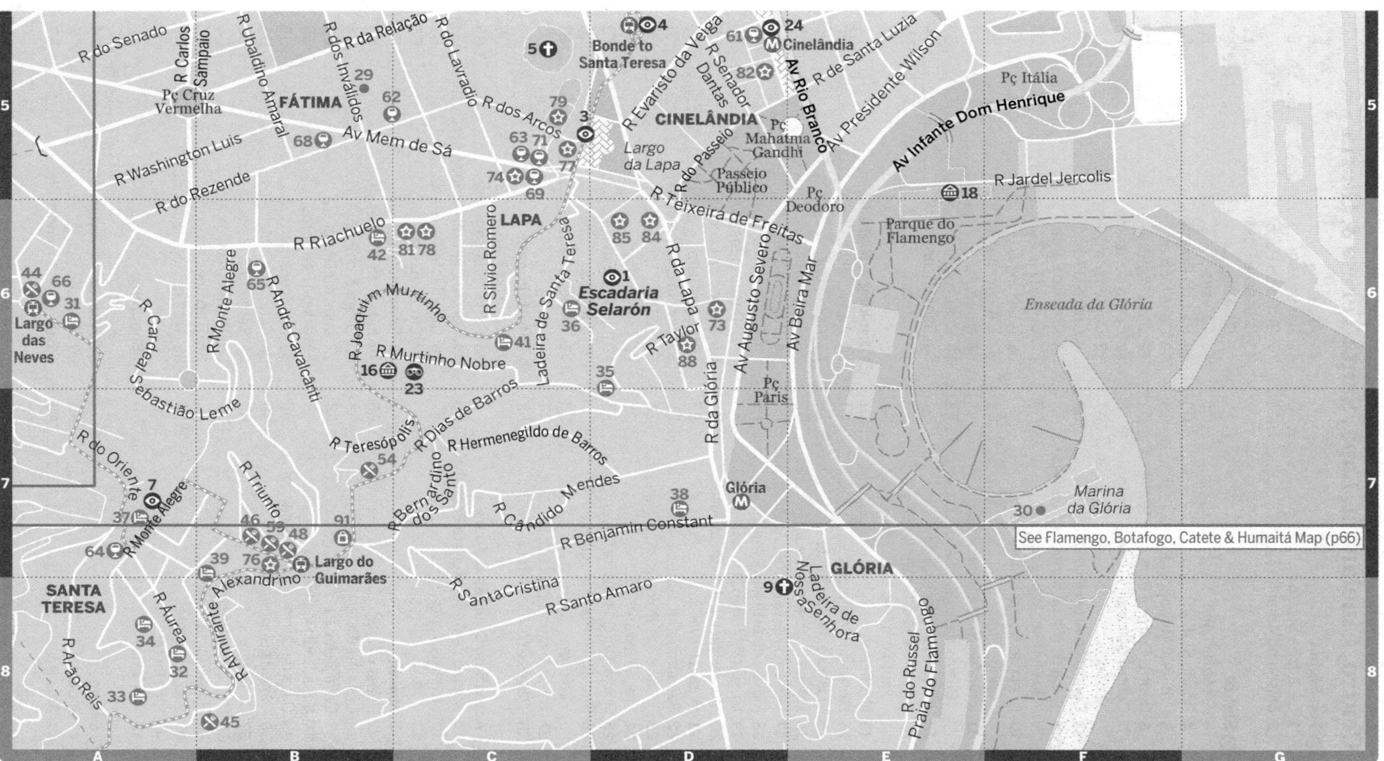

See Flamengo, Botafogo, Catete & Humaitá Map (p66)
Enseada da Glória
Marina da Glória
Parque do Flamengo
Pç Itália
Av Infante Dom Henrique
R Jardel Jercolis
Av Presidente Wilson
R de Santa Luzia
Av Rio Branco
Cinelândia
CINELÂNDIA
Pç Mahatma Gandhi
Passeio Público
Pç Deodoro
Av Beira Mar
Av Augusto Severo
Pç Paris
Glória
GLÓRIA
Ladeira de Nossa Senhora
R do Russel
Praia do Flamengo
R da Glória
R Senador Dantas
R do Passeio
R Evaristo da Veiga
R Teixeira de Freitas
R da Lapa
R Taylor
Escadaria Selarón
Bonde to Santa Teresa
Largo da Lapa
LAPA
Ladeira de Santa Teresa
R Silvio Romero
R dos Arcos
R do Lavradio
R da Relação
R dos Inválidos
FÁTIMA
Av Mem de Sá
R Riachuelo
R Joaquim Murtinho
R Murtinho Nobre
R Dias de Barros
R Hermenegildo de Barros
R Cândido Mendes
R Benjamin Constant
R Santo Amaro
R Santa Cristina
R Bernardino dos Santo
R Teresópolis
R André Cavalcânti
R Ubaldino Amaral
R Monte Alegre
R Triunfo
Largo do Guimarães
R Alexandrino
R Almirante
R Carlos Sampaio
Pç Cruz Vermelha
R Washington Luis
R do Rezende
R Cardeal Sebastião Leme
R do Senado
R do Oriente
R Áurea
R Arão Reis
SANTA TERESA
Largo das Neves

Centro, Cinelândia, Lapa, Santa Teresa & Glória

Top Sights

1 Escadaria Selarón D6
2 Museu do Amanhã C1

Sights

3 Arcos da Lapa C5
4 Bonde Station D5
5 Catedral Metropolitana C5
6 Centro Cultural Banco do Brasil D2
7 Centro Cultural Laurinda Santos Lobo A7
8 Centro de Arte Hélio Oiticica C3
9 Igreja de Nossa Senhora da Glória do Outeiro D8
10 Igreja de Nossa Senhora de Candelária D2
11 Igreja de Nossa Senhora do Carmo da Antiga Sé E3
12 Igreja São Francisco da Penitência & Convento de Santo Antônio D4
13 Ilha Fiscal G1
14 Morro da Conceição C1
15 Mosteiro de São Bento D1
16 Museu Chácara do Céu B6
17 Museu de Arte do Rio C1
18 Museu de Arte Moderna E5
19 Museu Histórico Nacional F3
20 Museu Nacional de Belas Artes D4
21 Museu Naval E3
22 Paço Imperial E3
23 Parque das Ruínas C6
24 Praça Floriano D5
25 Praça XV (Quinze) de Novembro E3
26 Real Gabinete Português de Leitura C3
27 Theatro Municipal D4
28 Travessa do Comércio E2

Activities, Courses & Tours

29 Núcleo de Dança Renata Peçanha B5
30 Saveiros Tours F7

Sleeping

31 Cama e Café A6
32 Casa Áurea A8
33 Casa Beleza A8
34 Casa Cool Beans A8
35 Casa da Carmen e do Fernando D6
36 Casa da Gente C6
37 Casalegre A7
38 Discovery Hostel D7
39 Hotel Santa Teresa B7
40 Pop Art Hostel C1
41 Rio Hostel C6
42 Vila Galé B6

Eating

43 AlbaMar F3
44 Alquimia A6
45 Aprazível B8
46 Bar do Mineiro B7
Bistrô do Paço .... (see 22)
47 Brasserie Rosário E2
Café Arlequim .... (see 22)
48 Cafecito B7
49 Cais do Oriente D2
50 Casa Momus C4
51 Casa Paladino C2
52 Cedro do Líbano B3
53 Confeitaria Colombo D3
Cristóvão .... (see 53)
54 Espírito Santa B7
55 Govinda D3
56 Imaculada C1
57 L'Atelier du Cuisinier D2
58 Mironga D1
59 Rústico B7
60 Santa Scenarium C4
Térèze .... (see 39)

Drinking & Nightlife

61 Amarelinho D5
62 Anexo Bar B5
63 Antônio's C5
64 Bar do Gomes A7
Bar dos Descasados .... (see 39)
65 Buraco da Lacraia B6
66 Goya-Beira A6
67 Jazz In Champanheria C1
68 La Paz B5
69 Leviano Bar C5
70 Samba Caffe E2
71 Sarau C5
72 Week B1

Entertainment

73 Beco do Rato D6
74 Carioca da Gema C5
75 Centro Cultural Carioca C3
76 Cine Santa Teresa B7
77 Circo Voador C5
78 Democráticus C6
79 Fundição Progresso C5
80 Ginga Tropical C4
81 Lapa 40 Graus C6
82 Odeon Petrobras D5
83 Rio Scenarium B4
84 Sala Cecília Meireles D6
85 Semente D6
86 Theatro Municipal D4
87 Trapiche Gamboa B1
88 TribOz D6

Shopping

Arlequim .... (see 22)
89 Feira do Rio Antigo C4
90 Granado E3
91 La Vereda Handicrafts B7

Arcos da Lapa AQUEDUCT

(Map p72; near Av Mem de Sá) A much-photographed symbol of Lapa, the arches date back to the mid-1700s, when the structure served as an aqueduct to carry water from the Carioca River to downtown Rio. In a style reminiscent of ancient Rome, the 42 arches stand 64m high. Today it carries the *bonde* (cable car) on its way between Centro and Santa Teresa.

Santa Teresa

Set on a hill overlooking the city, Santa Teresa, with its cobbled streets and aging mansions, retains the charm of days past and is Rio's most atmospheric neighborhood. Currently the residence of a new generation of artists and bohemians, Santa Teresa has colorful restaurants and bars and a lively weekend scene around Largo do Guimarães and Largo das Neves.

★**Bonde** CABLE CAR

(departures every 30min) The *bonde* that travels up to Santa Teresa from Centro is the last of the historic streetcars that once crisscrossed the city. Its romantic clatter through the cobbled streets has made it the archetype for bohemian Santa Teresa. Currently the *bonde* travels from the cable-car station in **Centro** (Map p72; Lélio Gama 65) over the scenic Arcos da Lapa and up as far as Largo do Curvelo. From there it's a 500m walk to Largo do Guimarães and the heart of Santa Teresa.

After a tragic accident in 2011, the *bonde* was taken out of commission, while much-needed improvements to the tracks were made. After more than four years, the line opened again – but only traveling 1.7km of the 10km of tracks. Work continues on the route, with full completion expected by 2017 at the earliest.

Museu Chácara do Céu MUSEUM

(Map p72; 3970-1126; www.museuscastromaya.com.br; Murtinho Nobre 93; adult/child R$2/free, Wed free; noon-5pm Wed-Mon) The former mansion of art patron and industrialist Raymundo Ottoni de Castro Maya contains a small but diverse collection of modern art, formerly Ottoni's private collection, which he bequeathed to the nation. In addition to works by Portinari, Di Cavalcanti and Lygia Clark, the museum displays furniture and Brazilian maps dating from the 17th and 18th centuries, and also hosts temporary exhibitions.

Parque das Ruínas VIEWPOINT

(Map p72; 2215-0621; Murtinho Nobre 169; 10am-8pm Tue-Sun) FREE This park contains the ruins – exterior brick walls and a newly built staircase – of the mansion belonging to Brazilian heiress Laurinda Santos Lobo. Her house was a meeting point for Rio's artists and intellectuals for many years until her death in 1946. There's a small gallery on the ground floor, but the real reason to come here is for the excellent panorama from the viewing platform up top.

Centro Cultural Laurinda Santos Lobo CULTURAL CENTER

(Map p72; 2215-0618; Monte Alegre 306; 10am-6pm Tue-Sun) FREE Built in 1907, this large mansion once served as a salon for artists from Brazil and abroad, as the location of parties hosted by socialite Laurinda Santos Lobo. Guests included Brazilian composer Heitor Villa-Lobos and American dancer Isadora Duncan. Today, as a cultural center, the building still plays an active role in the neighborhood by hosting exhibitions and open-air concerts throughout the year.

Zona Norte

The North Zone has a handful of attractions, including the Sambódromo, Maracanã Football Stadium and the sprawling market amusement of Feira Nordestina. You'll also find the Quinta da Boa Vista, a large park containing the Museu Nacional and the Jardim Zoológico (zoo).

Maracanã Football Stadium STADIUM

(Map p76; 8871-3950; www.suderj.rj.gov.br/maracana.asp; Av Maracanã, São Cristóvão; admission R$40-80, sports museum R$20; sports museum 9am-7pm Mon-Fri except game days) Rio's Maracanã stadium is hallowed ground among football lovers. The massive arena has been the site of legendary victories and crushing defeats – such as Brazil's gut-wrenching loss in the final game of the 1950 World Cup to Uruguay. More recently, Maracanã played a starring role in the 2014 World Cup when it hosted major games, including Brazil's opener. The stadium also hosts the opening and closing ceremony of the 2016 Summer Olympics, as well as the football final. But no matter who takes the field, the 78,600-seat open-air arena comes to life in spectacular fashion on game day.

São Cristóvão & Maracanã

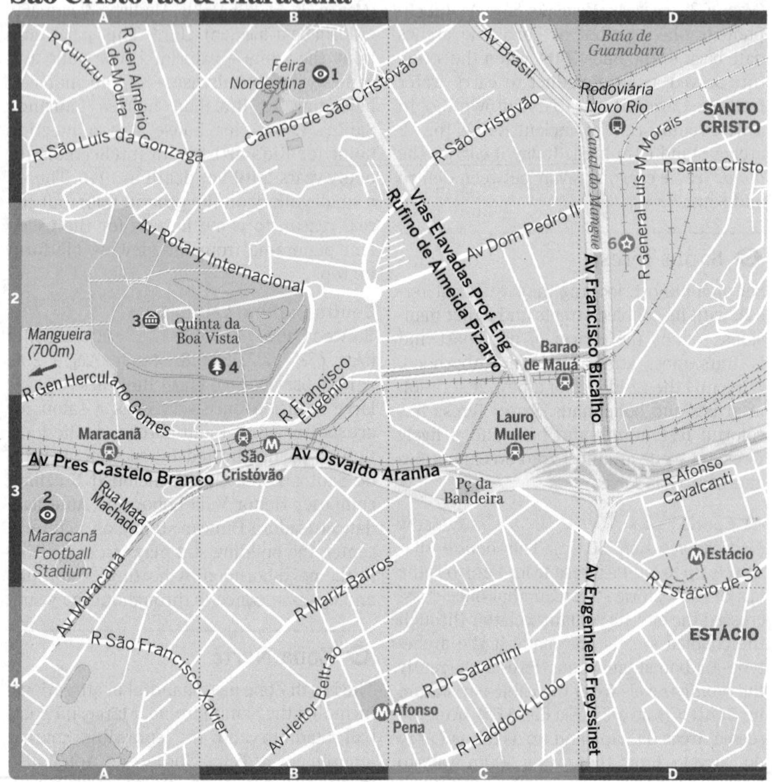

São Cristóvão & Maracanã

Sights

Quinta da Boa Vista PARK
(Map p76; ☎2562-6900; ⏰9am-5pm) Quinta da Boa Vista was the residence of the Portuguese imperial family until the republic was proclaimed. Today it's a large and busy park with gardens and lakes. On weekends it's crowded with football games and families from the Zona Norte. The former imperial mansion houses the Museu Nacional and Museu da Fauna. The Jardim Zoológico, Rio's zoo, is 200m away.

Museu Nacional MUSEUM
(Map p76; ☎3938-1100; Quinta da Boa Vista; adult/child R$6/3; ⏰noon-5pm Mon, 10am-5pm Tue-Sun) There are many interesting exhibits housed in the former imperial mansion: dinosaur fossils, saber-toothed tiger skeletons, beautiful pieces of pre-Columbian ceramics from the littoral and high plains of Peru, a huge meteorite, hundreds of stuffed birds, mammals and fish, gruesome displays of tropical diseases, and exhibits on the peoples of Brazil.

Feira Nordestina MARKET
(Map p76; ☎2580-5335; www.feiradesaocristovao.org.br; Campo de São Cristóvão; admission R$4, Tue-Thu free; ⏰10am-6pm Tue-Thu, 10am Fri to 9pm Sun) This enormous fair (32,000 sq meters with over 600 stalls) is not to be missed. It showcases the culture from

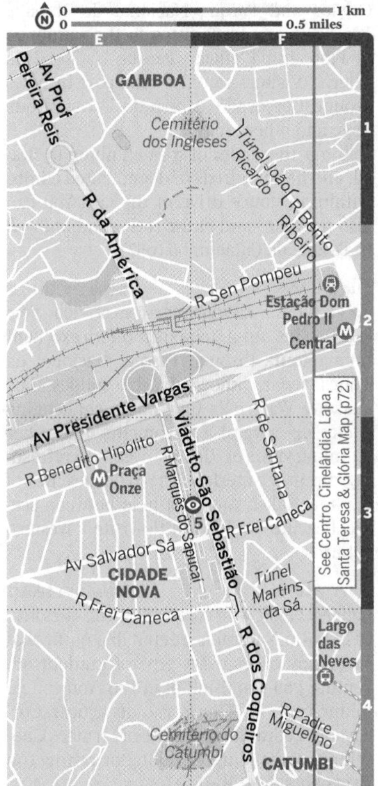

the Northeast, with *barracas* (food stalls) selling Bahian dishes as well as beer and *cachaça* (cane liquor), which flows in great abundance here. The best time to go is on the weekend, when you can catch live bands playing *forró,* plus samba groups and comedy troupes, MPB (Música Popular Brasileria) and *rodas de capoeira* (capoeira circles).

Sambódromo STADIUM

(Map p76; www.sambadrome.com; Marques do Sapuçai) The epicenter of Rio's Carnaval, the Sambódromo was designed by Oscar Niemeyer and completed in 1984. During the big parades, come for the fantastic views from the stands across elaborate floats, whirling dancers and pounding drum corps. The open-air arena received a makeover for the 2016 Olympics, with improved sight lines and a more symmetrical design in keeping with Niemeyer's original vision.

Barra da Tijuca & Western Rio

Ten kilometers west of Leblon, Barra da Tijuca (Barra) is the Miami of Rio, with malls and shopping centers set against the tropical landscape. It's also where many of the 2016 Summer Olympics take place. The beach here, a wide and lovely 15km-long stretch of shoreline, is the real attraction. Beyond this the region gets less and less urban. Some of Rio's most beautiful beaches lie out this way.

Praia da Barra da Tijuca BEACH

(Av Sernambetiba, Recreio dos Bandeirantes) The best thing about Barra is the beach. It stretches for 15km, with the lovely blue sea lapping at the shore. The first few kilometers of its eastern end are filled with bars and seafood restaurants.

Sítio Burle Marx GARDENS

(2410-1412; visitas.srbm@iphan.gov.br; Estrada da Barra de Guaratiba 2019, Guaratiba; admission R$10; tours 9:30am & 1:30pm Tue-Sat) This 35-hectare estate was once the home of Brazil's most famous landscape architect, Roberto Burle Marx. The estate's lush vegetation includes thousands of plant species, some of which are rare varieties from different corners of the globe. A 17th-century **Benedictine chapel** also lies on the estate, along with Burle Marx's original farmhouse and studio, where you can see displays of paintings, furniture and sculptures by the talented designer. Tours are by advance appointment only.

Casa do Pontal MUSEUM

(2490-4013; www.museucasadopontal.com.br; Estrada do Pontal 3295, Recreio dos Bandeirantes; admission permanent collection/temporary exhibits R$10/4; 9:30am-5pm Tue-Fri, 10:30am-6pm Sat & Sun) Owned by French designer Jacques Van de Beuque, this impressive set of more than 5000 pieces is one of the best folk-art collections in Brazil. The assorted artifacts are grouped according to theme, including music, Carnaval, religion and folklore. The grounds of the museum are surrounded by lush vegetation.

Parque Olímpico LANDMARK

This is the epicenter of the 2016 Summer Olympics and the Paralympic Games. You'll find seven arenas here: the tennis center, the aquatics stadium, the velodrome and separate arenas for basketball, judo and wrestling, handball, and fencing and tae kwon do. After the Olympics, the city has plans to convert some of the arenas into training facilities, while others will be dismantled and used to construct public schools.

Activities

Given the mountains, beaches and forests in their backyard, it's not surprising that *cariocas* are an active bunch. The coastline brings an array of options: jogging, hiking, walking, cycling and surfing. The mountains offer their own allure: you can hang glide off them or rock climb up them. Great hiking trails through Atlantic rainforest lie just outside the city.

Walking & Jogging

Good walking and jogging paths in the Zona Sul (the southern neighborhoods between Flamengo and Leblon) include Parque do Flamengo, which also has workout stations. A 7.5km track around Lagoa Rodrigo de Freitas provides a path for cyclists and joggers. Along the seaside, from Leme to Barra da Tijuca, there's a bike path and footpath. On Sundays the road is closed to traffic from 7am to 6pm. The road through Parque do Flamengo is also closed to vehicle traffic on Sundays.

Hiking & Climbing

In addition to access to nearby national parks such as Parque Nacional da Serra dos Órgãos and Parque Nacional do Itatiaia, Rio has many trails through the rainforest of Floresta da Tijuca (Parque Nacional da Tijuca). Visitors can also take part in hikes around Corcovado, Morro da Urca, Parque Lage and other areas.

Rio is the center of rock climbing in Brazil, and has hundreds of documented climbs within an hour's drive of the city. You can also try your hand at the rock-climbing wall in Parque da Catacumba (p57).

Jungle Me HIKING, GUIDED TOUR

(☎4105-7533; www.jungleme.com.br; tour from R$150) This top-notch outfit offers excellent hiking tours through Parque Nacional da Tijuca, led by knowledgeable guides. The Peaks & Waterfalls tour offers challenging walks up several escarpments that offer stunning views of Rio, followed by a refreshing dip in a waterfall. The Wild Beaches of Rio tour takes you on a hike between scenic beaches in Rio's little-visited western suburbs.

Rio Natural ADVENTURE SPORTS

(☎99992-1666; www.rionatural.com.br; hikes from R$190) Rio Natural is a reputable outfit that seemingly offers every type of outdoor adventure you can think of in Rio. You can go hiking (up Pico Tijuca, Pão de Açúcar, Corcovado, Pedra Bonita and Dois Irmãos), abseiling, paragliding, kayaking or rafting (on rivers outside of Rio).

BEACHES WEST OF RIO

Although Copacabana and Ipanema are Rio's most famous stretches of sand, there are many other stunning beaches in the area, some of which are in spectacular natural settings.

The first major beach you'll reach heading west of Leblon is **Praia do Pepino** in São Conrado, near where the hang gliders land. Note it's not the cleanest beach around. Further west is the small, lovely but well-concealed **Praia do Joatinga**, reachable by steep path down a rocky hillside. Be aware of the tides, so you don't get stranded.

Although it gets crowded on weekends, **Recreio dos Bandeirantes** is almost deserted during the week. The large rock acts as a natural breakwater, creating a calm bay. The 2km-long stretch of sand is popular with families.

The secluded 700m-long **Prainha** lies just past Recreio. It's one of the best surfing beaches in Rio, so it's always full of surfers. Waves come highly recommended here.

The most isolated and unspoiled beach close to the city, **Grumari** is quiet during the week and packed on weekends with *cariocas* looking to get away from the city beaches. It is a gorgeous setting, surrounded by mountains and lush vegetation.

From Grumari, a narrow road climbs over a jungle-covered hillside toward **Guaratiba**. West of here is a good view of the Restinga de Marambaia (the vegetation-rich strip between the beach and the mainland), closed off to the public by a naval base. *Cariocas* enjoy eating lunch at several of the seafood restaurants in the area.

WORTH A TRIP

PARQUE NACIONAL DA TIJUCA

The Floresta da Tijuca (another name for Parque Nacional da Tijuca) is all that's left of the Atlantic rainforest that once surrounded Rio de Janeiro. In just 15 minutes you can go from the concrete jungle of Copacabana to the 120-sq-km tropical jungle of **Parque Nacional da Tijuca** (Map p66; www.parquedatijuca.com.br; 8am-5pm). A more rapid and dramatic contrast is hard to imagine. The forest is an exuberant green, with beautiful trees, creeks and waterfalls, mountainous terrain and high peaks. It has an excellent and well-marked trail system, which includes the climb to the summit of **Pico da Tijuca** (1012m).

The heart of the forest is the Alto da Boa Vista area, which has many lovely natural and artificial features. Among the highlights of this beautiful park are several waterfalls (**Cascatinha Taunay**, **Cascata Gabriela** and **Cascata Diamantina**), a 19th-century chapel (**Capela Mayrink**) and numerous caves (**Gruta Luís Fernandes**, **Gruta Belmiro** and **Gruta Paulo e Virgínia**). Also in the park is a pleasant picnic spot (Bom Retiro) and several restaurants, which are near the **Ruínas do Archer** (the ruins of Major Archer's house). Tijuca wouldn't be the same without Archer – it was he who was tasked with replanting the forest in 1862 after years of clear-cutting for coffee and sugar-cane plantations.

It's best to get there by taxi, or to visit with an organized tour.

Rio Hiking HIKING
(99721-0594; www.riohiking.com.br; hikes from R$210) Founded by a mother-and-son team back in 1999, this popular outfit offers hiking trips that range from easy to strenuous and cover a variety of terrains around Rio. Popular tours include hikes up Pão de Açúcar, Corcovado and Pedra da Gávea. Other options: kayaking around Pão de Açúcar, surf lessons and all-day adventures outside of Rio (such as diving or hiking).

Crux Ecoadventure ROCK CLIMBING
(99392-9203, 3474-1726; www.cruxecoaventura.com.br) This reputable outfit offers a range of climbing excursions and other outdoor adventures. The most popular is the rock climb up Pão de Açúcar (R$375). Other possibilities include rappelling (abseiling) down waterfalls, full-day hikes through Floresta da Tijuca, and cycling and kayaking trips.

Climb in Rio ROCK CLIMBING
(2245-1108; www.climbinrio.com; half-day climbs R$230) This respected agency offers half- and full-day climbing trips led by experienced guides. Navigating more than 400 routes around Rio and the state, this is a good pick for climbing junkies.

Cycling

There are more than 300km of bike paths around Rio, with more planned in coming years. The best places to ride are around Lagoa Rodrigo de Freitas, along Barra da Tijuca and the oceanfront from Leblon to Leme. This last path also connects to Praia de Botafogo and Parque do Flamengo, running all the way to Centro. In the Floresta da Tijuca, a 6km cycle path runs from a Cascatinha Taunay waterfall to Açude museum. On Sundays the beach road from Leblon to Leme closes to vehicle traffic, as does the road through Parque do Flamengo.

You can rent bikes from a stand along the east and west sides of Lagoa Rodrigo de Freitas for R$15 per hour.

Rio by Bike BICYCLE TOUR
(96871-8933; www.riobybike.com; bike tour R$100-125) Two Dutch journalists operate this biking outfit, and their excellent pedaling tours combine a mix of scenery and cultural insight. It's a great way to get an overview of the city, with guides pointing out key landmarks and describing key events that have shaped Rio. Tours last three to four hours and travel mostly along bike lanes separated from traffic.

Velô Bike Store BICYCLE RENTAL
(Map p62; 3442-4315; Francisco Otaviano 20, Copacabana; per hr/day R$15/70, electric bike per hr R$30; 9am-7pm Mon-Fri, 9am-4pm Sat, 10am-4pm Sun) One of several shops conveniently located on the cycle path between Ipanema and Copacabana.

Hang Gliding

If you weigh less than 100kg (about 220lb) and can spare R$500, you can do the fantastic tandem hang glide off 510m-high Pedra

Bonita – one of the giant granite slabs that tower above Rio – onto Praia do Pepino in São Conrado. No experience is necessary; tandem riders are secured in a kind of pouch attached to the kite.

Flights typically last around 10 minutes, depending on weather and wind conditions. You can usually fly on all but three to four days per month, and conditions during winter are even better. If you schedule an early flight, you have more flexibility to accommodate weather delays. Prices include pickup and drop-off at your hotel. Travel agents also book tandem flights, but tack on their own fee. To cut out the middle person, call direct.

Delta Flight in Rio HANG GLIDING
(☎3322-5750, 99693-8800; www.riobyjeep.com/deltaflight) With more than 20 years' experience, Ricardo Hamond has earned a solid reputation as a safety-conscious and extremely professional pilot; he has flown more than 12,000 tandem flights.

Just Fly HANG GLIDING
(☎2268-0565; http://justflyinrio.blogspot.com) Paulo Celani is a highly experienced tandem flyer with more than 6000 flights to his credit.

Tandem Fly HANG GLIDING
(☎2422-6371, 2422-0941; www.riotandemfly.com.br) Two brothers – both very experienced pilots – run this outfit, and they also give lessons for those wanting to learn how to fly solo.

Surfing

Rio has some fine options when it comes to surfing, with some great breaks just outside the city. If you're not ready to leave the Zona Sul, though, Praia do Arpoador, between Copacabana and Ipanema, draws large flocks of surfers. Better breaks lie further west in Barra, Joatinga, Prainha and Grumari. Across the bay, Itacoatiara also has good breaks. For transportation to the western beaches, grab your board and hop on the **Surf Bus** (☎99799-5039; www.surfbus.com.br; one way R$10), a bright yellow-orange bus that makes four return trips daily (beginning at 7am) from Largo do Machado metro station (near Flamengo) to Prainha, with stops at beaches along the way.

If you don't have a board, you can hire or buy one in Arpoador at **Spirit Surfboards** (Map p62; Galeria River, Francisco Otaviano 67, Arpoador; surfboard hire per 1/2 days R$40/50); ⏲10am-6pm Mon-Sat), or hire on the beach.

You can also get out on the water on a stand-up paddleboard. Hire these out by the half-hour or take a lesson from rental outfits such as **Surf Rio** (Map p62; www.surfrio.com.br; Posto 6, Copacabana Beach; per hr R$50-60; ⏲7:30am-5pm), located at the southern end of Copacabana Beach. You can also rent a kayak off the beach in Praia Vermelha in Urca.

Beginners who want to learn to surf can take classes through informal *escolinhas* (schools) off Ipanema Beach and off Barra. You can also stay at the **Rio Surf 'n Stay** (☎3418-1133; www.riosurfnstay.com; Raimundo Veras 1140, Recreio dos Bandeirantes; dm/d from R$55/160; ❄📶) in Recreio dos Bandeirantes, which offers lessons (in English) and overnight accommodation.

Courses

Given the resurgent popularity of dance-hall samba throughout the city, it's not surprising that there are a number of places where you can learn the moves – then practice them – in Lapa.

Casa de Dança Carlinhos de Jesus DANCE
(Map p66; ☎2541-6186; www.carlinhosdejesus.com.br; Álvaro Ramos 11, Botafogo) At this respected dance academy in Botafogo, Carlinhos and his instructors offer evening classes in samba, *forró,* salsa and tango. On some Friday nights, open dance parties for students and guests are held. One of Botafogo's colorful *bloco* parties, Dois Pra Lá, Dois Pra Cá, begins from here during Carnaval.

Núcleo de Dança Renata Peçanha DANCE
(Map p72; ☎2221-1011; www.renatapecanha.com.br; Rua dos Inválidos 129, Lapa) A large upstairs studio on the edge of Lapa, this dance academy offers classes in *forró,* salsa, *zouk* (a slow and sensual dance derived from the lambada) and samba. Twice-weekly classes cost about R$140 per month.

Rio Samba Dancer DANCE
(Map p62; ☎98202-9810; riosambadancer.com; Barata Ribeiro 261A, Copacabana; group/private class R$70/150) English-speaking dance instructor Hélio Ricardo offers private and group dance classes in samba or *forró,* a popular music of the Northeast. To try out your new moves, sign up for a samba-class and night-tour combo: you'll take a one-hour crash course, then head out to Lapa for a night of dancing in a club (R$100 per person; cover charge not included).

Tours

Favela Tours

Favela Tour CULTURAL TOUR
(☎3322-2727; www.favelatour.com.br; tour R$90) Marcelo Armstrong's insightful tour pioneered favela tourism. His three-hour excursion takes in Rocinha and Vila Canoas.

Paulo Amendoim CULTURAL TOUR
(☎99747-6860; http://favelatourrio.com; tour R$75) Recommended guide Paulo Amendoim is the former president of Rocinha's residents association. He seems to know everyone in the favela, and leads a warm and personalized tour that helps visitors see beyond the stereotypes.

Be A Local CULTURAL TOUR
(☎99643-0366; www.bealocal.com; per person R$80) Offers daily trips into Rocinha (you'll ride up by moto-taxi, and walk back down), with stops along the way. It also organizes a night out at a *baile* (dance) funk party in Castelo das Pedras on Sunday.

City Walking Tours

Long guided hikes are also possible.

Free Walker Tours WALKING TOUR
(☎97101-3352; www.freewalkertours.com) This well-organized outfit runs a free walking tour that takes in a bit of history and culture in downtown Rio. You'll visit the Travessa do Comércio, Praça XV, Cinelândia, the Arcos da Lapa and the Selarón steps, among other places. Although it's free, the guide asks for tips at the end: by our reckoning, R$50 seems fair for the insightful three-hour walk.

The tour departs at 10:30am Monday through Saturday from Largo da Carioca (exit C out of Carioca metro station). Just show up (reservations aren't necessary). The same outfit also leads pub crawls in Ipanema and Lapa (each R$55), as well as a free Copacabana walking tour.

Lisa Rio Tours WALKING TOUR
(☎99894-6867; www.lisariotours.com; tour from US$41) Lisa Schnittger, a German expat who has lived in Rio for many years, leads a wide range of recommended tours. Some of her most popular excursions explore the colonial history of downtown, the bohemian side of Santa Teresa, and Afro-Brazilian culture in Rio.

Bay Tours

Saveiros Tours CRUISE
(Map p72; ☎2225-6064; www.saveiros.com.br; Marina de Glória, Glória; cruise from R$55) Saveiros leads daily two-hour cruises out over Baía de Guanabara in large schooners. The route follows the coastline of Rio and Niterói with excellent views of Pão de Açúcar, the MAC, Ilha Fiscal and the old fort of Urca. You'll sail under the Niterói bridge. Departs from the Marina de Glória.

Bem Brasil CRUISE
(www.bembrasilrio.com; Marina da Glória, Glória; cruise from R$70) Runs popular booze cruises in the bay from a two-floor sailboat soundtracked by well-known house DJ Andrew Gracie every Monday night at 11pm.

Other Tours

Most recommended outfits include round-trip transportation from your hostel/hotel in the price.

Be A Local TOUR
(☎99643-0366; www.bealocal.com; per person around R$140) Popular with backpackers, Be a Local offers group tours with a younger, edgier flavor. It offers favela tours, outings to football matches at Maracanã and trips to evening favela parties.

Brazil Expedition TOUR
(☎99998-2907; www.brazilexpedition.com; city tour R$120) The friendly English-speaking guides run a variety of traditional tours around Rio, including trips to Cristo Redentor, nightlife outings to samba schools,

COOK IN RIO

At long last, travelers finally have the opportunity to take a locally run cooking course. **Cook in Rio** (Map p62; ☎8761-3653; www.cookinrio.com; 2nd fl, Belfort Roxo 161; per person US$75) in Copacabana teaches aspiring chefs how to make some of Brazil's most famous dishes. Each one-day class runs from 11am to 4pm and includes the preparation of either *moqueca* (seafood stew) or *feijoada completa* (multi-dish black bean and pork stew), along with appetizers and side dishes, dessert and a masterful caipirinha. The best part is that you'll get to devour your creations afterwards.

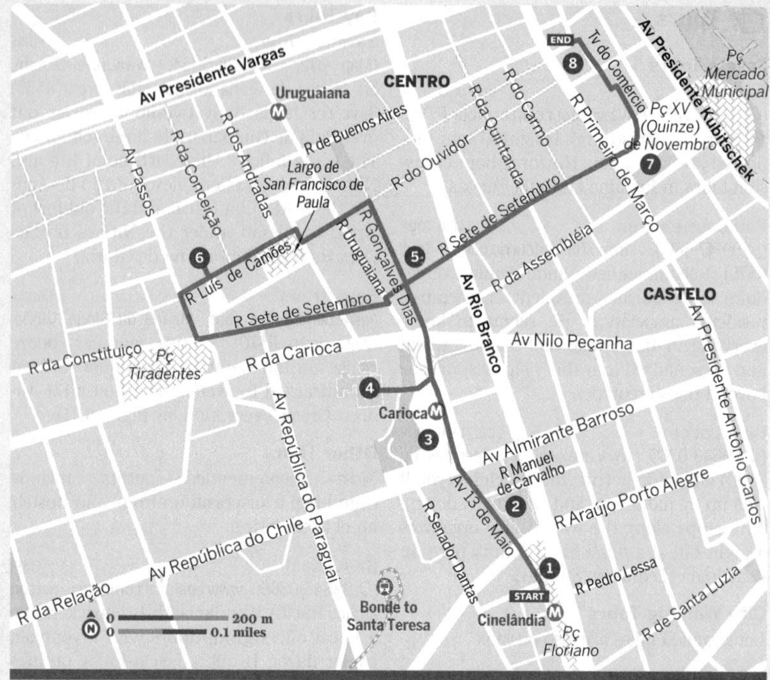

City Walk Rio on Foot

START PRAÇA FLORIANO
END TRAVESSA DO COMÉRCIO
LENGTH 3KM; FOUR HOURS

A mélange of historic buildings and skyscrapers, the center of Rio is an intriguing place to discover the essence of the city away from its beaches and mountains. This tour is best done during the week, as it gets rather deserted (and unsafe) on weekends.

Start at the **1 Praça Floriano** (p71), a scenic plaza set with several outdoor cafes. On the north side, the neoclassical **2 Theatro Municipal** (p71) is one of Rio's finest buildings, particularly after its R$65 million renovation. If you time it right, you can head inside on a guided tour.

Stroll north along Av 13 de Maio. You'll soon pass through the **3 Largo da Carioca**, a bustling area with a small market. Up on the hill is the **4 Igreja São Francisco da Penitência** (p70), a 17th-century church with a jaw-dropping gilded interior. You can reach the church via stairs or elevator near the Carioca metro station.

After taking in the views, go back down and make your way over to narrow Rua Gonçalves Dias to reach **5 Confeitaria Colombo** (p99) for a dose of caffeine, pastries and art nouveau.

From Rua Gonçalves Dias, turn left on Rua do Ouvidor, following it to Largo de San Francisco de Paula. Continue one block further to **6 Real Gabinete Português de Leitura** (p71), a historic reading room that seems straight out of 19th-century Portugal.

Turn right when exiting and pass by Praça Tiradentes, before heading over to Rua Sete de Setembro. Follow it until it ends near the **7 Paço Imperial** (p71). Once the seat of the Portuguese rulers in Brazil, the building today houses intriguing art exhibitions as well as several cafes.

Leaving the Paço, cross Praça XV (Quinze) de Novembro and take the narrow lane beneath the arch. You'll walk along one of Centro's oldest lanes, **8 Travessa do Comércio** (p71), where open-air restaurants and bars draw crowds around happy hour. It's a fitting end to the day's wander.

game-day trips to Maracanã Football Stadium, street-art tours and favela tours.

Helisight SCENIC FLIGHTS
(2511-2141; www.helisight.com.br; per person 6-/15-/30min flight R$260/650/900) Offering helicopter tours since 1991, Helisight has seven different itineraries, all giving gorgeous views over the city. There's a three-person minimum. Helipad locations are in Floresta da Tijuca facing Corcovado; on Morro da Urca, the first cable-car stop up Pão de Açúcar; and on the edge of Lagoa.

Jeep Tour DRIVING TOUR
(2108-5800; www.jeeptour.com.br; 4hr tour R$142) Tours go to the Floresta da Tijuca in a large, open-topped 4WD. It includes a stop at the Vista Chinesa, then on to the forest for an easy hike and a stop for a swim beneath a waterfall, before making the return journey.

Festivals & Events

Aside from Carnaval, there are many other exciting events happening throughout the year.

Festas Juninas CULTURAL
(Jun) The June Festival is one of the most important folkloric festivals in Brazil. In Rio, it's celebrated in various public plazas throughout the month, primarily on June 13 (Dia de Santo Antônio), June 24 (Dia de São João) and June 29 (Dia de São Pedro).

Portas Abertas CULTURAL
(www.artedeportasabertas.com.br; Jul) Santa Teresa's artists open their studios and the neighborhood becomes a living installation for a weekend each year in July.

Rio International Film Festival FILM
(www.festivaldorio.com.br; Sep-Oct) The festival is one of the biggest in Latin America. Some 250 films from more than 60 countries are shown at 20-odd theaters. It runs over two weeks, and kicks off either in September or October.

Reveillon & Festa de Iemanjá HOLIDAY, FESTIVAL
(Dec 31) New Year's Eve (Reveillon) in Rio is celebrated by millions of people. Tons of fireworks explode in the sky over Copacabana. New Year's Day coincides with the festival of Iemanjá, the sea goddess. Wearing white, the faithful carry a statue of Iemanjá to the beach and launch flowers and other offerings into the sea.

Sleeping

Rio has a wide mix of lodging options, including boutique hotels, hostels, B&Bs and plenty of cookie-cutter high-rise accommodations. If you want to be in the heart of the action and don't mind paying for it, stay in Ipanema or Leblon, where there are beautiful beaches and excellent restaurants, shopping and nightlife. Copacabana has many more options (and better prices), plus a great beach and many restaurants and bars. For a nonbeach alternative, take a peek at Santa Teresa's colonial guesthouses – the neighborhood is also close to the nightlife of Lapa. Other northern neighborhoods along the metro line (Botafogo, Flamengo and Catete) generally have cheaper options than the beachside southern neighborhoods.

Hotel rates are 30% higher during summer (from December to mid-March) and prices double or triple for New Year's Eve and Carnaval, when most places, including hostels, also require four- or seven-day minimum bookings.

Keep in mind that many hotels add a combined 15% service and tax charge, though cheaper places don't generally bother with this.

Ipanema & Leblon

Rio Hostel – Ipanema HOSTEL $
(Map p54; 2287-2928; www.riohostelipanema.com; Casa 1, Canning 18, Ipanema; dm/d from R$60/180; @) This friendly hostel is in a small villa on a peaceful stretch of Ipanema. A mix of travelers stay here, enjoying the clean rooms, the airy top-floor deck with hammocks, and the small front veranda. The location is fantastic: it's less than 10 minutes' walk to either Ipanema or Copacabana Beach.

Lemon Spirit Hostel HOSTEL $
(Map p54; 2294-1853; www.lemonspirit.com; Cupertino Durão 56, Leblon; dm R$70-90; @) One of Leblon's only hostels, Lemon Spirit boasts an excellent location one block from the beach. The dorm rooms (four to six beds in each) are clean and simple without much decor. There's a tiny courtyard in front, and the attractive lobby bar is a good place to meet other travelers over caipirinhas.

Hostel Harmonia HOSTEL $
(Map p54; 2523-4905; www.casadaharmonia.com; Casa 18, Barão da Torre 175, Ipanema; dm R$65-75; @) Run by a Californian,

Hostel Harmonia is a small but appealing hostel with a good traveler vibe. The lounge and rooms have two-toned wood floors, and quarters are clean and well maintained, with four to six beds in each room.

Leblon Spot Design Hostel HOSTEL **$$**
(Map p54; ☎2137-4310; www.leblonspot.com; Dias Ferreira 636, Leblon; dm weekday/weekend R$62/110, d R$260-350; ❄@📶) The location is outstanding: you're within a short stroll of some of Rio's best restaurants and liveliest drinking spots. The setting is a former house, with bright but rather cramped rooms with wood floors, a small lounge and a tiny veranda. Unlike other Rio hostels, there isn't much socializing here, and the staff isn't the friendliest.

Margarida's Pousada POUSADA **$$**
(Map p54; ☎2239-1840; www.margaridaspousada.com; Barão da Torre 600, Ipanema; d from R$300; ❄@📶) Those seeking something smaller and cozier than a high-rise hotel should try this superbly located Ipanema pousada (guesthouse). You'll find 11 pleasant, simply furnished rooms scattered about the low-rise building. Margarida also rents out several private, fully equipped apartments nearby.

Bonita HOSTEL **$$**
(Map p54; ☎2227-1703; www.bonitaipanema.com; Barão da Torre 107, Ipanema; dm R$60, d with/without bathroom R$270/220; ❄@📶🏊) This peacefully set converted house has history: it's where bossa nova legend Tom Jobim lived from 1962 to 1965 and wrote some of his most famous songs. Rooms are clean but simply furnished, and most open onto a shared deck overlooking a small pool and patio.

Arpoador Inn HOTEL **$$**
(Map p54; ☎2523-0060; www.arpoadorinn.com.br; Francisco Otaviano 177, Ipanema; r with/without view R$690/510; ❄📶) Overlooking Praia do Arpoador, this six-story inn is the only hotel in Ipanema and Copacabana that doesn't have a busy street between it and the beach. The rooms are small and basic, but the brighter 'deluxe' rooms have glorious ocean views. The hotel also has a good restaurant facing beachside.

Ipanema Hotel Residência APARTMENT **$$**
(Map p54; ☎3125-5000; www.ipanemahotel.com.br; Barão da Torre 192, Ipanema; d R$500, per month from R$7000; ❄📶🏊) Set on one of Ipanema's lovely tree-lined streets, this high-rise has large apartments with kitchen units, lounge areas and pleasant bedrooms. Each apartment has a veranda; some are larger than others. There's also a sunny rooftop pool surrounded by artificial grass, a sauna and a tiny workout room.

★ **Casa Mosquito** GUESTHOUSE **$$$**
(Map p54; ☎3586-5042; www.casamosquito.com; Saint Roman 222, Ipanema; r from R$650; ❄📶) Opened by two French expats, Casa Mosquito is a beautifully designed boutique guesthouse with luxuriously appointed rooms. The converted all-white 1940s mansion sits on a tranquil garden-filled property with scenic views of Pão de Açúcar and the Pavão-Pavãozinho favela. It's located on a steep, winding street about 10 minutes' walk from Praça General Osório. Meals are available by request.

Hotel Praia Ipanema HOTEL **$$$**
(Map p54; ☎2141-4949; www.praiaipanema.com; Av Vieira Souto 706, Ipanema; d from R$700; 🚭❄@🏊) With a view of Ipanema Beach, this popular 16-story hotel offers trim, comfortable rooms, each with a balcony. The design is sleek and modern, with off-white tile floors, recessed lighting and artwork on the walls. Stretch out on the molded white lounge chairs next to the rooftop pool or, better yet, enjoy a meal: the penthouse restaurant, Espaço 7zero6 (p93), is excellent.

Marina All Suites BOUTIQUE HOTEL **$$$**
(Map p54; ☎2172-1100; www.hoteismarina.com.br; Av Delfim Moreira 696, Leblon; ste from R$935; ❄@🏊) You'll find beautifully decorated rooms, doting service and all the creature comforts here. As per the name, all rooms are suites, meaning that between the comfy bedroom and the living room you'll have plenty of space in which to stretch out. The best rooms in the oceanfront hotel have splendid views of the shoreline.

Hotel Fasano HOTEL **$$$**
(Map p54; ☎3202-4000; www.fasano.com.br; Av Vieira Souto 80, Ipanema; d from R$1660; ❄@📶🏊) Designed by Philippe Starck, the Fasano has 91 sleek rooms set with Egyptian-cotton sheets, goose-down pillows and high-tech fittings. The best rooms have balconies overlooking the crashing waves of Ipanema Beach, which lies just across the road. Rooms without a view simply don't justify the price. The lovely rooftop pool

(open to guests only) is truly breathtaking – as are the room rates.

Ritz Plaza Hotel APARTMENT $$$
(Map p54; ☎2540-4940; www.ritzhotel.com.br; Av Ataúlfo de Paiva 1280, Leblon; r from R$620;) In one of Rio's most desirable areas, this stylish low-key hotel has attractive, uniquely designed rooms and common areas that give the Ritz a boutique feel. The best rooms have kitchen units and balconies – some offering partial ocean views – and all are trimmed with artwork, good lighting and spotless bedrooms. Amenities include an elegant (if often empty) bar, a sauna, a pool and a spa.

Gávea, Jardim Botânico & Lagoa

Pouso Verde GUESTHOUSE $$
(Map p56; ☎2529-2942; www.pousoverde.com; Caminhoá 14, Jardim Botânico; s/d R$240/300;) On a quiet cobblestone street in a charming corner of Jardim Botânico, Pouso Verde has elegant, comfortably furnished rooms, the best of which have views of Cristo Redentor. The historic house (which dates back to the 1890s) is packed with artwork, and the owners go out of their way to make guests feel at home. Excellent breakfasts.

Copacabana & Leme

Cabana Copa HOSTEL $
(Map p62; ☎3988-9912; www.cabanacopa.com.br; Travessa Guimarães Natal 12, Copacabana; dm R$40-80, d R$180-250; @) Top hostel honors go to this Greek-Brazilian-run gem in a colonial-style '50s house tucked away in a Copacabana cranny. Four- to 10-bed dorms prevail throughout the home, which is chock-full of original architectural details and a hodgepodge of funky floorings. There's a lively bar and common areas.

The hostel runs a brand-new all-suites building next door: a great option for travelers who want a private room without missing out on the social interaction of a hostel.

Che Lagarto – Suites Santa Clara BOUTIQUE HOSTEL $$
(Map p62; ☎3495-3133; www.chelagarto.com; Santa Clara 304, Copacabana; r with/without bathroom from R$220/170; @) On a tree-lined street in Copacabana's Bairro Peixoto neighborhood, this converted house has clean, simple and well-maintained rooms (all private rooms, no dorms), and a small downstairs lounge where you can meet other travelers. The friendly staff give out helpful advice, and can direct you to loads of activities.

Edificio Jucati HOSTEL, APARTMENT $$
(Map p62; ☎2547-5422; www.edificiojucati.com.br; Tenente Marones de Gusmão 85, Copacabana; d/q from R$230/290;) Near a small park and on a tranquil street, Jucati has large, simply furnished serviced apartments with slate floors and small but serviceable kitchens. Have a look at the layout before committing. Most apartments have just one bedroom with a double bed and a living room with a bunk bed. The small covered courtyard is a fine spot to unwind.

Hotel Santa Clara HOTEL $$
(Map p62; ☎2256-2650; www.hotelsantaclara.com.br; Décio Vilares 316, Copacabana; s/d/tr from R$250/280/320;) Along one of Copacabana's most peaceful streets, you'll find this attractive three-story hotel, with a white stucco facade and blue shutters. The front-facing upstairs rooms are best, and well worth the extra money, with wood floors, antique bed frames, writing desks and balconies. The rooms in back are a little gloomy.

Rio Guesthouse B&B $$
(Map p62; ☎2521-8568; www.rioguesthouse.com; Francisco Sá 5, Copacabana; d R$380-590;) The Australian-Brazilian hosts open up their home and rent out several

RIO FOR CHILDREN

Brazilians are very family-oriented. Some hotels let children stay free, although the age limit varies. Babysitters are readily available and most restaurants have high chairs.

There's plenty of good spade-and-sandbucket fun to be had on Rio's beaches, particularly Leblon's *posto* 12, known as Baixo for its mini-playground and all the moms and tots around. Other amusement for kids includes rainforest walks in **Parque Lage** (p57), pedal boats on **Lagoa** (p56), biking (and triking) from Parque dos Patins (on the west side of Lagoa), aquatic wonders at **AquaRio** (p69) and snacking at juice bars and markets all around town.

comfortable rooms at this split-level penthouse overlooking Copacabana Beach. The highlight is undoubtedly the outdoor patio, which has gorgeous views over Copacabana.

Copacabana Palace HOTEL **$$$**

(Map p62; ☎2548-7070; www.belmond.com; Av Atlântica 1702, Copacabana; d from R$1500; ❄@📶🏊) Rio's most famous hotel has hosted heads of state, rock stars and other prominent personalities – Queen Elizabeth once stayed here, as did the Rolling Stones. The dazzling white facade dates from the 1920s, when it became a symbol of the city. Today accommodations range from deluxe rooms to spacious suites with balconies.

Porto Bay Rio Internacional HOTEL **$$$**

(Map p62; ☎2546-8000; www.portobay.com.br; Av Atlântica 1500, Copacabana; d from R$750; ❄@📶🏊) One of Copacabana's top beachfront hotels, Porto Bay has stylish rooms with a light and airy feel that are painted in cool tones. Large white duvets, light hardwoods, elegant furnishings and simple artwork all complement each other nicely. Big windows let in lots of light, and most rooms have balconies.

Botafogo & Urca

Vila Carioca HOSTEL **$**

(Map p66; ☎2535-3224; www.vilacarioca.com.br; Estácio Coimbra 84, Botafogo; dm R$35-60, d R$130-320; ❄@📶) On a peaceful tree-lined street, this low-key and welcoming hostel has four- to 15-bed dorms in an attractively decorated house. The common areas are a fine spot to mingle with other travelers.

Oztel HOSTEL **$$**

(Map p66; ☎3042-1853; www.oztel.com.br; Pinheiro Guimarães 91, Botafogo; dm R$45-75, d R$240-300; ❄@📶) Evoking a Warholian aesthetic, Rio's coolest and most colorful hostel is like sleeping in an art gallery. The artsy front deck and bar is an inviting hangout lounge but the real coup are the private rooms: with a garden patio under the nose of Cristo Redentor, you'll be hard-pressed to find a groovier room in Rio.

Hotelinho Urca GUESTHOUSE **$$**

(Map p66; ☎3449-8867; www.hotelinho.com; Marechal Cantuária 10, Urca; r with/without bathroom from R$280/180; ❄📶🏊) One of the few lodging options in Urca, this quiet, low-key guesthouse has a range of clean, well-equipped rooms with attractive wood floors. The sunny veranda has views over the bay and is the best feature; there's also a tiny dip pool. Hotelinho Urca also rents several apartments nearby. You'll score a 5% discount if paying in cash.

Injoy Hostel GUESTHOUSE **$$**

(Map p66; ☎3593-6662; www.injoyhostel.com; Estácio de Coimbra 80, Botafogo; d from R$250; ❄@📶) Despite the name, this place feels less like a hostel and more like a small guesthouse. Injoy has 18 private rooms set in a lovely house at the end of a tree-lined lane. Rooms are modern, very clean and well maintained, and each is named after a major city, with iconic photos from that destination decorating one wall. Friendly staff.

O Veleiro GUESTHOUSE **$$**

(Map p66; ☎2554-8980; www.oveleiro.com; Mundo Novo 1440, Botafogo; R$240-380; ❄📶🏊) Surrounded by Atlantic rainforest, O Veleiro is a delightfully set guesthouse located on a cobblestone road uphill from Botafogo. The rooms are small and adequately furnished but the backyard is the real attraction, with hammocks, a small pool and pretty views (plus the occasional marmoset visitor).

On the downside, it's a bit of a trudge to get down to Botafogo (even more so on the way back uphill), but for a tranquil escape that's still inside central Rio, this is a decent option.

Flamengo & Around

Discovery Hostel HOSTEL **$**

(Map p72; ☎3449-0672; www.discoverhostel.com; Benjamin Constant 26, Catete; dm/d R$60/200; ❄📶) One of Rio's most socially minded hostels, Discovery is a great place to meet other travelers. While it's not on the beach, the attractive converted house is convenient for exploring the nightlife of Lapa, and it's an easy stroll to the metro. In addition to dorm rooms (a minus for the triple bunks), the hostel has a couple of colorful private rooms.

There's a bar, a lounge and a small plant-lined patio. The staff organize many activities for guests.

Casa Caminho do Corcovado B&B **$$**

(Map p66; ☎2557-2359; www.casacaminhodocorcovado.com.br; Filinto de Almeida 283, Cosme Velho; d R$240-390; ❄📶) On the Corcovado hillside, this idyllic place is surrounded by tropical rainforest, and feels like a peaceful escape from the city. Friendly knowledgeable hosts offer just two attractive rooms and one bungalow overlooking the garden; it's in high demand so book early. Fine views, and a relaxing air pervades.

Solar do Cosme GUESTHOUSE **$$**
(Map p66; ☎3596-0585; www.solardocosme.com; Ladeira do Ascurra 124, Cosme Velho; s/d R$234/260) Nestled at the foothill of Corcovado, this tranquil guesthouse earns high marks from guests for the kindhearted hosts, who are happy to share tips on making the most of Rio. The rooms are tidy and well maintained, and the lush grounds add to the value.

On the downside, it's a long way from the beach, though it's a short walk to the cog station leading up to Cristo Redentor.

Centro & Praça Mauá

Pop Art Hostel HOSTEL **$**
(Map p72; ☎2253-9069; www.poparthostel.com.br; Ladeira João Homem 56, Morro da Conceição; dm/d from R$40/130; ❄📶) Located in the pretty neighborhood of Morro da Conceição, this hostel has clean, modern rooms decorated with colorful artworks (though not necessarily pop art). The rooms lack windows, though there's a small, pleasant back terrace with views. It's a friendly spot,

FAVELA CHIC

Favela sleeps are nothing new – intrepid travelers have been venturing into Rio's urban mazes for nearly a decade – but as more and more of Rio's favelas (slums, informal communities) are pacified, hostels and pousadas (guesthouses) are popping up faster than the rudimentary constructions that make up the favelas themselves.

Our favorites:

Maze Inn (Map p66; ☎2558-5547; www.jazzrio.com; Casa 66, Tavares Bastos 414, Catete; dm R$90, s/d from R$175/225) Set in Tavares Bastos favela, the Maze Inn is a fantastic place to overnight for those looking for an alternative view of Rio. The rooms are uniquely decorated with original artworks by English owner and Renaissance man Bob Nadkarni, while the veranda offers stunning views of the bay and Pão de Açúcar.

Vidigalbergue (☎3114-8025; www.vidigalbergue.com.br; Casa 2, Av Niemeyer 314, Vidigal; dm R$45-60; ❄@📶) A 15-minute walk from Leblon brings you to this small hostel at the bottom of Vidigal favela, where these days there's even a tourist map to guide you around. The coup here is the stunning sea views from all the dorms and the hospitality of the two English-speaking best-friend owners, Luis and Andre.

Babilônia Rio Hostel (Map p62; ☎3873-6826; www.babiloniariohostel.com.br; Ladeira Ary Barroso 50, Leme; dm R$40-50, d R$140-170) Uphill from Leme, this place has five dorm rooms and two private rooms, including one much sought-after chamber (Quarto Vidigal) with air-conditioning and a sea view. It's a friendly place in a small, welcoming community and there are good eating and drinking options nearby.

Mirante do Arvrão (☎3114-1868; mirantedoarvrao.com.br; Armando de Almeida Lima 8, Vidigal; dm/s/d from R$58/158/400; ❄📶) A surprising find in Vidigal, the Mirante do Arvrão has beautifully set rooms, the best of which offer gorgeous views over the ocean. It's worth paying extra for a deluxe room with floor-to-ceiling windows and a private balcony. The hostel is built from sustainable materials and uses solar power to heat the showers.

Verandas do Vidigal (☎3114-3661; www.varandasdovidigal.com.br; Casa 3, Madre Ana Coimbra, Vidigal; dm R$38-45, d R$110-130; ❄📶) This friendly hostel has clean, Zen-like, tile-floored dorm rooms with four to 12 top-quality beds as well as a private double. The ocean views are mesmerizing, particularly from the laid-back veranda-bar. The friendly owner, who speaks English and hails from Rio Grande do Sul, has a deep affection for Vidigal and has a wealth of insight into the community.

Pousada Favelinha (Map p66; ☎98406-7764; www.favelinha.com; Almirante Alexandrino 2023, Santa Teresa; dm R$50, d R$110; @📶🐾) Located in the favela of Pereirão da Silva, Pousada Favelinha has four double rooms and a five-bed dorm, all with balconies that have stunning views over the city to Pão de Açúcar. There's also a terrace, a lounge, and lots of insider info available from the welcoming Brazilian-German owners.

and it's on one of Rio's most picturesque cobblestone lanes, just a short stroll to the sights of Praça Mauá.

Santa Teresa & Lapa

A growing number of budget and midrange hotels have opened in Santa Teresa in recent years, drawing travelers to this intriguing, arts-loving neighborhood. Do take care when walking around, day or night, as crime is still an issue.

Rio Hostel HOSTEL $
(Map p72; ☎3852-0827; www.riohostel.com; Joaquim Murtinho 361, Santa Teresa; dm/s/d from R$35/80/120; ❄@📶≈) This Santa favorite provides travelers with a home away from home. The backyard patio with its pool is a great place to meet other travelers, and there's also a kitchen for guests. Rooms are clean, and there are attractive doubles, including private suites with fine views behind the pool.

Casa da Gente GUESTHOUSE $
(Map p72; ☎2232-2634; www.casadagente.com; Gonçalves Fontes 33, Santa Teresa; s/d from R$125/185; 📶) 🍃 A short stroll from the top of the Escadaria Selarón, the Casa da Gente is a welcoming French-Brazilian-run guesthouse with a strong interest in sustainability. Rainwater catchment, solar panels, composting and a green roof are all part of the ethos. The rooms themselves are bright, clean and simply furnished.

The grassy terrace is a pleasant place to relax after exploring the city. It's not a bad spot for cat lovers, as there are three felines in residence.

★ **Casa Beleza** POUSADA $$
(Map p72; ☎98288-6764; www.casabeleza.net; Laurinda Santos Lobo 311, Santa Teresa; r R$260-450; ❄📶≈) This lovely property dates back to the 1930s and was once a governor's mansion. Tropical gardens overlook the picturesque pool, and you can sometimes spot toucans and monkeys in the surrounding foliage. It's a small and peaceful operation, with just four guestrooms and one peacefully set villa (complete with a rooftop deck offering panoramic views).

Casa Áurea GUESTHOUSE $$
(Map p72; ☎2242-5830; www.casaaurea.com.br; Áurea 80, Santa Teresa; d R$300-340, s/d without bathroom R$170/220; ❄📶) Set in one of Santa Teresa's oldest homes (1871), the two-story Casa Áurea has rustic charm, simple but cozy rooms and a large covered garden where you can lounge on hammocks, fire up the barbecue or whip up a meal in the open-air kitchen. Very welcoming and kindhearted hosts.

Cama e Café HOMESTAY $$
(Map p72; ☎2225-4366; www.camaecafe.com; Progresso 67, Santa Teresa; r R$196-300) A fine alternative to hotels and guesthouses, Cama e Café is a B&B network that allows travelers to book a room from local residents. There are several dozen options to choose from,

LONG-TERM RENTALS

If you're planning to stay in Rio for longer than a few nights, you might consider renting an apartment, which is often better value than staying in a hotel. Nightly rates start around R$200 for a studio apartment in Copacabana or R$350 in Ipanema; rates rise significantly during Carnaval and New Year's Eve. Airbnb.com has thousands of Rio listings all across the city.

Rio Spot Homes (Map p62; ☎3988-7613, 99188-3304; www.riospothomes.com; Office 214, Prado Junior 48, Copacabana) Professional outfit with dozens of great options around Copacabana, Ipanema and Barra.

Blame It on Rio 4 Travel (Map p62; ☎3813-5510; www.blameitonrio4travel.com; Xavier da Silveira 15B, Copacabana) Run by an expat from New York, this professional agency rents apartments and runs a full-service travel agency.

Ipanema for Rent (Map p54; ☎99603-2109, 7822-4684; www.ipanemaforrent.com.br; Sobreloja 29, Visconde de Pirajá 318, Ipanema; apt from R$150) Many choices, especially in Ipanema and Copacabana.

Rio Apartments (Map p62; ☎4042-6221; www.rioapartments.com; Santa Clara 98, Copacabana) A Swedish-run outfit with many apartment rentals in the Zona Sul.

with the majority of listings in Santa Teresa, and a few scattered options in Laranjeiras, the Zona Sul and Barra.

Casa da Carmen e do Fernando GUESTHOUSE **$$**

(Map p72; ☎2507-3084; www.bedandbreakfastrio.com.br; Hermenegildo de Barros 172, Santa Teresa; s/d from R$175/225;) This familial eight-room guesthouse attracts a laid-back crowd that feels right at home in the century-old building. The colorfully decorated lounge is adorned with artwork (including paintings by one of the owners) and has a comfy, lived-in feel; it's a fine place to watch a film, play music or enjoy the fine view through the oversized picture window.

Out the back is a small pool and a rustic terrace, which have equally impressive views. Rooms are simply furnished but enlivened with bright colors and likewise come with views.

Casalegre GUESTHOUSE **$$**

(Map p72; ☎98670-6158; www.casalegre.com.br; Monte Alegre 316, Santa Teresa; s R$150-250, d R$190-300;) Casalegre has a rustic, art-loving, bohemian vibe. Its rooms vary in size (the cheapest two share a bathroom), but all are decorated with different works of art and each is named after the artist whose work adorns its walls. There's a strong communal vibe here, and the owners often host parties, yoga classes and other activities.

Casa Cool Beans GUESTHOUSE **$$**

(Map p72; ☎2262-0552; www.casacoolbeans.com; Laurinda Santos Lobo 136, Santa Teresa; d R$250-400; @) Your expectations will easily be exceeded at this discreet 10-room B&B, where the American owner's mantra focuses on personalized service. Each colorful room in the renovated 1930s Spanish-style villa was designed by a different Brazilian artist; book room 9 for the best views. It also has a spacious sundeck and an enticing pool. No children allowed.

★**Hotel Santa Teresa** BOUTIQUE HOTEL **$$$**

(Map p72; ☎2222-2755; www.santa-teresa-hotel.com; Almirante Alexandrino 660, Santa Teresa; d from R$1000; @) What is probably the finest boutique hotel in Rio is set in a lavishly restored building that was part of a coffee plantation in the 19th century. It includes artfully designed rooms, an award-winning restaurant, a full-service spa, a stylish bar and a pool with fine views over the city.

Vila Galé BOUTIQUE HOTEL **$$$**

(Map p72; ☎2460-4500; www.vilagale.com; Riachuelo 124, Lapa; r R$360-800;) Breathing new life into ragged Lapa, Vila Galé – a high-end luxury chain from Portugal – invested some €35 million in this beautiful property. The spacious, well-appointed rooms are good value, and the best of them are set in a 19th-century building overlooking a lovely pool. The rooms are quiet despite having the best of Rio's nightlife right outside the door.

Eating

Rio has an impressive array of restaurants, serving up Brazilian regional cuisine along with international and fusion fare. In general, Ipanema and Leblon boast Rio's best dining, though every neighborhood has its gems.

Rio's quintessential dining experiences include feasting at a *churrascaria* (all-you-can-eat barbecued-meat restaurant), dining alfresco beside the lake in Lagoa, joining the fashion parade at a sidewalk cafe in Ipanema, chowing on local favorites at a neighborhood *boteco* (small open-air bar) and lingering over the views from a restaurant patio up in Santa Teresa.

To eat on the cheap, try per-kilo places and juice bars. Self-caterers should check out Rio's many *feiras* (produce markets).

Ipanema

Vero ICE CREAM **$**

(Map p54; ☎3497-8754; Visconde de Pirajá 260; ice creams R$11-16; 11am-midnight) This artisanal Italian-run gelateria whips up Rio's best ice cream. You'll find more than two dozen rich and creamy temptations, including *gianduia* (chocolate with hazelnut), *caramelo com flor de sal* (caramel with sea salt), *figo com amêndoas* (fig with almond) and classic flavors such as *morango* (strawberry). The selection changes daily.

Cafeína CAFE **$**

(Map p54; ☎2521-2194; www.cafeina.com.br; Farme de Amoedo 43; quiches R$10, sandwiches R$20-40; 8am-11:30pm;) In the heart of Ipanema, this inviting cafe with sidewalk tables is a fine spot for an espresso while watching the city stroll by. You'll also find freshly made sandwiches, salads, quiches and some very rich desserts.

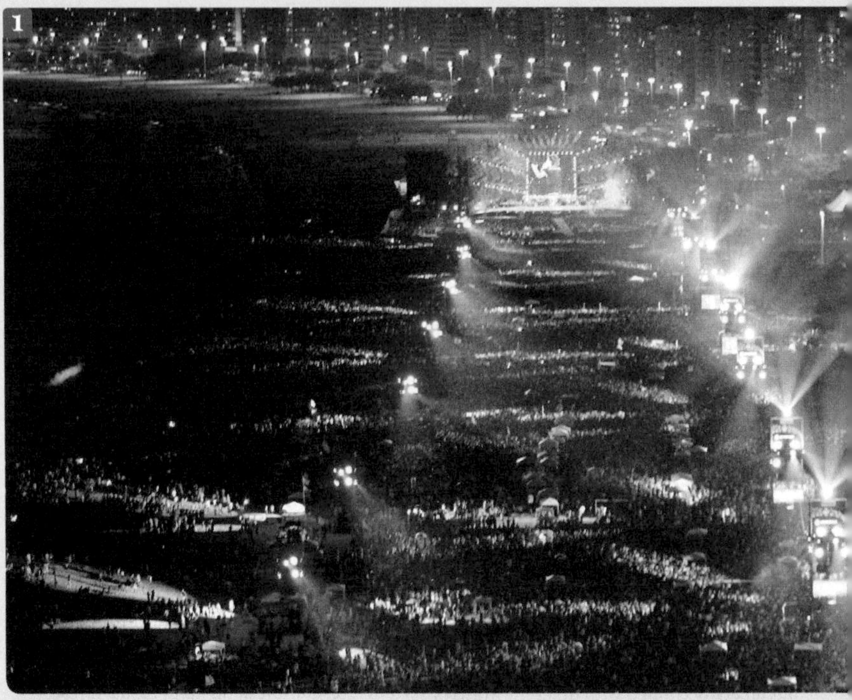
1

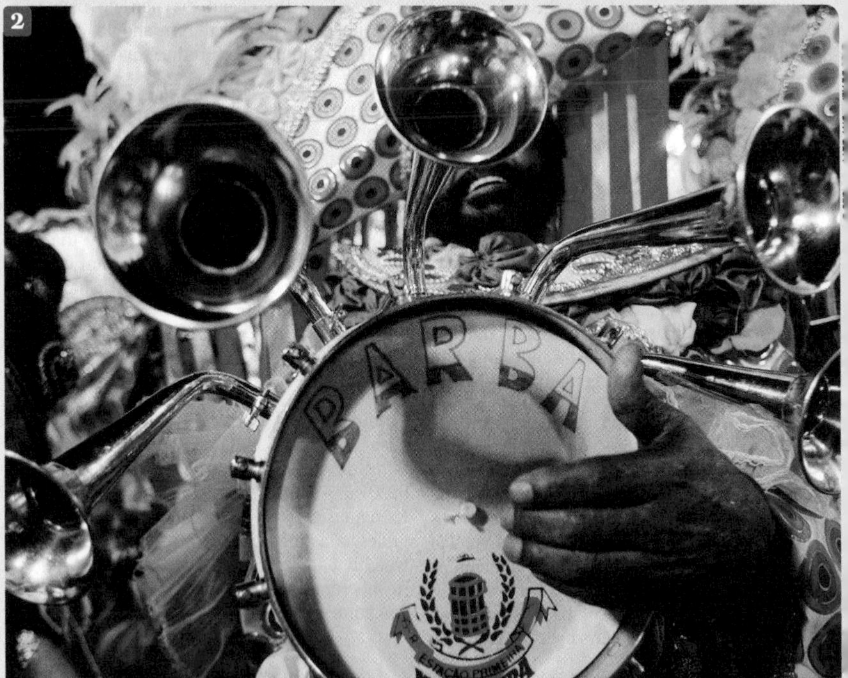
2
BARBA
ESTAÇÃO PRIMEIRA

CAIO LEAL/AFP / GETTY IMAGES ©

1. Concert, Copacabana Beach (p60) 2. Samba parade, Carnaval (p35), Rio de Janeiro 3. Gilberto Gil

Sounds of Rio

The city that gave the world Carnaval, samba and bossa nova offers dozens of ways to spend a sleepless night among the *cariocas* (locals).

Samba

Samba, the great soundtrack of Rio, plays all across town, though if you're looking for its heart you'll probably find it in the bohemian neighborhood of Lapa, where addictive rhythms spill out of old-fashioned dance halls, drawing music lovers from far and wide. Samba also takes center stage during Carnaval, with those percussive beats and singsong lyrics essential to the big fest. The top samba schools welcome visitors to their parties from September until Carnaval. These popular events are always a good time.

Bossa Nova & Jazz

Although bossa nova isn't much in fashion these days, there are still a few places where you can hear those rich, melancholic chords. Jazz also has its fans, and several venues around town have regular jazz nights.

Big Concerts

In addition to small bars and clubs, Rio has a few large concert halls that attract Brazilian stars such as Gilberto Gil and Milton Nascimento, as well as well-known international bands on world tours. During the warmer months, concerts are held periodically on the beaches of Copacabana and Ipanema, and the Marina da Glória is also a major venue.

TOP LIVE-MUSIC VENUES

- Samba: Democráticus (p109), Carioca da Gema (p109) and Rio Scenarium (p109)
- Bossa Nova: Vinícius Show Bar (p110)
- Jazz: TribOz (p109), Maze Inn (p110)

Uruguai SNACKS $

(Map p54; Posto 9, Ipanema Beach; sandwiches R$12-18; ⏲noon-5pm) Of the many *barracas* (food stalls) on the beach, Uruguai is a long-term favorite and serves scrumptious grilled chicken, beef or sausage sandwiches. Look for the blue-and-white striped Uruguayan flag flying high over the beach.

Koni Store JAPANESE $

(Map p54; ☎2521-9348; Maria Quitéria 77; hand rolls R$12-17; ⏲11am-2am Sun-Thu, to 6am Fri & Sat) Numbering almost two dozen branches in Rio, the Koni craze shows no sign of abating. The recipe is simple: *temaki* (seaweed hand roll) stuffed with salmon, tuna, shrimp, roast beef or a combination of ingredients, which can then be devoured at one of the tiny bistro tables.

Delírio Tropical BRAZILIAN $

(Map p54; ☎3624-8164; www.delirio.com.br; Garcia d'Ávila 48; salads R$15-22; ⏲11am-9pm Mon-Sat; ☑) Delírio Tropical serves a tempting array of salads, which you can enhance by adding grilled trout, salmon carpaccio, filet mignon and other items. The open layout has a pleasant, casual ambience, but you'll need to go early to beat the lunchtime crowds.

Laffa KEBAB $

(Map p54; ☎2522-5888; Visconde de Pirajá 175; sandwiches R$17-26; ⏲11:30am-midnight) A hit on the street-food scene, Laffa is a lively little eatery that whips up piping-hot grilled lamb or turkey shawarmas, falafel sandwiches or dessert concoctions such as apple strudel or sliced strawberries with Nutella. It's all served on laffa (pita bread) wraps, made fresh to order.

Azteka MEXICAN $$

(Map p54; Visconde de Pirajá 156; mains R$29-48; ⏲noon-11:30pm) A few steps from Praça General Osório, this small open-sided eatery fills a much lacking niche in Rio's food world: Mexican cuisine! Nibble on tortilla chips and guacamole before feasting on quesadillas and burritos. Try the Morelia (pulled pork in *tomatillo* sauce).

Via Sete INTERNATIONAL $$

(Map p54; ☎2512-8100; Garcia d'Ávila 125; mains R$42-75; ⏲noon-midnight; ☰) This restaurant on upscale Garcia d'Ávila serves a good selection of salads, burgers and unique appetizers such as calamari in manioc crust, as well as excellent grilled dishes such as tuna steak, rump steak, Black Angus and a fish of the day. You choose the side dishes and sauce to accompany your meal.

La Carioca Cevicheria PERUVIAN $$

(Map p54; ☎2522-8184; Garcia d'Ávila 173; sharing plates R$30-37; ⏲6:30pm-1am Mon-Fri, from 1pm Sat & Sun) True to its name, this Peruvian place specializes in ceviche and serves up more than a dozen varieties of the tangy, tender seafood dish. Other great plates for sharing include the *pulpo andino* (crispy octopus with potato salad and baked red pepper), *tiraditos* (fresh, thinly sliced fish) and *lomo saltado* (stir-fried steak and spices).

Venga! SPANISH $$

(Map p54; ☎2247-0234; Garcia d'Ávila 147; tapas R$18-40; ⏲noon-midnight) A festive spot to eat and drink, Venga! was Rio's first authentic tapas bar when it opened back in 2009. Classic wood details and a good soundtrack set the scene for noshing on *patatas bravas* (spicy potatoes), *pulpo a la Gallega* (grilled octopus), *gambas al ajillo* (garlic prawns) and other Iberian hits. Match those small plates with a glass of Spanish rioja. Also in Leblon.

Felice Caffè FUSION $$

(Map p54; ☎2522-7749; Gomes Carneiro 30; mains R$48-65, sandwiches R$35-45; ⏲noon-1am Mon-Fri, 10am-1am Sat & Sun; ❄☰) Half a block from the beach, Felice has a small shaded front terrace for taking in the passing parade of people. Head inside for air-conditioned splendor, where locals and travelers enjoy juicy grilled dishes such as sesame-crusted tuna fillet, plus risottos, steak burgers, bountiful salads, and, most importantly, rich Italian-style ice cream (R$12 for two scoops).

Terzetto Cafe CAFE $$

(Map p54; ☎2247-3243; Jangadeiros 28; mains R$43-65; ⏲8am-11:30pm Mon-Sat, to 10pm Sun) Fronting Praça General Osório, Terzetto is a lively, enticing cafe with an assortment of prepared salads and antipasti as well as focaccia, ravioli, bruschetta, grilled dishes, pizzas (after 4pm) and desserts. It's a great anytime spot with breakfast plates (such as egg dishes, fruit salad, granola and yogurt), lunch specials and decent coffees.

Frontera BUFFET $$

(Map p54; ☎3289-2350; Visconde de Pirajá 128; per kg R$60; ⏲11:30am-11pm) Run by a Dutch chef, Frontera offers more than 60 plates at its delectable lunch buffet, which features a mouthwatering assortment of grilled meats, baked casseroles and seafood pastas, plus salads, fresh fruits, grilled vegetables and desserts. Sushi and the dessert counter costs extra. Dark woods and vintage travel posters give it a cozier feel than most per-kilo places.

Brasileirinho BRAZILIAN **$$**
(Map p54; ☎2523-5184; Jangadeiros 10; mains R$38-59; ⏰noon-11pm) Facing Praça General Osório, this rustically decorated restaurant serves good, traditional *mineiro* cuisine. Favorites include *tutu a mineira* (mashed black beans with manioc), *carne seca* (dried beef) and *picanha* (rump steak). The *feijoada* (black bean and pork stew served with rice) here is tops – unsurprising given that Brasileirinho is run by the same owner as Ipanema's top-notch *feijoada* eatery Casa da Feijoada.

Gringo Cafe CAFE **$$**
(Map p54; www.gringocafe.com; Barão da Torre 240; breakfast R$22-34; ⏰8am-10pm; 📶) Tired of eating *feijoada*? This open-sided American-run diner dishes up remedies in spades for the homesick: waffles, pancakes, hash browns, mac and cheese, chili (both meat and vegetarian), barbecue ribs, milkshakes etc. It even smells like a US diner.

New Natural BRAZILIAN **$$**
(Map p54; ☎2287-0301; Barão da Torre 167; per kg R$55; ⏰8am-10:30pm; 🌿) Featuring an excellent lunch buffet of organic and vegetarian fare, New Natural was the first health-food restaurant to set up in the neighborhood. Fill up on fresh pots of soup, rice, veggies and beans at the healthy buffet.

Zazá Bistrô Tropical FUSION **$$$**
(Map p54; ☎2247-9101; www.zazabistro.com.br; Joana Angélica 40; mains R$60-86; ⏰7:30pm-midnight Mon & Tue, noon-midnight Wed-Fri, from 1pm Sat & Sun) Inside an art-filled and whimsically decorated converted house, Zazá serves beautifully prepared dishes with Asian accents, and uses organic ingredients when possible. Favorites include chicken curry with jasmine rice, flambéed prawns with risotto, and grilled fish served with caramelized plantain. Don't miss the cocktails.

Bazzar INTERNATIONAL **$$$**
(Map p54; ☎3202-2884; Barão da Torre 538; mains R$42-90; ⏰noon-1am Mon-Sat, to 5pm Sun) Set on a peaceful tree-lined street, this nicely designed restaurant with a relaxing front terrace serves creative, beautifully executed dishes. Current favorites include suckling pig with macadamia cream, grilled rock lobster and a vegetarian heart-of-palm *moqueca* (Bahian stew cooked in a clay pot with *dendê* oil, coconut milk and spicy peppers).

Espaço 7zero6 BRAZILIAN **$$$**
(Map p54; ☎2141-4992; http://espaco7zero6.com.br; Vieira Souto 706; set brunch/dinner R$72/175; ⏰noon-6pm Mon-Thu, 8am-2pm Fri-Sun & 7pm-midnight daily) From its location on the top floor of the Hotel Praia Ipanema, this place has a jaw-dropping view of Ipanema Beach. There's dinner most nights and lunch on weekdays, but the best time to come is for the weekend brunch, when the restaurant spreads a banquet of tropical fruits, yogurt, freshly baked breads and pastries, egg dishes and even waffles.

Casa da Feijoada BRAZILIAN **$$$**
(Map p54; ☎2247-2776; Prudente de Morais 10B; feijoada R$78; ⏰noon-midnight) Admirers of Brazil's iconic *feijoada* (black bean and pork stew served with rice) needn't wait until Saturday, the time it's traditionally eaten, to experience this meaty meal. The casual Casa da Feijoada serves the rich dish every day of the week.

Leblon

Kurt PASTRIES **$**
(Map p54; General Urquiza 117B; desserts R$7-12; ⏰8am-7pm Mon-Fri, 9am-6pm Sat) Extremely popular, Kurt spreads an array of irresistible temptations: flaky strudels, berry crumbles, and palm-sized tortes with strawberries and kiwifruit. There are a few outdoor tables where you can nibble on pastries and take in the street scene.

Armazém do Café CAFE **$**
(Map p54; ☎3874-5935; Rita Ludolf 87B; snacks R$6-12; ⏰8am-11pm) Dark-wood furnishings and the aroma of fresh-ground coffee lend authenticity to this Leblon coffeehouse. It serves waffles, snacks and desserts, and connoisseurs rate the aromatic roasts here much more highly than at neighboring cafes.

Zona Sul Supermarket SUPERMARKET **$**
(Map p54; ☎2259-4699; Dias Ferreira 290; ⏰6am-11pm Mon-Sat, 7am-10pm Sun) A Rio institution for nearly 50 years, Zona Sul supermarket has branches all over the city. This one is the best of the bunch, with

fresh-baked breads, imported cheeses and olives, wines, cured meats and other items. The adjoining pizza and lasagna counter serves decent plates. There's a handy **Ipanema branch** (Map p54; Prudente de Morais 49; 24hr Mon-Sat, 7am-8pm Sun) near Praça General Osório.

Vezpa PIZZA **$**
(Map p54; 2540-0800; Av Ataúlfo de Paiva 1063; slices around R$10; noon-2am Sun-Thu, to 5am Fri & Sat) Vezpa is a New York–style pizza place, with brick walls and high ceilings, where you can order pizza by the slice. The crusts are thin and crunchy and there are decent selections on hand – try the mozzarella with tomatoes and basil. Vezpa also has locations in Ipanema (on Farme de Amoedo) and Copacabana (on Djalma Ulrich).

Bibi Crepes CREPERIE **$**
(Map p54; 2259-4948; Cupertino Durão 81; crepes R$13-28; noon-1am) This small, open-sided restaurant attracts a young, garrulous crowd who enjoy the more than two dozen sweet and savory crepes available, as well as design-your-own salads (choose from 40 different toppings). Come early to beat the lunch crowds.

Talho Capixaba SANDWICHES **$**
(Map p54; 2512-8760; Av Ataúlfo de Paiva 1022; sandwiches around R$25-40; 7am-10pm) This deli and gourmet grocer is one of the city's best spots to put together a takeout meal. In addition to pastas, salads and antipasti, you'll find excellent sandwiches (charged by weight) made from quality ingredients. You can also dine inside or at the sidewalk tables in front.

Stuzzi ITALIAN **$$**
(Map p54; 2274-4017; Dias Ferreira 48; sharing plates R$22-55; 7pm-2am Mon-Sat, to midnight Sun) This buzzing, uberpopular Leblon spot specializes in creative Italian tapas (think roast lamb croquettes, and goat cheese, fig and honey bruschetta) and expertly mixed cocktails. The lively, candelit tables on the sidewalk are the place to be; come early to score one.

Vegetariano Social Club VEGETARIAN **$$**
(Map p54; 2294-5200; Conde Bernadotte 26L; buffet lunch R$41; noon-11pm Mon-Sat, noon-5:30pm Sun;) Vegetarians interested in sampling Brazil's signature dish should visit this small charmer on a Wednesday or a Sunday when tofu *feijoada* is served. At other times, it serves a 10-dish lunch buffet, while the more elaborate evening à la carte menu features risottos, *yakisoba* (Japanese grilled noodles), heart-of-palm stroganoff and other inventive dishes.

Prima Bruschetteria ITALIAN **$$**
(Map p54; 3592-0881; www.primab.com.br; Rainha Guilhermina 95; bruschetta R$9-17, mains R$41-53; noon-midnight) Prima showcases an Italian delicacy not often seen in these parts, using imaginative ingredients such as goat cheese, olive tapenade, prosciutto and smoked salmon to top its char-grilled bread. You'll also find fresh salads, antipasti plates and various risottos.

★ **CT Boucherie** FUSION **$$$**
(Map p54; 2529-2329; www.ctboucherie.com.br; Dias Ferreira 636; mains R$82-110; noon-4pm & 7pm-midnight Mon-Sat) Created by Claude Troisgros, Rio's most famous chef, this innovative Leblon restaurant takes the idea of the *churrascaria* (traditional barbecue restaurant) and turns it on its head. Instead of all-you-can-eat meat, you order a main course – say a beautifully turned out rack of lamb, duck breast or grilled fish – and you get as many sides as you wish, served *rodízio* style fresh from the kitchen.

Polenta with passion fruit, char-grilled vegetables, oven-roasted tomatoes, ratatouille with quinoa, and sweet-potato mash are among the many offerings. The setting is lively, and nicely designed (subway tiles, whimsical prints) with a welcome lack of pretension.

Zuka INTERNATIONAL **$$$**
(Map p54; 3205-7154; Dias Ferreira 233; mains R$70-110; 7pm-1am Mon, noon-4pm & 7pm-1am Tue-Fri, 1pm-1am Sat & Sun) One of Rio's best restaurants, Zuka prepares delectable, mouthwatering cuisine. Try zingy ceviche or the confection-like delicacy of Zuka's original foie gras to start, and follow with tender octopus over a roast potato crisp, honey-glazed duck breast with Moroccan couscous, grilled fish of the day with truffle sauce or many other outstanding dishes.

Brigite's BRAZILIAN **$$$**
(Map p54; 2274-5590; Dias Ferreira 247; mains R$65-95; 7pm-midnight Mon, noon-4pm & 7pm-midnight Tue-Sun) On restaurant-lined Dias Ferreira, Brigite's serves artfully prepared Franco-Italian fare in an inviting dining room with floor-to-ceiling windows, wood floors, white brick walls and a long

reflective bar. Come for pasta with clams, lamb and creamy polenta with porcini mushrooms, and good wines by the glass. A festive air prevails as the weekend nears.

Sushi Leblon JAPANESE **$$$**
(Map p54; ☎2512-7830; Dias Ferreira 256; mains R$60-90; ⊙noon-4pm & 7pm-1:30am Mon-Sat, 1pm-midnight Sun) Leblon's top sushi destination boasts a Zen-like ambience, with a handsome dark-wood sushi counter setting the stage for succulent cuisine. In addition to sashimi and sushi, you'll find grilled *namorado* (a type of perch) with passion-fruit *farofa* (garnish of manioc flour sautéed with butter), sea-urchin ceviche and refreshing sake to complement the meal.

Gávea, Jardim Botânico & Lagoa

During summer, live music fills the air at open-air restaurants around Lagoa Rodrigo de Freitas. Gávea has a few lively dining and drinking spots around Praça Santos Dumont, while Jardim Botânico has a sprinkling of eateries on Rua JJ Seabra and Rua Pacheco Leão.

★ **Volta** BRAZILIAN **$$**
(Map p56; ☎3204-5406; www.restaurantevolta.com.br; Visconde de Carandaí 5; mains R$40-60; ⊙noon-midnight Mon-Sat, to 6pm Sun) Set in a classy old villa with an outdoor patio on a peaceful corner of Jardim Botânico, Volta serves up playful, contemporary fare inspired by Brazilian comfort food. Start off with creative appetizers such as the sardine-topped tapioca crisp or the *coxinha* (cornmeal balls filled with chicken) with creamy Minas cheese, before moving on to sweet-potato gnocchi with pumpkin cream or a perfectly tender filet mignon.

The kitchen is helmed by two twenty-something identical twins, complete with matching tattoos. Book ahead for Tuesday nights, when there's live jazz.

La Bicyclette FRENCH **$$**
(Map p56; Jardim Botânico 1008; sandwiches R$18-33; ⊙8:30am-6pm Tue & Wed, to 8pm Thu-Sun; 📶✍) Just outside the entrance to the botanical gardens (but inside the gates off the busy roadway), La Bicyclette whips up creative sandwiches (named after French neighborhoods), hearty quiches, salads and desserts. It's set in a lovely colonial building and has outdoor seating on a peaceful veranda.

There's a second **location** (Map p56; Pacheco Leão 320; sandwiches R$18-33; ⊙8:30am-8pm; 📶) on the north side of the botanical gardens.

PLage Cafe CAFE **$$**
(Map p56; ☎2535-7336; off Jardim Botânico 414; mains R$26-54; ⊙9am-6pm; 📶✍) Inside the lush Parque Lage, this beautifully sited cafe serves a few hearty dishes, such as rich pork belly with lentils, plus salads, quiches, pastas such as eggplant lasagna, and changing daily specials like vegetarian cassoulet. On weekends it's a popular gathering spot for young families who come for brunch (R$27 to R$32), which features eggs Benedict, yogurt with granola and fruit plates.

Braseiro da Gávea BRAZILIAN **$$**
(Map p56; ☎2239-7494; www.braseirodagavea.com.br; Praça Santos Dumont 116; sandwiches around R$20, mains for 2 people R$50-110; ⊙noon-1am Sun-Thu, to 3am Fri & Sat) This family-style eatery serves large portions of its popular *linguiça* (garlicky pork sausage) appetizers, *picanha* (rump steak) and *galetos* (grilled chicken). On weekends the open-air spot fills with the din of conversation and the aroma of freshly poured *chope* (draft beer). As the evening wanes, a younger crowd takes over drinking late into the night.

Lagoon BRAZILIAN **$$**
(Map p54; ☎2529-5300; www.lagoon.com.br; Av Borges de Medeiros 1424; mains R$35-75; ⊙noon-2am) This lakefront eating and entertainment complex houses a handful of restaurants, as well as a cinema, and a bar and live-music venue. The best tables are on the 2nd floor, and offer photogenic views over the lake. Italian, seafood, bistro fare and traditional Brazilian cooking are among the options. No matter where you sit, you can order from all of the menus.

Arab da Lagoa MIDDLE EASTERN **$$**
(Map p56; ☎2540-0747; www.restaurantearab.com.br; Av Borges de Medeiros, Parque dos Patins; mains R$35-60; ⊙9am-1:30am) This is one of the lake's most popular outdoor restaurants. It serves up traditional Middle Eastern specialties such as hummus, baba ghanoush, tabbouleh, kibbe and tasty thin-crust pizzas. The large platters for two or more are good for sampling a tasty variety.

Bráz PIZZA **$$**
(☎2535-0687; Maria Angélica 129; pizzas R$50-80; ⊙6pm-midnight) The much-touted pizzeria

from São Paulo has had a huge *carioca* following since opening in Rio in 2007. Perfect crusts and superfresh ingredients are two of the components that make Bráz the best pizza place in town. This is no secret, so arrive early and plan on having a few quiet *chopes* (draft beers) on the front patio before scoring a table.

CT Trattorie ITALIAN $$$
(☎2266-0838; Av Alexandre Ferreira 66; mains R$68-98; ⊙noon-4pm & 7-11pm) This outstanding restaurant brought to you by top chef Claude Troisgros serves exquisite pasta dishes and northern Italian cuisine with Brazilian influences. Recent favorites: tender octopus carpaccio, fish with a cream sauce of *azedinha* (sorrel), and a rich spaghetti carbonara with *carne seca* (pulled dried beef).

It has a classy Old World design, with tile floors, oversized lights and black-and-white photos on the walls. Good wine selection.

Olympe FUSION $$$
(☎2539-4542; Custódio Serrão 62; mains R$90-125; ⊙noon-4pm Mon-Fri, 7:30pm-midnight Mon-Sat) Claude Troisgros, one of Rio's top chefs, and his son Thomas dazzle guests with unforgettable meals at this award-winning restaurant set in a peaceful villa on a quiet, tree-lined street. Originally from France, Troisgros mixes the Old World with the New in dishes such as duck with passion fruit, endive and foie gras or shrimp risotto with white-truffle oil and mushroom foam.

Copacabana & Leme

Supermarkets include **Pão de Açúcar** (Map p62; Av NS de Copacabana 493, Copacabana; ⊙24hr) and the fruit-filled **HortiFruti** (Map p62; Av Prado Junior 277; ⊙8am-9pm Mon-Fri, to 8pm Sat, to 2pm Sun).

Galeto Sat's BRAZILIAN $
(Map p62; ☎2275-6197; Barata Ribeiro 7; mains R$18-26; ⊙noon-5am) One of Rio's best roast-chicken spots, laid-back Galeto Sat's has earned many fans since its opening back in 1962. Grab a seat along the mirrored and tiled wall, order a *chope* (draft beer) and enjoy the scent of grilled spit-roasted birds before tucking into a filling meal. Price-wise you can't beat the R$50 feast for two.

Cervantes BRAZILIAN $
(Map p62; ☎2275-6147; Barata Ribeira 7; sandwiches R$15-30; ⊙noon-4am Sun & Tue-Thu, to 6am Fri & Sat) A Copacabana institution, the late-night Cervantes gathers *cariocas* who come to feast on Cervantes' trademark steak and pineapple sandwiches. This popular branch on busy Barata Ribeira attracts a mostly standing-room-only crowd. For the sit-down restaurant, head a few steps around the corner to Av Pradio Junior 335.

Boulangerie Guerin BAKERY $
(Map p62; ☎2523-4140; Av NS de Copacabana 920; pastries R$9-12; ⊙8am-8pm) Serving Rio's best croissants, *pains au chocolat* (chocolate-filled pastry) and eclairs, this French patisserie was an instant success upon opening in 2012. Prices for those delectable raspberry-covered tarts and creamy mille-feuilles are high, but so is the quality. You can can also enjoy baguette sandwiches and thick slices of quiche if you're craving something more substantial.

Nonna Ridolfi CAFE $
(Map p62; Ronald de Carvalho 161; sandwiches R$19-22; ⊙11am-9pm Tue, Wed, Fri & Sat, 4-10pm Thu, 11am-7pm Sun) This small, quaint cafe serves up tasty sandwiches, cheese and charcuterie plates, desserts and craft beers amid wooden shelves that evoke a bygone era. There's outdoor seating in front, offering a fine vantage point to take in this peaceful corner of Copacabana.

★El Born SPANISH $$
(Map p62; ☎3496-1780; www.barelborn.com.br; Bolívar 17; tapas R$15-40; ⊙5pm-2am Mon-Fri, from 3pm Sat & Sun) Named after Barcelona's hippest, foodie-loving neighborhood, El Born fires up some of Rio's best tapas plates: think Galician-style octopus, spicy prawns and tender Iberian ham. The setting channels a bit of old-world Spain, with rustic stone and brick walls, outdoor tables on the sidewalk and ample bar seating – the latter is a fine spot for watching the dexterous bartenders in action.

Don't order too much. Waiters emerge from the kitchen and make the rounds with freshly cooked tapas plates; if you see something you like, take it!

Bar do David BRAZILIAN $$
(Map p62; Ladeira Ary Barroso 66; appetizers R$20-30, mains around R$35; ⊙8am-10pm Tue-Sun) Located in Chapéu Mangueira favela, this simple open-sided eatery serves excellent snacks. The chef and owner David Vieira Bispo was formerly a fisherman, and his seafood *feijoada* (stew with rice) is out-

standing – but available weekends only. At other times, you can nibble on seafood *croquetes,* garlic shrimp, sausage with manioc, and other hits that go nicely with a caipirinha or two.

Cafe Colombo CAFE $$
(Map p62; ☎3201-4049; Forte de Copacabana, Praça Coronel Eugênio Franco; mains R$24-38; ⏰10am-8pm Tue-Sun) Far removed from the hustle and bustle of Av Atlântica, this cafe has magnificent views of Copacabana Beach. At the outdoor tables you can sit beneath shady palm trees, enjoying cappuccino, omelets, waffles, salads or sandwiches as young soldiers file past. To get here, you'll have to pay admission (R$6) to the Forte de Copacabana (p60).

Joaquina BRAZILIAN $$
(Map p62; ☎2275-8569; Av Atlântica 974; mains R$34-46; ⏰11:30am-midnight; 📶) Joaquina has much to recommend it: a great ocean-facing location with outdoor seating; excellent caipirinhas that don't stint on the fresh fruit; and tasty Brazilian fare served up at fair prices. On Sundays Joaquina serves *feijoada* (R$34); on Saturdays it's oxtail rice (also R$34). Arrive early before it runs out. Other hits: *moqueca* (seafood stew) for one, shrimp risotto and vegetarian stroganoff.

TT Burger BURGERS $$
(Map p62; Francisco Otaviano 67; mains around R$30; ⏰noon-midnight Sun-Wed, to 4am Thu-Sat) The son of famed local chef Claude Troisgros runs this high-end Brooklyn-style burger outpost, and has gained a strong following for his delicious burgers (the guava ketchup is outstanding), crispy fries and milkshakes. It's a charming spot, with subway tiles, framed photos, wood floors and a small front deck. There's a second location on Leblon's main drag (Av Ataúlfo de Paiva).

Bakers CAFE $$
(Map p62; ☎3209-1212; www.thebakers.com.br; Santa Clara 86; desserts R$7-10, mains R$25-45; ⏰9am-9pm; 📶) The Bakers is a fine spot for flaky croissants, banana Danishes, apple strudels and other treats. There are also waffles, omelets, salads, gourmet sandwiches (such as prosciutto and mozzarella on ciabatta), quiches (including ricotta with sun-dried tomatoes), and filling lunch specials such as grilled salmon or penne pasta.

Santa Satisfação BRAZILIAN $$
(Map p62; ☎2255-9349; www.santasatisfacao.com; Santa Clara 36C; mains R$27-46; ⏰10am-10:45pm Mon-Sat) Oozing farmhouse charm, this always-packed bistro is worth forking out a bit extra for outstanding daily lunch

THE KIOSKS OF COPACABANA

The *quiosque* (kiosk) has long been a presence on the beachfront of Rio. This is where cold drinks and snacks get doled out to *cariocas* on the move, with plastic tables and chairs providing a fine vantage point for contemplating the watery horizon. In recent years Copacabana Beach has seen a new crop of flashy kiosks replacing the old-fashioned wooden ones. Now it's possible to get a decent meal (the kitchens are cleverly concealed underground), an ice-cold draft beer or gourmet snacks without leaving the sand. Things are quite lively on weekends, when many kiosks host live music.

Here are a few current favorites:

Globo (Map p62; Copacabana Beach, near Miguel Lemos; snacks R$8-15; ⏰9am-midnight) Run by Brazil's major media network, Globo has a brightly illuminated kiosk with colorful seats near the new Museu do Imagem e Som. Aside from snacks and drinks, you can sometimes catch live programming here, such as mini concerts, televised interviews and public debates.

Cantinho Cearense (Map p62; near Duvivier; appetizers R$13-35, mains for 2 people R$63-100; ⏰9am-midnight) A popular gathering spot, Cantinho Cearense serves up cold *chope* (draft beer) and plenty of satisfying snacks, as well as heartier fare from the state of Ceará, including grilled seafood with fried cassava.

Espetto Carioca (Map p62; near Praça Julio de Noronha; snacks R$12-20; ⏰8am-midnight) At the northeast end of Leme, elevated over the beach, this peacefully set kiosk serves *espettos* (kebabs or skewers) of vegetables, meats and cheeses, which go nicely with drinks. Nearby, you can watch fearless *carioca* kids diving off the seawall. There's usually live music on weekends.

specials of upscale Brazilian comfort food and sophisticated sandwiches. Among the favorites: pasta with gorgonzola and sliced filet mignon, caprese salad, and an open-faced ham and brie sandwich.

Amir MIDDLE EASTERN **$$**
(Map p62; ☎2275-5596; Ronald de Carvalho 55C; mains R$43-58, sandwiches R$19-32; ⊙noon-midnight Mon-Sat, to 11pm Sun) Step inside Amir and you'll enter a world of delicate aromas and handsomely dressed waiters in embroidered vests. Daytime crowds come for the buffet (R$70 on weekdays, R$80 weekends), while at night the à la carte menu features all the favorites, including delicious platters of hummus, *kaftas* (spiced meat patties), falafel, kibbe and salads.

Churrascaria Palace CHURRASCARIA **$$$**
(Map p62; ☎2541-5898; Rodolfo Dantas 16; all you can eat R$110; ⊙noon-midnight) Hands down, this is one of the best *churrascarias* (traditional barbecue restaurants) in town. You'll find high-quality cuts of meat and attentive service at this elegantly set dining room. Waiters make frequent rounds with the goods; don't be shy about saying no, otherwise you'll end up with more than you could possibly eat.

Azumi JAPANESE **$$$**
(Map p62; ☎2541-4294; Ministro Viveiros de Castro 127; meals R$80-180; ⊙7pm-midnight Tue-Sun) Some claim Azumi is the bastion of traditional Japanese cuisine in the city. This laid-back sushi bar certainly has its fans – both in the *nisei* (second-generation Japanese born in Brazil) community and from abroad. Azumi's *sushiman* (sushi chef) masterfully prepares delectable sushi and sashimi, and the tempuras and soups are also excellent. Be sure to ask what's in season.

Botafogo & Urca

Cobal do Humaitá MARKET **$**
(Map p66; ☎2266-1343; Voluntários da Pátria 446, tafogo; ⊙7am-4pm Mon-Sat) The city's largest farmers market sells plenty of flowers, veggies and fruits; there are also cafes and restaurants on hand for those looking for a bit more.

Boua Kitchen & Bar BISTRO **$**
(Map p66; www.theboua.com.br; Nelson Mandela 102, Botafogo; burgers R$26-38) Behind the Botafogo metro station, this lively gastropub is one of more than a dozen eating and drinking spots along this lane. The microbrew selection is outstanding (with a rotating lineup of Belgian, German, American and Brazilian beers). You can sit outside and nosh on thick burgers, appetizers or steak and gorgonzola risotto while watching the passing people parade.

Meza Bar TAPAS **$$**
(Map p66; ☎3239-1951; www.mezabar.com.br; Capitão Salomão 69, Humaitá; tapas R$12-30; ⊙6pm-1am) Humaitá's see-and-be-seen hot spot serves up delectable, Brazilian-slanted tapas to a sophisticated and trendy crowd. Creative cocktails and delightful staff round out the fun.

Emporium Pax BRAZILIAN **$$**
(Map p66; ☎3171-9713; www.emporiumpax.com.br; Botafogo Praia Shopping, 7th fl, Praia de Botafogo 400, Botafogo; lunch buffet R$44-65; ⊙noon-midnight) One of many eateries at Botafogo Praia Shopping, Emporium Pax is a more polished affair than the adjoining food court and offers spectacular views of Pão de Açúcar and Baía de Guanabara. The big draw is the extensive lunch buffet, though for something lighter you can order salads, sandwiches and quiches, plus tasty desserts.

Miam Miam CONTEMPORARY **$$**
(Map p66; ☎2244-0125; www.miammiam.com.br; General Goés Monteiro 34, Botafogo; mains around R$60; ⊙7pm-midnight Tue-Fri, 8pm-1am Sat) Exposed brick walls and a mishmash of retro furnishings set the scene for dining in style at Botafogo's culinary darling. Chef Roberta Ciasca serves up her own brand of comfort food, which means smoked trout with roasted potatoes, pork with basmati rice and pineapple, eggplant lasagna with sheep's milk yogurt, and other unique dishes.

Oui Oui FRENCH, BRAZILIAN **$$**
(Map p66; ☎2527-3539; www.restauranteouioui.com.br; Conde de Irajá 85, Humaitá; small plates R$35-42; ⊙noon-3pm & 7pm-midnight Mon-Fri, 8pm-1am Sat) On a tranquil street in Humaitá, elegantly set Oui Oui serves innovative tapas plates designed for sharing – carmelized ribs with pumpkin puree, duck risotto, haddock croquettes, and zesty quinoa salad with truffle oil are perennial favorites.

Le Depanneur CAFE **$$**
(Map p66; Voluntários da Pátria 86, Botafogo; sandwiches R$22-32; ⊙8am-10:30pm; wi-fi)

This buzzing cafe and deli serves up juices, waffles, crepes, salads, antipasti plates and specialty sandwiches. On weekends the large plant-trimmed front patio fills with brunching locals and makes a good people-watching perch. There's also a self-serve bakery with croissants and other goodies, and plenty of other provisions for picnickers.

Julius Brasserie EUROPEAN $$
(Map p66; ☎3518-7117; Av Portugal 986, Urca; mains R$45-75; ⊙noon-midnight Tue-Sun) This elegant Dutch-Brazilian-run restaurant in Urca turns out a creative mix of grilled meats (rack of lamb, duck breast), seafood (shrimp curry with black rice), pastas and risottos in a quiet location on the edge of Praia da Urca. It makes a great lunch or dinner spot, followed by a stroll around the neighborhood.

Garota da Urca BRAZILIAN $$
(Map p66; ☎2541-8585; João Luís Alves 56, Urca; mains R$35-68; ⊙noon-1am Sun-Thu, to 2:30am Fri & Sat) Overlooking the small Praia da Urca, this neighborhood restaurant serves good-value weekday lunch specials, and you can enjoy views over the bay from the open-air veranda. By night, a more garrulous crowd converges for steak and *chope* (draft beer).

★**Lasai** FUSION $$$
(Map p66; ☎3449-1834; www.lasai.com.br; Conde de Irajá 191, Humaitá; prix fixe R$185-245; ⊙7:30-10:30pm Tue-Fri, 1-10:30pm Sat) Inside an elegant early-20th-century house in Humaitá, Lasai has dazzled critics and foodies for its deliciously inventive cuisine. The *carioca* chef Rafa Costa e Silva earned his chops in some of the world's best dining rooms (including Mugaritz in Spain), and he puts his skills to brilliant use here. Reservations essential.

There's no set menu: dishes are based on whatever is fresh for the day (and some ingredients are grown in the chef's own garden).

Flamengo & Around

Tacacá do Norte AMAZONIAN $
(Map p66; ☎2205-7545; Barão do Flamengo 35; tacacá R$22, juices R$8-17; ⊙9am-11pm Mon-Sat) In the Amazonian state of Pará, people order their *tacacá* late in the afternoon from their favorite street vendor. In Rio, you don't have to wait until the sun is setting. The fragrant soup of manioc paste, lip-numbing *jambu* (a Brazilian vegetable) leaves, and fresh and dried shrimp isn't for everyone. But then again, neither is the Amazon.

★**Ferro e Farinha** PIZZA $$
(Map p66; Andrade Pertence 42; pizzas R$30-40; ⊙7-11:30pm Wed-Sat, from 6:30pm Sun) Sei Shiroma, an expat from NYC, and a dexterous team of dough handlers serve up some of Rio's best pizza at this atmospheric and delightfully ramshackle spot in Catete. Seats are few, with just a handful of bar stools crowding around the pizza makers and oven at center stage, plus a few outdoor tables, so go early to try to beat the crowds.

Intihuasi PERUVIAN $$
(Map p66; ☎2225-7653; Barão do Flamengo 35D; mains R$60-80; ⊙noon-3pm & 7-11pm Tue-Sat, 12:30-5pm Sun) Colorfully decorated with Andean tapestries and artwork, this tiny Peruvian restaurant serves mouth watering ceviches, *papas rellenas* (meat-filled potatoes), seafood soups and other classic dishes from the Andes. For a break from caipirinhas, try a pisco sour or a nonalcoholic *chicha morada* (a sweet concoction made from purple corn).

Centro

Bistrô do Paço CAFE $
(Map p72; ☎2262-3613; Praça XV (Quinze) de Novembro 48, Paço Imperial; mains R$17-38; ⊙noon-7pm) On the ground floor of the Paço Imperial, this informal restaurant offers a tasty assortment of quiches, salads, soups and other light fare. Save room for the delicious pies and cakes.

Confeitaria Colombo BRAZILIAN $
(Map p72; ☎2505-1500; www.confeitariacolombo.com.br; Gonçalves Dias 34; pastries around R$9, sandwiches R$18-40; ⊙9am-7pm Mon-Fri, to 5pm Sat) Stained-glass windows, brocaded mirrors and marble countertops create a lavish setting for coffee or a meal. Dating from the late 1800s, the Confeitaria Colombo serves desserts – including a good *pastel de nata* (custard tart) – befitting its elegant decor. The restaurant overhead, **Cristóvão** (Map p72; Gonçalves Dias 34; buffet per person R$87; ⊙noon-4pm), spreads an extensive buffet of Brazilian dishes for those wanting to further soak up the splendor.

FOOD MARKETS

The *feiras* (produce markets) that pop up in different locations throughout the week are the best places to shop for *jabuticaba* (a native fruit that's grape-like), *acerola* (a type of cherry) and other fruits you won't find at home – not to mention delectable mangoes, papayas, passion fruit and more.

Cobal do Humaitá (p98) has flowers, veggies and fruits, and there are also restaurants on hand for those looking for a bit more. **Cobal do Leblon** (Map p54; ☎2239-1549; Gilberto Cardoso; ⏰6pm-1am Tue-Sun) is smaller but it doubles as an open-air eating-drinking spot in the evening.

Popular food markets by neighborhood:

Ipanema Mondays on Rua Henrique Dumont, Tuesdays on Praça General Osório and Fridays on Praça NS da Paz.

Leblon Thursdays on Rua General Urquiza.

Gávea Fridays on Praça Santos Dumont.

Jardim Botânico Saturday market on Rua Frei Leandro.

Copacabana Wednesdays on Praça Edmundo Bittencourt, Thursdays on Rua Ministro Viveiro de Castro and Rua Ronald de Carvalho, and Sundays on Praça Serzedelo Correia.

Leme Monday market on Gustavo Sampaio.

Urca Sundays on Praça Tenente Gil Guilherme.

Santa Teresa Fridays on Rua Felicio dos Santos.

Casa Paladino BRAZILIAN $
(Map p72; Uruguaiana 224; mains R$18-30; ⏰7am-8:30pm Mon-Fri, 8am-noon Sat) Going strong since 1906, this frozen-in-time delicatessen is lined with bottles, canned goods and other preserves. Find the hidden restaurant in the back for Paladino's famed sandwiches, such as the *triplo* (a pastrami, egg and melted cheese), and fluffy omelets with ingredients including cod, squid and octopus. It all goes nicely with an ice-cold draft beer.

Govinda VEGETARIAN $$
(Map p72; ☎3549-9108; 2nd fl, Rodrigo Silva 6; lunch R$32; ⏰11:30am-3:30pm Mon-Fri) Amid artwork and decorations from India, the always-welcoming Hare Krishnas whip up tasty vegetarian dishes made with care. Govinda is tucked down a narrow lane just off Rua São José and is always packed, so arrive early to get a seat.

Mironga BRAZILIAN $$
(Map p72; ☎2518-7727; Av Rio Branco 19; mains R$28-39; ⏰8am-10am & 11:30am-3:30pm Mon-Fri, noon-5pm Sun; 📶) With its tall ceilings, exposed Edison bulbs, lounge-like music and chunky wood tables, Mironga channels a Brooklyn vibe, which is unsurprising given the owner has deep NYC connections. Aesthetics aside, the food is excellent, with the focus on grilled dishes (rump steak, salmon and chicken breast) and burgers, with salads, ceviche and codfish snacks for those looking for something lighter.

Brasserie Rosário FRENCH $$
(Map p72; ☎2518-3033; Rua do Rosário 34; mains R$26-73; ⏰11am-9pm Mon-Fri, to 6pm Sat) Set in a handsomely restored 1860s building, this atmospheric bistro has a hint of old Europe about it. The front counters are full of croissants, *pain au chocolat* (chocolate-filled pastry) and other baked items, while the restaurant menu features roast meats and fish, soups, baguette sandwiches, quiche, cheese plates and the like.

Cedro do Líbano LEBANESE $$
(Map p72; ☎2224-0163; Senhor dos Passos 231; mains R$38-60; ⏰11am-4pm Mon-Sat) If you can get past the wedding-reception-like decor – white tablecloths with plastic chairs and tables – you can enjoy some excellent traditional Lebanese cooking at this long-running institution (opened in 1948). Kibbe, *kaftas* (spiced meat patties) and lamb are served tender and cooked to perfection.

Café Arlequim CAFE $$
(Map p72; ☎2220-8471; Praça XV (Quinze) de Novembro 48, Paço Imperial; mains R$27-44;

9am-8pm Mon-Fri, 10am-6pm Sat) In the middle of a shop selling books and CDs, this small, lively, pleasantly air-conditioned cafe is a fine spot to refuel, with Italian (Illy) coffee, sandwiches, salads, quiches, lasagna and desserts.

Imaculada BRAZILIAN **$$**
(Map p72; Ladeira do João Homem 7; mains R$25-40; 11am-4pm Mon, to 10pm Tue-Sat;) In the old neighborhood of Morro da Conceição, Imaculada is a Rio classic. The walls are adorned with artwork and the food is good. Come for daily lunch specials – *bobó de camarão* (manioc paste with dried shrimp, coconut milk and cashew nuts) on Thursdays or *feijoada* (bean and meat stew) on Fridays and Saturdays – and beer and appetizers at day's end.

Cais do Oriente BRAZILIAN **$$$**
(Map p72; 2233-2531; www.caisdooriente.com.br; Visconde de Itaboraí 8; mains R$55-85; noon-4pm Sun & Mon, to midnight Tue-Sat) Brick walls lined with tapestries stretch high to the ceiling in this almost-cinematic 1870s mansion. Set on a brick-lined street, hidden from the masses, Cais do Oriente blends elements of Brazilian and Mediterranean cooking in dishes such as duck breast with Brazil-nut *farofa* (garnish of manioc flour sautéed with butter) and açaí sauce. There's a back courtyard and an upstairs concert space that hosts periodic concerts.

AlbaMar SEAFOOD **$$$**
(Map p72; 2240-8378; Praça Marechal Âncora 186; mains R$78-132; noon-8pm) AlbaMar has long been one of Rio's best seafood destinations. Top picks are fresh oysters, grilled seafood with vegetables and *moqueca* (seafood stew cooked in coconut milk) dishes. The old-fashioned green gazebo-like structure offers excellent views of the Baía de Guanabara and the area of Niterói over the bay.

L'Atelier du Cuisinier FRENCH **$$$**
(Map p72; 3179-0024; Theophilo Otoni 97; mains R$60-70, 3-course lunch R$78; noon-3pm Mon-Fri) Set in a 19th-century building just off busy Av Rio Branco, this small 24-seat eatery serves some of the best cuisine in Centro. The menu is tiny (just a few options each day), but beautifully executed, with David Jobert creating recipes with fresh-from-the-market Brazilian ingredients.

Santa Teresa

Cafecito CAFE **$**
(Map p72; 2221-9439; www.cafecito.com.br; Paschoal Carlos Magno 121; sandwiches R$14-26; 9am-10pm Thu-Tue;) A few steps above street level, this open-air cafe attracts a mix of foreigners and neighborhood regulars; the Argentine owner is a longtime Santa Teresa resident. You'll find imported beers, desserts, cocktails (caipirinhas and mojitos), tapas plates and tasty ciabatta sandwiches with ingredients such as artichoke hearts, gorgonzola and prosciutto.

Nega Teresa BRAZILIAN **$**
(Map p66; Almirante Alexandrino 1458; mains around R$10; 5-10pm Thu-Sun) Bringing her Bahian delicacies to the people of Rio, Nega Teresa serves up scrumptious *acarajé* (a fritter filled with shrimp and spices) from a simple stand in the outer reaches of Santa Teresa, about 1km southwest of Largo do Guimarães. Connoisseurs rate Nega's street food among the city's best.

Alquimia CREPERIE **$**
(Map p72; Largo das Neves 11; crepes R$12-22; 5pm-midnight Thu-Sun) Beautifully set on tranquil Largo das Neves, Alquimia is a friendly Franco-Brazilian-run creperie that fires up delicious crepes, and it's also a charming spot to come for a drink in the evening. There's live music and occasional art exhibitions are held here.

Rústico BRAZILIAN **$$**
(Map p72; 3497-3579; Paschoal Carlos Magno 121; mains R$45-65; 6pm-midnight Mon, Thu & Fri, 1pm-midnight Sat, 1-10pm Sun;) In an old mansion overlooking the *bonde* (cable car) tracks, Rústico is a local favorite in Santa Teresa for its romantic outdoor terrace and first-rate cooking. A creative menu is designed by the Argentine owners. Among the crowd-pleasers: hearty salads with sundried figs, nuts and smoked salmon; boar leg in a white-wine sauce with carmelized apple and ginger; and vegetarian *moqueca* (traditionally a Bahian fish stew).

Bar do Mineiro BRAZILIAN **$$**
(Map p72; 2221-9227; Paschoal Carlos Magno 99; mains R$51-75; noon-2am Tue-Sat, to midnight Sun) Black-and-white photographs of legendary singers cover the walls of this old-school *boteco* (small open-air bar) in the heart of Santa Teresa. Lively crowds have been filling this spot for years to enjoy

traditional Minas Gerais dishes. The *feijoada* (bean-and-meat stew served with rice) is tops, and served every day, along with appetizers, including *pasteis* (savory pastries). Strong caipirinhas will help get you in the mood.

★ **Espírito Santa** AMAZONIAN $$$

(Map p72; ☎2507-4840; Almirante Alexandrino 264; mains R$50-88; ⊙noon-midnight Wed-Mon) Espírito Santa is set in a beautifully restored mansion in Santa Teresa. Take a seat on the back terrace with its sweeping views or inside the charming, airy dining room, and feast on rich, expertly prepared meat and seafood dishes from the Amazon and the Northeast.

★ **Aprazível** BRAZILIAN $$$

(Map p72; ☎2508-9174; Aprazível 62; mains R$70-110; ⊙noon-11pm Tue-Sat, to 6pm Sun) Hidden on a windy road high up in Santa Teresa, Aprazível offers beautiful views and a lush garden setting. Grilled fish and roasted dishes showcase the country's culinary highlights of land and sea. Standouts include orange-infused grilled fish with coconut rice, cashews and roasted plantains.

Térèze FUSION $$$

(Map p72; ☎3380-0220; Felicio dos Santos, Hotel Santa Teresa; mains R$80-130; ⊙noon-3:30pm & 7:30-11pm) Under the command of French chef Philippe Moulin, Térèze provides a memorable dining experience. All the elements are there, from the decadent menu to the suggested wine pairings and the superb views over the city. Choose from the likes of creamy codfish risotto with lobster bisque, suckling pig with mashed sweet potatoes and truffles, and eggplant gnocchi with cashew pesto.

Lapa

★ **Casa Momus** MEDITERRANEAN $$

(Map p72; ☎3852-8250; www.casamomus.com.br; Rua do Lavradio 11; mains R$40-60; ⊙11:30am-5pm Mon, to midnight Tue & Wed, to 2am Thu-Sat) One of the best and loveliest restaurants in Lapa, Casa Momus has a small, but well-executed menu of Mediterranean-influenced dishes. Start with prawn croquettes, fried polenta with spicy gorgonzola, or Moroccan lamb *kafta* (spiced meat patty) with tabbouleh and yogurt sauce; then feast on oxtail risotto with watercress, sesame-crusted tuna, pork tenderloin saltimbocca and other rich main courses.

Casa Momus is set in a beautifully decorated 19th-century building on a pedestrian-only stretch of Rua do Lavradio, with outdoor tables on the cobblestones.

Santa Scenarium BRAZILIAN $$

(Map p72; ☎3147-9007; www.santoscenarium.com.br; Rua do Lavradio 36; mains R$40-50; ⊙11:30am-midnight Tue-Sat, to 5pm Mon) Angels, saints and other sacred images adorn the exposed brick walls of this marvelously atmospheric restaurant on Lapa's antique row. Grilled meats and other Brazilian staples are on offer at lunchtime, while at night *cariocas* gather for cold beer, appetizers and sandwiches (such as the popular filet mignon with mozzarella and sliced pineapple). There's live music most nights.

Drinking & Nightlife

Ipanema, Leblon and Copacabana offer flashy nightspots as well as old-school watering holes. A youthful bar scene draws revelers to Gávea, while scenic Lagoa draws mostly couples. The narrow pedestrian streets of Centro near Praça XV (Quinze) de Novembro attract drinkers during weekday cocktail hours, and Santa Teresa is a laid-back spot for cocktails. Lapa is full of samba clubs and frenetic outdoor bars, and becomes a late-night street party on weekends.

Ipanema

★ **Canastra** WINE BAR

(Map p54; Jangadeiros 42; ⊙6:30pm-1am Tue-Sat) At first glance, Canastra looks like any other casual *boteco* (small open-air bar) on the back streets of Rio: sidewalk tables with a crowd milling about with drinks and snacks. But the food here is also outstanding, and the drink of choice is wine: perhaps unsurprising given that it's run by a trio of Frenchmen.

Their goal is to create a lively eating and drinking space without the pretension and high prices of so many other Rio locales. Its an admirable success. Come on Tuesdays for fresh oysters (a fine deal at R$40 a dozen).

Complex Esquina 111 COCKTAIL BAR

(Map p54; Maria Quitéria 111; ⊙noon-midnight Sun-Thu, to 3am Fri & Sat) This stylish, creative eating and drinking space has outdoor candlelit tables on a tranquil corner of Ipa-

LOCAL KNOWLEDGE

BARS WITH A VIEW

For first-rate drinks, friendly crowds and jaw-dropping views, head for the hills: great times await in Rio's favelas (slums, informal communities). The bars we recommend are located in safe areas. The only challenge is finding your way: first-timers should consider going by moto-taxi. You'll find drivers hanging out at the main entrance to each favela.

Estrelas da Babilônia (Map p62; Ladeira Ary Barroso; ⏲5-11pm Sun & Tue-Thu, to 3am Fri & Sat) In the uppermost reaches of the Babilônia favela, Estrelas da Babilônia has a picturesque open-air setting with an unrivaled view of the mountains and sea with the cityscape of Copacabana wedged between the two. It's a fun and welcoming spot, run by a Colombian-Belgian couple, with a lineup of live music, film screenings and other events. It's worth coming for the view alone.

Bar do Alto (Map p62; Ladeira Ary Barroso 57; ⏲1-10pm Wed-Sun) High up in the Babilônia favela, this friendly place has jaw-dropping views over Copacabana. It's an open-sided affair, with cool breezes, flickering candles on the tables, and a small menu with standouts such as fish or mixed-seafood *moqueca* (Bahian fish stew cooked in a clay pot with *dendê* oil, coconut milk and spicy peppers; around R$40), and *feijoada*-stuffed rolls – good for sharing.

Alto Vidigal (☎98741-3036; www.altovidigal.com; Armando de Almeida Lima 2; ⏲2pm-2am Tue-Sun) In the heights of the Vidigal favela this rustic, open-sided bar draws a fun, bohemian crowd to its weekend DJ fests (admission ranges from R$15 to R$60). Live bands sometimes play on Thursdays. Other nights of the week it's a fairly sedate spot for taking in that great hilltop view. You can take a taxi here, or catch a moto-taxi or van up from the Vidigal entrance.

nema. Try one of the signature sparkles (a champagne cocktail), while sharing a plate of tuna tartare, sliders or ceviche. It's a much-adored place by a good-looking neighborhood crowd, so come early to score an outdoor seat.

Bar Astor — BAR

(Map p54; www.barastor.com.br; Veira Souto 110; ⏲6pm-1am Mon-Thu, 1pm-3am Fri, noon-3am Sat, noon-10pm Sun) Won't make it to São Paulo? No problem. One of Sampa's best bars has now become a mainstay of postbeach revelry on prime real estate along the Ipanema shorefront. This gorgeous art deco bar does meticulously prepared caipirinhas, some 20 exotic flavors in all, and great food to help soak up the quality *cachaça* (sugarcane alcohol).

Barzin — BAR

(Map p54; Vinícius de Moraes 75; ⏲11am-3am Tue-Sun) Barzin is a popular spot for postbeach drinks; its open-sided ground-floor bar fills with animated chatter at all hours. Upstairs you can catch a changing lineup of bands playing surf rock, hip-hop and other popular Brazilian music (cover charge from R$30 to R$80).

Delirium Cafe — BAR

(Map p54; ☎2502-0029; Barão da Torre 183; ⏲5pm-1am) This small and cozy pub has more than 300 varieties of brew, with labels from across Europe, the US, Australia and beyond. If you've been to the original Delirium in Brussels, you might be a bit disappointed by their modest sister enterprise. You also have to be mindful of the cost. Nevertheless, it's a great destination for beer lovers.

Baretto-Londra — LOUNGE

(Map p54; ☎3202-4000; Av Vieira Souto 80; ⏲8pm-2am Thu-Sat) You'll find one of Rio's most glam bars here inside the Hotel Fasano, and it offers a vision of decadence matched by few of the city's nightspots. The intimate space, designed by Philippe Starck, has an enchantingly illuminated bar, leather armchairs and divans, and a DJ spinning world electronica.

Devassa — BOTECO

(Map p54; ☎2540-8380; Visconde de Pirajá 539; ⏲noon-2am) Devassa makes its own creamy brews and offers them up to chatty *cariocas* at this bar and restaurant; it's one of seven in the Rio chain. The choices: *loura* (pilsner), *sarará* (wheat beer), *ruiva* (pale ale), *negra* (dark ale) and *Índia* (India pale ale; IPA). The food menu features well-prepared pub fare: burgers, steak, pastas, grilled fish and lots of appetizers.

Empório BAR

(Map p54; ☎3813-2526; Maria Quitéria 37; ⏰8:30pm-late) A young mix of *cariocas* and gringos stirs things up over cheap cocktails at this battered old favorite in Ipanema. A porch out the front overlooks the street; it's a fine spot to stake out when the air gets too heavy with dubious '80s music. Don't come early; Empório doesn't get lively until after midnight.

Shenanigan's BAR

(Map p54; Visconde de Pirajá 112A; admission R$5-25; ⏰6pm-1am Mon-Sat, from 4pm Sun) Overlooking the Praça General Osório, Shenanigan's is an English-style pub with exposed brick walls, imported beers and a couple of tiny balconies perched above the street. Sunburnt gringos and the odd working girl mix it up over games of pool and darts to the backdrop of major games (Brazilian football, American NFL, NBA etc).

Leblon

Belmonte BAR

(Map p54; Dias Ferreira 521; ⏰11am-3am) An icon in Leblon, Belmonte always draws huge crowds: it's pretty much a massive street party every night, with beer-drinking revelers spilling onto the sidewalk from 8pm onward. If you can score a table, don't miss the delicious well-priced *pasteis* (dough that's filled then deep-fried) stuffed with crab, jerked beef with cheese, shrimp, heart of palm and other tasty ingredients.

Academia Da Cachaça BAR

(Map p54; ☎2529-2680; Conde de Bernadotte 26G; ⏰noon-1am) Although *cachaça* has a sordid reputation in some parts, at this bar the fiery liquor is given the respect it (nearly) deserves. Along with dishes of traditional Brazilian cooking, this pleasant indoor-outdoor spot serves more than 100 varieties of *cachaça;* you can order it straight, with honey and lime, or disguised in a fruity caipirinha.

Brewteco BAR

(Map p54; Dias Ferreira 420; ⏰11am-1am) A clear sign that the microbrew scene has arrived in Rio, Brewteco has scores of unique craft beers by the bottle from around the globe. California IPAs from Ballast Point, German hits such as Weihenstephaner, Belgian ales, and unique Brazilian options including Fraga Weiss, a wheat beer from Rio, draw the crowds.

Jobi BOTECO

(Map p54; ☎2274-0547; Av Ataúlfo de Paiva 1166; ⏰9am-5am) A favorite since 1956, Jobi has served a lot of beer in its day, and its popularity hasn't waned. The unadorned *botequim* (bar with table service) still serves plenty; grab a seat by the sidewalk and let the night unfold. If hunger beckons, try the tasty appetizers; the *carne seca* (jerked beef) and the *bolinhos de bacalhau* (codfish croquettes) are tops.

Usina CLUB

(Map p54; ☎2249-9309; www.usina47.com.br; Rita Ludolf 47; admission R$25-50; ⏰7pm-2am Mon-Sat, 6pm-midnight Sun) Usina gathers a young, attractive crowd, who sip brightly colored elixirs in its sleek and stylish main-floor lounge. Upstairs DJs break beats over the dance floor, and the occasional band makes an appearance.

Bar Veloso BOTECO

(Map p54; ☎2274-9966; Aristides Espínola 44; ⏰11am-1am) Named after the original bar (now Garota de Ipanema; p61) where Tom Jobim and Vinícius de Moraes penned the famous song 'The Girl from Ipanema', the open-sided Bar Veloso attracts a young, good-looking crowd, who spill out onto the sidewalk on busy weekends. Upstairs there's a quieter air-conditioned retreat where (mostly) men watch the game in peace.

Gávea, Jardim Botânico & Lagoa

Palaphita Kitch LOUNGE

(Map p54; ☎2227-0837; www.palaphitakitch.com.br; Av Epitácio Pessoa s/n; ⏰6pm-1am) A great spot for a sundowner, Palaphita Kitch is an open-air, thatched-roof wonderland with rustic bamboo furniture, flickering tiki torches and a peaceful setting on the edge of the lake. This is a popular spot with couples, who come for the view and the creative (but pricey) cocktails: the caipirinhas, made from unusual fruits from the Northeast and Amazonia, are a hit.

Bar do Horto BAR

(Map p56; ☎3114-8439; Pacheco Leão 780; ⏰noon-2am Tue-Sun) Colorful Bar do Horto is one of Jardim Botânico's most charming bars. The decor is festive and kitsch: walls covered with shimmering fabric and an interior that's festooned with brightly hued paper lanterns, butterfly appliqués, bottle-cap curtains and other recycled ephemera. At night the sidewalk tables gather a festive crowd that comes for cocktails and good cheer.

Hipódromo BAR
(Map p56; Praça Santos Dumont 108; ⏲noon-1am) In an area more commonly referred to as Baixo Gávea, Hipódromo is one of several bars responsible for the local residents' chronic lack of sleep. Most nights you'll find a college-age and twenty-something crowd celebrating here, with patrons spilling onto the facing Praça Santos Dumont.

Palaphita Gávea BAR
(Map p56; Bartolomeu Mitre 1314; ⏲6pm-4am) Overlooking the Joquei Clube (horse-racing track; p112), this sprawling open-air bar and party space is a wonderful mess of rustic wooden structures, thatch-roofed bars and scattered-about handmade furniture. It draws a young, animated crowd most nights and is a great place at which to end the night. On racing days, you can even place bets here and watch the horses thunder past.

00 (Zero Zero) LOUNGE, CLUB
(☎2540-8041; Av Padre Leonel Franca 240; cover R$40-80; ⏲11pm-5am Tue & Thu-Sat) Housed in Gávea's planetarium, 00 starts the evening as a stylish restaurant and transforms into a lounge and nightclub around 1am. DJs spin at rotating parties held here, and on Tuesday nights, party promoter Bem Brasil (www.bembrasilrio.com.br) throws a bash for the hostel crowd, making it a good place to be if you want to mingle with other travelers.

Copacabana & Leme

Escondido BAR
(Map p62; Aires de Saldanha 98, Copacabana; ⏲6pm-1am Tue-Sun) One of the top beer bars in Copacabana, Escondido has a rotating

GAY RIO

Rio has been a major destination for gay travelers since the 1950s. Back then the action was near the Copacabana Palace, where you'll still find remnants of this past (look for the rainbow-hued flag). Today, however, the party has mostly moved on, with the focal point of the LGBT (lesbian, gay, bisexual, transgender) scene, especially for visitors, being in Ipanema. The beach at the end of Rua Farme de Amoedo attracts a gay crowd (again, look for the rainbow flag), while bars and cafes of nearby streets – Rua Teixeira de Melo and Rua Farme de Amoeda – have a sprinkling of gay bars and cafes.

For more info on what's happening around town, check out www.riogayguide.com.

Buraco da Lacraia (Map p72; ☎2242-0446; André Cavalcante 58; admission R$40-45; ⏲10pm-5:30am Fri & Sat) An icon in Lapa, this is the place for a trashy good time, with bizarre drag shows, karaoke, a darkroom and other amusements.

Cafeína (p89) A popular Ipanema cafe that attracts a mix of gay and straight folk.

Fosfobox (p106) Small underground club that attracts a mixed crowd.

Galeria Café (Map p54; ☎2523-8250; www.galeriacafe.com.br; Teixeira de Melo 31; ⏲11pm-4am Wed-Sat) This bar with a mixed crowd has lovely decor.

Le Boy (Map p62; ☎2513-4993; www.leboy.com.br; Raul Pompéia 102, Copacabana; cover R$10-30; ⏲11pm-5am Tue-Sun) Open since 1992, Le Boy is Rio's gay temple. There are theme nights with drag shows and go-go boys.

Tô Nem Aí (Map p54; ☎2247-8403; cnr Farme de Amoedo & Visconde de Pirajá; ⏲noon-3am) On Ipanema's gayest street, this popular bar is a great after-beach spot.

TV Bar (Map p62; www.bartvbar.com.br; Shopping Cassino Atlântico, Av NS de Copacabana 1417, Copacabana; cover R$15-50; ⏲10pm-5am Thu-Sat, to 3am Sun) The trendy favorite in town; DJs spin amid an audiovisual assault in the space of a former TV station.

Week (Map p72; ☎2253-1020; www.theweek.com.br; Sacadura Cabral 135, Centro; 10pm-5am Sat) Rio's best gay dance club has a spacious dance floor, excellent DJs and go-go dancers.

selection of microbrews such as American Pale Ales (IPAs), stouts and ciders, including about two dozen on draft at any one time. It's a laid-back spot to head to with friends to sample a few brews and nibble on pub grub (including huge burgers).

Mais Que Nada CLUB
(Map p62; www.maisquenada-rio.com.br; Xavier da Silveira 34, Copacabana; 7pm-2am Wed-Sun) This small, festive club draws an equal mix of *cariocas* and gringos who come for a dance-loving lineup of samba, salsa and rock. Cover charge varies from R$10 to upwards of R$25. Wednesday nights (samba) are free.

As Melhores Cervejas do Mundo BAR
(Map p62; Ronald de Carvalho 154, Copacabana; 3-11pm Mon-Sat) This friendly new spot looks more like a bottle shop than a bar, but beer lovers shouldn't miss it. You'll find an impressive selection of brews from around the globe here, and there's always something going on: beer tastings, quiz nights, courses on beer and food pairings, and even a day (Saturday) when home brewers share their produce with one another.

Botequim Informal BOTECO
(Map p62; 3816-0909; Domingos Ferreira 215, Copacabana; noon-1am) Botequim Informal is a lively drinking spot with an elevated open-sided deck, frothy drafts and appetizers that include a good fried polenta with gorgonzola sauce. There are 10 other branches of Botequim Informal in Rio. This one lies amid half-a-dozen festive, open-sided bars in the Baixo Copa subneighborhood.

Sindicato do Chopp BAR
(Map p62; Av Atlântica 514, Leme) With a peaceful beachfront location, this casual bar is a relaxing and largely local spot to enjoy a draft or a filling meal.

Mud Bug BAR
(Map p62; 3547-8527; www.mudbug.com.br; Rudolfo Dantas 16, Copacabana; 5pm-3am) Mud Bug is a buzzing, warmly lit sports bar that has a rustic, all-wood interior where *cariocas* and foreigners mingle over football games, bar bites and a broad beer selection. There's also live music – typically classic rock – on weekends. A second, smaller Copacabana location is a few blocks west on Rua Paula Freitas, just north of NS de Copacabana.

Fosfobox CLUB
(Map p62; 2548-7498; www.fosfobox.com.br; Siqueira Campos 143, Copacabana; admission R$15-60; 11pm-4am Wed-Sat) This subterranean club is hidden under a shopping center near the metro station. Good DJs spin everything from funk to glam rock, and the crowd here is one of the more eclectic in the club scene.

Botafogo & Urca

Cabaret Lounge LOUNGE
(Map p66; 2226-4126; www.cabaretlounge.com.br; Voluntários da Pátria 449, Humaitá; cover R$15-40; 7pm-3am Tue-Thu, 9pm-5am Fri & Sat) The cozy Cabaret Lounge channels the look of an old-fashioned Parisian dance hall, with red walls, glittering chandeliers, velvet couches and armchairs, and gilt frames (containing video screens rather than sepia prints). Champagne and cocktails are the drinks of choice. As the evening progresses, it becomes more of a dance spot, with DJs spinning overhead.

Comuna BAR
(Map p66; 3029-0789; www.comuna.cc; Sorocaba 585, Botafogo; 6pm-2am Tue-Sun) This creative space is equal parts bar, art gallery and independent bookseller (and indie publishing house). There's always something afoot in the delightfully off-the-beaten-path locale, with workshops, music sessions, readings, exhibitions and fashion shows. It's also just a great spot for a bite (try one of the award-winning burgers) and a local microbrew.

Bar Urca BAR
(Map p66; 2295-8744; Cândido Gaffrée 205, Urca; 8am-11pm) This much-loved neighborhood bar and restaurant has a marvelous setting near Urca's bayside waterfront. At night, young and old crowd along the seaside wall to enjoy cold drinks, appetizers and fine views.

Caverna BAR
(Map p66; 3507-5600; www.espacocaverna.com; Assis Bueno 26; 6pm-1am Mon-Fri, 7pm-2am Sat) Yet another reason why Botafogo may be surpassing Ipanema in the cool factor these days, this always buzzing rock-and-roll loving bar and bistro serves up microbrews and juicy burgers amid a fun and festive atmosphere (though the music rocks a little loud some nights).

Crazy Cats BAR

(Map p66; www.facebook.com/crazycatsbistro; Sorocaba 19, Botafogo; ⌚7pm-1am Wed & Thu, 8pm-2am Fri & Sat, 5-11pm Sun) Vintage lovers shouldn't miss this imaginatively configured space in Botafogo. The owners must have raided every antique shop in Rio to assemble this curious collection, named after their four *gatos* (cats). Great sparkling cocktails, tasty snacks (like ceviche) and a classic rock-leaning soundtrack (plus the odd live band) all add to the appeal.

Cobal do Humaitá BAR

(Map p66; Voluntários da Pátria 446, Humaitá; ⌚8am-2am) A large food market in Humaitá, the Cobal transforms into a festive nightspot when the sun goes down, complete with open-air eating and drinking.

Bar Bukowski CLUB

(Map p66; ☎2244-7303; Álvaro Ramos 270, Botafogo; admission R$50; ⌚9pm-6am Fri & Sat) Paying homage to the bohemian American writer, this club has a downstairs dance floor and bar, and an upstairs level for live bands playing rock, pop and blues. It's a great scene, and usually attracts a fun crowd. There's also a pool table, darts and you can have a go at one of the water pipes.

Casa da Matriz CLUB

(Map p66; ☎2266-1014; www.facebook.com/casadamatriz; Henrique de Novaes 107, Botafogo; admission R$20-40; ⌚11pm-5am Wed-Sat) Artwork lines this space in Botafogo. With numerous rooms to explore (lounge, screening room, dance floors), this old mansion embodies the creative side of the *carioca* spirit. It usually attracts a student crowd. Check their Facebook page for party listings.

Champanharia Ovelha Negra BAR

(Map p66; ☎2226-1064; www.champanhariaovelhanegra.com.br; Bambina 120, Botafogo; ⌚5:30-11:30pm Mon-Fri) One of Rio's best happy-hour scenes, Ovelha Negra draws a mostly local crowd who come for the lively conversation and the 40 different varieties of champagne and prosecco – the specialties of the house.

Flamengo & Around

Bar do Zé BAR

(Map p66; Barão de Guaratiba 59, Catete; ⌚5pm-midnight Mon-Sat) Hidden down a narrow cobblestone side street off Rua do Catete, Bar do Zé has bohemian charm and remains little-known to most *cariocas*. You'll find just a few tables inside among the old bottle-lined shelves, low-playing samba on the radio and groups of friends gathered on the street out front.

Adega Portugália BAR

(Map p66; Largo do Machado 30, Catete; ⌚11am-midnight) Overlooking leafy Largo do Machado, Adega Portugália has an ideal location for enjoying a bit of open-air drinking and eating in an untouristy corner of Rio. In addition to a garrulous crowd and ice-cold *chope* (draft beer) you'll fine classic bar snacks such as *bolinhos de bacalhau* (codfish croquettes) and Portuguese-style sardines.

Belmonte BOTECO

(Map p66; ☎2552-3349; Praia do Flamengo 300, Flamengo; ⌚9am-2am) One of the classic *botecos* in Rio, Belmonte is a vision of Rio from the '50s. Globe lights hang overhead as patrons down ice-cold drafts from the narrow bar. Meanwhile, unhurried waiters make their way across the tile floors, carrying plates of *pasteis de camarão* (shrimp-filled pastries) or steak sandwiches. This hugely successful chain, born here, is now widespread across Rio.

Devassa BOTECO

(Map p66; ☎2556-0618; Senador Vergueiro 2, Flamengo; ⌚noon-1am) A particularly inviting branch of the growing Devassa network, this bar is set on a shaded square and serves the usual Devassa hits, including great drafts.

Centro

Samba Caffe BAR

(Map p72; Rua do Ouvidor 23, Centro; ⌚3:30pm-midnight Mon-Fri, noon-8pm Sat) Hidden in a narrow lane leading off Praça XV (Quinze) de Novembro, Samba Caffe is one of many photogenic open-air bars tucked into Rio's old colonial center. The narrow pedestrian lane is a popular meeting spot, and a festive air arrives at workday's end as *cariocas* fill the tables spilling onto the street.

Jazz In Champanheria BAR

(Map p72; Sacadura Cabral 63, Centro; ⌚6pm-1am Tue-Fri, 11pm-5am Sat) Set in a restored colonial building across from Praça Mauá, Jazz In draws a buzzing crowd that mingles among the art-covered walls, sipping bubbly (champagne and prosecco) and nibbling on bruschetta, sandwiches and other light fare. It's a lively after-work spot that morphs into a dance club as the evening progresses.

Amarelinho BOTECO
(Map p72; ☎3549-8434; Praça Floriano 55, Cinelândia; ⏰10am-1am) Easy to spot by its bright *amarelo* (yellow) awning, Amarelinho has a splendid setting on the Praça Floriano, with the Theatro Municipal in the background. Waiters serve plenty of *chope* (draft beer) here as they wander among the crowded tables. Amarelinho is a popular lunch spot but packs in even bigger crowds for that ever-important after-work brew.

Santa Teresa

Bar do Gomes BOTECO
(Map p72; ☎2232-0822; Áurea 26; ⏰noon-1am Mon-Sat, to 10pm Sun) Although the sign says 'Armazém do São Thiago', everyone calls the place Bar do Gomes. Regardless, this simple hole-in-the-wall has long been a favorite gathering spot, particularly on weekends, when young and old pack the few standup tables and bar front, and spill onto the sidewalk.

Bar dos Descasados LOUNGE
(Map p72; ☎3380-0200; Almirante Alexandrino 660; ⏰noon-midnight) Inside Hotel Santa Teresa, this stylish bar with outdoor seating has lovely views over the city (looking north). You can enjoy decadent cocktails (including a caipirinha made with tangerines grown on the property) and savory snacks such as salmon tartare while pondering the A-list crowd. The bar is fairly empty during the week but becomes a livelier destination, mostly for couples, on weekends.

Goya-Beira BAR
(Map p72; ☎2232-5751; Largo das Neves 13; ⏰6pm-midnight Sun-Thu, to 2am Fri & Sat) Small but charming Goya-Beira is one of Santa Teresa's gems, and has a peaceful view onto Largo das Neves. Owner Rose Guerra prepares intriguing *cachaça* infusions as well as pizzas and appetizers. Things are liveliest on weekends.

Lapa

Antônio's BOTECO
(Map p72; ☎2224-4197; Av Mem de Sá 88; ⏰4pm-3am Mon-Fri, from noon Sat & Sun) Antônio's in Lapa has lots of old-school charm with its hanging lamps, wrought-iron trim work and simple wooden tables. There are a few seats on the sidewalk for taking in the pulsing street scene. There are also plenty of other drinking spots nearby, if you feel like wandering.

Leviano Bar BAR
(Map p72; ☎2507-5967; www.levianobar.com.br; Av Mem de Sá 49; ⏰6pm-late) Near the entrance to Mem de Sá, the Leviano Bar is part of a new crop of slightly more upscale drinking and dance spots. Watch the passing people parade – and take in the great view of the Arcos da Lapa – from the outdoor area before heading to the upstairs dance floor, where DJs mix house, electro-samba, soul and reggae.

Sarau BAR
(Map p72; Av Mem de Sá 64; ⏰6pm-4am Tue-Sun) Just past the Arcos da Lapa and tucked inside a building covered with an enormous mural, this place is hard to miss. There's live music (samba and *forró,* popular music of the Northeast) from 7:30pm. It's also a great spot for having a few drinks at one of the many outdoor tables on the plaza in front and taking in the vertiginous street scene.

Anexo Bar BAR
(Map p72; Rua do Rezende 52; ⏰7pm-3am Tue-Sun) Tucked down a side street away from the Lapa mayhem, Anexo is an alternative space where you can find *boa gente* (good people). It's a friendly mixed crowd that comes for cocktails, good music and conversation among an art-filled interior. Owner Luiz and his crew make great drinks and tasty snacks (try the sausage and cheese sandwich).

La Paz CLUB
(Map p72; Rua do Rezende 82; admission R$10-30; ⏰11pm-6am Wed-Sat) For a break from samba, this popular nightspot provides a fine antidote, with a groove-loving dance floor provided by DJs spinning hip-hop, house and funk. It's a small and intimate club with an underground vibe; it has two dance floors, and a band that takes the stage on Friday and Saturday nights.

☆ Entertainment

Music & Dancing

Rio's music scene features talented performers playing in atmospheric settings to a democratic crowd. Lapa is the heart of samba, and its old clubs are a must-see for visitors. The widest assortment of music venues is along Av Mem de Sá.

Gafieiras (dance halls) are a big attraction in Lapa. Here you'll find restored colonial buildings hiding dance floors and large samba bands – along with their many admirers.

Rio Scenarium SAMBA
(Map p72; www.rioscenarium.com.br; Rua do Lavradio 20, Lapa; cover R$25-50; ⏲7pm-4am Tue-Sat) One of the city's most photogenic nightspots, Rio Scenarium has three floors, each lavishly decorated with antiques. Balconies overlook the stage on the 1st floor, where dancers keep time to the jazz-infused samba, *choro* or *pagode* (popular samba music) filling the air. Rio Scenarium receives much press outside of Brazil, and attracts at least as many foreigners as locals.

Carioca da Gema SAMBA
(Map p72; www.barcariocadagema.com.br; Av Mem de Sá 79, Lapa; cover R$25-40; ⏲7pm-2am Mon-Fri, from 9pm Sat & Sun) Although it's now surrounded by clubs, Carioca da Gema was one of Lapa's pioneers when it opened in 2000. This small, warmly lit club still attracts some of the city's best samba bands, and you'll find a festive, mixed crowd filling the dance floor most nights.

Democráticus SAMBA
(Map p72; ☎2252-1324; Rua do Riachuelo 93, Lapa; admission R$25-50; ⏲10pm-3am Wed-Sat) Murals line the foyer of this 1867 mansion. The rhythms filter down from above. Follow the sound up the marble staircase and out into a large hall filled with tables, an enormous dance floor and a long stage covered with musicians. A wide range of *cariocas* gathers here to dance, revel in the music and soak up the splendor of the samba-infused setting.

Lapa 40 Graus LIVE MUSIC
(Map p72; ☎3970-1338; www.lapa40graus.com.br; Rua do Riachuelo 97, Lapa; admission R$10-50; ⏲6pm-5am Wed-Sat) This impressive multistory music venue and pool hall has tables for lounging on the 1st floor, more than a dozen pool tables on the 2nd floor, and a small stage and dancing couples on the top floor. There are usually two shows nightly. Pop, rock, samba and *choro* kick off around 7pm and 11pm.

TICKET MATTERS

At most samba clubs and live-music bars (also self-serve restaurants) in Rio, you'll receive a ticket when you enter. Rather than paying for individual drinks, your ticket will be marked each time you order. At the end of the night, you'll head to the cashier and pay for your food and drinks, plus pay for any admission charge. The cashier will then give you another ticket to pass to the door attendant as you exit. Don't lose that ticket, as you'll be hit with a hefty fee (upwards of R$150). You'll see this system in many areas of Brazil.

Beco do Rato LIVE MUSIC
(Map p72; ☎2508-5600; http://becodorato.com.br; Joaquim Silva 11, Lapa; ⏲6pm-3am Tue, Thu & Fri) One of Lapa's classic bohemian spots, this tiny bar has excellent live groups playing to a samba-loving crowd. The outdoor seating and informal setting are an unbeatable mix. Marcio, the friendly owner, hails from Minas Gerais; to get the night started, ask him for a tasty *cachaça* from his home state.

TribOz JAZZ
(Map p72; ☎2210-0366; www.triboz-rio.com; Conde de Lages 19, Lapa; cover around R$30; ⏲6-8pm & 9pm-1am Thu-Sat) Not for lazy ears, this avant-garde jazz house, a little hidden gem among the sonic cognoscenti, is unique in Rio for its serious approach to performances. Run by an Australian ethnomusicologist, it sits in a shadier part of old Lapa in a signless mansion, which transforms into a beautiful showcase space for Brazil's most cutting-edge artists.

The crowd skews to over-thirties and/or music aficionados, who come for the evening's three 45-minute sets and good-value Oz-inspired grub. Reservations are essential two days in advance by phone only.

Bip Bip LIVE MUSIC
(Map p62; ☎2267-9696; Almirante Gonçalves 50, Copacabana; ⏲6pm-midnight Sun-Fri) For years Bip Bip has been one of the city's favorite spots to catch a live *roda de samba* (informal samba played around a table), despite it being just a storefront with a few battered tables. As the evening progresses the tree-lined neighborhood becomes the backdrop to serious jam sessions, with music and revelers spilling into the street.

Maze Inn LIVE MUSIC

(Map p66; ☎2558-5547; www.jazzrio.info; Casa 66, Tavares Bastos 414, Catete; admission R$25-50; ⏰10pm-3am, 1st Fri of month) Also known as the 'Casa do Bob' after owner Bob Nadkarni, this once-a-month event is well worth attending. It's set in the guesthouse of the same name high up in Tavares Bastos (one of Rio's safest favelas). There's a fun mix of *cariocas* and expats, with live jazz and fantastic city views.

Vinícius Show Bar LIVE MUSIC

(Map p54; ☎2523-4757; www.viniciusbar.com.br; 2nd fl, Prudente de Morais 34, Ipanema; admission R$35-50) Billing itself as the 'temple of bossa nova,' this place has been an icon in the neighborhood since 1989. The intimate space makes a fine setting to listen to first-rate bossa nova, and occasional Música Popular Brasileira (MPB) and samba. Shows typically start between 9:30pm and 11pm.

Trapiche Gamboa SAMBA

(Map p72; ☎2516-0868; Sacadura Cabral 155, Gamboa; admission R$15-25; ⏰6:30pm-1am Tue-Fri, 8:30pm-2am Sat) A charming live samba joint, Trapiche Gamboa is set in a multistory colonial edifice in Gamboa (just north of Centro) and has a friendly, mixed crowd and decent appetizers. It's a casual affair, with samba musicians gathering around a table on the ground floor, and dancers spilling out in front of them.

Beco das Garrafas LIVE MUSIC

(Map p62; http://becodasgarrafas.mus.br; Duvivier 37, Copacabana; admission R$30-40) Come to this club to connect to a small part of Brazilian history – and a big part of musical lore. It was on this lane where Tom Jobim and other innovators first unveiled bossa nova in the 1960s. Shuttered for years, the bar was brought back to life in 2014 and today hosts an excellent lineup of bossa and MPB singers.

SAMBA SCHOOLS

Starting around September, in preparation for Carnaval, most big samba schools open their rehearsals to the public. These are large dance parties, and provide a good chance to mingle with *cariocas*. Schools typically charge R$10 to R$40 at the door (prices are higher the closer you are to Carnaval).

Many samba schools are in the favelas (slums, informal communities), so use common sense when visiting.

You can visit the samba schools on a tour, or you can go by yourself. If going independently, catch a taxi there and back; there are always cabs outside the schools waiting to take people home. It's a good idea to confirm that the rehearsals are on before heading out. The most popular schools for tourists are Mangueira and Salgueiro.

Beija-Flor (☎2233-5889; www.beija-flor.com.br; Praçinha Wallace Paes Leme 1025, Nilópolis; ⏰9pm Thu)

Grande Rio (☎2671-3585; www.academicosdogranderio.com.br; Wallace Soares 5-6, Duque de Caixas; ⏰10pm Sat & 8pm Tue)

Imperatriz Leopoldinense (☎2560-8037; www.imperatrizleopoldinense.com.br; Professor Lacê 235, Ramos; ⏰8pm Sun)

Mangueira (☎2567-3419; www.mangueira.com.br; Visconde de Niterói 1072, Mangueira; ⏰10pm Sat)

Mocidade Independente de Padre Miguel (☎3332-5823; www.mocidadeindependente.com.br; Av Brasil 31146, Padre Miguel; ⏰10pm Sat)

Portela (☎2489-6440; Clara Nunes 81, Oswaldo Cruz; ⏰10pm Fri)

Rocinha (☎3205-3318; Bertha Lutz 80, São Conrado; ⏰10pm Sat)

Salgueiro (☎2238-9226; www.salgueiro.com.br; Silva Teles 104, Andaraí; ⏰10pm Sat)

Unidos da Tijuca (Map p76; ☎2516-2749; www.unidosdatijuca.com.br; Francisco Bicalho 47, Santo Cristo; ⏰10pm Sat)

Vila Isabel (☎2578-0077; Av Blvd 28 de Setembro 382, Vila Isabel; ⏰10pm Sat)

It's a small and intimate space, and a must-see for music fans.

Circo Voador CONCERT VENUE
(Map p72; ☎2533-0354; www.circovoador.com.br; Rua dos Arcos, Lapa; admission R$40-90) In a curvilinear building behind the Arcos da Lapa, Circo Voador hosts big-name Brazilian and international artists. The acoustics here are excellent, and after a show you'll find plenty of other musical options in the area. Check the website to see what's on. You can also take classes in capoeira, dance, percussion and yoga.

Fundição Progresso CONCERT VENUE
(Map p72; ☎3212-0800; www.fundicaoprogresso.com.br; Rua dos Arcos 24, Lapa; admission R$25-50) This former foundry in Lapa hides one of Rio's top music and theater spaces. A diverse range of shows is staged here: big-name acts such as Manu Chao and Caetano Veloso, plus theater, video arts and ballet. The foundation is one of Lapa's premier arts institutions, and you can study dance, capoeira and circus arts here.

Semente SAMBA
(Map p72; ☎9781-2451; Evaristo da Veiga 149, Lapa; admission R$20-40; ⏲8pm-2am) One of the few venues in Lapa that holds court on Sunday and Monday nights, Semente has longevity. Although it has closed and reopened a few times, it was one of the first places in Lapa to bring samba back to the city. Its current incarnation is small and intimate, with good bands and a crowd that comes for the music rather than the Lapa mayhem.

Centro Cultural Carioca SAMBA
(Map p72; ☎2252-6468; www.centroculturalcarioca.com.br; Rua do Teatro 37, Centro; admission R$20-40; ⏲7pm-1am Mon-Thu, 8:30pm-2am Fri & Sat) This carefully restored 19th-century building hosts an excellent musical lineup throughout the week, and it is a good option for those wanting to escape the crowds in Lapa, Rio's popular music district. The scene here is slightly more staid, which makes it a good choice for couples.

Ginga Tropical DANCE
(Map p72; ☎3588-6857; www.gingatropical.com.br; Praça Tiradentes 79, Centro; admission R$160; ⏲10pm Sun, Mon, Thu & Fri) For a look at Brazil's rich folkloric dances, book a ticket to an evening performance of Ginga Tropical. Some 16 different dance styles are represented, including a somewhat spooky Orixás performance, lightning-fast *frevo,* and a stunning acrobatically inclined capoeira group. Other highlights: twirling Amazonian *carimbó*, sultry Northeastern *forró*, and a wild and very rarely performed *boleadeira* from Rio Grande do Sul.

Miranda LIVE MUSIC
(Map p54; ☎2239-0305; mirandabrasil.com.br; Av Borges de Medeiros 1424, Lagoa; admission R$50-80) Situated on Lagoa Rodrigo de Freitas, Miranda is a classy but inviting bar and live-music venue that hosts a range of shows and events. These include *feijoada* (a bean-and-meat stew served with rice) and live samba on Sundays (R$70); Música Popular Brasileira (MPB) groups and well-known Brazilian artists such as Mart'nália and BossaCucaNova (a group that blends bossa nova with electronica).

Renascença Clube SAMBA
(☎3253-2322; www.renascencaclube.com.br; Rua Barão de São Francisco 54, Andaraí; ⏲5-10pm Mon & Sat) For an authentic slice of Rio, head to one of the massive open-air samba parties that happen several times a week in Andaraí. The set-up is simple: a handful of musicians gathered around a table playing samba, while huge dance-loving crowds (that join in on many of the songs) gather around. Monday nights (*samba do trabalhador*, or samba for the worker), which are lead by maestro Moacyr Luz, are excellent.

If you like samba, don't mind big crowds and are up for a bit of adventure, then this place is for you – it's well off the tourist circuit.

Classical Music, Theater & Dance

The city's most lavish setting for a performance is the beaux-arts **Theatro Municipal** (Map p72; ☎2332-9191; www.theatromunicipal.rj.gov.br; Manuel de Carvalho, Centro). You'll find a more exciting repertoire of modern dance, theater and performance art at the excellent **Espaço SESC** (Map p62; ☎2548-1088; www.sescrj.org.br; Domingos Ferreira 160, Copacabana). In Lapa the **Sala Cecília Meireles** (Map p72; ☎2332-9223; www.salaceciliameireles.com.br; Largo da Lapa 47, Lapa) is a splendid early-20th-century gem hosting orchestral concerts throughout the year.

Cinemas

Rio remains remarkably open to foreign and independent films, documentaries and avant-garde cinema. For listings and show times pick up *O Globo, Jornal do Brasil* newspapers or *Veja Rio* magazine. Ticket prices run from R$20 to R$32. Major shopping centers also have cinemas.

Cine Santa Teresa CINEMA
(Map p72; ☎2222-0203; www.cinesanta.com.br; Paschoal Carlos Magno 136, Santa Teresa) This small, single-screen theater is well located on Largo do Guimarães. Befitting the art-loving 'hood, the cinema screens a selection of independent and Brazilian films.

Estação Net Rio CINEMA
(Map p66; ☎2226-1986; Voluntários da Pátria 35, Botafogo) This two-screen cinema in Botafogo shows a range of films – Brazilian, foreign, independent, and the occasional Hollywood film. It has a lovely cafe inside, as well as a shop selling used records and books with a number of works focusing on the film arts.

Estação Net Botafogo CINEMA
(Map p66; ☎2226-1988; Voluntários da Pátria 88, Botafogo) One block from Estação Rio, this small three-screen theater shows a mix of Brazilian and foreign films. The small cafe in front is a good place to grab a quick *cafézinho* (small black coffee) before the movie.

Estação Net Ipanema CINEMA
(Map p54; ☎2279-4603; Visconde de Pirajá 605, Ipanema) On the 1st floor of a small shopping complex in Ipanema, this cinema screens popular contemporary films from Brazil and abroad. Its single theater seats 140.

Odeon Petrobras CINEMA
(Map p72; ☎2240-1093; Praça Floriano 7, Cinelândia) Rio de Janeiro's landmark cinema is a remnant of the once-flourishing movie-house scene that gave rise to the name Cinelândia. The restored 1920s film palace shows independent films, documentaries and foreign films, and sometimes hosts the gala for prominent film festivals.

Roxy CINEMA
(Map p62; ☎2461-2461; www.kinoplex.com.br; Av NS de Copacabana 945, Copacabana) Copacabana's only cinema is a fine retreat when the weather sours. The Roxy shows the usual films on wide release.

Spectator Sports

Rio's football stadiums are Maracanã, Estádio Olímpico João Havelange and Estádio de São Januário.

Maracanã Football Stadium STADIUM
(Map p76; ☎8871-3950; www.suderj.rj.gov.br/maracana.asp; Av Maracanã, São Cristóvão; admission R$40-80; ⏲9am-7pm; Ⓢ Maracanã) For a quasi-psychedelic experience, go to a *futebol* match at Maracanã, Brazil's temple to football (soccer). Matches here rate among the most exciting in the world, particularly during a championship game or when local rivals Flamengo, Vasco da Gama, Fluminense or Botafogo go head-to-head. Games take place year-round and generally happen on a Wednesday, Thursday, Saturday or Sunday.

Joquei Clube HORSE RACING
(Map p56; ☎3534-9000; www.jcb.com.br; Jardim Botânico 1003, Gávea; ⏲6-10pm Mon & Fri, 2-9pm Sat & Sun) One of the country's loveliest racetracks, with a great view of the mountains and Corcovado, the Joquei Clube (Jockey Club) seats 35,000. It lies on the Gávea side of the Lagoa Rodrigo de Freitas, opposite Praça Santos Dumont. Local race fans are part of the attraction – it's a different slice of Rio life.

Shopping

Rio has a wide range of shopping, from colorful markets to eye-catching Zona Sul boutiques. Some of the major strips in the city for window shopping include Av Ataúlfo de Paiva in Leblon, where you'll find boutiques sprinkled among cafes, bookshops and restaurants; Rua Visconde de Pirajá, Ipanema's bustling shopping strip; and Rua do Lavradio in Lapa, which has a long row of antique stores.

Rio's biggest market is found at the Feira Nordestina (p76) in São Cristóvão.

Ipanema & Leblon

Hippie Fair MARKET
(Map p54; Praça General Osório; ⏲9am-6pm Sun) The Zona Sul's most famous market, the Hippie Fair (aka Feira de Arte de Ipanema) has artwork, jewelry, handicrafts, clothing and souvenirs for sale. Stalls in the four corners of the plaza sell tasty plates of *acarajé* (croquettes made from mashed black-eyed peas, with a sauce of *vatapá* – manioc paste, coconut and *dendê* oil – and shrimp; R$9), plus excellent desserts (R$4). Don't miss it.

Toca do Vinícius MUSIC
(Map p54; ☎2247-5227; www.tocadovinicius.com.br; Vinícius de Moraes 129; ⏲11am-7pm Mon-Fri, 10am-6pm Sat, 3-6pm Sun) Bossa nova

fans shouldn't miss this store. In addition to its ample CD and vinyl selection (starting at R$40) of contemporary and old performers, it also sells music scores and composition books. Around the store you'll find memorabilia from great songwriters including Vinícius de Moraes and Chico Buarque.

Osklen CLOTHING
(Map p54; ☎2227-2911; Maria Quitéria 85; ⏰9am-8pm Mon-Fri, 10am-7pm Sat, 11am-5pm Sun) One of Brazil's best-known fashion labels outside the country, Osklen is notable for its stylish and well-made beachwear (particularly men's swim shorts and graphic T-shirts), sneakers and outerwear. The company was started in 1988 by outdoor enthusiast Oskar Metsavaht, the first Brazilian to scale Mont Blanc.

Gilson Martins ACCESSORIES
(Map p54; ☎2227-6178; Visconde de Pirajá 462; ⏰9am-8pm Mon-Sat) Designer Gilson Martins transforms the Brazilian flag and silhouettes of Pão de Açúcar and Corcovado into eye-catching accessories in his flagship store in Ipanema. This is the place for one-of-a-kind glossy handbags, wallets, passport covers, key chains and iPad covers. Products are durable and use recycled and sustainable materials – and are not available outside of Rio.

Maria Oiticica JEWELRY
(Map p54; ☎3875-8025; Shopping Leblon, Av Afrânio de Melo Franco 290; ⏰10am-10pm Mon-Sat, 1-9pm Sun) Using native materials found in the Amazon, Maria Oiticica has created some lovely handcrafted jewelry inspired by indigenous art. Seeds, plant fibers and tree bark are just some of the ingredients of her bracelets, necklaces, earrings and sandals. There are even sandals and handbags made from fish 'leather'.

10Aquim SWEETS
(Map p54; ☎2523-5009; Garcia d'Ávila 149; ⏰10am-6pm Mon-Sat) This artisanal chocolatier carefully sources its cacao from a single environmentally conscious grower in Bahia, and has garnered international awards for its high-quality (and delicious!) products. Stop by this jewel-box-sized store for rich truffles, macarons, chocolate cakes and mini tarts that look almost too lovely to eat.

Shopping Leblon SHOPPING CENTER
(Map p54; ☎2430-5122; www.shoppingleblon.com.br; Av Afrânio de Melo Franco 290; ⏰10am-10pm Mon-Sat, 1-9pm Sun) This glittering multistory shopping center packed with top-name Brazilian and foreign labels is the best shopping destination in Leblon. It has plenty of tempting stores that will drain your vacation funds, as well as good restaurants and a cinema.

Copacabana & Leme

Praça do Lido Market MARKET
(Map p62; Praça do Lido, Copacabana; ⏰8am-6pm Sat & Sun) Copacabana's response to Ipanema's widely popular Hippie Fair, this smaller weekend affair features handicrafts and souvenirs, soccer jerseys, jewelry stands and, from time to time, a man selling amazing slices of chocolate cake.

Loja Fla CLOTHING, ACCESSORIES
(Map p62; ☎2541-4109; Av NS de Copacabana 219, Copacabana; ⏰10am-6pm Mon-Fri, to 4pm Sat) With more than 30 million fans worldwide, Flamengo is one of the most-watched football (soccer) teams in all of Brazil. This shop sells all the Flamengo goods, including jerseys, logo-emblazoned socks and soccer balls, posters, iPhone covers and other memorabilia. The prices aren't cheap (jerseys run from R$90 to R$200), but that hasn't dented the popularity of this often-packed little store.

Bossa Nova & Companhia MUSIC
(Map p62; ☎2295-8096; Duvivier 37A, Copacabana; ⏰9am-7pm Mon-Fri, to 5pm Sat) Here you'll find a decent assortment of bossa, *choro* and samba CDs and LPs, as well as musical instruments, coffee-table books, sheet music and biographies of top Brazilian composers.

Galeria River SHOPPING CENTER
(Map p62; Francisco Otaviano 67, Arpoador; ⏰9am-8pm Mon-Sat) Surf shops, skateboard and rollerblade outlets, and shops selling beachwear and fashions for young nubile things fill this shopping gallery in Arpoador. Shorts, bikinis, swim trunks, party attire and gear for outdoor adventure are here in abundance. You can also rent surfboards (though for short rentals it's easier hiring on the beach).

Havaianas SHOES
(Map p62; ☎2267-2418; Xavier da Silveira 19, Copacabana; ⏰9am-8pm Mon-Sat, 10am-6pm Sun) If you're out of ideas for gifts to take home, head to this sizeable Havaianas

1
2

PAOLO COSTA / SHUTTERSTOCK ©

1. Maracanã Football Stadium (p75) 2. Football match (p682)
3. Fluminense supporters, Maracanã Football Stadium

Football Fever

Rio's Maracanã stadium, recently refurbished for the 2014 World Cup, is hallowed ground among football lovers. The massive arena has been the site of legendary victories and crushing defeats. But no matter who takes the field, the 78,600-seat open-air arena comes to life in spectacular fashion on game day.

The Spectacle

A game at Maracanã (p75) is a must-see for visitors. Matches here rate among the most exciting in the world, and the behavior of the fans is no less colorful. The devoted pound huge samba drums, spread vast flags across great swaths of the stadium, dance in the aisles and detonate smoke bombs in team colors. You'll hear – and feel – the deafening roar when the home team takes the field, and the wall of sound and palpable air of near-hysteria will surround you when a player slams the ball into the back of the net. Things are only slightly calmer since alcohol was banned inside the stadium back in 2003 (though with pressure from FIFA, an exception to the law was put in place for the 2014 World Cup).

The Clubs

Rio is home to four major club teams – Flamengo, Fluminense, Vasco da Gama and Botafago – each with a die-hard local following. Apart from several short breaks for the Christmas–New Year holiday and Carnaval, professional club competitions go on all year. The major event in Rio's sporting calendar is the *classico*, when the four hometown teams play each other. Expect intense and bitter rivalry, matched in excitement only by Rio and São Paulo competitions.

shop, where the ubiquitous Brazilian rubber sandal comes in all different styles, and sporting the flags of Brazil, Argentina, Portugal, England and Spain. There are snazzy designs for women, and even logo-bearing bags, key chains and beach towels.

Botafogo & Urca

Botafogo Praia Shopping SHOPPING CENTER
(Map p66; 3171-9872; Praia de Botafogo 400, Botafogo; 10am-10pm Mon-Sat, 2-9pm Sun;) Botafogo's large shopping center has dozens of stores, featuring Brazilian and international designers to suit every style – and clothe every part of the body. The 3rd floor's the best for top designers: check out stores such as Maria Filó, Reserva and Hope. The mall also has a cinema and several top-floor restaurants, such as Emporium Pax (p98), with great panoramic views.

Flamengo & Around

Pé de Boi HANDICRAFTS
(Map p66; 2285-4395; www.pedeboi.com.br; Ipiranga 55, Laranjeiras; 9am-7pm Mon-Fri, to 1pm Sat) Although everything is for sale here, Pé de Boi feels more like an art gallery than a handicrafts shop, owing to the high quality of the wood and ceramic works, and the tapestries, sculptures and weavings. This is perhaps Rio's best place to see one-of-a-kind pieces by artists from Bahia, Amazonia, Minas Gerais and other parts of Brazil.

Centro

Arlequim BOOKS, MUSIC
(Map p72; 2220-8471; Praça XV (Quinze) de Novembro 48, Paço Imperial, Centro; 10am-8pm Mon-Fri, to 6pm Sat) Bossa nova plays overhead at this charming cafe, bookstore and music shop. As well as new books (including foreign-language titles), Arlequim sells CDs covering bossa, samba and other styles. The cafe menu features salads, sandwiches and other light fare (mains R$20 to R$37).

Granado BEAUTY
(Map p72; 3231-6747; Primeiro de Março 14, Centro; 8am-8pm Mon-Fri, 10am-2pm Sat) A classic-looking apothecary with a name that's been around since 1870, Granado incorporates Brazilian ingredients in its all-natural products. Favorites include the Castanha do Brasil line of moisturizers, shampoos and conditioners (made from chestnuts from the Amazon).

Santa Teresa & Lapa

La Vereda Handicrafts HANDICRAFTS
(Map p72; 2507-0317; Almirante Alexandrino 428, Santa Teresa; 10am-8pm) La Vereda stocks a colorful selection of handicrafts from local artists and artisans in a spot near Largo do Guimarães. Handpainted clay figurines by Pernambuco artists, heavy Minas ceramics, delicate sterling silver jewelry and woven tapestries cover the interior of the old store.

Feira do Rio Antigo MARKET
(Map p72; 2224-6693; Rua do Lavradio, Lapa; 10am-6pm 1st Sat of month) Although the Rio Antiques Fair happens just once a month, don't miss it if you're in town. The colonial buildings become a living installation as the whole street fills with antiques, clothing and craft vendors, and food stalls, with samba bands adding to the festive air.

Information

DANGERS & ANNOYANCES

Rio has become slightly safer in recent years, although crime is still a problem, and tourists are sometimes targeted. To minimize your risk of becoming a victim, take some basic precautions. First off: dress down and leave expensive (or even expensive *looking*) jewelry, watches and sunglasses at home.

Copacabana and Ipanema Beaches have a police presence, but robberies still occur on the sands, even in broad daylight. Don't ever take anything of value with you to the beach. Late at night, don't walk on any of the beaches. Lapa and Santa Teresa are other areas well worth visiting but which have their share of crime. Avoid walking on empty streets; it's safest to stick to well-trafficked areas.

Take taxis at night (but never get into an unmarked car) to avoid walking along empty streets and beaches. That holds especially true for Centro, which becomes deserted in the evening and on weekends, and is better explored during the week.

Get in the habit of carrying only the money you'll need for the day, so you don't have to flash a wad of reais when you pay for things. Cameras and backpacks attract a lot of attention. Plastic shopping bags better disguise whatever you're carrying.

If you have the misfortune of being robbed, slowly hand over the goods. Thieves in the city are only too willing to use their weapons.

EMERGENCY

Report robberies to the **tourist police** (☎2332-2924; cnr Afrânio de Melo Franco & Humberto de Campos, Leblon; ⊙24hr).

Other useful numbers:

Ambulance (☎192)

Fire Department (☎193)

Police (☎190)

INTERNET RESOURCES

Rio Guia (www.rioguiaoficial.com.br) Riotur's comprehensive website.

Rio Times (www.riotimesonline.com) Online English weekly for news and current events.

www.ipanema.com This website has good tips for first-time visitors.

MEDIA

Rio's main daily papers are **Jornal do Brasil** (www.jbonline.com.br) and **O Globo** (www.globo.com.br). Both have entertainment and event listings, particularly strong on Fridays and Sundays. The national publication *Veja* has a *Veja Rio* insert on Sundays, which details weekly entertainment options.

MEDICAL SERVICES

For medical emergencies, the best hospital for foreigners is the **Clinica Galdino Campos** (☎2548-9966; www.galdinocampos.com.br; Av NS de Copacabana 492, Copacabana; ⊙24hr), which offers high-quality care and multilingual doctors.

There are scores of pharmacies in town, a number of which stay open 24 hours:

Drogaria Pacheco Branches in Ipanema (☎2511-7871; Av Visconde de Pirajá 455; ⊙7am-11pm) and Leblon (☎3875-3070; Av Ataúlfo de Paiva 1151; ⊙24hr). Has two branches in Copacabana (Av NS de Copacabana 698; ⊙24hr) and (Av NS de Copacabana 115; ⊙7am-11pm).

MONEY

ATMs and banks can be found throughout the city. Banco do Brasil, Bradesco and Citibank are the best banks to try when using a debit or credit card. At the airport, international ATMs and money exchange are located on the 3rd floor of Arrivals.

Banco do Brasil Branches in Centro (Senador Dantas 105, Centro) and two in Copacabana (Av NS de Copacabana 264) and (Av NS de Copacabana 1274).

Citibank Branches in Copacabana (Av NS de Copacabana 828), Ipanema (Visconde de Pirajá 260, Ipanema) and Centro (Rua da Assembléia 100, Centro).

TOURIST INFORMATION

Riotur (☎2541-7522; www.rioguiaoficial.com.br; Praça Pio X 119, Centro; ⊙9am-6pm Mon-Fri) is the Rio city tourism agency and is generally useful. Its handy multilingual website is a good source of information.

All Riotur offices distribute maps and the excellent (and updated) monthly *Rio Guide*, which lists the major seasonal events.

You'll find information posts in Copacabana, on Copacabana Beach and at Galeão airport.

Riotur Centro (Map p72; Candelária 6; ⊙9am-6pm Mon-Fri, to 3pm Sat)

Riotur Copacabana (Map p62; ☎2541-7522; Av Princesa Isabel 183; ⊙9am-6pm Mon-Fri, to 3pm Sat)

Riotur Galeão airport Terminal 1 (☎3398-4077; Terminal 1, Domestic Arrival Hall, Aeroporto Galeão; ⊙6am-11pm); **Terminal 2** (☎3367-6213; Terminal 2, International Arrival Hall, Aeroporto Galeão; ⊙6am-11pm)

Riotur Ipanema (Map p54; Visconde de Pirajá & Joana Angélica; ⊙8am-9pm)

Riotur Kiosk Copacabana Beach (Map p62; ☎2547-4421; Av Atlântica, near Hilário de Gouveia; ⊙8am-9pm)

Riotur Leblon (Map p54; Ataulfo de de Paiva & Dias Ferreira; ⊙8am-6pm)

Getting There & Away

AIR

Most flights depart from **Aeroporto Galeão** (GIG) also called Aeroporto Tom Jobim, 15km north of the center. Some flights to/from São Paulo and other Brazilian cities use **Aeroporto Santos Dumont**, east of the city center.

The following lists sample prices on Gol and TAM, Brazil's major carriers. Prices quoted are one-way and leave from Aeroporto Galeão. Given frequent specials and volatile prices, this information is subject to change.

DESTINATION	AIRLINE	COST (R$)
Belém	Gol	400-1100
Belém	TAM	400-1360
Fortaleza	Gol	570-950
Fortaleza	TAM	650-860
Iguaçu Falls	Gol	500-1050
Iguaçu Falls	TAM	690-830
Manaus	Gol	510-1010
Manaus	TAM	540-950
Recife	Gol	310-630
Recife	TAM	440-700
Salvador	Gol	450-690
Salvador	TAM	600-750
São Paulo	Gol	160-490
São Paulo	TAM	230-420

Some airlines:

Azul (AD; ☎4003-1118; www.voeazul.com.br)

Gol (G3; ☎0300-115 2121; www.voegol.com.br) All travel agents sell Gol tickets. Flies to/from Aeroporto Galeão and Aeroporto Santos Dumont

LATAM (KK; ☎4002-5700; www.latam.com)

BUS

Buses leave from the **Rodoviária Novo Rio** (Map p76; ☎3213-1800; Av Francisco Bicalho 1), about 2km northwest of Centro. Several buses depart daily from here to most major destinations, but it's best to buy tickets in advance. If you have a PayPal account, you can buy bus tickets online at www.clickbus.com.br or www.brasilbybus.com. After purchasing, you'll receive the booking reference and ticket number. At the bus station, you'll enter these at the self-service kiosks. A handful of travel agents also sell bus tickets. **Guanatur** (Map p62; ☎2548-3275; www.guanaturismo.com.br; Rua Dias da Rocha 16A, Copacabana; ⊙9am-6pm Mon-Fri, to noon Sat) and **Dantur** (☎2557-7144; www.dantur.com.br; Largo do Machado 29, loja 47, Flamengo; ⊙9am-6:30pm Mon-Fri, to 1pm Sat) sell tickets for many lines. The commission charge is R$6 per ticket.

The bus station is in a seedy area so it's a good idea to take a taxi to your hotel. To arrange a cab, go to the small booth near the Riotur desk on the 1st floor of the bus station. Average fares are R$50 to the international airport and R$40 to Copacabana or Ipanema.

In addition to the main tourist destinations, buses leave Novo Rio every 30 minutes or so for São Paulo (R$92 to R$198, six hours), operated by **Viação 1001** (☎4004-5001; www.autoviacao1001.com.br) and **Expresso Brasileiro** (www.expressobrasileiro.com).

Getting Around

TO & FROM THE AIRPORT

Rio's international airport, Aeroporto Galeão, is 15km north of the city center, on Ilha do Governador. Aeroporto Santos Dumont, used by some domestic flights, is by the bayside in the city center, 1km east of Cinelândia metro station.

Premium Auto Ônibus (www.premiumautoonibus.com.br; one way R$15) operates air-con buses from the international airport along

BUSES FROM RIO

DESTINATION	TIME (HR)	COST (R$)	FREQUENCY (PER DAY)	BUS COMPANY
International				
Buenos Aires, Argentina	46	450	1	Pluma (☎0800-646-0300), Crucero del Norte (☎21-3186-5466)
Santiago, Chile	62	486	1	Pluma (☎0800-646 0300), Crucero del Norte (☎21-3186-5466)
National				
Belém	54-60	600-700	10	Expresso Brasileiro (www.expressbrasileiro.com.br)
Belo Horizonte	7	95-200	8-19	Util (www.util.com.br)
Brasília	18	150-300	3	Util (www.util.com.br)
Buzios	3	66	8-16	Viação 1001 (www.autoviacao.com.br)
Curitiba	13	170-293	5	Penha (www.nspenha.com.br)
Florianópolis	18	230	1	Kaissara (www.kaissara.com.br)
Foz do Iguaçu	23	245	2	Pluma (www.pluma.com.br), Kaiowa (www.kaiowa.com.br)
Ouro Prêto	7	80-122	2	Util (www.util.com.br)
Paraty	4½	70	7-13	Costa Verde (www.costaverdetransportes.com.br)
Petrópolis	1½	20	25	Única-Fácil (www.unica-facil.com.br)
Porto Alegre	28	321	1	Penha (www.nspenha.com.br)
Recife	38	445	1	São Geraldo (www.saogeraldo.com.br)
Salvador	28	300-330	1-2	Aguia Branca (www.aguiabranca.com.br)
Vitória	8	110-130	9	Aguia Branca (www.aguiabranca.com.br)

several different itineraries. For the Zona Sul, take bus 2018, which heads southward through Glória, Flamengo and Botafogo, and along the beaches of Copacabana, Ipanema and Leblon to Barra da Tijuca (and vice versa) every 30 minutes from 5:30am to 11pm, stopping upon request. It takes 75 minutes to two hours depending on traffic. Bus 2018 also passes by Carioca metro station in Centro, where you can transfer to the metro. If you're going straight to Barra, it's faster to take bus 2918. There's also a bus that links to Santos Dumont airport (2101) and to the bus station (2145).

Heading to the airports, you can catch the Real Auto bus in front of major hotels and along the main beaches, but you have to look alive and flag it down.

From Aeroporto Galeão, yellow-and-blue *comum* (common) taxis cost around R$65 to R$90, depending on traffic, to reach Copacabana or Ipanema.

Keep in mind that traffic can lead to excruciatingly long delays on the return journey to the airport. Allow two hours from the Zona Sul at peak times (from 4pm to 7pm).

CAR

Driving in Rio can be frustrating, even if you know your way around. If you park your car on the street, it's common to pay the *flanelinha* (parking attendant) R$2 for looking after it. Some attendants work for the city; others are 'freelance'; regardless, it's a common practice throughout Brazil, and you risk their wrath by not paying!

Hire

Car-rental agencies can be found at both Galeão and Santos Dumont airports and are scattered along Av Princesa Isabel in Copacabana. At Galeão, **Hertz** (☎0800-701-7300; www.hertz.com), **Localiza** (☎0800-979-2000; www.localiza.com) and **Unidas** (☎2295-3628; www.unidas.com.br) provide rentals. In Copacabana **Hertz** (☎2275-7440; Av Princesa Isabel 500) and **Localiza** (☎2275-3340; Av Princesa Isabel 150) are among many outifts.

PUBLIC TRANSPORTATION

Metro

Rio's subway system (www.metrorio.com.br) is an excellent way to get around. One ride costs R$3.70. It's open from 5am to midnight Monday through Saturday and from 7am to 11pm on Sundays and holidays. During Carnaval the metro operates nonstop from Friday morning until Tuesday at midnight.

The main line goes from Ipanema-General Osório to Saens Peña, connecting with the secondary line to Estácio (which provides service to São Cristóvão and Maracanã). A new line (*linha* 4) connects Ipanema to Barra da Tijuca. It runs from General Osório to Jardim Oceânico and stops in Ipanema, Leblon and São Conrado. A spur to Gávea will eventually link it to the rest of the line.

You can purchase a *cartão pré-pago* (prepaid card) from a kiosk in any metro station using cash (no change given) with a minimum of R$5 or more. You can then recharge it at any kiosk.

Bus

Rio's new BRS (Bus Rapid System) features dedicated public transportation corridors in Copacabana, Ipanema, Leblon and Barra. Fares on most buses are around R$3.50. Every bus has its key destination displayed on the illuminated signboard in front. Hail a bus by sticking your arm straight out; drivers won't stop unless flagged down.

Light-Rail

Rio's new light-rail (the VLT), slated to begin operations in April 2016, runs from Aeropuerto Santos Dumont to the Rodoviária (bus station) via Praça Mauá. It's useful if you're catching an onward bus or staying near Praça Mauá. Another line from the airport to Centro may be added in the future, which would provide handy access to the metro.

TAXI & MOTO-TAXI

Rio's yellow taxis are handy for zipping around town. Metered taxis charge around R$5.20 flat rate, plus around R$2.05 per kilometer (R$2.50 at night, on Sundays and holidays). Radiotaxis are 30% more expensive than regular taxis. No one tips taxi drivers, but it's common to round up the fare.

If you have a smartphone, you can use a free app such as 99Taxis or Easy Taxi to hail a cab. Uber may also survive in Rio. Or you can call a radio-taxi company: **Coopertramo** (☎2209-9292), **Cootrama** (☎3976-9944) or **Transcoopass** (☎2209-1555).

In Rocinha and some other favelas, moto-taxis (a ride on the back of a motorcycle) are a handy way to get around; short rides (usually from the bottom of the favela to the top or vice versa) cost R$2 (though you may get the R$5 gringo rate).

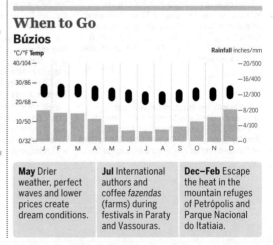

Rio de Janeiro State

POP 16 MILLION

Includes ➡

Best Places to Eat

- ➡ Rocka Beach Lounge (p161)
- ➡ Restaurante Alcobaça (p144)
- ➡ Rosmarinus Officinalis (p140)
- ➡ Linguiça do Padre (p148)
- ➡ Quintal das Letras (p134)
- ➡ Bacalhau do Tuga (p153)

Best Beaches

- ➡ Trindade (p135)
- ➡ Lopes Mendes (p124)
- ➡ Brava (p160)
- ➡ Aventureiro (p126)

Why Go?

If you thought Rio was just a city, think again! Right next door, the equally enticing *state* of Rio de Janeiro is home to some of Brazil's greatest treasures, all within an easy one- to four-hour journey from the Cidade Maravilhosa.

East along the coast are the dunes, lagoons, white sands and limpid blue-green waters of the Costa do Sol, an ever-popular playground for surfers, divers and suntan-seeking urban escapees.

Inland you'll find Itatiaia, Brazil's oldest national park, and the spectacular Serra dos Órgãos, whose whimsically shaped peaks test the mettle of international climbers and form the backdrop for the former imperial city of Petrópolis.

West lies the Costa Verde, a gorgeous patchwork of bays, islands, waterfalls and mountains. Highlights here include the 18th-century architecture of colonial Paraty and the vast island paradise of Ilha Grande, where dozens of hiking trails lead to more than 100 of Brazil's most secluded beaches.

When to Go

Búzios

°C/°F **Temp** — 40/104, 30/86, 20/68, 10/50, 0/32

Rainfall inches/mm — 20/500, 16/400, 12/300, 8/200, 4/100, 0

J F M A M J J A S O N D

May Drier weather, perfect waves and lower prices create dream conditions.

Jul International authors and coffee *fazendas* (farms) during festivals in Paraty and Vassouras.

Dec–Feb Escape the heat in the mountain refuges of Petrópolis and Parque Nacional do Itatiaia.

History

The Tupí and other indigenous groups inhabited modern-day Rio state for over two millennia before Europeans arrived in the 16th century. Early Portuguese activity was focused along the coast, but the discovery of gold in the late 17th century prompted construction of Brazil's first major overland thoroughfare, linking coastal Paraty with the valley of the Rio Paraíba and continuing into Minas Gerais. Another important chapter in Rio state's development was the establishment of coffee plantations here in the early 19th century. The crop was taken by mule train to new ports along the coast, and these roads were the main means of communication until the coming of the railways after 1855.

Modern Rio de Janeiro state is one of Brazil's economic powerhouses, fueled by oil, a steady tourist trade, and traditional industries such as steel and shipbuilding.

Getting There & Around

International and domestic flights fly into Rio de Janeiro's **Galeão** and **Santos Dumont** airports (see p 117), linking Rio state to cities throughout Brazil and the world.

Rio's long-distance bus station (p118) is a hub for virtually every bus line in the country, with fast, frequent service to nearby towns via well-maintained modern highways.

COSTA VERDE

West of Rio city is the Costa Verde (Green Coast), a captivating stretch of coastline where jungled mountainsides dotted with flowering trees dive precipitously into a blue-green sea. The sinuous shoreline here presents visitors with an ever-changing panorama of bays, islands, peaks and waterfalls. Tucked into this idyllic landscape, the 17th-century port of Paraty is famed both for its well-preserved historic center and for the legendary beauty of surrounding beaches such as Trindade and Sono. Just inland lies the Parque Nacional da Serra da Bocaina, which protects large tracts of endangered Mata Atlântica (Atlantic rainforest), along with sections of the 18th-century Caminho do Ouro (Gold Trail) once used to transport gold from Brazil's interior to the coast. Offshore lies another hiker's and beach lover's dream: Ilha Grande, a vast island with no vehicle traffic and very few settlements to disrupt its pristine natural splendor. Amazingly, all of this is right in Rio's backyard: hop a bus in the morning, and you can be spending the afternoon in tropical coastal paradise.

Ilha Grande & Vila do Abraão

☎ 0XX24 / POP 6100

The fabulous island retreat of Ilha Grande owes its pristine condition to its unusual history. First it was a pirates' lair, then a leper colony and, finally, a penitentiary where political prisoners were held alongside some of Brazil's most violent criminals. All that remains of those days are some half-buried stone foundations, but the island's unsavory reputation kept developers at bay for a long time. Consequently, beautiful tropical beaches and virgin Atlantic rainforest (now protected as state parkland) abound on Ilha Grande, and there are still only a few settlements on the island.

Boats from the mainland arrive at Vila do Abraão, the island's biggest town. Abraão was just a sleepy fishing village until the mid-1990s, when Ilha Grande's infamous penitentiary was destroyed and tourism on the island started in earnest. Over the years, a veritable thicket of pousadas (guesthouses), restaurants and bars has popped up, but this palm-studded beachfront town, with its tidy orange church, is still incredibly picturesque, and remains small by mainland Brazilian standards. Except for Abraão's lone garbage truck, fire engine and police vehicle, cars are not allowed in town, so the only transport here is by foot or boat. The village comprises a few dirt roads, and everybody congregates down near the docks and beach at night. On weekends and during high season it can get a bit claustrophobic in Vila do Abraão, but you can easily escape the crowds by hiking a few steps out of town in any direction.

Sights & Activities

The outdoor adventure options on Ilha Grande are endless. Posted around town are maps showing 16 different signposted trails leading through the lush forest to several of the island's 102 beaches. When visiting some beaches, it's possible to hike one way and take a boat the other.

Before hitting the trail, let people at your pousada know where you're going and when you'll be back, stock up on water and bug repellent, and bring a flashlight, as darkness comes swiftly under the jungle canopy.

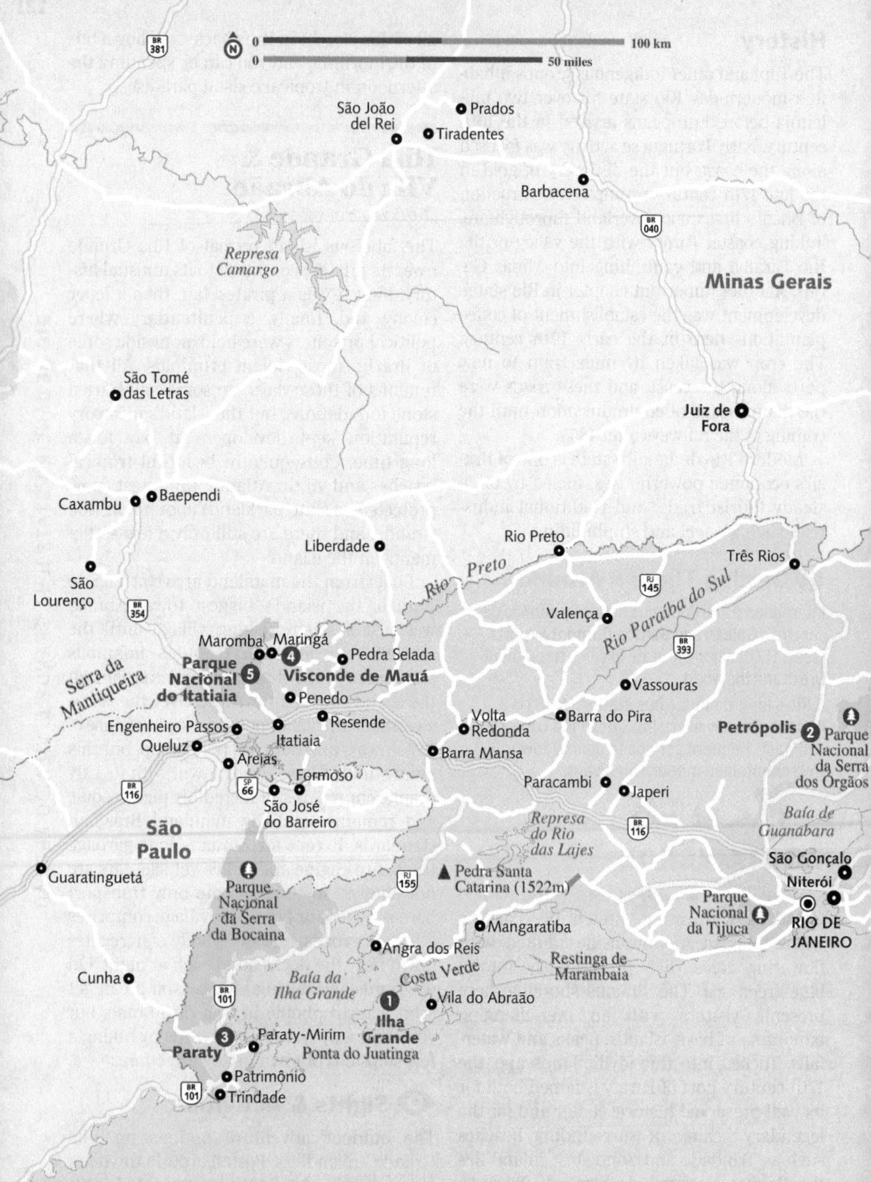

Rio de Janeiro State Highlights

1. On **Ilha Grande** (p121), surfing the south shore's wild waves, or chilling at the floating bar in a tranquil cove nearby.

2. Gliding across the polished wood floors of the **imperial palace** (p141) in Petrópolis, former home of Brazilian Emperor Dom Pedro II.

3. Snorkeling, swimming, sliding down waterfalls or learning to cook gourmet Brazilian food in picturesque colonial **Paraty** (p128).

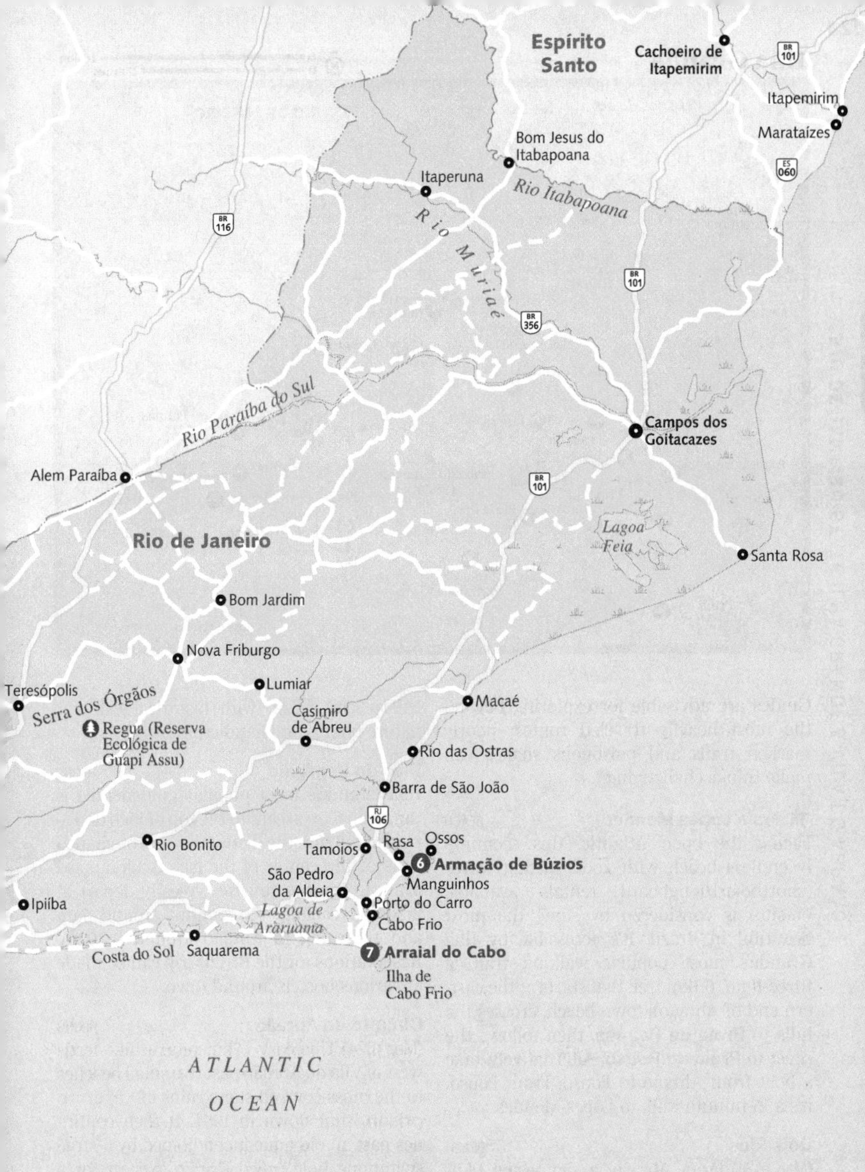

4 Relaxing to the rhythms of rushing water in the idyllic hidden valley of **Visconde de Mauá** (p138).

5 Climbing up craggy Pico das Agulhas Negras in **Parque Nacional do Itatiaia** (p136).

6 Strolling at sunset or partying all night on breezy beachfront Orla Bardot in **Armação de Búzios** (p156).

7 Watching for whales plying the sparkling waters off **Arraial do Cabo** (p152).

Ilha Grande

Guides are advisable for exploring beyond the most heavily traveled routes; poorly marked trails and poisonous snakes can make things challenging.

★ Praia Lopes Mendes BEACH

Facing the open Atlantic, this seemingly endless beach with good surfing waves (shortboard/longboard rentals available on-site) is considered by some the most beautiful in Brazil. It's accessible by Ilha Grande's most popular walking trail, a three-hour, 6.1km trek that starts at the eastern end of Abraão's town beach, crosses the hills to **Praia de Palmas**, then follows the coast to **Praia do Pouso**. Alternatively, take a boat from Abraão to Pouso. From Pouso, it's a 15-minute walk to Lopes Mendes.

Dois Rios BEACH

(Map p124) From Abraão, a signposted 6km dirt road leads to this picturesque beach where two separate rivers flow into the open Atlantic. Dois Rios served as the site of the **Colônia Penal Cândido Mendes**, Ilha Grande's last functioning prison, which held political prisoners during the military regime that took power in 1964, then got blown up by order of the state government in 1994. The reconstructed ruins house the small **Museu do Cárcere** (museucarcereuerj.blogspot.com; 9am-5pm) FREE, with historical exhibits, nature photos and handicraft displays.

Pico do Papagaio HIKING

Ilha Grande's most popular guided hike is the steep 6km ascent to the top of Pico do Papagaio (982m), the distinctive parrot-shaped peak at the center of the island. Organized tours to see the sunrise typically depart at 2:30am, reaching the summit around 6am and returning to Abraão around 9:30am. Reservations for the R$120 trip can be made at various hostels around town.

Circuito do Abraão HIKING

(Map p124) This easy 1.7km return hike leads west of Vila do Abraão past two small beaches to the moss-covered stone ruins of **Lazareto prison**, shut down in 1954. It then continues past an old aqueduct adjoined by a large swimming hole called **Poção**, perfect for a picnic and a dip. Along the way you'll hear birds and jungle creatures, and may run into local kids jumping into the water on their way home from school. Beyond the aqueduct, a more challenging trail leads to **Cachoeira da Feiticeira**, a lovely 15m waterfall, before continuing to the beach at **Saco do Céu**.

Elite Dive Center DIVING

(99936-4181; www.elitedivecenter.com.br; Travessa Buganville, Vila do Abraão) Offers courses and two-tank dives with English-speaking guides in some fantastic spots.

 Tours

There are a dozen-plus tour operators in town. Most offer identical prices for boat excursions including round-the-island tours (R$160), half-island tours (R$110), and daily trips to prime beaches and snorkeling spots such as Lopes Mendes (schooner/speedboat R$30/40), Feiticeira (R$50) and Lagoa Azul (R$60). Other services include bike, kayak and surfboard rentals and treks with bilingual guides.

Sleeping

Vila do Abraão is swarming with pousadas. Note that we quote prices for high season (December to March). Prices drop by as much as 50% between April and November.

Che Lagarto HOSTEL $
(3361-9669; www.chelagarto.com; Praia do Canto; dm R$39-75, d R$175-235;) Unbeatable location at the far eastern end of Abraão's main beach, a panoramic waterfront deck and a bar with free-flowing caipirinhas are the prime attractions at this hostel, part of South America's largest chain. Some boats from Conceição de Jacareí will drop you at the Aquário hostel next door; otherwise, it's a 10-minute walk from Abraão's town center.

Jungle Lodge GUESTHOUSE $
(99977-2405; www.ilhagrandeexpeditions.com; Caminho de Palmas 4; d R$140-160;) Tucked away above town in the rainforest, this rustic, five-room guesthouse and open-air chalet is run by a wild-haired Pantanal guide and his German wife. It's an entirely different experience than sleeping in Abraão, a 1.5km hike away. The view from the outdoor shower is miraculous.

Sitio Green Hostel HOSTEL $
(99906-5570; www.sitiogreenhostel.com; Francino Inácio Nascimento; dm/d R$70/200;) Appealing for nature lovers, this new hostel sits 10 minutes uphill from Abraão, with monkeys playing in the trees outside the glass-walled kitchen and lounge area. Two dorms are supplemented by a stand-alone double. It's a bit tricky to find; as you climb Rua Nascimento, branch right past two blue water tanks and follow the dirt path to its end.

Biergarten Hostel HOSTEL $
(3361-5583; Getúlio Vargas 161; dm from R$50, d with shared/private bathroom from R$150/170;) Just a stone's throw from the boat docks, this centrally located hostel is a good bet for those who seek easy walking access to – or stumbling access *from* – Abraão's nightlife.

★ **Pousada Manacá** POUSADA $$
(3361-5404; www.ilhagrandemanaca.com.br; Praia do Abraão 333; d R$280-320, tr R$360-400;) It's worth reserving ahead and paying the small surcharge for a front room with balcony and hammock at this French-run beachfront pousada. The ample breakfast is accompanied by sea views from the pleasant front terrace; other nice touches include in-room fridges, dependable solar hot water and a central patio for lounging. Septuagenarian owner Gerard speaks five languages.

★ **Pousada Naturalia** POUSADA $$
(3361-9583; www.pousadanaturalia.net; Praia do Abraão 149; r R$320;) One of Abraão's nicest midrange options, this comfortable pousada under the direction of French-Vietnamese owner Laurent sits amid giant boulders on a green hillside just inland from the beach. Its 12 spacious rooms all feature pretty ocean views and solar hot water.

Pousada d'Pillel POUSADA $$
(3361-5075; www.ilhagrandedpillel.com.br; Bicão; r R$160-290;) This friendly, family-run pousada, a few blocks from the beach, has a cool, shady garden with comfortable seating under a thatched roof out back. Additional amenities include DVD players in every room, a ping-pong table and free use of snorkeling equipment.

Aratinga Inn POUSADA $$$
(3361-9559; www.aratingailhagrande.com.br; Rua das Flores 232; r R$400-420, chalet R$450-490; closed May, Jun & Sep;) This cozy, gay-friendly, Australian-run pousada offers ultra-comfy chalets in a garden setting. Homey touches include complimentary use of iPads, beach towels and thermoses, a generous afternoon tea, and a 700-title movie library. New in 2015 is a welcoming lounge where guests can relax over music and board games and early arrivals can sip coffee or juice while awaiting their room.

Asalem POUSADA $$$
(99977-2675; www.asalem.com.br; Praia da Crena s/n; d/tr/ste R$560/672/740;) Despite its remote, immersed-in-nature atmosphere, Asalem is only a short boat ride from Abraão, or a 25-minute walk via a scenic beachfront trail. Owned by an internationally acclaimed

OFF THE BEATEN TRACK

THE QUIETER SIDE(S) OF ILHA GRANDE

Almost all travelers to Ilha Grande arrive and sleep in Abraão, the island's biggest town and only major port. But there's a whole world of other options out there for people wishing to get off the beaten track.

The easiest way to broaden your perspective is to take a round-the-island boat tour. These tours typically stop at some of Ilha Grande's most beautiful and remote swimming spots, including **Praia de Caxadaço**, **Praia de Parnaioca**, **Praia do Aventureiro**, **Lagoa Verde** and **Lagoa Azul**.

To really escape the crowds and get immersed in the island's wild natural beauty, consider staying at one of the following remote accommodations. All can provide transportation and meals.

Pousada Lagamar (☎3021-2738, 99978-4569; www.pousadalagamar.com.br; Praia Vermelha; d with garden/sea view R$230/250) Owners Ezequiel and Luciana have created this family-friendly pousada at beautiful Praia Vermelha on Ilha Grande's northwestern shore. It's a perfect place to kick back in nature for a few days and settle into a simpler rhythm: swimming, snorkeling, walking the nearby trails, lounging in your hammock with a good book, and enjoying dinners of freshly caught fish.

Cabanas Paraiso (☎99608-1987; www.cabanasparaiso.com; Praia Brava de Palmas; d with shared/private bathroom R$150/300) Low-key beachfront living is the norm at these simple fan-cooled bungalows on Praia Brava de Palmas, a small beach easily accessible from the popular Abraão–Lopes Mendes trail. Accommodations range from bare-bones units with shared bath to beachfront units with orthopedic mattresses, private bathrooms and sea-view verandas with hammocks.

Atlântica Jungle Lodge (☎99999-5577; www.atlanticajunglelodge.com.br; Praia do Pouso; room with forest/sea view R$789/847; ❄) Fall asleep to the sound of birds and jungle critters at this four-room eco-lodge, serenely situated near the island's southeast corner, between Pouso beach and the surrounding forest. From here, it's an easy 15-minute walk to Praia Lopes Mendes, Ilha Grande's most famous stretch of sand and surf. Guests get free use of kayaks, snorkeling equipment, beach towels and umbrellas.

photographer, it commands gorgeous bay and forest views from its hillside location. Price includes pick up and drop-off at Abraão pier, plus use of kayaks, canoes and the hotel's library of art books.

Eating

Restaurants abound along Rua da Praia, Rua Getúlio Vargas and the small pedestrian street Travessa Buganville. During busy periods you'll see sweets carts being pushed about.

Las Sorrentinas ARGENTINE, ITALIAN $
(www.facebook.com/Sorrentinas; Getúlio Vargas 638; mains R$24-27; ⏲6:30-10:30pm Mon-Sat) Superb homemade *sorrentinos* (ravioli-like stuffed pasta pockets) are the specialty at this breezy Argentine-run upstairs restaurant. Fillings range from gorgonzola, walnuts and mozzarella to ham, cheese and basil, accompanied by your choice of sauces. The place wins extra points for its friendly service and potent caipirinhas.

Biergarten BUFFET, VEGETARIAN $
(☎3361-5583; Getúlio Vargas 161; per kg R$55; ⏲noon-10pm Wed-Mon; 🌿) The self-serve buffet at this informal vegetarian-owned eatery includes everything from brown rice and soy protein to sushi and other seafood, with more vegetables than you'll see at most places around town.

Lua e Mar SEAFOOD $$
(Praia do Canto; mains for 2 R$80-155; ⏲11am-11pm Thu-Tue) Candlelit tables on the sand make a tranquil place to watch the crashing waves and scurrying crabs while you enjoy tasty *moqueca* (fish stew) and other seafood dishes for two.

Café do Mar BARBECUE $$
(www.cafedomar.com; Rua da Praia s/n; mains R$35-55; ⏲10am-midnight) Candlelit beach bar and lounge perfect for sundown cocktails and reasonably priced (by Ilha Grande standards!) meals.

Vila do Abraão

Activities, Courses & Tours
1 Elite Dive Center B2

Sleeping
2 Biergarten Hostel B2
3 Pousada d'Pillel C2
4 Pousada Manacá C1
5 Pousada Naturalia D1

Eating
6 Biergarten B2
7 Café do Mar D1
8 Dom Mário B2
9 Las Sorrentinas D1
10 Lua e Mar C1
11 O Pescador B2

Dom Mário SEAFOOD $$
(☎3361-5349; Travessa Buganville; mains for 2 R$65-119; ⏲5-11pm Mon-Sat) Long-time local chef Mário cooks up seafood specialties like *filé de peixe ao molho de maracujá* (fish fillet with passion-fruit sauce) and scrumptious desserts, including his trademark caramelized bananas.

O Pescador MEDITERRANEAN $$
(☎3361-5114; www.opescador.org; Rua da Praia 647; mains for 2 R$90-130; ⏲5pm-late) The Italian-run Pescador is one of the island's best choices for a fancy beachfront dinner, with mean caipirinhas, authentic Italian risotto and Mediterranean-style fish, meat and poultry dishes such as the *grigliata mista al salmoriglio* (fish and shrimp grilled with olive oil, lemon juice and oregano).

Orientation

Ferries from the mainland dock at a **cement pier** on the west end of Abraão's beach. Private speedboats and schooners dock at a separate **wooden pier** about 150m east.

In between the two piers lies the heart of Abraão village, with its main street, the cobbled Rua Alice Kuri da Silva, curving to become Rua Getúlio Vargas. West of the piers is the road to Praia Preta and the ruined Lazareto prison. East of the piers, at the far end of the town beach, Ilha Grande's most popular hiking trail leads to Praia de Palmas, Praia do Pouso and Praia Lopes Mendes.

Information

Note that there are no ATMs on the island, although many places accept credit cards and it's possible to change foreign cash in a pinch. Internet service is available at most accommodations but tends to be slow and intermittent.

TurisAngra (☎3361-5760; www.turisangra.com.br; Rua da Praia; ⏲7am-7pm) At the foot of the wooden pier, Ilha Grande's official tourist office offers general information about the island, including rudimentary maps of Abraão village and local trails.

Getting There & Away

The quickest and most hassle-free way to reach the island from Rio is via door-to-door shuttle services such as **Easy Transfer** (☎99386-3919; www.easytransferbrazil.com) – these will pick you up at any hostel, hotel or pousada in Rio and deliver you to the island (R$85, 3½ to 4½ hours), with a synchronized transfer from van to speedboat in the coastal town of Conceição de Jacareí. Easy Transfer also offers a similar service from Paraty (R$75, 3½ hours).

Reaching the island via public transport is slightly cheaper but more complicated, as you

OFF THE BEATEN TRACK

PARQUE NACIONAL DA SERRA DA BOCAINA – HIKING THE GOLD TRAIL

The historic Caminho do Ouro (Gold Trail), which connected Rio de Janeiro's coastline to the gold mines of Minas Gerais, passes through dramatic scenery in the Parque Nacional da Serra da Bocaina just north of Paraty. Paraty Tours (p132), Paraty Explorer (p132) and other operators offer two-hour hikes covering a very small fraction of the trail, near Penha.

For a more challenging and unique experience, consider the Trilha do Ouro backpacking adventure, a three-day, 53km hike through the wildest reaches of the national park, offered by **MW Trekking** (www.mwtrekking.com.br). This longer trek starts in São José do Barreiro in São Paulo state and visits a number of spectacular waterfalls en route towards Mambucaba, on the coast 45 minutes northeast of Paraty. The R$849 price includes transport to the trailhead, park fees, food, simple lodging and excellent local guide.

have to choose from multiple routes and buy two separate tickets (one for the bus, one for the boat).

Costa Verde (www.costaverdetransportes.com.br) runs buses from Rio to the three ports where boats for Ilha Grande depart: Conceição de Jacareí (R$49, 2½ hours, five buses daily), Mangaratiba (R$30, 2½ hours, four daily) and Angra dos Reis (R$49, three hours, hourly).

The most frequent boat crossings are from Conceição de Jacareí, where speedboats (R$30 to R$35, 20 minutes) and schooners (R$15 to R$20, 50 minutes) leave every hour or two between 8:30am and 6pm, returning from Abraão between 8am and 5:30pm. From Angra dos Reis, similar service is available by speedboat (R$40, 30 minutes) and schooner (R$25, 80 minutes). Boat companies operating along one or both routes include **Objetiva** (☎3361-5963; www.objetivatour.com), **Cambeba Flex** (☎3361-5662; www.cambebailhagrande.com), **Angra Flex** (☎3365-2125, 3365-4180; www.facebook.com/angraflex) and **Acquaflex** (☎3361-5156; www.aguavivatour.com.br).

More affordable but less frequent are the daily ferries to Ilha Grande operated by **CCR Barcas** (www.grupoccr.com.br/barcas), leaving from Angra dos Reis and Mangaratiba (R$14, 80 minutes from either port). Ferries depart Angra at 3:30pm weekdays and 1:30pm weekends, returning from Abraão at 10am daily. From Mangaratiba, ferries leave at 8am daily and 10pm Friday, returning from Abraão at 5:30pm daily. Extra ferries are sometimes added during high season; confirm locally before departure.

Angra is the most useful port for those traveling west from Ilha Grande. Colitur buses for Paraty (R$11.30, two hours) leave Angra's bus station, 1.5km east of the boat docks, at least hourly from 6am to 11pm daily.

Paraty

☎0XX24 / POP 38,000

Set amid jutting peninsulas and secluded beaches, with a backdrop of steep, jungled mountains plunging into an island-studded bay, Paraty is one of Brazil's most appealing destinations.

Paraty's colonial center is remarkable not only for its exquisitely preserved, centuries-old architecture, but also for its lack of automobile traffic. The irregular cobblestone streets are closed to motor vehicles, making it a delightful place to stroll about. Elegant white buildings adorned with fanciful multihued borders and latticed windows blend harmoniously with the natural beauty that envelops the town.

Dozens of pristine beaches are within a couple of hours of Paraty by boat or bus, while inland, the Parque Nacional da Serra da Bocaina provides protection for a lush remnant of Mata Atlântica (Atlantic rainforest). The Brazilian government has recognized Paraty as a National Historic Site since 1966.

Paraty is crowded and lively throughout the summer holidays, brimming with Brazilian and European vacationers. The town's cosmopolitan flavor is further enhanced by the large number of artists, writers and chefs, both Brazilian and foreign, who have settled here and opened shops, galleries and restaurants.

History

Paraty was inhabited by the indigenous Guaianás when Portuguese settlers first arrived here in the 16th century. With the discovery of gold in Minas Gerais at the end of the 17th century, Paraty became an obligatory stopover between Rio de Janeiro and the mines, as it was the only point where the escarpment of the Serra do Mar could be scaled.

As gold poured from the interior, Paraty became a busy, important port, and the wealthy built churches and fine houses. Paraty's glory days didn't last long. After the 1720s, a new road from Rio via the Serra dos Órgãos cut 15 days off the journey to Minas Gerais, and Paraty started to decline. In the 19th century, the local economy revived with the coffee boom, but until the mid-20th century the sea remained the only viable commercial route to Paraty. In 1954 a modern road was built through the steep Serra do Mar, passing the town of Cunha, 47km inland. Then in 1960 the coastal road from Rio, 253km away, was extended to Paraty and 330km beyond to São Paulo, ushering in a new era of tourism-based prosperity.

Sights

Hours and opening times at Paraty's historic churches seem to be in constant flux; check with the tourist office for up-to-the-minute details.

Casa da Cultura MUSEUM

(☎3371-2325; www.casadaculturaparaty.org.br; Dona Geralda 177; ⊙10am-10pm Tue-Sun) FREE In a beautiful colonial mansion, Paraty's Casa da Cultura hosts rotating exhibitions and events, with a focus on local culture. There are nice views of town from the main gallery upstairs.

Igreja Santa Rita dos Pardos Libertos CHURCH

(Praça Santa Rita; admission R$4 Wed-Sun, free Tue; ⊙10am-noon & 2-5pm Tue-Sun) Built in 1722, this was the church for freed mulattoes (persons of mixed black and white ancestry). It houses a tiny museum of sacred art and

Paraty Islands & Beaches

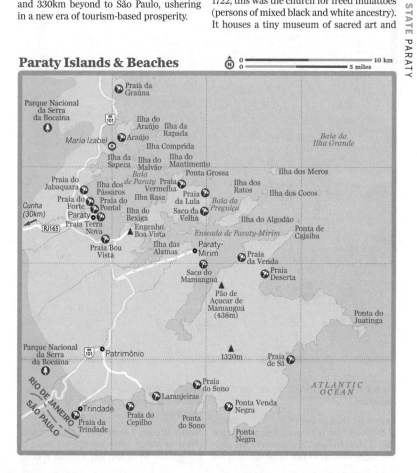

0 — 10 km
0 — 5 miles

Praia da Graúna
Parque Nacional da Serra da Bocaina
BR 101
Ilha do Araújo
Ilha da Rapada
Araújo
Maria Izabel
Ilha Comprida
Baía da Ilha Grande
Ilha da Sapeca
Ilha do Malvão
Ilha do Mantimento
Baía de Paraty
Ponta Grossa
Ilha dos Meros
Praia do Jabaquara
Ilha dos Pássaros
Praia Vermelha
Ilha dos Ratos
Ilha dos Cocos
Praia do Forte
Praia do Pontal
Ilha Rasa
Praia da Lula
Baía da Preguiça
Cunha (30km)
Paraty
Ilha do Bexiga
Saco da Velha
Ilha do Algodão
RJ165
Praia Terra Nova
Engenho Boa Vista
Enseada de Paraty-Mirim
Ponta de Cajaiba
Praia Boa Vista
Ilha das Alamas
Paraty-Mirim
Praia da Venda
Saco do Mamanguá
Praia Deserta
Pão de Açucar de Mamanguá (438m)
Ponta do Juatinga
Parque Nacional da Serra da Bocaina
BR 101
Patrimônio
1320m
Praia de Sá
RIO DE JANEIRO
SÃO PAULO
Praia do Sono
ATLANTIC OCEAN
Laranjeiras
Trindade
Ponta Venda Negra
Praia da Trindade
Praia do Cepilho
Ponta do Sono
Ponta Negra

Paraty

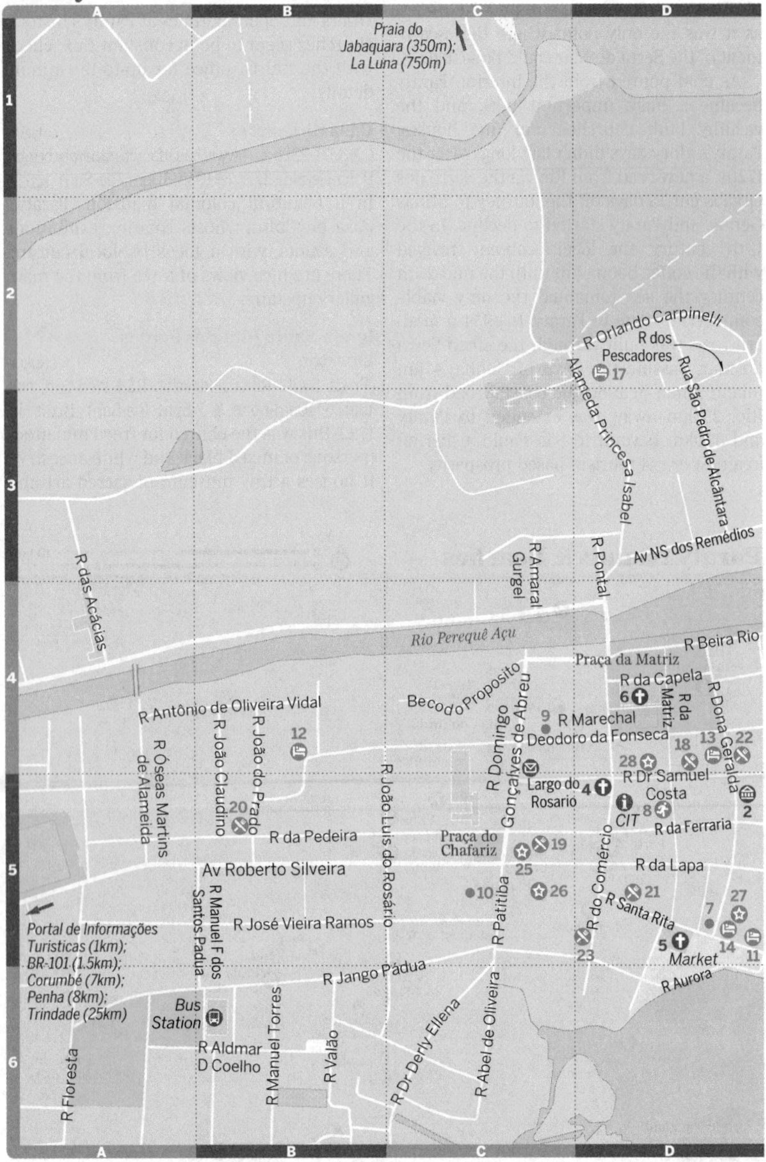

has some fine woodwork on the doorways and altars.

Capela de NS das Dores CHURCH
(R da Capela, btwn Dr Pereira & Fresca; admission R$4; ⏲1-6pm Fri-Sun) This church of the colonial white elite was built in 1800 and renovated in 1901. It houses a small art gallery and a fascinating cemetery in the inner courtyard.

Matriz NS dos Remédios CHURCH
(Praça da Matriz; admission R$4; ⏲9am-noon & 2-5pm Mon-Fri, to 4pm Sat) Built in 1787 on

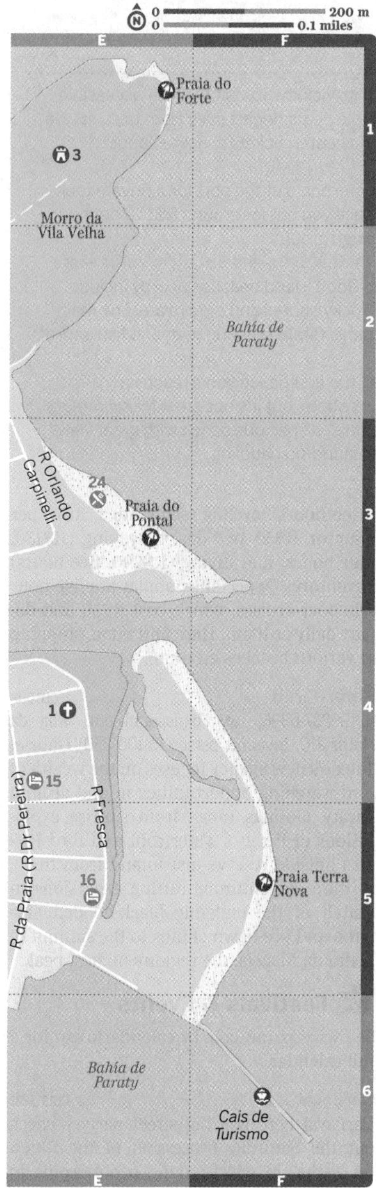

the site of two 17th-century churches, this church holds art from past and contemporary local artists. According to legend, the construction of the church was financed by pirate treasure found hidden on Praia da Trindade.

Paraty

Sights

1	Capela de NS das Dores	E4
2	Casa da Cultura	D5
3	Forte Defensor Perpétuo	E1
4	Igreja NS do Rosário e São Benedito dos Homens Pretos	D5
5	Igreja Santa Rita dos Pardos Libertos	D5
6	Matriz NS dos Remédios	D4

Activities, Courses & Tours

7	Academia de Cozinha e Outros Prazeres	D5
8	Birds Parati	D5
9	Paraty Adventure	C4
10	Paraty Tours	C5

Sleeping

11	Casa Turquesa	D5
12	Che Lagarto	B4
13	Hotel Solar dos Gerânios	D4
14	Pousada Arte Urquijo	D5
15	Pousada do Ouro	E4
16	Pousada Flor do Mar	E5
17	Pousada Morro do Forte	D2

Eating

18	Banana da Terra	D4
19	Casa do Fogo	C5
20	Manuê	B5
21	Oui Paraty	D5
22	Punto Divino	D4
23	Quintal das Letras	D5
24	Quiosque Dito e Feito	E3

Entertainment

25	Margarida Café	C5
26	Paraty 33	C5
27	Teatro Espaço	D5
28	Van Gogh Pub	D4

Igreja NS do Rosário e São Benedito dos Homens Pretos CHURCH
(cnr Dr Samuel Costa & Rua do Comércio; 9am-noon & 1-5:30pm Wed-Fri) FREE Built in 1725 by and for slaves, and renovated in 1857, the church has gilded wooden altars dedicated to Our Lady of the Rosary, St Benedict and St John.

Forte Defensor Perpétuo FORT
(7am-7pm) FREE For sweeping bay views, climb to this historic Portuguese fort. Built in 1703 and rebuilt in 1822, its original purpose was to defend the gold passing through Paraty's port from pirate raids. The fort's small museum is closed indefinitely for remodeling, but the grounds remain open; just heed the cryptic signs warning against

DON'T MISS

ISLANDS & BEACHES

Paraty has some 65 islands and 300 beaches in its vicinity. To visit the less-accessible beaches, take an organized schooner tour. Multiple boats depart daily from the **Cais de Turismo** at the southeastern edge of the historic center; tickets average about R$50 per person.

Alternatively, you can hire one of the small motorboats at the port for a private tour. Local captains know some great spots and will take you out for around R$100 per hour, which can be a good deal if you have a large enough group.

The closest fine beaches on the coast – **Vermelha**, **Lula** and **Saco da Velha** – are all east of Paraty, roughly an hour away by boat. Good island beaches nearby include **Araújo** and **Sapeca**; many other islands have rocky shores and are private. The mainland beaches tend to be better; most have *barracas* (stalls) serving beer and fish and, at most, a handful of beachgoers.

Back in Paraty, walking north across the river, the first beach you'll reach is **Praia do Pontal**. A cluster of open-air restaurants lines its shore, but it's not great for swimming. Another 2km further north is **Praia do Jabaquara**, a spacious beach with great views and shallow waters that's ideal for kayaking and stand-up paddling.

descending the steep slopes ('high index of accidents with oysters'!). It's 20 minutes north of town on Morro da Vila Velha (the hill past Praia do Pontal).

Tours

★Paraty Adventure OUTDOORS
(☎3371-6135; www.paratyadventure.com; Marechal Deodoro 12) Friendly Brazilians Alessandra and Edsom run this great little agency offering off-the-beaten-track opportunities for adventure and cultural immersion. Highlights include their all-day mountain-biking and hiking trip to Pedra da Macela, the region's highest peak (R$180), and a three-day trek to Ponta da Juatinga, the remote fishing village where Alessandra grew up (R$840, including food and accommodation in local homes).

★Paraty Explorer OUTDOORS
(☎99952-4496; www.paratyexplorer.com; Praia do Jabaquara) This agency on Jabaquara beach, run by friendly outdoors enthusiasts Paddy (from Ireland) and Rodrigo (from Brazil), specializes in sea kayaking, stand-up paddleboarding (SUP) and hiking adventures around Paraty Bay. Hiking destinations include dramatic Pão de Açúcar do Mamanguá, the historic Trilha do Ouro (Gold Trail) in Serra da Bocaina national park and remote beaches of the Costa Verde.

Paraty Tours OUTDOORS
(☎3371-1327; www.paratytours.com.br; Roberto Silveira 11) Paraty's longest-established commercial agency offers hiking (R$70 to R$200, six hours), horseback-riding (R$160, three hours), cycling (self-guided, R$10 per hour or R$50 per day), kayaking (R$130, four hours) and diving (R$290, five hours) adventures. Especially popular are five-hour schooner cruises, which cost R$50 and depart daily at 10am, 11am and noon, stopping at various beaches en route.

Birds Parati ECOTOUR
(☎99837-6396; www.birdsparati.com; Rua da Matriz 210; tours per person R$100-250) Gabriel Toledo's new agency focuses on the wealth of bird-watching opportunities in and around Paraty. Outings range from sunrise explorations of Paraty's waterfront and Bird Parati's hillside reserve just inland from town, to more adventurous rafting excursions in search of the endemic black-hooded antwren and pre-dawn climbs to the summit of Pedra da Macela, the region's highest peak.

Festivals & Events

See www.paraty.com.br/calendario.asp for a full calendar.

Carnaval CULTURAL
Carnaval here is a big street party – check out the Saturday procession of the **Bloco da Lama**, in which young people come in droves to cover themselves in mud and dance through the streets.

Semana Santa RELIGIOUS
Holy Week celebrations include the beautiful **Procissão do Fogaréu**, a torchlit procession through the historic center starting just past midnight on the Thursday before Easter. The **Festa do Divino Espírito Santo**

(seven weeks after Easter) and **Corpus Christi** (in June) are also magnificent, with processions and colorful street decorations.

FLIP CULTURAL

(Festa Literária Internacional de Paraty; www.flip.org.br; ⌚Jul) Since launching in 2003, Paraty's five-day international literary festival has grown into one of the year's biggest cultural events, bringing in authors from around the world.

Festival da Cachaça, Cultura e Sabores de Paraty FOOD

(Festival da Pinga; ⌚Aug) The Paraty region produces excellent *cachaça* (sugarcane alcohol), and in 1984 the town council inaugurated this annual four-day food-and-drink-fueled party.

Sleeping

From December to February, and during festivals, hotels fill up and room prices double, so reservations are advisable. The rest of the year, finding accommodations is relatively easy. Prices quoted here are high-season rates.

Budget-minded travelers will find several campgrounds and hostels along the Pontal and Jabaquara beachfronts (just north of town, across the pedestrian bridge).

★Happy Hammock HOSTEL $

(☎99994-9527; www.facebook.com/happyhammockparaty; Ponta Grossa; dm/d R$55/150) This Swiss-run waterfront hostel sits on isolated Ponta Grossa, 15 minutes by boat from Paraty. With no road access, limited generator-fueled electricity and gorgeous sea views, it's a dreamy end-of-the-line getaway where guests can lounge in hammocks, swim in phosphorescent waters or hike to nearby beaches before the tour boats arrive. Book dinners (R$15) and boat transfers (R$30) in advance.

Che Lagarto HOSTEL $

(☎3361-9669; www.chelagarto.com; Benina Toledo do Prado 22; dm R$39-56, r R$153-180; ❄@🛜🏊) Tucked down a backstreet between the bus station and the historic center, this good-time hostel is a social oasis, with a welcoming bar, barbecue, small pool area, zillions of organized activities and direct transfers to Rio, Ilha Grande and São Paulo; solitude seekers should ask for a room in the annex, which faces away from the commotion.

Hotel Solar dos Gerânios INN $$

(☎3371-1550; www.paraty.com.br/geranio; Praça da Matriz; s/d/tr R$120/180/240; @🛜) Run by the same family for decades, this rustic place on lively Praça da Matriz is the most affordable hotel in Paraty's colonial center. Wood and ceramic sculptures, stone walls and floors, columns and beamed ceilings, and a courtyard full of plants, cats and dogs all add character. Several rooms have balconies overlooking the square.

Pousada Flor do Mar POUSADA $$

(☎3371-1674; www.pousadaflordomar.com.br; Fresca 257; r R$350; ❄@🛜) Hidden away opposite Paraty's beachfront, this simple little pousada has clean, spacious rooms, a pretty front courtyard with hammocks and couches, and one of the historic center's quietest locations.

Le Gite d'Indaiatiba POUSADA $$

(☎3371-7174; www.legitedindaiatiba.com.br; Hwy BR-101, Km 558; d/tr R$200/250, d/tr/q bungalow R$250/300/350, d/tr loft R$600/700; ❄🛜🏊) In a gorgeous jungle setting 16km northwest of Paraty, well-traveled hosts Olivier and Valéria serve tasty Franco-Brazilian cuisine and rent out five units with fireplaces and panoramic verandas, including two 'lofts' with air-con, large bathtubs and DVD players. Activities include horseback riding, jungle treks, and relaxing stints by the pool, waterfall and riverside sauna. See website for driving directions.

Pousada Morro do Forte POUSADA $$$

(☎3371-1211; www.pousadamorrodoforte.com.br; Orlando Carpinelli 21; r R$350-480; ❄🛜🏊) This modern pousada enjoys incomparable vistas of the town and bay from its breakfast deck and pool. Perched on the Morro do Forte, a 10-minute climb from downtown, it has 10 comfortable rooms, the best of which are the upstairs units with panoramic balconies and hammocks. The owners speak English and German.

Pousada Arte Urquijo POUSADA $$$

(☎3371-1362; www.urquijo.com.br; Dona Geralda 79; s R$410-490, d R$490-590, ste R$670; 🛜🏊) This cozy little pousada is obviously a labor of love for the artist owners. Downstairs common areas include a spacious lounge and bar and a small pool. Especially nice is the Sofia Suite, with its deck, flowering tree and bay view.

Pousada do Ouro POUSADA $$$

(☎3371-4300; www.pousadaouro.com.br; Rua da Praia 145; d R$609-757, d/tr/q ste R$946/1239/1532; ❄@🛜🏊) It's easy to imagine bumping into Mick Jagger, Sônia Braga or Tom Cruise here – especially when you enter the lobby and see photos of them posing in front of the pousada! This centrally located hotel has everything – bar, pool, sauna and a gorgeous garden.

Casa Turquesa POUSADA $$$
(☎3371-1037; www.casaturquesa.com.br; Rua da Praia 50; d/ste R$1250/1450; ❄📶🏊) This luxuriously appointed, lovingly converted mansion near Paraty's waterfront is one of the most welcoming lodgings in town. Spacious rooms and suites with queen- or king-size beds and DVD players, inviting pool and lounge areas and copious breakfasts served any time of day invite guests to settle completely into relaxation mode.

Eating

Paraty has many pretty restaurants, but once your feet touch the cobblestones in the picturesque historic center, prices rise.

Manuê SANDWICHES, JUICE BAR $
(www.facebook.com/manueparaty; Rua João do Prado 1; sandwiches R$6-13, juices R$6-8; ⏲10am-11pm Wed-Mon; 📶) With good coffee, free wi-fi, two dozen varieties of juice and a delicious array of budget-friendly omelets and *dobrados* (toasted flatbread sandwiches), this little eatery draws a mixed crowd of locals and tourists.

Quiosque Dito e Feito SEAFOOD $$
(Praia do Pontal; mains for two R$50-90; ⏲10am-6pm) Ask locals where to find reasonably priced fresh seafood and they'll send you to this simple beachfront kiosk on Praia do Pontal. From straightforward fried fish to *moqueca* to the *caldeirada do mar* (a seafood stew for three), dishes are huge, but half-portions are available upon request.

Oui Paraty CREPERIE $$
(☎2122-2311; www.ouiparaty.com.br; Santa Rita 190; crepes R$25-40, other mains R$41-59; ⏲5:30-11:30pm Sun, Mon & Wed-Fri, 11am-11:30pm Sat) With a bona fide French chef in the kitchen, Oui Paraty stands out for its authentic Breton-style galettes made with buckwheat flour, alongside subtly sweet dessert offerings like nutella with homemade whipped cream or crêpe suzette flambéed in Grand Marnier.

Casa do Fogo BISTRO $$
(☎3371-3163; www.casadofogo.com.br; Comendador Jose Luiz 390; mains R$38-79; ⏲6pm-1am) The name says it all here – everything's on fire! The menu focuses on seafood set ablaze with the local *cachaça,* and desserts don't escape a fiery death either.

Punto Divino ITALIAN $$
(☎3371-1348; www.puntodivino.com; Marechal Deodoro da Fonseca 129; pizza R$30-49, mains R$36-83; ⏲noon-midnight) This cozy Italian restaurant has wonderful thin-crust pizzas and pastas. Live music adds to the romance.

La Luna ARGENTINE $$
(☎3371-6917; Praia do Jabaquara; mains R$42-74; ⏲6:30-11pm, closed Wed & Sun) Steak and a prime beachfront setting are the twin attractions at this Argentine-run eatery in Jabaquara, 2km north of Paraty's historic center. Everything from sirloin to *picanha* (rump steak) comes out sizzling on iron platters, accompanied by chimichurri sauce and all the trimmings. Moonrise views are spectacular, and there are beds where little ones can lounge while parents linger at the candlelit tables.

★**Quintal das Letras** FUSION $$$
(☎3371-2616; www.pousadaliteraria.com.br/quintal; Rua do Comercio 362; mains R$59-89; ⏲1-11pm Sun-Thu, noon-midnight Fri & Sat) Opened in 2014, this sophisticated eatery serves superb regional cooking with big-city flair. From amuse-bouches like a mushroom 'cappuccino' (frothy brown soup topped with a

CHEF FOR A DAY

Tired of eating out? How about cooking your own gourmet dinner tonight, with the help of acclaimed local chef and cookbook author Yara Roberts? Mixing theater with haute cuisine, chef Yara stages cooking classes in Portuguese, English, French and Spanish at **Academia de Cozinha e Outros Prazeres** (☎3371-6025; www.chefbrasil.com; Dona Geralda 288; cooking class incl dinner R$260), her home-based culinary academy. Guests learn about Brazilian regional cuisines, assist with the cooking (optional), then sit down to a leisurely dinner and an evening of lively conversation.

Groups are often international – residents of more than 60 countries have participated to date. The price includes cocktails, wine, desserts and recipes. Hungry for more? Chef Yara also organizes multiday programs that combine cooking classes with visits to local producers. See the website for details.

dollop of cream) to a sterling *moqueca de peixe* (fish stew) for one, and desserts like chocolate-hazelnut cake or fried bananas with homemade ginger ice cream, it's a class act all around.

Banana da Terra SEAFOOD **$$$**
(☎3371-1725; www.restaurantebananadaterra.com.br; Dr Samuel Costa 198; mains R$72-90; ⏲5pm-midnight Mon, Wed & Thu, noon-4pm & 7pm-midnight Fri-Sun) Chef Ana Bueno's creative taste combinations and artistic presentation make this one of Paraty's classiest restaurants. There's also an excellent wine list.

Drinking & Entertainment

A slew of bars spill tables out onto the tree-shaded cobblestones of Praça da Matriz from late afternoon to the wee hours.

Van Gogh Pub LIVE MUSIC
(Samuel Costa 22; ⏲9pm-late Thu-Mon) Paraty's new kid on the block keeps the old town hopping with five nights of live music per week, including reggae, samba, rock, jazz, blues and *forró*.

Margarida Café LIVE MUSIC
(☎3371-6037; margaridacafe.com.br; Praça do Chafariz; ⏲noon-midnight) This cavernous yet cozy bar with checkerboard tile floors and massive stone columns has great drinks and live music nightly, including MPB (Musica Popular Brasileira), bossa nova, jazz, *forró*, tango and more.

Paraty 33 LIVE MUSIC
(www.paraty33.com.br; Rua da Lapa 357; ⏲noon-1am Sun-Thu, to 4am Fri & Sat) With an early evening happy hour featuring MPB and bossa nova, and a late-night weekend mix of DJs and live acts, Paraty 33 is the historic center's liveliest nightspot.

Teatro Espaço THEATER
(☎3371-1575; www.ecparaty.org.br; Dona Geralda 327; admission R$45; ⏲shows 9pm Wed & Sat, plus Fri in summer) Now in its fifth decade, Paraty's internationally acclaimed Contadores de Estórias theater company presents puppetry, music and dance performances in this small playhouse.

Orientation

The historic center is small and easy to navigate, although street names and addresses can get confusing. Some streets have more than one name, and house numbers don't always follow a predictable pattern.

Information

Bradesco (Av Roberto Silveira) Multiple ATMs two blocks north of the bus station; more at Banco do Brasil next door.

CIT (☎3371-1222; Dr Samuel Costa 29; ⏲8am-8pm) Recently relocated to the historic center, Paraty's tourist office also has a second branch (☎3371-1897; Av Roberto da Silveira s/n; ⏲8am-8pm) just off highway BR-101.

Getting There & Away

The **bus station** (Rua Jango Pádua) is 500m west of the old town. **Costa Verde** ((www.costaverde transportes.com.br)) offers frequent services to Rio de Janeiro (R$66, 4¾ hours, 12 daily). Colitur has buses to Angra dos Reis (R$11.30, two hours, hourly from 5am to 8pm) and **Reunidas** (www.reunidaspaulista.com.br) buses head to São Paulo (R$58, 5¾ hours, six daily).

Around Paraty

The area surrounding Paraty is a nature-lover's paradise, offering some of southeastern Brazil's prettiest beach and mountain scenery. The region is also renowned for its excellent *cachaça* (sugarcane alcohol), and local *alambiques* (distilleries) offer tours.

Sights & Activities

★**Praia da Trindade** BEACH
About 25km south of Paraty, Trindade occupies a long sweep of stunningly beautiful coastline. Here you can lounge or hike along four of Brazil's most dazzling beaches (**Cepilho**, **Ranchos**, **Meio** and **Cachadaço**), with surging breakers, enormous boulders, vast expanses of mountain-fringed white sand, steep trails threading through the dense jungle, and a calm-watered natural swimming pool opposite the furthest beach, Cachadaço. Hourly Colitur buses (R$3.40, 45 minutes) serve Trindade from Paraty's bus station.

The town itself has the somewhat scraggly quality of a frontier outpost that's grown up too fast (indeed, 20 years ago there was only a small fishing village here), but the sizable cluster of pousadas, hostels, camping grounds and restaurants permits an overnight stay.

Saco de Mamanguá BAY
This gorgeous fjord-shaped inlet cuts a narrow 7km channel into the mountains southeast of Paraty. Various Paraty-based

tour companies offer boat trips here. Alternatively, hire a guide for the strenuous 2km hike up the dramatic peak known as **Pão de Açúcar do Mamanguá** (438m) for stunning views of the bays and islands below.

Praia de Paraty-Mirim BEACH

For accessibility, cost and beauty, this tranquil beach 17km southeast of Paraty is hard to beat. The adjacent chapel, dating to 1686, was the first constructed by the Portuguese in the Paraty region. *Barracas* (food stalls) on the beach here serve simple meals – don't miss the *pasteis de camarão* (fried dough pockets filled with locally caught shrimp) at **Quiosque do Xico** (snacks from R$5; 10am-6pm). Colitur runs buses here (R$3.40, 40 minutes) from Paraty's bus station.

Praia do Sono BEACH

This stunning beach, about 35km southeast of Paraty, is accessible only by foot or boat. Catch a Colitur bus to Laranjeiras (R$3.40, 40 minutes) and then follow the trail across the hills (about one hour). Paraty Tours (p132) and other local operators offer tours here.

Maria Izabel DISTILLERY

(Map p129; 99999-9908; www.mariaizabel.com.br; Sítio Santo Antônio, Corumbê; tours R$10; 10:30am-5pm Sat & Sun, by appointment Mon-Fri) This acclaimed *cachaça* distillery, 10km north of Paraty, often places within the top 10 or 20 in nationwide competitions. Call at least 24 hours in advance to arrange a visit, or sign up for a tour through a Paraty travel agency.

★ **Cachoeira Tobogã** SWIMMING

In the hills 8km inland from Paraty, this natural waterslide is a blast! The slick rock face sends swimmers plunging into an idyllic pool surrounded by lush jungle. Tourists who value their skulls should heed the posted warnings against surfing (ie standing instead of sitting), although local teenagers have mastered the technique and it's exciting (if terrifying!) to watch. Afterwards, grab a caipirinha at Bar do Tarzan, across the swinging bridge above the falls.

From Paraty, take a local Colitur bus to Penha (R$3.40, 30 minutes), get off at the church and follow signs 100m downhill.

ITATIAIA REGION

Originally settled by northern Europeans, the Itatiaia region of northwestern Rio de Janeiro state is a curious mix of Old World charm and New World jungle. The climate is alpine temperate and the chalets are Swiss, but the vegetation is tropical and the warm smiles are pure Brazilian. There are neatly tended little farms with horses and goats, and homes with clipped lawns and flower boxes side by side with large tracts of dense forest untouched by the machete. This is a wonderful place to tramp around green hills, ride ponies up purple mountains, splash in waterfalls and hike trails without straying too far from the comforts of civilization: a fireplace, a soft bed, a bottle of wine and a well-grilled trout.

Parque Nacional do Itatiaia

0XX24

Established in 1937, **Parque Nacional do Itatiaia** (3352-1292; www.icmbio.gov.br/parnaitatiaia/en; per day foreigners/Brazilians R$27/14; 8am-5pm) is Brazil's oldest national park, and one of its most ruggedly beautiful. Its lush, dark foliage contains more than 400 species of native bird and is also home to monkeys and sloths. Divided into upper and lower sections, the park features lakes, rivers, waterfalls, alpine meadows and primary and secondary Atlantic rainforests.

Don't let the tropical plants fool you; temperatures in the high country drop below freezing in June and, occasionally, the park even has a few snowy days. Bring warm clothes, even in summer.

Sights & Activities

Each section of the park (upper and lower) has its own entrance station. Park headquarters is 9km north of Itatiaia town, in the park's lower, tamer section. Here you'll find a **natural history museum**, along with easy trails leading to a lake, **Lago Azul** (Blue Lake), and three pretty waterfalls: **Poronga**, **Véu de Noiva** and **Itaporani**.

Climbing and trekking enthusiasts will want to pit themselves against the high country's more challenging peaks, cliffs and trails. The upper park's diminutive entrance station – almost two hours drive from Itatiaia town – is reached by way of a 15km, extremely rugged, unpaved road from a junction called Garganta do Registro, along

Itatiaia Region

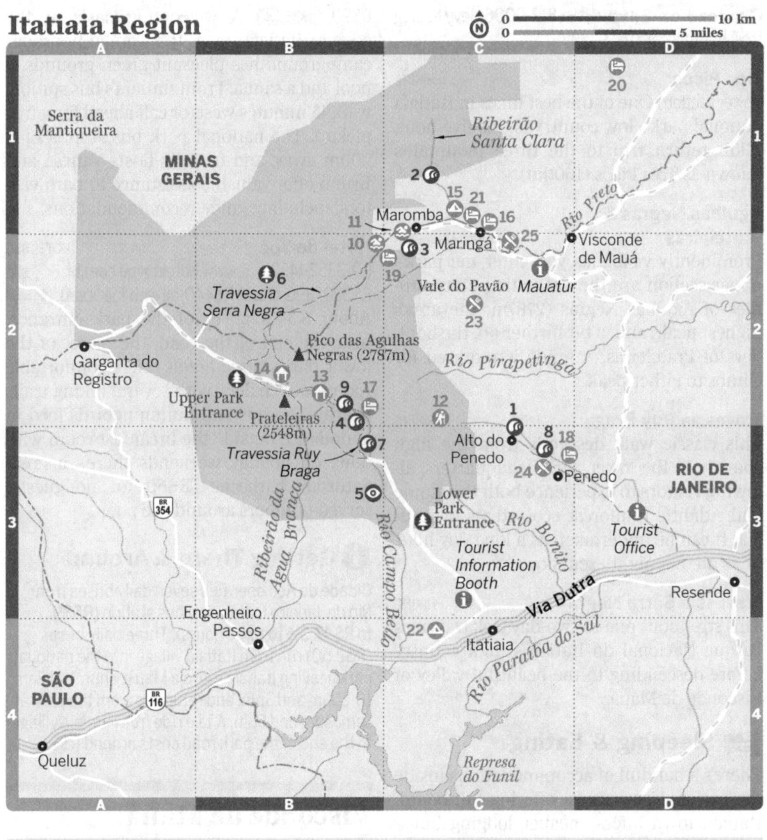

Itatiaia Region

Sights

1 Cachoeira de Deus C3
2 Cachoeira Santa Clara C1
3 Cachoeira Veu de Noiva C2
4 Itaporani Waterfall B2
5 Lago Azul B3
6 Parque Nacional do Itatiaia B2
7 Poronga Waterfall B3
8 Três Cachoeiras C3
9 Véu de Noiva Waterfall B2

Activities, Courses & Tours

10 Cachoeira do Escorrega B2
11 Poção C1
12 Três Picos C2

Sleeping

13 Abrigo Água Branca B2
14 Abrigo Rebouças B2
15 Fazenda Santa Clara Camping C1
16 Hotel Bühler C1
17 Hotel do Ypê B2
18 Pequena Suécia C3
19 Pousada Moriá C2
20 Quinta da Prata D1
21 Warabi Hotel C1
22 Ypê Amarelo C4

Eating

23 Babel C2
24 Koskenkorva C3
25 Rosmarinus Officinalis C2
Zorba Budda .... (see 21)

Hwy BR-354 at the border between Rio and Minas Gerais states.

Contact the **Grupo Excursionista Agulhas Negras** (www.grupogean.com), which organizes climbs throughout the year, or see the park's website ('Visitor's Guide' page) for a list of local guides; another excellent guide not on the park's list is **Levy**

Cardozo da Silva (98812-0006; levy.ecologico@hotmail.com).

Três Picos HIKING

(lower section) One of the best hikes in Itatiaia national park's low country is this five-hour, 15km return trip to the three mountains known as Três Picos (1600m).

Agulhas Negras & Prateleiras MOUNTAINEERING

Prominently visible as you enter the park's upper section are the dramatic pointy profiles of Agulhas Negras (2787m; the area's highest peak) and, a bit further on, the boulders of Prateleiras. A guide is required for climbs to either peak.

Travessia Ruy Braga HIKING

This classic walk descends from the high country to the lower park headquarters, allowing visitors to experience both the alpine and Atlantic rainforest ecosystems of Itatiaia. It can be undertaken as a long day hike, or as an overnight excursion.

Travessia Serra Negra HIKING

This strenuous one-to-two-day trek traverses Parque Nacional do Itatiaia's high country before descending to the beautiful valley of Visconde de Mauá.

Sleeping & Eating

There's a handful of accommodations inside the national park, most offering full board. Itatiaia town offers cheaper lodging but a less inviting atmosphere.

Abrigo Água Branca HUT $

(3352-2288; www.icmbio.gov.br/parnaitatiaia/reservas; dm R$10) Set amidst pretty high country scenery at 1700m, Parque Nacional do Itatiaia's newest hiker's hut is available for overnight use on the Travessia Ruy Braga trail.

Abrigo Rebouças HUT $

(3352-1292; www.icmbio.gov.br/parnaitatiaia/reservas; dm R$10) This hikers' shelter in the high country, with a gas stove and electricity, provides basic accommodations for up to 20 people but no food or other supplies. It was closed for repairs in 2015 but expected to reopen in 2016. Call ahead for current status, and reserve as far in advance as possible; the place fills up fast.

Ypê Amarelo CAMPGROUND, POUSADA $

(3352-1232; www.pousadaypeamarelo.com.br; João Mauricio Macedo Costa 352; campsite per person with/without breakfast R$50/35, r per person R$90;) A welcoming oasis at the edge of Itatiaia town, this combo pousada/campground has pleasant green grounds, a pool and a sauna. From Itatiaia's bus station, walk 15 minutes west, or call ahead for a free pickup. The national park bus stop is only 200m away, and friendly hosts Vanesa and Bruno offer valuable assistance to park visitors, including guide recommendations.

Hotel do Ypê HOTEL $$$

(3352-1453; www.hoteldoype.com.br; s/d R$320/390, chalet R$440, all with full board;) About 8.5km north of the park entrance, near the end of the road, the nicest of the lower park's three hotels offers comfortable rooms and chalets, with several hiking trails nearby. Toucans and hummingbirds feed in abundance outside the breakfast-room window; on holiday weekends there's a great Saturday barbecue (R$60 for nonguests) served outdoors around the pool.

Getting There & Around

Cidade do Aço operates seven daily buses from Rio de Janeiro to Itatiaia's bus station (R$39 to R$47, 2½ to three hours). Three daily buses (R$2.50) run from Itatiaia village into the national park, leaving Itatiaia's Igreja Matriz church at 7am, 10:20am and 3pm, and returning from the park at 1pm, 3pm and 5pm. A taxi ride from Itatiaia village to the end of the park road costs around R$55.

Visconde de Mauá

0XX24 / ELEV 1200M

With cozy chalets, forests, wildflower-fringed country lanes and the sound of rushing water, Visconde de Mauá is a river valley that feels like a world unto itself. Its isolation is largely thanks to the town's limited access routes; visitors must either switchback over precipitous mountaintops on the paved 27km route from Penedo, or take a series of rutted (but gorgeous) dirt roads from Liberdade, Minas Gerais.

The valley consists of three small villages a few kilometers apart along the Rio Preto, which forms the boundary between Rio de Janeiro and Minas Gerais states. The road passes first through **Mauá**, the largest village, then heads uphill to **Maringá**, 6km to the west, and **Maromba**, 2km further on, before petering out at the edge of the national park. Beyond Alto Maringá (upper Maringá village) the road remains unpaved; expect a bumpy ride!

Note that addresses in Maringá are marked 'RJ' or 'MG' to show whether they're on the Rio de Janeiro or the Minas Gerais side of the river.

Sights & Activities

Rio Preto, the cascading river dividing Minas Gerais from Rio state, has several small beaches and natural pools. It's possible to kayak the rapids. Horseback riding is also available from various private operators around town. Details are available at the tourist office.

Cachoeira Santa Clara WATERFALL
Among the nicest and most accessible of Mauá's dozen or so waterfalls, this one is a 10-minute drive or a 40-minute walk northwest of Alto Maringá on the Ribeirão Santa Clara. Cross the bridge to Minas Gerais about 1km west of Alto Maringá, then continue another 1km over a hill to a left-hand fork marked with signs for the waterfall.

Cachoeira Veu de Noiva WATERFALL
This very beautiful waterfall is 300m south of the main road, just west of Maromba.

★ **Cachoeira do Escorrega** SWIMMING
At the far western end of the valley, 2km west of Maromba on the border with Parque Nacional do Itatiaia, this natural water slide culminates in a gorgeous natural pool.

Poção SWIMMING
One of the valley's finest swimming spots is this giant, 7m-deep natural pool 1km west of Maromba.

Sleeping

The valley is jam-packed with cozy, chalet-style accommodations. Inexpensive, bare-bones rooms are also available near the bus stops in Mauá and Maromba; just ask around.

Fazenda Santa Clara Camping CAMPGROUND $
(☎3387-1508; www.viscondedemaua.com.br/campingsantaclaramaua.html; Estrada Maringá/Maromba, 1km; camping per person R$30, d cabana/chalet R$80/180) Occupying a grassy slope at the convergence of the Rios Preto and Santa Clara, this campground has a natural swimming hole and snack bar, plus two-person chalets and miniscule A-frame cabanas for those without a tent. The bus stop across the river is accessible via a pedestrian bridge.

★ **Pousada Moriá** POUSADA, CHALET $$
(☎3387-1505; www.pousadamoria.com.br; Estrada da Maromba s/n; ste R$290-350, d/q chalet from R$250/375;) At this welcoming end-of-the-road hideaway, eight chalets and three suites with whirlpool tubs straddle a hillside at the national park's edge. Cozy touches include fireplaces, electric blankets, a sauna, a DVD library and ample breakfasts served in a charming glass-walled cabin or on an outdoor deck within earshot of the waterfall. Owners are active in local reforestation efforts.

Warabi Hotel POUSADA $$
(☎3387-1143; www.viscondedemauaturismo.com; Alto Maringá, RJ; d midweek R$240-320, weekend R$300-440) Inviting features abound at this Japanese-Brazilian lodging just above Maringá: comfy futons, ofuro tubs and a spacious wooden deck overlooking the swimming pool, sauna and riverside lawn. Guests also appreciate the solar electricity, boats for floating downstream to a local swimming hole, and an on-site restaurant serving sushi, tempura, sukiyaki and other Japanese specialties (R$25 to R$59).

Hotel Bühler HOTEL $$$
(☎3387-1204; www.hotelbuhler.com.br; Maringá, MG; r midweek R$350, weekend incl half-board R$690; @) Founded in 1931, this German-style hotel with sprawling, verdant grounds, a stone's throw west of Maringá's restaurant row, is the valley's oldest lodging. Twenty fireplace-equipped chalets, including four larger ones suitable for families, are complemented by two swimming pools, a kids' wading pool, basketball and tennis courts, trails down to the river, a sauna and an on-site restaurant.

Quinta da Prata POUSADA $$$
(☎3294-2083; www.quintadaprata.com.br; Estrada do Vale da Prata, Km 3.5, Mirantão, MG; chalet incl full board R$600;) For a completely different perspective on Mauá, climb to this gorgeously sited, Brazilian-American mountain pousada 13km north near Mirantão. Two fireplace-equipped chalets are complemented by a spring-fed swimming pool, hot tub, art gallery, and whimsical multistory glass-walled loft with library, kitchen and computer/TV room. Three meals daily are included, and nearby trails lead to waterfalls and other natural wonders.

Eating

For over two decades, Mauá has hosted its renowned three-day culinary festival, the **Concurso Gastronômico** (www.mauagastronomico.com.br; mid-May), with special emphasis on the local trout and *pinhões*, giant nuts from the native *araucária* trees.

In Maringá, don't miss the Alameda Gastronômica (restaurant row), a street packed with restaurants for every taste along the Minas Gerais side of the Rio Preto. Here you'll find Italian and vegetarian eateries, a German beer garden, a jazz bistro and a restaurant whose menu revolves around local mushrooms.

Zorba Budda PIZZA **$$**
(☎3387-1170; Estrada Maringá-Marombá, Km 6, Alto Maringá, RJ; pizza R$36-75; ⏰8pm-1am Fri-Sun) A Mauá institution for over two decades, this pumpkin-colored pizzeria serves two dozen varieties of wood-fired, thin-crusted beauties. Perennial favorites include the *montanhesa* (with locally smoked trout), the *caliente* (tomato sauce, mozzarella, brie, mango slices and spicy pepper jelly) and the *selvagem* (with roasted garlic and hearts of palm).

Babel INTERNATIONAL **$$**
(☎9999-8121; www.babelrestaurante.com; Vale do Pavão; mains R$64-75, tasting menu R$185; ⏰1-10pm Fri & Sat, to 6pm Sun) Perched 3.5km up a mountainside along a steep, tortuous dirt road, this intimate glass-walled restaurant serves up divine views and refined international cuisine, from risotto and homemade fettuccine to lamb, duck and filet mignon. Chefs Dani Keiko and André Murray are renowned for their desserts (tiramisu, tarte tatin, ginger crème brûlée) and their decadent 'Tower of Babel' tasting menu.

★ **Rosmarinus Officinalis** MEDITERRANEAN **$$$**
(☎3387-1550; www.rosmarinus.com.br; Estrada Mauá-Maringá, Km 1; mains R$57-87; ⏰7-10pm Wed & Thu, 1-4pm & 7-11pm Fri & Sat, 1-5pm Sun) Food and setting are equally enticing at this sweet little house in the woods between Mauá and Maringá. Sporting a gorgeous new riverside deck, it's surrounded by meticulously tended gardens that provide veggies and herbs for some of Mauá's most memorable meals. Specialties include oatmeal-almond-breaded trout, brie-*pinhão* (giant pine nut) ravioli, and a sweet tomato, basil and mascarpone dessert 'salad.'

ℹ Information

Wi-fi is spotty and sometimes slow in the valley.

Mauatur (☎3387-1283; visiteviscondedemaua.com.br; ⏰10am-6pm Mon-Thu, 10am-10pm Fri, 9am-7pm Sat, 10am-4pm Sun) At the entrance to the village of Mauá, the valley's tourist information hut has brochures and photos of area accommodations; staff can help with room reservations upon request.

ℹ Getting There & Around

Visconde de Mauá has no bus station. Buses stop at the top of Mauá's main street and in the center of Maringá before ending their run at Maromba's town square.

All public transport into Mauá passes through Resende, a city on the national park's eastern outskirts. The most useful buses, operated by Resendense, run three to six times daily from Resende to Maromba (R$7.80, 1½ hours). Viação São Miguel also runs local buses from Resende but only goes as far as Mauá village (R$3, one hour). at 8:30am, 1:40pm and 7pm Monday through Saturday, plus 8am and 7pm Sunday.

Cidade do Aço (☎3354-2387; www.cidadedoaco.com.br) runs one direct bus weekly between Rio and Maromba (R$56, 4½ hours), leaving Rio at 7:30pm on Fridays and returning from Maromba at 4pm on Sundays and holidays. Otherwise, catch one of Cidade do Aço's frequent Rio–Resende buses (R$37 to R$49, 2½ hours) and transfer to a local Mauá-bound bus in Resende. Note that long-distance buses arrive on the upper level of Resende's bus station, while local buses leave from the lower level.

Penedo

☎0XX24 / POP 29,000 / ELEV 600M

Originally started as a Finnish colony in the early 20th century, Penedo has grown into a vacation resort that embraces all things non-Brazilian. In the more developed lower section of town, you'll find tourist traps capitalizing on the region's European heritage mixed in with authentic Old World influences such as the **Clube Finlândia** (☎3351-1374; clubefinlandiablog.blogspot.com; Av das Mangueiras 2601), which still hosts traditional Finnish dances the first Saturday of every month. In Alto do Penedo, the upper part of town, it's easier to appreciate the luxuriant natural beauty that lies just outside the city limits. Wherever you go, you'll be sure to appreciate the emphasis on the traditional Finnish sauna, found at most hotels.

Sights & Activities

Penedo's main attractions are the forest and waterfalls. Two especially worthwhile waterfalls are **Três Cachoeiras**, west of downtown Penedo along the main road just before it starts climbing to Alto do Penedo, and Cachoeira de Deus, about 20 minutes uphill from the bus turnaround in Alto do Penedo. Ask locally for directions, as signs are intermittent. About one hour of uphill hiking from the end of the asphalt in Alto do Penedo takes you into very dense forest with trails and opportunities to observe wildlife, including monkeys.

Sleeping & Eating

Penedo is expensive, due to the large number of weekend tourists who come up from Rio and São Paulo, but the accommodations and food are above average.

Pequena Suécia HOTEL $$
(3351-1275; www.pequenasuecia.com.br; Toivo Suni 33; d R$195-295, ste R$295-395, chalet R$395-695;) A Penedo classic, this red house in the woods has provided luxurious amenities in a rustic setting for over half a century. The on-site restaurant serves Scandinavian and vegetarian food, the spa offers massage and shiatsu treatments, and the attached club features live jazz music on weekends.

Koskenkorva FINNISH, GERMAN $$
(3351-2532; Av Três Cachoeiras 3955; mains R$50-70; noon-4pm & 7:30-10pm Thu-Tue) With a lovely outdoor seating area by a creek, Koskenkorva specializes in Finnish and German food. For a splurge, try the smorgasbord-like platter (R$140) featuring smoked trout, marinated salmon, herring, trout pâté and much more. Leave room for the fruit dessert crepes.

Information

Tourist Office (3351-1704; turismo@itatiaia.rj.gov.br; Av Casa das Pedras 766; 9:30am-5pm) Housed inside the town entrance portal; has brochures and information in Portuguese.

Getting There & Away

Cidade do Aço (www.cidadedoaco.com.br) operates three direct buses daily from Rio to Penedo (R$39, 3¼ hours). Alternatively, take one of its more frequent buses from Rio to Resende, then catch Viação Penedo's half-hourly Resende–Penedo bus (R$3.45, 45 minutes). The latter bus services the 3km-long main street and continues to the end of the paved road.

NORTH OF RIO DE JANEIRO

The mountains north of Rio rise up with shapes so improbable and dramatic, they catch your attention even from a great distance. Landing at Galeão international airport or surveying the northern skyline from the top of Rio's Pão de Açúcar (Sugarloaf), your eye is automatically drawn to the intriguing sawtooth ridge on the horizon. In the 19th century, the allure of these mountains led Brazil's imperial family to set up a summer residence in Petrópolis, and inspired the country's first Swiss immigrants to choose Nova Friburgo as their New World home.

More recently, climbers from all over the world have become enamored of the vertiginous rocky faces of the Serra dos Órgãos (Organ Pipe Range). To this day, the cooler climate and recreational opportunities, along with the region's imperial and immigrant legacy, continue to attract visitors from Rio and beyond.

Petrópolis

0XX24 / POP 296,000 / ELEV 809M

A lovely mountain retreat with a decidedly European flavor, Petrópolis is where Dom Pedro II's imperial court spent the summer when Rio got too muggy, and it's still a favorite weekend getaway for *cariocas* (residents of Rio city). The city center, with its picturesque parks, bridges, canals and old-fashioned street lamps, is easily explored on foot or by horse and carriage.

Sights & Activities

Most museums and other attractions are closed on Monday.

A fun way to get oriented is by taking a horse and carriage ride. Nineteenth-century *vitórias*, carriages of British design, leave from in front of the Museu Imperial and make 20- to 45-minute circuits of the downtown area (R$50 to R$60 for up to four people).

★ **Museu Imperial** PALACE, MUSEUM
(www.museuimperial.gov.br; Rua da Imperatriz 220; adult/student R$10/5; 11am-5:30pm Tue-Sun) Petrópolis' top draw is this impeccably preserved 19th-century palace. Felt slippers provided at the entrance help protect the fine wood floors – great fun to slide around

Petrópolis

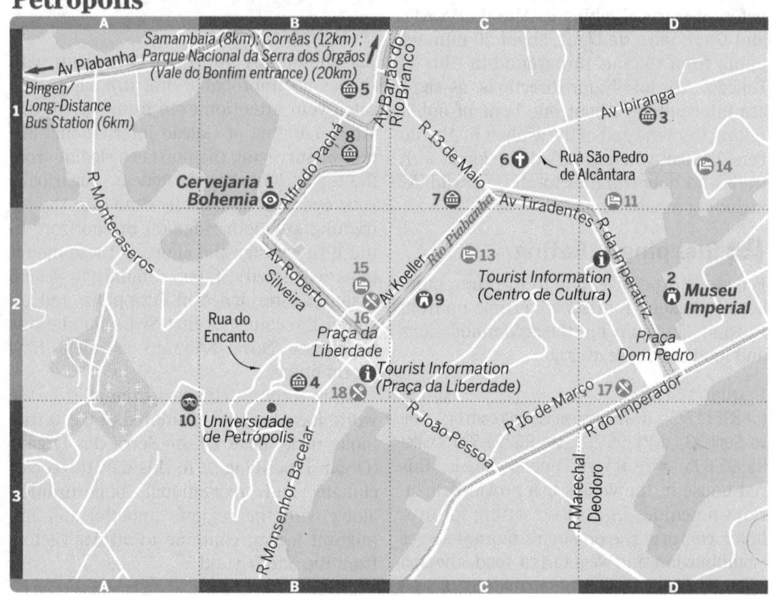

in! Displays include the 1.95kg imperial crown, with its 639 diamonds and 77 pearls, and the ruby-encrusted, feather-shaped gold pen used to sign the *Lei Aurea,* which freed Brazil's remaining slaves in 1888.

★Cervejaria Bohemia BREWERY

(www.bohemia.com.br; Alfredo Pachá 166; adult/student & senior R$27/13.50; ⏲1-4:30pm Tue-Thu, 10am-4:30pm Fri, 10am-6:30pm Sat & Sun) Petrópolis' newest attraction is the 90-minute tour (half self-guided, half guided) at Brazil's oldest brewery, where interactive exhibits trace beer-making history and nifty touch-screens let you explore brews from dozens of countries. Tours conclude with free samples of specialty beers that are only brewed here. The on-site bar-restaurant is the only spot in Brazil you can get Bohemia on draft.

Catedral São Pedro de Alcântara CHURCH

(Sao Pedro de Alcântara 60; ⏲8am-6pm) Petrópolis' cathedral houses the tombs of Brazil's last emperor, Dom Pedro II, his wife, Dona Teresa, and their daughter, Princesa Isabel. The **bell tower**, which offers fine views of the city, remained closed indefinitely at the time of research.

Palácio Rio Negro PALACE

(Av Koeller 255; ⏲1:30-5pm Wed-Sat) FREE Visitors are free to roam among the high-ceilinged, parquet-floored rooms of this grand yellow edifice, which served as a summer home for Brazil's presidents for decades before the capital moved to Brasília.

Casa da Ipiranga HISTORIC BUILDING

(☎2231-8718; casadaipiranga.blogspot.com; Av Ipiranga 716; admission R$10; ⏲2-6pm daily Jan & Jul, Fri-Sun rest of year) One of Petrópolis' finest mansions, the Casa da Ipiranga is open to visitors by guided tour. Other historical buildings can be viewed from the outside only, including the **Palácio da Princesa Isabel** (Av Koeller s/n) and the **Casa do Barão de Mauá** (Praça da Confluencia).

Casa de Santos Dumont MUSEUM

(Rua do Encanto 22; adult/concession R$8/4; ⏲9:30am-5pm Tue-Sun) This charming house was the summer home of Brazil's diminutive father of aviation and inventor of the wristwatch. Photos and exhibits document Dumont's many inventions.

Palácio de Cristal HISTORIC BUILDING

(Alfredo Pachá; ⏲9am-6pm Tue-Sun) FREE Built in France and imported in 1879, this ornate iron-and-glass structure was originally used

Petrópolis

Top Sights

Sights

Sleeping

Eating

as a hothouse for growing orchids. It's now a venue for evening cultural events.

Trono de Fátima VIEWPOINT

Enjoy great views of Petrópolis and the surrounding hills from this 3.5m Italian sculpture of the NS de Fátima Madonna. To reach it, turn right as you leave the Casa de Santos Dumont and continue walking uphill, always taking the right fork.

Trekking Petrópolis OUTDOORS

(2235-7607; www.rioserra.com.br/trekking) Organizes hiking and bird-watching trips in the nearby Mata Atlântica rainforest.

Sleeping

★Samambaia Hostel HOSTEL $

(2242-3478; www.isca.org.br; Estrada da Samambaia 138, Samambaia; dm R$75, d R$160;) Housed in a grand *fazenda* (plantation) mansion dating to 1723 and surrounded by Burle Marx–designed gardens, this unique hostel and environmental education center oozes character, with stone-slab floors, beamed ceilings and an 18th-century Portuguese chapel. School groups are a main focus, but independent travelers are also welcome. Reserve ahead for the four private rooms, which can also house families.

The hostel is 8km north of Petrópolis. From the Museu Imperial, take bus 300 (R$3.20) toward Terminal Corrêas and ask to get off at Samambaia (20 to 30 minutes).

★Pousada Paraiso Açu POUSADA $$

(2221-3999; pousadaparaisoacu.com.br; Estrada do Bonfim 3511; r weekend R$240-395, midweek R$150-300;) Outdoors enthusiasts need look no further than this end-of-the-road paradise, 20km northeast of Petrópolis at the entrance to Parque Nacional da Serra dos Órgãos. Surrounded by mountain peaks, with an attached restaurant serving home-brewed beer and local trout, it boasts cozy cabins and lounging areas, a spring-fed swimming pool, wood-fired sauna and ample recreation facilities for kids. Two-night minimum on weekends.

Pousada Imperial Koeller POUSADA $$

(2243-4330; www.pousadaimperialkoeller.com.br; Av Koeller 99; s R$195, d R$225-435;) This gabled gem, dating back to 1875, is right in the heart of things, along architecturally stunning Av Koeller. Its sister hotel **Pousada Monte Imperial** (info 2237-1664; www.pousadamonteimperial.com.br; José Alencar 27; r R$195-315;), in an old vine-covered house on the hillside above the Museu

Imperial, shares the same prices. Note that single rates are only available from Sunday through Thursday.

Pousada 14 Bis POUSADA **$$**
(☎2231-0946; www.pousada14bis.com.br; Buenos Aires 192; s/d with fan R$100/180, with air-con R$150/250; ❄) On a quiet residential street near the downtown bus station, the restored colonial Pousada 14 Bis has handsome, well-appointed rooms with comfortable beds. The best offer lovely wood floors and balconies overlooking the mountains or the garden out back.

Casablanca Imperial HOTEL **$$**
(☎2242-6662; www.casablancahotel.com.br; Rua da Imperatriz 286; s/d with fan R$230/266, with air-con R$266/319; ❄📶🏊) Almost next door to the Museu Imperial, the Casablanca has a range of rooms – the best feature high ceilings, old-fashioned shutters, large bathrooms with tubs, and antique furnishings.

Solar do Império HOTEL **$$$**
(☎2103-3000; www.solardoimperio.com.br; Av Koeller 376; r R$550-792 Fri & Sat, R$490-698 midweek; 📶🏊) Centrally located on Praça da Liberdade, with polished wood floors, 5m-high ceilings, grand fireplaces, a pool, sauna and spa, the meticulously restored Solar do Império will make you feel like a member of the imperial family.

Pousada da Alcobaça POUSADA **$$$**
(☎2221-1240; www.pousadadaalcobaca.com.br; Goulão 298, Corrêas; d from R$385; ❄📶🏊) Midway between Petrópolis and Parque Nacional da Serra dos Órgãos, this beautiful hotel has a pool, a sauna, a tennis court and lovely gardens crossed by a small river. There's also an excellent restaurant.

Eating

Restaurante Paladar BUFFET **$**
(www.paladarpetropolis.com.br; Barão do Amazonas 25; per kg R$56.90; ⏰11am-4pm Tue-Sun) Prices are higher than at your average per-kilo joint, but the atmosphere can't be beat at this classy converted mansion across from Praça da Liberdade. Watch the horse-drawn carriages clip-clop by as you enjoy classic Brazilian fare on the old-fashioned wraparound porch.

★ **Restaurante Alcobaça** BRAZILIAN **$$**
(☎2221-1240; Goulão 298, Corrêas; mains R$53-75) 🍃 Verdant, flowery grounds and a gorgeous mountain setting enhance the mood of relaxed elegance in the lovely glass-walled dining room of Pousada da Alcobaça, 12km outside Petrópolis. The locally sourced menu revolves around trout, steak, shrimp, chicken and pasta accompanied by fruit, veggies and herbs harvested from the pousada's own organic gardens. The Saturday *feijoada* (bean-and-meat stew) is legendary.

★ **Bordeaux** INTERNATIONAL **$$**
(☎2242-5711; www.bordeauxvinhos.com.br; Av Ipiranga 716; mains R$30-75, weekday lunch specials R$20-26, weekend buffet per kg $99; ⏰noon-4pm & 7pm-midnight Mon-Sat, noon-5pm Sun) On the picturesque grounds of the Casa da Ipiranga, these converted stables provide a pleasant backdrop for the menu of pasta, risotto, fish and meat dishes backed up by an extensive wine cellar.

Majórica Churrascaria BARBECUE **$$**
(☎2242-2498; www.majorica.com.br; Rua do Imperador 754; mains for two R$32-80; ⏰noon-11:30pm) This *churrascaria* (barbecue restaurant), a short distance from the Museu Imperial, is renowned throughout town for its excellent cuts of meat. Most dishes on the menu are designed to serve two to three people; solo travelers or those with smaller appetites can request half-portions.

Leopoldina BRAZILIAN **$$**
(www.solardoimperio.com.br/gastronomia; Av Koeller 376; mains R$42-72; ⏰7am-11pm) Tall windows flanked by murals of monkeys, capybaras and tropical foliage create a cheerful mood at this renowned restaurant attached to the Hotel Solar do Império. Chef Claudia Mascarenhas balances traditional recipes against more whimsical creations, using ingredients that range from lamb to lobster, figs to filberts. The midweek executive lunch (mains R$29.90) is especially good value.

Information

Bradesco (Rua do Imperador 268) One of many ATMs along Rua do Imperador.

Tourist Information (☎0800-024-1516, 2233-1217; www.visitepetropolis.com) Offices conveniently located at the long-distance bus station (Terminal Rodoviário Leonel Brizola; ⏰8:30am-5:30pm), Praça da Liberdade (Praça da Liberdade; ⏰8:30am-5:30pm) and at the Centro de Cultura (Rua da Imperatriz s/n; ⏰9am-6pm), across from the Museu Imperial.

Getting There & Around

Única/Fácil buses from Rio (R$25, 1½ hours, half-hourly from 5:30am to midnight) drop you at the Leonel Brizola bus station in Bingen, 6km outside downtown Petrópolis. To reach the downtown bus station (Terminal de Integração), transfer to local bus number 100 (R$3.20, 30 minutes, every 10 to 15 minutes).

Parque Nacional da Serra dos Órgãos

Created in 1939, this national park (2152-1100; www.icmbio.gov.br/parnaserradosorgaos; per day foreigners/Brazilians R$27/14; 8am-5pm) covers 118 sq km of mountainous terrain between Teresópolis and Petrópolis. The park's most distinctive features are the strangely shaped peaks of **Pedra do Sino** (2263m), **Pedra do Açu** (2230m), **Agulha do Diabo** (2020m), **Nariz do Frade** (1919m), **Dedo de Deus** (1651m), **Pedra da Ermitage** (1485m) and **Dedo de Nossa Senhora** (1320m). With so many peaks, it's no wonder that this is the mountain-climbing, rock-climbing and trekking center of Brazil.

The park has an extensive trail system, the most famous of which is the 42km, three-day traverse over the mountains from Petrópolis to Teresópolis. Hiring a guide for this and other local treks is easy. Inquire at the national park entrance or with Trekking Petrópolis (p143). The best time for walks is from May to October (the drier months).

The **main entrance** to the national park is at the south edge of the town of Teresópolis, off Hwy BR-116 from Rio, about 4km from the center. Walking trails, waterfalls, natural swimming pools and tended lawns and gardens make this a pretty place for a picnic. Other park entrances can be found at **Vale do Bonfim**, (20km northeast of Petrópolis) and **Guapimirim** (in the park's southeastern corner, off the Rio–Teresópolis highway).

From the Teresópolis entrance, the road extends into the park as far as Barragem Beija Flor. There are several good walks from near here. The highlight is the **Trilha Pedra do Sino** – a strenuous round-trip of about eight hours from the end of the park road (R$43 trail fee). The trail passes **Cachoeira Veu da Noiva**, the vegetation changes from rainforest to grassland, and the reward is a panoramic view stretching all the way to Rio de Janeiro and the Baía de Guanabara. For a shorter walk, take the 800m **Trilha Mozart Catão** (one hour round-trip from the park road) up to the Mirante Alexandre Oliveira (1100m) for nice views of Teresópolis – or follow the park's newest trail, the 1.2km **Trilha Cartão Postal**, up to a higher viewpoint (1320m) for spectacular perspectives on the distinctive Dedo de Deus and the entire Serra dos Órgãos range.

Getting There & Away

To get to the park's main entrance from the city center of Teresópolis, take the 'Soberbo' bus (R$3.30). Alternatively, take the more frequent 'Alto' bus and get off at the Praçinha do Alto, from where it's a 10-minute walk south to the park's main entrance. Both buses can be caught at multiple stops along Teresópolis' main drag, Av Almirante Lúcio Meira. A taxi ride from town to the park entrance costs about R$30.

Vassouras

0XX24 / POP 34,000 / ELEV 434M

Vassouras, a now-quiet town 118km north of Rio, was the most important city in the Paraíba valley in the first half of the 19th century. Local coffee barons, with titles of nobility granted by the Portuguese crown, built huge *fazendas* (plantations) in the surrounding hills. With the abolition of slavery in 1888, the depletion of the soil and the relocation of coffee production to São Paulo state, the importance of Vassouras diminished, but several historic buildings from the boom days still survive in the pleasant town center.

The area's biggest attractions are the coffee *fazendas* several kilometers outside of town, some of them on the scale of French châteaux and with gardens to match. To visit these, you really need your own vehicle; otherwise, you'll run up some hefty cab fares.

Sights

The town's large central square, known as the **Campo Belo**, is a picturesque grassy slope dotted with palm trees and a fountain. Twin roosters crown the spires of the **Matriz NS de Conceição** church at the top of the hill.

The countryside around Vassouras teems with old coffee *fazendas* protected by historical preservation institutes. Most are still privately owned, so prior permission is required before touring them; you'll generally pay a small admission fee. The most popular are the imposing **Fazenda do Secretário** (2488-0150; cnr Hwy RJ-115 & Estrada do Capim Angola), **Mulungú Vermelho** (99230-7772; www.facebook.com/mulunguvermelho; Barão Cananéia,

Vassouras), **Santa Eufrásia** (☎99994-9494; www.fazendasantaeufrasia.com; Hwy BR-393, Km 242, Barra do Piraí), **Cachoeira do Mato Dentro** (☎99992-7350; Hwy BR-393, Km 173), **São Luiz da Boa Sorte** (☎99250-9798; Hwy BR-393, Km 210) and **Cachoeira Grande** (☎2471-1264; www.fazendacachoeiragrande.com.br; Estrada Mendes-Vassouras, Km 43). Vassouras' tourist office has detailed information and can help arrange visits.

Museu Casa da Hera MUSEUM
(casadahera.wordpress.com; Dr Fernandes Jr 160; ⌚museum & grounds 10am-5pm Tue-Fri, 1-5pm Sat & Sun; grounds only 10am-5pm Mon) FREE Near Vassouras' tourist office, this museum displays antique hand-carved furniture and other colonial relics in the former mansion of aristocratic heiress Eufrásia Teixeira Leite. Guide Ramon Telles brings the building's history to life and sheds light on Vassouras' coffee-growing heritage with excellent free tours in English, French, German and Spanish. You can tour the surrounding farm seven days a week.

Festivals & Events

Café, Cachaça & Chorinho CULTURAL
(⌚Apr) In April, Café, Cachaça & Chorinho celebrates Vassouras' triple heritage of coffee, *choro* (improvised samba) music and *cachaça* production, with concerts and tastings throughout the region.

Festival Vale do Café CULTURAL
(www.festivalvaledocafe.com; ⌚Jul) For two weeks, Vassouras buzzes with more than just coffee during this annual festival. Daily concerts are scheduled, and some *fazendas* host dinners featuring period food and dress.

Sleeping & Eating

Mara Palace HOTEL $$
(☎2471-1993; www.marapalace.com.br; Raul Fernandes 121; s R$157-209, d R$197-247, ste R$259-305; ❄📶🏊) This centrally located three-star hotel has pools and a sauna. Rooms in the main building are preferable to the musty ones in the concrete annex out back.

Sabor do Vale BUFFET $
(☎2471-7657; Furquim 50; per kilo R$32.90; ⌚11am-3:30pm) Locals favor this per-kilo lunch place one block below the main square, with a warren of high-ceilinged rooms and a wood stove laden with *comida mineira* – meat, fish, rice, beans, kale and other classic fare from the neighboring state of Minas Gerais.

Hipólito BRAZILIAN $$
(☎2471-2805; Praça Barão do Campo Belo; mains per person R$39-69; ⌚7-11pm Tue-Fri, noon-4pm & 7-11pm Sat, noon-4pm Sun) For fine dining and a good wine list, Vassouras' top choice is this grand 19th-century mansion with a pleasant back patio just above the tourist office on the main square.

Information

Tourist Office (☎2491-9018, 99200-0989; www.visitevassouras.com; Memorial do Trem, Praça Martinho Nóbrega 40; ⌚10am-4pm Sat, Sun & holidays) Vassouras' new tourist office, in the old train station near the main square, has information about nearby coffee *fazendas*.

Getting There & Around

From the **bus station** (☎2471-1055; Praça Juiz Machado Jr), **Útil** (www.util.com.br) runs five to six daily buses to Rio (R$37, 2½ hours). **Viação Progresso** (www.viacaoprogresso.com.br) also runs a 7:50am bus to Petrópolis (R$40, 2¾ hours) Monday through Saturday.

To get to the *fazendas*, you'll need your own wheels or a taxi.

Teresópolis

☎0XX21 / POP 164,000 / ELEV 871M

Do as Empress Maria Tereza used to do and escape from the steamy summer heat of Rio to the cool mountain retreat of Teresópolis, the highest city in the state, nestled in the strange, organ-pipe rock formations of the Serra dos Órgãos. The gorgeous winding road from Rio to Teresópolis climbs steeply through a padded green jungle, with bald peaks towering dramatically overhead the entire way.

The Quebra Frascos, the royal family of the Second Empire, once resided here. Today the city's principal attraction is the surrounding landscape and its natural treasures.

Teresópolis's Comary neighborhood has long been the training base of Brazil's national football squad. Plans to move the team to a new training facility in Rio's Barra da Tijuca for the 2014 FIFA World Cup ultimately fizzled, meaning that you can still occasionally catch a glimpse of the team practicing here in town.

Sights & Activities

The area's main attraction is Parque Nacional da Serra dos Órgãos. The **Dedo de Deus** (God's Finger) is the town symbol, a dramat-

Teresópolis

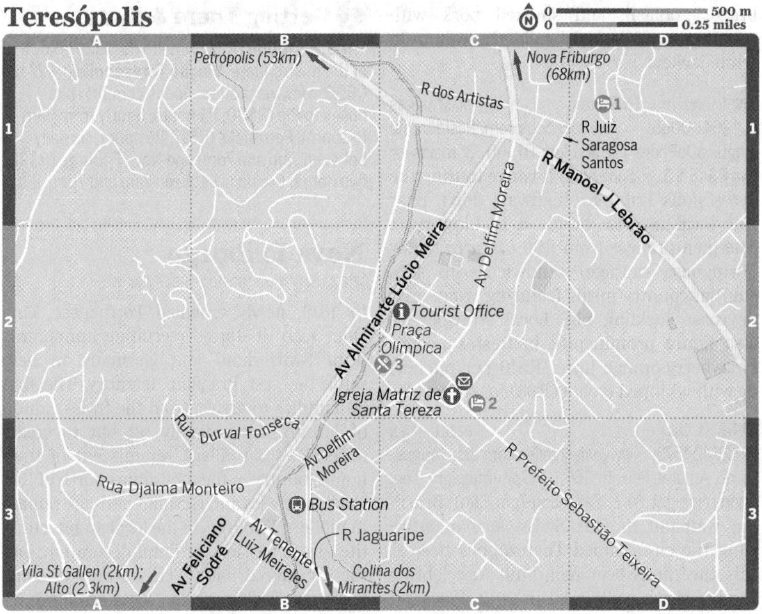

ic rock spire visible from all over town. **Colina dos Mirantes**, in the southern suburb of Fazendinha, is an especially good place to view the city and its mountain backdrop. On clear days you can see as far as Rio's Pão de Açúcar and the Baía de Guanabara.

Many more attractions lie outside town along the road to Nova Friburgo (p150) (also known as the 'Estrada Tere-Fri').

Teresópolis

Sleeping

1 Albergue Recanto do Lord D1
2 Várzea Palace Hotel C2

Eating

3 Taberna Alpina C2

Sleeping

Albergue Recanto do Lord HOSTEL $
(2742-5586; www.teresopolishostel.com.br; Luisa Pereira Soares 109; dm/d R$45/100; @) Designed to resemble an orange castle, this hostel on a steep hillside north of the center commands amazing views of the Dedo de Deus and other nearby peaks. Friendly owner Angela Inglez can provide a wealth of information about the surrounding area.

Várzea Palace Hotel HOTEL $
(2742-0878; hhotelvarzea@bol.com.br; Prefeito Sebastião Teixeira 41; s/d R$90/140, with shared bathroom R$60/80, ste R$170-220;) For a cheap sleep near the bus station, check out this crumbling relic of a hotel right off Teresópolis's main square – a local institution since 1916. Atmospheric touches include ornamental tiles, parquet wood floors and spacious, high-ceilinged rooms. The nicer suites have terraces.

Hotel Rosa dos Ventos HOTEL $$$
(2644-9900; www.hotelrosadosventos.com.br; Estrada Tere-Fri, Km 22.6; s/d incl breakfast from R$565/595, with full board from R$705/815;) Way up in the mountains, this luxurious alpine-style resort has its own lake and network of hiking trails. Magnificent views abound from the many terraces and on-site restaurants. It's 22km out of town along the road to Nova Friburgo.

Eating & Drinking

Taberna Alpina GERMAN $$
(2742-0123; Duque de Caxias 131; mains R$28-70; 8am-10pm Tue-Thu & Sun, to midnight Fri & Sat) The Taberna's cozy interior room, sporting wooden benches with heart-shaped cutouts, is reminiscent of the Alps. So is the menu, featuring German mustard, brown

bread, goulash, and smoked pork with sauerkraut, all served by elderly waiters in white jackets.

★**Linguiça do Padre** CHURRASCARIA $$
(☎2641-0065; www.facebook.com/RestauranteLinguicaDoPadre; Estrada Tere-Fri, Km 33; mains for two R$45-90; ⏰8am-8pm) If you're touring the Teresópolis–Friburgo highway, don't miss this local favorite beside a rushing river. The menu ranges from R$6 *linguiça* (spicy Portuguese sausage) sandwiches to substantial country meals featuring trout, goat or roast suckling pig. Local strawberries also figure prominently, in fresh-squeezed strawberry-orange juice (R$10 per pitcher) or with whipped cream (R$8) for dessert.

Vila St Gallen BEER GARDEN
(☎2642-1575; www.vilastgallen.com.br; Augusto do Amaral Peixoto 166; ⏰7pm-midnight Thu, noon-midnight Fri & Sat, noon-7pm Sun) Brazilian waitstaff in faux Swiss-German attire sling the city's famed Therezópolis beer at this cavernous beer hall, built to celebrate the brewery's centennial in 2012. Weekend patrons spill into the adjacent beer garden, bistro, fondue restaurant and kitschy chapel with piped-in Gregorian chants. There's international pub grub nightly, plus live rock and blues on Thursday and Friday.

Information

Bradesco (Av Delfim Moreira 556) One of several ATMs near the main square.

Tourist Office (☎2742-5561; www.teresopolis.rj.web.br.com/turismo; Praça Olímpica; ⏰9am-6pm Mon-Fri, 10am-3pm Sat) In the town center.

Getting There & Away

The **bus station** (Rua Primeiro de Maio) is south of the main square. **Viação Teresópolis** (☎2742-0606; www.viacaoteresopolis.com.br) runs buses to Rio (R$30, 1½ hours, hourly from 6am to 10pm), Petrópolis (R$17, 1½ hours, six daily between 7am and 7pm) and Nova Friburgo (R$22, two hours, five daily between 7am and 7pm).

Nova Friburgo

☎0XX22 / POP 182,000 / ELEV 846M

In 1818, newly crowned Portuguese King Dom João VI started recruiting immigrants from Switzerland and Germany to help settle his vast Brazilian territory. The first 30 families to arrive, from the Swiss canton of Friburg, immediately set out to create a perfect little village reminiscent of their home country in the mountains north of Rio. Traces of Swiss and German heritage remain in modern Friburgo, in the local architecture, the town's passion for floral decoration, and the fair-haired, blue-eyed features of some residents. Nowadays the local economy revolves around the lingerie industry, while tourism revolves around the region's natural attractions: waterfalls, woods, trails, sunny mountain mornings and cool evenings.

Sights & Activities

A **chairlift** (teleférico; ☎2522-4834; Praça do Teleférico; R$20; ⏰9:30am-5pm Tue-Sun) from town runs up to **Morro da Cruz** (1800m), offering fine panoramic views. Most other sights are a few kilometers out of town. One worthwhile vantage point is **Pico da**

THE TERESÓPOLIS–FRIBURGO SCENIC CIRCUIT

Pretty mountain vistas and European heritage are on full display along the **Circuito Turístico Tere-Fri** (www.terefri.com.br), a 68km scenic highway connecting the towns of Teresópolis and Nova Friburgo.

Starting from Teresópolis, highlights include the **Mulher de Pedra** (Woman of Stone) viewpoint at Km 12, where a distant mountain really *does* look like a reclining woman; the **Fazenda Geneve** (www.fazendageneve.com.br) at Km 16, where you can pet baby goats, buy local cheese, stroll the gardens or indulge in a fine French meal; the **Cachoeira dos Frades** turnoff at Km 21.5, where an unpaved side road leads through an idyllic valley to a waterfall with a swimming hole; **Hotel Rosa dos Ventos** (p147) at Km 22.6, one of many opulent hotels along the route; the **Linguiça do Padre** restaurant at Km 33; and **Queijaria Suiça** (☎2529-4000; www.frialpalimentos.com) at Km 49, where a Swiss cheese factory sits adjacent to a small museum tracing two centuries of Swiss culture in the Friburgo area.

Additional points of interest are indicated on a handy map available throughout the region. It's easiest to drive the route in your own car, although local buses travel through here and will let you off wherever you like.

Nova Friburgo

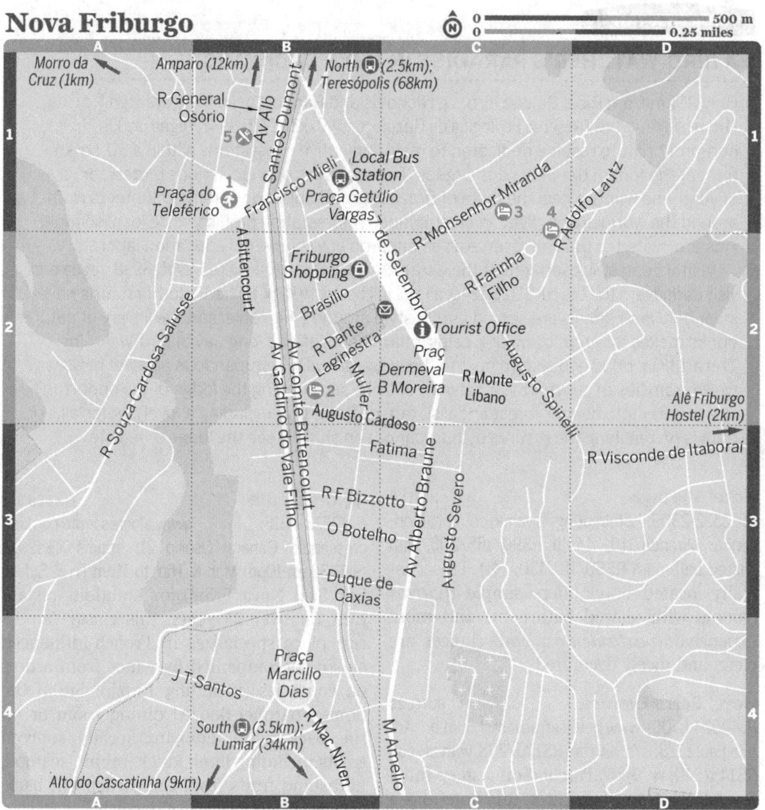

Caledônia (2310m), a popular launching site for hang gliders. It's a 6km uphill hike from the Alto do Cascatinha neighborhood; to reach the trailhead, take a local bus marked Cascatinha-Interpass (R$3.30, 15 minutes).

Ten kilometers to the north of town, you can hike (trail fee R$9) to **Pedra do Cão Sentado**, a rock formation resembling a sitting dog that serves as Friburgo's town symbol. To the southeast, **Lumiar** (34km from Nova Friburgo and reachable by local bus) is a popular destination for Brazilian ecotourists, with cheap pousadas, waterfalls, walking trails and white-water adventures centered on the Encontro dos Rios, the tumultuous confluence of three local rivers. Guided adventure tours of the area can be arranged through the Alê Friburgo Hostel.

Nova Friburgo

Activities, Courses & Tours
1 Chairlift B1

Sleeping
2 Hotel Alê B2
3 Hotel Maringá C1
4 Hotel Serra Everest C1

Eating
5 Crescente B1
Dona Mariquinha .... (see 3)

Sleeping & Eating

Alê Friburgo Hostel HOSTEL $
(2522-0540; www.friburgohostel.com; Bizzotto Filho 2; dm/s/d R$50/60/130;) This family-run hostel, 2km straight uphill from Friburgo's town square, compensates for its remote location with a friendly welcome and great amenities, including a pool, sauna and nice mountain views. The hostel's downtown affiliate, **Hotel Alê** (2526-3478; Dante Laginestra 89; dm/s/d R$50/70/140;), is more convenient for those using public transit, with a mix of dorms and old-fashioned, parquet-floored private rooms.

WORTH A TRIP

A BIRD-WATCHER'S PARADISE IN RIO'S BACKYARD

Only 80km from Rio's Galeão airport, Nicholas and Raquel Locke have created **Regua Nature Reserve** (Reserva Ecológica de Guapiaçu; ☎0xx21-2745-3947; regua.org), a non-profit nature reserve dedicated to restoring native ecosystems within a 50-sq-km tract at the foot of the Serra dos Órgãos. The reserve is open to serious birders, or anyone who wants a genuine taste of Brazil's remarkable biodiversity. Volunteers from around the world are engaged in an ambitious reforestation project, while local schoolkids are invited to use the reserve as a hands-on environmental education laboratory.

Visitors can stay overnight at the **Guapiaçu Bird Lodge** (☎021-2745-3998; regua.org/visit-us/lodge; s R$699, d R$1125-1240, all incl full board; ❄@🏊). The 10 comfy rooms have solar hot water, meals are served family-style around a big table, and the library of nature books makes for great browsing, caipirinha in hand, after a long day of bird-watching. The artificial pond ecosystem next to the lodge draws in a stupendous array of birds, as well as families of capybaras. A network of trails surrounding the lodge offers opportunities to enter into deeper forest and visit other attractions, including a lovely waterfall. For details on reaching the reserve by bus, car or van shuttle, see the lodge's website.

Hotel Maringá HOTEL **$**
(☎2522-2309; hotelmaringa@yahoo.com.br; Monsenhor Miranda 110; s/d/tr R$90/165/205, with shared bathroom R$60/110/130; 📶) This centrally located hotel offers simple *quartos* (rooms with shared bathroom) and more expensive *apartamentos*; both choices are clean and nicely decorated.

Hotel Serra Everest HOTEL **$$**
(☎2524-8700; www.hotelserraeverest.com.br; Adolfo Lautz 128; s/d with fan R$120/208, with air-con R$145/240; ❄📶🏊) Perched on a steep hill a few blocks from the center, this hotel has a pool and surprisingly good mountain views given its downtown location.

Hotel Auberge Suisse HOTEL **$$$**
(☎2541-1270; www.aubergesuisse.com.br; Rua 10 de Outubro, Amparo; chalet from R$525; ❄📶🏊) The luxury chalets here, 12km northeast of Nova Friburgo, all have wi-fi and minibars; most also have fireplaces and DVD players. The pretty landscaped grounds include indoor and outdoor pools, a sauna and a small collection of farm animals, whose milk is used to make cheese for the excellent on-site restaurant specializing in traditional Swiss cuisine: raclette, fondue and trout.

Dona Mariquinha BUFFET **$$**
(☎2522-2309; www.facebook.com/DonaMariquinha; Monsenhor Miranda 110; lunch buffet R$40; ⏲noon-3:30pm Tue-Sun, 7-9pm Mon-Fri) This friendly place features all-you-can-eat home cooking at lunchtime and all-you-can-eat soup for R$14 on weekday evenings.

★ **Crescente** FRENCH **$$$**
(☎2523-4616; www.elocrescente.com.br/crescente; General Osório 21; mains R$52-87; ⏲11:30am-10pm Mon & Thu, to 11pm Fri & Sat, to 5pm Sun) Nova Friburgo's standout restaurant for over 25 years, this classy family-run place specializes in French-influenced cuisine accompanied by wines from a dozen countries (including Brazil). Sit in the homey parquet-floored dining room or on the back patio, enjoying locally sourced treats including lamb, duck, rabbit, seafood, herbs and fruits from the garden out back, and a tempting range of desserts.

ℹ Information

Banco do Brasil (Praça Dermeval B Moreira 10) One of several ATMs downtown.

Tourist Office (☎2543-6307; circuito@pmnf.rj.gov.br; Praça Dermeval B Moreira; ⏲8am-8pm Mon-Sat, to 6pm Sun) Has maps, complete lists of hotels and restaurants, and excellent permanent staff, including the English-speaking Elaine and German-speaking Nair.

ℹ Getting There & Around

Nova Friburgo is a short jaunt from Rio, via Niterói, on bus line 1001. The ride is along a picturesque, winding, misty jungle road.

Nova Friburgo has two long-distance bus stations. From the **north bus station** (Rodoviária Norte; Praça Feliciano Costa), 2.5km north of the center, **Viação Teresópolis** (☎2522-2708; www.viacaoteresopolis.com.br) has buses to Teresópolis (R$22, two hours, five daily). From the **south bus station** (Rodoviária Sul; Ponte da Saudade), 4km south of the center, **Viação 1001** (☎2522-0400; www.autoviacao1001.com.br) has hourly buses to Rio (R$38 to R$48, 2½ hours) plus one direct bus to Cabo Frio on Saturday at 7am (R$68, 3¼ hours).

Local buses (R$3.30) connect both long-distance terminals to the central **local bus station** just north of Praça Getúlio Vargas. Local buses also go to just about all the tourist attractions. Ask for details at the tourist office.

EAST OF RIO DE JANEIRO

East of Rio, the mountains recede and the coastal strip becomes flatter, punctuated by the sparkling lagoons of the Região dos Lagos (Lakes Region) and the dazzling white sands of the Costa do Sol (Sunshine Coast). Some of Rio state's most beautiful beaches are found here. Only two hours from Rio by car, the area is a weekend playground for *cariocas*, with plenty of opportunities for nightlife and outdoor recreation.

Saquarema

☎0XX22 / POP 74,000

Straddling a spit of sand between a gorgeous lagoon and the open Atlantic, Saquarema is a laid-back little town 100km east of Rio. Polluting industries are forbidden in the municipality; the waters are clean, and fish and shrimp are abundant. Touted as the surfing capital of Brazil, its unmarred shoreline also attracts sportfishing enthusiasts and sun-worshipers. The surrounding area is a horse-breeding and fruit-growing center; you can visit the orchards and pick fruit, or rent horses or a jeep and take to the hills. Most local pousadas can arrange these activities.

Sights & Activities

NS de Nazaré CHURCH
(www.facebook.com/nazarethsaquarema; 8am-4pm) The stunning white church of NS de Nazaré (1837), perched on the hill near the entrance to the lagoon, is the town's focal point. From this strategic spot you can survey the long, empty beaches, the lagoon and the mountains beyond. The mass held here on September 7 and 8 attracts around 150,000 pilgrims, second only to the Nazaré celebrations of Belém.

Praia Itaúna BEACH
About 3km east of town is Praia Itaúna, Saquarema's most beautiful beach and one of the best surf spots in Brazil. National and international surfing competitions are held here each year, generally between May and October.

Festivals & Events

Quiksilver Pro Saquarema SPORTS
(pro-brasil.quiksilver.com; May) This six-day international competition is the highlight of Saquarema's annual surfing calendar.

Sleeping & Eating

Most of the best places are near the Itaúna beachfront.

Spazio Itaúna Hostel HOSTEL $
(☎2651-1748; www.spazioitauna.com.br; Rua das Garças 169a; dm R$60-70, tw R$140-165, d R$150-175, q R$270-310;) Directly opposite the beach at Itaúna, this new hostel offers spotless white dorms, twins, doubles and a family unit, each with mini-fridge and en suite bathroom. The guest kitchen, equipped with a four-burner stove and microwave, is perfect for cooking up post-surf snacks from the Mercado Itaúna market downstairs.

Maasai Hotel Beach & Resort HOTEL $$$
(☎2651-1092; www.maasai.com.br; Travessa Itaúna 17; garden-view/ocean-view d R$320/420, ste R$460;) If you're looking for cushy digs, this place is a no-brainer. Maasai has a stunning beachfront location, comfy sitting rooms, a sauna and swimming pool, and a pretty bar-restaurant overlooking the water.

Casa da Praia BRAZILIAN $$
(☎2651-7920; www.casadapraiaitauna.com.br; Av Oceânica 1564; mains per person R$28-49; 10am-6pm Mon-Thu, to midnight Fri & Sat, to

INDIGENOUS NAMES

Many place names in Rio state have their origins in indigenous words, including the following:

Geribá A kind of coconut palm.

Guanabara Arm of the sea.

Ipanema Place that gives bad luck or place of dangerous sea.

Itatiaia Many-pointed rock.

Mangaratiba Banana orchard.

Paraty A kind of fish.

Saquarema Lagoon without shells.

Tijuca Putrid-smelling swamp.

10pm Sun) This great little beachfront place, tucked behind a surf shop, serves its popular R$28 *prato do surfista* (surfer's special) till 6pm – grilled meat or fish accompanied by rice, beans and salad. After hours, it's all about seafood mains, cold beers and the sound of crashing waves.

Garota de Itaúna SEAFOOD **$$**
(☎2651-2156; Av Oceânica 165; mains per person R$31-70; ⏰11:30am-11:30pm Sun-Thu, to 1am Fri & Sat) The Girl from Itaúna's many attractions include a fabulous beachfront terrace and a wide variety of seafood specials. Enjoy the views but hang on to your beers – the wind can be vicious. The adjacent pousada rents simple rooms (single/double R$110/170).

Information

Centro de Atendimento ao Turista
(☎2651-2123; turismo@saquarema.rj.gov.br; Av Saquarema; ⏰9am-5pm Mon-Sat) Overlooking the lagoon, on the Itaúna side of the downtown bridge.

Getting There & Away

Viação 1001 (www.autoviacao1001.com.br) runs buses from Rio to Saquarema every hour or two throughout the day (R$30 to R$36, two hours). Saquarema's bus station is on the east side of the main bridge through town, about 800m north of the beach at Itaúna.

Montes Brancos (www.salineira.com.br) bus B145 runs direct from Saquarema to Cabo Frio four to five times daily (R$4.50, one hour). The main bus stop is just west across the bridge from the tourist office.

Arraial do Cabo

☎0XX22 / POP 28,000

Arraial do Cabo, 45km east of Saquarema, is surrounded by gleaming white sand dunes and offers breathtaking beaches without half the touristy fuss of neighboring Búzios. Arraial is home to a working fishing port, Porto do Forno, which lends it a welcoming working-class demeanor. Some of the best beaches – pristine swaths of gorgeous sand and bright-green waters – are within an easy 15-minute stroll of the downtown bus station, while others are just a short boat ride away. Arraial is a renowned diving destination, and it's also a good place to observe humpback whales, whose migration routes pass directly offshore.

Sights & Activities

Arraial's prime attractions lie along the shoreline. **Praia dos Anjos** has beautiful turquoise water but a little too much boat traffic for comfortable swimming. Just above the beach, look for the plaque commemorating Amerigo Vespucci's landing here in 1503. Vespucci left 24 men behind to start a settlement, making Arraial one of the first European toeholds in the Americas.

Favorite beaches within a short walking distance of town are **Prainha** to the north of town; **Praia do Forno** (accessed by a 1km walking trail from Praia dos Anjos) to the northeast; and the vast **Praia Grande** to the west, where wilder surf races in off the open Atlantic.

There are several other stunning beaches along the mountainous peninsula just south of town. For near-aerial views, and the best sunset in the area, climb up to **Pontal do Atalaia**, a popular viewpoint at the top of the peninsula that also makes an excellent spot for **whale watching** in July and August.

Ilha de Cabo Frio is accessed by boat from Praia dos Anjos (R$60 for the standard four-hour excursion). **Praia do Farol** on the protected side of the island is a gorgeous beach with fine white sand. From here it is a 2½-hour walk to the lighthouse. The **Gruta Azul** (Blue Cavern), on the southwestern side of the island, is another beautiful spot. Be alert, though: the entrance to the underwater cavern is submerged at high tide.

Arraial is one of Brazil's top scuba-diving spots. Tour operators that organize dives in these waters abound – the tourist office keeps a complete list. Dependable agencies include **PL Divers** (☎2622-1033; www.pldivers.com.br; Peçanha 57), **Sandmar** (☎2622-5703; www.sandmar.com.br; Epitácio Pessoa 21), **Ocean Sub** (☎2622-4642; www.oceansub.com.br; Luiz Corrêa 3) and **Rock 'n' Dive** (☎99873-7577, 99895-2191; rockndive.wix.com/rockndive).

Sleeping & Eating

Prices quoted here are for the high season. Discounts of up to 40% are common in the low season.

Marina dos Anjos Hostel HOSTEL **$**
(☎2622-4060; www.marinadosanjos.com.br; Bernardo Lens 145; dm/d with HI card R$60/164, without card R$64/180; @📶) One block back from Praia dos Anjos, this hostel is a wonderful base from which to explore the area. The helpful staff rent bicycles, canoes, snorkels,

surfboards and diving equipment, and help coordinate dives and boat tours. The central courtyard, with hammocks and pillows for lounging, is the venue for spontaneous evening barbecues and jam sessions.

Hotel Pousada Caminho do Sol HOTEL **$$**
(☎2622-2029; www.caminhodosol.com.br; Miguel Angelo 55; r R$210-395; ⓦ🏊) Right on Praia Grande, this pretty resort hotel with a pool and beautiful views is a big hit with visiting Brazilians looking for a romantic weekend.

Água na Boca BUFFET **$**
(☎2622-1106; Praça da Bandeira 1; per kg R$54; ⊙11:30am-4pm) A stone's throw from the bus station, this recommended self-serve includes plenty of seafood in its daily offerings.

★ **Bacalhau do Tuga** PORTUGUESE, SEAFOOD **$$**
(☎2622-1108; bacalhaudotuga.com; Santa Cruz 5, Praia dos Anjos; mains per person R$29-69; ⊙6-11pm Tue-Thu, from 1pm Fri-Sun) From humble origins selling codfish fritters from a beachside stand in 2008, the 'Tuga' (Portuguese guy) has ridden a wave of popular acclaim to open this full-fledged and ever-expanding restaurant near Praia dos Anjos. Super-fresh ingredients are incorporated into Portuguese classics, from seafood stews to custard tarts, served alongside local specialties like *peixe com banana* (grilled fish with bananas).

ℹ Information

Just around the corner from the bus station, you'll find a multibank ATM.

Tourist Office (☎2622-1949; turismo@arraial.rj.gov.br; Pórtico de Arraial do Cabo; ⊙8am-5pm) Housed within the town's formal entry portal, 3km northwest of the center, this office has English- and Spanish-speaking staff and provides a helpful map.

ℹ Getting There & Away

The Arraial do Cabo **bus station** (Praça da Bandeira) is situated in the town center. Direct buses operated by **Viação 1001** (☎2622-1488; www.autoviacao1001.com.br) run between Rio and Arraial every other hour (R$50 to R$66, three hours).

An alternative is to catch Salineira municipal bus B150 to Cabo Frio (R$4.50, every 15 minutes), then transfer to one of the half-hourly Rio-bound buses leaving from the Cabo Frio bus station.

For Búzios, take Salineira bus 414 (R$4.50, 1½ hours, six to seven daily).

Cabo Frio

☎0XX22 / POP 186,000

Sandwiched between sand dunes, lagoons and the sparkling Atlantic Ocean, Cabo Frio is the seventh-oldest city in Brazil. These days its historic charms and naturally gorgeous setting have been overshadowed by industry and overdevelopment, but on weekends and summer holidays its bars and beaches continue to draw throngs of happy-go-lucky Brazilians, whose merry-making spirit is the modern city's strongest attraction.

Sights & Activities

The three main focal points for tourists are **Praia do Forte**, a stunning stretch of white sand and green waters named after the 17th-century fort at its eastern end; the historic **Bairro da Passagem** neighborhood where the Portuguese first settled; and the restaurant-fringed **Canal do Itajuru**, which links nearby Lagoa de Araruama to the Atlantic Ocean.

There are three sand-dune spots in and about Cabo Frio. The dunes of **Praia do Peró**, a super beach for surfing and surf casting, are 6km north in the direction of Búzios, near Ogivas and after Praia Brava and Praia das Conchas. The **Dama Branca** (White Lady) sand dunes are on the road to Arraial do Cabo. The **Pontal** dunes of Praia do Forte town beach stretch from the fort to Miranda hill. Robberies can pose a danger at the dunes, so get advice from locals before heading out.

Forte São Mateus FORT
(⊙8am-5pm) FREE Forte São Mateus, a stronghold against pirates, was built between 1616 and 1620 to protect the lucrative brazilwood trade. You'll find it at the eastern end of Praia do Forte.

Sleeping & Eating

Pousada Boulevard POUSADA **$$**
(☎2643-1456; www.pousadaboulevard.com; Marechal Floriano 237; r R$250-450; ❄ⓦ🏊) Perfectly placed in Cabo Frio's canalside restaurant district, this newer pousada offers high-end amenities like satellite TV, a sauna and a plunge pool. The best five rooms have canal views.

CATARINA BELOVA / SHUTTERSTOCK ©

1. Praia dos Ossos (p160) 2. Boat tour, Paraty (p128)
3. Saquarema (p151) 4. Arraial do Cabo (p152)

BERTRAND GARDEL / GETTY IMAGES ©

Beaches of Rio de Janeiro State

Amerigo Vespucci said it best: 'If there were an earthly paradise, it wouldn't be far from here!' Tiny Rio state offers a stunning variety of beaches. Whether you're into surfing, diving, bronzing your bod or strutting your stuff on a seaside dance floor, you'll find it here.

Ilha Grande

A nature-lover's vision of tropical paradise, Ilha Grande (p121) has more trails than motorized vehicles, and endless stretches of secluded sands. Circumnavigate the island on foot, or hop from beach to beach on the classic round-the-island boat tour.

Paraty

Paraty's (p128) spectacular mosaic of bays, islands, mountains, waterfalls and beaches would be reason enough to visit; the colonial center's whitewashed houses, kaleidoscopic latticework and picturesque cobbled streets are like icing on the cake.

Saquarema

Laid-back and off the beaten track, Saquarema (p151) is best known to surfers, who flock here for international competitions; less-athletic types can admire its gorgeous 19th-century church, perched high on a promontory.

Arraial do Cabo

Even in Brazil, it'd be hard to find a cluster of beaches any prettier than this. Surrounded by prime diving and whale-watching spots, Arraial's (p152) white sands and blue-green waters are downright dazzling.

Búzios

If you'd like a few chic comforts and a little nightlife to go with that perfect tan, look no further than Búzios (p156). The preferred destination of Brazil's (and half of Argentina's!) beautiful people, this scalloped peninsula full of dreamy beaches is as luxurious and as decadent as it gets.

Malibu Palace Hotel HOTEL $$$
(☎2643-1955; www.malibupalace.com.br; Av do Contorno 900; r from R$460, with ocean view R$630;) For views and location, it's hard to beat this central place overlooking Cabo Frio's dazzling beachfront. Check online for discounted rates.

Restaurante Galápagos SEAFOOD, INTERNATIONAL $$
(☎2643-4097; Praça São Benedito 11; mains R$35-80; ⊙6pm-midnight Mon-Fri, noon-midnight Sat & Sun) Directly opposite the picturesque 17th-century white church on Cabo Frio's most historic square, this eatery in a colonial house serves sophisticated international fare, including a wide variety of seafood dishes, risotto with shrimp and asparagus or lobster and saffron, and lamb or beef with mashed potatoes and Madeira sauce.

Restaurante do Zé BARBECUE $$
(☎2643-4277; Blvd Canal 33; mains per person R$30-59; ⊙11am-midnight) The sidewalk tables at this animated eatery overlook the canal, one of the most picturesque spots in town. The house specialty is *picanha na chapa* (sizzling grilled steak).

Information

Bradesco (Av Assunção 904) One of several ATMs on this downtown thoroughfare.

Tourist Office (secretariaturismocabofrio@gmail.com; ⊙8am-6pm) At Cabo Frio's bus station; two additional branches along the Canal do Itajuru (☎2645-2505; Terminal de Barcos, Blvd Canal; ⊙8am-6pm) and in the historic Bairro da Passagem (☎2647-6227; Terminal de Transatlânticos, Av Assunção s/n, Bairro da Passagem; ⊙8am-6pm).

Getting There & Away

The **bus station** (Av Júlia Kubitschek) is 2km west of the center. Buses to and from Rio, operated by **Viação 1001** (☎2643-3778; www.autoviacao1001.com.br), leave half-hourly from early morning to late evening (R$44 to R$64, 2¾ hours).

Bus B150, operated by **Salineira** (☎2643-8144; www.salineira.com.br), runs to Arraial do Cabo every 15 minutes from the bus stop just to your left as you exit the bus station (R$4.50, 30 minutes). For Búzios, catch any Salineira bus marked 'Búzios' from the stop across the road (R$4.50, 45 minutes).

Búzios

☎0XX22 / POP 28,000

Beautiful Búzios sits on a jutting peninsula scalloped by 17 beaches. A simple fishing village until the early '60s, when it was 'discovered' by Brigitte Bardot and her Brazilian boyfriend, it's now one of Brazil's most upscale and animated seaside resorts, littered with boutiques, fine restaurants, villas, bars and posh pousadas. The Mediterranean touch introduced by the Portuguese has not been lost – indeed, the narrow cobblestone streets and picturesque waterfront contribute to Búzios' image as Brazil's St Tropez.

Búzios is not a single town but rather three settlements on the same peninsula – Ossos, Manguinhos and Armação de Búzios. Ossos (Bones), at the northern tip of the peninsula, is the oldest and most attractive. It has a pretty harbor and yacht club, plus a few hotels and bars. Manguinhos, on the isthmus, is the most commercial. Armação, in between, is the heart of town, with the most tourist amenities; it's here that you'll find Rua das Pedras, the hub of Búzios' nightlife, and Orla Bardot, the town's picturesque beachfront promenade.

Sights & Activities

The biggest draws in Búzios are the natural setting plus its endless array of opportunities for relaxation, nightlife, shopping and ocean sports.

Cobblestone **Rua das Pedras** is Búzios' main venue for shopping, dining and evening entertainment, overflowing with revelers on weekend nights. Its eastward continuation, **Orla Bardot**, is a delightful winding oceanfront promenade linking the two oldest and most picturesque sections of town (Armação and Ossos). As you walk along the beachfront, you'll notice several statues by sculptor Christina Motta, including representations of **Brigitte Bardot** and former Brazilian **president Juscelino Kubitschek**, plus some remarkably realistic-looking **fishermen** hauling in their nets.

Tours

Several operators offer tours to local beaches and islands. If you'd rather explore at your own pace, Búzios' *taxis marítimos* (water taxis) are an attractive alternative, charging R$6 to R$10 per person to individual

Búzios

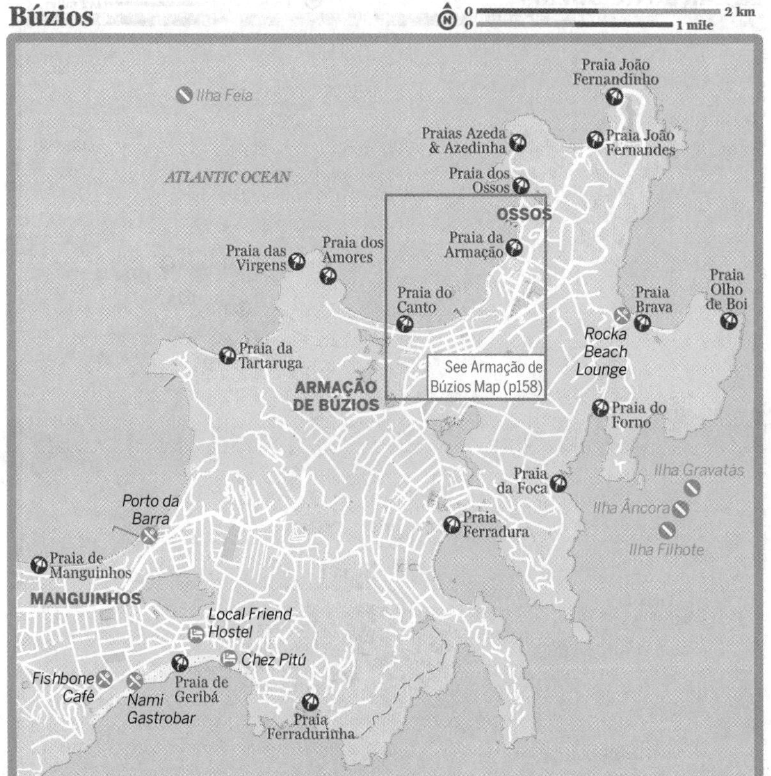

beaches around the peninsula (rates are posted on a board at Armação's main pier and elsewhere around town).

Tour Shop Búzios BUS TOUR, BOAT TOUR
(Map p158; ☎2623-4733; www.tourshop.com.br; Orla Bardot 550; tours from R$50) This agency runs the Búzios Trolley, an open-sided bus that visits 12 of the peninsula's beaches daily. Additional offerings include snorkeling, diving and rafting tours, along with excursions by schooner and glass-bottomed catamaran.

Búzios Divers DIVING
(Map p158; www.buziosdivers.com.br; Rua das Pedras 232) Offers a full range of diving courses and excursions to dive sites around Búzios.

Sleeping

Búzios caters to couples, so things can get pricey for solo travelers. Rates quoted here are for the high season: December through March, plus July.

★Local Friend Hostel HOSTEL $
(Map p157; ☎2623-0614; www.localfriendbuzios.com; Av Geribá 585; dm R$60-65, d/tr/q R$180/235/290) The name says it all at this brilliant new hostel one block from Geribá beach. After an eight-year round-the-world trip (New Zealand, Europe, USA) Rio Grande do Sul–born chef Eduardo Ghilardi has brought his infectious *gaúcho* hospitality to Búzios, inviting guests to disconnect from technology and enjoy human interaction: surfing, kayaking, playing board games or joining one of his regular cooking classes dinners.

The comfortable dorms come with unusually wide bunks; there are also family rooms and a delightful garden area complete with hummingbirds, fresh herbs and vegetables.

Armação de Búzios

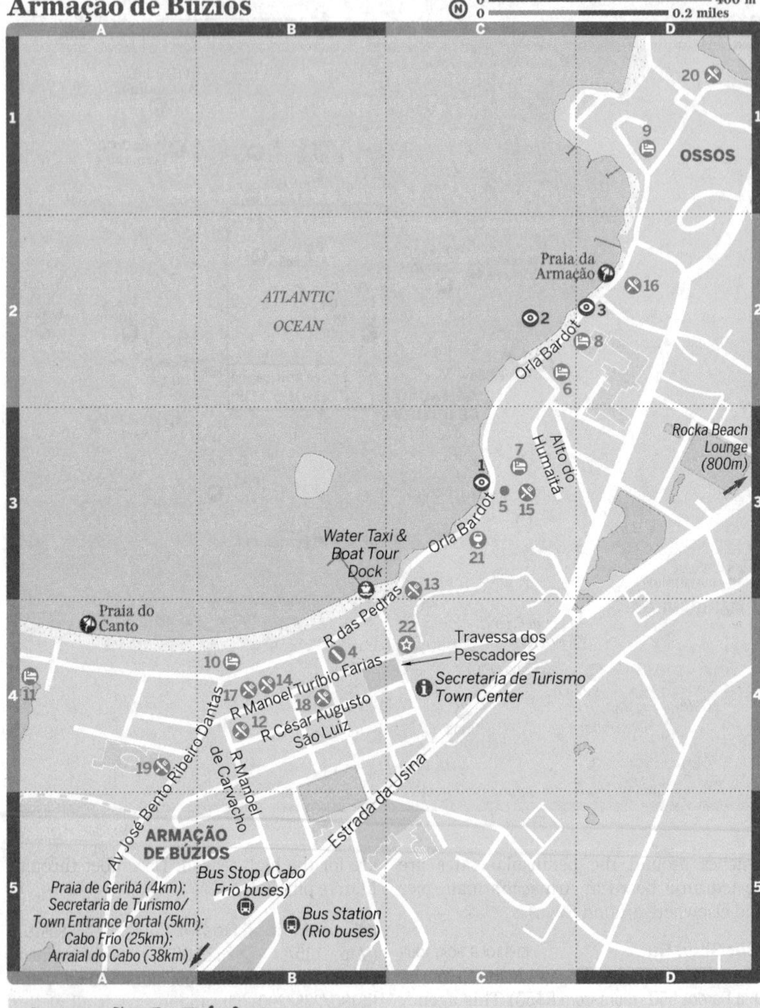

Armação de Búzios

Sights

1 Brigitte Bardot Statue C3
2 Fishermen Statues C2
3 President Juscelino Kubitschek Statue D2

Activities, Courses & Tours

4 Búzios Divers B4
5 Tour Shop Búzios C3

Sleeping

6 Casa Búzios C2
7 Casas Brancas C3
8 Cesar Apartamentos D2
9 L'Escale D1
10 Nomad Búzios B4
11 Villa Balthazar A4

Eating

12 Bananaland B4
13 Bar do Zé C3
14 Chez Michou Crêperie B4
15 Mistico Restaurante C3
16 O Barco D2
17 Primitivo B4
18 Restaurante do David B4
19 Salsa A4
20 Sukão D1

Drinking & Nightlife

21 Privilège C3

Entertainment

22 Gran Cine Bardot C4

★Nomad Búzios HOSTEL $
(Map p158; ☎2620-8085; www.nomadbuzios.com.br; Rua das Pedras 25; dm R$57-75, d R$200-325;) Búzios' best-positioned hostel boasts a seaside perch in the thick of the Rua das Pedras nightlife zone. The seven private doubles (four with terraces) enjoy gorgeous full-on ocean views. Meanwhile, the deck chairs and lounging bed on the waterfront terrace, coupled with R$7 caipirinhas in the bar downstairs, make life in the four- to 13-bed dorms pretty cushy as well.

L'Escale POUSADA $$
(Map p158; ☎2623-2816; www.pousadalescale.com; Travessa Santana 14, Ossos; r from R$280, with sea view R$340; closed May-Sep;) Book ahead for one of the three ocean-facing rooms with terraces and hammocks at this sweet, petite French-run pousada with a divine beachfront location in relaxed Ossos. Owners Sylvia and Francis also operate the eponymous restaurant downstairs serving fish soup, seafood and French specialties including beef bourguignon, sweet and savory crepes, and profiteroles.

Cesar Apartamentos APARTMENT $$
(Map p158; ☎2623-1349; www.cesarbuzios.com; Orla Bardot 974; r R$160, sea-view apt with/without terrace R$380/340;) One of Búzio's rare beachfront bargains, this family-run cluster of three modest rooms and four more spacious upstairs apartments boasts a prime Orla Bardot location. Budget-minded travelers will appreciate the motel-like cheapies downstairs; those with extra reais to spend should reserve ahead for one of the two front units with private terraces directly overlooking the water.

★Casa Búzios POUSADA $$$
(Map p158; ☎2623-7002; www.pousadacasabuzios.com; Alto do Humaitá 1; r R$470, ste R$560;) In a dream location just off Orla Bardot, this lovely older home surrounded by a sweet hillside garden is now a French-run pousada, offering six spacious and unique suites with high ceilings, pretty shutters, and wood and tile floors. Copious breakfasts are served on the poolside front patio, which affords picturesque views of boats bobbing in the harbor below.

★Villa Balthazar POUSADA $$$
(Map p158; ☎2623-6680; www.villabalthazar.com.br; Maria Joaquina 375; d R$390-475;) On a peaceful residential lane three blocks from Rua das Pedras, this stylish five-room pousada is a labor of love for youthful Swedish owners (and proud new parents) Petra and Felix, who have filled the place with family heirlooms and homey touches inspired by their own world travels. Guests love the in-room DVD players, swimming pool and delicious homemade breakfasts.

Casas Brancas BOUTIQUE HOTEL $$$
(Map p158; ☎2623-1458; www.casasbrancas.com.br; Alto do Humaitá 10; r R$1047-1815; ste R$1993-2147;) If you're honeymooning or just won the lottery, head straight for this top-end place on Alto do Humaitá hill. Pampering touches include stupendous ocean views from the poolside terrace (and all but the most basic rooms), massages in the on-site spa, free yoga and tai chi classes and a choice of two restaurants: the upscale Atlântico and the chilled-out Deck Pizzeria.

Prices quoted here are official high-season rates; look online for better deals.

Chez Pitú POUSADA $$$
(Map p157; ☎2623-6460; www.chezpitu.com.br; Aldeia de Geribá 10; r from R$546, with sea view from R$615;) Rooms are small and somewhat dated, but nothing can diminish the Geribá beachfront location of this colorful pousada, decorated with mosaics and brightly painted French doors. The breakfast room, poolside bar and lounge-chair-equipped front deck all offer tantalizing views of the ocean a few feet away. The nicest upstairs rooms sport small verandas tailor-made for watching Búzios' best sunset.

Eating

Most of the better restaurants are in or near Armação. For good seafood at more affordable prices, check out the little thatched-roof places on Ferradura and João Fernandes beaches.

Three kilometers west of town at Manguinhos, the trendy food complex **Porto da Barra** (Map p157; www.portodabarrabuzios.com.br) is also worth a look, featuring 14 bars and restaurants spread out along a tree-fringed waterfront boardwalk; it's a great place for a snack and a drink at sunset.

Chez Michou Crêperie CREPERIE $
(Map p158; ☎2623-2169; www.chezmichou.com.br; Rua das Pedras 90; crepes R$15-28; noon-late Thu-Tue, from 5pm Wed) Crowds flock here not only for the sweet and savory crepes, but

DON'T MISS

BÚZIOS' BEACHES

With nearly two dozen beaches to choose from in and around Búzios, it's hard to know where to start. In general, the southern beaches are trickier to get to, but they're prettier and have better surf. The northern beaches are more sheltered and closer to the towns.

Going counterclockwise from south of Manguinhos, the first beaches are **Geribá** and **Ferradurinha** (Little Horseshoe). These are beautiful beaches with good surf. Next on the coast is **Ferradura**, which is large enough for windsurfing, followed by **Praia da Foca** and **Praia do Forno**, which have colder water than the other beaches. **Praia Olho de Boi** (Bull's Eye) is the area's only nude beach. It's reached by a little trail from the long, clean beach of **Praia Brava**.

On the north side of the peninsula, both **João Fernandinho** and **João Fernandes** are good for snorkeling, as are **Azedinha** and **Azeda**, reached by a short trail from Ossos. **Praia dos Ossos**, **Praia da Armação**, **Praia do Canto** and **Praia dos Amores** are lovely to look at, but a bit public and not so nice for lounging on. **Praia das Virgens** and **Praia da Tartaruga** are quiet and pretty. **Praia de Manguinhos** is another town beach further west.

Offshore, the islands of **Âncora**, **Gravatás**, **Filhote** and **Feia** are especially good diving destinations.

also for mixed drinks at the outdoor bar, sports events on the big-screen TVs and the weekend DJ mixes (from 9pm).

Sukão SANDWICHES $

(Map p158; Praça dos Ossos; sandwiches R$12-22, juices R$10-14; ⏲10am-9pm) Half-liter goblets of fresh fruit juice and sandwiches piled onto four varieties of homemade bread make this Ossos corner eatery a tempting pit stop en route to the beach at Azeda or Azedinha.

★ **Nami Gastrobar** JAPANESE, FUSION $$

(Map p157; ☎2623-6637; www.facebook.com/namigastrobar; cnr Rua dos Namorados & Gerbert Perissé; mains R$33-89; ⏲6:30-11pm Wed-Fri, 12:30-11pm Sat, 12:30-5pm Sun) Near Geribá beach, this restaurant fuses traditional Japanese cuisine with Peruvian, Mexican and other influences to create a spectacularly eclectic international dining experience. Fresh seafood takes center stage in citrusy seviche, crunchy wasabi-salmon tacos, tempura shrimp and miso-marinated black cod, but meatier delights also abound, including delicate slices of grilled beef with sesame seeds or spare ribs with roasted corn.

O Barco SEAFOOD $$

(Map p158; Orla Bardot 1054; mains per person R$25-60; ⏲11am-11pm) This down-to-earth waterfront joint stakes its reputation on well-made, reasonably priced fish dishes – from fried fish with rice and salad to full-on seafood stews. Eight tables on a cute little terrace plus a few extra sidewalk seats offer excellent people-watching and ocean views. Solo diners will appreciate the menu's wealth of *pratos individuais* (individual dishes), a rarity in couples-oriented Búzios.

Fishbone Café SANDWICHES, BAR $$

(Map p157; ☎98134-0625, 2623-7348; www.facebook.com/fishbonebuzios; Av Gravatás 1196, Praia de Geribá; sandwiches R$26-35, mains R$45-58; ⏲10am-5pm Sun-Fri, to 7pm Sat) At this laid-back beach club on Praia de Geribá, the menu features everything from sandwiches to salads to a delicious *caldeirada de frutos do mar* (seafood stew), but plenty of people come just to drink, catch some rays and listen to tunes on the waterfront deck.

Restaurante do David SEAFOOD $$

(Map p158; ☎2623-2981; Manoel Turíbio de Farias 260; mains R$21-75; ⏲noon-midnight) Still going strong after 40 years, David's serves high-quality seafood at little wooden tables with red tablecloths in the heart of town.

Bananaland BUFFET $$

(Map p158; www.restaurantebananaland.com.br; Manoel Turíbio de Farias 50; per kg R$78.50; ⏲11:30am-10:30pm) Standing out among the several deluxe self-serve eateries on this street for its staggering variety of offerings, Bananaland offers something for everyone.

Salsa BUFFET $$

(Map p158; Av José Bento Ribeiro Dantas 94; per kg R$78.90; ⏲noon-5pm) Other per-kilo joints may offer a wider selection, but locals in the know swear by the unfailing freshness and quality of the self-serve fare at this health-food oriented lunchtime buffet.

Primitivo ITALIAN $$
(Map p158; primitivobuzios.com.br; Rua das Pedras 60; mains R$39-64, pizzas R$32-75; ⌚7-11:45pm) At this Italian-run place on Rua das Pedras, nine superb varieties of home-made gnocchi incorporate a tantalizing range of ingredients (Parma ham, mozzarella, parmesan, asparagus, eggplant, leeks, mushrooms, shrimp, thyme, nutmeg and cinnamon, to name a few). Pizzas here are also among the best in Búzios.

★ **Rocka Beach Lounge** SEAFOOD $$$
(Map p157; ☎2623-6159; www.rockafish.com.br; Praia Brava; mains R$72-89; ⌚11am-5:30pm, closed Tue in winter) Prime people-watching and some of Búzios' most creative cuisine are the twin draws at this casual-chic seafood eatery perched directly above Praia Brava. Rocka is a full-day event for most visitors, who linger long after lunchtime on the lounge chairs and beds spread out on terraced hillsides overlooking the beach. Reserve ahead for weekends, when things fill up fast.

★ **Mistico Restaurante** MEDITERRANEAN $$$
(Map p158; ☎2623-9046; www.abracadabrapousada.com.br; Alto do Humaitá 13; mains R$45-95; ⌚1-11pm) Perched high on the hill between Armação and Ossos, Pousada Abracadabra's restaurant enjoys one of Búzios' finest panoramic sea views, with poolside seating and an intimate glass-walled dining room. Amazingly, the food even outshines the setting, featuring reasonably priced, revelatory offerings such as the *seleção do mar*: grilled octopus, squid, salmon and shrimp with capers and Sicilian lemon cream (R$74).

Bar do Zé MEDITERRANEAN $$$
(Map p158; ☎2623-4986; Orla Bardot 382; mains R$46-126; ⌚6:30pm-late Mon, 1pm-late Tue-Sun) This classy restaurant with an open-air deck facing Orla Bardot is famous for its well-mixed drinks (classic caipirinhas, freshly minted mojitos), served alongside grilled fish, risotto, steak and seafood.

Drinking & Entertainment

A whole slew of bars and clubs lines Rua das Pedras and Orla Bardot, with the action continuing well past midnight.

Privilège CLUB
(Map p158; www.privilegebrasil.com/casa/buzios; Orla Bardot 550; ⌚11pm-late Thu-Sun) The star of Búzios' late-night scene is this sleek nightclub with two dance floors and four bars on the Orla Bardot waterfront.

Gran Cine Bardot CINEMA
(Map p158; ☎2623-1466; www.facebook.com/grancinebardot.buzios; Travessa dos Pescadores 88; admission R$26; ⌚Thu-Sun) Shows movies on weekend nights, including some in English with Portuguese subtitles. The adjacent cafe is a nice spot for snacks, coffee or caipirinhas before or after the show.

Information

Bradesco (Av José Bento Ribeiro Dantas 254) One of several downtown ATMs.

Hospital Municipal Rodolpho Perissé (☎2623-7959; Estrada Búzios-Cabo Frio) Just outside the town entrance portal along the road to Cabo Frio.

Secretaria de Turismo (www.buzios.rj.gov.br/informacoes_turisticas.aspx) Two well-staffed offices distribute city maps and hotel information, at the town entrance portal (☎2623-4254; Av José Bento Ribeiro Dantas; ⌚8am-9pm) and just off the main square in Armação (Map p158; ☎2623-2099; Travessia dos Pescadores 110, Armação; ⌚8am-9pm) .

Getting There & Around

The Búzios **bus station** (Map p158; Estrada da Usina 444) is a simple covered bus stop with no building attached, five blocks south of the Armação waterfront. **Viação 1001** (☎2623-2050; www.autoviacao1001.com.br) runs buses from Búzios to Rio's Novo Rio bus station (R$48 to R$61, 2¾ hours) at least 10 times daily between 6am and 8pm; the same company offers direct transfers four times daily to Rio's Galeão airport (R$80) and once daily to Copacabana and other Zona Sul beaches (R$90).

Municipal buses between Búzios and Cabo Frio (R$4.50, 45 minutes) travel along Av José Bento Ribeiro Dantas and Estrada da Usina; there's a convenient **stop** (Map p158; Estrada da Usina) directly opposite the Rio-bound bus stop.

Minas Gerais & Espírito Santo

Includes ➡

Best Places to Eat

- ➡ Xapuri (p171)
- ➡ Cantinho do Curuca (p214)
- ➡ Viradas do Largo (p194)
- ➡ Valsugana (p217)
- ➡ Kiko & Kika (p197)

Best Places to Stay

- ➡ Pouso do Chico Rei (p180)
- ➡ Pousada Santuário do Caraça (p206)
- ➡ Villa Magnolia Pousada (p189)
- ➡ Pousada do Capão (p204)
- ➡ Mandala das Águas (p197)

Why Go?

For those seeking a tangible sense of Brazilian history, no state compares with Minas Gerais. The cobblestone streets and splendid baroque monuments of Minas' colonial mining towns have seen it all, from the horrors of slavery to the fervor of Brazil's 18th-century independence movement.

Minas' natural wonders are equally alluring. The Serra do Espinhaço, a Unesco Biosphere Reserve running the length of the state, is just one of many refuges providing critical habitat for endangered species as well as exhilarating outdoor-recreation opportunities. Add to this the cosmopolitan charms of Belo Horizonte, the fabulous flavors of Minas' wood-fired cuisine, the intoxicating effects of Brazil's best *cachaça* (sugarcane alcohol) and the locals' legendary hospitality, and it's hard to resist Minas' seductive spell.

Neighboring Espírito Santo offers an attractive off-the-beaten-track counterpoint, with pretty beach and mountain scenery and some of Brazil's tastiest seafood.

When to Go

Belo Horizonte

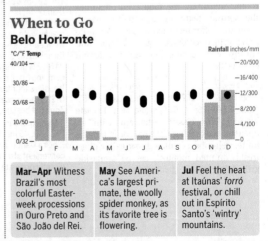

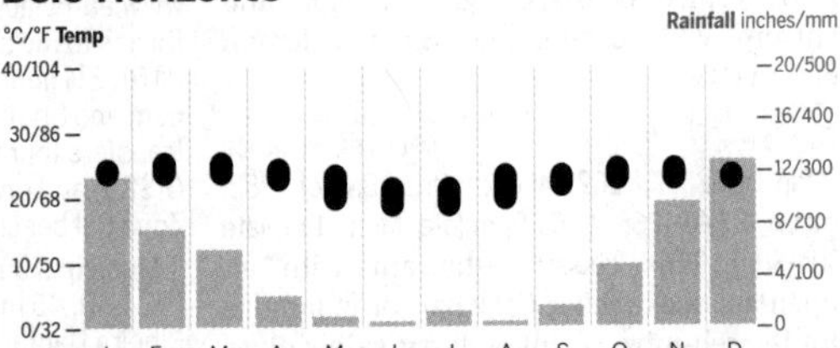

Mar–Apr Witness Brazil's most colorful Easter-week processions in Ouro Preto and São João del Rei.

May See America's largest primate, the woolly spider monkey, as its favorite tree is flowering.

Jul Feel the heat at Itaúnas' *forró* festival, or chill out in Espírito Santo's 'wintry' mountains.

History

Espírito Santo, like much of the Brazilian coast, was colonized in the 16th century, but the focus quickly turned inland In the late 1600s, when gold was discovered in Minas Gerais. Brazilians began flocking to Minas, while Portuguese flocked to Brazil. Slaves were brought from Bahia's sugar fields and the savannas of Angola, and until the last quarter of the 18th century, Minas' mines were producing half the world's gold.

Minas set the gold-rush standard – crazy, wild and violent – more than 100 years before the Californian and Australian gold rushes. Licentious living, disease and famine were rampant. Much of the gold wealth was siphoned off to Portugal; among the few lasting benefits to Brazil was the creation of the beautiful, church-clad mining cities that still dot Minas' hills. Nowadays, the Estrada Real (Royal Road) that connected these *cidades históricas* has become the state's most popular tourist route.

In neighboring Espírito Santo, coffee plantations were the prime source of income up until the 1960s. They've since been superseded by mining, shipping and – in the capital city, Vitória – Brazil's most famous chocolate factory.

Getting There & Around

Minas' capital city Belo Horizonte is the arrival point for most travelers. Pampulha and Confins airports handle domestic and international flights, while Belo's downtown bus station serves as a hub for ground transport. Direct buses from Rio and São Paulo also serve some of Minas' historic towns.

Vitória is Espírito Santo's largest city, with an international airport offering flights to major cities throughout Brazil. Buses run up and down the coastline, connecting Vitória with Bahia and Rio de Janeiro state, and also head inland to several cities in neighboring Minas Gerais.

MINAS GERAIS

POP 20 MILLION

Belo Horizonte

☎0XX31 / POP 2.4 MILLION / ELEV 858M

Known to the locals as Beagá (pronounced 'bay-ah-gah', Portuguese for BH), Belo Horizonte was named for its beautiful view of nearby mountains. Urban sprawl makes it harder to appreciate the natural setting nowadays, but Brazil's third-largest city still has considerable charm. Walk down the buzzing cosmopolitan streets of the Savassi neighborhood on a Saturday evening, eat at one of the fine restaurants in Lourdes, stroll through the densely packed stalls at Mercado Central, attend a weekend street fair or a concert at the Palácio das Artes, or visit the Inhotim art museum west of the city, and you'll see that Belo Horizonte has countless dimensions. Add to all this the friendly, welcoming nature of Beagá's people and you've got a winning combination. Stick around a few days – you might grow fond of the place.

History

In the late 19th century, as the Brazilian Republic was coming into its own, *mineiros* (residents of Minas Gerais state) began planning a new capital to replace hard-to-reach Ouro Preto, which had fallen out of favor as a symbol of colonialism. Belo Horizonte sprang up as an art nouveau city, influenced by the spirit of Ordem e Progresso (Order and Progress), the new slogan on the Brazilian flag.

In the 1940s Belo expanded northward. Then-mayor Juscelino Kubitschek commissioned young architectural-school graduate Oscar Niemeyer to design the brand-new Pampulha district. These two men are largely responsible for the city's wide avenues, large lakes, parks and jutting skyline.

More than 100 years after its founding, Belo Horizonte still has the young, contagious energy of a community reinventing itself. The city has undergone a major face-lift in recent years, with several new museums opening in Praça da Liberdade and a slew of government agencies moving 20km north to the Cidade Administrativa, a futuristic complex designed by the centenarian Niemeyer shortly before his death in 2012.

Beagá's role as a host city for the 2014 FIFA World Cup and the 2016 Olympics has prompted a whole new round of infrastructure improvements, including modern high-speed bus lines, an expansion of Confins international airport, and massive remodeling of the city's venerable football stadium, Mineirão.

Sights

Fans of modernist architect Oscar Niemeyer won't want to miss his creations dotted around a huge artificial lake in the Pampulha district, north of downtown. For

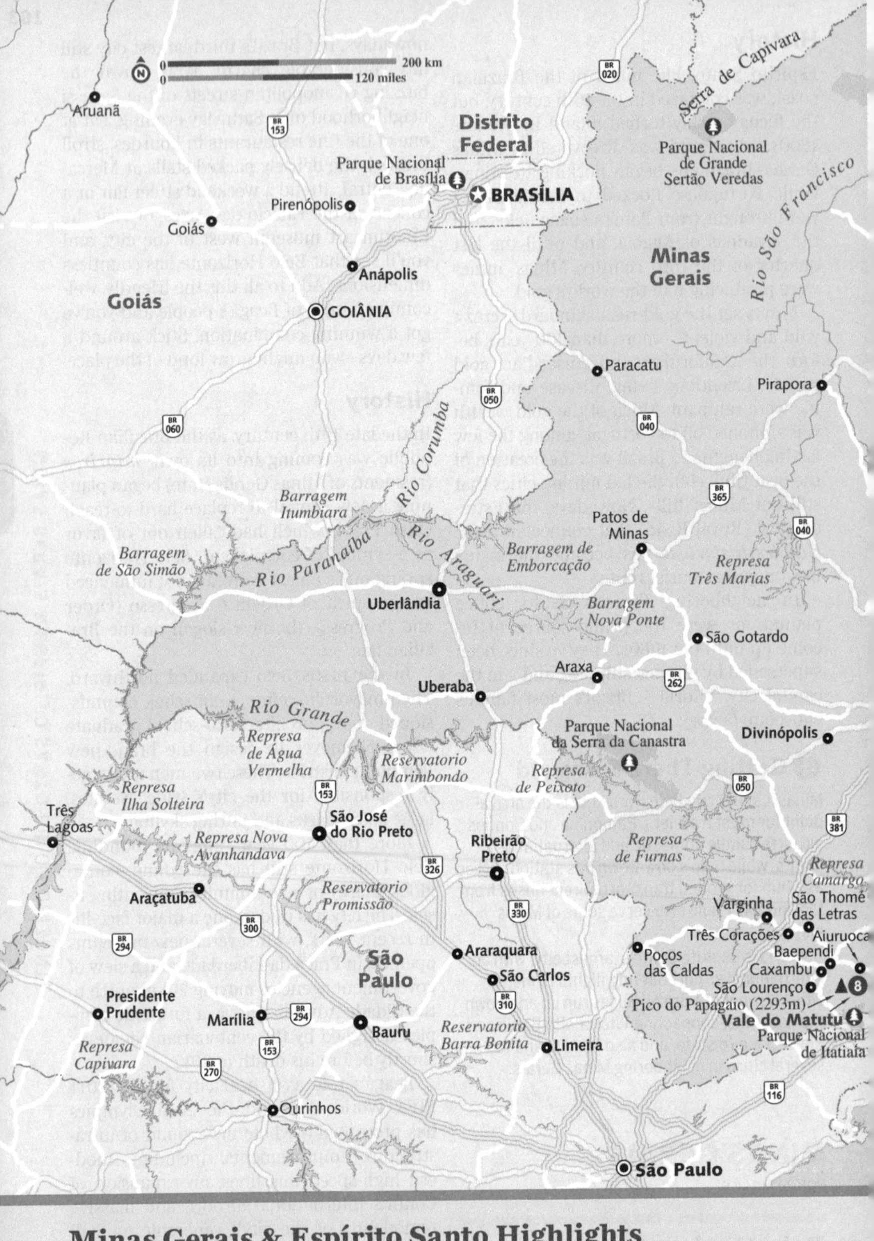

Minas Gerais & Espírito Santo Highlights

1. Checking out the 21 galleries of contemporary art at **Instituto de Arte Contemporânea Inhotim** (p175).
2. Wandering among the cobblestone streets and baroque architectural treasures of **Ouro Preto** (p175).
3. Climbing Brazil's third-tallest mountain, the 2892m Pico da Bandeira in **Parque Nacional de Caparaó** (p207).
4. Taking a tour or catching a match at **Mineirão football stadium** (p168) in Belo Horizonte, completely revamped for the 2014 World Cup.

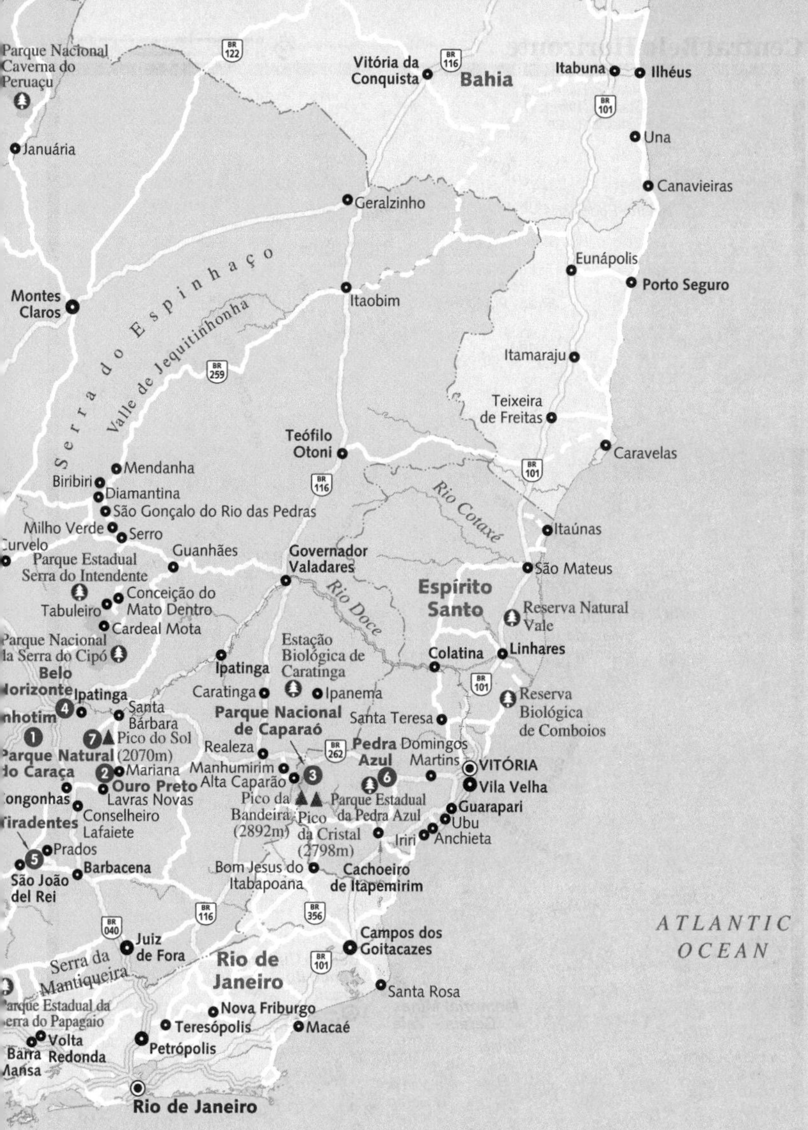

5 Taking a ride on a historic *Maria-Fumaça* **steam train** (p195) from Tiradentes.

6 Holding on to that rope as you scale the steep granite face of **Pedra Azul** (p216).

7 Waiting by starlight for the maned wolves to appear at the old monastery at **Parque Natural do Caraça** (p206).

8 Getting off the beaten track on the dirt roads and scenic mountain trails of the **Vale do Matutu** (p197).

Central Belo Horizonte

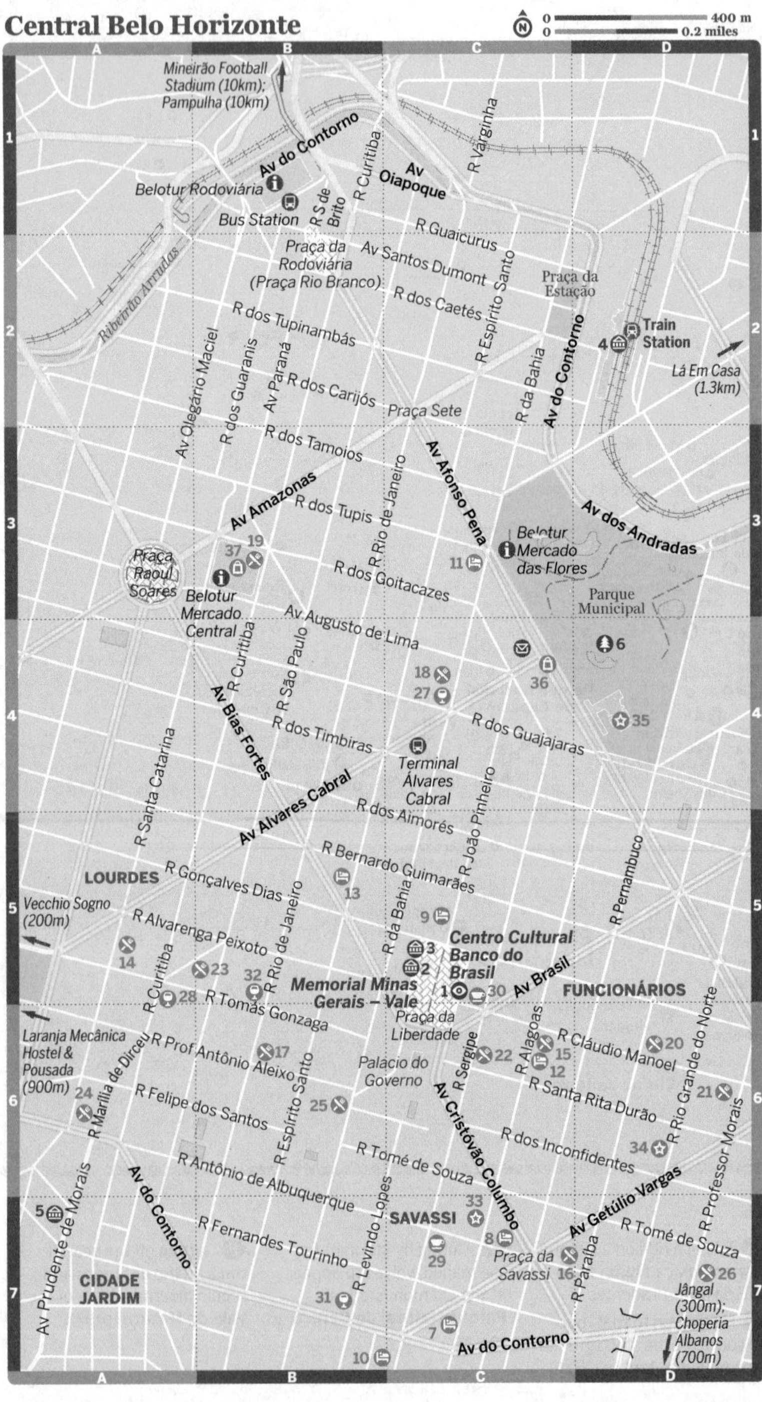

0 400 m
0 0.2 miles
Mineirão Football Stadium (10km); Pampulha (10km)
Av do Contorno
Belotur Rodoviária
Bus Station
R S de Brito
R Curitiba
Av Oiapoque
R Varginha
R Guaicurus
Praça da Rodoviária (Praça Rio Branco)
Av Santos Dumont
R Espírito Santo
Praça da Estação
R dos Caetés
Ribeirão Arrudas
R dos Tupinambás
Train Station
Lá Em Casa (1.3km)
R Olegário Maciel
R dos Guaranis
Av Paraná
R dos Carijós
Praça Sete
R da Bahia
R dos Tamoios
Av Afonso Pena
R Rio de Janeiro
Av Amazonas
R dos Tupis
Av dos Andradas
Belotur Mercado das Flores
Praça Raoul Soares
Belotur Mercado Central
R dos Goitacazes
Parque Municipal
Av Augusto de Lima
R Curitiba
R São Paulo
Av Bias Fortes
R dos Guajajaras
R dos Timbiras
Terminal Álvares Cabral
R João Pinheiro
Av Alvares Cabral
R dos Aimorés
R Santa Catarina
R Bernardo Guimarães
LOURDES
R Gonçalves Dias
R Pernambuco
Vecchio Sogno (200m)
R Alvarenga Peixoto
R da Bahia
Centro Cultural Banco do Brasil
Memorial Minas Gerais – Vale
Av Brasil
FUNCIONÁRIOS
R Tomás Gonzaga
Praça da Liberdade
Laranja Mecânica Hostel & Pousada (900m)
R Prof Antônio Aleixo
R Alagoas
R Cláudio Manoel
R Sergipe
Palácio do Governo
R Rio Grande do Norte
R Marília de Dirceu
R Santa Rita Durão
R Felipe dos Santos
R Espírito Santo
Av Cristóvão Columbo
R dos Inconfidentes
R Professor Morais
R Antônio de Albuquerque
R Tomé de Souza
Av Getúlio Vargas
Av Prudente de Morais
Av do Contorno
SAVASSI
R Levindo Lopes
R Tomé de Souza
R Fernandes Tourinho
Praça da Savassi
R Paraíba
CIDADE JARDIM
Jângal (300m); Choperia Albanos (700m)
Av do Contorno

Central Belo Horizonte

Top Sights
1 Centro Cultural Banco do Brasil C5
2 Memorial Minas Gerais – Vale C5

Sights
3 Museu das Minas e do Metal C5
4 Museu de Artes e Ofícios D2
5 Museu Histórico Abílio Barreto A7
6 Parque Municipal D4

Sleeping
7 Adrena Sport Hostel C7
8 Hostel Savassi C7
9 Hotel Ibis C5
10 Hotel Promenade Toscanini B7
11 Othon Palace C3
12 Royal Savassi Hotel C6
13 Samba Rooms Hostel B5

Eating
14 A Favorita A5
15 Amadeus C6
16 Baiana do Acarajé C7
17 Bar do Lopes B6
18 Cantina do Lucas C4
19 Casa Cheia B3
20 Casa Cheia Savassi D6
21 Domenico D6
22 Dona Lucinha II C6
23 Glouton B5
24 Marília Pizzeria A6
25 Restaurante do Minas Tenis Clube B6
26 San Ro D7

Drinking & Nightlife
27 Arcangelo C4
28 Bar Tizé A5
29 Café com Letras C7
30 Café com Letras – Centro Cultural Branch C5
31 CCCP B7
32 Choperia Albanos (Lourdes) B5

Entertainment
33 A Autêntica C7
34 A Obra D6
35 Palácio das Artes D4

Shopping
36 Feira de Arte e Artesanato C4
37 Mercado Central B3

information on all of Praça da Liberdade's new museums, including some not covered here, visit the website http://circuitocultur-alliberdade.com.br.

Praça da Liberdade & North

★Centro Cultural Banco do Brasil ARTS CENTER
(www.bb.com.br/cultura; Praça da Liberdade 450; 9am-9pm Wed-Mon) FREE Inaugurated in late 2013, this magnificent palace on Praça da Liberdade is one of Belo Horizonte's cultural gems. The vast 3rd-floor gallery hosts special exhibitions that rotate every couple of months, while the downstairs is dedicated to free or low-cost arts events including film, theater and dance; pick up a schedule on-site. The interior courtyard makes for a pleasant break anytime of day with its cafes, stained glass windows and retractable roof.

★Memorial Minas Gerais – Vale MUSEUM
(www.memorialvale.com.br; Praca da Liberdade s/n; 10am-5:30pm Tue, Wed, Fri & Sat, to 9:30pm Thu, to 3:30pm Sun) FREE The best element of Praça da Liberdade's 2010 makeover, this supremely cool contemporary museum chronicles Minas culture from the 17th to 21st centuries via three floors of cutting-edge interactive galleries and audiovisual installations.

Museu das Minas e do Metal MUSEUM
(MM Gerdau; 3516-7200; www.mmgerdau.org.br; Praça da Liberdade s/n; noon-6pm Tue-Sun, to 10pm Thu) FREE Opened in 2010, the Museu das Minas e do Metal traces the economic, cultural and social history of mining in Minas Gerais, with multiple floors of mineral exhibits and some interesting interactive displays.

Parque Municipal PARK
(Av Afonso Pena) One of Beagá's most appealing spots, this enormous sea of tropical greenery with artificial lakes and winding pathways is just 10 minutes southeast of the bus station. It's especially fun on Sunday, when everyone's out strolling and socializing.

Museu de Artes e Ofícios MUSEUM
(3248-8600; www.mao.com.br; Praça Rui Barbosa 600; adult/child R$5/2.50, free Sat & 5-9pm Wed & Thu; noon-7pm Tue & Fri, noon-9pm Wed & Thu, 11am-5pm Sat & Sun) Housed in Belo's historic train station, this museum displays a wide-ranging collection of objects used in the daily lives of *mineiros* past and present. There are interpretive cards in English adjacent to each exhibit.

DON'T MISS

FIVE ESSENTIAL BELO HORIZONTE EXPERIENCES

For a quintessential taste of Belo Horizonte, seek out at least one or two of these during your visit.

- Stroll through the cheerful chaos of market stalls and restaurants at Mercado Central (p173).
- Spend a Sunday morning at the open-air 'Hippie Fair', Feira de Arte e Artesanato (p173).
- Explore the 21 art galleries and magnificent grounds at Inhotim (p175).
- Take a stadium tour and visit the football museum at Mineirão (p168).
- Attend a performance or stop in for an evening drink at Centro Cultural Banco do Brasil (p167).

Savassi, Lourdes & South

Museu Histórico Abílio Barreto MUSEUM

(☎3277-8573; www.pbh.gov.br/cultura/mhab; Av Prudente de Morais 202, Cidade Jardim; ⏲10am-5pm Tue-Sun, to 9pm Wed & Thu) FREE The centerpiece of this museum, southwest of Savassi, is a renovated colonial farmhouse, the solitary remnant of Curral del Rey, the rural village destroyed in the 1890s to make room for Belo. The adjacent building features rotating exhibits focused on the culture of Belo Horizonte.

Pampulha

★**Mineirão & Museu Brasileiro de Futebol** STADIUM, MUSEUM

(☎3499-4300; www.minasarena.com.br/mineirao; Av Antônio Abrahão Caram 1001; adult/child stadium tour R$8/4, incl football museum R$14/7; ⏲9am-5pm Tue-Fri, to 1pm Sat & Sun) FREE An obligatory stop for football fans, Belo Horizonte's legendary 65,000-seat stadium was completely renovated for the 2014 World Cup, incorporating a brand-new football museum, esplanade and LEED-certified energy conservation enhancements. One-hour guided tours take in the locker rooms, showers, press room, stands and revamped playing field, with occasional wistful comments about Brazil's heartbreaking 7-1 World Cup loss to Germany here. Combined tickets include a self-guided museum visit, with exhibits covering the stadium's construction, famous games and players, and football history.

The stadium and museum are 10km north of Centro in Pampulha; take bus 5106 (R$3.40, 30 minutes) from Praça da LIberdade.

★**Igreja de São Francisco de Assis** CHURCH

(☎3427-1644; Av Otacílio Negrão de Lima s/n; admission R$2; ⏲8am-5pm Tue-Sat, 9am-2pm Sun) On the banks of Pampulha's artificial lake, Niemayer's striking modernist church is an architectural delight. Inside, the tiles and paintings by Portinari are equally striking.

Museu de Arte da Pampulha MUSEUM

(☎3277-7946; www.facebook.com/map.fmc; Av Otacílio Negrão de Lima 16585; ⏲9am-7pm Tue-Sun) FREE This art museum, with its cute garden designed by landscape architect Roberto Burle Marx, originally served as a casino and shows the obvious modernist influence of Le Corbusier.

Casa do Baile MUSEUM

(☎3277-7443; www.facebook.com/casadobaile.bh; Av Otacílio Negrão de Lima 751; ⏲9am-6pm Tue-Sun) FREE This former dance hall now holds all types of temporary art exhibits. Its lovely on-site cafe is a great place to take a break.

Sleeping

The World Cup in 2014 ushered in a glut of new hotels and hostels, offering travelers greater choice and more competitive prices. Large chain hotels, especially those aimed at business travelers, dominate the scene. Most hotels drop their rates significantly on weekends.

Praça da Liberdade & North

Samba Rooms Hostel HOSTEL $

(☎3267-0740; www.sambaroomshostel.com.br; Av Bias Fortes 368; dm R$35-55, s/d R$100/150, s/d without bath R$90/140; @📶) Within easy walking distance of Praça da Liberdade, Mercado Central and the airport bus stop, this friendly hostel in a historic building has five- to nine-bed dorms and pleasant common spaces including a spacious parquet-floored living room, a well-equipped guest kitchen and a cluster of open-air terraces.

Downsides are the street noise and the rather musty private rooms out back.

Royal Savassi Hotel HOTEL $$
(2138-0000; www.royalsavassi.com.br; Alagoas 699; r R$170-400;) Well-positioned just east of Praça da Liberdade, this business-oriented hotel offers good online deals year-round, especially on weekends, when prices can get slashed nearly in half. Amenities include plush beds, big flat-screen TVs, minibars, a rooftop Jacuzzi and the Amadeus restaurant, the sumptuous lunch buffet downstairs of which is complemented by one of Minas Gerais' best-stocked wine cellars.

Hotel Ibis HOTEL $$
(2111-1500; www.ibis.com.br; João Pinheiro 602; r R$145-215;) Midway between downtown and Savassi, and just steps from leafy Praça da Liberdade, this ultraconvenient chain hotel has comfortable if predictable rooms in an ugly high-rise behind a pretty 1930s town house. The optional breakfast (R$17) and parking (R$17) cost extra.

Othon Palace HOTEL $$
(2126-0000; www.othon.com.br; Av Afonso Pena 1050; r R$268-360;) The four-star Othon's many advantages include a great downtown location, multilingual staff, spacious rooms and spectacular views from the upper floors across the Parque Municipal. Don't miss the rooftop bar and pool, one of the best in the city, and feel free to bargain – suites are sometimes offered for the price of a standard room.

Savassi, Lourdes & South

★**Hostel Savassi** HOSTEL $
(3243-4771; www.hostelsavassi.com.br; Antônio de Albuquerque 626; dm R$45-50;) Opened for the World Cup in 2014, this hostel enjoys a dream location on a pedestrianized street in the heart of Savassi. The trio of six- to 12-person dorms offers individual reading lights and power outlets for every bed, while the bright upstairs guest kitchen and artistically decorated lounge/TV area invite travelers to stick around and mingle.

Adrena Sport Hostel HOSTEL $
(3657-8870; www.adrenasporthostel.com.br; Av Getúlio Vargas 1635; dm R$55, with HI card R$47, d with shared/private bathroom R$120/140;) This new HI-affiliated hostel in a 1950s Savassi town house is the brainchild of Pedro, who was born and raised in Belo Horizonte and owns the adventure-sports store downstairs. Six- to 10-bed sport-themed dorms with paragliding, skateboard and climbing-wall decor are complemented by a comfy living room and a back area where guests can linger over billiards and beer. An orderly, homey vibe prevails throughout.

Hotel Promenade Toscanini HOTEL $$
(3064-2200; www.promenade.com.br; Arturo Toscanini 61; s R$203-279, d R$226-310) Location is the main draw at this brand-new hotel with conservative cookie-cutter rooms at the southern edge of Savassi. Other perks include a weight room, wet and dry saunas, and discounts at the attached spa.

Pampulha

Pousada Sossego da Pampulha POUSADA $$
(3439-3250; www.sossegodapampulha.com.br; Av José Dias Bicalho 1258; s/d from R$188/218;) A stone's throw from Pampulha's lakeshore and the Mineirão football stadium, this pousada (guesthouse) is friendly, clean, well run and convenient for people arriving from the north. Amenities include a small pool and rooftop terrace with views of Belo Horizonte and the mountains. From Pampulha airport, 2km away, a taxi costs R$12.

Eating

Belo Horizonte is teeming with good food for every budget. The area between Praça Sete and Praça da Liberdade is best for cheap eats, with countless *lanchonetes* (snack bars), self-serve *por-kilo* restaurants and fast-food places. Further south, the Savassi and Lourdes neighborhoods constitute the epicenter of the city's fine-dining scene.

The lion's share of the city's non-*mineira* restaurants specialize in Italian food, although you can also find a world of other flavors if you look around.

Praça da Liberdade & North

Casa Cheia MINEIRA $
(3274-9585; www.restaurantecasacheia.com.br; Shop 167, Mercado Central; daily specials R$25-29; 11am-11:30pm Mon-Sat, to 5pm Sun) People line up by the dozen for a table at this long-established Mercado Central eatery, the name of which means 'full house'. A bevy of women prepare traditional favorites on a giant stove, including *pratos do dia* (low-priced daily specials) such as the not-to-be-missed Saturday *feijoada* (Brazil's

DON'T MISS

COMIDA MINEIRA: MINAS' FABULOUS FOOD

Ask any Brazilian what they like most about Minas Gerais, and they'll be sure to mention the food. Eating in Minas is an absolute treat. Wherever you go, you'll see signs advertising *comida mineira* – the hearty, high-calorie and extremely flavorful local cuisine, traditionally cooked on a *fogão a lenha* (wood stove) and revolving heavily around pork, sausage, beans, rice and kale.

Don't miss these specialties, which you'll see throughout the state:

feijão tropeiro – beans mixed with toasted manioc flour, crunchy pork rind, sausage, eggs, kale, garlic and onions

goiabada – sweet guava paste (like thick guava jelly) eaten as a dessert; often served together with Minas cheese under the romantic name *Romeo e Julieta*

queijo Minas – the traditional cow's milk cheese of Minas Gerais

tutu à mineira – a thick puree of mashed beans with garlic and onions, usually served alongside pork loin, crunchy pork rind, kale and/or rice

pão de queijo – chewy, cheesy and best enjoyed hot from the oven, Minas' famous cheese bread is made with tapioca flour, which accounts for its delightful consistency

Minas is also legendary for its *cachaça* (sugarcane alcohol) – don't leave the state without sampling it!

classic bean-and-meat stew). A new branch in **Savassi** (☎3234-6921; Cláudio Manoel 784; daily specials R$25-29; ⏰11am-11:30pm Mon-Sat, to 5pm Sun) offers the same menu and prices.

Cantina do Lucas MINEIRA, ITALIAN **$$**
(☎3226-7153; www.cantinadolucas.com.br; Av Augusto de Lima 233; mains R$21-64; ⏰11:30am-2am Mon-Thu, to 3am Fri & Sat, to 1am Sun) Tucked off a busy downtown street on the ground floor of the Maletta building, this beloved local institution has been feeding *belorizontinos* into the wee hours for over 50 years. Vest-and-tie-clad waiters navigate through a landscape of checked tablecloths and wood paneling, hefting trays of *mineira* food and pasta. Especially popular after the Sunday hippie fair in nearby Parque Municipal.

Savassi, Lourdes & South

San Ro ASIAN, VEGETARIAN **$**
(☎3264-9236; Professor Moraes 651; per kg R$53.90; ⏰11:30am-3pm Mon-Fri, to 3:30pm Sat & Sun; 🌿) If you're not a carnivore, or just need a break from Minas' meat-heavy repertoire, make a beeline for the buffet at this popular Asian-vegetarian, per-kilo place.

Bar do Lopes MINEIRA **$**
(☎3337-7995; www.facebook.com/bardolopes; Antônio Aleixo 260; lunch specials R$20, mains R$22-38; ⏰11:30am-3pm Mon, to midnight Tue-Sat, to 5pm Sun) With sidewalk seating under trees and awnings in the heart of Lourdes, this venerable corner bar is beloved for its filling, low-cost weekday *pratos executivos* (meat or fish with your choice of three accompaniments: rice, beans, potatoes and/or steamed veggies).

Amadeus BUFFET, SUSHI **$$**
(☎3261-4292; Alagoas 699; per kg lunch/dinner R$45.90/74.90; ⏰11:30am-3pm & 6pm-12:30am Mon-Sat, noon-5pm Sun) Attached to the Royal Savassi hotel, this airy glass-walled restaurant near Praça Liberdade boasts a a sumptuous per-kilo buffet and a 2500-label wine cellar that has been voted the best in Belo Horizonte by *Wine Spectator* magazine. Lunchtime offerings include sushi, *mineira* food and a tempting array of vegetables and desserts; dinner features Italian-style antipasti, cheeses and hot dishes.

Marília Pizzeria PIZZERIA **$$**
(☎3275-2027; www.mariliapizzeria.com.br; Marília de Dirceu 226; pizzas R$39-65; ⏰6pm-1am) With three dozen varieties of pizza, late hours and a floor-to-ceiling display of backlit bottles at its fashionable bar, Marília's has a trendy, youthful vibe and is routinely voted among the best pizzerias in Belo Horizonte.

Glouton FRENCH, FUSION **$$**
(☎3292-4237; glouton.com.br; Barbara Heliodora 59; mains R$55-77; ⏰7:30pm-midnight Tue-Thu, noon-3pm & 7:30pm-1am Fri, 1-5pm & 7:30pm-1am Sat, 1-5pm Sun) This intimate brick-walled bistro with a candlelit back patio is one of Belo's top addresses for a romantic dinner.

Award-winning chef Leonardo Paixão peppers his menu with French classics such as foie gras, onion soup and profiteroles, but hits his stride with more unique fusion recipes featuring Portuguese-Brazilian ingredients like suckling pig, codfish, manioc, okra, *malagueta* peppers and hearts of palm.

Restaurante do Minas Tenis Clube BUFFET **$$**
(☎3516-1310; Rua da Bahia 2244; all-you-can-eat buffet lunch weekday/Sat/Sun R$29/48/53, mains R$35-69; ⊙11:30am-11pm Mon-Sat, to 7pm Sun) For atmosphere and price combined, it's hard to beat the midday buffet at Belo's tennis club. Gorge to your heart's content in the parquet-floored dining room or on the palm-shaded back terrace overlooking the pool and water slides. The Saturday special is *feijoada*, while Sunday's more elaborate buffet includes shrimp. À la carte dinners are also served.

Domenico ITALIAN **$$**
(☎2516-2969; www.domenicopizzeria.com.br; Rua Cláudio Manoel 583; mains R$37-64; ⊙6.30pm-midnight Mon-Thu, 6.30pm-1am Fri & Sat, 6-11pm Sun) Housed in a low-lit, high-ceilinged historic building, this trendy trattoria serves fresh pasta, salads (niçoise, shrimp-asparagus or pear-gorgonzola) and risotto (with porcini, black squid ink, or figs and prosciutto), along with three dozen different pizzas featuring homemade tomato sauce. The owner, born in Naples and raised in Milan, also fills his menu with authentic Italian desserts such as tiramisu.

Dona Lucinha II BUFFET, MINEIRA **$$**
(☎3261-5930; www.donalucinha.com.br; Sergipe 811; all-you-can-eat buffet adult/child R$60/30; ⊙noon-3pm & 7-11pm Mon-Sat, noon-5pm Sun) The sumptuous buffet here features 50 traditional *mineira* dishes daily. It's fairly touristy, and prices have climbed thanks to the owner's publication of a best-selling cookbook, but the food is still outstanding.

Baiana do Acarajé BAHIAN **$$**
(☎3264-5804; http://baianadoacaraje.com; Antônio de Albuquerque 440; acarajé R$9-26, mains for two R$80-142; ⊙6pm-midnight Tue, noon-midnight Wed-Sat, noon-10pm Sun) A little slice of Bahia just off Praça da Savassi, this bright, lively and informal bar-restaurant specializes in tasty *acarajé* (shrimp-stuffed brown bean fritters) served alongside pricier and more substantial dishes like *moqueca* (Bahian seafood stew). A popular spot for people-watching over late-afternoon beers.

Vecchio Sogno ITALIAN **$$$**
(☎3292-5251; www.vecchiosogno.com.br; Martim de Carvalho 75; mains R$59-99; ⊙noon-12:30am Mon-Thu, noon-2am Fri, 6pm-2am Sat, noon-5:30pm Sun) Repeatedly voted Belo's best restaurant (not just its best Italian one), Vecchio Sogno is worth the splurge. Mains range from duck and wild rice risotto to shrimp flambéed in grappa. Reserve ahead.

A Favorita INTERNATIONAL **$$$**
(☎3337-5542; www.afavorita.com.br; Santa Catarina 1235; mains R$55-99; ⊙noon-12:30am Sun-Thu, to 2am Fri & Sat) Everything's superb at this classy, high-ceilinged restaurant in the heart of the chic Lourdes district. Specialties include grilled meat, decadent desserts and homemade pasta dishes.

Pampulha

★Xapuri MINEIRA **$$**
(☎3496-6198; www.restaurantexapuri.com.br; Mandacarú 260; mains per person R$49-70; ⊙noon-11pm Tue-Sat, to 6pm Sun) Dona Nelsa's local institution features fabulous *mineira* food served at picnic tables under a thatched roof, with hammocks close at hand for pre-meal children's entertainment or post-meal relaxation. The traditional wood stove blazes up front, while colorful desserts are attractively displayed in two long cases.

Drinking & Nightlife

Belo Horizonte is Brazil's self-proclaimed drinking capital, with thousands of *botecos* (neighborhood bars) sprinkled throughout the city. If you're visiting in mid-April to mid-May, don't miss the **Comida di Buteco festival** (www.comidadibuteco.com.br), in which dozens of places compete to see who makes the best bar food. Originating right here in 1999, it has since expanded to over a dozen other Brazilian ciites.

Late-night club- and pub-based nightlife gravitates toward Savassi, which is full of trendy dance clubs.

★Café com Letras CAFE
(☎3225-9973; www.cafecomletras.com.br; Antônio de Albuquerque 781; ⊙noon-midnight Mon-Thu, to 1am Fri & Sat, 5-11pm Sun; 📶) With live jazz on Sundays, DJs Thursday through Saturday, and a bohemian buzz between sets, this bookstore-cafe is a fun place to kick back over light meals (R$22–60) and drinks, browse the shelves and enjoy the free wi-fi. Check out its new branch in the **Centro Cultural**

OFF THE BEATEN TRACK

SABARÁ

Sabará, 25km southeast of Belo Horizonte, was one of the world's wealthiest cities in the 18th century, when it produced more gold in one week than the rest of Brazil produced in a year. Now just a workaday suburb, it still retains many churches, mansions, statues, fountains and sacred art from those gold-mining glory days.

All colonial attractions are signposted from central Praça Santa Rita. Most charge small admission fees, and all are closed Mondays. Highlights include the following:

Matriz de NS de Conceição (Praça Getúlio Vargas; 9am-noon & 2-5pm Tue-Sun) This triple-naved church was finished in 1720 and is a fascinating blend of Asian and Portuguese baroque styles.

Igreja de NS do Ó (Largo NS do Ó; 9am-noon & 2-5pm Tue-Sun) Diminutive and jewel-like, decorated in gold, red and blue and dedicated to the Virgin Mary in her role as protector of pregnant women.

Igreja NS do Carmo (Rua de Carmo; 9-11:30am Tue-Sun) Aleijadinho's work predominates here, especially in the faces of São Simão and São João da Cruz.

O Teatro Imperial (Rua Dom Pedro II; 8am-noon & 1-5pm Tue-Sun) Sabará's elegant 1770 opera house.

Museu do Ouro (3671-1848; Rua da Intendência; admission US$1; noon-5pm Tue-Sun) A 1730s gold foundry filled with historical artifacts.

Igreja NS do Rosário dos Pretos (Praça Melo Viana; 8-11am & 1-5pm) Started and financed by slaves, this half-finished church now stands as a memorial to slavery's abolition.

Buses to Sabará (R$3.85 to R$5.10, 40 minutes) run every 10 to 15 minutes from a street corner on the south side of Belo's main bus station. Return buses leave from the bus stop on Av Victor Fantini in Sabará.

Banco do Brasil (Centro Cultural Banco do Brasil, lower level; 10am-9pm). It also sponsors jazz performances at the annual **Savassi Festival** (www.savassifestival.com.br; mid-Sep).

Jângal BAR
(http://jangalbh.com; Rua Outono 523; 6pm-1am Tue-Fri, 2pm-1:30am Sat, 2-10pm Sun) With an ever-evolving lineup of three dozen creative mixed drinks and nightly musical offerings that run the gamut from samba to electronica, this relaxed garden bar has become a local fixture since opening in 2013.

Arcangelo BAR
(2nd fl, Ed Maletta, Rua da Bahia 1148; 6pm-midnight Tue-Sat) The best bar of many inside the indie-intellectual Maletta building in Centro, with great views from its consistently packed 2nd-floor open-air balcony. Voted Beagá's best happy hour.

CCCP PUB
(Cult Club Cine Pub; www.cultclubcinepub.com.br; Levindo Lopes 358; 6pm-3am Mon-Fri, to 4am Sat) With a dozen-plus Brazilian and international beers on tap, plus occasional movies and live music on Tuesday, Thursday, Friday and Saturday nights, this pub is a Savassi favorite.

Choperia Albanos PUB
(www.albanos.com.br; Pium-i 611, Sion; 6pm-1am Mon-Fri, noon-1am Sat, noon-8pm Sun) This beloved, award-winning brewpub with its spacious tile-floored interior serves some of Beagá's best beer and is always buzzing at happy hour. There's a second branch in **Lourdes** (Rio de Janeiro 2076; 6pm-1am Mon-Fri, noon-1am Sat, noon-8pm Sun).

Bar Tizé BAR
(3337-4374; www.bartize.com.br; Curitiba 2205, Lourdes; 5pm-12:30am Mon-Fri, noon-12:30am Sat & Sun) Since 1967, this strategically located corner bar with tables spilling onto a long island of sidewalk has been drawing crowds with ice-cold buckets of beer and award-winning *comida di buteco*.

☆ Entertainment

Belo Horizonte is a cosmopolitan town with a vibrant arts scene and plenty of nightlife. Online entertainment listings are available at www.soubh.com.br, guiabh.com.br and www.divirta-se.uai.com.br. Weekly entertainment calendars can also be found in the 'Divirta-Se' section of the *Estado de Minas* newspaper.

Theater

Palácio das Artes PERFORMING ARTS

(☎3236-7400; http://fcs.mg.gov.br/espacos-culturais/palacio-das-artes; Av Afonso Pena 1537) Near the southern end of Parque Municipal, this arts complex with multiple performance spaces and galleries is the hub of Belo's theater, dance and music-concert scene. Current shows are listed in the Art and Culture section of the free guide put out by Belotur, the municipal tourist bureau.

Live Music

Bar do Museu Clube da Esquina LIVE MUSIC

(☎2512-5050; www.bardomuseuclubedaesquina.com.br; Paraisópolis 738; ⏰7pm-1am Mon-Sat) Locals pack into this intimate Santa Tereza bar for live performances celebrating the legacy of the Clube da Esquina, Belo Horizonte's groundbreaking musical movement of the 1960s and 1970s. Family members and musical associates of the Clube's revered cofounders make regular appearances.

O Alambique LIVE MUSIC

(☎3296-7188; http://alambique.com.br; Av Raja Gabaglia 3200; ⏰10:30pm-4am Tue & Thu-Sat, 7pm-midnight Sun) With a capacity of 1200, this venerable nightspot 6km south of the center has panoramic city views, five themed bars, 70 different *cachaça*-based drinks, and enough samba, *sertanejo* and *forró* (popular music from the Northeast) to keep things lively all night long.

A Obra LIVE MUSIC

(www.aobra.com.br; Rio Grande do Norte 1168; ⏰10pm-late Wed-Sat) One of Savassi's best dance clubs, A Obra hosts live rock and indie shows.

A Autêntica LIVE MUSIC

(www.aautentica.com.br; Rua Alagoas 1172; ⏰9pm-late Tue-Sat) This up-and-coming Savassi club hosts an eclectic mix of live music, from samba to blues to jazz to alternative rock; live shows start around 10:30 on Tuesday, Thursday, Friday and Saturday nights.

Sports

Three football teams call Belo Horizonte home: América, Atlético Mineiro and Cruzeiro. The latter two teams play regularly in the city's legendary 65,000-seat stadium, Mineirão; its fame attained international proportions when it was selected as a venue for the 2014 FIFA World Cup and 2016 summer Olympics. Even if you don't get a chance to see a match, it's well worth touring the stadium and its recently opened football museum (p168).

Shopping

Don't leave Belo Horizonte without visiting its wonderful street markets. Locals also favor the many high-rise shopping centers downtown and Savassi's high-end boutiques.

★ Feira de Arte e Artesanato MARKET

(Feira Hippie; www.feirahippiebh.com; Av Afonso Pena; ⏰7am-2pm Sun) A Belo Horizonte classic, this Sunday street fair attracts massive crowds searching for clothing, jewelry, street food and more. Located between Rua da Bahia and Rua das Guajajaras, and bordered by the soothing greenery of the Parque Municipal, it's a fun place to wander and enjoy a slice of city life, even if you're not in a shopping mood.

★ Mercado Central MARKET

(cnr Curitiba & Rua dos Goitacazes; ⏰7am-6pm Mon-Sat, to 1pm Sun) You'll find everything from parrots to peppers to perfume at this indoor market, a true Belo Horizonte institution. Sample the delicious local produce, socialize with locals at one of the bars or just roam the aisles aimlessly.

Orientation

Central Belo Horizonte has a grid of large *avenidas* (avenues), with another smaller grid superimposed at a 45-degree angle. The boundaries of the original planned city are defined by the ring road called Av do Contorno. It's a hilly town, so trips are sometimes less straightforward than they appear on the map.

The main drag is Av Afonso Pena, which runs diagonally from northwest to southeast, starting at the bus station at the northern end of downtown and running past leafy green Parque Municipal. From northwest to southeast, there are three pivotal *praças* (squares): bustling Praça Sete, just southeast of the bus station; serene Praça da Liberdade, heart of the government-turned-museum district; and trendy Praça da Savassi, the center of Belo nightlife and cafe society.

Outside of downtown, Pampulha (8km north) is the neighborhood with most cultural attractions and tourist amenities.

Information

EMERGENCY

Ambulance (☎192)

Fire department (☎193)

Police (☎190) For nonurgent matters, call ☎3330-5200.

MONEY

Banks with ATMs are clustered downtown between Praça Sete and Parque Municipal, and along Av do Contorno in Savassi.

Banco do Brasil (Av do Contorno 5722)
Bradesco (Rua da Bahia 951)

TOURIST INFORMATION

Belo Horizonte's municipal tourist bureau, **Belotur** (belotur@pbh.gov.br), is among the best in Brazil. Its numerous offices distribute the free *Guia Turístico*, an exceptionally helpful trilingual guide (English, Spanish, Portuguese) cataloging the city's restaurants, museums, cultural events and other tourist attractions, with instructions on how to get around using local buses. The *Guia Turístico* also includes a city map, airline and bus-company information, and everything else you ever wanted to know about Belo.

Alô Turismo (☎ from Belo Horizonte 156, from elsewhere 3429-0405; ⏲ 24h) Belotur's tourist-inquiry hotline.

Belotur Confins Airport (☎ 3689-2557; ⏲ 8am-10pm Mon-Fri, to 5pm Sat & Sun) At the main airport exit, outside baggage claim.

Belotur Mercado Central (☎ 3277-4691; ⏲ 9am-5:20pm Mon, 8am-4:20pm Tue, 8am-5:20pm Wed-Sat, 8am-1pm Sun) On the ground floor of Belo's famous indoor market.

Belotur Mercado das Flores (☎ 3277-7666; Av Afonso Pena 1055; ⏲ 9am-6pm Mon-Fri, 8am-3pm Sat & Sun) At the flower market on the western edge of Parque Municipal.

Belotur Pampulha Airport (☎ 3246-8015; ⏲ 8am-5pm Mon-Fri, 8am-4pm Sat, 1-5pm Sun)

Belotur Rodoviária (☎ 3277-6907; Praça Rio Branco; ⏲ 8am-6pm Mon-Fri, to 5pm Sat & Sun) Inside the bus station.

Getting There & Around

AIR

Belo Horizonte has two airports. International flights use the recently renovated and expanded **Aeroporto Confins**, 40km north of the city. The **Aeroporto da Pampulha**, 10km north of the city center, is more conveniently located but only has domestic flights.

Flights from the two airports serve most locations in Brazil. A full list of airline offices, with phone numbers, appears in the front of the free Belotur guide.

AIRPORT BUSES

Expresso Unir (☎ 3689-2415; www.conexaoaeroporto.com.br) runs frequent, comfortable Conexão Aeroporto buses between downtown and Belo's two airports (Pampulha and Confins). The *convencional* bus (R$10.70 to either airport) leaves Belo's bus station every 15 to 45 minutes between 3:45am and 10:45pm (slightly less frequently on weekends). Travel time is approximately 30 minutes to Pampulha airport, 70 minutes to Confins. Buses return from Confins between 5:15am and 12:15am.

Unir also runs an *executivo* bus to Confins airport (R$23.70, 50 minutes) from the **Terminal Álvares Cabral** (☎ 3224-1002; Alvares Cabral 387), just southwest of Parque Municipal, every 25 to 40 minutes between 3:15am and 9:30pm, returning from Confins between 5:40am and 12:30am. See Unir's website for complete schedules.

REGIONAL BUSES

Belo's long-distance **bus station** (☎ 3271-3000; Praça Rio Branco 100) is near the northern end of downtown. The free Belotur guide lists bus company phone numbers in the front pages.

LOCAL BUSES

Belo Horizonte's local buses, operated by **BHTrans** (☎ 3429-0405; www.bhtrans.pbh.gov.br), are color-coded. Blue buses (R$3.40) go up and down main avenues in the city center, green express buses (R$3.40) only stop at select points, red-and-beige buses (R$3.40 and up, depending on distance) connect outlying suburbs to downtown, and yellow buses (R$2.45) have circular routes through the city.

BUSES FROM BELO HORIZONTE

DESTINATION	COST (R$)	TIME (HR)	COMPANY
Brasília	145-164	11-12	União (www.expressouniao.com.br), Kaissara (www.kaissara.com.br)
Diamantina	88	5	Pássaro Verde (www.passaroverde.com.br)
Ouro Preto	30	2	Pássaro Verde (www.passaroverde.com.br)
Rio de Janeiro	93-159	7	Útil (www.util.com.br), Cometa (www.viacaocometa.com.br)
Salvador	259	23	Gontijo (www.gontijo.com.br)
São João del Rei	55	3½	Sandra (www.viacaosandra.com.br)
São Paulo	116-202	8¼	Cometa (www.viacaocometa.com.br)
Vitória	103-113	8¾	São Geraldo (www.saogeraldo.com.br), Kaissara (www.kaissara.com.br)

DON'T MISS

THE WORLD-CLASS MUSEUM IN BELO'S BACK YARD

Instituto de Arte Contemporânea Inhotim (☎3571-9700; www.inhotim.org.br; Rua B, Inhotim, Brumadinho; adult/student Tue & Thu R$25/12.50, Fri-Sun R$40/20, free Wed; ⊙9:30am-4:30pm Tue-Fri, to 5:30pm Sat & Sun) is the world's largest open-air contemporary-art museum, and greater Belo Horizonte's standout attraction. The sprawling complex of gardens dotted with 21 world-class modern-art galleries and numerous outdoor sculptures lies 50km west of the city, near the town of Brumadinho. Much of the international artwork on view is monumental in size, with galleries custom-built to display it. The constantly expanding gardens, opened to the public in 2006, boast over 4000 different species of plant (including one of the world's most extensive collections of palm trees) and lakes with swans.

You can wander at will, or attend daily scheduled programs led by guides trained in visual arts and natural science. Ten on-site eateries serve everything from hot dogs to gourmet international fare. Wednesday's a great day to visit, as the museum is free; weekends can get crowded, but offer a wider range of guided tours.

From Tuesday through Sunday **Saritur** (☎3479-4300; www.saritur.com.br) runs direct buses (R$53.40 round-trip, 1½ hours each way) from Belo Horizonte to Inhotim at 8:15am, returning at 4:30pm weekdays, 5:30pm Saturday and Sunday.

The city's newest public transport innovation, introduced for the 2014 FIFA World Cup, is the fleet of brand-new greenish-yellow buses painted with the MOVE logo. Designed to cut travel times in half, MOVE buses enjoy the use of exclusive new bus lanes and loading platforms and offer special facilities for carrying bicycles, but still cost the same as regular city buses (R$3.40). Downtown corridors for MOVE buses run along Av Paraná and Av Santos Dumont, with the main northbound line to Pampulha traveling along Av Antônio Carlos and Av Dom Pedro I.

TRAIN

Companhia Vale do Rio Doce (☎0800-285-7000; www.vale.com/brasil/EN/business/logistics/railways/trem-passageiros;) operates a daily train to Vitória in Espírito Santo state (*econômica/executiva* class R$62/95), departing at 7:30am from Belo Horizonte's **train station** (Praça da Estação), just north of Parque Municipal, and arriving at Cariacica/Pedro Nolasco train station on Vitória's western outskirts at 8:30pm. The return run leaves Vitória at 7am, reaching Belo Horizonte at 8:10pm.

Ouro Preto

☎0XX31 / POP 70,000 / ELEV 1179M

Of all the exquisite colonial towns scattered around Minas Gerais, Ouro Preto is the jewel in the crown. Significant historically as a center of gold mining and government, and as the stage for Brazil's first independence movement, the city remains vital in modern times as a center for education and the arts, and is one of Brazil's most visited tourist destinations.

Built at the feet of the Serra do Espinhaço, Ouro Preto's colonial center is larger and has steeper topography than any other historical town in Minas. The narrow, crooked streets of the upper and lower towns tangle together and in places are too rough and precipitous for vehicles. Navigating the vertiginous cobblestone slopes on foot can be exhausting, but the views of 23 churches spread out across the hilly panorama are spectacular. The city is a showcase of outstanding *mineiro* art and architecture, including some of Aleijadinho's finest works.

History

Legend has it that a servant in an early expedition exploring Brazil's interior pocketed a few grains of an odd black metal he found while drinking from a river near the current site of Ouro Preto. It turned out to be gold, and the local deposits were soon discovered to be the largest in the New World.

Gold fever spread fast. In 1711 Vila Rica de Ouro Preto was founded, and in 1721 it became the capital of Minas Gerais. Gold bought the services of baroque artisans, who turned the city into an architectural gem. At the height of the gold boom in the mid-18th century, there were 110,000 people (mainly slaves) in Ouro Preto, compared with 50,000 in New York and about 20,000 in Rio de Janeiro.

In theory, all gold was brought to *casas de intendências* (weighing stations), and a *quinto do ouro* (royal fifth) was set aside for the Portuguese crown. The greed of the Portuguese led to sedition, as the miners found it

Ouro Preto

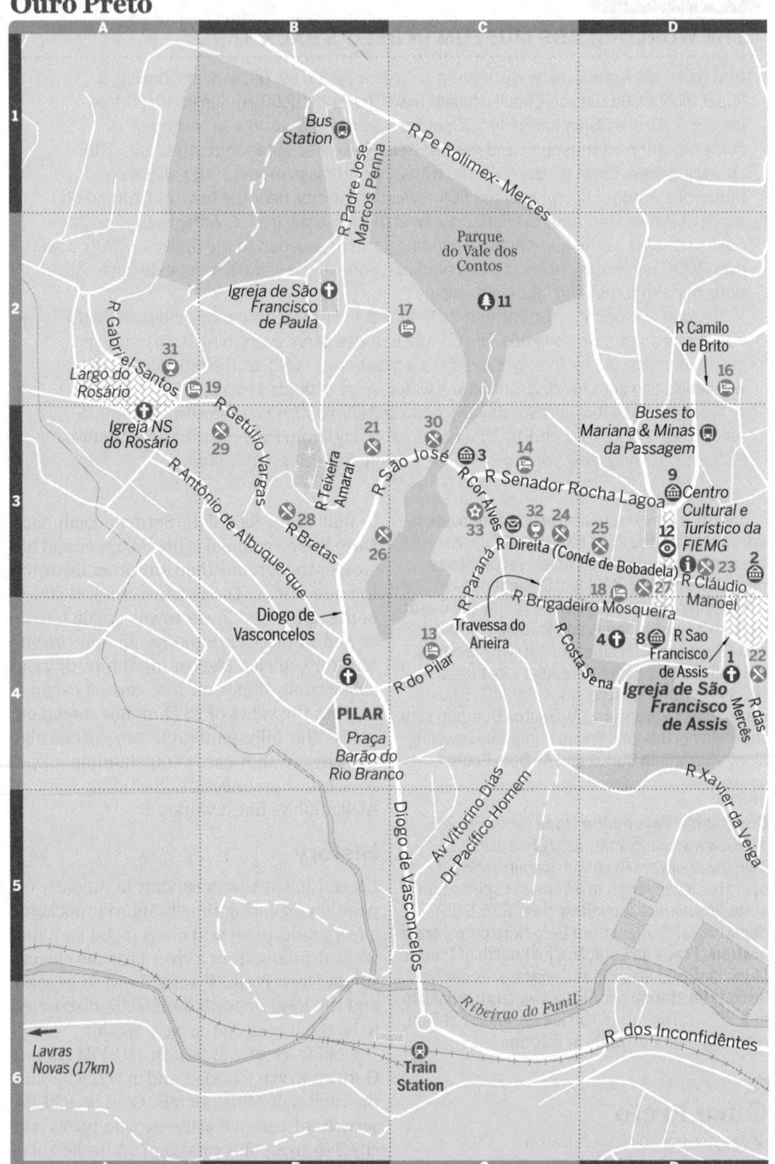

increasingly difficult to pay ever-larger gold taxes. In 1789 poets Claudio da Costa, Tomás Antônio Gonzaga, Joaquim José da Silva Xavier (nicknamed Tiradentes, meaning 'Tooth Puller,' for his dentistry skills) and others, full of French Revolutionary philosophies, hatched an uprising against Portuguese colonization known as the Inconfidência Mineira. The rebellion was crushed in its early stages by agents of the crown. Gonzaga was exiled to Mozambique and Costa did time in prison. Tiradentes was jailed for three years, then drawn and quartered in Rio de Janeiro. His head was paraded around Ouro Preto,

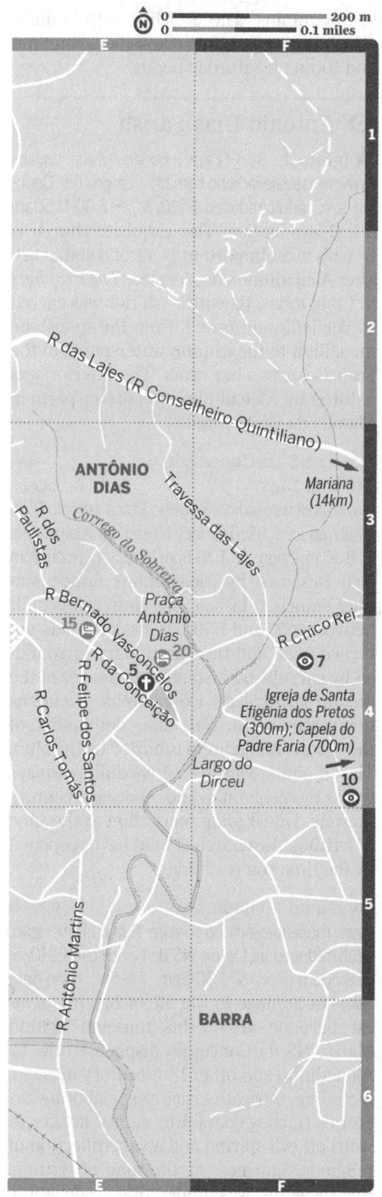

Ouro Preto

Top Sights

1 Igreja de São Francisco de Assis D4

Sights

2 Casa de Tomás Antônio Gonzaga D3
3 Casa dos Contos C3
4 Igreja NS do Carmo D4
5 Matriz NS da Conceição de Antônio Dias E4
6 Matriz NS do Pilar B4
7 Mina do Chico-Rei F4
8 Museu da Inconfidência D4
9 Museu de Ciência e Técnica da Escola de Minas D3
Museu do Aleijadinho .... (see 5)
Museu do Oratório .... (see 4)
10 Oratório Vira-Saia F4
11 Parque do Vale dos Contos C2
12 Praça Tiradentes D3

Sleeping

13 Goiabada com Queijo C4
14 Grande Hotel Ouro Preto C3
15 Pousada dos Meninos E4
16 Pousada Nello Nuno D2
17 Pousada São Francisco C2
18 Pouso do Chico Rei D3
19 Solar do Rosario A2
20 Trilhas de Minas Hostel E4

Eating

21 Adega Ouro Preto B3
22 Bené da Flauta D4
23 Café e Livraria Cultural D3
24 Café Geraes & Escadabaixo C3
25 Casa do Ouvidor D3
26 Chafariz B3
27 Chocolates Ouro Preto D3
28 Chocolates Ouro Preto B3
29 Hannah B3
30 O Passo C3

Drinking & Nightlife

31 Barroco e Barraco A2
32 Cervejaria Porão C3

Entertainment

33 Cine Vila Rica C3

his house demolished and its grounds salted to ensure that nothing would grow there.

In 1897 the state capital was shifted from Ouro Preto to Belo Horizonte, decisively preserving the city's colonial flavor. In 1980 Ouro Preto was enshrined as Brazil's first Unesco World Heritage site.

Sights

There are virtually no 20th-century buildings to defile this stunning colonial town. As you wander, watch for informative historical plaques that have been placed on 150 houses around town to heighten visitors' curiosity and expand their knowledge of the city's treasures – part of a citywide cultural initiative known as Museu Aberto/Cidade Viva.

Ouro Preto is divided into parishes, each with its own Matriz (mother church). If you stand in Praça Tiradentes facing the Museu da Inconfidência, the parish of Pilar is to the right (west), the parishes of Antônio Dias and Santa Efigênia to the left (east).

For a panoramic view of the churches and rooftops, head northeast out of Praça Tiradentes and walk for five minutes along Conselheiro Quintiliano toward Mariana.

Praça Tiradentes & Around

Praça Tiradentes is the heart of town, surrounded by some of Ouro Preto's finest museums and churches.

Museu da Inconfidência MUSEUM
(www.museudainconfidencia.gov.br; Praça Tiradentes 139; adult/child R$10/5; ⏲10am-5:20pm Tue-Sun) This historical museum is housed in Ouro Preto's old municipal headquarters and jail, an attractive building built between 1784 and 1854 on the south side of Praça Tiradentes. It contains the tomb of Tiradentes, documents of the Inconfidência Mineira, torture instruments and important works by Manuel da Costa Ataíde and Aleijadinho (p186).

Museu do Oratório MUSEUM
(www.museudooratorio.org.br; Adro da Igreja do Carmo 28; adult/reduced R$5/2.50; ⏲9:30am-5:30pm) This museum features a fabulous collection of hand-carved *oratórios* (miniature home altars and portable devotional shrines) dating back to the 17th century. It's housed in the Casa do Noviciado, a triple-level colonial building where Aleijadinho is said to have lived while working on the adjacent Igreja NS do Carmo.

Igreja NS do Carmo CHURCH
(Brigadeiro Mosqueira; admission R$3; ⏲8:30-11:10am & 1-5pm Tue-Sat, 10am-3pm Sun) Built between 1766 and 1772, this lovely church was a group effort by the area's most important artists. It features a facade and two side altars by Aleijadinho.

Museu de Ciência e Técnica da Escola de Minas MUSEUM
(Praça Tiradentes; adult/reduced R$6/3; ⏲noon-5pm Tue-Sun) In the old governor's palace above Praça Tiradentes, this museum features dazzling gemstones from around the world. Even if you skip the museum itself, it's worth climbing to its front terrace for spectacular views of Praça Tiradentes backed by mountains. The attached astronomical observatory offers free shows between 8pm and 10pm on Saturday nights.

Antônio Dias Parish

★ **Igreja de São Francisco de Assis** CHURCH
(www.museualeijadinho.com.br; Largo de Coimbra s/n; adult/reduced R$10/5; ⏲8:30-11:50am & 1:30-5pm Tue-Sun) This exquisite church is Brazil's most important piece of colonial art, after Aleijadinho's masterpiece *The Prophets* in Congonhas. Its entire exterior was carved by Aleijadinho himself, from the soapstone medallion to the cannon waterspouts to the Franciscan two-bar cross. The interior was painted by Aleijadinho's long-term partner, Manuel da Costa Ataíde.

Matriz NS da Conceição de Antônio Dias CHURCH
(www.museualeijadinho.com.br; Praça Antônio Dias; adult/reduced R$10/5 incl Museu do Aleijadinho; ⏲8:30am-noon & 1:30-5pm Tue-Sat, noon-5pm Sun) Designed by Aleijadinho's father, Manuel Francisco Lisboa, this church was built between 1727 and 1770. The eagle with downturned head and the Virgin Mary surrounded by cherubs both stand atop images of the moon, Portuguese iconographic elements that symbolize the Christians' domination of the Moors. Aleijadinho is buried by the altar. The adjoining Museu do Aleijadinho displays works by Aleijadinho and other 18th-century masters. Undergoing renovation at the time of writing, the church should have reopened by the time you read this.

Museu do Aleijadinho MUSEUM
(www.museualeijadinho.com.br; Rua da Conceição; adult/reduced incl Igreja NS da Conceição R$10/5; ⏲8:30am-noon & 1:30-5pm Tue-Sat, noon-5pm Sun) An homage to the life of Brazil's greatest baroque artist, this museum behind Matriz NS da Conceição displays works by Aleijadinho and other 18th-century masters, including intricate crucifixes, elaborate oratories (niches containing saints' images to ward off evil spirits) and a vast collection of religious figurines. At the time of writing, the museum was undergoing renovation, with its most important pieces temporarily moved to the Igreja de São Francisco.

Mina do Chico-Rei MINE
(☎3552-2866; Dom Silvério 108; admission R$15; ⏲8am-5pm) Near Matriz NS da Conceição de Antônio Dias is the abandoned mine of Chico-Rei (p181). There's little to see as you

stoop through the low passageways, but it's the perfect place to meditate on the fascinating story of this famous king-turned-slave-turned-king-again.

Casa de Tomás Antônio Gonzaga HISTORIC BUILDING
(Cláudio Manoel 61) Marked with a plaque, this 18th-century building is the spot where Gonzaga and the other Inconfidentes conspired to put an end to Portuguese rule in Brazil.

Pilar Parish

Matriz NS do Pilar CHURCH
(Praça Monsenhor Castilho Barbosa; adult/reduced R$10/5; 9-10:45am & noon-4:45pm Tue-Sun) On the southwest side of town, this is Brazil's second-most-opulent church (after Salvador's São Francisco). It has 434kg of gold and silver and is one of the country's finest showcases of artwork. Note the wild-bird chandelier holders, the scrolled church doors and the hair on Jesus (the real stuff, donated by a penitent worshipper).

Casa dos Contos MUSEUM
(São José 12; 10am-5pm Tue-Sat, to 3pm Sun) FREE This 18th-century treasury building doubled as a prison for members of the Inconfidência. The renovated mansion now houses displays on the history of gold – and money in general – in Brazil.

Parque do Vale dos Contos PARK
(www.valedoscontos.com.br; 7am-5pm) Built on the site of Ouro Preto's 18th-century botanical garden, this lovely, verdant public park snakes downhill along a creek from the bus station to the Pilar church, passing en route under the bridge adjacent to Casa dos Contos. It's a tranquil spot with pretty views, great for a break from the crowds and the cobblestones. It's occasionally closed due to heavy rains or landslides; inquire locally if you find the gate locked.

Santa Efigênia Parish

Igreja de Santa Efigênia dos Pretos CHURCH
(3551-5047; Santa Efigênia 396; adult/reduced R$5/2.50; 8:30am-4:30pm Tue-Sun) Financed by gold from Chico-Rei's mine and built by the slave community, this mid-18th-century church honors Santa Efigênia, princess of Nubia. The exterior image of NS do Rosário is by Aleijadinho. Slaves legendarily contributed to the church coffers by washing their gold-flaked hair in baptismal fonts, or smuggling gold powder under fingernails and inside tooth cavities.

Capela do Padre Faria CHURCH
(Rua da Padre Faria s/n; adult/reduced R$5/2.50; 8:30am-4:30pm Tue-Sun) Built between 1701 and 1704 and named after one of the original *bandeirantes* (roaming adventurers who spent the 17th and 18th centuries exploring Brazil's interior), Ouro Preto's oldest chapel sits at the far eastern edge of town, behind a triple-branched papal cross (1756) representing the pope's temporal, spiritual and material powers. Because of poor documentation, the artists here are anonymous.

Oratório Vira-Saia SHRINE
(cnr Barão do Ouro Branco & Ladeira de Santa Efigênia) This is the most famous of several *oratórios* built on street corners around town by early-18th-century Ouro Preto residents to keep evil spirits at bay. Others can be found on Rua dos Paulistas and Antônio Dias.

Tours

AGTOP WALKING TOUR
(3551-2655; 4hr tour up to 10 people in Portuguese R$140, in English, French or Spanish R$220) Official guided city tours are available at the tourist office (p183). Note that prices quoted here are from the official table; you may be able to negotiate better rates with individual guides. The office can also help organize treks and horseback rides into the surrounding hills.

Festivals & Events

Semana Santa (Holy Week; March/April) processions in Ouro Preto are quite a spectacle (p180).

There are also festivities associated with Congado, the local expression of Afro-Christian syncretism (similar to Candomblé in Bahia or Quimbanda in Rio). The major **Congado celebrations** are for NS do Rosário (October 23 to 25, at the Capela do Padre Faria), for the New Year and for May 13 (the anniversary of abolition).

Carnaval CULTURAL
(www.carnavalouropreto.com; Feb/Mar) Thanks in part to Ouro Preto's huge student population, Carnaval here is boisterous and fun. The town government hosts free live music on multiple stages in the historic center, while dozens of *blocos* (drumming and dancing processions) parade through

SEMANA SANTA IN OURO PRETO

Semana Santa (Holy Week) is celebrated all over Brazil, but Ouro Preto's festivities are especially dazzling. For four days the town becomes a giant stage, starting with Thursday night's ceremonial washing of feet and the deposition of Christ from a giant cross in front of Igreja de São Francisco on Good Friday.

The most memorable event is saved for the wee hours preceding Easter Sunday. Around midnight Saturday, locals begin opening bags of colored sawdust on street corners all over town, unleashing an all-night public art project in which 3km of Ouro Preto's cobblestone streets are covered with fanciful designs, a giant carpet marking the route for the following morning's Easter processions. Until the early 1960s, Ouro Preto observed the old Portuguese tradition of decorating Easter-parade routes with flowers and leaves. More recently, colored scraps of leather, sand, coffee grounds and sawdust have become the media of choice for these *tapetes coloridos* (colored carpets).

Tourists are welcome to participate in laying out the designs, but be prepared for a late night. Things really don't get going until well after midnight. Music and general merrymaking erupt unpredictably all night long, and a few stragglers stick around till dawn to put finishing touches on Praça Tiradentes, the last spot cleared of vehicle traffic. If you prefer your beauty rest, go to bed early Saturday evening, then wake up at 5am Sunday to see the magic that's unfolded while you slept. It's like awakening to a Technicolor snowfall!

The designs – some religious, some profane – change every year and only last a few short hours. Within moments of the procession's passing, the public-works crew is out in force with brooms and shovels to clean the streets, until next year.

the streets throughout the week; Balanço da Cobra and Bloco do Caixão are among the best.

Tiradentes Day CULTURAL
(Apr 21) Ouro Preto reclaims the symbolic role of state capital once a year.

CineOP FILM
(www.cineop.com.br; Jun) Annual film festival in mid-June.

Festival de Inverno CULTURAL
(www.festivaldeinverno.ufop.br; Jul) This two-week arts festival features music, dance, theater, cinema and kids' activities at various venues throughout Ouro Preto and Mariana.

Sleeping

Praça Tiradentes & Around

★**Pouso do Chico Rei** INN $$
(3551-1274; www.pousodochicorei.com.br; Brigadeiro Musqueira 90; s R$210-250, d R$240-290, tr R$310-370, q R$400-450; s/d/tr without bathroom from R$100/175/260;) Easily Ouro Preto's best midrange option, this beautifully preserved 18th-century mansion directly opposite the Carmo church is all colonial charm, with creaky wood floors and a breakfast room full of hand-painted antique cupboards. Each room is unique, and most have period furniture and fabulous views. The three least-expensive rooms share a bathroom. Well worth booking ahead.

Antônio Dias Parish

Trilhas de Minas Hostel HOSTEL $
(3551-6367; www.trilhasdeminashostel.com; Praça Antônio Dias 21; dm R$45-50, d R$120;) Boasting in-your-face views of NS de Conceição across the street, this three-room hostel has another unique perk: the owners run an adventure travel agency that offers local excursions with a strong emphasis on cultural immersion. Friendly pets, a permaculture garden out back and furniture built from reclaimed wood reflect the owner's passions for sustainability and animal rescue.

Pousada Nello Nuno POUSADA $
(3551-3375; www.pousadanellonuno.com.br; Camilo de Brito 59; s R$125-130, d R$160-200, tr R$200-273;) In a quiet location just northeast of Praça Tiradentes, this family-run pousada has clean and airy *apartamentos* (rooms with private bathroom) with lots of artwork around a cute flagstoned courtyard. French and English spoken.

Pousada dos Meninos POUSADA $$$
(3552-6212; www.pousadadosmeninos.com.br; Rua do Aleijadinho 89; d R$269-380, ste R$450, apt for 3/4/5 people R$362/483/582;)

Tucked directly behind NS da Conceição, this spiffy new pousada offers beautifully renovated rooms in an old mansion with original parquet wood floors. The spacious master suite comes with its own kitchenette, and there's also a two-room apartment sleeping up to five people. The tiled breakfast room downstairs is a cheerful spot to start the day.

Pilar Parish

Goiabada com Queijo HOSTEL $

(3552-3816; www.facebook.com/HostelGoiabadacomQueijo; Rua do Pilar 44; dm R$35-45;) Midway between Praça Tiradentes and the train station, this sweet and simple three-room hostel is a labor of love for well-traveled owner Lidiane, who makes guests feel at home with her solid command of German and English and her enthusiasm for showing off Ouro Preto's hidden treasures.

Pousada São Francisco HOSTEL, GUESTHOUSE $

(3551-3456; www.pousadasaofranciscodepaula.com.br; Padre Pena 201; dm R$40, s R$70-150, d R$100-180, tr R$200-230, q R$250;) Hidden away on a leafy hillside full of chirping birds, this hostel-like guesthouse has friendly multilingual staff and a guest kitchen. The two upstairs rooms with panoramic views are the best of the bunch. From the bus station, follow signs five minutes downhill, turning left just before Igreja São Francisco de Paula. After-dark arrivals should phone for an escort.

Grande Hotel Ouro Preto HOTEL $$

(3551-1488; www.grandehotelouropreto.com.br; Rua das Flores 164; s/d R$195/235, s/d ste from R$230/290;) Oscar Niemeyer's Grande Hotel is not as nice to look *at* as it is to look *from*. Very central, with a pool and bar area overlooking the town, it's the only modernist structure for miles and is something of an eyesore. The two-level suites offer views and are better value than the bland, rather cramped standard rooms.

Solar do Rosario HOTEL $$$

(3551-5200; www.hotelsolardorosario.com.br; Getúlio Vargas 270; d R$325-615, ste R$590-980;) With an enviable position facing the Rosário church, this four-star hotel is the finest new hotel to open in Ouro Preto in recent years. Ample rooms in the original 18th-century mansion are complemented by luxurious suites in the colonial-style modern annex and countless amenities spread over pretty terraced grounds out back, including indoor and outdoor pools, a sauna and more.

Eating

Plenty of budget eateries are clustered along lively Direita, São José and Praça Tiradentes.

Praça Tiradentes & Around

Café e Livraria Cultural CAFE $

(3551-1361; http://cafeculturalop.com.br; Cláudio Manoel 15; light meals R$14-20; 9am-7pm) Tucked away just below the tourist office, this laid-back little cafe with exposed stone walls has simple food, fancy coffee drinks, and an extensive beer and wine list. A good place to pore over the map and get your bearings.

Chocolates Ouro Preto CAFE $

(www.chocolatesouropreto.com.br; Praça Tiradentes 111; snacks R$5-15; 9am-7pm) Best known for its hot chocolate and other sinful indulgences, Ouro Preto's hometown chocolate factory also serves sandwiches, soups and other savory snacks. Its **second branch** (Getúlio Vargas 66) keeps the same hours and prices.

Café Geraes & Escadabaixo INTERNATIONAL $$

(3551-5097; www.escadabaixo.com.br; Direita 122; mains R$26-69; noon-12.30am Mon, Wed, Thu & Sun, to 1:30am Fri & Sat) Well-heeled

CHICO-REI

Brazil's first abolitionist was Chico-Rei, an African tribal king. In the early 1700s, amid the frenzy of the gold rush, an entire tribe, king and all, was captured in Africa, sent to Brazil and sold to a mine owner in Ouro Preto.

The king, Chico-Rei, worked as the foreman of the slave miners. Working Sundays and holidays, he finally bought his freedom from the slave master, then freed his son Osmar. Together, father and son liberated the entire tribe.

This collective then bought the fabulously wealthy Encardadeira gold mine, and Chico-Rei assumed his royal functions once again, holding court in Vila Rica and celebrating African holidays in traditional costume. News of this reached the Portuguese king, who immediately prohibited slaves from purchasing their freedom. Chico-Rei is now a folk hero among Brazilian blacks.

students and artists favor this trendy spot to sip wine, talk shop and linger over creatively prepared salads, pasta, salmon and steak dishes. On weekdays, there's a good-value *prato executivo* lunch: main dish, salad, dessert and coffee for R$25. Its downstairs space **Escadabaixo** serves the exact same menu, but with more of a cellar beer-hall atmosphere.

Casa do Ouvidor MINEIRA **$$**
(☎3551-2141; www.casadoouvidor.com.br; Direita 42; mains R$24-51; ⏲11am-3pm & 7-10pm) Just downhill from Praça Tiradentes, Ouvidor has garnered numerous awards for its *comida mineira* (p170). At night, low lighting enhances the rustic charm of the ancient upstairs dining room. Definitely come with an empty stomach – portions are immense.

Antônio Dias Parish

Bené da Flauta INTERNATIONAL **$$$**
(☎3551-1036; www.benedaflauta.com.br; São Francisco de Assis 32; mains R$40-98; ⏲noon-11pm Mon-Sat, to 10pm Sun) Occupying two levels of a gorgeous colonial *sobrado* (mansion) just below Igreja de São Francisco, this upscale restaurant is ideal for a romantic dinner, with pretty views of Ouro Prêto's hillsides, candlelight reflecting off tall multi-paned windows, and Brazilian jazz on the sound system. The menu of trout, steak, pasta and *mineira* specialties is complemented by a good wine list.

Pilar Parish

Adega Ouro Preto SELF-SERVE **$**
(Teixeira Amaral 24; all-you-can-eat R$30, per kg R$42; ⏲11am-4pm) The cavelike Adega is a great deal at lunchtime, when *mineira* specialties are sold by the kilo or on an all-you-can-eat basis.

★**O Passo** ITALIAN **$$**
(www.opassopizzajazz.com; São José 56; pizzas R$32-69, mains R$39-79; ⏲noon-midnight Sun-Thu, to 1am Fri & Sat) In a lovely 18th-century building with intimate candlelit interior, this local favorite specializes in pizza, pasta and salads complemented by a good wine list. Outside, the relaxed creekside terrace is ideal for an after-dinner drink. On Tuesday nights, don't miss the *rodizio de pizzas* (all-you-can-eat pizza, R$35.90). There's live jazz on Thursdays and Friday evenings, and during Sunday lunch.

Chafariz BUFFET **$$**
(☎3551-2828; São José 167; all you can eat R$52; ⏲noon-4pm Tue-Sun) Eclectically decorated with old photos, religious art, Brazilian flags and antiques, this local institution serves one of Minas' tastiest (if priciest) buffets. The menu showcases traditional local favorites such as *lombo* (roasted pork loin) and *feijão tropeiro* (beans mixed with toasted manioc flour, pork rind, sausage and eggs and kale), followed by Minas cheese and *goiabada* (guava paste) for dessert. Postmeal shots of *cachaça*, coffee and *jabuticaba* liqueur are included in the price.

Hannah JAPANESE, MIDDLE EASTERN **$$**
(☎3551-7128; www.hannahop.com.br; Getúlio Vargas 241; mains R$28-74; ⏲6:30pm-midnight Tue-Thu, to 1am Fri & Sat, noon-4:30pm & 7pm-midnight Sun) Hannah serves an unconventional but tasty mix of Japanese and Middle Eastern food, from tempura, *yakissoba* (fried noodles) and *temakis* (sushi cones) to lamb with couscous or *kofta* (meatballs) in tomato sauce. The Wednesday and Thursday evening buffet features all-you-can-eat sushi and other Japanese treats for R$59.90.

Drinking & Entertainment

At night and on weekends, students assemble in Praça Tiradentes and crowd the bars along nearby Direita.

Cervejaria Porão PUB
(Direita 160; ⏲6-11pm Sun-Wed, to midnight Thu, to 1am Fri & Sat) On Ouro Preto's main street, this stone-walled cellar pub with back patio keeps its youthful clients happy with 80 different varieties of beer, cheap eats and loud music.

Barroco e Barraco BAR
(www.facebook.com/barrocoebarraco; Gabriel Santos 16; ⏲2-10pm Mon-Thu, 4pm-late Fri & Sat) Locals convene at this artsy bar every afternoon and evening to sip wine and enjoy homemade bar snacks, seated at sidewalk tables or on cushions along the stone wall overlooking Igreja NS do Rosário. The attached shop sells local artwork, and there's live music most Friday and Saturday nights.

Cine Vila Rica CINEMA
(☎3552-5424; www.facebook.com/Cine.Teatro.Vila.Rica; Praça Reinaldo Alves de Brito; admission weekday/weekend R$5/10) With an ever-changing film lineup (including frequent classic films in English), this small community movie theater and its attached A Pérola cafe make for an enjoyable night out.

Orientation

Many streets in town have two names: the official one and another used by locals because the official one is too long. For example, Conde de Bobadela, the major thoroughfare descending from Praça Tiradentes, is commonly known as Rua Direita, and Conselheiro Quintiliano, the road to Mariana, is also Rua das Lajes. Adding to the confusion, street names are rarely posted.

Information

Banco do Brasil (São José 189)
Bradesco (Praça Tiradentes 44) Bank
Centro Cultural e Turístico da FIEMG (3559-3269; turismo@ouropreto.mg.gov.br; Praça Tiradentes 4; 9am-6pm) Offers information in English, Spanish and French, including a leaflet listing museum and church hours and a rough town map.

Getting There & Away

BUS

Long-distance buses leave from Ouro Preto's main **bus station** (3559-3252; Padre Rolim 661), a 10-minute uphill walk from Praça Tiradentes at the northwest end of town. During peak periods, buy tickets a day in advance.

Pássaro Verde (www.gabrasil.com.br) provides service to Belo Horizonte (R$29, two hours, hourly from 6am to 8pm); **Útil** (3551-3166; www.util.com.br) goes to Rio (R$115, 7¾ hours, 8am and 10pm daily) and São Paulo (R$140, 11 hours, 9am and 7pm daily); the São Paulo bus stops en route at São João del Rei (R$60, 4½ hours).

To get to Mariana or Minas de Passagem, catch a local **Transcotta** (p185) bus (R$3.70, every 20 minutes from 6am to 11pm) from the local bus stop just northeast of Praça Tiradentes.

TRAIN

Ouro Preto-Mariana Tourist Train (www.vale.com/brasil/EN/business/logistics/railways/trem-turistico-ouro-preto-mariana; 1 way/round-trip R$40/56, in air-conditioned panoramic car R$60/80) The Vale mining company operates the renovated historic tourist train on weekends between Ouro Preto and Mariana, leaving Ouro Preto's **train station** (3551-7705; Praça Cesário Alvim 102) twice daily Friday through Sunday. The 18km, one-hour journey is pretty but slow, snaking along a river gorge the whole way. Best views are from the right side leaving Ouro Preto, and the left side leaving Mariana.

Getting Around

Viação Turin runs a small bus (R$2.40) between the bus station and Capela do Padre Faria on the eastern side of town, making various stops in the historic center along the way.

Mariana

0XX31 / POP 54,000 / ELEV 712M

Graced with fine colonial architecture and two of Minas' prettiest squares, Mariana, founded in 1696, was one of the state's earliest settlements and its first capital. Only 14km from Ouro Preto, Mariana makes an easy day trip or can even be used as a base to explore both cities. Its compact historical center is easier to navigate than Ouro Preto's, not only because of its smaller size, but also because the hills are less steep. The ground floors of many historic mansions have been transformed into stores, boutiques and artists' workshops where you're invited to wander at will.

Sights

All the sights are close together. Two blocks uphill from the tourist information office and the Ouro Preto bus stop, Praça Minas Gerais boasts one of the state's nicest arrangements of public buildings on a single square.

Igreja São Francisco de Assis CHURCH
(Praça Minas Gerais; admission R$2; 9am-noon & 1-4pm Tue-Sun) Mariana's loveliest church was designed by Aleijadinho, whose work can also been seen in the pulpits and other interior details. The gorgeous ceiling panels in the sacristy were painted by Mariana's native son Ataíde, who lies buried here with 94 other lucky souls.

Praça Gomes Freire SQUARE
One block downhill from Praça Minas Gerais, this leafy square is an inviting place to sit and watch the world go by, with a pond, a gazebo and park benches shaded by grand old trees.

Catedral Basílica da Sé CHURCH
(3558-2785; www.orgaodase.com.br; Praça Cláudio Manuel; church admission R$2.50, organ concerts R$30; 8am-6pm Tue-Sun, organ concerts 11:30am Fri, 12:15pm Sun) The star attraction at Mariana's cathedral is its fantastic German organ dating from 1701, painted with designs from the then-Portuguese colony of Macau and adorned with carved wooden angels. Organ concerts are held twice weekly.

Museu Arquidiocesano de Arte Sacra MUSEUM
(3557-2581; Frei Durão 49; admission R$5; 8:30am-noon & 1:30-5pm Tue-Sun) This museum features sculptures by Aleijadinho, paintings by Ataíde and other religious objects.

WORTH A TRIP

MINAS DA PASSAGEM

Halfway between Ouro Preto and Mariana, **Minas da Passagem** (☎3557-5000; www.minasdapassagem.com.br; adult/child R$39/31; ⏰9am-5pm Mon & Tue, to 5:30pm Wed-Sun; 👪) is an ancient gold mine founded by the Portuguese in 1719 and definitively decommissioned in 1985. Guided tours descend in a rickety antique cable car, covering the mine's history and local gold-extraction methods, then visiting a subterranean lake and a shrine to the many black slaves who died here dynamiting into the rock. Any Ouro Preto–Mariana bus can drop you here (R$3.70, 15 minutes from either town).

Igreja NS do Carmo CHURCH
(Praça Minas Gerais; ⏰9-11:45am & 1-4pm) On Mariana's central square, this church was severely damaged by fire in 1999, but still retains its original rococo chancel (the only element to have survived unscathed).

Cia Navegante Teatro de Marionetes THEATER
(☎3557-3927; www.cianavegante.com.br; Seminário 290; ⏰9am-6pm) At this longstanding marionette theater founded by local artist Catin Nardi, you can see new puppets under construction, plus old ones that have appeared on Brazilian national TV miniseries.

Sleeping & Eating

Pouso da Typographia POUSADA $$
(☎3557-1577; Praça Gomes Freire 220; s/d R$180/296; 📶) This pousada's central location on Mariana's prettiest square can't be beat, although front rooms can get noisy on the weekends. It's worth a peek just to see the antique printing presses in the foyer.

Hotel Providência HOTEL $$
(☎3557-1444; www.hotelprovidencia.com.br; Dom Silvério 233; s/d R$125/230; 📶🏊) Guest rooms in this 1849 building, two blocks uphill from Praça Minas Gerais, are airy and inviting, with clean white sheets and lovely high ceilings. It shares a semi-Olympic-size swimming pool with the Catholic school next door.

★ **Lua Cheia** SELF-SERVE $
(☎3557-3232; Dom Viçoso 58; per kg R$35; ⏰11am-3pm Mon-Fri, to 4pm Sat & Sun) Mariana's best per-kilo place, one block south of Praça Gomes Freire, offers a sumptuous buffet spread, along with atmospheric seating in a high-ceilinged colonial building or on the umbrella-shaded back patio.

Bistrô INTERNATIONAL $$
(☎3557-4138; Salomão Ibrahim 61a; mains R$34-65; ⏰6pm-midnight Mon-Sat, 11:30am-midnight Sun) Tucked down a side street from Praça Gomes Freire, this bright and cheery two-level eatery serves everything from steak to seafood to pizza, all accompanied by a good beer and wine list.

O Rancho BUFFET, PIZZERIA $$
(☎3558-1060; http://ranchorestaurante.com.br; Praça Gomes Freire 108; buffet R$26, pizzas R$33-49; ⏰11am-3pm & 6-11pm Tue-Fri, 11am-11pm Sat & Sun) This cozy, low-key eatery specializes in hearty *mineira* fare, with soups bubbling on the wood-fired stove every night; there's also pizza for those needing a break from rice and beans.

Information

Bradesco (Av Salvador Furtado) ATMs one block below the cathedral square.

Tourist office (☎3558-2314, 3558-1062; http://mariana.org.br; Rua Direita 91-93; ⏰8am-6pm) A block above the square where buses from Ouro Preto stop, Mariana's newly relocated tourist office offers city information and tours.

Getting There & Away

There are regular Transcotta buses between Ouro Preto and Mariana (R$3.70, 30 minutes, at least twice hourly from 6am to 11pm). In Mariana, the bus stop is across from Praça Tancredo Neves just outside the historic centre; in Ouro Preto catch the bus from the local bus stop northeast of Praça Tiradentes.

Mariana's long-distance bus station, Rodoviária dos Inconfidentes, is located about 2km outside of town. Passaro Verde runs buses to Belo Horizonte (R$33, two hours) every hour or two, and Útil operates a daily 6:30pm bus to São Paulo (R$144, 11 hours). The Transcotta bus from Ouro Preto also stops here en route to downtown Mariana.

Mariana's picturesque peach-and-white-colored train station is just two blocks away from the local bus stop for buses to Ouro Preto. **FCA** (☎0800-285-7000; www.trensturisticos.fcasa.com.br) runs a tourist train from Mariana to Ouro Preto (oneway/return from R$40/50) twice daily Friday through Sunday. There's a museum and kids' playground to keep everyone occupied while you wait.

Lavras Novas

0XX31 / POP 1000 / ELEV 1510M

Lavras Novas, named for the new gold strikes discovered here in 1704, sits on a high plateau 17km from Ouro Preto. When the gold started running out in the late 18th century, this hamlet became home to a small community of freed slaves, and many of their descendants have remained to this day. Surrounded by wide-open mountain scenery, its cobblestone main street runs between colorful single-story houses to the town's focal point, the **Igreja NS dos Prazeres**.

The rapid influx of visitors over the past decade, coupled with the recent paving of Lavras' access road, have led to a small boom in new pousadas and ecotourism agencies; on busy weekends it can sometimes feel like outsiders outnumber locals. For lower prices and a taste of the town's traditional off-the-beaten-path tranquility, consider visiting midweek.

Activities

Several companies around town offer guided hikes and horseback-riding tours to local attractions, including the waterfalls **Três Pingos** and **Namorados**. An alternative resource for independent hikers is the rudimentary free trail map distributed at pousada Palavras Novas.

Sleeping & Eating

Pousadas empty out during the week, but reservations are advisable on weekends and holidays, when there's often a two-night minimum.

Taberna Casa Antiga e Chalés Galo do Campo CHALET **$$**
(9957-8189; www.lavrasnovas.com.br/galodocampo; Alto do Campo 213; d midweek R$220-250, weekend R$270-320) Nestled among trees at the edge of town are these cute chalets with views of horse pastures and mountains. The rustic-chic restaurant next door is filled with candlelight, cozy couches and curtain-draped nooks; it serves a varied international menu and hosts live blues bands on weekends.

Palavras Novas POUSADA **$$$**
(3554-2025; www.pousadapalavrasnovas.com.br; NS dos Prazeres 1110; d/chalet midweek from R$250/380, weekend from R$325/425;) With fireplaces, afternoon tea, whirlpool tubs, in-room DVD players, a sauna, spa and heated pool, nice mountain views and live music on weekends, Palavras Novas caters to a luxury-minded crowd. The pousada leads group hikes every weekend.

Getting There & Away

Transcotta (3551-2385) runs daily buses to Lavras Novas (R$5.80, 45 minutes) from in front of the Ouro Preto train station (*not* the bus station). There are three departures in each direction Monday through Friday, and one each on Saturday and Sunday.

Congonhas

0XX31 / POP 49,000 / ELEV 871M

This small industrial town has been saved from complete obscurity by the beautiful, brooding presence of Aleijadinho's extraordinary *The Prophets* at the Basílica do Bom Jesus de Matosinhos. The dramatic statues almost seem to be performing a balletic dance and it's a wondrous experience to be able to walk freely among them. They are Aleijadinho's masterpiece and Brazil's most famed work of art. It's worth taking the trouble to get to Congonhas just to see them.

Congonhas is 72km south of Belo Horizonte, 3km off Hwy BR-040. The city grew up with the search for gold in the nearby Rio Maranhão, and the economy today is dominated by iron mining in the surrounding countryside.

Sights

The Prophets PUBLIC ART
(Praça do Santuario) Already an old man, sick and crippled, Aleijadinho sculpted *The Prophets* between 1800 and 1805. Symmetrically placed in front of the **Basílica do Bom Jesus de Matosinhos**, each of the 12 Old Testament figures was carved from one or two blocks of soapstone. Each carries a message in Latin: some are hopeful prophecies, others warn of the end of the world.

Much has been written about these sculptures – their dynamic quality, the sense of movement (much like a Hindu dance or a ballet), how they complement each other and how their arrangement prevents them from being seen in isolation. The poet Carlos Drummond de Andrade wrote that the dramatic faces and gestures are 'magnificent, terrible, grave and tender' and commented on 'the way the statues, of human size, appear to be larger than life as they look down upon the viewer with the sky behind them.'

ALEIJADINHO

Antônio Francisco Lisboa (1738–1814), known worldwide today as Aleijadinho (Little Cripple), was the son of a Portuguese architect and a black slave. His nickname was given to him sometime in the 1770s, when the artist began to suffer from a terrible, debilitating disease. It might have been syphilis or possibly leprosy – either way, he lost his fingers and toes and the use of his lower legs.

Undaunted, Aleijadinho strapped hammers and chisels to his arms and continued working, advancing the art in his country from the excesses of the baroque to a finer, more graceful form known as Barroco Mineiro.

Mineiros (residents of Minas Gerais state) have reason to be proud of Aleijadinho – he is a figure of international prominence in the history of art. He studied European baroque and rococo traditions through pictures, but went on to develop his own unique style, using only native materials such as soapstone and wood. Aleijadinho's angels have his stylistic signature: wavy hair, wide-open eyes and big, round cheeks.

For many years Manuel da Costa Ataíde, from nearby Mariana, successfully collaborated with Aleijadinho on several churches. Aleijadinho would sculpt the exterior and a few interior pieces, and Ataíde would paint the interior panels. With his secretly concocted vegetable dyes, Ataíde fleshed out many of Aleijadinho's creations.

Aleijadinho was buried in Ouro Preto's **Matriz NS da Conceição de Antônio Dias** (p178), within 50 paces of his birth site. He was named patron of Brazilian arts by federal decree in 1973. *The Prophets* in Congonhas, the Igreja de São Francisco de Assis and the facade of the Igreja de NS do Carmo, both in Ouro Preto, were all carved by Aleijadinho, as were innumerable relics in Mariana, Sabará, Tiradentes and São João del Rei.

Before working on *The Prophets*, Aleijadinho carved (or supervised his assistants in carving) the wooden statues that were placed in the six little chapels below. The **chapels** themselves – also of Aleijadinho's design – and their placement on the sloping site are superb. The way the light falls on the pale sculpted domes against the dark mountain backdrop is truly beautiful.

Each chapel depicts a scene from Christ's passion, and several portray Jesus with a red mark on his neck. While little is known of Aleijadinho's politics, some local historians interpret this to mean that Aleijadinho intended to draw parallels between the martyred Christ and slain independence fighter Tiradentes. Aleijadinho's sculptures of Roman soldiers lend support to this theory – they all have two left feet and sport ankle boots, a shoe style favored by the colonizing Portuguese.

Festivals & Events

Holy Week RELIGIOUS

(Mar/Apr) Processions in Congonhas are famous, especially the dramatizations on Good Friday.

Jubileu do Senhor Bom Jesus do Matosinhos RELIGIOUS

(Sep 7-14) One of Minas' great religious festivals; every year approximately 600,000 pilgrims arrive at the basilica to make promises, do penance, receive blessings, and give and receive alms.

Sleeping & Eating

It's possible to catch an early bus into Congonhas and another one out that same afternoon. Since there's little to see beyond Aleijadinho's artwork, most people don't spend the night. One pleasure of staying over is the opportunity to see the statues in the early-morning light, when they're especially beautiful.

Hotel Colonial HOTEL $

(3731-1834; www.hotelcolonialcongonhas.com.br; Praça da Basílica 76; s/d R$80/150;) Conveniently situated right across the street from Aleijadinho's masterpieces, this hotel still wears faded remnants of its former glory in the huge hallways and immensely high ceilings. Most rooms are spacious and the bathrooms surprisingly modern.

Cova do Daniel MINEIRA $$

(3731-1834; Praça da Basílica 76; mains for two R$60-80; 11am-11pm Tue-Sun, 9am-6pm Mon) This restaurant specializes in *mineira* classics such as *feijão tropeiro* and *tutu à mineira* (black-bean *feijoada*). It's a convenient lunch option for day-trippers.

Getting There & Away

Congonhas is on the direct bus route between Belo Horizonte and São João del Rei, so these two towns make the best starting points for a day trip. **Viação Sandra** (www.viacaosandra.com.br) serves this route several times daily (R$27, 90 minutes from Belo Horizonte; R$31, two hours from São João).

Getting Around

The long-distance bus station is on Av Júlia Kubitschek, across town from the sites of interest. From here local buses for the basilica and *The Prophets* (R$2.60, 15 minutes) leave every 30 to 60 minutes. For the best approach and first view of the statues, get off just after the bus passes the church (as it heads downhill). The same bus returns you to the bus station, or you can take a taxi (R$15, 10 minutes).

São João del Rei

☎0XX32 / POP 84,000 / ELEV 898M

Set between mountain ridges near the southern end of the Serra do Espinhaço, São João del Rei affords a unique look at a *cidade historica* that didn't suffer a great decline when the gold boom ended in the 1800s. Present-day São João has the unselfconscious urban vitality of a modern city, which can come as a welcome contrast to the preserved-in-amber quality of neighboring Tiradentes. Downtown there are plenty of high-rises and other trappings of 21st-century Brazil, yet around every corner lurk unexpected colonial surprises. The historic city center, which is protected by Brazil's Landmarks Commission, features two good museums, several of the country's finest churches and some gorgeous old mansions – one of which belonged to the late and still popular never-quite-president Tancredo Neves. Floodlights illuminate the churches every night, adding to the city's aesthetic appeal.

São João is bisected by the Córrego do Lenheiro – really just a glorified creek in a concrete channel. Two lovely 18th-century stone bridges serve as convenient landmarks, roughly delineating the boundaries of the colonial center.

Sights

★ **Igreja de São Francisco de Assis** CHURCH
(Padre José Maria Xavier; admission R$3; ⏲8am-4pm Mon, to 5pm Tue-Sat, to 2pm Sun) This exquisite 1774 baroque church, fronted by a palm-shaded, lyre-shaped plaza, is home to two Aleijadinho sculptures (second altar to the left) and one of Minas' finest facades, based on Aleijadinho's design. Out back, arrows lead to politician Tancredo Neves' grave, a pilgrimage site for Brazilians. The local Ribeiro Bastos orchestra and choir perform sacred baroque music Sundays at 9:15am.

Museu Regional São João del Rei MUSEUM
(☎3371-7663; http://museuregionaldesaojoaodelrei.blogspot.com; Praça Severiano Resende s/n; ⏲9:30am-4pm Tue-Fri, 9am-1pm Sat & Sun) FREE One of the best regional museums in Minas Gerais, this 19th-century colonial mansion houses three floors of antique furniture, sacred art and assorted cultural relics.

Museu de Arte Sacra MUSEUM
(☎3371-7005; www.museudeartesacra.com.br; Praça Embaixador Gastão da Cunha 8; adult/reduced R$5/2.50; ⏲noon-5pm Mon-Fri, 9am-1pm Sat) In a building that served as the public jail between 1737 and 1850, this museum has a small but impressive collection of art from the city's churches.

Igreja de NS do Carmo CHURCH
(Getúlio Vargas; admission R$2; ⏲7am-noon & 2-5pm Mon-Sat, 7am-noon & 5:30-7pm Sun) This 18th-century church, dominating a lovely triangular *praça* (plaza), was designed by Aleijadinho, who also did the frontispiece and the sculpture around the door. In the second sacristy is a famous unfinished sculpture of Christ.

Catedral de NS do Pilar CHURCH
(Getúlio Vargas; ⏲8:30-11am & 1-8pm) Begun in 1721, São João's cathedral has exuberant gold altars and fine Portuguese tiles. Two of the city's famous orchestras can be heard here at the 7pm Mass: on Wednesdays it's the Lira Sanjoanense orchestra, and on Thursday and Friday it's the Ribeiro Bastos orchestra.

Igreja de NS do Rosário CHURCH
(Praça Embaixador Gastão da Cunha; ⏲8:30-10:30am) This simple church was built in 1719 to honor the patron saint who was protector of the slaves.

Festivals & Events

Someone's always celebrating something in São João. There are literally dozens of festivals, both religious and secular; stop by the tourist office for a full calendar.

Carnaval RELIGIOUS
(⏲Feb/Mar) Locals boast, credibly, that their Carnaval is the best in Minas Gerais.

São João Del Rei

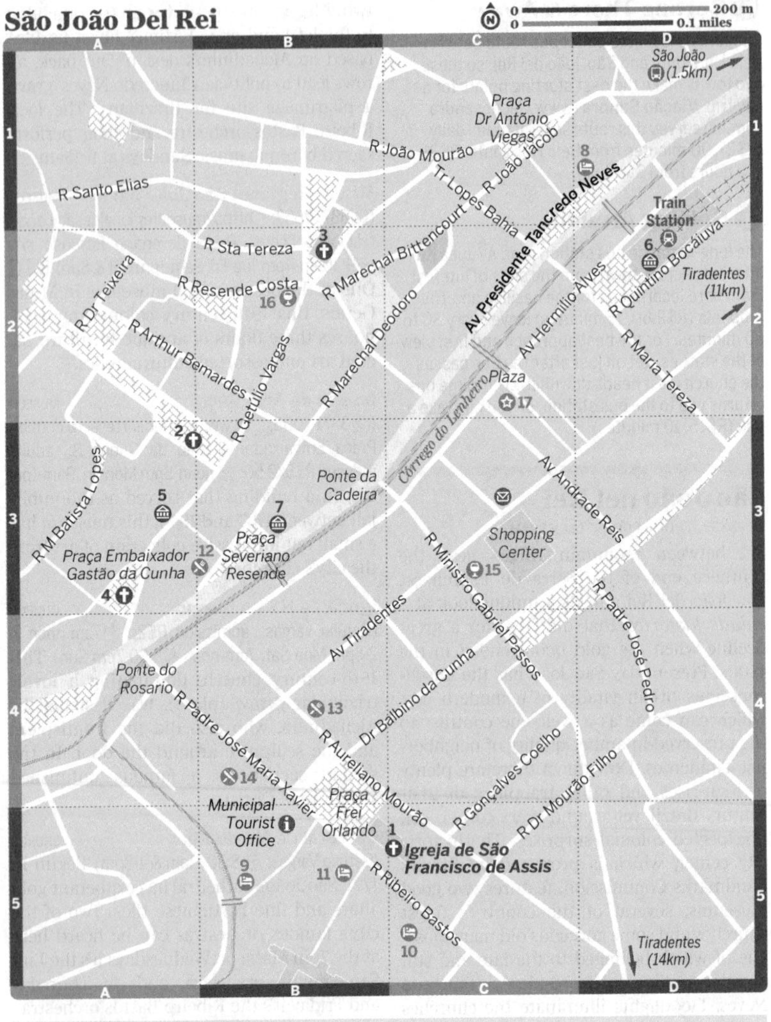

São João Del Rei

Top Sights
1 Igreja de São Francisco de Assis C5

Sights
2 Catedral de NS do Pilar A3
3 Igreja de NS do Carmo B2
4 Igreja de NS do Rosário A3
5 Museu de Arte Sacra A3
6 Museu Ferroviário D2
7 Museu Regional São João del Rei B3

Sleeping
8 Hotel Brasil D1
9 Pousada Beco do Bispo B5
10 Pousada Casarão C5
11 Villa Magnolia Pousada B5

Eating
12 Churrascaria Ramon B3
13 Dedo de Moça B4
14 Restaurante Villeiros B4

Drinking & Nightlife
15 Del Rei Cafe & Chopperia C3
16 Taberna de Omar B2

Entertainment
17 Teatro Municipal C2

Holy Week RELIGIOUS
(Mar/Apr) Semana Santa processions are especially colorful, preserving centuries-old Portuguese traditions and incorporating the music of the city's two baroque orchestras, who have been performing here uninterruptedly since the 1700s.

Semana da Inconfidência CULTURAL
(Apr 15-21) Celebrates Brazil's first independence movement, culminating in a horseback procession between São João and Tiradentes.

Sleeping

Book ahead in December, when the town is filled with students sitting for exams, and during holidays such as Carnaval and Easter.

Hotel Brasil HOTEL $
(3371-2804; Av Presidente Tancredo Neves 395; per person R$45, without bathroom R$35;) The management is as ancient as the infrastructure at this funky, rambling 19th-century relic with high-ceilinged, bare-bones rooms, some facing the river; it's straight across the pedestrian bridge from the train station. No breakfast.

Villa Magnolia Pousada POUSADA $$
(3373-5065; www.pousadavillamagnolia.com.br; Ribeiro Bastos 2; s/d midweek from R$166/207, weekend from R$202/253;) A delightful refuge just across from Igreja de São Francisco, this stylishly renovated 19th-century mansion features pure cotton bedding, oversized towels, spacious rooms, a large pool, shade trees and common areas filled with art books.

Pousada Beco do Bispo POUSADA $$
(3371-8844; www.becodobispo.com.br; Irmã Eugênia Luz Pinto 93; s/d midweek R$150/230, weekend R$180/250;) Tucked down a peaceful dead-end street a block from Igreja de São Francisco, this pousada has cheerful, ultracomfy rooms with queen- and king-sized beds, fine cotton sheets, international TV channels and a pool with palm trees. Friendly multilingual owner Nitza has lived in Italy and the United States and enjoys sharing her love of São João with visitors.

Pousada Casarão POUSADA $$
(3371-7447; www.pousadacasarao.net.br; Ribeiro Bastos 94; s/d/ste R$100/170/190;) In a refurbished mansion behind the Igreja de São Francisco, this pousada tastefully blends old with new; many rooms are decorated with antiques, yet all have modern bathrooms. The French doors in the breakfast room overlook the pool.

Eating

Restaurante Villeiros SELF-SERVE $
(3372-1034; www.villeiros.com.br; Padre José Maria Xavier 132; per kg R$39.90; 11am-3:30pm) A fabulous self-serve place with great variety near the Igreja de São Francisco, Villeiros is very popular with locals and has a cheerful patio out back.

Dedo de Moça BRAZILIAN $$
(www.facebook.com/dedodemoca.sjdr; Aureliano Mourão 101; mains per person R$27-44; noon-3pm Thu-Tue, 6:30pm-midnight daily) This popular downtown spot is part bar, part restaurant, with a menu that offers intriguing new twists on traditional *mineira* cuisine. Local favorites include *acarajé mineira* (black-eyed-pea fritters with various fillings including local cheese, sausage, dried beef and lemongrass) and *filé catauá* (steak with melted Catauá cheese and fresh tomato-basil sauce).

Churrascaria Ramon CHURRASCARIA $
(3371-3540; Praça Severiano Resende 52; mains for two R$36-76; 11am-6pm) Ramon prides itself on perfectly cooked meats and all the traditional *mineira* favorites. For a bargain, try the *prato comercial* (meat, beans, rice, salad and potato salad) for R$20.

Drinking & Entertainment

Most of the city's nightlife is on the south side along Av Tiradentes.

Taberna de Omar BAR
(Getúlio Vargas 242a; 6pm-midnight Wed-Fri, 11am-midnight Sat, 11am-4pm Sun) This popular hole-in-the-wall directly opposite the Carmo church serves everything from artisanal beers and *cachaça* to mixed drinks, coffee, tea and juices. It's especially revered for its fresh-baked whole grain breads served with local cheese, *doce de leite* (milk caramel) and homemade jam. There's occasional live music.

Del Rei Cafe & Chopperia BAR
(3371-1368; www.facebook.com/delreicafe; cnr Av Tiradentes & Gabriel Passos; 11am-11pm Sun-Wed, to 1am Thu-Sat) This busy corner bar, with numerous sidewalk tables, is great for people-watching. Locals congregate here daily for early-evening beers and late-night snacks.

Teatro Municipal PERFORMING ARTS

(www.facebook.com/teatrosaojoaodelrei; Av Hermilio Alves) Constructed in 1893, this grand old theater in the heart of town stages occasional performances throughout the year (many free of charge).

Information

Bradesco (Av Hermilio Alves 200)

Municipal Tourist Office (☎3372-7338; www.facebook.com/sjdr.cultura.turismo.esporte.lazer; Praça Frei Orlando 90; ⏰8am-5pm) Opposite Igreja São Francisco de Assis.

Getting There & Away

BUS

São João's **bus station** (☎3373-4700; Rua Cristóvão Colombo) is 1.5km northeast of the center.

Frequent buses connect São João and Tiradentes. Vale do Ouro buses (R$3.80, 30 minutes) follow the scenic (but bumpy!) Estrada Real, while Presidente buses (R$3.35, 20 minutes) take the faster paved road.

TRAIN

The wonderful Maria-Fumaça **tourist train** (p195) runs on weekends and holidays between São João del Rei and Tiradentes. The **train station** (☎3371-8485; Av Hermílio Alves 366) is just east of the city center.

Getting Around

Local Presidente buses (gray with red letters) run between the bus station and the center (R$2.40, 10 minutes). Exiting the bus station, you'll find the local stop to your left and across the street (in front of the Drogaria Dose Certa).

Alternatively, catch a traditional taxi for R$15 or **motorbike taxi** (☎3371-6389) for R$4 just outside the bus station.

Returning from the center to the bus station, the most convenient local bus stop is in front of the train station.

Tiradentes

☎0XX32 / POP 7000 / ELEV 927M

Perhaps nowhere else in Minas do the colonial charm and picturesque natural setting blend so harmoniously as in Tiradentes. Quaint historic houses, fringed by exuberant wildflowers, stand out against a backdrop of pretty blue mountains threaded with hiking trails. If you can, visit midweek, when the town's abundant attractions are most easily appreciated. On weekends, the swarms of visitors who come to gawk at Tiradentes' antique stores and boutiques can make the place feel a bit like a theme park, and the sudden increase in horse-drawn carriages creates some strong aromas!

History

Originally called Arraial da Ponta do Morro (Hamlet on a Hilltop), Tiradentes was renamed to honor the martyred hero of the Inconfidência, who was born at a nearby farm. In recent years the town, which sits at the center of a triangle formed by Brazil's three largest cities, has become a magnet for artists and other urban escapees. Today the historic center is home to only a couple dozen original Tiradentes families, intermingled with new arrivals from around the world.

Sights

Tiradentes' center is a compact and photogenic cluster of cobbled streets. The town's colonial buildings run up a hillside from the main square, **Largo das Forras**, culminating in the beautiful Igreja Matriz de Santo Antônio. From the terrace in front of the church there's a stunning view of the terracotta-tiled colonial houses, the green valley and the towering wall

BUSES FROM SÃO JOÃO DEL REI

DESTINATION	COST (R$)	TIME (HR)	BUS COMPANY
Aiuruoca	58	4¾	Sandra (www.viacaosandra.com.br)
Belo Horizonte	55	3½	Sandra (www.viacaosandra.com.br)
Caxambu	53	3½	Sandra (www.viacaosandra.com.br)
Congonhas	31	2	Sandra (www.viacaosandra.com.br)
Ouro Preto	63	4	Útil (www.util.com.br)
Petrópolis	62 to 84	4½	Paraibuna (www.paraibunatransportes.com.br)
Rio	70 to 95	5½	Paraibuna (www.paraibunatransportes.com.br)
São Paulo	96	7½	Gardénia (www.expressogardenia.com.br)

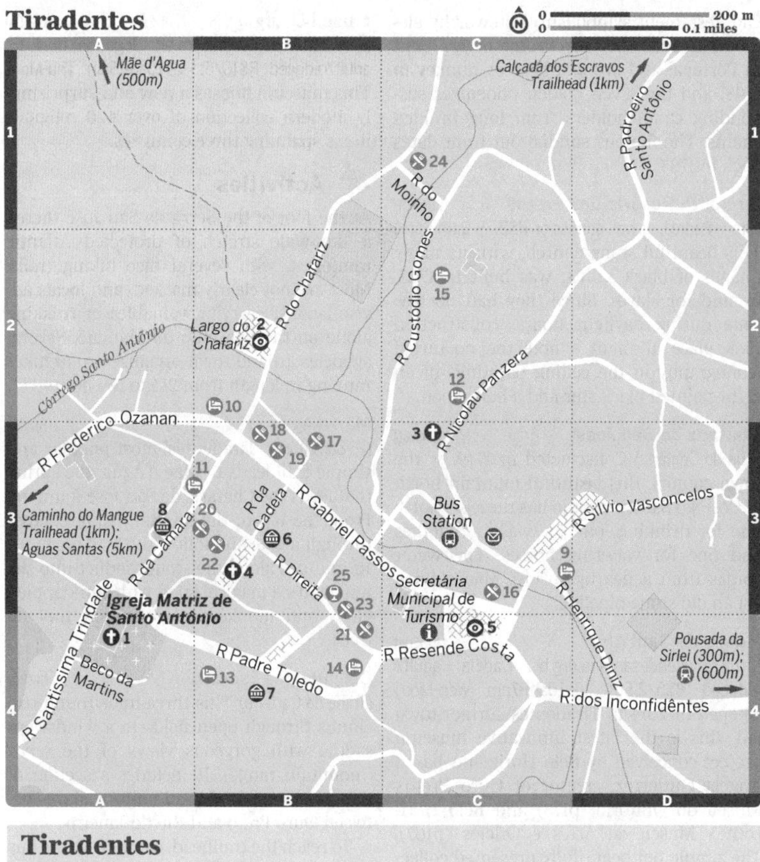

Tiradentes

Top Sights
1 Igreja Matriz de Santo Antônio A4

Sights
2 Chafariz de São José B2
3 Igreja de São Francisco de Paula C3
4 Igreja NS Rosário dos Pretos B3
5 Largo das Forras C4
6 Museu de Sant'Ana B3
7 Museu do Padre Toledo B4
8 Museu Liturgia A3

Sleeping
9 Hotel Solar da Ponte C3
10 Pousada da Bia B2
11 Pousada do Ó B3
12 Pousada Pé da Serra C2
13 Pousada Richard Rothe B4
14 Pousada Três Portas B4
15 Pouso Alforria C2

Eating
16 Bar do Celso C3
17 CasAzul B3
18 Divino Sabor B3
19 Estalagem do Sabor B3
20 Gourmeco B3
21 Luth Bistrô B4
22 Tragaluz B3
23 Uai Thai B3
24 Viradas do Largo C1

Drinking & Nightlife
25 Entrepôt du Vin B3

of stone formed by the Serra de São José. For another picture-postcard view of town, climb the hill just above the bus station to the grassy square in front of **Igreja de São Francisco de Paula**.

★ **Igreja Matriz de Santo Antônio** CHURCH
(Padre Toledo s/n; admission R$5; ⌚9am-5pm) Named for Tiradentes' patron saint, this gorgeous church is one of Aleijadinho's last designs. The dazzling gold interior is rich in

Old Testament symbolism. Noteworthy elements include the polychrome organ, built in Portugal and brought here by donkey in 1798, and the seven golden phoenixes suspending candleholders from long braided chains. The famous sundial out front dates back to 1785.

Igreja NS Rosário dos Pretos CHURCH
(Praça Padre Lourival; admission R$3; ⌚9am-5pm) This beautiful stone church, with its many images of black saints, was built in 1708, by and for slaves. Since they had no free time during daylight hours, construction took place at night - note the nocturnal iconography in the ceiling paintings of an eight-pointed black star and a half-moon.

Chafariz de São José FOUNTAIN
(Rua do Chafariz) Constructed in 1749 by the town council, this beautiful fountain north of Córrego Santo Antônio has three sections: one for drinking, one for washing clothes and one for watering horses. The water comes from a nearby spring, Mãe d'Agua, via an old stone pipeline.

Museu de Sant'Ana MUSEUM
(http://museudesantana.org.br; Cadeia; adult/reduced R$5/2.50; ⌚10am-7pm Wed-Mon) Opened in 2014 in Tiradentes' former town jail, this is the latest innovative museum project conceived by Belo Horizonte–based Angela Gutierrez, creator of Ouro Preto's Museu do Oratório (p178) and Belo Horizonte's Museu de Artes e Ofícios (p167). The simple but beautifully presented collection features 270 images of St Anne in wood, stone and terracotta, from the 17th century to the present. Bilingual exhibits trace the importance of St Anne imagery throughout Brazil and its evolution through the baroque and rococo periods.

Museu do Padre Toledo MUSEUM
(Padre Toledo 190; adult/reduced R$10/5; ⌚10am-5pm Tue-Fri, to 4.30pm Sat, 9am-3pm Sun) Dedicated to 18th-century Brazilian priest and revolutionary hero Padre Toledo, this recently renovated museum occupies the 18-room house where Padre Toledo himself once lived and where the Inconfidentes first met. The collection features regional antiques and documents from the 18th century, along with some fine ceiling paintings artistically reflected in floor-mounted mirrors.

Museu Liturgia MUSEUM
(www.museudaliturgia.com.br; Jogo de Bola 15; adult/reduced R$10/5; ⌚10am-5pm Thu-Mon) This museum houses a new and surprisingly modern collection of over 420 religious items spanning three centuries.

Activities

At the foot of the Serra de São José there's a 1km-wide stretch of protected Atlantic rainforest, with several nice hiking trails. Most are not clearly marked, and locals advise against carrying valuables or trekking alone on the Caminho do Mangue. Several agencies around town organize group hikes ranging in length from 2½ to 5½ hours.

Mãe d'Agua HIKING
(⌚8am-4pm) Tiradentes' most popular and simple trail leads to Mãe d'Agua, the spring that feeds the Chafariz de São José fountain. From the top of the fountain square, cross through a gate and follow the trail north for 10 minutes along the stone viaduct into the jungle. It's a magical spot, with sun-dappled glens and monkeys cavorting in the tall trees.

Calçada dos Escravos HIKING
(Trilha do Carteiro) This three-hour round-trip climbs through open fields to a windswept saddle with gorgeous views of the *serra* (mountain range). It includes a section of the old stone-paved road built by slaves between Ouro Preto and Rio de Janeiro.

To reach the trailhead, climb from the bus station to Igreja de São Francisco de Paula, then follow the cobbled road north, continuing straight at the first intersection and bearing slightly left at the second, following the brown sign for Serra São José/Trilha do Carteiro. Shortly after passing Pousada Recanto dos Encantos on your right, take the right (uphill) fork and continue straight another few hundred meters; after passing house No 878 (left side), cross through a gate and look for a signpost indicating the Calçada dos Escravos. Fork left on the rickety bridge over the stream, then start climbing toward the saddle.

Caminho do Mangue HIKING
This two-hour walk, best undertaken with a guide, heads up the *serra* from the west side of town to Aguas Santas. There you'll find a mineral-water swimming pool and a simple Portuguese-owned restaurant.

Festivals & Events

Tiradentes is popular as a center for national events. Two of the biggest and longest established are the **Mostra de Cinema** (www.mostratiradentes.com.br; Jan), held in the second half of January, and the 10-day **Festival de Cultura e Gastronomia** (www.farturagastronomia.com.br/tiradentes; Aug), in the second half of August, respectively bringing international films and world-class chefs to Tiradentes. In late June classic-motorcycle buffs pack the streets, celebrating **Bike Fest Tiradentes** (www.grupoberg.com.br; Jun) with beer, food, blues, and rock and roll. Other recently launched events include the **Festival de Fotografia** (fotoempauta.com.br/festivais; Mar).

Sleeping

Tiradentes caters to a well-heeled crowd and couples looking for romance. Budget-minded and/or solo travelers can save money by visiting midweek, when some pousadas grant discounts.

Pousada da Bia POUSADA **$$**
(3355-1173; www.pousadadabia.com.br; Ozanan 330; s/d midweek R$180/240, weekend R$200/260;) Just outside Tiradentes' historical center, French- and English-speaking owner Bia runs this pleasant pousada with a sunny breakfast house, fragrant herb garden and relaxing pool area. Rooms to the right of the garden offer nicer views but less privacy than those on the left. There are also two spacious new deluxe rooms (R$180–R$200 per couple, plus 30% per extra person).

Pousada da Sirlei INN **$$**
(3355-1440; www.facebook.com/PousadadaSirlei; Antonio de Carvalho 113; s/d R$100/200; P@) Five minutes' walk from the cobblestones and bus station but kitty-corner to a pleasant plaza, this quaint inn is long on mismatched flooring and doting grandmotherly charm.

Pouso Alforria POUSADA **$$**
(3355-1536; www.pousoalforria.com.br; Custódio Gomes 286; s/d R$300/350; @) This classy, secluded pousada, tucked up a flagstoned driveway five minutes' walk north of the center, features eight rooms in modern style, a reading room full of art books and some nice views of the Serra de São José. English and French are spoken.

Pousada do Ó POUSADA **$$**
(3355-1699; www.pousadadoo.com.br; Chafariz 25; d R$200-320;) Set in an 18th-century house, Pousada do Ó enjoys a privileged location two blocks below the church in the heart of colonial Tiradentes. The original pousada, featuring seven snug rooms around a small garden, is supplemented by four larger rooms in the building above. Rooms 8 and 11 are the best of the bunch.

Pousada Três Portas POUSADA **$$**
(3355-1444; www.pousadatresportas.com.br; Direita 280a; r R$265-420;) This pousada in a historic building just above Tiradentes' main square features rooms with beautiful antiques and hardwood floors, some with four-poster beds. The cheery upstairs sitting room with fireplace enjoys nice views of town and the mountains beyond; other amenities include a covered swimming pool and sauna.

Pousada Pé da Serra POUSADA **$$**
(3355-1107; www.pedaserra.com.br; Nicolau Panzera 51; d weekday/weekend R$228/248;) This family-run place sits on a ridge just above the bus station. The nine small but spotless rooms have panoramic views – the location, garden and pool area make up for the otherwise simple decor.

★ **Hotel Solar da Ponte** POUSADA **$$$**
(3355-1255; www.solardaponte.com.br; Praça das Mercês; r midweek R$596-860, weekend R$745-1075; @) Right in the heart of town, this magnificent re-creation of a colonial mansion is one of Brazil's finest hotels, with first-rate food and service across the board. The rooms have fresh flowers, beautiful antiques, and comfortable chairs and beds. There's a reading room, complete with fireplace, and complimentary afternoon tea is served in the garden.

Pousada Richard Rothe POUSADA **$$$**
(3355-1333; www.pousadarichardrothe.com.br; Padre Toledo 124; r midweek/weekend R$350/380; @) On a picturesque street in the historic center, this stylish pousada has spacious suites, an elegant reading room with fireplace, and a small protected forest out back where monkeys come to play at dawn.

Eating

Divino Sabor SELF-SERVE **$**
(Gabriel Passos 300; per kg R$41.90; 11:30am-2:30pm Tue-Sun) Very popular with

locals for its self-serve offerings, including grilled meats and the normal range of *mineira* specialties.

Bar do Celso MINEIRA **$**

(Largo das Forras 80a; mains R$20-36; noon-8pm Wed-Mon) On the main square, this locally run restaurant specializes in down-to-earth *mineira* fare at reasonable prices. Folks with less voracious appetites will appreciate the R$18 *prato mini*, a smaller plate designed for one person.

Gourmeco ITALIAN **$$**

(3355-1955; www.gourmeco.com.br; Direita 10b; mains R$40-45) Authentic Italian pasta and risotto dishes, coupled with a prime corner location just below Tiradentes' beautiful Matriz church, make this one of the best new eateries in town. Pugliese Slow Food aficionado Umberto and chef Juliana whip up classics ranging from *orecchiette* (ear-shaped pasta) with Bolognese *ragù* (meat sauce) to superb tiramisu.

Uai Thai THAI **$$**

(9927-9903; www.uaithai.com.br; Direita 205a; mains R$40-65; noon-3pm & 7-11pm Mon, Tue, Thu & Fri, noon-5pm & 8pm-midnight Sat, noon-5pm Sun) Chef Ricardo Martins mixes Asian and Brazilian influences at this fusion eatery on restaurant-happy Rua Direita. Specialties include lemon-crusted *surubim* (freshwater fish) with sautéed veggies and cashews, and a Thai-influenced variation on Romeu e Julieta, the classic *mineira* dessert of guava paste and cheese – this one incorporating curry, mint and a scoop of homemade ice cream.

Tragaluz REGIONAL **$$**

(3355-1424; www.tragaluztiradentes.com; Direita 52; mains R$48-75; 7-10:30pm Sun, Mon, Wed & Thu, to 12:30am Fri & Sat) Set in a romantic, candlelit space with exposed stone and brick walls, Tragaluz prides itself on home cooking served with artistic flair. The innovative dishes range from yam and sugar beet soup to *pintada* (the restaurant's trademark guinea fowl) with veggies, mushrooms and homemade ravioli, and divine desserts like *cachaça* mousse, lemon sorbet and fried guava paste.

CasAzul MEXICAN, BRAZILIAN **$$**

(8511-4501; www.facebook.com/casazulbistro; Cadeia s/n; mains R$35-55; noon-4pm Fri-Sun, 8-11pm Tue-Sat) Crepes, salads and homemade chicken enchiladas share the menu with a good drinks list at this trendy Latin-themed bistro with vividly painted walls, rustic furniture and artsy lighting.

Pau de Angu REGIONAL **$$**

(9948-1692; Estrada para Bichinho Km 3; mains for 2/4 people from R$79/129; noon-5pm Wed-Mon) In a peaceful country setting between Tiradentes and the artsy community of Bichinho, this is a great spot for homemade *linguiça* (garlicky pork sausage), hot sauces and all things *mineira*. Portions are huge and meant to be divided among two to five people.

Luth Bistrô INTERNATIONAL **$$**

(9966-2819; www.facebook.com/luthtiradentes; Direita 224; mains R$40-80; 8pm-midnight Thu & Fri, 12:30-5pm & 8pm-midnight Sat, 12:30-5pm Sun) The gorgeous walled garden setting is the big draw at this recently opened gastropub near the heart of town. Spacious, verdant grounds surrounding a pond provide a pleasant backdrop for sipping local beer and test-tasting European-Brazilian fusion dishes such as *fondue mineiro* (made with local Minas cheese) or risotto with *cachaça*-flambéed *linguiça*.

Estalagem do Sabor MINEIRA **$$$**

(3355-1144; Gabriel Passos 280; mains R$65-99; 11am-8pm) One of Tiradentes' finest restaurants, Estalagem specializes in meat and *comida mineira* supplemented by a good wine list.

★**Viradas do Largo** MINEIRA **$$$**

(3355-1111; www.viradasdolargo.com.br; Rua do Moinho 11; mains R$34-96; noon-10pm Wed-Mon) Tucked down a peaceful lane far from the relative bustle of downtown Tiradentes, this is one of the region's standout restaurants for traditional *mineira* cuisine. Crowds pack into it on weekends, spilling over into the pleasant outdoor patio and garden area.

Drinking & Entertainment

A trio of popular bars with outdoor seating and occasional live music vie nightly for visitors' attention on Largo das Forras.

Entrepôt du Vin WINE BAR

(Direita 205; 3pm-late Mon-Fri, noon-late Sat, 10am-4pm Sun) This convivial little wine bar with its 18th-century frescoed ceiling makes an agreeable spot to sip a glass or two.

DON'T MISS

SMOKING MARY

Sure, there are buses that will get you back and forth between São João del Rei and Tiradentes, but how can they compare with a trip on a 19th-century steam train in pristine condition? Jump aboard as this little engine hisses and belches its way through the winding valley of the Serra de São José to Tiradentes. The tracks pass through one of the oldest areas of gold mining in Minas and you'll see the remnants of 18th-century mine workings all around. Keep a sharp eye out for modern *garimpeiros* (gold panners) still hoping to strike it rich.

Built in the 1880s as the textile industry began to take hold in São João, the Maria-Fumaça ('Smoking Mary,' as the steam train is locally known) was one of the first rail lines in Brazil. More history is available at the **Museu Ferroviário** (admission R$3, free with train ticket; ⌚9-11am & 1-5pm Wed-Sat, 9am-1pm Sun) inside São João's train station.

Now operated by **Trilhos de Minas** (☎3355-2789; www.trilhosdeminas.com; R$40/56 one-way/round-trip, half price for kids six to 12 and adults over 60), trains run twice daily in each direction on Fridays, Saturdays, Sundays and holidays. When leaving São João the best views are on the left side. If you need more time in Tiradentes than the train schedule allows, you can always bus back (there are regular connections between the two cities).

A similar historic train travels between Mariana and Ouro Preto.

Organ Concerts CLASSICAL MUSIC
(☎3355-1238; Igreja Matriz de Santo Antônio; adult/reduced R$35/20) On Friday nights at 8pm, live concerts are performed on the 18th-century organ amid the glittering gold interior of Igreja Matriz de Santo Antônio (p191).

Information

Bradesco (Passos 43) Multiple ATMs, near the main square.

Secretária Municipal de Turismo (☎3355-1212; tiradentes.net; Resende Costa 71; ⌚9am-5pm) On the main square; provides maps, information on hotels and guided tours.

Getting There & Away

BUS

Tiradentes' **bus station** is just north of the main square, across the stream. Two companies, Presidente (R$3.35, 20 minutes) and Vale do Ouro (R$3.80, 30 minutes), run regular buses between Tiradentes and São João del Rei. Thanks to this friendly rivalry, you'll never wait longer than 45 minutes for a bus during daylight hours. Between 7pm and 10pm, only Vale do Ouro operates, and departures are less frequent. If you miss the last bus, a taxi costs about R$60.

With advance planning, it's possible to catch a bus directly from Tiradentes to Rio. The morning **Paraibuna** (www.paraibunatransportes.com.br) bus originating in São João del Rei (8am Monday to Saturday, 10am Sunday) will pick passengers up in front of the Tiradentes train station – not the bus station – but you must buy your ticket in São João and indicate that you're boarding in Tiradentes. Coming from Rio, you can do the same thing in reverse: take Paraibuna's 7am bus Monday through Saturday (or the 2pm bus on Sunday) and indicate that you want to disembark in Tiradentes when buying your ticket; make sure to inform the driver as well.

TRAIN

The Maria-Fumaça tourist train connects Tiradentes with São João del Rei. Tiradentes' train station is about 700m southeast of the main square.

Caxambu

☎0XX35 / POP 22,000 / ELEV 895M

Long before Perrier hit Manhattan singles bars, Caxambu water was being celebrated on the international circuit, winning gold medals at the 1903 Victor Emmanuel III Exposition in Rome and the St Louis International Fair of 1904.

Caxambu remains the most venerable of several mineral spa towns in southern Minas (collectively known as the Circuito das Águas), although its turn-of-the-century glory has faded gradually toward dowdiness. Even so, it's a convenient transport hub for other southern Minas attractions, and worth a look for curiosity's sake if you're passing this way.

Sights

Parque das Águas PARK, SPRING
(admission R$5, plus individual attractions R$5-40; ⌚7am-6pm) A rheumatic's Disneyland,

OFF THE BEATEN TRACK

A MYSTICAL RETREAT IN SOUTHERN MINAS

If you're into mysticism or superstition, or just looking for a cheap, fun and idyllic place to relax, consider a detour to the quaint village of **São Thomé das Letras** (population 7000, elevation 1291m, phone code 35). High on a plateau north of Caxambu, with a bird's-eye view of the surrounding farmland, São Thomé feels like a world apart. Perhaps this accounts for its reputation among Brazilian mystics as one of the seven sacred cities of the world, and the many sightings of flying saucers and extraterrestrials reported here.

The word 'Letras' in São Thomé's name refers to the puzzling inscriptions found in local caverns such as **Carimbado** and **Chico Taquara** (both 3km outside town) and the **Gruta de São Thomé**, a small cave in the heart of town. More down-to-earth attractions include the nearby waterfalls **Euboise** (3km), **Prefeitura** (7km) and **Véu de Noiva** (12km) and the town's buildings, made from beautiful slabs of quartzite. There are two nice churches: **Igreja Matriz de São Thomé** (1785), on leafy Praça da Matriz, and the raw-stone **Igreja de Pedra**, downhill toward the bus station. For great mountain views at sunset and sunrise, head up to the **lookout** 500m above town.

During the third or fourth weekend in August the three-day **Festa de Agosto** draws lots of pilgrims with live music and other festivities.

The town is filled with reasonably priced pousadas and restaurants. One block uphill from the Gruta de São Thomé, **Pousada Serra Branca** (3237-1200; www.pousadaserrabranca.com.br; João de Deus 7; s R$60, d R$110-130;) offers bargain-priced *apartamentos* (rooms with private bathroom); just downhill, in an old stone building, **Pousada Arco Iris** (3237-1212; www.pousarcoiris.com.br; João Batista Neves 225; s/d from R$190/250;) is the prettiest of São Thomé's budget pousadas, with a sauna and pool. For tasty treats in the heart of town, try the excellent per-kilo *mineira* cuisine at family-run **Restaurante da Sinhá** (3237-1348; Capitão Pedro José Martins 31; per kg R$39.90; noon-11pm) or the wood-fired pizzas at **Ser Criativo** (3237-1266; Praça Getúlio Vargas 18; pizzas R$33-56; 6pm-midnight).

São Thomé's **tourist information office** (3237-1276; turismo@saotomedasletras.mg.gov.br; José Cristiano Alves 20; 9am-noon & 2-5pm Mon-Sat, 9am-noon Sun) is just off the main square, Praça da Matriz. It provides a brochure in Portuguese with a rudimentary map of town and can point you to surrounding natural attractions.

From São Thomé's bus station, 1km north of the center, **Coutinho** (3341-5040) runs once daily to/from Caxambu along a rugged but scenic dirt road, in good weather only (R$18.55, 2¼ hours, leaving Caxambu at 2:15pm, returning from São Thomé at 7:30am).

this vast park in the center of town has lovely gardens, tree-shaded canals, a geyser, a spring-fed outdoor swimming pool, a chairlift climbing 800m to the Christ statue atop Morro Cristo hill, and the ornate 1912-vintage **Balneário Hidroterápico**, where you can soak in a hot bath, take therapeutic showers or relax in a sauna.

Sleeping & Eating

If you're in Caxambu outside peak holiday times you can get some good deals. The fancier hotels include meals, and many have spas and offer massages.

Locally produced honey, homemade fruit liqueurs and preserves are sold all over town.

Palace Hotel HOTEL $

(3341-3341; www.palacehotel.com.br; Dr Viotti 567; d incl breakfast/full board R$155/267;) This colonial establishment is one of the best deals in town. The pool out back has a waterslide, and the card-playing rooms downstairs exude 19th-century charm.

Hotel Caxambu HOTEL $$

(3341-9300; www.hotelcaxambu.com.br; Major Penha 145; s/d incl breakfast from R$160/200, incl all meals R$280/350;) The historic facade here hides a slew of modern amenities. There's a pool and a good restaurant, and it's located right in the center of town.

Coreto SELF-SERVE $

(www.facebook.com/RestauranteCoreto; Praça 16 de Setembro 59; per kg R$33.90; 11am-2.30pm) Organic salads and *mineira* cuisine cooked over the wood fire are the specialties at Caxambu's newest self-serve place, which enjoys a nice location directly across from the bandstand in the town's central square.

Information

Bradesco (Dr Viotti 566)

Secretaria de Turismo (www.caxambu.mg.gov.br; Praça 16 de Setembro 24; ⌚8am-6pm Mon-Fri) In the town hall, adjacent to the Parque das Águas.

Getting There & Away

The bus station is about 1km south of the center on Praça Cônego José de Castilho Moreira.

Expresso Gardénia (www.expressogardenia.com.br) offers service to Belo Horizonte (R$112, six hours) at 8:10am daily and 10:40pm Sunday to Friday. **Cometa** (www.viacaocometa.com.br) goes to São Paulo (R$63, 5½ to 6½ hours) four times daily. For Rio de Janeiro (R$58 to R$71, five hours) and Resende (R$28 to R$34, 2½ hours), gateway to Parque Nacional de Itatiaia, **Cidade do Aço** (www.cidadedoaco.com.br) runs a daily *executivo* bus at 8am, plus a midnight service Sunday to Friday.

Aiuruoca & the Vale do Matutu

☎0XX35 / POP 6200 / ELEV 989M

About an hour east of Caxambu is the Vale do Matutu, a lush green valley flanked by waterfalls and mountains. Most prominent among the surrounding peaks is photogenic Pico do Papagaio (2293m), which forms the centerpiece of the Parque Estadual da Serra do Papagaio. There's some great hiking in the region. Access to the valley is via a very rough dirt road running 20km south from the small town of Aiuruoca. You could easily linger here for a few days, relaxing into the rhythms of nature, reading a good book, hiking and swimming.

Sights & Activities

At the far end of the valley is the attractive century-old Casarão do Matutu, the headquarters of AMA-Matutu, a community organization dedicated to sustainable tourism. If somebody's home, they can provide information about the valley and nearby hiking opportunities.

Guides are strongly recommended and can be arranged through the Casarão or through Pousada Mandala das Águas. Destinations include the nearby waterfall Cachoeira do Fundo (a moderate four-hour, 10km round-trip), or the valley's standout attraction, Pico do Papagaio (a challenging eight-hour, 13km round-trip with 800m elevation gain, from R$75 per person).

Sleeping & Eating

Throughout the valley, pousadas and hotels have sprouted like mushrooms in recent years; most serve meals.

Pousada Dois Irmãos POUSADA $

(☎3344-1373; Coronel Oswaldo 204, Aiuruoca; s/d R$60/120) This simple hotel near Aiuruoca's main square is the best option if you arrive at night and just need a place to lay your head. The attached restaurant serves good *mineira* food (per kilo R$32.90)

★**Mandala das Águas** POUSADA $$

(☎9948-5650; www.mandaladasaguas.com.br; Vale do Matutu, Km 15; d/ste with half-board R$300/370; 📶) Near the valley's far end, the delightfully tranquil Mandala features spacious rooms, verandas with hammocks, panoramic views of Pico do Papagaio and trails to secluded swimming holes in the gorgeous river below. The American-Brazilian owners use produce from their garden in the hearty homemade meals, and breakfast includes some of the best *pão de queijo* (balls of cheese-stuffed tapioca bread) you'll find anywhere in Minas.

★**Kiko & Kika** BRAZILIAN $$

(☎9927-4853; Estrada Aiuruoca/Alagoa, Km 1.8; mains R$35-68; ⌚noon-4pm Fri & Sun, to 5pm Sat) For fine dining in a rural setting, try this sweet little restaurant just 2km south of Aiuruoca. Run by a couple with roots in France and Switzerland, it specializes in trout – both fresh and smoked – along with earthy touches such as wooden utensils and fresh herbed lemonade. Dinner is available upon request on Friday and Saturday nights (7pm to 9pm).

Getting There & Away

Aiuruoca's bus stop is on the central Praça Côn José Castilho. Viação Sandra operates one daily bus (R$16, one hour) from Caxambu to Aiuruoca at 6:20pm, plus a 10am departure on weekdays only. Buses return to Caxambu at 5:20am and 11:15am on weekdays, 5:20am on Saturday and 6:20am on Sunday.

To reach the more remote pousadas in the Vale do Matutu, you'll need your own car (beware the rough road) or a **taxi** (☎9944-1601, 3344-1601; www.ajuru.com.br/taxi). Once settled in the valley, walking is the most pleasant way to get around.

Colonial Towns of Minas Gerais

Minas' standout attraction, the *cidades históricas* (colonial towns) collectively constitute one of Brazil's most appealing and accessible tourist circuits. Baroque masterworks built with 18th-century mineral wealth, they all share a common ancestry, yet each has unique charms.

Ouro Preto

Ouro Preto (p175) tops the list as Minas' most magnificent and best-preserved colonial gem. Its two dozen churches and cobblestoned streets have benefited from more than 80 years of conservation efforts.

Mariana

A pearl inside the surrounding 21st-century oyster, Mariana (p183) is home to two of Minas' most harmonious squares and an 18th-century organ that still plays weekly concerts. Hop aboard the scenic train from Ouro Preto for a perfect day trip.

Tiradentes

With winding alleys decked in flowers, a photogenic mountain backdrop, and atmospheric restaurants and boutiques on every corner, cute-as-a-button Tiradentes (p190) wins the prize for romantic charm.

Diamantina

A remote, rugged setting and unadulterated architectural integrity give Diamantina (p200) a 'lost in time' quality. Prefer something sleepier but just as picturesque? Follow the Estrada Real southeast to São Gonçalo, Milho Verde and Serro.

São João del Rei

A colonial-modern hybrid, bustling São João (p187) is peppered with enough 18th-century churches to hold their own against the encroaching high-rises.

Congonhas

Colonial Minas' ugly duckling, urbanized Congonhas (p185) remains a must-see thanks to Aleijadinho's brilliant sculptures of *The Prophets*, the crowning masterpiece of Minas' greatest baroque artist.

1. *The Prophets* (p185), Congonhas **2.** Cobblestone streets, Ouro Preto (p175) **3.** Igreja Matriz de Santo Antônio (p191), Tiradentes

2

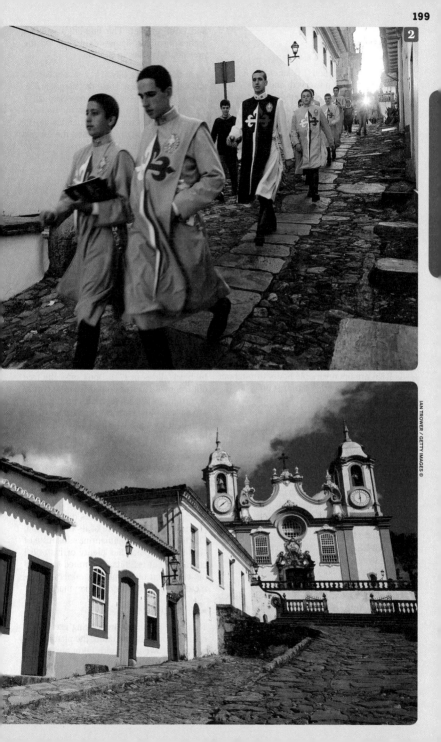

IAN TROWER / GETTY IMAGES ©

Diamantina

☎0XX38 / POP 46,000 / ELEV 1113M

Isolated but fabulous, Diamantina is one of Brazil's best preserved and least visited colonial towns. Surrounded by desolate mountains, it was the most remote mining town in Minas and the starting point for the Estrada Real, the old road to the coast built with the sweat, blood and tears of thousands of African slaves. Diamantina's fine mansions and winding streets haven't changed much in the last 200 years. Designated a Unesco World Heritage site in 1999, this *cidade histórica* is also the birthplace of Juscelino Kubitschek, former Brazilian president and founder of Brasília.

As with most *mineiro* cities, Diamantina is built on precipitous slopes. The bus station sits high on a bluff, so the 500m descent into town can be tough on the knees, and the return climb is a true workout. The central square is Praça Conselheiro Mota, dominated by **Santo Antônio cathedral** – both colloquially known as Sé.

Sights

Diamantina's churches (admission to each is R$3) are open variable hours throughout the year; check with the tourist office for the current schedule.

Casa de Juscelino Kubitschek MUSEUM
(☎3531-3607; São Francisco 241; admission R$5; ⏲8am-5pm Tue-Sat, to 1pm Sun) Casa de Juscelino Kubitschek, childhood home of the former president, is full of historical memorabilia that reflect his simple upbringing as the grandson of poor Czech immigrants. Kubitschek himself believed that his early life in Diamantina influenced him greatly.

Museu do Diamante MUSEUM
(☎3531-1382; http://museudiamante.blogspot.com; Direita 14; admission R$1; ⏲10am-5pm Tue-Sat, 9am-1pm Sun) Between Praça JK and the cathedral is the house of Padre Rolim, one of the Inconfidentes. It's now the Museu do Diamante, exhibiting religious art, old photos, furniture, weapons and other relics of the diamond days.

Mercado Municipal MARKET
(Municipal Market; Praça Barão Guaicuí) Built by the army in 1835, this public market is a popular community gathering place on Friday evenings, when there's live music, and on Saturday mornings for the weekly food and craft market. The building's wooden arches inspired Niemeyer's design for the presidential palace in Brasília.

Casa da Chica da Silva HISTORIC BUILDING
(☎3531-2491; Praça Lobo de Mesquita 266; ⏲noon-5:30pm Tue-Sat, 8:30am-noon Sun) FREE This fine colonial mansion was the home of diamond contractor João Fernandes de Oliveira and his longtime partner, the former slave Chica da Silva. Upstairs, paintings and poems (in Portuguese only) evoke the lifestyle of the extravagant mulatto.

Igreja de NS do Carmo CHURCH
(Rua do Carmo) Adorned with rich, golden carvings and a gilded organ made in Diamantina, this is the town's most opulent church. Constructed between 1760 and 1765, its tower was reputedly built at the rear at the request of locally renowned personage Chica da Silva, so that she might sit in the front pews (Portuguese law at the time denied blacks the right to pass 'beyond the belltower').

Igreja de NS do Rosário dos Pretos CHURCH
(Largo do Rosário) Downhill from the center you'll find Diamantina's oldest church, built by black slaves in 1731. Don't miss the tree out front with a cross embedded in its trunk; according to legend, it sprang up here as a divine sign to prove the innocence of an 18th-century slave who was falsely accused of stealing diamonds.

Casa da Glória MUSEUM
(☎3531-1394; Rua da Glória 298; admission R$1; ⏲1-6pm Tue-Sun) Connected by a vivid-blue 2nd-story passageway, these two houses on opposite sides of the street were originally the residence of Diamantina's diamond supervisors and the palace of its first bishop. Currently housing Diamantina's Institute of Geology, the place has plenty of historical character, but exhibits are limited to a ragtag collection of old photos, mineral specimens and 19th-century German maps.

Activities

There are numerous interesting excursions near Diamantina, including the picturesque historical town of **Biribiri**, 14km north via a scenic dirt road through Biribiri State Park; along the way are some red-hued cliff paintings and a beautiful multilevel waterfall – **Cachoeira da Sentinela** – with pools for swimming.

Diamantina

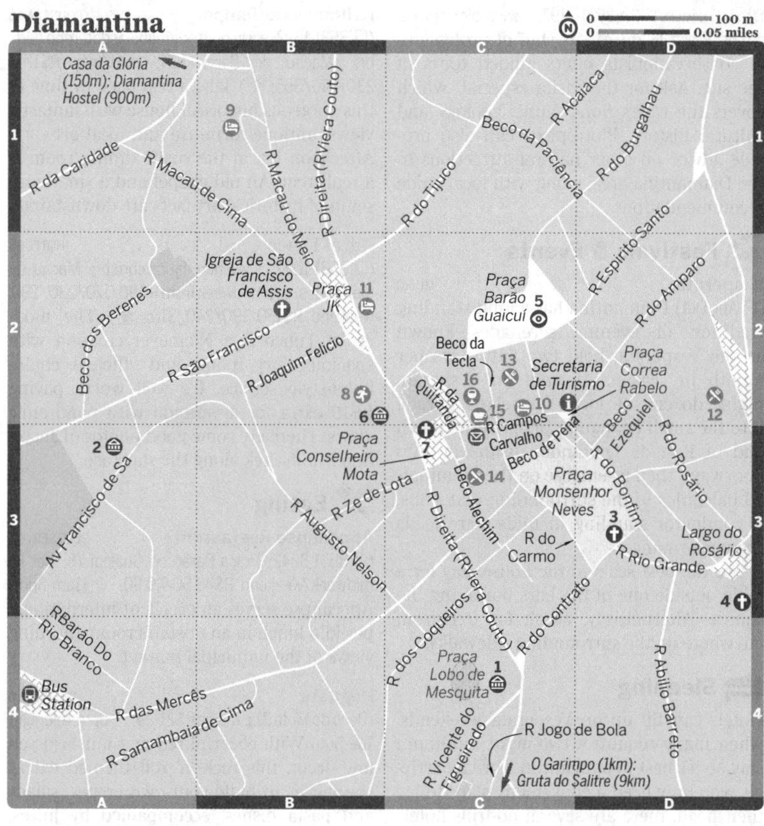

Diamantina

Sights
1 Casa da Chica da Silva C4
2 Casa de Juscelino Kubitschek A3
3 Igreja de NS do Carmo D3
4 Igreja de NS do Rosário dos Pretos D3
5 Mercado Municipal C2
6 Museu do Diamante B2
7 Santo Antônio Cathedral C3

Activities, Courses & Tours
8 Biotrópicos B2

Sleeping
9 Hotel Tijuco B1
10 Pousada Capistrana C2
11 Relíquias do Tempo B2

Eating
12 Al Árabe D2
13 Apocalipse Restaurante C2
14 Deguste C3

Drinking & Nightlife
15 Livraria Café Espaço B C2
16 Recanto do Antônio C2

Caminho dos Escravos HIKING
Accessed via a trailhead 3km north of town, this stone-paved road built by slaves passes through rugged high country between Diamantina and Mendanha, 20km to the northeast. The walk is best undertaken with a guide (get contact info from the tourist office), as the trail is intermittent and poorly signposted.

Gruta do Salitre CAVE
(⏲9am-noon & 2-5pm Sat, 9am-noon Sun) This lovely quartzite cave 9km southeast of Diamantina (near the village of Curralinho) is administered by local environmental NGO

Biotrópicos (3531-2197; www.biotropicos.org.br; Praça JK 25) ; its staff of professional conservationists offers guided tours of the site. Ask for the 'visita especial,' which covers the cave's flora, fauna, geology and cultural history. Biotrópicos can also provide advice on other natural attractions in the Diamantina area, along with local guide recommendations.

Festivals & Events

Vesperata MUSIC
(Apr-Oct) Diamantina has a long-standing tradition of evening serenades known as the Vesperata, held two Saturdays per month in season. At 8pm on Vesperata night, dozens of local musicians parade into the small triangular praça at the north end of Rua da Quitanda, disappear into doorways, then re-emerge on the illuminated balconies of the surrounding mansions. A conductor standing in midsquare leads the performance.

For the best seats in the house, pay for a table outside one of the bars bordering the square. Alternatively, watch for free from anywhere on the surrounding sidewalks.

Sleeping

Hotels can fill up on Vesperata weekends, when many require a two-night minimum stay, so it's best to plan ahead. For late arrivals who only need a convenient place to lay their head, there are several no-frills hotels directly across from the bus station.

Pousada Capistrana POUSADA $
(3531-6560; www.pousadacapistrana.com.br; Campos Carvalho 35; s/d from R$70/140; P) Rooms here are a bit cramped, but the location smack in the middle of Diamantina's historic district is hard to beat. Parking is available.

Diamantina Hostel HOSTEL $
(3531-2003; www.diamantinahostel.com.br; Rua do Bicame 988; dm R$40-60, d R$96-140;) Diamantina's hostel sits on a residential hillside, 1km northwest of the bus station and within a 15-minute walk of the historic center. Dorms and doubles are very simple, but most come with ensuite bathrooms, and there are pretty views from the upstairs breakfast room and guest kitchen. Laundry facilities are also available.

Relíquias do Tempo POUSADA $$
(3531-1627; www.pousadareliquiasdotempo.com.br; Macau de Baixo 104; s/d/tr/q R$175/230/310/365;) Take a trip back in time at this gorgeous historical house with fantastic views, antique furniture and local artwork. Afternoon tea in the rustic dining room is a real treat. An old chapel and a small museum of historical artifacts are downstairs.

Hotel Tijuco HOTEL $$
(3531-1022; www.hoteltijuco.com.br; Macau do Meio 211; s/d/tr midweek from R$90/170/230/290, weekend R$150/190/240/310;) The modernist Tijuco is a Niemeyer creation with spacious, airy rooms and efficient chain-hotel-style service. It's well worth paying R$10 extra for a veranda with panoramic views. There are some good photos of Juscelino Kubitschek along the staircase.

Eating

Apocalipse Restaurante SELF-SERVE $
(3531-3242; Praça Barão do Guaicuí 78; per kg midweek/weekend R$43.50/49.90; 11am-3pm) Apocalipse serves an excellent international per-kilo lunch in an upstairs room affording views of the municipal market.

Deguste CREPERIE $
(Beco do Mota 31a; mains R$21-29; 6pm-midnight Tue-Sun) With cheerful red and mustard yellow decor, this rock 'n' roll–themed eatery specializes in build-your-own crepes, salads and pasta dishes, accompanied by juices, milkshakes and ice-cream treats. It's hidden on a backstreet just above the cathedral.

Al Árabe LEBANESE $$
(3531-2281; www.restaurantealarabe.com.br; Praça Dr Prado 124; sandwiches R$21.50, mains R$35-50; 10am-11pm Mon-Sat;) From simple snacks (starting at R$5) to more elaborate dishes for two, Al Árabe's Lebanese-Brazilian chef offers an enticing line-up of Middle Eastern specialties, including many vegetarian options.

O Garimpo MINEIRA $$
(3531-1044; www.pousadadogarimpo.com.br; Av da Saudade 265; mains for two R$58-120; 6-10pm Mon-Fri, noon-10pm Sat, noon-4pm Sun) Famous for its regional dishes, the restaurant at Pousada do Garimpo challenges the heftiest of appetites with its house specialty *bambá do garimpo,* a high-calorie concoction dating back to the diamond-mining days that includes pork chops, beans, rice, fine-

ly chopped kale and *angu* (corn porridge). There's also an occasional all-you-can-eat weekend buffet for R$60 including desserts.

Drinking & Nightlife

On Friday evenings from 6pm onwards, visit Diamantina's Mercado Municipal for **Sexta Nossa**, a community happy hour where locals unwind with drinks and regional food, accompanied by live *chorinho* (informal instrumental music), samba and blues music.

Another classic weekend event is **Café no Beco**, held Sunday mornings from 8am to 1pm along the Beco da Tecla, a pedestrianized street between the cathedral and the market square. Locals sell baked goods, play live music and offer free coffee and tea to passers-by.

★**Livraria Café Espaço B** CAFE
(☎3531-6005; Beco da Tecla 31; ⏲9am-midnight Mon-Thu, to 2am Fri & Sat, to 2pm Sun; wi-fi) This bookstore-cafe is a relaxing spot to mingle with Diamantina's bohemian set. You can browse books (including a few in English), use the free wi-fi and linger over coffee, tea, wine and light meals ranging from salads to pasta, trout and fondue.

Recanto do Antônio BAR
(☎3531-1147; Beco da Tecla 39; ⏲11am-4pm & 6pm-late Tue-Sun) With stone walls and wood beams, this cozy and convivial bar-restaurant features live music on weekends, and its *sanduiche de filé* (steak sandwich) is one of the tastiest bar snacks around.

Information

Banco do Brasil (Praça da Sé) Behind the cathedral.

Bradesco (Praça Barão do Guaicuí) Just below the Mercado Municipal.

Secretaria de Turismo (☎3531-9532; http://diamantina.mg.gov.br/turismo; Praça Antônio Eulálio 53; ⏲9am-6pm Mon-Sat, to 2pm Sun) Distributes a Portuguese-language town map and guide.

Getting There & Away

From Diamantina's bus station at the top of town, Pássaro Verde (p183) runs eight daily buses to Belo Horizonte (R$88, five hours) and two to the neighboring historical town of Serro (R$26, two hours). A taxi between the bus station and the center costs around R$15.

Serro & Around

☎0XX38 / POP 21,000 / ELEV 781M

Founded in 1714, the charming colonial town of Serro snakes down a hillside in beautiful rural country south of Diamantina. While quite popular with Brazilians, this region remains little visited by foreigners and therefore retains a tranquil and traditional *mineiro* air. Its cheese is considered the best in Minas.

Heading north from Serro toward Diamantina, the tranquil high-altitude hamlets of **Milho Verde** and **São Gonçalo do Rio das Pedras** (less than 35km away) also make lovely stopovers, with access to some fabulous hiking opportunities, including some of the most scenic stretches of the original Estrada Real (the 18th-century 'Royal Road' that connected Diamantina to the Rio de Janeiro coast).

Sights

Serro's main attractions are its historic buildings. Several 18th-century churches are worth a visit, including the **Igreja de NS do Carmo** (admission R$3; ⏲variable), the **Igreja do Bom Jesus do Matozinhos** (admission R$3; ⏲variable) and the **Capela de NS do Rosario** (admission R$3; ⏲variable). Note that hours change frequently for all of these attractions; check with the tourist office for the latest schedule.

Capela de Santa Rita CHURCH
(admission R$3; ⏲variable) The most striking building in town is the graceful, single-steepled Capela de Santa Rita, straight uphill from the main square via a steep series of steps.

Chácara do Barão do Serro HISTORIC BUILDING
(⏲variable) FREE Just downhill from town, the Chácara do Barão do Serro is a lovely old mansion affording a glimpse of 19th-century baronial life in Serro.

Festivals

Festa de NS do Rosário CULTURAL
In early July Serro hosts one of Minas' oldest festivals, the Festa de NS do Rosário, dating back to 1728. Townspeople representing Brazil's three traditional social groups parade through the streets in colorful attire: *caboclos* (the mixed descendants of indigenous peoples and Portuguese) beat out rhythms on bows and arrows, holding mock

confrontations with sword- and guitar-wielding *marujos* (Europeans), while *catopês* (Africans) speak in ancient dialect and beat on instruments symbolizing empty plates.

Sleeping & Eating

Serro is full of low-cost eateries, most serving *comida mineira*, but its selection of hotels is limited. The towns of São Gonçalo and Milho Verde, with their rural tranquility, are nicer places to spend the night, and pousadas in both towns often include meals in their rates.

Refúgio dos Cinco Amigos POUSADA $
(3541-6037; www.pousadarefugio5amigos.com.br; Largo Félix Antônio 160, São Gonçalo; r per person incl breakfast/all meals R$80/$120;) This charmingly rustic Swiss-run pousada next to the church green and bus stop has been welcoming guests to São Gonçalo for over three decades. Simple but delicious meals are cooked on the wood stove, and there's a spacious reading room with a fireplace for chilly nights.

Pousada do Capão POUSADA $$
(3541-6068; www.pousadacapao.com; Rua da Nascente 550, São Gonçalo; d incl breakfast/half-board R$180/240, 2-person chalet incl breakfast/half-board 220/280;) Rooms and chalets encircle a spacious green area at this lovely pousada hidden just outside São Gonçalo. Trained chef and American expatriate Peter and his Brazilian wife Marcia are consummate hosts, plying guests with superb homemade liqueurs, baked goods, international comfort food and insiders' advice on local attractions, including hikes to numerous nearby waterfalls.

Information

Centro de Informações Turísticas
(3541-2754; http://serro.mg.gov.br; Nagib Bahmed 3; 8am-5pm Mon-Sat, to noon Sun) hands out a useful map of Serro's old mansions and churches and also provides information about São Gonçalo and Milho Verde.

Getting There & Away

Both Pássaro Verde (p183) and **Serro** (3201-9662; www.serro.com.br) offer long-distance bus service from Serro's **bus station** (3541-1366), one block downhill from the historical center. Destinations include Belo Horizonte (R$72 to R$97, 5½ hours, four daily), Conceição do Mato Dentro (R$21, 1½ hours, one daily) and Diamantina (R$25, 2¼ hours, two daily).

Milho Verde and São Gonçalo do Rio das Pedras can be reached from either Serro or Diamantina. From Serro, TransFacil's two daily buses (R$8) pass first through Milho Verde (one hour) before continuing to São Gonçalo (1½ hours). From Diamantina, Diamantinense's lone daily bus (3pm Monday to Saturday, 6pm Sunday) goes first to São Gonçalo (R$12, two hours), then to Milho Verde (R$15, 2½ hours).

Parque Nacional da Serra do Cipó

0XX31

Some 100km northeast of Belo Horizonte, **Parque Nacional da Serra do Cipó** (3718-7151; www.icmbio.gov.br/parnaserradocipo; Hwy MG-10, Km 97) FREE is one of the most beautiful parks in Minas. Most of the park's vegetation is cerrado (savanna) and grassy highlands, straddling the Serra do Espinhaço that divides the water basins of the São Francisco and Doce rivers. At lower elevations there are waterfalls and lush, ferny river valleys containing a number of unique orchids. Fauna here includes maned wolves, tamarin monkeys, banded anteaters, jaguars, bats and the small, brightly colored *sapo de pijama* (pyjama frog).

The park is vast, and the most popular trails involve multiday traverses of the *serra* (mountain range). Information and trail maps are available at park headquarters a few kilometers southeast of the town of Cardeal Mota. Two especially worthwhile day hikes are the 16km round-trip from headquarters to a 70m waterfall called **Cachoeira da Farofa**, and the 24km round-trip to the 80m-deep gorge called **Cânion da Bandeirinha**.

Local tour operators offering hiking, climbing, stand-up-paddling, rafting, horseback-riding and mountain-biking excursions to the park include **Bela Geraes Turismo** (3718-7394; http://serradocipogeraes.com.br) and **Cipoeiro Expedições** (9611-8878; www.cipoeiro.com.br).

Sleeping & Eating

Véu de Noiva CAMPGROUND $
(3718-7096; www.acmmg.com.br/veudanoiva.html; Hwy MG-010, Km 99.5; campsites per person R$37;) Camping in the park is not permitted, but this campground along the main road 5km north of park headquarters is a great alternative. There's a freshwater swimming pool, snack bar and direct access to

OFF THE BEATEN TRACK

SAFE HAVEN FOR AN ENDANGERED PRIMATE

The *muriqui* (woolly spider monkey), largest primate of the New World, is a stunning creature. Adult males stand roughly 1.5m tall, and their movements and physical presence can be startlingly humanlike. The animal's photogenic qualities have made it a poster child for wildlife preservation in Brazil, but actually seeing one in the wild can be challenging. At the time of writing, there were only a few thousand left in the world – including only 1200 of the rarer northern *muriqui* – down from an estimated 400,000 at the time of Portuguese colonization.

Three factors explain the *muriquis'* drastic drop in numbers: destruction of their native Mata Atlântica (Atlantic rainforest) habitat, their own docile nature (their Tupi name means 'easygoing folks') and the slow pace of their reproductive cycle. Female *muriquis* generally give birth to a single baby after a gestation period of eight months, and newborns stay with their mothers for up to three years, during which time no new mating occurs. *Muriquis* are slow moving and less combative than most other primates – indeed, they spend most of their time eating, playing and hugging each other! So they've historically been easy targets for hunters.

Estação Biológica de Caratinga (☎3322-2540; www.preservemuriqui.org.br/estacao.htm), a remote and little-visited nature reserve in eastern Minas, is the easiest place to spot *muriquis* in the wild. The reserve has played a critical role in rescuing the northern *muriqui* from extinction. There were only eight *muriquis* on record here in 1944, when local coffee farmer Feliciano Abdalla committed himself to preserving a large chunk of the native Atlantic rainforest on his property. Forty years later, the Estação Biológica was established, and in the three decades since, research and preservation efforts have led to greater understanding of the *muriqui* and an impressive resurgence of its numbers. Today there are approximately 450 northern *muriquis* living within the reserve, representing roughly a third of the world's population.

Seeing the primates in their natural habitat is an amazing experience, and visitors have a better-than-average chance of a sighting, thanks to the expert skills of local guides. To arrange a day visit (R$150 to R$200 per person depending on group size, plus R$40 for optional lunch), call or email the park office. Bring sturdy shoes for quick scrambles up the hillside, and don't wear red – *muriquis* take this as a sign of aggression. May is an especially good month to visit, as the *muriquis'* favorite food source, *Mabea fistulifera*, is in flower and the animals may linger in a single spot for long periods feeding on the nectar.

Ipanema and Caratinga are the transport hubs nearest the park. Pássaro Verde (www.passaroverde.com.br) runs two daily buses from Belo Horizonte to Ipanema (R$116, eight hours), and one early-morning bus from Ouro Preto to Caratinga (R$78, 5¼ hours). São Geraldo (www.saogeraldo.com.br) also runs a direct service from Vitória (Espírito Santo) to Caratinga (R$57, 6¾ hours, daily at 10:25pm).

From either Caratinga or Ipanema, take a Rio Doce bus (R$17, two hours from Caratinga; R$8, one hour from Ipanema) and ask to be let off at the Estação Biológica. From the bus stop, it's a 2km walk up a dirt road to park headquarters.

Ipanema is your best bet for an overnight stay. The centrally located hotel **Italia Palace** (☎3314-1793; www.italiapalacehotel.com; Av 7 de Setembro 383; s/d with fan R$65/110, with air-con & minibar R$110/160;) offers excellent value.

the lovely Véu de Noiva waterfall via a 200m footpath. Buses will drop you at the entrance upon request.

Grande Pedreira POUSADA **$$**
(☎8492-7548, 3718-7007; http://pousadagrandepedreira.com.br; Rua da Pedreira 100; d R$190) Set on a pretty green hillside across the road from the Véu de Noiva waterfall, this pousada is surrounded by giant boulders tailor-made for practicing your rappelling technique. Owners speak English and Spanish.

Hotel Cipó Veraneio HOTEL **$$$**
(☎3718-7000; www.cipoveraneiohotel.com.br; Hwy MG-10, Km 94; d R$472-585;) The most convenient place to stay if you're arriving by bus and want easy access to park

headquarters, Cipó Veraneio is right on the road but has great facilities, including an acclaimed restaurant and a pool.

Getting There & Away

Serro (p204) and Saritur (p175) run buses to the park from Belo Horizonte (R$26, 2½ hours, several daily from 6am to 4pm). For park headquarters, get off at the Hotel Cipó Veraneio (R$25, 2¼ hours), then walk or hitch 3km east down the signposted dirt road on your right, just past the hotel but before the Rio Cipó bridge.

For camping, continue 5km further north through the town of Cardeal Mota.

Tabuleiro

☎0XX31

North of Parque Nacional da Serra do Cipó, but still within Unesco's Serra do Espinhaço Biosphere Reserve, is Cachoeira Tabuleiro, Brazil's third-highest waterfall (273m). Access is via the small town of Tabuleiro, approximately 180km north of Belo Horizonte.

To get to the falls, proceed west through downtown Tabuleiro approximately 3km to **Parque Estadual Serra do Intendente** (☎3868-2878; admission R$10; ⊙8am-2pm). From the entrance station, a well-marked 2km-long trail descends steeply to the river, then peters out, requiring you to boulder-hop the rest of the way upstream. The views of the waterfall are spectacular the whole way. During the dry season you can swim in the natural pool at the foot of the falls.

Five kilometers east of the falls, the **Tabuleiro Eco Hostel** (☎3654-3288; http://tabuleiro-eco-hostel8.webnode.com; Joaquim Costinha 1b, Vila do Tabuleiro; campsites/dm/d R$30/60/150; 📶) offers grassy terraces for camping, plus dorms and private rooms in a series of colorful buildings running down the hillside. Facilities include a DVD library, kitchen and laundry facilities and an on-site snack bar–restaurant. The hostel owners organize climbing excursions plus hikes and horseback rides to nearby cliff paintings, waterfalls, canyons and swimming holes. There are also some pousadas and simple restaurants in town.

The first part of getting to Tabuleiro is easy: take a Serro (p204) bus from Belo Horizonte to Conceição do Mato Dentro (R$51, four hours, six daily from 6am to 4pm). The trick is getting from Conceição to Tabuleiro; local buses only leave at 3pm on Monday, Wednesday and Friday, and at 2pm on Saturday, returning from Tabuleiro at 8am the same days (R$10, one hour). A one-way taxi between Conceição and Tabuleiro costs R$80.

More convenient are the transfers offered (with advance notice) by the Tabuleiro hostel. From downtown Belo Horizonte or Confins airport, the trip to Tabuleiro costs R$400 for up to four people.

Parque Natural do Caraça

☎0XX31 / ELEV 1297M

Some 100km east of Belo Horizonte in the heart of the Serra do Espinhaço, the Parque Natural do Caraça is a blissful spot. Isolated from the rest of the world by a mountain ridge, the park encompasses 110 sq km of transition zone between the Mata Atlântica (Atlantic rainforest) and cerrado ecosystems. The park's centerpiece, nestled in a bowl-shaped valley, is a former monastery and boarding school attended by several Brazilian presidents. Now converted to a pousada, it's still owned and run by the Catholic congregation who use the neo-Gothic church for services.

The surrounding countryside includes several mountains – including **Pico do Sol** (at 2070m, the highest point in the Serra do Espinhaço) – as well as creeks forming waterfalls and natural swimming pools. The hillsides are lined with easily accessible hiking trails, all marked on a useful map provided at the park entrance. Most, including the easy 30-minute walk to the falls and pools at **Cascatinha** or the four-hour round-trip to the gorgeous **Cascatona waterfall**, can be undertaken solo. More treacherous trails require you to hike with a local guide (see www.santuariodocaraca.com.br/guias for a list of guides and their contact info).

Sleeping & Eating

★**Pousada Santuário do Caraça** POUSADA **$$**
(☎8978-3179; www.santuariodocaraca.com.br; r per person R$143-212, without bathroom R$102, all incl full board; @📶) Rooms at this peaceful, one-of-a-kind pousada range from simple *quartos* (rooms with shared bathrooms) off the garden courtyard to larger *apartamentos*, the best of which are in the Ala do Santuário (Sanctuary Wing). All rates include three awesome *mineira* meals

DON'T MISS

THE MANED WOLVES OF CARAÇA

The maned wolf – *lobo guará* in Portuguese – is South America's largest wild canine, living happily in the protected cerrado (savanna) environment of the Parque Natural do Caraça. A few years back, one of Caraça's priests had the idea of befriending the wolves, St Francis–style. After two years of patient work gradually tempting them toward the church with offerings of food, he gained the wolves' trust.

Nowadays the feeding has become a nightly ritual, open to overnight guests at the Pousada Santuário do Caraça. After dinner in the monastery's old stone refectory, people drift out to the patio. The ceremonial tray of scraps for the wolves is placed on the flagstones just past sunset, while popcorn, herb tea, and *cachaça* (sugarcane alcohol) are provided for the humans. Then the waiting begins.

Even on nights when a wolf never comes, the meditative pleasure of sitting under the stars, trading conversation and soaking up Caraça's tranquility is a magical memory that most visitors will carry with them for a long time. But wait patiently enough and you may be rewarded...with the patter of feet, the sudden hush rippling through the crowd, the scamper up the steps, and the wild eyes of this beautiful creature come to steal a quick meal and then vanish again into the night.

featuring local produce. The big highlight of staying here is the nightly feeding of the wolves. Advance reservations required.

Visit midweek if you can, as room rates are 10% cheaper and it's easier to see the wolves and appreciate Caraça's isolation and tranquility without the crowds of weekend escapees from Belo. During less-crowded periods, breakfast is served in the more intimate downstairs dining room, where you can fry your own eggs on the wood-fired stove. Kids under seven stay for free, and those aged seven to 11 pay half-price, making this a superb deal for families.

Getting There & Away

The two towns nearest the park are Barão de Cocais and Santa Bárbara.

Pássaro Verde (www.passaroverde.com.br) operates frequent buses from Belo Horizonte to Barão de Cocais (R$32, two hours, every two hours from 6am to 8:30pm). From Ouro Preto, **Vale do Ouro** (☎3551-5679) runs two buses Monday through Saturday to Santa Bárbara (R$31, 2½ hours, 7:25am and 1:45pm).

Vale's daily Belo–Vitória train also makes a stop just outside Barão de Cocais, in Dois Irmãos (regular/*executivo* R$15/32, leaving Belo Horizonte at 7:30am and arriving at 9am).

From Barão de Cocais or Dois Irmãos, the 30-minute taxi ride to Caraça costs around R$90; from Santa Bárbara, it's R$110. To reserve a taxi ahead of time, call **Célio do Táxi** (☎9689-3098). Note that the park gate is only open from 7am to 5pm (or to 9pm for pousada guests).

Parque Nacional de Caparaó

☎0XX32

This 250-sq-km national park contains southern Brazil's highest mountains, including **Pico da Cristal** (2798m), **Pico do Calçado** (2766m) and the third-highest peak in the country, **Pico da Bandeira** (2892m). Popular with climbers and hikers from all over Brazil, it affords panoramic views of the Caparaó Valley that divides Minas Gerais and Espírito Santo. The wide-open, rocky highlands that predominate here are complemented by a few lush remnants of Mata Atlântica (Atlantic rainforest) at lower elevations.

The **park entrance** (www.icmbio.gov.br/parnacaparao; admission foreigner/Brazilian R$25/12.50; ⏲7am-10pm) is 2km straight uphill from the nearest town, Alto do Caparaó. Between November and January there's lots of rain. The best time for clear weather is between June and August – although these are the coldest months. Bring warm clothes!

Activities

Pico da Bandeira HIKING

The classic hike to the summit of Pico da Bandeira can be made without climbing gear or a guide, as the trail is gradual and well marked. It costs between R$70 and R$100 for a taxi from town to the trailhead at Tronqueira, 8km up a steep dirt road from the park entrance. Cars are prohibited beyond

Tronqueira. From here, a gradual 9km climb leads to the summit.

Most people go straight up and back to Alto do Caparaó the same day, but with your own tent, you can cross over to the Espírito Santo side of the park, camp overnight, and retrace your steps the following day. The drop-off from Pico da Bandeira on the Espírito Santo side is steeper than on the Minas side, making for some very dramatic views, and there are three waterfalls with idyllic swimming holes – **Farofa**, **Aurélio** and **Sete Pilões** – near the last campground, Macieira.

Sleeping & Eating

Caparaó National Park Campsites CAMPING $
(3747-2086; reservaspnc@icmbio.gov.br; per site R$6) The Minas Gerais side of the park offers one official campsite, **Tronqueira**, at the trailhead for the 9km climb to the summit. On the Espírito Santo side of the park are two additional campsites: **Casa Queimada**, 4.5km below the summit by trail, and **Macieira**, 4.5km further by dirt road. Bring food and gear, and reserve sites by phone or email. All sites have flush toilets and cold showers. The Minas side has a second campsite, **Terreirão**, 4.5km below the summit at the halfway point of the climb from Tronqueira but it was closed indefinitely at the time of writing.

Pousada Querência HOSTEL $
(3747-2566; www.picodabandeiratur.tur.br/querencia.htm; Av Pico da Bandeira 1061; s/d R$90/130, with shared bathroom R$50/100) Despite its inconvenient location at the bottom of town, this friendly former hostel has good facilities, including a guest kitchen. It organizes sunrise hikes to Pico da Bandeira and other local excursions.

Pousada do Bezerra POUSADA $$
(3747-2538; www.pousadadobezerra.com.br; Av Pico da Bandeira; s/d incl breakfast R$129/199;) The lodging option closest to the park entrance has a sauna for soothing weary muscles and serves trout at its attached restaurant.

Caparaó Parque Hotel HOTEL $$$
(3747-2559; www.caparaoparquehotel.com.br; Av Pico da Bandeira; s R$266-276, d R$349-399;) Above town near the park entrance, the region's spiffiest hotel offers comfortable rooms and chalets amid manicured grounds. It also has two pools, a sauna, a natural swimming hole in the adjacent Rio Caparaó, an on-site restaurant and a pizzeria. It's a civilized spot to unwind after a day in the wild.

Getting There & Away

To reach Caparaó by bus from Belo Horizonte or Vitória (Espírito Santo), head first to the tiny town of Manhumirim, 25km outside the park. **Pássaro Verde** (www.passaroverde.com.br) operates three daily buses from Belo to Manhumirim (R$93 to R$102, 5½ to seven hours). From Vitória, **Águia Branca** (www.aguiabranca.com.br) runs a daily 5:50pm bus direct to Manhumirim (R$43, 4¼ hours).

Rio Doce runs nine daily buses from Manhumirim to Alto Caparaó (R$5.55, 45 minutes, from 6:30am to 8pm, returning 6:25am to 9:10pm). Alternatively, it's a half-hour taxi ride (about R$60). Manhumirim's **Palace Hotel** (0xx33-3341-2255; Av Lauro Silva 656; s/d R$70/100, without bathroom R$45/80;), diagonally across from the bus station, is perfectly adequate if you're stuck here overnight.

An alternate option from Vitória is Águia Branca's 7:20am bus to Manhuaçu (R$44, 4¼ hours), where eight daily Rio Doce buses connect to Alto Caparaó (R$11.20, 1½ hours).

ESPÍRITO SANTO

POP 3.5 MILLION

Vitória

0XX27 / POP 328,000

Espírito Santo's capital doesn't have much to show from its colonial past; indeed, the first thing visitors are likely to notice nowadays is Vitória's modern industrial port. Even so, the beaches east of the center are pleasant, the locals (known as *capixabas*) are warm and friendly, and the city has a flourishing economy, which means many bars, universities, nightclubs, restaurants and hotels.

The remnants of old Vitória, built on an island just off the coast, are connected to the mainland via a series of bridges.

Sights

The city's best beaches are Canto and Camburí to the north, and the renowned Praia da Costa to the south, in the sister city of Vila Velha.

City Center

Anchieta Palace PALACE
(3636-1032; www.facebook.com/palacioanchieta; Praça João Clímaco; 9:30am-5pm Tue-Fri,

OFF THE BEATEN TRACK

GREEN DETOURS IN ESPÍRITO SANTO

Espírito Santo offers a handful of off-the-beaten-track attractions for nature-lovers. All are easily accessible by car as day trips from Vitória, or can be combined into a longer itinerary progressing north toward Bahia.

Museu de Biologia Professor Mello Leitão (☎0xx27-3259-1182; www.museudebiologia melloleitao.gov.br; José Ruschi 4, Santa Teresa; 8am-5pm Tue-Sun) In the pretty mountain town of Santa Teresa, 82km northwest of Vitória, this museum celebrates the work of local ecologist Augusto Ruschi (1915–86), who conducted pioneering studies on the region's remarkable variety of hummingbirds and orchids and was a strong early proponent of environmental protection in Brazil. The verdant grounds are a peaceful oasis, and offer a chance to observe many local plant and hummingbird species.

Reserva Biológica de Comboios (☎0xx27-3274-1209; www.projetotamar.org.br/base.php?cod=23; 8am-noon & 1-5pm Tue-Sun) Reached by a 23km dirt road from the city of Linhares, on the northern coast of Espírito Santo, this reserve is the state headquarters for the turtle-conservation organization Tamar. Here you can observe giant sea turtles in the reserve's aquarium, or continue north 7km to visit the beach community of Regência, where residents earn their living from a combination of fishing and turtle-conservation work.

Reserva Natural Vale (☎0xx27-3371-9703; www.vale.com/rnv; Hwy BR-101, km 121, Linhares; 8:30am-4:30pm) North of Linhares toward the Bahia border, this privately protected 218-sq-km expanse of Atlantic rainforest has earned it a place on Unesco's World Heritage list for its tremendous biological diversity. Visitors can stay overnight at the reserve's simple but comfortable **lodge** (☎0xx27-3371-9797; s/d midweek R$133/160, weekend R$181/208, holiday R$293/320;) and explore the surrounding network of trails.

to 4pm Sat & Sun) FREE Vitória's grandest historic building is this former Jesuit college and church, now the seat of state government. Free guided 40-minute tours include the original 16th-century foundations, artifacts discovered during renovation, and the tomb of Padre José de Anchieta (1534–97), an early missionary hailed as the 'Apostle of Brazil'. Weekend tours (50 minutes) visit additonal rooms reserved for government functions on weekdays.

Parque Moscoso PARK

(Av Cleto Nunes) *Capixabas* like to walk and relax in the leafy Parque Moscoso, just west of the city center.

Vila Velha

Across the river and south of Vitória sits Vila Velha, the first place in Espírito Santo to be colonized.

Convento da Penha CONVENT

(http://conventodapenha.org.br; Rua Vasco Coutinho; 5:15am-4:45pm Mon-Sat, from 4:15am Sun) A must-see is this 16th-century convent atop the densely forested Morro da Penha. The panoramic city views are magnificent, and the chapel (founded in 1558) isn't too bad either. It's a major pilgrimage destination – around Easter expect massive crowds paying homage to NS da Penha, some climbing the hill on their knees.

Garoto CHOCOLATE FACTORY

(☎3320-1708; www.garoto.com.br; Praça Meyerfreund 1; shop 9am-6pm Mon-Fri, 8:30am-2pm Sat) Brazil's best chocolate is made and sold right here, at Garoto's factory and store just off Rodovia Carlos Lindenberg; take bus 500 to Vila Velha, then transfer to bus 525 or 526. Reserve ahead for 90-minute **factory tours** (☎3320-1709; tour R$17) in Portuguese, which include a chocolate tasting.

Beaches

Praia da Costa BEACH

This Vila Velha beach is the city's nicest. It has fewer hotels and restaurants than Camburí, but you can swim and bodysurf. Keep a close eye on the horizon – huge supertankers often pop up with surprising speed!

Praia do Camburí BEACH

This 5km stretch of beach is punctuated by kiosks, restaurants, nightspots and midrange hotels. Don't swim near the bridge – it's polluted.

Sleeping & Eating

Staying out at the beach is a much more attractive option than downtown, which is deserted after nightfall. Vitória receives a lot of midweek business travelers; on non-holiday weekends many hotels drop their rates. Decent budget options are scarce.

Make sure you try the regional specialty known as *moqueca capixaba*, a savory stew made from fish, shellfish, tomatoes, peppers and cilantro cooked in a *panela de barro* (earthenware casserole dish).

Cannes Palace Hotel HOTEL $
(3232-7200; www.hotelcannes.com.br; Av Jerônimo Monteiro 111; s/d R$115/135;) Not quite as decrepit as it looks from the outside, this aging high-rise is downtown's best budget option. Close to both the bus station and the Anchieta Palace, its rooms come with air-con and patterned wood floors.

Ibis Vitória HOTEL $$
(2104-4850; www.ibis.com.br; João da Cruz 385, Praia do Canto; r weekend/midweek R$144/169;) Well priced given its prime location, this chain hotel sits right at the edge of the Triângulo das Bermudas, Vitória's nightlife hub, and is only a few blocks from Praia do Canto. Breakfast is available for an extra charge. There's another Ibis with identical prices 1.5km north on the Camburí beachfront.

Senac Ilha do Boi HOTEL $$$
(3345-0111; www.hotelilhadoboi.com.br; Bráulio Macedo 417; r R$330-505;) For a real night of luxury, this is an excellent choice. It's located on top of a hill with fabulous views of the bay. The service is impeccable and the amenities delightful, including a tennis court, solarium, piano bar, pools and saunas.

★**Pirão** SEAFOOD $$$
(3227-1165; www.piraovitoria.com.br; Joaquim Lírio 753, Praia do Canto; mains for two R$98-190; 11am-4pm & 6-11pm Mon-Fri, 11am-5pm Sat & Sun) With award-winning *moquecas* and *torta capixaba* (seafood frittata with olives and hearts of palm), Pirão has earned a reputation as one of the city's finest restaurants.

Lareira Portuguesa PORTUGUESE $$$
(3345-0329; www.lareiraportuguesa.com.br; Av Saturnino de Brito 260, Praia do Canto; mains for two R$190-235; 11:30am-3pm & 6:30pm-midnight Mon-Sat, 11:30am-4:30pm Sun) A gorgeous garden and beautiful Portuguese tiles make this a sexy and sophisticated location. Delicious fish dishes form the backbone of the menu, but you'll also find Old World classics like roasted goat and plenty of Portuguese desserts.

Drinking & Entertainment

Capixabas like the nightlife – check out the Triângulo das Bermudas, a neighborhood packed with bars, eateries and nightclubs centered on the intersection of Joaquim Lírio and João da Cruz. Crowds also gather at Curva da Jurema, populated by shacks that serve snacks and food into the wee hours.

Theatro Carlos Gomes THEATER
(http://secult.es.gov.br; Praça Costa Pereira) Drawing its architectural inspiration from La Scala in Milan, this classy theater stages national-caliber productions at very reasonable prices. Check the website to see what's currently playing (click the 'Espaços culturais' link).

Information

ATMs for several banks are clustered together inside the bus station.

Vitória's city government operates two conveniently located **tourist information booths**: in the arrivals hall at the airport (www.vitoria.es.gov.br/turista/informacoes-turisticas; 3235-6350; 7am-8:30pm) and opposite track 6 at the bus station (3203-3666; Av Alexandre Buaiz 350; 6am-9:50pm Mon-Fri, to noon Sat).

Getting There & Away

AIR

Eurico Salles Airport (VIX; 3235-6300) is 10km northeast of the city center, in

BUSES FROM VITÓRIA

DESTINATION	COST (R$)	TIME (HR)	BUS COMPANY
Belo Horizonte	95-122	8¾	São Geraldo (www.saogeraldo.com.br), Kaissara (www.kaissara.com.br)
Porto Seguro	106-149	9-11	Águia Branca (www.aguiabranca.com.br)
Rio	93-172	7½-9	Águia Branca (www.aguiabranca.com.br), Kaissara (www.kaissara.com.br)
Salvador	150-190	21	Águia Branca (www.aguiabranca.com.br)

Goiabeiras. Flights leave regularly for Belo Horizonte, Rio, São Paulo and other Brazilian cities.

BUS

Vitória's teeming, modern bus station is just west of the old town center.

TRAIN

Companhia Vale do Rio Doce (p175) runs a daily train to Belo Horizonte (*econômica/executiva* R$62/95, 13 hours) from Estação Ferroviária Pedro Nolasco, 5km west of downtown Vitória in Cariacica.

Getting Around

Between the airport and the city center, take the local bus marked '*aeroporto/rodoviária*' (R$2.55). Taxis from the airport cost around R$25 to Praia do Canto or R$35 to the city center.

Local buses (R$2.55) run from the various stops outside the bus station; the route is written on the side of each bus. For the center, catch any bus that goes along Av Vitória and get off after you pass the yellow Anchieta Palace on your left. For Praia do Camburí, catch any bus that goes along Av Dante Michelini. For Praia do Canto and Triângulo das Bermudas, take any bus that goes along Av Saturnino de Brito. To Vila Velha and Praia da Costa catch any bus marked Praia da Costa.

Itaúnas

0XX27 / POP 2500

Surrounded by a majestic state reserve and encroaching sand dunes, Itaúnas masquerades as a sleepy fishing village most of the year. However, around New Year's Eve and Carnaval (February/March), and again in July, it's a party-mad town filled with young Brazilians who come for the lively *forró* dance parties as much as for the beautiful surroundings.

Near the Bahia border 270km north of Vitória, Itaúnas is one of those rare places that manages to retain a low-key 'end of the road' feel despite the intermittent barrage of tourists. Many visitors fall under the town's easygoing spell and end up staying longer than they expected.

Fifty years ago, sand dunes engulfed the original village of Itaúnas, which was set about 1km closer to the ocean than it is now – these days the old church tower and other ruins lie completely buried in sand, marked only by a small sign.

Sights & Activities

★ Parque Estadual de Itaúnas PARK
(3762-5196; pei@iema.es.gov.br; 8am-5pm) The 36.7-sq-km Parque Estadual de Itaúnas extends for 25km along the coast and has impressive 20m- to 30m-high sand dunes that afford magnificent views of the Atlantic Ocean and the surrounding mangrove forest and wetlands. The wilderness here is home to monkeys, sloths, *jaguatiricas* (wildcats) and sea turtles, who come onshore from September to March to lay eggs. The park office, in the village next to the Rio Itaúnas bridge, has informative displays about the local flora, fauna and culture.

Trilha das Dunas WALKING
(Dunes Trail) Close to the town of Itaúnas, this is the state park's most popular hike. The 1km trail crosses the dunes to a series of beachside *barracas* (stalls selling beer and seafood). From town, simply cross the bridge over the Rio Itaúnas, follow the dirt road until the dunes slope down to meet it, then start climbing. At the crest of the first dune, panoramic views of the ocean unfold.

Trilha do Tamandaré WALKING
This easy 700m nature trail starts just across the bridge from the state-park office, weaving along the Rio Itaúnas and through the dunes to the beach. Birds and butterflies abound along this route.

Riacho Doce WALKING
More ambitious hikers can follow the long, flat beach 8km north from Itaúnas to Riacho Doce, a small river that forms the border between Espírito Santo and Bahia. You'll know you've arrived when you see the handpainted sign on the other side 'Sorria – voce está na Bahia!' (Smile – you're in Bahia!). Here you'll find Pousada do Celsão, the attached restaurant of which serves tasty home-cooked meals. (Just beware the intrepid pet parrot – he'll try to climb in the hammock with you!)

For the return trip, retrace your steps down the beach (best done at low tide), or hitch a ride with one of the pickup trucks or school buses that occasionally drive the 16km road back to town.

Casinha de Aventuras OUTDOORS
(Av Bento Daher; 9am-6:30pm daily Jan & Jul, 9am-noon Tue-Sat rest of year) Near the bus stop in the center of town, this well-established outfit arranges kayaking trips along the Rio Itaúnas, horseback and dune-buggy excursions, bike rentals and more.

Festivals & Events

Reveillon (New Year's Eve) draws up to 10,000 visitors annually. Carnaval also draws a festive, youthful crowd.

FENFIT MUSIC
(Festival Nacional de Forró; www.forrodeitaunas.com; late Jul) For 10 days in late July, Itaúnas hosts this national festival celebrating *forró* (popular music of the Northeast). Big-name performers pour in from all over Brazil, and there's music and dancing all day and night.

Sleeping

Pousada Ponta de Areia POUSADA $
(99713-3170; itaunasbixao@gmail.com; Honório Pinheiro da Silva; s/d R$50/70) This delightfully simple and welcoming pousada is hidden on a backstreet and not prominently signposted. To find it, ask locals for Bixão, the gracious and well-traveled owner, who is also an excellent resource for cyclists headed up or down the coast.

Hospedaria Cosanostra B&B $
(99627-1138; www.mapadavilaitaunas.com.br/pousada-cosanostra.html; Leite da Silva; d R$80-100, tr/q from R$110/140;) Directly across from the church on Itaúnas' main square, this simple but welcoming place run by an Italian-Brazilian couple has eight fan-cooled rooms with private bath, plus a yard with hammocks and barbecue. The attached restaurant serves homemade pizza and *piadine* (flatbread from Italy's Romagna region).

Pousada & Camping A Nave POUSADA, CAMPGROUND $
(3762-5102; www.anave.tur.br; Ítalo Vasconcelos; campsites per person R$30, s/d from R$80/120;) Rustic rooms with carved wooden doors abound at this attractive pousada, which is a labor of love for its sculptor and owner, Júlio. The attached campground, overlooking a mangrove forest and sand dunes, is also attractive.

Casa da Praia POUSADA $$
(99902-0533, 3762-5133; www.pousadacasadapraiaitaunas.com.br; Dercilio Ferreira da Fonseca; r R$150-220;) This is one of Itaúnas' loveliest pousadas, on a backstreet with a deck overlooking the river. The owners take great pride in keeping the grounds and rooms spotless.

Pousada Zimbaue POUSADA $$
(3762-5023; www.guiaitaunas.com.br/zimbaue.html; Cabral da Silva 6; s R$90-190, d R$120-240, tr R$170-290;) This cheerful pousada just off the main square has clean white sheets, free bicycles for guests' use and a spacious common area with DVD player and internet access.

Pousada dos Corais POUSADA $$
(3762-5200; www.pousadadoscorais.com.br; Barcelos 154; d/tr R$250/320;) If you're suffering from the heat, try this friendly pousada with its air-con rooms, comfortable sitting areas and pool.

Eating

There are plenty of inexpensive eateries around Itaúnas. Especially appealing are the three *barracas* out at the beach – Sal da Terra, Tartaruga and Itamar – serving seafood and beer with ocean views. Note that hours are seasonal and prone to change.

Dona Tereza SEAFOOD $$
(3762-5031; www.facebook.com/restaurantedonateresa; Leite da Silva; mains R$24-74; 11am-midnight, to 8pm low season) This highly recommended restaurant with a breezy front terrace is a family affair; don't be surprised if the eight-year-old grandson takes your order! The *prato feito* (plate of the day, listed simply as 'pf' on the menu) is a great deal, including fish, rice and beans for only R$24. From the central square, go one block toward the river.

Dona Pedrolina SEAFOOD $$
(3762-5296; Lionório Lisboa Vasconcelos; mains R$24-70; 11:30am-11pm) At this excellent family-run place, simple meals of fish, rice, beans and salad are very affordable, or you can splurge on *moqueca de camarão* (shrimp stew), which feeds three people for R$129.

A Casa di Berê BRAZILIAN $$
(99986-1228; Lionório Lisboa Vasconcelos; mains R$29-55; 4:30-11pm Tue-Sun) An instant hit since opening in late 2014, this colorfully decorated eatery is suffused with the friendly presence of owner Berê, who works the tables with a smile and cooks up delicious homemade pasta dishes. Don't miss her trademark frozen dessert, made with local white cheese, then topped with warm guava paste and a sprig of mint.

Restaurante Sapucaia INTERNATIONAL **$$**
(98143-9345; www.sapucaiaitaunas.com.br; Barcelos; mains R$35-69; 7-11pm) Open only in high season, this well-regarded restaurant has built its reputation on inventive seafood and pasta dishes such as *ravioli de camarão e banana* (ravioli stuffed with shrimp, ricotta and bananas). Don't miss the specialty: house-smoked fish carpaccio.

Drinking & Entertainment

During high season the pounding beats of *forró*, reggae and *axé* (an Afro-Brazilian pop style incorporating samba, rock, soul and other influences) spill from every open window and doorway in Itaúnas. Things don't really start swinging till after midnight, and the party lasts till dawn.

Bar da Ponte BAR
Right next to the Rio Itaúnas bridge, this place hosts live reggae and some samba during New Year, Carnaval and in July.

Bar Forró LIVE MUSIC
(www.forrodeitaunas.com) This ever-popular *forró*-themed bar is the center of the action during New Year's, Carnaval and the Festival do Forró in July.

Buraco do Tatu LIVE MUSIC
(www.facebook.com/buracodotatu; Vasconcelos 20) Host to Itaúnas' first-ever reggae festival in October 2015, the 'Armadillo's Lair' offers a mix of *forró* and reggae throughout the year.

Orientation

The main road into town loops around the village square and back out again. Buses stop just a few yards from the square, and most stores, restaurants and pousadas are concentrated nearby. The beach is 1km east, across the bridge over the Rio Itaúnas. The village's handful of dirt streets are not signposted, but a pair of handy maps, posted on the square and near the bridge to the dunes, can help you get oriented.

Information

Although most businesses accept credit cards, there are no banks in Itaúnas; bring some cash.

Getting There & Away

The closest place you can make long-distance bus connections is in Conceição da Barra, 23km south. **Águia Branca** (www.aguiabranca.com.br) runs three buses daily from Vitória to Conceição (*convencional/executivo* R$55/73, five hours).

From Conceição a local Mar Aberto bus goes to Itaúnas (R$6.20, 40 minutes) at 7am, 12:30pm and 3:30pm daily, returning to Conceição at 8am, 1:30pm and 4:30pm. There's an additional 10:30am bus to Itaúnas on Monday and Friday throughout the year (returning at 11:30am), plus multiple extra buses in summer. If you get stuck overnight in Conceição, there are several pousadas to choose from.

To head north into Bahia, first catch an Águia Branca bus from Conceição out to São Mateus on the main highway (R$8.10, one hour, eight daily). From there, buses run to Porto Seguro (*convencional/executivo/semi-leito* R$67/78/91, 5¼ to 6½ hours, two to three daily).

Guarapari

0XX27 / POP 105,000

About an hour south of Vitória, Guarapari is a favored resort destination for Brazilians and, as such, retains a relaxed, fun and family-friendly atmosphere. There are 23 beaches in the municipality, each with an attractive mountain backdrop.

The center sits on a little peninsula, 500m south and across the bridge from the bus station; the beach is 200m further east.

Sights

The best beach is **Praia do Morro**, north of the city (be aware that its so-called healing black monazitic sand is, in fact, said to be radioactive!). Back in the center, from north to south, you'll find **Praia dos Namorados** (small but surrounded by rocks creating beautiful pools), **Praias Castanheiras** and **Areia Preta** (more radioactive sand but crystal-clear waters), **Praia do Meio**, aka Siribeira (great rock pools with gorgeous snorkeling), **Praia Enseada Azul** (a long stretch with lots of natural beauty) and **Praia dos Padres** (accessible only by trail from Enseada Azul, with stunning green waters). At the far southern end of town is **Meaípe**, best known for its beachfront eateries.

Sleeping

Camping Club do Brasil CAMPGROUND **$**
(3262-1325; www.campingclube.com.br/es_01.htm; Praia de Setiba; camping per person/tent R$46.50/11.70) This camping spot a few kilometers north of town is just a stone's throw from lovely Setiba beach.

Hotel Atlântico HOTEL $$
(☎3361-1551; www.hotelatlanticoguarapari.com.br; Av Edísio Cirne 332; d R$210-295; ❄@🛜≋) Just across from Praia dos Namorados in the heart of Guarapari, this well-equipped hotel offers comfy rooms with panoramic terraces, plus perks including a sauna, poolside bar and free beach umbrellas.

Porto do Sol HOTEL $$$
(☎3161-7100; www.hotelportodosol.com.br; Av Beira Mar 1; s R$228-387, d R$281-479; ❄@🛜≋) Surrounded by water on three sides, this high-end hotel has an unbeatable location between downtown and Praia do Morro. All rooms have panoramic ocean views, with wi-fi, DVD and whirlpool tubs in the deluxe suites. Sea turtles sometimes come up onto the rocks directly below the rooms.

Eating

Up and down all the beaches, but particularly on Praia do Morro, you'll find dozens of *barracas* selling inexpensive fresh seafood and regional dishes. The classic spot to enjoy *moqueca capixaba* (Espírito Santo's famous seafood stew) is Meaípe, 10km south of town.

Restaurante Dom de Barro SELF-SERVE, MINEIRA $
(☎3262-8825; Getúlio Vargas 125; per kg R$42.90; ⏱11am-3pm Mon-Fri) Atmospherically decked out with bright murals, shelves of *cachaça* bottles and an old wood stove, this high-ceilinged downtown self-serve place specializes in fine *comida mineira*.

★**Cantinho do Curuca** SEAFOOD $$$
(☎3272-2000; www.cantinhodocuruca.com.br; Av Santana 96, Meaípe; mains for 2 R$87-215; ⏱11am-10pm) The *moqueca* at this beachfront eatery in Meaípe has been voted the best in Brazil multiple times. Everything from fish to squid and shrimp to bananas finds its way into the dozens of clay pots bubbling away in the cavernous kitchen. Early arrivals can grab one of the limited front tables facing the water.

Restaurante Gaeta SEAFOOD $$$
(☎3272-1202; Av Santana 47, Meaípe; moqueca for two R$85-209; ⏱11am-10pm) Jostling for the title of the region's best seafood restaurant, this beachside eatery offers a dazzling array of savory stews. Sizzling clay *panelas* (casserole dishes) come laden with everything from *moqueca de camarão pequeno* (featuring tiny shrimp) to the trademark *moqueca de banana* (invented here) to the house specialty *moqueca das três ilhas* (lobster, prawns and sea bass).

Information

There are several banks with ATMs along Joaquim da Silva Lima in the center.

The **Tourist Office** (☎3262-8759; seltur@guarapari.es.gov.br; Paulo de Águiar 68; ⏱8am-6pm) is in the center just west of the bridge; it has maps and information in Portuguese.

Getting There & Away

Planeta (☎3223-5761) runs buses from Vitória to Guarapari's **bus station** (João Gomes de Jesus 50) roughly hourly from 7:30am to 9:30pm (R$13.40, 1¼ hours).

THE GOITACÁ WARRIORS

Early European explorers reported encounters with the fearsome, long-haired, tall, robust and formidable Goitacá warriors, coastal dwellers of the Rio state–Espírito Santo border region. The tribe had long resisted invasions by rival Tupi nations and, despite the technological advantage of guns, the Europeans found the Goitacá almost impossible to capture. The Goitacá were excellent runners and swimmers, and seemed by all reports to be equally at home on land and in the water. When chased, they were so fast through the waters and jungle that nobody could catch them on foot, on horseback or by boat.

According to legend, a Goitacá could run after a wild deer and capture it with his arms, and could catch a shark using only a piece of wood. (This was accomplished by forcing a stick inside the shark's mouth to stop the jaws from closing, and pulling its guts out by hand until it died.) The Goitacá nation (around 12,000 people), never defeated in battle, was exterminated at the end of the 18th century by a smallpox epidemic – a disease deliberately introduced by the Portuguese for that very purpose.

Beaches South of Guarapari

📞 0XX28

Within a 45-minute drive of Guarapari, you'll find a trio of beach communities worthy of an afternoon's jaunt: **Ubu** (20km south of Guarapari), a sleepy little seaside town with a picturesque waterfront; **Anchieta** (8km further south), one of Espírito Santo's oldest settlements with a 16th-century sanctuary founded by famed Jesuit priest José de Anchieta; and **Iriri** (8km south of Anchieta), an agreeable coastal getaway very popular with *mineiros*, who come in droves during the summer months (especially Carnaval), turning it into an upbeat, family-focused resort.

Sights

Santuário Nacional Padre Anchieta CHURCH

(admission R$5; ⏲8am-5pm Tue-Sun) Dominating Anchieta town from its impressive hillside location, this striking blue-and-white church dates back to the 16th century. A graceful 150-year-old chestnut tree shades the pretty plaza out front. The adjacent museum contains relics uncovered during restoration, and highlights the evangelical work of Jesuit priest José de Anchieta.

Praia de Ubu BEACH

This long, picturesque stretch of sand has a cliff at one end and a mermaid statue marking the beach's midpoint.

Praia de Iriri BEACH

Lined with beachfront eateries and pousadas, Iriri's pretty crescent-shaped beach is tucked into a sheltered cove flanked by rocky ledges on either side.

Festivals & Events

Every year, devoted followers of Padre Anchieta participate in the **Passos de Anchieta** (Steps of Anchieta; www.abapa.org.br; ⏲Jun), a four-day, 100km pilgrimage along the beach from Vitória to Anchieta.

Sleeping & Eating

★ **Recanto da Pedra** POUSADA $$

(📞3534-1599; www.recantodapedra.com.br; Av Beira Mar 16; s/d R$132/175; ❄📶) Hands down the best value along this stretch of coast, Recanto da Pedra is picturesquely sited on rocks at the northern end of Iriri beach. Many rooms have terraces with bird's-eye views of the gracefully curving shoreline. The attached restaurant serves excellent food, and swimmers occasionally pop up out of the water for a quick drink at the bar.

Restaurante do Português SEAFOOD $$

(📞3534-1222; Alpoim 558; mains for two R$40-100; ⏲11am-9pm) Generous portions of tasty local seafood are served at this unpretentious eatery half a block from the beach, including a R$14 *prato individual* for solo diners. There are also a few bare-bones rooms upstairs (per person R$50) for penny-pinchers.

Moqueca do Garcia SEAFOOD $$$

(📞3536-5050; www.peixadadogarcia.com.br; Praia de Ubu; mains for two R$78-199; ⏲11am-5pm Mar-Nov, to 11pm Dec-Feb) Down by the waterfront in Ubu, celebrating half a century in business, this acclaimed restaurant serves top-notch *capixaba* cuisine, with a strong focus on *moquecas*.

Getting There & Away

From Guarapari, Planeta runs half-hourly buses to Ubu (R$4, 30 minutes), Anchieta (R$5.70, 40 minutes) and Iriri (R$7, one hour).

Domingos Martins

📞 0XX27 / POP 32,000 / ELEV 542M

The landscapes get more dramatic, the Old World influences more pronounced and the temperatures cooler as you leave Espírito Santo's coast for the mountainous interior. High season here is May to August, when Brazilians flock inland for a rare taste of winter comforts – chilly nights, fondue and a blazing fire.

Tucked into the highlands of the Serra Capixaba, the pretty little German-style town of Domingos Martins – also referred to as Campinho by locals – makes a good base for exploring the nearby forests, streams and mountains. The town's Germanic roots are evident in the bilingual signs scattered around town, the German-influenced cuisine found on many local menus and the orderly layout of the main square, a pretty gathering spot with benches, trees, well-tended flowers and an old Lutheran church.

Sights

Casa da Cultura MUSEUM
(3268-2550; www.domingosmartins.es.gov.br; Av Presidente Vargas 531; 8am-5pm Tue-Sun) FREE Opposite the first bus stop in town, this place serves as an unofficial tourist office, offering a wealth of advice about Domingos Martins and the surrounding area. The museum upstairs features photos, documents and household objects dating from 1847, when Pomeranians first settled this colony.

Instituto Reserva Kautsky GARDENS
(3268-2300; http://institutokautsky.blogspot.com.br; admission R$10; by arrangement) FREE Flora-lovers should head out to this lovely mountainside reserve, established by dedicated botanist Roberto Kautsky, who cultivated more than 100 species of orchids at his home at the southern end of town. To arrange a visit, phone weekdays between 8am and 5pm, or contact Cristine Feitosa at assessoria.ik@gmail.com.

Festivals & Events

Sommerfest CULTURAL
(www.facebook.com/SommerfestDomingosMartins; late Jan/early Feb) Domingos Martins celebrates its German heritage with music, dance and food during the four-day Sommerfest.

Festival Internacional de Inverno MUSIC
(Jul) In the second half of July, the Festival Internacional de Inverno is an annual 10-day gathering of Brazilian and international musicians who offer daily classes and nightly concerts on Domingos Martins' main square.

Sleeping & Eating

Solar da Serra POUSADA $$
(3268-1691; Gerhardt 91; r with fan R$140-230, with air-con R$170-250;) Up a steep hill a couple of blocks from the main square, this modern German-style pousada has spacious, clean rooms, the best of which offer pleasant views of the surrounding hillsides. Back rooms are a steal midweek, when prices drop 30% to 50% below weekend rates quoted above.

Sabor Café Expresso CAFE $
(3268-3263; Lazer 54; strudel R$8, fixed-price meals R$15.50; 8:30am-10pm Mon-Sat, to 5pm Sun) Homemade cakes, apple (or banana!) strudel and hot chocolate are the specialties at this lively sidewalk cafe in the heart of the pedestrian zone. Inexpensive *pratos feitos* offer fantastic value.

Choperia Fritz Frida GERMAN $$
(3268-1808; Av Presidente Vargas 782; mains per person R$49-74; 11am-11pm Wed-Mon) This half-timbered building with a big upstairs window overlooking the main square serves pizza, beer and old German favorites. Half portions cost 70% of full-portion price.

Getting There & Away

Águia Branca (www.aguiabranca.com.br) runs five direct buses daily (R$11.50, one hour) along the 42km route from Vitória to Domingos Martins' **bus station** (3268-1243; Rua Bernardino Monteiro). Upon request, any bus between Vitória and Belo Horizonte will also stop on the main highway just outside the town entrance gate, where you can call a **taxi** (99917-4959) for the 3km, R$15 ride to the town square.

Pedra Azul

Towering dramatically above the surrounding green hills, 50km west of Domingos Martins along Hwy BR-262, is one of Espírito Santo's quintessential attractions – **Pedra Azul** (500m), a massive rock outcropping tinted by a bluish moss that changes color with the sun's shifting rays, making for some fabulous photo ops. Even if you only spend a day here, it's well worth the trip.

Sights & Activities

★ **Parque Estadual da Pedra Azul** PARK
(guided walk reservations 99739-8005, park 3248-1156; pepaz@iema.es.gov.br; park 8am-5pm, guided walks by arrangement) FREE If you've made it to Espírito Santo, don't miss this gorgeous state park. Rangers lead guided walks affording magnificent views of Pedra Azul and the surrounding forest and farmland, with stops at the rock's nine natural pools. Bring a swimsuit and sturdy shoes – the climb is moderately difficult, and there's a short section where ropes are used to scale a steep rock face. The round trip takes three hours; book ahead, as schedules vary according to demand.

Note that independent climbing and camping are not permitted in the park.

Fjordland Cavalgada Ecológica HORSE RIDING
(3248-0076; www.fjordland.com.br; Rota do Lagarto, Km 2.2; 20/100min trail rides R$40/90;

8am-5pm) This outfit leads leads horseback excursions around the foot of Pedra Azul on beautiful Fjorde horses from Norway.

Sleeping & Eating

The area is dotted with fancy resort hotels, many offering the option of full board.

Tre Fiori CHALET $$
(3248-1124; pousadatrefiori@gmail.com; Rota do Lagarto, Km 3, Aracê; d chalet midweek/weekend R$230/250) Tucked into a green valley at the foot of Pedra Azul, 3km from the main highway along winding Rua do Lagarto, these four simple duplex chalets and four additional rooms with panoramic terraces offer great views. The owner, with family ties to Italy's Trento region, recently opened the attached **Don Lorenzoni Due** (mains R$50 to R$85) restaurant.

Pousada Peterle POUSADA $$
(3248-1171; www.pousadapeterle.com.br; Hwy BR-262, Km 88; d midweek/weekend from R$230/275;) Directly opposite the Águia Branca bus stop and 2km below the park entrance, Pousada Peterle has attractive log cabins with fireplaces and balconies. On weekends, prices rise and a two-night minimum stay is often required.

Pousada Pedra Azul POUSADA $$$
(3248-1101; www.ppazul.com; Rota do Lagarto, Km 1.5; d R$350-495, ste R$663;) Set in lovely gardens only 500m from park headquarters, this high-end pousada is one of the region's oldest. The main brick-and-wood building with Alpine-style balconies and pagoda-like roofs was designed by Brazilian architect Zanine. Amenities include a pool, sauna, tennis courts, lake and waterfall. The spacious, recently renovated guest rooms have high ceilings, big tubs and armchairs.

★ **Valsugana** ITALIAN $$
(3248-1126; www.restaurantevalsugana.com.br; off Hwy BR-262, Km 89.5; mains R$39-69; 11:30am-3:30pm & 7-10:30pm Sat, 11:30am-3:30pm Sun year-round, plus 7-10:30pm Fri Apr-Sep) Hearty Italian fare and pretty perspectives on Pedra Azul make this one of the area's nicest restaurants. Classics such as saltimbocca (prosciutto-and-sage-stuffed veal escalope) or spinach ravioli with ricotta and walnuts are interspersed with more inventive recipes, all featuring fresh local produce. The wine list is also excellent.

Getting There & Away

Águia Branca buses pass within 2km of the park entrance. In Vitória, buy a ticket for Fazenda do Estado (R$22, two hours, hourly from 5am to 6:20pm), and ask to be let off at Km 88. The Km 88 bus stop is directly opposite Peterle's pousada and restaurant. From here, it's a 2km uphill walk to the park entrance along a lovely winding cobblestone road, Rota do Lagarto.

São Paulo State

11 / POP 41.2 MILLION

Includes ➜

Best Places to Eat

- ➜ Maní (p241)
- ➜ Patuá da Baiana (p244)
- ➜ Mocotó (p245)
- ➜ Cantinho da Lagoa (p257)
- ➜ Marukuthai (p261)

Best Places to Stay

- ➜ Pousada Picinguaba (p257)
- ➜ Hotel Emiliano (p237)
- ➜ We Hostel Design (p236)
- ➜ Na Mata Suites (p259)
- ➜ Guest Urban (p238)

Why Go?

Speaking of São Paulo state without using superlatives is difficult. The southern hemisphere's largest city! Its finest museums! Its best restaurants! Its worst traffic! (Well, you can't have everything.) São Paulo city – Sampa to locals – serves as Brazil's Boom Town, commercially, financially, industrially and culturally, and an explosion of sophisticated travelers descending on the city's extraordinary restaurants, art galleries, bars and cultural centers has ensured the sprawling city remains a must-stop for urban-addicted sophisticates.

Inland from the cityscape, the Serra da Mantiqueira's 2500m peaks play the novel Alpine-esque getaway role, while Iporanga sits tucked away in pristine Brazilian Atlantic Forest. And out to sea, some of southeastern Brazil's finest beaches cling both to the mountainous stretch of rainforest-backdropped coastline near Ubatuba; and to nearby Ilhabela, which relishes its position as São Paulo's cosmopolitan island escape.

When to Go

São Paulo

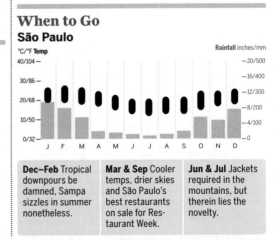

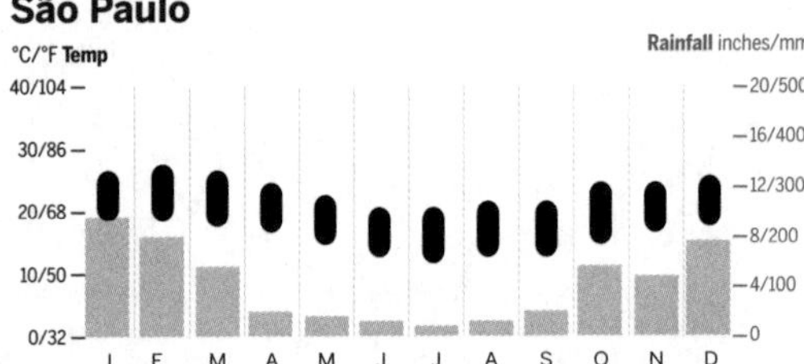

Dec–Feb Tropical downpours be damned, Sampa sizzles in summer nonetheless.

Mar & Sep Cooler temps, drier skies and São Paulo's best restaurants on sale for Restaurant Week.

Jun & Jul Jackets required in the mountains, but therein lies the novelty.

Getting There & Around

The state's capital, São Paulo city, is Brazil's principal hub for international travel. Dozens of airlines have direct international services to São Paulo's newly-expanded Guarulhos airport, and there are direct bus services from neighboring countries. The city is also a major center for domestic air travel. The state's highway system is among the best in South America, making driving a good option, though São Paulo city itself can be maddening because of poor signage and horrendous traffic. Alternatively, there are also frequent and good long-distance bus services to destinations across the country.

SÃO PAULO CITY

0XX11 / POP 11.3 MILLION (CITY), 19.9 MILLION (METRO) / ELEV 760M

São Paulo is a monster. Enormous, intimidating and, at first glance at least, no great beauty. It's a difficult city for the traveler to master and one that may not seem worth the sweat. Even the most partisan *paulistano* – resident of São Paulo city – will rail about the smog, the traffic, the crumbling sidewalks and the gaping divide between poor and rich.

But in the same breath they'll tell you they'd never live anywhere else. Let them guide you to their favorite haunts and the reason for this will begin to unfold. Maybe they will introduce you to the city's innumerable art-house cinemas and experimental theaters. If they're gourmands, you'll focus on the smart bistros and gourmet restaurants that make the city a world-renowned foodie haven. If they're scenesters, double up on espresso before embarking on a tour of raucous underground bars and the 24/7 clubbing scene. Whatever pleasures you might covet, Sampa – as the city is known – probably has them in spades.

This fertile cultural life is supported by Brazil's biggest and best-educated middle class and further enriched by literally hundreds of distinct ethnic groups – including the largest community of people of Japanese descent outside Japan, the largest population of Italian descendants outside Italy and a significant Arab community fueled mostly by Lebanese and Syrian immigration. There are one million people of German stock, as well, sizable Chinese, Armenian, Lithuanian, Greek, Korean, Polish and Hungarian communities; and, most recently, growing numbers of Peruvians, Bolivians, Haitians and Africans. São Paulo also has the largest openly gay community in Latin America.

An estimated 20 million people live in greater São Paulo, making it the third-largest metropolis on earth. Besides a dizzying avalanche of first-rate museums, cultural centers, experimental theaters and cinemas, Sampa's nightclubs and bars are among the best on the continent (15,000 bars make for one hell of a pub crawl) and its restaurants are among the world's best. Its relentless, round-the-clock pulse – a close cousin of New York or Tokyo – can prove taxing even for the fiercest hipster. Then again, it may just deliver the charge you need to discover one of the world's great cities.

History

The history of the city of São Paulo largely mirrors that of the state. For the first three centuries after the arrival of Jesuits here in 1554, the city grew only gradually as a posting station for fortune hunters heading for the interior, and growers from nearby sugar plantations.

Upon Brazil's independence in 1822, São Paulo was declared a state capital, a decision that in turn led to the founding of the College of Law – arguably Brazil's first public institution of higher learning. An increasingly important political and intellectual center, the city was soon leading the fight both to end slavery and to found the republic.

The city's fortunes began to rise in the late 19th century when the region's planters began replacing sugar with the world's new, favorite cash crop: coffee. Some of the coffee barons' mansions still line Av Paulista today. The millions of descendants of immigrants who came to work those plantations – especially Italians and Japanese – are another legacy of the coffee boom.

When coffee prices plummeted at the beginning of the 20th century, there was enough capital left over to transform the city into an industrial powerhouse. Factory jobs attracted immigrants from around the world, and the city's population practically doubled every decade between 1920 and 1980. In the 1980s, foreign immigration slowed, but laborers streamed in from the drought-stricken Northeast. Many found work building the city's new skyscrapers. Unfortunately, growth far outpaced investment in the city's infrastructure. Today, serious traffic, crime and pollution still flummox city leaders and remain serious problems, but the dynamism of its culture and economy is still attracting the best and brightest from all over Brazil.

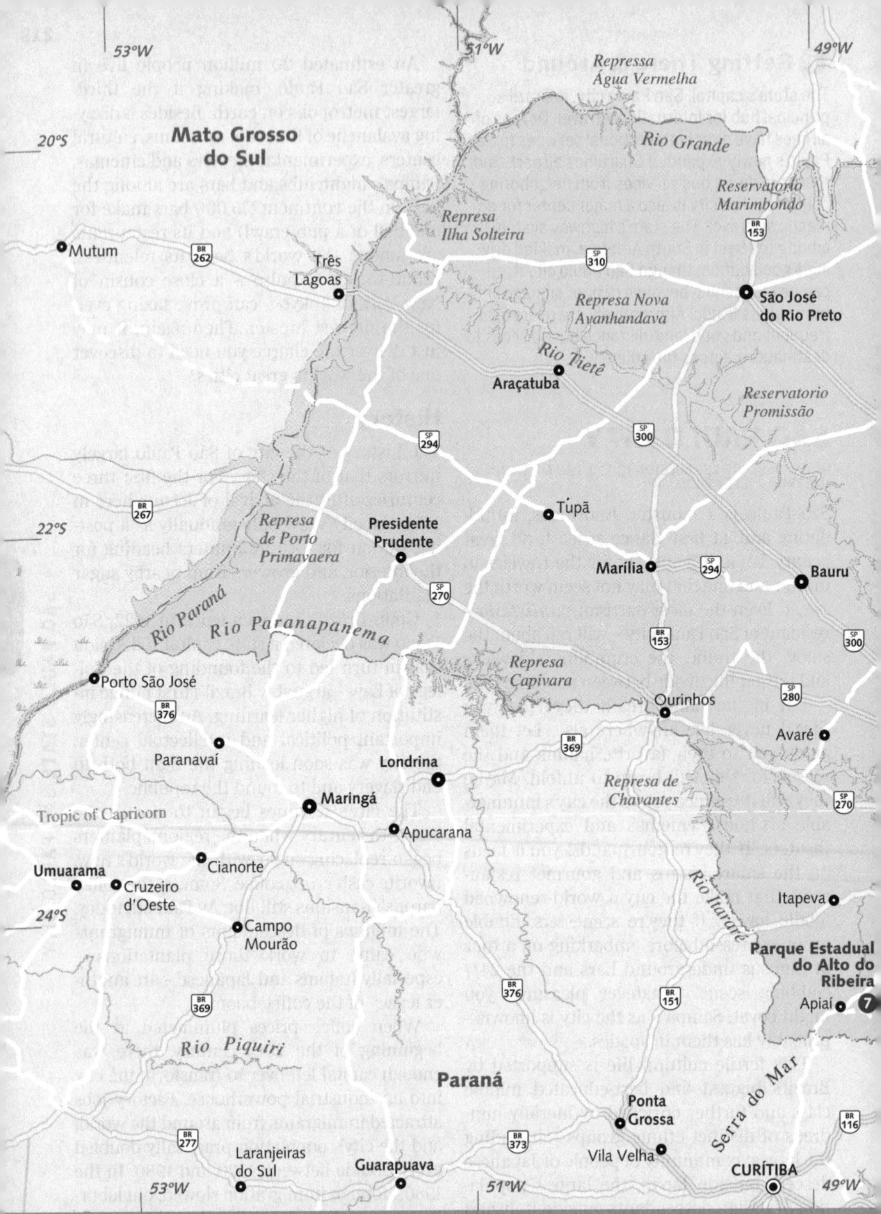

53°W
51°W
49°W
20°S
22°S
24°S

Mato Grosso do Sul
Mutum
BR 262
Três Lagoas
Represa Água Vermelha
Rio Grande
Reservatorio Marimbondo
BR 153
Represa Ilha Solteira
SP 310
São José do Rio Preto
Represa Nova Avanhandava
Rio Tietê
Araçatuba
Reservatorio Promissão
SP 294
SP 300
BR 267
Tupã
Represa de Porto Primavaera
Presidente Prudente
Marília
SP 294
Bauru
SP 270
Rio Paraná
Rio Paranapanema
BR 153
SP 300
Represa Capivara
Porto São José
BR 376
Ourinhos
SP 280
Avaré
Paranavaí
BR 369
Londrina
Represa de Chavantes
SP 270
Maringá
Tropic of Capricorn
Apucarana
Cianorte
Umuarama
Cruzeiro d'Oeste
Rio Itararé
Itapeva
Campo Mourão
Parque Estadual do Alto do Ribeira
BR 376
BR 151
Apiaí
7
BR 369
Rio Piquiri
Paraná
Serra do Mar
Ponta Grossa
BR 116
BR 277
BR 373
Vila Velha
Laranjeiras do Sul
Guarapuava
CURÍTIBA
53°W
51°W
49°W

São Paulo State Highlights

1. Driving one of the world's most stunning coastal routes along the Costa Verde from **São Sebastião** (p258) to Rio de Janeiro.

2. Overwhelming yourself with cuisine, culture, cafe and craziness in **São Paulo** (p219) city.

3. Gawking at São Paulo city's eye-popping skyline from the top of the **Banespa** (p229) building.

4. Seeking out wild, deserted beaches where mountains meet the sea north of **Ubatuba** (p255).

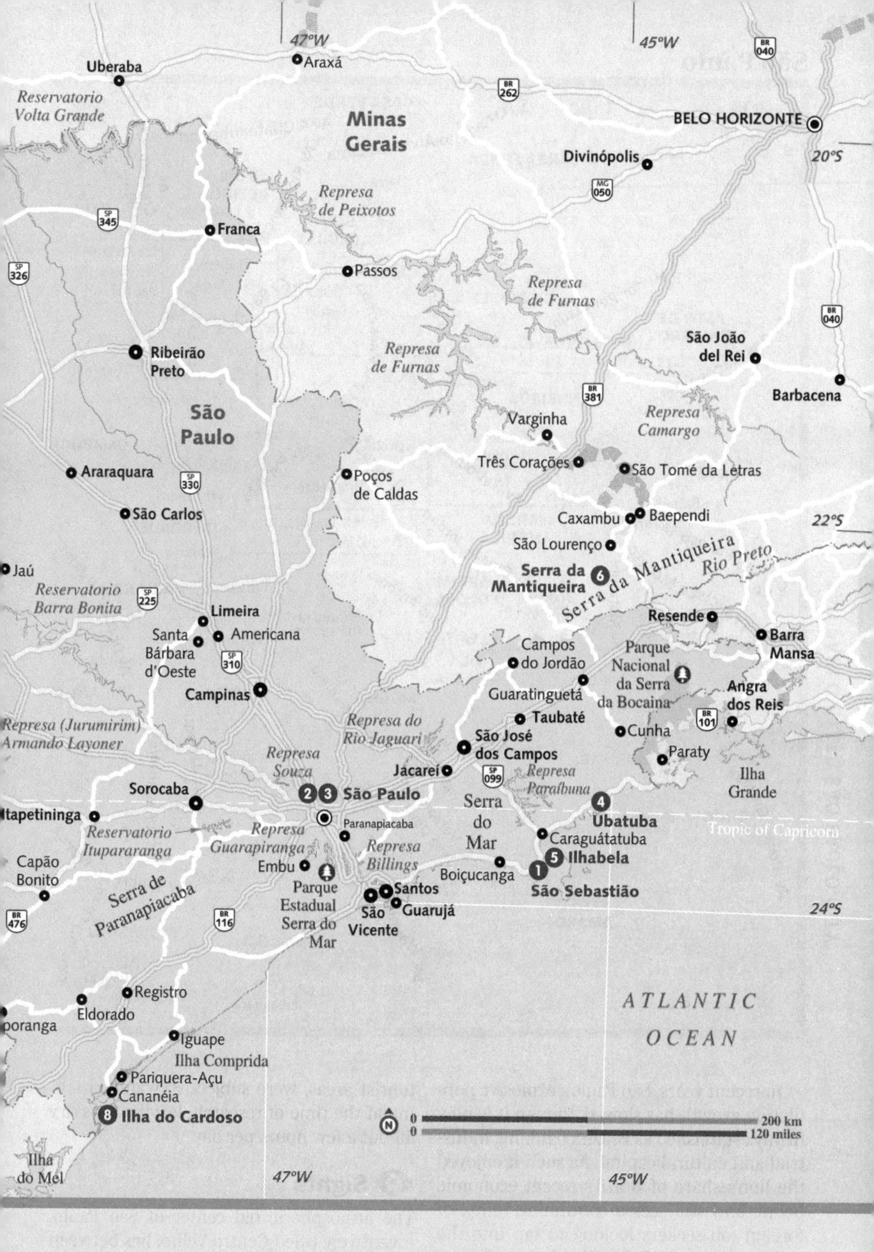

5 Escaping to **Ilhabela** (p259), São Paulo's idyllic island getaway for the rich and famous.

6 Hiking amid the green peaks of the **Serra da Mantiqueira** (p238), São Paulo's Alpine wonderland.

7 Caving in pristine Brazilian Atlantic Forest in **Parque Estadual do Alto do Ribeira** (p260) near Iporanga.

8 Going wet and wild in off-the-grid **Ilha do Cardoso** (p254).

São Paulo

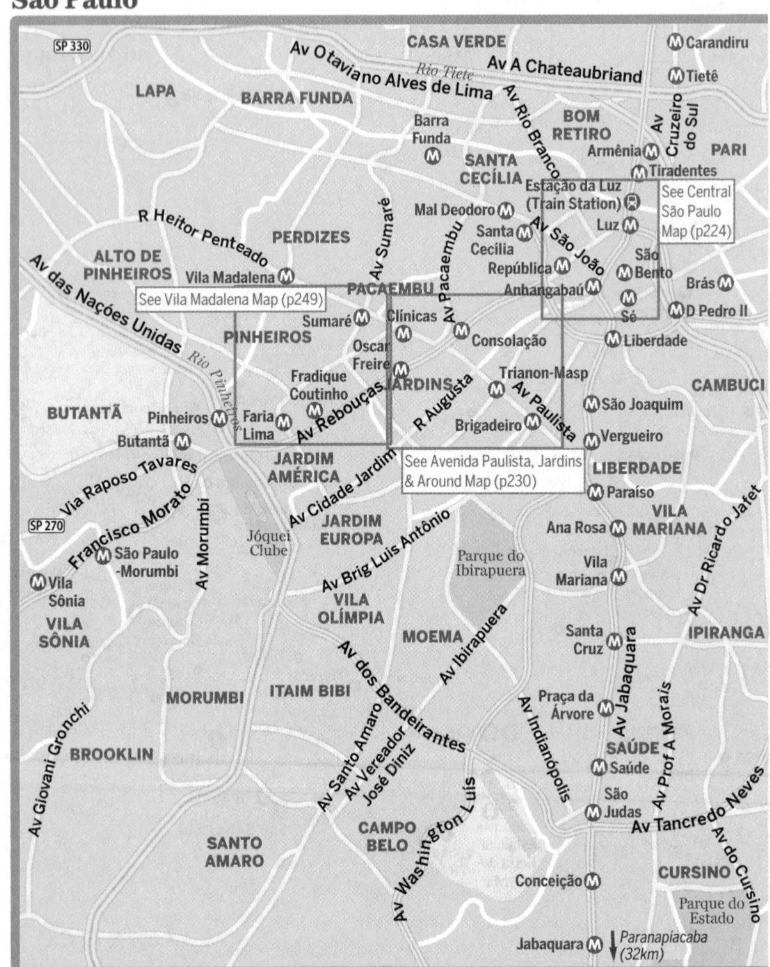

In recent years, São Paulo's explosive population growth has slowed, though it is now firmly established as Brazil's banking, industrial and cultural capital. As such it enjoyed the lion's share of Brazil's recent economic boom, and still sees a continuing influx of foreign job seekers looking to tap into the action. Post-2014 FIFA World Cup, Sampa continues to make strides toward modernizing its infrastructure, including significant expansions of its metro, suburban train and highway systems. That said, the city was in the middle of a very serious water shortage in 2015. Many parts of the city, including tourist areas, were subject to water rationing at the time of research, leaving taps dry all but a few hours per day.

Sights

The atmospheric old center of São Paulo, inventively titled Centro Velho, lies between Praça da Sé, Luz metro station and Praça da República. It's a pedestrianized maze offering a fascinating cornucopia of architectural styles (always look above the ground floor, where all charm has been lost to everyday shops).

Praça da Sé & Around

The old heart of the city, **Praça da Sé** (literally, 'Cathedral Square') has seen better days, but still draws animated crowds, from street hawkers and nose-down business types to – unfortunately – more than its fair share of pickpockets and homeless people. Crowning the square is the domed **Catedral da Sé** (Map p224; www.catedraldase.org.br; Praça Da Sé s/n, Centro; 8am-7pm Mon-Fri, to 5pm Sat, to 6pm Sun), a huge neo-Byzantine concoction that, for better or worse, replaced the original 18th-century structure in the 1920s.

On the other side of Praça da Sé stands the more modest but also more authentic **Igreja do Carmo** (Map p224; Av Rangel Pestana 230, Centro; 8am-5pm Mon-Fri, to noon Sat & Sun), which dates to the 1630s and still preserves its original high altar.

About 700m north of the cathedral, **Rua 25 de Março** is the traditional preserve of the city's Lebanese merchants and remains a lively, crowded wholesale shopping district.

★Mercado Municipal MARKET
(Mercadão; Map p224; www.oportaldomercadao.com.br; Rua da Cantareira 306; 6am-6pm Mon-Sat, to 4pm Sun) This covered market is a belle-époque confection of stained glass and a series of vast domes. Inside, a fabulous urban market specializes in all things edible. It's also a great place to sample a couple of classic Sampa delights: mortadella sandwiches at Bar do Mané and *pasteis* (pockets of dough stuffed with meat, cheese or fish and then fried).

Páteo do Colégio LANDMARK
(Map p224; 3105-6899; www.pateodocolegio.com.br; Praça Páteo do Colégio; adult/student R$6/3; 9am-4:45pm Tue-Fri, to 4:30pm Sat) Occupying the exact spot where São Paulo was founded in 1554 by Jesuit brothers José de Anchieta and Manoel da Nóbregra, this mission is actually a 1950s replica of the monastery that once stood here.

Inside, you'll find a nice little collection of original relics from the city's first days, as well as an interesting set of drawings that chart the city's growth over the last five centuries, and a tranquil cafe.

Caixa Cultural BUILDING
(Map p224; 3321-4400; www.caixacultural.com.br; Praça da Sé 111; 9am-9pm Tue-Sun) FREE This cultural center occupies a grand neoclassical-style building with an imperious facade of black marble. Temporary exhibits of major Brazilian artists are shown; and the executive office suite on the 6th floor is an oddly fascinating museum of the bank's history that can be seen on Wednesdays, Saturdays and Sundays at 11am and 4pm or by appointment.

Solar da Marquesa HISTORIC BUILDING
(Map p224; www.museudacidade.sp.gov.br; Roberto Símonsen 136; 9am-5pm Tue-Sun) FREE Down a set of narrow downtown side streets stands one of the city's last surviving 18th-century residences. This simple but

Central São Paulo

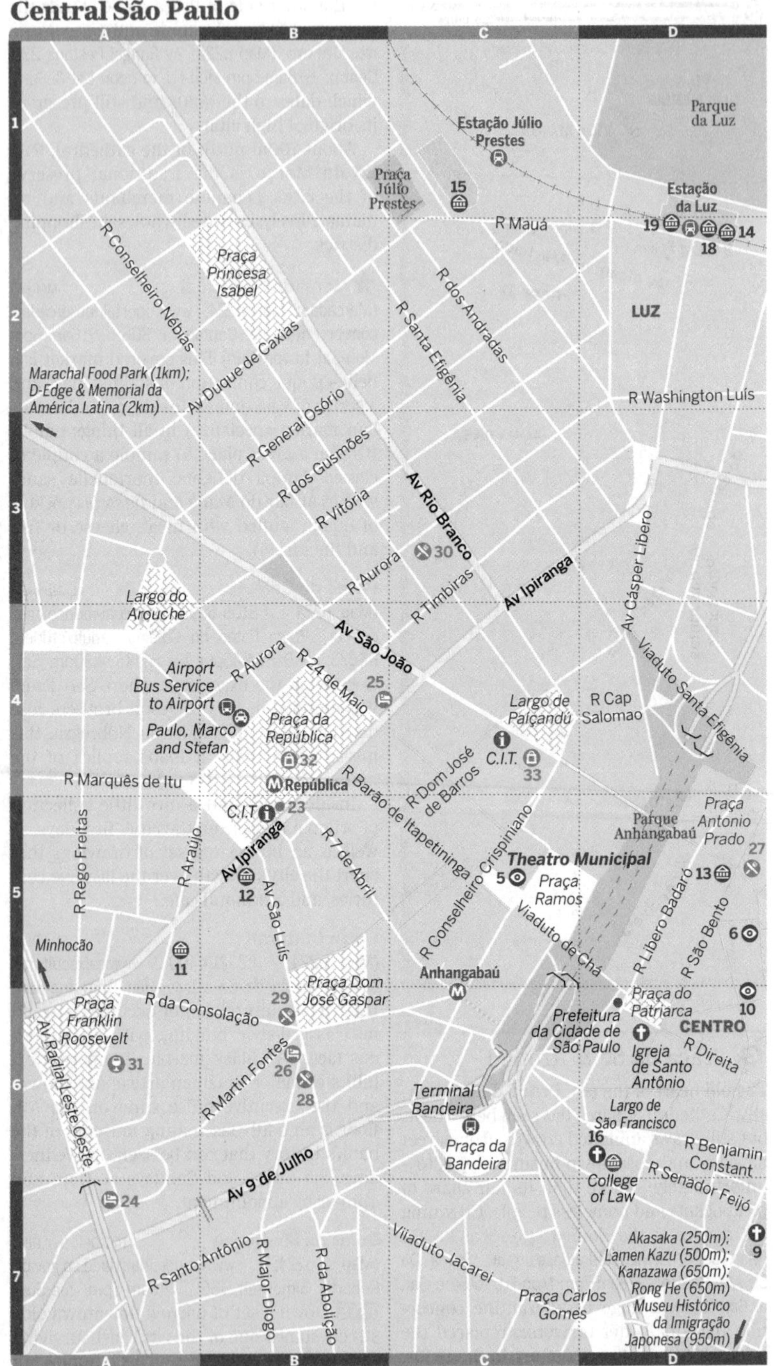

Central São Paulo

Top Sights

1 Banespa ... E5
2 Mercado Municipal ... F4
3 Mosteiro São Bento ... E4
4 Pinacoteca do Estado ... E1
5 Theatro Municipal ... C5

Sights

6 BM&FBovespa ... D5
7 Caixa Cultural ... E6
8 Casa da Imagem ... E6
9 Catedral da Sé ... D7
10 Centro Cultural Banco do Brasil ... D6
11 Edifício Copan ... A5
12 Edifício Itália ... B5
13 Edifício Martinelli ... D5
14 Estação da Luz ... D2
15 Estação Júlio Prestes ... C1
16 Igreja de São Francisco de Assis ... D6
17 Igreja do Carmo ... E6
18 Memorial da Resistência ... D2
19 Museu da Língua Portuguesa ... D2
20 Páteo do Colégio ... E6
21 Praça da Sé ... E7
22 Solar da Marquesa ... E6

Activities, Courses & Tours

23 SP Free Walking Tour ... B5

Sleeping

24 155 Hotel ... A7
25 Hotel Marabá ... B4
26 Novotel Jaraguá São Paulo ... B6

Eating

27 Casa Mathilde ... D5
28 Estadão ... B6
29 Ramona ... B6
30 Rinconcito Peruano ... C3

Drinking & Nightlife

Alberta #3 ... (see 29)
Bar da Dona Onça ... (see 11)
31 Lekitsch ... A6

Entertainment

Sala São Paulo ... (see 15)
Theatro Municipal ... (see 5)

Shopping

32 Feira da República ... B4
33 Galeria do Rock ... C4

delightful villa was once home to a lover of Emperor Dom Pedro I; it now houses the restrained **Museu da Cidade de São Paulo**, a multi-location museum devoted to the city's history.

LOCAL KNOWLEDGE

MINHOCÃO

A 3.4km elevated highway from downtown (Rua da Consolacão near Praça Franklin Roosevelt) west towards Barra Funda, Minhocão (officially Via Elevada Presidente Costa e Silva) is a free-for-all for cyclists, skateboarders, walkers and runners between 9:30pm and 6am, and all day Sunday. The nickname comes from a mythical earthwormlike creature that slithers around Central and South American forests.

Igreja de São Francisco de Assis CHURCH
(Map p224; Largo de São Francisco 133, Centro; ⏲7:30am-6:30pm) Built in the 17th and 18th centuries, this classic example of Portuguese baroque just west of the cathedral is one of the best-preserved colonial structures in the city (note that two churches stand adjacent to each other, each with the same name; the church to the right also dates to the 17th century but is less architecturally important).

Triângulo & Anhangabaú

Just north of Praça da Sé lies the **Triângulo**, a triangle bounded roughly by **Praça da Sé**, **Mosteiro São Bento** and the **Prefeitura** (city hall). It has narrow, pedestrian-only streets and towering office buildings that in the late 19th and early 20th centuries served as the city's commercial heart.

Heading west from Praça do Patriarca, you'll cross the 1892 **Viaduto de Chá**, which crosses the **Vale do Anhangabaú**, along with the **Viaduto Santa Efigênia** a little to the north and dating from the same era. Both of these elaborate cast-iron bridges were long synonymous with São Paulo's cultural and economic ascendancy. In the Tupi-Guarani language, Anhangabaú means Demon's Valley, and indigenous peoples believed evil spirits dwelled there. The area is dicey after dark.

★**Theatro Municipal** THEATER
(Map p224; ☎3397-0300; www.theatromunicipal.org.br; Praça Ramos de Azevedo) São Paulo's most splendid construction, this theater was begun in 1903 in the style of Paris' Palais Garnier. Its heavily ornamented facade seems to combine every architectural style imaginable, from baroque to art nouveau, and its interior is clad in gold and marble. Free English tours run twice daily Tuesday to Friday at 11am and 5pm, and Saturday at noon.

Edifício Martinelli HISTORIC BUILDING
(Map p224; ☎3104-2477; www.prediomartinelli.com.br; São Bento 405; ⏲tours half-hourly 9:30-11:30am & 2-4pm Mon-Fri, 9am-1pm Sat) FREE São Paulo's first skyscraper, in a gorgeous 1929 Beaux Arts building, features a mansion built on top of its 26th-floor viewing terrace. The terrace and its incredible views are now open for free visits. You must arrive on the half-hour during the above stated hours to gain entrance.

Centro Cultural Banco do Brasil BUILDING
(Map p224; www.culturabancodobrasil.com.br/portal/sao-paulo; Álvares Penteado 112; cinema & exhibitions from R$4; ⏲9am-9pm Wed-Mon) FREE Housed in an extraordinarily and lovingly restored Beaux Arts building, this cultural center holds innovative exhibitions of contemporary art as well as excellent film series and theater performances, some of which have an entrance fee.

BM&FBovespa NOTABLE BUILDING
(Map p224; ☎3272-7373; www.bmfbovespa.com.br; Rua XV (15) de Novembro 275, Centro; ⏲10am-5pm Mon-Fri) FREE Latin America's largest stock exchange. There is no longer a live trading floor to visit, but the lobby serves as a de facto museum, with small artifacts, a mock trading floor and an eight-minute self-congratulatory explanation of the Brazilian stock exchange in 3D!

Praça da República & Around

Just a few blocks northwest of Anhangabaú lies **Praça da República**, an always lively square that turns into an open-air market on Saturday and Sunday, specializing in crafts, paintings, coins and gemstones. The area north of the square has become a center popular with the gay community, while to the south lies a dense nest of business hotels, huge office buildings and, especially along **Avenida São Luís**, what were once some of the city's most prestigious apartment buildings.

For Caetano Veloso fans, a visit to the corner of **Avenida Ipiranga** and **Avenida São João**, which features in his beloved song 'Sampa,' is mandatory. There are no sights to speak of, but the bustling intersection does do a good job of summing up the city.

Edifício Copan HISTORIC BUILDING
(Map p224; www.copansp.com.br; Av Ipiranga 200) Copan was designed by late modernist master Oscar Niemeyer. The building's serpentine facade and narrow *brises soleil*

(permanent sunshades) have become a symbol of the city. You can visit its snaking, sloping ground-floor shopping arcade and hip restaurants, but the upper floors are private apartments and thus off-limits.

Note that the leftist architect designed the building to bring together all classes by including sprawling apartments for the rich as well as tiny studios for the working poor – a real rarity in class-conscious São Paulo.

Edifício Itália HISTORIC BUILDING
(Map p224; ☎2189-2997; www.edificioitalia.com.br; cnr Avs São Luís & Ipiranga; ⏰3-4pm Mon-Fri) FREE With 46 stories, this skyscraper just south of the Praça da República is the tallest in the city center. Its top-floor restaurant, **Terraço Italia**, offers some of the best views of São Paulo.

Views are free during the above stated window; otherwise, you'll need to shell out for an overpriced *guaraná* soda during restaurant-bar hours (skip the food!).

Luz

Located in a tough area just north of the city center, Luz has become an unlikely cultural hub thanks to major restoration of a series of grand turn-of-the-century buildings around the **Parque da Luz**.

Across the street from the park sits **Estação da Luz** (Map p224; Praça da Luz), a restored late-Victorian train station constructed with materials entirely shipped in from Britain and completed in 1901. It services São Paulo's extensive suburban lines, with a long tunnel linking it to Metrô Luz.

★**Pinacoteca do Estado** MUSEUM
(Map p224; www.pinacoteca.org.br; Praça da Luz 2; adult/student Estação Pinacoteca R$6/3, Sat free; ⏰10am-6pm Tue-Sun) This elegant neoclassical museum houses an excellent collection of Brazilian – and especially Paulista – art from the 19th century to the present, including works by big names such as Portinari and Di Cavalcanti. There is a lovely cafe that faces adjacent Parque da Luz.

Museu da Língua Portuguesa MUSEUM
(Map p224; www.museudalinguaportuguesa.org.br; Praça da Luz; adult/student R$6/3) This fascinating museum, with exhibits documenting the rise of the Brazilian language, closed after a horrible fire in late 2015. Thankfully much of its collection is digitized and the museum is expected to be rebuilt in time. Check the website for updates.

Estação Júlio Prestes HISTORIC BUILDING
(Map p224; Largo General Osório 66) This grand turn-of-the-century Beaux Arts–style working railway station (actually completed in the 1930s) is the **Estação Pinacoteca** (☎3324-1000; www.pinacoteca.org.br; adult/student incl Pinacoteca do Estado R$6/3; ⏰10am-6pm Tue-Sun), an annex of the Pinacoteca do Estado hosting Sampa's three best contemporary art halls and an excellent permanent collection of modernist Brazilian art. Also here is the powerful **Memorial da Resistência** (Map p224; www.memorialdaresistenciasp.org.br; ⏰10am-5:30pm Tue-Sun) FREE, occupying cells where dissidents were tortured during Brazil's military dictatorship.

Museu de Arte Sacra MUSEUM
(Museum of Sacred Art; www.museuartesacra.org.br; Tiradentes 676; adult/student R$6/3, Sat free; ⏰9am-5pm Wed-Fri, 10am-6pm Sat & Sun) The best of its kind in Brazil, this museum includes works by renowned 18th-century sculptor Antônio Aleijadinho, along with some 200 other ecclesiastical works from the 17th to the 20th centuries. The museum is housed in the 18th-century Luz monastery, which is one of São Paulo's best-preserved buildings of the period.

A newer annex houses an amazingly large and elaborate Neapolitan manger scene, plus a collection of other manger scenes from around the world. It's 50m from Metrô Tiradentes.

Liberdade

Liberdade – a short walk south of Praça da Sé – has long been the traditional center of Sampa's massive Japanese community. Though most new Asian immigrants these days come from China and Korea, the gritty neighborhood is still lined with traditional Japanese shops and eateries and is full of hidden gems of Asian culture.

Praça da Liberdade is the neighborhood's main square and also the location of its metro stop. It hosts an open-air market on Sunday. A short walk south on Galvão Bueno takes you past many Asian shops and restaurants as well as some rather neglected Japanese-style gardens.

Museu Histórico da Imigração Japonesa MUSEUM
(Museum of Japanese Immigration; ☎3209-5465; www.bunkyo.bunkyonet.org.br; São Joaquim 381; adult/student R$7/3.50; ⏰1:30-5:30pm Tue-Sun) This modest but fascinating museum, on

the 7th floor of a Liberdade office building, documents the arrival and integration of the Japanese community. Photos, period objects and a full-scale reconstruction of a typical immigrant's farm lodging tell a poignant story, from the arrival in Santos of the first 781 settlers aboard the *Kasato-Maru* in 1908 through to today. Bring ID.

Higienópolis, Pacaembu & Barra Funda

Northwest of Av Paulista lies the leafy neighborhood of **Higienópolis**, one of the most traditional of the city's upscale neighborhoods and a good spot for a stroll. Praça Buenos Aires, a tree-filled, European-style square, serves as the neighborhood's lungs and playground. As you continue northwest, you pass through **Pacaembu**, a low-rise neighborhood of ramblingly luxurious homes reminiscent of upscale Los Angeles. Finally, you reach **Barra Funda**, a more workaday neighborhood that at night comes alive with some of the city's trendiest nightclubs.

Museu do Futebol MUSEUM
(Map p230; www.museudofutebol.org.br; Praça Charles Miller s/n, Pacaembu; adult/student R$6/3, Thu free; 9am-5pm Tue-Sun;) Tucked under the bleachers of colorfully art-deco Pacaembu Stadium, this fantastic museum is devoted to Brazil's greatest passion – football (soccer). Its multimedia displays over two floors manage to evoke the thrill of watching a championship game, even for nonfans.

Catch bus 177C-10 (Jardim Brasil), 917M-10 (Morro Grande) or 6232-10 (Barra Funda) from Av Dr Arnaldo 500 outside Metrô Clínicas and get off in front of Pão de Açúcar grocery store on Av Pacaembu.

Avenida Paulista, Jardins & Around

Once the domain of coffee barons and their sprawling manses, **Avenida Paulista** (often known simply as 'Paulista') began to go 'Manhattan' in the 1950s and today is lined with towering modernist office buildings. Though few of these buildings have much architectural merit, the sum of the parts is impressive. It's also a lively area both day and night, packed with restaurants, shops, theaters and cafes. Just off Paulista, across from the Museu de Arte de São Paulo (MASP), lies **Parque Siqueira Campos** (Map p230; Peixoto Gomide 949, Jardins; 6am-6pm), a beautifully designed and maintained park that re-creates the Atlantic rainforest that was leveled to build São Paulo. It's a remarkably tranquil refuge just off the city's busiest street.

Along Rua Augusta north of Paulista, **Baixo Augusta** was São Paulo's traditional red-light district; however, the area has been commandeered over the last decade by a combination of gay, fashion-forward and alternative crowds (often all three), and its bars and nightclubs are packed after 10pm with alterna-scensters.

On the southern slope of Paulista lies **Jardins**, the city's leafiest and most chic central neighborhood. This is where you will find some of the city's most over-the-top living and shopping and, above all, **Rua Oscar Freire** (Brazil's Rodeo Dr and the eighth most luxurious street in the world), with its showstopping series of boutiques and super-refined eateries.

★**Museu de Arte de São Paulo** MUSEUM
(MASP; Map p230; www.masp.art.br; Av Paulista 1578, Bela Vista; adult/student R$25/12, Tue all day & Thu after 5pm free; 10am-6pm Tue & Thu-Sun, to 8pm Wed) Sampa's pride, this museum possesses Latin America's most comprehensive collection of Western art. Hovering above a concrete plaza that turns into an antiques fair on Sunday, the museum, designed by architect Lina Bo Bardi and completed in 1968, is considered a classic of modernism by many and an abomination by a vocal few.

The collection, though, is unimpeachable, and ranges from Goya to El Greco to Manet. The impressionist collection is particularly noteworthy. There are also a few great Brazilian paintings, including three fine works by Cândido Portinari. Regrettably, the museum seems rather neglected by its guardians, with public areas looking shabby in places. More shocking was the theft in 2007 of paintings by Portinari and Picasso, which revealed that a museum with a billion-dollar collection lacked motion detectors or cameras with infrared capabilities. Fortunately, the two paintings were eventually recovered.

Casa Amarela MUSEUM
(Map p230; www.casaamarela.art.br; José Maria Lisboa 838, Jardins; 10am-7pm Mon-Fri, to 6pm Sat) FREE Relatively unknown and blissfully uncrowded, this unassuming yellow home is part NGO handicraft shop, part two-table romantic cafe and part tiny museum boasting one the world's best collections of

SÃO PAULO STATE SÃO PAULO CITY

artifacts from Irmãos Villas-Bôas, a three-brother Brazilian activist team who were the first white men to ever come in contact with upper Xingu river indigenous communities of the Amazon.

They were responsible for the preservation of South America's first indigenous reserve, Parque Indígena do Xingu, in 1961.

Parque do Ibirapuera

The biggest green space in central São Paulo, Parque do Ibirapuera makes a fine escape from the city's seemingly infinite stretches of concrete. In addition, the leafy 2-sq-km park serves as a thriving center of the city's cultural life, with a series of museums, performance spaces and the grounds for São Paulo's renowned Bienal (p233).

Inaugurated in 1954 to commemorate the city's 400th anniversary, the park was designed by renowned landscape architect Roberto Burle Marx. A series of buildings in the park are the work of Oscar Niemeyer; most of them are linked by a long and distinctively serpentine covered walkway. At the north entrance stands Victor Brecheret's huge **Monumento Bandeiras**, erected in 1953 in memory of the city's early pioneers.

To get to the park, take the metro to Vila Mariana station and then bus 775-A 'Jardim Aldagiza.' There are snack stands and a full-service restaurant at the Museu de Arte Moderna; or pick up a great and cheap burger off the southwest corner of the park at **Bullguer** (www.bullguer.com; Diogo Jácome 606, Vila Nova Conceicão; burgers R$16-28; noon-3pm & 6:30pm-midnight Mon-Fri, noon-5pm &

FREE SP!

There's no sugarcoating it: Brazil is expensive and São Paulo is the beast of the bunch. But that doesn't mean you can't have fun on a shoestring budget. Our favorite freebies:

Banespa (Edifício Altino Arantes; Map p224; João Brícola 24; 10am-3pm Mon-Fri) For one of Sampa's best panoramas, head to the top of this 161m-high skyscraper, Brazil's version of the Empire State Building, completed in 1939. Ride free to the observation deck on the top floor for views of the city.

Note: you will need some form of ID to sign in. You'll need to hurry up and wait: first to sign in, then for an elevator to the 26th floor, then a second elevator and finally for the spiral staircase to the top. The five-minute maximum visit is enforced heavy-handedly, but the view will floor you.

Mosteiro São Bento (Map p224; 2440-7837; www.mosteiro.org.br; Largo de São Bento s/n; 6am-6pm Mon-Wed & Fri, 6am-8am Thu, 6am-noon & 4-6pm Sat & Sun) Among the city's oldest and most important churches, São Bento dates to 1598, though its neo-Gothic facade dates only to the early 20th century. Step inside the church to view its impressive stained glass. Mass (7am weekdays, 6am on Saturday and 10am Sunday) includes Gregorian chanting.

There's a legendary, culturally-rich brunch of monk and top chef delicacies – including Prosecco! – on the second and last Sunday of each month – booking required well in advance (R$187 per person; reservations at brunchnomosteiro@multiplaeventos.com.br).

Casa da Imagem (Map p224; 3106-5122; www.casadaimagem.sp.gov.br; Roberto Simonsen 136-B, Centro; 9am-5pm Tue-Sun) Beautifully curated from some 84,000 historical photographs, this museum inside a restored colonial downtown mansion is a must for those interested in the São Paulo of days gone by. Themed exhibitions change every three months; and original frescoes from the 1880s were uncovered during the building's restoration.

SP Free Walking Tour (Map p224; www.spfreewalkingtour.com; 11:30am Mon, Wed & Sat) Culls over 450 years of Sampa history into a long but fascinating 'Old Downtown' walk three times a week at 11:30am. The tour meets next to the C.I.T. at Praça da República and ends 3½ hours later at Largo São Bento; and there are walk-exclusive discounts to be had along the way.

An Paulista Av tour covers the modern city every Thursday and Sunday at 3:30pm, leaving from Banco do Brasil at the corner of Paulista and Rua Augusta on the Jardins side and ending 3¼ hours later at Praça Oswaldo Cruz. An artsy, graffiti-heavy tour in Vila Madalena leaves from outside Fradique Countinho metro station on Tuesdays and Sundays at 11am.

Avenida Paulista, Jardins & Around

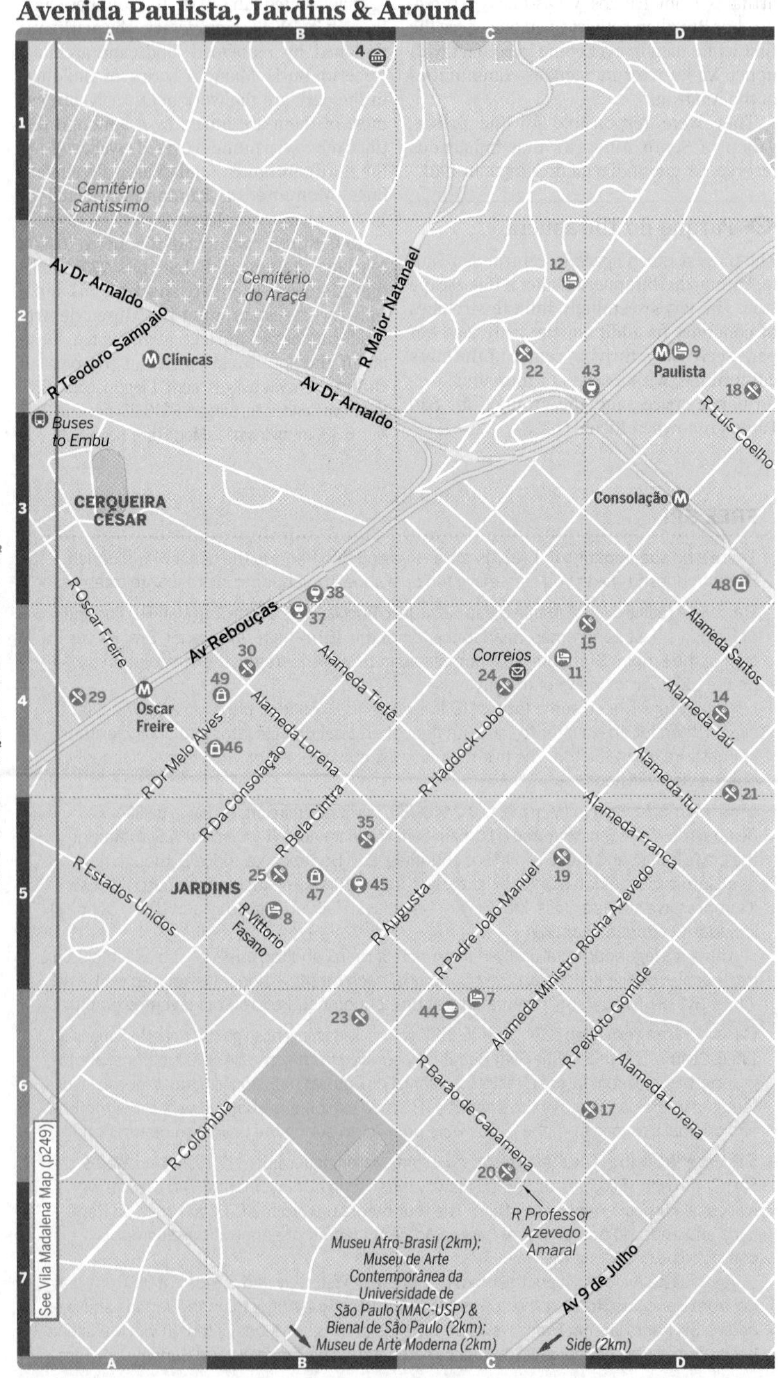

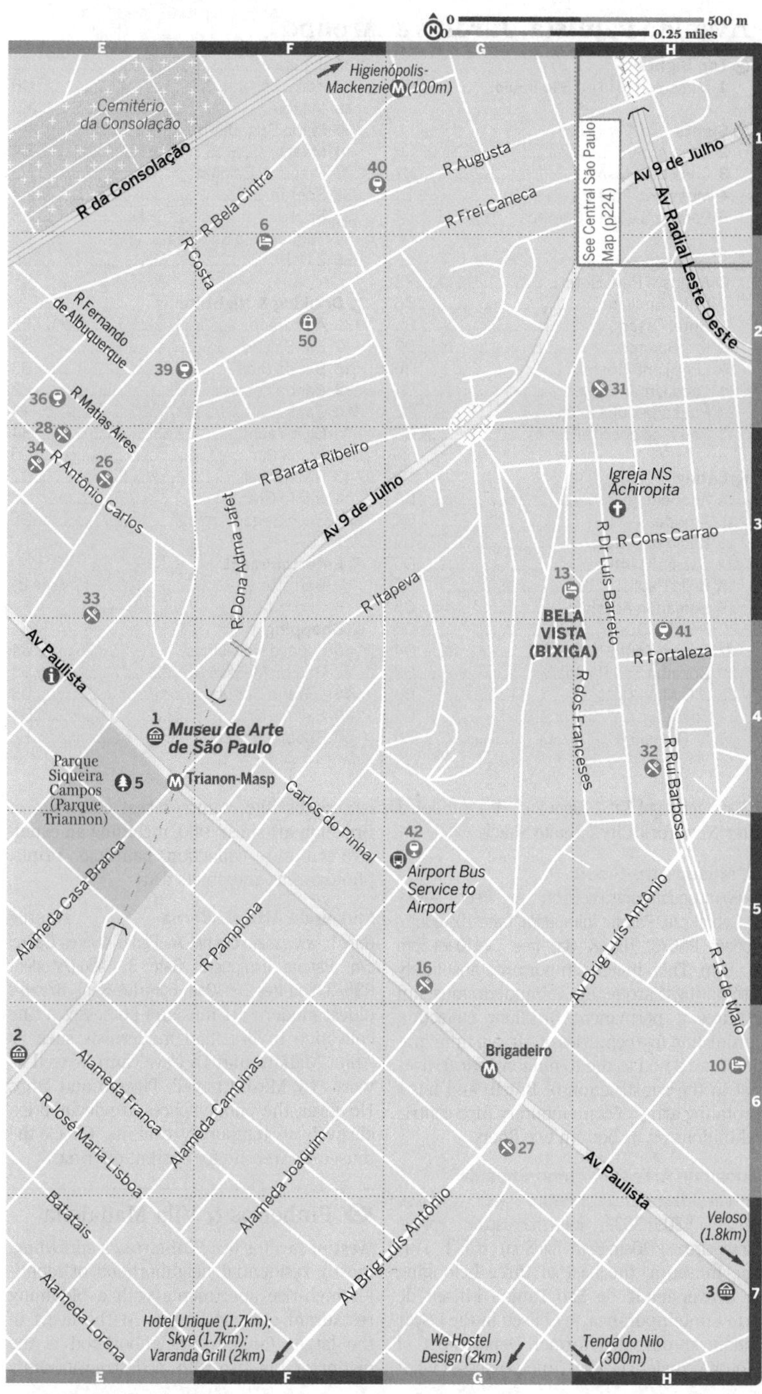
0 500 m
0 0.25 miles
Higienópolis-Mackenzie (100m)
Cemitério da Consolação
R da Consolação
R Bela Cintra
R Costa
R Augusta
R Frei Caneca
See Central São Paulo Map (p224)
Av 9 de Julho
Av Radial Leste Oeste
R Fernando de Albuquerque
R Matias Aires
R Antônio Carlos
R Barata Ribeiro
Av 9 de Julho
R Dona Adma Jafet
R Itapeva
Igreja NS Achiropita
R Dr Luís Barreto
R Cons Carrao
BELA VISTA (BIXIGA)
R Fortaleza
R dos Franceses
Av Paulista
Museu de Arte de São Paulo
Parque Siqueira Campos (Parque Triannon)
Trianon-Masp
Carlos do Pinhal
R Rui Barbosa
Airport Bus Service to Airport
Alameda Casa Branca
R Pamplona
Av Brig Luís Antônio
R 13 de Maio
Brigadeiro
Alameda Franca
Alameda Campinas
R José Maria Lisboa
Alameda Joaquim
Av Paulista
Batatais
Av Brig Luís Antônio
Veloso (1.8km)
Alameda Lorena
Hotel Unique (1.7km); Skye (1.7km); Varanda Grill (2km)
We Hostel Design (2km)
Tenda do Nilo (300m)
SÃO PAULO STATE SÃO PAULO CITY

Avenida Paulista, Jardins & Around

Top Sights
1 Museu de Arte de São Paulo E4

Sights
2 Casa Amarela E6
3 Casa das Rosas H7
4 Museu do Futebol B1
5 Parque Siqueira Campos E4

Sleeping
6 Augusta Park Hotel F2
7 Hotel Emiliano C6
8 Hotel Fasano B5
9 Ibis Budget D2
10 LimeTime Hostel H6
11 Lobo Urban Stay C4
12 Pousada Dona Ziláh C2
13 Pousada dos Franceses G3

Eating
14 Aconchego Carioca D4
15 Amadeus D4
16 Bacio di Latte G5
17 Bacio di Latte D6
18 Bella Paulista D2
19 Benjamin Abrahão C5
20 Brasil a Gosto C6
21 Capim Santo D4
22 Cozinha São Paulo C2
23 D.O.M. B6
24 Epice C4
25 Ici Brasserie B5
26 Jiquitaia E3
27 Kan G6
28 Madhu E3
29 Maria Brigadeiro A4
30 Meats B4
31 Patuá da Baiana H2
32 Speranza H4
33 Spot E3
34 Taquería La Sabrosa E3
35 Z Deli B5

Drinking & Nightlife
36 Astronete E2
37 Bar Balcão B4
38 Bar da Dida B3
39 Bar da Lôca E2
40 Caos F1
41 Club Yacht H4
42 Frank Bar G5
43 Riviera Bar D2
44 Santo Grão C6
45 Suco Begaço B5

Entertainment
Barretto .... (see 8)

Shopping
46 Espaço Havaianas B4
47 Galeria Melissa B5
48 Livraria Cultura D3
49 Salinas Off B4
50 Shopping Frei Caneca F2

6:30pm-midnight Sat, 1-10pm Sun;), modeled after New York City's Shake Shack.

★ **Museu Afro-Brasil** MUSEUM
(www.museuafrobrasil.com.br; Av. Pedro Alvares Cabral s/n, Parque Ibirapuera, Gate 10; adult/student R$6/3, Thu & Sat free; 10am-5pm Tue-Sun) This hugely important, absolutely fascinating Parque do Ibirapuera museum features a permanent 3rd-floor collection chronicling five centuries of African immigration (and a nod to the 10 million African lives lost in the construction of Brazil) and hosts a rotating array of contemporary Afro-centric exhibitions on its bottom two floors.

Museu de Arte Contemporânea da Universidade de São Paulo MUSEUM
(MAC; 3091-3039; www.mac.usp.br; Parque Ibirapuerra; 10am-6pm Tue-Sun) FREE This fine museum, the best of three belonging to Universidade de São Paulo's Museu de Arte Contemporânea, is housed in the Oscar Niemeyer–designed former Department of Motor Vehicles (Detran) and possesses what is arguably the country's best collection of Brazilian art since 1960, including an extensive sculpture collection, paintings, prints, photographs and objets d'art.

Museu de Arte Moderna MUSEUM
(MAM; www.mam.org.br; Av Pedro Alvares Cabral s/n, Parque Ibirapuera, Gate 3; adult/student R$6/3, Sun free; 10am-6pm Tue-Sun) Brazil's oldest modern-art museum possesses a fine collection of Brazilian modernists such as Anita Malfatti and Di Cavalcanti as well as works by Miró, Chagall, Picasso and Dufy. However, the public spaces are devoted exclusively to temporary exhibits. Check the museum's website for current offerings.

Pinheiros & Vila Madalena

West of Jardins lies **Pinheiros**, a sprawling, mostly residential neighborhood of identikit high-rise apartments with a blooming restaurant and arts scene. At the heart of the larger Pinheiros neighborhood is the distinctly low-rise and pedestrian-friendly

Vila Madalena. Long a Bohemian enclave, it has in recent years become a popular alternative to the high-end, attitude-heavy clubs and restaurants of nearby Vila Olímpia. The epicenter of the bar and restaurant scene is the corner of Rua Mourato Coelho and Rua Aspicuelta, which are crowded at happy hour and, on weekends, stay that way until the wee hours. There are also a number of interesting shops, cafes and art galleries.

Galeria Milan GALLERY
(Map p249; ☎3031-6007; www.galeriamillan.com.br; Fradique Coutinho 1360; ⏲10am-7pm Tue-Fri, 11am-6pm Sat) Displays the work of some of the city's most cutting-edge contemporary artists, both well-established names and up-and-coming newbies.

Instituto Tomie Ohtake MUSEUM
(Map p249; ☎2245-1900; www.institutotomieohtake.org.br; Brigadeiro Faria Lima 201, Pinheiros; ⏲11am-8pm Tue-Sun) FREE This cultural institute, founded by Ruy Ohtake, São Paulo's most prominent contemporary architect, is dedicated to his Japanese-born mother, one of São Paulo's most illustrious painters. An attractive gallery space features changing exhibits of prominent, mostly local artists.

South & East of Jardins

Extra-wide Av Brigadeiro Faria Lima (called just 'Faria Lima') marks the southwestern edge of the Jardins neighborhoods. Faria Lima is also the main corridor connecting Pinheiros with the ritzy residential neighborhoods of **Morumbi**, **Vila Olímpia**, **Itaím Bibi** and **Moema**. All of these areas are composed largely of congested streets, forbidding luxury high-rises and glittering complexes that house the majority of the city's most profitable businesses, from banking to technology. That said, there are plenty of fine restaurants, nightclubs and shopping opportunities that die-hards may want to seek out.

Museu da Casa Brasileira MUSEUM
(☎3032-3727; www.mcb.org.br; Brigadeiro Faria Lima 2705, Pinheiros; adult/student R$6/3, Sat & Sun free; ⏲10am-6pm Tue-Sun) Occupying an extravagant Palladian-style villa built by a local tycoon and his wife in the 1940s, this small but charming museum is dedicated to architecture and design and offers a hodgepodge collection of Brazilian furnishings from the 17th to the 20th centuries. There's also a cafe-restaurant with lovely outdoor seating.

Fundação Maria Luisa e Oscar Americano MUSEUM, GARDENS
(☎3742-0077; www.fundacaooscaramericano.org.br; Av Morumbi 4077, Morumbi; adult/student R$10/5; ⏲museum & cafe 10am-5:30pm Tue-Sun) Home of the couple who developed the leafy, upscale suburb of Morumbi, this fine retreat hosts impressive gardens and a lovely collection of painting, sculpture and objets d'art from the 18th to the 20th centuries. The 1950s house-turned-museum is a small masterpiece of Brazilian modernism, and there's also a lovely cafe that serves traditional high tea for R$58.

Museu Paulista MUSEUM
(www.mp.usp.br; Parque de Independência, Ipiranga; adult/student R$6/3, 1st Sun of month free; ⏲9am-5pm Tue-Sun) Set amid Versailles-like gardens in the eastern suburb of Ipiranga, this museum began its life as a memorial to Brazil's independence from Portugal. According to legend, Dom Pedro declared independence on the shores of a nearby stream. The gardens and palace are the real treat here, as are the fine vistas that its hilltop position affords.

Courses

Polyglot LANGUAGE COURSE
(☎3744-4397; www.polyglot.com.br; Eng Luiz Carlos Berrini 96, Brooklyn) One of the most respected language schools for Portuguese.

Tours

Flaviz Liz di Paolo CULTURAL, SHOPPING
(☎98119-3903; www.flavializ.com) Personal guide Flavia Liz is an enthusiastic, multilingual São Paulo specialist who offers customized guiding services throughout the city and surroundings. Whether you want to dig into architecture, shopping, art galleries, graffiti, favelas or any other niche, she is your woman.

Festivals & Events

The city's two biggest events are the Bienal de São Paulo and the Gay Pride events (p247). In 1997, São Paulo's first Gay Pride parade drew a meager 3000 people. In less than a decade, it has grown into the world's largest Pride event, attracting as many as five million.

Bienal de São Paulo ART
(www.bienal.org.br; Parque do Ibirapuera, Moema) Modeled on the Venice Biennale, the Bienal de São Paulo, founded in 1951, has grown

into one of the world's most important arts events. Many of the participants are working artists who have been nominated by their home country.

The event is held during even-numbered years, generally from October to December, in a sprawling pavilion designed by modernist master Oscar Niemeyer in the leafy **Parque do Ibirapuera** (www.parqueibirapuera.org). In recent years, admission has been free, though this is subject to funding.

São Paulo Restaurant Week FOOD
(www.restaurantweek.com.br; lunch/dinner R$37.90/49.90; ⏲ Feb/Mar & Aug/Sep) More than 100 restaurants offer special menus and promotional prices for two weeks, twice a year.

Virada Cultural MUSIC
(www.viradacultural.prefeitura.sp.gov.br; ⏲ Apr/May) A nonstop, free 24-hour party of cultural, especially musical, events around the city.

São Paulo International Art Fair ART
(www.sp-arte.com; ⏲ Apr) This national and international art fair is one of the world's largest.

Mostra Internacional de Cinema FILM
(www.mostra.org; ⏲ Oct) The country's largest film festival, with screenings throughout the city.

Reveillon NEW YEAR
(⏲ 31 Dec) Av Paulista turns into a big outdoor party to ring in the new year.

Sleeping

São Paulo's only true traveler-like quarter is the bohemian *bairro* of Vila Madalena, 6km west of Praça da Sé, which boasts a bona fide hip hostel scene in addition to being the city's long-standing cradle of artsy boutiques, cutting-edge galleries and boisterous nightlife. The leafy, upscale district of Jardins, 5km southwest of Centro, is pricier but also very pleasant. There's a solid concentration of hostels around the residential neighborhoods of Paraíso and Vila Mariana off the southeastern end of Av Paulista – a little out of the way but near good metro connections. If you opt for Centro, the areas surrounding Estação da Luz train station and central downtown are rife with cheap hotels,, but also crime and prostitution – use extreme caution and don't walk around at night. Stick to the safe-ish immediate area around Praça da República.

City Walk Sampa's Centro Velho

START PRAÇA DA REPÚBLICA
END PRAÇA DA REPÚBLICA
LENGTH 3.5KM; TWO HOURS

Downtown São Paulo is a vibrant living museum of architectural gems and glory days gone by. Head out on a weekday (weekends and nights are a little too dicey) on this pleasant Centro stroll.

Start at 1 **Praça da República**, head down Av Ipiranga and then turn left onto Av São Luís to get a look at what's still one of the tallest buildings in town – the 46-story 2 **Edifício Itália** (p227). Continuing down Av São Luís, check out the rather squat, gray building at the end of the small park on the left. It looks like a prison, but it's the 3 **Mario de Andrade Municipal Library**, housing the largest book collection in the city.

Turning left onto Rua Xavier de Toledo, keeping the library on your left, follow the road downhill toward the Anhangabaú metro station a few blocks away. Follow Toledo until the 4 **Theatro Municipal** (p226) appears – this baroque building, with its art-nouveau features, is the pride of the city. Opposite the theater, on the right, is the 5 **Viaduto de Chá**, a metal bridge built in 1892 and named after an old tea plantation that used to be in the area. Pedestrian traffic became too heavy for the old bridge and a new one was inaugurated in 1938.

Crossing the bridge, look out over the 6 **Parque Anhangabaú** on the left. At the other side of the bridge, enter 7 **Praça do Patriarca** straight ahead. Here you'll find the 8 **Igreja de Santo Antônio**, the central church of the settlement of São Paulo at the start of the 17th century, and rebuilt in the 18th century.

Turn right some 20 paces beyond on Rua São Bento, leading to 9 **Largo de São Francisco**, a triangular plaza that is home to twin churches, both known as 10 **Igreja de São Francisco de Assis** (p226), and the well-respected 11 **College of Law**. Just beyond the con-

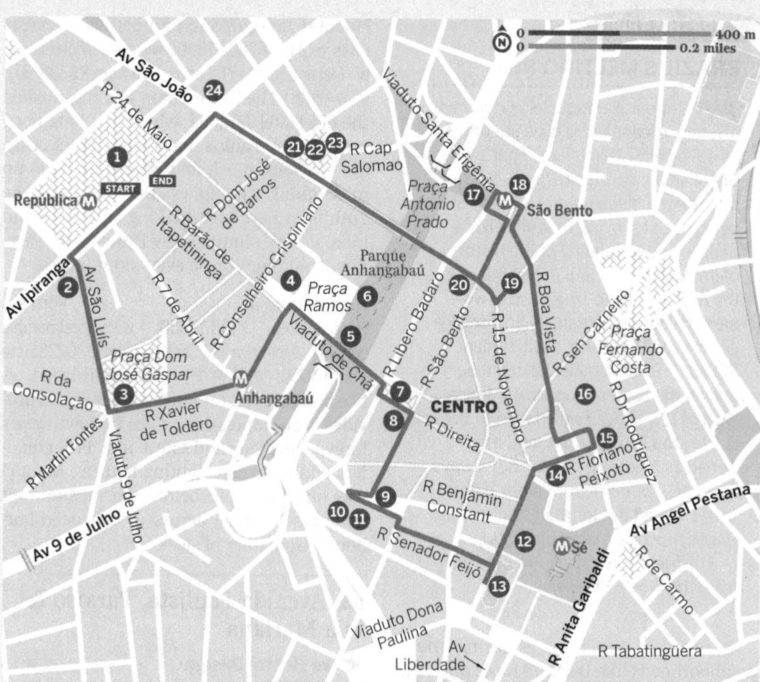

troversial statue of a Frenchman kissing an indigenous woman in front of the College of Law is Senador Feijó, leading to the famous 12 **Praça da Sé** (p223). Soak up the joyous vibe in the square, but watch your pockets. Step inside the enormous 13 **Catedral da Sé** (p223).

As you exit the cathedral, head down the plaza and continue toward the 14 **Caixa Economica Federal**, home to the city's coffers and also a great cultural center (Caixa Cultural) that features Brazilian artists. Turning right onto Rua Floriano Peixoto, walk to the end and feast your eyes upon the pinkish-colored 15 **Solar da Marquesa** (p223). Follow the street around to the left to 16 **Praça Páteo do Colégio** (p223), the actual site where São Paulo was founded in 1554.

Directly in front of this plaza is Boa Vista. Following it away from Praça da Sé to the end, where you'll find 17 **Largo de São Bento**, home to the 18 **Mosteiro São Bento** (p229), a monastery and basilica built in an eclectic style and still putting on Gregorian-chant concerts.

Leaving the square, walk up the pedestrianized Rua São Bento to Av São João. Turn left at São João and another quick left at the next street, where on the right stands the art-deco 19 **Banespa building** (p229). Head to the top floor for a sweeping view of São Paulo. Backtrack to São Bento and then keep heading straight down Av São João. On the left just past São Bento stands 20 **Edifício Martinelli** (p226). You are now crossing the Vale do Anhangabaú that you saw earlier from the Viaduto de Chá.

Head up São João as far as 21 **Largo de Paiçandú**. Behind the pretty 22 **NS do Rosário dos Homens Pretos** is the magnificent 23 **Monumento á Mãe Preta** (Monument to the Black Mother). This heart-wrenching statue depicts an African slave woman suckling a white child, and the poem underneath gives voice to her lament for her own children who must go hungry.

To wrap up a long day, continue forward and you will end up at the 24 **intersection of Av São João and Av Ipiranga**, a corner that is considered the most famous in all of São Paulo and was immortalized in Caetano Veloso's beautiful ode to the city, 'Sampa.' Turn left and you will be back where you started at Praça da República.

WORTH A TRIP

BRAZIL'S MELTING POT

Brazil's unparalleled racial and ethnic diversity means there is no such thing as a typical Brazilian face. That's why Brazilian passports are highly sought after on the black market – many faces could pass for being Brazilian. For a deeper understanding of the history of immigration to São Paulo, head to the **Memorial do Imigrante** (www.memorialdoimigrante.sp.gov.br; Visconde de Paraiba 1316, Moóca; adult/student R$6/3; ⊙9am-5pm Tue-Sat, 10am-5pm Sun) in the eastern suburb of Moóca. Built in 1887, it was called the **Hospedaria dos Imigrantes**, and functioned as a holding place – not always friendly – for immigrant labor before they shipped out for their first jobs in Brazil, mostly on large plantations.

The memorial is a five-minute walk from the Metrô Bresser.

Be wary of lower prices luring you to neighborhoods like Belém, Moóca and Parada Inglesa – they might be cheaper, but you'll be a long haul from the action and sleeping in the city's two least desirable zones, north and east, which are more prone to crime.

Central São Paulo

Akasaka HOTEL $
(☎3207-1500; www.akasakahotel.com.br; Praça da Liberdade 149, Liberdade; s/d/tr/q R$150/155/180/250; ❄📶) Conveniently located across from the metro on Praça Liberdade, this triumphantly no frills (no wi-fi! no breakfast!) budget option offers 40 simple but clean rooms. It's a convenient choice for those especially interested in the city's Japanese and Korean subcultures.

155 Hotel BOUTIQUE HOTEL $$
(Map p224; ☎3150-1555; www.155hotel.com.br; Martinho Prado 173, Consolacão; d/tr/ste R$195/293/297; ❄@📶) This gay-friendly, 76-room, affordable boutique hotel between Centro and the alterna-hipster bars of Baixo Augusta is steeped in minimalist blacks and grays in the ultra-sleek suites; regular rooms aren't quite as hip but are still top value all things considered, with tight bathrooms but hardwood floors and writing desks.

Novotel Jaraguá São Paulo BUSINESS HOTEL $$
(Map p224; ☎2802-7000; www.accorhotels.com.br; Martins Fontes 71, Centro; s/d from R$308/371; P❄@📶) The Accor chain has refurbished the old Hotel Jaraguá, which had long been central São Paulo's most chic hotel. Digs are spacious, plush and cheerfully done up in soothing cafe tones. Rooms above the 20th floor have breathtaking city views and there's a free shuttle to Av Paulista, Av Faria Lima and Praça de Sé every 30 minutes.

Hotel Marabá HOTEL $$$
(Map p224; ☎2137-9500; www.hotelmaraba.com.br; Av Ipiranga 757, Centro; s/d R$330/385, ste from R$750; P❄@📶) This refurbished office building just off Praça da República provides is an impressive choice in downtown's hiply-gentrifying and safest area. From quality bedding to chic lighting fixtures, Marabá was only just here before the hipsters but manages to come across as the neighborhood's Godfather of sleek.

Avenida Paulista, Paraíso & Vila Mariana

★**We Hostel Design** HOSTEL $
(☎2615-2262; www.wehostel.com.br; Morgado de Mateus 567, Vila Mariana; dm R$57-73, d without bathroom R$160-210; ❄@📶) Simply gorgeous, São Paulo's best hostel sits inside a beautiful 100-year-old historic white mansion on a quiet Vila Mariana residential corner. From the guest kitchen to the hammock-strewn, quasi-wraparound porch to the kitschy living room, everything here has been designed with expert connoisseurship of retro furniture and coveted antiques.

Pousada dos Franceses POUSADA $
(Map p230; ☎3288-1592; www.pousadadosfranceses.com.br; Rua dos Franceses 100, Morro dos Ingleses; dm R$55, s/d/tr R$100/160/200, s/d without bathroom R$92/140; @📶) On a quiet, almost suburban street, yet just a short walk to Av Paulista, this veteran hostel offers decent communal digs, bright and pleasant common areas, and private rooms of varying sizes and comfort.

LimeTime Hostel HOSTEL $
(Map p230; ☎2935-5463; www.limetimehostels.com; 13 de Maio 1552, Bela Vista; dm from R$35, r without bathroom R$120; @📶) This superbly located, graffiti-slathered hostel is well-worn but within walking distance of Av Paulista, Metrô Brigadeiro and the airport bus stop at Hotel Maksoud Plaza. Power-equipped

lockers and flat-screens give it a hi-tech edge, while the owner, a wild-haired DJ named Bebeto, is a perfect ambassador for the city. You'll trade breakfast for one free caipirinha per night, though that won't make up for being charged for towels *even in private rooms.*

Augusta Park Hotel HOTEL **$$**
(Map p230; ☎3124-4400; www.augustapark.com.br; Augusta 922, Consolação; s/d R$235/280; ❄📶🏊) Set amid the action of Baixo Augusta, the Augusta Park offers some of Sampa's best-value, if slightly dated, rooms and a convenient location (especially if you managed to snag the promotional rates, some R$50 cheaper than those above).

Ibis Budget HOTEL **$$**
(Map p230; ☎3123-7752; www.ibishotel.com; Rua da Consolação 2303, Consolação; r R$180-255; ❄@📶) Somewhat soulless but boasting with a great location and price, this modern budget chain is worth considering. Dormitory-like rooms are spartan, but you are 30m from Metro Paulista.

Avenida Paulista, Jardins & Around

Lobo Urban Stay GUESTHOUSE **$$**
(Map p230; ☎3569-7198; www.lobourbanstay.com; Haddock Lobo 839, Jardins; dm/s/d/tr R$60/150/200/250; @📶) This quiet, design-forward newcomer easily offers the best location for money in the city, located smack dab in the middle of São Paulo's most fashionable environs. Run by two journalists, there's one eight-bed dorm with its own private bath; and two spacious private rooms (especially good-value for solo travelers).

Pousada Dona Ziláh POUSADA **$$**
(Map p230; ☎3062-1444; www.zilah.com; Minas Gerais 112, Higienópolis; r/tr R$315/390; @📶) A move after 30 years in Jardins to this new Paulista-adjacent 1932 mansion in Higienópolis spells the end of an era, but not the end of the charm. These six new rooms offer upgraded comforts, especially where the bathrooms are concerned, and extensive gardens that are watered with filtered shower and sink water.

Hotel Emiliano BOUTIQUE HOTEL **$$$**
(Map p230; ☎3068-4399; www.emiliano.com.br; Oscar Freire 384, Jardins; d from R$1878; P❄@📶🏊) Sleek, bright and minimalist, Emiliano is the city's best hotel, steeped in refined luxury with local touches such as the lobby's lush suspended orchid garden, impeccable service and a sun-drenched rooftop pool, all without taking itself too seriously. It nails the combo of cool (not too in your face) and opulent (but not too stuffy).

And then there's that decadent R$159 weekend brunch. Divine.

Hotel Unique DESIGN HOTEL **$$$**
(☎3055-4710; www.hotelunique.com.br; Av Brigadeiro Luis Antônio 4700, Jardim Paulista; d from R$1520; P❄@🏊) Designed by Ruy Ohtake, the slice of watermelon–reminiscent Unique is certainly the city's most architecturally ambitious hotel, as well as a favorite of rock stars and fashionistas. Rooms, with their portal-like windows, are elegantly minimalist, and the rooftop bar (p247) and pool offer some of the city's very best views.

Hotel Fasano BOUTIQUE HOTEL **$$$**
(Map p230; ☎3896-4000; www.fasano.com.br; Vittorio Fasano 88, Jardins; d from R$2507; P❄@🏊) This ultra-refined 60-room hotel behind an English red-brick facade evokes a bygone era of Modernist glamour, with muted gray travertine marble set off with exquisite 1930s-era antiques in rooms and common areas, and a reserve, formality and discreetness rare in Brazil (only four rooms per floor).

The Zen-like rooftop pool area and intimate jazz bar alone are worth the price of admission.

Vila Madalena, Pinheiros & Around

★**Guest 607** POUSADA **$**
(☎2619-6007; www.guest607.com.br; João Moura 607, Pinheiros; dm R$45, d R$210, d/tr without bathroom from R$130/158; ❄@📶) This colorful six-room gastro-guesthouse turned a two-story townhouse into a design-forward and food-centric spot to rest your weary head. Rooms are smallish, but the whole place is packed with personality and there's a sophisticated bistro serving three meals a day.

It's just an 800m walk to the beginning of Oscar Freire in Jardins.

Ô de Casa HOSTEL **$**
(Map p249; ☎3063-5216; www.odecasahostel.com; Inácio Pereira da Rocha 385, Vila Madalena; dm R$50-60, r R$150, r without bathroom R$130; ❄📶) This artsy and colorful hostel is one of the neighborhoods oldest and nicest, with a sociable bar and rooftop terrace that gives way to shotgun-style in four-, six- and eight-bed mixed dorm configurations and

WORTH A TRIP

SERRA DA MANTIQUEIRA

About 180km northeast of São Paulo, the beautiful green peaks of the Serra da Mantiqueira are a hotbed of mountain biking and trekking for *paulistanos*, and are a hugely popular winter weekend getaway for Paulistas who enjoy the novelty of wearing woolens. **Campos do Jordão**, Brazil's highest city, is a kitschy and comfortable base from which to explore the nearby peaks, which are home to some of the last remaining virgin *araucária* (Paraná pine) forests and proffer spectacular views of the Paraíba valley.

Popular attractions in the area are **Horto Florestal State Park** (reception desk 3663-3762; per vehicle R$6; 9am-4pm), 14km east from Campos and home to the largest *araucária* reserve in the state. It offers fine walks of varying levels of difficulty. One of the most popular climbs in the surrounding mountains is the 1950m **Pedra do Baú**. **Altus** (3663-4122; www.altus.tur.br; Roberto Simonsen 1724, Vila Inglesa) organizes groups for hiking, rock climbing, mountain biking and other outdoor adventure activities.

Campos itself is a well-heeled getaway. The peak tourist period is July, when the town receives up to a million tourists (expect a minimum one-week stay at this time; there are steep discounts on weekdays and outside winter months). The town also fancies itself a bit of a gastronomic hub and in fact is second only to São Paulo for starred restaurants in the state, but dining out here is expensive and the majority of spots are more show than substance. Don't miss the award-winning **Harry Pisek** (3663-4030; www.salsicharia harrypisek.blogspot.com.br; Pedro Paulo 857; mains R$41-83; 10am-5pm Sun-Fri, to midnight Sat;), whose Chef Pisek studied the art of sausage-making in Germany and is celebrated for his homemade productions. can be filed under expensive, but worth it.

Campos is served by **Pássaro Marron** (www.passaromarron.com.br), which goes to São Paulo (R$46.43, three hours, six daily); and **Viacão Sampaio** (www.viacaosampaio.com.br), which heads once daily to Rio de Janeiro (R$64, five hours, 4:45pm).

well-kept bathrooms. An annex across the street houses quieter private rooms, which attract couples looking for privacy and shorter bathroom waits, without sacrificing the hostel atmosphere.

LimeTime Hostel HOSTEL $
(Map p249; 3798-0051; www.limetimehostels.com; Mourato Coelho 973, Vila Madalena; dm from R$35, d R$110;) Vila Madalena's most sociable hostel and the better of LimeTime's two in the city, thanks to the courtyard bar that is open to the general public and superb location within the neighborhood's nightlife and arts scenes. Digs are dorm-only, but each has its own private bath, and there's a dilapidated rooftop patio that oozes potential. No breakfast, no free towels.

Sampa Hostel HOSTEL $
(Map p249; 3031-6779; www.hostelsampa.com.br; Girassol 519, Vila Madalena; dm from R$47, s/d/tr/q R$130/160/225/280;) This veteran of the Vila Madalena's hostel scene is one of its best, offering four-, six- and eight-bed dorms (the latter a bit cramped), a few sparse private rooms and a funky TV room and kitchen facilities. A new sundeck/barbecue area was being installed at time of research.

★ **Guest Urban** BOUTIQUE HOTEL $$
(3081-5030; www.guesturbansp.com.br; Lisboa 493, Pinheiros; s/d from R$253/273;) This 1930s mansion, opened in late 2015, holds 14 suites reeking of industrial-chic (exposed brick and beams, unfinished steel and concrete) offset by a sunny open patio and cutting-edge art (reprints for sale in lobby). It's one block from Praca Benedito Calixto in the heart of hip Pinheiros.

Eating

São Paulo's dining scene is as vast as the city itself – and is one of the best in the southern hemisphere. Thanks to the rise of world-famous chefs such as Alex Atala (D.O.M.) and Helena Rizzo (Maní), contemporary Brazilian cuisine is having a moment on the world's culinary stage; and Sampa, its gastronomic epicenter, is catering to a growing number of gastronomic tourists. The 2015 release of the *Michelin Guide* to São Paulo and Rio de Janeiro marks the coveted culinary bible's first foray into Latin America.

Latin foods from previously unseen Spanish-speaking countries (Peru, Colombia, Bolivia) have made considerable inroads as well, while the gourmet burger battle has now given way to the food truck, gourmet Italian gelato and/or Mexican popsicle wars. You won't go hungry!

For the frugal, there are the ubiquitous *lanchonetes* – corner bars offering beer to the thirsty and, for the hungry, full meals for between R$10 and $20 (look for chalkboard *prato feito* offerings). Plus, literally hundreds of ethnic groups each have their offerings, from Lebanese to African cuisine.

Although restaurants open by 7pm, most don't fill up until 9pm or so on weekdays, and later on weekends, when many kitchens take orders to 1am or later. There are also lots of very good 24-hour options for late-night munchies.

TheFork (www.thefork.com.br), **Restorando** (https://sao-paulo.restorando.com.br) and **Table 4** (www.table4.com.br) are the most common real-time restaurant reservation services.

Central São Paulo

Estadão FAST FOOD **$**
(Map p224; www.estadaolanches.com.br; Viaduto 9 de Julho 193, Centro; specialty sandwiches R$14-29; 24hr) This classic Centro *lanchonete* (snack bar) serves working folk's meals at all hours, but its signature *pernil* (pork loin) sandwich, smothered in the cheese of your choice (provolone!) and sautéed onions, is one of Sampa's gastronomic musts.

Rong He CHINESE **$**
(www.ronghe.com.br; Rua da Glória 622; Liberdade; mains for 2 people R$14-45; 11:30-3pm & 6-10:30pm Mon-Fri, 11:30am-10:30pm Sat & Sun) A Liberdade institution and the city's best Chinese. First and foremost, expect surly service; second to that, the *gyoza* (pan-fried Japanese dumplings) and the house-made Chinese noodle dishes, are served in great-value portions *yakisoba*-style or in soupy, hot caldrons (*ensopada*) to out-the-door lines of devoted patrons. You can watch the dough masters at work through the show kitchen window.

Rinconcito Peruano PERUVIAN **$**
(Map p224; www.rinconcitoperuano.com.br; Aurora 451, Centro; mains R$18-40; noon-5pm Mon, to 11pm Tue-Sat, to 9pm Sun) Success has been good to the little Peruvian restarant that could. Expanded, remodeled and borderline too classy for the dicey neighborhood (though still unsigned!), this is a wonderful spot for great-value Peruvian classics such as seviche and *lomo saltado*.

You'll need to keep your guard up arriving here (it's fine during the day, but keep in mind that this is Sampa's Cracolândia), but Peruvian cooks, waitstaff and clientele means it's the real deal.

Kanazawa SWEETS **$**
(www.kanazawa.com.br; Galvão Bueno 379, Liberdade; sweets R$3; 8am-8:30pm) Pop into this Japanese convenience store in Liberdade for tasty *sakura moti* (sweets made from red kidney bean paste, rice and cherry blossom leaves).

Casa Mathilde SWEETS **$**
(Map p224; www.casamathilde.com.br; Praça Antônio Prado 76, Centro; sweets R$3-8; 9am-7:30pm Mon-Fri, 9:30am-4:30pm Sat;) Overwhelm yourself on the traditional sweets of Portugal, laid out here in a dizzying and mouth watering 15m-long display case.

★**Lamen Kazu** JAPANESE **$$**
(www.lamenkazu.com.br; Tomás Gonzaga 51, Liberdade; mains $22-48; 11am-3pm & 6-10:30pm Mon-Sat, 11am-3pm & 6-9pm Sun;) It's not as famous (or cheap) as its nearby rival Aska, but take the hint: the 99% Japanese clientele should tell you something. The fiery Kara Misso Lamen (spicy broth and spiced pork in addition to the usual condiments; R$35), doused with the house-made chili sauce, is a revelation, as is everything on the menu.

Ramona BRAZILIAN, FUSION **$$**
(Map p224; www.casaramona.com.br; Av São Luís 282, Centro; mains R$40-63; noon-midnight Mon & Tue, to 2am Wed-Fri, 1pm-2am Sat, 1-5pm Sun;) This República hot spot has given *paulistanos* a reason to venture into Centro at night. The legitimately retro space, fueled by a holier-than-thou indie soundtrack, excels at memorable grub like spicy bacon-jalapeno cheeseburgers or more sophisticated dishes like *baru* nut-crusted catch of the day; great cocktails, including the elusive Bloody Mary; and delicious desserts.

Avenida Paulista, Jardins & Around

Jardins is your place to splurge; it offers an incredibly dense collection of some of Brazil's most illustrious restaurants, plus some surprisingly reasonable choices to boot. Stop by the lovely **Cozinha São Paulo** (Map p230; www.cozinhasp.org; Praça dos Arcos; R$15; noon-3pm Tue-Sun), a food stand/social project offering affordable organic meals by monthly changing invited suburban chefs at the tailend of Av Paulista.

Meats BURGERS $
(Map p230; www.restaurantemeats.com.br; Alameda Lorena 2090; burgers R$22-34; noon-midnight Mon-Thu, to 1am Fri & Sat, 1pm-midnight Sun;) Denver Bronco–obsessed Paulo Yoller is the city's tattooed Beastie Boy of burgers and often regarded as Sampa's most creative grillman. This new and smaller Jardins location adds to his flagship in **Pinheiros** (www.restaurantemeats.com.br; Rua dos Pinheiros 320, Pinheiros ; burgers R$22-47; noon-midnight Mon-Thu, to 1am Fri-Sat, 1pm-midnight Sun;). Our go-to is the Hooligan, with cheddar, pickles, bacon and horseradish mayo. It morphs into an after-hours bar from midnight to 3am Wednesday to Sunday.

★**Bacio di Latte** GELATO $
(www.baciodilatte.com.br; gelato from R$10) Jardins (Map p230; Oscar Freire 136; 11am-11pm Sun-Fri, to midnight Sat;) Vila Madalena (Map p249; Harmonia 337, Vila Madalena; 11am-10pm Mon-Fri, to 11pm Sat, to 10pm Sun;) Av Paulista (Map p230; Av Paulista 854; 9am-9:45pm Mon-Sat, from 10am Sun) A Scotsman and two Italians were the first to do what nobody outside Buenos Aires could previously do: produce amazing Italian gelato in South America. It's often voted as the city's best ice cream, and is one of Brazil's best as well.

Maria Brigadeiro SWEETS $
(Map p230; www.mariabrigadeiro.com.br; Capote Valente 68, Pinheiros; sweets R$3.75-4.20; 11am-7pm Mon-Sat;) *The* place to come for *brigadeiro* (chocolate bonbons of condensed milk, butter and chocolate powder), served in sweet-tooth-satiating gourmet versions like pistachio, *doce de leite* with walnuts and *cachaça* (sugarcane alcohol). The adorable workshop, Brazil's first atelier dedicated to its most iconic sweet, serves espresso for those eating in, but it's a zoo of takeaway chocolate ecstasy.

It's just a block away from Metrô Oscar Freire, 'scheduled' to open in 2016.

Benjamin Abrahão PADARIA $
(Map p230; www.benjaminabrahao.com.br; José Maria Lisboa 1397, Jardins; sandwiches R$10-39, buffet R$23-32; 6am-8:30pm;) The French-born Brazilian running the show at one of the city's best *padarias* started making bread when he was 13, taught by Austrian, Swiss and German immigrants. You can't go wrong with sandwiches here, or anything baked, or that *brigadeiro* carrot cake (*bolo de cenoura com brigadeiro*)!

Kan SUSHI $$
(Map p230; 3266-3819; Manoel da Nóbrega 76, Jardins; omakase R$230-280; 11:30am-2pm & 6-10pm Tue-Sat, 6-10pm Sun) Sushi superman Keisuke Egashira speaks broken Portuguese, arriving a few years back after 23 years at Tokyo's Sushi-Kan. This uneventfully simple raw fish powerhouse hidden away in a nondescript shopping plaza off Av Paulista evokes *Jiro Dreams of Sushi*–level authenticity. It's generally pricy but the eight-piece set lunches are a steal (R$50). Japanese menu only.

Get there bang at opening to snag a sushi-bar seat without a reservation.

★**Aconchego Carioca** BRAZILIAN $$
(Map p230; 3062-8262; Alameda Jaú 1372, Jardins; mains for 2 people R$56-86; 6-11pm Mon, noon-midnight Tue-Sat, noon-6pm Sun;) A *boteco* (small open-air bar) import from Rio, Aconchego Carioca quickly gained an avid following in Sampa due to its undivided attention to specialty Brazilian microbrews, creative *bolinhos* (fried finger foods – try *virado à paulista*, with beans, kale, sausage, beef and egg; or the *feijoada* version) and fabulous, well-portioned takes on traditional dishes such as *bobó de camarão* (shrimp in manioc puree; feeds three!).

Capim Santo BRAZILIAN, SELF-SERVE $$
(Map p230; 3089-9500; www.capimsanto.com.br; Alameda Ministro Rocha Azevedo 471, Jardins; dinner mains R$49-89, lunch buffet weekday/weekends R$58/88; noon-3pm & 7:30pm-midnight Tue-Fri, 12:30-4pm & 8pm-midnight Sat, 12:30-5pm Sun;) Top chef Morena Leite turns out excellent regional Brazilian fare, with an emphasis on local and organic ingredients, served in a relaxed, beautifully Brazilian indoor-outdoor space. The excellent weekday buffet is the affordable way into this higher end spot.

Tenda do Nilo MIDDLE EASTERN $$
(Oscar Porto 638, Paraíso; dishes R$29.50-64; noon-3pm Mon-Sat) This criminally small, sidewalk-simple joint epitomizes the city's indelible Lebanese and Syrian links, two huge immigrant forces who thankfully didn't leave their food behind. Get here early and wait. Then wait some more for fabulous stuffed grape leaves, falafel and the star of

WORTH A TRIP

TUDO BEM, Y'ALL?

When the South lost the American Civil War in 1865, Brazil's Emperor Dom Pedro II saw dollar signs. Offering cheap land to planters in exchange for the state-of-the-art techniques for growing cotton that they would bring with them, he lured as many as 10,000 Southerners to his country.

Most of the new immigrants settled in central São Paulo state, where they found growing conditions remarkably similar to those of the southern US. They planted pecans, peaches, corn and cotton, just as they had in their native soil. They also made a concerted effort to stay aloof from Brazilian culture, venerating the Confederate flag and preserving their language and many of their customs. However, they did have to forgo one luxury: slavery, the institution they had fought so hard to defend. Research indicates that only a few former Confederates actually owned slaves in Brazil.

In the neighboring towns of **Americana** and **Santa Bárbara d'Oeste**, both about 100km northwest of São Paulo, you can still hear descendants of the *confederados* speaking English with a distinctly Southern lilt. And every year, the Fraternity of American Descendants – the community's main social institution – holds a picnic, complete with fried chicken, biscuits and peach pie.

Piracicabana (www.piracicabana.com.br) has direct services to and from São Paulo's Tietê bus station (R$33.30 to R$35.25, two hours).

the show: *fatteh* (toasted pita bread, beef, chickpeas, fresh curd, garlic and cashews). Superb!

The sister-run show includes being referred to as *Habib* ("beloved" in Arabic) and unsolicited dining lessons!

Spot INTERNATIONAL **$$**

(Map p230; ☎3283-0946; www.restaurantespot.com.br; Alameda Ministro Rocha Azevedo 72, Bela Vista; mains R$43-69; ⏲noon-3pm & 7-11pm Mon-Thu, noon-3pm & 7pm-midnight Fri, noon-5pm & 7pm-midnight Sat, noon-5pm & 7-11pm Sun) Hidden behind the scrap and steel of Av Paulista skyscrapers, upscale diner Spot is the self-consciously sophisticated domain of celebrities, hip gays, artists, performers and journalists. The menu is simple, with classic but well-prepared pastas and grilled meats, and the people-watching patio is a superb oasis for whiling away a weekend afternoon with a pitcher of clericot.

Z Deli DELI **$$**

(Map p230; www.zdelisanduiches.com.br; Haddock Lobo 1386, Cerqueira César; sandwiches R$25-55; ⏲noon-midnight Mon-Thu, to 1am Fri & Sat, to 11pm Sun) Servers can barely maneuver within this tiny deli that has capitalized on the city's odd combination of storied Jewish history but lack of the food that normally goes with it. Here you'll find juicy burgers, gourmet pastrami and roast beef sandwiches, bagels and lox, and authentic cheesecake.

Ici Brasserie MODERN FRENCH **$$**

(Map p230; ☎2883-5063; www.icibrasserie.com.br; Bela Cintra 2203, Jardins; mains R$39-88; ⏲noon-3pm & 6:30-11pm Mon, noon-3pm & 6:30pm-midnight Tue-Thu, to 1am Fri, noon-11pm Sun; 📶) This modern Jardins brasserie is a good-time, casual spot for well-done classics like *steak frites*, *boeuf Bourguignon* and other French staples, with a particular emphasis on craft beer, featuring a carefully curated menu with several brewed just for the house. The chef, Benny Novak, is one of Sampa's most well known for non-Brazilian kitchens. Don't skip the *pain perdu*!

★**Maní** BRAZILIAN **$$$**

(☎3085-4148; www.manimanioca.com.br; Joaquim Atunes 210, Jardim Paulistano; mains R$65-97; ⏲noon-3pm Tue-Sat, 8-11:30pm Tue-Thu, from 8:30pm Fri & Sat, noon-4:30pm Sun) Maní will astound you. This rustic-chic restaurant, run impeccably by the 2014 Veuve Cliquot World's Best Female Chef, Helena Rizzo, is often touted as Sampa's best Brazilian restaurant, and rightly so. The inventive slow-cooked egg (1½ hours at 63°C) is more famous, but the deconstructed Waldorf salad and the house-cooked potato chips topped with filet Mignon are true culinary coups.

The contemporary Brazilian dishes are best savored when your taste buds acquiesce to the five-course seasonal menu (R$195) or the far more dramatic *degustação* (with/without wine R$380/560).

Pizza Paulistana

Swarms of Italian immigrants settled in São Paulo in the late 19th century, giving the city one of the largest Italian populations in the world outside Italy and one of South America's best-kept culinary secrets. Locals say the pizza is so good, even the Italians are jealous!

Bráz Pizzaria

The experience at **Bráz** (Map p249; www.brazpizzaria.com.br; Vupabussu 271, Pinheiros; pizza R$49-75; ⏲6:30pm-12:30am Sun-Thu, to 1:30am Fri & Sat; 👪📶) will leave you thinking, 'Italy, schmataly.' Do as Brazilians do and order a Brahma draft beer (*chope*) followed by an appetizer of warm sausage bread (*pão de calabresa*) dipped in spiced olive oil, then let the feast commence. Bráz has a number of locations in both São Paulo and Rio de Janeiro; visit the website for details.

Speranza

One of the oldest and most traditional pizzerias, **Speranza** (Map p230; www.pizzaria.com.br; Treze de Maio 1004, Bixiga; pizza R$44-86; ⏲6pm-1am Sun-Thu, to 1:30am Fri & Sat; 👪) is in the Italian neighborhood of Bixiga, where the Famiglia Tarallo has been serving serious pizza since 1958. Perfect meal: the life-changing bruschetta appetizer followed by a fiercely traditional margarita pizza. No, wait: those calzones are insanely good, too.

Leggera Pizza Napoletana

At **Leggera Pizza Napoletana** (www.pizzerialeggera.com.br; Diana 80; pizza R$30-38; ⏲7-11pm Sun & Tue-Thu, to 11:30pm Fri & Sat; 📶), Brazilian-Italian-American *pizzaiolo* Andre Guidon imports everything humanly possible from Italy – and this small, family-run affair epitomizes the Brazilian-Italian diaspora. The 12 individual-sized, uncut pies here (plus a few calzones) are easily Sampa's best. They emerge from one of just 500 or so Neapolitan pizzeria ovens in the world certified by the Associação Verace Pizza Napoletana. Reservations prudent.

1. Pizza at Leggera Pizza Napoletana **2.** Bráz Pizzaria
3. Bráz Pizzaria **4.** Pizza at Speranza

KEVIN RAUB ©

KEVIN RAUB ©

★ Patuá da Baiana BAHIAN $$$

(Map p230; ☎98312-5302, 3115-0513; www.facebook.com/patuadabaiana; Luis Barreto 74A, Bela Vista; mains R$57-180; ⏰by reservation) It's expensive; we probably shouldn't even include it, but the experience at Bahian beauty Bá's 'secret' underground restaurant in her own home is just too priceless. You must call ahead and know someone who knows someone. If Bá digs your vibe, she greets you with open arms and treats you to a night of scrumptious Bahian specialties.

She chooses the dishes, not you. And all the while Bá pulls off a one-woman show as a caipirinha extraordinaire as well. It's a night you won't soon forget.

Amadeus SEAFOOD $$$

(Map p230; ☎3061-2859; www.restaurante-amadeus.com; Haddock Lobo 807, Jardins; mains R$52-138; ⏰noon-3pm & 7-11pm Mon-Thu, noon-4pm & 7pm-midnight Fri & Sat, noon-5pm Sun) Brazilian seafood isn't the first thing to come to mind due to São's Paulo inland location, but Chef Bella Masano's classic, family-run seafooder does an outstanding job in that regard, especially where shrimp is concerned (she even boasts an entire shrimp tasting menu). The Old School decor isn't as inviting, but you soon won't care.

Varanda Grill STEAK $$$

(☎3887-8870; www.varandagrill.com.br; Mena Barreto 793, Jardins; steaks R$69-290; ⏰noon-3pm & 7-11pm Mon-Thu, noon-3:30pm & 7-11pm Fri, noon-6pm & 7pm-midnight Sat, noon-5:30pm Sun; 📶) This top-quality casual grill (there's a more formal location at gastronomy-heavy Shopping JK (p251)) serves the city's best steak – don't let anyone tell you otherwise. Argentine and American cuts feature heavily in the exceptional beef (from Brazil, Argentina, Uruguay on over to Kobe); and one of Brazil's most extraordinary wine list follows suit.

Brasil a Gosto BRAZILIAN $$$

(Map p230; ☎3086-3565; www.brasilagosto.com.br; Azevedo do Amaral 70, Jardins; mains R$39-95, tasting menu R$155; ⏰7pm-midnight Tue-Thu, noon-5pm & 7pm-midnight Fri & Sat, noon-5pm Sun; 📶) This Jardins staple lures both tourists galore and discerning Brazilians (and ex-President Lula, a big fan) for some of the city's finest for homegrown cuisine. Chef Ana Luiza Trajano specializes in innovative takes on iconic ingredients and regional dishes. Sit upstairs for winter wall garden views and order the crunchy shrimp in manioc sauce.

Epice BRAZILIAN $$$

(Map p230; ☎3062-0866; www.epicerestaurante.com.br; Haddock Lobo 1002, Jardins; mains R$77-95, tasting menu R$290; ⏰noon-2:30pm & 8-11pm Tue-Thu, noon-2:30pm & 8pm-midnight Fri, 1-3:30pm & 8pm-midnight Sat; 📶) Few top-end restaurants have taken Sampa by storm like Alberto Landgraf's Epice. Casual in appearance but complex in culinary circles, Landgraf calls on radical flavor combinations and traditionally rejected ingredients to confuse and surprise the city's fussiest foodie palettes. Off-menu prix-fixe dishes like lamb neck with shredded sun-dried beef shock and awe.

D.O.M. BRAZILIAN $$$

(Map p230; ☎3088-0761; www.domrestaurante.com.br; Barão de Capamena 549, Jardins; tasting menus R$280-570, with wine R$590-857; ⏰noon-3pm & 7pm-midnight Mon-Fri, 7pm-midnight Sat) Brazilian celebrity chef Alex Atala's small and deceptively casual contemporary Brazilian restaurant serves up some of the finest food in Sampa, which is saying a lot. Indeed, it placed ninth on the 2015 *S. Pellegrino World's 50 Best Restaurants* list, which foodies fawn over relentlessly.

For a blow-out, cutting-edge Brazilian meal, some say this is the spot, though we have never been personally blown away by it. Reservations mandatory.

Baixo Augusta

Taquería La Sabrosa MEXICAN $

(Map p230; www.facebook.com/taquerialasabrosasp; Augusta 1474, Consolação; mains R$14-19, lunch combos R$20-24; ⏰noon-midnight Mon-Thu, noon-2am Fri, 1pm-2am Sat, 1pm-midnight Sun) An authentic *taqueria*, previously rarer than a *chupacrabra* sighting in São Paulo! This colorful Mexican-Brazilian operation – the same couple who runs higher-end Oba in Jardins – churns out tacos, tostadas, *carnitas*, guacamole and spicy salsas, all of which were only previously available in these parts as badly imitated Tex-Mex. This is Mex-Mex!

Madhu INDIAN $

(Map p230; ☎3262-5535; www.madhurestaurante.com.br; Augusta 1422, Consolação; meals R$14-26; ⏰noon-10:30pm Mon-Wed, to 11:30pm Thu, to 12:30am Fri, 1pm-1am Sat, 1-10:30pm Sun; 📶🌿) Brazil's first Indian fast-food joint, this simple-with-a-dash-of-style spot serves up good and cheap curries, *kathi* rolls and *masala dosa* amid Augusta's bustle.

★Jiquitaia BRAZILIAN $$

(Map p230; ☎3262-2366; www.jiquitaia.com.br; Antônio Carlos 268 , Consolação; mains R$43-68; ⏰noon-3pm Mon, 7-11:30pm Tue-Fri, noon-11:30pm Sat) Accolades abound for upstart Brazilian chef Marcelo Bastos and his affordable entry-level into contemporary Brazilian cuisine – pick any three courses at this cute and cozy bistro-style restaurant to create-your-own set menu (R$69), including – drum roll, please! – the elusive *moqueca* (Bahian fish stew) for one person! Sister Nina admirably handles the excellent fresh fruit caipirinhas.

Vila Madalena, Pinheiros & Around

Underdog Meat & Beers BURGERS, STEAK $

(João Moura 541, Pinheiros; burgers from R$20; ⏰6:30-11pm Mon-Sat) A humble Argentine is behind the grilled perfection that emerges from this tiny and trendy newcomer, where the perfectly charred meat – add cheese, grilled jalapeños and bacon to experience what is easily the city's most outstanding burger – will overwhelm you with decadent goodness. The mostly standing room-only crowd (the bar stools inside are too hot, anyway) spills onto the street and leans towards indie rock and double IPAs.

Butantan Food Park FOOD TRUCK $

(www.butantanfoodpark.com.br; Agostinho Cantu 47, Butantã; mains R$15-25; ⏰11am-4pm Mon-Wed, to 10pm Thu-Sat, noon-7pm Sun) The best spot to dive into the city's exploding food truck scene is this permanent parking lot, which hosts a daily revolving door of 15 to 35 vendors (food trucks, carts, bikes and craft-brewer tents) – no two visits are the same. On weekends, it's a full-on foodie fest. It's 650m from Metrô Butantã on the yellow line.

A second location, **Marachal Food Park** (www.facebook.com/Marechalfoodpark; Albuquerque Lins 505 ; mains R$15-25; ⏰11am-9pm Tue-Sun), has opened beside Metrô Marachal Deodoro.

Sanpo Bentô Deli JAPANESE $

(www.facebook.com/sanpobentodeli; Fradique Coutinho 166, Pinheiros; mains R$16-25; ⏰noon-9pm Mon-Fri, to 4pm Sat; 📶) This great little fast-casual Japanese does authentic *onigiri* (triangular rice balls), *donburi* (rice bowls – try the pork!) and bento boxes (single-portion meals) with great sides such as the house eggplant and potato salad with *edamame* (soybeans), all of which is pretty stunning at these prices.

Mercearia São Pedro BOTECO $

(Map p249; Rodésia 34, Vila Madalena; appetizers for 2 people R$22-42; ⏰8am-midnight Mon-Sat, 8am-6pm Sun) This independently minded *boteco* (traditional bar) is slammed at night, when packs of sexy bohemians swill properly chilled bottled beer, fresh *pastels* (stuffed, fried pastries; R$5), and excellent, down-to-earth fare such as *picanha* (rump roast) with sautéed onions. You'll have a great time here without – as the Brazilians say – leaving your pants.

A Queijaria DELI $

(Map p249; www.aqueijaria.com.br; Aspicuelta 5, Vila Madalena; per kg R$48-160; ⏰9am-8pm Mon-Sat) It's easy to tire of Brazil's uneventful cheese, but this revelatory cheesemonger – a Sampa first – features small production artisanal and farmstead cheeses, mostly from Minas Gerais and São Paulo states, that will kill your *saudades* (longing) for European and North American *queijo*. Add wine, bread and olive oil, too, and make it a picnic.

★Feijoada da Lana BRAZILIAN $$

(Map p249; Aspicuelta 421, Vila Madalena; feijoada weekday/weekend R$42/74; ⏰noon-3:30pm Tue-Fri, 12:30-5pm Sat & Sun) Lana, a journalist by trade, offers her hugely popular version of *feijoada*, Brazil's national dish, inside a smallish Vila Madalena house. Production here isn't as elaborate as at more expensive options or fancy hotels, but it's long on smiling service, hearty goodness and (included on weekends!) *batidinhas de limão*, a sort of shaken caipirinha. In our humble opinion – and Anthony Bourdain's! – it's the best *feijoada* for the buck in town, and you don't have to wait until Saturday to enjoy it.

Greater São Paulo

★Mocotó BRAZILIAN $$

(☎2951-3056; www.mocoto.com.br; Nossa Senhora do Loreto 1100, Vila Madeiros; mains R$30-47; ⏰noon-11pm Mon-Sat, to 5pm Sun) It's worth the trek to Zona Norte for a meal at this darling of regional restaurants, where the city's most likeable and impressive young chef took over his father's simple emporium and started churning out Northeastern specialties. Suddenly, Rodrigo Oliveira's kitchen found itself a destination restaurant for *paulistanos* who otherwise couldn't have told you where the hell Vila Madeiros was.

For weekend lunches, it's a full-on gastro-party, with everyone digging into seriously homey comfort food at friendly prices chased by hundreds of artisan *cachaças*. Take the metro blue line until the end at Tucuruvi; from there, it's a R$18 to R$25 taxi ride.

Drinking & Nightlife

Coffee in São Paulo is generally excellent by Brazilian standards, thanks largely to the city's Italian heritage. Santo Grão (p248) and Coffee Lab (p250) serve some of Brazil's best beans – mountain-grown arabicas, mostly from Minas Gerais.

Traditional bar neighborhoods are Vila Madalena, which skews mainstream; along Rua Mario Ferraz in Itaim Bibi, where the rich, bold and beautiful play; and Baixo Augusta, where the GLS scene (Portuguese slang for Gay, Lesbian and Sympathetics) mingles with artsy hipsters in the city's edgiest-nightlife district. Artists, journalists and upper middle-class bohemians have embraced Pinheiros of late, immediately southeast of Vila Madalena.

Ave Paulista is also very lively at happy hour along the sidewalk bars near Joaquim Eugênio de Lima. República, near Centro, is the latest to gentrify, with waves of cool spots finally giving *paulistanos* a reason to go downtown at night.

Partying in Sampa isn't cheap: clubbing prices here rival those of New York or Moscow. Nightclubs don't open until midnight, don't really get going until after 1am, and keep pumping until 5am or later. Then there are the after-hours places. The hottest districts are Vila Olímpia (flashy, expensive, electronica) and Barra Funda/Baixo Augusta (rock, alternative, down-to-earth). Some clubs offer a choice between a cover charge or a pricier *consumação* option, recoupable in drinks. Most clubs offer a discount for emailing or calling ahead to be on the list. Keep the card they give you on the way in – bartenders record your drinks on it, then you pay on the way out.

Check out the Portuguese-language *Guia da Folha* (http://guia.folha.uol.com.br) as well as a supplement in the Friday edition of *Folha de São Paulo* newspaper.

Central São Paulo

★Bar da Dona Onça BAR, BRAZILIAN

(Map p224; ☎3129-7619; www.bardadonaonca.com.br; Av Ipiranga 200, Centro; mains R$42-64; ⊙noon-11:30pm Mon-Thu, to 12:30am Fri & Sat; 📶) In the striking Copan building, Dona Onça is one of downtown's best bars, not only for the packed crowds and excellent drinks – lauded chef Janaina Rueda's kitchen here churns out extraordinary Brazilian-heartland fare (chicken with okra, a fabulous pork calf, and an artistic *feijoada* on Saturday).

Alberta #3 BAR

(Map p224; www.alberta3.com.br; Av São Luís 272, Centro; cover R$15-35; ⊙7pm-late Tue-Sat) This three-story hipster hideout off Praça da República draws inspiration from '50s-era hotel bars and lobbies, and rides a soundtrack steeped mostly in classic rock, jazz and soul (DJs often spin vinyl on the small dance floor).

Choperia Liberdade KARAOKE

(Rua da Glória 523, Liberdade; consumação Tue-Sun R$15; ⊙7pm-5am, to 6am Fri & Sat) For karaoke the old-fashioned way, head to this kitsch classic, which is decked out in Christmas lights, party favors, plug-in paintings and glowing aquariums. The crowd runs the gamut: scenesters, serious Japazillion songsters, Brazilian baby boomers and curious twentysomethings on a birthday binge.

Avenida Paulista, Jardins & Around

★Veloso BOTECO

(www.velosobar.com.br; Conceição Veloso 56, Vila Mariana; ⊙5:30pm-12:30am Tue-Fri, from 12:45pm Sat, 4-10:30pm Sun) Arrive early to this outstanding *boteco* a quick walk from Vila Mariana's metro station – crowds fight over tables for some of the city's best caipirinhas, in exotic flavors (*jabuticaba*, starfruit with basil, tangerine with *dedo-de-moça* pepper; R$18 to R$30), and shockingly good *coxinhas* (battered and fried shredded chicken, *catupiry* cheese and spices; R$27.60).

The house-made hot sauce is the best we've found in the country. Put your name on the list, but you'll be drunk and full before you get a table, though an expansion next door has relieved some of the long wait times.

Frank Bar COCKTAIL BAR

(Map p230; www.facebook.com/frankbarsp; Alameda Campinas 150, Bela Vista; cocktails R$29-33; ⊙6pm-2am; 📶) Re-issue! Re-package! Re-evaluate the cocktails... São Paulo's most old-school luxury hotel, Maksoud Plaza,

GAY & LESBIAN SÃO PAULO

Latin America's largest and most visible gay community supports a dizzying array of options, day and night. There are not only gay bars and discos but also restaurants, cafes, even a shopping center – **Shopping Frei Caneca** (Map p230; ☎3472-2000; www.freicanecashopping.com; Frei Caneca 569, Baixo Augusta; ⏰10am-10pm Mon-Sat, 2-8pm Sun), known as 'Shopping Gay Caneca,' has a largely gay clientele. And **São Paulo Pride** (www.gaypridebrazil.org/sao-paulo), usually celebrated in mid-June, is by most estimates the largest gay gathering in the world. São Paulo is also the only city in Brazil where same-sex public displays of affection are a fairly common sight, at least in certain 'safe' neighborhoods. These include the area just north of Praça da República, which tends to be more working class; Rua Frei Caneca just north of Av Paulista, which attracts an alternative crowd; and Rua da Consolaçao in Jardins, largely the domain of Sampa's upscale gays.

Don't miss the bars surrounding **Feira Benedito Calixto** (p251) in Pinheiros on Saturday afternoons after the street fair; **Bar da Lôca** (Map p230; cnr Frei Caneca & Peixoto Gomide, Baixo Augusta; ⏰6am-1am) where the early-evening pre-party spills into the streets; and **Bella Paulista** (Map p230; ☎3214-3347; www.bellapaulista.com; Haddock Lobo 354, Cerqueira Cesar; sandwiches R$24-34; ⏰24hr; 📶), the 24-hour restaurant where everyone ends up after the clubs close.

Other gay and lesbian venues:

Club Yacht (Map p230; ☎3111-6330; www.facebook.com/clubyacht; Treze de Maio 703, Bela Vista; ⏰11:30pm-5am Wed & Thu, midnight-5am Fri, midnight-9am Sat) This maritime-themed gay/mixed nightclub mixes mirror balls and blue walls with nautical overload. Two large mezzanines stand sentinel above the large dance floor – for those who like to watch – and the whole space is bedazzled with encrusted shells throughout. The most glamorous choice *du moment*.

Bar da Dida (Map p230; Rua Melo Alves 98, Jardins; ⏰6pm-1am Tue-Sun) This tiny, intimate *boteco* is a casual, well-regarded gay gathering spot, especially during *lusco fusco* (twilight), when the bar's sidewalk seating is flooded with attractive and stylish folks, fresh off their jobs in the glamorous boutiques, galleries and salons in the hood.

Lekitsch (Map p224; Praça Franklin Roosevelt 142, Consolação; ⏰6pm-2am Tue-Thu, to 3am Fri, 1pm-3am Sat, 1pm-midnight Sun) Eclectic and funky, Lekitsch is the creative cradle of Praça Roosevelt, which has become a weekend gay gathering point of late. Walls peppered in kitsch (doll heads, retro Simon Says games) surround a wildly mixed crowd of alterna-hipsters and creative types.

has turned over its old piano bar to Spencer Jr, the city's most heralded mixologist, in a plea to return to relevance. The result is Frank Bar, a dark and intimate barman's bar paying meticulous attention to cocktails. Bar bites by Paulo Yoller (of Meats (p240) fame) are not to be missed.

Skye — BAR

(www.unique.com.br; Av Brigadeiro Luis Antônio 4700, Jardim Paulista; ⏰noon-1am) Dress up a little for the rooftop bar of the Hotel Unique (p237), whose sleek design and unparalleled views make it the perennially perfect place for a sundowner.

Bar Balcão — BAR

(Map p230; ☎3063-6091; Doutor Melo Alves 150, Jardins; ⏰6pm-1am) Good wine, light meals and a simple but elegant design built around a cleverly serpentine bar, this Jardins delight is especially popular with well-heeled designers, foreign correspondents and artists.

Riviera Bar — COCKTAIL BAR

(Map p230; www.rivierabar.com.br; Paulista 2584, Consolação; ⏰noon-midnight Mon-Wed & Sun, to 1am Thu, to 2am Fri & Sat) Steeped in *paulista* history, Riviera was the epicenter of the intellectual counterculture for more than 50 years before falling on hard times and shutting in 2006. Reopened and reimagined, the new and sophiticated Riviera hosts live jazz and bossa nova in a space draped in mid-century Modern furnishings.

★Santo Grão CAFE

(Map p230; ☎3062-9294; www.santograo.com.br; Oscar Freire 413, Jardins; coffee R$5.60-15.10; ⏲9am-1am Mon, 7:30am-1am Tue-Thu, to 2am Fri, 8am-2am Sat, 8am-midnight Sun; 📶) This Kiwi-run, top-end coffee haunt serves cappuccinos that are as good as those in Italy. Beans are roasted out back while the little terrace reverberates with caffeine-fueled conversation. There's a fab bistro menu and insane people-watching.

Suco Begaço JUICE BAR

(Map p230; www.sucobagaco.com.br; Haddock Lobo 1483, Jardins; juice R$8-15; ⏲9am-9pm Mon-Sat, noon-8pm Sun; 👪) The flagship of this rapidly expanding juice chain burns through 600 glasses daily, mixed with water, orange juice, tea or coconut water. Also offers awesome-value, build-your-own salads and sandwiches.

🍷 Baixo Augusta

★Caos BAR

(Map p230; www.facebook.com/caosaugusta; Augusta 584, Baixo Augusta; consumacão R$30-50; ⏲8pm-2am Tue-Fri, 9pm-3am Sat) Antique bicycles, hubcaps, household appliances, keychains – you name it, it's stuffed inside this alternative hangout that's a microcosm of all that's great about the neighborhood: among the junkyard aesthetic, you get lip-locked lesbians, beer fiends downing Brazilian microbrews, hot-rod gearheads arguing pinstripe width and gringos taking it all in. Good times.

Astronete BAR, CLUB

(Map p230; www.astronete.com.br; Matias Aires 183, Baixo Augusta; admission R$20-40; ⏲10pm-5am Thu-Sat) A few years in and still a favorite among the counterculture: freaks, geeks and gaggles of *alternativos* gather over rock, electro, indie and soul at what could now be considered a Baixo Augusta classic.

🍷 Barra Funda

D-Edge CLUB

(☎3665-9500; www.d-edge.com.br; Auro Soares de Moura Andrade 141, Barra Funda; cover R$30-140; ⏲11pm-late Mon & Wed-Sat) With one of the city's most remarkable sound systems and a roster of world-famous DJs, this mixed gay-straight club is an elder statesmen of the club scene, but remains a 'don't miss' for fans of electronica.

🍷 Vila Madalena, Pinheiros & Around

São Cristóvão BOTECO

(Map p249; www.facebook.com/barsaocristovao; Aspicuelta 533, Vila Madalena; mains R$32-84) This wildy atmospheric *boteco* is spilling over with football memorabilia from the owner's collection, more than 3500 pieces in all.

Empório Alto de Pinheiros BAR

(www.altodospinheiros.com.br; Vupabussu 305, Alto de Pinheiros; ⏲noon-midnight Sun-Wed, to 1am Thu-Sat; 📶) This neighborhood beer emporium evolved into a full-on gourmet craft beer bar as the brew scene in Brazil exploded. *Cerveza* geeks fret nervously over more than 400 bottled or 33 choices on draft, including rarer Brazilian microbrews. You'll need a few drinks to tolerate the service.

Delirium Cafe BAR

(www.deliriumcafesp.com.br; Ferreira de Araújo 589, Pinheiros; draft beers R$12-28; ⏲6pm-1am Mon-Wed, to 2am Thu-Sat, 2-10pm Sun; 📶) Run by Belgium's recognizable pink elephant beer of the same name, this good-time craft beer bar is predictably heavy on Belgian beers, but is also notable for its domestic microbrew selection. All in all, there's 24 on tap and more than 420 by the bottle; and knowledgeable bartenders to boot. A good time.

Boca de Ouro COCKTAIL BAR

(www.bocadeouro.com.br; Cônego Eugênio Leite 1121, Pinheiros; cocktails R$8-24; ⏲6pm-midnight Mon-Thu, to 2am Fri & Sat; 📶) Classic cocktails mixed with the methodicalness of art restoration and a distinctly un-Brazilian setup (an actual belly-up-to bar behind a Brownstonelike facade that could easily pass for Brooklyn with a little imagination), Boca de Ouro feels novel and attracts an artistic crowd. Good bottled craft beer and excellent bar grub like *bolovo* – a Brazilianized Scotch egg – round out this neighborhood-y choice nicely.

★SubAstor COCKTAIL BAR

(Map p249; ☎3815-1364; www.subastor.com.br; Delfina 163, Vila Madalena; ⏲8pm-3am Tue-Sat) This dark and speakeasy-sexy bar sits below a *boteco* called Astor (extraordinarily great as well for food and caipirinhas), hence the name: SubAstor ('Below Astor'). Sincere mixology goes down here, from creative takes on classics like *caju amigo* (*cachaça* and cashew juice) to far more cutting-edge liquid art.

Vila Madalena

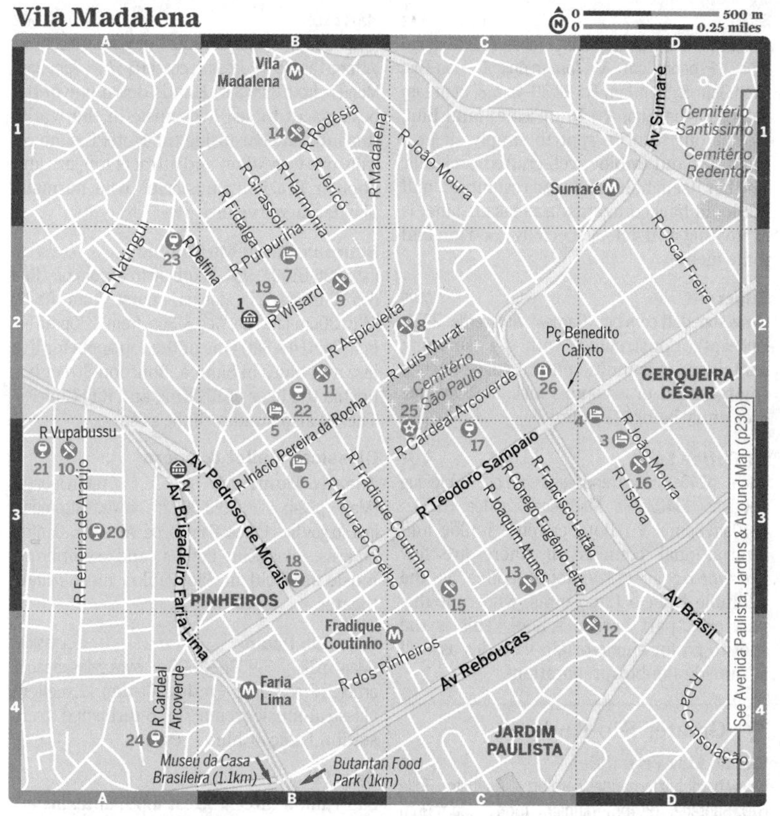

Vila Madalena

Sights
1 Galeria Milan....B2
2 Instituto Tomie Ohtake....A3

Sleeping
3 Guest 607....D3
4 Guest Urban....D2
5 LimeTime Hostel....B2
6 Ô de Casa....B3
7 Sampa Hostel....B2

Eating
8 A Queijaria....C2
9 Bacio di Latte....B2
10 Bráz Pizzaria....A3
11 Feijoada da Lana....B2
12 Maní....D4
13 Meats....C3
14 Mercearia São Pedro....B1
15 Sanpo Bentô Deli....C3
16 Underdog Meat & Beers....D3

Drinking & Nightlife
17 Boca de Ouro....C3
18 Cervejaria Nacional....B3
19 Coffee Lab....B2
20 Delirium Cafe....A3
21 Empório Alto de Pinheiros....A3
22 São Cristóvão....B2
23 SubAstor....A2
24 Superloft....A4

Entertainment
25 Ó do Borogodó....C3

Shopping
26 Feira Benedito Calixto....C2

Cervejaria Nacional MICROBREWERY
(www.cervejarianacional.com.br; Av Pedroso de Morais 604, Pinheiros; 5pm-midnight Mon-Wed, noon-midnight Thu, to 1:30am Fri & Sat;) A microbrewery with an alternative edge, this is the best of Sampa's local craft-suds factories.

SÃO PAULO STATE SÃO PAULO CITY

Side COCKTAIL BAR
(www.siderestaurante.com.br; Tabapuã 830, Itaim Bibi; noon-3pm & 7pm-midnight Mon-Thu, noon-3pm & 8pm-1am Fri, 12:30-4pm & 8pm-1am Sat, 12:30-4pm Sun;) In upscale Itaim Bibi, Side is our favorite spot to simply sit at a great bar and imbibe well-crafted cocktails. The bar itself, half inside the restaurant, half outdoors backed against a pleasant lane, is as inviting as it gets. Especially good gin and tonic menu.

Superloft CLUB
(www.superloft.com.br; Cardeal Arcoverde 2926, Pinheiros) Constructed with 34 shipping containers, this multi-cultural space hosts a smorgasbord of art and music/club events. Free entry before 12:30am.

★ **Coffee Lab** CAFE
(Map p249; www.raposeiras.com.br; Fradique Coutinho 1340, Vila Madalena; coffee R$5-12; 10am-8pm ;) Both caffeine junkie and international connoisseur, there are few *brasileiras* as crazy about coffee as the adorable Isabela Raposeiras, who runs this part cafe, part barista school. This is the spot to go for single-origin varieties as well as outside-the-box preparations.

Greater São Paulo

Bar do Luiz Fernandes BAR
(www.bardoluizfernandes.com.br; Augusto Tolle 610, Santana; 4pm-midnight Tue-Fri, 11am-9pm Sat, 11am-6pm Sun) Friendly, supremely local and quintessentially São Paulo, it's worth traipsing into the North Zone for this authentic *boteco* to chase Doña Idalina's house-specialty *bolinhos* (croquettes; try the beef version, splashed with spicy vinaigrette and fiery *malagueta* pepper sauce) with ice-cold Original and Serramalte beers – something locals have adored for 50 years. It's a 2km taxi from Metrô Santana.

Entertainment

Live Music

Ó do Borogodó SAMBA
(Map p249; 3814-4087; Horácio Lane 21, Vila Madelena; cover R$25; 9pm-3am Mon-Fri, from 1pm Sat, 7pm-midnight Sun) Probably the best spot in town for live samba, *chorinho* and *pagode* (popular samba music), uneven floors and cramped space notwithstanding, especially when you combine the serious muscianship on display here with cheap caipirinhas and the rump-shaking, sweat-soaked crowd of sexy revelers.

Barretto MPB, JAZZ
(Map p230; 3896-4000; www.fasano.com.br; Vittorio Fasano 88, Jardins; cover R$37; 7pm-3am Mon-Fri, from 8pm Sat) Hands down one of the best places to see live music in the world, this intimate bar inside the Hotel Fasano recalls pre-war Milan and attracts top jazz and popular Brazilian musicians who normally play far larger venues.

Bourbon Street Music Club JAZZ, SALSA
(5095-6100; www.bourbonstreet.com.br; Rua dos Chanés 127, Moema; cover from R$32; 10:30pm-late Tue, Wed & Sun, from 8:30pm Thu, from 9pm Fri & Sat) One of the top spots for live jazz and blues in Sampa, Bourbon Street has hosted the likes of BB King and Ray Charles. There's also Sunday night salsa.

Classical, Ballet & Opera

Theatro Municipal THEATER, OPERA
(Map p224; 3223-3022; www.teatromunicipal.sp.gov.br; Praça Ramos de Azevedo, Centro) Operas, classical ballets and symphonic music are held in São Paulo's most ornate theater.

Sala São Paulo CLASSICAL
(Map p224; 3367-9500; www.salasaopaulo.art.br; Praça Júlio Prestes, Centro) Excellent classical-music venue in refurbished train station Estação Júlio Prestes.

Sports

São Paulo's three biggest football teams are **São Paulo FC** (www.saopaulofc.net), who play at the 67,428-capacity **Estádio do Morumbi** (a 2016 Olympic Games venue); **Palmeiras** (www.palmeiras.com.br), who play in the new 43,600-capacity **Allianz Parque** near Barra Funda; and **Corinthians** (www.corinthians.com.br), who play at the new **Arena Corinthians**, 24km east of Centro.

Shopping

For high fashion and high-end home furnishings, wander Rua Oscar Freire and surrounding streets in the Jardins district.

Espaço Havaianas SHOES
(Map p230; 3079-3415; www.havaianas.com; Oscar Freire 1116, Jardins; 10am-8pm Mon-Sat, noon-6pm Sun;) You will find flip-flops in every imaginable design and hue – and at quite reasonable prices – at the flagship store for Brazil's favorite beach footwear, boldly designed by Isay Weinfeld.

★Casa da Vila HANDICRAFTS, HOMEWARES
(☎5575-2757; www.casadavila.com.br; Capitão Calvalcanti 82, Vila Mariana; ⏰1-7pm Mon-Fri) This gorgeously preserved 1929 mansion on a quiet residential street, walking distance from Metrô Vila Mariana, is Sampa's best spot for high-quality, affordable Fair Trade handicrafts from all 26 Brazilian states (plus Distrito Federal!). A must.

Feira Benedito Calixto ANTIQUES
(www.pracabeneditocalixto.com.br; Praça Benedito Calixto, Pinheiros; ⏰9am-7pm Sat) Open-air market for handicrafts, antiques and food stalls Sunday, plus live *chorinho* in the afternoon.

Galeria Melissa SHOES
(Map p230; ☎3083-3612; www.melissa.com.br; Oscar Freire 827, Jardins; ⏰10am-7pm Mon-Fri, to 5pm Sat) This temple to high-end plastic footwear offers bold and unique designs by an international potpourri of creative folk including Vivienne Westwood, Zaha Hadid and Karim Rasheed. But it is as notable for its consistently changing facade, which is a freestyle canvas for an ever-changing rotation of acclaimed Brazilian artists and designers – each new shoe line brings a completely new storefront.

Galeria do Rock CLOTHING
(Map p224; www.galeriadorock.com.br; São João 439, Centro; ⏰10am-6pm Mon-Sat) This seven-floor shopping center is an anthropologically fascinating gathering point for São Paulo's underground communities, from punks to goths to metal heads. Shops are divided among three concepts: art, music and attitude.

Livraria Cultura BOOKS
(Map p230; ☎3170-4033; www.livrariacultura.com.br; Av Paulista 2073, Bela Vista; ⏰9am-10pm Mon-Sat, noon-8pm Sun; 👪) Spread out over three stores on the ground floor of the Conjunto Nacional building, this is hands-down the city's best bookstore. There is a large selection of both English-language books and travel guides, plus a pleasant cafe.

Feira da República HANDICRAFTS
(Map p224; Praça da República; ⏰8am-6pm Sun) This open-air market specializes in handicrafts and painting.

Salinas Off SWIMWEAR
(Map p230; www.salinascompras.com.br; Doutor Melo Alves 344, Jardins; ⏰10am-7pm Mon-Fri, to 6pm Sat) Always dreamed of hitting the beach wearing virtually nothing? Salinas is one of the country's trendiest bikini brands. Pick up last year's collections on the cheap at this outlet-style location, where two-pieces run between R$49 and R$193.

Shopping JK Iguatemi MALL
(www.jkiguatemi.com.br; Av Juscelino Kubitschek 2041, Vila Olímpia; ⏰10am-10pm Mon-Sat, 2-8pm Sun) South America's most luxurious high-end shopping mall is worth a stroll for the sheer opulence of it all and some very good restaurants.

WORTH A TRIP

EMBU

Founded in 1554, Embu spent most of its life as a quiet colonial village until, in the 20th century, it was swallowed up by São Paulo, whose center sits about 30km to the west. Yet Embu has managed to retain much of its colonial core, thanks largely to the hippies, artists and intellectuals who made the town their refuge from São Paulo's concrete jungle, starting in the 1970s. Today the town makes a popular weekend retreat for *paulistanos*, when local artisans offer their wares at the outdoor **feira** (Market; Largo dos Jesuitas; ⏰9am-6pm Sat & Sun). The area around the *feira* is full of antique and crafts shops that make good browsing on other days of the week.

From São Paulo, catch the EMTU bus 033 'Embu' (R$4.10, one hour, about 15 minutes) from the stop at **Teodoro Sampaio 323** (Map p230), about 100m down the street from Metrô Clínicas.

ℹ Orientation

Because it grew at dizzying speeds and without a master plan, São Paulo has no single grid of streets, but rather a hodgepodge of grids in more or less concentric circles that radiate out from the historic center. This, together with a dearth of easily identifiable landmarks, means it's easy to get hopelessly lost.

Sitting atop a low ridge lined with skyscrapers, Av Paulista is the city's main drag, dividing its largely working-class Centro from tonier neighborhoods to the south. At its western end, Av Paulista is crossed by the corridor made up of Av Rebouças and Rua da Consolação, which roughly divides the city's eastern and western halves.

To the north of Av Paulista lies what is generally called Centro, including Praça da República and around; the traditionally Italian Bela Vista

WORTH A TRIP

A TRAIN! A TRAIN!

Founded by the British-owned São Paulo Railway Company, the pretty town of **Paranapiacaba** may sit amid the Atlantic rainforest of the Serra do Mar, about 40km southeast of São Paulo, but it still retains distinctly English traits, right down to a rough replica of Big Ben. Because of its remoteness, the town has been remarkably well preserved, with a neat grid of streets populated by English-style buildings of wood and brick. The home of the railway's chief engineer, a classically Victorian wood construction known as 'Castelinho,' has been converted into the **Museu do Castelo** (Caminho do Mendes; admission R$2; ⌚10am-4pm Sat & Sun), a small museum with period furnishings and fine views. Paranapiacaba also makes a good base for day hikes into the **Parque Estadual Serra do Mar.**

The best way to arrive in Paranapiacaba is on the '50s-era **Expresso Turístico Paranapiacaba** (☎0800 055 0121; www.cptm.sp.gov.br; 1/2/3 people R$34/51/68; 👪) tourist train, which runs from São Paulo's Estação Luz at 8:30am on Sunday to Estação Paranapiacaba. Definitely book ahead – trains are a novelty in Brazil and this one, the country's second-oldest locomotive in operation, is very popular, especially in summer. Trains do not run on every Sunday – check the website for schedules.

area (also known as Bixiga); Luz, a newly refurbished cultural hub; the traditionally Japanese Liberdade; and the old commercial and historic core around Praça da Sé and its cathedral, including Triângulo and Anhangabaú.

Extending for about 10 blocks south of Paulista is the leafy neighborhood known as Jardins (the neighborhood's official name is Jardim Paulista), which has the lion's share of the city's higher end restaurants and boutiques. Further south is the leafy, low-rise and exclusively residential area known as Jardim Europa and also the slightly less exclusive Jardim America. Southeast of Jardim Europa is sprawling Parque do Ibirapuera, while to the west lie the upscale neighborhoods of Pinheiros and Vila Madalena. South of Jardim Europa lie the upmarket bastions of Vila Olímpia and Itaim Bibi, both of which are increasingly important business centers.

Tourist offices offer a free user-friendly map covering all of the city's most relevant neighborhoods.

ℹ Information

Crime is an issue in São Paulo, though the majority is limited to the city's periphery, and tourists aren't often targeted unless they're the unlucky victim of an *arrastão*, when armed bandits rob an entire restaurant of patrons in the blink of an eye. General rules of thumb include being especially careful in the center at night and on weekends (when fewer people are about) and watching out for pickpockets on buses, around Praça da Sé and on Linhas 1 (blue) and 3 (red) of the metro. Otherwise, maintain the same common-sense vigilance you would in any developing-world metropolis.

ATMs are widely available throughout the city. Bradesco and Banco do Brasil are feeless and the most foreign-friendly. Note that most are closed from 10pm to 6am for security reasons. Always use ATMs inside banks to avoid cloning.

C.I.T (Map p224; ☎3331-7786; www.cidadedesaopaulo.com; Praça da República; ⌚9am-6pm) with branches at GRU Airport (Terminals 1 & 2; ⌚8am-8pm), Mercado Municipal (Map p224; Rua da Cantareira 306, Rua E, Portão 4; ⌚8am-5pm Mon-Sat, 7am-4pm Sun), Paulista (Map p230; Av Paulista 1853; ⌚9am-6pm), Olido (Map p224; São João 473; ⌚9am-6pm), Tietê Bus Station (Av Cruzeiro do Sul 1800, Rodoviário Tietê, Santana; ⌚6am-10pm) and Congonhas Airport (Av Washington Luis s/n, Congonhas Airport, Vila Congonhas; ⌚7am-10pm). São Paulo's tourist-information booths all have good city maps, as well as helpful walking maps for individual neighborhoods.

They also offer monthly events listings, LGBT and other themed guides and maps, many of which are also available for download in English and Spanish on the website.

Correios (Map p230; www.correios.com.br; Haddock Lobo 566, Jardins; ⌚9am-5pm) A particularly convenient location; one of Sampa's many post offices.

Deatur Tourist Police (☎3120-4417; Rua da Cantareira 390; ⌚8am-7pm) A special police force just for tourists, with English-speaking officers, located at Mercado Municipal.

Einstein Hospital (☎2151-1233; www.einstein.com.br; Albert Einstein 627, Morumbi) Located on a southwestern corner of Morumbi, Einstein is one of Latin America's best hospitals.

Polícia Federal (☎3538-5000; www.dpf.gov.br; Hugo Dantola 95, Lapa; ⌚8am-4:30pm Mon-Fri) For visa extensions, head to this office about 4km west of the Metrô Barra Funda.

Sírio-Libânes Hospital (☎3394-0200; www.hospitalsiriolibanes.org.br; Dona Adma Jafet 91, Bela Vista) State-of-the-art hospital near Av Paulista.

Getting There & Away

AIR

São Paulo is the Brazilian hub for many international airlines and thus the first stop for many travelers. Before buying a domestic ticket, check which of the city's airports the flight departs from, as the international airport also serves many domestic flights.

GRU Airport (☎2445-2945; www.gru.com.br; Rod Hélio Smidt s/n), the international airport, is 25km east of the center. Most domestic flights depart from newly renamed Terminal 2 in the main building, but Azul/Trip and Passaredo operate out of the newer Terminal 1, 2km to the southwest. Most international flights now operate out of the new Terminal 3 (connected to T2 by corridor and people-mover), an impressive world-class terminal that opened in 2014. Exceptions include mid-haul flights from Central and South America and the Caribbean (Aerolíneas Argentinas/Austral, Aeromexico, Avianca/Taca, Boliviana de Aviacion, Copa, Tame etc) and a few stragglers from Africa (Ethiopian, Royal Air Maroc, TAAG) and Europe (Air Europa) – but check ahead, the migration to T3 will continue over the life of this guide.

Frequent free shuttle connect the terminals 24 hours a day.

The domestic-only airport, **Congonhas** (CGH), 14km south of the center, services many domestic destinations, including the majority of flights to Rio (Santos Dumont Airport), which depart every half-hour (or less).

BUS

São Paulo has four long-distance bus stations, all accessible by metro. Each terminal tends to specialize in a certain set of destinations, but there are no hard-and-fast rules, unfortunately. If you need to check which terminal services your destination, see the Consulta De Viagens section of **Socicam** (www.socicam.com.br).

The main terminal and South America's largest, Terminal Tietê, 4.5km north of Centro, offers buses to destinations throughout the continent. Avoid bus arrivals during early morning or late afternoon – traffic jams are enormous.

Buses to Santos leave about every half-hour from a separate bus station – the Terminal Intermunicipal do Jabaquara, which is at the end of the southern metro line (Metrô Jabaquara). Terminal Bresser, near the Memorial do Imigrante in the east-zone district of Brás, services south

BUSES FROM SÃO PAULO

DESTINATION	STARTING FARE (R$)	TIME (HR)	BUS COMPANY
Angra dos Reis	70	7½	Reunidas Paulista (www.reunidaspaulista.com.br)
Asunción (PY)	184.50	20	Pluma (www.pluma.com.br)
Belo Horizonte	102	8	Cometa (www.viacaocometa.com.br)
Brasília	171	15	Real Expresso (www.realexpresso.com.br)
Buenos Aires (AR)	370.50	36	Pluma (www.pluma.com.br)
Curitiba	75	6	Cometa (www.viacaocometa.com.br)
Florianópolis	126	11	Catatrinense (www.catarinense.net)
Foz do Iguaçu	114.50	15	Pluma (www.pluma.com.br)
Montevideo (UY)	390	32	TTL (www.ttl.com.br)
Pantanal (Campo Grande)	193	13½	Andorinha (www.andorinha.com)
Pantanal (Cuiabá)	247	26	Andorinha (www.andorinha.com)
Paraty	54	6	Reunidas Paulista (www.reunidaspaulista.com.br)
Recife	436	45	Itapemirim (www.itapemirim.com.br)
Rio de Janeiro	78	6	1001 (www.autoviacao1001.com.br)
Salvador	326	32	São Geraldo (www.saogeraldo.com.br)
Santiago (CH)	405	54	Pluma (www.pluma.com.br)
Santos	22	1¼	Cometa (www.viacaocometa.com.br)

Click Bus (www.clickbus.com.br) is a good app for consulting departures times, fares and purchases (with foreign cards!) and there's a dedicated pick-up booth inside Tietê bus terminal.

OFF THE BEATEN TRACK

SÃO PAULO SEASHORE ESCAPES

There's a lot more beach on São Paulo's coast than our pages could possible cover. In addition to the beach towns we feature, consider escaping the city and digging your toes into these additional sands, several of which won't be quite so crowded.

Santos

Though it never receives a star for cleanliness, Santos is the closest beach to the city of São Paulo, just over an hour away on a good traffic day. Due to oil money, it's a fun town in its own right, with lots of great bars and restaurants. Locals consider Boqueirão, between canals 3 and 4, to be the city's best beach. Santos' beachfront garden, clocking in at 5335m, is in the record books for the largest in the world.

Cometa (www.viacaocometa.com.br) buses to Santos leave frequently from Terminal Intermunicipal do Jabaquara in São Paulo (R$21.25, 1¼ hours).

Guarujá

With its fine beaches along the stretch of coast closest to São Paulo, once-glamorous Guarujá has suffered from overdevelopment. Still, if you can't get further afield, it retains some charm as a quick getaway – even if concrete towers line the beaches, which get packed with weekend day-trippers. Surfers should note that there are good waves along Praia do Tombo and Praia do Éden (reached by a downhill trail from the road to Pernambuco or Iporanga beaches) that are a good bet for beating the crowds.

Ultra (www.viacaoultra.com.br) buses to Guarujá (R$28, 1¼ hours) leave throughout the day from Terminal Intermunicipal do Jabaquara in São Paulo.

Boiçucanga & Around

The laid-back surfer town of Boiçucanga makes a good base to explore the stretch of coast that runs almost due west from São Sebastião. The variety of beaches, many backed by the steeply rising Serra do Mar, is remarkable, and there's good surf at nearby Camburi and Maresias, which have also developed into major party towns. Juqueí is popular with families.

Boiçucanga is reached from São Paulo Tietê (R$43.45, four hours, four daily), Guarujá (R$27, two hours, three daily) and São Sebastião (R$10.60, 40 minutes, three daily) with **Litorânea** (www.litoranea.com.br).

Ilha do Cardoso

As wild as it gets in São Paulo state, this ecological reserve near the state's southern border with Paraná offers gorgeous natural pools, waterfalls and untouched beaches, and is home to only 400 residents and no cars. Dark sands and brownish-grey sea don't sway the nouveau hippies, who love these beaches due to their isolation.

Two **Intersul** (www.intersul-transporte.com.br) buses per day leave São Paulo's Barra Funda bus station for Cananéia (R$60.10, five hours, 2:30pm and 8:30pm), from where a number of private operators offer boat service to the island along the waterfront. Prices vary, but expect to pay around R$20 to R$30 per person (four-person minimum). You can also reach Cananéia from Iguape (R$21.80, 1¾ hours) via Pariquera-Açu.

of Minas Gerais state. Terminal Barra Funda, in the west zone, near the Memorial da Ámerica Latina, services destinations in São Paulo state, including Iguape and Cananéia, Paraná and all buses to the Pantanal.

Getting Around

TO/FROM THE AIRPORT

CPTM Linha 13 (Jade) is currently under construction, which will connect GRU Airport with Engenheiro Goulart station in northeast São Paulo and *may* be ready during the lifespan of this guide. Until then, **Passaro Marron** (www.passaromarron.com.br) operates two airport buses. The **Airport Bus Service** (www.airportbusservice.com.br; one-way from R$42) is the most efficient way to/from GRU Airport, making stops at Aeroporto Congonhas, Barra Funda, Tiête, Praça da República and various hotels around Av Paulista and Rua Augusta (look for a family of taxi drivers, **Paulo, Marco and Stefan** (Map p224; ☎ 99236-2670), hanging around outside the Praça da República stop – they'll take you faster in a shared taxi for the same price).

The *cheapest* way is to catch suburban Airport Bus Service line 257 (299 as well but it takes a lot longer and is best avoided) to/from Metrô Tatuapé (R$5.15, 30 to 45 minutes; easily confused with the flashier aforementioned Airport Bus Service – they depart right next to each other outside Terminal 2), which departs every 15 minutes between 5am and 12:10am. To the airport, exit Tatuapé to the left towards Shopping Metrô Boulevard Tatuapé and the buses are on the street below to the left as you cross the pedestrian bridge.

Guarucoop (☎2440-7070; www.guarucoop.com.br) is the only taxi service allowed to operate from the international airport and charges vacation-spoiling prices to the city (R$135.64 to Av Paulista, R$161.04 to Vila Madalena).

Uber was cleared to operate out of GRU Airport in early 2015. Uber Black is generally R$30 to R$40 cheaper than Guarucoop (and UberX some R$50 to R$60). They cannot pick you up on the near curve, however; you must meet the driver on the far curve.

To the airport, São Paulo taxis are now authorized to charge a 50% surcharge for crossing municipalities – one more reason to bypass them.

For Congonhas, catch bus 875A-10 'Perdizes-Aeroporto' from Metrô São Judas or catch a regular taxi (R$40 to R$60 to/from most neighborhoods of interest).

BUS

São Paulo's immense public-transport system, run by **SPTrans** (☎toll-free 156; www.sptrans.com.br), is arguably the world's most complex, boasting more than 15,000 buses and 1333 lines. Buses (R$3.50) are crowded during rush hours and can be prone to pickpockets. Watch your valuables, especially phones in pockets or backpack side pockets. The city tourist-information booths are excellent sources of information about buses.

BIKE

There are sporadic bike paths around the city, though the grand R$112 million, 400km bike path plan of São Paulo mayor Fernando Haddad had been halted by a court order at time of research, pending further usability and practicality studies. The one exception being along Av Paulista, the construction of which was allowed to continue (in addition to the 2015 announcement that the entire avenue would be closed to vehicles on Sundays between 9am and 5pm). Both Bradesco-sponsored **CicloSampa** (☎3184-3000; www.ciclosampa.com.br; per 30 min R$5, 1st 30 min free; ⏲6am-10pm) and Itaú-sponsored **Bike Sampa** (☎4003-6055; www.mobilicidade.com.br/bikesampa.asp; per hr R$5, first hr free; ⏲6am-10pm) have bike hire stations around town, but it remains a bike-at-your-own risk city.

METRO

You can reach many places on the excellent **Metrô São Paulo** (www.metro.sp.gov.br), the city's rapidly expanding subway system (2015 marked the opening of Brazil's first monorail, the Linha-15 Prata and it's integrated commuter rail counterpart, **CPTM** (www.cptm.sp.gov.br). The metro is cheap, safe and fast and runs from 4:40am to midnight on most lines. A single ride costs R$3.50. Refillable Bilhete Único (R$3.50) cards are worthwhile for discounts transferring between bus and subway.

TAXI

All taxis should be metered – if your driver doesn't turn the meter on, be sure to mention it. If the driver still doesn't, ask to be let out. The **99Taxis app** (www.99taxis.com) is the preferred app by local taxi drivers and is far and away more convenient and safer than calling for a taxi or hailing one in the street.

PAULISTA COAST

São Paulo's coast, known in Portuguese as the *Litoral Paulista*, is most spectacular in its northern reaches, especially around Ubatuba, thanks to the jungle-covered peaks of the Serra do Mar that reach all the way down to the Atlantic.

Ubatuba

☎0XX12 / POP 79,000

Draped with the rich flora of the Mata Atlântica, the peaks of the Serra do Mar provide a dramatic, emerald-green backdrop to the winding Ubatuba coastline. This region has become a pre-eminent resort for well-heeled *paulistanos*, with its elegant beach homes and a number of stylish hotels and pousadas, especially south of the town. Heading north toward neighboring Paraty in the state of Rio de Janeiro, beaches tend to be harder to reach but also wilder and more pristine, and the little-visited Parque Nacional da Serra da Bocaina spans both São Paulo and Rio de Janeiro states. The area is especially agreeable in winter, when temps remain high enough, less rain bucks the town nickname (Uba*chuva* meaning Uba*rain*) and far fewer people.

The town itself, known simply as 'Centro,' is perhaps uninspiring, save for its handsome waterfront promenade, pretty bay views and a few small beaches, but there is no shame in basing yourself here while you explore the northern and southern coastlines – and there's plenty of action at night along Rua Guarani, the main drag.

Sights & Activities

The town's prettiest beaches are best reached by bike (Ubatuba is well equipped with bike lanes) and the scenic bay has become a popular spot for stand-up paddling. The real trick, though, is to get to the remote beaches and picturesque islands outside the city. The tourist office can also offer information about hikes and guided visits to the adjacent state park, with good hiking trails into the thickly forested coastal range.

Ubatuba is also a major bird-watching hot spot, especially in October.

Boat Trips

Boat trips leave from Itaguá for the most popular island trip, **Ilha Anchieta** (around R$75 plus R$12 island tax, three to four hours). This protected nature reserve offers rare glimpses of fish and birds undisturbed in their natural habitats, but there are loads more less explored choices as well. These minicruises offer enviable views of the coast and its beautiful, deep-green waters. You can make reservations at the tourist office or many hotels and guesthouses. Alternatively, deal directly with operators who set up tables along the promenade in front of Itaguá beach. Cruise operators also leave from the Enseada and Saco da Ribeira neighborhoods. You can also see the local **Projecto Tamar** (www.tamar.org.br), which protects native turtles and their eggs.

Beaches

Within the district of Ubatuba there are some 74 beaches and 15 islands spread across 100km. The best two beaches in town are **Vermelha** (good for surfing) and **Cedro** (more secluded), both reachable on foot or by bike.

Regular buses run along the coastal road. Some of the best beaches south of Ubatuba include **Praia Vermelha** (3km), **Enseada** (8km), **Flamengo** (12km, on the Ponta do Flamengo), **Lázaro** (16km) and **Domingos Dias** (18km). The big, loud party scene is 6km south of Ubatuba at **Praia Grande**.

North of town, the beaches are hidden away down steep hillsides. They're harder to find but good for boogie boarding and surfing and well worth the effort. Among the best are **Vermelha do Norte** (9km), **Itamambuca** (15km), **Félix** (17km), **Prumirim** (23km), **Ubatumirim** (33km) and **Picinguaba** (43km).

Sleeping

If you're without a car, Centro is the most convenient place to stay. From here you can catch local buses (R$3.40) to the beaches.

Green Haven Hostel HOSTEL $
(☎3832-7277; www.greenhavenhostel.com; Av Governador Abreu Sodré 1245, Perequê-Açu; dm R$40-60, r R$150-200;) Vini, both an ex-lawyer and former semi-pro rugby player in Malta, and his brother, Tulio, an eco-architect, are the personalities behind this good-time hostel on one of Ubatuba's best beaches for novice surfers. Sustainable touches abound (earthen-brick bungalows, solar-heated showers, mud-fashioned front desk, toothpaste-tube mattress supports) and there's an excellent wrap-around balcony where the magic happens.

Dorms come in six-, eight- and 14-bed configurations, the latter boasting the best views and sunrises. A Jacuzzi is on the way and bicycles, surfboards and inspirational bathrooms are available.

Ecotrip Hostel HOSTEL $
(☎3833-4036; www.ecotriphostel.com.br; Dom Joao III 573, Centro; dm R$50-60, s/d from R$100/160;) The friendly English-speaking Malu runs this welcoming centrally located hostel. Situated just five blocks from the water, it's a simple but well-managed spot, with a nice outdoor kitchen, a small pool and, in season, breakfast fruits directly from Malu's secret fruit garden.

Hotel Solar das Águas Cantantes HOTEL $$
(☎3842-0178; www.solardasaguascantantes.com.br; Estrada Saco da Ribereira 951, Lázaro; s/d from R$264/293;) With quarters ranged around a lush courtyard, this grand, whitewashed colonial affair run by the son of the original Austrian owner sits a short walk from the stunning (if crowded) Praia do Lázaro. The high-ceilinged rooms have an austere elegance. The hotel's often-starred restaurant, renowned for its seafood stews (mains for two people R$72 to R$165), is excellent.

Torre del Mar POUSADA $$
(☎3832-2751; www.pousadatorredelmar.com.br; Milton de Holanda Maia 210, Itagua; r R$200-320;

) This widely adored Mediterranean-white pousada is tucked away a few blocks from the main drag and receives rave reviews for its accomodating, English-speaking owners. The 18 rooms are smallish but well maintained, and great common areas include a fabulous interior garden and perfect little rooftop pool and patio.

A Pousadinha POUSADA **$$**
(3832-2136; www.ubatuba.com.br/pousadinha; Guarani 686, Itaguá; r R$180-250;) This former boarding house offers just seven small and simple but airily stylish rooms that make for palpable value on this expensive stretch of coast.

★ **Pousada Picinguaba** POUSADA **$$$**
(3836-9105; www.picinguaba.com; Picinguaba; r incl dinner R$1480, ste R$2180;) Tucked away in a small fisherman's village north of Ubatuba is one of the region's most charming pousadas, a 10-room, sustainably run gem owned by a French-Portuguese couple. Everything here, from the original artworks and furniture to the outdoor poolside tables overlooking the calm bay, is subtle, meticulously curated and designed to instill a sense of place without going overboard.

It also now offers horseback rides across the Parque Estadual da Serra do Mar to their countryside sister property, Fazenda Catuçaba. Brazil at its finest!

Eating

Don't miss *azul-marinho,* a delicious local stew of fish and green bananas that gets its purplish-blue color from a chemical reaction between the latter and the iron cauldrons they're cooked in; and banana sweets from **Tachão de Ubatuba**.

O Limoeiro BRAZILIAN **$**
(Praça Theoforico de Oliveira 08, Ilha dos Pescadores; mains for 2 people R$48-78; 4pm-midnight Mon-Sat;) This laid-back riverside spot – open on Mondays! – is walking distance from Centro and does some shockingly cheap Brazilian food (a *moqueca* for two for R$48 that's actually good? *Sim!*) and excellent caipirinhas. The house-specialty lemandarin, lemongrass, honey and aged *cachaça* is like Lay's potato chips – you can't have just one!

Integrale BAKERY **$**
(www.padariaintegrale.com.br; Esteves da Silva 360, Centro; sandwiches R$7.50-15.50; 7:30am-8:30pm Mon-Sat, to 7pm Sun;) This beautiful natural bakery is definitely a rare breed along this coast. Choose from a very long list of wholegrain, chemical and preservative-free breads, salads, sandwiches, quiches, snacks and strong organic coffee, then tuck into it all on the lovely and lush patio.

★ **Cantinho da Lagoa** BRAZILIAN, SEAFOOD **$$**
(www.cantinhodalagoa-ubatuba.blogspot.com.br; Prumirim; mains for 2 people R$49-170; 9am-6pm, closed Tue) The sophisticated dishes emerging from this excellent beach shack perched on top of the rocks at one of the region's prettiest beaches (Prumirim) are the result of the owner's stint in London kitchens. Fabio, who's from the village, invented one of the best dishes on this coast, the *cajutapu* (palm-heart pasta with grilled shrimp and *juçara* fruit sauce; R$47).

Terra Papagalli SEAFOOD **$$$**
(Xavantes 537, Itaguá; mains for 2 people R$139-158; noon-11pm daily Dec & Jan, Thu-Sun Mar-Nov) This intimate restaurant along the waterfront manages to be both the least touristy and the most creative along this string of mostly carbon-copy options. A few dishes each night are served, depending on the catch (we scored *dourada* with a lovely tamarind sauce and Brazil-nut rice), and it all goes down very romantically among the candlelit tables.

Peixe com Banana SEAFOOD **$$$**
(3832-1712; Guarani 255, Itaguá; mains for 2 R$98-145; noon-11pm, closed Mon-Thu Mar-Nov) Don't be fooled by the plastic tablecloths or the touristy seafront location. This is one of the region's most popular seafood joints, famed for its excellent version of *azul-marinho (*R$118 for two), fresh fish and *moquecas*.

A Taberna SEAFOOD **$$$**
(3832-5663; www.atabernaubatuba.com; Av Leovigildo Dias Veira 958, Itaguá; mains R$57.50-122; noon-11pm Mon & Wed-Thu, to midnight Fri & Sat, to 10pm Sun;) This well-regarded Portuguese-Brazilian seafooder does *bacalhau* (cod) 16 ways, but we are partial to the excellent seafood *feijoada* or the congac-braised calamari. Though the previous Portuguese owners are long gone, Brazilians have maintained the menu and Old World atmosphere and there's a pleasant patio with ocean views.

Entertainment

Blues on the Rocks LIVE MUSIC

(www.bluesontherocks.com.br; Chico Santos 17, Itaguá; cover R$5-15; ⌚7pm-late Dec-Feb, Wed-Sat Mar-Nov) This wildly popular rock, blues and jazz venue is consistently voted the best live-music spot on the Paulista coast.

Information

Banco do Brasil (www.bb.com.br; Conceição 138) Visa/Mastercard ATM.

C.I.T. (☎3833-9123; cnr Conceição & Iperoig, Centro; ⌚8am-6pm) Housed inside the colonial blue-and-white Paço da Nóbrega building along the waterfront. Has useful maps of surrounding beaches and good local info.

Getting There & Around

Ubatuba has two intercity bus stations. For São Paulo (R$58.40, four hours, eight daily), São Sebastião (R$23.25, 70 minutes, hourly; change in Caraguátatuba) and other destinations within the state, head to **Litorânea bus station** (☎3832-3622; www.litoranea.com.br; Maria Victória Jean 381, Centro), located at the edge of the town center, about 1.5km from the tourist office and beach.

For buses to Paraty (R$11.80, 1½ hours, four daily) and Rio de Janeiro (R$75.20, five hours, 11am and 11:40pm), head to the **São Jose bus station** (Thomaz Galhardo 513, Centro), on the main street a few blocks from the beach.

Local buses (R$3.40, about hourly from 7am to 8pm) head up and down the coastal highway and come within hiking distance of most beaches. The main stop in the center is at Hans Staden 488, between the two long-distance stations.

São Sebastião

One of the only towns on the Paulista coast that has preserved a portion of its colonial charms, São Sebastião sits on a dramatic channel dividing the mainland from Ilha de São Sebastião (popularly known as 'Ilhabela'), a 15-minute ferry trip away. Prices in town are moderate by local standards, but for good reason. There are no beaches at hand, and the town is also a major oil depot, with huge tankers somewhat diminishing the natural beauty. Still, it makes a fine stopover if you're traveling to Ilhabela.

Sleeping

Hostel São Sebastião HOSTEL $

(☎3892-2684; www.saosebastiaohostel.com.br; Eduardo Cássio 77; dm R$40-55, s/d/tr from R$90/125/160; ❄📶🏊) Totally soulless, but the cheap town hostel occupies a sprawling hillside home 2km from the historical center and ferry to Ilhabela. Dorms feature specious bathrooms and there's a nice pool with views. A towel kit costs R$5 extra.

★ **Pousada da Ana Doce** POUSADA $$

(☎3892-1615; www.pousadaanadoce.com.br; Expedicionários Brasileiros 196; s/d from R$200/250; ❄📶🏊) It's so hard to choose at this colonial center gem, the most charming inn in town. One of the 16 neat, cheerful little rooms arranged around a charming, plant-filled courtyard in the main structure, or one of 10 that surround a pool in a newly-built annex next door (two of which offer French doors opening right into the pool!). Book ahead.

Eating

Be sure to try the excellent locally made Rocha-brand *sorvete* (ice cream) and *picolês* (popsicles), available most famously at Altino Arantes 90. Flavors like *milho verde* (sweet corn), *coco quemado* (burnt coconut) and *banana caramelada* (caramelized banana) are unforgettable.

Atobá BUFFET $$

(www.facebook.com/atobarestaurante; Praça Major João Fernandes 218; per kg weekday/weekend R$50.80/57.60; ⌚11:30am-4pm; 👪) In a colonial building on the town's main square, Atobá offers a high-quality per-kilo buffet for lunch. Small extras like a good selection of seeds and piles of roasted garlic give it a leg up in these parts.

Information

C.I.T. (Secretaria de Turismo e Cultura; ☎3892-2206; www.turismo.saosebastiao.sp.gov.br) For information, head to the tourist offices, one of which is in an elaborated waterfront kiosk in the colonial center of town (Altino Arantes s/n; ⌚11am-8pm, closed Mon & Tue Jun-Aug); or a second at the bus station (Praça Vereador Venino Fernandes Moreira 10; ⌚8am-5pm Mon-Fri).

Getting There & Away

The **bus station** (Rodoviária Municipal; ☎3893-4340; Praça Vereador Venino Fernandes Moreira 10) is located just off the main coastal highway and a short walk from the colonial center. **Litorânea** (☎3893-2475; www.litoranea.com.br) has frequent service to São Paulo (R$52.55, 3½ hours, eight daily), as well as direct service to Guarulhos International Airport (R$53, four hours, four daily), Boiçucanga (R$10.60, 40 minutes, seven daily) and other stops along the coast to Santos. **Util** (☎3892-6233; www.util.com.br) offers service to Rio (R$89.45, seven hours, 9am and 10pm), with a stop in Paraty (R$35.60, 3½ hours).

Ilhabela

☎0XX12 / POP 28,000 (WINTER), 120,000 (SUMMER)

Rising steeply from the narrow strait that divides it from the continent, the 350-sq-km Ilhabela (Beautiful Island) earns its name from its volcanic peaks, beautiful beaches, dense tropical jungle and some 360 waterfalls. Almost 85% of the island has been turned into a park and Unesco-protected biosphere, which shelters a remarkable profusion of plant and animal life, including toucans and capuchin monkeys. A haunt of pirates in the 16th and 17th centuries, its waters are scattered with shipwrecks, many of which make for excellent diving. The island also proffers jungle hiking, windsurfing and beach-lazing.

Be aware that in the height of summer the bugs are murder, especially the little bloodsuckers known as *borrachudos*. Use plenty of insect repellent at all times. Summer is also when the island is packed with vacationing *paulistas*. Also try to avoid arriving on Friday evening and/or leaving on Sunday evening, especially in summer, as traffic, the line for the ferry and spikes in accommodations prices can tarnish your experience of paradise.

Sights

Vila Ilhabela, on the northwestern part of the island, has quite a few well-preserved colonial buildings, including the slave-built **Igreja NS da Ajuda** (founded 1532); the **Fazenda Engenho d'Agua** in Itaquanduba (founded 1582); and **Fazenda Santa Carmen** at Feiticeira beach. Two kilometers inland from Perequê beach (near the ferry terminal), **Cachoeira das Tocas** has various small waterfalls with accompanying deep pools and waterslides.

Beaches

Of the sheltered beaches on the north side of the island, **Praia Jabaquara** is recommended. It can be reached by car via a dirt road. On the eastern side of the island, where the surf is stronger, try beautiful **Praia dos Castelhanos** (good for camping and surfing), which is backed by the steeply rising jungle. From the town of Borrifos at the southern end of the island, you can take a four-hour walk to **Praia Bonete**, a windy surf beach that you will share mostly with a local community of fisher folk.

Activities

Maremar Aventura Turismo OUTDOORS
(☎3896-3679; www.maremar.tur.br; Praça Elvira Storace 12, Perequê; ⏰8:30am-6pm, to 8pm Dec-Apr) Near the ferry, this recommended agency organizes all kinds of outdoor activities, including schooner trips around the island (from R$60 per person), full-day trips to the idyllic fishing village and beach of Bonete (by advance booking only) and Jeep/boat tours to Praia de Castelhanos (R$150 per person); and rents bikes (per half-day/full day R$35/50). They also have a second **Kiosk** (Av Princesa Islabel 90, Perequê; ⏰9am-6pm, to 10pm Dec-Apr).

Sleeping

Making a reservation is a good idea on weekends – mandatory on summer weekends. Prices are high, so some travelers choose to stay in São Sebastião, where rates are more reasonable.

Hostel Central HOSTEL **$**
(☎3896-6363; www.hostelcentral.com.br; Irene R Barbosa 116, Perequê; dm from R$50-60, r/q from R$150/250; ❄📶🏊) This HI hostel, well-located in Perequê, is easily the island's best. The space, with a small but inviting pool surrounded by jungly exposed brick, is a little oasis in itself and the former home of the English-speaking owner, who is a Bonete expert (his nickname is Daniel Bonete!).

Good-value private rooms have patios with hammocks and there are nine-bed (male) and eight-bed (female) dorms.

★**Na Mata Suites** POUSADA **$$**
(☎3895-8771; www.namatasuites.com.br; Benedicto Mariano Leite 690, Barra Velha; d weekday/weekend R$225/250; P❄@📶🏊) Tucked away in a small thatch of lush neighborhood rainforest, you'll find an absolutely lovely four-bungalow trove of hospitality, originally converted from private jungle into a discerning getaway by Anglo-Brazilian owners, who have now leased the property to an equally hospitable couple of Portuguese-Brazilian architects who are carrying on the consummate traveler vibe.

Each well-appointed bungalow comes with a rustic terrace that's perfect for breakfast (if you don't take it by the pool); and their select positioning ensures privacy for all.

WORTH A TRIP

PARQUE ESTADUAL DO ALTO DO RIBEIRA (PETAR)

Nestled in the Vale do Ribeira in the hills near the São Paulo–Paraná border, Iporanga was founded in 1576 after gold was discovered here. Today, the surrounding region remains one of the least-disturbed stretches of the Brazilian Atlantic Forest and is of international importance for its biodiversity. It also makes a good base for visiting the **Parque Estadual do Alto do Ribeira**. This 357-sq-km state park, with its 400 cataloged caves, is known as Brazil's Capital das Grutas (Cave Capital).

PETAR's Núcleos de Visitação are excellent visitors centers with information on cave trips, guides and campgrounds. There are four Núcleos: **Núcleo de Santana** (www.petaronline.com.br/conheca-o-petar/nucleos/nucleo-santana; per person R$12, plus per vehicle R$6), 18km northwest of town, has good facilities for visitors and campers, including a coffee shop and exhibition hall, five caves and a 3.5km-long trek to a beautiful waterfall; **Núcleo Ouro Grosso** (13km northwest of town) has basic accommodations for groups and offers cooking facilities, two caves and a walking trail; **Núcleo Casa de Pedra** (9km by road plus 3km by walking trail, northwest from town) is the base for visiting the Casa de Pedra, famous for its 215m-high entrance and pristine Atlantic forest; and **Núcleo Caboclos** (www.petaronline.com.br/conheca-o-petar/nucleos/nucleo-caboclos; entrance/camping R$12/18), centrally located in the park, 86km by road from town, has good camping facilities, basic visitors' lodgings and several caves.

For information as well as camping and caving reservations, contact **PETAR** (Parque Estadual do Alto do Ribeira; ☎15-3552-1875; www.petaronline.com.br). The trustworthy **Ecocave** (☎15-3556-1574; www.ecocave.com.br) organizes expeditions to the caves, as well as hiking, rappelling and inner-tubing along the local river.

From São Paulo's Barra Funda bus station, **Transpen** (www.transpen.com.br) offers service to Apiaí (R$69, five hours, three daily), where you can catch a **Princesa dos Campos** (www.princesadoscampos.com.br) 3pm bus to Iporanga (R$4.60, 1¾ hours), returning at 7am.

Pousada Canto Brava POUSADA $$

(☎3896-5111; www.pousadacantobravo.com.br; r R$170-520; @ 📶) Unplugged and mostly candlelit, this sustainably slanted pousada hidden away on in Bonete beach is Ilhabela's most romantic escape. It's a haul to arrive on foot – a 12km hiking trail from Sepituba – but you'll share sand with nobody beyond local fisherman (sweating for your dinner, which will be spruced up by their organic gardens!) and undaunted surfers.

Pousada Catamarã Brasil POUSADA $$

(☎3894-1034; www.pousadacatamarabrasil.com.br; José Batista dos Santos 273, Curral; r R$145-340; ❄ 📶 🏊) Hidden up an inauspiciously rutted side street, this colorful and pristinely maintained inn offers very comfortable rooms, plus a small but pretty pool hidden in a lush garden. Good value but little warmth or hospitality.

Pousada Mariola POUSADA $$

(☎3896-4141; www.pousadamariola.com.br; Chico Reis 304, Saco da Capela; s/d from R$185/200; P ❄ 📶 🏊) An engineer owns this fabulous choice implanted into giant granite stones perched high on a view-riffic hillside and reached via a charming street with upright palms shooting straight from the cobblestones. The 15-room boutique inn offers spacious rooms with Asian aesthetics and patios that take full advantage of the expansive vistas of the sailboat-strewn sea below.

DPNY Beach BOUTIQUE HOTEL $$$

(☎3894-3000; www.dpnybeach.com.br; José Pacheco do Nascimento 7668; r weekday/weekend from R$760/980; P ❄ @ 📶 🏊) Set right on the sands of Praia Curral, this über-trendy getaway for São Paulo fashionistas isn't subtle: the Mediterranean-on-overdrive aesthetic would be jarring if the crowd here didn't subscribe to the more-is-more line of trendsetting decorating.

Rooms are exquisitely appointed, with extra touches like Nespresso machines; there's a huge pool and harem-like spa that surely gets out of hand (in a good way) on busy nights. Miami-style ambient music pumps throughout the property. It is also home to Hippie Chic Beach Bar, the island's fanciest bar-lounge, and Tróia, its most gourmet restaurant (mains R$39 to R$86).

Eating

Note that some places tend to close early during low season when crowds are thin, so plan for a backup.

Cheiro Verde BRAZILIAN $

(☎3896-3245; www.cheiroverdeilhabela.com.br; Rua da Padroeira 109, Vila; meals R$23.80; ⏰11:30am-5pm Mon, Wed & Thu, to 11pm Fri-Sun; 📶👶) The best place in Vila for a generous *prato feito* (plate of the day) with grilled meat or fish, plus rice, beans and salad, this simple but clean and airy place attracts tourists and locals alike. Each day's menu awaits on a monitor by the door.

Cura BUFFET $

(☎3896-1341; Princesa Isabel 337, Perequê; per kg R$49.90; ⏰11:30am-4pm Mon-Fri, to 6pm Sat & Sun; 👶) The island's best per-kilo restaurant, set in a large and homey space across from the sands of Perequê.

Capitano ITALIAN $$

(☎99770-9581; www.pastadelcapitano.com.br; Pedro Paula de Moraes 703, Saco de Capela; mains R$42-65; ⏰7pm-1am Wed-Sun, daily Jul & Nov-Feb) Chef Fabio Piscioto hails from São Paulo's most traditional Italian neighborhood and was destined to return to his pasta-making roots after 30 years as a graphic designer. Everyone raves about the simple, clean pasta dishes here, and we, too, are in awe: the squid-ink tagliatelle with shrimp grew better and better as it aged on our plate.

Prainha do Julião SEAFOOD $$

(☎3894-1867; www.prainhadojuliao.com.br; Riachuelo 5370, Julião; mains R$35-72; ⏰10am-6pm Mon-Thu, to 6:30pm Fri-Sun; 📶) Hidden from the main road along the island's southside is this upscale beach shack, firmly planted into the sands of Ilhabela's best accessible beach, Julião. Creative seafood with actual vegetables are served on a pristine stretch of beach dug into only by those in the know, who imbibe in the all-day bar scene as well.

O Borrachudo BURGERS $$

(☎3896-1499; www.borrachudo.com.br; Carvalho 20, Vila; sandwiches R$9.60-28.70; ⏰4pm-12:30am Sun, Wed & Thu, to 1:30am Fri & Sat) In a colonial building right on Vila's waterfront, this relaxed cafe-bar proudly serves excellent burgers of all kinds (including ostrich and Guinness-soaked top sirloin), as well as other gourmet sandwiches and 30 beers.

★ Marukuthai THAI $$$

(☎3896-5874; www.marakuthai.com.br; Av Força Expedicionária Brasileira 495, Indaiá; mains R$48-129; ⏰8pm-12:30am Thu-Sat, daily Jan; 📶) Dine on the sands overlooking romantic, yacht-filled seas at Ilhabela's best gourmet restaurant, the domain of darling local chef Renata Vanzetto and her tropical take on Brazilianized Thai. Her best acts pilfer from both cuisines, such as a jasmine rice risotto with shrimp, calamari, sake, coconut milk, red peppers and lime; and slow-cooked octopus with *pimenta-biquinho* vinaigrette.

Drinking

Ponto das Letras CAFE

(Dr Carvalho 146, Vila; coffee R$3.80-9; ⏰10am-8pm Mon-Thu, to 11pm Fri-Sun; 📶) Extremely pleasant cafe and bookshop in the historic district, easily the island's best. It's not hard to figure out this is the domain of paradise's cultured species.

Hippie Chic Beach Bar LOUNGE

(www.dpnybeach.com.br; DPNY Beach, José Pacheco do Nascimento 7668, Curral; 📶) With quietly thumping lounge music, hip-tropical decor and table service on the sand, the island's fanciest bar attracts rich *paulistas* eager to show off this season's designer gear. Specialty cocktails are R$25 to R$30.

Orientation

The ferry arrives from the mainland in the Barra Velha neighborhood, which blends seamlessly with the town of Perequê just to the north. About 7km north lies the historic town of Vila. Good roads run along the western coast of the island; however, the south and east coasts are reachable only by boat or on foot except for a rough road accessible by 4WD that reaches Praia dos Castelhanos on the west coast. The road is controlled (a daily limit of 40 cars, 80 jeeps and 60 motorcycles is enforced; no entry after 2pm).

Information

For those bringing a car to the island, avoid huge lines waiting for the Dersa **ferry** (☎0800-773-3711; www.dersa.sp.gov.br) on summer weekends by booking in advance (return weekdays/weekends R$88.40/132.60). ATMs in Barra Velha, Perequê and Vila Ilhabela (Vila) accept international bank cards.

Tourist Office (Sectur; ☎3895-7220; www.ilhabela.sp.gov.br; Praça Vereador José Leite dos Passos 14, Barra Velha; ⏰9am-6pm) The tourist office is located about 100m from the ferry terminal in Barra Velha.

Getting There & Around

The 15-minute ferry trip between São Sebastião and Ilhabela runs 24/7 every half-hour from 5:30am to 10:30pm and more or less hourly after that. Cars cost R$15 weekdays and R$22.50 on weekends, motorcycles cost R$7.50 weekdays and R$11.30 on weekends; pedestrians ride free. Returning to the mainland, you pay an environmental tax only (R$2.50 for motorcycles, R$6.50 for cars).

A local bus (R$3.40, every 30 minutes, 5:35am to 1:40am) runs the length of the island, including a stop at the ferry. **Chame Taxi** (☎3895-8587) are usually waiting at the ferry.

A decent road runs the length of the western coast. Another unsealed road (22km) crosses the island. To get to the other side of the island requires either a 4WD, a boat or a good strong pair of hiking legs.

Iguape & Around

☎0XX13 / POP 29,000

Founded by the Portuguese in 1538 to defend Brazil from the Spanish, Iguape is one of the oldest towns in Brazil and one of the few along São Paulo's coast to retain its colonial contours. An ongoing federal initiative is helping to restore the old city center, which has long been neglected. While beaches are a bit of a hoof, the town makes a tranquil base from which to explore the region.

Sights

Boasting impressive buildings and few foreign tourists, Iguape is good for those who appreciate their colonial architecture in various shades of preservation and decay. The town's colonial charms are clustered around the whitewashed main plaza, **Largo da Basílica**, and the 18th-century **basilica** (8am-8pm). About 1.5km along the road to Barra do Ribeira is a turnoff to the **Mirante do Morro do Espia**, a lookout with a good view of the port and region.

Iguape looks across a narrow strait to **Ilha Comprida**, a long, skinny island (86km by 3km) that shelters Iguape from the open ocean. The island is covered with a combination of mangrove and Atlantic rainforest, and has an uninterrupted beach that stretches the entire Atlantic-facing length of the island. A toll bridge connects Iguape with the island.

Sleeping & Eating

There are a number of inexpensive pizzerias and other eateries on Largo da Basílica.

Silvi Hotel HOTEL $

(☎3841-1421; www.silvihotel.com.br; Sandoval Trigo 515; s R$95-165, d R$170-240, tr R$240-285;) Humble but efficient motel-style accommodations in a leprechaun-green building. Rooms are plain but in perfect working order, and the staff is both helpful and friendly.

Pousada Solar Colonial POUSADA $$

(☎3841-1591; solarcolonial@terra.com.br; Praça da Basílica 30; s/d/tr R$110/160/200;) Occupying an historic and handsome colonial building right on the town's main square, this inn offers simple but clean, refurbished rooms, plus breakfast in a bright room with French windows onto the main square. Rooms have fans only, but this spot is a steal.

Panela Velha SEAFOOD $$$

(☎3841-1869; 15 de Novembro 190; mains for 2 people R$76-200; 11am-11pm;) Considered the best option in town, this trim, tiny, spotless little place specializes in simple but expertly prepared local seafood in the form of stews like *moquecas* and *caldeiradas*, grilled fresh from the sea or river (nothing farmed here) and paella. It's all good.

Information

P.I.T. (Largo da Basilica 63; 8am-6pm Mon-Fri) Tourist information on the main square, next to the basilica. You'll find foreign-friendly ATMs behind the basilica.

Getting There & Around

Intersul (www.intersul-transporte.com.br) offers five daily buses from Iguape to São Paulo (R$52.95, 3½ hours). For Cananéia (R$21.80, 1¾ hours), switch in Pariquera-Açu. Local buses cross the bridge to Ilha Comprida. If you have a 4WD, it is possible to drive along the long, flat beach on Ilha Comprida and take the ferry across to Cananéia (per vehicle weekday/weekend R$9.70/14.60, passengers free), though you must time your trip for low tide.

Paraná

POP 10.4 MILLION

Includes ➜

Best Places to Eat

- Manu (p268)
- Barolo (p267)
- Mar e Sol (p275)
- Fim da Trilha (p277)
- Casa do Barreado (p272)

Best Places to Sleep

- Hotel das Cataratas (p281)
- Tetris Container Hostel (p280)
- Motter Home (p265)
- Hostel Natura (p280)
- Astral da Ilha (p275)

Why Go?

Since its 1853 succession from São Paulo state, Paraná has been endlessly compared with its larger neighbor to the north. Indeed, the two share a slew of superlatives, rating among Brazil's highest standards of living and best educated populations.

With its efficient public transportation, innovative architecture and outstanding urban parks, the capital, Curitiba, exemplifies the state's successes. Though no tourism magnet, the city's air of European culture and excellent restaurants make for a nice dose of Brazil at its most developed. Sunbathers and surfers sigh for Ilha do Mel and Parque Nacional do Superagüi, where large swaths of unspoiled rainforest and pristine coastline make for some of the least developed and most idyllic beaches in southern Brazil.

But it's Iguaçu Falls that has always earned the wonder and admiration of travelers, from indigenous tribes to Jesuit missionaries to modern-day tourists. The awe it inspires cannot be overstated.

When to Go

Foz do Iguaçu

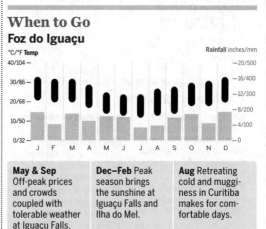

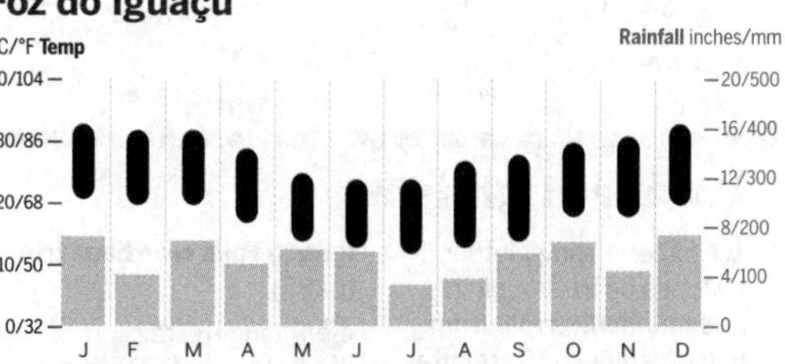

May & Sep Off-peak prices and crowds coupled with tolerable weather at Iguaçu Falls.

Dec–Feb Peak season brings the sunshine at Iguaçu Falls and Ilha do Mel.

Aug Retreating cold and mugginess in Curitiba makes for comfortable days.

History

Like much of southern Brazil, Paraná was neglected by the Portuguese colonists; even a brief gold rush in the 17th century withered when bigger finds were discovered in Minas Gerais. When Paraná seceded from São Paulo in 1853, the economy was based on cattle and *erva maté* (tea), and the government encouraged Italian immigration to develop the economy. Waves of Germans, Ukrainians and Poles followed. With immigration and railroad construction, Curitiba developed into one of the country's richest cities.

Getting There & Around

Curitiba is the state's transportation hub, with bus and air services to every major city in Brazil. A passenger train links Curitiba with the coastal town of Paranaguá. Foz do Iguaçu also has a small international airport and direct bus services to São Paulo, Rio de Janeiro and every big city in the South.

CURITIBA

0XX41

While not necessarily sexy, Curitiba has long garnered praise for being one of the world's best models of urban planning. If it weren't for the bold initiatives of its three-term mayor, Jaime Lerner, whose daring moves in early 1970s – transforming a six-block length of the downtown into a pedestrian zone (done in secret under the cover of darkness), creating five express-bus avenues with futuristic tubular boarding platforms, encouraging recycling and sustainable design long before it was fashionable, and planting trees and creating parks on an enormous scale – Curitiba would probably resemble any other Brazilian city.

Instead, it's the envy of urban planners the world over and Brazil's most efficient city. Today, it's easier to get around Curitiba than any other large city in Brazil. The city has also taken innovative approaches

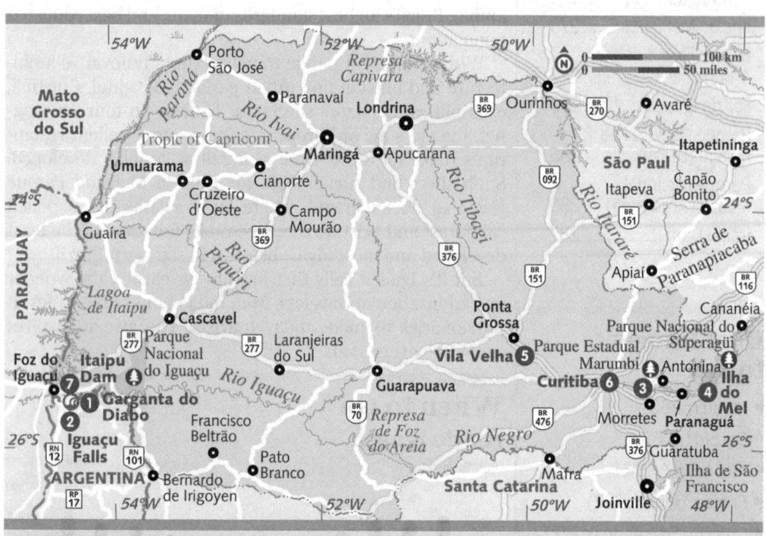

Paraná Highlights

1. Experiencing Mother Nature's heart-stopping and thunderous roar from above and below **Garganta do Diabo** (p285) at Iguaçu Falls.
2. Drenching yourself under one of world's most magnificent waterfalls on an **Iguaçu Falls riverboat trip** (p285).
3. Riding the rails on the **Serra Verde Express** (p270) to Morretes, one of Brazil's last great train rides.
4. Lazing about the wild beaches and sandy trails of car-free **Ilha do Mel** (p273).
5. Marveling at the ancient 'stone city' of **Vila Velha** (p109).
6. Appreciating art and eye-popping architecture at Curitiba's **Museu Oscar Niemeyer** (p265).
7. Admiring the jaw-dropping engineering feat of **Itaipu Dam** (p287).

to urban ills such as homelessness, pollution and poverty. Today, the city ensures an above-average quality of life for Brazil. With its abundant green spaces, sophisticated population and well-heeled infrastructure, Curitiba is not a bad spot to recharge your batteries and soak in Brazil at its functioning best.

Sights & Activities

The focal point of Curitiba's downtown is Rua das Flores, officially known as XV de Novembro, a 500m pedestrian mall ideal for shopping and strolling. At its eastern end sits Praça Santos Andrade, dominated by the impressive Federal University of Paraná. North of Rua das Flores is Praça Tiradentes, site of the founding of the city. Today its most prominent landmark is the cathedral on the northeast corner. Just beyond is Largo da Ordem and Praça Garibaldi, the city's atmospheric colonial heart.

★Museu Oscar Niemeyer MUSEUM
(MON; ☎3350-4400; www.museuoscarniemeyer.org.br; Marechal Hermes 999; adult/child R$9/4.50; ⏰10am-6pm Tue-Sun) Designed by and named for the architect responsible for much of Brasília, this exotic, eye-shaped museum is painted with whimsical dancing figures in bold colors. Rotating exhibits highlight Brazilian and international artists of the 20th and 21st centuries; and there's an excellent permanent exhibit on Niemeyer himself.

There's free admission on the first Sunday of the month and after 6pm on the first Thursday of the month (when the museum closes at 8pm).

Jardim Botânico GARDENS
(www.jardimbotanicocuritiba.com.br; Eng Ostoja Roguski s/n; ⏰6am-8pm Apr-Nov, to 9pm Dec-Mar) In the far south of the city, the Jardim Botânico is a vast, flower-filled expanse, studded with sculpture and crisscrossed by walking paths. The centerpiece glass-and-metallic greenhouse is more interesting as a decorative showpiece than as a botanical wonder.

Largo da Ordem PLAZA
Curitiba's old colonial heart. The pedestrian-only cobblestone streets are lined with beautifully restored buildings, many of which now house trendy art galleries, pubs and cafes. On Sunday, it fills up along with adjacent Praça Garibaldi for a lively art and artisan market (Praça Garibaldi; ⏰9am-2:30pm Sun) with more than 1000 stalls.

Oi Torre Panorâmica OBSERVATION DECK
(Castro Vellozo 191; adult/child R$3.50/1.75; ⏰10am-6:30pm Tue-Sun) For an overview of Curitiba, head to the 109m-high Torre Panorâmica, offering 360-degree views from its observation deck.

Federal University of Paraná HISTORIC BUILDING
The neoclassical headquarters of the Federal University of Paraná is home to MusA-UFPR (www.proec.ufpr.br; 1st fl, 15 de Novembro 695; ⏰9am-6pm Mon-Fri, 9am-1pm Sat) FREE, the university's museum, which features rotating exhibitions, along with a small permanent collection of Tupi-Guarani artifacts.

Tours

Linha Turismo CITY TOUR
(www.urbs.curitiba.pr.gov.br/transporte/linha-turismo; tours R$35; ⏰every 30min 9am-5:30pm Tue-Sun Mar-Oct, every 15min 8:45am-6pm Nov-Carnaval) This double-decker city tour bus is a convenient way to see the sights both inside and outside Curitiba's downtown. It starts at Praça Tiradentes and you can hop-off/hop-on up to four times along the 25-sight route. Stops are announced in English and Spanish and you can use your hop-offs any day you wish.

Sleeping

★Motter Home HOSTEL $
(☎3209-5649; www.motterhome.com.br; Desembargador Motta 3574; dm R$44-48, r R$140; @📶) In leafy Mercês – 15 minutes' walk from Largo da Ordem – Curitiba's top hostel choice makes artistic use of a striking canary-yellow, turret-style mansion from the '50s, with striking art, retro-sophisticated common areas and original hardwood floors.

There's an unwillingness to accommodate solo travelers privately without charging them for two (or at least knock off one of the breakfasts), but otherwise the place is fun and gorgeous.

Curitiba Casa HOSTEL $
(☎3044-7313; www.curitibacasahostel.com; Brasílio Itiberê 73; dm R$44-52, r R$145; @📶) Despite its odd location 15 minutes east of the *rodoferroviária* (bus and train station), this hostel has more fans than *futebol*. Clean, colorful and classy.

Garden Curitiba Hotel HOTEL $$
(☎3222-2524; www.gardencuritiba.com.br; Ébana Pereira 405; s/d/tr R$155/199/263; @📶) This

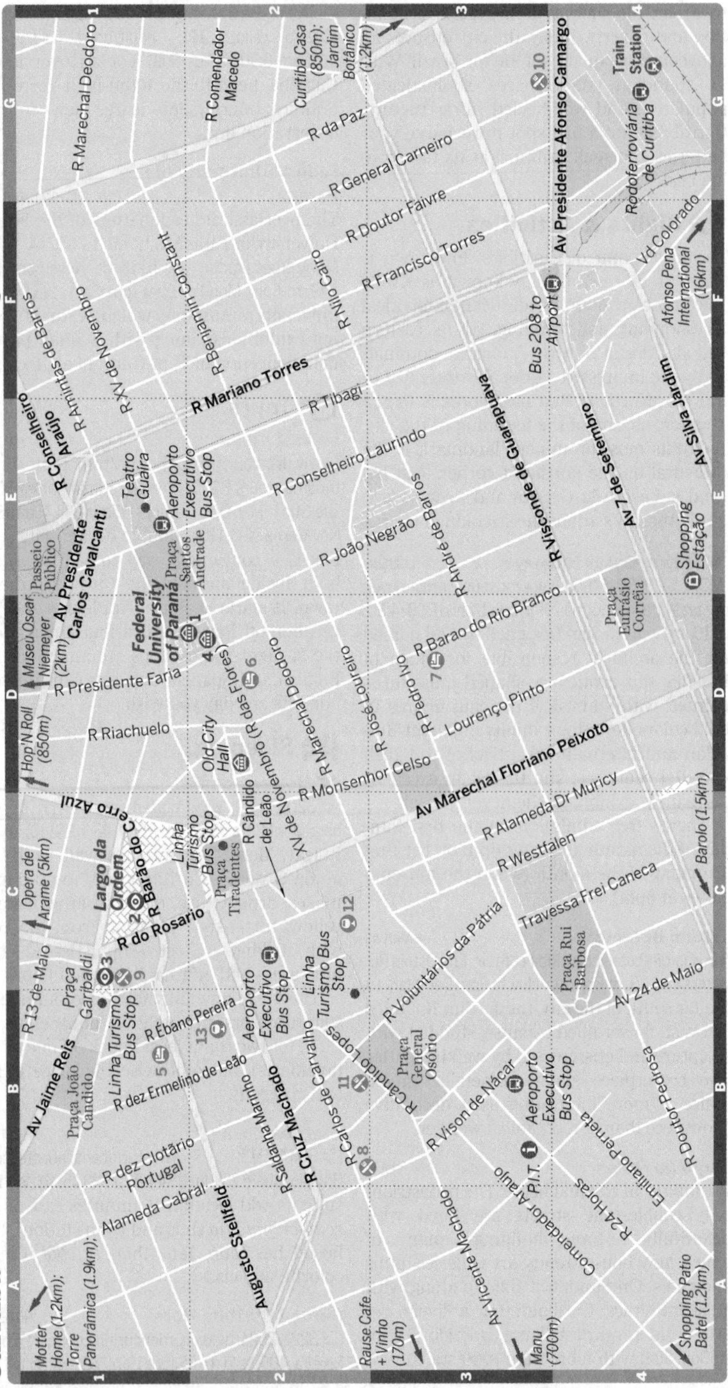

Curitiba

0 — 400 m
0 — 0.2 miles

Motter Home (1.2km); Torre Panorâmica (1.9km);
R 13 de Maio
Opera de Arame (5km)
Hop'N Roll (850m)
Museu Oscar Niemeyer (2km)
Passeio Público
Av Jaime Reis
Praça João Candido
Praça Garibaldi
Linha Turismo Bus Stop
Largo da Ordem
R Barão do Cerro Azul
R do Rosario
R Riachuelo
R Presidente Faria
Av Presidente Carlos Cavalcanti
R Conselheiro Araújo
R Amintas de Barros
R Marechal Deodoro
R XV de Novembro
Teatro Guaíra
Federal University of Paraná
Praça Santos Andrade
Aeroporto Executivo Bus Stop
Alameda Cabral
R dez Clotário Portugal
R dez Ermelino de Leão
R Ébano Pereira
Linha Turismo Bus Stop
Praça Tiradentes
Old City Hall
R Cândido de Leão
XV de Novembro (R das Flores)
R Mariano Torres
R Benjamin Constant
R Comendador Macedo
Augusto Stellfeld
R Saldanha Marinho
Aeroporto Executivo Bus Stop
R Cruz Machado
R Carlos de Carvalho
Linha Turismo Bus Stop
R Marechal Deodoro
R Monsenhor Celso
R Conselheiro Laurindo
R Tibagi
R Nilo Cairo
R da Paz
Curitiba Casa (850m); Jardim Botânico (1.2km)
Rause Cafe + Vinho (170m)
R Cândido Lopes
Praça General Osório
R Voluntários da Pátria
R José Loureiro
R João Negrão
R Pedro Ivo
R Barao do Rio Branco
R André de Barros
R Francisco Torres
R Doutor Faivre
R General Carneiro
Av Vicente Machado
R Vison de Nácar
Av Marechal Floriano Peixoto
Lourenço Pinto
R Visconde de Guarapuava
Manu (700m)
P.I.T.
Aeroporto Executivo Bus Stop
Comendador Araújo
R Westfalen
R Alameda Dr Muricy
Bus 208 to Airport
Av Presidente Afonso Camargo
Praça Rui Barbosa
Travessa Frei Caneca
R 24 Horas
Emiliano Perneta
Av 24 de Maio
Praça Eufrásio Corrêia
Av 7 de Setembro
Rodoferroviária de Curitiba
Train Station
R Doutor Pedrosa
Shopping Patio Batel (1.2km)
Barolo (1.5km)
Shopping Estação
Av Silva Jardim
Afonso Pena International (16km)
Vd Colorado
1 2 3 4 5 6 7 8 9 10 11 12 13

Curitiba

cozy little hostelry is as good as it gets for the price in Brazil and is one of the more pleasant places to stay. Thanks to its small size and homey decor, as well as very pleasant and helpful staff, the Garden Curitiba offers an air of small-town intimacy otherwise lacking in this big city.

Book and pay ahead for substantial discounts off rates listed here.

L'Avenue Apart Hotel HOTEL **$$**
(3222-5525; www.lavenueaparthotel.com.br; XV de Novembro 526; s/d/tr R$150/190/230;) One of the few places to stay on Rua das Flores, this tasteful but not-too-trendy hotel has 63 dated suites, all with kitchenettes and sitting areas, some in better condition with better layouts than others. Great value if you aren't fussed about decor.

San Juan Johnscher BOUTIQUE HOTEL **$$$**
(3302-9600; www.sanjuanhoteis.com.br; Barão do Rio Branco 354; s/d R$255/305, ste from R$380;) Behind a beautiful neoclassical facade, this renovated hotel retains much of its original architectural detail, but does not skimp on modern amenities. Stained-wood floors, painted moldings and black-and-white photos give the 24 rooms an aura of understated elegance. The lobby, designed with a Jenga-like aesthetic of stacked *imbuia* (Brazilian walnut) wood support beams and fireplace, is a sight to see.

Eating

Rua 24 Horas, near Praça General Osório, is an atmospheric street-turned-enclosed-food-court (not open 24 hours!).

Rause Cafe + Vinho CAFE **$**
(www.rausecafe.com.br; Carlos de Carvalho 696; items R$4.50-27.50; 8am-8pm Mon-Fri, to 2pm Sat;) At its heart, a smart coffeehouse (choose from specialty Bahia and Minas coffees, prepared by Chemex, Aeropress, V60, as a Greek frappe etc), but there's a great selection of eats as well (osso buco risotto, fig confit and Brie crepes) plus wine and beer. Tack on a fun chalkboard menu hovering over a retro vibe and it's your caffeine-fueled hideaway.

Mercado Municipal MARKET **$**
(www.mercadomunicipaldecuritiba.com.br; 7 de Setembro 1865; 7am-2pm Mon, to 6pm Tue-Sat, to 1pm Sun) Curitiba's excellent urban market, full of food stalls, cafes, gourmet emporiums and Brazil's first organic food court.

Bouquet Garni BUFFET **$**
(www.restaurantebouquetgarni.com; Carlos de Carvalho 271; buffet weekday/weekend R$24/30; 11am-3pm;) Most of the ingredients at this all-organic vegetarian restaurant come from the owners' farm. The menu changes daily according to what's fresh and what's in season. Rock up on a bike for a 10% discount.

★ **Barolo** ITALIAN **$$**
(3243-3430; www.barolotrattoria.com.br; Av Silva Jardim 2487; pasta for 2 R$68-137.80; noon-2:30pm & 7pm-midnight Mon-Sat, to 4pm Sun;) It's not located in Curitiba's touristy Italian neighborhood, but this upscale trattoria is the real deal. The pastas – pick your type, then pick your sauce (priced separately) – served in cast-iron pans, are an absolute revelation. We went for barolo (red pepper, cream, broccoli and tomato). Reservations are a good idea for dinner. File under 'Better than Italy.'

Swadisht INDIAN **$$**
(3015-1056; www.swadisht.com.br; Av Vicente Machado 2036; mains for 2 R$60-104; 7-11:30pm Mon-Thu, to midnight Fri & Sat;) Hankering for a fiery curry? This upscale Indian restaurant

WORTH A TRIP

VILA VELHA

Located in Campos Gerais, 93km west of Curitiba, **Parque Estadual de Vila Velha** (☎042-3228-1138; www.pontagrossa.pr.gov.br/parque-estadual-vila-velha; Brazilians/foreigners R$18/25; ⏲8:30am-3:30pm Wed-Mon) is known as the 'stone city'. The park's centerpieces are the 23 *aretinhas* (sandstone pillars), created over millions of years. The mysterious red-earth rock formations – some taking recognizable shapes such as boots and bottles – create striking silhouettes against the blue sky and green foliage.

Within the boundaries of the same park, visitors can witness another geological marvel: a series of *furnas* (craters) that are the result of underground erosion. A 90-minute bus tour stops first at the Lagoa Dourada, a lovely lagoon that attracts ample birdlife. The next stop features two yawning craters that reach depths of 54m.

From Curitiba, catch a **Princesa dos Campos** (www.princesadoscampos.com.br) bus to Vila Velha (R$27.42, 1½ hours, 7:45am or 5:15pm); morning buses to Ponta Grossa will stop here, but you'll need to catch an early morning departure to arrive early enough to see the whole park. Stop first at the park center, where you can watch an introductory video and buy tickets for the various tours.

in Batel is easily Brazil's (and maybe South America's) best. The Indian owner, manager and kitchen staff are not afraid to light you up if you beg for 'Indian spicy' (well off their three-level heat chart for locals) and our kadai chicken packed a wallop indistinguishable from India. Truly satisfying.

Yü ASIAN $$
(www.yurestaurante.com.br; Praça General Osório 485; per kg R$72.90; ⏲11:30am-3pm Mon-Fri, noon-3:30pm Sat & Sun; 📶) Reflecting Curitiba's significant Asian immigration, this pricier *por-kilo* does outstanding Korean, Chinese and Japanese dishes, including sushi, sashimi and fantastic *lula apimentada* (spicy squid salad), and a long list of other top-quality Far East fare.

Madero BURGERS $$
(www.restaurantemadero.com.br; Kellers 63; burger & fries R$29-39; ⏲11:45am-2:30pm & 6-11:30pm Mon-Thu, 6:15pm-midnight Fri, 11:45am-midnight Sat, 11am-11:30pm Sun; 📶) Now a full-fledged chain around Brazil, this award-winning burger joint started here. It's all about the crunchy bun and better-than-sex *doce de leite* petit gâteau dessert, both of which ensure your happy ending here.

★ **Manu** BRAZILIAN $$$
(☎3044-4395; www.restaurantemanu.com.br; Dom Pedro II 317; 8-/13-/17-course menu R$155/200/240, with wine R$88/122/154; ⏲8-11:30pm Tue-Sat; 📶) Not so much a meal as a journey. Manoella Buffara is Curitiba's hottest chef and her pedigree backs up her impressive menus, which come in three tasting versions in three price ranges nightly and rely heavily on regional farm co-operatives and the restaurant's own organic nursery.

'Manu' – short for Manoella – counts stints in two of the world's most famous kitchens, Noma (Copenhagen) and Alinea (Chicago), as inspiration and impetus behind her ever-evolving dishes, which often get unorthodox pairings with outside-the-box wines (São Paulo's Guaspari Syrah, for example). This is the South's only spot where gourmands can gather and gaggle over subtle culinary feats, a two-star Michelin-quality equivalent for a lot less than €300! Reservations essential.

La Varenne Gastranomia FRENCH, BRAZILIAN $$$
(☎3044-6600; www.lavarenne.com.br; Av. do Batel 1868, Shopping Pátio Batel; mains R$51-99; ⏲noon-4pm & 7pm-midnight Mon-Sat, noon-4pm Sun) Inside Curitiba's chicest shopping mall, this gourmet newcomer has seized the city's foodie brigade. Pernambucano chef Ivo Lopes' heart (and kitchen!) pumps French-Italian blood running through Brazilian veins. The results are impressive: A gorgeous *bacalhau* (cod) ravioli, perfect with a hint of a kick and free-range egg yolk; or black cod in basil sauce on a bed of supreme *mandioquinha* (a root vegetable) mashed. Stunning!

Drinking & Nightlife

On warm nights, revelers spill out of pubs and cafes onto the streets around Praça Garibaldi and Largo da Ordem, and you'll find the city's most happening nightlife around the corner of Av Vincent Machado and Alameda Taunay in trendy Batel.

★**Hop'N Roll** BAR
(www.hopnroll.com.br; Mateus Leme 950; pints R$13-29; ⏲5:30pm-1:30am Mon-Thu, to 2:30am Fri & Sat; 📶) The hophead assault on this excellent craft-beer bar's 32 draft options – served in proper pints – is relentless. Aficionados will find the lion's share of local and Southern Brazil's artisanal beers (if not on draft then on the 130+ bottle menu) and select imports – and they brew their own as well. Book ahead if you want a seat.

Txapela BAR
(www.txapela.com.br; Ébano Pereira 269; tapas R$5.50-39.90, cover Fri & Sat R$5-15; ⏲6pm-12:30am Mon-Wed, to 1:30am Thu-Sat; 📶) Two locals ran off to Spain, returned with dreams of tapas and *jamón serrano* dancing in their heads, and voila! This Spanish-themed hotspot is great for cocktails but there's an inexplicable lack of local beers for which Curitiba is known.

Bar Triângulo BAR
(XV de Novembro 36; ⏲10am-11:30pm) Don't miss the people-watching at this nearly 80-year-old bar.

☆ Entertainment

Opera de Arame THEATER
(João Gava, Parque Pedreira Paulo Leminski; ⏲8am-10pm Tue-Sun) Constructed from wire with a glass roof, this theater is among Curitiba's most unusual and enigmatic landmarks. It is surrounded by the stone quarry park, which contains an outdoor stage hosting national acts throughout the year.

ℹ Information

Wi-fi is well employed through Curitiba's hotels, restaurants and bars.

Banco do Brasil (Praça Tiradentes 410) Visa/Mastercard ATM.

Bradesco (www.bradesco.com.br; XV de Novembro 155) Visa/Mastercard ATM.

P.I.T. (Postos de Informações Turísticas, Tourist Information; ☎3225-4336; www.turismo.curitiba.pr.gov.br; Rua 24 Horas; ⏲9am-6pm) Curitiba's tourist information offices are stocked with glossy brochures and maps and are well staffed with willing and helpful employees who speak a little English as well. You'll find branches at the airport (Airport Arrivals Hall; ⏲7am-11pm) and also at Oi Torre Panorâmica (☎3339-7613; Castro Vellozo 19 , Oi Torre Panorâmica; ⏲10am-6:30pm Tue-Sun).

ℹ Getting There & Away

AIR

There are direct flights from newly expanded **Afonso Pena International Airport** (CWB; ☎3381-1515; Av Rocha Pombo s/n, São José dos Pinhais), 18km southeast of Centro, to cities throughout Brazil.

BUS & TRAIN

Curitiba's long-distance bus and train stations form a single three-block complex called the **rodoferroviária** (☎3320-3000; www.urbs.curitiba.pr.gov.br/comunidade/rodoferroviaria; Av Pres Affonso Camargo 330), which sits 2km southeast of downtown and received a World Cup 2014 makeover. Access to the departures areas is now restricted to ticket holders. Ticket counters for interstate bus travel *(interestadual)* sit on the 2nd floor of the first block; bus

BUSES FROM CURITIBA

DESTINATION	STARTING FARE (R$)	TIME (HR)	BUS COMPANY
Asunción (PY)	163	15	Pluma (www.pluma.com.br)
Buenos Aires (AR)	366	32	Pluma (www.pluma.com.br)
Florianopólis	74	5	Catarinense (www.catarinense.net)
Foz do Iguaçu	155	10	Catarinense (www.catarinense.net)
Joinville	28	2	Catarinense (www.catarinense.net)
Morretes	22	1½	Graciosa (www.viacaograciosa.com.br)
Paranaguá	27	1¾	Graciosa (www.viacaograciosa.com.br)
Rio de Janeiro	162	13	Penha (http://vendas.nspenha.com.br)
Santiago (CL)*	396	54	Pluma (www.pluma.com.br)
São Paulo	80	7	Itapemirim (www.itapemirim.com.br)

* Departs every 15 days only

companies for destinations within Paraná (*estadual*) are located on the 2nd floor of the second block. The train station block sits behind the two bus station blocks.

The Serra Verde Express train between Curitiba and Morretes via the Serra do Mar is one of the marvels of travel in Brazil.

Getting Around

URBS (www.urbs.curitiba.pr.gov.br) runs Curitiba's space-age bus system, made up of integrated station pods, known as *tubos*. City buses, several of which are electric/biodiesel buses called Hibribuses, cost R$3.30 (R$1.50 on Sundays).

TO & FROM THE AIRPORT

Bus 208 (Ligeirinho/Aeroporto) serves Centro every 30 minutes (R$3.30, 30 minutes). Catch it heading east on Av 7 de Setembro. The classier, wi-fi-enabled **Aeroporto Executivo** (☎3381-1326; www.aeroportoexecutivo.com.br; one way R$13) goes direct every 15 minutes between 5:15am (starting from *rodoferroviária*; from 6am Sunday) to 12:30am (last bus from airport) along select, well-marked Centro stops, including Teatro Guaíra, Receita Federal, Biblioteca Nacional and Rua 24 Horas. An express bus follows the same schedule but only goes between the airport, *rodoferroviária* and Estação Shopping.

MORRETES

☎0XX41 / POP 16,000

Founded in 1721 on the banks of the Rio Nhundiaquara, this calm and collected colonial town rests on an emerald-green plain at the foot of the Serra do Mar. The loveliest colonial buildings are clustered around Praça Lamenha Lins and along Rua das Flores, the cobblestone walkway that runs along the river.

The region's culinary gift to the world is *barreado*, a rib-sticking meat stew cooked in a clay pot. Originally it served to keep revelers nourished over the course of several days of Carnaval (February/March), but you can test its sustaining qualities any time of year.

Sights & Activities

The Rio Nhundiaquara is navigable by inner tube, which you can rent at the Pousada do Oasis in the village of Porto de Cima.

Parque Estadual Marumbi NATURE PARK
(☎3462-3598; 🕒7am-7pm) FREE Besides the quaint colonial center, the biggest attraction in Morretes is the Parque Estadual Marumbi, a paradise for rock climbers and nature-lovers. It contains a network of old pioneer trails that were the only connections

DON'T MISS

ALL ABOARD!

The **Serra Verde Express** (☎3888-3488; www.serraverdeexpress.com.br; Estação Ferroviária) between Curitiba and Morretes offers sublime views of threatening mountain canyons, tropical green lowlands and the vast, blue Atlantic. As you descend, watch as the climate and environment change – the weather becoming hotter and muggier, the vegetation lusher and greener.

The train leaves Curitiba at 8:15am daily, descending 900m through the lush Serra do Mar to the historic town of Morretes, arriving at noon and returning at 3pm (arriving back in Curitiba at 6:30pm). There are three classes of service. One-way economy/tourist/executive class tickets cost R$79/99/149. Executive class includes a bilingual guide (and beer!).

Views are most spectacular from the left side of the train (right side on the return trip), but the democratic computer ticketing system prevents requests – it takes turns between left and right (good luck!). Reservations are highly recommended during summer. Prices and times change frequently, so be sure to stop by the train station or check the website in advance.

If you want to make the ride a little more interesting (and start drinking at 7am!), **Cervejaria Bodebrown** (☎3082-6354; www.bodebrown.com.br; Carlos de Laet 1015; Beer Train R$370), one of Brazil's leading craft-beer breweries, runs the Beer Train on the same route three or four times per year. The trip isn't cheap, but includes unlimited tastings of five beers (usually unique or new offerings paired with bread and cheese), lunch and transport. Trust us – it's a good time!

between the coast and the highland in the 17th and 18th centuries.

Calango Expedições ADVENTURE TOUR
(☎3462-2600; www.calangoexpedicoes.com.br; Carneiro 6; ⊙9am-6pm) These eco-correct adventure-tour specialists in the historic center will get you out and about. Options include kayaking (R$90, 1½ hours), mountain biking (R$90, three hours) and Jeep tours (R$90, three hours) in the stunning surrounding scenery.

Sleeping & Eating

Most of the restaurants are along Largo Dr José Pereira on the riverfront and are open for lunch only; everyone's got *barreado*.

Hotel Nhundiaquara POUSADA $
(☎3462-1228; www.nundiaquara.com.br; General Carreiro 13; s/d R$100/165, s/d without bathroom R$80/100;) Outside, the oldest building in town sits in pristine condition front and center on the riverfront; inside, plain, wood-paneled rooms with high ceilings and cramped bathrooms with low water pressure are what you get, but there's an antiquated air about the place amongst the warped flooring and storybook setting.

The on-site restaurant is famous for its *barreado* (R$41.90), served on the breezy colonial-style terrace overlooking a lovely bend in the Rio Nhundiaquara.

Pousada do Oasis POUSADA $
(☎3462-1888; www.pousadadooasis.com.br; Estradas das Prainhas, Porto de Cima; s/d R$90/165, chalets R$175-335;) A lush walkway leads to these sweet, spacious chalets surrounded by forest, flowering bushes and tropical goodness. It makes a great base for exploring the Parque Estadual Marumbi and you can also rent inner tubes here. Transport from Morretes is erratic – you're better off in a taxi (R$15 to R$20) or make arrangements with the pousada.

★**Villa Morretes** BRAZILIAN $$
(☎3462-2140; www.barreado.com.br; Frederico de Oliveria 155; mains for 2 R$59-120; ⊙11:30am-3pm Wed-Thu & Mon, to 4pm Sat & Sun;) Amid lush gardens and babbling fountains on the more tranquil side of the river sits this scenic restaurant, a great and friendly option for regional specialties, including *barreado* (R$59.50 to R$67, depending on the seafood pairing) or fish with *maracujá* (passion-fruit) sauce.

Sit on the riverside and don't miss their version of *bolinho de chuva* on Saturdays, a sort of banana-flavored funnel cake. It's 100m on the left after you cross the bridge from the more touristy options.

Information

Tourist Office (☎3462-1024; Praça dos Imigrantes; ⊙Sat & Sun) The tourist office occupies a small kiosk just beside the riverbank near Pousada Nhundiaquara.

Getting There & Away

The Morretes train station is on a pretty square in the center of town. The **Serra Verde Express** runs to Curitiba daily at 3pm.

The bus station is about 1km from the center of town. **Viação Graciosa** (☎3462-1115; www.viacaograciosa.com.br) has seven daily buses to Curitiba (R$17.90, 1½ hours) and one to Paranaguá (R$9.73, one hour, 10:40am).

PARANAGUÁ

☎0XX41 / POP 140,500

This colorful old port, sitting serenely on the banks of the Rio Itiberê, has an appealing atmosphere of tropical decadence. Commercially important since the late 18th century, the city has some impressive churches and other public buildings, many of which are being carefully restored. For travelers, Paranaguá serves primarily as a point of departure to Ilha do Mel and Parque Nacional do Superagüi.

Sights

The city's colonial churches are simple but striking. Several churches were constructed during the 18th century, including **Igreja São Francisco das Chagas** (XV Novembro s/n; ⊙9-11am & 2-6pm Mon-Sat, 2-6pm Sun) and **Igreja São Benedito** (Conselheiro Sinimbu s/n; ⊙8am-6pm Mon-Fri, to 4pm Sat, to 5pm Sun), built specifically for the town's slaves.

Museu de Arqueologia e Etnologia MUSEUM
(Archeology & Ethnology Museum; www.facebook.com/MAEUFPR; XV de Novembro 575; ⊙8am-8pm Tue-Sun) FREE Housed in an 18th-century Jesuit college, this surprisingly great, free museum displays indigenous artifacts, primitive and folk art, and old tools and machines.

Igreja de NS do Rosário CHURCH
(Marechal Deodoro de Fonseca; ⊙7am-9pm) The oldest of the city's colonial churches is Igreja de NS do Rosário, parts of which date to 1578.

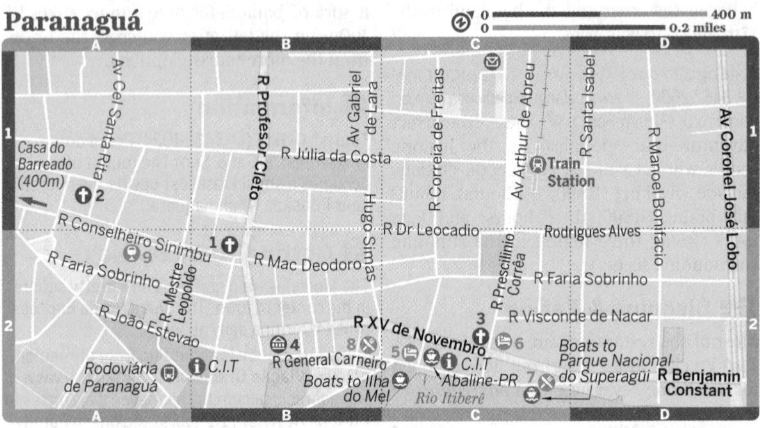

Paranaguá

Sights

1 Igreja de NS do Rosário B2
2 Igreja São Benedito A1
3 Igreja São Francisco das Chagas C2
4 Museu de Arqueologia e Etnologia B2

Sleeping

5 Hostel Continente C2
6 Hotel Ponderosa C2

Eating

7 Danubio Azul C2
8 Mercado do Café B2

Drinking & Nightlife

9 Toca do Barril A2

Sleeping & Eating

For a variety of cheap eats in a colonially draped food court, head inside the **Mercado do Café** (Carneiro 458; meals R$10-55; ⏲7am-6pm).

Hotel Ponderosa HOTEL **$**
(☎3423-2464; Prescilinio Corrêa 68; s/d R$60/80, d with view R$90; ❄📶) Occupying a restored colonial building on a prominent corner, the simple Ponderosa evokes a grand past, with its high ceilings and wide-plank wood floors. The rooms facing the port are particularly pleasing, with lots of light and lovely views of the waterfront.

Hostel Continente HOSTEL **$**
(☎3423-3224; www.hostelcontinente.com.br; General Carneiro 300; dm R$50, s/d/tr R$80/140/165; ❄📶) This HI hostel has clean if cramped dorms and doubles in an enviable location across from the ferry dock. Facilities include laundry and a communal kitchen.

★ **Casa do Barreado** BRAZILIAN **$$**
(☎3423-1830; www.casadobarreado.com.br; José Antônio da Cruz 78; per person incl dessert R$40; ⏲noon-3pm Sat & Sun) In her own home a few blocks behind the historic district, Norma cooks up real-deal *barreado* (meat stew) true to its original recipe (simmered for 24 hours in an earthen clay pot), a less commercialized version than you will find in Morretes. This weekend-only affair has earned a culinary star 15 years running. A true local experience.

Do not miss *chico balanceado*, a concoction of bananas, meringue and *manjar branco* (coconut pudding)!

Danubio Azul BRAZILIAN, SEAFOOD **$$**
(www.restaurantedanubioazul.com.br; XV de Novembro 95; mains for 2 R$32-170, per kg R$62.90; ⏲11am-3pm & 7pm-midnight Mon-Sat, to 3pm Sun) The town's best restaurant does excellent fish preparations and a tasty signature filet mignon among bland decor, but stretching water views. At lunch it's a high-quality *por-kilo* buffet.

Drinking & Nightlife

Toca do Barril BAR
(www.facebook.com/tocadobarril; Conselheiro Sinimbu 210; ⏲7pm-late Tue-Sat; 📶) This cozy cantina is Paranaguá's best, serving up a surprisingly good mix of bottled craft beers from Curitiba and Santa Catarina and live music to a wildly mixed crowd.

Information

Banco do Brasil (www.bb.com.br; Faria Sobrinho 324) Visa/Mastercard ATM.

C.I.T (Centro de Informaçãos Turísticas; www.fumtur.com.br; General Carneiro s/n, Palácio Mathias Böhn; ⏲8am-5:30pm) Bus Station (Centro de Informaçãos Turística; ☎3420-2785; www.fumtur.com.br; Praça dos Povos Arabes; ⏲8am-6pm) The two most convenient of Paranaguá's municipal tourism information booths, well equipped with brochures, maps and Ilha do Mel info.

Getting There & Away

Abaline-PR (☎3455-2616; www.abaline.com.br; General Carneiro 258) runs boats to Ilha do Mel throughout the day (R$40 return), with stops at both Nova Brasília (1½ hours) and Encantadas (two hours). In high season, there are departures from Paranaguá at 8:30am, 9:30am, 11am, 1pm, 3pm, 4:30pm and 6pm (these dwindle down to 9:30am and 3:30pm in low season). Buy tickets in advance inside Palácio Mathias Böhn accross from the dock.

Three boats – **Megatron** (☎3482-7131), **Superagüi** (☎3482-7152) and **Silvano** (☎3482-7150) – alternate runs to Parque Nacional do Superagüi (R$60 return, one hour) at 3pm Monday to Saturday, from four docks northeast of Ilha do Mel's dock.

From the **bus station** (☎3420-2925; Ponta do Caju) on the waterfront, **Viação Graciosa** (☎3462-1115; www.viacaograciosa.com.br) has 15 buses per day to Curitiba (R$25, 1½ hours) and one to Morretes (R$11.50, one hour, 5pm).

ILHA DO MEL

☎0XX41 / POP 1100

This hourglass-shaped island at the mouth of the Baía de Paranaguá is the most pristine and picturesque beach resort in all of southern Brazil, offering mostly wild beaches, good surfing waves and scenic coastal walks. The island's tranquility and lack of development are thanks in part to its isolation. Accessible only by boat, Ilha do Mel is traversed by sandy paths and has not a single car, so traffic jams throughout the island's scenic sandy lanes consist of surfboard-toting Brazilians on bicycles and bedazzled foreigners in their new Havaianas.

The fatter, northern half of the island is an ecological preserve, closed to inland exploration. The hillier southern portion is the locale of three small villages: Nova Brasília and Praia do Farol near the isthmus; and Encantadas at the far southern tip. They can be rowdy during the summer holidays, when young crowds descend on the island. But for the most part, Ilha do Mel, or 'honey island,' is the territory of surfers, campers, and beachcombers in search of serenity.

Sights

Fortaleza de NS dos Prazeres FORT

(Fort of Our Lady of the Pleasures) This fort, which dates to the 1760s, is a 3km hike from Nova Brasília via Praia da Fortaleza. Inspect the deserted fortress before climbing up to the lookout for an incredible vista of the bay.

Farol das Conchas LIGHTHOUSE

(Conchas Lighthouse) Built in 1872 on orders from Dom Pedro II, this lighthouse stands picturesquely atop a hill at the island's most easterly point. From here you have panoramic views of the island, the bay and the Serra do Mar. It's a popular spot to watch the sun drop below the horizon – don't miss it.

Grutas das Encantadas CAVES

Legend has it that these small caves at the island's southern tip are inhabited by beautiful mermaids who enchant all who come near. Signs clearly mark the way to the caves from Encantadas and Praia da Fora.

Activities

You can hire boats to explore the islands. For Ilha do Superagüi (return R$400, 40 minutes) and Ilha das Palmas (R$150 return), Táxi Náutico (☎3426-8043) leaves from Praia do Farol; for Ilha das Peças, boats (R$250, four to five hours) leave from the same dock as the inter-island ferry in Nova Brasília.

Surfing & Swimming

Ilha do Mel has no shortage of beaches. Those facing the bay enjoy warm waters gently lapping at the white sand, while those facing the ocean boast the big surf. But almost all of them are unspoiled, marked only by windswept dunes, forested hills and rocky outposts. Praia da Fora and Praia Grande are a 20-minute walk (2km) from Nova Brasília and a 40-minute walk (4km) from Encantadas. According to local surfers, in winter these beaches have the best waves in Paraná.

Praia do Farol is the long stretch of sand between the Nova Brasília dock and the Farol das Conchas. It is backed by the swampy, grassy protected area of the *restinga* (a tropical and subtropical moist broadleaf forest

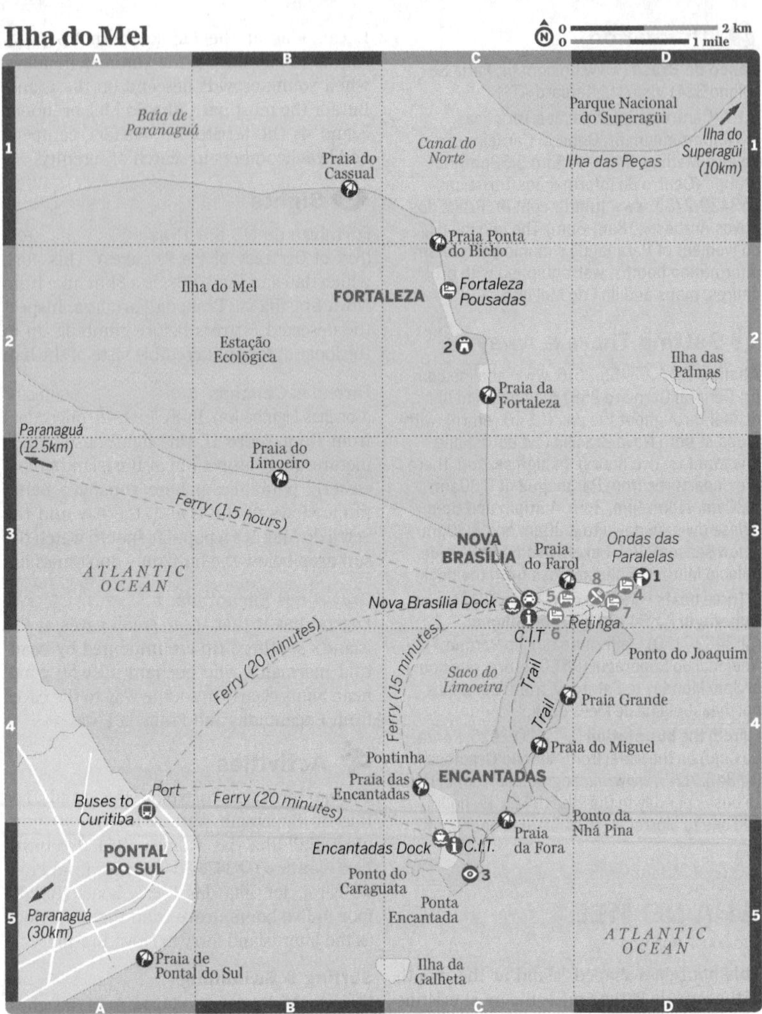

Ilha do Mel

Sights

1 Farol das Conchas....D3
2 Fortaleza de NS dos Prazeres....C2
3 Grutas das Encantadas....C5

Sleeping

4 Enseada das Conchas....D3
5 Pousada das Meninas....C3
6 Pousadinha Ilha do Mel....C3
7 Treze Luas....D3

Eating

8 Ilha do Mel Cafe....D3

unique to Brazil), which also preserves the natural beauty of the beach. Surfers congregate at the base of the hill and ride the legendary **Ondas das Paralelas**.

If you didn't bring your surfboard, you might prefer the calmer, warmer waters of the beaches that face the shallow bay. In the north, **Praia da Fortaleza**, often nearly deserted, allows you to bathe in the shadow of the 18th-century Portuguese fort. The best beach near the settlement of Encantadas is **Praia da Fora**, which has big waves and a few stalls selling *cervejas* (beers) and *sucos* (fruit juices).

Astral da Ilha Surf Club WATER SPORTS
(☎3426-8196; www.astraldailha.com.br; ⏰9am-6pm) This well-organized outfit based out of Pousada Astral da Ilha in Vila do Farol is the spot to come for surf lessons and stand-up paddle instruction (per hour R$80 to R$100) and surfboard (per hour/day R$25/50) and SUP (per hour/day R$50/100) rentals.

Cycling

Biking is a great way to beat the heat and land on the sand faster. Note that you cannot take bikes to Encantadas due to large rocks in the path.

Pura Vida BICYCLE RENTAL
(☎3426-8138; Caminho do Farol s/n, Nova Brasília; per hr/day R$15/60; ⏰9am-8pm) Tony and his English-speaking partner rent the best single-gear beach cruisers on the island. It's on your left just past the ferry dock.

Sleeping & Eating

To escape the summer crowds, head to the few **pousadas** around Fortaleza, though you are a good one-hour, 3km hike from the Nova Brasília pier. Prices listed are for the summer high season – book ahead for holidays and any November-to-March weekend. Bare-bones rooms go for as little as R$80 per person – try the perfectly clean **Farol das Estrelas** (☎3426-8158; r per person R$80). Expect discounts of 20% to 50% between April and October.

Nova Brasília & Praia do Farol

Pousadinha Ilha do Mel POUSADA $
(☎3426-8026; www.pousadinha.com.br; Caminho do Farol s/n, Nova Brasília; r from R$140, r without bathroom from R$80; ❄📶) A newer annex of chic rooms built from local hardwoods and outfitted with hammocks and solar-heated water are the best bet, though the cheaper rooms are the most comfortable and best-value for money for centavo-pinchers. The Pousadinha has a popular **restaurant** serving pastas and seafood (mains R$56 to R$96 for two people) open to non-guests.

★ **Pousada das Meninas** POUSADA $$
(☎3426-8023; www.pousadadasmeninas.com.br; s/d without bathroom R$232/310, with bathroom R$320/400, chalets R$460, all incl dinner; ❄📶) 🍃 Built from driftwood and recycled material, this pousada offers the charm of a guesthouse and the friendliness of family. Hung with hammocks and chock-full of cutesy kitsch around every turn, the simple but tasteful rooms are set around a cozy garden. From December 15 to March 1, organically-inclined half-board meal plans are obligatory.

Enseada das Conchas POUSADA $$
(☎3426-8040; www.pousadaenseada.com.br; s/d/tr R$270/363/495; ❄📶) This quaint pousada has four well-appointed guestrooms painted in striking colors and decorated according to themes ('Sunrise,' 'Sea Blue' etc). A wide deck is shaded by a thatch roof and scattered with lounge chairs and 14-some odd cats. It's steps from the lighthouse and the island's best surf beach, and homespun hospitality comes courtesy of veteran innkeepers Carlos and Sueli.

Ilha do Mel Cafe CAFE
(☎3426-8065; www.pousadailhadomelcafe.com.br; Farol das Conchas; crepes R$12-25; ⏰9am-6pm Mon-Thu, to 9pm Fri-Sun; 📶) This charming blue house is on the path between Nova Brasília and Farol das Conchas. It offers charged wi-fi for non-paying customers (per hour R$3), average food, the island's best espresso (R$4.50), rooms for rent (from R$400) and information about the island. It's about the atmosphere.

★ **Mar e Sol** SEAFOOD $$
(Praça Felipe Valentim, Farol dos Conchas; meals R$18-30; ⏰11am-10pm; 📶) En route to the lighthouse, Mar e Sol serves spectacular fish, shrimp or crab *moquecas* (R$87 to R$125 for two), seafood risottos and cheaper daily specials in individual portions. Junior, the local pet parrot, offers recommendations.

Praia Grande & Praia da Fora

★ **Astral da Ilha** POUSADA $$$
(☎3426-8196; www.astraldailha.com.br; Praia de Fora; r from R$450, with meals from R$690; ❄📶) 🍃 Their own craft beer? Hibiscus caipirinhas? In-house masseuse? Surf/SUP school? Jazz Festival on premises every August? They are doing things a little differently at this internationally-themed (Bali, Africa, Hawaii) and sustainable top-end choice – all said and done, the island's best. Bungalows, fashioned 100% from recycled woods, feature fireplaces and sinks made from giant seashells and tree trunks. The more jungly and discreet Suites da Figeira are flanked by a 100-year-old fig tree.

Treze Luas POUSADA $$$
(☎3426-8067; www.pousadatrezeluas.com.br; s/d from R$340/425; ❄📶) Brightened by

OFF THE BEATEN TRACK

PARQUE NACIONAL DO SUPERAGÜI

Composed of the Superagüi and Peças islands, this national park in the Baía de Paranaguá is covered by mangroves and salt marshes, which support an amazing variety of bird and plant life. The national park is part of the 4700 sq km of Atlantic forest reserves in Paraná and São Paulo states that were given Unesco World Heritage status in 1999.

The park is famous for its array of orchids. Hummingbirds and toucans live here, not to mention the roseate spoonbill and the stunning Brazilian tanager. Every evening at sunset, hundreds – sometimes thousands – of red-tailed parrots return to roost in the canopy on **Papagaio Island**. Dolphins are often sighted in the waters between Ilha do Superagüi and Ilha do Mel. Other mammals are more elusive, but include agoutis, pacas, deer, howler monkeys and pumas. The park is also home to the endangered black-faced lion tamarin, though it is rarely sighted.

The national park is not open to visitors, although boats are allowed to motor around the islands. Boat trips depart from Ilha do Mel and the tiny fishing village of **Barra do Superagüi**, one of the few settlements within the confines of the protected area. It's worth spending a day in the village to get a taste of life in a place still relatively untouched by tourism.

There is one boat to Ilha do Superagüi from Paranaguá ($60 return, three hours) Monday to Saturday at 3pm. Expect prices upwards of R$280 to hire a private boat for up to four people. To make transportation arrangements in advance, contact Dalton at **Pousada Superagüi** (☎3482-7149; www.pousadasuperagui.com.br; Principal s/n; r per person R$60; @).

whimsical artwork and bold-colored linens, this charming pousada offers shiny stained-wood walls and cool tile floors (some rooms have private verandas) and newer beachfront rooms. A common porch overlooks a makeshift Zen garden flocked by striking-red Brazilian tanagers.

Encantadas

Encantadas is less charming than Nova Brasília; there is a party scene on the beach itself, which has more infrastructure than other beaches, and the contrasting atmosphere is otherwise a quieter mash-up of simpler residential abodes with vaguely hippy-dippy transients, campers and backpackers. The walk from Nova Brasília to Encantadas is about 4.5km and is exposed to bright sun.

Hostel Encantadas Ecologic HOSTEL $
(☎9678-6428; www.facebook.com/hostelcantadasecologic; Encantadas; camping per person R$20, dm R$35, with bathroom R$45, d with/without bathroom R$110/80;) The island's cheapest hostel is a colorful though extremely rustic choice, with rickety dorms and private rooms. Breakfast is R$10.

★ **Bob Pai e Bob Filho** POUSADA $$
(☎3426-9006; www.pousadabobpaibobfilho.com.br; Praia de Encantadas s/n; r R$270; @) 'Father Bob and Son Bob' easily wins the island personality contest with nine unadorned but well-equipped rooms (flat-screen TVs, mini bars, beach kits – some with hammock-strewn patios) surrounding the atmospheric Captain's Bar and knickknack-peppered gardens.

Recanto Francês POUSADA $$
(☎3426-9105; www.recantodofrances.com.br; s/d with fan R$120/200;) Though the French have now departed, the charming Luciane has taken over this pousada steps from Mar do Fora beach and is ensuring the rustic but colorful clapboard rooms surrounding a pleasant garden remain good hospitality for money. Her *crepiocas* (a mix between a crepe and tapioca) at breakfast are a nice touch.

Shams MIDDLE EASTERN $
(mains R$14-28; 7-11pm Tue-Sun May-Sep, 7pm-midnight Thu-Tue Oct-Apr) Yassir, a first-generation Lebanese descendant, threw down a couple of plastic tables in the sand and now churns out great shawarma, falafel, homemade burgers and – drumroll, please – banoffee pie!

Praça de Alimentação SEAFOOD $
(Mar da Fora; meals from R$20; 9am-6pm Mar-Nov, 8am-7pm Dec-Feb;) This beachside restaurant complex located south of

Encantadas serves simple, fresh and cheap dishes for lunch, along with a dose of *forró* (popular music of the Northeast) til late on Friday and Saturday nights in summer.

★ **Fim da Trilha** BRAZILIAN, SPANISH **$$**
(☎3426-9017; www.fimdatrilha.com.br; mains R$37-53; ⌚noon-3pm & 7-10:30pm; 📶) One of the island's best restaurants is a definitive don't-miss for its real-deal spicy, Spain-indistinguishable paellas served – stop the presses! – in individual portions (R$41 to R$53), including a vegetarian option. Decent beers (Baden Baden, Eisenbahn) are available, but the most interesting chaser is the *caipikult*, a caipirinha made with Yakult, a milky probiotic drink. Try it!

ℹ Orientation

Most of the hotels are clustered in the village of Nova Brasília, which occupies the isthmus linking the two ends of the island, and Praia do Farol, the beach that stretches east from here. The landmark lighthouse sits atop a *morro* (hill) on its easternmost point. Another, smaller settlement, Encantadas, at the southern end of the island, is the closest point to the mainland. A 6km trail on the east coast links the two towns, traversing a series of undeveloped beaches including Praia da Fora, Praia do Miguel and Praia Grande.

ℹ Information

There are no banks, ATMs or pharmacies on the island, so plan ahead. The post office, health center and Polícia Militar are clustered together near the ferry dock in Nova Brasília.

C.I.T (Centro de Informaçãos Turística; www.fumtur.com.br; Arrival Dock, Nova Brasília; ⌚8am-7pm, to 8pm Nov-Mar) Encantadas (Centro de Informaçãos Turística; www.fumtur.com.br; Encantadas; ⌚8am-noon & 2-6pm, closed Mon & Tue) Helpful tourist information booths.

ℹ Getting There & Away

Abaline-PR (☎3455-2616; www.abaline.com.br; General Carneiro 258) runs boats (R$40 return) at 8:30am, 9:30am, 11am, 1pm, 3pm, 4:30pm and 6pm in summer (these dwindle down to 9:30am and 3:30pm in low season) from the jetty opposite Paranaguá's tourist office, stopping first in Nova Brasília (1½ hours), and afterwards in Encantadas (two hours). Back to the mainland, boats depart Nova Brasília for Paranaguá in summer at 7:30am, 10am, 1:30pm, 3:30pm, 4:30pm, 6:30pm and 7pm. In low season, departures are 8am and 5pm during the week and 10am and 5pm on weekends. All boats leave a half hour earlier from Encantadas.

Alternatively, **Viação Graciosa** (☎3462-1115; www.viacaograciosa.com.br) runs six daily buses from Curitiba to Pontal do Sul (R$34.50, 2½ hours), on the mainland opposite Encantadas, where you can embark for the 20-minute crossing to Nova Brasília or Encantadas (R$30 return). In high season, boats leave every half-hour from 8am to 8pm from Pontal and 7am to 8pm from Ilha do Mel; in low season, every hour.

If you arrive with clunky wheeled luggage, a battalion of wooden cart-wielding sand porters have your back: from Nova Brasília, it's R$30 as far as Farol and R$40 to Praia Grande.

ℹ Getting Around

It's a 1½-hour walk along the coast from Nova Brasília to Encantadas; otherwise, grab the island ferry from one village to the other (R$10, 15 minutes, seven to nine daily).

IGUAÇU FALLS & AROUND

☎0XX45 / POP 256,000

Rising in the coastal mountains of Paraná and Santa Catarina, the Rio Iguaçu snakes west for 600km, picking up a few dozen tributaries along the way. It widens majestically and sweeps around a magnificent forest stage, before plunging and crashing in the tiered cascades known as Iguaçu Falls.

Thousands of years before they were 'discovered' by Europeans, the falls were a holy burial place for the Tupi-Guarani and Paraguas tribes. Spaniard Don Alvar Nuñes happened upon the falls in 1541, dubbing them 'Saltos de Santa María.' But this name didn't stick and the Tupi-Guarani name, Iguaçu (Great Waters), did. In 1986, Unesco declared the region a World Heritage site; a New Seven Wonders of Nature accolade followed in 2011.

ℹ IGUAZÚ/IGUAÇU TOURIST CORRIDOR

Mercosul (South American free trade zone) nationals can enter Argentina in the area around Iguazú Falls for less than 72 hours without a visa. Although citizens from most western European countries do not need a visa, citizens of the United States, Australia and Canada must pay a reciprocity tax in advance, even for day trips to the Argentine side of the falls. If you need a visa for Brazil, you will need it to visit the falls from Argentina, even on an organized day trip.

Iguaçu Falls

Nearly nothing wows like the breathtaking roar of the Rio Iguaçu splicing the edge of Brazil and Argentina, creating the spectacular Iguaçu Falls. Encompassing some 275 individual falls occupying an area more than 3km wide and 80m high, it's wider than Victoria Falls, higher than Niagara and more beautiful than both.

Brazilian Side

The main event of Parque Nacional do Iguaçu in Brazil is the Trilha das Cataratas, or 'Waterfall Trail.' This 1200m trail follows the shore of the Iguaçu river, providing innumerable photo ops and a grand overview of the falls along the way. It terminates at the bottom of Garganta do Diabo, or 'Devil's Throat,' the most spectacular part of the falls. A manmade walkway allows you to go out to the middle of the river so the force of rushing water seemingly surrounds you. Expect to be dazzled – and doused.

Argentine Side

Argentina's Parque Nacional Iguazú offers the single-most heart-stopping moment at Iguaçu Falls: as the 2km elevated plank walkway from Estación Garganta del Diablo culminates at the top of Garganta del Diablo, Mother Nature's absolute ferocity very suddenly and shockingly leaps from the stuff of legend to very real indeed. The sound and the fury is nothing short of electrifying.

Boat Trips

While admiring the falls from above, you will surely spot fearless adventurers experiencing the falls from below. You can get closer to Garganta do Diabo on

TCYUEN / GETTY IMAGES ©

EMILY RIDDELL / GETTY IMAGES ©

1. Iguaçu Falls
2. Viewing platform, Iguaçu Falls
3. Toucan

RMNUNES / GETTY IMAGES ©

boat tours on the Argentine side, but the Brazilian version is more elaborate. Plus Brazilian boats have a backup motor and are Navy-inspected. See Macuco Safari (p285) and Iguazú Jungle Explorer (p280).

Outdoor Adventures

Parque Nacional do Iguaçu covers 550 sq km of rainforest, most of which is inaccessible to anybody but the wildlife. Hiking is more rewarding in the morning, when the weather is cooler and birds and animals are more active. Look for butterflies, parrots, parakeets, woodpeckers, hummingbirds, toucans, lizards and spiders, among more elusive creatures such as monkeys, deer, sloths and anteaters. A worthwhile activity to tack on your day is a visit to the 5-hectare Parque das Aves, home to 800-plus species of birds, living in 8m-high aviaries that are constructed right in the forest, some of which you can walk through.

Aerial Views

While the Brazilian side gives the grand overview of the falls and Argentina the up-close-and-personal look, no view is quite as memorable as fitting the entire motherlode into one panoramic camera frame. Helisul, next to the entrance to Parque Nacional do Iguaçu, offers 10-minute helicopter tours of the falls for up to four or seven people at a time.

Foz do Iguaçu

The Brazilian city of Foz do Iguaçu went through a period of frenzied growth during the 18 years that Itaipu Dam was under construction (completed in 1982), when the population increased more than fivefold. It was an edgy place then, but it has since settled down.

Tours

There are no tours offering both sides of the falls in the same day, but it can be done. Be on the Brazilian side bang at opening at 9am, get out of there on a Rio Uruguay (www.riouruguaybus.com.ar) bus to Puerto Iguazú's bus station (eight departures per day, you'll want the 10am, 11am, noon or 1pm to make it happen) and transfer to the local bus to the falls. Be sure to be on a bus back to Brazil by 6pm.

Almost all the hotels in Foz do Iguaçu offer tours to the Argentine park for around R$150 (you'll save R$25 or so and a few hours if you opt to go independently).

Macuco Ecoaventura/ Safari BOAT TOUR, HIKING
(3574-4244; www.macucosafari.com.br; Brazil) Boat tours and hiking on the Brazilian side.

Iguazú Jungle Explorer BOAT TOUR
(03757-421696; www.iguazujungle.com) Offers three combinable tours: most popular is the short boat trip leaving from the Paseo Inferior that takes you under one of the waterfalls for a high-adrenaline soaking (AR$350). The Gran Aventura combines this with a jungle drive (AR$650), while the Paseo Ecológico (AR$200) is a wildlife-oriented tour in inflatable boats upstream from the falls.

Sleeping

Av das Cataratas on the way to the falls is lined with chain and convention-style hotels. Don't be shy about trying to negotiate a lower price if the hotel is not full.

★ **Tetris Container Hostel** HOSTEL $
(Map p282; 045-3132-0019; www.tetrishostel.com.br; Av das Cataratas 639; dm R$35-40, d from R$160;) Brazil's coolest hostel is crafted from 15 shipping containers – even the pool is a water-filled shipping container! – and makes full use of other industrial byproducts as well, like sinks made from oil drums. Colorful bathrooms brighten the dorms (a four-bed female plus 10- and 12-bed mixed) and the patio/bar area is tops. Adorable staff to boot.

★ **Hostel Natura** HOSTEL $
(3529-6949; www.hostelnatura.com; Av das Cataratas Km 12.5; camping/dm per person R$28/50, s/d/tr without bath R$105/130/154, d/tr R$140/150;) This hostel is set on a gorgeous piece of land, amid two small lakes and lush scenery. The rooms themselves are pleasant and tidy, and there's ample outdoor lounge space, a restaurant and a fun bar. The hostel is 12km from town on the way to the falls. Cash only.

Pousada Sonho Meu GUESTHOUSE $
(Map p282; 045-3573-5764; www.pousadasonhomeufoz.com.br; Mem de Sá 267; s/d R$160/210;) What from the outside looks like an administrative building becomes a delightful oasis barely 50m from the local bus terminal. Rooms are newly upgraded and simply decorated with bamboo; there's a standout pool (complete with a mini waterfall!), breakfast area and outdoor guest kitchen; and a warm welcome throughout.

Maricá Bed & Breakfast B&B $
(9102-8900; www.maricabedbreakfast.com; Gregório Dotto 118; r R$160-300;) For something more personal, the friendly innkeeper at this intimate guesthouse runs a one-woman show to the tune of all sorts of traveler accolades. There are four-themed rooms, all colorful and classic, and a spiffy little pool and walled garden. She's none too fond of walk-ins, so reserve ahead. It's a 3.5km walk to the action on Av Jorge Schimmelpfeng.

Hotel Rouver HOTEL $
(Map p282; 3574-2916; www.hotelrouver.com.br; Av Jorge Schimmelpfeng 872; s/d/tr from R$90/120/165;) This recently renovated budget hotel has a boutiquey feel and a lot on offer for the price, including free airport pickup, cable TV and a good continental breakfast. No need to spring for higher categories unless you're just dying for a minibar and small terrace.

Hotel Del Rey HOTEL $$
(Map p282; 045-2105-7500; www.hoteldelreyfoz.com.br; Tarobá 1020; s/d R$255/270;) Friendly, spotless and convenient hotel, more intimate than most of the big guns around. The completely modernized rooms are spacious and comfortable, facilities are excellent and the breakfast buffet is huge.

Iguazú Falls

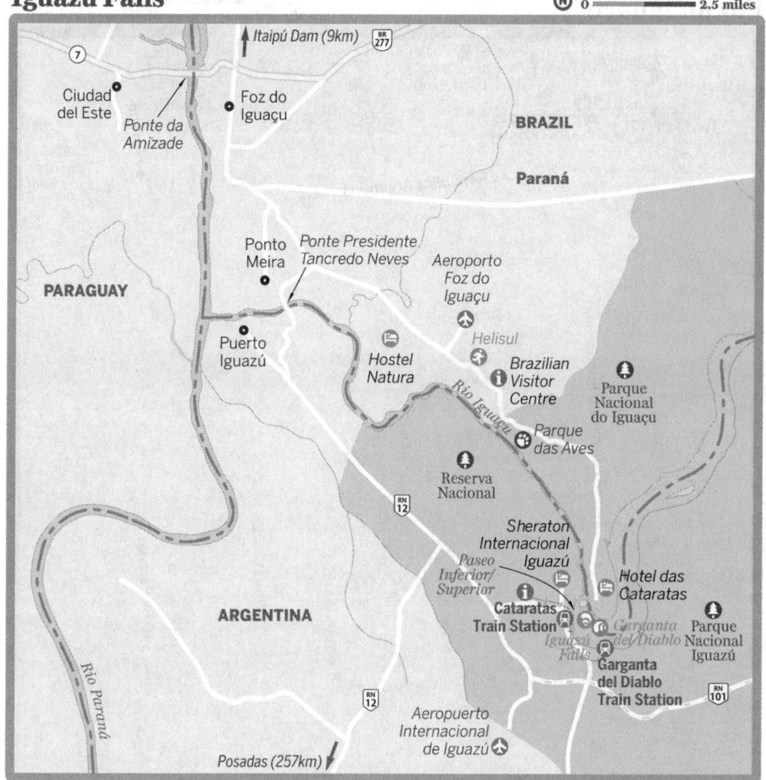

Hotel Rafain Centro HOTEL $$
(☎045-3521-3500; www.rafaincentro.com.br; Marechal Deodoro da Fonseca 984; s/d rack rate R$347/435, discounted R$170/215;) Much more appealing than some of the hulking megahotels around town, the Rafain is an excellent value, four-star businesslike hotel with plenty of style, artistic detail and friendly staff. Rooms are simple with large balconies and there's a cracking pool and terrace. Nice poolside happy hour and Saturday *feijoada* (R$37).

★**Hotel das Cataratas** HOTEL $$$
(Map p281; ☎045-2102-7000; www.belmond.com; BR469, Km32; r without/with view from R$1966/2317, ste from R$2136;) You'll find spectacular views from the Sheraton on the Argentine side, but nowhere on either side of the falls is as delightful, delicious and deluxe as this 193-room, pink-as-peppercorns Belmond luxury hotel. The grand colonial edifice is located within Parque Nacional do Iguaçu, just across from the main trail to the falls.

The coup of staying here is access to the park after hours, which includes the Trilha das Cataratas – the waterfall is your oyster! There's a spa, fitness center and the classiest restaurant in the region by an incalculable margin. The dinner-only **Itaipu** (mains R$71 to R$126), which serves fine-dining rarities in these parts like rabbit, lobster tail and *pirarucu*, a farm-controlled Amazonian fish. (Non-guests are welcomed for dinner with reservations). There's a classic bar with American-style jazz and, if you're not tired of getting wet, the pool ain't too shabby, either.

Eating

True gourmands will find the best dining experiences – and service – in Puerto Iguazú in Argentina. Start with La Rueda.

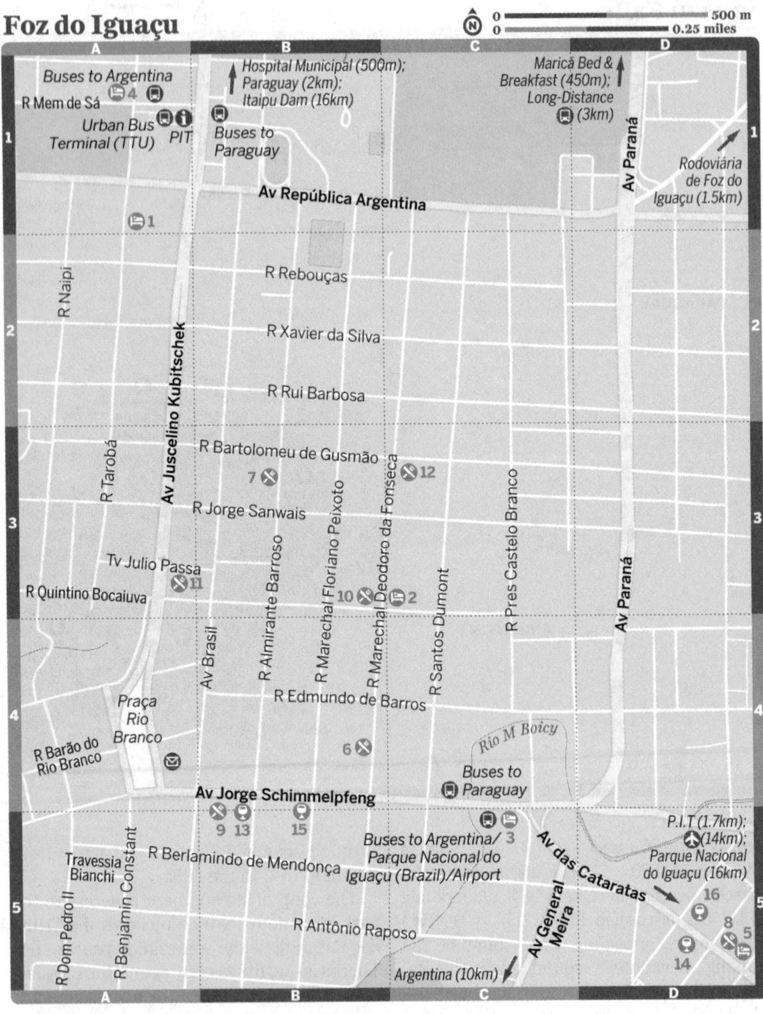

Foz do Iguaçu

Sleeping

1 Hotel Del Rey A1
2 Hotel Rafain Centro C3
3 Hotel Rouver C5
4 Pousada Sonho Meu A1
5 Tetris Container Hostel D5

Eating

6 Beduinos B4
7 Chef Lopes B3
8 Empório com Arte D5
9 Oficina do Sorvete B5
10 Trapiche B3
11 Tropicana A3
12 Vó Bertila C3

Drinking & Nightlife

13 Capitão Bar B5
14 Cervejario D5
15 Rafain Chopp B5
16 Zeppelin Old Bar D5

Tropicana CHURRASCARIA $

(Map p282; www.pizzariareopicana.com.br; Av Juscelino Kubitschek 228; buffet R$26; ⏲11am-3:30pm & 6:30-11:30pm; 📶) This all-you-can-eat shoestring savior offers absolutely ridiculous taste for money. Expect a madhouse.

Oficina do Sorvete CAFE $

(Map p282; www.oficinadosorvete.com.br; Av Jorge Schimmelpfeng 244; per kg sandwiches/ice cream R$44.50/45; ⏲1pm-12:30am; 📶👪) Take a dive into nearly 50 colorful, beat-the-heat ice-cream flavors on hand, from decadent *(doce de leite, caramelo, coco quemado)* to exotic fruits *(jabuticaba)* to inebriating (caipirinha).

Beduinos MIDDLE EASTERN $

(Map p282; www.beduinos.com.br; Marechal Deodoro de Fonseca 755; mains R$9-23; ⏲6pm-midnight Tue-Sun) Foz's Lebanese community is second in size only to São Paulo, and this Arab cheapie is a nice by-product of that immigration. Great shawarma, a long line of *esfihas* (ground beef pastries with veggies) and hummus are staples here. They aren't much for decor, but there's a pleasant and popular patio.

★ **Vó Bertila** PIZZA $$

(Map p282; www.vobertilla.com.br; Bartolomeu de Gusmão 1116; pizza R$22-68, pasta for 2 R$48-82; ⏲6:30pm-12:30am, closed Mon) This informal, family-run cantina churns out wood-fired pizza – even in personal sizes! – and authentic pastas in heaping portions. All homey and hardwoods, it's the kind of down-home Italian spot Brazil does so very well. Expect it to be packed.

Empório com Arte CAFE $$

(Map p282; www.facebook.com/emporiocomarte; Av das Cataratas 569; mains $28-62; ⏲1-11pm Mon-Sat, 2-10pm Sun; 📶) This welcomed edition to the Foz scene ('scene' used loosely) is full of country charm and swarming with town sophisticates gossiping among a potpourri of regional art and antiques. It's mainly a cafe, serving decent espresso, sweets etc, but there are a few more elaborate main courses (think duck confit in dark beer reduction) for a rustic-romantic meal.

Trapiche BRAZILIAN, SEAFOOD $$

(Map p282; ☎3527-3951; Marechal Deodoro de Fonseca 1087; mains for 2 R$65-150; ⏲6pm-midnight; 📶) The *moqueca* and other outstanding seafood stews here are big enough to sate at least a couple of big appetites, and when the kitchen is on, they're damn good. A wealth of seafood awaits and the highest priced items include lobster. There's a substantial nightly seafood buffet (R$90) in case you just can't make up your mind amid this dizzying sea of options.

Chef Lopes BRAZILIAN $$$

(Map p282; www.cheflopes.com.br; Barroso 1713; mains R$28-120; ⏲11:30am-3:30pm & 6-11pm; 📶) Intimate it's surely not, but this super-sized dining room churns out the town's best *por-kilo* lunch buffet (weekday/weekend R$47/57) with a sinister dessert spread and, for dinner, a top-end menu loaded with Argentine-cut steak options like *bife do chorizo* and non-farmed local fish like *congrio* and *surubi.*

Drinking & Nightlife

Nightlife is hopping along Av Jorge Schimmelpfeng, where you will find breezy beer gardens for early evening, lively outdoor patio bars and hot-to-trot nightclubs that stay open late. Good starting points/outdoor drinking dens include **Rafain Chopp** (Map p282; www.rafainchopp.com.br; Av Jorge Schimmelpfeng 450; mains R$34-50; ⏲4pm-2am; 📶) and **Capitão Bar** (Map p282; www.capitaobar.com; Av Jorge Schimmelpfeng 288; ⏲noon-2am Mon-Thu, to 2:30am Fri & Sat, noon-1am Sun; 📶).

★ **Zeppelin Old Bar** LIVE MUSIC

(Map p282; www.zeppelinoldbar.com; Raul Mattos 222; live-music cover R$6-30; ⏲6:30pm-midnight Tue, 6pm-1am Wed, 9pm-2am Thu-Sat; 📶) Outstanding bar serving up excellent cocktails and live music. The beautiful people congregate from Thursday onwards.

Cervejario BAR

(Map p282; www.cervejario.com.br; Av das Cataratas 428; ⏲2-10pm Tue-Sat) Great selection of regional craft beers, to drink in or take away.

Orientation

Av Brasil is the town's main street, running north to south. The long-distance bus station is located 4.5km to the northeast, but the local bus station – just north of Av República Argentina – serves the airport (15km southeast) and Parque Nacional do Iguaçu (17km southeast).

Just south of town, the junction of the Paraná and Iguaçu rivers forms the tripartite Paraguay–Brazil–Argentina border (marked by obelisks). The Ponte Presidente Tancredo Neves crosses the Rio Iguaçu about 6km from the center of town, connecting Brazil with the Argentine town of Puerto Iguazú. Just north of the center, the

Ponte da Amizade spans the Rio Paraná, crossing to the shabby Paraguayan town of Ciudad del Este aka Brazilian Shopping Paradise!

Information

Wi-fi is ubiquitous at hotels and restaurants.

Banco do Brasil (www.bb.com.br; Av Brasil 1377) Visa/Mastercard ATM.

Bradesco (www.bradesco.com.br; Av Brasil 1202) Visa/Mastercard ATM.

Correios (www.correios.com.br; Praça Getúlio Vargas 72 ; 9am-5pm Mon-Fri) Postal sevices.

Hospital Municipal (3521-1951; Adoniran Barbosa 370; 24hr)

Polícia Federal (3576-5500; www.dpf.gov.br; Av Paraná 3471) For immigration procedures.

P.I.T (0800-45-1516; www.pmfi.pr.gov.br/turismo; Av das Cataratas 2330, Vila Yolanda; 7am-11pm) Provides maps and detailed info about the area. The main office is in Vila Yolanda, out of town on Av das Cataratas towards the falls, reachable on bus 120. Other branches are at the airport (0800-45-1516; www.pmfi.pr.gov.br/turismo; Aeroporto Internacional de Foz do Iguaçu/Cataratas; 8am-10pm), long-distance bus station (0800-45-1516; www.pmfi.pr.gov.br/turismo; Av Costa e Silva 1601; 7am-6pm) and local bus station (0800-45-1516; www.pmfi.pr.gov.br/turismo; Kubitschek 1310; 7:30am-6pm).

Getting There & Away

AIR

Daily flights link **Foz do Iguaçu/Cataratas International Airport** (IGU; 3523-4244) to Lima and several major Brazilian cities. Sit on the left-hand side of the plane on arrival for good views of the falls.

BUS

The **long-distance bus station** (045-3522-3336; Av Costa e Silva 1601) is 4.5km northeast of the center of town.

Getting Around

Local bus fare is R$2.90. The local transport terminal is known as **TTU** (Terminal Turístico Urbano; 2105-1385; Av Juscelino Kubitschek 1385; 5am-midnight).

TO/FROM THE AIRPORT

Bus 120 'Aeroporto/Parque Nacional' runs to the airport (R$2.90, 30 minutes) and the Brazilian side of the waterfalls (40 minutes) every 22 to 30 minutes from 5:25am to midnight. Catch it at the local bus terminal or any stop along Av Juscelino Kubitschek south of Barbosa. Bus 120 'Centro/TTU' goes from the airport to Centro (exit to the far left end and look for blue 'Ônibus' sign).

Taxis run around R$20 to the falls and R$50 to Centro.

TO/FROM THE BUS STATION

City buses 105 and 115 (R$2.90) cover the 6km between the long-distance bus station and the local terminal downtown. Taxis cost R$55 to the Brazilian side of the falls, R$60 to the Argentine border and R$50 to the Paraguayan border.

TO/FROM THE FALLS

For the Brazilian side of the falls, catch the 'Aeroporto/P Nacional' bus (R$2.90) to the park entrance. You can catch it in the local bus terminal, or at stops along Av Juscelino Kubitschek and Av Jorge Schimmelpfeng.

To get to the Argentina side, catch a Puerto Iguazú bus (R$4, one hour) on Mem de Sá across from the local bus terminal or along Av das Cataratas, closer to most hostels. They pass every 30 minutes or so between 6:15am and 7:15pm (fewer on Sunday). At Puerto Iguazú bus station, Río Uruguay (www.riouruguaybus.com.ar) services the falls (AR$100 return, 30 minutes) frequently between 7:20am and 8:50pm.

BUSES FROM FOZ DE IGUAÇU

DESTINATION	STARTING FARE (R$)	TIME (HR)	BUS COMPANY
Asunción	55	6½	Sol del Paraguay (www.soldelparaguay.com.py)
Buenos Aires	290	18	Crucero del Norte (www.crucerodelnorte.com.ar)
Campo Grande	140	13	Eucatur (www.eucatur.com.br)
Curitiba	154	10	Catarinense (www.catarinense.net)
Florianópolis	185	16	Catarinense (www.catarinense.net)
Rio de Janeiro	274	24	Kalowa (www.expressokaiowa. com.br)
São Paulo	196	16	Kalowa (www. expressokaiowa.com.br)

Parque Nacional do Iguaçu (Brazil)

You can't miss the shiny entrance to the Parque Nacional do Iguaçu (☎3521-4400; www.cataratasdoiguacu.com.br; adult foreigners/Mercosul/Brazilians R$52.30/41.30/31.30, child R$8; ⊙9am-5pm), which houses bathrooms, ATMs, lockers, souvenir shops and vast parking facilities. You can purchase your ticket in advance on the web site and pick it up in the preferential line at the ticket windows. Once ticketed, you will be directed to board a free double-decker bus.

To visit the falls, take the bus to the third stop, site of Hotel das Cataratas (p281). Here you can pick up the Trilha das Cataratas, or 'Waterfall Trail,' a 1200m trail following the shore of the Iguaçu river, terminating at the Garganta do Diabo. From here, take the panoramic elevator to get a view of the falls from above. At the top, a short walk along the road leads to Porto Canoas station, where you will find a nice restaurant with an excellent lunch buffet (R$58) and a food court and cafe with less expensive options. Both have seating on a pleasant outdoor terrace overlooking the flats of the river.

Remember, it's always wet at the falls, and water attracts sunlight. Pack rain gear *and* sunblock. Bug repellent is a must on the walking trails. Also note that lighting for photography is best in the morning on the Brazilian side.

WARNING: PESOS, POR FAVOR!

In a tremendous feat of retrogression, credit cards are not accepted to purchase your entry ticket to Parque Nacional Iguazú (Argentina), nor dollars, euros or reais. Your options are to exchange in Foz, stop at the Banco de la Nación cash machine at the initial entrance gate to the park (often not working) or ask to be let past the ticket takers to try the Macro cash machine 200m inside the park across from Freddo (doesn't work with all cards). Your last resort is overpaying significantly for an item in the souvenir shop to the left of Banco de la Nación with dollars, euros or reais in order to receive pesos in change. Moral of the story? Exchange in Foz – your best rates are at Scappini Câmbio (Rua 24 de Março 386, Supermercado Super Muffata; ⊙8am-10pm Mon-Sat, to 8pm Sun) or hit the cash machine in Puerto Iguazú.

Activities

Boat Trips

Many claim that the way to truly experience the falls is to feel their wrath raining down on you. Boats from both sides of the border take adventurous passengers under the falls.

Macuco Safari (☎045-3574-4244; www.macucosafari.com.br; adult/child R$179/89.50) offers the Brazilian side's spectacular opportunity to get up close, personal and wet at the base of the falls. The excursion starts with a 3km ride through the jungle, with an English-speaking guide pointing out the park's flora and fauna. The second phase is a short hike (600m) to a small waterfall called Salto de Macuco (no swimming allowed). Finally, climb aboard a Zodiac for a 4km journey over flat water and rapids, and under the falls known as the Three Musketeers. You *will* get soaked. The boat ride is 30 minutes, but the whole excursion takes about two hours. Buy a protective camera/phone sleeve if you want your own photos.

To reach Macuco, get off the double-decker bus at the second stop.

Hiking

You can explore a few hiking trails in the company of a guide provided by the park (English-speaking guides are available). The Trilha Poço Preto (☎045-3529-9665; www.macucosafari.com.br; per adult/child R$278/139), run by Macuco Safari (p285), is a 9km trail that starts near the entrance (get off the bus at the first stop) – you choose to go on foot, bikes or eletric carts – and leads to the Lagoa do Poço Preto, a small lagoon that attracts birdlife. A quick boat ride and an optional paddle in a kayak complete the well-choreographed outing. The return trip is via the Trilha das Bananeiras, but you can get a lift.

Parque Nacional Iguazú (Argentina)

Parque Nacional Iguazú (☎03757-491469; www.iguazuargentina.com; adult foreigners/Mercosul/Argentines AR$260/200/160, child AR$65/50/40, parking AR$70; ⊙8am-6pm) has plenty to offer, and involves a fair amount of walking. The spread-out complex at the entrance has

GETTING TO ARGENTINA & PARAGUAY

Many nationalities can enter Argentina without a visa, but double-check before you arrive or at the **Argentine Consulate** (045-3574-2969; www.cpabl.mrecic.gov.ar; Travessia Bianchi 26; 10am-3pm Mon-Fri) in Foz do Iguaçu. Overland-traveling citizens of the United States (10 years $160), Australia (single entry $100) and Canada (single entry/five years $75/150) must pay a reciprocity tax in advance through **Provincia NET** (https://reciprocidad.provincianet.com.ar); click 'Sign Up' just under 'Log In,' follow the steps to register and pay and print out your receipt to take along with you. For Paraguay, Americans ($160), Australians ($135) and Canadians ($75 to $150) need a visa (though not unless you go beyond Ciudad del Este). Get this in advance at home or from the **Paraguayan Consulate** (045-3523-2898; fozconsulpar@mre.gov.py; R Marechal Deodoro da Fonseca 901; 9am-1pm Mon-Fri) in Foz.

To Puerto Iguazú, Argentina

If traveling by bus, at Brazilian immigration in either direction, most bus drivers won't wait around while you finish formalities. Officially, you must get a pass from the driver, get your passport stamped, then wait and reboard the next bus *from the same bus company*. The reality is that some wait, some don't; and some give you a pass and some don't. You may need to pay again. On the Argentine side, most drivers wait, but some don't; you may also need to pay again here, meaning with luck you can do this for R$4, and if you are prone to the blues, R$12. Welcome to tri-border anarchy!

It's important you pay attention as drivers ask if anyone needs to stop at immigration on the Brazilian side – but in Portuguese (or Spanish), if at all. Many travelers miss it and end up with serious immigration hassles later (ie hefty fines).

On day trips to the Argentine side of the falls, do not forget your Brazilian entry card, you are officially leaving the country and will need to leave this with Brazilian authorities. You will be issued with a new one upon return. At Argentine immigration, the bus always stops and usually waits for everyone to be processed. Both borders are open 24 hours but bus service ends around 7:15pm. The last bus you can catch is the second-to-last bus back to Brazil. If you don't, there will be no bus coming after yours to scoop you up after you finish with border formalities.

To Ciudad del Este, Paraguay

To get to the border, take a bus (R$5, 30 minutes) from Av Juscelino Kubitschek across from TTU (p284), or bus 101 or 102 from inside TTU, which pass by Ponte da Amizade, or a taxi. At the border, get your passport stamped, then catch the next bus or taxi to Ciudad del Este, or walk across the Ponte da Amizade (Friendship Bridge). If traveling further into Paraguay, you'll need to complete formalities with Brazil's Polícia Federal and the Paraguayan immigration authorities at the consulate in Foz.

various amenities, including lockers, two ATMs and a restaurant. The complex ends at a train station, where a train runs every half-hour to the Cataratas train station, where the waterfall walks begin, and the elevated walkway at **Garganta del Diablo.**

Activities

Boating

Iguazú Jungle Explorer (p280) offers two versions of this adventure for those 12 years of age and up. The Gran Aventura (AR$520) is a one-hour excursion that includes an 8km ride through the jungle on the back of a jeep and a 6km ride down the Iguazú river. The trip culminates in an up-close-and-personal tour of Salto San Martin and Garganta del Diablo. This excursion departs every 1½ hours from the visitors center near the entrance.

If your primary interest is the so-called 'waterfall baptism,' you can opt for the abbreviated Aventura Nautica (AR$270). The 12-minute trip departs from the dock opposite Isla San Martín (every 20 minutes), giving passengers a quick tour of the canyon and a sousing shower. Protective bags are provided for cameras and other gear; anything not contained therein – including you – will get wet.

Buy tickets just past the park entrance or at the Iguazú Jungle Explorer office near Estación Cataratas.

Hiking

To explore the rainforest in the national park, stop at the **Centro de Visitantes** (☎054-3757-49-1445; ⊙8am-5:45pm) near the entrance and inquire about the Sendero Macuco. This 7km trail is a rare opportunity to explore the park independently. Six interpretive stations explain the flora, including bamboo, palmitos and pioneer plants. The white-bearded manakin and toco toucan live in these parts, as does a troupe of brown capuchin monkeys. The trail's end point is the Arrechea Waterfall, a 20m cascade that has gouged out a lovely natural pool below.

Early morning is the best time for hiking. Departure before 4pm (3pm in winter) is required.

Itaipu Dam

On the Paraná river 14km north of Foz, **Itaipu Dam** (☎0800-645-4645; www.turismoitaipu.com.br; Tancredo Neves 6702; regular/special tour R$27/68; ⊙regular tour hourly 8am-4pm) trades jaw-dropping statistics with Three Gorges Dam in China for the accolade of largest hydroelectric power plant on the planet.

The statistics are startling. The dam's structures stretch for almost 9km and reach a height of more than 200m. The concrete used in its construction would be sufficient to build a two-lane highway from Moscow to Lisbon. At the height of construction, crews worked at a blinding pace, equivalent to building a 20-story office building every hour. No wonder it cost US$18 billion. The plant provides 17% of the electric energy consumed in Brazil, and 75% of the energy consumed in Paraguay. Even more extraordinary is the massive size of the construction that spans the river, the palpable power of the water rushing out of the spillway, and the endless array of power lines emanating from the plant.

Construction of the dam was controversial. Critics estimate that 700 sq km of forest was lost or compromised, with several species of plant life being driven into extinction. Many native Guarani and Tupi settlements were destroyed, as were the impressive Sete Quedas waterfalls. On the other hand, the dam's generating capacity is 14,000 megawatts of clean energy. To produce an equivalent amount in oil-burning thermoelectric plants, you'd need 434,000 barrels of oil per day. That's a lot of carbon dioxide emissions.

For its part, the Itaipu Binacional – a joint Brazilian–Paraguayan agency that administers the dam – has been sensitive to criticisms. Innovative programs have relocated animals displaced by flooding, reforested the land along the reservoir's banks, and compensated communities affected by the construction. Itaipu's public relations team is eager to publicize accomplishments, if not the downsides. So expect a barrage of propaganda when you take the regular tour *(visita panorâmica)*. A short film is followed by a visit to the central observation deck, providing a panoramic view of the complex. All information is in Portuguese and English. For a more technical tour, you'll want to indulge yourself in the truly fascinating **special circuit** (*circuito especial*; minimum age 14; 8am, 8:30am, 10am, 10:30am, 1:30pm, 2pm, 3:30pm and 4pm). This in-depth, 2½-hour tour is fascinating for anyone with engineering tendencies.

If you're wondering how this massive feat of engineering affected the local flora and fauna, check out the **Ecomuseu** (www.turismoitaipu.com.br/pt/atracoes/ecomuseu; adult/student R$10/5; ⊙8am-4:30pm Tue-Sun). If you just want to ogle it all with a pretty sunset, try the new evening catamaran tour (R$60).

To get to the Itaipu Dam, catch bus 101, 102 or, in the afternoons from 2pm to 6:38pm, 104 (R$2.90, 30 minutes), which leave every 20 to 25 minutes from Foz do Iguaçu's TTU terminal (p284).

Santa Catarina

POP 6.25 MILLION

Includes ➡

Best Places to Eat

- ➡ Bistrô Santa Marta (p297)
- ➡ Restaurante Lagoa Azul (p297)
- ➡ Urucum (p312)
- ➡ Black Sheep (p291)
- ➡ Abendbrothaus (p307)

Best Places to Stay

- ➡ Janela de Márcia (p297)
- ➡ Pousada Natur Campeche (p299)
- ➡ Pousada La Roca (p312)
- ➡ Quinta do Bucanero (p312)
- ➡ Tucano House (p296)

Why Go?

Life's a beach. At least in sunny Santa Catarina, which boasts 560km of spectacular coastline. If you like your beach deserted, there is a spot of sand for you in the south of Ilha de Santa Catarina. If you prefer a party scene, head further north on that same island. If you're all about big surf, it's up in Guarda do Embaú and Praia do Rosa, two absolutely stunning surf villages south of Florianópolis.

Sun and sand aside, the inland regions are also where Santa Catarina exhibits the profound influence of its German ancestry, most evident during Oktoberfest, Blumenau's huge festival for folk dancing, accordion playing and beer drinking (mostly beer drinking). But the alpine architecture and fresh-brewed beer are here to enjoy year-round.

Like the other southern states, Santa Catarina enjoys some of Brazil's highest standards of living, with sound infrastructure and a blonde-haired, blue-eyed population that often feels more European than Latin.

When to Go

Florianópolis

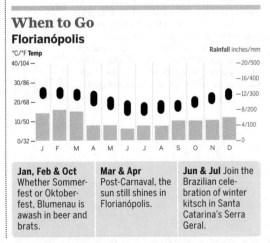

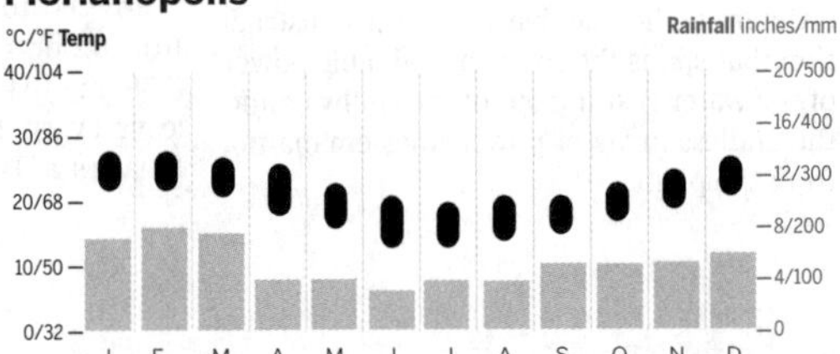

Jan, Feb & Oct Whether Sommerfest or Oktoberfest, Blumenau is awash in beer and brats.

Mar & Apr Post-Carnaval, the sun still shines in Florianópolis.

Jun & Jul Join the Brazilian celebration of winter kitsch in Santa Catarina's Serra Geral.

History

In the 1820s, a newly independent Brazil realized the strategic importance of this region on the frontier between the Spanish and Portuguese Americas. The emperor invited German-speaking immigrants to develop the land and serve as a buffer against Spanish insurgency. The German immigrants – and Italians who followed – never adopted the plantation culture of the Northeast. Instead, the economy was based on small, family-owned farms, a legacy that lives on in the region's egalitarian politics and equitable distribution of income.

Getting There & Around

Florianópolis is the state's transportation hub, with direct bus and air services to every major city in Brazil. Joinville also has direct air services to São Paulo, with connections to other major cities. Most destinations within Santa Catarina are accessible from Florianópolis by bus; services are extensive and dependable.

ILHA DE SANTA CATARINA

Ilha de Santa Catarina has a vibrant and varied coastline, from the calm, crowded bays of the north, to the wild, cliff-hugging beaches of the south. But it's not just the beaches that make this island so enchanting. A forest of protected pines shelters the east coast, while the dunes near Praia da Joaquina create a lunar landscape. The spine of mountains, luxuriant with the Mata Atlântica (Atlantic rainforest), drops precipitously down to the lovely Lagoa da Conceição.

Though technically speaking, the whole island is Florianópolis, it's downtown Floripa, known as Centro, that is both the political capital of Santa Catarina, the cultural capital of southern Brazil and the gateway to the rest of the island. The island's *bairros* (districts) can feel like completely different towns, with their own distinct personalities and infrastructure.

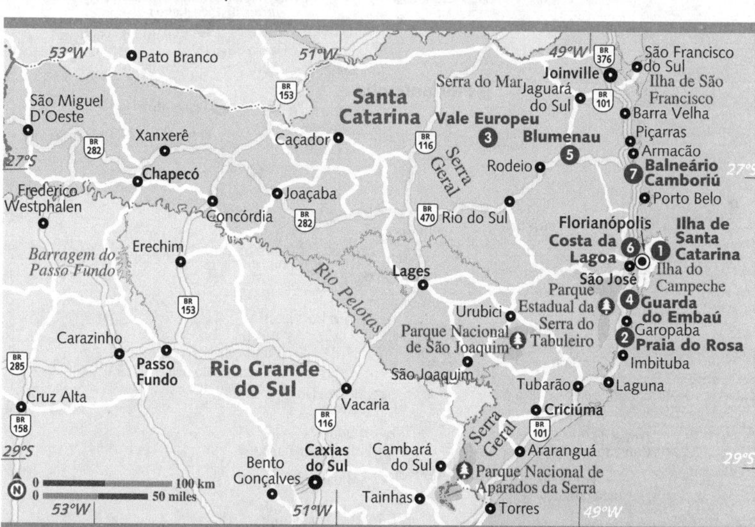

Santa Catarina Highlights

1. Sunning, surfing and snorkeling around the wild sands of beautiful **Ilha de Santa Catarina** (p289).
2. Sucking up the sophisticated surfer atmosphere in stunning **Praia do Rosa** (p312).
3. Drinking your way through Santa Catarina's rich beer culture in the **Vale Europeu** (p309).
4. Joining the parade of surfers and sun-worshipers wading through the Rio da Madre to the stunning beach at **Guarda do Embaú** (p310).
5. Saying *Prost!* to the world's third-largest Oktoberfest in **Blumenau** (p303).
6. Losing a day gorging on fresh seafood and cold beer on the waterfront in **Costa da Lagoa** (p297).
7. Beach-hopping via the fun-packed Parque Unipraias in **Balneário Camboriú** (p308).

Ilha de Santa Catarina

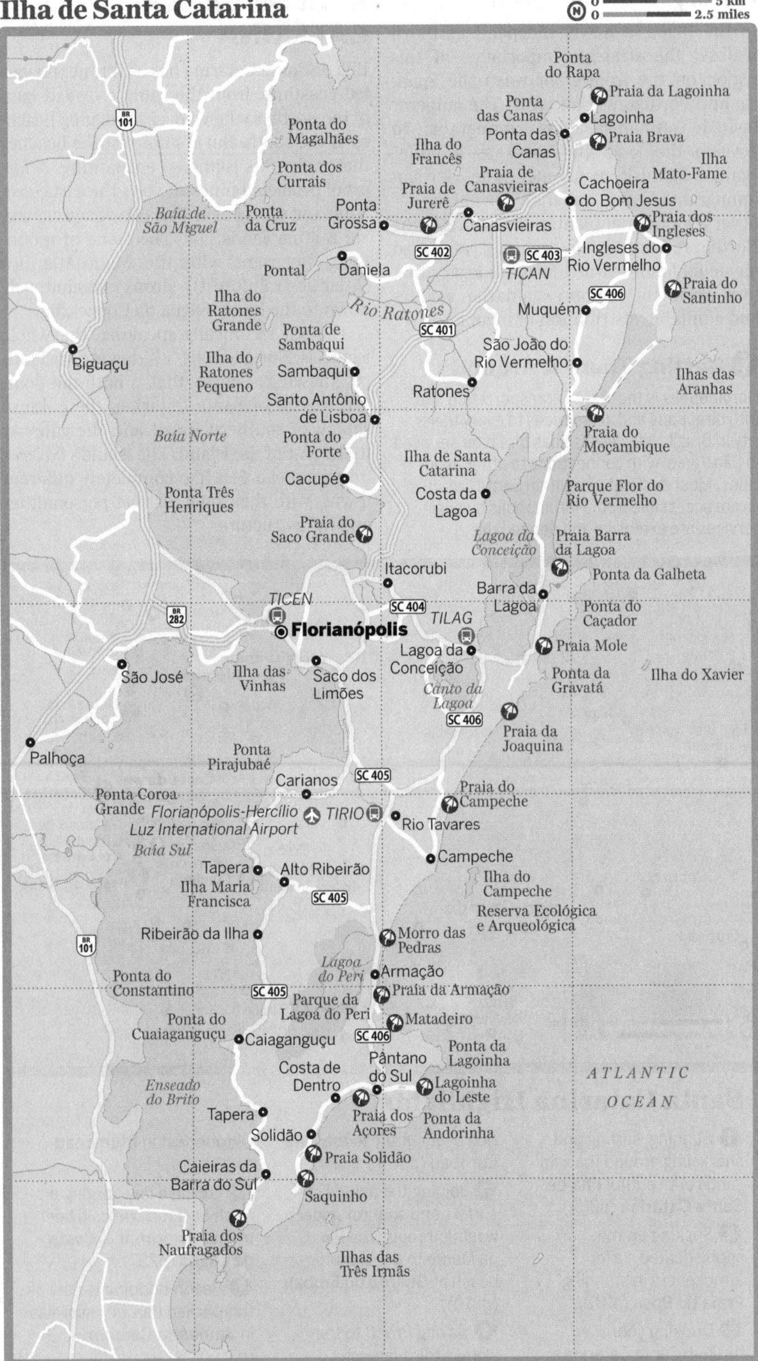

Florianópolis

☎0XX48 / POP 421,000

There are two faces to Florianópolis (Floripa). On the mainland, the industrial zone occupies the districts of Estreito and Coqueiros. Across the bay, the island holds the historic center and the chic district of Beira-Mar Norte. Two picturesque bridges link these halves. The old suspension bridge, the Ponte Hercílio Luz, is no longer open to traffic, but it still lights the night sky, acting as the defining feature of Floripa's spectacular skyline.

Sights & Activities

The center of town is the inviting **Praça XV de Novembro**, with its shady walks and nearly 150-year-old fig tree.

★Museu Histórico de Santa Catarina — MUSEUM

(Palácio Cruz e Sousa; ☎3028-8091; www.mhsc.sc.gov.br; Praça XV de Novembro 227; admission R$5; ⏲10am-6pm Tue-Fri, to 4pm Sat & Sun) Formerly the colonial governor's palace, this gorgeous must-see building boasts ornate parquetry floors and extravagant 19th-century ceilings.

Sleeping

Florianópolis suffers from a lack of budget sleeping options, although prices drop dramatically outside high season (December to March), making many midrange places more affordable. Most folks spend little more than a night in downtown itself.

Centro Sul Hotel — HOTEL $

(☎3222-9110; www.centrosulhotel.com.br; Av Hercílio Luz 652; s/d/tr R$98/148/188; ❄@📶) CSH – as it is called – is a comfortable, kitschy, budget-friendly option. Everything is a bit worn with age, but the rooms are clean and well priced, even in high season. It's the best option for a cheap overnight.

★Cecomtur Executive — HOTEL $$

(☎2107-8800; www.cecomturhotel.com.br; Arcipreste Paiva 107; s/d R$189/219; ❄@📶🏊) This efficient business hotel isn't fancy, but it's got everything you need: modern, spotless, spacious rooms; congenial, English-speaking service and a few perks besides. It's our pick for great value, especially since in reality it charges about R$30 below the rack rate.

Eating

O Padeiro de Sevilha — BAKERY $

(www.opadeirodesevilha.com.br; Esteves Júnior 2144; items R$2.50-10, bread per kg R$10.50-30; ⏲6:50am-8:30pm Mon-Fri, 7am-2pm Sat; 📶) Considered one of the top 30 bakeries in Brazil, this social magnet features an 11m-long communal table flanked by a self-serve cornucopia of fresh-baked artisanal breads and both savory and sweet treats selected from some 200 recipes.

Central — BUFFET $

(www.centralrestaurante.com.br; Vidal Ramos 174; per kg weekday R$50; ⏲11am-3pm Mon-Fri; 📶) This outstanding, award-winning *por-kilo* buffet concentrates on a more subtle selection of daily dishes, each and all focused on high-quality, home-cooked goodness. Lines out the door: not uncommon. The **Esteves Júnior** (www.centralrestaurante.com.br; Esteves Júnior 242; per kg weekday/weekend R$49.90/59.90; ⏲11am-3pm Mon-Sat) branch is open on Saturday.

★Forneria Catarina — PIZZA $$

(☎3333-0707; www.forneriacatarina.com.br; Esteves Júnior 604; pizza R$41-68; ⏲6-11:50pm; 📶) Considering it's located far, far outside São Paulo city limits, this upscale Sampa-style pizzeria does an absolute bang-up job with pizza *paulistana* – at far more accommodating prices. We reckon half *rustica* (arugula, Parma ham), half *siciliana* (grilled eggplant, smoked mozzarella) is the perfect combination.

Box 32 — SEAFOOD $$

(www.box32.com.br; Mercado Público; mains R$34.50-69; ⏲10am-8pm Mon-Fri, to 4pm Sat) You'll often find local celebrities at this historic bar and restaurant in the Mercado Municipal (now dressed in newly-expanded digs) indulging in a happy hour of frothy house-brewed beer, fresh seafood and *pata negra* ham imported from Spain.

★Black Sheep — JAPANESE $$$

(☎9189-9015; www.theroof.com.br; Majestic Palace Hotel, Av Beira Mar 2746; omakase R$125, rolls R$13-44; ⏲7:30pm-midnight Wed-Sat; 📶) Korean/Japazilian chef Emerson Kim and his Latvian wife/hostess honed their skills at Nobu (yes, *that* Nobu). You will find a grand total of *zero* items with cream cheese; but perhaps more surprising are the shockingly fair prices. The R$125 *omakase* (chef's

Florianópolis

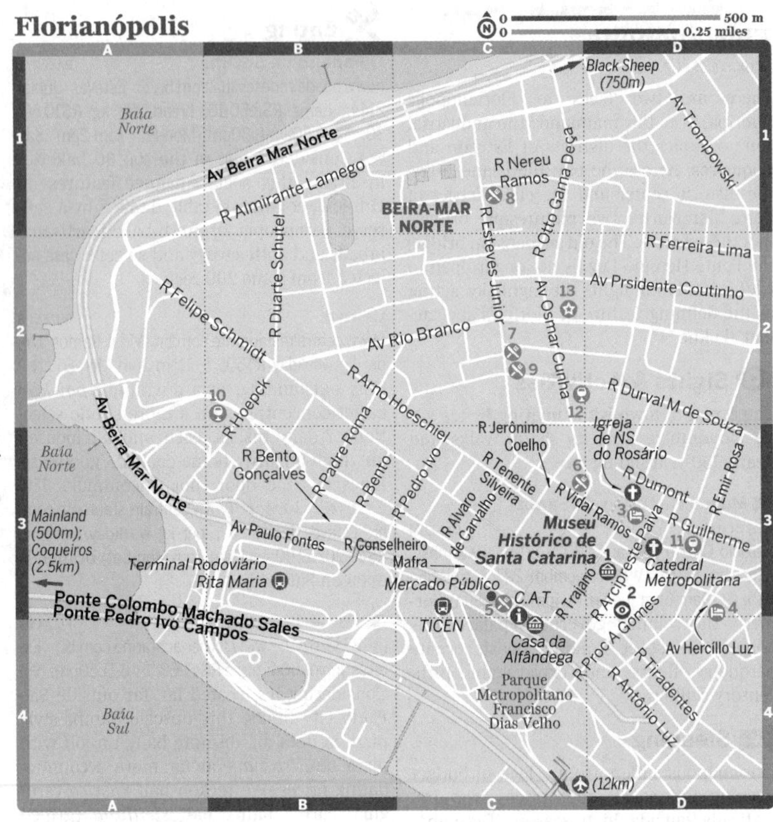

Florianópolis

Top Sights
1 Museu Histórico de Santa Catarina D3

Sights
2 Praça XV de Novembro D3

Sleeping
3 Cecomtur Executive D3
4 Centro Sul Hotel D3

Eating
5 Box 32 ..... C3
6 Central C3
7 Central C2
8 Forneria Catarina C1
9 O Padeiro de Sevilha C2

Drinking & Nightlife
10 1007 Boite Chik B2
11 Gato Mamado D3
12 Jivago Social Club C2

Entertainment
13 Concorde Club C2

menu) is not only extraordinary, but extraordinary value.

It's tucked away on The Roof, a sleek nightclub on the rooftop of one of Floripa's most upscale hotels. Reservations essential.

Drinking & Nightlife

While many people flock to Lagoa for its nightlife, Centro has a few hotspots too.

★ **Boteco Zé Mané** BOTECO
(www.facebook.com/botecozemane; Desembargador Pedro Silva 2360; mains R$27-41;

6pm-midnight Sun-Thu, to 1:30am Fri & Sat;) It's worth the trek to the mainland for this fantastic *boteco* (small neighborhood bar) along the Via Gastrônomica in Coqueiros. Jazzed-up caipirinhas (R$18) like bergamot, basil and pink peppercorn; and our fave, *jabuticaba* (an intense, native grape-like fruit) with basil, fuel the raging scene here in a revamped colonial house overlooking the waterfront.

It's eight minutes away on buses 664 'Itaguaçu' or 665 'Abraão' (R$3.10) from TICEN Platform B.

Gato Mamado BAR
(www.gatomamado.com.br; Saldanha Marinho 351; 6pm-midnight Mon-Fri. 8pm-1am Sat) Revelers spill out onto the sidewalk at this tiny bar that is king in Centro for happy hour. Rarely seen craft beers on draft (Schornstein, Bierland, Bodebrown, Das Bier; R$8) are available. The crowd tends toward bohemian, especially on Thursday when it swells with journalists and artists.

Information

Banco do Brasil (www.brb.com.br; Praça XV de Novembro 329) Visa/Mastercard ATM.

Bradesco (www.bradesco.com.br; Praca XV De Novembro 298) Visa/Mastercard ATM.

C.A.T (3228-1095; www.vivendofloripa.com.br; Rodoviária; 8am-6pm) Airport (Centro de Atendimento ao Turista; www.santur.sc.gov.br; Florianópolis-Hercílio Luz International Airport; 8am-8pm) Mercado Público (3240-4407; www.vivendofloripa.com.br; Conselheiro Mafra 255, Mercado Público; 8am-6pm Mon-Fri, 9am-noon Sat) Floripa has three government-run tourist info booths of interest to tourists, one at the airport run by the state; and two more in the city run by the municipality.

Polícia Militar (3229-6000; www.pm.sc.gov.br)

Getting There & Away

AIR

Daily flights from **Florianópolis-Hercílio Luz International Airport** (FLN; 3331-4000; Rod Deputado Diomício Freitas 3393, Bairro Carianos), 12km south of Florianópolis, serve Buenos Aires, Santiago, Montevideo, Brasília, Campinas, Porto Alegre, Rio de Janeiro and São Paulo, among others, depending on the season.

To reach the airport, bus 183 'Corredor Sudoeste' (35 minutes) and 186 'Corredor Sudoeste Semi-Direto' (25 minutes) leave from **TICEN** (p294) terminal frequently between 5:20am and 12:30am. **Cooperativa Aerotaxi** (3331-4182; Florianópolis-Hercílio Luz International Airport), a pre-paid taxi scheme at arrivals, charges R$39 to Centro, R$48 to Lagoa da Conceicão and R$65 to Barra da Lagoa.

BUS

The **long-distance bus station** (3212-3508; Av Paulo Fontes 1101) lies a few blocks west of the Praça XV de Novembro. Buses link Florianópolis with every major city in southern Brazil. There are buses to Asuncion daily at 3pm, Buenos Aires daily at 10:15pm and Santiago Tuesday at 12:35am. For Montevideo, buses depart at 11am on Saturday.

BUSES FROM FLORIANÓPOLIS

DESTINATION	STARTING FARE (R$)	TIME (HR)	BUS COMPANY
Asunción (PY)	190	21	Pluma (www.pluma.com.br)
Blumenau	39	3	Catarinense (www.catarinense.net)
Buenos Aires (AR)	314	25	Pluma (www.pluma.com.br)
Curitiba	57	5	Catarinense (www.catarinense.net)
Foz do Iguaçu	179	14	Catarinense (www.catarinense.net)
Garopaba	22	2	Paulotur (www.paulotur.com.br)
Guarda do Embaú	13.50	1½	Paulotur (www.paulotur.com.br)
Joinville	53	2½	Catarinense (www.catarinense.net)
Montevideo (UY)	275	18	EGA (www.ega.com.uy)
Porto Alegre	83	6	Eucatur (www.eucatur.com.br)
Rio de Janeiro	214	17	Itapemirim (www.itapemirim.com.br)
Santiago (CL)	420	44	Pluma (www.pluma.com.br)
São Paulo	133	12	Catarinense (www.catarinense.net)

GAY FLOR-EE

Floripa is Brazil's second gay capital. Its Pride celebration, Parada da Diversidade (www.facebook.com/floripa diversidade), has grown into one of Brazil's biggest and draws over 100,000 revelers annually. Check out Guia Gay Floripa (www.guiagayfloripa.com.br). Popular GLS (Gays, Lesbians and Sympathetics) hotspots of the moment include **Jivago Social Club** (☎3028-0788; www.jivagosocialclub.com; Leoberto Leal 4; ⏲8pm-4am Thu-Sat) and, skewing younger, **1007 Boite Chik** (☎3204-6175; http://1007brasil.com; Alameda Adolfo Konder 1007). And, of course, the trashier **Concorde Club** (☎3024-4969; www.conca.com.br; Av Rio Branco 729; ⏲midnight-8am Sat) remains a hardcore standby. At the beaches, you'll find nightclub institution **The Week** (☎3868-9944; www.theweek.com.br; Rod Jornalista Manoel de Menezes 1666) at Praia Mole – it's especially hot during Carnaval.

ℹ Getting Around

The city is a convenient transportation hub, with all of the island's 42 beaches within an hour's drive.

BUS

Local buses run on an integrated scheme called SIM – *Sistema Integrado de Mobilidade*. Buses leave from the **TICEN** (Terminal de Integração Centro; Av Paulo Fontes s/n) terminal, one block east of Florianópolis' long-distance bus station. Connections to the island's beaches are made via three outlying terminals: TIRIO (Rio Tavares Terminal), TILAG (Lagoa Terminal) and TICAN (Canasvieiras Terminal).

For southern beaches, including Armação, Pântano do Sul and Costa de Dentro, catch bus 410 'Rio Tavares' (Platform B), then transfer at TIRIO to bus 563.

For eastern beaches, catch bus 330 'Lagoa da Conceição' (Platform A), then transfer at TILAG for a second bus to your final destination, for example bus 360 to Barra da Lagoa.

For Canasvieiras and northern beaches, catch bus 210 'Canasvieiras Direto' (Platform B) from TICEN to TICAN.

A single fare of R$3.10 (paid at the TICEN ticket booth) covers your initial ride plus one transfer.

CAR

Inova (☎3225-7779; www.alugueinova.com.br; Silva Jardim 495; ⏲7:30am-7pm Mon-Fri, 8am-noon Sat) For daily rentals starting at R$85 (including unlimited mileage and insurance), it's worth the R$12 taxi ride from the bus station to rent from this Santa Catarinense rental car company.

North Island

From Praia de Jurerê – a requisite stop on the international clubbing scene – to Praia dos Ingleses, the north of the island is designed for mass tourism: calm, family-friendly waters; newly widened roads that provide easy access to the international airport; and lots of anonymous hotels and restaurants.

Santo Antônio de Lisboa

On the west coast, Santo Antônio de Lisboa is among the oldest communities on the island. An old-fashioned, fishing-village atmosphere is complemented by cobblestone streets and Azorean architecture. The most prominent edifice is the **Igreja da NS da Necessidade**, dating from 1750.

Santo Antônio's seaside setting and fishing heritage guarantee delicious seafood.

Eating

Fairyland Cafe CAFE $
(www.facebook.com/FairyLandCupcakes; Caminho dos Açores 170; cupcakes R$4.50-7, sandwiches R$19-21.50; ⏲2-8pm Tue-Sun, closed 1st Tue of month; 📶) An adorable cafe along a quieter section of town. Does good coffee, cupcakes and light bites for a see-and-be-seen crowd.

Marisqueira Sintra SEAFOOD $$
(www.marisqueirasintra.com.br; XV de Novembro, 147; mains for 2 R$65-125; ⏲noon-5:30pm & 7:30-11:30pm Mon & Wed-Sat, noon-5pm & 7:30-11:30pm Sun) Does wonderful things with octopus and Portuguese *cataplanas* (seafood stews) in a postcard waterfront setting.

Canasvieiras

Canasvieiras is not the most attractive place on the island, but it has easy access to **Praia de Jurerê** and **Praia de Canasvieiras**. Both beaches offer options for windsurfing, fishing and jet-skiing. Nightlife in town is hopping, as crowds of young people flock to local bars and clubs. Outside the season, however, it's sleepy, and many hotels are closed altogether.

Sleeping

Floripa Hostel – Canasvieiras HOSTEL $
(☎3266-2036; Dr João de Oliveira 517; dm with/without air-con R$60/50, r R$100-110;) This vaguely institutional HI hostel subscribes to all the hostel norms: friendly, English-speaking reception; bunk beds and lockers; shared bathrooms, kitchen and TV room. It's two blocks from the beach.

Praia da Lagoinha & Praia Brava

The northeastern tip of the island is a slender peninsula, accessed by slow-moving roads that wind around the hills to the beach. These towns are ritzier than their neighbors, though the beaches are still overbuilt. **Praia da Lagoinha** is a crescent-shaped patch of sand, surrounded on three sides by rocky cliffs that keep the water calm. Further south, **Praia Brava** has wilder waves that attract a steady stream of surfers.

Sleeping

Villabella Villaggio POUSADA $$
(☎3284-2017; www.villabellavillaggio.com.br; Av Epitácio Bittencourt 470, Praia Brava; d R$350-470, chalets from R$350; closed Jun-Sep; @) Santa Catarina's Italian heritage is lovingly showcased in the design and decor at the luxurious Villabella Villaggio. Every guestroom has an expansive view toward either Praia da Lagoinha or Praia Brava, and the dark hardwood chalets (some fashioned from reforested eucalyptus) are dressed up in sophisticated country decor.

Pousada da Vigia POUSADA $$
(☎3284-1789; www.pousadadavigia.com.br; Cônego Walmor Castro 291, Lagoinha; d from R$345;) The pink Pousada da Vigia overlooks Praia da Lagoinha – and what a miraculous view it is! With only 10 guestrooms scattered around lovely gardens, service is attentive and reaches to the beach, which is accessible by a 200m footpath. Room 4 knocked us out.

Praia dos Ingleses & Praia do Santinho

Once among the island's finest beaches, **Praia dos Ingleses** has suffered from its popularity. It's now crowded with high-rise hotels and overpriced restaurants.

Further south, **Praia do Santinho** is quieter, thanks to the protected area of dunes behind it. Santinho is the north island's best surfing beach, acclaimed for its consistent waves and uncrowded conditions.

Sleeping

Pousada do Atobá POUSADA $$
(☎3269-2560; www.pousadadoatoba.com.br; Servidão Ipê do Costão 146; r from R$300;) Superb value awaits at this gem of a guesthouse with airy, bright rooms looking onto well-kept gardens. The English-speaking family that runs the place takes exceptionally good care of guests. Bus 264 'Ingleses' from TICAN stops just 30m away.

Solar do Santinho POUSADA $$$
(☎3269-4168; www.pousadasolardosantinho.com.br; Estrada Vereador Onildo Lemos 2197; s/d R$280/320;) This 16-room pousada is tucked away in leafy surrounds 100m from the beach. Bi- and tri-level rooms are spacious, with kitchenettes, balconies and tasteful art. Buddha statues are peppered throughout the property, which treats its own waste water and runs solar-heated showers.

East Coast

Facing the open ocean, the east coast boasts the island's cleanest waters, longest beaches and most challenging surf.

Barra da Lagoa & Around

In the north, **Praia do Moçambique** merges with **Praia Barra da Lagoa** to form a stunning, 14km strand. The beach is hidden from the road by a thriving pine forest. Surfing is sweet all along here: Praia Barra da Lagoa has gentle swells and shallow waters that are good for beginners, while the long stretch of Moçambique has more challenging peaks. Praia do Moçambique is protected, so the only construction is around the town of Barra da Lagoa. Restaurants, bars and pousadas are plentiful, but you'll need to go back to Lagoa town for a foreign-friendly ATM.

Sleeping

Backpackers Share House HOSTEL $
(☎3232-7606; www.backpackersfloripa.com; Servidão da Prainha 29; dm R$55, d/tr without bathroom R$180/210; @) Across the pedestrian bridge from Barra da Lagoa beach, that

crazy white fortress with the souped-up motorcycle on the roof is the Backpackers Share House. It attracts an international party crowd with amenities including free caipirinhas, use of surfboards and other beach toys, and evening barbecues.

Floripa Hostel – Barra da Lagoa HOSTEL **$$**
(☎3232-4491; www.floripahostel.com.br; Inelzyr Bauer Bertoli s/n; dm R$65, d R$165;) This purpose-built hostel is just 150m from the beach and is a welcome respite from the high-priced Lagoa options. Well-equipped private rooms are a highlight here, with tasteful art, and the numerous dorms sleep no more than four. A pool is on the way.

Pousada Oceanomare CHALET **$$**
(☎3269-7200; www.pousadaoceanomare.com.br; Rodovia João Gualberto Soares 5158; s/d R$300/350, lofts R$500;) A great option north of Praia do Moçambique for families. The island's best pool and sundeck and numerous distractions for the kiddos mean adults here can enjoy the contemporary hardwood chalets that climb up the forested hillside worry-free.

Praia Mole

Praia Mole is famous for its world-class waves and internationally heralded party scene, especially among the gay and lesbian community. The beach is absolutely beautiful, as are most of the bodies sunning and surfing here. It does get crowded, but that's part of the appeal.

Sleeping

Bangalôs da Mole CHALET **$$**
(☎3232-0727; www.bangalosdamole.com.br; Rodovia Jornalista Manoel de Menezes 1007; bungalows R$265-360;) Directly across from the beach, this place has spacious suites and bi-level bungalows, all with cool tile floors and high ceilings.

Praia da Joaquina

About 3km south of Praia Mole, the huge white dunes of 'Joaca' are visible for miles. These massive sandy mounds have inspired a new sport: sand surfing. Rent a sandboard (per hour R$20) and haul it up to the top of the dune, from where it is a fast, dirty ride down.

Good old-fashioned surfing is still the number-one activity at Praia da Joaquina, which boasts long, fast, powerful waves that are up to 3m high. Stop in at **Swell** (☎3232-0366; www.swellcasadesurf.com; Estrada Geral da Joaquina 834; ⊙9am-7pm) surf shop for information and gear.

Sleeping

Cris Plage Hotel HOTEL **$$**
(☎3232-5380; www.crisplagehotel.com.br; Estrada Geral da Joaquina 1; r/tr R$210/270, with seaview R$260/395;) Wins points for its prime beachfront location and contemporary touches that contrast nicely with the otherwise aging 30-year-old property.

Lagoa da Conceição

For spectacular scenery, exhilarating water sports or all-night parties, Lagoa da Conceição is a popular alternative to the beaches. Forested hills form a fabulous backdrop for the pretty lagoon. The town of Lagoa, often packed with tourists, sits on a sandbar that divides the two halves of the lagoon and is the island's action-packed center.

Get off the beaten track by hiking along the lagoon's undeveloped west coast. From the center of town, it is 6km to the tiny village of Costa da Lagoa, which is otherwise accessible only by boat.

Activities

Surfing, kitesurfing, diving and stand-up paddle outfits line the shores at Lagoa da Conceição as well as Barra da Lagoa on the island's eastern shore. Ecotourism is gaining a strong foothold as well - there are some wonderful treks around the island.

Reefifi SURFING, BICYCLE RENTAL
(Henrique Veras do Nascimento 151; ⊙10am-9pm) A nice surf shop renting boards (per day R$35), bikes (per day R$35) and stand-up paddles (per day R$150), and can arrange surf lessons.

Sleeping

Loads of pousadas are along the southern shore of the lake. Drive over the bridge and continue east on Rua das Rendeiras. Prices drop between 15% and 40% outside high season.

★**Tucano House** HOSTEL **$**
(☎3207-8287; www.tucanohouse.com; Rua das Araras 229; dm R$55-70, r with/without bathroom R$220/$200; ⊙closed Mar 15–Nov;)

Siblings Lila and Caio are your delightful hosts at this eco-forward hostel in the heart of the Lagoa action. Their childhood home now features solar-heated showers, recycled rainwater cistern and amenities like free use of bikes and surfboards, and island adventures in a decked-out VW van.

Vintage Hostel HOSTEL $
(3236-0278; www.facebook.com/vintagehostel florianopolis; Altenor Viêira 197; dm R$50, r with/without bathroom R$120/140;) This quiet hostel in a residential street just a few steps from the action is owned by friendly Sander, who has traveled the world and brought back a few knickknacks like Russian matryoshka dolls, which he uses to color this private home otherwise teeming with vintage family heirlooms.

★ **Janela de Márcia** B&B $$
(9958-1782; www.janelademarcia.com; Dr Alfredo Daura Jorge 131; r R$325;) Brazilian returnee Márcia and her big, hospitable personality run the show at this intimate B&B – don't call it a pousada! – hidden away in an upscale residential neighborhood five minutes' walk from TILAG. Márcia's keen eye for art and design triumphs with restraint in her three cozy guestrooms; and the marvelous breakfast comes in part from her own gardens.

Pousada Ilha da Magia CHALET $$
(3232-5038; www.pousadailhadamagia.com.br; Av Acácio Garibalde São Tiago 23; s/d/tr R$220/260/340;) Across from the lagoon, these cute and classic cottages come in a variety of styles, from alpine to A-frame, all recently refurbished after 40 years. Mid-century modern–style Brastemp minibars add a wonderful retro touch. No breakfast.

Eating

Lagoa is the center for gastronomy and nightlife on the island. Check out the good-time **Food Truck Parking Lot** (www.foodtruckparkinglot.com.br; Henrique Veras do Nascimento 190; 6pm-midnight Wed-Fri, 4pm-midnight Sat & Sun) for a variety of cheap eats in a nice, open-air atmosphere.

Gelateria Max ICE CREAM $
(www.maxgelateria.com.br; Av Afonso Delambert Neto 619; ice cream from R$10; noon-6:30pm Tue-Fri, 12:30-7pm Sat & Sun) Italian training and equipment ensure the creamy gelato produced here is some of Brazil's best. Killer flavors include pistachio and *doce de leite* (milk caramel).

> DON'T MISS
>
> ### COSTA DA LAGOA
>
> The west coast of Lagoa de Conceicão (inaccessible by car) is home to a string of atmospheric seafood restaurants owned by fishermen and makes for a fabulous day trip from Lagoa town. **Cooperbarco** (3232-8266; Ivo D'Aqunio 14; return R$15) runs the local transport boats to the restaurants in the village of Costa da Lagoa hourly or so between 7:10am and 4:18pm weekdays and between 8am and 1pm on Saturday and Sunday, leaving from near the bridge across the lagoon in Lagoa de Conceicão. Skip the crowded first pier stop and head to the excellent **Restaurante Lagoa Azul** (www.restaurantelagoaazul.com.br; Servidão Caminho Costa da Lagoa 177, Pier 17; mains for 2 R$70-110; 10am-6:30pm Mar-Nov, to 8pm Dec-Feb;) , plop down picnic-table-style next to the water and order a freshly caught *carapeva* fish – available only in Costa da Lagoa. Paradise found!

Café Cultura CAFE $$
(www.cafeculturafloripa.com.br; Severino de Oliveira 669; coffee R$4-11, mains R$18-43; 9am-midnight;) Breakfast until 1pm, waffles, salads, paninis, sophisticated mains and specialty java served by various methods – there is something for everyone at Floripa's best cafe, brought to you by a Californian ex-Starbucks barista and his Brazilian coffee-heiress wife. It's always packed – expect unapologetically exasperating service.

★ **Bistrô Santa Marta** BRAZILIAN $$$
(3371-0769; www.bistrosantamarta.com.br; Laurindo Januário da Silveira 1350; mains R$57-110; 8pm-midnight Mon-Sat;) Extraordinary service greets those willing to escape Lagoa town for Canto da Lagoa about 2km from town. This adorable, eight-table contemporary bistro works with a limited but excellent menu (filet mignon, lobster, octopus, lamb) set to moody lounge music at perfect volume.

The honest-to-goodness hospitality is delivered by *gaúcho* couple Milene (kitchen)

WORTH A TRIP

GO NORTH, YOUNG SUNSEEKER

While the stellar beaches south of Florianópolis might hog the most pristine sands and charming beach towns, it's no monopoly. The northern Santa Catarina coast has its own charms as well. Here are a few additional spots worth checking out.

Ilha de São Francisco

The lovely city of **São Francisco do Sul**, 45km east of Joinville, is Brazil's third oldest, founded in 1504 by the French (only Bahia and São Vicente are older). The historical center is on the Patrimônio Histórico (National Heritage list) for its decadent, colonial feel. The city acts as a gateway to the rest of the Ilha de São Francisco, a popular destination for sun-worshipers and surfers. **Viacão Verdes Mares** (www.vmares.com.br) runs regular buses to Ilha de São Francisco from Joinville (R$11.20 to R$13.70).

Penha & Armação

These two villages are side by side along the north shore of a peninsula that juts out into the ocean, 110km north of Florianópolis. The crescent-shaped beach wraps around a bay dotted with colorful fishing boats. The idyllic village atmosphere changes slightly on summer weekends, however, when the main beachfront turns into one big *festa*. Regardless, these twin towns feel more like fishing villages than holiday resorts. **Catarinense** (www.catarinense.net) runs a few buses a day to Penha from Blumenau (R$23, two hours) and several from Joinville (R$18, 1½ hours), calling at Piçarras (6km north).

Porto Belo, Bombas & Bombinhas

A small peninsula fans out from Porto Belo about 60km north of Florianópolis. Here, clear, emerald-green waters offer some of the best diving in southern Brazil.

The town of **Porto Belo** is a developed fishing village, so its beach is dominated by a big dock and boats moored in the bay. The principal swimming beaches are **Praia Bombinhas** (9km from Porto Belo) and the adjacent **Praia Bombas** (3km). These sandy stretches are also lined with small-scale hotels and seafood restaurants.

From Balneário Camboriú, **Praiana** (www.praiana.com.br) runs numerous buses to Porto Belo (R$4.70, one hour), where you can switch for Bombinhas (R$3, 20 minutes). Frequent Porto Belo intermunicipal buses also depart throughout the day from Santa Catarina, next to Camboriú's bus station. **Viação Navegantes** (www.viacaonavegantes.net) also runs six buses per weekday from Florianópolis (R$13.50, 1¾ hours), fewer on weekends.

and Branco (wine and service). As a duo, they'll leave you with a meal you won't soon shake from your consciousness. Reservations essential.

Drinking & Nightlife

Books & Beers BAR

(www.booksbeers.com; Ivo D'Aquino 103; beers R$7-45.50; 5pm-midnight Tue-Fri, from noon Sat, noon-10:30pm Sun;) An outrageous craft-beer list awaits at this trendy newcomer, beautifully laid out in a hardcover menu that looks and reads like a long-lost treasured tome of taste. There's more than 125 labels by the bottle to drink in the *Old Man and the Sea*-inspired library vibe with sunset views.

★ **Black Swan** PUB

(www.theblackswan.com.br; Manuel Severino de Oliveira 592; mains R$18.50-34.50; 5pm-midnight Mon-Fri, 11am-late Sat, to 8pm Sun;) A proper English-run pub and garden pouring a wide range of proper pints – R$24.50 to R$27.50, all rarer than the pub's namesake – and pub grub, all served up alongside 12 TVs, screening your sporting heart's desire, and live music from Thursday to Saturday and Monday (jazz).

Entertainment

John Bull Pub LIVE MUSIC

(www.johnbullfloripa.com.br; Rua das Rendeiras 1046; 10pm-4am Tue-Sat Dec-Mar, closed Wed Apr-Nov) Famous for live rock, with bonus views over the lagoon.

Information

Banco do Brasil and Bradesco both sit at the corner of Moacyr Pereira Junior and José Henrique Veras.

A.C.I.F. (3232-0185; www.acif.org.br; Nossa Senhora da Conceição 30; 2-6pm Mon-Fri) This private organization promotes tourism in Lagoa and is your best bet for well-rounded tourism information.

Correios (Henrique Veras do Nascimento 82; 9am-5pm Mom-Fri) Postal services.

Polícia Militar (3665-4980; www.pm.sc.gov.br; Av das Rendeiras 966)

South Island

With white-sand beaches and mountains that drop into the sea, the south is the most pristine and picturesque part of the island. But south-island residents are engaged in the inevitable struggle between developers and preservers: the former see the potential for more tourists and big bucks; the latter fear that their piece of paradise will soon resemble the north. The balance is delicate and ever shifting.

For now, these towns retain their idyllic appeal. The beaches are less crowded (the hottest surf spots excepted) and the vibe is more laid-back than other island destinations.

At the southern tip, Praia dos Naufragados is accessible only by hiking 4km on a flat, shady trail from the village of Caieiras da Barra do Sul. Your reward is a picturesque lighthouse and a fantastic vista of the islands in the vicinity.

Ribeirão da Ilha

More than any other town, the tiny village of Ribeirão da Ilha has preserved its Azorean heritage, evident in its cobblestone streets and colorful tile-roof houses. The main square centers on the lovely Igreja NS da Lapa do Riberão, which dates to 1806.

Eating

Ostradamus SEAFOOD $$$

(3337-5711; www.ostradamus.com.br; Rod Baldicero Filomeno 7640; oysters R$38-45, mains for 2 R$92-169; noon-11pm Tue-Sat, to 5pm Sun;) Given the village's location overlooking the tidal flats, it is no surprise that the local specialty is oysters. Sit on the dock at this incredibly atmospheric place and slurp a dozen or two.

Campeche

Campeche is a bohemian outpost, home to artists, massage therapists and other freethinkers seeking to escape the crowds of the city and the tourist hotspots.

The 5km Praia do Campeche is protected, so the beach is completely undeveloped, yet those condo complexes have managed to creep in as close as the law allows. Desolate dunes and pounding surf – stretching for miles in either direction – offer relative solitude for swimmers and sunbathers. At the southern end of the beach, catch a boat (R$80 round-trip) to Ilha do Campeche, an ecological reserve with opportunities for hiking and snorkeling; or, alternatively, save R$20 by catching one from the fishermen cooperative at Armação Beach.

Sleeping

★**Pousada Natur Campeche** POUSADA $$$

(3237-4011; www.naturcampeche.com.br; Servidão Nunes 59; s/d from R$280/350;) The owner of this endlessly charming, socially aware pousada has traveled the world, foraging treasures to decorate the country-themed rooms. Exotic and steeped in carbon-footprint-erasing touches like solar-heated showers, the unique rooms are spread deceptively about the property, surrounded by hammocks, lush gardens and artistically fed common areas. It's just 100m from Praia do Campeche. Pretty perfect.

Armação

This little town dates to the 18th century, when it served as a whaling center. The impressive Igreja Santa Ana still stands from those days. While whaling is no longer practiced, the fishing industry still thrives here.

Armação provides access to three beaches, all excellent surfing spots. North of town, Morro das Pedras is popular for its consistent right, but you'll probably have to fight for a chance to ride it. Further south, Praia da Armação is a surfer's delight, especially at the northern end of the beach. For a little adventure, follow a winding trail along the rocky coastline to the gorgeous Matadeiro, a near-deserted beach surrounded by lush greenery.

Inland from Armação, the Lagoa do Peri is a pretty lake surrounded by parkland. Lesser-known and less visited than Conceição, it offers wonderful opportunities for swimming and hiking. The jumping-off point for the lake is about 1km south of Praia de Armação on the main road approaching the town – you can't miss the large park entrance.

Sleeping

Pousada Alemdomar POUSADA $$
(3237-5600; www.alemdomar.com.br; Tulia de Olivera 403; s/d/tr R$190/230/260;) After passing Hiper Bom Supermarket, follow the unpaved Euclides João Alves about 400m south from the Lagoa do Peri park entrance and take your first left to find this little plot of New-Age paradise. Six simple guestrooms evoke tranquility and harmony with nature.

Pântano do Sul

Fishermen of Azorean descent still inhabit the village of Pântano do Sul, so its beach is dotted with fishing boats and seafood shacks. Ringed by mountains, the protected cove contains calm, cool waters that are ideal for sunning and swimming.

From here, you can catch a lift from a local fisherman or hike about 1½ hours to the deserted beach of **Lagoinha do Leste**. The hike is hot, so leave early and bring plenty of water. Lagoinha do Leste offers some of the island's most consistent and powerful waves, so don't be surprised when surfers run past you on the trail.

Eating

Bar do Arante SEAFOOD $$
(www.bardoarante.com.br; Abelardo Otácilio Gomes 254; mains for 2 R$75-168, weekend buffet per person R$55; 11:30am-midnight) The rustic seafood shack Arante has become an island institution, its walls covered with poetry and artwork that patrons have doodled over the years.

Costa de Dentro & Around

This is the end of the road, and it feels like it. These tiny towns are home to a handful of places to stay and eat, but they are left largely to their fishing and farming residents. Costa de Dentro has access to the lovely, calm waters of the **Praia dos Açores** – making this a good escape from the surfing scene – or continue all the way to **Praia Solidão** or **Saquinho**.

Sleeping

★**Pousada Sítio dos Tucanos** INN $$
(3237-5084; www.pousadasitiodostucanos.com; Estrada Rosália Ferreira 2776; s/d from R$180/295, chalet R$360;) About 1.5km past Costa de Dentro, this multilingual, German-run pousada sits tucked away high up in isolated and peaceful farm country, the domain of nature-and-animal lovers. Extremely cozy, it offers rustic but comfortable rooms, most with balconies; common areas are flooded with light from tall French doors.

If coming by bus 563, call ahead for pick-up at the bus stop 800m away.

THE MAINLAND

North and south of Florianópolis, fine sand and big surf attract beachcombers, sunbathers and surfers. Inland, the Serra Geral runs parallel to the coast, protecting some of southern Brazil's most remote destinations. This is where Santa Catarina's German and Italian heritage endures most tenaciously.

Joinville

0XX47 / POP 515,000

While Joinville does not have the historic center (or the beer festival) of Blumenau, it does have its own claims to fame. It's the only city outside Moscow with a school of the Bolshoi Ballet, a coup that goes hand in hand with its annual **dance festival** (www.festivaldedanca.com.br; held in July), one of the largest and most renowned in the world; and it relishes its own decidedly German roots. They are evident in the city's nouveau-alpine architecture and well-manicured parks. The economy thrives on metallurgy, plastics and information technology, but this industrial activity is tucked neatly away from the eyes of visitors. The result is a big city with small-town manners.

Sights & Activities

★**Museu Nacional da Imigração e Colonização** MUSEUM
(National Museum of Immigration & Colonization; www.museudeimigracao.blogspot.com.br; Rio Branco 229; 9am-5pm Tue-Fri, noon-6pm Sat & Sun) FREE In an elegant palace dating from 1870,

Joinville

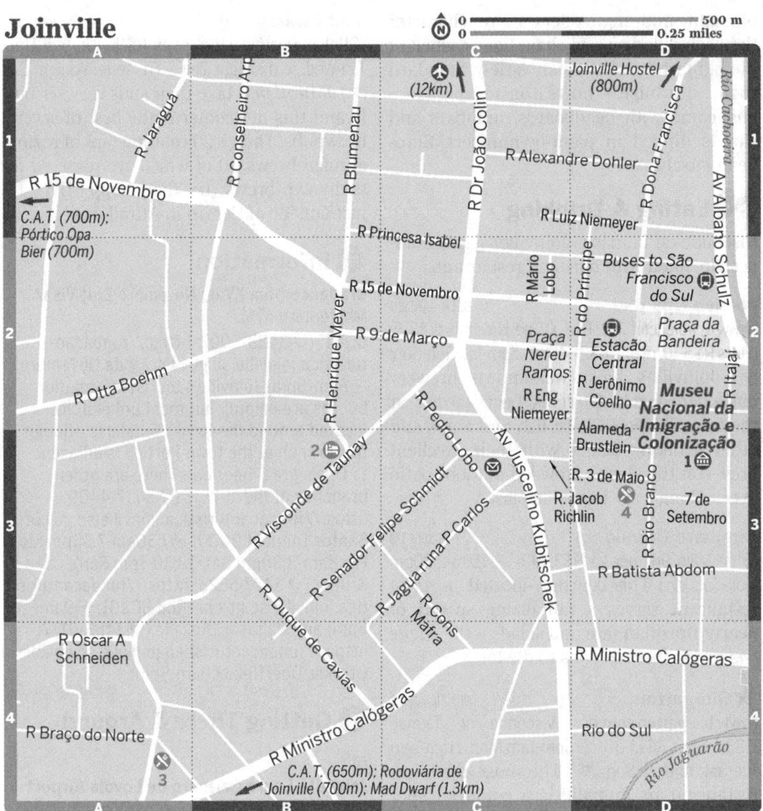

this museum documents the history of immigration to Santa Catarina. The impressive stand of palms along **Alameda das Palmeiras** will lead you there.

Barco Príncipe III BOAT TOUR
(☎3455-4444; www.barcoprincipe.com.br; Baltazar Buschle 3870; adult/child incl lunch R$146/73; ⊙tours 10:30am;) This famous boat cruise offers tours around the Baía da Babitonga, stopping in São Francisco do Sul for 1½ hours. It departs from the Espinheiros neighborhood, 10km from the center, but only when they have 100 people or more. Pricey, but everyone raves about it.

Sleeping

Joinville Hostel HOSTEL $
(☎3424-0844; www.joinvillehostel.com.br; Dona Francisca 1376; dm from R$63, s/d R$100/125, without bathroom R$85/110; @) If you like your HI hostel to feel like home, this one, run by the immediately likable Kely, is for you. It boasts large green spaces, a little garden and a good bit more attention to detail and decor than the norm – Kely has created a homespun vibe just a 10-minute walk from Centro.

Hotel Tannenhof HOTEL $$
(www.tannenhof.com.br; Visconde de Taunay 340; s/d from R$235.40/269.50; @) This

Joinville

Top Sights

Sleeping

Eating

pleasant midrange offers more character than Joinville's myriad chain hotels, albeit of the old-fashioned German variety. Standard rooms are huge – no reason to upgrade – and come with headboards, minibars and closets dipped in paint-by-numbers European kitsch.

Eating & Drinking

Visconde de Taunay is Joinville's gastronomic strip, lined with bars and restaurants.

Pórtico Opa Bier BEER GARDEN
(www.opabier.com.br; Rua XV de Novembro 4315; beers R$5-10, mains R$27-49; 5pm-late Tue-Sun;) Joinville's most well-known brewery has opened this fabulous beer garden at the town Pórtico. Chase fish and chips and other drinking dishes with their excellent brews on the always-crowded outdoor patio overlooking leafy Expoville park.

Tempeiro Crioulo BUFFET $
(3 de Maio 94; per kg R$32.90; 11am-2:30pm Mon-Sat;) This centrally-located *por-kilo* restaurant serves a tantalizing spread of hearty Brazilian fare and salads – the *carne ensopada* (beef stew) is to die for.

★ **Biergarten** BRAZILIAN $$
(www.biergarten.com.br; Visconde de Taunay 1183; mains R$13-80; 5pm-1am Mon, 11am-1am Tue-Sat, to 8pm Sun;) The most agreeable restaurant in Joinville is a convivial spot to sample regional specialties like *marreco* (stuffed garganey, a kind of small duck; R$95 for two), washed down with its own *chope* (draft beer) called Zeit (Munique Helles is best). It draws a lively crowd, which fills up the good-time space of upscale rustic picnic tables, especially on Sunday.

Mad Dwarf BREWERY
(Ottokar Doerffel 1112; pints R$15-40; 5-11pm Tue-Wed, to midnight Thu & Fri, 4pm-midnight Sat;) *Joinvilense* take their suds very seriously and this newcomer is the best of several brewpubs. There's 20 rotating taps of regional microbrews, 10 of which are reserved for their own brews (try their hoppy IPA). It's just outside of Centro in Atiradores.

Information

Bradesco (Rua XV de Novembro 214) Visa/Mastercard ATM.

C.A.T. (3433-5007; https://fundacaoturistica.joinville.sc.gov.br; XV de Novembro; 8am-6pm) Joinville's tourist information booths are helpful, but most unhelpfully located around the town's outskirts, though this branch at the town Pórtico is adjacent to Opa's great beer bar. There are other branches at the airport (3427-4409; https://fundacaoturistica.joinville.sc.gov.br; Santos Dumont 9000; 7:30am-7:30pm Mon-Fri, 8am-3:30pm Sat, 12:30-7pm Sun), Casa Krüger (3427-5623; https://fundacaoturistica.joinville.sc.gov.br; Rod SC301; 9am-6pm) and Baltasar Buschle (3453-0177; https://fundacaoturistica.joinville.sc.gov.br; Ottokar Doerffel; 9am-5pm).

Getting There & Around

AIR

Joinville-Lauro Carneiro de Loyola Airport (JOI; 3481-4000; Av Santos Dumont 9000) is 13km north from the city; To reach the airport, catch bus 800/Iririú (R$3.25) from Box 3 at the local city bus terminal and switch at Terminal Iririú for the Cubatão bus to the airport. Regular flights go to Campinas, Porto Alegre, São Paulo and Rio.

BUS

The **bus station** (3433-2991; Paraíba 769) is 2km southwest from the city center. Local

BUSES FROM JOINVILLE

DESTINATION	STARTING FARE (R$)	TIME (HR)	BUS COMPANY
Blumenau	27	2	Catarinense (www.catarinense.net)
Curitiba	26	2	Catarinense (www.catarinense.net)
Florianópolis	49	2½	Catarinense (www.catarinense.net)
Foz do Iguaçu	120	13	Pluma (www.pluma.com.br)
Porto Alegre	115	9	Catarinense (www.catarinense.net)
Rio de Janeiro	182	17	Penha (http://vendas.nspenha.com.br)
São Paulo	101	9	Catarinense (www.catarinense.net)

SPRECHEN SIE DEUTSCH?

The first German immigrants arrived here in the 1820s at the behest of Dom Pedro I. The southern part of the newly independent Brazil was still disputed by Argentina and Uruguay, and the emperor wanted to populate the region with loyal followers. Successive waves of immigrants arrived in the 1850s and the 1890s, then again around the two world wars. Contrary to popular imagination, most Germans who arrived in the 1940s were political and economic refugees, rather than Nazi leaders on the run.

For a century, German was the dominant language in many parts of southern Brazil. German speakers came from different regions of Germany and spoke different dialects, so they faced their own linguistic Babel. They often resorted to a kind of Creole, which incorporated Portuguese and local Indian languages. Italians, facing a similar problem, relied on 'Taliã,' an amalgamation of dialects based mainly on those of the Veneto region.

The 20th century took a toll on the German language in Brazil. The world wars led to the suppression of German in public institutions like schools and government. Industrialization and increasing economic integration brought the region into closer contact with Portuguese speakers. Finally, the arrival of radio and TV, dominated by national networks, reinforced the use of Portuguese, especially among the young.

In the town of Pomerode, a confluence of forces has ensured the preservation of the German language. Only in the last generation have decent roads linked Pomerode to Blumenau, so the town remained physically isolated from its neighbors. In addition, nearly all of its original settlers spoke the same dialect (Pomeranian), so there was no need to resort to Portuguese as a *lingua franca*. And the settlers were Lutheran, so German remained their language of worship. These days, a growing movement is preserving Brazil's bilingual communities.

buses go every 15 minutes to the city center (R$3.70). **Viacão Verdes Mares** (www.vmares.com.br) runs regular buses to Ilha de São Francisco, both from the bus station (R$13.70), and, more conveniently and cheaply, from Centro (R$11.20).

Blumenau

☎0XX47 / POP 309,000

Blumenau is not the only city in Santa Catarina that was founded by German settlers who transplanted their beer-brewing expertise and their taste for alpine architecture to South America. But it is the best known, thanks in part to its uninhibited, over-the-top Oktoberfest. The annual beer-drinking extravaganza is among Brazil's largest street parties, second only to Carnaval in Rio.

Oktoberfest is what makes Blumenau famous, but it is not what makes the city German. Throughout the historic city center, the architecture is dominated by Germanic themes. Local restaurants specialize in *eisbein* (cured ham hock) and *kassler* (smoked pork chop), and numerous beer brands are brewed locally. Most telling, perhaps, is the tall, fair population, many of whom often speak German in their homes.

Sights

Blumenau's major festivals are held at **Parque Vila Germânica** (www.parquevilagermanica.com.br; Alberto Stein 199; ⌚10am-8pm Mon-Fri, to 6pm Sat, 11am-5pm Sun), part huge convention hall, part kitschy alpine village, which is worth a look-see even when events aren't on, as there are several good restaurants, bars, gourmet shops and a whole lot of *lederhosen*. To get there, catch buses 30 or 31 from Av Beira Rio.

Rua XV Novembro NEIGHBORHOOD

Rua XV Novembro is home to the city's best examples of Germanic architecture, including the **Castelinho da XV** (now a Havan department store), a replica of the city hall of Michelstadt, Germany.

Museu de Família Colonial MUSEUM

(☎3381-7516; www.arquivodeblumenau.com.br; Alameda Duque de Caxias 78; admission R$3; ⌚10am-4pm Tue-Sun) Learn about Blumenau's beginnings in this group of houses that were

Blumenau

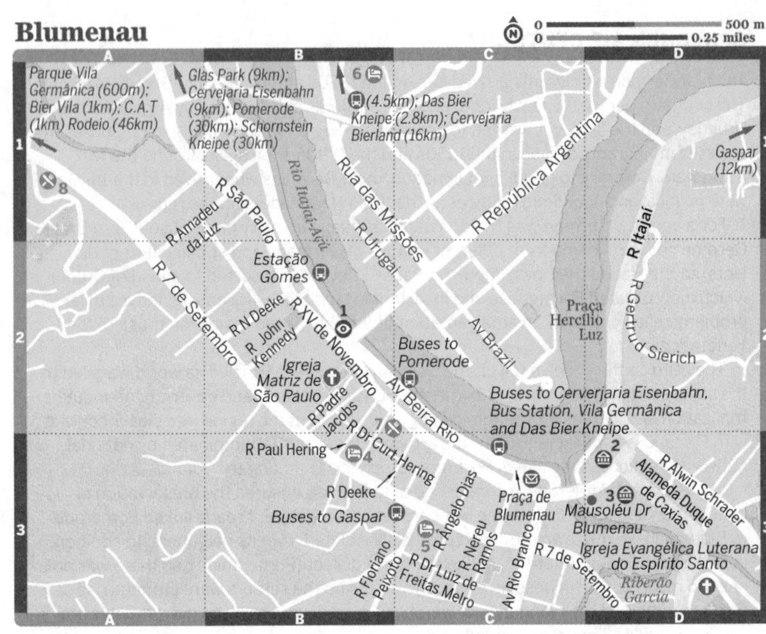

Blumenau

Sights

1 Castelinho da XV........B2
2 Museu da Cerveja........D3
3 Museu de Família Colonial........D3

Sleeping

4 Hotel Glória........B3
5 Hotel Hermann........C3
6 Pousada Brigite Hostel........B1

Eating

7 Basement English Pub........B2
Cafehaus Glória........(see 4)
8 Don Peppone........A1

occupied by the city's founder, Herman Bruno Otto Blumenau, in the 1850s. His daughter's cat cemetery – where lies interred Pepito, Mirko, Bum, Putzi, Schnurr and other beloved feline companions – is a nice spot of contemplation in the rambling backyard garden.

Museu da Cerveja MUSEUM
(Praça Hercilio Luz; 9am-5pm Mon-Fri, 10am-6pm Sat & Sun) FREE The small Museu da Cerveja is dedicated to the city's long-entwined history with the beer-brewing process.

Festivals & Events

Oktoberfest BEER
(3326-6901; www.oktoberfestblumenau.com.br; Vila Germânica; admission per day R$10-30) A festive parade kicks off nearly 20 days of folk music, dancing and beer drinking. This is the 'biggest German party in the Americas' (well, second biggest after Ontario, but who's keeping track?). A smaller Sommerfest takes place in January.

Sleeping

Book accommodations well in advance for Oktoberfest or Sommerfest.

Hotel Hermann POUSADA $
(3322-4370; www.hotelhermann.com.br; Floriano Peixoto 213; s/d/tr R$85/135/185, with air-con R$99/153/205;) Optimal budget choice, inside a historic timber-frame home replete with creaky hardwood floors throughout. Rooms are simple but well maintained and the cozy feel of Blumenau of old permeates the entire premises. Note there are no double-bed rooms with fans.

Pousada Brigite Hostel HOSTEL $
(3232-1175; www.pousadabrigitehosel.com.br; Venezuela 335; dm R$60, s/d R$120/147;) A well-meaning, strong-willed eccentric is the

namesake host at this budget find perched on a downtown hill with beautiful Blumenau views and guavas falling from the trees. Upstairs dorms are spiffy and clean, downstairs private rooms follow suit, with Senhora Brigite's comfortable home in-between.

Brigite is deeply involved with tourism in the region and proudly offers an excellent selection of local artisanal beers, though this is a far cry from a party hostel.

★**Hotel Glória** HOTEL **$$**

(3326-1988; www.hotelgloria.com.br; 7 de Setembro 954; d/tr from R$192/242;) With its wood-paneled entrance, stained glass and traditional German *kaffeehaus* (coffeehouse) attached, this Blumenau classic has modernized 70% of its fleet of rooms in the past few years but maintains its Old World flair. Upgraded rooms boast restrained style and explosive showers. Breakfast is extraordinary.

Eating & Drinking

Cafehaus Glória CAFE **$**

(www.cafehaus.com.br; 7 de Setembro 954; buffet from R$22; 8am-8pm Mon-Sat;) This Old World coffeehouse is a consistent madhouse, famous for its can't-miss *café colonial,* an afternoon buffet (*por-kilo* R$34; Monday to Saturday 3pm to 8pm) that features cakes, pastries and sandwiches similar to British high tea. Lunchtime means a quality but more traditional Brazilian buffet (*por-kilo* R$42).

★**Basement English Pub** PUB FOOD **$$**

(www.basementpub.com.br; Paul Hering 35; mains R$16.90-47.50; 6pm-midnight Mon-Sat;) Easily one of Brazil's best bars in a gorgeous authentic English pub atmosphere. It does a good job with homesick-remedy pub grub like burgers and fish and chips that hit the spot among a blitzkrieg of brats. Live music often.

Don Peppone ITALIAN **$$**

(www.donpepponeexpress.com.br; 7 de Setembro 2013; mains for 2 R$66-94, pizza R$60-90; 11:30am-2pm & 6pm-midnight;) Fancier than its logo suggests, Dom Peppone is an upscale anecdote to sausages and sauerkraut and a fine example of Blumenau's 'other' ethnic cuisine.

Bier Vila BEER GARDEN

(www.biervila.com.br; Alberto Stein 199, Parque Vila Germânica; beers R$7.20-15; 11am-11pm;) With 12 options on draft and 400 local and regional craft beers by the bottle, this is easily Blumenau's best drinking den for enthusiasts. Typical German fare on offer as well, but it's about the suds.

Shopping

Blumenau produces high-quality crystal and glassware.

Glas Park/Museu do Cristal CRYSTAL

(3327-1261; www.cristaisdimurano.com.br; Rudolf Roedel 233; 9am-6pm Mon-Fri, 9am-1pm Sat) An on-site crystal museum shows the history of the industry and the art, and fascinating demonstrations are given between 9am and 1pm.

Information

Bradesco (www.bradesco.com.br; XV de Novembro 849) Visa/Mastercard ATM.

C.A.T (Centro de Atendimento ao Turista; 3331-7726; www.turismoblumenau.com.br; Albero Stein 199; 10am-7pm Mon-Fri, to 4pm Sat & Sun) Helpful tourist information about Blumenau and the Vale Europeu, located inside Parque Vila Germânica. A second location operates on Rua Itajaí (3222-3176; www.turismoblumenau.com.br; Itajaí 3435; 8am-4pm Mon-Fri) at the eastern entrance to town.

Correios (Post Office; www.correios.com.br; Praça Dr Blumenau; 8am-6pm Mon-Fri) Postal services.

BUSES FROM BLUMENAU

DESTINATION	STARTING FARE (R$)	TIME (HR)	BUS COMPANY
Balneário Camboriú	19	1½	Catarinense (www.catarinense.net)
Curitiba	45	4	Catarinense (www.catarinense.net)
Florianópolis	42	3	Catarinense (www.catarinense.net)
Joinville	28	2	Catarinense (www.catarinense.net)
Piçarras	21	2	Catarinense (www.catarinense.net)

Vale Europeu

Italian and German immigrants from the 1830s settled the picturesque Vale Europeu, a collection of towns and villages tucked amid bucolic vistas in the Itajaí River valley around Blumenau. Today, much of their original European culture is alive and well, from striking traditional German *enxaimel* houses to Reinheitsgebot-brewed *bier*.

Towns & Villages

For a profound insight into the region's Germanic roots, head 30km north of Blumenau to Pomerode, where an estimated 70% of the population speaks German. The Festa Pomerana celebrates its northern German heritage every January, and the **Museo Pomerano** (☎3387-0408; Harmann Weege 111; adult/child R$2/1; ⏰10-11:30am & 1-5pm Tue-Fri, 10am-4pm Sat & Sun) explores the town's history in loving detail. The region's Italian heritage is alive in Nova Trento, 61km south of Blumenau, which celebrates local gastronomy during the Grape Festival in January and is home to the important pilgrimage site Santuário Santa Paulina, an imposing modern church with a dramatic slalom-like sloping ceiling. Some 40,000 pilgrims and tourists visit this church *per month*. Timbó, founded by both Germans and Italians, is brimming with verdant gardens and is considered by the UN to be one of the best places to live in Brazil.

Festivals

Blumenau's massive Oktoberfest (p304) is nearly 20 days of folk music, dancing and beer drinking – lots of beer drinking. This is the 'biggest German party in

1

the Americas' (well, second biggest after Ontario, but who's counting?).

Outdoor Adventures

The Vale Europeu – like Europe itself – lends itself to beautiful countryside pedaling. See the Circuito Vale Europeu website (www.circuitovaleeuropeu.com.br) for an excellent self-guided bike tour. The helpful website www.valeeuropeu.com.br, and the comprehensive booklet *Vale Europeu*, which can be picked up at the tourist office in Blumenau, both cover ecotourism opportunities in the valley.

Best Place to Stay

A pleasant place to lay your head in Pomerode is **Pousada Bergblick** (☎3387-0952; www.bergblick.com.br; Georg Zeplin 120; s/d R$188/288, s/d with balcony & Jacuzzi R$258/388; ❄@📶), which has gigantic rooms with mountain views and an alpine feel.

Best Restaurant

The feast at **Abendbrothaus** (☎3378-1157; www.abendbrothaus.blogspot.com; Henrique Conrad 1194, Vila Itoupava; meals R$69; ⏲11:30am-4pm Sun) in Vila Itoupava, 25km north of Blumenau, is the most coveted table in Santa Catarina for *marreco* (stuffed garganey, a kind of small duck).

Best Microbrewery

Schornstein Kneipe's (p309) pilsners, India pale ale, weiss, bock and imperial stout all cure 'homebeersickness'; and it has the best tasting room of the bunch as well. It's a must on the artisanal beer trail.

BELISARIO ROLDAN / 500PX ©

1. Blumenau (p303)
2. Pomerode countryside
3. Oktoberfest (p304), Blumenau

DIRCINHASW / GETY IMAGES ©

DIRCINHA WELTER / GETY IMAGES ©

Getting There & Around

The **bus station** (☎3323-2155; Av 2 de Setembro 1222) is 6km west of the center. To get into the center of town, take bus 11 or 17 (R$3.30) from the far side of Av 2 de Setembro to Estação Gomes, or take a taxi for R$18. Heading back, the same buses leave from Estação Dr Blumenau.

For the Vale Europeu, hourly **Volkmann** (www.turismovolkmann.com.br) buses head from Av Beira Rio to Pomerode (R$4.95). From the bus station, **Expresso Presidente** (☎3323-2077; www.expressopresidente.com.br) has seven daily buses making the 30km jaunt from Blumenau to Timbó (R$9.50, one hour). **Reunidas** (☎3323-3207; www.reunidas.com.br) has four buses from Blumenau to Nova Trento (R$17, two hours).

North of Florianópolis

Varied and inviting, the beaches along the coast north of Florianópolis are both its blessing and its curse. The blessing is the crystalline waters and fine sand, not to mention the endless days of sun. The curse is the high-rise hotels and condominiums that are more prominent than the forested hillsides and rocky outposts.

Balneário Camboriú

☎0XX47 / POP 108,000

Balneário Camboriú is considered a poor man's Rio – indeed it boasts a giant Christ statue, beautiful beaches, hopping nightlife and a long stretch of skyscraper-lined sand that suspiciously mirrors Copacabana right down to its name – Av Atlântica – all for a fraction of Copacabana prices. Truth be told, Camboriú is really a carbon copy of Copacabana except for one caveat: it's much newer, so the city's infrastructure, from gaudy high-rise hotels to trendy street-level bars, is all in much better shape. But the vibe – forced and unsophisticated at times – can often feel like it's dripping in Copacabana cliché.

The summer population swells to nearly a million, as Argentines, Paraguayans and Brazilians flood in to enjoy one of Brazil's hottest party scenes. Camboriú is known for being as gay-friendly as Rio, and also for its *teleférico* (cable car) connecting a large central *morro* (hill) with not one, but two beaches – apparently the only one of its kind in the world.

Sights

Families like Camboriú for its kid-friendly attractions like Unipraias and proximity to **Beto Carrero World** (☎3261-2222; www.betocarrero.com.br; Inácio Francisco de Souza 1597; adult/child R$105/88; 9am-6pm;), Latin America's largest theme park.

★ **Parque Unipraias** NATURE RESERVE
(☎3404-7600; www.unipraias.com.br; Av Atlântica 6006; 9am-8pm Dec-Feb, 9:30am-6pm Mar-Nov;) Camboriú's pride and joy is this 6-hectare urban reserve. In addition to 500m of walking trails, the real coup is its amusements: the **bondinho** (cable car; adult/child R$39/19;), an Italian-built cable-car system that connects three stations between Barra Sul up to the 240m-high Morro da Aguada and back down to Praia Laranjeiras on a spectacular 3.2km, 30-minute ride over Atlantic rainforest.

At the top, the park also operates the kid-tastic **Yoohooo!** (tickets R$28;) roller coaster, which plunges 700m at 60km per hour, and **ZipRider** (tickets R$45), a thrilling 750m plunge to Praia Laranjeiras. Both are a blast!

The park is mostly weekends only in June and August, so check ahead if you're coming through then.

Beaches

Praia Laranjeiras, the busiest and closest beach to town, and six beaches extending south along the Costa Brava have crystalline waters and views of forested hills in the background. Four kilometers north, on the road to Itajaí, **Praia dos Amores** has good surf conditions, as does **Praia Atalaia** in Itajaí, 10km north of Camboriú.

Cristo Luz Statue LANDMARK
(☎3367-4042; www.cristoluz.com.br; Indonésia 800; before/after 7pm R$13/25; 4pm-midnight Mon-Sat, from 10am Sun) The 33m Cristo Luz statue holds a sombrero from which a spotlight illuminates the city at night, sometimes in streaming colors. During summer, live music is often staged from 7pm.

Sleeping

Discounts range up to 50% outside of the packed summer months.

Rezende House HOSTEL $$
(☎3361-1008; www.rezendepousada.com.br; Rua 3100, 780; dm/s/d/tr R$83/209/259/339; @) In the middle of the beach and nightlife

DON'T MISS

EIN BIER, POR FAVOR!

Brazil's mainstream brews – Skol, Brahma and Antarctica – are fine for staving off the tropical heat, but let's face it: taste is not their strong suit. Luckily, in the last few years, the craft-beer revolution has kicked off throughout Brazil, but German immigrants from the Vale Europeu have had a handle on this for decades! There is a true beer culture here dating back to the mid-1800s. The following are some of the region's best breweries, all with tasting rooms in and around Blumenau.

Cervejaria Eisenbahn (☎3488-7307; www.eisenbahn.com.br; Bahia 5181, Blumenau; draft beers R$5-16.50; ⏰4pm-midnight Mon-Sat) Though the craft-beer movement has dethroned Eisenbahn as the best and most famous artisanal Brazilian beer, the long-standing brewer has stepped up its game since being acquired by Schincariol, remodeling its formerly lame brewpub into a comfortable diner-like drinking den with a great outdoor patio.

The taproom features 15 beers (four on draft). To get there, grab the bus marked 'Passo Manso' from the Estação Dr Blumenau stop on Av Beira Rio (R$3.30) and ask to get off at Eisenbahn. Tours had been indefinitely suspended at time of research due to ongoing renovations.

Schornstein Kneipe (☎3333-2759; www.schornstein.com.br; Hermann Weege 60, Pomerode; beers R$7.50-14, mains for 2 R$60-89; ⏰5pm-midnight Wed-Fri, from 11am Sat; 📶) This truly excellent microbrewery producer two types of pilsner as well as an Indian pale ale (our fave!), weiss, bock and an imperial stout. Call ahead to arrange a brewery tour. To reach the brewery, grab an hourly Volkmann bus from Av Beira Rio to Pomerode (R$4.95).

Cervejaria Bierland (☎3323-6588; www.bierland.com.br; Gustavo Zimmermann 5361, Blumenau; draft beers R$6-9.90; ⏰11am-2pm Mon, 11am-2pm & 4pm-midnight Tue-Sat) Don't judge a beer by its label – Bierland's brews are much better than their packaging. Ten in total are brewed here, including a pale ale, bock, golden ale and Viennese-style ale, with six on draft at any given time, along with finger foods to chase them with. It's 12km from Centro in Itoupava Central.

Cervejaria Das Bier (☎3397-8600; www.dasbier.com.br; Bonifácio Haendchen 5311, Gaspar; draft beers R$6.50-14.20; ⏰5pm-midnight Wed-Fri, 3pm-midnight Sat, 11am-7pm Sun) Das Bier brews its two pilsens according to *Reinheitsgebot* (Germany's 1516 beer purity law) and follows those with a brown ale, weiss, pale ale, roggen Kölsch and a dark laced with *rapadura* (unrefined whole cane sugar). It also offers the most serious eats of the breweries listed here. Tours by appointment. Verde Vale runs buses to Gaspar every half-hour from an intermunicipal stop across from Hotel Plaza Blumenau (R$3.40).

If you can't make it to Gaspar, it has opened **Das Bier Kneipe** (www.dasbier.com.br; Via Expressa Paul Fritz Kuehnrich 1600, Shopping Park Europeu; beers R$7.10-14.80; ⏰10am-10pm Mon-Sat, to 8pm Sun; 📶), 5km from central Blumenau in Shopping Park Europeu, with six choices on draft. Catch bus 15 from Estacão Blumenau (R$3.30).

action, a few blocks back from the sand, this HI hostel fills up fast in high season. Acoustics are an issue, though, especially next to the breakfast room (avoid room 107). Room rates can drop significantly off the high-season walk-up rates posted here.

Pousada Villa Atlântica POUSADA $$
(☎3081-3331; www.villa-atlantica.com.br; Rua 3300, 415; r R$340; ❄📶) For something more quaint, this good-value pousada, just two blocks from the beach in Barra Sul, has simple but clean rooms accented in light colors and some surprising mod-cons, like flat-screen TVs.

Felissimo Exclusive Hotel BOUTIQUE HOTEL $$$
(☎3360-6291; www.felissimoexclusivehotel.com.br; Ales Blaun 201 , Praia dos Amores; r R$959-1570; ❄📶🏊) This refined, 10-room pousada is a worthwhile spot to break the bank in Camboriú. Classic white dominates the decor, all designed by the discerning, hands-on owner, and some of the tuck-away-forever

rooms feature outdoor bathtubs; Nespresso machines and Bose Sounddocks are standard.

If you do leave the room, it's likely for the heated pool, the outdoor Japanese ofuro bath, or the excellent bistro with impressive patio views – easily one of the top dining spots in town (open every day but Sunday for non-guests; mains R$64 to R$130). It's 500m from Praia dos Amores.

Eating

Madero BURGERS $
(www.restaurantemadero.com.br; cnr Av Atlântica 3180; burgers R$23-38; ⊙11:45am-2:30pm & 6:15-11:30pm Mon-Thu, to midnight Fri, 11:45am-midnight Sat & Sun;) Curitiba's top burger joint landed itself on some prime beachfront real estate for its trendy Camboriú outlet. Madero does great burgers between even greater buns; but save room for the sinister *doce de leite* petit gâteau dessert.

Mundo Selvagem BRAZILIAN $
(Av Atlântica 2186; per kg R$46.90; ⊙11:30am-3pm & 6pm-12:30am Mon-Fri, 11:30am-12:30am Sat & Sun) This Buddhist-on-safari-themed *por-kilo* restaurant, complete with politically correct animal taxidermy, is one of Balneário's top-quality buffet lunch choices. Save room for dessert; we didn't and walked away wallowing in regret.

Bistrô Palatare FRENCH, ITALIAN $$
(☎3366-3699; www.palatare.com.br; Rua 2550, 699; mains R$41-68; ⊙7:30pm-midnight Fri & Sat;) A hands-on couple runs the best contemporary restaurant in town, specializing in Franco-Italian dishes that only hit their eight tables on Friday and Saturday nights. Zé Eduardo handles the kitchen, where mains like duck confit with soft polenta and mustard sauce or Uruguayan beef are dished up; his wife, Margeret, runs the dining room. Yes, you need reservations.

Drinking & Nightlife

Nightlife in Camboriú is king; the city boasts some of the world's most renowned clubs. They swing in and out of favor like a game of Pong and crowds here can swell to concert-level. **Green Valley** (☎3360-8097; www.greenvalley.art.br; Rio Mamoré 1083) and **Warung Beach Club** (☎3348-7643; www.warungclub.com.br; Av. José Medeiros Viêira 350, Praia Brava, Itajaí) are both mega. Tickets can usually be purchased from www.ingresso nacional.com.br, www.aloingressos.com.br or www.blueticket.com.br.

For something more low-key, pop into any number of great bars lining Av Atlântica.

Information

Portal Turístico (☎3367-8005; www.secturbc.com.br; Blvd do Estado 5041; ⊙7am-10pm, to midnight Dec-Feb) Balneário Camboriú's tourist information is helpful though inconveniently located at the entrance to town, 2km southwest of Av Atlântica.

Getting There & Away

Catarinense (www.catarinense.net) runs frequent buses to Florianópolis (R$24, 1½ hours), Joinville (R$28, 1½ hours) and Blumenau (R$20, 1½ hours).

For Bombinhas, **Praiana** (☎3367-1224; www.praiana.com.br) buses between Itajaí and Porto Belo pass the intermunicipal bus stop on Rua Santa Catarina next to the bus station between 16 and 24 times per day (R$4.70, one hour). Once in Porto Belo, you must switch to a Bombinhas-bound bus (R$3, 20 minutes).

It's a R$20 taxi ride from the bus station to Av Atlântica.

The **Bondindinho** (R$4), a colorful modified bus, combs Av Atlântica, Pontal Norte, Av Brasil and Via Gastronômica every 15 minutes. It operates 24 hours a day in summer.

South of Florianópolis

The waves have put this stretch of coastline on the map. Long gone are the quiet fishing villages and near-deserted beaches that once dotted the coast south of Florianópolis. While the local population is still largely descended from Azorean fishermen, you'll be hard-pressed to find them amid the suntanned surfers and bikini-clad beauties. The beaches that don't have big surf – and there are a few – are given over to fun-seeking families who show up every summer for their fix of sun and sand.

Guarda do Embaú

☎0XX48

Famous for its excellent left that breaks at the mouth of the river, Guarda do Embaú often makes the list of Brazil's best surfing beaches. But it's much more than that. When the river meets the sea in this laid-back, bohemian surf village, it creates one of southern Brazil's most postcard-perfect settings: surfers and sun-worshipers wading

OFF THE BEATEN TRACK

SERRA GERAL

High in the mountains of the Serra do Rio do Rastro (an offshoot of the Serra Geral), **São Joaquim** is about 290km southwest of Florianópolis. This little town in the Rio Canoas valley is famous for its apple orchards, many of which were planted by the local Japanese population. São Joaquim's other claim to fame is its snowfall: come in early July for the annual Festival de Inverno (Winter Festival). **Reunidas** (☎3224-1740; www.reunidas.com.br) has one daily bus from Florianópolis to São Joaquim (R$63, 5½ hours, 6:30pm). **Nevatur** (☎3222-5012; www.nevatur.com.br) makes the run on Monday, Wednesday, Friday and Sunday (R$77, 3:30pm).

Bom Jardim da Serra, founded in the 1870s by *gaúchos* (cowboys), is known as the 'capital of the water' and does indeed boast many lakes and waterfalls. About 45km south of São Joaquim, it also serves as the start of the hair-raising and spectacular winding road known as the **Estrada da Serrado Rio Rastro**, which switchbacks through high-mountain scenery toward the **Parque Nacional de São Joaquim**. The park boasts a breathtaking landscape of grassy highlands, thick *araucária* (Paraná pine) forests and Santa Catarina's highest peak, **Morro da Igreja** (1822m). The park lacks infrastructure, but hiking trails lead to panoramic lookouts and free-falling waterfalls. Nevatur has one 3:30pm bus to Bom Jardim da Serra (R$66, five hours, Monday, Wednesday, Friday and Sunday).

The nicest town is **Urubici**, 60km northeast of São Joaquim, famous for being near Morro da Igreja, where you'll find **Pedra Furada**, a large, naturally carved stone 30m in circumference. The area is a hotbed of adventure sports (hang gliding, rappelling) and cold weather – it recorded Brazil's chilliest day on historical record: -17.8°C in 1996! Reunidas services Urubici once daily from Floripa (R$48, four hours, 6:30pm).

back and forth across the beautiful Rio da Madre between town and Guarda's gorgeous sun-toasted sands. It's an excellent destination for wave riders and other bohemian types.

The tiny village has several restaurants, a lot of well-stocked surf shops and some jazzy boutiques. For more information on Guarda, see www.guardadoembau.com.br.

Sleeping & Eating

There are a half-dozen or so cocktail and sandwich *barracas* (stalls) on the beach in high season. In low season, the village is all but shut.

Nascer do Sol Suítes ACCOMMODATION SERVICES $
(nascerdosolsuites@outlook.com; Cumbatá 31; s/d R$110/160, with kitchen R$130/200; ❄📶) These simple budget rooms are perfectly comfortable and located on the 2nd floor of an emporium smack dab in the center of the action. There are no services, but the English-teaching owner, a *carioca* transplant, provides linguistic rescue services if needed.

Canto da Guarda POUSADA $$
(☎3283-2375; www.pousadacantodaguarda.com.br; Inês Maria de Jesus s/n; s/d from R$170/190, with air-con from R$210/230; ❄📶) A very cute and tasteful midrange choice offering just 10 rooms with English-speaking owners. There's little reason to upgrade above the bi-level standards, which are great value and perfectly comfortable with lovely hammock-strewn verandas.

Zululand CHALET $$
(☎3283-2093; www.zululand.com.br; Servidão Emerenciana s/n; d without air-con R$310, bungalows with air-con from R$380; ❄📶🏊) Owned by well-known model/actor/surfer Paulo Zulu, Zululand is a collection of funky-shaped bi-level bungalows well equipped with tasteful art and flat-screen TVs, all set about a property flush with lush tropical foliage.

Big Bamboo SEAFOOD $$$
(www.bigbamboo.com.br; Beira do Rio da Madre; mains for 2 R$62-180; ⏰11:30am-midnight Dec-Mar, 11:30am-midnight Wed-Sat, to 5pm Sun Apr-Nov) A solid choice for seafood with organic leanings and good microbrews in a seaside setting with views of the river and beach. It's owned by the father of Brazilian footballer

Fernando Prass, whose memorabilia decorates the bar.

Getting There & Away

Paulotur (www.paulotur.com.br) has buses throughout the day from Florianópolis to Guarda (R$13.50, two hours). To continue south to Praia do Rosa, catch an hourly Paulotur bus in the village back to Hwy BR-101 (R$3.10, 10 minutes), flag down a Garopaba-bound bus (R$7.50, 30 minutes) from the southside bus stop near the underpass, and get off at the Praia do Rosa turnoff on the road to Garopaba and catch a local bus (R$2.20) to town or taxi to your pousada (R$10 to R$20).

Praia do Rosa

☎0XX48

Santa Catarina's swankiest seaside town, Praia do Rosa, is about 15km south of Garopaba. The beach here, all 3km of it, is the stuff of models and photo shoots – one of Brazil's storybook destinations, backed by small sand dunes and flanked by outcrops of lush Mata Atlântica (Atlantic rainforest). Besides the stunning beach, Rosa has two things going for it: a cultured, eco-conscious population; and waves that propelled the town, which sits high on a bluff above the beach, from a modest fishing hamlet in the '70s to one of Brazil's most sophisticated surf villages.

In winter, the bay becomes a breeding ground for southern right whales, and mothers and calves can be seen from the beach.

There are no banks in Praia do Rosa – Garopaba or Imbituba are the nearest ATMs. And you'll need a map – it's a complicated labyrinth of dirt roads layered over various hillsides, most of which eludes Google maps.

Activities

Turismo Vida Sol e Mar WHALE WATCHING

(☎3355-6111; www.vidasolemar.com.br; Estrada Geral da Praia do Rosa; tours per person weekend/weekday R$140/90; ⊙tours 8am & 11am) Every winter, between June and October, hundreds of southern right whales return to the Santa Catarina coast. For a close encounter, these ecologically sound whale-watching tours leave from Garopaba and last for 90 minutes or more. Each boat has an IBF – Right Whale Institute scientist on board, but whale sightings are (obviously!) not guaranteed.

Sleeping

The highest road in town, Caminho do Rei, is home to accommodations options with sweeping views.

★ **Pousada La Roca** POUSADA $$

(☎3355-7020; www.pousadalaroca.com.br; Caminho do Rei; s/d R$320/380; ⊙closed Jul & Aug;) Argentine owners are constantly improving the best-value pousada along Caminho do Rei. Cool stone walls and shiny wood floors evoke an eco-stylish atmosphere and the new and improved shared balcony – complete with stylish lounge furniture – offers ocean views from the upper floors, while the lower floors are engulfed in greenery. Go for rooms 4 to 7 for extra privacy.

Albergue Explorer HOSTEL $$

(☎3355-7403; www.albergueexplorer.com.br; Francisco Marques; dm/d R$50/220;) There are better-value privates out there, but the dorms here, all with private bath and one with a private kitchen, are in good shape. Enjoy expansive views from the common patio, a small pool with waterfall, and the hospitality of Paulo and Francis, who speak English and Spanish, respectively.

★ **Quinta do Bucanero** POUSADA $$$

(☎3355-6056; www.bucanero.com.br; Estrada Geral da Praia do Rosa; r R$650-850, ste R$1390-1800;) Built Bedrock-style literally in and around the rocky cliffside, Rosa's most charming option is a 12-room gem of hospitality in jungly surrounds. Rooms are dressed in light colors and feature five-star comforts and view-riffic patios (new suites take that mantra to stupendous levels).

The gorgeous pool and new infinity-style, water-framed patio overlook the lagoons and the beach below, while the pousada has it's own exclusive path and boat for beach access.

Eating & Drinking

There are goods bars on the beach, but development has been restrained for the most part.

★ **Urucum** SEAFOOD $$

(☎3355-7330; www.restauranteurucum.blogspot.com; Estrada Geral da Praia do Rosa; mains for 2 R$96-134; ⊙1pm-midnight;) Chef Rafael Miralha hails from Espírito Santo and trained in Southern California before setting up shop in Rosa, *capixaba* (Espírito Santo) recipes in hand. He specializes in *moquecas* (seafood stews) done up in the style of his home state (healthier and lighter than the Bahian version). Alongside eye-popping views, his scrumptious creations are served in well-worn clay cookware and do not disappoint.

Tigre Asiático ASIAN **$$$**
(☎3355-7045; www.tigreasiaticorestaurante.com.br; Centrinho do Rosa; mains R$48-77; ⏲7-11pm; 📶) Considered Santa Catarina's best beach restaurant outside Floripa, the Asian Tiger, located in town, is an Indonesian-Thai fusion trip by way of local Brazilian ingredients. In a romantic candlelit space with no shortage of Buddhas minding your menu choices, your best bets are the seasonal dishes; the fiery four-pepper octopus will light you up!

ℹ Getting There & Away

From a stop in Centrinho diagonally opposite to Tigre Asiático, local buses run to Garopaba (R$3.70, 20 minutes), from where you can continue on to Florianópolis (R$22, two hours) with **Paulotur** (www.paulotur.com.br); and Imbituba (R$3.75, 40 minutes), from where **Santo Anjo** (www.santoanjo.com.br) and **Eucatur** (www.eucatur.com.br) go to Porto Alegre (R$69, six hours) six times per day.

Rio Grande do Sul

POP 10.7 MILLION

Includes ➡

Best Places to Eat

- ➡ Valle Rustico (p322)
- ➡ Belle du Valais (p325)
- ➡ Mamma Gema (p322)
- ➡ Atelier das Massas (p318)
- ➡ Per Voi (p325)

Best Places to Stay

- ➡ Parador Casa da Montanha (p329)
- ➡ Pousada Borghetto Sant'Anna (p321)
- ➡ Jardim Secreto Pousada (p325)
- ➡ Vila Ecológica (p328)
- ➡ Hostel Britanico (p324)

Why Go?

From the jaw-dropping forest-covered canyons of the national parks near Cambará do Sul, and cascading river valleys near cozy Brazilian alpine villages like Gramado, to the stunning Vale dos Vinhedos, where Italian-descended vintners produce wines to rival those of Chile and Argentina, the Rio Grande do Sul defies notions of typical Brazil.

Brazil's southernmost state is its most culturally distinct, home to an independently minded population steeped in cattle herding and cowboy culture. *Gaúchos*, as residents of Rio Grande do Sul are known, are a fiercely proud and traditional lot. In the countryside, it is not unusual to see old-timers sporting wide-brimmed hats and other traditional dress. Grilled meat, or *churrasco*, is still the state's favorite food, and everywhere – even in the cosmopolitan capital of Porto Alegre – locals suck down *chimarrão*, the distinctive, traditional tea made from the *maté* plant.

When to Go

Porto Alegre

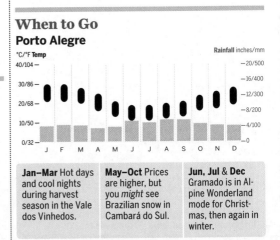

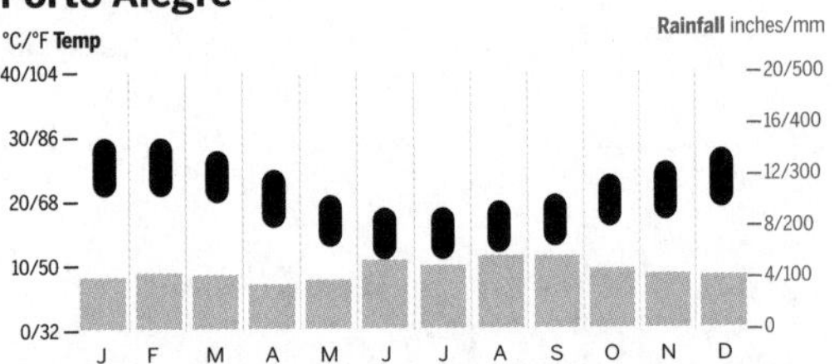

Jan–Mar Hot days and cool nights during harvest season in the Vale dos Vinhedos.

May–Oct Prices are higher, but you *might* see Brazilian snow in Cambará do Sul.

Jun, Jul & Dec Gramado is in Alpine Wonderland mode for Christmas, then again in winter.

History

Living on land long disputed by the Spanish and Portuguese, the people of Rio Grande do Sul used the conflict to create an identity distinct from the rest of Brazil. The region even declared its independence during the ill-fated Guerra dos Farrapos, a decade-long civil war ending in 1845. A wave of immigrants, mostly German, Italian and Swiss, began arriving in the late 19th century, reinforcing the region's cultural differences.

Getting There & Around

Porto Alegre is the state's transportation hub, with air and bus services to every major city nationwide. Excellent roads and efficient regional bus service make traveling relatively easy, with most long-distance routes originating in Porto Alegre.

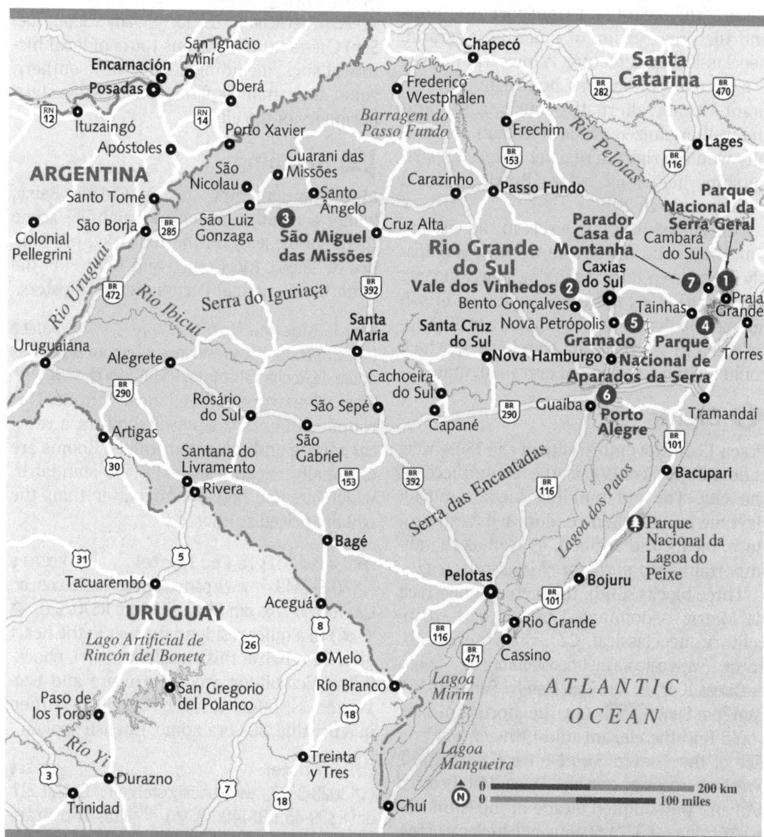

Rio Grande do Sul Highlights

1. Peering over the edge of the Cânion da Fortaleza in **Parque Nacional da Serra Geral** (p328).
2. Tasting your way through the New World's emerging wine region in the gorgeous **Vale dos Vinhedos** (p326).
3. Wandering the stunning grounds of the ruined Jesuit mission at **São Miguel das Missões** (p319).
4. Looking skyward in wonder while tackling the stunning Trilha do Rio do Boi through **Parque Nacional de Aparados da Serra** (p328).
5. Exploring the Swiss mountain village of **Gramado** (p323), where fondue flows freely throughout a gorgeous Brazilian winterscape.
6. Learning to sip *gaúcho* tea with a *chimarrão mestre* in **Porto Alegre** (p322).
7. Holing up in splurge-worthy tented luxury at the gorgeous **Parador Casa da Montanha** (p329).

PORTO ALEGRE

0XX51 / POP 1.4 MILLION

On the banks of the huge freshwater Lagoa dos Patos, Porto Alegre is southern Brazil's most important port city and a key player in Mercosul (the South American free trade agreement).

The downtown area has benefited from a thoughtful approach to development, including the creation of transportation hubs and the preservation of much of its grand, neoclassical architecture. A long tradition of progressive politics has helped nurture vibrant arts and alternative music scenes, and the well-organized gay and lesbian community won the right to register domestic partnerships here long before Brazil legalized gay marriage in 2013.

Unfortunately, crime levels in the city are concerning and the downtown area is palpably seedy, even during the day, when the city has a grittier feel than most southern Brazilian metropolises. Plans are in place to 'Lisbonize' the city's waterfront warehouses, which could revitalize the area if ever inaugurated.

Sights

Praça 15 de Novembro, site of the 1869 Mercado Público (p319), is the centerpiece of the city. The old building bustles during daytime hours, when vendors sell fresh produce, meats and seafood, as well as the all-important *erva maté* for *chimarrão* (tea).

Three blocks south, the picturesque Praça da Matriz is dominated by the early-20th-century, neoclassical **Catedral Metropolitana** (www.catedralmetropolitana.org.br; Duque de Caxias 1047; 7am-7pm Mon-Fri, 9am-7pm Sat, 8am-7pm Sun) FREE. On the northern side, you'll find the elegant mid-19th-century edifice of the **Teatro São Pedro** (3227-5100; www.teatrosaopedro.com.br; Praça Mal Deodoro s/n) and the sculpted facade of the **Biblioteca Público** (3224-5045; www.bibliotecapublica.rs.gov.br; cnr Riachuelo & General Câmara).

Museu de Arte do Rio Grande do Sul MUSEUM
(www.margs.rs.gov.br; Praça da Alfândega; 10am-7pm Tue-Sun) FREE A pedestrian promenade runs into Praça da Alfândega, the leafy square that is home to the Museu de Arte do Rio Grande do Sul. The neoclassical building is an impressive venue for regional artists. On the ground floor, the inviting Bistrot de MARGS takes advantage of the leafy setting, which is a lovely spot for lunch.

Museu Histórico Júlio de Castilhos MUSEUM
(www.museujuliodecastilhos.blogspot.com; Duque de Caxias 1205; 10am-5pm Tue-Sat) FREE Near the Praça da Matriz is Museu Histórico Júlio de Castilhos, displaying *gaúcho* artifacts in a typical 19th-century home.

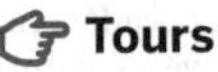

Tours

Linha Turismo CITY TOUR
(www.portoalegre.travel; Travessa do Carmo 84; weekday/weekend R$25/30; 9am-5:30pm Tue-Sun) Offers 90-minute bus tours of local historical sites, including a *zona sul* (southern zone) tour that explores the southeastern periphery of the city.

Sleeping

Most travelers now stay in Cidade Baixa, where a healthy hostel and nightlife scene thrive; or the leafy northern districts of Moinhos de Vento, Rio Branco and Bom Fim, the latter the domain of Porto's Alegre's hipsters.

Eko Residence Hotel HOTEL $
(3215-7600; www.residencehotel.com.br; Av Des André da Rocha 131; r from R$149;) This 97-apartment hotel near Parque Farroupilha offers solar-power showers, a vertical garden and rainwater toilets. Rooms are criminally cheap, especially the standards, which are far bigger and better than the equally-priced studios.

★ **Porto Alegre Eco Hostel** HOSTEL $
(3019-2449; www.portoalegreecohostel.com.br; Luiz Afonso 276; dm R$49, s/d from R$70/120;) In a quiet residential street in the heart of Cidade Baixa, this excellent hostel, chock-full of demolition wood furniture and eco-awareness, offers a lovely backyard garden in a pristine '30s-era home. English spoken.

Brick Hostel HOSTEL $
(3028-3333; www.brickhostel.com; Cabral 217; dm R$39-45, r R$140;) This Rio Branco hostel is walkable to Parque Farroupilha, Moinhos de Vento and Centro but offers a quiet respite from both the latter and the more rambunctious Cidade Baixa. Dripping in retro funk, there's an artsy common area (hipster local art for sale) and dorms with individual lockers, reading lights and electrical outlets, and a few minimalist privates.

Hotel Laghetto Viverone BOUTIQUE HOTEL $$
(2102-7272; www.hotellaghettomoinhos.com.br; Dr Vale 579; s/d from R$274/319, ste from R$691;) Porto Alegre's best boutique hotel is built off an exquisite 1937 mansion (hous-

Porto Alegre

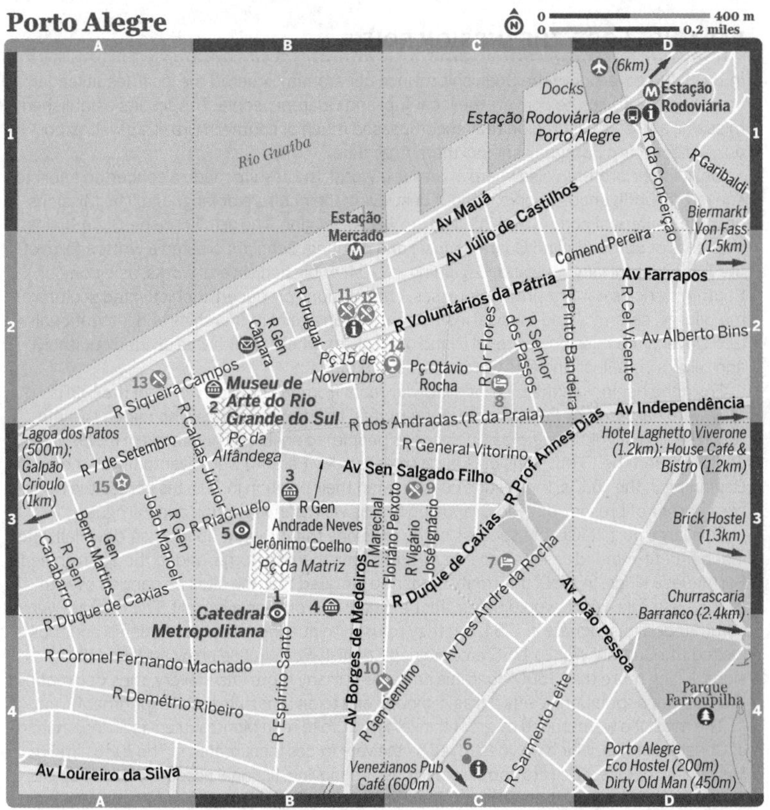

Porto Alegre

Top Sights

1 Catedral Metropolitana B3
2 Museu de Arte do Rio Grande do Sul B2

Sights

3 Biblioteca Público B3
4 Museu Histórico Júlio de Castilhos B3
5 Teatro São Pedro B3

Activities, Courses & Tours

6 Linha Turismo C4

Sleeping

7 Eko Residence Hotel C3
8 Hotel Continental Business C2

Eating

9 Atelier das Massas C3
Banco 40 .... (see 11)
Bar Gambrinus .... (see 11)
10 Boteco Natalicio C4
11 Café do Mercado B2
12 Mercado Público B2
13 Sabor Natural A2

Drinking & Nightlife

14 Chale da Praça XV C2

Entertainment

15 Casa da Cultura Mario Quintana A3

ing the lobby, bar and restaurant) with a glass atrium connecting the 132-guestroom tower to the historic property. Muted grey rooms are modern, minimalist and comfortable, while the three themed suites are worth the splurge for huge mirrors, sink-in bathtubs and unique design (we dig Nuptials and NYC).

It's in the upscale and leafy Moinhos de Vento, across the street from an intriguing historic, Versailles-inspired water treatment plant and gardens.

PARADISE LOST: THE MISSION ROUTE

In 1608, the governor of the Spanish province of Paraguay ordered the local Jesuit leader, Fray Diego de Torres, to convert the local Tupi and Guarani people. The Jesuits established missions across a vast region that encompassed much of southern Brazil, as well as portions of southern Paraguay and northern Argentina.

Unlike their brethren elsewhere in the New World, the Jesuits made a concerted effort to convert the indigenous people without destroying their culture or language. The missions became centers of culture and intellect, as well as religion. The arts flourished, combining elements of European and Guarani music and painting. Scholars created a written form of the Tupi-Guarani language and, beginning in 1704, published several works, using one of South America's earliest printing presses. The missions produced sophisticated sculpture, metallurgy, ceramics and musical instruments. In an age of monarchies and institutionalized slavery, the missions were an island of idealism, where wealth was divided equitably, and religion, intellect and arts were cultivated in tandem.

From the beginning, the missions faced threats from the outside world. In the 1620s they were harassed by Portuguese *bandeirantes,* bands of *paulistas* who raided the interior in search of gold and *índios* (indigenous people) to enslave. Thousands of *índios* were captured, and the 13 missions of Guayra (present-day Paraná) were eventually abandoned. Beginning in the 1630s, the Jesuits consolidated their position in 30 sites across the northwest corner of present-day Rio Grande do Sul, as well as in Argentina and Paraguay.

To a large part, it was the success of the missions that brought about their downfall. The independent-minded Jesuits became an embarrassment to Rome, and to the Spanish and Portuguese kings. In 1750, the Treaty of Madrid dictated that the sites be handed over to Portuguese rule, which would not protect the natives from enslavement. The Guarani were commanded to evacuate in 1754, but they refused to abandon their settlements and thus incited the Guarani War. In 1756, a combined Spanish-Portuguese army attacked the missions, killing more than 1500 Guaranis and selling many more into slavery, thus decimating the Guarani population. It was a tragic, bloody end to an amazing social experiment.

The missions were lauded by great thinkers from Voltaire to Montesquieu as an incarnation of Christian utopia, which was destroyed by the very forces that created it. The 1986 film *The Mission,* with Robert De Niro and Jeremy Irons, is a moving, fictional account of these events.

Today, all 30 missions are in ruins. Together, they form the **Rota Missões**, or 'Missions Route,' a network of pilgrimage sites for the faithful and the curious. Seven are in Brazil (in

Hotel Continental Business BUSINESS HOTEL **$$**
(☎3027-1600; www.hotelcontinentalbusiness.com.br; Praça Otávio Rocha 49; s/d weekend R$159/179, weekday R$179/199; ❄@📶) It's short on charm, but this 126-room hotel offers good-value rooms and professional service.

Eating

Sabor Natural BUFFET **$**
(Siqueira Campos 890; buffet R$20; ⏱11am-3pm Mon-Fri; 🌿) Vegetarians will delight at this all-organic, beef-free, all-you-can-eat buffet that caters to the downtown lunch crowd. Enjoy limitless soups, salads and other mostly herbivore-leaning fare.

★ **Atelier das Massas** ITALIAN **$$**
(☎3255-8888; www.atelierdemassas.com.br; Riachuelo 1482; pasta R$30-54; ⏱11am-2:30pm & 7-11:30pm Mon-Sat; 📶) Crammed with atmosphere as much as artisanal pastas, put this dive-like pasta bar on your immediate to-do list and never mind the curmudgeon old-school servers. There's an irresistible antipasti buffet and a very long list of delectable homemade pastas.

House Café & Bistro BRAZILIAN **$$**
(☎3407-7371; www.housecafebistro.com.br; Dona Laura 19; mains R$42-90; ⏱11:30am-2:30pm Tue, 11:30am-2:30pm & 7-11pm Wed-Sat; 📶) Housed in an eclectic 1917 Rio Branco mansion amid grand pianos and wine art, this funky bistro serves an extraordinarily good-value executive lunch for R$37, voted the best deal in the city under R$50 by *Veja*. Ana Celina dos Santos is a contemporary Brazilian whiz, using organic ingredients where possible.

Boteco Natalicio BOTECO **$$**
(www.botecionatalicio.com.br; Genuíno 217; mains R$20-55; ⏱11:30am-2:30pm & 5pm-1am Mon-Fri,

the northwestern part of Rio Grande do Sul), eight are in southern Paraguay and 15 are in northeastern Argentina.

The small, pleasant city of **Santo Ângelo** is the regional transportation hub and jumping-off point for exploring the Brazilian missions. The impressive cathedral, on Praça da Catedral, is a contemporary replica of the church at São Miguel das Missões and casts a gorgeous rust-orange glow over the center of town at sunrise. From here you can organize tours with **Caminho das Missões** (3312-9632; www.caminhodasmissoes.com.br; Antunes Ribas 984) or **Marino Theobald** (9961-3826; marino_theobald@yahoo.com.br; per site R$60-80) or, ideally, rent your own vehicle – try **Pontual** (3313-6000; www.pontualautolocadora.com.br; Marquês do Herval 1845; per day from R$110; 8:30am-noon & 2-6pm Mon-Fri, 9am-noon Sat).

The most striking of the missions is **Sítio Arqueológico São Miguel Arcanjo** (adult/child R$5/2.50; 9am-noon & 2-6pm, closed Mon) in São Miguel das Missões, 53km southwest of Santo Ângelo. The elegant church, designed by an Italian architect who was also a Jesuit friar, earned Unesco World Heritage status in 1984. It is surrounded by the mystical ruins of the Jesuit settlement, which evokes the feeling of 'paradise lost.' On a beautiful day, snapping pics will drain your iPhone battery. The archaeological site also includes the excellent little **Museu das Missões** (3381-1291; www.museudasmissoes.blogspot.com). Designed by Lúcio Costa, of Brasília fame, the museum contains an impressive collection of religious artifacts that were rescued from the ruins. A spectacular, if campy, sound-and-light show illustrates the history of the missions, coming soon in English and Spanish as well. Additional ruined missions in the region worth visiting include **São João Batista** (Entre-Ijuís; 9am-5pm) FREE, **Santuário de Caaró** (505-7427; 8-11:30am & 1:30-6pm Mon-Fri, or by appt) FREE, **São Lourenço Mártir** (8am-noon & 1:30-6pm) FREE and **São Nicolau** (8am-noon & 2-6pm Mon-Fri, 2-6pm Sat & Sun) FREE. For an excellent overview of the Brazilian missions see the website of the Rota Missões (www.rotamissoes.com.br).

From Santo Ângelo, **Unesul** (3313-2618; www.unesul.com.br) has three buses (fewer on Sunday) to Bento Gonçalves (R$93, 7½ hours, 10am, 2pm and 8:55pm). **Ouro e Prata** (www.viacaoouroeprata.com.br) buses run frequently between Santo Ângelo and Porto Alegre (from R$110, seven hours, up to 10 per day). **Antonello Turismo** (3312-2184; www.turismoantonello.com.br) has four daily buses to São Miguel das Missões (R$10.20, 1½ hours, 7:15am, 11am, 3:30pm and 4:45pm) Monday to Friday, three on Saturday (10am, 1:30pm and 3:30pm) and two on Sunday (9:30am and 6:20pm).

5pm-1am Sat;) The walls of this lively, bi-level *boteco* (open-air bar) straddling Centro and Cidade Baixa is covered in some 200-odd musings of comedians and locals, and packs a wild punch to *chope* (draft beer) starved locals, here to preempt the beer with regional delicacies like honey-smoked pork ribs and crunchy shrimp sandwiches with *coalho* cheese. Saturday *feijoada* (bean-and-meat stew), too (male/female R$40/35).

Churrascaria Barranco BARBECUE $$
(3331-6172; www.churrascariabarranco.com.br; Av Protásio Alves 1578; mains R$27-67; 11am-2am;) Seasoned just so for nearly 50 years, this always-crowded temple of beef offers no cowboy shows or endless skewers of speared meat, but this is where locals go for their *carne* (meat) fix. The huge outdoor patio is packed with lively patrons washing back prime cuts of Angus with selections from the nearly 300-label wine list while dodging the insistent salad carts. It's in Petrópolis, 4km southwest of Centro.

Mercado Público MARKET $$
(www2.portoalegre.rs.gov.br/mercadopublico; 7:30am-7:30pm Mon-Fri, to 6:30pm Sat) Porto Alegre's bustling public market offers a wealth of eats. Recommended options include **Banco 40** (www.banca40.com.br; Mercado Público; 8am-7:30pm Mon-Fri, to 6:30pm Sat), home of the incomparable *super bomba royal* (a showy ice cream and fruit salad concoction; R$15); **Gambrinus** (www.gambrinus.com.br; Mercado Público; mains R$36-85; 11:30am-8:30pm Mon-Fri, to 4pm Sat), an old-world seafood restaurant; and **Café Do Mercado** (www.cafedomercado.com.br; Mercado Público; coffee R$4-13.50; 8am-7:30pm Mon-Fri, 9:30am-5pm Sat), one of the city's best cafes.

Drinking & Nightlife

Cidade Baixa and upscale Moinhos de Vento are Porto Alegre's nightlife hubs. The city also has a very active gay and lesbian social scene – try **Astro** (www.astroclub.com.br; Av Goethe 141; ⊙11pm-7am Fri & Sat) or **Venezianos Pub Café** (www.venezianos.com.br; Joaquim Nabuco 397; ⊙7pm-3am Tue-Sat) or take your pick from a number of hotspots on Rua de República between Lima e Silva and João Pessoa in Cidade Baixa, especially on Sunday evenings.

★Biermarkt Von Fass BAR
(www.biermarkt.com.br; Barão de Santo Ângelo 497; beers R$9-48; ⊙6-11:30pm Mon-Sat; 📶) With its 38 taps, this Moinhos de Vento drinking den is said to offer the most beers on draft in all of Latin America. We're not sure about that, but it is the stomping ground of craft-beer fiends with a strong emphasis on local breweries, including co-brews by Seasons (with San Diego's Green Flash) and Tupiniquim (with Copenhagen's Evil Twin).

Dirty Old Man BAR
(www.dirtyoldman.com.br; Lima e Silva 956; ⊙from 7pm Tue-Sun; 📶) This awesomely named bar (a nod to Bukowski) is Cidade Baixa's best. Draft Baldhead IPA and English Bitter Ales, along with cool cocktails (R$12 to R$17), fuel the good time, while the crowd swilling it down is as eclectic and rare as the environment itself.

Chale da Praça XV BRAZILIAN
(www.chaledapracaxv.com.br; Praça 15 de Novembro; mains R$31-60; ⊙11am-11pm; 📶) Housed in a pleasant, Victorian-style garden house and surrounded by a sprawling terrace, this Porto Alegre institution buzzes with activity. Great Sunday bet.

☆ Entertainment

Casa da Cultura Mario Quintana CINEMA
(☎3221-7147; www.ccmq.rs.gov.br; Rua dos Andradas 736; ⊙2-9pm Mon, from 9am Tue-Fri, from noon Sat & Sun) The cultural center in this pink baroque building has a cinema and two busy cafes. The 7th-floor Café Santo de Casa is a lovely place to listen to live music and watch the sunset over Lagoa dos Patos.

ℹ Information

Banco do Brasil (www.bb.com.br; Av Uruguaí 185) Visa/Mastercard ATM.

Bradesco (www.bradesco.com.br; Siqueira Campos 1163) Visa/Mastercard ATM.

Brigada Militar (www.brigadamilitar.rs.gov.br; Rua dos Andradas 522) Military police command.

C.A.T. (www.turismo.rs.gov.br) Rio Grande do Sul state tourism board runs two helpful tourist information centers, one in Rodoviária (Centro de Atencão ao Turista; ☎3225-0677; ⊙8am-4pm

BUSES FROM PORTO ALEGRE

DESTINATION	STARTING FARE (R$)	TIME (HR)	BUS COMPANY
Buenos Aires (AR)	249.50	21	Pluma (www.pluma.com.br)
Cambará do Sul	36	6	Citral (www.citral.tur.br)
Canela	29	3	Citral (www.citral.tur.br)
Chuí	101.50	7	Planalto (www.planalto.com.br)
Curitiba	126	13	Penha (http://vendas.nspenha.com.br)
Florianópolis	86	6	Santo Anjo (www.santoanjo.com.br)
Gramado	27	3	Citral (www.citral.tur.br)
Montevideo (UY)	205.50	12	TTL (www.ttl.com.br)
Pelotas	50	3½	Embaixador (www.expressoembaixador.com.br)
Rio de Janeiro	295	26	Penha (http://vendas.nspenha.com.br)
Rio Grande	73	5	Planalto (www.planalto.com.br)
Sânto Angelo	110	7	Ouro e Prata (www.ouroeprata.com)
São Francisco de Paula	22	3	Citral (www.citral.tur.br)
São Paulo	213	19	Penha (http://vendas.nspenha.com.br)
Torres	36	3	Unesul (www.unesul.com.br)

Mon-Fri, to 1pm Sat & Sun) and one at the Airport (Arrivals Hall, Terminal 1; 7:30am-10pm).

C.I.T (Centro de Informações Turísticas; 3211-5705; www.portoalegre.travel; Mercado Público; 9am-6pm Mon-Sat) Cidade Baixa/Linha Turismo (Centro de Informações Turísticas; 3289-6765; www.portoalegre.travel; Travessa do Carmo 84; 8am-6pm) Airport (Centro de Informações Turísticas; 3358-2048; www.portoalegre.travel; Arrivals Hall, Terminal 1; 8am-10pm) Three of the most convenient and well-organized municipality tourist information booths.

Correios (www.correios.com.br; Siqueira Campos 1100; 9am-6pm Mon-Fri, to noon Sat) Postal services.

Polícia Federal (3235-9000; www.dpf.gov.br; Av Ipiranga 1365; 8am-6pm Mon-Fri) Visa extensions.

Getting There & Away

AIR

Terminals 1 and 2 of Porto Alegre's **Salgado Filho International Airport** (POA; 3210-0101; Av Severo Dulius), 6km from downtown, are connected by a free shuttle. The majority of airlines operate out of Terminal 1, but Azul/Trip departs from the older Terminal 2. In addition to major destinations throughout Brazil, international destinations include Buenos Aires, Lima, Lisbon, Miami, Montevideo, Panama City and Santiago. Take a taxi (R$25 to R$30, 15 minutes) or ride the metro (R$1.70, 30 minutes).

BUS

The busy **long-distance bus station** (3210-0101; www.rodoviaria-poa.com.br; Largo Vespasiano Julioveppo 70), 1.5km northeast of Centro, is accessible by metro; alternatively, a taxi downtown costs R$10 or so from the pre-paid **Ponte do Taxi** (3221-9371; Rodovíaria). If your baggage is considered large, they will tack on an additional R$6.55.

Two day and two overnight buses go to Chuí on the Uruguayan border during the week (two fewer on weekends); otherwise you can connect in Pelotas.

Getting Around

Porto Alegre's metro, **Trensurb** (www.trensurb.gov.br; one way R$1.70; 5am-11:20pm), has convenient stations at Estação Mercado (by the port), Estação Rodoviária (the next stop) and the airport (three stops beyond). For Cidade Baixa, catch bus T5 from the airport or 282, 2821, 244 or 255 from the bus station (R$3.25). Both the metro and the bus stop sit between Terminals 1 and 2 (closer to 2). The free **Aeromóvel** (Brazil's first atmospherically-powered people mover) connects the metro with the terminals every 10 to 15 minutes.

SERRA GAÚCHA

The scenic stretch of mountains north of Porto Alegre is known as the Serra Gaúcha. This lovely landscape – particularly beautiful between Nova Petrópolis and Gramado – is characterized by forested hillsides and unexpected rocky cliffs, often sparkling with waterfalls.

The region was first settled by Germans (beginning in 1824) and later by Italians (starting in the 1870s), and this heritage is still a source of pride and fascination. Although the mountains don't reach much more than 1000m, Gramado and Canela resemble Swiss villages in their architecture and atmosphere. In Bento Gonçalves and the nearby Vale dos Vinhedos, fountains flow with *vinho*, as descendants of Italian immigrants continue fostering momentum within the wine industry.

Bento Gonçalves

0XX54 / POP 107,200

Considering the region's Italian heritage and its dry, mountainous landscape, it makes sense that Rio Grande do Sul would be Brazil's wine epicenter. The command post for this burgeoning wine industry is Bento Gonçalves, 124km north of Porto Alegre – a distinctly indistinct middle-class Brazilian city that does not offer much beyond convenient access to the region's vineyards. The entrance to town leaves no doubt to its allegiances: a gigantic 'wine barrel' known as Pórtico da Pipa straddles the street.

Sleeping & Eating

There is little reason to stay in Bento proper, with a wealth of beautiful inns in the countryside just steps away in Vale dos Vinhedos. It's more convenient, however, if you're dependent on public transportation.

Hotel Vinocap BUSINESS HOTEL **$**

(3455-7100; www.vinocap.com.br; Barão do Rio Branco 245; s/d from R$159/279;) Perfectly agreeable, centrally located business hotel, which is well equipped for wine tourism.

★Pousada Borghetto Sant'Anna POUSADA **$$$**

(3453-2355; www.borghettosantanna.com.br; Linha Leopoldina 868; ste R$380, cottages R$450-500;) About 4km from Bento, perched above the Vale dos Vinhedos, this cluster of romantic stone houses gives a fantastic view of the valley below. Reminiscent of Tuscany, the lodgings mix rustic charm with sumptuous comfort and unobtrusive construction, right down to large portions of sedentary rock in the showers. Breakfast is simpler than expected, but views make up for it.

Mamma Gema ITALIAN $$
(☎3459-1392; www.mammagema.com.br; Estrada RS 444, Km18.9; mains for 2 R$73-105; ⏲11am-3:30pm Tue-Fri, to 4pm Sat & Sun) Unlike many of the trattorias in the region, Mamma focuses on quality, not quantity, and is a mainstay in Vale dos Vinhedos. The owner, an ex professional footballer, harvests his own wild mushrooms for use in his perfectly executed pastas and risottos.

At night, all eyes turn to its downstairs pizzeria, **Pizza Entre Vinhos** (☎3459-1392; www.mammagema.com.br; Estrada RS 444, Km18.9; pizzas R$63-77; ⏲7-10:30pm Thu-Thu, to 11pm Fri & Sat; 📶), where the best pizza in the region is served alongside the best selection of Vale dos Vinhedos wines in one spot.

★Valle Rustico BRAZILIAN $$$
(☎8123-0080; www.vallerustico.com.br; Linha Marcílio Dias s/n; prix-fixe with/without wine R$150/100; ⏲7:30-10pm Wed-Sat, noon-3:30pm Sun; 📶) Wine country's best restaurant sits down a lonely and dark Vale dos Vinhedos dirt road – don't worry, it's open – where you'll find an atmospheric beamed-wooden-ceiling dining room in the basement of a house. Local chef Rodrigo Bellora offers a nightly-changing seasonal 'experience' menu (eight to 11 courses; clocking in at 85% organic), optionally paired with Vinhedos wines. Reservation essential.

Canta Maria ITALIAN $$$
(☎3453-1099; www.cantamaria.com.br; RST-470, Km217; buffet R$62/75; ⏲11:30am-3:30pm & 7-11pm Mon-Sat; 📶) This classic near Pórtico da Pipa serves the '*Gaúcho* Happy Meal,' a brought-to-table buffet of *comida típica italiana*: *cappelletti* (chicken) soup, salad, pasta, *galeto* (rotisserie spring chicken), *linguiça* (garlicky pork sausage), pork ribs, polenta and fried cheese for R$62; tack on a *rodízio* (smorgasbord) of grilled meats and lamb for R$75 (unnecessary unless you've got a real hankering). Call ahead for free transport.

Drinking & Nightlife

Doppio Malto BAR
(www.facebook.com/doppiomaltobirreria; Rua 15 de Novembro 122; ⏲5:30-11pm Tue-Sat; 📶) Yes, this is wine country, but this bar is worth a try for its half-dozen or so craft beers on draft (most hail from their own brewery). This is genuine drinking man's territory, with proper pints and some of the best suds we tried in the South.

Information

You'll find Visa/Mastercard ATMs at Banco do Brasil and Bradesco, both located on Praça Walter Galassi.

C.A.T. (Centro de Atendmiento ao Turista; ☎3453-6699; www.bentogoncalves.rs.gov.br; Marechal Deodoro 70; ⏲9am-5pm Mon-Fri, to 3pm Sat & Sun) is a good tourism office with a must-have Vale dos Vinhedos map. There's another branch at Pórtico da Pipa (Centro de Atendmiento ao Turista; ☎3453-2555; Travessa Carazinho s/n, Pórtico da Pipa; ⏲8am-5:30pm Mon-Fri, 9am-5pm Sat & Sun).

CHEERS TO CHIMARRÃO

It was the indigenous Guarani who taught Spanish settlers the pleasures of *chimarrão* (tea from the *maté* plant) and how to sip it, not from a cup but through a *bomba* (straw) stuck into a hollowed-out *cuia* (gourd). Also known as *erva maté*, this tea-like beverage is made from the leaves of the *maté* tree, which is native to the *pampas* (grassy plains) that extend from Argentina and Uruguay through southern Brazil.

The original *gaúchos*, the men who tended the region's vast cattle herds, quickly became addicted to *maté*'s pleasurable effects, which are at once energizing and calming. *Chimarrão* is an acquired taste and a serious addiction, but these days, this ancient tradition is getting a boost from scientists and pseudoscientists alike, who make claims about *maté*'s health benefits, from lower blood pressure to increased intelligence. Hard results are yet to come.

Anyone you meet with a gourd (read: that's nearly everyone!) will offer you some, or pop into touristy *churrascaria* **Galpão Crioulo** (www.churrascariagalpaocrioulo.com.br; Parque Maurício Sirotsky Sobrinho; buffet lunch/dinner R$62.50/79; ⏲11:30am-3pm & 7:30pm-midnight) and begin your own personal case study with the in-house master!

Getting There & Around

The **long-distance bus station** (☎3452-1311; www.rodoviariabento.com.br; Gomes Carneiro 19) is about 1km north of the center. **Bento** (☎3452-1311; www.bentotransportes.com.br) has hourly service to Porto Alegre (R$29.60, 2½ hours); for Caxias do Sul (R$8.15, 1¼ hours). **Ozelame** (☎3452-3777; www.ozelame.com.br) departs hourly as well. For Canela, Gramado or Cambará do Sul, connect in Caxias. **Unesul** (☎3903-1710; www.unesul.com.br) has three daily buses to Santo Ângelo (R$93, 7½ hours, 10am, 2pm and 8 :55pm).

For Vale dos Vinhedos, **Transportes Monte Bello** (☎3457-1100) can get you onto Via Trento four times a day (R$5.05, 30 minutes, 10:30am, 11:45am, 4:30pm and 6pm), but renting your own vehicle or a **local tour** (p326) are best.

Pinto Bandeira

Sleepy Pinto Bandeira, just 15km northeast of Bento Gonçalves, is a separate wine appellation from the more established Vale dos Vinhedos but boasts soil arguably more suited for sparkling wines. It has its own fair share of charming places to sleep and taste.

For more information on Pinto Bandeira, see www.asprovinho.com.br.

Sights

Cave Geisse — WINERY

(☎3455-7461; www.vinicolageisse.com.br; Linha Jansen s/n; tastings R$20-45, ATV tour R$70; ⏲9-11:30am & 1-5pm Mon-Fri, 10am-5pm Sat, 10am-4pm Sun) Founded by famed Chilean winemaker Mario Geisse, Cave Geisse produces Brazil's most internationally heralded sparkling wines and is a cult favorite abroad. Reservations are best.

Don Giovanni — WINERY, POUSADA

(☎3455-6293; www.dongiovanni.com.br; Linha Amadeu Km12; tastings R$15, r R$375-450; ⏲9-11:30am & 1-5pm Mon-Fri, 9am-5:30pm Sat, 9am-1pm Sun) Both a winery and a homey pousada, Don Giovanni is a one-stop shop in Pinto Bandeira. The eight rooms here are large and feed off a rustic upscale aesthetic, with expansive views of 50 hectares of vineyards. It's most famous for sparkling wines.

Getting There & Away

Bento (☎3452-1311; www.bentotransportes.com.br) services Pinto Bandeira four times a day (R$8.15, one hour, 10:30am, 11:40am, 4pm and 5:45pm), passing the turnoffs for many of the wineries.

Gramado

☎0XX54 / POP 32,200

Gramado isn't as sexy as Ipanema or as alluring as the Amazon, but this tiny mountain resort, which bills itself as 'naturally European,' is one of Brazil's nicest. It does indeed feel like a Swiss mountain village – boutiques sell avant-garde glassworks and gourmet chocolate, local restaurants specialize in fondue, hotels are decked out like Swiss chalets – while infrastructure, safety and scenery all meet the standards of similar size towns in North America or Europe (pedestrian crosswalks are respected!). At times the insistence on *fahrvergnügen* crosses over into kitsch, and there is very little in the way of culture, but the overall effect is pleasant, and the standard of living in this little piece of alpine paradise is unparalleled in Brazil.

Sights & Activities

Três Coroas, 24km south of Gramado, is one of Brazil's whitewater-rafting hotspots.

Lago Negro — LAKE

About 1.5km southeast of the center, Lago Negro is an attractive, artificial lake surrounded by hydrangeas and crowded with swan boats.

Snowland — SNOW SPORTS

(☎3295-6000; www.snowland.com.br; RS 235, 9009; adult/child R$99/60; ⏲10am-5pm Mon-Fri, 9am-6pm Sat & Sun) Latin America's first snow park, opened in 2013, is an artificial winter wonderland of skiing, snowboarding, snowmobiling, tubing and ice skating, as well as bars and restaurants. It's 6km west of Centro.

Tours

Passeio Panorâmico Gramado — CITY TOUR

(☎3286-9324; www.jardineiradashortensias.com.br; Av das Hortênsias 1710; adult/child R$20/10; ⏲10:30am, 2pm & 4pm) This two-hour bus tour gives an overview of the town's history, architecture and nature highlights.

Festival & Events

Festival de Gramado — FILM

(www.festivaldegramado.net; Av Borges de Medeiros 2697, Palácio dos Festivais; tickets R$15-30; ⏲Aug) Gramado hosts the nine-day Festival de Gramado, Brazil's most prestigious film festival.

Gramado

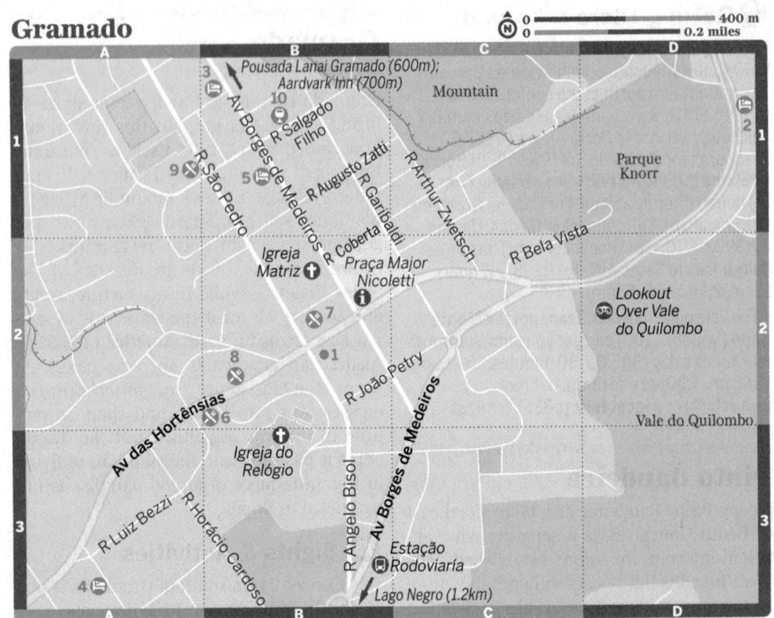

Gramado

Activities, Courses & Tours
1 Passeio Panorâmico Gramado B2

Sleeping
2 Hostel Britanico D1
3 Hotel Vovó Carolina B1
4 Jardim Secreto Pousada A3
5 Pousada Metodista B1

Eating
6 Belle du Valais B2
7 Josephina Café B2
8 Per Voi B2
9 Serra Grill A1

Drinking & Nightlife
10 Taberna MF B1

Sleeping

We list prices here for Gramado's high seasons – weekends in winter (June to August). Rates can rise significantly over Christmas and during the film festival.

★ **Hostel Britanico** HOSTEL $
(☎3286-6250; www.britanico.com; Arthur Reimann 1; dm R$75, d/q R$179/399; ❄📶) This outstanding newcomer – call it a 'poshtel' – is an eight-minute stroll from central Gramado on the road to Canela. Dorms are of a standard previously unseen in Brazil, with reading lights, electricity outlets and privacy curtains (there are even a few double-bed dorms for you and yours!); private rooms and common areas are better than many hotels. English spoken.

Pousada Metodista POUSADA $
(☎3286-2299; Av Borges de Medeiros 2889; r with/without bathroom from R$250/90; 📶) Seven rooms in the hallowed halls behind the Methodist church have big, industrial-style bathrooms; a recent remodeling has added new box-spring beds and cozy comforters. If you're looking for hostel prices but peace and quiet, you'll find salvation here.

Hotel Vovó Carolina HOTEL $$
(☎3286-2433; www.vovocarolina.com.br; Av Borges de Medeiros 3129; s/d from R$230/290; ❄📶) Right in the center, this 19-room hotel has smallish, carpeted rooms, no-nonsense service and cake-laden breakfasts.

Aardvark Inn POUSADA $$
(☎3286-0806; www.aardvarkinn.com.br; Mestre 18; s/d from R$270/300; ❄📶) This residential small-scale inn tips the warm-and-fuzzy to value scale in your pleasant favor. Accented with refurbished wood throughout, rooms

are large with whitewashed adobe walls and several have a private garden entrance.

Pousada Lanai Gramado POUSADA **$$**
(☎3295-1120; www.pousadalanaigramado.com.br; Travessa Corsan 19; s/d from $280/310; ❄@📶) Two combined residential mansions 1.5km from the main square house a range of upscale, borderline-meretricious private rooms, but the real coup is the stupendous views on offer at breakfast (and those *doce de leite*-stuffed pastries).

★ **Jardim Secreto Pousada** POUSADA **$$$**
(☎3286-2023; www.pousadajardimsecreto.com.br; F G Bier 110; r from R$490; ❄📶) An English-speaking, twenty-something sibling threesome runs the hospitality at this triumphantly lovely pousada just 800m from the main square. Extensive gardens surround the property, which is dotted with gnomes, birdhouses and other rustic-chic knickknacks. If there's a downside, it's the four- to five-night minimum in high season (and two-night weekend minimum otherwise).

Eating

Gramado has no shortage of Italian, German and Swiss cuisine, reflecting the ethnic makeup of the region's original settlers. Rua Coberta is lined with sidewalk cafes. Many restaurants shut down for up to a month after Carnaval and some are only open Thursday to Sunday outside peak season.

Serra Grill BUFFET **$**
(São Pedro 567; per kg R$47.90; ⏲11am-2:30pm Mon-Fri, to 3pm Sat & Sun; 📶) People line up around the corner to get at this high-quality buffet, which features an excellent, varied selection of grilled meats, well-done pastas and heartier regional mains, as well as good veggie options (we even spotted wheat berries!).

Josephina Café CAFE **$$**
(www.josephinacafe.com.br; Pedro Benetti 22; mains R$21-52; ⏲11:30am-11pm Tue-Sun; 📶) Gramado's best cafe is short on forced touristy schtick, long on charm. Come for espresso (proper to-go cups!), sweets, more sophisticated bistro fare or just drinks.

★ **Per Voi** ITALIAN **$$**
(☎3286-0803; www.pervoigramado.com.br; Av das Hortênsias 1511; buffet R$62, pastas R$32-39; ⏲noon-3pm & 7-11pm Tue-Sun; 📶) Per Voi isn't Gramado's most famous joint specializing in the Italian-*gaúcho* tradition of bottomless *cappelletti* (chicken) soup, *galeto* (rotisserie chicken) and a series of pasta dishes, but it's the best and most welcoming. Top-notch servers and a charismatic owner glide about the warm-hearted ambiance, ensuring it feels less like a chicken factory and more like an intimate Italian restaurant.

The pastas, made in-house, are wonderful and the *galeto* comes in several variations. Eat here instead.

Belle du Valais SWISS **$$$**
(☎3286-1744; www.belleduvalais.com.br; Av das Hortênsias 1432; mains R$80-130; ⏲7pm-midnight Mon-Fri, noon-3pm Sat & Sun; 📶) Fondue is as common as the cold in Gramado, but this old-school-elegant hotspot is considered one of Brazil's best. The menu is rounded out by filets cooked on volcanic rocks and a wealth of impressive meat and fish preparations, all finely pairable with local wines, including Lidio Carraro, one of Brazil's most heralded.

Service? Impeccable. Reservations? Recommended.

Drinking & Nightlife

Taberna MF BAR
(www.facebook.com/legadoMF; Salgado Filho 170; ⏲5-11pm; 📶) Yes, the 'MF' stands for 'Motherfucker' (we asked!). As if that's not reason enough to pop in, you'll find 30 taps of craft beer here, including a concentration of Belgian-style ales and a great IPA.

Purists may scoff, but it also features blends, mixing different styles into one beer glass – an unorthodox but bold move to say the least. With 170ml and 300ml serving sizes in crystal from Blumenau, this is a spot *lupelomaníacos* ('hopheads' in Portuguese!) can settle in for a long and festive evening.

Information

Bradesco (www.bradesco.com.br; Av das Hortênsias 1929) Visa/Mastercard ATM.

C.A.T (Centro de Atendimento ao Turista; ☎3286-1475; www.gramado.rs.gov.br; Av Borges de Medeiros 1646; ⏲9am-7pm) Well-stocked tourist information office.

Getting There & Around

The town is small enough to get everywhere by foot. From the **bus station** (☎3286-1302; Av Borges de Medeiros 2100), **Citral** (www.citral.com.br) runs buses all day to Porto Alegre (from R$27, 2½ hours) and Canela (from R$4.35, 20 minutes); and at least seven daily to Caxias do Sul (from R$13.40, two hours).

1

Vale dos Vinhedos

Brazil isn't the first country that rolls off the tongue of passionate oenophiles engulfed in wine-fueled debates, but those in the know are starting to rave about the outstanding award-winning sparkling wines, merlots and chardonnays produced in southern Brazil's Vale dos Vinhedos.

Wine Tasting

Hard work, innovation and cooperative earth has catapulted mostly Italian immigrant families from novelty winemakers in the 1870s to heralded vintners 150 years later – Vale dos Vinhedos was named one of 2013's 10 Best Wine Travel Destinations by *Wine Enthusiast* magazine. More than 30 wineries, rural inns and restaurants dot the Estrada do Vinho and Via Trento, a picturesque loop.

Vinícola Almaúnica

Almaúnica's (☎3459-1384; www.almaunica.com.br; RS 444, Km17.35; tastings R$30; ⏲8am-noon & 1:30-5:30pm Mon-Fri, 10am-noon & 1:30-5:30pm Sat, 10am-1pm Sun) Syrahs and Quatro Castas blends are some of the region's most highly awarded reds, and the owner is often in the tasting room.

Casa Valduga

One of Brazilian wine's big guns, **Valduga** (☎2105-3154; www.casavalduga.com.br; Via Trento 2355; tasting & tour R$40, s/d from R$220/300; ⏲9:30am-6pm Mon-Sat, 9:30am-5pm Sun) offers free tastings as well as tours of its striking winery and pousada (hourly from 9:30am to 4:30pm).

Vinícola Miolo

At **Vinícola Miolo** (☎2102-1540; www.miolo.com.br; Estrada do Vinho, km21; tastings R$15;

LELIA VALDUGA / GETTY IMAGES ©

SAMBAPHOTO/GEYSON MAGNO / GETTY IMAGES ©

1. Caminhos de Pedra
2. Vineyard
3. Grape harvesting

ANDREA PISTOLESI / GETTY IMAGES ©

⌚9am-4:30pm) champagnes are notable, as well as cabernet sauvignon and merlot. The huge complex spreads out from an artificial lake and tours are run every half-hour.

Gastronomy

Valle Rustico (p322) sits down a lonely and dark dirt road – don't worry, it's open – where you'll find an atmospheric dining room in the basement of a local house. Local chef done good Rodrigo Bellora culls as many ingredients as possible from the restaurant's own organic gardens. Unlike many trattorias in the region, Mamma Gema (p322) focuses on quality, not quantity.

Tours

Vale das Vinhas (☎3451-4216; www.valedasvinhastur.com.br; Barão do Rio Branco 245; per person from R$85 incl tastings; ⌚8:15am & 1:15pm) runs three-hour tours that visit three wineries in the Vale dos Vinhedos, as well as a full-day option. **Caminhos de Pedra** (☎3455-6333; www.caminhosdepedra.org.br; Linha Palmeiro s/n) organizes fascinating self-guided tours of architectural relics from the 19th century.

Best Places to Stay

The cluster of romantic stone houses at Pousada Borghetto Sant'Anna (p321) gives a fantastic view of the valley below. Reminiscent of Tuscany, the lodgings mix rustic charm with sumptuous comfort.

Hotel & Spa do Vinho Caudalie (☎2102-7200; www.spadovinho.com.br; RS 444, Km21; r/ste from R$487/R$587; ❄@📶🏊) boasts unobstructed views of the vineyards, which you can ogle from the hotel's pool and wine-barrel spa to the upscale restaurant.

Cambará do Sul

☎0XX54 / POP 6500

Cambará do Sul is a dusty frontier town built on cattle ranching with an authentic *gaúcho* aura. Located 186km northeast of Porto Alegre, it serves as a base for both Parque Nacional de Aparados da Serra and Parque Nacional da Serra Geral, the national parks that are somewhat capriciously described as the 'Brazilian Grand Canyon.'

At an altitude of 1000m, Cambará receives more snowfall than any other destination in Rio Grande do Sul, making it a popular destination during winter months (May to October), when prices are higher.

Cambará do Sul claims to be the 'capital of honey,' and you can sample this local delicacy all over town.

Sights & Activities

Parque Nacional de Aparados da Serra CANYON

(☎3251-1227; admission R$7; ⏲8am-5pm Tue-Sun) Located 18km from the town of Cambará do Sul, this magnificent park occupies 102.5 sq km on the border between Rio Grande do Sul and Santa Catarina states. It's here that vast, uninspired pasturelands give way to a series of stunning canyons, where the earth opens up and drops to depths of 720m.

The park preserves one of the country's last *araucária* (Paraná pine) forests, earning it its protected status. But the main attraction is the **Cânion do Itaimbezinho**, a narrow, 5800m-long canyon with sheer parallel escarpments, ranging from 600m to 720m. Two waterfalls drop into this incision in the earth.

Three trails wind through the park. **Trilha do Vértice** runs for 2km to an observation point for the canyon and the Cascata do Andorinhas. **Trilha Cotovelo** is a 3km trail (2½ hours round-trip) passing by the Véu de Noiva waterfall, with wonderful vistas of the canyon.

For a completely different perspective, **Trilha do Rio do Boi** follows the base of the canyon for 7km, from the Posto Rio do Boi entrance. This last route is most easily accessed from the town of Praia Grande in Santa Catarina. A professional guide is required for the challenging, loose, rocky trail. During rainy season it is closed because of the danger of flooding.

Parque Nacional da Serra Geral CANYON

FREE Parque Nacional da Serra Geral, 23km from Cambará do Sul, contains canyons that rival Itaimbezinho. The **Cânion da Fortaleza** is an 8km stretch of escarpment with 900m drops. A gently inclining **Trilha do Mirante** leads about 7km to the edge of the canyon, yielding incredible views of the **Cachoeira do Tigre Preto** waterfall.

The **Pedra do Segredo** is a tower of rocks that balances precariously on this precipice. **Cânion Malacara** is formed by the river of the same name; the **Trilha Piscina do Malacara** leads to a natural pool with cool, crystal waters and wonderful views.

Tours

Local companies provide transportation and guides for the canyons. Horseback-riding and mountain-climbing expeditions are also available. Some agencies belong to ABETA, Brazil's strict ecotourism association.

Cânion Turismo HIKING, ADVENTURE TOUR

(☎3251-1027; www.canionturismo.com.br; Getúlio Vargas 876; ⏲8am-7pm) Pop into this excellent agency and check out the scale model of the canyons for a much-needed perspective on the area. Guided treks like Trilha do Rio do Boi are around R$426 for one person, dwindling down to R$147 per person within a group of 10 people. Also offers recommended two- or four-hour horseback-riding excursions to a potpourri of different canyons and waterfall circuit treks.

Sleeping

Cambará has many economical, family-run inns, while higher-end options are outside of town. Camping in the parks is strictly prohibited, but the tourist information office can help you locate municipal campgrounds.

Prices quoted here are for the high season (July and November to February). In other seasons, expect a discount of 25% or more.

Pousada Oliveira POUSADA $

(☎3251-1544; pousada.oliveira2011@hotmail.com; RS 020 148; s/d R$100/165;) The best deal for backpackers, these bright-green A-frame cabins evoke a more local feel than elsewhere and are as welcoming as can be for the price, kept cozy by a fireplace (we prefer the back ones facing the *araucária* forest). It's 800m or so outside town.

★ **Vila Ecológica** POUSADA $$

(☎3251-1351; www.vilaecologica.blogspot.com.br; João Pazza 1166; r R$200; @) Vila Ecológica sits colorfully but most ordinarily on a hill behind Casa do Turista. You wouldn't look twice. But closer inspection reveals Cambará's best-value hospitality. Rooms are

WORTH A TRIP

CANELA & PARQUE ESTADUAL DO CARACOL

While lacking Gramado's sophistication, neighboring Canela has a small-town charm of its own. Centered on a leafy green square, the village center is lined with shops and cafes and is anchored at one end by the impressive Gothic **Catedral de Pedra** (stone cathedral). Canela offers cheaper accommodations and more convenient access to the state parks, which are popular hiking spots. The major attraction near town is the **Parque Estadual do Caracol** (☎3278-3035; RS 466; adult/child R$18/9; ⏲8:45am-5:45pm), 7km northeast of Canela, and its spectacular **Cascata do Caracol**, a 130m free-falling waterfall. For tourist information, stop by **C.I.T.** (Central de Informações Turísticas; ☎3282-2200; www.canelaturismo.com.br; Largo da Fama 77; ⏲8am-7pm) in central Canela.

Citral (☎3282-1185; www.citral.tur.br) runs buses to/from Gramado every 20 minutes (from R$4.35, 20 minutes). Buses go to São Francisco de Paula (R$8.05, one hour), where you can connect to Cambará do Sul (R$14.80, 1½ hours); and to Caxias do Sul (R$22.65, two hours), where you can connect to Bento Gonçalves (R$8.15, 1½ hours) with Ozelame (p330). Frequent buses go to Porto Alegre (from R$28.65, 2½ hours). **Viação Canelense** (☎3282-2326) operates three buses a day to Parque Estadual do Caracol (R$2.30, 20 minutes) at 8:15am, 12:10pm and 5:30pm, returning to Canela at 8:35am, 12:25pm and 6pm. A taxi from Canela's bus station is R$35.

equipped with heaters/air-con and cable TV and were constructed from ecologically savvy materials. There's a small and tasty restaurant (mains R$16 to R$32) for guests only, English is spoken and there's even craft beer. Touché!

Pousada Corucacas POUSADA $$
(☎3251-1123; www.corucacas.com; RS 020, Km1; camping per person R$15, r per person incl breakfast & dinner R$135; 📶) About 1km from town on the road to Ouro Verde, this working farm has rustic rooms and a big-sky setting, flush with lakes and *araucária* trees. Endless opportunities for horseback riding and hiking are just out the back door, and a fireplace heats up the common room in the evening.

Estalagem da Colina CHALET $$
(☎3251-1746; www.estalagemdacolina.com.br; Av Getúlio Vargas 80; d R$287-329, q R$515; @📶) Offers 10 stylish wooden chalets, with Sky TV, minibars and heaters (some with hydrobathtubs). In the main lodge, guests can congregate around the fire in winter – it's the romantic choice.

★**Parador Casa da Montanha** CAMPGROUND $$$
(☎3295-7575; www.paradorcasadamontanha.com.br; r incl afternoon tea R$747-1750) Midway between Cambará and Itaimbezinho, the poshest place in the region is modeled after luxurious African safari camps. Overlooking *araucária* forest and a cackling waterfall, Brazil's only heated, elevated tents are perched amid tranquil postcard-envy scenery and combine creature comforts with rusticity.

Eating & Drinking

Dining options are limited, though some cute cafes and bistros have sprung up.

Sendero Bistro CAFE $
(www.senderobistro.com.br; Antonio Raupp 419; mains R$25-46; ⏲11:30am-4pm & 7-10:30pm, closed Wed; 📶) An intimate bistro and best-bet alternative to the town's typical all-you-can-eat fare. A young couple does jazzed-up versions of typical staples (filets, risottos, stroganoff) with above-par service for Cambará. Monday to Saturday, there's a *por-kilo* (R$37) lunch buffet.

Galpão Costaneira BUFFET $
(Dona Úrsula 1069; buffets R$27-43; ⏲11:30am-3pm & 7:20-10:30pm Mon-Sat, to 3pm Sun; 📶) A hearty local buffet served in a rustic farmhouse setting that's at its best when you choose tabletop-cooked *picanha* (beef), spicy *linguiça* (garlicky pork sausage) and cheese.

★**O Casarão** BUFFET $$
(☎3251 1711; www.galeteriacasarao.com.br; João Francisco Ritter 969; buffets R$47.50-67.50; ⏲11:30am-2pm & 6:30-9pm Tue-Sat, 11am-3pm Sun) Set amongst homey hardwoods, this excellent restaurant serves the homey food of Brazil's Italian colonists. A buffet of organic salads, house-made pastas and soups accompanies house-specialty *galeto* or farmed trout. Local wines and grappas are served as well.

Du Perau Pub BAR
(www.facebook.com/duperaupubbar; Av Getúlio Vargas 80; 📶) A gaggle of local boys done good.

This nightlife hotspot serves 55 types of craft beer, every one of them from Rio Grande do Sul, as well as Gramado's Gram Bier pilsen on draft. It's housed in an atmospheric clapboard structure dotted with vinyl on the Estalagem da Colina end of the main road.

Information

The nearest foreign-friendly ATM is in Gramado (no, seriously!)

Casa do Turista (☎3251-1320; www.cambaradosul.rs.gov.br; Av Getúlio Vargas 1720; ⏰8am-6pm) is on the far end of town on the road to Fortaleza. No English.

Getting There & Around

The tiny **bus station** (☎3251-1567; Dona Úrsula s/n) is right in town, though rarely staffed. **Citral** (www.citral.tur.br) offers one bus from Porto Alegre for Cambará do Sul (R$36, 5½ hours) at 6am Monday to Saturday. Returning, you must catch a 6:30am or 1:30pm bus to São Francisco de Paula (R$14.80, one hour) and switch there for Porto Alegre (from R$21.60, three hours), Canela (from R$7.90, one hour) or Gramado (from R$9.15, one hour).

Expresso São Marcos (www.expressosaomarcos.com.br) has two buses going to Caxias do Sul (from R$24.95, three hours, 7:45am and 10:45am) on Monday, Tuesday, Wednesday and Friday (10:45am only on Thursday, 7:30am only on Saturday, 5:30pm only on Sunday), where you can connect hourly to Bento Gonçalves (R$8.15, 1¼ hours) with **Ozelame** (☎3228-4088; www.ozelame.com.br; Rodoviária de Caxias do Sul). If you are coming from the north, you can connect from Torres via Tainhas or via Criciúma.

The parks are not serviced by public buses. A taxi to Parque Nacional de Aparados da Serra costs R$100 round-trip. Local tour companies are a reasonable alternative, especially if they can hook you up with a small group.

LITORAL GAÚCHO

On paper, it sounds amazing: a 500km strip of Brazilian coastline that forms one seemingly endless beach, stretching from Torres on the Santa Catarina border, all the way to Chuí at the Uruguayan border. Unfortunately, the reality is less enticing. The water tends to be murky and the beaches are undistinguished, but there's good surf and alluring culture.

Torres

☎0XX51 / POP 34,600

On the border with Santa Catarina, Torres is the exception to the state's uninviting coastline. It's not thrilling, but the pleasant town, 205km north of Porto Alegre, has attractive (if crowded) beaches punctuated by basalt rock formations, vegetative dunes and a boardwalk bursting with crepes and churros – it's all vaguely reminiscent of a countrified British seaside town, its *gaúchos*-digging-their-toes-in-the-sand culture unique in Brazil.

Praia Grande, the town's main beach, is quite calm and is bookended by the smaller Prainha to the south and Praia dos Molhes to the north, a famous surf spot where the Rio Mampituba dramatically enters the sea. Praia da Cal, 2km south of Praia Grande, also draws serious surfers.

In winter, Antarctic currents bring cold, hard winds to the coast; the crowds disappear, and some hotels shut down from May to November.

Sights & Activities

Parque Estadual da Guarita NATURE RESERVE
(Benjamin Constant 154; cars R$5; ⏰8am-8pm Dec-Feb, to 5:30pm Mar-Nov) The gardens of Parque Guarita, 2km south of Av Beira Mar, make for a gorgeous natural setting, while

WORTH A TRIP

PRAIA GRANDE

The oddly-named **Praia Grande** (It's not big and there's no beach!) sits just across the border in Santa Catarina at the bottom of the canyons that make up Parque Nacional de Aparados da Serra and Parque Nacional da Serra Geral and offers an alternative perspective to Cambará do Sul. In this blossoming ecotourism destination, a wealth of waterfalls and natural swimming pools are at your disposal, as are hiking, tree climbing, rappelling and ziplines. Bed down at the wonderful **Refúgio Ecológico Pedra Afiada** (☎051-3532-1059; www.pedraafiada.com.br; Estrada Geral Vila Rosa s/n, Praia Grande; d incl meals R$350-1080; 📶) 🌿 and take in the canyons from a whole new perspective.

There is one daily bus from Cambará do Sul to Praia Grande (9:45am Monday to Saturday); as well as service from Porto Alegre in Rio Grande do Sul and Criciúma and Araranguá in Santa Catarina. For more info, see www.praiagrande.sc.gov.br/turismo.

the nearby beach of the same name is considered the most beautiful in Torres, a true stunner reminiscent of rocky British Isle beaches.

Felipe Raupp Escola de Surf SURFING
(☎9991-4049; www.frsurf.com.br; 5-course packages from R$750) Internationally renowned Raupp is the man to get you up in Torres, offering serious, multiday surf courses.

Tours

Marina BOAT TOUR
(☎3626-2933; www.barcosmarina.com.br; adult/child R$40/25; ⏱11am, 3pm & 5pm Jan-Apr) Marina offers boat trips to Ilha dos Lobos, an ecological reserve that is home to a colony of sea lions, between January and April. In season, there is a booth at the beginning of Av Beira Mar.

Festivals & Events

★**Festival Internacional de Balonismo** HOT-AIR BALLOONING
(International Hot-Air Balloon Festival; www.festivaldebalonismotorres.com.br; ⏱Apr) Torres' hot-air balloon festival is a spectacular sight.

Sleeping & Eating

We've listed prices for summer (December to February) – expect discounts of 20% to 40% between March and November and a 25% hike during the hot-air-balloon festival.

Recanto da Prainha HOTEL $$
(☎3626-5229; www.recantodaprainha.com.br; Alferes Feirreira Porto 138; s/d R$180/210, with air-con R$230/280;) This amicable hotel with its colonial-green exterior is a block from the quiet beach at Prainha.

★**Solar Inn** POUSADA $$
(☎3626-3731; www.solarinn.com.br; Av Beira Mar 1713; r from R$300, with seaview R$350-400;) Excellent beachfront location, partial Germanic architecture and welcoming staff; you can't beat this spartan inn perched across from Prainha beach, or its inviting patio.

Monsieur Café CAFE $
(www.facebook.com/monsieurcafetorres; Av Benjamin Constant 23; coffee R$4-13.50, items R$2-15; ⏱10am-8pm Mon-Fri, to 9pm Sat, 1-8pm Sun Mar-Dec 14, 9am-10pm Mon-Sat, 1:30-8pm Sun Dec 15-Feb;) Easily Torres' best and swarming with charm – save the TripAdvisor reviews as window decor – this cafe and its welcoming patio sit just off the lagoon a few blocks back from Prainha. Great espresso, teas and *pão de queijo* (balls of cheese-stuffed tapioca bread) pressed panini – and an absolutely unrelenting choice of sweets and cakes.

Cantinho do Pescador SEAFOOD $$
(www.cantinhodopescador.com; Av Cristóvão Colombo 210; mains for 2 R$33-102; ⏱10am-midnight;) This always-packed, partly open-air seafooder does a commendable job with local fish at the Praia dos Molhes end of town, with panoramic Rio Mampituba views. The crab in its own shell *(siri na casca)* is wildly popular and the pineapple stabbed with skewers of shrimp is just wild.

Information

There is a Banco do Brasil at Rua 15 de Novembro 236.

Bradesco (www.bradesco.com.br; Júlio de Castilhos 324) Visa/Mastercard ATM.

Casa do Turista (☎3626-9150 ext 710; www.torres.rs.gov.br; Av Barão do Rio Branco 315; ⏱8am-12:30pm & 1-7pm Mon-Fri, 9am-2pm Sat, 2-7pm Sun) Excellent municipal tourism office.

Getting There & Around

The town is small and all conveniences are accessible by foot, including the **bus station** (☎3664-1787; www.rodoviariatorres.com.br; Av José Bonifácio 524). Destinations include Porto Alegre (from R$38, three hours) and Florianópolis (R$48, five hours, one to two daily). For Cambará do Sul, **Expresso São Marcos** (www.expressosaomarcos.com.br) goes to the dusty one-horse town of Tainhas (R$20.75, two hours, 9am and 3pm Monday to Saturday, 9:30am and 3pm Sunday) where you can connect with **Citral** (☎3244-1315; www.citral.tur.br; Frederico Tedesco 602) buses leaving São Francisco de Paula at 9:15am and 5pm Monday to Saturday (11am on Sunday), passing through Tainhas for Cambará (R$6.85, 45 minutes) around 30 to 45 minutes later.

Alternatively, call the only taxi (R$80, 30 minutes) in town, **Alex Offmann** (☎054-8438-3200; Tainhas).

Rio Grande

☎0XX53 / POP 197,200

Located at the mouth of Lagoa dos Patos, Rio Grande was founded in 1737 to guard the disputed southern border of the Portuguese empire. The region's oldest city, it blossomed during the 19th century, when its port became a vital link in the profitable beef trade. Rio Grande has a charming historic center that is home to some interesting colonial and neoclassical buildings.

GETTING TO URUGUAY

Located 245km south of Rio Grande, the border town of Chuí/Chuy is the end of the Brazilian line. The city is both Brazilian and Uruguayan, respectively. The main drag acts as the border: on the northern (Brazilian) side it is Av Uruguaí, while on the southern (Uruguayan) side it is Av Brasil. The Uruguayan side has grown over the last decade to be synonymous with duty-free shops, which are flooded with Brazilians from open to close. It's not interesting but increased security in recent years means it's relatively safe as far as border towns go. Those who linger usually only do so to take advantage of cheaper accommodations when visiting Uruguayan attractions further afield. If you stay, the best value for money is at **Etnico Hostel** (+5984474-2281; etnicohostelchuy@gmail.com; Liber Seregni 299; dm UR$400, s/d UR$800/1200;), three blocks into Uruguay, where trilingual host Rodrigo is eager to help, and bakery-fresh breakfast pastries are a nice touch.

Brazilian **immigration** (3265-2523; www.dpf.gov.br; BR-471, Km 650; 24hr) is on the main highway, several kilometers north of town. You do not need a visa or entry or exit stamp to visit the town; however, if you are continuing into Uruguay, you will need to tell the driver to stop at the border post for an exit stamp. In Uruguay, **immigration** (+598-4474-2072; https://migracion.minterior.gub.uy; Ruta 9; 24hr) is 2.5km south of town. The bus will stop again for the Uruguayan officials to check your Brazilian exit stamp. Uruguay maintains a **consulate** (3265-1151; www.emburuguai.org.br; Venezuela 311; 9am-3pm Mon-Fri) in Chuí, though most nationalities do not need a visa for Uruguay.

Pop into Chuy's **Centro de Informes** (+5984474-3627; www.turismorocha.gub.uy; Gral Artigas esq Arachanes; 10am-6pm Tue-Sat Mar-Dec, 9am-7pm Jan-Feb) for helpful Uruguayan tourist info – you are not far from **Parque Nacional Santa Teresa** (+5984477-2101; sepae.webnode.es; Ruta 9, Km 302; 8am-8pm Dec-Mar, to 6pm Apr-Nov) FREE.

Chuí is serviced by **Embaixador** (3265-1498; www.expressoembaixador.com.br; Av Argentina 192) with five daily buses from Pelotas (R$47.35, four hours, 6am, 9:30am, 1pm, 4pm and 6:30pm) and two from Rio Grande (R$43.75, four hours, 7am and 3:30pm); and **Planalto** (www.planalto.com.br), with two buses from Porto Alegre (from R$101.50, seven hours, 1pm and 11:30pm). The Brazilian **bus station** (3265-1498; Venezuela 247) is about three blocks in from Av Brasil.

To carry on to Montevideo and other Uruguayan destinations, bus companies line Calle Leonardo Oliveira near Av Brasil on the Uruguayan side. **Rutas del Sol** (+598-4474-2048; www.rutasdelsol.com.uy; Leonardo Oliveira 121), with services at 1am, 5am, 8am, 12:45pm, 6:15pm and 11pm, and **Cot** (+598-4474-4697; www.cot.com.uy; Leonardo Oliveira 111), with 4am, 11am and 8pm departures, are your best bets for Montevideo (UR$558, five hours).

Sights

Museu Oceanográfico MUSEUM

(3231-3496; www.museu.furg.br/museu_oceanografico.html; Capitão Heitor Perdigão 10; admission R$5; 9-11:30am & 2-6pm Tue-Sun) The excellent Museu Oceanográfico is one of the best in Latin America.

Sleeping & Eating

★ **Paris Hotel** HISTORIC HOTEL $

(3231-3866; www.hotelvillamoura.com.br; Marechal Floriano Peixoto 112; s/d R$87.50/125, without bathroom R$62.50/100;) The oldest in Rio Grande do Sul, this hotel, built in 1826, exhibits a bygone grandeur in its high ceilings, antique furnishings and leafy courtyard. At this price, it would be silly not to sleep in an antique bed and lounge in a 19th-century patio that once hosted Dom Pedro II.

Casa Europa Gastrobar BISTRO $$

(3035-6257; www.facebook.com/casaeuropagb; Benjamin Constant 460; mains R$20-55; 6:30pm-midnight Mon-Sat;) A sophisticated little surprise for Rio Grande, this Euro-style bistro does a small but great selection of mostly Italian and French dishes backed by sweet service.

Getting There & Away

From the **bus station** (3232-8444; www.rodoviariariogrande.com.br; Vice-Almirante Abreu 737), buses connect Rio Grande with all major cities in southern Brazil. **Embaixador** (www.expressoembaixador.com.br) has two departures for Chuí (R$46.60, four hours, 7am and 3:30pm) on the Uruguayan border as well as Pelotas (from R$11.75, one hour, every 30 minutes), which is the major transportation hub. **Planalto** (www.planalto.com.br) has at least 14 buses most days to Porto Alegre (from R$73.15, five hours).

Brasília & Goiás

Includes ➡

Best Places to Eat

- ➡ Taypá (p345)
- ➡ Olivae (p345)
- ➡ Fazenda Babilônia (p356)
- ➡ Universal Diner (p346)
- ➡ Jambalaya (p359)

Best Places to Stay

- ➡ Baguá Pousada (p360)
- ➡ Brasília Palace Hotel (p344)
- ➡ Pouso, Café e Cultura (p355)
- ➡ Taman Baru (p356)
- ➡ Pousada do Ipê (p353)

Why Go?

Brasília was conceived as a workable, utopic answer to modern, urban chaos. The purpose-built city is lauded by many for its futuristic architecture and avant-garde design but knocked by detractors who bemoan the impracticality of the uberorganized, themed city blocks. As Brazil's seat of government, bureaucrats rule, but a thriving city is there, the first in the world constructed in the 20th century to achieve World Cultural Heritage designation by Unesco.

Enveloping the Distrito Federal (DF), Goiás is Brazil's 'road less traveled,' though not for good reason: fiery red sunsets over the lush, rolling hills of the dramatic cerrado (savanna) landscape set the stage for unparalleled postcard-perfect views. Almost criminally overlooked by many tourists, Goiás is easy to get lost in for a few weeks. Major attractions include the picturesque colonial villages of Cidade de Goiás and Pirenópolis, and the rivers, waterfalls and forest trails of Parque Nacional da Chapada dos Veadeiros.

When to Go

Brasília

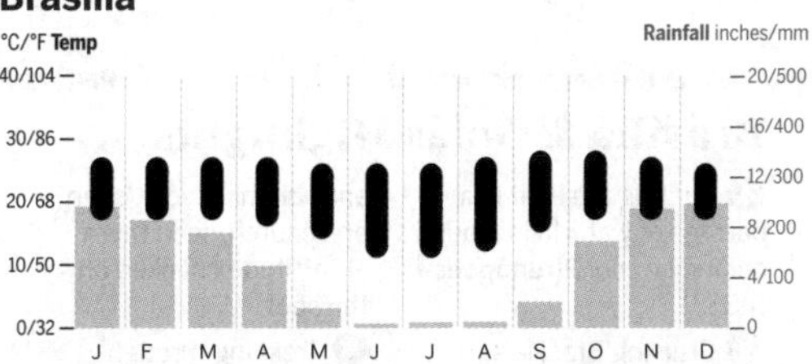

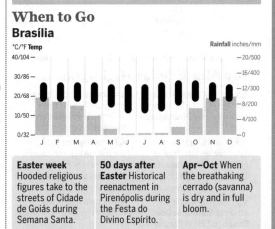

Easter week Hooded religious figures take to the streets of Cidade de Goiás during Semana Santa.

50 days after Easter Historical reenactment in Pirenópolis during the Festa do Divino Espírito.

Apr–Oct When the breathaking cerrado (savanna) is dry and in full bloom.

History

On the heels of the gold discoveries in Minas Gerais, *bandeirantes* (groups of roaming adventurers who explored the interior) pushed further inland in search of more precious metals and, as always, indigenous slaves. In 1682, a *bandeira* headed by Bartolomeu Bueno da Silva visited the region. The indigenous Goyaz people gave him the nickname *anhanguera* (old devil) when, after burning some *cachaça* (sugarcane alcohol) – which the Goyaz believed to be water – he threatened to set fire to all the rivers if they didn't show him where their

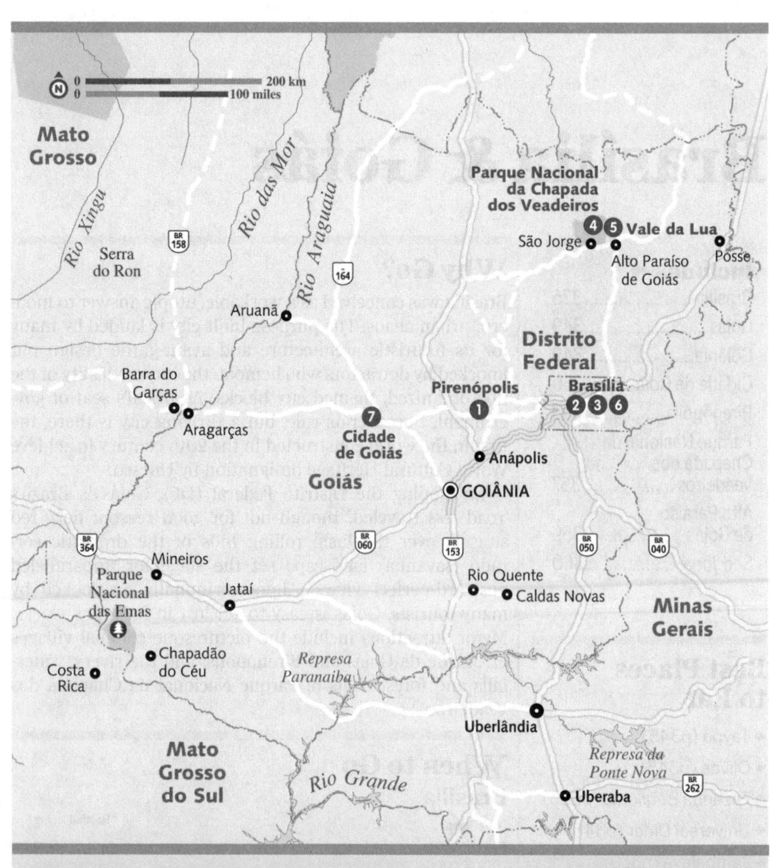

Brasília & Goiás Highlights

❶ Beating the heat in a barrage of waterfalls around colonially cool **Pirenópolis** (p353).

❷ Cruising Brasília's futuristic architecture at night when the **Praça dos Três Poderes** (p339) takes on an otherworldly glow.

❸ Stepping inside the ethereal **Santuário Dom Bosco** (p338) in Brasília and watching your 'seen one church, seen them all' attitude checked on the spot.

❹ Trekking through the unique high-cerrado (savanna) flora in **Parque Nacional da Chapada dos Veadeiros** (p358).

❺ Rock-hopping the naturally formed lunarscape at **Vale da Lua** (p359), near Chapada dos Veadeiros.

❻ Losing yourself in the excellent **bars and restaurants** (p345) of Brasília's unique *superquadras*

❼ Lazily wandering the cobblestone streets of **Cidade de Goiás** (p350) in a sugar-induced coma.

gold mines were. Three years later, the old devil returned to his native São Paulo with gold and indigenous slaves from Goiás. Given the difficulties caused by the isolation of the region, its gold rush was essentially over before it had begun.

Goiás achieved official statehood in 1889 but went about its business quietly until the mid-1950s, when a portion of it was carved out to build Brasília. The concept of an inland capital dated back to 1823 and the Brazilian statesman José Bonifácio, who believed that moving the capital from Rio de Janeiro was central to capitalizing on the country's vast inland resources. The idea didn't gain many followers, however, until Dom Bosco, a Salesian priest living in Turin (Italy) prophesied that a new civilization would emerge in Brazil, somewhere between the 15th and 20th parallels. Suddenly it seemed like a good idea and land was allocated in the 1891 constitution for a new capital.

Still, it wasn't until 1955 that Brasília started to become a reality: President Kubitschek ordered work to begin, and architect Oscar Niemeyer took on the challenge. With millions of poor peasants from the Northeast working around the clock, the city was built, incredibly, in just three years. The capital was officially moved from Rio to Brasília on April 21, 1960.

The new capital became a symbol of the country's determination to become a great economic power and distracted attention from ongoing social and economic problems. Goiás too thrived, this time on the back of a 'green-gold' rush, a colossal soy and sugar boom, that made many farmers millionaires almost overnight. Today, Goiás remains one of Brazil's most prosperous and comfortable states.

In 1989, due to the vastness of its borders, Goiás once again forfeited some of its land, when half of the state was split off to become the separate state of Tocantins.

BRASÍLIA

☎061 / POP 2.6 MILLION

Well into middle age, Brazil's once-futuristic capital remains an impressive monument to national initiative. Brasília replaced Rio de Janeiro as Brazil's center of government in 1960, under the visionary leadership of President Juscelino Kubitschek, architect Oscar Niemeyer, urban planner Lucio Costa and landscape architect Burle Marx.

From the air, Brasília's millennial design evokes the image of an airplane, with each of its architectural marvels strategically laid out along the Eixo Monumental (which forms the fuselage), and its residential and commercial blocks along its outspread wings (*asas*).

With long distances and harrowing six-lane highways connected by spaghetti junctions to negotiate, Brasília presents challenges for walkers. Though renting a car is trial by fire, the big picture becomes all the more clear from behind a steering wheel. Those up for the adventure will find a lively city hidden behind the futuristic facade, one that that's not only a pilgrimage for architecture and design buffs but foodies, night owls and those seeking an unarguably unique travel experience.

Sights

Brasília's major edifices are spread along a 5km stretch of the Eixo Monumental. At the bottom end are the most interesting government buildings. Sights are listed here in order along the Eixo Monumental. To visit them on public transport, combine local buses 104 and 108 with some long walks.

'Tail' End of the Eixo Monumental

Though maps of Brasília invariably figure the airplane design with the cockpit at the bottom and the tail at the top, the tail end of the Eixo Monumental is actually in the northwest of the city. From the local bus station take buses 312, 331 or 343 from platforms C8 to C10 to get here (R$3, every 20 minutes).

Memorial JK MUSEUM

(Map p336; ☎3226-7860; www.memorialjk.com.br; Praça do Cruzeiro; adult/child R$10/5; 9am-6pm Tue-Sun) The tomb of JK (President Juscelino Kubitschek) lies underneath eerily beautiful stained glass by French artist Marianne Peretti inside the Memorial JK. The museum houses JK's 3000-book-strong personal library as well as a pictorial history of Brasília. Don't miss JK's 1973 Ford Galaxie!

Museu dos Povos Indígenas MUSEUM

(Map p336; Praça Buriti; 9am-5pm Tue-Fri, 10am-5pm Sat & Sun) FREE Opposite the

Brasília

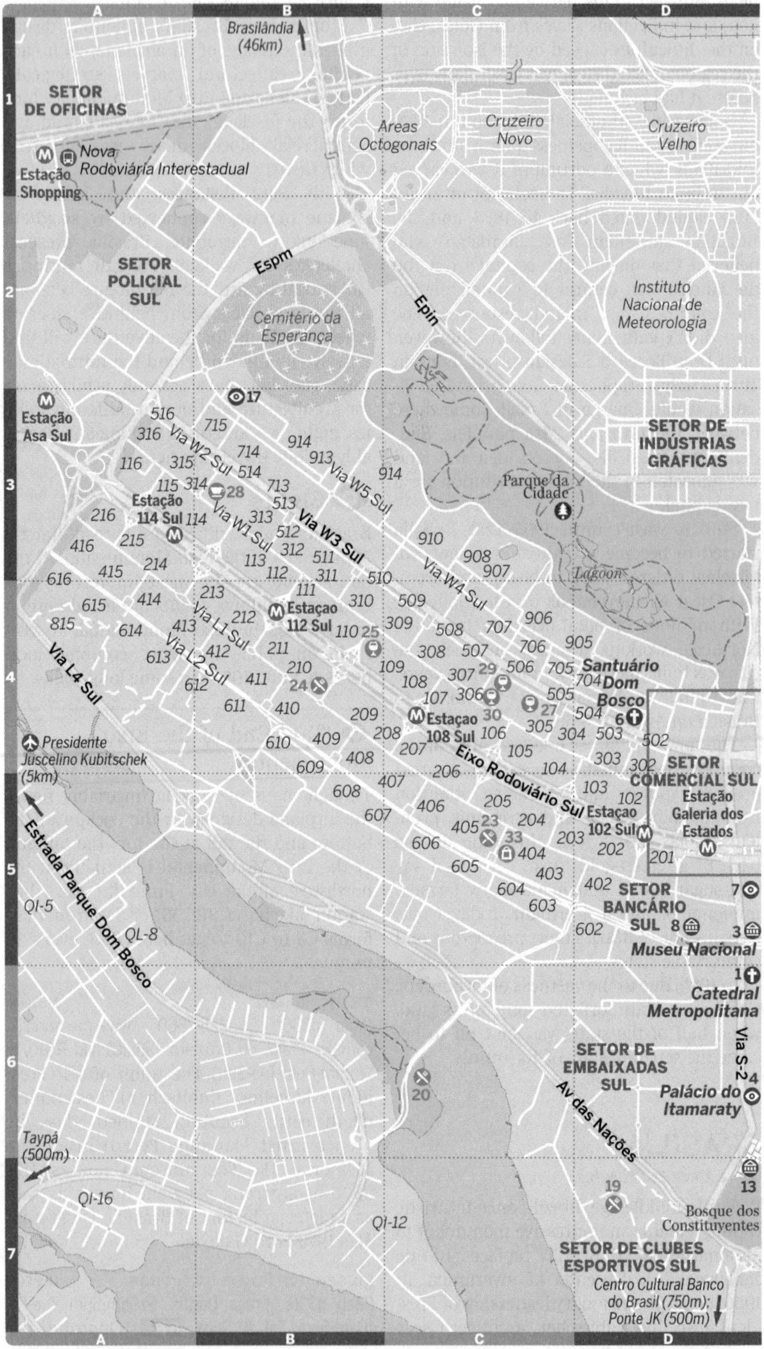

A
B
C
D
1
2
3
4
5
6
7
Brasilândia (46km)
SETOR DE OFICINAS
Nova Rodoviária Interestadual
Estação Shopping
Areas Octogonais
Cruzeiro Novo
Cruzeiro Velho
SETOR POLICIAL SUL
Espm
Epin
Cemitério da Esperança
Instituto Nacional de Meteorologia
Estação Asa Sul
17
SETOR DE INDÚSTRIAS GRÁFICAS
Via W2 Sul
Via W5 Sul
Via W3 Sul
Via W1 Sul
Via W4 Sul
Parque da Cidade
Lagoon
Estação 114 Sul
28
Via L1 Sul
Via L2 Sul
Via L4 Sul
Estaçao 112 Sul
25
24
29
27
30
Santuário Dom Bosco
6
Estaçao 108 Sul
Eixo Rodoviário Sul
Presidente Juscelino Kubitschek (5km)
SETOR COMERCIAL SUL
Estação Galeria dos Estados
Estaçao 102 Sul
23
33
Estrada Parque Dom Bosco
QI-5
QL-8
SETOR BANCÁRIO SUL
7
8
3
Museu Nacional
1
Catedral Metropolitana
Via S-2
SETOR DE EMBAIXADAS SUL
20
Av das Nações
4
Palácio do Itamaraty
Taypá (500m)
QI-16
QI-12
19
13
Bosque dos Constituyentes
SETOR DE CLUBES ESPORTIVOS SUL
Centro Cultural Banco do Brasil (750m); Ponte JK (500m)

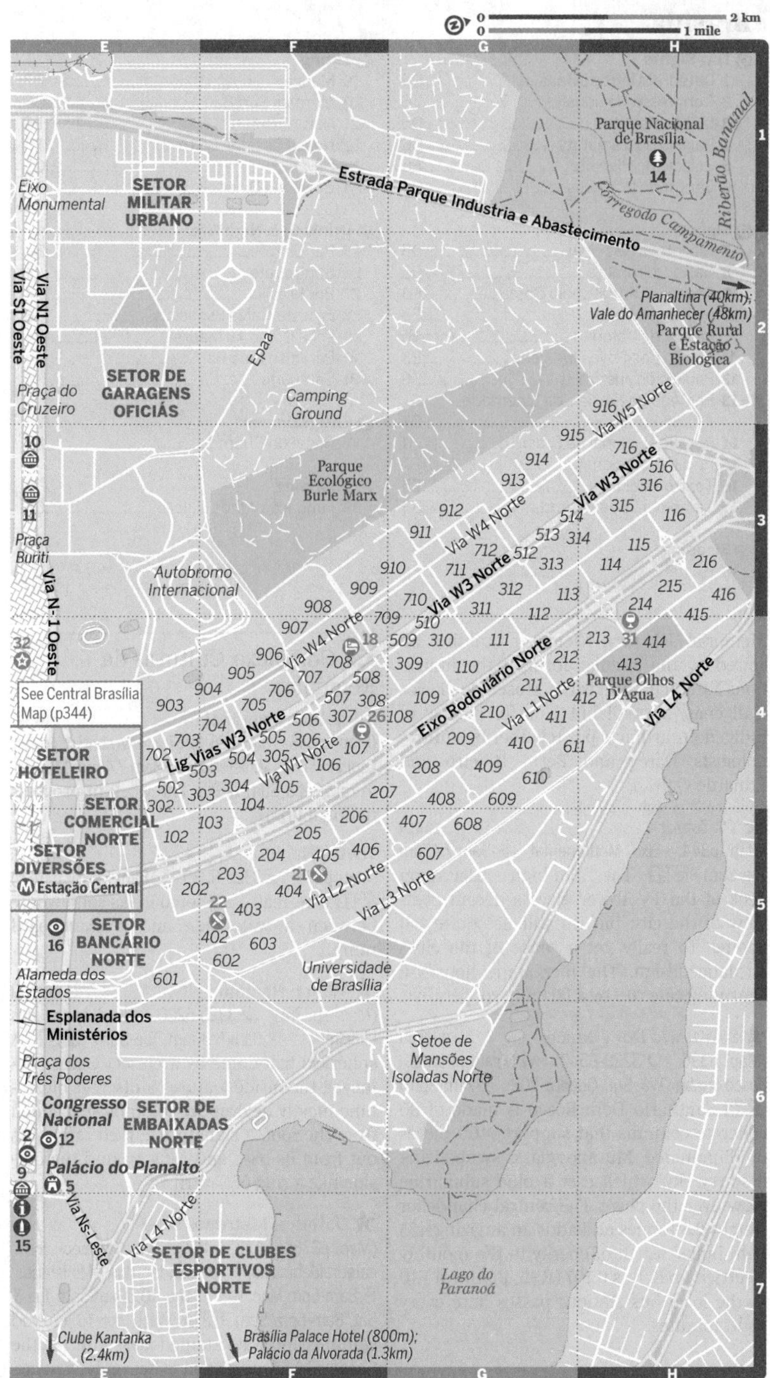

0 2 km
0 1 mile
Parque Nacional de Brasília
14
Ribeirão Bananal
Córrego do Campamento
Estrada Parque Industria e Abastecimento
Eixo Monumental
SETOR MILITAR URBANO
Via N1 Oeste
Via S1 Oeste
Planaltina (40km); Vale do Amanhecer (48km)
Parque Rural e Estação Biologica
Epaa
SETOR DE GARAGENS OFICIÁS
Praça do Cruzeiro
Camping Ground
Via W5 Norte
Via W3 Norte
Via W4 Norte
Parque Ecológico Burle Marx
10
11
Praça Buriti
Via N-1 Oeste
Autobromo Internacional
Via W3 Norte
32
Eixo Rodoviário Norte
Via W4 Norte
18
31
Parque Olhos D'Agua
Via L4 Norte
Via L1 Norte
See Central Brasília Map (p344)
Lig Vias W3 Norte
26
Via W1 Norte
SETOR HOTELEIRO
SETOR COMERCIAL NORTE
SETOR DIVERSÕES
Estação Central
21
Via L2 Norte
Via L3 Norte
22
16
SETOR BANCÁRIO NORTE
Universidade de Brasília
Alameda dos Estados
Esplanada dos Ministérios
Praça dos Três Poderes
Setoe de Mansões Isoladas Norte
Congresso Nacional
SETOR DE EMBAIXADAS NORTE
2
12
9
Palácio do Planalto
5
15
Via Ns-Leste
Via L4 Norte
SETOR DE CLUBES ESPORTIVOS NORTE
Lago do Paranoá
Clube Kantanka (2.4km)
Brasília Palace Hotel (800m); Palácio da Alvorada (1.3km)

Brasília

Top Sights

1	Catedral Metropolitana	D6
2	Congresso Nacional	E6
3	Museu Nacional	D5
4	Palácio do Itamaraty	D6
5	Palácio do Planalto	E6
6	Santuário Dom Bosco	D4

Sights

7	Biblioteca Nacional	D5
8	Caixa Cultural	D5
9	Espaço Cultural Lucio Costa	E6
10	Memorial JK	E3
	Museu de Valores	(see 8)
11	Museu dos Povos Indígenas	E3
12	Palácio da Justiça	E6
13	Panteão da Pátria e da Liberdade Tancredo Neves	D7
14	Parque Nacional de Brasília	H1
15	Pavilhão Nacional	E7
16	Teatro Nacional	E5
17	Templo da Boa Vontade	B3

Sleeping

18	Hostel 7	F4

Eating

19	Mangai	D7
20	Mormaii Surf Bar	C6
21	Naturetto	F5
22	Nossa Cozinha Bistrô	F5
23	Olivae	C5
24	Universal Diner	B4

Drinking & Nightlife

25	Bar Beirute	B4
26	Bar Beirute	F4
27	Bar Brasília	C4
28	Ernesto Cafés Especiais	B3
29	Loca Como Tu Madre	C4
30	Paradiso Cine Bar	C4
31	Santuário	H4

Entertainment

32	Clube do Choro	E4

Shopping

33	Fundacão Athos Bulcão	C5

Memorial JK, in a Niemeyer building inspired by the circular form of the indigenous Yanomani hut, is the Museu dos Povos Indígenas, a small but colorful display of indigenous artifacts put together by anthropologists Darcy and Berta Ribeiro and Eduardo Galvão.

★TV Tower TOWER

(Map p344; Eixo Monumental; ⏲9am-7:45pm Tue-Sun) FREE The 75m-high observation deck of the TV Tower gives a decent overview of the city, but it's still not quite tall enough to really get a sense of the city's airplane design. The mezzanine houses a charming cafe run by a farming cooperative.

★Santuário Dom Bosco CHURCH

(Map p336; ☎3223-6542; www.santuariodombosco.org.br; W3 Sul, Quadra 702; ⏲7am-8pm) FREE Santuário Dom Bosco is made of 80 concrete columns that support 7400 pieces of illuminated Murano glass, symbolizing a starry sky, which cast a blue submarine glow over the pews. The central chandelier weighs 2.5 tonnes and adds an amazing 435 light bulbs' worth of energy to the monthly electricity bill. Bus 0.107 (R$2; platform E10 in the local bus station) passes here every eight minutes.

Complexo Cultural da República

Biblioteca Nacional LIBRARY

(Map p336; ☎3325-6257; www.bnb.df.gov.br; Esplanada dos Ministérios; ⏲8am-7:45pm Mon-Fri, to 2pm Sat & Sun) FREE The work-in-progress national library.

Teatro Nacional THEATER

(Map p336; ☎3325-6239; ⏲8am-6pm Mon-Fri) FREE The Teatro Nacional looks somewhere between a waterslide and a skateboard ramp.

★Museu Nacional MUSEUM

(Map p336; ☎3325-5220; Esplanada dos Ministérios; ⏲9am-6:30pm Tue-Sun) FREE A spherical half-dome by architect Oscar Niemeyer, the inside features a discreet mezzanine mostly held up by columns suspended from the roof. A signature curved ramp juts out from its base and runs around the outside like a ring of Saturn.

★Catedral Metropolitana CHURCH

(Map p336; ☎3224-4073; www.facebook.com/catedraldebrasilia; Esplanada dos Ministérios; ⏲8am-5pm Mon, Wed & Thu, 10:30am-5pm Tue & Sat, 8am-6pm Sun) FREE With its 16 curved columns and wavy stained-glass interior, the Catedral Metropolitana is heavenly viewing.

At the entrance are the haunting *Four Disciples* statues carved by Ceschiatti, who also made the aluminum angels hanging inside.

Setor Bancário Sul

Brasilía's banking sector may not be the first place you would think of going to for cultural enrichment, but there are a couple of museums here and guess what? They're free!

Caixa Cultural MUSEUM

(Map p336; 3206-9450; www.caixacultural.com.br; SBS Q4, Lote 3/4; 9am-9pm Tue-Sun) FREE The lobby of the Caixa Cultural is a small museum of financial bits and pieces, ranging from old lottery tickets through to wooden safes. The exhibits themselves are of only passing interest, but the gorgeous stained-glass murals, each one representing a Brazilian state, makes it worth the visit.

Museu de Valores MUSEUM

(Map p336; 3414-2093; www.bcb.gov.br/?MUSEU; 10am-6pm Tue-Fri, 2-6pm 1st Sat of month only) FREE Numismatists may be interested in a visit to the money museum in the Banco Central do Brasil HQ. On show is cash from around the world, the world's largest gold nugget (56.6kg!), as well as a complete set of Brazilian currency (including a 1,000,000-cruzeiro note). You'll need to show your passport to get in.

Praça dos Trés Poderes

Down in the cockpit, you'll find the most interesting buildings surrounding the Praça dos Trés Poderes. It's a synthesis of the ideas of architects Niemeyer and Costa, combining various monuments, museums and federal buildings. The space includes striking sculptures, including Bruno Giorgi's *Os Candangos,* Alfredo Ceschiatti's *A Justiça* and Niemeyer's *O Pombal* (which looks like a clothes peg).

It's worth visiting the praça (plaza) during the day and again at night for two very different experiences. After dark, surreal lighting casts an eerie glow across the futuristic buildings, as though they are being lit up by the landing lights of an alien spacecraft. Robberies have been reported here at night, though, so have a taxi wait for you while you visit. Note that you will not be allowed to enter government buildings during weekdays in shorts, sandals, sleeveless/crop-top shirts or short skirts.

Espaço Cultural Lucio Costa MUSEUM

(Map p336; Praça dos Trés Poderes; 9am-6pm Tue-Sun) FREE Down a concealed flight of steps on the praça itself is the Espaço Cultural Lucio Costa. Inside you will find a 170-sq-meter scale map of the *Plano Piloto,* plus images of the city during its construction and early occupation. There is even a map of the city in braille.

★**Palácio do Itamaraty** GOVERNMENT BUILDING

(Palace of Arches; Map p336; 3411-8051; www.itamaraty.gov.br; Esplanada dos Ministérios, Bloco H; 9am-11am & 2-6pm Mon-Fri, 9-11am & 1-6pm Sat & Sun) FREE Palácio do Itamaraty is home to the Foreign Ministry and is one of the most impressive buildings – a series of arches towering over a reflecting pool and floating gardens landscaped by Burle Marx. Outside, the Bruno Giorgi sculpture *Meteor* consists of five marble blocks, each representing a continent.

Palácio da Justiça GOVERNMENT BUILDING

(Map p336; 3216-3216; Esplanada dos Ministérios; 2-4pm Mon-Fri, 10am-3pm Sat & Sun) Water cascades between the arches of the Palácio de Justicia into a koi fish pond. Access is from outside only.

★**Congresso Nacional** GOVERNMENT BUILDING

(Parliament; Map p336; 3216-1771; www.congressonacional.leg.br; Praça dos Três Poderes; 9am-5pm) FREE Featuring the photogenic 'dishes' and twin towers, the Congresso Nacional is one of the more interesting buildings on the inside as well. In addition to the color-coded chambers of the Senate (blue) and House of Representatives (green), there is an architecturally interesting 'Tunnel of Time' and an exhibit of antique Senate benches and microphones from 1867.

The convex dome on the roof of the House of Representatives is supposed to signify that membership is open to all ideologies. Visits on Tuesday, Wednesday and Thursday (or for non-Portuguese guides) must be scheduled.

★**Palácio do Planalto** PALACE

(Map p336; 3411-2042; www2.planalto.gov.br; 9:30am-2pm Sun) FREE The Palácio do Planalto is another Niemeyer design that's worth seeing, inside and out. From the curved lines of the exterior to the lustrous columns and sweeping curved ramp inside, it's one of the best examples of architectural

Niemeyer's Brasília

Oscar Ribeiro de Almeida Niemeyer Soares Filho passed away just 10 days short of his 105th birthday on December 5, 2012, but his legacy lives on in Brazil's futuristic capital. As the creative genius behind the 'free-flowing, sensually-curved' designs of Brasília's civic buildings, as well as some of Brazil's most eye-catching edificies elsewhere, the great architect had a unique gift for turning reinforced concrete into artistic masterpieces.

Niemeyer was visited in September 1956 by Brazilian president Juscelino Kubitschek, who was an admirer of his work. With the words 'Oscar, we are going to build the capital of Brazil,' a legendary partnership began, and with the addition of Lucio Costa as the landscaper, the dream soon became a reality. The completion of the city took place remarkably quickly and Brasília was ready for business on April 21, 1960. Niemeyer later lamented the rush, but to the nonperfectionist, the results were still outstanding.

Though an atheist himself, the 'crown of thorns' form of the Catedral Metropolitana (p338) is widely recognised as one of his most cutting-edge designs, with long stained-glass panels 'to connect the people to the sky, where their Lord's paradise is.' The heavens theme continues nearby at the simple but stunning Museu Nacional (p338), a white dome with a circumnavigating ramp leading to the entrance that recalls Saturn and its

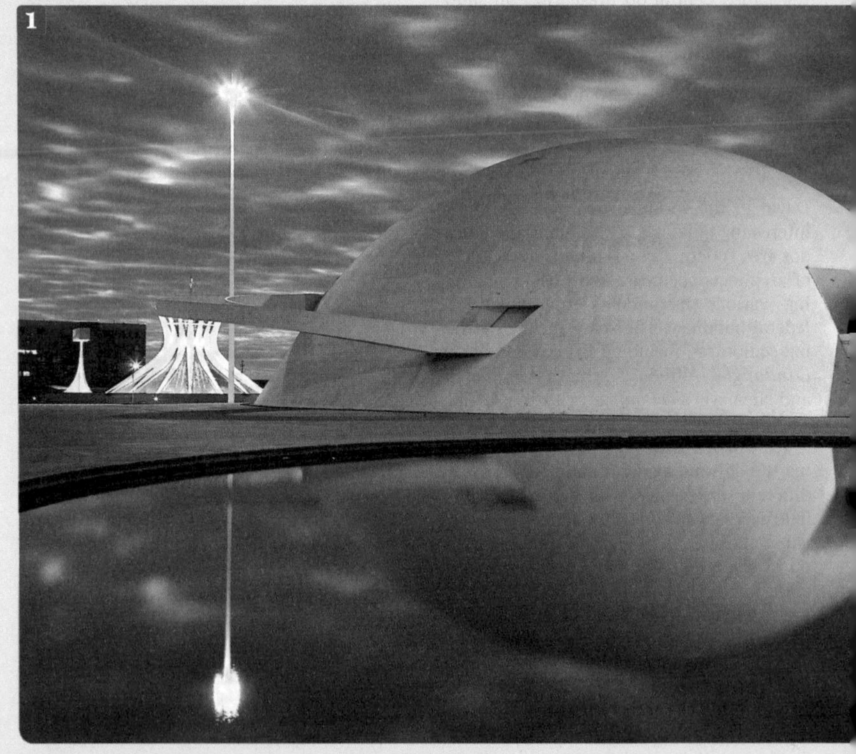
1

rings. Less visually striking, the design of the domes on the roof of the Congresso Nacional (p339) represents an openness of government to all political ideologies and reflected the optimistic future that Brasília would embody. Inspired by the words of Kubitschek 'What is Brasília, if not the dawn of a new day for Brazil?,' Niemeyer created the modernist Palacio da Alvorada (Palace of the Dawn; p343) as the official residence of the president, its simplistic layout turning its nose up at the excesses of previous incumbents of Brazil's top job.

Niemeyer was politically leftist and designed Brasília along socialist principles, with similar apartment blocks to prevent the emergence of wealthy neighborhoods. He was a friend of Fidel Castro, who once said 'Niemeyer and I are the last communists on this planet.' His political beliefs led to persecution under the military dictatorship of the 1960s and he was driven into exile, returning only when the country returned to democratic principles in the mid-1980s. Niemeyer continued to work right up to his death and lived to see Brazil finally beginning to fulfil the promise it promised with the building of Brasília.

Though he never cared for eulogies, it is hard to disagree with the words of President Dilma Roussef that marked his passing 'Brazil today lost one of its geniuses. It's a day for mourning.'

JANE SWEENEY / GETTY IMAGES ©

1. Congresso Nacional (p339) **2.** Catedral Metropolitana (p338) **3.** Palácio da Alvorada (p343)

RUY BARBOSA PINTO / GETTY IMAGES ©

FRANCISCO ARAGÃO / GETTY IMAGES ©

modernism in the world. The tour even lets you peek into the president's office.

There is a ceremonial changing of the guard outside the gates every hour on weekends and every two hours during the week.

Panteão da Pátria e da Liberdade Tancredo Neves MUSEUM

(Map p336; ☎3325-6244; ⏲9am-6pm Tue-Sun) FREE A newer tribute to the principal heroes of Brazilian history, including a set of vertiginous steps to an eternal flame in memory of Tancredo Neves, the elected president who died before he could assume power. The flame is slightly dangerous in a stiff breeze, but it's worth the risk for the aerial view of the Praça dos Trés Poderes.

Pavilhão Nacional MONUMENT

(Map p336) On the first Sunday of the month the ceremonial changing of Brasília's tallest and largest flag, a 286-sq-meter banner on the Pavilhão Nacional flagpole takes place. Conceived by Sergio Bernardes, it consists of 24 separate flagpoles welded together, each one symbolizing a Brazilian state.

ADDRESSES FOR THE LOGICAL MIND

Believe it or not, Brasília's addresses – a series of numbers and letters that pinpoint an exact location – are designed to make your life easier (once you know what all the acronyms mean!).

For example, the address SQS 704, Bloco Q, Casa 29. That means it's in Super Quadra South 704, *bloco* (building) Q, *casa* (house) 29. The first digit in the address (7) shows the position east or west of the Eixo Rodoviário (the main north–south arterial road): odd numbers to the west and even to the east, increasing as they move away from the center. The last two digits (04) show the distance north or south of the Eixo Monumental. So the place you are looking for is four blocks to the south of the Eixo Monumental and four blocks east of the Eixo Rodoviário (1, 3, 5, 7). The higher the number of the Super Quadra, the further it is from the center.

Get to know these acronyms:

Asa Norte/Asa Sul The two 'wings' of the city, connected by main roads, *eixo rodoviários*. The N (Norte) or S (Sul) after an acronym indicates on which side of the Eixo Monumental it's located.

SBN/SBS (Setor Bancário Norte/Sul) The banking areas either side of the Eixo Monumental.

SCEN/SCES (Setor de Clubes Esportivos Norte/Sul) The main recreational zone on the shores of Lago do Paranoá.

SCLN/SCLS (Setor Comércio Local Norte/Sul) The main shopping blocks between the *superquadras*.

SCN/SCS (Setor Comercial Norte/Sul) The commercial office-block areas next to the main shopping centers.

SDN/SDS (Setor de Diversões Norte/Sul) The main *conjuntos* (shopping centers) either side of the Eixo Monumental.

SEN/SES (Setor de Embaixadas Norte/Sul) The embassy sectors.

SHIN/SHIS (Setor de Habitações Individuaís Norte/Sul) The residential areas around the lake. SHIN is reached on the Eixo Norte. SHIS is accessed via the bridges off Av das Nações.

SHN/SHS (Setor Hoteleiro Norte/Sul) The hotel sectors each side of the Eixo Monumental.

SMHN/SMHS (Setor Médico Hospitalar Norte/Sul) The hospital sectors each side of the Eixo Monumental, next to the SCN and SCS, respectively.

SQN/SQS (Super Quadras Norte/Sul) The individual *superquadras* in the main residential wings of the *plano piloto*.

Got it?!

Setor de Clubes Esportivos (SCE)

★**Centro Cultural Banco do Brasil** GALLERY
(CCBB; 3310-7087; www.culturabancodobrasil.com.br; SCES, Trecho 2, Conjunto 22; 9am-9pm Tue-Sun) FREE Brasília's most important contemporary museum houses fascinating exhibitions in two galleries, an indie cinema, a cafe and a bookstore. A free bus runs every 90 minutes (varying hours from 11am to 11pm) along the Eixo Monumental (look for the painted bus that says CCBB).

Behind the CCBB you can see the triple-arched **Ponte JK** across Lago do Paranoá, a design presumably inspired by the Loch Ness monster.

★**Palácio da Alvorada** PALACE
(Palace of the Dawn; 3411-2317; www2.planalto.gov.br; SCEN; 3-5pm Wed) FREE The official presidential residence, the Palácio da Alvorada is a Niemeyer building. It was the first edifice in the city to be inaugurated, in 1958, predating the inauguration of the city itself by two years. The name translates as 'Palace of the Dawn,' in reference to JK's description of Brasília as 'a new dawn in Brazilian history.'

The gates are marshaled by dapper Dragões da Independência (Dragons of the Independence) guards, from a special regiment of soldiers who date back to the War of Independence. Arrive early for one-hour Wednesday tours (cancelled if it's raining). Take bus 0.104 (R$1.50, every 30 minutes) from platform A16 in the local bus station.

North of the City

Parque Nacional de Brasília PARK
(Map p336; 3465-2013; Brazilian/foreigner R$8/16; 8am-4pm) In the northern reaches of the city limits, the 30-sq-km Parque Nacional de Brasília is a good place to relax. It has natural swimming pools and is home to a number of threatened animals, including deer, anteaters, giant armadillos and maned wolves. Bus 128 from box E12 in the city bus station goes past the front gate.

Activities

Clube Kantanka WATER SPORTS
(8172-5233; www.katanka.com.br; SCES, Trecho 4, Conjunto 11; 8:30am-5:30pm) Stand-up paddleboarding has caught on in Brasília. These folks give lessons and rent equipment on Lago Paranoá.

Tours

★**Experimente Brasília** BICYCLE TOUR, WALKING TOUR
(www.experimentebrasilia.com.br) Go local with this excellent upstart agency, determined to show you a side of Brasília that will surprise you, whether that be on foot or two wheels. The most fascinating of the unique tours explores deep into *superquadra* life.

Billy Deeter TOUR
(8112-3434; www.mrbrasilia.com) For themed multilingual tours, Billy Deeter, who was born in the USA but has lived in Brasília since he was a child, organizes group and/or private customized tours, which include some off-the-beaten-track points of interest.

Sleeping

Bank on spending more than you'd like to in Brasília – during the business week, 'budget' here means 'midrange' elsewhere. Characterless high-rise chain hotels are the norm, crammed into the central Setor Hoteleiro with its ubiquitous traffic noise. Those in the SHN (Setor Hoteleiro Norte) are more conveniently located for the shopping centers, but those in the SHS (Setor Hoteleiro Sul) are better value. The less floors the hotel, the cheaper.

Prices listed are Monday to Friday – prices can drop as much as 75% on weekends.

Hostel 7 HOSTEL $
(Map p336; 3033-7707; www.hostel7.com.br; SCLRN 708, Bloco I, Loja 20; dm R$80-90;) Brasília's best hostel is an all-dorm affair, coming in three mixed variations of eight or 12 beds and one female-only dorm. The rooms are basic, but have lockers, air-con and bathrooms, while the common spaces are tight. There's a nice covered courtyard/bar area in the back. Local art and historic photos of the city add a nice local touch.

Econotel HOTEL $$
(Map p344; 3204-7337; www.hoteleconotel.com.br; SHS, Quadra 3, Bloco B; s/d/tr from R$139/239/309;) The closest thing to a budget hotel in the SHS, though the rooms are newer, fresher and better equipped and the hallways a tad brighter than many of the other stagnant options in a higher range. Pricier 'luxury' rooms are spacious and more modern, and the front desk steps up the professionalism compared with similar SHN options.

Central Brasília

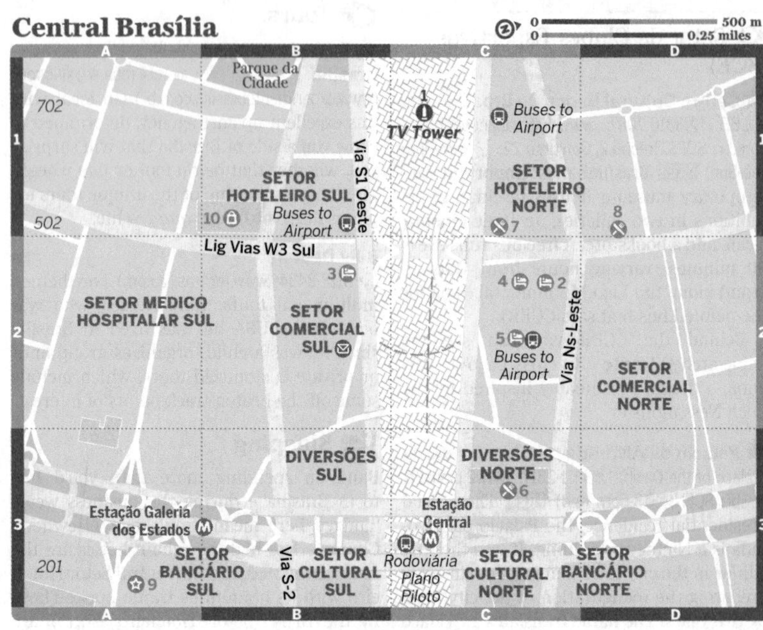

Central Brasília

Top Sights
1 TV Tower ... C1

Sleeping
2 Aristus Hotel ... C2
3 Econotel ... B2
4 Hotel Diplomat ... C2
5 Kubitschek Plaza ... C2

Eating
6 Conjunto Nacional ... C3
7 Marietta ... C1
8 Shopping Brasília ... D1

Entertainment
9 Outro Calaf ... A3

Shopping
10 Pátio Brasil ... B1

Aristus Hotel HOTEL $$
(Map p344; ☎3328-8675; www.aristushotel.com.br; SHN, Quadra 2, Bloco O; s/d from R$250/300; ❄@📶) If you spend any time in Brasília, you'll eventually get sick of elevators. The friendly Aristus is comfortably squat with only two floors, so you won't need one. Recently given a makeover, rooms are fine and simple, a lone window being the only difference in the more expensive rooms.

Hotel Diplomat HOTEL $$
(Map p344; ☎3204-2010; www.diplomathotelbrasilia.com; SHN, Quadra 2, Bloco L; s/d/tr from R$199/239/279; ❄📶) Near the TV Tower, this updated cheapie wins votes for its ample breakfast, free wi-fi and substantial weekend discounts (basement rooms are the cheapest). There's also train compartment-sized cabins for solo travelers.

★ **Brasília Palace Hotel** HISTORIC HOTEL $$$
(☎3306-9000; www.brasiliapalace.com.br; SHTN, Trecho 1, Lote 1; s/d R$495/570; ❄@📶🏊) Despite being gutted by fire and closed for nearly 30 years, Brasília's first hotel is still its best. Designed by Oscar Niemeyer in 1957, common spaces here are a living mid-century-modern treasury, with furniture and art by Niemeyer and Athos Bulcão and others around every turn, all shaded by an exterior blanketed with massive movable shutters.

Many of the 152 rooms, set along astonishingly long and wide corridors, offer views over Lago Sul, and the whole experience here screams one mantra: *This* is Brasília!

Kubitschek Plaza HOTEL $$$
(Map p344; ☎3329-3333; www.kubitschek.com.br; SHN, Quadra 2, Bloco E; s/d R$680/816; P ❄ @ ⓦ ≋) The halls and lobby of this classic choice feature wonderful art by local artists and famous photographs of Juscelino Kubitschek's administration, giving it a leg up from the hotel sector competition on local character. Rooms include gorgeous hardwood floors and earth-toned headboards.

Eating

Brazilians may say that Brasília is boring, but foodies flock here with abandon – the capital has one of the highest concentrations of starred restaurants in the country. The best selections are around SCLS 209/210, 409/410 and 411/412, which forms a sort of 'gourmet triangle' (it is also home to some of the city's most lively nightlife). Another good selection of restaurants is clustered in SCLS 405 and SCLN 412/413.

Elsewhere, Brazilians in need of sustenance head to the shopping malls. Three centrally located oases – **Shopping Brasília** (Map p344; www.brasiliashopping.com.br; Quadra 5, Asa Norte SCN; ⊙10am-10pm Mon-Sat, 2-8pm Sun), **Pátio Brasil** (Map p344; www.patiobrasil.com.br; Asa Sul, W3 SCS; ⊙10am-10pm Mon-Sat, noon-8pm Sun) and **Conjunto Nacional** (Map p344; www.conjuntonacional.com.br; SDN CNB, Conjunto A; ⊙10am-10pm Mon-Sat, noon-8pm Sun) – all have food courts with enough variety to cater to most tastes.

Mormaii Surf Bar BRAZILIAN $
(Map p336; SHIS, Quadra do Lago 10, Bloco E, Lote 8; açaí R$14.90-28.90; ⊙noon-midnight Mon, from 10am Tue-Thu, to 1am Fri-Sun; ⓦ) Though there's sushi, salads and sandwiches, locals park themselves on the outdoor lakeside patio every afternoon for the house specialty, *açaí na tigela,* a refreshing sorbetlike meal of blended palmberries, guaraná syrup, bananas and honey that's normally eaten at the beach.

The waterfront location (in the Pontão) is Brasília's beach! On weekends, it attracts a roaring nightlife crowd as well.

Naturetto BRAZILIAN $
(Map p336; www.naturetto.com.br; CLN 405, Block C; per kg R$46.90; ⊙11:30am-3pm & 6:30-9:30pm Mon-Fri, 11:30am-4pm Sun; ⓦ🖉) This excellent, near-vegetarian (there's fish) *por-kilo* restaurant is worth seeking out for creative dishes and the rustic, inner-city environment in which to enjoy it all. Nutritionists are on hand, overseeing the food and answering questions; it's packed at lunch.

Marietta SANDWICHES $
(Map p344; www.marietta.com.br; 2nd fl, Shopping Brasília; sandwiches R$14.50-28; ⊙10am-10pm Mon-Sat, 2-8pm Sun) This sandwich shop turns out the capital's best: a triangular triple-decker of arugula, buffalo mozzarella and sun-dried tomatoes. It has prizewinning juices and killer salads as well.

★Olivae BRAZILIAN $$
(Map p336; ☎3443-8775; www.olivaerestaurante.com.br; SCLS 405, Bloco B, Loja 6; mains R$62-73; ⊙noon-3pm Mon, noon-3pm & 7-11pm Tue-Thu, noon-3pm & 7pm-midnight Fri & Sat; ⓦ) With a disciple of Brazilian superchef Alex Atala running the show, this classy newcomer has everyone's taste buds doing a happy dance, including *Veja* magazine, which showered it with Chef of the Year, Best New Restaurant and Best Varied Restaurant awards in 2014–15.

The three-course lunch special for R$51 is an astonishing deal; and there are prix-fixe dinners (R$82 or R$110) and weekend grills as well.

Mangai NORTHEASTERN $$
(Map p336; www.mangai.com.br; SCES, Trecho 2, Conjunto 41; per kg R$62.90; ⊙noon-3pm & 6-10pm Mon-Thu, noon-10pm Fri & Sat, 11am-9pm Sun) With culinary stars, this Northeastern *por-kilo* restaurant offers a culinary experience like no other. An assembly line of tempting creative dishes will totally overwhelm you – and that's just the salad section. The space itself is gargantuan and full of Brazilian character. It's down by the Ponte JK and gets very busy at lunch.

Nossa Cozinha Bistrô FUSION $$
(Map p336; ☎3326-5207; www.nossacozinhabsb.blogspot.com.br; SCLN 402, Bloco C; mains R$32-57; ⊙11.30am-3pm & 7.30pm-midnight Mon-Sat; ⓦ) At this near-makeshift bistro tucked away on Bloco C's backside, superb value awaits. The US-trained chef excels at gourmet treats like the signature pork ribs (velvety! chocolaty! tasty!). For Brazil, the check is a pleasant shock.

★Taypá PERUVIAN $$$
(☎3248-0403; www.taypa.com.br; SHIS QI 17, Bloco G, Loja 208; mains R$47.80-84.80; ⊙noon-3pm

& 7pm-midnight Mon-Fri, noon-4pm & 7pm-midnight Sat, noon-5pm Sun;) It's worth a trip to the edges of Lago Sul – a R$30 or so taxi fare – for Marco Espinoza's authentic upscale Peruvian. His whole team hails from Peru and it shows: the fabulous ceviche *criollo*, drowning in creamy *leche de tigre* (citrus-marinated ceviche), and the decadent *suspiro de limeño* (milk caramel and meringue), were the best we've ever had outside Peru. Great *pisco* cocktails, too.

Universal Diner INTERNATIONAL **$$$**
(Map p336; 3443-2089; www.restauranteuniversal.com.br; SCLS 210, Bloco C, Loja 18; dishes R$59-98; noon-3pm & 7pm-midnight Mon-Thu, to 1am Fri & Sat;) A junkyard-chic aesthetic greets patrons at this hypereclectic kitsch freak-out of an eatery (it's overflowing with funky bric-a-brac and antique knickknacks), another of the city's Brazilicious culinary gems and easily its biggest personality. The mouthwatering tenderloin *au poivre* (peppered) is fantastic, as is the gnocchi, served on vinyl LP placemats. Come for Thursday-night burgers, grilled up streetside from 6pm.

Drinking & Nightlife

For cheap drinks with the university crowd, head to SCLN 408/9 for a collection of options.

Bar Beirute BOTECO
(Map p336; www.facebook.com/barbeirute; SCLS 109, Bloco A; 11am-1am Sun-Wed, to 2am Thu-Sat) This Brasília institution has a massive outdoor patio packed with an edgier crowd than most. It's a GLS point – the clever Brazilian acronym for gay, lesbian and sympathetic people – but it's really a free-for-all, the most classic drinking experience in the city and no better spot for a mug of teeth-numbing cold Beira – Beirute's own brand of beer! There's another branch at Asa Norte (Map p336; SCLN 107, Bloco B).

Loca Como Tu Madre PUB
(Map p336; www.locacomotumadre.com.br; SCLS 306, Bloco C, Loja 36; 6pm-12:30am Mon-Thu, to 1:30am Fri & Sat;) 'Crazy Like Your Mama' boasts a great outdoor space that caters to well-heeled *brasiliense* imbibing to the sounds of nightly DJs spinning pop and

BRASÍLIA – CAPITAL OF THE THIRD MILLENNIUM

In 1883 an Italian priest, John Bosco, prophesied that a new civilization would arise between parallels 15 and 20, and that its capital would be built between parallels 15 and 16, on the edge of an artificial lake. Many consider Brasília to be that city, and a number of cults have sprung up in the area. If you tire of Brasília's architectural monuments, a visit to one of the cults may be part of your destiny.

About 45km east of Brasília, near the satellite city of Planaltina, you'll find the **Vale do Amanhecer** (Valley of the Dawn; 3388 0537; 10am-midnight), founded in 1959 by a clairvoyant, Tia Neiva. The valley is actually a small town where you can see (or take part in) Egyptian, Greek, Aztec, Indian, Roma, Inca, Trojan and Afro-Brazilian rituals. The mediums in the town believe that a new civilization will come during the 3rd millennium. The town's main temple was inspired by spiritual advice received by Tia Neiva. In the center is an enormous Star of David, which forms a lake, pierced by an arrow. Get there by bus 617 from the center of Brasília.

About 63km west of Brasília, near the town of Santo Antônio do Descoberto (Goiás), is the **Cidade Ecléctica** (Eclectic City; 3626-1391; 8am-6pm). Founded in 1956 by Yokanam, who was once an airline pilot, the group's aim is to unify all religions on the planet through fraternity and equality. You're welcome to attend its ceremonies, but there are strict dress regulations. Women cannot wear long pants (skirts only) and men cannot wear shorts. If you're not dressed suitably, you'll be given a special tunic to wear.

The **Templo da Boa Vontade** (Temple of Goodwill; Map p336; 3114 1070; www.tbv.com.br; SGAS, Quadra 915, Lotes 75/76; entrance to most of its rooms is free; 24hr) was created by the Legion of Goodwill in 1989 as a symbol of universal solidarity. It incorporates seven pyramids, joined to form a cone that is topped with a 21kg crystal. To view it, you must take off your shoes and walk along the spiraling inner circle via the black path. You must return on the white path (do not screw this up). It's all a bit dizzying. There is also an interesting Egyptian room for meditation that will make you feel like King Tut (of course, they take all of this very seriously, so let's keep these jokes between us). Get there on bus 105 or 107 from the city bus station.

musica popular brasileira at pleasant sound levels around tables arranged under suspended box pallets. Upstart Chef Renata Carvalho's trendy pub grub is lauded here as well.

Paradiso Cine Bar COCKTAIL BAR
(Map p336; www.paradisocinebar.com.br; SCLS 306, Bloco B, Loja 4 ; cocktails R$15-29; ⏲4pm-1am Mon-Wed, to 2am Thu-Sat) The classic cinema theme here is a little gimmicky, but this new bar's riveting and inventive cocktail list has taken Brasília by storm. A definite don't miss for connoisseurs of craft cocktails, and there's live jazz or blues upstairs every Tuesday (R$15).

Santuário BAR
(Map p336; www.facebook.com/SantuarioCC; SCLN 214, Bloco C, Loja 27; ⏲2pm-midnight Mon, noon-1am Tue & Wed, noon-1am Thu-Sat; 📶) Craft-beer fiends flock to this bar/shop on the wingtip of Asa Norte for 12 daily-rotating drafts of domestic and international microbrews, cool music and the city's best overall beer experience.

But charging R$8 to R$12 for 'tasting' size samples when folks just want a sip before they commit is outrageous and contrary to standing operating procedures for similar establishments around the world.

Bar Brasília BAR
(Map p336; ☎3443-4323; SCLS, Quadra 506, Bloco A, Loja 15A; ⏲11am-midnight Mon-Sat, to 5pm Sun) In the same vein as the classic bars from Rio and São Paulo, complete with a hardwood bar relocated from a pharmacy in 1928, and antique tiled floors. It's great for draft beer and weekend *feijoada* (bean-and-meat stew; R$45.50).

Ernesto Cafés Especiais CAFE
(Map p336; www.facebook.com/ErnestoCafes Especiais; SCLS 115, Bloco C, Loja 14; coffee R$5-16; ⏲8am-11pm Tue-Sat, to 10pm Sun; 📶) Easily Brasília's best coffee experience, this very serious java joint offers specialty microlot coffees from Minas Gerais and is hopping with locals day or night, whether over breakfast (fresh baked bread, good tapiocas) or simply losing an afternoon entrenched in conversation on the pleasant back patio.

☆ Entertainment

Check the online listings of *Diverte-se Mais* (www.df.divirtasemais.com.br) by *Correio Brasiliense* newspaper for live music and cultural events.

Clube do Choro LIVE MUSIC
(Map p336; ☎3224-0599; www.clubedochoro.com.br; Setor de Divulgação Cultural, Bloco G; cover R$20; ⏲8pm-midnight Tue-Sat) A wildly mixed crowd of serious music aficionados – No talking! No standing! – descend on this locals' secret walkable from the hotel sectors, a showcase for some of the country's most magnificent *choro* (improvised samba). Reserve the best seats online. Food and drinks are (quietly) served.

On the first Saturday of the month, students from the affiliated *choro* school form an impromptu orchestra of Brazilian musicianship under the trees outside from 10am to 2pm...for free!

Outro Calaf LIVE MUSIC
(Map p344; ☎3325-7408; www.outrocalaf.com.br; SBS, Quadra 2, Bloco Q, Edifício João Saad; cover R$10-30; ⏲9pm-2am Mon-Fri, 2:30pm-midnight Sat, 4pm-midnight Sun) After a lengthy court battle with his former building, Venceslau Calaf, long heralded as Brasília's top dog for live music, bolted from the original Bar do Calaf and opened Outro Calaf pretty much right next door. His audiences followed, all of whom rate the excellent live samba, *pagode* (popular samba) and *choro* as the city's best.

Shopping

Fundacão Athos Bulcão ARTS & CRAFTS
(Map p336; www.fundathos.org.br; SCLS 404, Bloco D, Loja 1; ⏲9am-6pm Mon-Fri, 10am-5pm Sat) Painter/sculptor Athos Bulcão was the only artist allowed to colorfully spruce up Niemeyer and Costa's grand plan, and his iconic designs are as much a part of Brasília history as his more well-known counterparts. Pick up art, coffee mugs, beach towels and the like.

ℹ Information

Brasília has a large chunk of real estate devoted to embassies and consulates, most located between Quadras 801 and 810 in the Setor de Embaixadas Sul (Embassy Sector South).

There are banks with moneychanging facilities in the Setor Bancário Sul (SBS; Banking Sector South) and Setor Bancário Norte (SBN; Banking Sector North). Both sectors are close to the city bus station. All the major malls, bus stations and the airport have a variety of ATMs, most with Cirrus/MasterCard/Visa networking, but you should avoid using freestanding machines due to rampant card-cloning in Brazil.

LOCAL KNOWLEDGE

TAXI TALK

Always carry a taxi phone number with you in Brasília. They are as scarce as snow in the *superquadras*. With **Unitaxi** (☎3325-3030) or **Rádio Táxi Alvorada** (☎3321-3030; www.radiotaxi33213030.com.br), you are entitled to a 20% to 30% discount off the meter if you call (not always announced to foreigners). Remind both the dispatcher *and* the driver: '*Com o desconto, por favor.*' You can also download their apps.

C.A.T Airport (www.vemviverbrasilia.df.gov.br; Presidente Juscelino Kubitschek International Airport; ⏲8am-6pm) Tres Poderes (Centro Atendimento ao Turista; Map p336; ☎8693-2542; Praça dos Três Poderes; ⏲8am-6pm) The city's two most helpful tourist-information booths.

Correios (Map p344; www.correios.com.br; SHS, Quadra 2, Bloco B; ⏲9am-5pm Mon-Fri) Postal services. There are also branches in the arrivals hall of the airport and at the main malls.

De Base do Distrito Federal (☎3315-1200; www.saude.df.gov.br; SMHS 101)

Santa Lúzia (☎3445-6000; www.hsl.com.br; SHLS, Quadra 716, Conjunto E)

Getting There & Away

Brasília has a large daily influx of sightseers and lobbyists, so the international airport connects with all major Brazilian cities.

AIR

Brasília's shiny new **Aeroporto Presidente Juscelino Kubitschek** (BSB; ☎3364-9037; www.aeroportobrasilia.net) is 12km south of the center.

You can book flights and rental cars through the travel agencies in the Hotel Nacional complex, but if you prefer to contact the airlines directly, they all have offices at the airport.

BUS

From the flashy new long-distance bus station, **Rodoviária Interestadual** (Map p336; ☎3234-2185; SMAS, Trecho 4, Conjunto 5/6), 3km southwest off the edge of Asa Sul, buses go almost everywhere in Brazil.

Getting Around

The easiest way to or from the airport is **Ônibus Executivo Aeroporto** (Bus 113; ☎3344-2769; www.tcb.df.gov.br; fare R$8; ⏲6:30am-11pm), which does a loop from the airport to the Rodoviária Plano Piloto (local bus station), the entirety of the Esplanada dos Ministérios and both SHS (45 minutes) and SHN (30 minutes) every 30 minutes between 6:30am and midnight (11pm on weekends). It departs just outside the arrivals hall to the far right. Taxis to the airport cost around R$52 and local bus 0.102/102.1 is R$2 (40 minutes).

Estação Shopping of the **Metrô DF** (www.metro.df.gov.br; weekends/weekdays R$2/3; ⏲6am-11:30pm Mon-Fri, 7am-7pm Sat & Sun) connects the Rodoviária Interestadual with the local **Rodoviária Plano Piloto** (Map p344) bus station (Estacão Central) in the city center, as does local bus 108.8 (R$2, 20 minutes). It's worth picking up a frequent rider card, called a Cartão Cidadão, for local buses from **DFTrans** (www.dftrans.df.gov.br) from the Sistema Bilhetagem Automatica (SBA) window downstairs and to the left of the Metro entrance. The Metro offers a similar subway-only product, Cartão Flex, but unfortunately there is not one integrated transport card for all forms of transport. If you can navigate the Portuguese, the DFTrans web site is also useful for finding out bus routes from the local bus station – a confusing maze of mess.

BUSES FROM BRASÍLIA

DESTINATION	STARTING FARE (R$)	TIME (HR)	COMPANY
Belém	358	35	Transbrasiliana (www.transbrasiliana.com.br)
Campo Grande	255	19	Motta (www.motta.com.br)
Cuiabá	178	20	Expresso São Luiz (www.expressosaoluiz.com.br)
Goiânia	28	3	Araguarina (www.araguarina.com.br)
Porto Velho	332	42	Andorinha (www.andorinha.com)
Rio de Janeiro	195	17	Itapemirim (www.itapemirim.com.br)
Salvador	150	22	Real Expresso (www.realexpresso.com.br)
São Paulo	189	14	Real Expresso (www.realexpresso.com.br)

The Metrô DF is only really useful for access to restaurants and bars in the Asa Sul. It runs from the city bus station to the huge suburbs of Ceilândia and Samambaia, with a predictably named station (102 Sul, 104 Sul etc) every two blocks or so from the central station. Last service is at 11:30pm. Metrô expansion projects to the airport and the entirety of Asa Norte – a game-changing proposition for city transport – as well as a light rail network (South America's first modern tramway) remain in various stages of longer-term planning and implementation.

Its (☎2196-7834; www.itsrentacar.com.br; Aeroporto Internacional de Brasília) rents cars for as little as R$82 per day with a kilometer cap.

GOIÁS

POP 6 MILLION

Goiás is a vast and wild state of green hills and deep valleys, dominated by the picturesque cerrado so typical of central Brazil. Agriculture is big business here, with soya, biodiesel and ethanol industries making this one of the wealthiest states in the country, albeit at the expense of the landscape. Fortunately, its unrelenting natural beauty is preserved in a series of jaw-dropping national parks, while a series of handsome colonial towns (www.cidadeshistoricasgoias.com.br) are perfect places to try the much-lauded regional cuisine.

Getting There & Around

The gateway to Goiás is Brasília, with daily flights to all major Brazilian cities. If you don't mind spending days on buses it's also possible to travel overland: from the coast via scenic Minas Gerais or from the Pantanal portals of Cuiabá and Campo Grande.

Goiás offers many attractions and is a popular stopover for travelers crossing the interior of the country. Regular bus services connect all the major towns and cities. Road conditions are generally good and renting a car is a viable option.

Goiânia

☎0XX62 / POP 1.3 MILLION

The capital of Goiás, Goiânia is the state's other planned city, predating Brasília by almost 30 years. Planned by urbanist Armando de Godói and founded in 1933, it's a pleasant enough combination of parks, leafy avenues and high-rise buildings laid out around circular streets. There's not much to see here, but it's a major transport nexus and if you're touring the state, you'll inevitably find yourself passing through more than once.

Sleeping

There are a million places to stay for all budgets close to the gigantic bus station. Midrange and top-end hotels drop as much as 50% off their prices when business is slow.

Hostel 7 HOSTEL $
(☎3877-6077; www.hostel7br.com; Av T2, Quadra 107, Lote 4, Setor Bueno; dm from R$80, s/d with fan R$80/100; @☎☒) The strengths of Goiânia's first hostel, an HI-affiliate, are design-oriented: a minimalist asthetic in a well-to-do/lively residential neighborhood southwest of Centro, with such striking accents as carved-out Volkswagen buses and hip common spaces. But charging for bath towels and leaving bed dressing to guests in cramped private rooms is a definite overreach.

Rodohotel HOTEL $
(☎3224-2664; www.rodohotelgo.com.br; Rua 44 554; s/d/tr with fan R$80/120/180, with air-con R$100/160/240; ❄☎) Opposite the bus station's northern exit, this almost-cheapie will do for an overnight stay before catching an early bus. Opt for a modernized 3rd-floor room.

Goiânia Palace HOTEL $$
(☎3224-4874; www.goianiapalace.com.br; Av Anhanguera 5195; s/d/tr from R$105/140/175; ❄☎) Pretty in pink! Art deco brick-and-wood *apartamentos* with new wardrobes and full-length mirrors and made-to-order eggs for breakfast. Very friendly, centrally located and English/French are sometimes spoken.

Eating & Drinking

There is some great regional food to try as well as some thriving nightlife.

★**Chão Nativo I** GOIANO $$
(☎3233-5396; www.chaonativo1.com.br; Av República do Líbano 1809, Setor Oeste; fixed-price meals from R$33.90, per kg from R$48.90; ⏲11am-3:30pm Mon-Fri, to 4pm Sat & Sun) Mathematize your hunger by choosing between pay-by-weight or all-you-can-eat at this smorgasbord of bubbling cauldrons of Goiânian concoctions, often voted the city's best for local cuisine.

Piquiras INTERNATIONAL $$$
(☎3281-4344; www.piquiras.com; Rua 146 464, Setor Marista; mains R$46-110; ⏲5pm-midnight

Mon-Fri, 11am-1am Sat & Sun;) A Goiânia institution serving great examples of local fare. South of downtown, the expansive outside deck is packed with the city's young and fun on weekends.

★**Mönch Bier** BAR

(Rua 144 665, Qd 51, Lt02, Sector St Marista; 4pm-3am Tue-Sun;) Goiânia's best bar, with an unparalleled domestic craft-beer list, including 10 daily-rotating taps of brews rarely seen outside the bottle. Tack on a great crowd, friendly waiters and management, and cool music, and this wins top spot for hopheads.

Celsin & Cia BAR

(www.celsinecia.com.br; Rua 22 475, Setor Oeste; 5pm-2am Mon-Fri, 11am-2am Sat & Sun) *Goianos* of all ilks drink in droves at this traditional *boteco*, filling the 65 outdoor tables under illuminated almond trees day and night.

Information

If you're just passing through pretty much everything you are likely to need, from food to ATMs to a post office, is in the monster-size bus station-mall. If you're traveling on to the national parks or colonial towns, it is wise to get money here.

C.I.T. (Centro de Informação Turística; 3524-5060; www4.goiania.go.gov.br; Aeroporto de Santa Genoveva/Goiânia; 7am-11pm) Friendly municipal tourist info booth outside airport terminal.

Getting There & Around

Aeroporto de Goiânia (3265-1500; Praça Capitão Frazão 913) is 6km northeast of the city center. You can fly to Rio, São Paulo and other major Brazilian cities, but it's usually cheaper (not to mention more convenient) to fly to nearby Brasília. From the airport, bus 256 (R$3.30, hourly) heads into the center, but Goiânia buses do not accept cash. You must buy paper tickets (only option for tourists) or refillable cards from **Sitpass** (0800-648-2222; www.sitpass.com.br; Rua 4 515, Edifício Parthenon Center, Setor Central) at numerous newsstands and other locations around town; or beg for tourist mercy!

BUS

Buses depart from the huge **bus station-mall** (3240-0000; www.rodoviariadegoiania.com; Rua 44 399, Setor Central). In addition the services below, there are departures to Alto Paraíso (R$79.50, seven hours) operated by **Empresa São José do Tocantins** (3224-8330; Rodoviária de Goiânia), leaving at 8:20pm daily and 12:10pm Tuesday, Thursday and Saturday.

Many buses arriving in Goiânia stop first at the Campinas subterminal. If the station doesn't look ridiculously huge, then stay on board. You're not there yet!

Cidade de Goiás

0XX62 / POP 24,700

Straddling the Rio Vermelho and surrounded by the rugged Serra Dourada, Cidade de Goiás is a sleepy town of lamplit cobblestone streets and whitewashed colonial homes. The former state capital, once known as Vila Boa (and briefly later on as Goiás Velho and sometimes today only as Goiás), was awarded Unesco World Heritage status in 2002. Its gorgeous baroque churches shine and the town's population swells during Semana Santa (Holy Week). Every July 25, the anniversary of the town's founding in 1727, the state governor visits Cidade de Goiás, which becomes the state capital for three days.

Sights

Strolling through town, you quickly notice the magnificent 18th-century colonial architecture, much of which is home to narrow streets and low houses hawking the region's famous *frutas cristalizados* (sugar-coated

BUSES FROM GOIÂNIA

DESTINATION	STARTING FARE (R$)	TIME (HR)	COMPANY
Brasília	27.68–51.83	3	www.viacaogoiania.com.br, www.araguarina.com.br
Caldas Novas	31.32	2½	www.nacionalexpresso.com.br
Cidade de Goiás	28	3	www.empresamoreira.com.br
Cuiabá	144.82	16	www.expressosaoluiz.com.br
Pirenópolis	15	2½	www.viacaogoianesia.com.br

OFF THE BEATEN TRACK

SOME LIKE IT HOT!

Suffering from high blood pressure after Brasília? Poor digestion after your visit to a truck-stop cafe in Minas? Exhausted after your extended Carnaval in Salvador? Then **Caldas Novas**, with more than 30 curative hot springs, may be just the place for you. The population of this upmarket resort town, located 160km southeast of Goiânia, swells during the holidays, when 200,000 people can descend on the town in search of curative Eden.

Nearly everyone in Caldas Novas has a thermal pool to cure what ails ya, but not all of them are open to the public. Besides the hotels and pousadas, there are a few good options in and around the city for day use only. Working your way from the city center out, **SESC Caldas Novas** (www.sescgo.com.br; Av Ministro Elias Bufaiçal 600; day use R$40; 8am-8pm Mon-Sun) is the most conveniently located and favorably priced. The 11 thermal pools in the SESC complex are well maintained and within walking distance of Praça Matriz. A little further out is **di Roma Acqua Park** (3455-9393; http://www.diroma.com.br/index.php/diroma-acqua-park; São Cristóvão 1110; adult/child R$70/45; 8am-7pm), an all-out aquatic extravaganza featuring the world's first thermal wave pool, waterslides, lazy river, restaurants and numerous therapeutic waters.

For something even more wet and wild, the aquatic playground of Rio Quente, 22km from Caldas Novas, is home to the world's only thermal-water river and enough water-themed entertainment to ensure you'd rather drown by the time it's all over. **Hot Park** (3512-8040; www.hotpark.com; Fazenda Água Quente s/n; adult/child R$130/100; 9:30am-5pm, closed Thu in low season) is the epicenter of the fun, a sort of waterlogged Disney World for bronzed Brazilian beauties. Its 22,000 sq meters of slippery amusement includes a R$2.5-million mega half-pipe imported from Canada, the only one of its kind in Latin America.

During holidays and long weekends the town is packed, so reservations are advisable. Chain hotels dominate and rooms in all categories tend to be nearly identical; pick based on hot-springs action – and expect to break your budget in high season. **Nacional Expresso** (62-3416-8181; www.nacionalexpresso.com.br) makes the trip from Goiânia once daily (R$31.32, three hours, 8:30am). During high season it also offers buses from São Paulo (from R$150.20, 12 hours).

fruit concoctions that come in a plethora of flavors). Fuel up and make your way around the town's seven churches.

★Museu das Bandeiras MUSEUM
(3371-1087; Praça Brasil Caiado; admission R$4; 9am-5pm Tue-Fri, 9am-noon & 1:30-5pm Sat, 9am-1pm Sun) The fascinating Museu das Bandeiras is an old jail (1766–1950) that's full of interesting antiques and original furniture – the 1.5m-thick cell walls, originally made of weak *taipa de pilão* wood and reinforced with much stronger *aroeira* (pepper-tree) wood, are a museum piece in themselves. Outside in the square, the **Chafariz de Cauda fountain** (1778) is perfectly preserved, save the water.

Museu de Arte Sacra MUSEUM
(admission R$3; 9am-5pm) In the old Igreja da Boa Morte, this just-renovated museum has a good selection of 19th-century works by renowned Goiânian sculptor Viega Vale.

Casa de Cora Carolina MUSEUM
(3371-1990; Dom Cândido Penso 20; admission R$6; 9am-4.45pm Tue-Sat, to 3pm Sun) The Casa de Cora Carolina is the birthplace and home of the area's renowned poet.

Palácio Conde dos Arcos PALACE
(3371-1200; Praça Castelo Branco; admission R$4; 8am-4pm Tue-Sat, to 1pm Sun) The Palácio Conde dos Arcos is the restored colonial governor's residence.

Igreja São Francisco de Paula CHURCH
(Praça Zaqueu Alves de Castro; 1-5pm Tue-Thu, 9am-1pm Sat & Sun) FREE The most impressive of the town's seven churches is the oldest, built in 1761. There's a humble religious museum inside (R$2).

Festivals & Events

Semana Santa RELIGIOUS
The highlight of the week before Easter is the Wednesday-night procession re-enacting

Cidade de Goiás

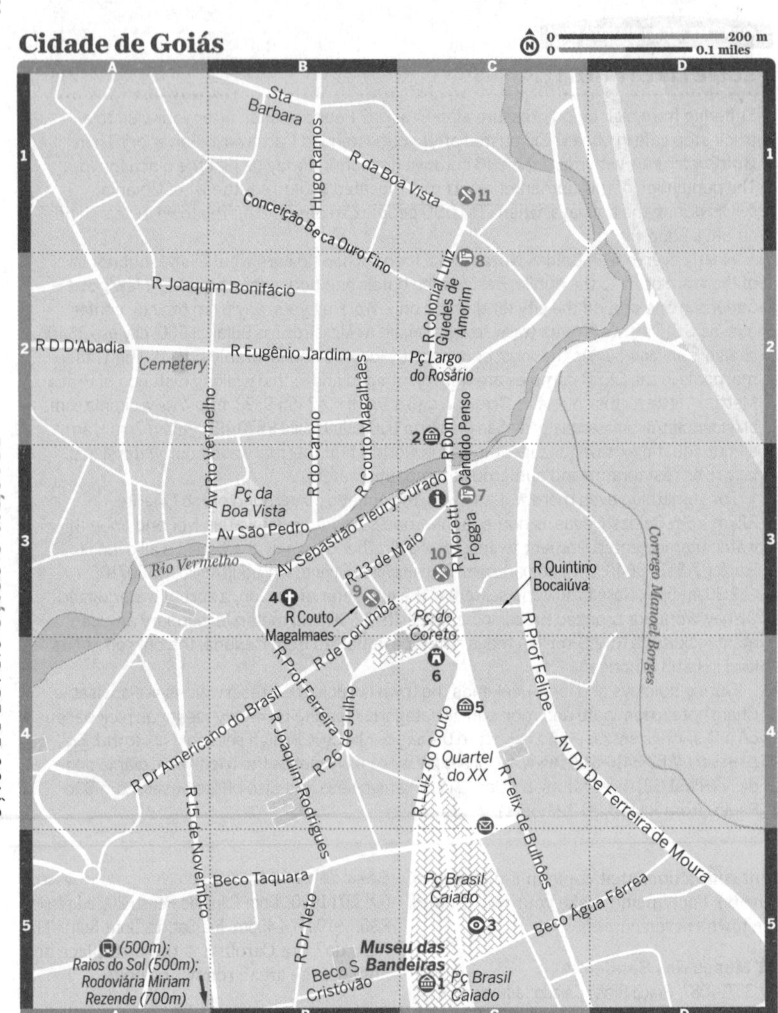

the arrest of Christ. The streetlights are turned off and thousands march through the streets carrying torches, led by 40 eerie, pointy-hooded figures (the *farricocos*), whose colorful dress harks back to the days of the Inquisition.

Festival International de Cinema e Video Ambiental FILM
(www.fica.art.br) The largest environmental film festival in the world, usually held in June or August.

Sleeping

Cidade de Goiás is a popular getaway from Goiânia, so book ahead if you're arriving on a weekend. The town is packed during Semana Santa and for the Festival International de Cinema e Video Ambiental, when prices rise.

Raios de Sol HOTEL $
(3371-3161; www.hotelraiodesol.com; Av Dario de Paiva Sampaio s/n; s/d without air-con R$55/100, with air-con R$65/120;) Maybe not the ray of sunshine you were looking for in your life, but this hotel next to the bus station is good

Cidade de Goiás

Top Sights

1 Museu das Bandeiras.........C5

Sights

2 Casa de Cora Carolina.........C2
3 Chafariz de Cauda Fountain.........C5
4 Igreja São Francisco de Paula.........B3
5 Museu de Arte Sacra.........C4
6 Palácio Conde dos Arcos.........C4

Sleeping

7 Casa da Ponte.........C3
8 Pousada do Ipê.........C2

Eating

9 Casa do Doce.........B3
10 Casarão.........C3
11 Flor do Ipê.........C1

value and saves you the hike to the center if you arrive late.

★**Pousada do Ipê** POUSADA $$
(☎3371-2065; www.pousadadoipe.com; Colonial Luiz Guedes de Amorim 22; s/d apt R$216/238, chalets R$221/271; ❄☎≋) The most charming place to stay, the pousada (guesthouse) is a tranquil property set around a lush courtyard and swimming pool. Enjoy the sugar-laden breakfast of local jams and jellies in a room just off the old-style kitchen.

Casa da Ponte HOTEL $$
(☎3371-4467; casadapontehotel_@hotmail.com; Moretti Foggia s/n; s/d without air-con R$110/198, with air-con R$165/275; ❄☎) There's no accounting for taste with regard to the floral bedspreads, but this kitschy hotel is on a nice corner overlooking the Rio Vermelho.

Eating

The *empadão* reigns here – the tasty savory pie that's filled with meat, vegetables, cheese, olives and sometimes egg is served just about everywhere. Equally ubiquitous are *frutas cristalizados.*

★**Flor do Ipê** GOIANA $
(www.restauranteflordeipe.com; Rua da Boa Vista; dishes for 2 R$20-60; ⏲noon-3pm & 7-11pm Tue-Sun; ☎) For lunch, there's a wealth of regional choices laid out in fiery-hot clay pots for R$30. In the evenings, the shady garden setting fills up quickly for excellent à la carte local dishes.

Casarão GOIANA $
(Moretti Foggia 2; dishes R$8-12; ⏲8am-8pm Mon-Thu, to midnight Fri & Sat) Up a rickety wooden staircase, this unconventional spot is tops in town to try piping-hot *empadão,* served in traditional ceramic crockery.

Casa do Doce SWEETS $
(Maximiliano Mendes 1; sweets per kg R$25-30; ⏲9am-5pm Mon-Fri, to 6pm Sat & Sun) You'll find the colorful display of 28 crystallized fruits here too much to walk away from.

Information

C.A.T (Centro Atendimento ao Turista; ☎3371-7713; www.cidadedegoias.com.br; Moretti Foggia; ⏲8am-6pm Mon-Fri, 9am-11pm Sat, 9am-1pm Sun) Friendly and helpful municipal tourist info.

Correios (www.correios.com.br; Aguavi; ⏲9am-noon & 1-5pm Mon-Fri) Postal services.

Getting There & Away

The **bus station** (Av Dario de Paiva Sampaio s/n) is 500m south of Praça Brasil Caiado. **Empresa Moreira** (☎3018-9500; www.empresamoreira.com.br) runs frequent buses between Cidade de Goiás and Goiânia (R$29.35, three hours), from where you can connect to pretty much everywhere else in the state.

Pirenópolis

☎0XX62 / POP 23,000

A curious mix of art deco and Portuguese colonial architecture first strikes visitors to 'Piri,' but that's far from the only odd thing about this quirky town which has been on the Patrimonio Nacional (National Heritage) register since 1989. Set on striking red earth astride the Rio das Almas, it's another colonial gem with a history steeped in gold, though quite different from others in the state.

An alternative movement took hold here in the '70s and remains today. There is a New Age, vaguely hippie vibe to this laid-back spot, and the streets are lined with artist workshops each trying to out-kook their neighbor. You'll be sick of waterfalls by the time you leave, but it's an excellent base from which to explore the 73 found around the area.

Sights & Activities

★**Museu do Divino** MUSEUM
(☎3331-1460; Bernardo Sayão; admission R$2; ⏲9am-5pm Mon-Sat, to 3pm Sun) The municipal Museu do Divino exhibits the masks and costumes used during the Festo do Divino Espírito Santo. These masks were made by local craftsmen using methods passed down from generation to generation.

Pirenópolis

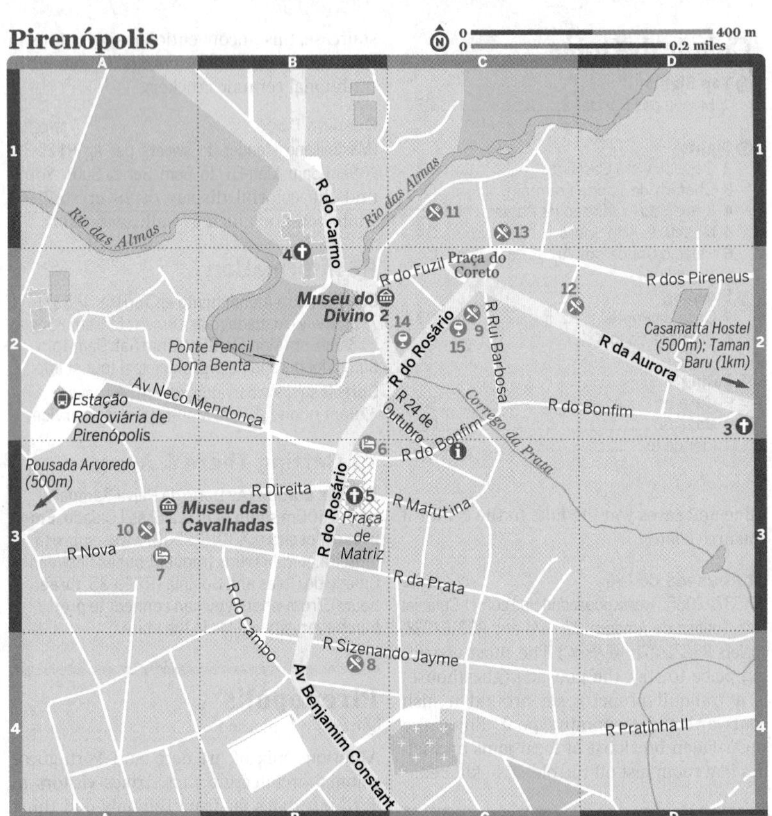

Pirenópolis

Top Sights

1 Museu das Cavalhadas ... A3
2 Museu do Divino ... B2

Sights

3 Igreja NS do Bonfim ... D2
4 Igreja NS do Carmo & Museu de Arte Sacra ... B2
5 Igreja NS do Rosário Matriz & Museu da Matriz ... B3

Sleeping

6 Pousada Cavalhadas ... B3
7 Pouso, Café e Cultura ... A3

Eating

8 As Flor ... B4
9 Bacalhau da Bibba ... C2
10 Boca do Forno/Boca Santa ... A3
11 Montserrat Gastronomia ... C1
12 Pedícafé ... C2
13 Pireneus Café ... C1

Drinking & Nightlife

14 Cachaçaria do Dil ... C2
15 Rosário 26 ... C2

★Museu das Cavalhadas MUSEUM
(☎3331-1166; Direita 39; admission R$2; ⏲10am-5pm) The privately owned Museu das Cavalhadas is cluttered with bright and colorful artifacts brought to life in a guided tour from the owner. The sign says to ring the doorbell if the museum appears to be closed.

Igreja NS do Carmo & Museu de Arte Sacra CHURCH, MUSEUM
(Rua do Carmo; admission R$2; ⏲2-6pm Wed-Sat, 10am-5pm Sun) Reopened in October 2009, the town's most famous church, Igreja NS do Carmo (1750), houses the Museu de Arte Sacra.

Igreja NS do Rosário Matriz & Museu da Matriz CHURCH, MUSEUM
(Praça de Matriz; admission R$2; ⏲8am-noon & 2-6pm Wed-Sun) The oldest church in Goiás, the 1728 Igreja NS do Rosário Matriz was tragically gutted by fire in 2002 (arson is suspected). Inside, the Museu da Matriz explains the history and ongoing renovation. The new altar was restored and brought in from the former slave church, a necessary house of worship since slaves were banned from this one.

Igreja NS do Bonfim CHURCH
(Rua do Bonfim; admission R$2; ⏲noon-6pm Thu-Sat, 9am-noon Sun) Full of charisma, the Portuguese-built Igreja NS do Bonfim (1750) is a simple, rectangular adobe church with wooden floors and ceiling, flanked by two lateral chapels. The recently restored gilded turquoise altar and wooden pulpit are worth a look.

Santuário de Vida Silvestre – Fazenda Vagafogo WILDLIFE RESERVE
(Vagafogo Farm Wildlife Sanctuary; ☎3335-8515; www.vagafogo.com.br; guided walk R$20; ⏲9am-5pm) Six kilometers northwest of town, this is a 44-hectare private nature reserve. It's a great place to spot wildlife and even if you don't see much, the light hike is a welcome retreat from the heat (there are two natural pools for swimming). To walk here from town, head north along Rua do Carmo and follow the signs. The cafe at the visitors center does a ridiculously good weekend brunch (R$45; 9am to 4pm), with a rainbow coalition of homemade wild cerrado fruit preserves. Try them all.

Reserva Ecológica Vargem Grande WATERFALL
(☎3331-3071; www.vargemgrande.pirenopolis.tur.br; Rua do Frota 888; admission R$25; ⏲9am-5pm) This 360-hectare park on private land contains two impressive waterfalls – **Cachoeira Santa Maria** and **Cachoeira do Lázaro**. There are small river beaches and natural pools for swimming. If you're here for waterfalls, these are the ones to see. The reserve is 11km east of town on the road to Serra dos Pireneus.

You don't need a guide to enter, but unless you have a car, you'll need a ride from one.

Parque Estadual da Serra dos Pirineus PARK
(☎3265-1320; www.semarh.goias.gov.br/site/conteudo/parque-estadual-dos-pirineus-pep; ⏲8am-5pm, 9am-8pm summer) Pireneus, 18km northeast of town, is the Brazilian form of the word 'Pyrenees' and the top spot in the state for bouldering and mountain climbing. There are waterfalls and interesting rock formations to see along the way, some dating back to Gondwanaland. You'll need an accredited guide to enter; ask at a local agency.

On the first full moon in July, locals celebrate the **Festa do Morro** with a procession to the Morro dos Pireneus (some to pray, some to play), where there is a small chapel on Pai. The festival is a modern tradition, more New Age than religious, and serious partying ensues.

Sleeping

You can't walk more than 100m without finding a pousada in Pirénopolis, but book ahead at weekends and during festivals (when prices can triple!).

Casamatta Hostel HOSTEL $
(☎3331-2483; www.casamattahostel.com; Luiz Gonzaga Jaime 109; dm R$60, s/d without bathroom R$80/140;) Piri's best hostel is home to a supreme seven-hammock patio, high-pressure showers and a small pool for a refreshing dip to ward off the cerrado heat. There's liberal use of stone throughout, from tables to flooring, which also helps keep temps manageable. Rubens, the friendly owner, offers bicycles for rent and transport to surrounding waterfalls in his Volkswagen van.

Pousada Cavalhadas POUSADA $
(☎3331-1261; www.pousadacavalhadas.com.br; Praça do Matriz 1; s/d/tr R$150/200/270;) Facing the Igreja Matriz, this is a basic, conveniently located option with some muted character. It won't win any awards, but it's about the best (and most secure) of the cheapies around the praça.

★**Pouso, Café e Cultura** POUSADA $$
(☎3331-3647; www.pousocafecultura.com.br; Santa Cruz 32; chalet weekday/weekend R$220/450;) This lengthy historic home once belonged to a Brazilian ambassador – his collection of antiques and knicknacks from around the world pepper the lush and gorgeous property, adding a sense of historical character missing elsewhere. The 12 chalets are draped by floral paths through a well-kept garden and feature beautiful hardwood flooring and vintage Brastemp minibars.

Pousada Arvoredo POUSADA **$$**
(☎3331-3479; www.arvoredo.tur.br; Av Abercio Ramos Qd 17 Lt 15; weekend r from R$350, weekday s/d R$130/190;) This excellent-value pousada is steeped in sustainable tourism (all the bricks were recycled from old homes in Goiânia) and offers lovely verandas and large rooms full of natural handicrafts.

★**Taman Baru** BUNGALOWS **$$$**
(☎3331-3880; www.tamanbaru.com.br; Estrada dos Pireneus, Km 2; r R$300-400, bungalows R$450; P@) A romantic retreat with the occasional Balinese touch set inside a forest, located just east of town. The colorful bungalows and gorgeous infinity pool both offer outstanding views across the cerrado. It's worth springing for the midrange rooms, which don't share walls with others. Best for couples.

Eating

Rua do Rosário, aka Rua do Lazer, is the main restaurant-cafe strip and turns into a pedestrianized free-for-all of outdoor tables and lively city dwellers on weekends. Most restaurants close on Monday, and some only open on weekends.

★**Pireneus Café** CAFE **$**
(www.pireneuscafe.com.br; Rua dos Pireneus 41; sandwiches R$12-28; 5-11pm Wed-Fri, 9am-midnight Sat, 9am-11pm Sun) A sophisticated spot overlooking Praça do Coreto for life-changing grilled focaccia sandwiches, first-rate coffee and the town's most interesting craft-beer selection.

Pedícafé CAFE **$**
(Aurora 21; items R$3-18; 1-9pm Wed-Sun;) Easily the most adorable and best coffeehouse in town, but don't discount the sweet treats that could accompany your espresso or unique tea blends, with *brigadeiro* (*doce de leite* covered with chocolate) in traditional farmer's cups and the guava cake topping the list.

As Flor BRAZILIAN **$**
(Sizenando Jaime 16; weekday/weekend R$25/28; 11:30am-3:30pm) Come on an empty stomach to this simple lunch spot for regional delights, an outrageous amount of which will be slapped on the table in front you for a ridiculously cheap price. The chicken and pork are especially tasty, and there's a plethora of interesting vegetables and local side dishes like *jiló* and *feijão tropeiro*.

Boca do Forno/Boca Santa PIZZERIA **$**
(Travessa Santa Cruz s/n; pizzas R$31-55, rodízio R$25; noon-4pm Mon-Fri & 6pm-midnight Tue-Sun;) The owner of this cozy pizzeria is from Brazil's pizza capital, São Paulo. If that means nothing to you, it will once you try the pizza. Wednesday's pizza *rodízio* (all you can eat) is a real treat. During weekdays, it moonlights as Boca Santa, a great vegetarian restaurant (one of the few in town). Each day, a set two-course meal runs R$15.

Montserrat Gastronomia ITALIAN, SPANISH **$$**
(☎9985-8489; www.montserratpirenopolis.blogspot.com; Ramalhuda 10; mains R$32-54; 7pm-

CAFÉ COLONIAL: THE FOOD OF THE TROPEIROS

After the *bandeirantes* (groups of adventurers who explored the interior) swept Goiás clean of its gold, the *tropeiros* (the famed muleteers of Brazil) followed in their path, conquering the region and bringing slaves from Brazil's coast. Food was scarce en route, so the *tropeiros* adapted various foods from Afro-Brazilian, Portuguese and indigenous cultures to allow for the lengthy journey without refrigeration.

This long-lost subculture of Brazilian cuisine has been resurrected at **Fazenda Babilônia** (☎9291-1511; www.fazendababilonia.com.br; GO 431A, Km 24; 8am-5pm Sat & Sun), a sugar plantation established in 1800 and *fazenda* (farm) on the Patrimonial Nacional (National Heritage) register since 1965. Every weekend, this restored *fazenda*, 24km southwest of Pirenópolis, breaks out the historical gastronomy for a fascinating breakfast called Café Colonial. Hearty meats, cheeses and pastries highlight the near-endless options. *Carne de porco* (a succulent pork dish stored in its own fat for conservation), *mané pelado* (a sweet cake of grated manioc, eggs, cheese and coconut milk) and *matula galinha* (chicken with saffron, eggs, aromatic peppers and toasted corn wrapped in a corn husk) highlight an absolutely thrilling banquet that includes nearly 30 dishes that you're not likely to have seen before. The whole thing costs R$72, including a fascinating tour of the *fazenda* itself.

FESTA DO DIVINO ESPÍRITO SANTO

Pirenópolis is famous for performing the story of Festa do Divino Espírito Santo, a tradition begun in 1819 that is more popularly known as As Cavalhadas.

Starting 50 days after Easter, for three days the town looks like a scene from the Middle Ages as it celebrates Charlemagne's victory over the Moors. A series of medieval tournaments, dances and festivities, including a mock battle between the Moors and Christians in distant Iberia, takes place. Combatants ride decorated horses, kitted out in bright costumes and bull-head masks. The Moors are defeated on the battlefield and convert to Christianity, 'proving' that heresy doesn't pay in the end.

The festival is a happy one, and more folkloric than religious. If you're in the neighborhood, make a point of seeing this stunning and curious spectacle, one of the most fascinating in Brazil.

midnight Fri, noon-4pm & 7pm-midnight Sat, noon-4pm Sun;) This small Catalonian-run choice serves a cautiously-creative menu that leans Italian, with occasional nods to the Iberian Peninsula (both Catalunya and Basque dishes make appearances). Taper your expectations – this ain't San Sebastián – but it's a pleasant evening out for the food and wine brigade. Cash only.

Bacalhau da Bibba SEAFOOD **$$$**
(3331-2103; Rua do Rosário 42; dishes for 2 people R$180-190; noon-4pm & 7-11:30pm) Oh my cod! A restaurant that serves nothing but *bacalhau*! That's not the only thing that's slightly surreal about this place either. It doubles as an antiques shop!

Drinking

Rosário 26 BAR
(Rosário 26; 5:30pm-midnight Tue-Thu, 5pm-2am Fri-Sun;) One of the few actual bars to belly up to along action-packed Rua do Rosário 26. Small craft beer selection, including Goiás' own, Colombina.

Cachaçaria do Dil BAR
(Rua do Rosário 17; cachaça R$5-36; 11am-midnight) More than 350 different *cachaças* to choose from.

Shopping

Ruas Aurora and Rosário and Rui Barbosa are lined with places selling commercialized handicrafts from the region – everything from silver and ceramic pots to colorful cloths and statues of slaves. If you are looking for something more unique, then it's worth visiting the artist workshops on the Circuito de Criação (pick up a leaflet from the C.A.T office).

Information

Banco do Brasil (www.bb.com.br; Sizenando Jayme 1) Visa/MasterCard ATM.

Bradesco (www.bradesco.com.br; Sizenando Jayme 5) Visa/Matercard ATM.

C.A.T (Centro de Atendimento ao Turista; 3331-2633; www.pirenopolis.com.br; Rua do Bonfim 14; 8am-6pm Mon-Sat, to 3pm Sun) Friendly tourist info.

Hospital Estadual Ernestina Lopes Jaime (HEELJ; 3331-1666; Rua Pireneus s/n) Piri's public hospital is now the best option in town.

Getting There & Around

The **bus station** (3331-1080; Av Neco Mendonça s/n) is 500m northwest of Igreja Matriz. **Goianésia** (3331-2763; www.viacaogoianesia.com.br) offers five daily buses to Brasília (R$26, three hours), one to Goiânia (R$15.50, three hours, 9:15am) and Anápolis (R$8.70, 1½ hours, 9:15am), where you can also catch a connection to Goiânia. There are also up to five more Anápolis departures throughout the day on São José do Tocantins (tickets purchased on bus). Pirénopolis is foot friendly.

Parque Nacional da Chapada dos Veadeiros

This spectacular national park in the highest area of the Central West showcases the unique landscape and flora of high-altitude cerrado across 650 sq km of pristine beauty (with a near doubling of protected area in the works).

With high waterfalls, raging canyons, natural swimming pools and oasislike stands of wine palms, the park is a popular destination for ecotourists. In fact, the whole area is beautiful, with its big skies, exotic flora and dramatic hills rising up like waves breaking across the plains.

The sublime landscape, much of it based on quartz crystal and multihued sandstone, has also attracted New Agers who have established alternative communities and a burgeoning *esoturismo* (alternative, new agey tourism) industry in the area. It is also noticeably well maintained – you won't find a Skol beer can within kilometers.

Travelers visiting the park base themselves in one of two nearby towns: Alto Paraíso de Goiás, 38km from the park; or tiny-but-growing São Jorge, 2km from the entrance and connected to Alto Paraiso by a newly-paved road. The best time to visit the park is between April and October, before the rivers flood during the rainy season and access becomes very slippery. You'll need two days to see the main attractions.

Sights & Activities

Guides are no longer required to visit the **park** (☎3455-1116; www.chapadadosveadeirosoficial.com.br; ⊙8am-6pm Tue-Sun, entry until noon only) **FREE**, but are highly recommended. Private guides can be organized at the visitors' center, through the local guide association, ACV-CV, or at hotels in Alto Paraíso or São Jorge. At time of research, the park was free, but there was talk of reimplementing the admission charges that were dropped in 2013.

The best guides run full-day tours (R$150 to R$180 depending on language skills) to the park's three main attractions: *canions* (canyons) and *cariocas* (rocks), which are usually combined as they traverse the same trail in the park, and *cachoeiras* (waterfalls). The tours are included in the price of the guide and can be divided by up to 10 people.

The **canions-cariocas tour** weaves along the Rio Preto, which runs through the middle of the park. The river has cut two large canyons (imaginatively named Canyon I and Canyon II) through sandstone, with sheer, 20m-high walls on either side. It's a spectacular sight. There are natural platforms for diving into the cold water at the bottom of the rushing river. Canyon I

UNIQUE CERRADO

Calling cerrado 'the South American savanna' is to oversimplify an extremely complex and varied ecosystem. True, it may look like bushy grassland for part of the year, but visit at the right time and it is converted into an immense flower garden of breathtaking scale and beauty. Nor is it strictly even grassland; in fact, in some areas it is a type of forest. Confused? Let us explain!

Cerrado can be classified into four distinct types, each of which mesh together to form a mosaic of savanna-like habitat. *Cerradão* is dry cerrado forest, either in solid blocks or in small forest islands; *campo limpo* (clean field) consists entirely of grass; *cerrado sensu stricto* is composed of low, bushy vegetation with no grass at all; and *campo sujo* (dirty field) is a mix of all the other types into one. The different types are quite easily distinguishable to the naked eye, even to non-specialists, but when you consider that the plant species that make up each of these broad classifications may differ dramatically from one area to the next, you begin to get an idea of the immense biodiversity that the cerrado harbors. In fact, of the 10,000 or more species of plants found in the cerrado, 44% are found nowhere else in the world.

But it's not just the plants that make the cerrado so important for conservation. Besides providing a home for some of Brazil's most spectacular and threatened mammal species, such as the maned wolf, giant armadillo, pampas deer and giant anteater, it also protects a number of highly threatened and localized birds, such as the white-winged nightjar, dwarf tinamou, lesser nothura and the gorgeous yellow-billed blue finch, all of which depend on this unique habitat for their continued survival.

Sadly, that struggle for survival is getting harder with every passing year. Since the 1970s, vast tracts of native cerrado vegetation have been converted to make space for soybean, rice, corn, wheat and cattle production – only 20% of the original vegetation is left. The rate of habitat loss makes it one of the world's fastest disappearing eco-regions, and the destruction shows no sign of abating.

Though the natural vegetation of most of Goiás state is cerrado, Parque Nacional Chapada das Guiamaraes and Parque Nacional da Chapada dos Veadeiros showcase it in dramatically beautiful surroundings, with the picturesque habitat framed against a stunning backdrop of rocky mountainsides and craggy cliffs.

is usually flooded from September to May and inaccessible. The **cariocas** (named for two girls from Rio who went missing here in the '80s) picks up at the end of the river valley on the trail from Canyon II and leads to interesting rock formations and a huge cascading waterfall.

The more difficult (and rewarding) **cachoeiras tour** takes in Salto do Rio Preto I and II, two spectacular waterfalls (80m and 120m, respectively) that cascade to the ground just 30m apart. The falls are set in a picturesque valley at the end of a trail that weaves through a classic cerrado landscape of meadows and gallery forests. There is a small lake for swimming under II, where the sun creates a dazzling celestial effect under the water. Take loads of water and sunscreen; it's about a 6km ascent all the way back and the sun can be brutal.

The park's newest offering is the 23km **Trilha de Sete Quedas**, a two-day traverse of the park with overnight camping, which was previously banned. Tents are pitched in a magical spot with seven small waterfalls near the Rio Preto.

Vale da Lua VALLEY
(Moon Valley; admission R$20; 7am-5:30pm) Over millions of years, the rushing waters of the Rio São Miguel have sculpted rock formations in the lunar landscape of Vale da Lua. An ethereal metaconglomerate of rocks containing quartz, sand and clay reflect a rainbow of colors and the chilly emerald waters add to the otherworldly atmosphere.

Vale da Lua is outside the national park and subject to flash floods during the rainy season. There's a signed turnoff about 4km outside São Jorge along the newly paved road from Alto Paraiso. Take sunscreen and water with you.

Alto Paraíso de Goiás

0XX61 / POP 7000

Crystals, dreadlocks and dirty feet are ubiquitous in Alto Paraíso, 38km from the park. It is one of Brazil's kookiest towns, but besides unleashing your inner hippy, crystal shopping or planning your trip to Chapada dos Veadeiros, there is not much else to do here except chill your boots and zone out to New Age cultural overwhelm.

Tours

Though most travelers stay in the village of São Jorge, it is in fact easier (if ever so slightly more expensive) to arrange visits to Chapada dos Veadeiros in Alto Paraíso.

★ **Travessia Ecoturismo** ADVENTURE TOUR
(3446-1595; www.travessia.tur.br; Av Ari Valadão Filho 979; 9am-6pm Mon-Fri, to noon Sat & Sun) An excellent eco-agency on the main road in Alto Paraíso that can arrange everything in Chapada, including zip-lining and more adventurous canyoning and rappelling trips. Prices include transportation and English-speaking guides.

Sleeping & Eating

Alto Paraíso has a wide range of accommodations, with several good options to rest and refuel here. For lunch, two dueling vegetarian buffets are worth your time: **Alquimia do Sabor** (Av Ari Valadão Filho s/n; per kg R$42.90; noon-4pm Wed-Mon;) has the best food, while **Organika** (Pouso Alta 113; per kg R$45.50, items R$3.50-27.50; noon-8pm Tue-Sat, to 5pm Sun;) is wins for ambiEnce and diverse cafe options.

Pousada Veadeiros POUSADA $
(3446-1820; das Nascentes 129; s/d/tr R$80/100/150;) Hard-to-beat value is the calling at this cool and kitschy pousada not far from the bus station. Each apartment is named after a native bird and decorated in its colors (you'll need a bit of imagination to associate the bird with some of them!) and nearly all of the breakfast comes from the property or is made in-house.

Buddy's Hostel HOSTEL $
(www.buddysalto.com; dm/s/d R$40/90/110; Av João Bernardes Rabelo Lt 01 Qd 01;) Our favorite hostel is owned by a Brazilian-French-American Circue du Soleil acrobat and run by his sweet mother, who lived in France for two decades. Three five-bed dorms and a few privates open out onto a small patch of grass with a *palapa* (thatched) hut. It's just a few steps from the main street, on the opposite end from the bus station.

Breakfast is coffee only. Cash only.

★ **Jambalaya** INTERNATIONAL $$
(3446-1775; Rua dos Colibris s/n; mains R$29-49; 7:30-11:30pm Mon-Tue, 12:30-11:30pm Wed-Sun;) A contemporary gem tucked away in a residential neighborhood a short walk from the main road, tables are shrouded in candlelit romanticism surrounding a pleasant garden. Flavors occasionally stray international (Thai, Arab, Cajun) but mainly this

kitchen churns out excellent risottos, filets, fish and chicken preparations that punch above the town's weight class. Cash only.

Information

Banco do Brasil (Av Ari Valadão Filho 690; 10am-3pm Mon-Fri) Visa/MasterCard ATM.

C.A.T (Centro Atendimento ao Turista; 3446-1159; www.chapadadosveadeirosoficial.com.br; Av Ari Valadão Filho s/n; 8am-8pm) On the main street, 200m from the bus station.

Getting There & Away

From Goiânia, São José do Tocantins (p348) heads to Alto Paraiso (R$79.50, seven hours, 8:20pm daily and 12:10pm Tuesday, Thursday and Saturday), with one daily bus doing the reverse leg at 11pm and another at 1:30pm Monday, Wednesday and Friday (R$76.75).

Real Expresso (2106-7144; www.realexpresso.com.br) has three daily buses from Brasília to Alto Paraíso (R$43.10, 4½ hours, 10am, 7pm and 9pm). Returns to Brasília leave at 2am, 3:30am and 2:15pm (R$44, 4½ hours).

São Jorge

0XX61 / POP 1200

With sandy streets (for now) and a laid-back vibe, the former crystal-mining hamlet of São Jorge (2km from the national-park entrance) has the feel of a beach town, despite its inland location. Though logistically Alto Paraíso is more convenient for arranging trips to Parque Nacional da Chapada dos Veadeiros (and has more going on), many travelers prefer to stay in São Jorge because it is prettier, closer to the park and has more of a village atmosphere.

Sleeping & Eating

Quality pousadas are plentiful and usually very fairly priced, though prices rise considerably at weekends. The best restaurant is inside Pousada Casa das Flores.

Pousada Flor do Cerrado POUSADA **$**
(9998-5384; s/d/tr R$120/180/220;) Small, cozy and the best of the cheaper options in town, with all wood furniture, earthy decoration and hammocks for lounging in the shade.

Pousada Bambu Brasil POUSADA **$$**
(3455-1004; www.bambubrasil.com.br; Rua 1 Quadra 1; weekday/weekend r R$220/280;) Great value for couples, this charming pousada with hand-painted furniture and poolside hammocks is a stylish place to relax. No children under 12.

★**Baguá Pousada** POUSADA **$$$**
(3455-1046; www.baguapousada.com.br; Rua 1 Qd 16; bungalows weekday/weekend R$360/504;) Massive (82 sq meters!), breathtakingly classy bungalows at this designer eco-pousada have raised the bar on sophistication in Goiás, while safari-chic lounge furnishings in the common area should suit Brazil's fashion cognoscenti. It's closest to the park's entrance as well.

Lua de São Jorge PIZZERIA **$$**
(Rua 1 Qd 1; pizzas R$28.60-51.70; 6pm-midnight Thu-Tue) Intensely researched conclusion: the best of the numerous wood-fired pizzerias in town.

Information

C.A.T (Centro Atendimento ao Turista; 3455-1090; 8am-6pm) There is a small tourist desk near the entrance to town that can help you find a guide.

Getting There & Away

Ironically, the road to São Jorge is now paved – with a beautiful bike path to boot – but at the time of research, there were no buses between São Jorge and Alto Paraiso, leaving carless folks at the mercy of taxi drivers, who charge R$60 to R$100 depending on your negotiation skills. Mototaxis charge half that if you're traveling light. The trip takes about 30 minutes.

Mato Grosso & Mato Grosso do Sul

Includes ➡

Best Places to Eat

- ➡ Mahalo (p366)
- ➡ Gaucho Gastão (p384)
- ➡ Casa do Peixe (p384)
- ➡ A Casa do João (p395)
- ➡ Morro dos Ventos (p369)

Best Places to Stay

- ➡ Refúgio Ecológico Caiman (p381)
- ➡ Cristalino Jungle Lodge (p371)
- ➡ Pousada Araras Eco Lodge (p380)
- ➡ Casa da Quineira (p369)
- ➡ Pousada Galeria Artes (p394)

Why Go?

Mato Grosso was once Brazil's wild west, a land known only to explorers, indigenous hunters, poachers, gold seekers and naturalists. Today, some of Brazil's most photogenic wildlife and incredible scenery make it a prime destination for ecotourists and anglers.

The Pantanal, one of the most important and fragile ecosystems on the planet, truly shines as Brazil's top destination for animal-spotting and bird-watching. The attractions don't stop there: the crystal-clear rivers and cave lakes around Bonito and Bom Jardim allow you to explore a remarkable underwater world by donning a scuba tank or snorkeling mask.

In the far-north town of Alta Floresta, the cerrado (savanna) morphs into the Amazon; in the south near Bonito, the Serra da Bodoquena is a breathtakingly beautiful, watery wonderland. In between the two, the Parque Nacional da Chapada dos Guimarães boasts some of the most commanding plateau views in Brazil.

When to Go

The Pantanal

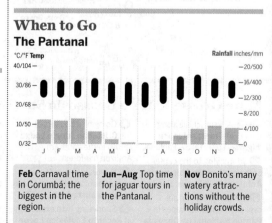

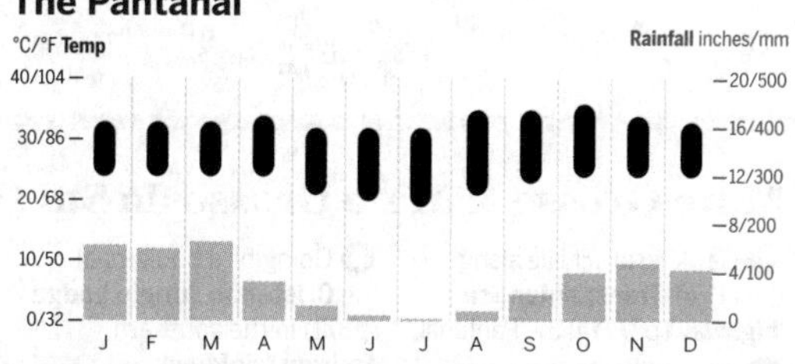

Feb Carnaval time in Corumbá; the biggest in the region.

Jun–Aug Top time for jaguar tours in the Pantanal.

Nov Bonito's many watery attractions without the holiday crowds.

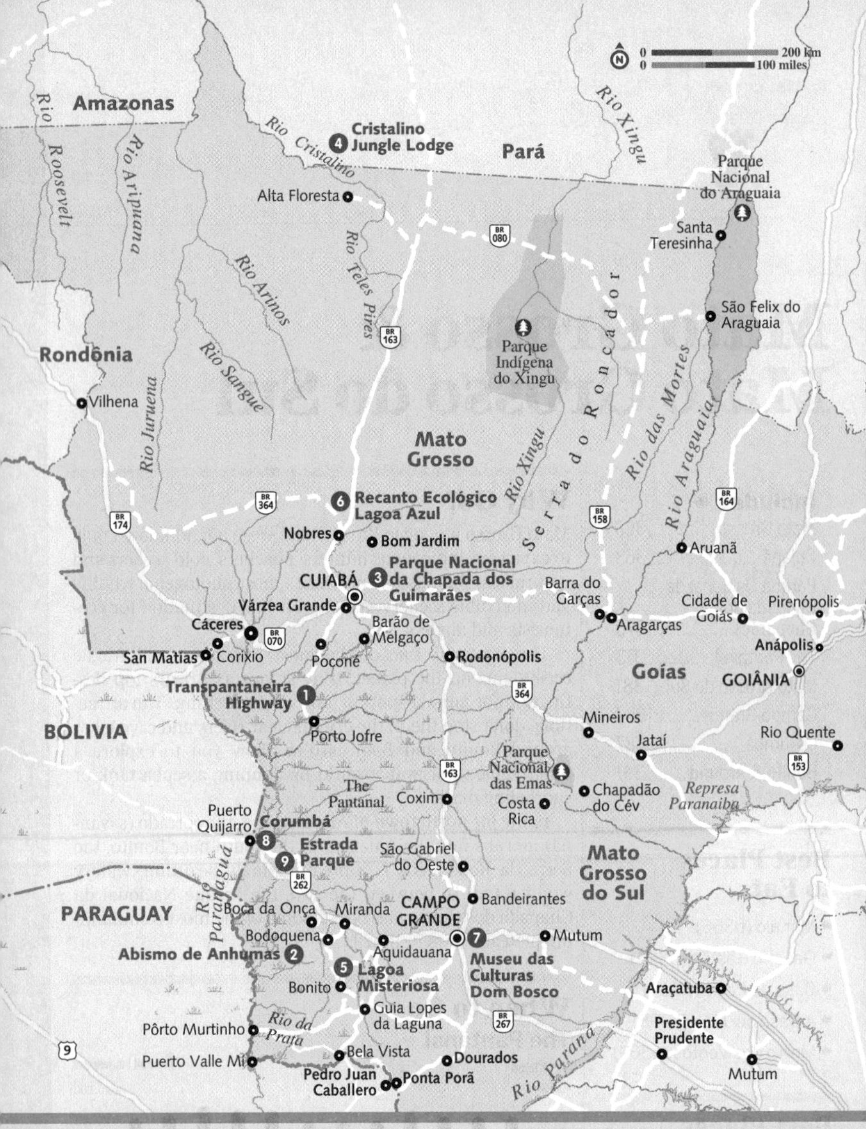

Mato Grosso & Mato Grosso do Sul Highlights

1. Gawking at wildlife along the 145km **Transpantaneira 'highway'** (p377) in the Pantanal.
2. Journeying to the center of the earth at the **Abismo de Anhumas** (p392) near Bonito.
3. Watching the sun set over dramatic landscapes in **Parque Nacional da Chapada dos Guimarães** (p370).
4. Going bird bonkers at the **Cristalino Jungle Lodge** (p371) in the southern Amazon rainforest.
5. Exploring the underwater mysteries of a bottomless cave at **Lagoa Misteriosa** (p393).
6. Snorkeling with exotic fish at **Recanto Ecológico Lagoa Azul** (p372).
7. Delving into Mato Grosso do Sul's indigenous culture at the **Museu das Culturas Dom Bosco** (p382).
8. Dancing in the streets during Corumbá's **Carnaval** (p389), Mato Grosso–style.
9. Fishing, canoeing and caiman-spotting off **Estrada Parque** (p379).

History

According to the Treaty of Tordesillas, the remote state of Mato Grosso belonged to Spain, not Portugal. For years its exploration was limited to occasional expeditions by adventurers and Jesuit missionaries, but with the discovery of gold in the early 18th century, it was invaded by thousands of fortune hunters. Reaching Cuiabá meant crossing the lands of several indigenous groups, many of whom were formidable warriors. They included the *caiapó* (who even attacked the settlement at Goiás), the *bororo* of the Pantanal, the *parecis* (who were enslaved to mine gold), the *paiaguá* (who caused periodic panic in Cuiabá) and the *guaicuru* (skilled riders and warriors). As the gold rush tailed off, however, Mato Grosso again slipped into obscurity and isolation, its inhabitants eking out a living from subsistence farming and fishing. As late as the 19th century, the only access to Mato Grosso from Rio de Janeiro was by ship via the Rio Paraguai, a journey of several weeks.

Mato Grosso's isolation helped fuel the birth of several separatist movements but, with the coming of the republic in 1889, the telegraph in the early 20th century and the opening of a few rough roads, it slowly reconnected with the world. The government policy of developing the interior in the 1940s and '50s and the construction of the new capital Brasília in 1960 brought waves of migrants from the Northeast and the South back to the region, participating in an agricultural boom that continues today. In 1979 the massive area of Mato Grosso was cut in half, creating the new state of Mato Grosso do Sul. Agriculture pays the bills in both states, with huge cattle, sugarcane and soy plantations peppering whatever landscape isn't legally protected.

Mato Grosso is still home to many indigenous groups, several living as they have for centuries. The *erikbatsa*, noted for their fine featherwork, live near Fontanilles and Juima; the *nhambikuraa* are near Padroal; and the *cayabi* live near Juara. There are also the indigenous *cinta larga* of Parque Indígena Aripuanã and the tribes under the care of Fundação Nacional do Indio (Funai) in the Parque Indígena do Xingu, which was set up in the 1950s as a safe haven for several indigenous groups.

ℹ Getting There & Away

The gateway cities to the region are Cuiabá and Campo Grande, with daily flights to Rio, São Paulo and Brasília. There is also the handy hop from São Paulo to Bonito. The majority of travelers coming from Bolivia take the scenic train journey from Santa Cruz to Quijarro and cross into the Brazilian town of Corumbá, which is connected by road to all points east. Mato Grosso do Sul also borders Paraguay to the south. There are regular bus services to the Paraguayan border from Campo Grande and Bonito.

MATO GROSSO

Mato Grosso means 'thick forest.' Part of the highland plain that runs through Brazil's interior, it's a dusty land of rolling hills, endless plantations, abundant savannas and some of the best fishing rivers in the world. Three of Brazil's major ecosystems – the Pantanal, Amazon and cerrado – meet within its borders.

Cuiabá

☎0XX65 / POP 569,000

Cuiabá is a boomtown basking in the relentless Mato Grosso sun. The city is actually two sister cities separated by the Rio Cuiabá: Old Cuiabá and Várzea Grande (where the airport is located).

The town's name is an indigenous *bororo* word meaning 'arrow-fishing,' though it was first gold and later agriculture that led to the city becoming one of the fastest-growing capitals in Brazil over the last 30 years. A lively place with a vibrant dining scene and some beautiful colonial architecture around its main square, Cuiabá is an excellent starting point for excursions to the Pantanal, Chapada dos Guimarães and Bom Jardim.

History

In 1719 a *paulista*, Pascoal Moreira Cabral, was hunting indigenous groups along the Rio Cuiabá when he found gold. A gold rush followed, but many of the fortune hunters never reached the new settlement at Cuiabá. Traveling more than 3000km from São Paulo by river took five months; along the way, gold seekers found little food, many mosquitoes, dangerous rapids, lengthy portages, disease and incredible heat.

With the end of the gold boom and the decay of the mines, Cuiabá would have disappeared, except that the soil along the Rio Cuiabá allowed subsistence agriculture, while the river itself provided fish.

Central Cuiabá

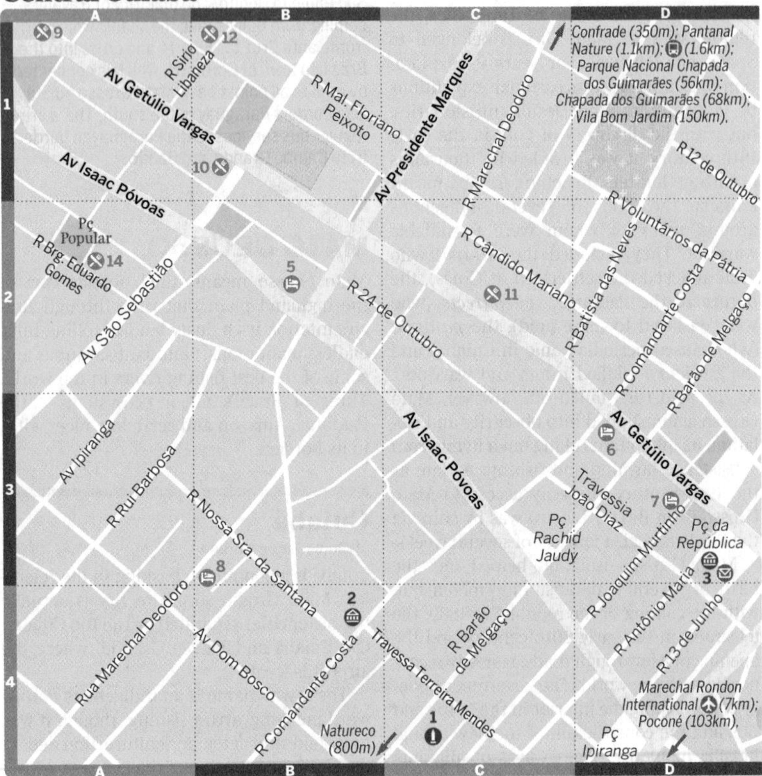

By 1835 the town was the capital of Mato Grosso but, apart from a brief resurgence as a staging point for the war against Paraguay in the 1860s, it remained a backwater. Today, thanks mostly to a massive agri-economy and the popularity that came from hosting the 2014 FIFA World Cup, Cuiabá has finally been propelled into the modern world.

Sights

Museu Histórico de Mato Grosso MUSEUM

(3613-9234; http://museuhistoricodemt.blogspot.com; Praça da República 131; 8am-8pm Tue-Fri, to 3pm Sat) FREE Inside a restored colonial building, this museum is an interesting stroll through the state's history. Exhibits range from reproductions of prehistoric rock art and books of sales from the slave trade to vibrant paintings illustrating the war with Paraguay and other historical events, 19th-century silverware and the original typewriter belonging to Rubens de Mendonça – Brazilian poet, historian and journalist.

Museu Rondon MUSEUM

(3615-8489; Av Fernando Correia da Costa) FREE The small Museu Rondon has exhibits on indigenous culture and is well worth a visit to check out the ornate headdresses and weaponry. Located on the grounds of the Federal University of Mato Grosso (UFMT), the museum is behind the swimming pool and was under extensive renovation when we visited. To get here, catch a 103 Jd Universitário bus (R$3) on Av Tenente Coronel Duarte.

Museu do Morro da Caixa D'Agua Velha MUSEUM

(3617-1274; Comandante Costa; 8am-5pm Mon-Fri) FREE The city's oddest museum brings together a variety of frankly weird water-themed trinkets, from old tubes to showerheads, housed inside a beautifully lit

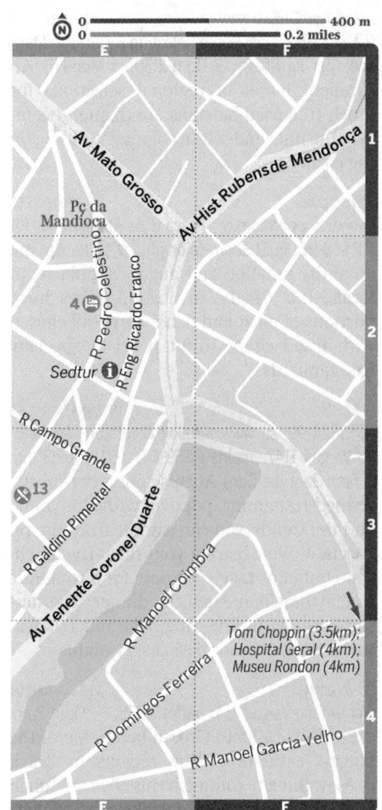

stone tunnel. Far more interesting than the display is the construction itself: this was the city's former water tank, built in the style of a Roman aqueduct in 1882.

Centro Geodésico da America do Sul MONUMENT

(Barão de Melgaço) An obelisk here allegedly marks the center of the continent, calculated before the invention of satellite mapping. Tell locals that the actual geographical center of South America lies 67km away near Chapada dos Guimarães and it's unlikely you'll win any popularity contests.

Tours

Cuiabá is the major gateway to the northern Pantanal, in particular the Transpantaneira road, as well as Parque Nacional Chapada dos Guimarães and the aquatic attractions in the area around Bom Jardim. City tour operators (p378) offer trips to all these places.

Central Cuiabá

Sights

1 Centro Geodésico da America do Sul ... C4
2 Museu do Morro da Caixa D'Agua Velha ... B4
3 Museu Histórico de Mato Grosso ... D3

Activities, Courses & Tours

Ecoverde Tours ... (see 4)

Sleeping

4 Hostel Pousada Ecoverde ... E2
5 Hotel Deville Prime Cuiabá ... B2
6 Hotel Mato Grosso ... D3
7 Mato Grosso Palace Hotel ... D3
8 Pantanal Backpacker ... B3

Eating

9 Choppão ... A1
10 Getúlio ... B1
11 Ki-Nutre ... C2
12 Mahalo ... B1
13 Mistura Cuiabana ... E3
14 Pizza na Pedra ... A2

Festivals

Festa de São Benedito CULTURAL

The Festa de São Benedito takes place during the first week of July at the Igreja NS do Rosário and the Capela de São Benedito. The holiday has a more Umbanda (white magic) than Catholic flavor; it's celebrated with colorful, traditional dances and regional foods such as *bolos de queijo* (cheese balls) and *bolos de arroz* (rice balls).

Sleeping

Discounts are common during the week and out of season (November to May).

★Hostel Pousada Ecoverde POUSADA $

(☎3624-1386; www.ecoverdetours.com.br; Celestino 391; s/d without bathroom R$50/80; wi-fi) A rustic pousada (guesthouse) in a 100-year-old colonial house with a tranquil, hammock-hung minijungle out back, filled with cats, chickens and guinea fowl. Friendly owner and local wildlife expert Joel Souza of Ecoverde Tours is one of the founders of ecotourism in the area and his pousada consists of five fan-cooled rooms that share four external bathrooms.

A rustic jungle camp near Porto Jofre is in the works, due to have a main house and tents; ask Joel for details.

Pantanal Backpacker HOSTEL $

(☎9939-6152; www.pantanalbackpacker.com; Av Mal Deodoro 2301; dm R$40-60, tw 150; ❄@🛜🏊) Positively luxurious budget crash pad, a 10-minute walk from the main nightlife area, complete with waterfall and pool. A lot of thought has gone into what backpackers need – a kitchen, bathrooms and lockers in every room, comfy bunks, attentive staff – and it's all present and correct. Organized tours to Nobres and beyond get good feedback.

Mato Grosso Palace Hotel BUSINESS HOTEL $

(☎3614-7000; www.hotelmt.com.br; Joaquim Murtinho 170; s/d from R$127/149) This former Best Western sits in a you-couldn't-be-more-central-if-you-tried location. Expect helpful staff (some English spoken), cable TV and an ample breakfast buffet. Our one quibble is that the hot water occasionally runs out. Good online discounts.

Gran Odara Hotel BUSINESS HOTEL $$

(☎3616-2014; www.hotelgranodara.com.br; Av Miguel Sutil 8344, Ribeirão da Ponte; s/d from R$290/309; P❄@🛜🏊) With its exquisite reception area, the Gran Odara makes an impact as soon as you walk in, and the tasteful rooms are along the same lines – all dark wood and creams. It's a little removed from the center but if you're only in town for the night, it's worth the splurge to enjoy the spa, rooftop pool and other perks. Wi-fi is somewhat unreliable.

Hotel Mato Grosso HOTEL $$

(☎3614-7777; www.hotelmt.com.br; Costa 643; s/d/tr R$148/194/228; P❄🛜) For basic comfort in a central location, the simple but clean rooms here are good value.

Hotel Deville Prime Cuiabá LUXURY HOTEL $$$

(☎3319-3000; www.deville.com.br; Ac Isaac Póvoas 1000; s/d from R$297/344; ❄🛜🏊) This smart five-star hotel tower has filled the 'luxury digs within a five-minute walk of Cuiabá's best nightlife' niche very nicely. Post-Pantanal pampering beckons, in the form of spa, pool, elegant surroundings, spacious rooms bursting with mod cons, varied dining and on-the-ball service.

Eating

The center is where locals work during the day, making it almost deserted at night. The biggest concentration of decent restaurants is around Praça Popular and along Av Getúlio Vargas nearby.

Mistura Cuiabana SELF-SERVE $

(☎3624-1127; cnr Pedro Celestino & Cândido Mariano; per kg R$28; ⏰11am-2:30pm Mon-Fri) An excellent buffet of regional selections for lunch (the fried bananas are divine). It's inside the blue-and-white colonial building on the corner.

Choppão BOTECO $$

(www.choppao.com.br; Praça 8 de Abril; mains for 2 R$58-90; ⏰11.30am-midnight; 🛜) Occupying an entire junction and hugely popular with locals, this Cuiabá institution offers huge portions of meat and fish for two, all chased with frigid *chope* (draft beer) in specially iced tankards.

Getúlio INTERNATIONAL $$

(☎3624-9992; www.getuliogrill.com.br; Av Getúlio Vargas 1147; mains R$39-65; ⏰11am-2:30pm & 5pm-2am Tue-Sun) At this sports-bar-meets-refined-restaurant, popular with the young and the trendy, you can sample from the respectable wine list, eat your fill at the lunchtime buffet or take your date for a romantic Italian/Brazilian/Japanese dinner. The desserts are worth lingering over and DJs feature on the outdoor patio every night.

Ki-Nutre VEGETARIAN $$

(Av Getúlio Vargas 714; buffet R$38; ⏰11am-2pm; closed Sat; 🖉) Mato Grosso being one of the biggest cattle-producing regions in Brazil does nothing to diminish this cheerful lunch spot's popularity. The loyalty of local fans has been won with excellent fruit juices, a fully stocked veggie buffet and the ability to work wonders with tofu and pulses (beans and lentils).

Pizza na Pedra PIZZERIA $$

(☎3622-0060; Praça Popular 45; pizza R$37-68; ⏰6pm-midnight Tue-Sun; 🖉) A lively pizzeria with an extensive menu and a pizza *rodízio* (all you can eat) on Wednesdays – though some old-timers complain that the choice isn't as good as it used to be. The ridiculous dessert pizzas give you the opportunity to pile carbs on top of carbs.

★ **Mahalo** FUSION $$$

(☎3028-7700; www.mahalocozinhacriativa.com.br; Presidente Castelo Branco 359; mains from R$45; ⏰11am-2.30pm & 7.30pm-midnight Mon-Sat) Inside a converted mansion, the city's big splurge is one of Brazil's top restaurants, thanks to the efforts of Parisian-trained chef Ariani Malouf. Go for the set three-course weekday lunch or else choose from the likes of pintado (giant catfish) encrusted with Brazil nuts or a perfectly seared rack of lamb with sweet potato puree. Dress nicely and book ahead.

Drinking & Nightlife

There are two main nightlife clusters in town: the buzzy sports bars with ample outdoor seating around the lovely Praça Popular (aka Praça Eurico Gaspar Dutra) and more establishments along Av Getúlio Vargas. For something a bit more 'local', head for the tiny Praça da Mandioca, where you'll find regulars getting drunk on Skols at three virtually identical bars, with live bands on weekends.

Tom Choppin BAR

(☎3627-7227; www.tomchoppin.com.br; Rua das Laranjeiras 701; ⏰5pm-late Mon-Sat) Outstanding brews and views are the draw for Cuiabá's well-to-do at this open-air Música Popular Brasileira bar perched high above the city. Its name is a pun on the name of famous Brazilian musician Tom Jobim. Music veers between samba, *choro,* bossa nova and MPB. It's halfway between *centro* and the zoo.

Confrade BAR

(☎3027-2000; www.confrade.com.br; Av Mato Grosso 1000; ⏰5pm-late; 👪) No longer a microbrewery, but still serving a wide range of beers, Confrade is a massive bar with an outdoor terrace where Cuiabá's young and trendy gather nightly. We prefer their cocktails to their brews and there's live MPB every night of the week.

Information

EMERGENCY

Ambulance (☎192)

Fire Department (☎193)

Police (☎190)

MEDICAL SERVICES

Hospital Geral (☎3363-7000; 13 de Junho, cnr Thogo da Silva Pereira) University hospital with 24-hour emergency services.

MONEY

There are ATMs (open until 10pm) outside the airport for Visa/MasterCard withdrawals.

Banco do Brasil (Av Getúlio Vargas 915; ⏰11am-4pm Mon-Fri) ATM accepts foreign Visa/MasterCard.

POST

Post office (Praça da República 101; ⏰9am-5pm Mon-Fri, 8am-noon Sat)

TOURIST INFORMATION

Sedtur (☎3613-9300; www.sedtur.mt.gov.br; Voluntários da Pátria 118; ⏰9am-6pm

FLIGHTS FROM CUIABÁ

DESTINATION	TIME (HR)	FREQUENCY	AIRLINE
Alta Foresta	1¼	2 daily	Azul (www.voeazul.com.br)
Belo Horizonte	2½	daily except Sat	Azul (www.voeazul.com.br)
Brasília	1½	up to 8 daily	Avianca (www.avianca.com.br), Azul (www.voeazul.com.br), GOL (www.voegol.com.br), TAM (www.tam.com.br)
Campo Grande	1¼	3-5 daily	Avianca (www.avianca.com.br), Azul (www.voeazul.com.br), GOL (www.voegol.com.br)
Goiânia	2½	3-4 daily	Azul (www.voeazul.com.br), Passaredo (www.voepassaredo.com.br)
Foz do Iguaçu	1¾	daily except Sat	Azul (www.voeazul.com.br)
Londrina	1¾	daily except Sat	Azul (www.voeazul.com.br)
Maringá	1¾	daily except Sun	Azul (www.voeazul.com.br)
Porto Velho	2	2-4 daily	Azul (www.voeazul.com.br), GOL (www.voegol.com.br)
Ribeirão Preto	3¾	daily except Sun	Azul (www.voeazul.com.br), Passaredo (www.voepassaredo.com.br)
São Paulo	2¼	9-11 daily	Avianca (www.avianca.com.br), Azul (www.voeazul.com.br), GOL (www.voegol.com.br), TAM (www.tam.com.br)

Mon-Fri) has some helpful maps and brochures in Portuguese.

Getting There & Away

AIR

Marechal Rondon International Airport (☎3614-2511) is in Várzea Grande, 7km from Cuiabá.

BUS

Cuiabá's **bus station** (☎3621-3629) is 3km north of the center on the highway toward Chapada dos Guimarães.

Getting Around

From the airport, bus 24 (R$3.10) runs to town from outside the Las Velas Hotel; turn left as you leave the airport and walk 100m to Av Getúlio Vargas. A taxi costs around R$35. Buses back to the airport depart from Praça Ipiranga and the corner of Avenida Coronel Duarte and Avenida Getulio Vargas.

From inside the bus terminal, you can get a Centro bus to Praça Alencastro (R$3.10). More frequent buses marked 'Centro' leave from outside the bus station and drop you along Av Isaac Póvoas; get off in front of the CAT office. A taxi from inside the bus station costs around R$30. Bus 7 runs between the airport and the bus station.

Referência (☎3682-6689; www.referencia.com.br) and **Localiza** (☎3682-7900; www.localiza.com) are a couple of reliable car-rental companies with offices in the airport. The best car for the Pantanal is one with high clearance, though any car can make it during dry season. In the wet season (November to March) you'll need a 4x4 and off-road driving experience, and some sections may be impassible anyway.

Chapada dos Guimarães

☎0XX65 / POP 18,700

The area around Chapada dos Guimarães is as little known as it is spectacular, reminiscent of the American southwest and surprisingly different from the typical Mato Grosso terrain. The town is 800m higher than state capital Cuiabá and provides a cool and convenient base for exploring the surrounding areas. It is also home to one of the lushest central squares in Brazil.

The area surrounding the Parque Nacional Da Chapada has numerous attractions. On the way from Cuiabá to Chapada town, you pass **Rio dos Peixes**, **Rio Mutaca** and **Rio Claro**, which are popular weekend bathing spots for *cuiabános*, and three commanding valleys, **Vale do Salgadeira**, **Vale**

BUSES FROM CUIABÁ

DESTINATION	COST (R$)	TIME (HR)	FREQUENCY	COMPANY
Alta Floresta	197	14	6 daily	Verde Transportes (www.viagemverde.com.br)
Bom Jardim	41	5	daily at 2pm	TUT Transportes (☎3321-4326)
Brasília	178-196	23	7 daily	Viação São Luiz (www.viacaosaoluiz.com.br), Eucatur (www.eucatur.com.br)
Cáceres	42-53	3¾	6 daily	Verde Transportes (www.viagemverde.com.br), Eucatur (www.eucatur.com.br)
Campo Grande	93-116	12	17 daily	Motta (www.motta.com.br), Eucatur (www.eucatur.com.br), Nova Integração (www.novaintegracao.com.br), Andorinha (www.andorinha.com), Viação São Luiz (www.viacaosaoluiz.com.br)
Chapada dos Guimarães	28	1¼	9 daily	Expresso Rubi (☎3621-2188)
Goiânia	115-149	18	8 daily	Viação São Luiz (www.viacaosaoluiz.com.br), Eucatur (www.eucatur.com.br)
Poconé	12	2½	6 daily	TUT Transportes (☎3321-4326)
Porto Velho	156-185	23-26	10 daily	Eucatur (www.eucatur.com.br), Gontijo (www.gontijo.com.br), Expresso Itamariti (www.expressoitamarati.com.br), Nacional Expresso (www.nacionalexpresso.com.br)

do Paciência and Vale do Rio Claro. The sheer 80m drop called Portão do Inferno (Hell's Gate) is also unforgettable – it was formerly the town 'prison' in the early 1900s (use your imagination!).

Sights

Mirante de Geodésia VIEWPOINT

The *mirante* (lookout), marked with a modest concrete square, is the geographic center of South America. While the monument is underwhelming, the views are magnificent! Off to your right you can see the Cuiabá skyline, and beyond that, the flatlands that eventually become the Pantanal. To get here, follow Route 251 through Chapada and head east for 7km; a cycle path connects the viewpoint to the town. The rim of the canyon is a couple of hundred meters away.

Sleeping

Pousada Bom Jardim POUSADA $

(3301-2668; www.pousadabomjardim.com.br; Praça Dom Wunibaldo; s/d/q with fan R$80/120/180, s/d/tr with air-con from R$100/150/190;) There's little reason to spring for air-con at this cheapie right in the main square – the fans are high-octane. A favorite with backpackers. Rooms are a bit dingy but spotless.

Pousada Villa Guimaraes POUSADA $$

(3301-1366; www.pousadavillaguimaraes.com.br; Neco Siqueira 41; r with/without bathroom R$305/185;) Ideally located near the main square, this cheerful yellow pousada is all heavy wooden furniture and colorful accents. The breakfast is by far the best in town.

Casa da Quineira LODGE $$$

(3301-3301; www.casadaquineira.com.br; Frei Osvaldo 191; d/tr/q from R$460/590/810;) Tucked away down a quiet street near the heart of Chapada, this is the closest the town gets to a stately mansion. Contemporary art merges seamlessly with extensive scuplted grounds, hammocks on the veranda and high-tech gadgets. On cooler nights, guests can gather by the fireplace, and the Saturday night dinners are the stuff of legend.

Pousada do Parque Eco Lodge LODGE $$$

(3391-1346; www.pousadadoparque.com.br; Estrada do Parque Ecológico Km 52; r R$425;) This intimate eco-choice borders 150 hectares of newly preserved parkland and is the closest accommodations to the national park's entrance (4.5km). Delicious, home-cooked food and a knowledgeable wildlife guide enhance your stay here, miles away from the nearest neighbor. It's down a fairly rough road that leads to the Waterfall Circuit; inquire in advance about the gate key. Book in advance.

Eating

There's a good lunchtime restaurant on the premises of Parque Nacional Da Chapada Dos Guimarães. A couple of dessert places offer homemade ice cream in tempting local fruit flavours on the town's main square.

Felipe BUFFET $

(Cipriano Curvo 596; meals per kg R$36; noon-11pm) Fill your boots without emptying your pockets at this per-kilo extravaganza just off the main square.

Pomodori ITALIAN, BRAZILIAN $$

(Caldas 60; mains R$28-39; from 4pm Mon-Fri, from noon Sat & Sun) Surely the cutest restaurant in the center, with checkered tablecloths, serving a handful of select Italian plates nightly and equally good fishy mains, such as pintado with passion-fruit sauce. It is also renowned for its empanadas (stuffed pastries) with savoury fillings.

★ **Morro dos Ventos** BRAZILIAN $$

(3301-1030; www.morrodosventos.com.br; Rodovia MT 251, Km 1; mains from R$38; 11am-4pm;) Fantastic takes on regional cuisine, from perfectly grilled *picanha* (fillet steak) with a full entourage of *farofa* (garnish of manioc flour sautéed with butter) with banana, rice and beans and tangy tomato vinaigrette, and rice slow-cooked with chunks of pork to great slabs of grilled pintado and fantastic fruit juices. The vibe? Plantation in the antebellum era. Near the restaurant is a viewpoint with dizzying glimpses of the valley below.

★ **Bistro da Mata** INTERNATIONAL $$$

(3301-3483; www.bistrodamata.com.br; turnoff on Estrada do Mirante Km 1; dishes R$50-98; 8pm-2am Fri, 11am-2am Sat, 11am-5pm Sun;) A romantic bistro with stupendous views, rough-hewn stone walls and an appealing outdoor terrace. The creative daily menu incorporates the likes of bacon-wrapped veal medallions with wild mushroom risotto, and grilled pintado with olive pesto; the homemade pasta buffet on Sunday is worth telling your grandchildren about.

Information

C.A.T. (☎3301-2045; Penn Gomes s/n; ⏰8am-5pm Mon-Sat) The semihelpful official tourist office occasionally dishes out cartoonish maps of the area, useful if you're driving.

Banco do Brasil (Praça Dom Wunibaldo) Accepts foreign cards.

Bradesco (Fernando Corréia da Costa 868) Accepts foreign cards.

Post office (Fernando Corréia da Costa 848; ⏰8am-4pm Mon-Fri) A block from the main square.

Getting There & Away

Expresso Rubi (☎3621-2188) buses leave Cuiabá's bus station for Chapada town (R$18, 1¼ hours, nine daily) between 6:30am and 7pm. The miraculous views are out the right-side window from Cuiabá.

In the other direction, the first bus leaves Chapada town at 5:30am and the last at 7pm. Chapada's bus station is two blocks from the main plaza (Praça Dom Wunibaldo).

Parque Nacional da Chapada dos Guimarães

☎0XX65

Only receiving national-park status in 1989, the outstanding Parque Nacional da Chapada dos Guimarães remains under the mass-tourism radar, though it's hard to see why. Picture the scene: red rock buttresses soaring up from a green valley; lines of palm trees marking the location of clear rivers and pools for snorkeling; waterfalls ranging from immense and admired from afar to petite and swimmable; dusty hikes through parched land, observed only by yellow-eyed burrowing desert owls; mysterious caves to explore... The park sits high on a plateau, meaning that evening and morning temperatures are mercifully cooler than elsewhere in Mato Grosso.

Véu de Noiva is the only part of the park you can visit independently. Otherwise, a certified guide is required.

Sights

Véu de Noiva WATERFALL

(Bridal Veil; ⏰9am-4pm; last entry at noon) FREE The impressive Véu de Noiva, an 86m free-falling waterfall, provides the park's characteristic postcard moment. A small trail leads to the lookout, perched on top of rocks with the canyon below. This is one of Chapada's most dazzling spots; no guide necessary.

It is around 9km west of the town of Chapada. You can get off the bus from Cuiabá at the park turnoff, spend a couple of hours, then flag down the next bus coming through to Chapada.

Tours

Most visitors join one of the tour circuits, though it's possible to visit the area's attractions on a custom-made tour; inquire about recommended, certified guides at your lodgings in Chapada dos Guimarães. You can also organize tours at the park office (near the restaurant), though you're better off arranging things in town.

While most tours start around 9am, you can arrange visits for earlier in the day (if you're a keen bird-watcher, for instance), in which case your guide can pick up the relevant key from the office the day before. Regular tours should be reserved in advance, especially in July, August and September. Tours include transportation but not meals.

Cidade de Pedra MOUNTAIN

(Stone City; per person from R$180; ⏰9am-4pm) Cidade de Pedra provides Guimarães' most transcendent moment. Jagged red sandstone rock formations reminiscent of those in Utah and Arizona jut up into the sky from the tops of enormous cliffs that drop down into the vast green valley beneath. You follow the short footpath that skirts the edge of the cliff through scrubland, peering at the abyss below. Morning is the best time to visit, when the sunlight illuminates most of the cliffs. It's 20km north of Chapada.

Circuito das Cachoeiras WATERFALL

(Waterfall Circuit; per person from R$160) The Waterfall Circuit involves a gentle 6.5km trek through a parched red landscape, covered with scrubland and low trees, with six waterfall stops en route; the whole thing takes four to six hours, depending on how easy you want to take it. The first waterfall is the highest, while the others are better for swimming, with deep pools and cascades forming natural Jacuzzis. Access to some involves negotiating steep steps.

Roteiro da Caverna Aroe Jari e Lagoa Azul CAVE

(Aroe Jari Cave Circuit; per person from R$230) This tour focuses on Brazil's largest sandstone cave, reachable via a hiking trail

WORTH A TRIP

CRISTALINO PRIVATE NATURAL HERITAGE PRESERVE

The uninspiring town of **Alta Floresta**, 873km north of Cuiabá, is the end of the road: north of here is the vast expanse of the Amazon jungle. There is one excellent reason for heading out here, and that is to visit the Cristalino Private Natural Heritage Preserve, considered one of Amazonia's best for spotting rare birds and mammals, including the endangered white-nosed bearded saki monkey, lowland tapir, giant otter and five species of macaw.

On the banks of the Rio Cristalino (39km north of Alta Floresta) in an area rich in Amazon flora and fauna, the revamped **Cristalino Jungle Lodge** (066-3521-1396; www.cristalinolodge.com.br; s US$420-650, d per person US$360-530;) offers two 50m-high observation towers and over 20km of good bird- and animal-watching trails (it is considered one of the top 50 spots in the world for birding). The new VIP bungalows flash creature-comfort luxe. Rates include transfers, gourmet meals, expert multilingual guides, excursions and insurance. Book well ahead if you want to stay in high season.

If you are short on time or money and can't spend the night at the Cristalino Jungle Lodge, it's possible to stay at the comfortable **Floresta Amazônica Hotel** (066-3512-7100; www.cristalinolodge.com.br; Av Perimetral Oeste 2001; r R$200;) in Alta Floresta and organize a day visit with the Cristalino Jungle Lodge directly for US$200 per person. While the trip includes transfers, a guide, a nature walk and lunch at the lodge, we found it to be poor value. It takes 1½ hours to reach the reserve from Alta Floresta, meaning that day visitors don't get to the reserve before 11am, when it's already too hot to see the wildlife – the reserve's main attraction. They are then whisked back off to Alta Floresta at around 3pm or 4pm, with guides and transfers worked around guests staying at Cristalino Jungle Lodge. A night or two at the Cristalino Jungle Lodge is a much better proposition.

From Cuiabá, Verde Transportes (www.viagemverde.com.br) runs bus services north to Alta Floresta (R$197, 13¼ hours, six daily). Azul (www.voeazul.com.br) offers daily flights.

through scrubland and featuring unusual rock formations and a startling, mirrorlike cave lake.

Circuito Vale de Rio Claro SNORKELING
(Rio Claro Valley Circuit; per person from R$180) A steep scramble takes you to a viewpoint overlooking the lush valley and the razor-thin rock formations in front of you. Then you swim and snorkel in clear, deep, rapid-fed pools in the forest before embarking on a 500m float, following your guide along the twists and turns of the narrow river, the sombre underwater world stretching beneath you.

Morro São Jerônimo HIKING
(per person from R$230) The flat, tablelike summit of Morro São Jerônimo rises above the southern edge of the national park, affording spectacular 360-degree views of Chapada's rock formations, the Pantanal and the valleys below. It's an excellent and not particularly difficult day hike, though it is 18km round-trip. Bring plenty of water and sturdy shoes.

Chapada Explorer ECOTOUR
(3301-1290; www.chapadaexplorer.com.br; Praça Dom Wunibaldo 57; 8-11am Mon-Sat) An excellent Chapada-based agency run by locals who have grown up around ecotourism and are actively involved in teaching the benefits of low-impact tourism to locals. It runs excursions to all of the area's attractions in groups up to a maximum of 10, as well as multiday Pantanal excursions. Bring your own food; prices do not include admission costs.

Bom Jardim

0XX65 / POP 11,500

The watery attractions around Bom Jardim – a parched one-street town 150km north of Cuiabá – are similar to those of Bonito in Mato Grosso do Sul, albeit on a smaller scale and minus the crowds. Crystalline rivers overloaded with tropical fish, caves, waterfalls and macaws make this an extremely rewarding place to spend some time, whether you take a tour from Cuiabá or overnight in the town proper.

Sights & Activities

You'll need to be accompanied by a guide to visit the main attractions. Tour companies in Cuiabá run these excursions, but you can also contract a guide locally if you prefer to travel independently, though you'll need your own wheels. If staying the night in Bom Jardim, it can be cheaper to book both accommodation and tour together.

★Recanto Ecológico Lagoa Azul SNORKELING
(full day incl lunch R$100) The number-one attraction is this underground-spring-fed Aquário Encantado, with incredible visibility down to its maximum depth of 6m and schools of fish that mill about as you explore the underwater world. 'Aquarium' aside, you can float and snorkel for 850m along the Rio Salobra that cuts across the land of the same *fazenda* (farm). It's 10km from town.

Rio Triste SNORKELING
(snorkeling R$75) At Rio Triste, 17km from Vila de Bom Jardim, you're delivered to the start of the forest trail by tractor. With any luck, you may spot some monkeys before floating face to face with red-finned piraputanga fish in a deep, clear pool. Then float downriver behind your guide, dodging submerged tree trunks and trying to spot sand-colored freshwater stingrays.

Cachoeira da Serra Azul WATERFALL, SNORKELING
(SESC Serra Azul, Rosario Oeste; snorkeling R$50) Twenty kilometers from town, this is the most impressive of the area's numerous waterfalls. A 50m-high cascade plunges into an 8m-deep, vivid blue, natural pool, with some excellent *flutação* (flotation) to be had here.

Lagoa das Araras BIRD-WATCHING
(R$15; from 5pm) A 15-minute walk signposted from Bom Jardim's main street leads to Lagoa das Araras, a tranquil sunken forest of palm trees. Sunset is the best time to observe dozens of cawing blue and yellow macaws coming noisily to roost; you'll see a handful during the day too.

Sleeping & Eating

Pousada Bom Jardim POUSADA $$
(3102-2018; www.pousadabomjardim.com; Rodovia MT 241, Km 65; s/d/tr R$145/220/280; P) In the heart of Vila Bom Jardim, this friendly pousada doubles as a tour agency. Rooms have crimson accents, and hammocks surround a tranquil green space out back.

Pousada Rota das Aguas POUSADA $$
(3102-2019; www.rotadasaguas.tur.br; Rodovia 241, Km 65; s/d/tr R$150/200/330;) Right in town, the colorful rooms at this appealing pousada face a green inside courtyard, complete with pet macaw. The owner is happy to share his knowledge of the area but the pousada and travel-agency staff seem rather disinterested.

Balneario Estivado SELF-SERVE
(buffet R$20; 11am-5pm) A couple of kilometers out of town, toward Rio Triste, this thatched restaurant comes with an additional attraction: snorkeling in a crystal-clear pool filled with fish (R$10). The buffet showcases regional dishes.

Getting There & Away

One **TUT Transportes** (3317-2200) bus a day runs from Cuiabá to Bom Jardim at 2pm (R$41, five hours) with the return leaving at 6am. Transport is included in guided tours from Cuiabá.

Poconé

0XX65 / POP 23,300

This dusty frontier town is a place travelers invariably have to pass through on their way to the Transpantaneira 'highway.' It's so sleepy that, as one local put it, 'In Poconé, even the restaurants close for lunch!' This place is unlikely to detain you for longer than a meal stop, though those driving themselves to a lodge along the Transpantaneira might consider overnighting here to get an early start and catch the wildlife in action on the way.

Pousada Pantaneira (3345-3357; www.pousadapantaneira.com.br; Rodovia Transpantaneira Km 0; rodizio R$35;) is a justifiably popular *churrascaria* that sits at the top of the Transpantaneira. The different cuts of meat are gut-bustingly good, as is the extensive buffet of *pantaneiro* sides. There are also some simple rooms as well (single/double/triple R$70/120/150).

The **Banco do Brasil** (Campos Sales) has a Visa/MasterCard ATM, but don't bet your life on it working.

There are TUT Transportes buses from Cuiabá to Poconé (R$12, 2½ hours, six daily) from 6am to 7pm, and six in the opposite direction from 6am to 7:30pm. In Poconé they stop at the bus station about 10 blocks from the center of town, then continue on to Praça da Matriz.

THE PANTANAL

While the Amazon gets the press coverage, the Pantanal is a better place to see wildlife. The dense foliage of the Amazon makes it difficult to observe the animals, unlike the open marshes of the Pantanal. These marshes are home to an immense variety of life, from jaguars to jabiru storks, so if you like to see animals in their natural environment, the Pantanal is an unmissable destination.

Located in the heart of South America, the world's largest wetland is 20 times the size of the famed Everglades in Florida – it covers some 210,000 sq km. Less than 100,000 sq km of this is in Bolivia and Paraguay; the rest is in Brazil, split between the states of Mato Grosso and Mato Grosso do Sul.

The Pantanal has few people and no towns. Distances are so great and ground transport so poor that people get around in small airplanes and motorboats; car travel is restricted by the seasons. The principal access road that runs deep into the Pantanal is the **Transpantaneira**. This raised dirt road sectioned by small wooden bridges ends 145km south of Poconé, at Porto Jofre. The much-mooted road connection of Porto Jofre to Corumbá (at the border with Bolivia) has long been shelved due to concerns about the general absurdity of having a road that's underwater for half the year.

The **Parque Nacional do Pantanal Matogrossense** occupies 1350 sq km in the southwest of the region, but most of the Pantanal is privately owned. Cooperation between ecotourism and the landowners in the region (mostly cattle ranchers) has contributed to the sustainable conservation of the environment. By providing ranchers with an income that encourages their coexistence with wildlife, it covers the shortfall created by the seasonal flooding of the area, which would otherwise be covered by more intensive (and hence more destructive) ranching efforts. The national park and three smaller private nature reserves nearby were given Unesco World Heritage listing in 2000.

PANTANAL PACKING LIST

You can't buy much in the Pantanal, so come prepared. The dry season is also the cooler season. Don't forget the following:

- ☐ Quick-dry, light-colored long-sleeved shirts; leave behind red (it scares animals), yellow (mosquitoes love it) and black clothing (it's too hot and mosquitoes love it too)
- ☐ Neutral-colored long pants
- ☐ Sneakers or walking boots
- ☐ Rain poncho
- ☐ Flip-flops or water sandals
- ☐ Sun hat
- ☐ Swimwear
- ☐ Fleece or sweater
- ☐ Day pack
- ☐ Mosquito repellent with plenty of DEET
- ☐ Sunscreeen
- ☐ Sunglasses
- ☐ Binoculars
- ☐ Strong flashlight or headlamp
- ☐ Camera with good zoom lens
- ☐ Flask or reusable water bottle

The Pantanal

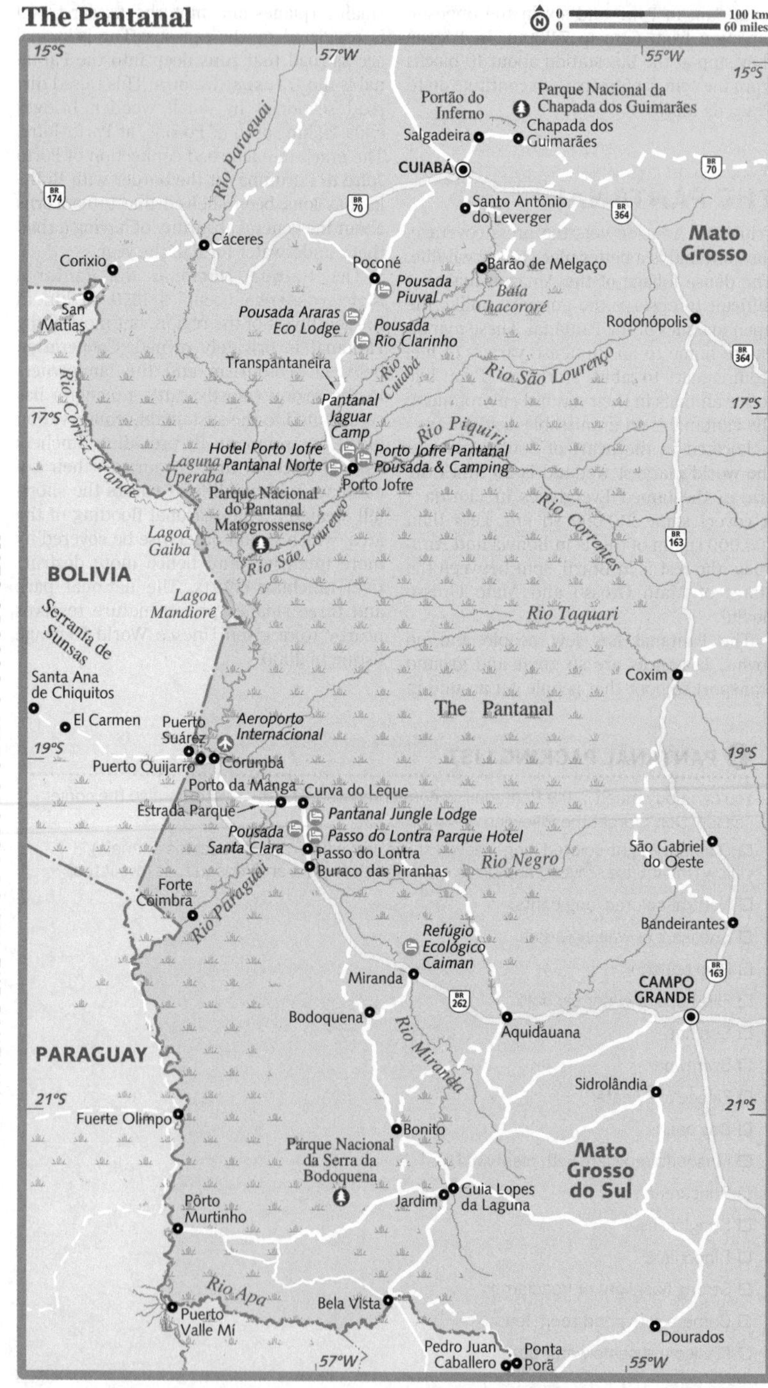

Geography & Climate

Although *pantano* means 'swamp' in both Spanish and Portuguese, the Pantanal is not a swamp but a vast alluvial plain. In geological terms, it is a sedimentary basin of quaternary origin, but its vastness led the early settlers to mistake it for a sea, which they called the Xaraés. This began to dry out, along with the Amazon Sea, 65 million years ago.

The Pantanal – 2000km upstream from the Atlantic Ocean yet just 100m to 200m above sea level – is bounded by higher lands: the mountains of the Serra de Maracaju to the east, the Serra da Bodoquena to the south and the Serra dos Parecis and Serra do São Geronimo to the north. From these highlands the rains flow into the Pantanal, forming the Rio Paraguai and its tributaries (which flow south and then east, draining into the Atlantic Ocean).

During the wet season (November to March), the rivers flood their banks, inundating much of the low-lying Pantanal and creating *cordilheiras* (vegetation islands above the high-water level), where the animals cluster together. The waters reach their high mark – up to 3m – in January or February, then start to recede in March. This seasonal flooding has made systematic farming impossible and has severely limited human incursions into the area. However, it does provide an enormously rich feeding ground for wildlife.

The floodwaters replenish the soil's nutrients, which would otherwise be very poor, due to the excessive drainage. The waters teem with fish, and the ponds provide protective niches for many animals and plants. Enormous flocks of wading birds gather in rookeries several square kilometers in area.

Later in the dry season, the water recedes, the lagoons and marshes dry out and fresh grasses emerge on the savanna (the Pantanal's vegetation includes savanna and forest which blend together, often with no clear divisions). The hawks, storks and caiman *(jacaré)* compete for fish in the remaining ponds. As the ponds shrink and dry up, the caiman crawl around for water, sweating it out until the rains return.

Planning

When to Go

It's possible to visit the Pantanal year-round, but it's best to go during the dry season (May to September). The best time to watch birds is from July to September, when the waters have receded and the bright-green grasses pop up from the muck. If you are on the trail of the elusive jaguar, then you will need to visit June to August, when it is access-all-areas and you can probe deeper into the wilderness.

PANTANAL CUISINE

Pantaneiros – the local Pantanal folks – make good use of regional ingredients in preparing their delicacies. You'll find lots of restaurants offering regional specialties on your travels in the area – stop in and try some.

In the northern Pantanal, the cuisine is decidedly fishy. Pacu, dourado and pintado are the most consumed fish, and they come *frito* (fried), *grelhado* (grilled), *assado* (baked) or *defumado* (smoked). Both dourado and pacu have lots of small bones, but they separate easily when baked slowly. Pacu is often baked and served with an *escabeche* sauce consisting of onions, tomatoes and peppers. Another favorite fish is pintado, excellent when spiced with rough salt and pepper and grilled. One specialty is *peixe à urucum*, where the chosen fish is served topped with spices, condensed milk, coconut milk and melted mozzarella. Piranha soup is also popular and considered an aphrodisiac by the *pantaneiros*.

On farms and in southern Pantanal, the dishes are more strongly influenced by the cattle and grains produced in the area. Specialties include *carne seca com abobora* (sun-dried beef with pumpkin) and *paçoca-de-pilã* (sun-dried beef with manioc flour), the latter eaten with bananas and unsalted rice. There's also *arroz de carreteiro* (rice with sun-dried beef served with fried manioc and banana) and *galinha caipira* (chicken served with white rice). Popular Pantanal desserts include *furrundu* – a mixture of papaya trunk (not the fruit), sugarcane juice and coconut – and ice cream made from *bocaiúva*, a local fruit.

1

2

NIGEL PAVITT/ JOHN WARBURTON-LEE PHOTOGRAPHY LTD / GETTY IMAGES ©

1. Jaguar 2. Water lilies, the Pantanal 3. Wooden bridge, the Pantanal

Driving the Transpantaneira

In 1970 the government decided to push a road through the Pantanal from Cuiabá to Corumbá. After struggling as far as Porto Jofre, 145km from Poconé, they then made the wise choice of stopping and questioning the wisdom of traversing an area that was under water for six months a year. The result, or remnant, is the Transpantaneira, a raised dirt road that extends deep into the Pantanal, though the fanciful plans of completion still haunt the nightmares of local ecologists.

Wildlife is plentiful along the roadside and you'll see *jacarés* (caiman), capybaras and lots of birds. There are several places to stay along the Transpantaneira.

If driving from Cuiabá, head out around 4am to reach the Transpantaneira by sunrise, when the animals come to life. Weekdays are better for driving, as there's less traffic kicking up dust. The road officially starts in Poconé, though many consider the wooden sign and guard station 17km south as the beginning of the Transpantaneira. Fill up your tank in Poconé. Though you should be able to make it to Porto Jofre and back on one tank, better safe than sorry as the gas station at Hotel Porto Jofre charges twice the going rate if you miscalculate.

Heading south, you'll navigate over 125 little wooden bridges and around countless meter-wide potholes. Notice the interesting carved statue of Sào Francisco, Protector of Ecology, around Km 18. He was installed by a priest in Poconé a few years back. At Km 32 is the small bar Barara, where you can stop for a beer and *galinhada* (boneless chicken and rice) or fried fish. You can also purchase a ticket here to go to the top of the lookout tower next door at Pousada Araras Eco Lodge (p377), a treat even if you're not staying.

After Km 105, the landscape changes, with denser vegetation and an altogether wilder feel – it's jaguar country! Even if you don't spot one, you are rewarded for your efforts once you hit Campo do Jofre, just north of Porto Jofre.

Flooding, incessant rains and heat make travel difficult during the wet season (November to April), though this time is not without its special rewards – this is when the cattle and wildlife of the Pantanal clump together on the *cordilheiras*. However, the islands are covered with dense vegetation that can make spotting wildlife difficult. The heaviest rains fall in February and March. Roads become impassable and travel is a logistical nightmare.

From June to August, the driest months, the chances of spotting jaguars rise dramatically. The heat peaks from December to February, when temperatures higher than 40°C (104°F) are common, roads turn to breakfast cereal, and the mosquitoes are out in force. Many hotels close at this time and in the northern Pantanal tour companies effectively take a break.

Fishing is best during the first part of the dry season (April to May), when the flooded rivers settle back into their channels, but locals have been known to lasso 80kg fish throughout the dry season. This is some of the best fishing in the world. There are three species of piranha, as well as the tasty dourado (known locally as the river tiger) that reaches upwards of 9kg. Other excellent catches include pacu, suribim, bagre, piraputanga, piapara, cachara, pirancajuva and pintado, to name but a few.

Although hunting is not allowed, fishing – with the required permits – is encouraged between February and October. It is, however, prohibited during the *piracema* (breeding season), running any time between November and March. Banco do Brasil branches issue permits valid for three months for fishing in the Pantanal, but you'll need to print off the application form at www.imasul.ms.gov.br first. National fishing permits valid for one year are also available from Ibama offices in **Campo Grande** (☎067-3317-2952; Padre João Crippa 753; ⏲9am-5pm Mon-Fri), **Corumbá** (☎067-3231-6096; Firmo Matos 479; ⏲9am-5pm Mon-Fri) and **Cuiabá** (☎065-3648-9100; Av Historiador Rubens de Mendonça 5250; ⏲9am-5pm Mon-Fri).

Health

There is no malaria in the Pantanal, but dengue fever occasionally breaks out in the region. Preventative measures are usually rapidly taken by authorities and the vector mosquito is, regardless, generally associated with urban areas and not the countryside. If you're concerned, consult a travel-health expert for the latest information before you leave home. For more on these and other travelers' health concerns, check out Lonely Planet's *Healthy Travel – Central & South America* by Drs Gheradin and Young.

There are medical services available in Cuiabá, Corumbá and Campo Grande.

Tours

The principal access towns where you can arrange tours are Cuiabá in the north (for the Transpantaneira) and Campo Grande in the south (for the Estrada Parque), with Corumbá on the Bolivian border more of a sideshow these days.

Tours from Cuiabá tend to be slightly more expensive, but more professional with smaller groups and better-trained guides than those from either Campo Grande or Corumbá. They also go deeper into the Pantanal. If time is a problem and money isn't, contact Focus Tours (www.focustours.com) in the US, who are nature tour specialists active in trying to preserve the Pantanal.

From Cuiabá

From Cuiabá, the capital of Mato Grosso, small tour operators arrange safaris along the Transpantaneira that include transportation, ranch accommodations on farms and guides. Guides are English-speaking and well-trained on the whole, and smaller groups increase your chances of seeing the shier animals. Fortunately, while there is healthy competition between tour operators in Cuiabá, it's not as intense as in Mato Grosso do Sul and some operators share the same Pantanal camps.

Tours here are well organized and quite comfortable, starting from around R$500 per day – if you are serious about seeing animals they are worth the extra money. Some companies also offer 'jaguar tours' for around R$1000 per day, with an excellent chance of seeing this magnificent feline in the Porto Jofre area from June to November.

★**Pantanal Nature** NATURE TOUR
(☎0xx65-9994-2265, 0xx65-3322-0203; www.pantanalnature.com.br; Professor Francisco Torres 48; per day high/low season R$700/450) Superb agency run by Ailton Lara that has quickly built up a sterling reputation for its professional tours and expert guides. It also runs

the Panatal Jaguar Camp near Porto Jofre, with excellent success rates in seeing the animal in the dry season.

Pantanal Explorer NATURE TOUR

(☎065-3682-2800; www.pantanalexplorer.com.br; Av Governador Ponce de Arruda 670, Várzea Grande) Owner Andre Von Thuronyi has been working with sustainable tourism in the area for over 30 years and fights harmful government interference in the Pantanal with ferocity. He is actively involved in saving the hyacinth macaw and giant otter. Affiliated with Pousada Araras Eco Lodge (p380).

Ecoverde Tours NATURE TOUR

(☎065-9638-1614, 0xx65-3624-1386; www.ecoverdetours.com.br; Pedro Celestino 391; per day R$500-700) Top-notch company with 25 years of service and experienced guides. Working with local pousadas toward an ecofriendly approach, Joel Souza can guide you in English, German, French, Portuguese or Spanish. You can find him at Hostel Pousada Ecoverde.

From Campo Grande

Southern gateways to the Pantanal are the cities of Corumbá, Campo Grande, Aquidauana and Miranda. Most backpackers head to Campo Grande. Corumbá, Aquidauana and Miranda are popular with Brazilian anglers and high-end travelers.

Budget tour operators working in Mato Grosso do Sul offer packages at camps along Estrada Parque, a 117km stretch of dirt road through the region known as Nhecolândia. Estrada Parque is actually closer to Corumbá than to Campo Grande, but the vast majority of companies have long relocated to Campo Grande, a travel hub convenient for onward travel to other parts of Brazil. If you are visiting Bonito, go to the Pantanal first as the tours end in Buraco das Piranhas, closer to Bonito than Campo Grande.

Campo Grande has made a big effort to clean up its act in recent years, with local government closing down the lodges that didn't comply with ecological legislation and tightening the screws on dodgy operators. Problems persist, but things are definitely moving in the right direction. The cheapest tours are rough-and-tumble affairs and groups are often large, but with prices starting at around R$400 per day it is an economical way to see the Pantanal and its wildlife.

Pantanal Viagens & Turismo NATURE TOUR

(☎067-3321-3143; www.pantanalviagens.com.br; room 09, old bus terminal, Joaquim Nabuco 200) A nice agency working with Pousada Passo

CHOOSING A GUIDE IN THE PANTANAL

Pantanal tourism is big business and in the past some companies have been guilty of employing underhand tactics in the race to hook in clients. Though measures have finally been taken to clamp down on the worst offenders, it is still worth bearing a few suggestions in mind to have a safe and enjoyable trip.

- Resist making a snap decision, especially if you've just climbed off an overnight bus.
- Do not make your decision based on cost. Cheaper very rarely means better, but even expensive tours can be a letdown.
- Go on forums. Read online reviews. Speak to other travelers. What was their experience like? In Campo Grande some of the tour companies are quick to badmouth others. Get your advice straight from the horse's mouth.
- Compare your options, but remember that the owner or salesperson is not always your guide, and it's the guide you're going to be with in the wilderness for several days. Ask to meet your guide if possible. Ascertain your guide's linguistic abilities.
- Don't hand over your cash to any go-betweens or buy bus tickets that somebody other than the person you give your money to is going to give you.
- If you are even remotely concerned about sustainable tourism, do not use operators and lodges that harm this fragile environment. That means no picking up the animals for photographs or touching them whatsoever.
- Group budget tours focus squarely on the spectacular and easy-to-see species. Serious wildlife-watchers should be prepared to pay more for a private guide.

do Lontra and other Pantanal lodgings that has worked hard to maintain its excellent reputation. Caters for mid- to high-range budgets, but offers professional and reliable packages.

Pantanal Discovery NATURE TOUR
(☎067-9163-3518; www.gilspantanaldiscovery.com.br; Hotel Nacional, Dom Aquino 610; per 3 days dm/r R$900/1000) A perennial operator with a polished sales pitch; owner Gil is assertive and helpful and is the pick of budget operators in town.

Sleeping

Pantanal accommodations are divided into roughly three types: pousadas, which include all meals and range from simple to top end; *fazendas*, which are ranch-style hotels that usually have horses and often boats for use; and *pesqueiros*, which cater for anglers and usually have boats and fishing gear for rent. If you have doubts about roughing it on the budget tours, it is better to spend a bit more money for basic comforts – a bed, running water and some hope of avoiding a million mosquito bites. It rarely costs much more and the investment is worth it for a good night's sleep.

If you travel independently, you can rent a car and book a stay at various Pantanal lodges. Transportation is almost never included in the room rates and can take a sizable chunk out of your budget if you don't have your own wheels. From Cuiabá, transfers in and out may require any combination of 4WD, boat, horseback and plane, depending on the season.

For this reason, it is almost always cheaper – not to mention logistically less stressful – to go in under the services of a tour operator. Transportation in and out is then included and they often have access to more remote lodges.

Along the Transpantaneira

Accommodations along the Transpantaneira are plentiful and there is a good variety of choices, from fairly rustic to high end.

Porto Jofre Pantanal Pousada & Camping POUSADA, CAMPING $$
(☎065-9971-3699; www.portojofrepantanal.com.br; s/d/tr/q R$280/500/660/800, camping R$35; ❄📶) Right at the end of the Transpantaneira, this pousada, a budget-tour favorite, has a wonderful riverfront location – ideal for wildlife-spotting boat tours – as well as excellent food, spartan, air-conditioned rooms and clean showers for campers. Meals are included in room price (campers pay extra). You have to bring a guide with you if you're not part of a tour.

★**Pousada Araras Eco Lodge** LODGE $$$
(☎065-3682-2800; www.araraslodge.com.br; Transpantaneira Km 32; s/d R$990/1545; ❄@📶🏊) This pioneering ranch offers the most comfort and luxury along the Transpantaneira. Rooms have lovely artisanal bedspreads and nice patios with hammocks separated by bamboo curtains. There is a treetop tower for bird-watching (hyacinth macaws are always around) and owners André and his wife are focused on sustainability (solar panels, growing most food on their own farm).

Pousada Rio Clarinho FAZENDA $$$
(☎065-9977-8966; www.pousadarioclarinho.com.br; Transpantaneira Km 40; s/d/tr incl meals & excursions R$250/420/600; ❄) An avian symphony is your wake-up call at this rustic *fazenda* right on the Rio Clarinho (there's a river platform for swimming). With an extensive area of forested trails, there are more than 260 species of bird on the property, as well as capybaras and giant otters. The food is authentic *pantaneiro* and the owners' warmth transcends the language barrier.

Pousada Piuval POUSADA $$$
(☎065-3345-1338; www.pousadapiuval.com.br; Transpantaneira Km 10; s/d with full board R$375/560; ❄📶🏊) It's a trade-off at the first pousada along the Transpantaneira: it's more commercial (feeding caimans) but also more comfortable. It sits on 70 sq km and is popular with European travelers and bird-watchers. The pool is wonderful, as are sunset boat rides. It offers horseback riding, trekking and night safaris as well. Day visits to the pousada available.

Pantanal Jaguar Camp LODGE $$$
(www.pantanaljaguarcamp.com.br; s/d R$300/670; 📶) Intimate, solar-powered wilderness lodge with private bathrooms, comfortable beds and an on-site restaurant. This is a great Porto Jofre base for jaguar-seeking boat trips that is affiliated with Pantanal Nature (p378). Other activities include night safaris on the Transpantaneira and bird-watching.

Hotel Porto Jofre Pantanal Norte LODGE $$$
(☎065-3637-1593; www.portojofre.com.br; Transpantaneira Km 145; s/d R$407/684; ⊙Mar-Oct; ❄@≋) This is a luxury hotel-lodge at the end of the road, catering almost exclusively to sport fishers on expensive packages. There's an airstrip, a marina and a nice restaurant, all of this right on the Rio São Lourenço.

Around Miranda

There are several excellent, high-end hotel-*fazendas* in this area.

Refúgio Ecológico Caiman LODGE $$$
(☎011-3706-1800, 067-3242-1450; www.caiman.com.br; r incl meals R$2570-3075; ❄≋) An ecopioneering lodge 36km north of Miranda and a private Pantanal for a privileged few. There are two lodges: Cordilheiro is the most remote and rustic with a great lookout tower, while Baiazinha is more playful, with a pool deck and position for spotting jaguars. Tours are led by on-site multilingual guides. An environmental charge of R$150 per guests applies.

There are an estimated 40 jaguars and 300 macaws on the property. Prices include meals and numerous activities, from canoeing to horseback riding; there is a three-night minimum in high season.

Along Estrada Parque

Estrada Parque runs off the main Campo Grande–Corumbá road (Hwy BR-262) at Buraco das Piranhas, 72km from Corumbá and 324km from Campo Grande. The first stretch of Estrada Parque penetrates 47km into the Pantanal, before it doglegs back toward Corumbá.

To get to the Estrada Parque you can take the Campo Grande–Corumbá bus and arrange for your lodge to pick you up (for a small fee) at the Buraco das Piranhas intersection.

Pousada Santa Clara POUSADA $$
(☎067-3384-0583; www.pantanalsantaclara.com.br; Office 12, Campo Grande bus station; 3-day package per person camping R$440, dm/d R$660/770; ❄≋) This is one of the most popular budget lodges in the southern Pantanal. A host of activities (hikes, piranha fishing, night safaris, horseback riding), accommodations to suit all budgets and hearty *panatneiro* cooking have clinched its popularity with the backpacker market. Expect large groups.

Pantanal Jungle Lodge LODGE $$$
(☎067-3325-8080; www.pantanaljunglelodge.com.br; 3-day, 2-night package in dm/d per person R$900/1100; ❄≋) This brand-new lodge is set to become another backpacker favorite, thanks to its enviable riverside location and well-organized activities – from canoeing and piranha fishing to night safaris on the river and wildlife-spotting treks. Lodge either in one of the breezy dorms or in a private room with air-conditioning.

Passo do Lontra Parque Hotel LODGE $$$
(☎067-3245-2407; www.passodolontra.com.br; Estrada Parque Km 10; chalet/apt R$400/520; ❄≋) A comfortable place with large *apartamentos* (rooms with private bathroom) and riverside chalets in an accessible location near the beginning of the Estrada Parque. Safaris along Rio Miranda are the focus.

Getting There & Away

Cuiabá is the main gateway to the northern Pantanal. Campo Grande is the principal southern launch point into the Pantanal, while Corumbá is a convenient point of access only if you are arriving from Bolivia. The route to Corumbá from Campo Grande runs via Aquidauana and Miranda.

There are direct flights to Cuiabá (p367), Campo Grande (p387) and Corumbá (p390) from other Brazilian destinations.

Getting Around

Roads in the Pantanal are unsurfaced, few in number and are frequently closed by rain. Since the lodges are the only places to sleep, drink and eat, and public transportation is very limited, independent travel is difficult. Unless you have extensive off-road experience, hiring a car is an option in the dry season only. Only the Transpantaneira in Mato Grosso and Estrada Parque in Mato Grosso do Sul go deep into the region. If you're not hiring a car, you have to arrange transportation in advance through a lodge.

MATO GROSSO DO SUL

Mato Grosso do Sul was created in 1977 when the military government decided it would be the best way to administer and develop such a large region (cynics claimed it was to provide more high-paying bureaucratic jobs for cronies). But even before the split, the area had a different economic and social makeup from the northern Mato Grosso.

In the late 19th century, many migrants from the south and southeast of Brazil arrived in the area, so Mato Grosso do Sul has a greater number of smaller farms and much more intensive agriculture when compared to the large farms and ranches in the north. All this is thanks to the rich, red earth, known as *terra roxa*.

The wealth created by the *terra roxa* has helped develop the state's modern agricultural sector. The main crop is soy, but there's also lots of corn, rice and cotton production and cattle farms. Mato Grosso do Sul also encompasses two-thirds of the Pantanal and the Serra da Bocaina, two wonderful natural areas that are popular with both Brazilian and foreign travelers.

Campo Grande

☎0XX67 / POP 842,000

Known as the Cidade Morena for its red earth rather than for its beautiful women (*morena* also means 'brunette'), Campo Grande is the capital of Mato Grosso do Sul and the main gateway to the southern Pantanal. It's a vast, modern metropolis, where high-rises tower above the shopping malls and streets are lined with restaurants – contrasting with the source of its wealth, which mainly lies in cattle and farming. Home to no less than four universities, Campo Grande is young at heart, its large student population producing an almost insatiable demand for nocturnal entertainment (hence the proliferation of bars and live-music venues).

Founded around 1875 as the village of Santo Antônio de Campo Grande, Campo Grande really began to grow when the railway came through in 1914. The city was declared the capital of Mato Grosso do Sul by decree of military president Ernesto Giesel in 1977.

Sights

Most of the city's attractions are found inside the immense Parque das Nações Indígenas, an ecological reserve with a lake, cycling and jogging track and a scattering of monuments and museums. You may spot capybaras by the river.

★Museu das Culturas Dom Bosco MUSEUM

(☎3326-9788; www.mcdb.org.br; Parque das Nações Indígenas; adult/child R$5/2.50; ⏲8am-4.30pm Tue-Sun) Built on the site of a *bororo* burial ground, this superb museum is divided into two parts. One is a collection of over 10,000 insects and stuffed flora and fauna, while the other is a visually striking, unmissable introduction to the indigenous people of the Mato Grosso region, with subtly lit underfloor and suspended-glass displays showcasing shaman paraphernalia, weaponry, everyday tools, splendid adornments made of feathers and funerary objects. The enlarged black-and-white photos are almost equally striking.

Look out for *xavante* coming-of-age ritual objects, elaborate clay figures illustrating the creation myth of the *karajá*, gorgeous macaw feather headdresses of the *bororo* and the rare funerary masks of the peoples from the Ulaupés River.

Aquario do Pantanal AQUARIUM

(Parque das Nações Indígenas) Originally slated for completion in June 2014, this ambitious aquarium/research center was still a long way from opening to the public at the time of writing. Eventually it will be the biggest freshwater aquarium in the world, housing 263 species of Pantanal fish and other native wildlife in gigantic walk-through tanks holding an incredible 6.6 million liters of water, as well as other freshwater fish from around the world.

The construction of the aquarium has been plagued with problems: it already costs four times more than the original estimate and 80% of its fish died during a cold snap because they couldn't be transferred from their holding tanks to the aquarium tanks, which should have been completed but weren't.

Museu de Arte Contemporânea de Mato Grosso do Sul (MARCO) MUSEUM

(Av Maria Coelho 6000; admission R$10; ⏲7.30am-5.30pm Tue-Fri, 2-6pm Sat & Sun) Just outside the northern gate of Parque das Nações Indígenas, this compact but well-presented modern-art museum showcases a permanent collection of works by local talent and temporary exhibits by other Brazilian artists.

Feira Central MARKET
(http://feiracentralcg.com.br; Av Calógeras & 14 de Julho; 5pm-late Wed-Fri, noon-late Sat & Sun) A great market worth a stroll, this massive open-air food and shopping court is lined with Japanese soba-noodle joints and other eateries, as well as some indigenous crafts and leatherwork. It's packed with revelers on weekends.

Sleeping

Hauzz Hostel HOSTEL $
(8118-7270; www.hauzzhostel.com; Piratininga 1527 ; s/d R$70/140;) A quiet, secure hostel with snug, fan-cooled rooms that share several bathrooms, run by delightful hostess Christina, who does her best to help in spite of the language barrier. A three-block walk to Shopping Campo Grande and handy for visiting Parque das Nações.

Oka Hostel HOSTEL $
(3026-7070; www.okabrasilhostel.com.br; Jeriba 454; dm/d R$65/150;) Several blocks south of Shopping Campo Grande, this lively backpacker hangout in a converted mansion scores points for its helpful English-speaking staff and common areas that encourage camaraderie between guests. The downside includes cramped dorms, air-con that struggles during the hottest time of year, the ratio of guests per bathroom and a location somewhat removed from the action.

Hotel Nacional HOTEL $
(3383-2461; Dom Aquino 610; s/d with air-con R$70/140, without air-con R$65/80;) A basic budget choice hugely popular with international backpackers and Brazilian student groups. Choose between simple digs with shared facilties and plusher ones with air-con, bathrooms and TV.

Turis Hotel HOTEL $$
(3382-2461; www.turishotel.com.br; Allan Kardec 200; s/d/tr R$151/226/275;) Modern and minimalist, this excellent option is entirely too trendy for its location and is very good value. Great breakfast, and the staff go out of their way to be helpful in spite of limited English.

Hotel Internacional BUSINESS HOTEL $$
(3027-0200; www.hotelintermetro.com.br; Allan Kardec 245; s/d/tr from R$150/175/220;) Good-value downtown hotel with snug rooms and a fantastic breakfast spread.

Bahamas Apart Hotel HOTEL $$
(3303-9393; www.bahamasaparthotel.com.br; José Antônio 1117; s/d/tr from R$236/331/383;) Sleek high-rise hotel with aquamarine window panes offering spacious two-story *apartamentos* with kitchenette, living and dining areas, bathtubs in the bathrooms and balconies overlooking the city. However, the plumbing can be temperamental and wi-fi comes and goes like a stray cat.

Grand Park Hotel BUSINESS HOTEL $$$
(3044-4444; www.grandparkhotel.com.br; Av Afonso Pena 5282; s/d/ste R$360/445/940;) The swishest option in the park area, with half the rooms rooms overlooking said park. Boons include spacious, spotless rooms with climate control, satellite TV, rooftop pool and a generous breakfast buffet. One for treating yourself after roughing it in the Pantanal.

Eating

Campo Grande boasts the third-highest Japanese population in Brazil and soba noodles feature prominently on some menus as well as at the Feira Central.

Restaurante da Gaucha SELF-SERVE $
(Allan Kardec 238; buffet R$13; 11.30am-11pm) Handy cheapie right near several central hotels, a backpacker favorite due to its rock-bottom prices and all-you-can-gobble, delicious buffet dishes.

Cantina Romana ITALIAN $$
(3324-9777; www.cantinaromana.com.br; Rua da Paz 237; mains for 2 R$38-60; 11am-2pm & 6-11pm) Shock-value old school Italian cantina and pizzeria, going strong since 1978. Attentive service, mega portions and authentic surroundings to indulge yourself in. We're big fans of its *gnocchi alla siciliana*. If you graze at the weekday lunchtime buffet, you won't need dinner.

Guacamole MEXICAN $$
(3201-3225; http://guacamolemex.com.br; Av Afonso Pena 3883; mains from R$30; 7pm-2am;) The owners have opted for an uber-Mexican theme (think primary colors and psychedelic cacti) and decided to run with it a few kilometers. Luckily, the dishes (chalupas, tacos, enchiladas, *alambres*, ceviche...) are all reasonably authentic. Late in the evening this becomes the place to be seen if you're a Campo Grande fashionista;

Campo Grande

a mariachi band provides entertainment (cover R$10).

Varandas do Pantanal PANTANEIRO **$$**
(Av Bom Pastor 306; mains R$13-45; 6pm-midnight Tue-Sat) At this very local spot, homesick Corumbá transplants gather for true *pantaneiro* cuisine. Standout dishes include *sarrabulho* (a hearty stew made with hearts, kidneys and liver) and *arroz pantaneiro* (rice cooked with sun-dried beef and sausage typical of the region), accompanied by fried banana. Wash it down with strong caipirinhas to the accompaniment of live music (Thursday to Saturday; cover R$6).

★**Gaucho Gastão** CHURRASCARIA **$$$**
(www.gauchogastao.com.br; Dr Zerbine 48; rodízio R$59; 11.30-2.30 & 6.30-midnight Mon-Sat, 11.30am-3pm Sun) On weekends in particular, this family-run *churrascaria* heaves with local families while the waiters are a whirlwind of skewers featuring succulent cuts of beef and pork, chicken hearts, grilled pineapple and all the other ingredients that add up to the perfect meat *rodízio*. Its signature melt-in-the-mouth *costela* (boneless beef rib) alone is worth the trip. *Por-kilo* available.

★**Casa do Peixe** SEAFOOD **$$$**
(3382-7121; www.casadopeixe.com.br; Dr João Rosa Pires 1030; mains from R$44; 11am-2pm & 6.30-11pm Mon-Sat, 11am-3pm Sun) This place rightfully deserves its reputation as the best *peixaria* (fish restaurant) in town, with a superior buffet accompanying the hearty mains. The *rodízio* is an awesome way to acquaint yourself with pintado, pacu and other fish of the Pantanal, cooked many sublime ways, while the inclusion of sushi and sashimi pays homage to the city's large Japanese population.

Campo Grande

Sights
1 Feira Central B1

Activities, Courses & Tours
2 Pantanal Viagens & Turismo A3

Sleeping
3 Bahamas Apart Hotel D3
4 Hotel Internacional A3
5 Hotel Nacional A3
6 Turis Hotel A3

Eating
7 Cantina Romana F2
8 Guacamole F3
9 Restaurante da Gaucha A3

Drinking & Nightlife
10 Muchachos D4
11 Territorio do Vinho F2

Shopping
12 Casa do Artesão B4
13 Feria de Artesanato de Artistas Sul Mato Grossenses C4

Drinking & Nightlife

Campo Grande's nightlife knows no evening off, especially beyond the 3900 block of Av Afonso Pena, east of downtown where there is a cluster of happening bars.

Cachaçaria Brasil BAR

(☎3313-6731; www.cachacariabrasilms.com.br; Av Fernando Correa da Costa 165; ⏲5pm-2am Mon-Sat) Samba, over 100 kinds of *cachaça* (sugarcane alcohol), an extensive food and drink menu, pool tables, nightly live music and live *futebol* (football) make this Campo Grande's in place for a crowd of all ages.

Territorio do Vinho WINE BAR

(☎3029-8464; www.territoriodovinho.com.br; Euclides da Cunha 485; ⏲7pm-1am Mon-Sat, plus 11am-3pm Sat & Sun) Stylish, jazz-tinged wine bar and restaurant by night and equally classy lunch spot on weekends, Territorio do Vinho is the place to acquaint yourself with Brazilian wines (though you can choose from hundreds of other vintages from its iPad menu). The menu? Gourmet Italian-Brazilian fusion. Dress nicely.

Muchachos SPORTS BAR

(José Antônio Pereira 509; ⏲5-11pm; closed Mon) Informal, lively bar where you can watch football on the big screen with a mixed expat and local crowd while sipping a Corona and sampling from the extensive Tex-Mex menu.

Café Mostarda BAR

(☎3301-9990; www.cafemostarda.com.br; Av Afonso Pena 3952; ⏲6pm-late Tue-Sun) The rich and beautiful practically trip over themselves onto Av Afonso Pena at this trendy outdoor cafe, with live rock music nightly.

Shopping

Casa do Artesão ARTS & CRAFTS

(☎3383-2633; Av Calogeras 2050; ⏲8am-6pm Mon-Fri, 9am-noon Sat) An excellent selection of indigenous arts, including colorful Terena ceramics and Kadiwéu wooden carvings depicting mythical figures, as well as 'jungle jewellery' that makes use of seeds and locally brewed liquor.

Feria de Artesanato de Artistas Sul Mato Grossenses HANDICRAFTS
(Praça Dos Imigrantes; ⏲9am-6pm Mon-Fri, 8am-noon Sat) High quality leatherwork and embroidery by local craftspeople.

Shopping Campo Grande MALL
(www.shoppingcampogrande.com.br; Av Alfonso Pena; ⏲10am-10pm Mon-Sat, 2-8pm Sun) Large shopping mall with multiplex cinema that screens international releases.

Information

MEDICAL SERVICES

Clínica Campo Grande (☎3323-9000; Marechal Rondon 1703) For medical emergencies.

MONEY

Banco do Brasil (Av Afonso Pena 2202; ⏲11am-4pm Mon-Fri) Visa/MasterCard ATM and money exchange.

Bradesco (Av Afonso Pena 1828; ⏲11am-4pm Mon-Fri) Visa/MasterCard ATM.

TRANSPORT FROM CAMPO GRANDE

Flights

DESTINATION	TIME (HR)	FREQUENCY	AIRLINE
Brasília	1¾	2-3 daily	Avianca (www.avianca.com.br), GOL (www.voegol.com.br), TAM (www.tam.com.br)
Cuiabá	1¼	2-5 daily	Avianca (www.avianca.com.br), Azul (www.voeazul.com.br), GOL (www.voegol.com.br)
Curitiba	1¼	daily except Sun & Mon	Azul (www.voeazul.com.br)
Londrina	1½	daily except Sun & Mon	Azul (www.voeazul.com.br)
Maringá	1¼	1-2 daily	Azul (www.voeazul.com.br), GOL (www.voegol.com.br)
Santa Cruz, Bolivia	1½	Mon & Fri	Amaszonas (www.amaszonas.com)
São Paulo	1¾	8-14 daily	Azul (www.voeazul.com.br), GOL (www.voegol.com.br), TAM (www.tam.com.br)

Buses

DESTINATION	TIME (HR)	FREQUENCY	COST (R$)	BUS COMPANY
Bonito	6½	2 daily	55	Cruzeiro do Sul (www.cruzeirodosulms.com.br)
Brasília	23½-24½	2 daily	238-261	Motta (www.motta.com.br), Viação São Luiz (www.viacaosaoluiz.com.br)
Corumbá	6	8 daily	105-125	Andorinha (www.andorinha.com)
Cuiabá	10-13	18 daily	92-123	Andorinha (www.andorinha.com), Eucatur (www.eucatur.com.br), Motta (www.motta.com.br), Nova Integração (www.novaintegracao.com.br), Viação São Luiz (www.viacaosaoluiz.com.br)
Foz do Iguaçu	18	5.40pm	150	Nova Integração (www.novaintegracao.com.br)
Ponta Porã	6	10 daily	80	Expresso Queiroz (www.expressoqueiroz.com.br), Cruzeiro do Sul (www.cruzeirodosulms.com.br), Viação São Luiz (www.viacaosaoluiz.com.br)
Rio de Janeiro	24	2 daily	303-317	Andorinha (www.andorinha.com)
São Paulo	15½	7 daily	207-223	Andorinha (www.andorinha.com), Motta (www.motta.com.br)

POST

Post office (cnr Av Calógeras & Dom Aquino; ⏲8am-5pm Mon-Fri, 8-11:30am Sat)

TOURIST INFORMATION

There are small tourist kiosks at the **bus station** (☎3314-4448; Rodoviária; ⏲6am-10pm), **airport** (☎3363-3116; ⏲6:15am-midnight) and the **Feira Central** (☎3314-3872; Feira Central; ⏲6-10pm Wed-Sun).

CAT Morada dos Bais (☎3314-9968; Av Afonso Pena; ⏲8am-6pm Tue-Sat, 9am-noon Sun) This helpful tourist office offers an excellent city map and an extensive database with information about the state and staff organize city tours. They won't recommend Pantanal tour companies though!

Getting There & Away

AIR

Aeroporto Internacional de Campo Grande (☎3368-6050; Av Duque de Caixas) The airport is 7km west of town.

BUS

Nondirect intercity buses to Corumbá stop in Miranda and Aquidauana, and can drop you at the intersection with Estrada Parque.

Campo Grande's plush **bus station** (☎3313-8707; Av Gury Marques 1215) is inconveniently located 6km west of the center on the road to São Paulo.

Vanzella (☎3255-3005; www.vanzellatransportes.com.br) has a handy minibus service that offers hotel pickup and runs to Bonito via Campo Grande airport at 9.30am, 2.30pm, 6pm and 11pm daily (R$100, four to five hours). Return services are at 7.30am, 10am, 12.30pm and 6.30pm.

Getting Around

TO/FROM THE AIRPORT

To get to the airport from the bus station, the Expreso Mato Grosso (R$9, hourly) is your best bet. To get a bus to the center from the airport, walk out of the airport to the bus stop on the main road and catch the 409 or the 441 (R$3). A taxi costs around R$40.

BUS

Local buses 61 and 87 (R$3) connect the long-distance bus station to the city center. There's also the hourly Expreso Mato Grosso (R$9) door-to-door service. To use city buses you need to buy an an Assetur *passe de ônibus* (bus pass) from newsstands, pharmacies or bus-stop kiosks. They come as one-time use (*unitario*) or rechargable (*recarregável*). A taxi to the center will cost around R$30.

Corumbá

☎0XX67 / POP 97,900

'Corumbaly' (old Corumbá) is a gracefully aging port city close to the Bolivian border. Known as Cidade Branca (White City), it is 403km northwest of Campo Grande by road. The city sits atop a steep hill overlooking the Rio Paraguai; on the far side of the river, a huge expanse of the Pantanal stretches out on the horizon. Divided into two parts, the upper city contains most of the commerce, and the lower city is the old port area.

Founded in 1776 by Captain Luis de Albuquerque, by 1840 it had become the biggest river port in the world. The impressive, brightly painted buildings along the waterfront reflect the wealth that passed through the town in the 19th century before Corumbá went into decline with the coming of the railway.

Sights & Activities

★Muhpan — MUSEUM

(Museu de História do Pantanal; ☎3232-0303; www.muhpan.org.br; Manoel Cassava 275; ⏲1-6pm Tue-Sat) FREE On the waterfront, this partially interactive museum tells the story of the formation of the Pantanal and 10,000 years of human habitation in the region. Exhibits range from presentations on the flora and fauna in different parts of the great wetlands to the history of European exploration of this hard land and the founding of Corumbá. Look out for a splendid *bororo* headdress of macaw feathers, and some wonderful vintage photos of indigenous people and Pantaneiro *gaúchos* herding cattle.

Forte de Coimbra — FORT

(⏲8.30-11am & 1.30-4pm) FREE Located some 80km downriver from Corumbá along Rio Paraguai, this large fort was built in 1775 to repel invaders from Paraguay, which it failed to do quite spectacularly in 1864, when it was overrun by the Paraguayan army. As the fort is on Brazilian army territory, tour agencies have to obtain visiting permission. Tours are done either by boat – a spectacular journey that passes by two impressive caves – or by driving to Porto Morrinho and then continuing by boat. Expect to pay around R$300 for a tour; lunch is included.

Cristo Rei do Pantanal — VIEWPOINT

Easily reachable via a short but steep walk or taxi ride uphill, Corumbá's answer to

Corumbá

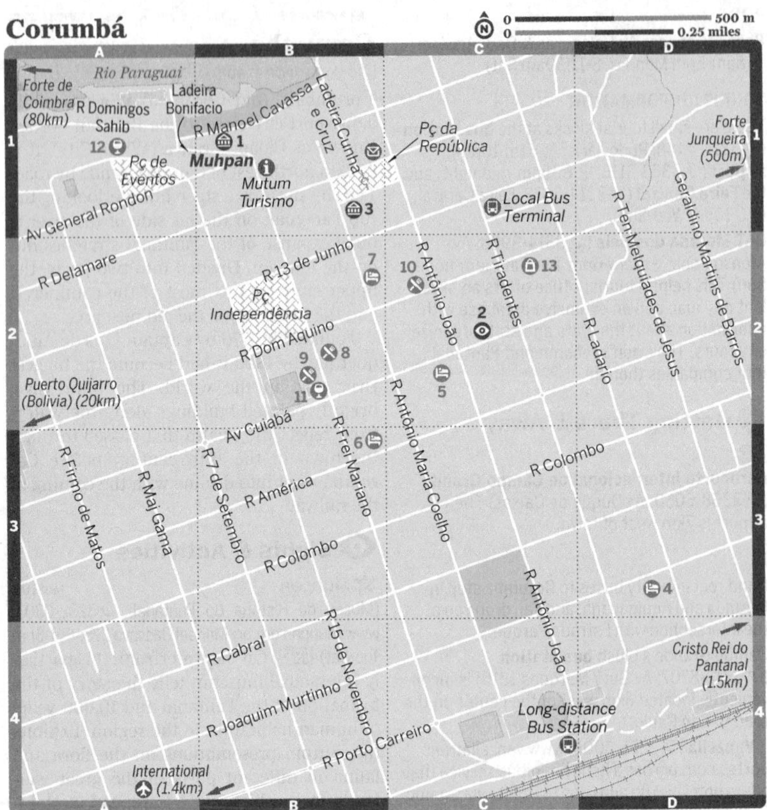

Corumbá

Top Sights
1 Muhpan ... B1

Sights
2 Art Izu ... C2
3 Museu de Corumbá ... B1

Sleeping
4 Hostel Pantanal ... D3
5 Hotel Laura Vicuña ... C2
6 Hotel Nacional ... B3
7 Santa Mônica Palace Hotel ... B2

Eating
8 Avalom Grill ... B2
9 Laço do Ouro ... B2
10 Peixaria do Lulu ... C2

Drinking & Nightlife
11 Dolce Cafe ... B2
12 Vivabella ... A1

Shopping
13 Casa de Artesão ... C2

Cristo Redentor presents you with sweeping views of the town and the Pantanal in the distance. Clear mornings are best.

Forte Junqueira FORT
(☎3231-5828; Cáceres 425; ⏰9:30-11am & 2-4pm Mon-Fri) FREE Forte Junqueira is a tiny hexagonal fort with 50cm-thick walls. The real highlight here is the excellent view of the Rio Paraguai and the Pantanal in the distance. To get here, go east along Dom Aquino and turn left at the athletics ground. Once you hit the waterfront, continue east for another 10 minutes. The entrance is an unmarked door to the left of the main gate.

Museu de Corumbá MUSEUM
(Instituto Luiz de Albuquerque; ☎3231-5757; Delamare 939) FREE The Instituto Luiz de Albuquerque houses the Museu de Corumbá, which contains a reasonably interesting collection of indigenous artifacts and local modern art. It was closed for renovation for an unspecified period of time during our last visit.

Art Izu BUILDING
(Av Cuiabá 558; ⏲8-11am & 1-5pm Mon-Fri) Art Izu is home to one of Corumbá's premier artists, Izulina Xavier. You can't miss it – the giant bird sculptures and bronze statue of São Francisco in the front yard are stunning and the crazy paving in front is, well, crazy. You can purchase some handicrafts inside.

Festivals

Carnaval CARNAVAL
(www.carnavaldecorumba.com.br; ⏲Feb/Mar) One of Brazil's biggest and best Carnavals really makes this hot, sleepy backwater come to life. The tradition was imported here by naval officers, many from Rio, who found themselves stationed here and felt the need to liven things up.

Sleeping

Hotel Laura Vicuña HOTEL $
(☎3231-5874; www.hotellauravicuna.com.br; Av Cuiabá 775; s/d/tr R$90/130/168; ❄📶) Cheapish central option with everything you are likely to need (clean, compact rooms, air-con, good wi-fi, hot showers) without being the sort of place that memories are made of.

Hostel Pantanal HOSTEL $
(☎9641-5524; Joaquin Murtino 359; dm/d R$40/130; 📶) These bargain basement backpacker digs have only two saving graces: proximity to the bus station and an English-speaking owner who can help arrange onward passage to Bolivia.

Hotel Nacional HOTEL $$
(☎3234-6000; www.hnacional.com.br; América 936; s/d R$195/260; ❄📶🏊) The swishest option in town, popular with visiting fishers. Amenities include gym and pool, but the mattresses could be comfier, the breakfast more generous and you're likely to see ladies of negotiable affection haunting the lobby.

Santa Mônica Palace Hotel BUSINESS HOTEL $$
(☎3234-3000; www.hsantamonica.com.br; Coelho 345; s/d R$183/231; ❄📶🏊) A favorite with tour groups, this is a partially revamped hotel in the center of town with antiquated telephones and minibars. Rooms are compact, but breakfast is extensive, albeit with lines during peak time as there are not enough tables.

GETTING TO/FROM BOLIVIA

The Fronteira bus (R$3, 15 minutes) goes from Corumbá's Praça Independência to the Bolivian border every 25 minutes from 6am to 7pm. A taxi from the center to the border is around R$40 while groups of two or less traveling light are better off using a moto-taxi (R$24).

All Brazilian exit formalities must be completed with the **Polícia Federal** (☎3234-7822; www.dpf.gov.br; ⏲8-11am & 2-5pm Mon-Fri, 9am-1pm Sat & Sun) at the border. Both countries work limited matching office hours, so be prepared to overnight in Corumbá if you are crossing outside of them. To enter Bolivia, most countries do not need a visa, but citizens of the United States must obtain a visa (US$135) from abroad or at the **Bolivian Consulate** (☎3231-5605; consuladoboliviacorumba@gmail.com; cnr Porto Carrero & Firmo de Matos; ⏲8am-12:30pm & 2-5:30pm Mon-Fri) in Corumbá.

In Bolivia *colectivos* (B$5) and taxis (around B$30) run the 3km between the border and Quijarro train station for onward travel to Santa Cruz. There are two options: the faster and more comfortable Ferrobus which departs at 6pm on Tuesday, Thursday and Saturday (13 hours, B$235), arriving at 7am, and the cheaper Expreso Oriental that leaves at 1pm on Tuesday, Thursday and Sunday (16¾ hours, B$70), arriving at 5.40am. Buy tickets in advance if you can. The Ferrobus makes the return journey from Santa Cruz on Monday, Wednesday and Friday at 6pm, arriving at 7am, while the Expreso Oriental departs on the same days at 1.20pm, arriving at 6.02am.

The road from Puerto Quijarro to Santa Cruz is in decent condition and bus journeys take about half the time of train journeys.

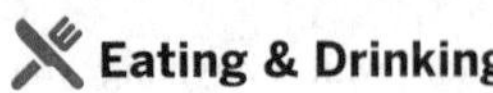

Eating & Drinking

Avalom Grill INTERNATIONAL $$

(☎3231-4430; Frei Mariano 499; mains R$19-50; ⊙11am-3pm & 7-11pm Mon-Sat; ☑) Upscale Avalom's popularity may be waning, but its menu still pays homage to the diverse groups of Corumbá's settlers, with indigenous, Portuguese, French, Spanish and Italian dishes, some of which are executed better than others. Fig salad with gorgonzola and homemade pizza are excellent. Steaks? Thumbs down.

Laço do Ouro CHURRASCARIA $$

(☎3231-7371; Frei Mariano 556; rodízio R$39; ⊙10am-2am) *Corumbaense* flock to this unpretentious, family-run *churrascaria* for the best meat *rodízio* in town at lunchtimes; dinner is à la carte.

Peixaria do Lulu SEAFOOD $$

(☎3232-7855; Dom Aquino 738; mains R$38-50; ⊙11am-3pm & 6:30-11pm Mon-Sat) Friendly, family-run Lulu is the fried-fish king in Corumbá. Don't let the humble appearance fool you – the pacu and pintado dishes are terrific.

Vivabella BAR

(☎3232-3587; Arthur Mangabeira 1; ⊙6pm-late Mon-Sat) Vivabella is perched precariously on a hillside over the Rio Paraguai. Watch the sunsets over the Pantanal on the outdoor deck while sipping beer or caipirinhas, or turn up later for live music.

Dolce Cafe BAR

(Frei Mariano 572; ⊙5.30-11pm) Locals with huge tankards of beer pack the outdoor tables at this hugely popular cafe in the evenings. The food – fried chicken, burgers and more – is the ideal accompaniment to watching soccer on the big screen.

Shopping

Casa de Artesão ARTS & CRAFTS

(Dom Aquino 405; ⊙8:30-11am & 2-5pm Mon-Fri) The old prison has swapped inmates for artists, who hawk their wooden carvings, baskets and leatherwork from former cells.

Information

EMERGENCY

Federal Police (☎3231-5848; Praça da República 51; ⊙8.30-11:30am & 1:30-5pm Mon-Fri)

MEDICAL SERVICES

Hospital Santa Casa (☎3231-2441; 15 de Novembro 854)

MONEY

If you're crossing to or from Bolivia, the money changers at the border give a much better rate than those in town. All banks listed have ATMs that accept foreign cards.

Banco do Brasil (Rua 13 de Junho 914)

Bradesco (Delamare 1067)

POST

Post office (Delamare 708; ⊙8:30am-5pm Mon-Fri, 8-11:30am Sat)

TRAVEL AGENCIES

Pantanal tours, and boat and fishing tours of the Corumbá environs, are available from all travel agencies or by consultation in the boat offices along the port road Manoel Cassava.

Mutum Turismo (☎3231-1818; www.mutumturismo.com.br; Frei Mariano 17; ⊙8am-6pm Mon-Fri, to 1pm Sat) A reliable and long-established travel agency for Pantanal river cruises. Can recommend reputable guides.

Getting There & Away

AIR

Corumbá International Airport (☎3231-3322; Santos Dumont) is 3km west of the town center. Currently it only serves São Paulo with Azul (two hours; Monday, Wednesday and Friday).

BUS

The **long-distance bus station** (☎3231-2033; Porto Carreiro) is 10blocks south of the center. A taxi to the center costs around R$20, a moto-taxi around R$7.

BUSES FROM CORUMBÁ

DESTINATION	COST (R$)	TIME (HR)	FREQUENCY	COMPANY
Bonito	81	5	daily at 7am	Cruzeiro do Sul (www.cruzeirodosulms.com.br)
Campo Grande	103-123	6	8 daily	Andorinha (www.andorinha.com)
Ponta Porã	130	12	daily at 7am	Cruzeiro do Sul (www.cruzeirodosulms.com.br)

Getting Around

The hourly Popular Nova bus to the airport runs from the **local bus terminal** (Rua 13 de Junho).

A taxi from the center to the airport costs around R$30; taxis use meters.

Bonito & Around

☎0XX67 / POP 17,000

Bonito is *the* ecotourism model for Brazil. This small aquatic playground in the southwestern corner of Mato Grosso do Sul has few attractions of its own, but the natural resources of the surrounding area are spectacular, and local authorities have taken the high road in their regulation and maintenance. There are caves with lakes and amazing stalactite formations, beautiful waterfalls and incredibly clear rivers surrounded by lush forest where it's possible to swim eyeball to eyeball with hundreds of fish.

Since Bonito exploded on the ecotourism map in the early 1990s, the number of visitors has risen dramatically every year, leading to the creation of the 76-sq-km Serra da Bodoquena national park in 2000. Though some of the attractions are within the park boundaries, the vast majority of the protected area is off-limits to visitors.

Bonito is a one-street town. Coronel Pilad Rebuá is a 3km stretch that is home to everything you are likely to need during your stay.

Sights & Activities

There are few things to do around town, although the surrounding area has become more accessible now that more and more places are renting bicycles. For most activities, a guided tour is mandatory.

Project Jibóia SNAKE SHOW

(☎8419-0313; www.projetojiboia.com.br; Nestor Fernandes 610; admission R$25; ⏲7pm) Project Jibóia is a one-man crusade to change the world's opinion of snakes by showing that they're not necessarily dangerous and can be lovable. You're treated to a 90-minute stand-up show in Portuguese with audience participation, complete with boa constrictors that you nearly swap spit with by the end of the night. You'll either love it or hate it.

Aquario do Bonito AQUARIUM

(Rua 24 de Fevereiro 2083; admission R$25; ⏲9am-11pm) If you can't tell a pacu from a piraputanga, wade through this makeshift aquarium of Pantanal *peixes*. A rainy-day activity.

Balneário Municipal SWIMMING

(admission R$25; ⏲8am-6pm) One of the few natural attractions that doesn't need a guide is the Balneário Municipal, a natural swimming pool on the Rio Formoso with clear water, nice beach and lots of fish, 7km southeast of town. You can spend the whole day here and have lunch at the kiosks. Get there by cycling or else moto-taxi (around R$10 one way).

Tours

The local government has strict regulations in place for visiting the area's natural attractions, partly because many are on private land and partly to minimize the impact on some pristine areas. Most attractions have a daily limit on the number of visitors they will accept, and an authorized, locally registered guide must accompany visitors at all sites. Not all guides speak English.

BONITO: A BEAUTIFUL WATER WORLD

If you've never tried freshwater snorkeling in Bonito (or Bom Jardim) before, it's a remarkable experience. You peer at the curious fish surrounding you, the tiny fish nibbling on your skin, marvel at how you can make out the detail of every dead leaf lining the bottom of the river in HD clarity, or suck in your belly as the current carries you over the obstacle course of dead tree trunks. But how did this happy accident of nature happen? The river waters spring from subterranean sources in a limestone base, almost entirely free of clay, which releases calcium carbonate into the water. The calcium carbonate calcifies all impurities in the water, which then sink to the riverbed (this is the reason you're asked to stay afloat and not touch the bottom during river tours). The result is an area filled with natural aquariums surrounded by lush forest – a beautiful environment in which to study the abundant and fascinating fish of the rivers and streams.

Bonito

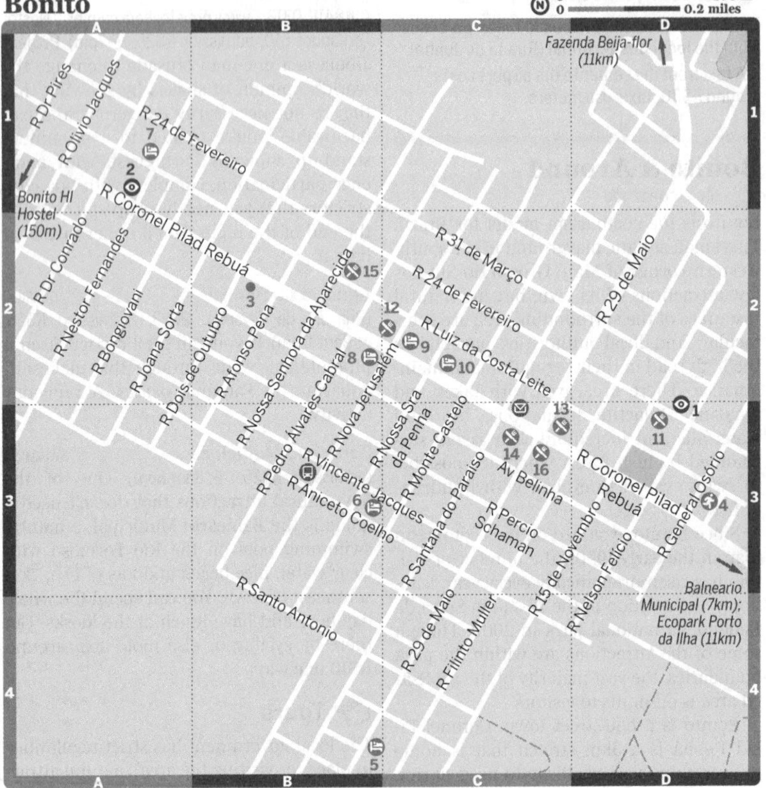

Prices of attractions are regulated by their owners, so it makes no difference, price-wise, which company you book your tour through. However, transport is usually only included in the cost when you book through a hotel, not an agency, but it sometimes depends on group size and you should ask in advance.

Snorkeling and *flutação* (flotation) in Bonito's incredibly clear waters are the main attractions, but remember that sunscreen and insect repellent are not allowed. Rappelling at the Abismo de Anhumas involves completing a course the day before at its **rappelling training center** (General Osório; 9am-6pm), while the Boca da Onça Ecotour requires you to rappel first at its own **training center** (Coronel Pilad Rebuá; 8.30am-6pm) if you wish to take part in that particular activity. Many of the best tours take a full day and will include lunch.

In the high season, the most popular tours must be booked in advance. You'll need a solid three days to take in the best of Bonito.

★ **Abismo de Anhumas** ADVENTURE TOUR

(www.abismoanhumas.com.br; rappelling R$633, scuba diving R$891) You rappel into a gigantic, beautiful cave that culminates in an underground lake. Nothing stands between you and the 72m drop apart from your safety harness and the rope you're clipped to. After you make it down, it's time for a spin around the lake to admire the beautiful rock formations. Then you dive or snorkel in the frigid underwater world (visibility is 30m), with phallic pinnacles rising from the depths, before climbing the rope back out. A heart-stopping experience.

The whole thing is otherworldly – Bonito's most unforgettable attraction by a landslide, limited to 18 visitors per day.

Bonito

Sights
1 Aquario do Bonito ... D3
2 Project Jibóia ... A1

Activities, Courses & Tours
3 Boca da Onça Training Center ... B2
4 Rappelling Training Center ... D3

Sleeping
5 Hotel Pousada Águas de Bonito ... B4
6 Papaya Hostel ... B3
7 Pousada Galeria Artes ... A1
8 Pousada Muito Bonito ... B2
9 Pousada Remanso ... C2
10 Pousada São Jorge ... C2

Eating
11 A Casa do João ... D3
12 Cantinho do Peixe ... C2
13 O Casarão ... C3
14 Pantanal Grill ... C3
15 San Marino Pizza ... B2
16 Vicio da Gula Café ... C3

Drinking & Nightlife
Taboa Bar ... (see 13)

★Rio da Prata SNORKELING
(www.riodaprata.com.br; 5hr trip incl lunch R$218; 6:30am-2pm) The marvelous Rio da Prata, 56km south of Bonito, includes a trek through rainforest and some great snorkeling. The latter involves a 3km float downstream along the Rio Olha d'Agua, amazingly crystal clear and full of fish; and Rio da Prata, a little foggier but still fantastic for viewing massive pacu and big, scary dourado.

Lagoa Misteriosa DIVING, SNORKELING
(www.lagoamisteriosa.com.br) No one know the true depth of this crystal-clear cenote; researchers have only reached a depth of 200m and that's not the cave lake's deepest part. You can snorkel and marvel at the seemingly infinite blue, interspersed with drowned tree trunks, but it's scuba divers and cave divers (appropriate certification mandatory) who get the best of this watery world.

Lagoa Misteriosa is only open for several months per year and can get rather crowded.

Nascente Azul SNORKELING
(www.nascenteazul.com.br; full day incl lunch adult/5-11yr R$172/53) This fabulous *flutação* attraction, 29km from town, begins with a 1900m forest trek that culminates in your arrival at the breathtakingly beautiful *nascente* (spring), an indigo-colored gateway to the center of the earth. From here you leisurely float your way back to base along a crystal-clear forest stream teeming with fish.

Gruta do Lago Azul CAVE
(half-day excursion R$45) The centerpiece of this large, vaulted cave is a luminous underground lake with incredibly clear water and seemingly immeasurable depths (over 70m by the current estimates). The cave lies 20km west of Bonito and is worth visiting for the strange stalactite formations alone. It's truly miraculous in late December and early January, when the sun shines in at just the right angle, illuminating the lake. Wear sturdy footwear.

Boca da Onça Ecotour SWIMMING
(3268-1711; www.bocadaonca.com.br; trekking incl lunch adult/6-11yr R$183/145, incl rappelling R$399; 9:30am-6pm) The Boca da Onça Ecotour, 59km northwest of Bonito, is a manicured 4km trail through the forest to a series of 11 waterfalls, a few of which you can take a chilly dip in. It all culminates with the 156m Boca da Onça waterfall, an impressive cascading waterfall that takes the state's highest honors. Rapelling is possible from reportedly the highest platform in Brazil here, and there is an excellent lunch and hang time by a fantastic natural river-water pool.

Buraco das Araras BIRDWATCHING
(www.buracodasararas.com.br; admission R$55) A sunset visit to Buraco das Araras, the world's largest sinkhole, is usually tagged on to a day out at Rio da Prata and Laguna Misteriosa. It's a 1km walk, complete with two viewpoints, that allows you to watch dozens of scarlet macaws flying home to roost, their cries piercing the air. An impressive spectacle.

Ecopark Porto da Ilha WATER SPORTS
(3255-3021; www.portodailha.eco.br; Coronel Pilad Rebuá 18900) Twelve kilometers south of town, you can paddleboard next to waterfalls, go rafting or floating in an inner tube down gentle rapids, go canoeing and try your hand (or foot) at slacklining over a deep, clear pool. The restaurant serves large plates of solid local dishes and hamburgers.

CROSSING THE BORDER TO PARAGUAY

Brazilian formalities take place at the **Federal Police** (☎3437-0500; Av Presidente Vargas 70; ⏰9am-noon & 1-4pm Mon-Fri) in the town center. Outside of working hours, if you can prove your need to travel is urgent, they will stamp you. The **Paraguayan immigration office** (☎3431-6312; Guia Lopes; ⏰7am-9pm) is five blocks away from the Brazilian Federal Police office.

From the bus station on Alberdi in Pedro Juan Caballero, there are hourly buses to Asunción (eight to 10 hours) and Concepción (five hours).

Fazenda Beija-flor BIRDWATCHING
(☎3255-4844; www.apiariobeijaflor.com.br) On the banks of Rio Mimoso, 11km south of Bonito, this former cattle grazing ground has been transformed into a private conservation area. On the grounds of this *fazenda* you can spot a great variety of birds, particularly several different species of hummingbirds. Horseback riding is also available.

Sleeping

Bonito's stupendous popularity during peak season (December to March) means that you should book ahead to get the lodgings you want. Out of season, higher-end options may slash their prices by as much as 50%.

Papaya Hostel HOSTEL $
(☎3255-4690; www.papayahostelbonito.com; Vicente Jacques 1868; dm/d R$50/150; ❄@🛜🏊) This papaya-colored hostel, handily located near the bus station, is the kind of place where backpackers find themselves delaying their departure, seduced by the poolside chill-out area, communal barbecues, fellow travelers to chat with while cooking and a plethora of tours organized by the helpful, English-speaking owner.

Bonito HI Hostel HOSTEL $
(☎8180-7231; www.bonitohostel.com.br; Lúcio Borralho 716; dm R$48, d with/without air-con R$135/115; ❄@🛜🏊) 🍃 One of Brazil's top HI hostels, this well-oiled backpacker haunt is a bit far from the action, but perks include hammocks, pool, large lockers, kitchen, laundry, bikes for hire and multilingual staff. Dorms come with private bathrooms, and the private rooms with air-con (a must in summer!) are hotel standard. The owner is unlikely to win any congeniality prizes.

Pousada São Jorge INN $
(☎3255-4046; Coronel Pilad Rebuá 1605; dm/s/d/tr R$33/100/130/150; ❄@🛜) There's decent English spoken and a really good breakfast at this budget option, run by an extremely friendly couple who can help you organize your stay. Some rooms are a little dark and the dorms would benefit from mosquito-proofed windows.

Pousada Galeria Artes POUSADA $$
(☎3255-4843; www.pousadagaleriaartes.com.br; Luiz da Costa Leite 1053; s/d/tr/f R$185/285/365/455; 🚭❄🛜🏊) Run by the delightful, multilingual and well-traveled proprietor Maria, this peaceful haven a few blocks from the center is set around a pool. Rooms are a little on the dark side but comfortable and spotless, breakfast ingredients come from a nearby farm and the pousada makes a point of exhibiting contemporary art.

Pousada Muito Bonito POUSADA $$
(☎3255-1645; www.hotelmuitobonito.com.br; Coronel Pilad Rebuá 1444; s/d/tr R$180/250/230; P❄@🛜) 🍃 You will struggle to find better value than at this excellent budget pousada in the center. Administered by the second generation of the pioneering Doblack family, it offers revamped, well-appointed budget rooms around a small courtyard. These guys also run one of the most popular tour agencies in town and are happy to provide plenty of information on the area.

Pousada Remanso HOTEL $$
(☎3255-1137; www.pousadaremanso.com.br; Coronel Pilad Rebuá 1515; s/d/tr from R$137/209/279; P❄🛜🏊) Good-value, midrange hotel right in the heart of town, with leather hammocks, nicely maintained landscaping and a small pool and hot tub.

Hotel Pousada Águas de Bonito HOTEL $$
(☎3255-2330; www.aguasdebonito.com.br; Rua 29 de Maio 1679; r R$389-706; ❄🛜🏊) A little out of the center, this two-story retreat comes with a recommended restaurant, peaceful surroundings and generally helpful staff (even though not all speak English). Rooms are modern and spacious; the ones on the second level have pleasant patios.

Eating

Vicio da Gula Café BURGERS **$**

(☎3255-2041; Coronel Pilad Rebuá 1852; burgers R$13-24; ⊙noon-2am) Popular corner spot for great burgers, fries and *açaí na tigela* (a berrylike fruit, in a bowl). The cake display may delay your exit.

San Marino Pizza PIZZERIA **$$**

(☎3255-2656; Luiz da Costa Leite 1543; pizzas R$29-43; ⊙6pm-midnight Wed-Mon; 🄴) The cheese-laden pizza pie from this outlet of the Campo Grande pizzeria is the best in town. The *calabresa* and the veggie-friendly *paulista* are our favorites. The sweet dessert pizzas are an acquired taste.

O Casarão BUFFET **$$**

(☎3255-1970; Coronel Pilad Rebuá 1835; buffet R$35; ⊙11.30am-2.30pm & 6.30-10.30pm Mon-Sat, 11.30am-3pm Sun) Bouncing buffet joint on the main drag. Hugely popular with locals on Sundays, when most other places are closed.

Cantinho do Peixe SEAFOOD **$$**

(☎3255-3381; Coronel Pilad Rebuá 1437; mains R$25-62; ⊙11am-3pm & 6-11pm; 📶) Pintado (giant catfish), fresh from Rio Miranda, ends up on plates 15 different ways at this simple restaurant. Start with the piranha soup and move on to *pintado á urucum*, a lasagna-like dish, or else opt for the *moqueca* (claypot stew) with all the trimmings.

Pantanal Grill CHURRASCARIA **$$**

(☎3255-2763; Coronel Pilad Rebuá 1808; mains R$30-65; ⊙10am-11pm Mon-Sat; ❄) 🍃 Got a craving for capybara with bacon? What about peccary with pineapple? Fancy some grilled caiman? Pantanal Grill's got it all, as well as succulent bacon-wrapped veal medallions for more traditional palates. Don't worry, the meat (caiman notwithstanding) is farmed, not wild.

★**A Casa do João** SEAFOOD **$$$**

(☎3255-1212; www.casadojoao.com.br; Nelson Felicio 664a; mains R$28-54; ⊙11:30am-2:30pm & 6-11:30pm) 🍃 Top spot in town for fish dishes, especially famous for its *traíra* (a predatory fish), which comes in a range of sizes and styles: soup, grilled and served with passion-fruit sauce. All the furniture here is made from reclaimed wood from fallen trees in the area.

Drinking

Taboa Bar BAR

(☎3255-1862; www.taboa.com.br; Coronel Pilad Rebuá 1837; ⊙5pm-late) A graffiti-clad institution on the main drag where locals and travelers converge over the house special: *pinga (cachaça)* with honey, cinnamon and guaraná. The food ain't bad, either.

ℹ Information

Lodgings have all the tourist information you need and will waste no time in telling you what your options are.

Some travel agencies are more helpful than others and can organize English-speaking guides.

Banco do Brasil (Luiz da Costa Leite 2279; ⊙9am-2pm) Accepts foreign Visa and MasterCard.

Bradesco (Colonel Pilad Rebuá 1942) Handy for cash withdrawals.

Hospital Darci Bigaton (☎3255-3455; Pedro Apóstolo 201)

Post office (Coronel Pilad Rebuá 1759; ⊙8-11:30am & 1-4pm Mon-Fri)

BUSES FROM BONITO

DESTINATION	COST (R$)	TIME (HR)	FREQUENCY
Campo Grande (bus)	55	6	noon & 6pm
Campo Grande (minibus)	100	5	7.30am, 10am, 12.30pm & 6.30pm
Corumbá (bus)	81	6	12.30pm
Corumbá (minibus)	120	5	2-3 weekly
Estrada Parque (minibus)	100	3½	1 daily
Foz do Iguaçu (minibus)	200	12	2 weekly
Ponta Porã (bus)	64	7½	noon

Getting There & Away

AIR

There are two weekly flights with **Azul** (www.voeazul.com.br) between Bonito and São Paulo (Campinas) airport on Sundays and Wednesdays (1½ hours); more operate during high season.

BUS

The bus station is handily located three blocks south of the main street.

Cruzeiro do Sul (www.cruzeirodosulms.com.br) is the only bus company that serves Bonito. For Foz do Iguaçu you can either head to Campo Grande and catch a direct bus from there or get a direct minibus transfer from Bonito.

Vanzella (☎3255-3005; www.vanzellatransportes.com.br) offers door-to-door van service to Campo Grande, Estrada Parque in the southern Pantanal, Foz do Iguaçu and the Bolivian border, passing through Corumbá.

Getting Around

Many of Bonito's attractions are a fair hike from town, and there's no public transport. Some guesthouses lend their guests bicycles, or you can rent a decent mountain bike along the main street for around R$30 per day. Hotels often provide transport, but not always. If you find yourself looking for transport, try the local shuttle service, Vanzella which will take you to any excursion provided there is a minimum of four people.

If you are part of a group, it might end up being more economical to hire a taxi for the full day (R$80 to R$180 depending on the distance) from any Ponto de Táxi. If you are on your own take your friendly neighborhood moto-taxi: to the Rio Sucuri (38km round-trip) and Gruta do Lago Azul (38km round-trip) costs R$56; to Abismo Anhumas (41km round-trip) costs R$60; to Rio da Prata (100km round-trip) costs R$120; and to Boca da Onça (120km round-trip) R$140. The drivers can either wait around or come back for you.

Ponta Porã

☎0XX67 / POP 69,000

It's a strange feeling to cross a street and change countries, but you can do just that in Ponta Porã, a bustling little border town divided from the Paraguayan town of Pedro Juan Caballero by Av Internacional. The beer changes from Skol to Pilsen, you see flasks of *tereré* (iced maté) and prices on electronics are slashed – other than that, it's hard to even notice there is a border here (Portunhol vernacular is rampant). There are only two reasons to come: because you are a member of the hordes of Brazilian bargain hunters, or because you are crossing the border to Paraguay. Extra caution is a good idea at night.

Avenida Internacional is lined with a plethora of restaurants. If you must stay the night, **Hotel Barcelona** (☎3437-2500; www.hotelbarcelona.com.br; Guia Lopes 50; s/d R$189/270; P ❄ @ 🛜 ≋) is centrally located, with big rooms (aged furniture free of charge) that could use better maintenance and a nice pool. **Hotel Internacional** (☎3431-1243; www.grupointerhoteis.com.br; Av Internacional 2604; r from $R120; P ❄ 🛜) is also central but its rooms are cheaper and fan-cooled.

The **bus station** (☎3431-4145) is 4km out of town. A local bus (R$3) runs between the main bus station and the central local bus station every 45 minutes until 10pm.

For Foz do Iguaçu, take a bus from the station on Alberdi in Pedro Juan Caballero (Paraguay) to Ciudad del Este (six hours, three daily), just across the border from Foz. You don't need a Paraguayan visa to transit through Paraguay on your way to Foz do Iguaçu, but you do need an entry stamp.

BUSES FROM PONTA PORÃ

DESTINATION	TIME (HR)	FREQUENCY	COST (R$)	COMPANY
Bonito	6½	daily at 6am	64	Cruzeiro do Sul (www.cruzeirodosulms.com.br)
Campo Grande	5½-6	10 daily	61-80	Cruzeiro do Sul (www.cruzeirodosulms.com.br), Expresso Queiroz (www.expressoqueiroz.com.br), Viação São Luiz (www.viacaosaoluiz.com.br)
Corumbá	12½	daily at 6am	130	Cruzeiro do Sul (www.cruzeirodosulms.com.br)
São Paulo	21	3 daily	245-307	Motta (www.motta.com.br)

Bahia

POP 15 MILLION

Includes ➡

Best Places to Eat

- Rabanete (p452)
- Caranguejo de Sergipe (p416)
- Lampião (p462)
- Restaurante do Senac (p415)
- Paraíso Tropical (p416)

Best Beaches

- Trancoso (p451)
- Morro de São Paulo (p431)
- Itacaré (p437)
- Praia do Espelho (p452)
- Arraial d'Ajuda (p449)

Why Go?

Africa meets South America in the staggeringly beautiful northeastern state of Bahia. The heady blend of two seemingly disparate cultures – classic Portuguese architecture and African drum beats, Catholic churches and Candomblé (Afro-Brazilian religion) – is unique, and for most travelers, truly intoxicating. Bahia's centerpiece is Salvador, a jewel-box colonial city with gilded churches, cobblestone streets, lively festivals, powerful percussion reverberating off old stone walls and capoeiristas battling against the backdrops of 16th-century buildings. The Afro-Brazilian capital is especially traveler-friendly these days: Salvador underwent a minor face lift before serving as a World Cup host city in 2014. Beyond the city limits, Bahia awaits with more than 900km of coastline, World Heritage–listed sites, deserted beaches and paradisaical islands. In the south, idyllic coastal villages attract vacationers and divers, while inland, the spectacular Parque Nacional da Chapada Diamantina features waterfalls and quiet hiking paths waiting to be explored.

When to Go

Salvador

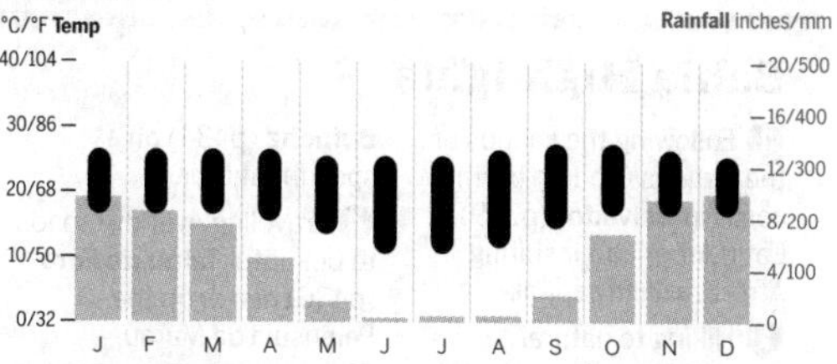

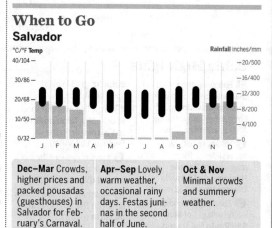

Dec–Mar Crowds, higher prices and packed pousadas (guesthouses) in Salvador for February's Carnaval.

Apr–Sep Lovely warm weather, occasional rainy days. Festas juninas in the second half of June.

Oct & Nov Minimal crowds and summery weather.

History

Prior to the Portuguese arrival, the region known today as Bahia had a wide variety of ethnic groups scattered inland and along the coast, speaking dozens of languages. Many of the tribes were wiped out by the Portuguese, though some – like the Pataxó – are still around today. The indigenous tribes practiced some form of agriculture, raising manioc, sweet potatoes and maize, and practiced hunting and fishing, while gathering fruits from the forests. Little else is

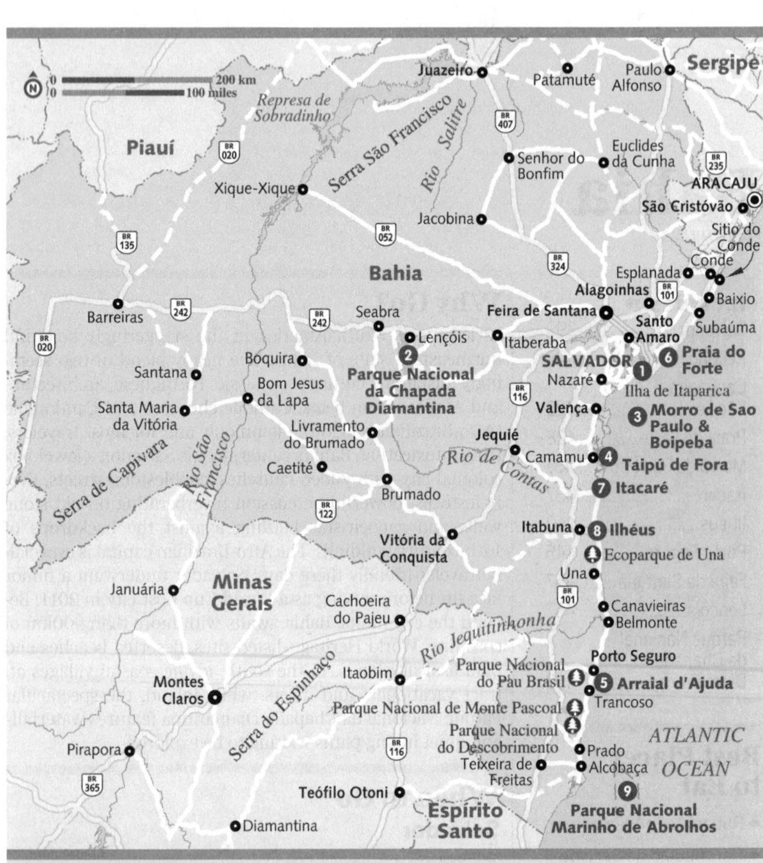

Bahia Highlights

1. Following the sounds of the famous Olodum drum corps in **Salvador** (p399), Latin America's inspiring Afro-Brazilian capital.
2. Hiking to natural waterslides in the magnificent **Parque Nacional da Chapada Diamantina** (p462).
3. Zooming around the island villages of **Morro de São Paulo** (p431) and **Boipeba** (p434) on a speedboat tour.
4. Traveling over dirt roads to beautiful **Taipu de Fora** (p436) beach on the Peninsula de Maraú.
5. Lingering over alfresco meals and coastal strolls in **Arraial d'Ajuda** (p449).
6. Watching tiny sea turtles hatch on the sand in **Praia do Forte** (p428).
7. Catching a wave or taking a capoeira lesson on the sand in surfer-happy **Itacaré** (p437).
8. Tracing the footsteps of Brazil's literary great, Jorge Amado, in **Ilhéus** (p440).
9. Diving beneath the deep in the remote **Parque Nacional Marinho de Abrolhos** (p456).

known of the area's native population, who, for the most part, disappeared following the European arrival.

Portuguese sailors first made landfall near Porto Seguro in 1500, but it wasn't until one year later – All Saints' Day (November 1), according to legend – that Italian navigator Amerigo Vespucci sailed into Salvador's bay and named it Baía de Todos os Santos. Two generations later, in 1549, Tomé de Souza returned under orders of the Portuguese crown to found Brazil's first capital, Salvador da Bahia.

To fuel this new country, the colonists grew sugarcane and later tobacco in the fertile Recôncavo region (named after the concave shape of the bay) that surrounds the Baía de Todos os Santos. The Portuguese enslaved the indigenous people to work these fields, and when they proved insufficient, they brought over Africans in staggering numbers. From 1550 to 1850, at least 3.6 million slaves were brought from Africa to Brazil, and the great majority of them ended up in the Northeast.

In such numbers, the slaves managed to maintain much of their African culture. When their own religious practices were prohibited, for instance, slaves moved their Candomblé *terreiros* (venues) underground and syncretized their gods with Catholic saints. African food and music enriched the homes of both blacks and whites, and the African culture deeply influenced the newly developing Brazilian culture.

Throughout the life of the colony, the Portuguese utilized a harsh plantation system that would keep African slaves tied to the land until their emancipation in 1888. In addition to sugar and tobacco, the Portuguese created cattle ranches, which spread inland, radiating west into the *sertão* (backlands) and Minas Gerais, then northwest into Piauí.

Primary products were shipped out, while slaves and European luxury goods were shipped in. Bahia was colonial Brazil's economic heartland, with Salvador da Bahia the capital of colonial Brazil between 1549 and 1763. The city was the center of the sugar industry, which sustained the prosperity of the country until the collapse in international sugar prices in the 1820s. During the gold and coffee booms in the south, Salvador continued its decline.

Industrialization in Bahia began in the mid-19th century and continued slowly, with developments in banking and industry, as new rail lines brought goods from the interior to Salvador's large port. Factories appeared and the economy, once a monoculture of the sugarcane industry, diversified. The most important event of the late 19th century was the emancipation of slaves, which brought freedom for many of Bahia's inhabitants.

In the 20th century, oil discoveries in the 1940s helped bring Bahia out of economic stagnation and contributed to the state's continued modernization. Today, Salvador remains an important port, exporting soy, fruit, cocoa, petrochemicals and sugarcane – which is once again achieving prominence for its role as a highly efficient biofuel. In recent decades, tourism has emerged as an important industry and, with the influx of cash, the state has invested in much-needed infrastructure and public-health projects.

Getting There & Around

Bahia's primary airport (p420) is located in its capital, Salvador, though Porto Seguro also has frequent and inexpensive flights.

Hwy BR-101 skirts the Bahian coastline. It is the main thoroughfare through the state and the chosen route of most long-distance buses.

Transportation is usually a snap in Bahia: there's always some way to get where you want to go. Aside from buses run by official lines to and from bus stations, Kombi vans and *bestas* (vans that run a specific route and will stop anywhere to drop off or pick up passengers) are common, as are collective taxis.

SALVADOR

0XX71 / POP 2.68 MILLION

Salvador da Bahia has an energy and unadorned beauty that few cities can match. Once the magnificent capital of Portugal's great New World colony, Salvador is the country's Afro-Brazilian jewel. Its brilliantly hued center is a living museum of 17th- and 18th-century architecture and gold-laden churches. More importantly, Salvador is the nexus of an incredible arts movement. Wild festivals happen frequently, with drum corps pounding out powerful rhythms against the backdrop of colonial buildings almost daily. At night, capoeira circles form on plazas and open spaces, while the scent of *acarajé* (bean and shrimp fritters) and other African delights fill the evening air. Elsewhere in town, a different spirit flows through the crowd as religious followers celebrate and reconnect with African gods at mystical Candomblé ceremonies. In fact, there's no other place in the world where descendants

Salvador

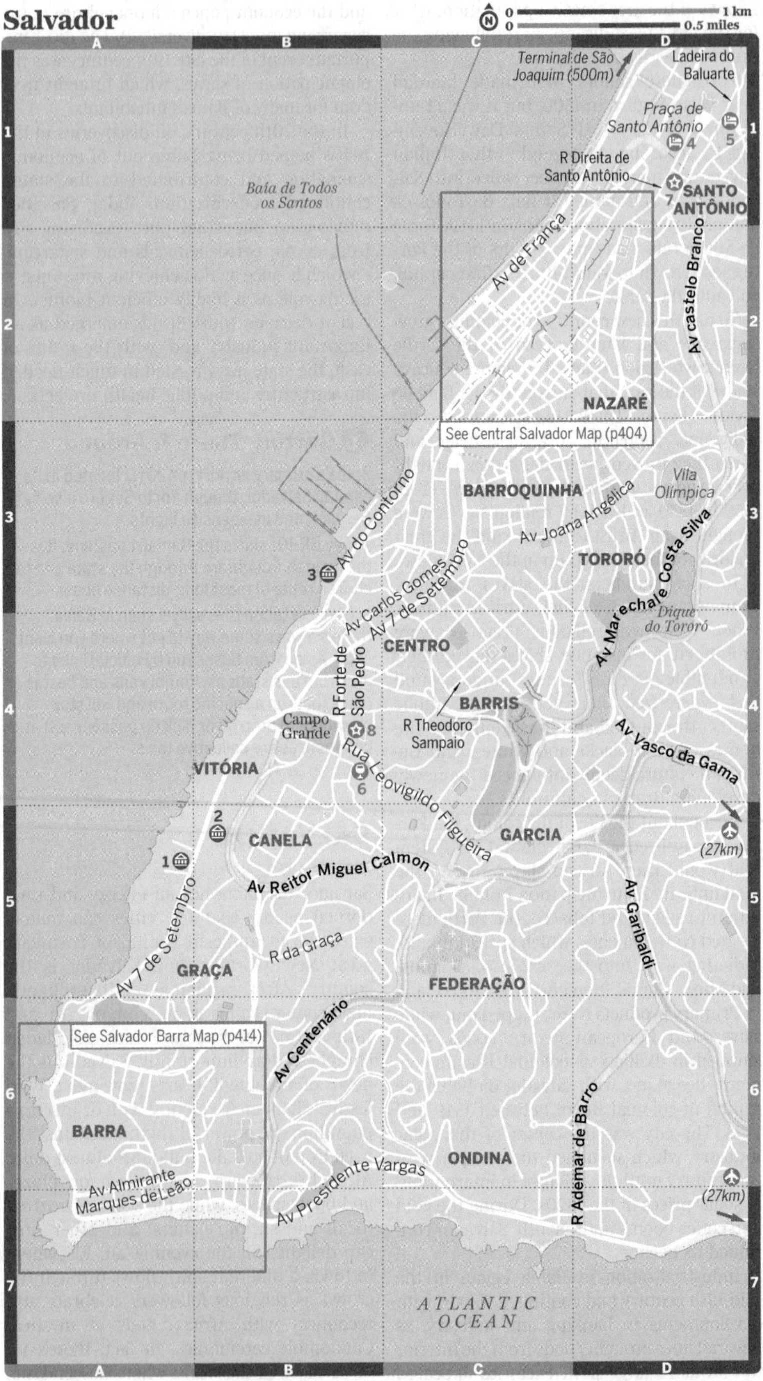

0 — 1 km
0 — 0.5 miles

Terminal de São Joaquim (500m)
Ladeira do Baluarte
Praça de Santo Antônio
R Direita de Santo Antônio
SANTO ANTÔNIO
Baía de Todos os Santos
Av de França
Av castelo Branco
NAZARÉ
See Central Salvador Map (p404)
Av do Contorno
BARROQUINHA
Av Joana Angélica
Vila Olímpica
TORORÓ
Av Marechale Costa Silva
Dique do Tororó
Av Carlos Gomes
Av 7 de Setembro
CENTRO
R Forte de São Pedro
BARRIS
R Theodoro Sampaio
Campo Grande
Rua Leovigildo Filgueira
Av Vasco da Gama
VITÓRIA
CANELA
GARCIA
(27km)
Av Reitor Miguel Calmon
Av 7 de Setembro
Av Garibaldi
R da Graça
GRAÇA
FEDERAÇÃO
Av Centenário
See Salvador Barra Map (p414)
BARRA
R Ademar de Barro
ONDINA
Av Almirante Marques de Leão
Av Presidente Vargas
(27km)
ATLANTIC OCEAN

Salvador

Sights

Sleeping

Drinking & Nightlife

Entertainment

of African slaves have preserved their heritage as well as in Salvador – from music and religion to food, dance and martial-arts traditions. Aside from the many attractions within Salvador, gorgeous coastline lies right outside the city – a suitable introduction to the tropical splendor of Bahia.

As one of Brazil's 12 host cities for the 2014 FIFA World Cup, Salvador has undergone significant changes in recent years, including the development of pedestrian-only promenades in Barra and the construction of a useful (if limited) Metro line, not to mention the inauguration of Itaipava Arena Fonte Nova football stadium. Thanks to the influx of international tourists, public-transportation options have improved, and there's an affordable and user-friendly shuttle running between the airport and the city.

History

In 1549 Tomé de Souza landed on Praia Porto da Barra under Portuguese royal orders to found Brazil's first capital, bringing city plans, a statue, 400 soldiers and 400 settlers, including priests and prostitutes. He founded the city in a defensive location: on a cliff top facing the sea. After the first year a city of mud and straw had been erected, and by 1550 the surrounding walls were in place to protect against attacks from hostile *índios* (indigenous people). Salvador da Bahia remained Brazil's most important city for the next three centuries.

During its early years, the city depended upon the export of sugarcane and later tobacco from the fertile Recôncavo region at the northern end of Baía de Todos os Santos. Later, cattle ranching was introduced, which, coupled with gold and diamonds from the Bahian interior, provided Salvador with immense wealth, as is visible in the city's opulent baroque architecture.

African slaves were first brought to Salvador in the mid-1500s, and in 1587 historian Gabriel Soares tallied an estimated 12,000 whites, 8000 converted *índios* and 4000 black slaves. The number of blacks eventually increased to constitute half of the city's population, and uprisings of blacks threatened Salvador's stability several times.

After Lisbon, Salvador was the most important city in the Portuguese empire. It was the glory of colonial Brazil, famed for its many gold-filled churches, beautiful mansions and numerous festivals. It was also renowned as early as the 17th century for its bawdy public life, sensuality and decadence – so much so that its bay won the nickname Baía de Todos os Santos e de Quase Todos os Pecados (Bay of All Saints and of Nearly All Sins)!

Salvador remained Brazil's seat of colonial government until 1763, when, with the decline of the sugarcane industry, the capital was moved to Rio.

In 1798 the city was the stage for the Conjuração dos Alfaiates (Conspiracy of the Tailors), the beginning of a wave of battles between Portuguese loyalists and those wanting independence. It was only on July 2, 1823, with the defeat of Portuguese troops in Cabrito and Pirajá, that the city found peace. At that time, Salvador numbered 45,000 inhabitants and was the commercial center of a vast territory.

For most of the 19th and 20th centuries the city stagnated as the agricultural economy foundered on its disorganized labor and production. Today, Salvador is Brazil's third-largest city, and it has only begun moving forward in the last few decades. New industries such as petroleum, chemicals and tourism have brought wealth to the city's coffers, but the rapidly increasing population is still faced with major economic and social problems.

Sights

The Cidade Alta (Upper City, made up of the Pelourinho and Carmo) is packed with the city's most impressive sights, though you'll also find worthwhile museums in Vitória, a wonderfully scenic lighthouse in Barra and other fascinating attractions scattered about the city.

Pelourinho

Regardless of what the tourist information offices tell you, or even what's posted outside, Pelourinho's churches keep sporadic opening hours – don't plan your day around getting inside one, or you may be disappointed.

★Pelourinho NEIGHBORHOOD

(Map p404) The centerpiece of the Cidade Alta is the Pelourinho (or Pelô), a Unesco-declared World Heritage site of colorful colonial buildings and magnificent churches. As you wander the cobblestone streets, gazing up at the city's oldest architecture, you'll realize that the Pelô is not just for tourists. Cultural centers and schools of music, dance and capoeira pack these pastel-colored 17th- and 18th-century buildings.

The area has undergone major restoration work – which remains ongoing – since 1993 thanks to Unesco funding. Admittedly, the Pelô has lost a lot of its character in the process, but to say that it is now safer and better preserved is an understatement.

★Elevador Lacerda HISTORIC BUILDING

(Map p404; ☎3322-7049; fare R$0.25; ⏱7am-11pm) The beautifully restored, art deco Elevador Lacerda connects the Cidade Alta with Comércio via four elevators traveling 72m in 30 seconds. The Jesuits installed the first manual rope-and-pulley elevator around 1610 to transport goods and passengers from the port to the settlement. In 1868 an iron structure with clanking steam elevators was inaugurated, replaced by an electric system in 1928.

Facing the elevator are the impressive arches of the Câmara Municipal, the 17th-century city hall, which occasionally puts on cultural exhibitions.

Largo do Pelourinho SQUARE

(Map p404; Pelourinho) Picture-perfect Largo do Pelourinho is a sloping, triangle-shaped square, once the site of the *pelourinho* (whipping post) – one of several nearby locations where slaves were exposed and punished. After slavery was outlawed in 1835, the neighborhood fell into disrepair; in the 1990s major restoration efforts uncovered the original splendor of the cobblestone square's colonial houses and churches. Today, the square is the heart of Salvador's historic center.

Igreja e Convento São Francisco CHURCH

(Map p404; Cruzeiro de São Francisco; admission R$3) One of Brazil's most magnificent churches, the baroque Igreja e Convento São Francisco is filled with displays of wealth and splendor. An 80kg silver chandelier dangles over ornate wood carvings smothered in gold leaf, and the convent courtyard is paneled with hand-painted azulejos (Portuguese tiles). The complex was finished in 1723.

Terreiro de Jesus SQUARE

(Map p404; Praça 15 de Novembro) A colorful intersection of vendors, tourists, capoeiristas and colorful locals, the Terreiro de Jesus is a historic site of religious celebra-

AFRICAN SLAVE ARTISANS

African slaves played a key role in building the beautiful Pelourinho. Forced to work on their masters' churches, and prohibited from practicing their own religion, slave artisans expressed themselves through their work. At Igreja e Convento São Francisco, the faces of the cherubs are distorted, and some angels are endowed with huge sex organs, while others appear pregnant. Most of these creative touches were chastely covered by 20th-century sacristans. The polychrome figure of São Pedro da Alcântara by Manoel Inácio da Costa shows a figure suffering from tuberculosis – just like the artist himself. One side of the saint's face is more ashen than the other, so he appears to become more ill as you walk past him. José Joaquim da Rocha painted the entry hall's ceiling using perspective technique, a novelty during the baroque period.

Meanwhile, over at Igreja da Ordem Terceira do Carmo (p405), the artist known as O Cabra (Half-Caste) was hard at work on his infamous statue of Nossa Senhora do Carmo. O Cabra was a slave with no artistic training, and he was reportedly besotted with Isabel II, daughter of the rich landholder Garcia d'Ávila. He supposedly modeled the Virgin in Isabel II's likeness, and gave African facial features to the Christ child cradled in the statue's arms. Could this be what O Cabra imagined their love child would look like? O Cabra took eight years to finish the life-size image of Christ (1630), with blood made from 2000 rubies. It's on display in the church's small museum.

WORTH A TRIP

IGREJA NOSSA SENHORA DO BONFIM

This is where all those colorful ribbons come from: on the Itapagipe Peninsula, north of most of Salvador's main sights, the famous 18th-century church **Igreja Nossa Senhora do Bonfim** (3316-2196; Praça Senhor do Bonfim; 6:30am-noon & 2-6pm Tue-Thu & Sat, 5:30am-noon & 2:30-6pm Fri & Sun) is a proud symbol of Bahia. Bonfim's fame derives from its power to effect miraculous cures, making it a popular shrine. The *fitas* (colored ribbons) you see everywhere in Salvador (and everywhere in Brazil) are a souvenir of the church. If you tie a *fita* around your wrist, you are making a commitment that lasts for months. With each of the three knots a wish is made, which will come true by the time the *fita* falls off. Cutting it off is inviting doom.

In the **Sala dos Milagres** (Room of Miracles) on the right side of the church, devotees leave photos, letters and ex votos (wax replicas of body parts representing those that were cured or need curing). Due to Candomblistas' syncretization of Jesus Christ (Nosso Senhor do Bonfim) with Oxalá, their highest deity, Bonfim is their most important church. Huge services are held here on Friday, Oxalá's favorite day of the week.

To get there, take a taxi, or try the 25-minute city bus journey. At the base of Elevador Lacerda, heading north along Av Jequitaia, look for the 204 bus labeled with the destination 'Ribeira'; the bus stops near the church.

tions, and is ringed by four churches, as well as the 19th-century **Faculdade de Medicina Building**. The plaza feeds into the **Cruzeiro de São Francisco**, named for the cross in the square's center.

Fundação Casa de Jorge Amado MUSEUM
(Map p404; 3321-0070; www.jorgeamado.org.br; Largo do Pelourinho 51; admission R$3, Wed free; 10am-6pm Mon-Fri, to 4pm Sat) Literary types shouldn't miss a quick visit to the Fundação Casa de Jorge Amado, offering an overview of the life of one of Brazil's best-known writers. A wall of Amado's book covers in every major language demonstrates his widespread popularity, while the museum café serves a menu of appetizers and desserts as described by the writer in his novels.

Praça da Sé SQUARE
(Map p404) The history of Praça da Sé reveals intriguing details about Salvador's development. From 1552 to 1933, the square was the site of the grand Sé Primacial cathedral, overlooking the bay. Sadly, the cathedral and its cemetery were razed in the '30s – roped-off remnants remain today – part of a plan to make wider avenues where streetcars could travel. By the 1950s, Praça da Sé was the home of Salvador's main bus terminal. Today, the plaza sees mostly tourist traffic.

Museu Afro-Brasileiro MUSEUM
(Map p404; 3283-5540; www.mafro.ceao.ufba.br; Terreiro de Jesus; adult/child R$6/3; 9am-5:30pm Mon-Fri, 10am-5pm Sat) Holding one of Bahia's most important collections, the Museu Afro-Brasileiro exhibits wood carvings, baskets, pottery and other artwork and crafts linking Brazilian and African artistic traditions. The highlight of the museum is a room lined with 27 huge, breathtaking carved wooden panels by Argentine-born Carybé, who is perhaps Salvador's most renowned 20th-century fine artist.

Catedral Basílica CHURCH
(Map p404; Terreiro de Jesus; admission by donation) The Catedral Basílica dates from 1672 and is a marvelous example of Jesuit architecture. The interior is elegant and simple, with marble-covered walls and towering pillars. The sacristy has a beautiful carved jacaranda archway and a painted dome and floor.

Museu da Cidade MUSEUM
(Map p404; 3321-1967; Largo do Pelourinho 3; admission R$3; 10am-5pm Mon-Fri) Rather like the city itself, Museu da Cidade contains an eclectic assortment of the old and the modern, the sacred and the profane. Exhibits include *orixá* (deity of Candomblé) costumes and traditional rag dolls enacting quotidian colonial life.

Igreja NS do Rosário dos Pretos CHURCH
(Map p404; Largo do Pelourinho; admission by donation) The king of Portugal gave the Irmanidade dos Homens Pretos (Brotherhood of Black Men) the land for the periwinkle-blue Igreja NS do Rosário dos Pretos in 1704. Building in their free time, it took these slaves and freed slaves almost 100 years to complete it.

Central Salvador

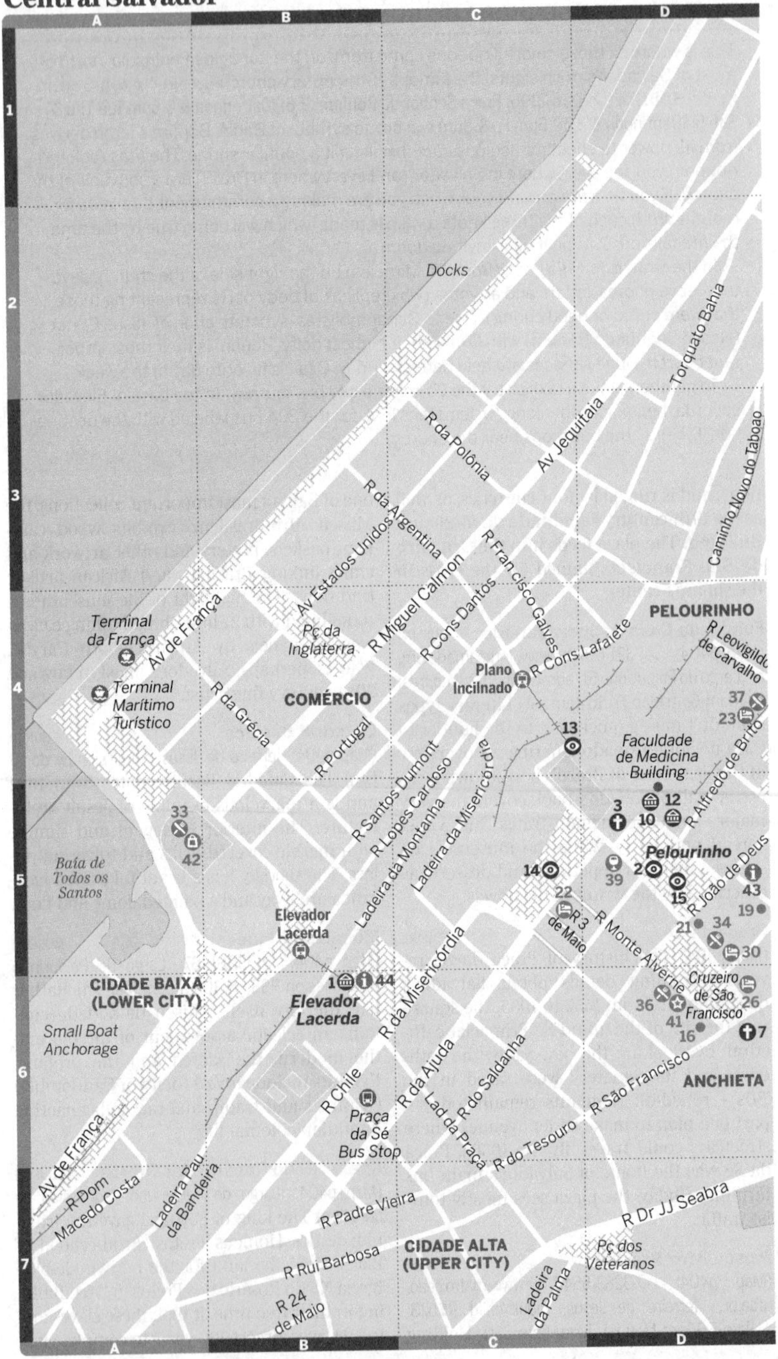

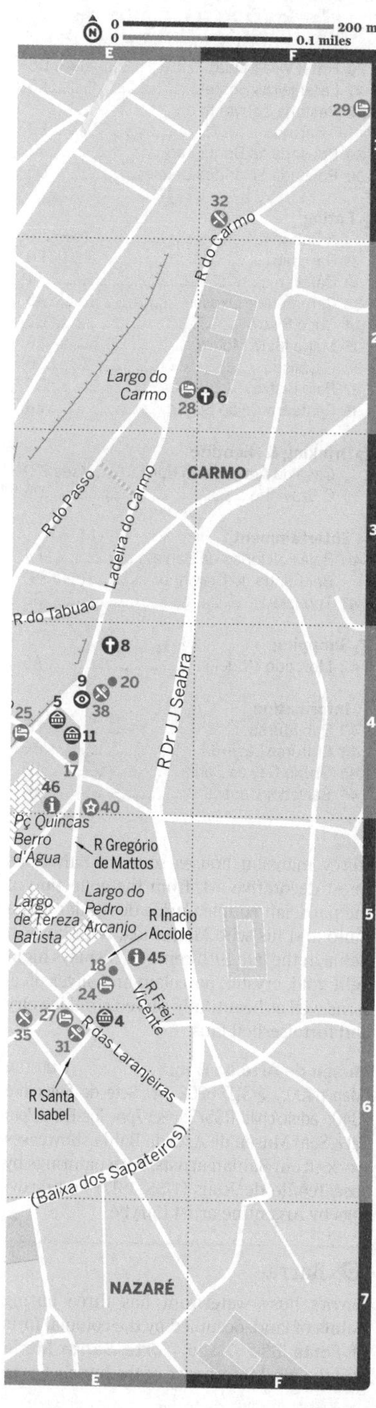

Plano Inclinado Gonçalves CABLE CAR

(Map p404; Praça da Sé & Guindaste dos Padres, Comércio; R$0.15; ⌚7am-7pm Mon-Fri, to 1pm Sat) After sitting, unused, for almost three years, the 1874 funicular railway Plano Inclinado Gonçalves reopened in 2014. The newly restored line connects Comércio and Cidade Alta on steep tracks, a scenic alternative to the nearby Elevador Lacerda.

Museu de Arqueologia e Etnologia MUSEUM

(Archaeology & Ethnology Museum; Map p404; ☎3283-5530; www.mae.ufba.br; Faculdade de Medicina, Terreiro de Jesus; admission R$6; ⌚10am-5pm Mon-Fri) Below the Museu Afro-Brasileiro (one admission ticket gets you into both), the Museu de Arqueologia e Etnologia exhibits indigenous Brazilian pottery, bows and arrows, masks and feather headpieces. Also tucked between the building's arching stone foundations is 19th-century glass and porcelain found during the excavations for the metro.

Carmo

Igreja da Ordem Terceira do Carmo CHURCH

(Map p404; Largo do Carmo; admission by donation) The original church, founded in 1636, burnt to the ground; the present neoclassical structure dates from 1828. The nave has a French organ and a baroque altar with a scandalous statue of NS Senhora do Carmo. Church historians claim the statue was modeled in the likeness of Isabel II, daughter of Garcia d'Ávila, the largest landholder in the Northeast.

Cidade Baixa/Comércio

Interspersed between the Comércio's modern skyscrapers is some fantastic 19th-century architecture in various stages of decay.

Mercado Modelo MARKET

(Map p404; www.mercadomodelobahia.com.br; Praça Visconde de Cayru; ⌚9am-7pm Mon-Sat, to 2pm Sun) The original 1861 Customs House was partly destroyed in a fire in 1986. After reconstruction, it was transformed into the Mercado Modelo. When shipments of new slaves arrived into port, they were stored in the watery depths of this building while awaiting auction. Fun fact: night guards report ghostly activities after closing hours.

Solar do Unhão HISTORIC BUILDING

(Map p400; ☎3117-6139; Av Contorno s/n; ⌚1-6pm Tue-Sun) FREE This wonderfully preserved 18th-century complex served as a

Central Salvador

Top Sights
1 Elevador Lacerda B6
2 Pelourinho D5

Sights
3 Catedral Basílica D5
4 Escola Olodum E6
5 Fundação Casa de Jorge Amado E4
6 Igreja da Ordem Terceira do Carmo F2
7 Igreja e Convento São Francisco D6
8 Igreja NS do Rosário dos Pretos E4
9 Largo do Pelourinho E4
Mercado Modelo .... (see 42)
10 Museu Afro-Brasileiro D5
11 Museu da Cidade E4
12 Museu de Arqueologia e Etnologia D5
13 Plano Inclinado Gonçalves C4
14 Praça da Sé C5
15 Terreiro de Jesus D5

Activities, Courses & Tours
16 Associação Artística e Cultural Diaspora D6
17 Associação Brasileira de Capoeira Angola E4
18 Atelier Mestre Lua Rasta E5
19 Fundação Mestre Bimba D5
20 SENAC E4
21 Toursbahia D5

Sleeping
22 Bahiacafé Hotel C5
23 Casa do Amarelindo D4
24 Hostel Galeria 13 .... E5
25 Hostel Solar dos Romanos E4
26 Hotel Villa Bahia D6
27 Laranjeiras Hostel E6
28 Pestana Convento do Carmo E2
29 Pousada do Boqueirão F1
30 Pousada Solar dos Deuses D5

Eating
A Cubana .... (see 25)
31 Bar Zulu E6
32 Cafélier F1
33 Camafeu de Oxossi A5
34 Cuco Bistrô D5
35 Maria Mata Mouro E6
36 O Coliseu D6
37 Pelô Bistrô D4
38 Restaurante do Senac E4

Drinking & Nightlife
Casa do Amarelindo Bar .... (see 23)
39 O Cravinho D5

Entertainment
40 Balé Folclórico da Bahia E4
Bar Fundo do Cravinho .... (see 39)
41 Topázio D6

Shopping
42 Mercado Modelo A5

Information
43 Bahiatursa D5
44 Emtursa Lacerda B6
45 Grupo Gay da Bahia E5
46 Salvador Central E4

transfer point for sugar shipments: legend says it's haunted by the ghosts of murdered slaves. Today, the building houses the **Museu de Arte Moderna** (Map p400; ☎3117-6139; www.mam.ba.gov.br; Contorno s/n; adult/child R$6/3; ⏲1-7pm Tue-Fri & Sun, to 9pm Sat) FREE, with a changing display of avant-garde exhibits, a hillside sculpture garden, and popular Saturday-evening jazz and bossa nova concerts (JAM no MAM; p418) with stunning views over the bay. Take a taxi – the area is known for tourist muggings.

Vitória

The main artery of this leafy suburb is a well-traveled boulevard between Barra and the Pelourinho.

Museu Carlos Costa Pinto MUSEUM
(Map p400; ☎3336-6081; www.museucostapinto.com.br; Av Sete de Setembro 2490; admission R$5; ⏲2:30-7pm Mon & Wed-Sat) This lovely two-storey mansion houses some of Salvador's finest decorative art, from the collection of the patrician couple Carlos de Aguiar Costa Pinto and his wife Margarida, both born in Bahia in the late 19th century. Displays highlight gold, crystal, porcelain and silver pieces, as well as beautifully carved coral jewelry and tortoiseshell fans.

Museu de Arte da Bahia MUSEUM
(Map p400; ☎3117-6902; Av Sete de Setembro 2340; adult/child R$5/3; ⏲1-7pm Tue-Fri, 2-7pm Sat & Sun) Museu de Arte da Bahia showcases works from Bahian artists, with paintings by José Teófilo de Jesus (1758–1817) and drawings by Argentine artist Carybé.

Barra

Barra's busy waterfront has three jutting points of land, occupied by the colonial forts of **Forte São Diogo**, **Forte Santa Maria** and the most impressive of the bunch, **Forte** de Santo Antônio da Barra (Map p414; Largo do Farol da Barra s/n). Built in 1698, Bahia's oldest fort is more commonly called the Farol da Barra for the lighthouse – South America's oldest – within its walls. Today the striking structure houses the excellent nautical museum. As you join the locals gathering to catch the sunset from the grassy ledge behind the fort, notice how Salvador's peninsula is the only location in Brazil where the sun appears to set over the ocean.

★ **Museu Náutico da Bahia** MUSEUM
(Nautical Museum of Bahia; Map p414; ☎3264-3296; www.museunauticodabahia.org.br; Largo do Farol da Barra s/n, Forte de Santo Antônio da Barra; adult/student R$15/7.50; ⏰9am-6pm Tue-Sun, daily Jan & Jul) In addition to having superb views, the Forte de Santo Antônio da Barra contains the excellent nautical museum, with relics and displays from the days of Portuguese seafaring, plus fascinating exhibits on the slave trade. All information is offered in both Portuguese and English – a rarity in Bahia. If you only have time for one museum in Salvador, this is the one.

Beaches

When locals talk about going to a city beach, they're usually referring to Barra. The neighborhood is undergoing a makeover that started before the 2014 World Cup: the waterfront road is now pedestrian-only, at least along the most popular stretch extending from either side of Forte de Santo Antônio da Barra. This change has resulted in cleaner, quieter city beaches. **Praia Porto da Barra**, on a horseshoe-shaped stretch of coast, is small, picturesque, usually crowded, loaded with vendors selling everything imaginable, and a great place to be at sunset. The bay's waters are clear and calm, and the people-watching is fantastic. To the left of the lighthouse, **Praia do Farol da Barra** has a beach break popular with surfers at high tide, and tidal pools popular with children and families at low tide.

Smaller crowds and an unpolluted Atlantic are about 40 minutes' bus travel east from the center (or more with traffic). Calm seas lap on flat, white sands with *barracas* (stalls) and swaying palms at popular beaches **Piatã** (25km) and **Itapuã** (27km). As you reach the beaches of **Stella Maris** (31km) and **Flamengo** (33km), the waves get progressively stronger, *barracas* begin to space out, and sand dunes and more greenery create a more natural setting. Catch an Itapuã, Aeroporto or Praia do Flamengo bus, making sure it goes up the coast *(via orla)* and as far as you are going.

Courses

Capoeira, Dance & Percussion

Classes in capoeira, African dance and percussion are easily arranged through hostels and pousadas (guesthouses) in the Pelourinho. Course prices vary depending on season, availability and the number of people in your party, but generally you can expect to pay around R$35 per hour for a class.

Associação Artística e Cultural Diaspora DANCE
(Diáspora Art Center; Map p404; ☎3323-0016; 3rd fl, Cruzeiro de São Francisco 21; prices vary; ⏰10am-6pm Mon-Fri) Stop in to inquire about the latest schedule of classes in traditional and contemporary Afro-Brazilian dance, capoeira and percussion.

Associação Brasileira de Capoeira Angola CAPOEIRA
(Map p404; ☎9266-7881; www.abca.portalcapoeira.com; Gregório de Mattos 38; ⏰classes 1-3pm Tue & Wed; 👪) This friendly capoeira association (known as ABCA) runs classes open to all ages, including children five and older. Be sure to wear comfortable, loose-fitting pants you can move around in.

Atelier Mestre Lua Rasta MUSIC
(Map p404; ☎3488-3600; www.atelierlua.com.br; Acciole 3) To set up a percussion class, pass by this shop of instruments handmade by the *mestre* (master) himself; Mestre Lua can also set you up with a capoeira class. He also provides overnight accommodations for R$40 per person, per night.

Fundação Mestre Bimba CAPOEIRA
(Map p404; ☎3322-5082; www.capoeiramestrebimba.com.br; Laranjeiras 01) A school run by the son of the founder of Capoeira Regional, Mestre Bimba.

Cooking

Senac COOKING
(Map p404; ☎3186-4000; www.ba.senac.br; Largo do Pelourinho 13-19; from R$30; ⏰9am-5pm Mon-Sat) A must-see for foodies, Senac is a Bahian culinary school where both locals and tourists take cooking classes; one course focuses solely on the preparation of popular street foods like *acarajé* (Bahian fritters made of brown beans and dried shrimp fried in palm oil). Inside this lovely colonial building, there's also a free

Baía de Todos os Santos & Recôncavo

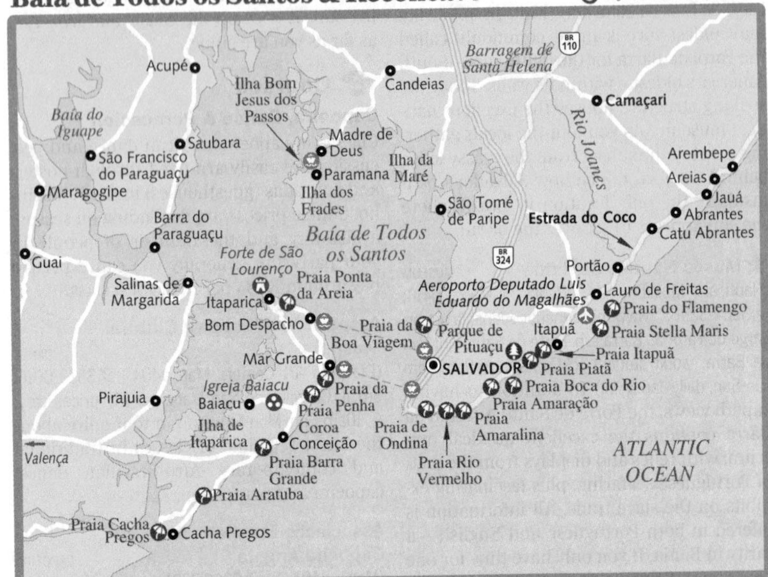

museum dedicated to Bahian gastronomy, and a pair of eateries – the student-run buffet *típico* (p415) is particularly excellent.

Language

Hostels and pousadas in Salvador can recommend language courses – a minimum one-week commitment is common – and private teachers. Prices start around R$400 a week for a spot in a group class. Check the schools' websites for the latest details and promotions.

Diálogo LANGUAGE
(Map p414; ☎3264-0053; www.dialogo-brazilstudy.com; Dr João Pondé 240, Barra; ⏲9am-6pm Mon-Sat) Language classes here get mixed reviews from travelers, though some teachers are reportedly excellent. Benefits include language exchange with Brazilian students, city excursions and samba classes. Diálogo also specializes in arranging homestays with local families.

Idioma Escola de Português LANGUAGE COURSE
(Map p414; ☎3267-7012; www.portugueseinbrazil.com; Greenfeld 46, Barra; ⏲8am-6pm Mon-Fri) Convenient if you're staying in Barra, this language school offers group classes and private sessions in addition to cultural excursions like Bahian cooking workshops and scuba-diving classes.

Tours

Salvador Bus BUS TOUR
(Map p414; ☎3356-6425; www.salvadorbus.com.br; Av Sete de Setembro s/n; adult/child R$55/40; ⏲9:30am-6:45pm Mon-Sat) If you're short on time, climb aboard the open-air Salvador Bus at Farol da Barra, the Mercado Modelo or a number of other downtown destinations; the hop-on, hop-off sightseeing bus offers multilingual tours.

Toursbahia TOUR
(Map p404; ☎3320-3280; www.toursbahia.com.br; Cruzeiro de São Francisco 4, Pelourinho; ⏲9am-6pm Mon-Sat) Toursbahia is a multilingual agency offering local and national tours.

Festivals & Events

Salvador delights in its wild festivals, which have links to both Catholicism and Candomblé. Although Carnaval steals the show, there are numerous festivals, particularly in January and February.

Procissão do Senhor Bom Jesus dos Navegantes RELIGIOUS
(⏲Jan 1) A maritime procession transports the image of Bom Jesus from Igreja NS da Conceição in Cidade Baixa north along the bay to Igreja de NS da Boa Viagem. A festival ensues on Praia da Boa Viagem.

Festas de Reis RELIGIOUS
(Jan 6) On the Dia de Reis, a procession of the *reis magos* (wise men) statues travels to a crèche in the Igreja da Lapinha.

Lavagem do Bonfim RELIGIOUS
(2nd Thu in Jan) Salvador's biggest festival outside of Carnaval honors the saint with Bahia's largest following; Senhor do Bonfim, associated with Candomblé. A procession of *baianas* (women dressed as Bahian 'aunts') in ritual dress carrying buckets of flowers walks 6km from Cidade Baixa to Igreja NS do Bonfim.

Festa de Iemanjá RELIGIOUS
(Feb 2) Perhaps Candomblé's most important festival, the event pays homage to the *orixá* Iemanjá, goddess of the sea and fertility. In the morning, devotees descend on Praia Rio Vermelho, where ceremonies are held to bless offerings of flowers, cakes, effigies and bottles of perfume. The ensuing street festival is packed with people and some of Salvador's best bands and lasts into the night.

Festa de São João da Bahia RELIGIOUS
(www.saojoaobahia.com.br; late Jun) Pyrotechnics, street parties, and *forró*, performances spring up all over town for a week near the end of June. Bahia's so-called 'festas juninas' (June celebrations) take place in Salvador and throughout the state.

Festa de NS da Conceição RELIGIOUS
(Dec 8) Candomblistas honor the saint's *orixá* alter ego, Iemanjá, with a procession and ceremonies in Cidade Baixa.

Passagem do Ano Novo NEW YEAR
(Dec 31) New Year's Eve is celebrated with all the zest of Carnaval, especially on the beaches.

SALVADOR'S CARNAVAL

Carnaval in Salvador is billed as 'the world's largest party.' It's a debatable distinction, but as the organizers explain, while Rio de Janeiro's Carnaval may draw more people, Salvador's Carnaval occupies more physical space (several kilometers at a time) than its sister party in A Cidade Maravilhosa. Either way, it's a huge party, attracting upwards of two million revelers for six straight days of revelry before Ash Wednesday. Each day, the festivities kick off around 5pm every afternoon and wind down around 5am.

The focus is on music, namely nationally famous city bands playing *axé* and *pagode* (Bahia's pop music) atop creeping *trios elétricos* (long trucks loaded with huge speakers). Between them march a few *blocos afros* (groups with powerful drum corps promoting Afro-Brazilian culture) and *afoxés* (groups tied to Candomblé traditions). A *trio elétrico*, together with its followers grouped in a roped-off area around it, form a *bloco*. People pay big bucks for the *abadá* (outfit) for their favorite band, mostly for prestige and the safety of those ropes. Choosing to *fazer pipoca* (be popcorn) in the street is still a fine way to spend Carnaval, as you'll see a variety of music and be spared the hassle involved with picking up the *abadá*.

There are three major parade circuits: Dodô, between Barra and Ondina along Av Oceânica; Osmar or 'the Avenidas,' between Campo Grande and Praça Castro Alves along Av Sete de Setembro; and Batatinha in the Pelourinho.

Crowds pose the greatest threat during Carnaval, so be aware of your surroundings. A large police presence helps to keep violence to a minimum. On the Barra–Rio Vermelho circuit, avoid the section where the coastal road narrows near the Morro do Cristo – the tension heats up there.

Otherwise, if you're planning on spending Carnaval in Salvador, the best thing to do is to plan ahead: many hostels and pousadas (guesthouses) offer packages, but they tend to fill up quickly. It's advisable to look closely at a city map before committing to anything: some city neighborhoods can be so noisy during Carnaval that you wouldn't be able to sleep if you wanted to. Many locals living in the Barra neighborhood clear out completely for Carnaval, renting out their apartments and houses to tourists, which is another accommodation option if you're up for the adventure.

For more information and details on specific events and schedules, log onto the official online portal for Salvador's Carnaval at www.carnaval.salvador.ba.gov.br. For English-language background on the music at the center of the event, check out the helpful page at www.bahia-online.net/Carnival.htm.

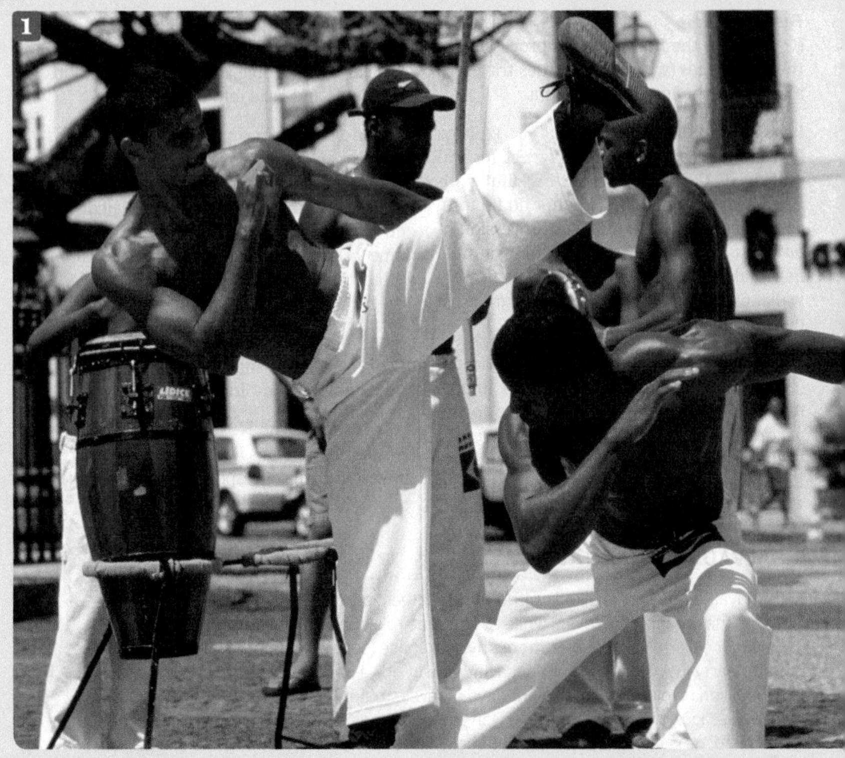

Capoeira

Combining elements of the fight, the game and the dance, capoeira was developed by Afro-Brazilian slaves more than 400 years ago as a means of maintaining a ready self-defense against their masters. Today, it remains a uniquely Bahian art form.

Origins

Capoeira is said to have originated from a ritualistic African dance. Capoeira was prohibited by slave owners and banished from the *senzalas* (slave barracks), forcing slaves to practice clandestinely in the forest. Later, in an attempt to disguise this act of defiance from the authorities, capoeira was developed into a kind of acrobatic dance. The clapping of hands and striking of the *berimbau*, a one-string musical instrument that looks like a fishing rod, originally served to alert fighters to the approach of the boss and subsequently became incorporated into the dance to maintain the rhythm.

As recently as the 1920s, capoeira was still prohibited. In the 1930s Mestre Bimba changed the emphasis of capoeira from a tool of insurrection to a form of artistic expression that's become an institution in Bahia.

Traditions & Variations

Today, there are two schools of capoeira: the slow and low Capoeira de Angola, originally led by Mestre Pastinha, and the more aggressive Capoeira Regional, initiated by Mestre Bimba. The former school believes capoeira came from Angola; the latter says it was born in the plantations of Cachoeira and other cities of the Recôncavo region.

BRUCE YUANYUE BI / GETTY IMAGES ©

HUW JONES / GETTY IMAGES ©

1. Capoeira performance, Salvador
2. Capoeira dance school, Natal
3. Capoeira instruments

MEGATRI / GETTY IMAGES ©

The movements are always fluid and circular, the fighters always playful and respectful as they exchange mock blows. Capoeira is typically practiced by two fighters at a time inside a *roda* (circle) of spectators/fighters who clap and sing. In addition to the *berimbau*, other instruments such as the *pandeiro* (tambourine), *agogô* (bell) and *atabaque* (drum) provide musical accompaniment. Capoeira gains more followers by the year, both nationally and abroad. Throughout Brazil – particularly Bahia – you will see people practicing their moves on the beach and street *rodas* popping up in touristy areas.

Watching Capoeira

At night in the Pelourinho, you'll hear music spilling out of capoeira studios clustered in the area of Teatro San Miguel Santana. Take a peek inside and don't be surprised if you're asked to pay a small fee to observe – you're supporting the studio. It's more authentic than the capoeira you'll see in touristy areas: linger to watch the performers in the Terreiro de Jesus and the ground level of the Mercado Modelo, and you'll be hustled for cash within moments. More professional capoeira is on proud display in folkloric shows like Salvador's famous Balé Folclórico da Bahia (p419).

Capoeira Classes

In Salvador, capoeira classes (p407) are held in the Pelourinho. Elsewhere in Bahia, capoeiristas often advertise lessons at youth hostels. Expect to pay around R$35 for a one-hour class; wear comfortable, loose-fitting pants you can move around in.

Sleeping

Staying in the Pelourinho means being close to the action, but the beach suburbs are mellower (and just a short bus or taxi ride away). Santo Antônio is a peaceful neighborhood with classy pousadas (guesthouses) in renovated old buildings just a short walk from the Pelourinho. Reservations during Carnaval are essential.

Pelourinho

★Hostel Galeria 13 HOSTEL $
(Map p404; ☎3266-5609; www.hostelgaleria13.com; Acciole 23; dm/d from R$35/140; ❄📶🏊) Located in an old colonial house complete with a swimming pool and a Moroccan-style lounge – rarities at any hostel, but especially in one at such a great location in the middle of the historic center – Galeria 13 is a huge hit with backpackers. Breakfast is served till noon, and nonguests are welcome to hang out. It's affiliated with the excellent Bar Zulu (p415), just around the corner.

Hostel Solar dos Romanos HOSTEL $
(Map p404; ☎3321-6812; www.hostelsolardosromanos.com; Portas do Carmo 14; dm R$35-50, d R$100-120; ❄📶) This clean and affordable hostel boasts an unusual combination: both a location in the heart of the Pelourinho and a terrace with bay views. Doubles are simple; perks include 24-hour kitchen access.

Laranjeiras Hostel HOSTEL $
(Map p404; ☎3321-1366; www.laranjeirashostel.com.br; Rua da Ordem Terceira 13; dm R$40-48, s from R$65, d R$96-115, tr from R$150; ❄@📶) This cheerful yellow colonial mansion-turned-hostel is one of the best budget options in the Pelô. High-ceilinged rooms range from dorms to comfortable suites – save cash by choosing a room with a fan instead of air-conditioning. Perks include kitchen access, laundry facilities, and an on-site creperie.

Bahiacafé Hotel BOUTIQUE HOTEL $$
(Map p404; ☎3322-1266; www.bahiacafehotelsalvador.com; Praça da Sé 22; d R$199-239) This chic but low-key boutique hotel has fashionably outfitted rooms and an excellent location close to the center of the action in the Pelourinho. The lobby cafe, filled with locally produced artwork and open to the public, is the perfect spot for a quick cappuccino during an afternoon of sightseeing.

★Casa do Amarelindo BOUTIQUE HOTEL $$$
(Map p404; ☎3266-8550; www.casadoamarelindo.com; Portas do Carmo 6; d R$420-550, d with balcony & view R$505-670; ❄📶🏊) Inside a 10th-century colonial mansion on a historic block, this charming boutique hotel is truly a gem. Ten impeccably outfitted guest rooms have first-class bedding, hot tubs or rainfall showers, and huge windows; there's an adorably petite rooftop swimming pool, a popular bistro and a small fitness center. No children under age 14 are permitted.

Pousada Solar dos Deuses POUSADA $$$
(Map p404; ☎3322-1911; www.solardosdeuses.com.br; Largo Cruzeiro de São Francisco 12; d R$490; ❄📶) Design-minded guests rave about the charming details of this petite pousada: think exposed stone and brick walls, decorative wrought-iron headboards, wood-carved furniture inspired by Bahia's Candomblé tradition, and a picture-perfect breakfast served in your room. French, English and Spanish are spoken.

Hotel Villa Bahia BOUTIQUE HOTEL $$$
(Map p404; ☎3322-4271; www.en.lavillabahia.com; Largo do Cruzeiro de São Francisco 16; d R$610-678; ❄📶🏊) 🌿 Occupying a pair of restored Portuguese-style colonial houses, this sustainably run boutique hotel (practices

REVIVING A LANDMARK

An art deco landmark immortalized in literature, the Palace Hotel has been closed for more than a decade. But it was the pinnacle of glamour in its heyday. The hotel opened in 1934 and hosted famous guests from Orson Welles to Carmen Miranda; Jorge Amado chose its ballroom as the setting for a memorable scene in his novel *Dona Flor e Seus Dois Maridos* (Dona Flor and Her Two Husbands.)

Now, the Palace Hotel was set to reopen in 2016 after a multi-milllion-dollar restoration overseen by the Brazilian entrepreneur Antonio Mazzafera and the noted Scandinavian architect Adam Kurdahl. The hotel will have around 100 guest rooms and suites, two restaurants and a swimming pool with views over the bay. It's part of a larger effort to revive the neighborhood – keep your eye on this pocket of the old city that's being called the 'Bahia Design Destrict.'

include recycling and employment of local craftspeople) has 17 rooms with hardwood floors, shuttered windows, and antique furnishings ranging from heavy armoires to twinkling chandeliers. There's a panoramic terrace and plunge pool, plus a good organic restaurant that's open to the public.

Carmo & Santo Antônio

Many of the city's most charming (and best-value) pousadas are located in this neighborhood. It pays to look around online before booking a room.

Pousada Baluarte POUSADA $
(Map p400; 3327-0367; www.pousadabaluarte.com; Ladeira do Baluarte 13; d R$130-190, tr R$250;) Run by a friendly French-Brazilian couple, Baluarte feels like a B&B, with a welcoming, homelike ambience and just five rooms with hardwood floors and beautiful block prints by a local artist. A delicious breakfast is served on the veranda; the Pelourinho is a 10-minute walk away.

Pousada do Boqueirão POUSADA $$
(Map p404; 3241-2262; www.pousadaboqueirao.com.br; Direita de Santo Antônio 48; d with/without bathroom from R$360/320, ste from R$540;) Two early-20th-century houses have been joined together to form this elegant guesthouse, tastefully decorated with antiques and artwork. Spacious common rooms back onto a porch with a fantastic bay view, where breakfast is served.

Pestana Convento do Carmo HOTEL $$$
(Map p404; 3327-8400; www.pestana.com/en/pestana-convento-do-carmo; Rua do Carmo 1; d from R$650;) Set in a restored 17th-century convent, this magnificent hotel has elegantly furnished rooms with old-world details and modern comforts, and even more impressive common areas. There's a stone chapel and arched walkways around the cloister.

Aram Yami Hotel BOUTIQUE HOTEL $$$
(Map p400; 3242-9412; www.aramyamihotel.com; Direita de Santo Antonio 132; ste from $550) How about taking in the sunset from an infinity pool overlooking the bay? The dream is a reality at the exclusive Aram Yami Hotel, a chic urban getaway that's practically a vacation in itself. The terraces offer spectacular views, six suites are spacious and plush, and the staff is particularly helpful with planning cultural excursions.

Barra & Coastal Suburbs

Of all the beachside suburbs, happening Barra attracts the majority of visitors due to its proximity to the Pelourinho.

★ **Open House Barra** POUSADA $
(Map p414; 3264-0337; www.openhousebarra.com; Bernardo Catarino 137, Barra; dm R$44, d with/without bathroom R$132/110;) This fantastically colorful and homey place is run by professional artists with deep connections with the local music, dance and film community. Musicians and capoeira demonstrations periodically take place at the hostel, especially during Carnaval, when the guesthouse offers one of Salvador's most memorable party experiences.

Âmbar Pousada POUSADA $
(Map p414; 3264-6956; www.ambarpousada.com.br; Afonso Celso 485; dm/s/d R$50/120/135; @) A favorite among budget-minded travelers, this easygoing hostel and guesthouse has a welcoming atmosphere. Dorms are quiet, and doubles are small – note that some of the private bathrooms are only separated by a partition, not a door – but there's ample public space, and it's a two-minute walk to the beach.

Che Lagarto HOSTEL $
(Map p414; 3235-2404; www.chelagarto.com; Av Oceânica 84, Barra; dm R$28-32, d R$90-130;) Occupying a coveted spot of real estate just across the street from the beach, this spacious branch of the Che Logarto hostel chain is a good place to meet other travelers. But let the buyer beware: travelers complain about poor service and the ongoing need for better maintenance.

Pousada Estrela do Mar POUSADA $$
(Map p414; 3264-4882; www.estreladomarsalvador.com; Afonso Celso 119, Barra; d R$190-225;) This white stucco house with dark-blue shutters – very Portugal-meets-the-tropics – is surrounded by greenery, while inside plain white walls set off bright Bahian paintings and vibrant blue tilework. The location is close to the beach on a mellow, tree-shaded street.

Pousada Noa Noa POUSADA $$
(Map p414; 3264-1148; www.pousadanoanoa.com; Av Sete de Setembro 4295, Barra; d R$160-220;) The buzzy oceanfront terrace and bar – an ideal spot from which to watch the sunset with a cocktail in hand –

Salvador Barra

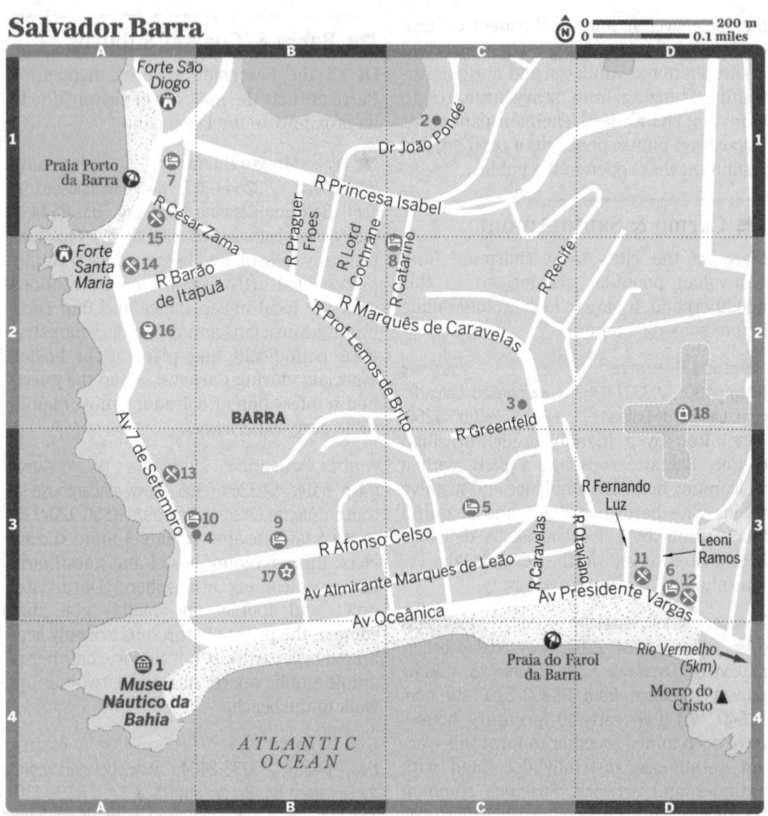

Salvador Barra

Top Sights

1 Museu Náutico da Bahia A4

Sights

Forte de Santo Antônio da Barra .... (see 1)

Activities, Courses & Tours

2 Diálogo C1
3 Idioma Escola de Português C2
4 Salvador Bus B3

Sleeping

5 Âmbar Pousada C3
6 Che Lagarto D3
7 Hit Hotel A1
8 Open House Barra C2
9 Pousada Estrela do Mar B3
10 Pousada Noa Noa A3

Eating

11 Caranguejo de Sergipe D3
12 Caranguejo do Porto D3
13 Empada Brasil A3
14 Ola Cevicheria A2
15 Portal do Mar A1

Drinking & Nightlife

16 Pereira A2

Entertainment

17 Off Club B3

Shopping

18 Shopping Barra D2

is the key selling point of this welcoming guesthouse. Of 15 simply furnished guest rooms, only a few have ocean views, and the others are on the dark side.

Hit Hotel HOTEL **$$**
(Map p414; 3264-7433; www.hithotel.com.br; Av Sete de Setembro 3691; d R$169-209;) New on Barra's waterfront, this modern ho-

tel is low-key, offering basic but comfortable rooms. Many have bay views, as does the breakfast area.

Eating

Dining out is a delight in Salvador. Traditional Bahian cuisine has a heavy African influence, featuring ingredients like coconut cream, tomato, seafood, bell pepper and spices of ginger, hot peppers and coriander. Check local listings and promotions for **Food Park Salvador**, a brand-new festival featuring food trucks and live music on select weekends. The youthful event is just getting off the ground: the most recent edition was held in Ondina.

Pelourinho

The Pelourinho is packed with restaurants; some feel uncomfortably touristy, while others are wonderfully charming. Be aware that sidewalk seating, while allowing unparalleled people-watching opportunities, makes you an easy target for salespeople and children asking for money.

★Bar Zulu INTERNATIONAL $

(Map p404; Laranjeiras 15; mains R$14-30; 1pm-1am Wed-Mon, closed Tue;) This laid-back corner bar and eatery has outdoor tables and serves a wide range of Spanish tapas, Bahian classics and international dishes, plus Argentine wine by the glass and cocktails like the colorful 'Galeria 13,' made with lemon, watermelon and *cachaça* (sugarcane alcohol). Try the house burger, Thai curry, or one of the rice-based dishes – like a lighter take on *moqueca* (fish stew).

A Cubana ICE CREAM $

(Map p404; www.acubana.com.br; Portas do Carmo 12; cones from R$9; 9am-10pm) One of Salvador's oldest and best ice-cream shops, with two popular locations in the Pelourinho; the other one is located at the top of the Elevador Lacerda.

★Restaurante do Senac BUFFET $$

(Map p404; www.ba.senac.br; Largo do Pelourinho 13; buffet per kilo R$35, buffet típico R$48 ; buffet per kilo 11:30am-3:30pm Mon-Fri, buffet típico 11:30am-3:30pm daily;) The best Bahian buffet in town. The cooking school Senac spreads a tempting array of regional dishes, including several varieties of seafood, *moqueca,* and traditional desserts. The impressive buffet típico is on the top floor, not to be confused with the street-level buffet per kilo, which is also good for a quick lunch.

O Coliseu BAHIAN $$

(Map p404; 3321-5585; www.ocoliseu.com.br; 2nd fl, Cruzeiro de São Francisco 9; per kg R$35, dinner R$160; 11:30am-4pm & 7-8:30pm Mon-Sat;) This vegetarian-friendly restaurant offers a spread of regional dishes, buffet-style. It's pay-as-you-go at lunch, and a dinner-and-show package at night, with the popular Topázio (p419) folkloric show. Dinner begins at 7pm, the show starts at 8:30pm.

Cuco Bistrô INTERNATIONAL $$

(Map p404; 3322-4383; Largo do Cruzeiro de São Francisco 6; mains R$35-55; noon-3pm & 8pm-midnight Mon-Sat, noon-3pm Sun) Don't be deterred by the fact that this bistro doubles as an internet café: it's a favorite among locals and tourists alike for its Mediterranean-influenced cuisine and modern takes on Bahian dishes. At lunchtime, try the frequently changing set menu (R$49), including an appetizer and dessert.

Maria Mata Mouro BRAZILIAN $$$

(Map p404; 3321-3929; www.mariamatamouro.com.br; Ordem Terceira 8; mains for 2 R$65-120; 11:45am-11pm) The picture-perfect garden patio and elegant dining room are fine settings to enjoy one of Pelô's top menus. You'll find Bahian classics, fresh seafood and Portuguese dishes prepared with a gourmet twist, plus a varied wine list and a talented bartender shaking up unique cocktails.

Pelô Bistrô BRAZILIAN $$$

(Map p404; www.casadoamarelindo.com; Hotel Casa do Amarelindo, Portas do Carmo 6; mains R$45-70; 11:30am-10:30pm;) The lovely bistro at Hotel Casa do Amarelindo (p412) is a sure thing for a gourmet lunch or dinner: the seafood-focused menu features grilled salmon with passion fruit and sautéed shrimp with pineapple rice, plus a good South American wine list.

Carmo

★Cafélier CAFE $

(Map p404; 3241-5095; www.cafelier.com.br; Rua do Carmo 50; snacks & light meals R$8-25; 2:30-9:30pm Mon-Tue & Thu-Sat, 2:30-8pm Sun, closed Wed) This quaint hideaway café, located inside an antique house that's positioned dramatically on a cliff top over the ocean, is one of a kind. Come for the views, plus beautifully prepared cappuccino, rich chocolate cake, savory snacks and wines by the glass.

Cidade Baixa/Comércio

In the Comércio, cheap *lanchonetes* (snack bars) and self-service restaurants abound. For something more memorable, head south along the bay, where there are several fine (if expensive) restaurants with views over the water.

Camafeu de Oxossi BAHIAN $
(Map p404; ☎3242-9751; Mercado Modelo, Praça Cayru; mains R$18-45; ⏲9am-6pm Mon-Sat, to 2pm Sun) A standard Bahian menu is available at this casual spot on the upper terrace of the Mercado Modelo. Though it's touristy and the food isn't particularly notable, many shoppers or travelers waiting to take the ferry to Morro stop here for coffee, juice, snacks, *moqueca* or cold beer with lovely views over the bay.

Barra & Coastal Suburbs

Budget-minded travelers will find plenty of self-serve eateries, sandwich shops, tapioca stands and supermarkets in Barra.

Empada Brasil BRAZILIAN $
(Map p414; www.empadabrasil.com.br; Av Sete de Setembro 4191, Barra; mains R$4-25; ⏲10am-10pm) This branch of the Brazilian chain is nothing fancy, but it offers porch seating, inexpensive takeout and a decent buffet spread featuring a small range of Bahian dishes.

★ **Caranguejo de Sergipe** SEAFOOD $$
(Map p414; ☎3248-3331; Av Oceânica & Fernando Luz, Barra; mains R$22-40; ⏲11am-2am Tue-Sun, from 4pm Mon) A local favorite, this always-packed eatery is known for fresh crabs and platters of grilled seafood and vegetables. Don't miss the expertly prepared *maracujá* caipirinha (passion fruit cocktail) – perhaps the most delicious drink on the beach.

★ **Paraíso Tropical** BAHIAN $$
(☎3384-7464; www.restauranteparaisotropical.com.br; Edgar Loureiro 98B, Cabula; mains R$30-65; ⏲noon-10pm Tue-Sat, to 5pm Sun, closed Mon) Though it's far off the beaten path in the residential neighborhood of Cabula, foodies don't mind the detour to Paraíso Tropical: the classic Brazilian restaurant has long been considered one of Salvador's top choices for beautifully prepared Bahian cuisine with a gourmet twist. Come for a leisurely lunch; expect long waits on weekends.

Ola Cevicheria PERUVIAN $$
(Map p414; ☎3264-2519; Sete de Setembro 3807, Barra; mains R$32-52; ⏲6pm-midnight Mon-Sat) This modern but casual Peruvian eatery on Barra's waterfront offers a refreshing change of pace from the traditional Bahian seafood scene. The menu offers eight varieties of seviche, plus a short list of heartier dishes focused on beef or duck. Frosty pisco cocktails and breezy outdoor seating add to the appeal.

Caranguejo do Porto SEAFOOD $$
(Map p414; ☎3245-9197; Av Oceânica 819, Barra; mains R$22-59; ⏲noon-late Mon-Sat) Another of Barra's seaside hot spots for traditional Bahian food; think *moqueca*, fresh crabs, *pasteles* (empanada-like pastries stuffed with meat and other savory fillings), cold

A NIGHT OUT IN RIO VERMELHO

The coastal neighborhood of Rio Vermelho has always been culturally significant to the city of Salvador: Portuguese sailors wrecked their ship offshore in 1510, famed writer Jorge Amado lived here and the important Candomblé festival Festa da Iemanjá (p409), honoring the goddess of motherhood and fertility, takes place on its shores. But in recent years, the neighborhood has also emerged as a hub of nightlife.

Arrive around sunset and take your pick from the sea of plastic tables and chairs set up on the lively plaza of Largo de Santana. Several casual bars serve cold beer to these outdoor tables, but the real attraction is the traditional street food prepared by colorfully dressed Bahian women at stands around the square. Particularly legendary are the *acarajé* (balls of dough fried in *dendê* – palm oil – and served with spicy sauces and shrimp).

On any given evening, there are cultural events and free concerts in the square, at the cultural center **Casa de Mãe Iemanja** (☎3334-3041; Guedes Cabral 81, Rio Vermelho; ⏲2pm-2am Fri-Sun) FREE, and around the waterfront market Mercado do Peixe. Afterward, go for drinks at nearby Póstudo (p417), then catch some live music at Commons Studio Bar (p418). After midnight, hit the dance floor at San Sebastian.

Rio Vermelho is about a 30-minute walk along the coast, or a short bus ride from Barra on any bus marked 'Orla' (waterfront).

beer and caipirinhas (cocktails) this lively eatery transitions into a casual bar scene as the night rolls on.

Portal do Mar BRAZILIAN **$$**
(Map p414; Sete de Setembro 510; mains R$24-65; ⌚10am-midnight) Open all day, with outdoor tables just across the street from the beach, this is an appealing spot for a sunset caipirinha or an easygoing dinner – the staff boldly call themselves the *moqueca* experts, but they also serve pasta, steak and grilled fish.

Drinking & Nightlife

The Pelourinho is Salvador's nightlife capital: bars with outdoor tables and live music spill onto the cobbled streets. It's the place to be every week on Terça da Benção (Blessed Tuesday), when street parties kick off after evening Mass.

In Barra, find relaxed ambience and music along Av Almirante Marques de Leão and the waterfront around the Farol da Barra. Bohemian Rio Vermelho has one of the more interesting nightlife scenes in the region.

GAY & LESBIAN VENUES

Salvador's gay nightlife scene may be subdued compared to those of other Brazilian capitals, but these off-the-beaten-path venues are worth seeking out.

A young, gay-friendly crowd flocks to **Beco dos Artistas** (Artist's Alley; Map p400; Av Cerqueira Lima, Garcia), a lively alley with several bars popular for preclubbing drinks. Take a taxi and enter from Rua Leovigildo Filgueira. After midnight In Rio Vermelho, good-looking **San Sebastian** (www.sansebastianoficial.com.br; Paciência 88, Rio Vermelho; admission R$35; ⌚11:45pm-5am Fri-Sun) draws the LGBT crowd with three floors, four bars and two dance floors. In Barra, near the beach, **Off Club** (Map p414; ☎3267-6215; R Dias D'Ávila 33, Barra; ⌚10pm-6am Thu-Sun) is another hot spot for dancing, bringing in top-name DJs.

Check www.guiagaysalvador.com.br for the latest listings and events.

Pelourinho & Carmo

Many restaurants and cafés on the side streets of the Pelourinho offer live music at night.

O Cravinho BAR
(Map p404; www.ocravinho.com.br; Terreiro de Jesus 3; ⌚11am-11:30pm) This friendly neighborhood bar specializes in flavored shots of *cachaça*, including its trademark clove-infused variety. Decorated with barrels and packed with a vibrant mix of locals and tourists and featuring live music many evenings of the week, it's an atmospheric place to stop in for a quick drink while sightseeing in the Pelourinho.

Casa do Amarelindo Bar COCKTAIL BAR
(Map p404; ☎3266-8550; www.casadoamarelindo.com; Hotel Casa do Amarelindo, Portas do Carmo 6; ⌚noon-late) The chic tropical-style bar at the lovely Pelô Bistrô (p415) at Casa do Amarelindo is the ideal spot for a nightcap; better still is the panoramic terrace where a skilled bartender shows up after dark to mix classic cocktails.

Barra & Coastal Suburbs

★ **Pereira** BAR
(Map p414; ☎3264-6464; www.pereirarestaurante.com.br; Sete de Setembro 3959, Barra; ⌚noon-4pm & 5pm-1am Tue-Sun) Up a staircase from the seaside road that curves around the tip of Barra, Pereira is a stylish restaurant and wine bar. Excellent *chope* (draft beer) is on tap and the sunset views over the ocean are beautiful.

Póstudo BAR
(☎3334-0484; João Gomes 87, Rio Vermelho; ⌚11am-3am) This perpetually cool bar and restaurant, right in the middle of Rio Vermelho nightlife action, has ocean views and a long drinks menu.

Entertainment

Bars and clubs tend to come and go in Salvador, so ask around to see what's hot at the moment, or log onto the agenda of parties, concerts and performances at Festa da Semana (www.festadasemana.com.br/salvador).

Live Music

Salvador is the pulsing center of an incredible music scene, where a blend of African and Brazilian traditions has produced mind-blowing forms of percussion that *salvadorenos* mix into their reggae, pop and rock, *pagode* and *axé*. The city has also produced unique styles such as *afoxé* and samba reggae. Since hardly a bar or restaurant in the city lacks live music at least one night of the week, catching some of Salvador's talented artists isn't hard.

During the high season, there are almost nightly concerts in the inner courtyards of the Pelourinho, with cover charges ranging from free to R$30. Take a stroll by the following places and find out what's on for the evening: Largo de Tereza Batista, Largo do Pedro Arcanjo and Praça Quincas Berro d'Água (all usually free). There are also occasional concerts on the Terreiro de Jesus and you can frequently hear drum corps, which rehearse by walking through the Pelourinho, blocking traffic and gathering a following as they go.

Traditional groups (characterized by strong Afro drum corps) to be on the lookout for include Ilê Aiyê (the first exclusively black Carnaval group), the all-female Dida, Muzenza and Male Debalê. More pop and with strong percussion sections are world-famous Olodum (Tuesday-night Pelourinho institution), Araketu and Timbalada, brainchild of master composer and musician Carlinhos Brown. The queens of Salvador pop music – Margareth Menezes, Ivete Sangalo and Daniela Mercury – also often 'rehearse' publicly.

For the biggest acts, keep your eye on Salvador's finest venue, the **Teatro Castro Alves** (Map p400; www.tca.ba.gov.br; Praça 2 de Julho, Campo Grande); its amphitheater has weekly concerts throughout summer.

★Jam no MAM LIVE MUSIC
(Map p400; www.jamnomam.com.br; Museu de Arte Moderna, Av Contorno s/n; adult/child R$7/3.50; ⌚6-9pm Sat) Saturday-evening jazz and bossa nova at MAM (Museu de Arte Moderna; p406) is a must for music lovers. Go early to see the museum first and catch the views at sunset. Though the venue is located within walking distance of the Pelourinho, muggings are common along the quiet stretch; taking a taxi is recommended.

Bar Fundo do Cravinho LIVE MUSIC
(Map p404; www.clubedosamba.com.br; Terreiro de Jesus 5, Pelourinho; cover charge varies; ⌚4-11pm) Live samba nightly starting around 8pm, down an alley behind the eponymous bar.

Commons Studio Bar LIVE MUSIC
(www.commons.com.br; Doutor Odilon Santos 224, Rio Vermelho; cover from R$10) Rustic-chic, with state-of-the-art equipment, this cool venue is a relatively new addition to Salvador's nightlife scene. Commons hosts the up-and-coming Brazilian musical acts and runs community-focused programming, from workshops to special events. Log onto the website for the schedule, and click on the 'Lista Amiga' section for reservations and discounted tickets.

D'Venetta LIVE MUSIC
(Map p400; www.dvenetta.com.br; Rua dos Abodes 12, Santo Antônio; some events free, cover charges vary; ⌚6pm-1am Wed-Fri, 11:30am-7pm Sun, closed Mon-Tue) This buzzed-about cultural center, bar and art space in Santo Antônio features live samba, *samba de roda* and jazz.

Folkloric Shows & Capoeira

The chance to see a folkloric performance that showcases the unique range of Bahian music and dance – including live percussion and vocals, the dances of the *orixás, maculêlê* (stick dance), samba and capoeira – shouldn't be missed. You can also catch some authentic capoeira in the Pelourinho, where studios charge a few reais for watching a class (often called a 'show') and for taking pictures.

OLODUM

Walking around in Salvador, the bold symbol of a red, yellow and green peace sign is everywhere: it's the iconic symbol of Olodum, an Afro-Brazilian cultural group founded in 1979 by percussionist Neguinho do Samba. Originally, the objective was to curb racism and create opportunities for Bahia's marginalized youth. The organization still works toward these aims, primarily through music: the Olodum school is famous for developing its leader's signature style of *afro bloco*, also known as samba reggae, which takes inspiration from the musical styles of Caribbean reggae, salsa and Brazilian samba.

Today, Olodum runs a school, and the official band records music with big-time Brazilian musicians; during Carnaval, Olodum features prominently on the musical lineup. The colorful band of percussionists has also made waves in the international pop-culture scene: Michael Jackson filmed his 1996 music video for the single 'They Don't Care About Us' with the Olodum troupe in the streets of the Pelourinho. Log onto www.olodum.com.br for more on the organization, or take a peek into the **Escola Olodum** (Map p404; ☎3321-4154; www.olodum.com.br; Gregório de Mattos 22; tours by donation, workshops free; ⌚10am-6pm Mon-Fri) in the Pelourinho.

★ **Balé Folclórico da Bahia** PERFORMING ARTS

(Map p404; ☎3322-1962; www.balefolclorico dabahia.com.br; R Gregório de Mattos 49, Teatro Miguel Santana; admission R$40; ⌚shows 8pm Mon-Sat) The most astounding professional show is put on by this world-renowned folkloric ballet company.

Topázio PERFORMING ARTS

(Map p404; ☎3321-6918; www.capoeiratopazio.com.br; 2nd fl, Cruzeiro de São Francisco 9; incl buffet dinner R$160; ⌚8:30pm Mon-Sat) The popular show that used to be staged at the Solar do Unhão, featuring 18 dancers, musicians, and capoeiristas, now happens after dinner at O Coliseu (p415). Dinner starts at 7pm and the show begins around 8:30pm. Reserve ahead.

Shopping

For most visitors, shopping opportunities in Salvador fall into one of two camps: the artisan crafts and traditional Bahian souvenirs of the Pelourinho and the Mercado Modelo, and large shopping centers such as **Shopping Barra** (Map p414; ☎3264-4566; Av Centenário 2992, Barra, SAC) and **Shopping da Bahia** (www.shoppingdabahia.com.br; Av Tancredo Neves s/n, Iguatemi), busy with Brazilian fashionistas and bustling food courts, across from the bus station, previously known as Shopping Iguatemi.

Mercado Modelo HANDICRAFTS

(Map p404; www.mercadomodelobahia.com.br; Praça Cayru, Cidade Baixa; ⌚9am-7pm Mon-Sat, to 2pm Sun) This two-story market – once the site where slaves were held – has dozens of tourist-oriented stalls selling local handicrafts, plus food stands frequented by locals.

Orientation

Salvador sits at the southern tip of a V-shaped peninsula at the mouth of the Baía de Todos os Santos. The city can be difficult to navigate as there are many one-way, no-left-turn streets that wind through Salvador's hills and valleys. The center of the city is on the bay side of the peninsula and is divided by a steep bluff into two parts: Cidade Alta (Upper City) and Cidade Baixa (Lower City).

The heart of historic Cidade Alta is the Pelourinho (or Pelô), which is also the heart of Salvador's tourism and nightlife. This roughly refers to the area from Praça da Sé to Largo do Pelourinho.

From Praça Castro Alves, Av 7 de Setembro runs through the Centro to the wide Praça Campo Grande, then continues southwest through the well-to-do Vitória neighborhood, and down to the mouth of the bay. Here, at the tip of the peninsula, is the affluent Barra district, with its lighthouse, forts and popular beach.

A main thoroughfare, which constantly changes names (one being Av Presidente Vargas), snakes east from Barra along the Atlantic coast. It cuts inland briefly around Forte de Santo Antonio (where pedestrian-only promenades have been recently built), then passes through the coastal neighborhoods of Ondina and Rio Vermelho, continuing through a chain of middle-class beachfront suburbs all the way to Itapuã.

Cidade Baixa contains the Comércio (the city's commercial and financial center), the ferry terminals and port. North, the land curves around the bay to create the Itapagipe Peninsula, including the Bonfim and Boa Viagem neighborhoods. The suburbs along the bay are poor, and the level of poverty generally increases with the distance from the center.

VINTAGE SALVADOR

History buffs and photography enthusiasts shouldn't miss a virtual visit to Salvador Antiga (www.salvador-antiga.com), an excellent online resource for old photos and watercolor renderings of the city in days gone by. Images are helpfully categorized according to neighborhood.

Information

EMERGENCY

Delegacia do Turista (Tourist Police; ☎3116-6817; Cruzeiro de São Francisco 14, Pelourinho) Any crime involving a tourist must be handled by the city's tourist police. A few speak English or French.

Pronto Socorro (Ambulance; ☎192)

INTERNET ACCESS

It's easy to get online in Salvador. Internet cafés are everywhere (R$4 to R$8 per hour); most pousadas and many restaurants offer wi-fi.

Baiafrica Internet Café (Praça da Sé 8, Pelourinho; ⌚9am-10pm Mon-Sat) Fast internet and flat-screen monitors, each outfitted with Skype and a webcam.

MEDICAL SERVICES

Hospital Espanhol (Av Sete de Setembro 4161, Barra) One of the city's main hospitals (and a lovely architectural landmark too.)

MONEY

Banco do Brasil (Cruzeiro de São Francisco 11, Pelourinho) Also in the airport and scattered around Barra.

WORTH A TRIP

ILHA DE ITAPARICA

The Baía de Todos os Santos, occupying 1000 sq km, is Brazil's largest bay, containing 56 islands rich with lush vegetation and historic architecture. The most popular escape for residents of Salvador is the island of Itaparica. The shores are lined with vacation homes, and while the beaches are only average, many travelers enjoy taking a day trip to the bars, restaurants and relaxed atmosphere of the likable island town of Mar Grande, 9km south of the transport hub of Bom Despacho.

Guarding the northern tip of the island, the **Forte de São Lourenço** (1711) was built by Dutch invaders and figured prominently in Bahia's battle for independence in 1823. In the center of the island, a huge tree wraps its roots around and grows through the ruins of the **Igreja Baiacu** church. The clear waters of **Praia Barra Grande**, in front of the village, is Itaparica's finest public beach. It has clear water and weekend homes, and lies in front of its namesake village. Plenty of casual restaurants, clustered near the ferry dock, serve Bahian-style seafood with bay views.

The boat journey from Salvador is half the fun. Passenger ferries (R$3, 40 minutes, every 30 minutes from 6am to 6pm, to 6:30pm on weekends) run between Salvador's Terminal Marítimo Turístico and Mar Grande's terminal. It's wise to buy your return ticket ahead of time on summer days.

Bradesco (Mattos s/n, Pelourinho) With international ATMs. Also in the Barra, at the bus station and in the airport.

Toursbahia (☎3320-3280; www.toursbahia.com.br; Cruzeiro de São Francisco 4, Pelourinho) Changes cash and traveler's checks; nearby outfits do the same.

SAFE TRAVEL

In the center, tourist police maintain a visible presence, particularly in the Pelourinho. Crime in the Pelô increases during the high season (especially around Carnaval) and on crowded Tuesday nights, and pickpocketing is common on buses and in crowded places where tourists are easily singled out. To minimize risks, dress down, keep jewelry to a minimum, carry just enough cash for your outing and only a photocopy of your passport, and try to be roughly oriented before you set out.

If you must carry a bank card, take only one – and use ATMs inside banks instead of freestanding machines that are more susceptible to hackers.

The Pelourinho shifts quickly into sketchy areas, so avoid wandering off the beaten path. Cidade Baixa is deserted and unsafe at night and on weekends, and the *ladeiras* (steep roads) that connect it to Cidade Alta should never be taken on foot.

On the beaches, keep a close eye on juvenile thieves – or *capitães d'areia* (captains of the sand) – who are quick to make off with unguarded possessions.

Don't hesitate to use taxis after dark or in areas where you feel apprehensive, though taking buses in the evening is not necessarily unsafe.

TOURIST INFORMATION

You can also find plenty of tourist information at the many travel agencies throughout the city.

Bahiatursa (Map p404; ☎3321-2463; www.bahiatursa.ba.gov.br; Rua Francisco Muniz Barreto 12, Pelourinho; ⏰8:30am-9pm Mon-Thu, to 10pm Fri-Sun) The tourism authority is friendly if not terribly organized. The Pelourinho office, which has maps and listings of what's happening around town, is your best bet. There are also desks at the bus station and the airport, and a city tourist office (Emtursa Lacerda; Map p404; ☎3321-3127; www.emtursa.salvador.ba.gov.br; Elevador Lacerda, Cidade Alta). Also see www.bahia.com.br.

Grupo Gay da Bahia (Map p404; ☎3322-2552; www.ggb.org.br; Frei Vicente 24, Pelourinho; ⏰9am-6pm Mon-Fri) A cultural center for gay, lesbian and transgender people.

Quatro Cantos Turismo (☎3264-2000; www.4cantosturismo.com.br; Marquês de Caravelas 154, Barra; ⏰9am-6pm Mon-Fri) This travel agency is a helpful stop for maps, tourist information and trip planning; the agents can also help you buy plane tickets.

Salvador Central (Map p404; ☎3321-0536; www.salvadorcentral.com; João de Deus 22, Pelourinho; ⏰10am-7pm Mon-Sat) This apartment-rental agency and tourist-information desk also runs an English-language website that's an excellent resource for anyone interested in the region's music culture.

ℹ Getting There & Away

AIR

Aeroporto Deputado Luis Eduardo do Magalhães (SSA; ☎3204-1010; São Cristóvão) is served by domestic airlines like **Gol** (☎3204-1603; www.voegol.com.br; airport), **TAM** (☎3365-2324; www.tam.com.br; airport), and Azul (www.voeazul.com.br). American

Airlines (www.aa.com) now offers a direct flight to Miami, and **Aerolineas Argentinas** (☎1-800-333-0276; www.aerolineas.com.ar) has a new direct flight to Buenos Aires. But generally speaking, flights to international destinations go via São Paulo or Rio.

BOAT

Boats to Morro de São Paulo and points on Baía de Todos os Santos leave from the **Terminal Marítimo Turístico** (Map p404; Av da França s/n, Comércio), also known as the **Terminal da França** (Map p404), behind the Mercado Modelo, and the **Terminal de São Joaquim** (☎3633-1248; Av Oscar Pontes 1051), a 10-minute taxi ride north. Note that at the airport or bus station, these boats are often referred to by the English phrase 'ferry boat'.

BUS

For shorter trips, you can buy bus tickets at the time of travel. For longer journeys, especially during peak travel times, you'll want to book ahead to make sure you have a spot. The easiest way to purchase bus tickets is at the main train station – but Salvador's bus station is a long haul from the center. So it's best to plan your strategy and buy tickets when you're passing through; unlike with plane tickets, most travel agencies in town don't sell bus tickets.

Brazilians often reserve online, a privilege not extended to foreigners, with a few exceptions. A few bus lines are starting to offer the option to use a foreign credit card, and you might have luck through new websites like www.clickbus.com.br or www.busbud.com. When in doubt, ask the staff at your hotel or hostel: they're often willing to help make travel arrangements, or at least give advice.

Note that, in addition to the fees listed below, for many bus tickets out of Salvador, you are also required to buy an Interestadual card (R$4.50) at the time of ticket purchase. Swipe it at the departure gates for access to the bus platforms.

Getting Around

TO/FROM THE AIRPORT

The airport is located about 30km east of the center. For a taxi going to Barra or the Pelourinho, you'll pay around R$122 in advance at the airport – the official **Taxi Comtas** and **Taxi Coometas** stands inside the arrivals hall accept credit cards, which is convenient if you're not carrying local currency. The trip takes 40 to 60 minutes. You'll pay slightly less if you hail a taxi outside, though you might not see any available cars. Follow the signs for 'taxi comum'.

A new executive bus called First Class (www.firstclassbus.com.br) travels between the airport and key tourist points, including Praca da Sé (in the Pelourinho) and a handful of large beach hotels in Barra. The flat fee is R$30 per person and buses leave from the airport, roughly every 40 minutes, all day and into the evening. Look for the First Class desks: there's one in the baggage-claim area, and another in the arrivals hall. The same service takes you back to the airport: check the First Class website for information on pickup times and places.

There are also public buses (R$3, running 5:30am to 10pm, with fewer departures on weekends) that provide access to the center. For Barra or the Pelourinho (or Terminal Marítimo Turístico for the ferry to Morro de São Paulo, accessible from the Cidade Alta via Elevador Lacerda), take the bus marked 'Praça da Sé-Aeroporto'. For the ferry to Bom Despacho, take the Aeroporto–São Joaquim bus, which also stops at the Rodoviaria (bus station). The ride to the center takes anywhere between 90 minutes and two hours, depending on traffic.

The same buses make the return journey. Buses to the airport depart regularly from the so-called Praça da Sé bus stop, a block southeast of Praça Municipal. Supposedly they leave every 30 minutes, but the schedule isn't fixed, so leave plenty of time. You can pick up the same bus in Barra.

BUSES FROM SALVADOR

DESTINATION	TIME (HR)	COST (\$R)	FREQUENCY	BUS COMPANY
Aracaju	4-6	58-80	10 daily	Águia Branca & Rota
Ilhéus	8	76-156	5 daily	Águia Branca
Lençóis	7-8	65-78	4-5 daily	Real Expresso
Maceió	11	117-145	4 daily	Rota
Natal	25	212	2 daily	São Geraldo
Penedo	10	85	daily	Águia Branca
Porto Seguro	11	176	daily	Águia Branca
Recife	16	161	daily	Águia Branca
Rio de Janeiro	30	299	daily	Águia Branca
São Paulo	32	372	daily	São Geraldo
Vitória	21	189	daily	Águia Branca

TO/FROM THE BUS STATION

Salvador's **bus station** (☎3616-8300) is 8km east of the city center. A taxi to Cidade Alta or Barra runs R$25 to R$45, depending on traffic.

Buses (R$3) marked 'Praça da Sé' go to the center from in front of Shopping Bahia (previously known as Shopping Iguatemi), just across the footbridge in front of the bus station. Going to the bus station, any bus that's labeled 'Shopping Bahia' or 'Iguatemi' will get you to the vicinity.

PUBLIC TRANSPORTATION

Linking Cidade Alta (the Pelourinho) and Cidade Baixa (Comércio and the ferry terminals) are the Elevador Lacerda (p402) and the Plano Inclinado Gonçalves (p405).

Public buses crisscross the city; particularly useful to tourists are those that run between Barra and Praça da Sé (R$3).The destinations are clearly labeled on the front of the bus.

Note that passengers board the bus through the rear door (and pay the attendant seated there), then disembark from the front door of the bus (near the driver). There are two main city bus terminals in the center that can serve as destinations or transfer points: Terminal da França in the Comércio, and Lapa, behind Shopping Lapa and Shopping Piedade. If heading north to the Igreja NS do Bonfim, catch a bus from the stop at the base of the Elevador Lacerda.

Taxis can be taken at meter price (legal) or negotiated, but you might not get to choose which.

RECÔNCAVO

A region of green, fertile lands surrounding the Baía de Todos os Santos, the Recôncavo brought riches to Salvador (and the Portuguese crown) with its sugar and tobacco crops. The profits reaped off these lands also spurred the growth of once-rich towns like Cachoeira, which is resplendent with colonial architecture and history.

Cachoeira & São Félix

☎0XX75 / POP 46,400

Cachoeira, affectionately known as the jewel of the Recôncavo, is a sleepy place, full of colorful, mostly preserved colonial architecture uncompromised by the presence of modern buildings. The town sits below a series of hills, strung along the banks of the Rio Paraguaçu in a face-off with its twin, São Félix – the two towns are connected by a striking British-built bridge divided for cars and pedestrians. A steady trickle of tourism flows through the area, attracted by Brazil's best tobacco, its reputation as a renowned center of Candomblé and a strong wood-sculpting tradition. It's possible to see both Cachoeira and São Félix on a long day trip from Salvador, but it makes more sense to detour here (using Feira de Santana as a hub) on your way to or from Parque Nacional Chapada Diamantina.

History

Diego Álvares, the father of Cachoeira's founders, was the sole survivor of a ship bound for the West Indies that was wrecked in 1510 on a reef near Salvador. This Portuguese Robinson Crusoe was saved by the indigenous Tupinambá of Rio Vermelho, who dubbed the strange white sea creature Caramuru, (Fish-Man). Álvares lived 20 years with the indigenous group and married Catarina do Paraguaçu, the daughter of the most powerful Tupinambá chief. Their sons João Gaspar Aderno Álvares and Rodrigues Martins Álvares killed off the local indigenous people, set up the first sugarcane *fazendas* (ranches) and founded Cachoeira.

By the 18th century, tobacco from Cachoeira was considered the world's finest, sought by rulers in China and Africa. The 'holy herb' also became popular in Brazil, taken as snuff, chewed or smoked in a pipe.

Sights & Activities

Cachoeira is one of Candomblé's strongest and perhaps purest spiritual and religious centers. On Friday and Saturday nights, ceremonies are often held in small homes and shacks in the hills. Travelers who are especially interested in learning more should contact the tourist office for information about local guides who specialize in this particular scene.

The town also maintains a strong tradition of African-influenced wood carving. Stop in on the ateliers (studios) of two of the best sculptors in town, **Doidão** (cnr 25 de Junho & 7 de Setembro, Cachoeira) and **Louco** (Rua 13 de Maio, Cachoeira), to get a sense of the local style; they operate roughly from 10am to 4pm Monday to Friday.

Note that, as elsewhere in Bahia, churches are sometimes closed even when their posted opening hours indicate otherwise. Admission is by donation.

Igreja da Ordem Terceira do Carmo CHURCH

(Praça da Aclamação, Cachoeira) The Igreja da Ordem Terceira do Carmo has a gilded baroque altar, paneled ceilings and azulejos (handmade tiles imported from Portugal), and dates from 1702.

Igreja Matriz NS do Rosário CHURCH
(Nery s/n, Cachoeira) The church dates to between 1693 and 1754. It has beautiful azulejos and a ceiling painted by Teófilo de Jesus. On the 2nd floor, the Museu das Alfaias contains remnants from the abandoned 17th-century Convento de São Francisco do Paraguaçu.

Museu Regional da Cachoeira MUSEUM
(☎3425-1123; Praça da Aclamação 4, Cachoeira; admission R$2; ⊙8am-noon & 2-5pm Mon-Fri, 8am-noon Sat & Sun) Housed in an 18th-century colonial mansion, the humble Museu Regional da Cachoeira displays colonial furnishings and priestly vestments.

Casa da Câmara e Cadeia HISTORIC BUILDING
(Prefecture & Jail; Praça da Aclamação, Cachoeira; ⊙8am-4pm Mon-Fri) FREE At the Casa da Câmara e Cadeia, organized criminals ran the show upstairs and disorganized criminals were kept behind bars downstairs. The building dates to 1698 and served as the seat of the Bahian government in 1822.

Museu Hansen Bahia MUSEUM
(☎3425-1453; www.hansenbahia.com.br; 13 de Maio, Cachoeira; ⊙9am-5pm Tue-Fri, to 2pm Sat & Sun) FREE Karl Heinz Hansen (1915-76) was a German artist who emigrated to Brazil in 1949. He felt such an affinity with his new home that he had his surname changed to 'Hansen Bahia'. Today, this museum displays his powerful block prints and paintings, many showing the influence of Cachoeira's wood-carving tradition. The striking building is the birthplace and former home of Brazilian heroine Ana Nery, who organized the nursing corps during the Paraguay War.

Festivals & Events

Festa de São João FOLKLORIC
(⊙3rd week of June) The largest popular festival of Bahia's interior, celebrated with folklore, music, dancing and a generous amount of food and drink.

Festa de NS do Rosário RELIGIOUS
(⊙mid-Oct) A religious festival featuring great music and food.

Festa de NS D'Ajuda RELIGIOUS
(⊙mid-Nov) Features a ritual *lavagem* (washing) of the church and a street festival.

Sleeping & Eating

On Cachoeira's waterfront plazas, vendors sell cold beer, popcorn and regional treats such as *caldo de cana* (sugarcane juice). Several large supermarkets in town are convenient for self-catering.

Pousada do Convento do Carmo POUSADA $
(☎3425-1716; www.pousadadoconvento.com.br; Praça da Aclamação, Cachoeira; s/d from R$72/105; ❄📶🏊) The 18th-century convent attached to the Igreja da Ordem Terceira do Carmo has been converted into a comfortable guesthouse. Rooms are spacious, with tall ceilings and heavy wood floors. The classy on-site restaurant, **A Confraria**, is open to the public between 11am and 10pm.

Pousada Treze de Março POUSADA $
(☎3425-5124; www.pousadatrezedemarco.com.br; Conegundes Barreto 9; s/d R$90/150; ❄📶) There's a vaguely institutional feel to this tidy guesthouse and its boxy tiled rooms. But the location is good, and the price is right.

Pousada Paraguassú POUSADA $
(☎3438-3369; www.pousadaparaguassu.com.br; Salvador Pinto 3, São Félix; s/d from R$100/170; ❄📶) Located on the riverfront in São Félix, Paraguassú has basic, cozy rooms surrounding a small garden. The riverside terrace is a breezy place to enjoy the ample breakfast buffet, or, at night, Bahian food or pizza in its restaurant.

Aclamação Restaurante BRAZILIAN $
(☎3425-3428; Praça da Aclamação 2; mains R$6-38; ⊙11am-10pm) This busy corner eatery offers a range of great-value sandwiches, acai and traditional Bahian dishes. Try the sandwich named after the nearby river, Rio Paraguaçu, piled high with bacon, cheese, grilled chicken, beef, tomatoes and lettuce.

Pizzaria Recanto Misticismo PIZZERIA $
(☎3425-3414; Inocência Bonaventura, Cachoeira; mains R$12-30; ⊙6-10pm) This popular pizzeria has brick walls, a varied menu and nicely lit tables with views onto the plaza. It fills up in the evening with groups of students and local couples and families.

Restaurante Rabbuni BRAZILIAN $
(Praca Aclamacão; per kg R$30; ⊙noon-3pm Mon-Fri) A cheerful buffet lunch spot on the square.

Baiana's Point BAR
(☎3425-4967; Virgílio Reis, Cachoeira; ⊙5-10pm) Perched on scenic stilts over the river, this place makes a great setting for an

Cachoeira

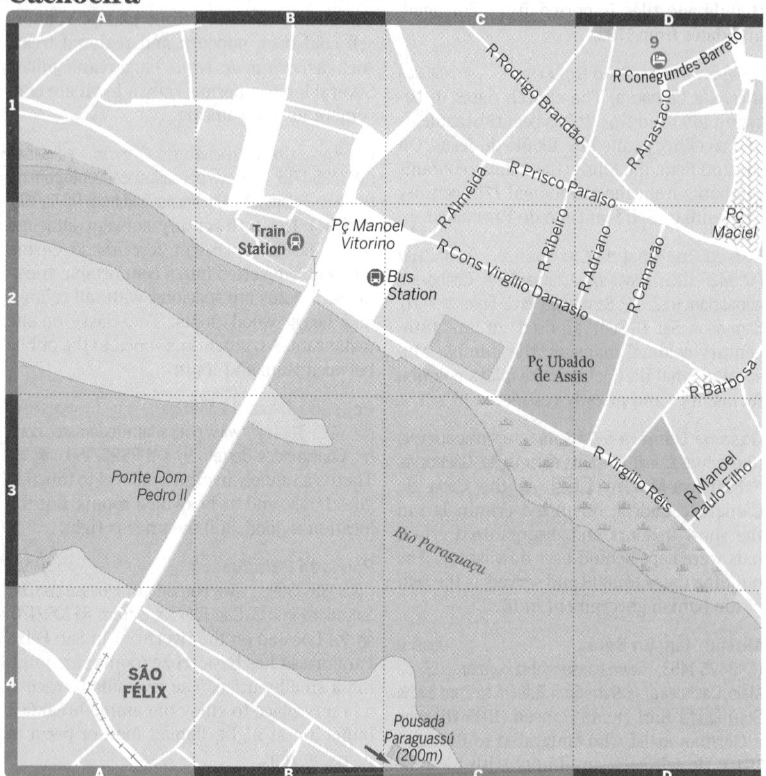

early-evening drink – if you can get anyone to serve you (service is painfully slow).

Bar do Reggae BAR
(Virgilio Réis s/n; ⏲5pm-late) On warm evenings, everyone and his brother is sitting at these sidewalk tables, drinking beer and enjoying a starlit view of the river.

Information

Both São Félix and Cachoeira have banks with ATMs. For more information on the towns' history, river excursions or church visits, stop into the helpful **tourist office** (Tourist Information; R Ana Nery 4; ⏲8am-5pm Mon-Fri) in Cachoeira.

Getting There & Away

These twin towns are served by nearly identical bus stations, positioned directly across the river from each other at each base of the bridge: most trips commence on the São Félix side, stopping to pick up passengers in Cachoeira before continuing out of town.

Numerous daily buses operated by **Transporte Santana e São Paulo** (☎3450-4951) run to Salvador (R$23, 2½ hours, 5:30am to 7pm), stopping in Santo Amaro (1½ hours) along the way.

To make connections north, south or west, you can also catch one of Transporte Santana's various daily services to Feira de Santana (R$6, 1½ hours, 12 daily).

Santo Amaro

☎0XX75 / POP 58,000

Santo Amaro is a friendly colonial sugar town that sees very few tourists and has an unpretentious charm. It is most well known for being the hometown of the brother-sister pair Caetano Veloso and Maria Betânia, two of Brazil's most popular singers (who often put in an appearance during Carnaval). The center bustles with people, especially around the small outdoor market. Paper production has replaced sugar as

Cachoeira

Sights
1 Casa da Câmara e Cadeia ... F4
2 Doidão ... E4
3 Igreja da Ordem Terceira do Carmo ... F4
4 Igreja Matriz NS do Rosário ... E3
5 Louco ... E3
6 Museu Hansen Bahia ... E3
7 Museu Regional da Cachoeira ... F4

Sleeping
8 Pousada do Convento do Carmo ... F4
9 Pousada Treze de Março ... D1

Eating
10 Aclamação Restaurante ... E4
11 Pizzaria Recanto Misticismo ... F4
12 Restaurante Rabbuni ... E4

Drinking & Nightlife
13 Baiana's Point ... E4
14 Bar do Reggae ... E4

the major industry, visible in the invasion of bamboo on the hillsides where sugarcane once flourished, and a large paper mill outside of town.

The decrepit sugar-baron mansions along the old commercial street, Rua General Câmara, and the numerous churches are reminders of Santo Amaro's prosperous days. The ornate **Matriz de NS da Purificação** (1668) is the largest church, with azulejos and a painted ceiling. Unfortunately, a gang of thieves stole most of the church's holy images and exported them to France.

The **Lavagem da Purificação** (January 23 to February 2) is celebrated by a procession and ritual washing of the church steps by *baianas* (Bahian 'aunts' in traditional dress), before bands and *trios elétricos* (long trucks loaded with huge speakers) take over the streets.

Buses leave Salvador for Santo Amaro (R$15, one hour) almost every 30 minutes from 5:30am to 7pm. Most continue on to Cachoeira/São Félix (R$12, one hour).

NORTH OF SALVADOR

Bahia's northern coast is not as startling as its southern, but the beaches here are still lovely, boasting tall bluffs with rustling palms and white sands (that grow finer the further north you go), which front a mix of calm inlets and wild surfable breaks. Keep in mind that when *salvadorenos* want a day at the beach, they naturally head for Bahia's northern coast. As a result, the sands close to the city get packed on weekends. To escape the crowds, head further north, where there are many kilometers of deserted pristine shoreline.

The Estrada do Coco (Coconut Hwy) runs as far north as Praia do Forte, where the Linha Verde (Green Line) picks up, continuing all the way to the Sergipe border. You may feel that you are going against the grain if you are trying to access this coast heading north to south. Grassy medians in the highways require buses to pass town entrances and then double back, so few do. Instead, they drop passengers on the highway, leaving you to walk or pick up other transportation into the small towns and fishing communities along this stretch of coast. Traveling from south to north is a much smoother process.

Candomblé

The wild and little-understood Candomblé religion is deeply rooted in Bahian culture and connects countless Afro-Brazilians to a long line of West African ancestry.

African Origins

Candomblé is the most orthodox of the religions brought from Africa by the Nago, Yoruba and Jeje peoples. Candomblé is an African word denoting a dance in honor of the gods. Afro-Brazilian rituals are directed by a *pai de santo* or *mãe de santo* (literally 'saint's mother or father' – the Candomblé priests) and practiced in a *casa de santo* or *terreiro* (house of worship). The ceremonies are conducted in the Yoruba language.

Orixás

The religion centers around *orixás* (deities). Like the gods in Greek mythology, each *orixá* has a unique personality and history. Candomblé followers believe that every person has a particular deity watching over them – from birth until death. A person's *orixá* can be identified when a *pai* or *mãe de santo* makes successive throws with a handful of *búzios* (shells), in a divination ritual known as Jogo dos Búzios (Casting of Shells). The position of the shells is used to interpret one's luck, one's future and one's past relationship with the gods. Although *orixás* are divided into male and female types, there are some that can switch from one sex to the other, such as Logunedé, son of two male gods, Ogun and Oxoss.

Candomblé in Practice

To keep themselves strong and healthy, followers of Candomblé give food or other offerings to please their respective *orixás*. For example, to Iemanjá, the goddess or queen of the sea, one should give perfumes, flowers, combs and mirrors. Oxúm, god of fresh waters and waterfalls, is famous for his vanity, and is honored with earrings, necklaces, champagne and honey. In Bahia and Rio, followers of Afro-Brazilian cults turn out in huge numbers for the festival held during the night of December 31 and on New Year's Day – and in Salvador, on February 2. Millions of Brazilians go to the beach at this time to pay homage to Iemanjá. Flowers, perfumes, fruits and even jewelry are tossed into the sea to please the mother of the waters, or to gain protection and good luck in the New Year.

Attending a Candomblé Ceremony

Ceremonies take place in richly decorated halls called *terreiros*. Drummers pound out powerful rhythms while the mostly female dancers, chanting in Yoruba, glide in a counterclockwise circle, representing the rolling back of the centuries, as they reach out to their ancestors. A festive, celebratory atmosphere prevails, with the *mãe de santo* or *pai de santo* presiding. The chiming of bells conjures the spirits: when a spirit arrives, those dancing may take on the attributes of the *orixá* in question. A good list of *terreiros* can be found at www.salvadorcentral.com.

JAN SOCHOR / LATINCONTENT / GETTY IMAGES ©

1. Festa de Iemanjá, Ilha de Itaparica (p420)
2. Candomblé devotees
3. Candles and flowers given to Iemanjá

DANIELA GAMA / GETTY IMAGES ©

DANIELA GAMA / GETTY IMAGES ©

Praia do Forte

☎0XX71 / POP 1800

Beloved by tourists, upmarket Praia do Forte is an attractive and somewhat ecologically sensitive beach village overflowing with stylish restaurants and shops. The main drag, Alameda do Sol, is a pedestrian walkway that leads to an incredibly picturesque and pint-sized church, a sea-turtle reserve and fantastic, palm-lined beaches with sparkling white sands that fill up on weekends. Surrounding the village are castle ruins, a lagoon for canoeing and the Sapiranga forest reserve, which has hiking and biking trails and a zip-line. If you can, time your visit for the full moon and walk along the beach past the resort at sunset, when the sun turns the waters of the Rio Timeantube red as the moon rises over the sea.

Sights & Activities

Castelo do Garcia d'Ávila RUINS

(☎3676-1133; www.fgd.org.br; Avenida do Farol 1540; admission R$10; ⏲8:30am-noon & 2-6pm Mon-Fri) Dating from 1552, the Castelo was the first great Portuguese edifice in Brazil. Desperate to colonize, the king of Portugal granted lands to merchants, soldiers and aristocrats; a farmer named Garcia d'Ávila, endowed with this tract of land, chose this ocean-view plot for his home. Today, it's an impressive ruin with sweeping views. It's 7km outside of town – take a taxi.

Reserva da Sapiranga HIKING

(☎9985-3349; www.fgd.org.br; admission R$10, guided hikes R$5-15; ⏲8am-5pm) A turnoff from the road to Castelo do Garcia d'Ávila leads down a dirt track to the Reserva da Sapiranga, where guides take visitors along trails skirting through 600 hectares of secondary Atlantic rainforest. Hikes range from 30 minutes to five hours, with one of the more popular hikes leading down to the Rio Pojuca (bring your swimsuit).

Tours

Worthwhile tours in the area include hiking and bird-watching treks, canopy tours, kayaking and whale-watching (in season). A handful of professional outfitters such as **Portomar** (☎3676-0101; www.portomar.com.br; Rua da Aurora 1; ⏲9am-7pm) handle these trips and run popular excursions at low tide to nearby *piscinas naturais* (natural pools), where you can snorkel or scuba dive around a colorful coral reef.

Sleeping

Praia do Forte has an abundance of attractive midrange guesthouses that fill to capacity on summer weekends. Prices here are more expensive than many other destinations in Bahia, though you'll save by visiting during the week. Rua da Aurora, parallel to Alameda do Sol, has a handful of more affordable pousadas.

Praia do Forte Hostel HOSTEL $

(☎3676-1094; www.albergue.com.br; Aurora 155; dm/d R$62/160; ❄📶) This popular HI hostel has a convenient location, clean rooms facing onto a grassy courtyard, and a good breakfast spread. Rental bikes and surfboards are available too. Air-con is available in some rooms, and not others: read the fine print if it's the middle of summer.

★**Casa Verde Apart** APARTMENT $$

(☎3676-1531; www.casaverdeapart.com; Peixe Espada 100; apt for 2/4 people from R$240/300; ❄📶) In a leafy setting near the beach, these six attractive and spacious apartments are complete with well-equipped kitchens and balconies with hammocks. The place is managed by a gracious couple. Breakfast is available on request, for an extra fee.

Pousada dos Artistas POUSADA $$

(☎3676-1147; www.pousadadosartistas.tur.br; Praça dos Artistas s/n; d/tr R$249/324; ❄📶) This friendly guesthouse – run by a dancer and a painter-sculptor, as the name suggests – offers lovely colonial-style rooms (each with a private balcony and hammock) looking out over a lush tropical garden.

Shanti House Apart APARTMENT $$

(☎3199-0103; www.shantihouse0.tripod.com; Maria Mole 14; studio for 2 with/without balcony R$210/190, duplex for 4 R$280; 📶🏊) One of the better deals in a town that's getting increasingly expensive, this guesthouse is close to the beach and features four apartments with kitchenettes. With the exception of the most standard studio, all apartments also feature a private balcony with hammock. A duplex apartment sleeps four and has a larger terrace. All include access to the central swimming pool.

Pousada Ogum Marinho POUSADA $$

(☎3676-1165; www.ogummarinho.com.br; Alameda do Sol s/n; d/tr R$300/375; ❄📶) One block from the beach, Ogum Marinho has attractive rooms with stone-slab floors, comfortable furnishings and private decks strung with hammocks.

DON'T MISS

THE SEA TURTLES OF TAMAR

There are only five remaining species of sea turtle left in the world – and all of them live on the Bahian coast. A true highlight of any trip through the region is a visit to the sea-turtle reserve that's dedicated to protecting loggerhead, hawksbill, olive ridley and green turtles – and their adorably tiny babies.

The nonprofit organization **Projeto TAMAR** (☎3676-0321; www.tamar.org.br; admission R$20; ⏰8:30am-5:30pm) runs 18 stations in Bahia (the name is an abbreviation for the Portuguese word for sea turtle, *tartaruga marinha*). Of these. the Praia do Forte is perhaps the most impressive, exhibiting pools with marine turtles of various sizes and species, as well as urchins, eels and other sea life.

Outside the station itself, the most important action happens on the shoreline during the turtles' nesting season (September to March). Tamar researchers protect around 550 nests a year along 50km of coast close to Praia do Forte. The moist, leathery, ping-pong-ball-size eggs are buried in the sand when laid and either left on the beach or brought to the hatcheries for incubation. When they hatch, the baby turtles are immediately released into the sea. Though this system allows some 500,000 baby turtles to hatch each year in Bahia, only several hundred will reach adulthood.

A trip to the reserve, located just behind the church on Praia do Forte's main square, is interactive and family friendly; take your time and have an outdoor lunch beside the ocean at Souza Bar (p429), located inside the project station.

Tivoli Ecoresort RESORT $$$
(☎3676-4000; www.tivolihotels.com; Av do Farol s/n; d incl half-board from R$1170; ❄📶🏊) 🌿 It's all luxury at this lavish beachfront resort, where walkways wind through groomed gardens past eight swimming pools to the beach. Rooms all have verandas, the cuisine is top-notch and the spa offers a wide range of treatments. Although there's nothing particularly 'eco' about the design, the hotel does contribute to social and educational programs.

Eating

Countless attractive eateries line the town's pedestrian walkways, but prices are high and the food, generally speaking, is nothing special. If you're in the market for a quick lunch or a beach picnic, grab a deli sandwich or stock up on snacks at the supermarket. For the best atmosphere and value, explore side streets and the casual cafes around the central plaza, where cold beer flows freely at night.

★**Souza Bar** BAHIAN $
(☎9987-8638; Alameda do Sol s/n, Projeto Tamar station; small plates R$10-20; ⏰10am-1am Mon-Fri, 10am-6pm Sat) Festive Souza Bar inside the Projeto Tamar station, has a dramatic setting along the rocky coastline. It's a sure bet for fresh clams, crispy *bolinho de peixe* (fried fish balls) and caipirinhas. A second location, near the bus drop-off, hosts live music on Friday and Saturday evenings.

Casa da Nati BUFFET $
(☎3676-1239; Alameda do Sol s/n; mains R$18-42; ⏰7-10:30am & 11:30am-10pm) A longtime Praia do Forte favorite, Casa da Nati spreads an excellent self-serve lunch buffet, plus a good menu of à la carte dishes all day and into the evening. It's also a good spot for breakfast if you're staying in an apartment. At night, the glow of lanterns illuminates the pretty outdoor dining area.

Vila Gourmet BRAZILIAN $$$
(☎3676-1088; www.sobradodavila.com.br; Alameda do Sol; mains for 2 R$62-95; ⏰8am-10pm) This stylish tropical-style eatery (connected to the centrally located Pousada Sobrado da Vila) serves regional cuisine that's a cut above the rest; thanks to organic vegetables and eggs sourced from a private farm.

Orientation

Buses stop at the northern end of the main pedestrian thoroughfare, Alameda do Sol (also called Av ACM). Though beaches are often crowded in front of the plaza and church, find a peaceful spot under the palm trees by walking south along the coast for five to 10 minutes.

Information

Several ATMs are located near the bus stop. Travel agencies scattered around town can help you arrange area excursions or book onward travel.

Getting There & Around

Praia do Forte is 3km off the highway. **Linha Verde** (☎3460-3636) has regular departures to Praia do Forte from Salvador's bus station (R$10, 1¾ hours). Four daily departures go directly to Praia do Forte (at 9am, 9:45am, 6pm and 7pm at the time of writing) though other buses can get you there too: just ask at the Linha Verde desk. Buses make the return journey regularly between 7am and 6:30pm. Informal Kombi vans make the same trip to Salvador for the same price; wait near the bus stop for pickup.

Praia do Forte to Sítio do Conde

Imbassaí is a rustic beach town 16km north of Praia do Forte. A tall sand dune and the peaceful Rio Barroso, which runs parallel to the beach, separate the village from a pretty beach with rough surf. Most guesthouses in town are midrange and top-end options. Even the HI option, **Imbassaí Eco Hostel Lujimba** (☎3677-1056; www.hihostels.com/hostels/imbassai-eco-hostel-lujimba; Rua P, Quadra 21, Imbassai; dm/d from R$90/250;), is expensive for a hostel, but is well-liked for its pleasant wooden-floor rooms in a rustic, thatched-roof guesthouse amid greenery. Hammocks, fruit trees and excursions add to the allure.

A few kilometers north of Imbassaí, along the river, lies the more rustic town of **Diogo**, which sees fewer visitors and retains the charm of village life. For those looking to unwind, the relaxing **Pousada Too Cool** (☎9952-2190; www.toocoolnabahia.com; chalet for 2 from R$330;) is a destination in itself with colorfully designed chalets with verandas overlooking the lush surroundings. The friendly owner can arrange kitesurfing, kayaking, horseback riding and other activities.

To reach most places between Praia do Forte and Sítio do Conde, take a **Linha Verde** (☎3460-3636) bus from Salvador's bus station (almost hourly between 5am and 6pm) and alert the driver to your destination.

Sítio do Conde

☎0XX75

Wet lowlands full of cattle surround this quiet, working-class beach retreat. While there's little to the town itself – just a few main streets and a sleepy central plaza – Sítio has a lovely beach with pounding surf (located 1km from the plaza). North or south along the coast quickly leads to a deserted shore with churning seas and flat sands backed by bluffs topped with coconut trees.

Sleeping & Eating

B&B Bela Bahia B&B $$
(☎3449-7037; www.bela-bahia.com; R Principal, Poças; d from R$220;) Travelers rave about the personalized attention (in English) and paradise-like setting at B&B Bela Bahia, run by a laid-back Belgian-Brazilian couple. It's just outside of Conde, in the village of Poças.

Zecas & Zecas BAHIAN $
(☎3449-1298; Praça Arsênio Mendes 51; mains for 2 R$25-55; ⊙noon-10pm Mon-Sat) Zecas & Zecas, on the main square, is a colorful seafood restaurant serving the town's best *moqueca*.

Getting There & Away

Direct transportation to Sítio do Conde is infrequent: the meandering trip can take four or more hours from Salvador on bus lines São Luís and Oliveira (R$50, several daily). Area pousadas like B&B Bela Bahia also offer private transportation from the Salvador airport (R$640 round-trip per carload).

Mangue Seco

☎0XX75

Mangue Seco is a tiny, beautifully rustic riverfront village at the tip of a peninsula formed by the Rio Real, which delineates the Bahia–Sergipe border. The town itself is just a scattering of simple dwellings along sandy paths, a tiny church and plaza, a modern lighthouse (yielding lovely views for intrepid climbers) and a few friendly guesthouses and restaurants. The town ends at the edge of an enormous expanse of tall white sand dunes, beyond which the wide, flat sands of the Bahian coast stretch to the south. Mangue Seco's remote location prompts most visitors to come on guided day tours, preventing rapid growth and leaving nights decidedly quiet. It's about a 1.5km walk to the ocean, which has a handful of simple *barracas* strung with hammocks.

Sleeping & Eating

Mangue Seco's culinary specialty is *aratu*, a tiny red shellfish sometimes prepared in *moquecas*. In addition to the pousadas' excellent restaurants, visitors can sample seafood at low-key outdoor eateries along the riverbank.

Resort Recanto da Natureza HOTEL $$
(☎9881-8761; www.resortrecantodanatureza.com.br; Sítio Angelin; ste from R$320;) Don't let the word 'resort' fool you: travelers from far and wide sing the praises of the laid-back atmosphere at Resort Recanto da Natureza. It's more like a rustic-chic country hotel with a great swimming pool and attentive staff.

Pousada O Forte POUSADA $$$
(☎3445-9039; www.pousadaoforte.com; Praia da Costa s/n; d from R$350;) Located just outside the village center on the riverfront, on the way to the beach, this ecofriendly French-Brazilian-owned guesthouse occupies an isolated spot overlooking the river. With pretty bungalows and a lovely swimming pool, it's family friendly, too.

Recanto de Dona Sula CAFE $
(☎3445-9008; snacks R$6-18; 8:30am-7pm) At this local favorite, homemade candies, ice creams and liqueurs are made from regional fruits; the coffee is excellent, too. Both charming and environmentally conscious (recycling is a priority), this sweet cafe is located next to the church.

Getting There & Away

Mangue Seco is remote; unless you're hiring private transportation or coming on a day trip from Salvador, getting here requires a combination of bus, taxi and boat.

Most travelers arrive in Mangue Seco as follows: from the south, a **Rota** (☎3251-2181) bus from Salvador (R$46 to R$60, five daily) to Estância; from the north, a Coopertalse (www.coopertalse.com.br) bus from Aracaju to Estancia (R$10, several daily.) A taxi from Estancia to Pontal (R$65) takes you to the speedboat between Pontal and Mangue Seco (around R$50 for up to four people). If you can manage to catch one, vans also make the trip from Pontal (R$10, 90 minutes) to Estância. It helps to consult with your accommodation before traveling for tips on your travel strategy.

Especially if you're traveling with others, it's worthwhile to ask your accommodations in Mangue Seco if it offers more direct transportation. Pousada O Forte, for example, offers service from Salvador (R$400 to R$450 for up to four people) and Aracaju (R$190 for up to four people).

SOUTH OF SALVADOR

Morro de São Paulo

☎0XX75

As postcard-pretty as any Mediterranean island village, Morro de São Paulo has long been a favorite weekend getaway for travelers and Salvador locals alike. Though Morro is overtly touristy, many visitors don't care, since it's also a fabulous tropical paradise with sandy lanes, calm waters and a candlelit nightlife scene.

Remotely perched at the northern tip of the Ilha de Tinharé, Morro's appeal stems from its relaxed pace – no cars are allowed on the island – and unique geography: three jungle-topped hills on a point at the meeting of the mangrove-lined Canal de Taperoá and a clear, shallow Atlantic.

During the high season the village booms, dozens of vendors mix fresh-fruit caipirinhas on the sand, and lighthearted dancing and music enliven the beaches every night.

Sights & Activities

The town's icon is a 17th-century carved-stone **fortress gate**, which welcomes each arrival from its position above the dock.

Around the corner at the point are the **fort ruins** (1630). Catching the rare sight of the sun setting over the river and mangroves from the fort is a visitor ritual. The **lighthouse** (1835) above the fort affords a fantastic view over Morro's beaches.

Down a sandy lane from the main square, the **Fonte Grande** (Great Fountain), in operation since the 17th century, is a good example of an old urban water-supply system in Bahia.

The waters of Morro's four conveniently named main beaches are mostly calm, shallow and warm, and their sands are narrow and swallowed by the high tides. Tiny **Primeira Praia** is lined with pousadas, occasionally hosts lively football matches on the sand and has a decent surf break. Deep **Segunda Praia** (500m) is the 'action' beach, with pousadas, restaurants, nightclubs and a sea of tables and chairs. Pousadas and anchored boats dominate one end of **Terceira Praia** (1km). Once you pass a pair of restaurants, **Quarta Praia** (2km) is a long, lovely stretch of sand graced by tall, swaying palms. For even more isolated peace, continue on at low tide to **Praia do Encanto** (5km) or further down the island to **Garapuá**.

Tours

A daylong boat trip around the island (R$100 to R$130), with stops at the Garapuá and Moreré offshore reefs and the villages of Boipeba and historical Cairu, is obligatory. You'll fly over waves in a speedboat, past gorgeous beach and mangrove scenery, jump off the boat for swimming and snorkeling, stop at a floating oyster bar, and walk around historic island villages. Many agencies in town, like **Zulu Turismo** (☎3652-1358; www.morrodesaopaulobahiabrasil.com; Rua da Mangaba 98), run the trip. It doesn't matter which agency you book with: they all redirect travelers to the same boats.

Another popular daylong excursion (R$65 to R$80) takes travelers to Garapuá via 4WD vehicle. It's a good way to enjoy the natural pools at a more leisurely pace.

Scuba enthusiasts can log onto the website or stop into the local office of **Companhia do Mergulho** (☎3652-1200; www.ciadomergulho.com; Prainha s/n, Primeira Praia), located on the path to the beach.

Sleeping

Since Morro is a popular getaway from Salvador, prices vary wildly: during peak Brazilian vacation times, prices skyrocket and pousadas book up well ahead of time. Reservations for Morro's numerous pousadas are required for all major holidays, especially Carnaval and the days before and after. Be forewarned that staying on Segunda Praia during summer means sleeping to the nightclubs' pounding beats; the least expensive pousadas are in town.

Che Lagarto Hostel HOSTEL $
(☎3652-1018; www.chelagarto.com; Fonte Grande 11; dm with/without breakfast from R$40/R$65, d with/without breakfast from R$112/R$125; ❄📶) Convenient to the ferry dock and local nightlife, yet with a middle-of-the-jungle feel thanks to its forest-shrouded wooden sundeck, this chain hostel is geared to those looking for a youthful party vibe.

★ **Pousada Porto de Cima** POUSADA $$
(☎3652-1562; www.pousadaportodecima.com.br; Porto de Cima 56; d/tr/q from R$209/280/355; ❄📶) Shabby-chic cabins set in a lush jungle-like garden over the sea, along the path to Porto de Cima Beach. Watching electric-blue hummingbirds and the occasional monkey from the vantage point of your porch hammock is about as relaxing as it gets around here, and the breakfast is downright picturesque.

Pousada Natal POUSADA $
(☎3652-1059; Caminho da Praia s/n; d from R$120; ❄📶) This laid-back main-street budget spot has basic rooms and friendly staff; it's well positioned between the harbor and the beaches. To get here, just follow the crowds heading to the beaches from the port – it's about midway between the plaza and Primeira Praia.

Villa dos Graffitis POUSADA $$
(☎3652-1803; www.villadosgraffitis.com.br; Segunda Praia; d R$230) As the name suggests, modern art is the focus at this cool, sustainably built new guesthouse with more personality than any other on Morro's beachfront. The owners commissioned Brazilian street artists to paint murals in guest rooms and public spaces, including around the stylish swimming pool, hot tub and solarium, and the hipster-friendly billiards room.

Pousada Bahia Bacana POUSADA $$
(☎3652-1674; www.pousadabahiabacana.com.br; Prainha 35, Primera Praia; d R$199-349; ❄📶🏊) An excellent addition to the Morro's pousada scene, Bahia Bacana features a small but extremely memorable swimming pool perched high over the beach. Guest rooms are bright and welcoming, with hardwood floors; many have private balconies with hammocks and sea views.

Le Terrace Beach Hotel HOTEL $$
(☎3652-1308; www.leterrace.com.br; Segunda Praia ; R$250-320; ❄📶) Tucked into the trees on the far end of Segunda Praia, Le Terrace has, well, plenty of terraces: one for breakfast with an ocean view, another off your guest room. These spacious apartments are well-equipped and stylish. The only downside is that it can be noisy at night: those earplugs are provided for a reason.

Pousada Colibri POUSADA $$
(☎3652-1056; www.pousada-colibri.com; Porto de Cima 7; d/ste from R$205/235; ❄📶🏊) In a marvelous hilltop position, the lushly landscaped Colibri has pretty cabins and suites with verandas and hammocks. Surrounding jungle assures quiet, but it's a bit of a hike from the beach – luckily, rates include round-trip baggage transfer from the harbor. To reach it, take the path to the spring, then turn right up a quiet forested lane.

Pousada O Casarão POUSADA $$

(☎3652-1022; www.pousadaocasarao.com; Praça Aureliano Lima 190; d R$210-370;) Reigning over the main plaza, this beautifully renovated colonial mansion – dating from 1906 – has lovely rooms with classic furnishings and large windows, plus hillside bungalows with private balconies. Amenities include two swimming pools: one, with a bar, for adults, and another for children.

Villa das Pedras POUSADA $$$

(☎3652-1075; www.villadaspedras.com.br; Segunda Praia; d R$350-520;) This eye-catching guesthouse, with vibrant hues and clean, modern lines, wins the most style points on busy Segunda Praia. The lavish breakfast spread, swimming pool and bar, and location directly across from the beach make it worth the splurge; the downside to the central location is that the area can be loud at night.

Eating & Drinking

Restaurants in Morro are priced for well-off vacationers, and quality varies – not to mention that most eateries price their main dishes for two, making eating out expensive for solo travelers. Luckily, casual dining options abound on the island. Sample crepes and pasteles (thin square of dough stuffed with meat, cheese or fish, then fried) and freshly squeezed juices at the food stands along the beaches. The path leading from the main square to Fonte Grande is lined with good-value bakeries and lunch spots. At night, Segunda Praia is alive with restaurants competing for your business – it's a prime opportunity to dine with the sand between your toes.

After dark, don't miss dexterous vendors along Rua Caminho da Praia and on Segunda Praia mixing delicious caipirinhas (cocktails) – made with a wide range of fresh fruits, many of which you've probably never heard of. Outdoor bars are scattered along Segunda Praia.

★ **Pedra Sobre Pedras** CAFE $

(Segunda Praia; mains R$8-15; 24hr) This little cafe is on a wooden deck perched high over Segunda Praia, just off the pedestrian walkway. Pull up a stool and enjoy crepes, well-mixed caipirinhas and gorgeous views over the beach action.

ARRIVING ON THE ISLAND

No matter how you arrive on the island, you'll pay a fee (R$15) to enter. Most visitors arrive by boat and are ushered directly to the payment kiosks before leaving the dock. You'll pay another R$1 when you leave.

Tia Lita BAHIAN $

(www.pousadatialita.com.br; Terceira Praia; mains R$15-35; 11am-10pm) This casual and popular down-home restaurant serves grilled fish, chicken or beef with rice and salad, plus sandwiches and *moqueca*. It's located down a narrow lane off Terceira Praia.

Alecrim SELF-SERVE $$

(Caminho da Praia; per kg R$39; noon-11pm) This popular per-kilo place on the main pedestrian street – conveniently open at night as well as during the day, unlike many restaurants of this sort – serves basic but well-prepared Bahian dishes, plus a few less standard offerings like paella with shrimp.

Andina LATIN AMERICAN $$

(☎8326-7555; www.andinacocinalatina.com; Porto de Cima 44; mains R$22-40; 7-11pm Tue-Sun) Creative Latin American cuisine and cocktails in a lovely treehouselike setting. Andina is a newcomer to the island's dining scene, and a bit of a hidden gem: to get there from the main square, step through the archway closest to the O Casarãao mansion. When you reach the historic fountain, hang a right and walk uphill to the restaurant.

Minha Louca Paixão BRAZILIAN $$

(www.minhaloucapaixao.com.br; Terceira Praia; mains R$30-68; 5-11pm;) Well-prepared seafood dishes served at elegant (and quiet) waterfront tables make this sophisticated eatery, located at an upscale pousada of the same name, one of the more romantic dining options along the beaches. It's a great option for a special occasion.

Café das Artes BRAZILIAN $$

(☎3652-1057; www.solardasartes.net; Praça Aureliano Lima; mains R$15-60; 11am-11pm) This pretty café-restaurant doubles as an art space; the patio overlooking the square is a sweet spot for a little night music. House specialties include seafood risotto and shrimp cooked in green coconut sauce. It's located at a popular pousada, Solar das Artes.

Bianco e Nero PIZZERIA $$

(☎ 3652-1097; Caminho da Praia; mains R$20-55; ⏰ noon-11:30pm Tue-Sun, from 5:30pm Mon) This fashionable Italian pizzeria and eatery is hugely popular for its fresh seafood pastas, oven-fired pizzas, rich Italian desserts and wines by the glass, all served on a large terrace above the main pedestrian thoroughfare. Service can be lax; you're paying for the stylish atmosphere.

★ **Portaló Bar & Restaurante** COCKTAIL BAR

(www.hotelportalo.com; Hotel Portaló; ⏰ noon-10pm) This hotel's terrace is the place to be at sunset for glorious views over the harbor, a DJ-spun soundtrack and festive drinks served with the flourish of tropical flowers. There's a full dinner menu, too, if you want to make an evening of it. Look for it when you're stepping off the boat upon arrival on the island.

Orientation

At the dock, wheelbarrow valets wait to help you transport your luggage and lead you to your accommodations, which is especially useful for travelers without rolling luggage (be sure to negotiate the price beforehand).

Uphill lies the main square (Praça Aureliano Lima) in the Vila, with an information office and a few restaurants. To reach the beaches, take a left at the square; this passes along the main street, Rua Caminho da Praia, and is lined with restaurants and shops. Continue downhill to access the shores, reaching Primeira Praia (First Beach), then Segunda Praia, and so on. Heading right from the main plaza, you'll go through an archway down Rua da Fonte and pass the spring-fed fountain that was once the village's freshwater source.

Information

There are a few ATMs on the island, but it's wise to bring necessary funds with you from the mainland, especially during high season, when tourists deplete the ATMs' cash supplies. Many establishments also accept credit cards. Pharmacies and internet cafés are plentiful (R$4 to R$7 per hour).

At the top of the hill up from the dock and along the path to the beach, several travel agencies sell boat and domestic airline tickets, organize excursions and distribute maps.

Getting There & Away

Two small airlines have daily flights between Salvador and Morro (R$200, 25 minutes). Contact **Aerostar** (☎ in Salvador 071-3377-4406; www.aerostar.com.br), **Addey Taxi Aéreo** (☎ in Salvador 071-3204-1393; www.addey.com.br) or a travel agency.

A handful of operators run catamarans and small ferries (R$75 to R$80) between Morro and the Terminal Marítimo Turístico in Salvador. There are five to seven daily departures each way. For reservations, contact **Biotur** (☎ 3641-3327; www.biotur.com.br), **Farol do Morro** (☎ 3652-1083; www.faroldomorrotour.com), **IlhaBela** (☎ in Salvador 071-9195-6744; www.ilhabelatm.com.br) or **Lancha Lulalu** (☎ 9917-1975), or stop into a travel agency on the island. The ride can be rough – come with travel-sickness medication if you're especially prone to seasickness – and it's common for passengers to get wet on smaller boats.

If you're heading directly to Salvador's airport from Morro, contact **Cassi Turismo** (☎ 4101-9760; www.cassiturismo.com.br). The agency sells a transfer package (R$85 to R$90, five daily) involving a short boat ride from Morro to Ponto do Curral, then a 1½ hour van ride to Mar Grande on Ilha Itaparica, a 40-minute ferry to Salvador, and finally, a ride to the airport.

Catamarans (R$50 to R$60, one daily each way) go to Boipeba. There are also daily boats to Valença (R$10, 1½ hours), convenient if you're heading to the Peninsula Marau or points south.

Boipeba

☎ 0XX75

South of the Ilha da Tinharé, across the narrow Rio do Inferno, sits the Ilha de Boipeba. The village of Boipeba, on the northeastern tip of the island, is quiet, rustic and said to be what Morro was 20 years ago – though this is slowly changing as more travelers hear about this little paradise. The island's coastline is pristine, with more than 20km of beautiful, deserted beaches, including **Ponta de Castelhanos**, known for its diving.

Sleeping & Eating

Expanding tourist infrastructure has brought a range of excellent new pousadas to Boipeba; most have charming tropical-themed bars and restaurants that are open to the public. More eateries serving fresh seafood line the beach where the river meets the sea.

Abaquar Hostel HOSTEL $

(☎ 3653-6263; www.abaquarhostel.com; R do Areal s/n; dm/d with fan R$40/110, with air-con R$50/135; 📶) Paradise for the backpacker set. Abaquar has four- and six-bed dorms, each with its own bathroom and balcony, plus tidy doubles with views of the gardens. There are plenty of hammocks to choose from in this quiet, palm-tree-shaded setting. Children age 12 and up are welcome.

Pousada Pérola do Atlântico POUSADA $$
(☎3653-6096; peroladoatlanticoboipeba@hotmail.com; Rua da Praia s/n; s/d/tr from R$120/160/220; ❄📶) On the beach, this welcoming guesthouse has lush gardens with winding pathways leading through the tranquil setting. Guest rooms offer private patios with hammocks.

Pousada Santa Clara POUSADA $$$
(☎3653-6085; www.santaclaraboipeba.com; Travessa da Praia 5; d from R$260; ❄📶) A 10-minute walk from the town center, this restful guesthouse truly feels like a getaway. Santa Clara has lush foliage and large, cheerful rooms; the wonderful breakfast and on-site restaurant (open to the public Tuesday to Sunday), both using local produce, are particularly beloved by repeat guests.

Getting There & Away

Getting to Boipeba can be complicated. The easiest way to arrive is by speedboat from Valença (accessible from Salvador by a combination of ferry and bus via Bom Despacho.) From Valença's ferry dock, catch a speedboat (R$38, one hour, hourly between 10am and 4pm) to Boipeba. There are other options between Valença and Boipeba, including a bus-boat combination via Torrinha, but the direct speedboat is easier to plan. Accommodations owners in Boipeba are helpful resources as you're planning your travel strategy to or from the island.

From Morro de São Paulo, catamarans (R$50 to R$60, 1½ hours) leave for Boipeba in the morning – 9:30am at the time of writing, but be sure to double check – then turn around and make the return journey to Morro. You can also negotiate a ride to Boipeba with one of the many tour companies running day trips, or arrive overland on a 4WD vehicle (R$95, two daily).

Check www.boipebatur.com.br or www.ilhaboipeba.org.br for more details on these and other transportation options.

Valença

☎0XX75 / POP 97,300

Valença is a colonial fishing town on the banks of the Rio Una, historically the site of Portuguese struggles with both indigenous tribes and the Dutch. For most it is simply the gateway to Morro de São Paulo, but locals know it as a center of shipbuilding: 15th-century techniques have been so well maintained that the town was chosen to produce a replica of the Spanish galleon *La Niña* for the American epic film *1492* (1992) about Christopher Columbus' journey.

To see the building of traditional fishing boats in action, wander to the far end of the port, where the smell of sap and sawdust, old fish and sea salt mingles with the wonderful odor of nutmeg drying in the sun. For a good walk and a beautiful view, follow the river's left bank upstream toward the **Igreja NS de Amparo** (1757) on the hill.

From the port, walk straight uphill to reach the pedestrian center of town. Keep going straight up along this main street, Rua Governador Gonçalves, to reach the bus station, about 1km from the port. There are several banks and internet cafés around town.

Sleeping & Eating

Casual outdoor bar-snack stands are scattered along the riverfront near the bridge.

Hotel Portal Rio Una HOTEL $$
(☎3641-5050; www.portalhoteis.tur.br; Maestro Barrinha s/n; d/tr R$199/259; ❄📶🏊) This large, attractive hotel has Valença's finest restaurant and rooms, each with verandas overlooking the river. It's 1km from the river, on the opposite side of the port.

Mega Chic BRAZILIAN $
(www.restaurantemegachic.com.br; Maçônica 11; mains R$18-35; ⏰11:30am-4pm) Across the bridge from the center, Mega Chic offers a self-serve buffet and an à la carte menu of pastas, salads, sandwiches and cocktails.

Getting There & Away

There are daily boat services to Boipeba, Gamboa and Morro de São Paulo from the port in the center. Most travelers arrive to the port on one of the frequent Cidade Sol (www.viacaocidadesol.com.br) buses (R$13 to R$20, 16 daily) that run between Bom Despacho (on the island of Itaparica, where the ferry leaves for Salvador) and the port of Camamu (with connections to Barra Grande on the Peninsula Marau). Valença is about midway between the two, roughly a two-hour bus ride from both Bom Despacho and Camamu. Buses stop at the port. Águia Branca (www.aguiabranca.com.br) runs the same route, with fewer departures. The **bus station** (☎3641-4894; Av Abel Aguiar Queiroz s/n), a 1km hike or a R$20 taxi ride from the port, has additional options for onward travel.

Camamu

0XX73 / POP 31,055

On the mainland, shielded from the open ocean by the Peninsula de Maraú, Camamu is primarily the jumping-off point for Barra Grande. The town is the port of call for the many tiny fishing villages in the region and overlooks a maze of mangrove-filled islets and narrow channels. If you need to spend the night, there are a few inexpensive, family-run pousadas and simple cafés around the boat dock.

There is no real bus station here; buses stop near the port. Cidade Sol (www.viacaocidadesol.com.br) goes to Itacaré (R$10, one hour), with six departures daily from 7am to 8pm. Santana (www.empresasantana.com.br) also makes the trip.

Cidade Sol and **Aguia Branca** (3255-1823; www.aguiabranca.com.br) run to and from Bom Depacho several times daily (R$29 to R$33). Cidade Sol has more frequent departures. Aguia Branca also goes to Ilhéus (R$21, three hours, two daily.)

Barra Grande

0XX73

Deliciously off the beaten path on the northern tip of the Peninsula de Maraú, laid-back Barra Grande is a remote fishing village with sandy streets, tree-shaded magic and a tiny, picturesque center. Though it remained a relatively desolate paradise for decades, it's slowly becoming more of a vacation getaway for Brazilian families. The village remains a great place from which to explore the rest of the peninsula.

Separating the peninsula from the mainland is the island-riddled Baía de Camamu, Brazil's third-largest bay. One long, bumpy dirt road (often impassable after rain) heads down the peninsula, providing access to stunning beaches with crystal-clear water, such as **Praia Taipu de Fora** (7km, rated among Brazil's top beaches), and a handful of very small fishing villages. Pricey excursions to **Lagoa Azul**, viewpoints, bay islands and down the Rio Maraú are offered by local providers.

Other lovely destinations are accessible on foot from Barra, though visitors should note that, although the town center is small, the surrounding area is not: many beaches are a hike from the pousadas.

At the base of the village, where the boats arrive from Camamu, is the 2km-long **Barra Grande beach**, where the calm waters are fine for swimming and those traveling with children. A short walk along the beach leads to the **Ponta da Mutá**, the northeastern point of the peninsula, with a lighthouse marking the bay's entrance. Around the rocky point, you access a long stretch of coast, with **Praia da Bombaça** the next notable beach (3.5km from Barra Grande), before reaching Praia Taipús de Fora (located 3.5km further).

Sleeping & Eating

A range of new pousadas have opened to accommodate the influx of visitors in the last few years: it pays to shop around before committing to one. There are several supermarkets around the main plaza and a string of casual beach bars serving food and drinks along Praia Barra Grande. Note that opening hours are more limited in the low season.

Flat Barra APARTMENT **$$**
(3258-6124; www.flatbarra.com.br; Jose Melo Pirajá s/n; apt for 2/3 people R$168/225;) Staying at this lovely property is like renting your own beach apartment. The place looks like a pousada – complete with tropical foliage, a lavish breakfast spread and a swimming pool – but instead of regular guest rooms, these accommodations have full kitchens, private balconies and separate sleeping and living areas.

Taipabas Hotel POUSADA **$$**
(3258-6177; www.taipabashotel.web2007.uni5.net; Vivaldo Monteiro 20; d/tr R$210/262;) This charming family-run hotel offers treehouselike guest rooms with private hardwood balconies that overlook a central swimming pool, plus one of the best breakfasts in town.

Ponta do Mutá POUSADA **$$**
(3258-6028; www.pousadapontadomuta.com.br; Anjo s/n; d with/without sea view from R$395/345;) This welcoming gueshouse's primary selling point is its location right on the beach, near the boat dock, and its grassy lawn dotted with chaise longees facing the water. Pleasantly decorated rooms each feature a veranda and hammock; many have sea views.

Pousada Porto da Barra POUSADA $$
(☎3258-6349; www.pousadaportodabarra.wix.com/pousada; Av Vasco Neto 13; d/t R$220/300; ❄📶) Near the dock, Porto da Barra offers standard rooms with tile floors and hammocks strung outside the doors. The sea breezes and leafy, palm-tree-dotted grounds, just steps from the beach, are the main draw.

Pousada Barrabella POUSADA $$
(☎3258-6285; www.pousadabarrabella.com.br; Av Vasco Neto 3; d R$280; ❄📶🏊) This pretty guesthouse, decorated with furnishings made by local craftspeople, offers tranquil rooms with sea or bay views and private balconies, an excellent restaurant, an inviting swimming pool with a waterfall, and a cocktail bar that overlooks the ocean.

★**Praça da Taínha** BRAZILIAN $
(Jose Melo Pirajá; mains R$10-35; ⏲5pm-late) This grassy open-air plaza is home to several casual, budget-friendly eateries – look for crepes, pizzas, sandwiches, tapioca, *moqueca*, ice cream and cocktails – and a stage where live musicians often perform. The pretty lights and festive atmosphere make the place extremely appealing at night.

A Tapera BAHIAN $$
(☎3258-6119; www.atapera.com.br; Doutora Lili s/n; mains for 2 R$30-60; ⏲1-11pm) Just off the plaza, this traditional Bahian restaurant – considered by many to be the best on the peninsula – serves fresh seafood, including a fine *moqueca*. Dine outside under the trees for the best atmosphere.

Information

Get funds before going to Barra Grande, as there are no banks. There's a tourist-information kiosk near the entry to the boat dock on Praia Barra Grande; check www.barragrande.net for the complete lowdown on the area.

Getting There & Around

Though slower passenger ferries also make the trip, most travelers make the quick trip between Barra Grande and Camamu by speedboat (R$30, 30 minutes). Two companies offer the service; Camamu Adventure (www.camamuadventure.com.br) has the most frequent departures, with boats leaving on the hour between 7am and 5pm. From Camamu, catch a bus south to Itacaré or, if you're headed to Salvador, a bus to Bom Despacho, then a ferry across the bay.

Four-wheel-drive *jardineiras* (pick-up trucks with bench seating in the back) park near the main plaza in town, and leave for the beaches as soon as they have a full load. The most common destination is Taipu de Fora (40 minutes, R$12.50 one way). Look for the 'Ponto das Jardineiras' sign and the drivers in yellow T-shirts. From the same spot, you can also arrange for travel to the beaches by taxi or moto-taxi, though the former can be expensive and the latter can be messy if it starts to rain, or it the road is muddy.

Itacaré

☎0XX73 / POP 27,500

Beautiful Itacaré has long been sought out by hippies and surfers mesmerized by wide stretches of virgin Atlantic rainforest, picturesque beaches and reliable surf breaks. Countless pousadas and restaurants now pack the streets; still, a mellow, youthful vibe prevails, surf culture reigns supreme, and many establishments in the area are committed to environmentally friendly practices (look for the Carbon Free Tourism sign proudly posted around town).

Activities

The closest beach to town is **Praia da Concha**. Though not overly remarkable, it features the most services – beach cabanas serve drinks and food and rent lounge chairs – and calm waters ideal for those traveling with children.

The lovely coast south of Itacaré is characterized by rough surf, better for surfing than for swimming. **Resende**, **Tiririca** and **Ribeira** beaches are set in coves separated by rainforest-covered hills. Offering palm-tree shade and basic services, they're located within 1.5km of town – just follow the signs (and the parade of surfers.)

Slightly beyond these is the idyllic Prainha, reachable by trail from Praia do Ribeira, and further, the paradise-like Engenhoca, Hawaizinho and Itacarezinho beaches (p439), located 12km south of town. Many travel agencies offer day trips to the area, as well as a range of excursions: canoe trips upriver, rafting, mountain biking, rappelling, hiking and horseback riding. A popular excursion is the daylong adventure up to the Peninsula de Maraú (R$75), with stops at **Lagoa Azul** and **Praia Taipús de Fora**.

Surfboard rentals and surf lessons are easily arranged through outfitters around town.

Brazil Trip Tour ADVENTURE TOUR
(☎9996-3331; www.braziltriptour.com; R Pedro Longo 235) One of several reliable agencies

offering excursions, surf lessons, transfers and tours, Brazil Trip Tour specializes in English-speaking guides and eco-minded tours.

Easy Drop SURFING
(☎3251-3065; www.easydrop.com; R João Coutinho 140; 1-day class R$210, 1-week package from R$1795) This well-established surf camp, offering a week-long surfing experience with classes and accommodations, gets great reviews from travelers.

Sleeping

The majority of guesthouses are scattered along Rua Pedro Longo/Pituba. For a quieter stay that's still close to the action, try a pousada (guesthouse) on a side street instead of one that's located right on the main drag.

★ **Pousada Ilha Verde** POUSADA $
(☎3251-2056; www.ilhaverde.com.br; Ataíde Setúbal 234; s/d from R$100/140, chalet for 4 R$360;) In a lush setting, Ilha Verde has uniquely decorated rooms inspired by the owners' world travels. Features include private patios, an inviting swimming pool, abundant outdoor lounge space for luxuriating in the greenery, and a fair-trade shop with handicrafts made from Brazilian straw and shells.

Pousada dos Anjos POUSADA $
(☎3251-2482; www.luciakobayashi.wix.com/pousadadosanjos; R Joao Coutinho 185; d with/without fan from R$140/120;) A laid-back guesthouse with a boho-chic twist, not to mention gorgeous views and perhaps the most adorable breakfast in town. Located inside a restored colonial building away from the noise of Pituba, it has six rooms with mosquito nets and hardwood floors; some look out over the water. The open-air terrace is the perfect place to relax with a book.

Pousada Maresia POUSADA $
(☎3251-2338; www.maresiapousada.com.br; Pedro Longo 388; d/tr from R$120/180;) Simple rooms and a leafy garden courtyard – a memorable setting for breakfast – are part of the charm of this budget-friendly guesthouse that's focused on sustainable tourism. It's well positioned between the beach path and the heart of the action in the village.

Casarão Verde Hostel HOSTEL $
(☎3251-2037; www.casaraoverdehostel.com; Castro Alves s/n; dm R$30, d without bathroom from R$70;) Budget travelers rave about the friendly reception and pristine, spacious rooms at this lovely colonial house – painted pale green, as the name suggests – that's been smartly converted into a hostel.

Pousada Casa Tiki POUSADA $
(☎9810-6098; www.pousadacasatiki.com.br; Rua C, Praia da Concha; d with/without bathroom from R$130/115;) The home-away-from-home vibe is what makes this small guesthouse special: there are only four rooms, leisurely breakfasts happen around a communal table, and the owners, a young English-speaking couple, mix potent cocktails and offer travel advice.

Albergue O Pharol HOSTEL $
(☎3251-2527; www.albergueopharol.com.br; Praça Santos Dumont 7; dm/d from R$32/85, apt for 4 from R$190;) A favorite among backpackers, this centrally located and low-key hostel has tidy rooms, some with private balconies. There's a shared kitchen and a guest laundry area; the only downside is that there's no breakfast.

Che Lagarto HOSTEL $
(☎3251-3019; www.chelagarto.com; R Pedro Longo 58; dm/d from R$32/120;) Centrally positioned on the main street, this multistory hostel has its own pub, plenty of hammock space, and a communal kitchen and outdoor grill space. The place is pretty much a party in itself.

Concha Tropical Flat APARTMENT $
(☎3251-3426; www.conchatropical.com.br; Rua B, Praia da Concha; apt for 2/4 people R$150/240;) Ideal for self-caterers, these modern apartments are equipped with kitchens, flat-screen televisions and private balconies with ocean views. There's no breakfast included; communal facilities include a barbecue area.

Eating & Drinking

A browse up and down Itacaré's main thoroughfare is the best way to discover what's on offer; look for pop-up food stands and makeshift caipirinha stands at night.

Tio Gu Café Creperia CREPERIE $
(www.tiogu.com; Pedro Longo 488; mains R$15-30; 5pm-midnight Tue-Sat, to 11pm Sun;) This eco-conscious surfers' hangout has a loyal local following thanks to its perfectly prepared crepes (including delicious dessert options like chocolate and kiwi) and healthy fruit and vegetable infusions.

OFF THE BEATEN TRACK

LITTLE HAWAII

Hawaizinho means 'Little Hawaii' in Portuguese – and it's just one of the paradise-like beaches south of Itacaré, popular destinations for intrepid surfers and sunbathers alike. Some of the following beaches are located within easy walking distance of the highway, while others require a hike through the woods.

You can reach the access points on any of the buses that make the regular trip between the bus stations of Itacaré and Ilhéus. Drivers are used to dropping people off: just make sure to advise the driver where you'd like to disembark, and be sure to bring your own food and water, as there's little infrastructure along this stretch.

The beaches listed below are ordered from north to south, starting after Itacaré and the beaches of Prainha and São José, located immediately to Itacaré's south.

Jeribucaçu Strong waves, plenty of shade and a few places to eat.

Engenhoca Popular with surfers. Has coconut-water and tapioca vendors.

Hawaizinho & Camboinha Reefs, strong waves. Accessible from the highway by the same path as Engenhoca.

Itacarezinho The longest beach in the area; sea turtle mating ground. There's a bar-restaurant on the sand.

Bastante Elefante BURGERS $

(www.bastanteelefante.com.br; Pedro Longo s/n; mains R$22-25; 7-10:30pm Thu-Tue, closed Wed;) New to Itacaré's main thoroughfare is this stylish burger joint that (surprise!) also specializes in vegetarian and vegan options. It's both hipster- and kid-friendly, with a few outdoor tables, and a full cocktail list, too.

Tapiocaria Bem Bahia BAHIAN $

(Praça Santos Dumont 32; mains R$10-25; noon-11pm) This casual eatery on the main square specializes in delicious tapioca pastries stuffed with your choice of fillings. With a few outdoor tables, sandwiches, fresh juices and caipirinhas, it's a great budget pick for lunch or dinner.

Alamaim MIDDLE EASTERN $

(www.restaurantealamaim.com.br; R Pedro Longo 204; mains R$15-35; 2:30-10pm Mon-Sat;) Get your hummus fix here: this cool but casual eatery specializes in vegetarian Middle Eastern food, from falafel to couscous, and has relaxing lounge space where you can kick back after a day of surfing or swimming.

Mar e Mel BAR

(3251-2358; www.maremel.com.br; Rua D, Praia da Concha; mains R$20-38; 5pm-midnight) This is the place to hear (and dance to) live *forró* three nights a week (Tuesday, Thursday and Saturday at 9pm). There's a spacious wooden deck and abundant seafood and drink choices.

Orientation

Itacaré lies at the mouth of Rio de Contas, where the river meets the sea. A short walk east of the working-class neighborhoods around the fishing port leads to the area known as Pituba, which is essentially one long street, Rua Pedro Longo, lined with pousadas, restaurants and shops. Follow this road east out of town to access Itacaré's prettiest beaches. North of the Pituba strip is known as Condomínio Conchas do Mar, and has higher-end restaurants and pousadas in a more verdant setting. The neighborhood ends at the small beach of Praia da Concha.

Information

There are several exchange offices, internet cafés, and an ATM around the main plaza. Visit www.itacare.com.br for an overview.

Getting There & Around

Itacaré's **bus station** (3288-2019) is just out of the center, but it's a bit of a hike from many of the pousadas. A wheelbarrow-pushing guide (R$7 to R$10 per load of luggage) is helpful for guiding you to your hotel or hostel.

Many travelers arrive in Itacaré from points north – from Salvador, taking the ferry to Bom Despacho and then connecting to a bus – or from Camamu, the jumping-off point for Barra Grande and the Peninsula Maraú. From Camamu, Cidade Sol (www.viacaocidadesol.com.br) makes the trip to Itacaré six times daily (R$10, one hour.) Santana (www.empresasantana.com.br) also makes the trip. Buses depart from the

WORTH A TRIP

BAHIA FOR CHOCOLATE LOVERS

Take a break from the beach and head into the forest to **Vila Rosa** (www.vilarosaitacare.wix.com/vilarosaitacare; tour with transportation adult/child R$85/60, without transportation R$50/25), a beautifully restored cocoa farm. Guided tours take visitors around the plantation to see the collection, fermentation and drying of cocoa beans, then into the chocolate factory to taste the final product. The farm is located 20km away from Itacaré: the best way to arrive is to make a reservation on Vila Rosa's shuttle, which leaves Itacaré between 9am and 10am.

Have lunch in the charming café, go for a dip in the stone pools, or take a kayak out on the reservoir. You can even stay the night in one of the five guest rooms of the old colonial manor.

bus companies' offices, around the corner from the port where boats depart for Barra Grande.

Coming or going from the south, Rota (p431) has around 15 daily departures to Ilhéus (R$14, 1¾ hours, from 5am to 7:45pm). The same buses will drop you at the access points to the beaches between Itacaré and Ilheús – make sure to tell the driver where you'd like to be let off. Rota also has one early-morning bus to Porto Seguro (R$74, eight hours). You'll have more options for the same trip if you're willing to switch buses in Ilheús.

Rental cars and private taxi services advertised around town are useful for transfers to Ilheus (R$120 to R$180) and Camamu (R$140).

Ilhéus

0XX73 / POP 220,900

Bright, early-20th-century architecture and oddly angled streets lend a vibrant and rather playful air to slightly rough-around-the-edges Ilhéus. The town's fame comes from its history as a prosperous cocoa port, as well as being the hometown of Jorge Amado, the famous Brazilian novelist, who used it as the setting for one of his best novels, *Gabriela, Cravo e Canela* (Gabriela, Clove and Cinnamon). Though not a primary tourist attraction, the city is worth a quick stopover.

History

Ilhéus was a sleepy place until cacao was introduced into the region from Belém in 1881. With the sugar plantations in the doldrums, impoverished agricultural workers and freed or escaped slaves flocked from all over the Northeast to the hills surrounding Ilhéus to participate in the new boom: cacao, known as the *ouro branco* (white gold) of Brazil.

Sudden, lawless and violent, the scramble to plant cacao displayed all the characteristics of a gold rush. When the dust settled, the land and power belonged to a few ruthless *coroneis* (so-called 'colonels') and their hired guns. The landless were left to work, and usually live, on the *fazendas* (plantations), where they were subjected to a harsh and paternalistic labor system. This history is graphically told by Amado, who grew up on a cacao plantation, in his book *Terras do Sem Fim* (published in English as *The Violent Land*).

In the early 1990s, the *vassoura de bruxa* (witch's broom) disease left cacao trees shriveled and unable to bear fruit, hurting the area's economy dramatically. Though the disease persists to this day, you can still see cacao *fazendas* and rural workers like those Amado described throughout the lush, tropical hills.

Sights & Activities

The best thing to do in Ilhéus is explore the old streets. The center has several quaint antique buildings and pedestrian-only thoroughfares, an ideal setting for photographers to wander.

Casa de Jorge Amado MUSEUM

(3634-8986; Amado 20; admission R$2; 9am-noon & 2-6pm Mon-Fri, 9am-1pm Sat) The Casa de Jorge Amado, where the eponymous writer lived with his parents while working on his first novel, has been restored and turned into a lovely and informative museum honoring Amado's life. Not many writers can boast this sort of recognition while still alive, but he became a national treasure well before his death in 2001.

Catedral de São Sebastião CHURCH

(Praça Dom Eduardo; 10am-8pm) The Catedral de São Sebastião is the city's icon – construction began in 1931 – and is a unique, eclectic mix of architectural styles. For an unforgettable view of the fairy-tale-like spires, walk out onto the beach at sunset and look back at the cathedral silhouetted against the clouds.

Igreja de São Jorge CHURCH
(Praça Rui Barbosa; admission by donation; ⌚10am-6pm Tue-Sun) The Igreja de São Jorge is the city's oldest church, dating from 1556, and houses a small sacred-art museum.

Beaches

City beaches aren't the cleanest (though that doesn't stop local surfers from taking to the waves). Your best bet is to head south, but even then you'll find that the area's broad, flat beaches are best for soccer games, and it takes kilometers for the water to lose the muddy color of the river outflow. **Praia dos Milionários** (7km) has some *barracas* and is popular with locals.

Tours

Trips to a tree-sloth recuperation center, Primavera Fazenda (where you'll be taken through the process of cacao production) and Lagoa Encantada, a state-protected area of Atlantic rainforest with waterfalls and wildlife, can all be arranged through local travel agencies like **Órbita Turismo e Expedições** (☎3234-3250; www.orbitaexpedicoes.com.br; R Leite Mendes, 71).

Festivals & Events

As any Amado fan would guess, Ilhéus has highly spirited festivals. One of the best is the **Festa de São Sebastião** from January 11 to 19.

Sleeping

Note that Ilhéus' best hotels, located south of the historic center and the Pontal neighborhood, are convenient only for those traveling by car.

Lagoa Encantada II POUSADA **$**
(☎3632-5675; Italia 156, Pontal; d R$90; ❄📶) Located south of the center, near the airport and the beach, this quiet guesthouse is ideal for budget travelers, if a bit hard to find. During the day, it's pleasant to walk the 5km into the center; mostly along the waterfront. At night, take the bus or a R$30 taxi ride to and from downtown.

Pousada Pier do Pontal POUSADA **$**
(☎3221-4000; www.pierdopontal.com.br; Lomanto Junior 1650, Pontal; s/d from R$120/150; ❄📶🏊) This guesthouse could use a face lift. On the plus side, it's on the waterfront and has a swimming pool. It's a long stroll or a short taxi or bus ride to the historic center.

Ilhéus Praia Hotel HOTEL **$$**
(☎2101-2533; www.ilheuspraia.com.br; Praça Dom Eduardo, Centro; s/d from R$132/165; ❄📶🏊)

BAHIA'S FAVORITE SON

Nobody is more responsible for bringing Bahian culture to the rest of the world than Jorge Amado, Brazil's most famous modernist author. Amado's tales have been translated into 49 languages and read the world over.

Born in 1912, Jorge spent his youth in Ilhéus, the scene of many of his later novels. After secondary studies in Salvador, Amado studied law in Rio, but instead of going into practice he decided to become a writer. He surprised critics and the public by publishing his first novel, *O País do Carnaval*, when he was only 19 years old.

An avowed communist, Amado participated in the rebel literary movement of the time, launching two romances set in the cacao zone around Ilheús: *Cacau* and *Suor*. The first novel was banned by the fascist-leaning Vargas government, which only increased Amado's popularity. Sent to prison several times for his beliefs, Amado was elected a federal deputy for the Brazilian communist party (PCB) in 1945, but he lost his seat after a disagreement with the party several years later. He left Brazil and lived for more than five years in Europe and Asia, finally breaking ties with the communist party after the crimes of Stalin were revealed to the world.

With *Gabriela, Cravo e Canela* (Gabriela, Clove and Cinnamon), published in 1958, he entered a new writing phase, marked by a romantic and playful style that intimately described the colorful escapades of his Bahian heroes and heroines. This and his later novel *Dona Flor e Seus Dois Maridos* (Dona Flor and Her Two Husbands), set in Salvador, were both adapted into popular films.

Amado died in Salvador in August 2001, just short of his 89th birthday.

Ilhéus

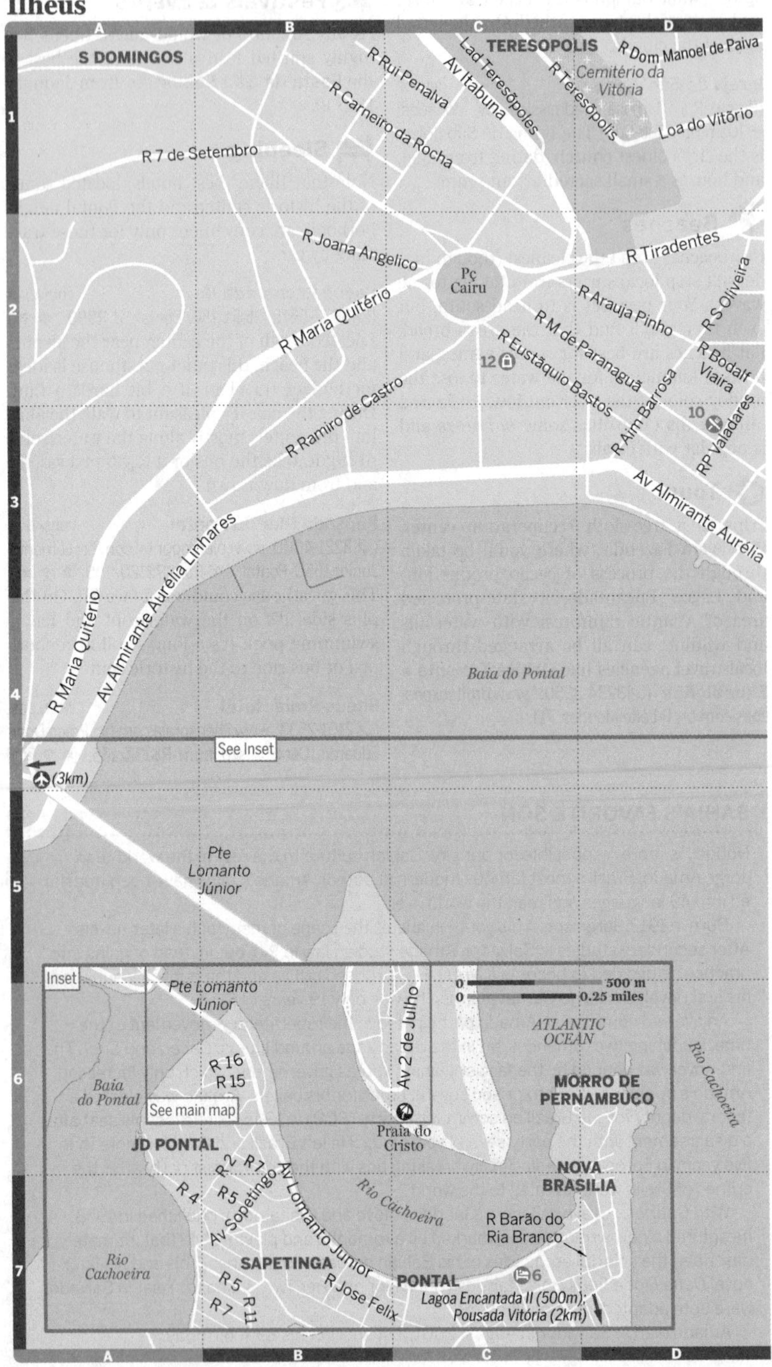
S DOMINGOS
TERESOPOLIS
R Rui Penalva
Av Itabuna
Lad Teresõpoles
R Teresõpolis
Cemitério da Vitória
R Dom Manoel de Paiva
Loa do Vitõrio
R Carneiro da Rocha
R 7 de Setembro
R Joana Angelico
Pç Cairu
R Tiradentes
R S Oliveira
R Arauja Pinho
R Maria Quitério
R M de Paranaguã
R Eustãquio Bastos
R Bodalf Viaira
12
10
R Aim Barrosa
RP Valadares
R Ramiro de Castro
Av Almirante Aurélia
Av Almirante Aurélia Linhares
R Maria Quitério
Baia do Pontal
See Inset
(3km)
Pte Lomanto Júnior
Inset
Pte Lomanto Júnior
R 16
R 15
See main map
Av 2 de Julho
Praia do Cristo
0 500 m
0 0.25 miles
ATLANTIC OCEAN
Rio Cachoeira
MORRO DE PERNAMBUCO
Baia do Pontal
JD PONTAL
R 2
R 7
Av Lomanto Junior
R 4
R 5
Av Sopetingo
Rio Cachoeira
NOVA BRASILIA
R Barão do Ria Branco
Rio Cachoeira
SAPETINGA
R 5
R 7
R 11
R Jose Felix
PONTAL
6
Lagoa Encantada II (500m); Pousada Vitória (2km)

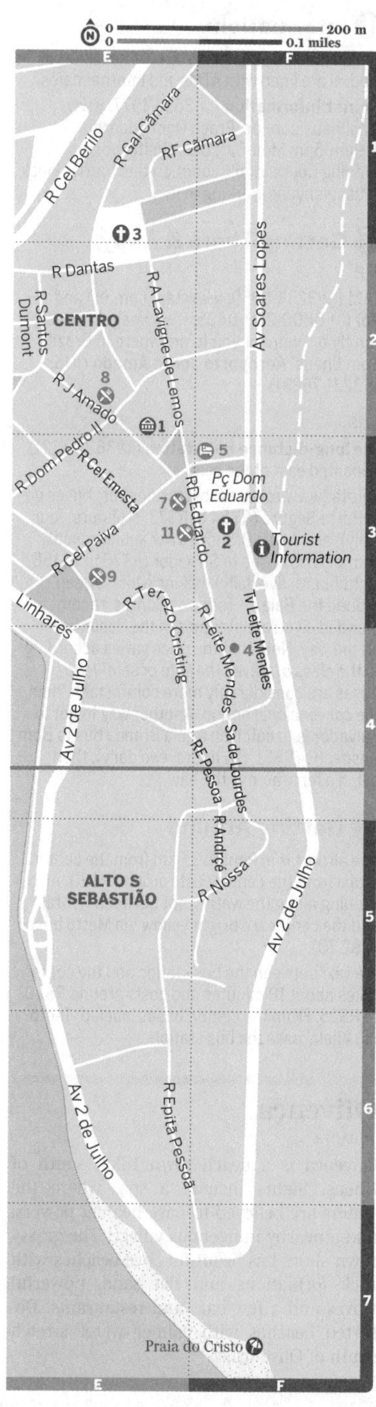

Ilhéus

Sights

1 Casa de Jorge Amado E2
2 Catedral de São Sebastião F3
3 Igreja de São Jorge E1

Activities, Courses & Tours

4 Órbita Turismo e Expedições F4

Sleeping

5 Ilhéus Praia Hotel F3
6 Pousada Pier do Pontal C7

Eating

7 Bar Vesúvio E3
8 Barrakítika E2
9 Bataclan E3
10 Berimbau D3
11 Grão Amado E3

Shopping

12 Mercado de Artesanato C2

This high-rise hotel is fraying around the edges, but many rooms have fine views of the cathedral across the plaza. The relatively high prices don't seem in line with these average rooms, but it's extremely convenient for an overnight stay if you're hoping to sightsee in the historic center.

Eating & Drinking

For inexpensive sandwiches and cold drinks during daylight hours, try the stands along the pedestrian streets downtown. At night, visit the vendors selling tapioca and other treats across from the cathedral on the waterfront. For a quick pick-me-up, try the coffee stand on the main square across from the cathedral.

Berimbau CAFE **$**

(cnr Paranaguá & Valadares; mains R$12-28; 10am-5pm Mon-Fri) Berimbau is stuck in the past, in the best sense of the phrase: the classic corner diner looks like the setting for a '60s-era Brazilian film. By morning, the café serves up coffee, sandwiches and pastries to the downtown business crowd, and there's a busy buffet at lunchtime. It's the place to soak up a little local culture in Ilheús.

Grão Amado CAFE **$**

(Praça Dom Eduardo; mains R$12-25; 10am-7pm Mon-Sat) This contemporary coffee shop offers delicious and beautifully presented pastries, cakes and crepes alongside a thorough coffee menu. It's perfect for breakfast or a late-afternoon snack at one of a few outdoor tables.

★ **Bar Vesúvio** BAHIAN $$
(☎3634-2164; www.barvesuvio.com; Praça Dom Eduardo 190; mains R$33-66; ⏰11am-midnight Mon-Sat, 5pm-midnight Sun) This landmark bar and restaurant attracts Amado fans (two of the novelist's fictional protagonists met here) for *moquecas* and cold beer served at the outdoor tables facing the cathedral, which is beautifully illuminated at night. Start with a few *pasteles arabes* (Middle Eastern-style pastries stuffed with spicy meat).

★ **Bataclan** BRAZILIAN $$
(☎3634-0088; www.bataclan.com.br; Av 2 de Julho 77; mains R$28-65; ⏰10am-5pm Mon-Sat, event times vary) Once a cabaret frequented by cocoa tycoons (and one of the settings for Amado's *Gabriela*), this colonial building was restored to its original brilliance in 2004. Now it serves as a restaurant and cultural center staging concerts and art exhibitions. There's a lunch buffet from 11:30am to 2:30pm on weekdays.

Barrakítika BRAZILIAN $$
(☎3231-8300; www.barrakitika.com.br; Amado 39; mains R$25-60; ⏰11am-midnight Mon-Sat) This casual and hugely popular restaurant has outdoor tables, inexpensive set lunches from *feijoada* (bean-and-meat stew) to *peixe frito* (fried fish), and a full menu with everything from steak to pizza. At night, Barrakítika hosts a lively bar scene; look for live music on weekends.

Shopping

Mercado de Artesanato MARKET
(Praça Eustáquio Basto 2; ⏰8:30am-10pm) This bustling artisan market, showcasing the lovely white dresses, crocheted textiles and beaded jewelry typical of the region, is a great place to pick up a few Bahian souvenirs.

Orientation

The city center is located on a beach-lined point that reaches into the mouth of the Rio Cachoeira, and is sandwiched between two hills. On the southern side of the S-curving river mouth is the modern neighborhood of Pontal; catch a taxi over the bridge to reach it.

Information

The downtown pedestrian streets near the cathedral are lined with ATMs and internet cafés.

Tourist Information (☎3634-1977; www.brasilheus.com.br; Praça Dom Eduardo; ⏰9am-5pm Mon-Sat) Despite the posted opening hours, don't count on this tourist kiosk to have anyone working in it.

Getting There & Away

AIR

TAM (☎3234-5259; www.tam.com.br) and **Gol** (☎0800-280-0465; www.voegol.com.br) can fly or connect you to anywhere in Brazil from Ilhéus' **Aeroporto Jorge Amado** (IOS; ☎3231-7629).

BUS

The **long-distance bus station** (☎3634-4121) is located east of the center.

Rota (www.rotatransportes.com.br) buses go to Porto Seguro (R$54 to R$73, six hours, four daily), and Aguia Branca (www.aguiabranca.com.br) has buses to Salvador (R$76 to R$156, eight hours, five daily) making a long sweep around the Baía de Todos os Santos, recommended if you are stopping in the Recôncavo on the way. Note that the price varies according to the class of travel: the *leito* or *semi-leito* buses are considerably more comfortable than the *convencional* option. Another way to get to Salvador is to catch an Aguía Branca bus to Bom Despacho (R$51, 6½ hours, two daily), then catch a ferry across the bay.

Getting Around

The airport is in Pontal, 3.5km from the center. A taxi from the center costs around R$20. Also running along the waterfront between Pontal and the center are bright yellow Via Metro buses (R$2.70).

A taxi between the bus station and the center takes about 10 minutes and costs around R$20 to R$25. From the center, buses labeled 'Teotônio Vilela' pass the bus station.

Olivença

☎0XX73

Olivença is a beach town 16km south of Ilhéus. Sights include a spa, where the waters are believed to have healing powers, and a nearby indigenous village. The grassy town shore has beautiful cove beaches with rock formations and flat sand, powerful waves and a few bars and restaurants. Deserted beaches with calmer water stretch south of Olivença.

Most visitors come here, though, for the great waves just north of town at **Backdoor**, one of Brazil's best surf breaks. Make a night or weekend of it by checking into **Back Door Village** (☎3269-1141; www.villagebackdoor.com.br; Rodovia Ilhéus–Olivença, Km 13.5; d/tr from R$180/270; ❄📶🏊), a pleasant beach hotel with a swimming pool and thatched-roof, '60s-style bungalows. It's located just outside of Olivença, on the road to Ilhéus. Also in the vicinity is the touristy but family-friendly beachfront complex of **Batuba Beach** (www.batubabeach.com.br; 👪), where you can do everything from dining on the sand (mains R$18–35) to catching live music to taking a surf lesson. Check the website for more details.

City buses leave every 30 minutes from the Ilhéus bus station (passing the city bus terminal) for Olivença (30 minutes) from 6am to 11pm. The bus travels close to the beaches, so you can hop off when you see one you like, or just tell the driver your destination. Private transfer can also be arranged through Ilhéus travel agencies (around R$80 for up to four people).

Porto Seguro

☎0XX73 / POP 145,000

Historically, Porto Seguro is significant: it's the point where Portuguese sailors first landed in the land now known as Brazil. But apart from its small historic center and colorful colonial houses, the city is rougher than many others in Bahia – not that the hordes of Brazilian and Argentinian package tourists, here for beach action and nightlife, really care. Due to the city's raucous nightlife, the streets are quiet and even run-down during the day, as though the whole city is experiencing a hangover the morning after the party. Many travelers linger in town only long enough to catch the ferry toward the lovely coastline and mellow village of nearby Arraial d'Ajuda.

History

Pedro Cabral's landing 16km north of Porto Seguro (Safe Port) at Coroa Vermelha is officially considered the first Portuguese landfall in Brazil. The sailors stayed just long enough to stock up on supplies. Three years later Gonçalvo Coelho's expedition arrived and planted a marker in what is now Porto Seguro's Cidade Histórica (Historic City). Jesuits on the same expedition built a church, now in ruins, in Outeiro da Glória. In 1526 a naval outpost, convent and chapel (Igreja NS da Misericórdia) were built in the present-day Cidade Histórica.

The Tupininquin, not the Pataxó, were the indigenous tribe around the site of Porto Seguro when the Portuguese landed. They were rapidly conquered and enslaved by the colonists, but the Aimoré, Pataxó, Cataxó and other inland tribes resisted Portuguese colonization and constantly threatened Porto Seguro. Military outposts were built along the coast in Belmonte, Vila Viçosa, Prado and Alcobaça to defend against both European attacks by sea and *índio* attacks by land.

Sights & Activities

Motivation is required to climb the stairs to the Cidade Histórica; sweeping views over the coastline make the hike worthwhile. The historic center features remnants of Brazil's early settlement, the colonial era and indigenous life. Opposite the museum is **Gonçalo Coelho's marker stone**, now encased in glass and ringed with a fence. Other reminders of the past are old stone churches such as the **Igreja NS da Misericórdia** (1526), the **Igreja NS da Pena** (1772) and the **Capela de São Benedito**, dating from the 16th century. Note that while the area is beautifully illuminated at night, the steps are not safe after dark – it's best to take a taxi.

Back down by the beach, just north of town, the **Memorial da Epopéia do Descobrimento** (☎3268-2586; www.memorialdodescobrimento.com.br; Av Beira-Mar 800; admission R$6; ⏰8:30am-12:30pm & 1:30-5pm Mon-Sat) is a worthwhile stop. The park features a replica of the Portuguese ship that first landed on Brazilian shores. The surrounding botanical gardens also feature a replica of an indigenous village; the guides are descendants of the Pataxó.

Beaches

North of town is one long bay dotted with *barracas* and clubs with invisible divisions creating the Orla Norte (North Coast): **Praia Curuípe** (3km), **Praia Itacimirim** (4km), **Praia Mundaí** (6km), **Praia de Taperapua** (7km) and **Praia do Mutá** (10km.) The sands are white and fluffy, backed by green vegetation lapped by a tranquil sea, and are dotted with big beach clubs like Tôa-Tôa (p448),

Porto Seguro

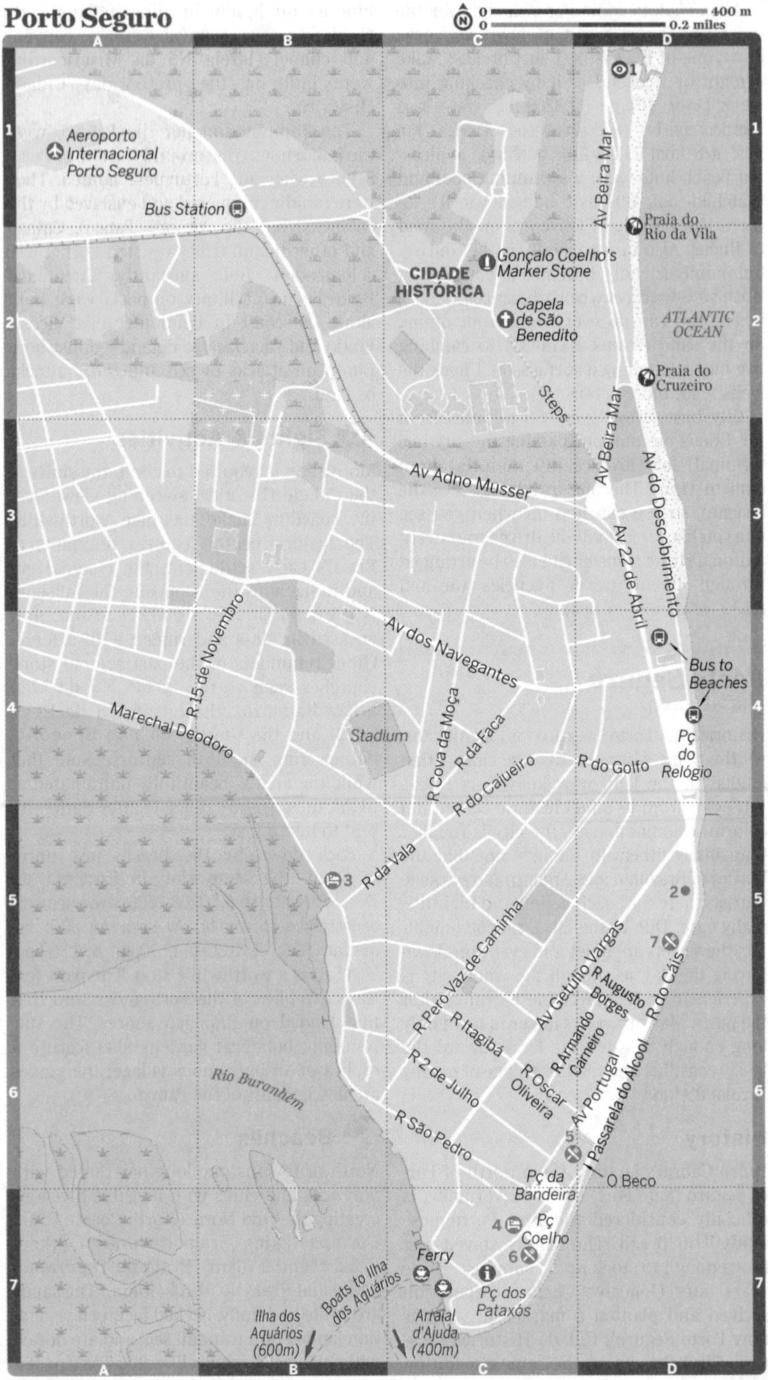

0 400 m
0 0.2 miles

A B C D

Aeroporto Internacional Porto Seguro
Bus Station
CIDADE HISTÓRICA
Gonçalo Coelho's Marker Stone
Capela de São Benedito
Steps
Av Beira Mar
Praia do Rio da Vila
ATLANTIC OCEAN
Praia do Cruzeiro
Av Adno Musser
Av do Descobrimento
Av 22 de Abril
Av dos Navegantes
R 15 de Novembro
Bus to Beaches
Marechal Deodoro
Stadium
R Cova da Moça
R da Faca
R do Cajueiro
R do Golfo
Pç do Relógio
R da Vala
R Pero Vaz de Caminha
Av Getúlio Vargas
R Augusto Borges
R do Cáis
R Itagibá
R Armando Carneiro
R 2 de Julho
R Oscar Oliveira
Av Portugal
Passarela do Álcool
Rio Buranhém
R São Pedro
O Beco
Pç da Bandeira
Pç Coelho
Ferry
Boats to Ilha dos Aquários
Pç dos Pataxós
Ilha dos Aquários (600m)
Arraial d'Ajuda (400m)

1 2 3 4 5 6 7

Porto Seguro

where MCs and dancers lead Brazilian crowds through popular dances.

Tours

Several travel agencies – try **Pataxó Turismo** (☎3288-1256; www.pataxoturismo.com.br; Shopping Rio Mar, loja 3) – offer full-day tours to Praia do Espelho and Praia do Curuípe (R$55) as well as Trancoso (R$45) and other destinations south. Half-day excursions to the offshore reefs of Recife de Fora and Coroa Alta (R$80), fantastic locales for snorkeling with a wide variety of bright tropical fish, are very popular. Unfortunately, since visitors are encouraged to walk over coral reefs in order to enter internal pools, we don't officially recommend it.

Festivals & Events

Porto Seguro's **Carnaval**, Bahia's most famous after Salvador's, is relatively small and safe, consisting of a few *trios elétricos* cruising the main drag blasting *axé*. These days, just as many tourists come for the parties across the way in Arraial d'Ajuda.

Sleeping

Porto Seguro overflows with hotels but receives a surprisingly high number of visitors on package tours, meaning decent low-cost rooms are difficult to find during high season. Note that many hotels listing a Porto Seguro address are not in town, but north of town on the coast – nice, but potentially problematic if you want to be in the center of the nighttime action. Alternatively, catch the ferry to Arraial d'Ajuda and stay in a nicer hotel for the same price – transportation between the two towns is quick and easy, but Arraial's accommodations are superior.

Hotel Estalagem BOUTIQUE HOTEL $
(☎3288-2095; www.hotelestalagem.com.br; Marechal Deodoro 66; r R$110-165;) One of the more stylish options in Porto Seguro, this affordable boutique hotel is housed inside a colonial building dating from 1801; check out the antique stones, sourced from the coral reef and originally joined together with whale oil, in the entryway. Today, renovated guest rooms are understated and comfortable, with private balconies overlooking the swimming pool below.

Pousada Brisa do Mar POUSADA $
(☎3288-1444; Praça Coelho 180; d/tr/q R$70/85/120;) This basic guesthouse, in a long, narrow house near the waterfront, is nothing fancy. But as Porto Seguro accommodations go, the location is good: it's close to restaurants, the Passarela do Álcool (Alcohol Walkway) and the ferry to Arraial.

Eating & Drinking

Most dining and drinking options are found around the Passarela do Álcool. At night, the *passarela* has craft stalls and street performers, with live music spilling onto the plazas. Look for fresh-fruit cocktail stands making *capeta* (guaraná, cocoa powder, cinnamon, sweetened condensed milk and vodka) – just the thing to kick off the evening.

★ **Portinha** BUFFET $
(☎3288-2743; Saldanha Marinho 33; per kg R$36; ⊙noon-10pm) One of the classiest per-kilo eateries around, Portinha puts out a mouthwatering buffet of gourmet dishes, from pasta with sun-dried tomatoes and basil to fresh fish fillets. Both the leafy patio tables and the stylish rustic interior offer plenty of atmosphere. Look for other locations in Arraial and Trancoso.

O Beco BRAZILIAN $
(cnr Beco & Rua do Cáis; mains R$12-30; ⊙5pm-late Tue-Sun) Not sure where to eat? Just walk over here. This quaint little open-air galleria, just around the corner from the Passarela do Álcool, is lined with small bistros and cafés where you'll find everything from sushi to crepes to Portuguese-style baked goods.

Tia Nenzinha BAHIAN $$
(Av Portugal 170; mains for 2 R$35-70) A classic in Porto since 1976, no-frills Tia Nenzinha serves an assortment of Bahian dishes.

Entertainment

Young partiers selling club and party tickets (R$25 to R$75) around the Passarela let you know what's happening on any given night. The major beach clubs all put on weekly nighttime *luaus* (parties); the one at **Barramares** (3679-2980; www.barramares.com.br; Av Beira Mar, Km 6, Praia de Taperapuã) is the most stunning. It's about 6km north of town, and several other good nightspots are on the way, including **Tôa-Tôa** (3679-1555; www.portaltoatoa.com.br; Av Beira Mar, Km 5, Praia de Taperapuã). On a river island between Porto Seguro and Arraial, the **Ilha dos Aquarios** (3268-2828; www.ilhadosaquarios.com.br; Ilha Pacuio, office in Porto Seguro, Av Conselheiro Luiz Viana Filho 278; adult/child under 10 R$65/free; 8pm-late Fri, box office 8pm-5am Tue-Sun) complex also offers a good party.

Information

Banco do Brasil ATM (Av 22 de Abril)

Bradesco ATM (Av dos Navegantes)

Bradesco ATM (Praça do Relógio)

Tourist Information Kiosk (Praça dos Pataxós; 10am-6pm Mon-Sat)

Getting There & Away

AIR

Gol (3268-4460; www.voegol.com.br), **Azul** (www.voeazul.com.br) and **TAM** (3288-3399; www.tam.com.br) can connect you anywhere in Brazil from **Aeroporto Internacional Porto Seguro** (BPS; 3288-1880), a short drive outside of town. Taxis cost around R$35 to the port or the city center.

BOAT

The *balsa*, a quick car and passenger ferry, connects Porto Seguro to Arraial d'Ajuda (R$3.50, 10 to 15 minutes). From Arraial's port, you can catch buses into town, or to points further south like Trancoso.

BUS

The **bus station** (3288-1914) is 1.5km outside town; taxis cost around R$30 to the ferry or the center.

Rota (www.rotatransportes.com.br) buses go to Ilhéus (R$54 to R$73, six hours, four daily). Rota also has one daily bus to Itacaré (R$74, eight hours). You'll have more options for the same trip if you're willing to switch buses in Ilheús. Águia Branca (www.aguiabranca.com.br) offers one daily departure to Salvador (R$176, 11 hours), an overnight bus at the time of writing. Águia Branca also runs the long haul to Rio de Janeiro (R$207, 22 hours, including a connection in Vitória).

For more frequent connections, three companies run buses to Eunápolis (R$10, one hour, every 30 minutes from 5:30am to 10pm).

Getting Around

If you're heading to beaches north of Porto Seguro, look for Riacho Doce, Alto do Mundaí, Campinho–Barramares or Cabrália buses (R$2.70) that pick up passengers at a bus stop on Praça do Relógio, among other places. Taxis are widely available throughout the city: a cab from the bus station to the ferry costs around R$20.

FRIDAY NIGHT ON ILHA DOS AQUÁRIOS

Everywhere you go in Porto Seguro, you'll see ads and promotions for Ilha dos Aquários – and down by the water, a dedicated boat dock next to the Arraial d'Ajuda ferry. But what *is* Ilha dos Aquários (travelers often wonder, staring down at the brochure)? Is it an aquarium or a nightclub? Both, in fact. It's one of those quintessentially Brazilian entertainment complexes that wears a few hats, catering to the stroller-set earlier in the evening and the up-all-night party crowd after midnight.

As the name indicates (*ilha* means 'island'), you can't walk or drive here: all guests arrive by a quick boat ride, included with the entrance fee. The illuminated shark aquariums and family-oriented shows are fun for all ages; there's also a food court and a number of different dining and drinking venues. There's a certain novelty to the fact that it's only open on Friday evenings after dark. After the families head out, the party kids start coming in, and the island morphs into a huge party with live *forró*, house music, specially invited DJs and Bahian music.

South of Porto Seguro

South of Porto Seguro, the Bahian coastline is particularly lovely, lined with pristine sands, colorful cliffs and charming beach villages that become increasingly rustic (and less touristy) as you head south.

Arraial d'Ajuda

☎0XX73 / POP 12,000

Atop a bluff overlooking an enchanting stretch of coastline, Arraial d'Ajuda is a peaceful tourist village with indisputable appeal. Its narrow paved roads and dusty lanes wind beneath large, shady trees, with lovely pousadas and open-air restaurants hidden among the greenery. Solid, brightly painted facades surround its plazas, and the air remains tinged with the scent of tropical vegetation. In the past, Arraial was the playground of the wealthy, which isn't far removed from the upmarket tourists the town tends to attract: the place is an extremely popular vacation spot for well-off Argentinians. More recently, however, a new wave of international backpackers and nouveau hippies have brought a little diversity to the idyllic surroundings.

Sights & Activities

Arraial's beaches are sheltered by offshore reefs, making the clear water particularly appealing (and family friendly) at low tide. stand-up paddling (SUP) is currently all the rage here, with classes and rental equipment available at several spots along the coast. **Praia Mucugê** is Arraial's main beach and is crowded with *barracas*, though the crowds thin out considerably if you hang a left and continue past the Eco Parque entrance. Heading south, **Praia do Parracho** is also built up, but with beach clubs and a few condominium complexes. Around the point, beautiful **Praia Pitinga** has red-striped sandstone cliffs, pretty, calm waters and a few *barracas*. South of Pitinga, **Praia da Lagoa Azul** and **Praia Taípe** are backed by tall cliffs, and face stronger waves.

Coral Vivo MUSEUM

(www.coralvivo.org.br; Mucugê 402; ⏲4-11pm Mon-Sat) FREE This colorful minimuseum offers exhibits of the five varieties of coral found in Bahia, including fire coral and the aptly named *corais cérebro* (brain coral), plus general information on the region's marine biodiversity. Down on the beach, there's another location with impressive coral tanks inside Arraial d'Ajuda Eco Parque, accessible by admission to the park (10am to 5pm.)

Eco Parque WATER PARK

(☎3575-8600; www.arraialecoparque.com.br; Estrada da Balsa, Km 4.5; adult/child R$100/60; ⏲10am-5pm; 👪) Occupying a huge piece of land on the coast, this family-friendly water park has long, twisting waterslides, a wave pool and a 'lazy river' you can float down on rafts. There's also a *tiroleza* (zip line), kayaks for rent and a host of other outdoor activities, plus live music and entertainment.

Tours

Several travel agencies organize day trips to beautiful beach villages south of Arraial. Popular excursions include the trip to **Praias Espelho and Curuípe**, including a stop in Trancoso, a long day's outing to **Caraíva** and a snorkeling trip to the offshore reef of **Recife de Fora**. If you're visiting between July and October, ask about humpback-whale-watching tours.

Arraial Trip Tur TOUR

(☎3575-2805; www.arraialtriptur.com.br; Mucuge s/n) Offers excursions to Praia do Espelho (R$50), Trancoso (R$40), Caraíva (R$70), plus whale-watching (R$180) and scuba tours (prices vary.) Check the website for details to help you plan your time: many trips are scheduled for specific days of the week. The agency also rents bicycles for R$35 per day.

Arco-Íris Turismo TOUR

(☎3575-1672; Mucugê 199) Arco-Íris Turismo organizes schooner and van trips to Caraíva, Praias Espelho and Curuípem, and the offshore reefs Recife de Fora and Coroa Alta. It also occasionally runs three-day catamaran trips to the Parque Nacional Marinho de Abrolhos.

Sleeping

Arraial is home to a large number of lovely pousadas where you'll probably want to stay for a week. You'll see plenty of options on the road from the ferry dock to the center (frequent buses and vans run the route), but most visitors find the village to be more convenient for its access to dining, shopping and nightlife.

Art Hotel Aos Sinos Dos Anjos POUSADA $
(☎3575-1176; www.aossinosdosanjos.com; Ipê 71; s/d from R$110/140;) A unique gem in Arraial d'Ajuda, this guesthouse is entirely decorated with the works of local artists and filled with colorful mosaics, healing crystals, seashells and sculptures. Two levels of suites, each with its own patio and hammock, face the pretty swimming pool. It's tucked away on a side street that runs parallel to Rua Mucugê.

Arraial d'Ajuda Hostel HOSTEL $
(☎3575-1192; www.arraialdajudahostel.com.br; Campo 94; dm/d from R$48/145; @) This colorful HI hostel offers well-equipped private rooms as well as dorm-style accommodations in a funky Greco-Bahian-style building with a courtyard swimming pool. Travelers like the communal outdoor kitchen and the location near the beach.

★ **Pousada Catamarã** POUSADA $$
(☎3575-1556; www.pousadacatamara.com.br; Alameda dos Oitis 90; s/d from R$180/205;) The inviting outdoor pool, festive thatched-roof pool bar, comfortable guest rooms with private verandas, and proximity to the beach make this guesthouse a top choice. It's located downhill from the village on a side street just before you reach Praia Mucugê.

Pousada Erva Doce POUSADA $$
(☎3575-1113; www.ervadoce.com.br; Mucugê 200; d from R$240;) Squarely in the center of the village on a cobblestone plaza lined with boutiques and cafes, this peaceful guesthouse has spacious, thoughtfully designed rooms. Surrounding the small swimming pool is a leafy tropical garden with an open-air bar and hammocks, ideal for lazing away the afternoon. The hotel's sushi restaurant is a local favorite.

Vila do Beco POUSADA $$
(☎3575-1230; www.viladobeco.com.br; Beco dos Jegues 173; d with/without sea view from R$250/185;) This tranquil property spreads toward the edge of the bluff – white buildings are spread through lush grounds, ending at a pool with jaw-dropping ocean views. Many guest rooms, outfitted with rustic wood furnishings and romantic mosquito nets, offer two levels and a terrace.

Atmosphera Pousada POUSADA $$
(☎3575-1954; www.atmospherapousada.com.br; Estrada do Mucugê 735; d from R$235, bungalows R$495;) This smart and sustainably built guesthouse is set in a pretty tropical garden just steps from Praia Mucugê. Each guest room features a private balcony with hammock, and a solar-powered shower.

Eating

Arraial has no shortage of excellent restaurants, many offering atmospheric outdoor seating. For something more casual, head to the main square at night for inexpensive crepes, tapioca, caipirinhas and traditional Bahian plates of rice, beans and grilled steak, or stop at one of the gourmet ice-cream stands along Rua do Mucugê.

★ **Portinha** BUFFET $
(www.portinha.com.br; Mucugê s/n; per kg R$36; noon-5:30pm Tue-Sun;) Just by looking, you'd never guess this good-looking eatery is a self-service spot: with elegant outdoor tables and a style-conscious crowd, it looks like any of Arraial's upscale restaurants. Like its sister locations in Porto Seguro and Trancoso, Portinha serves an impressive spread of seafood, salads, stews and grilled meats, all kept hot over a wood fire.

Piazza del Caffé CAFE $
(www.piazzadelcaffe.com.br; Mucugê 200; mains R$12-24; 6pm-late) On a picturesque plaza in the center of the village, this café turns out delicious espresso and cappuccino, rich chocolate cakes, freshly baked *pão de queijo* (cheese bread) and gourmet sandwiches. Outdoor tables on the veranda are perfectly positioned for people-watching over the village's main thoroughfare.

Beco das Cores BRAZILIAN $
(cnr Mucugê & Beco das Cores; mains R$15-45; 5pm-late) This lively galleria is a big draw for its atmosphere and variety: you'll find good sushi, crepes, pizza and more gourmet fare; there's live music on summer weekend nights, and it's a cozy spot for cocktails on balmy evenings.

Manguti ITALIAN $$
(☎3575-2270; www.manguti.com.br; Mucugê 99; mains R$25-50; 6-11pm) This Italian classic, housed in a sweet, old-fashioned house on the main drag, is known for its hearty portions of homemade gnocchi. Also on the menu: excellent grilled fish.

Rosa dos Ventos BRAZILIAN $$
(☎3575-1271; Alameda dos Flamboyants 24; mains R$25-50; 4pm-midnight Mon-Tue & Thu-Sat,

1-10pm Sun) Considered one of Arraial's finest restaurants, Rosa dos Ventos offers a short menu of exquisite grilled seafood, perfect cocktails and decadent desserts; the candle-lit front patio is the ideal place to linger over a bottle of wine. It's located on a road that runs parallel Rua do Mucugê.

Aipim BRAZILIAN **$$**
(☎3575-3222; www.arraialdajuda.tur.br/aipim; Beco do Jegue 131; mains R$28-55; ⏲6pm-midnight Mon-Sat) A first-rate locale for a romantic evening out in Arraial: this stylish eatery exudes tropical chic with its Old World decor, New World music, superb grilled seafood and wines by the glass.

Entertainment

Arraial has lively nightlife options throughout the summer, when beach clubs host huge parties (cover R$25 to R$50); you'll see promoters everywhere, and local travel agencies can also provide the latest details. Another popular option for night owls is the Ilha dos Aquarios (p448) nightclub complex on an island between Porto Arraial and Porto Seguro.

Morocha Club CLUB
(www.morochaclub.com; Mucugê 260; cover generally free; ⏲6pm-late, event times vary) In town, Morocha is ground zero for nightlife, particularly in summer and around Carnaval. A popular local hangout and restaurant, it's relaxed and loungelike earlier in the evening, then busy with concerts, dancing, DJs and theme parties late at night.

Information

There are several ATMs around town. For tourist information, stop by the well-stocked kiosk in the main plaza at the top of Rua do Mucugê; the attendants distribute maps and brochures for all of the major excursions and tours from Arraial.

Getting There & Around

Car and passenger ferries (p448) travel almost constantly between Porto Seguro and Arraial d'Ajuda between 7am and midnight, with hourly boats running from midnight through the early morning. Prices for the *balsa* vary slightly depending on which way you're going, and which ferry you happen to get on: passengers either travel for free, or pay R$3.50, while cars cost between R$10 and R$12. The ride takes 10 to 15 minutes. From the boat dock, jump on a bus or Kombi van to the center of Arraial d'Ajuda (R$2.70). Depending on where you're staying, you can also ask the driver to drop you off at one of the many pousadas located along the road into town. It's also possible to walk the 4km along the beach, but be cautious about carrying valuables or walking alone during hours when the beaches are deserted.

From Arraial's ferry port, you can also catch a van or **Aguia Azul** (☎3668-1347, 3575-1170) bus (R$10, one hour) to Trancoso. If you're trying to catch a van to Trancoso from the center of Arraial, simply walk to the main north–south road (helpfully labeled 'Estrada para Trancoso') and hail a van or bus (usually marked 'Trancoso–Balsa') as it goes by.

Bicycles, motorbikes, cars and beach buggies are all available for rental from agencies in Arraial. Just be sure to have a good map before you set out for an excursion, as many dirt roads heading south aren't marked.

Trancoso

☎0XX73

Sitting atop a grassy bluff overlooking fantastic beaches, Trancoso embodies a certain rustic sophistication that captivates style-minded travelers – indeed, much of the village looks straight out of a *Travel & Leisure* spread. It's a favorite destination for jetsetters who want to get away from it all while still having access to a few fashionable venues for dining and shopping.

Trancoso is smaller in scale than Arraial, with a relaxed air, an assortment of pretty guesthouses, a postcard-worthy church overlooking the ocean, and irresistible open-air bars and restaurants surrounding the grassy (and car-free) Quadrado (the main square). Though the place caters to rich tourists, the sight of the candlelit Quadrado at night remains magical.

The beach is a 15-minute walk downhill from the cliff-top village: if you're standing in the Quadrado (official name: Praça de São João) and facing the ocean, the start of the path is located to the right of the church.

Sleeping

Reservations are a must during January and major holidays. New pousadas are opening all the time to meet increased tourist demand.

Café Esmeralda Albergue Pousada POUSADA **$**
(☎3668-1527; www.trancosonatural.com; Praça São João 272; d from $90; ❄📶) The cheapest overnight on the Quadrado is a friendly multilingual guesthouse with basic,

WORTH A TRIP

PRAIA DO ESPELHO

Rated among Brazil's top 10 beaches, Praia do Espelho (Beach of the Mirror; so named for the reflections on the still surface of the water) is 27km south of Trancoso and 14km north of Caraíva. Protective offshore reefs create calm, warm, transparent waters, while reefs closer to shore create natural pools at low tide. The shore is thick with coconut palms. White and orange cliffs divide Espelho from **Praia do Curuípe**, its neighboring beach, which has a collection of top-end pousadas (guesthouses).

Tour agencies in Arraial d'Ajuda and Trancoso offer day trips to these beaches (recommended, as the roads are bumpy and arriving on your own is a challenge) or you can catch one of Aguia Azul's two to three daily buses between Trancoso and Praia do Espelho. Visit www.praiadoespelho.net.br for the latest departure times and additional information about this remote and beautiful destination.

fan-cooled rooms; you'll pay slightly more one of the air-conditioned 'superior' rooms (from R$120). It's behind the café of the same name, which is convenient, as breakfast isn't included in the room rate.

Bom Astral POUSADA **$**
(☎3668-1270; www.bomastral.net; Praça São João 298; d/apt for 2 from R$130/230; ❄📶) Decent value on the Quadrado, Bom Astral has pleasant, simple rooms, small but well-maintained. Apartments have extras like TVs, kitchenettes and patios with hammocks.

★**Pousada Jacarandá** POUSADA **$$**
(☎3668-1155; www.pousadajacaranda.com.br; Vieira 91; bungalows for 2 from R$220; ❄📶🏊) 🌿 This ecofriendly guesthouse features six freestanding bungalows built with natural, locally sourced materials, plus a lovely swimming pool and art-filled interiors. It's a short walk from both the Quadrado and the beach, but the quiet location is a benefit if you're looking to relax.

Pousada Samambaia POUSADA **$$**
(☎3668-1774; www.samambaiatrancoso.com; Viera s/n; d from R$250; ❄📶) Space and tranquality are major selling points at this lovely guesthouse, consisting of 10 pretty chalets with kitchens, patios and hammocks. The central swimming pool, fringed with palm trees, is the perfect place to take a break from the beach.

Pousada Quarto Crescente POUSADA **$$**
(☎3668-1014; www.quartocrescente.net; Mangabeiras 30; d from R$290; ❄📶🏊) At this popular guesthouse, just a short walk from the Quadrado, gardens surround a picturesque wooden deck and swimming pool. Guest rooms have private patios with hammocks; pricier options include kitchenettes and Jacuzzis. There's also a well-stocked library with helpful travel books and maps, and an excellent breakfast spread.

Pousada Mundo Verde POUSADA **$$**
(☎3668-1279; www.pousadamundoverde.com.br; Telegrafo 43; d from R$285; ❄🏊) A swimming pool with a spectacular view is the crowning glory of this peaceful guesthouse, set on a quiet bluff overlooking the ocean, not far from the Quadrado. Stylish Mundo Verde has spacious, airy rooms with mosquito nets; each has a private balcony or patio with hammock, table and chairs.

Eating

In the evening colorful glowing lanterns illuminate the restaurants around the Quadrado – each looks prettier than the one before – but the dining scene here is known for high prices and hit-or-miss quality and service. In this town, you're paying first and foremost for the atmosphere. You can find more casual snacks, ice cream and tapioca pastries in the small plaza behind the main square, where taxis and buses drop off.

★**Rabanete** SELF-SERVE **$**
(www.portinha.com.br; Praça São João s/n; per kg R$44; ⏲noon-8pm, to 10pm Jan & Feb) This Trancoso classic, which was known as Portinha until a recent change in ownership, woos diners with a sumptuous buffet (don't miss the dessert spread) and atmospheric seating at tree-shaded picnic tables on the Quadrado. It's one of only a few places open for lunch.

Uxua Praia Bar BRAZILIAN **$$**
(www.uxua.com; Praia dos Nativos; mains R$35-50; ⏲11:30am-dusk) Even if you're not lucky enough to be staying in Trancoso's top-of-the-line Uxua Casa Hotel & Spa, you

can pay a visit to the hotel's stylish but relaxed beach bar. During the day, it's the hippest spot on the sand for cocktails and seafood plates. Just look for the big wooden boat, cleverly converted into a bar.

Maritaca ITALIAN $$
(☎3668-1258; Telégrafo 388; mains R$50-75; ⏰7-11pm Tue-Sun, to 2am Jan & Feb) Elegant and airy Maritaca does delicious thin-crust pizzas – the carpaccio is a standout – as well as Italian pastas and rich desserts made with top-end imported ingredients. The prices are lofty for a pizzeria; then again, this is Trancoso.

Capim Santo BRAZILIAN $$
(www.capimsanto.com.br; Quadrado; mains R$26-48; ⏰5-11pm Mon-Sat) Dining on the impossibly quaint porch of this old house – or in the beautifully illuminated garden beside it – makes for a memorable evening. Part of the pousada of the same name, Capim Santo specializes in fresh, innovative juice infusions and traditional Bahian seafood dishes with an international twist.

O Cacau BAHIAN $$$
(www.ocacautrancoso.com.br; Quadrado; mains R$60-100; ⏰4-11:30pm Tue-Sun, 4pm-1:30am daily Jan & Feb) This beautifully appointed eatery is a haven for foodies interested in Bahian cuisine. Look for light, modern takes on classic dishes from *acarajés* to *moqueca* and grilled lobster. O Cacau has a great wine list (especially for Brazil) and to-die-for desserts, with prices to match.

☆ Entertainment

There's always live music somewhere on the Quadrado at night. If local legend Elba Ramalho, called 'The Queen of Forró,' is giving a show, don't miss it. One venue that she recently performed at is **Pára-Raio** (www.pararaiotrancoso.com.br; Carlos Alberto Parracho 50; no cover; ⏰7pm-late), an ambient restaurant with outdoor tables under massive trees and an enclosed dance space where DJs spin. During summer, there are some happening nighttime beach parties with pumping trance music and psychedelic decor; look for promoters handing out flyers.

ℹ Information

At the small plaza tucked behind the Quadrado, find ATMs, a few internet cafés, supermarkets and a taxi stand. There's a tourist office on the plaza too, offering maps and information (at least when it's open, which it often isn't outside of the peak summer months).

ℹ Getting There & Away

Hourly Aguia Azul buses connect Trancoso with Arraial d'Ajuda and the ferry dock – some continue to Porto Seguro – and run from 6am to 8:30pm (R$10, one hour). Some buses leave from the Quadrado area, but to catch most of the departures, walk inland from the square towards the main road that runs in and out of town. Kombi vans run the same route for around the same price.

Caraíva

☎0XX73

Time moves slowly in the remote and beautiful village of Caraíva, where roads and cars don't exist (neither did electricity before 2007). The easygoing atmosphere has long attracted hippies and those looking for a quiet pace of life. Today, even though there's cell-phone reception and even internet access, locals say Caraíva feels like Trancoso did a couple of decades ago. Power outages are all too common – noisy generators light up the shops and restaurants lining the sand streets, and most importantly, keep the *forró* hopping on Friday night.

The dreamily rustic village is strung along the eastern bank of the mangrove-lined Rio Caraíva and deserted beach kissed by strong waves. Boat trips upriver, south to Parque Nacional de Monte Pascoal or Corumbau, and north to Praia do Espelho and Praia do Curuípe, are easily organized through your accommodations (around R$85 per person).

Most visitors make the short journey to **Barra Velha**, the indigenous Pataxó village, 6km away from town; you can walk, catch a boat or even hire a horse to get there. When going to the village, bring lots of water and small bills in case you'd like to purchase handicrafts. On the edge of the river, the **Centro Cultural de Tradições Indígenas** (⏰hours vary) offers exhibits, performances and more information on the Pataxó. Visit www.caraiva.com.br for more information.

Sleeping & Eating

★ **Pousada Cores do Mar** POUSADA $$
(☎3668-5090; www.pousadacoresdomarcaraiva.com.br; Rua da Praia 850; cottages for 2/4 people from R$250/350; ❄📶) At this heavenly oceanfront getaway, palm trees tower over freestanding cottages and inviting chaise

THE PATAXÓ

Bahia's largest indigenous group, the Pataxó (pa-ta-*sho*), who number roughly 3000, are among Brazil's many indigenous groups facing an uncertain future. Historically, the Pataxó are survivors. They were a strong tribe who held out against the Portuguese, and up until the 1800s were one of the most feared indigenous groups of the interior. Their resistance hindered frontier expansion, though by the early 19th century their power had waned.

Today, the Pataxó practice subsistence agriculture in the south of Bahia, supplemented by hunting, fishing and gathering. Similar to Amazonian indigenous groups, the Pataxó utilize local plants as their pharmacy, with the rainforests of southern Bahia providing a vital source for traditional medicine. The region boasts incredible biodiversity, with many of its plants and animals found nowhere else on earth. In all, the Pataxó use more than 90 different plant species to treat colds, asthma, fever, toothaches, rheumatism, anemia and dozens of other illnesses.

Despite the wide acceptance of the healer's powers within the community, the Pataxó are struggling to maintain their traditions. As elsewhere in indigenous communities, the youth are not actively embracing the customs of the older generation. Traditional healers *(curandeiros)*, who can be male or female, haven't passed their knowledge down to the next generation. In Barra Velha, the largest Pataxó community (numbering some 1800), all of the healers are over 60, meaning that if nothing changes, their knowledge will be lost within two decades. Today's *curandeiros* may be the final generation of traditional healers in Pataxó culture.

Sadly, the issues of Pataxó health were in the news for a different reason in 2012, when the family of a gravely ill indigenous child fought for treatment in the hospital in Porto Seguro, and then Salvador. Though the child survived, the treatment was delayed due to bureaucratic struggles over who should pay for her health care, and the case caught the attention of a large number of Bahians.

In addition to internal struggles, the Pataxó face severe threats from outside. As Bahia's population grows, farmers have pushed them off their lands, leading to violent skirmishes. In 2007, 15 indigenous Pataxó went to Brasília to settle the matter of their land rights. Yet whether the tribe can flourish – and successfully preserve its customs – may be a matter less for government officials to decide than for Pataxó youth, who will be instrumental in ensuring the tribe's longevity.

longues facing the water. Travelers rave about the peaceful interiors, complete with top-end bed linens and private terraces with sea views, and the ample breakfast spread.

Pousada Lagoa POUSADA **$$**
(☎3668-5059; www.lagoacaraiva.com.br; Rua da Lagoa 1900; d/bungalows from R$225/315;) At this eco-minded place (it recycles, composts, and employs local workers), choose between simple but stylish cottages with small verandas, or slightly cheaper suites. The restaurant-bar is a popular nighttime hangout, and open to the public: in addition to fresh fish and homemade bread, the eatery serves produce sourced from the guesthouse's own garden.

Pousada Caraiva Guest House POUSADA **$$**
(☎9967-3848; www.caraivaguesthouse.squarespace.com; Sete de Setembro 1300; s/d from R$165/180;) Set in a beautifully landscaped garden near the beach, this guesthouse is a traveler's favorite, thanks in part to the friendly service. Even the most standard rooms are spacious, with private patios, and the alfresco breakfast is a delight.

Boteco do Pará BAHIAN **$$**
(www.botecodoparacaraiva.com.br; mains for 2 R$45-80; ⊗11am-6pm Tue-Sun, closed Jun) A Caraíva classic for more than three decades, Boteco do Pará is the best of several casual eateries specializing in fresh seafood. It's a lovely rustic venue for relaxing by the river and feasting on traditional *moqueca* and cold beer. Bonus: unlike many other eateries, it's open year-round (except June).

Mangue Sereno ITALIAN **$$**
(☎9991-1711; www.caraivapousadamanguesereno.com.br; mains R$28-45; ⊗7-11:30pm Dec-Mar)

Homemade pastas and creative seafood dishes are locally famous at this lovely restaurant at the pousada of the same name; the romantic, low-key setting is a great spot for a leisurely dinner.

Getting There & Away

Two daily buses run by **Aguia Azul** (☎3668-1347, 3575-1170) travel between Caraiva and the ferry in Arraial d'Ajuda (R$20, two hours) stopping in Trancoso along the way. At the time of writing, buses left Arraial for Caraíva at 7am and 3pm, leaving Caraíva for the return journey at 6:20am and 4pm.

On arrival in Caraíva, hop on a canoe (R$4) to cross the river into the village. Wheelbarrow-pushers (R$20 per load) await on the other side if you need help with your luggage, or, more likely, help finding your accommodations.

Parque Nacional de Monte Pascoal

In 1500 the Portuguese, sailing under the command of Pedro Álvares Cabral, sighted the broad hump of Monte Pascoal, their first glimpse of the New World. They called the land Terra da Vera Cruz (Land of the True Cross).

Now a 225-sq-km national **park** (☎3294-1870; www.icmbio.gov.br; admission R$5, tours for groups of up to 10 people R$40), the area contains a variety of ecosystems: Atlantic rainforest, swamplands, shallows, mangroves, beaches and reefs. Wildlife includes several monkey species, two types of sloth, anteaters, rare porcupines, capybara, deer, jaguars and numerous species of bird.

The northeastern corner of the park, below Caraíva, is home to a small number of indigenous Pataxó people, who took over control of the park in 2000. They allow visitors access to a few trails while accompanied by a guide (settle fees before setting out); one of the trails climbs the mountain. While there is no fee to enter the park, there are access fees (ranging between R$40 and R$60 per group of one to six people) for certain areas.

The coastal side of the park is accessible by boat or on foot from Caraíva. Though there are no direct buses to the park, buses run from Porto Seguro to Itamaraju (30km from the park), and from Friday to Monday, buses go from Itamaraju to the park entrance.

Caravelas

☎0XX73 / POP 22,500

Caravelas is a calm fishing town on the banks of the mangrove-lined Rio Caravelas; the primary reason visitors come here is to visit the Parque Nacional Marinho de Abrolhos and other offshore reefs.

Sights & Activities

To get a feel for the town's thriving fishing industry, wander along the riverfront where the fishers return with the day's catch. When the locals go to the beach, most head north for **Praia Grauçá** (7km) or the more isolated **Praia Iemanjá** (20km). Both have calm water colored brown with river silt. Reachable by boat are **Praia Pontal do Sul** (across Rio Caravelas) and the island beach **Coroa da Barra** (30 minutes offshore).

Tours

Travel agencies offer snorkeling day trips to nearby reefs and islands such as Parcel das Paredes, Sebastião Gomes and Coroa Vermelha. Since most tourists head for Abrolhos, these trips rarely meet the minimum number of people required (five) for departure – you'll have better luck if you're already traveling in a group.

Sleeping & Eating

The restaurants at Praia Grauçá are your best bet for fresh seafood.

Hotel Marina Porto Abrolhos HOTEL $$
(☎3674-1060; www.marinaportoabrolhos.com.br; Rua da Baleia 333, Praia Grauça; d from R$260;) The nicest hotel in town is located 7km from Caravelas, and has round, thatched-roof, beachfront chalets surrounding a gigantic pool. There are also tennis courts, a pool bar, gym and library.

Pousada Liberdade POUSADA $$
(☎3297-2415; www.pousadaliberdade.com.br; Nogueira 1551; s/d from R$95/170;) This conveniently located guesthouse offers accommodations in small cottages with a few creature comforts like televisions and minibars; there's also a pool and trundle beds, making it suitable for families. It's a good place to base yourself while you figure out your plans for heading into the park.

Carenagem BRAZILIAN $$
(☎3297-1280; Av das Palmeiras 210; mains R$20-32; ⊙noon-11pm Mon-Sat) Basic but good value, this popular meeting spot has an extensive menu of seafood and meat dishes as well as classic cocktails and live music on weekends. There are several other good dining options on Av das Palmeiras.

Information

Banco do Brasil (Praça Dr Imbassaí) Has ATMs.

Getting There & Around

Carvelas and Abrolhos aren't very easy to get to: many travelers find it more convenient to visit with an organized excursion like those run by Porto Seguro's Pataxó Turismo (p447). The one-day (10-hour) trip costs R$150 per person, including transportation, but it's a long way to go for a single day. Prices for the more appealing two- and three-day excursions vary depending on the size of the group and the accommodations. Contact Pataxó for more information.

Renting a car in the Porto Seguro area and driving to Caravelas/Abrolhos is a popular option. Otherwise, unless you're willing to shell out for an expensive round-trip taxi, you're stuck with the limited bus schedule. Aguia Branca (www.aguiabranca.com.br) goes to Salvador (R$139, 16 hours) by way of Itabuna, with more frequent departures in summer and only a few times weekly in low season. Otherwise, access to Caravelas is via Teixeira de Freitas, 74km west. The **bus station** (☎3297-1422) is in the center of town.

Local buses do a round-trip between Caravelas and the neighboring village of Barra (providing access to Praia Graução), leaving every 30 minutes from 6:30am until 10:30pm.

Parque Nacional Marinho de Abrolhos

It is thought that the name of Brazil's first marine park comes from a sailor's warning: when approaching land, open your eyes *(abre os olhos)*. Abrolhos covers an area of

GREAT CREATURES OF THE SEA

One of the world's great migratory animals, the humpback whale travels up to 25,000km each year. Massive in scale, adults can reach 17m long and weigh up to 36,000kg. Although they were hunted to near extinction by the turn of the 20th century, the population is slowly recovering following a moratorium on whale hunting in 1966. Biologists estimate that 30,000 to 60,000 now remain.

Identified by their long pectoral fins, distinct humps and knob-covered heads, the humpbacks feed only during the summer in polar waters on a diet of krill and small fish. In the winter they migrate from the poles to tropical waters, where mating occurs. Thus, the austral winter (June to September) is the best time to observe them off the coast of Brazil, when they come in large numbers to mate and give birth.

During this time, the humpbacks fast and live off their fat reserves. Competition for females is intense, with groups of two to 20 males (called escorts) sometimes trailing a lone female. To win her over, each male competes to establish dominance – tail slapping, charging and parrying over the course of several hours.

The whale song is perhaps one of the most fascinating and least understood attributes of these mammals. Whales within an area sing the same song – or variations of the same song – while those from different regions sing entirely different songs. Performed only by males, each song lasts 10 to 20 minutes and can be repeated over several hours (some scientists have recorded whales singing continuously for over 24 hours). The songs are staggeringly complex. One research team from the Universidade Estadual de Campinas studied whales off Abrolhos in Bahia one winter and identified 24 note types, organized in five themes.

No one knows the purpose of the song, which changes from year to year, though scientists originally thought it had a role in mating (observations of males singing far from the presence of a female has thrown doubt onto this).

In Bahia, whale-watching is a growing tourist industry, with numerous places from which to embark on a seagoing observation trip. During the winter, they can often be observed outside of Salvador, while Parque Nacional Marinho de Abrolhos is among the world's best places to observe them.

913 sq km, including reefs noted for the variety of colors and a five-island archipelago that Charles Darwin, aboard the HMS *Beagle,* visited in 1832. These days the primary residents of the archipelago are migrating birds and humpback whales (June to October), which come here to rest and give birth. Only the Ilha de Santa Bárbara has a handful of buildings, including a lighthouse built in 1861.

In these crystal-clear waters, visibility can reach 20m in the dry season (May to September).

Getting There & Around

Abrolhos is located 80km offshore from Caravelas, the primary gateway, where travel agencies offer one- to four-day trips to the park. Day trips start around R$300 per person, depending on availability and what onboard amenities are included. Schooner tours lasting from two to four days, with overnight stays and meals onboard, are offered by small outfitters like **Catamarã Sanuk** (3297-1344; www.abrolhos.net; Estrelas 80, Caravelas). Prices start around R$1100 per person for scuba/snorkeling trips; you can also rent equipment here.

WEST OF SALVADOR

The great attraction in Bahia's interior is the Parque Nacional da Chapada Diamantina, a verdant area of scenic plateaus, grassy valleys, waterfalls and rushing rivers. Opportunities for trekking and outdoor adventures abound. In contrast to this verdant area, the rest of this region comprises the bizarre moonscapes of the *sertão* (backlands of the Northeast), a vast and parched land on which a struggling people eke out a living raising cattle and tilling the earth.

Feira de Santana

0XX75 / POP 617,000

After Salvador, Feira de Santana is the second-largest city in Bahia. It's a major cattle-trading center, but not a tourist draw: there's not much to see here. Still, many travelers pass through the bus station on their way to Chapada Diamantina or the Recôncavo.

Festivals & Events

Feira invented the now-widespread concept of **Micareta**, an out-of-season Carnaval. In 1937 a flood caused the city's Carnaval to be celebrated late, a tradition the citizens decided to adopt and rename. In April or early May, thousands of spectators fill the city to see Salvador's best *trios elétricos* parade for four days along with local samba schools and folklore groups. For those who missed out on Carnaval in Salvador, this could be the next best thing. Log onto www.micaretafeira.com.br for more information.

Sleeping & Eating

There are several cheap lodging options near the bus station. Several bars, cafés and restaurants are scattered around the town, many that feature live music and *forró* at night.

Hotel Acalanto HOTEL $$
(3612-6700; www.hotelacalanto.com.br; Torres 77; d R$190;) This comfortable business-style hotel, a stone's throw from the bus station, is a solid bet if you have a layover in Feira.

O Picuí BAHIAN $
(3221-1018; www.restaurantepicui.com.br; Av Maria Quitéria 2463; mains R$15-33; 11am-midnight Mon-Sat, to 7pm Sun) A local favorite serving hearty regional dishes from grilled steaks to salmon glazed with *maracuja* (passion-fruit) sauce.

Getting There & Away

At the crossroads of three major highways, Feira is a major transportation hub. Frequent buses go to Salvador (R$20 to R$25, two hours) and Cachoeira (R$10, 1½ hours). Real Expresso buses running between Lençóis and Salvador also pass through Feira de Santana.

Lençóis

0XX75 / POP 11,400

If you want to see a flip side to surf-and-sand Bahia, or have time for only one excursion into the Northeastern interior, this is it. Lençóis is the prettiest of the old diamond-mining towns in the Chapada Diamantina, a mountainous wooded oasis in the dusty *sertão.* While the town itself has charming cobbled streets, brightly painted 19th-century buildings, and appealing outdoor cafés and restaurants, the surrounding areas are the real attraction. Caves, waterfalls, idyllic rivers and panoramic plateaus

Lençóis

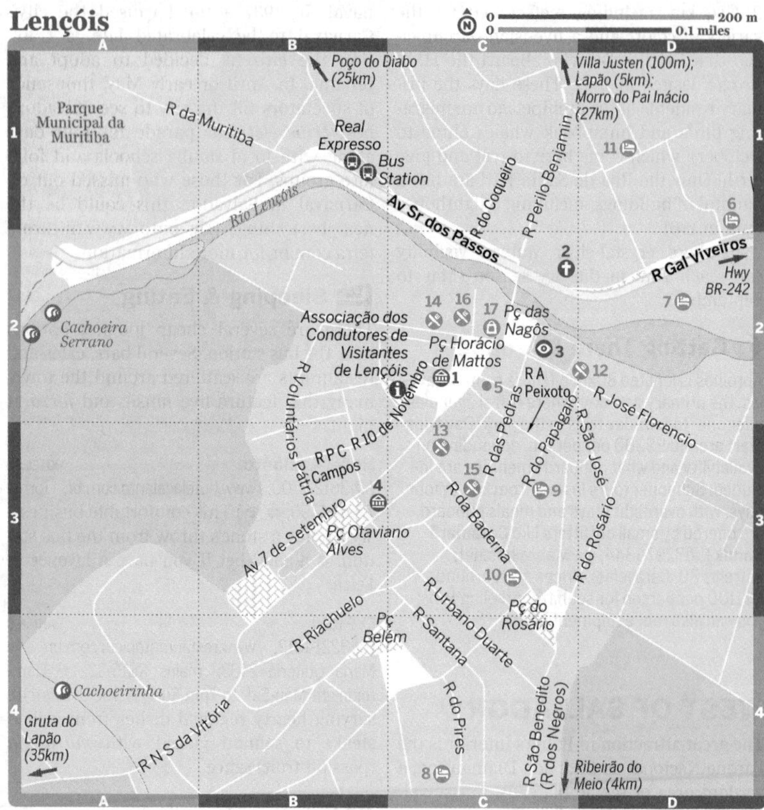

Lençóis

Sights
1 French Vice-Consulate Building ... C2
2 Igreja Senhor dos Passos ... C2
3 Mercado Cultural ... C2
4 Prefeitura Municipal ... B3

Activities, Courses & Tours
5 Chapada Adventure David ... C2
H2O Travel Adventures ... (see 8)

Sleeping
6 Alcino Estalagem & Atelier ... D1
7 Pousada Canto das Águas ... D2
8 Pousada dos Duendes ... C4
9 Pousada Lua de Cristal ... C3
10 Pousada Safira ... C3
11 Vila Serrano ... D1

Eating
12 Burritos y Taquitos ... D2
13 Cafeteria São Benedito ... C3
14 Cozinha Aberta ... C2
15 Lampião ... C3
16 O Bode ... C2

Shopping
17 Dos Irmãos ... C2

set the stage for some fantastic adventures, with the town of Lençóis serving as a base for treks into the surrounding Parque Nacional da Chapada Diamantina and for sights outside the park.

History

The history of Lençóis epitomizes the story of the diamond boom and subsequent bust. After earlier expeditions by *bandeirantes* (*paulista* explorers and hired guns) proved fruitless, the first diamonds were found in

Chapada Velha in 1822. After large strikes in the Rio Mucujê in 1844, a motley collection of prospectors from across Brazil arrived seeking their fortunes.

Miners began searching for diamonds in alluvial deposits. They settled in makeshift tents, which, from the hills above, looked like bedsheets drying in the wind – hence the town's name: Lençóis (Sheets). The tents of these diamond prospectors grew into villages: Vila Velha de Palmeiras, Andaraí, Piatã, Igatu and Lençóis. Exaggerated stories of endless riches in the Diamantina mines precipitated mass migrations, but the area proved rich in clouded industrial stones, not display-quality gems.

At the height of the diamond boom, the French – who purchased diamonds and used them to drill the Panama Canal (1881–9), St Gothard Tunnel and London Underground – built a vice-consulate in Lençóis. French fashions and bons mots made their way into town, but with the depletion of diamonds, the falloff in French demand and the newly discovered South African mines, the boom went bust at the beginning of the 20th century.

Despite these developments, mining held on. Powerful and destructive water pumps were introduced in the 1980s, which increased production until they were finally banned in 1995. The few remaining miners have returned to traditional methods to extract diamonds from the riverbeds. With the establishment of the national park in 1985, the town's economy turned instead to tourism, which continues to be the major industry of Lençóis.

Sights

You'll notice a few historic buildings during a quick stroll around town. At the 19th-century **French vice-consulate building** (Praça Horácio de Mattos), diamond commerce was negotiated. The lovely **Prefeitura Municipal** (Praça Otaviano Alves; ⌚10am-5pm Mon-Fri) FREE, built in 1860, was the mansion of Colonel César Sá – the neoclassical details were reportedly added to please his wife. The adobe **Igreja Senhor dos Passos** (Av Senhor dos Passos 220; ⌚10am-5pm) honors the patron saint of miners – and was built by slaves.

For handicrafts made of local wood and stone, clay soaps and semiprecious jewelry, stop by the beautiful old **Mercado Cultural** (Praça Aureliano Sá; ⌚8am-11pm Mon-Sat). Perched above the river on the main square, the market began construction in the 19th century.

Activities

Numerous local agencies offer a wide range of outdoor activities, including hiking, rappelling, climbing, kayaking, mountain biking and horseback riding, in Chapada Diamantina national park. There are also great hikes leaving from town that the adventurous can undertake without a guide.

One such hike is a 3km walk out of town, following the Rio Lençóis upstream. You first pass a series of rapids known as **Cachoeira Serrano**; off to the right is the **Salão de Coloridas Areias** (Room of Colored Sands), where artisans gather material for bottled-sand paintings. You then pass Poço Halley (Swimming Hole), before seeing **Cachoeirinha** (Little Waterfall) on a tributary to your left. Continuing upriver, **Cachoeira da Primavera** (Spring Waterfall) is on another tributary on your left. (When the water is low, you can start this hike by climbing up the rocky slope on the right side of the stream. When the water is higher, you'll have to cut through the woods – the 'trail,' if you can call it that, should start at the traffic turnaround and run parallel to the river.)

Another relaxing 4km hike is to **Ribeirão do Meio**, a series of swimming holes with a natural waterslide. It's not a long journey from town, but the path is hardly marked, so it can be a little tricky to access. To begin, follow Rua São Benedito (known as Rua

FOLK ART

Bahia has some of Brazil's best artisans, who usually have small shops or sell in the local market. You can buy their folk art in Salvador, but the best place to see or purchase the real stuff is in the town of origin. Feira de Santana is known for its leatherwork. Maragojipinho, Rio Real and Cachoeira produce earthenware. Caldas do Jorro, Caldas de Cipo and Itaparica specialize in straw crafts. Rio de Contas and Muritiba do metalwork. Ilha de Maré is famous for lacework. Jequié, Valença and Feira de Santana are woodworking centers. Santo Antônio de Jesus, Rio de Contas and Monte Santo manufacture goods made of leather and silver.

NAVIGATING LENÇÓIS

In the past few years, almost all of Lençóis' streets have been officially renamed. The locals, of course, continue to use the original names, causing confusion for tourists. Note that while some businesses have embraced using their new addresses, many have not: you might have trouble when you're asking for directions. Luckily, Lençóis is small and easy to navigate, but if you're arriving at night, you should look at the map so you know where you're going when you arrive at the bus station. It's also common for staff from pousadas (guesthouses) and hostels to meet the buses arriving from Salvador: ask ahead if you'd like some help getting from the station to your destination.

dos Negros) from Pousada & Camping Lumiar. Continue past the pousada's entrance and keep walking out of town. When you see the sign for Pousada Solar Moraes, you know you're in the right place. Continue onto the red stone and dirt path that leads uphill. Five to 10 minutes later, the trail levels off and you'll see a sign for Ribeirão do Meio. Keep going along the dirt road until you see the archway entrance for Pousada Luar do Sertão. The trail to Ribeirão do Meio really starts here, to the left of the pousada entrance, on a stone staircase that leads down through the woods. Keep following the trail until you reach a ridge overlooking Rio Ribeirão. There's no 'right way' to scramble down to a series of swimming holes and the natural waterslide, but there are easier ways and harder ways – just use common sense. Avoid injury by climbing the dry rocks (not the slide's wet ones) before launching off.

For more swimming, catch the morning bus to Seabra and hop off at Mucugêzinho (25km). About 2km downstream is **Poço do Diabo** (Devil's Well), a beautiful swimming hole on the Rio Mucugêzinho with a 25m waterfall.

Tours

The Chapada Diamantina, and the areas surrounding it, are a natural wonderland; unspoiled, in part, because they lack the tourist infrastructure of many national parks. Given the lack of marked trails and public transportation, the easiest way to explore is by going on a tour or a longer trek through a local agency.

Note that most of the major attractions in the park have individual entrance fees of R$15 to R$20; these days, the fees are often included in the quoted tour price (and include packed lunches), but ask before committing to anything.

One popular tour (R$170, plus optional R$20 for snorkeling) visits Rio Mucugêzinho and its swimming hole Poço do Diabo, Gruta da Lapa Doce (an 850m-long cave, formed by a subterranean river, with an impressive assortment of stalagmites and stalactites), Gruta da Pratinha (a cave and river with clear, light-blue waters) and Morro do Pai Inácio (an 1120m peak affording an awesome view over a plateau-filled valley).

Tours to Poço Encantado (the Lençóis poster child: a cave filled with stunningly beautiful blue water) and Poço Azul (another rainwater-filled cave you can swim in) are also offered (R$170). Before planning this one, ask the agency about the expected quality of the light; after rains, the water remains murky.

Other popular outings include the trip to Fumaça Waterfall (R$140) and the trip to the Marimbus wetlands (R$170, plus optional R$35 for kayaking).

If you're not interested in going on a formal tour, consider going into the park with a guide: they're affordable (plan on R$150 to R$180 per day for groups of up to six people), they're incredibly knowledgeable about local flora and fauna, and they can find the best swimming holes – all priceless in a park with few signs or official trails. For multiday treks, guides also arrange basic lodging and meals in local homes for the bargain price of around R$70 per person, per day.

There are numerous tour agencies available in town.

Chapada Adventure David OUTDOORS
(☎3334-1933; www.chapadaadventure.com; Praça Horácio de Matos 114; ⏰8am-10pm) A friendly agency with multilingual staff.

H2O Travel Adventures OUTDOORS
(☎3334-1229; www.h2otraveladventures.com; Pousada dos Duendes, Rua do Pires s/n; ⏰10am-9pm) Both day trips and treks are offered; the website offers detailed descriptions of each excursion's attractions and level of difficulty.

Festivals & Events

The weeklong **Festa de Senhor dos Passos**, the festival honoring the patron saint of miners, begins on January 23. Celebrated the week of June 23, the lively **Festa de São João** is a huge street party with traditional *forró* dancing, bonfires outside every house and delicious street food. One of the biggest cultural events of the year is the **Festival de Lençóis** in September or October; in the past, big-name acts like Gilberto Gil and Gal Costa have performed.

Sleeping

Lençóis' best pousadas are famous for their fantastic breakfast spreads. Note that many of the accommodations located on the same side of the river as the bus station – ie not in the so-called 'center' of Lencois – are only accessible by a fairly steep uphill hike, and most streets aren't labeled. Many pousadas will offer to have someone meet you at the bus station on your arrival: after dark, when it's confusing to navigate, it's wise to take them up on it.

★Pousada Lua de Cristal POUSADA $
(☎3334-1658; www.pousadaluadecristal.com.br; Patriotas 27; s/d/tr R$120/150/200; wifi) Run by an exceptionally kind owner, this charming new guesthouse offers sweet, simple rooms with antique stained-glass windows, many opening to views over the town. Outdoor breakfast tables are an added bonus.

Pousada Safira POUSADA $
(☎3334-1443; www.pousadasafira.com; Miguel Calmon 124; d with/without bathroom R$110/90; wifi) This down-to-earth guesthouse is run by Dona Eulina, something of a local legend for her motherly warmth and hospitality. Basic but cozy, it's a travelers' favorite.

Pousada dos Duendes HOSTEL $
(☎3334-1229; www.pousadadosduendes.com.br; Rua do Pires s/n; dm R$50-70, d R$150-260; @ wifi) With a relaxed atmosphere, open-air lounge space, a garden with hammocks, and a vegetarian-friendly eatery on-site, Duendes is a backpacker institution. You can arrange everything here – park tours, excursions on horseback, kayak trips – and the kitchen will even pack your lunch on request. It's a five-minute walk outside of town.

Alcino Estalagem & Atelier INN $$
(☎3334-1171; www.alcinoestalagem.com; Tomba Surrão 139; d R$280; air-con wifi) This lovely yellow mansion, filled with antiques and hand-painted tile, was designed and built by a local artist. Staying here is like being a guest in a private home. Peruse the library or relax in the charming interior patio; the extensive breakfast is rightfully famous.

Vila Serrano POUSADA $$
(☎3334-1486; www.vilaserrano.com.br; Alto do Bonfim 8; d/bungalows from R$270/340; wifi) In a lush setting, the classy and environmentally conscious Vila Serrano comprises spacious apartments, designed according to the principles of feng shui with romantic drapery, rustic wooden accents and private verandas where hammocks swing.

Villa Justen POUSADA $$
(☎3334-1522; www.vilajusten.blogspot.com.ar; Sao Felix 44; d/tr R$165/260) A newer option in town, Villa Justen features a handful of smartly outfitted chalets. Each has a patio and hammock, plus a kitchen that's more well-equipped than the usual: a full-sized refrigerator, pots and pans, even a couple of wine glasses. It's tucked away on the hill behind the bus station, about a 10-minute walk away.

Pousada Canto das Águas POUSADA $$$
(☎3334-1154; www.lencois.com.br; Av Senhor dos Passos 1; d from R$345; air-con wifi pool) At the river's edge, this family-friendly, sustainably designed hotel has a sophisticated but earthy look – think stone, hardwood and large windows facing the trees. There's a swimming pool; the sound of the river's flowing water fills guest rooms at night. The hotel's excellent coffee shop and restaurant, São Benedito Cafeteria and Azul, respectively, are open to the public.

Eating

Lençóis has a number of bakeries and basic minimarkets catering to hikers. At night, the town's atmosphere is wonderfully charming as many restaurants on Praća Horácio de Matos and Rua das Pedras put candlelit tables out on the cobblestone walkways.

★Cafeteria São Benedito CAFE $
(Rua da Baderna 29; mains R$12-25; ⊙5-11pm Wed-Mon; menu) This modern coffee shop is a welcome newcomer to Lençóis, serving good coffee, gourmet sandwiches, soups and wraps, and homemade desserts that hit the spot after a day of hiking. The original

location is inside Pousada Canto das Águas, but this central café is easier for most travelers to access.

★**O Bode** BUFFET $
(☎9913-0722; Beco do Rio; per kg R$24; ⊙noon-5pm, to 10pm during peak tourist times) On an open-sided terrace over the river, this pleasant, well-liked per-kilo restaurant spreads a small but enticing buffet that includes meats, pasta and salads. By night, it's an inviting pizzeria.

Burritos y Taquitos MEXICAN $
(☎3334-1083; José Florencio 3; mains R$12-32; ⊙6-10pm Tue-Sun) It's a rare chance to get your Mexican fix in rural Bahia: popular with locals, this casual restaurant does reasonably authentic burritos, tacos and guacamole, and has a back patio overlooking the river.

★**Lampião** BRAZILIAN $$
(☎3334-1157; Baderna 51; mains R$28-40; ⊙noon-11pm) This popular eatery specializes in cuisine from Brazil's Northwest – think grilled meats, fishes and chicken, served at cute alfresco tables for two – and offers a good-value set lunch.

Cozinha Aberta FUSION $$
(☎3334-1321; www.cozinhaaberta.com.br; Barbosa 42; mains R$28-44; ⊙12:30-10:30pm) This gourmet bistro, specializing in slow food, serves eclectic fusion dishes from Thai noodles to Indian curries and Italian pastas. The setting is charming and homelike, with daily specials spelled out on chalkboards.

Shopping

Lençóis has several small boutiques and shops where you can pick up locally produced artwork, crafts and artisanal liqueurs.

Dos Irmãos OUTDOOR EQUIPMENT
(☎3334-1405; www.doisirmaos.com.br; Praça Horácio de Matos 3; ⊙10am-late) This outdoor outfitter sells backpacks, water bottles, camping equipment and hiking boots.

Information

The online portal of Guia Lençóis (www.guialencois.com.br) is a great resource for tourist information. Another excellent resource – especially for those heading into the park for a few days – is the English-language *Guia Turistico Chapada Diamantina* (R$29), an excellent information booklet with color photos, maps and detailed descriptions of area hikes. It's for sale at the tourist office and at businesses around town.

Associação dos Condutores de Visitantes de Lençóis (☎3334-1425; cnr Baderna & 7 de Setembro; ⊙8am-noon & 2-8pm) Information about tour guides. Guides may also be hired through the town's various outfitters and travel agencies.

Banco do Brasil (Praça Horácio de Mattos 56) Has ATMs.

Getting There & Away

BUS

If coming from the south, the journey, though indirect, will be a lot quicker if you route through Salvador. **Real Expresso** (☎3334-1112; www.realexpresso.com.br) buses for Salvador (R$65 to R$78, seven to eight hours) leave four to five times daily. Buses stop in Feira de Santana (R$50), where connections can be made to just about anywhere, including Cachoeira and Santo Amaro. Be sure to bring a sweater for the journey: these buses are notorious for blasting the air-conditioning.

CAR

Lençóis is 13km off Hwy BR-242, the main Salvador–Brasília route. There's a gas station 22km east of Lençóis on Hwy BR-242, in Tanquinho. The drive from Salvador to Lencois takes about five to six hours.

Parque Nacional da Chapada Diamantina

Within this national park's 1520 sq km, waterfalls cascade over the Sincora Range's mountains and plateaus, dropping into rivers and streams that wind their way through grassy valleys and clean swimming holes. An endless network of trails is dotted with cactus and strawflowers in some places, and the philodendrons, velosiaceas, orchids and other bromeliads that have escaped poaching in others. Several species of monkey swing through trees where *araras* (macaws) perch. *Veados* (deer) pick their way past gaping caves, while *mocós* (native rodents) and *cutia* (agouti) scurry underfoot. Even an *onça pintada* (jaguar) or two sharpens its claws on a towering tree, but you're much more likely to cross paths with a cute *quati* (small, furry carnivore with a brown-and-yellow-ringed tail).

The region's unique natural beauty and the tranquility of its small colonial towns have attracted a steady trickle of Brazilian and foreign travelers for several decades;

some have never left. These introduced residents, moved by the degradation of the environment and depletion of the wild-animal population, spearheaded an active ecological movement in direct opposition to the extractive mentality of diamond miners and many locals. After six years of bureaucratic battles, biologist Roy Funch helped convince the government to create the Parque Nacional da Chapada Diamantina in 1985.

The park has little infrastructure for visitors. Bus services are infrequent and scarce, particularly to the remote parts of the park. However, camping or sleeping in the park's small caves is free and can be done without a permit. You'll want gear such as backpacks, sleeping bags or tents, which can easily be rented in Lençóis, and reasonably warm clothes.

Serious hikers will want to pick up a detailed guide to sprawling Chapada Diamantina, available for purchase in Lençóis.

Geology

According to geologists, the diamonds in Chapada Diamantina were formed millions of years ago near present-day Namibia (Bahia was contiguous with Africa before continental drift). The diamonds were mixed with pebbles, swept into the depths of the sea that covered what is now inland Brazil, and imprisoned when the seabed turned to stone. Ultimately this layer of conglomerate stone was elevated, and the forces of erosion released the trapped diamonds, which then came to rest in the riverbeds.

Day Hikes & Trips

The most popular day trip into the park is to the top of Brazil's tallest waterfall, **Cachoeira da Fumaça** (Smoke Waterfall), so named because before it has plummeted the entire 420m, the water evaporates into mist. This 6km hike requires a guide, so contact an agency in Lençóis. Alternatively, you can originate from the closest village, **Capão** (80km west of Lençóis by road), which has a number of pousadas and a few travel agencies. The nearby mystical Vale do Capão, or **Caeté-Açu**, has attracted an international community of folks interested in an alternative, back-to-the-land lifestyle.

Up the road and outside the park, **Palmeiras** (54km west of Lençóis by car) is a drowsy little town with a scenic riverside position. The streets are lined with colorful houses and a couple of budget-friendly pousadas.

Hikers may want to take the trail along Barro Branco between Lençóis and **Morro do Pai Inácio**, an 1120m peak affording a brilliant view over a plateau-filled valley. Allow four or five hours one way for the hike.

Just southwest of Lençóis, upstream from Ribeirão do Meio, is the lovely **Cachoeira do Sossêgo** waterfall, with a deep pool at its base and rock ledges for diving. The 7km hike involves a great deal of stone-hopping along the riverbed and should not be attempted without a guide, or when rain or high water has made the lichen-covered rocks slippery.

Gruta do Lapão is probably the largest sandstone cave in South America and is just a 5km hike north of Lençóis. A guide is required as access is tricky.

'Chapada's Pantanal', or **Marimbus**, is a marshy microregion 94km south of Lençóis where you can canoe or kayak while fishing for *tucunaré* (peacock bass) and keeping a lookout for capybaras and *jacarés* (caimans). H2O Travel Adventures (p460) and other Lençóis agencies offer kayak tours here.

Longer Hikes

Navigating the correct routes for the longer treks in the park can be very difficult, so using a guide is strongly recommended. Treks organized with a guide can last anywhere from two to eight days, and can be custom-fitted to the group. They usually involve a combination of camping and staying in local homes and pousadas.

The Base of Fumaça

This extremely beautiful yet tiring 36km trek traverses the park from Lençóis to Capão in three days. Detours to other waterfalls are taken along the way, in addition to reaching the base of **Cachoeira da Fumaça**. An extra day can be added walking back to Lençóis or you can continue with the Grand Circuit (p464). Be forewarned that the area around Fumaça's base gets extremely crowded at times, so you may find yourself sharing your sleeping cave with unexpected companions.

Vale do Patí

This recommended hike starts and ends in Vale do Capão, and can last from four to six days depending on detours. You are likely to have the trails to yourself here, and the views over the plains and Chapada's table mountains are spectacular. Stopping in at a local home for a meal or a night is a possibility: it's much easier to negotiate if you're traveling with a local guide.

Grand Circuit

The Grand Circuit of the park covers about 100km, best done in a counterclockwise direction. It takes about five days, but at least eight days are required to include side trips. Especially if you're not carrying all of your own camping equipment and food, it's best to go with a knowledgeable guide, who can arrange overnight stays and meals in locals' homes along the way.

On the first day, make the hike from Lençóis to Vale do Capão (25km, about seven hours); on the way, you can take a side trip to the top of **Cachoeira da Fumaça**. In the visitor-friendly Vale do Capão, you can camp or stay at a pousada such as the eco-minded **Pousada Pé no Mato** (www.penomato.com.br; Ladeira da Vila, 2, Caeté-Açú; dm/s/d from R$50/130/156), offering peaceful and affordable dorms, private rooms and free-standing cabins, plus an on-site tour agency that can help you plan almost any adventure in the park.

From the Bomba neighborhood of Vale do Capão, continue on to cross the beautiful plains region of Gerais do Vieira and the Rio Preto highlands to the **Vale do Patí**. You can camp overnight on the plains; if you're with a guide, you'll probably stay overnight in a local home.

You can power on in one day to Andaraí, or take a recommended day or two to explore the Vale do Patí, checking out the gorgeous waterfall **Cachoeirão** and the **Morro do Castelo** mountain before moving on.

Once in Andaraí, side trips to **Poço Encantado** (56km from Andaraí) and the intriguing diamond-era stone ruins in **Igatu** (12km from Andaraí) are highly recommended. In Andaraí, either camp or check into the cozy **Pousada Sincorá** (075-3335-2210; www.sincora.com.br; Paraguaçu 120; s/d/tr R$63/115/145), renowned for its delicious breakfast. You can go for a dip at the nearby river beaches along the **Rio Paraguacu** or take the short hike to **Cachoeira do Ramalho**, a 90m waterfall.

In Igatu, take the two-hour hike along the **Rampa do Caim** for sweeping views over the Vale do Patí. You can spend the night at the charming **Flor de Açucena** (075-3335-7003; https://sites.google.com/site/igatur; Nova s/n; campsites per person R$30, s/d from R$80/100), offering campsites, guest rooms built into the rocky hillside, abundant greenery and striking views, with a trail leading down to the river.

Most choose to drive from Andaraí to Lençóis as the walk is on an uninteresting dirt road. If you decide to walk, allow two days, camping the first night near Rio Roncador.

Tours

Many reputable travel agencies offer group tours into the park.

For multiday trips, an even better option is contracting your own guide, an experience that greatly enhances any trip into the park. In Lençóis, you can find a guide by heading to the Associação dos Condutores de Visitantes de Lençóis or asking at any of the big tour agencies or even at reputable pousadas. The going rate at the time of writing was R$170 per day for a group of up to six travelers, though prices vary. In addition to offering expertise on the park's trails and the local flora, fauna, history and geology, a guide can arrange meals and overnight stays in local homes along the way (around R$60 per person, per day).

Whether or not you take a guide, do not go into the park alone.

Sergipe & Alagoas

Includes ➡

Best Places to Sleep

- ➡ Pousada da Amendoeira (p481)
- ➡ Pousada Ricardinho do Frances (p478)
- ➡ Maceió Mar Hotel (p474)
- ➡ Pousada Olho D'água (p482)

Best Off the Beaten Track

- ➡ São Miguel Dos Milagres (p481)
- ➡ Laranjeiras (p471)
- ➡ Praia Do Francês (p478)
- ➡ Pontal de Coruripe (p478)

Why Go?

Overshadowed by big Bahia to the south, the tiny states of Sergipe and Alagoas have long been overlooked by travelers. But it's a tendency that's changing – in the past few years, the thoroughly likable coastal city of Maceió has emerged as a buzzing vacation destination for Brazilian tourists. Still, despite the influx of ecofriendly pousadas (guesthouses) and stylish restaurants, there remain plenty of isolated, paradiselike stretches of white sand, emerald waters, swaying palms and quaint villages along Alagoas' coast.

Inland travel appeals to history-minded travelers: Penedo is a charming riverfront town with picturesque colonial churches and hilly cobblestone streets. Further south, Sergipe's provincial capital has fewer attractions of its own, but Aracaju serves as a gateway to more sleepy colonial towns. In these off-the-beaten-path hamlets, historic 17th-century churches attest to the region's prominence in the early days of European settlement in Brazil.

When to Go

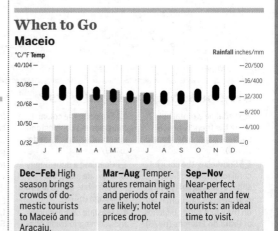

Maceio

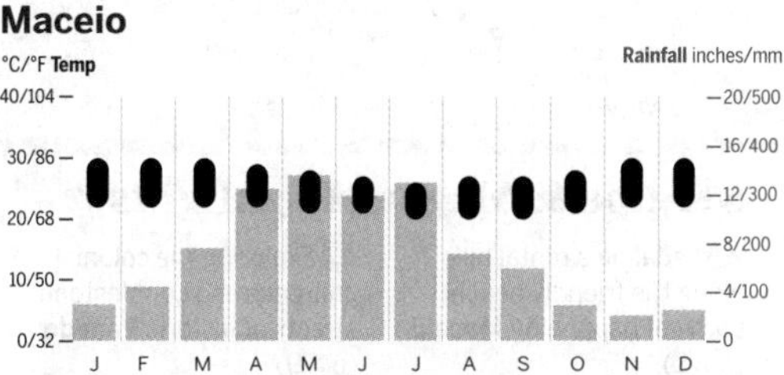

Dec–Feb High season brings crowds of domestic tourists to Maceió and Aracaju.

Mar–Aug Temperatures remain high and periods of rain are likely; hotel prices drop.

Sep–Nov Near-perfect weather and few tourists: an ideal time to visit.

History

During the invasion by the Dutch in 1630, many slaves took advantage of the confusion and escaped to the mountains behind the coasts of northern Alagoas and southern Pernambuco. Where the Alagoan towns of Atalaia, Capela, Viçosa, União dos Palmares and Porto Calvo stand today, virgin forests with fruit and wildlife once provided for colonies of runaway slaves. Palmares, the mightiest republic of escaped slaves, led by the former African king Zumbi, covered present-day Alagoas and Pernambuco. In the 18th and 19th centuries, sugarcane and cotton brought the region prominence; today, sugarcane is still an important crop

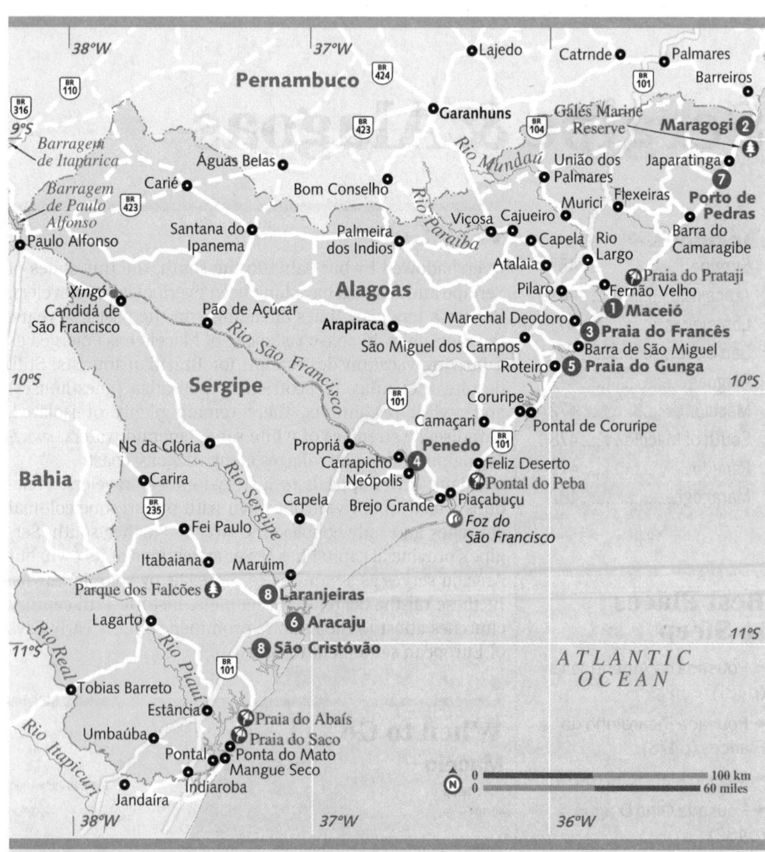

Sergipe & Alagoas Highlights

1. Pedaling a rental bike along the friendly beach paths of happening **Maceió** (p472).
2. Snorkeling the colorful coral reefs miles off the shore of **Maragogi** (p482).
3. Getting away from it all on the white sandy beaches of **Praia do Francês** (p478).
4. Exploring the colonial churches and cobblestone streets of historic **Penedo** (p479).
5. Boarding a dune buggy for a joyride along the smooth white sands of **Praia do Gunga** (p479).
6. Feasting on fresh crabs and listening to traditional *forró* music in the open-air eateries of **Aracaju** (p467).
7. Slowing down to discover **Porto de Pedras** (p481) and the laid-back beach villages north of Maceió.
8. Stepping back in time in Sergipe's colonial gems of **Laranjeiras** (p471) and **São Cristóvão** (p471).

in the area, alongside oranges and cassava, though tourism is making inroads in Maceió. Unfortunately, the states are also known for extreme poverty in the interior and rampant corruption.

Getting There & Away

Hwy BR-101 skirts the coastline of both Sergipe and Alagoas between 25km and 50km inland. It is the main thoroughfare through the region and the chosen route of most long-distance buses. The main airports in the region are in the capital cities, Aracaju and Maceió.

Getting Around

As is the norm in the Northeast, there is always some form of transportation between where you are and where you need to go: buses, Kombi vans (aka *bestas*) and *taxis colectivos* (collective taxis). In this area, it pays to be communicative and flexible, as transportation is less formal than in some other areas of Brazil.

SERGIPE

Brazil's smallest state, Sergipe is a land of sugarcane fields with a coastline of swamp, mangrove and sandy shores. In addition to attractive beaches just south of Aracaju, the state capital, Sergipe, is home to the sleepy, picturesque colonial towns of São Cristóvão and Laranjeiras.

Aracaju

0XX79 / POP 571,000

Though Aracaju's coastline attracts Brazilians for weekend getaways, the city isn't much of a draw for international tourists. Still, many travelers spend a night or two here while in transit between Alagoas and Bahia. Apart from the picturesque main square with its towering cathedral, the historic center is slightly run-down. The outlying beaches boast a seemingly endless number of restaurants and hotels to accommodate summertime crowds.

History

The seat of state government was moved from São Cristóvão to Aracaju in 1855, in part because of its good, deep harbor – badly needed to handle large ships transporting sugar to Europe – and because residents of the old capital were on the verge of armed revolt. Within a year, an epidemic broke out and decimated Aracaju's population, which the residents of São Cristóvão naturally saw as an omen that the new capital had a doomed future. The city received a makeover in the early 1900s with the advent of streetcars and other urbanizing elements.

Sights & Activities

Oceanário AQUARIUM

(3243-3214; www.tamar.org.br; Santos Dumont 1010, Atalaia; adult/child R$16/8; 9am-9pm) The Tamar Project's small, interesting Oceanário has tanks with sea turtles, rays and eels as well as examples of specific local freshwater environments and their species.

Mercado Municipal MARKET

(José do Prado Franco s/n, Centro; 6am-6pm Mon-Sat, to noon Sun) At the colorful Mercado Municipal, locals sell and barter a wide range of goods; if you're passing through downtown around lunchtime, stop in for a casual meal and people-watching.

Beaches

With rustling palms and a relative lack of buildings, **Praia Atalaia Nova** (6km across the Rio Sergipe, southeast of the center) is generally calmer than the city beaches to the south, namely **Praia dos Artistas** (7km), **Praia Atalaia** (9km) and **Praia Aruana** (11km). These beaches are heavily developed but are popular with locals; they are also good sources of inexpensive seafood. Further south, **Praia do Refúgio** (18km) is the prettiest and most secluded beach nearby.

Tours

Local travel agencies offer a variety of day tours, including catamaran trips on the Rio São Francisco to the green waters of the canyon of **Xingó**, or to the **Foz do São Francisco**, where the river meets the sea. A tour is also a pretty good way to check out difficult-to-reach **Mangue Seco**, on the border with Bahia. Exotic-bird enthusiasts will enjoy a visit to the **Parque dos Falcões** (www.parquedosfalcoes.com.br), a reserve located 45km from Aracaju; contact **Ecotur** (3224-9115; www.ecotur.tur.br) for details.

Nozes Tur OUTDOORS

(3243-7177; www.nozestur.com.br; Santos Dumont 340, Atalaia; 9am-7pm) Offers a range of day tours. The office is well-located on Atalaia's waterfront; tour reservations are also available online.

Festivals & Events

On January 1 a huge fleet of fishing boats sails along the Rio Sergipe following the image of their patron saint to celebrate **Bom Jesus dos Navegantes**. The largest festival of all is the **Festa de São João**, which runs for the entire month of June and includes live *forró* (a music and dance style of the Northeast) bands and *quadrilha* (a type of square dancing) presentations.

Sleeping

The majority of Aracaju's hotels are on Atalaia, the waterfront, which is a bit of a trek from the bus station and the center – travelers who are only passing through for a night may find downtown accommodations more convenient. If you're staying on the beach, remember that the coastline is several kilometers long. Most visitors are happiest staying on the far northern end in the district of Coroa de Meio, or on the far southern side near the Passarela do Caranguejo, though there are plenty of pousadas in between.

Casa da Vovó Guida GUESTHOUSE **$**
(3243-1847; http://casa-da-vovo-guida.blogspot.com; José F Albuquerque 174, Atalaia; d from R$90;) A top budget pick in Aracaju, this 18-room hotel, a block away from the beach and a five minutes' walk north of Passarela do Caranguejo, is spotlessly clean and family run. The guesthouse doors close at 10pm – and breakfast isn't included – but the owner speaks perfect English.

Pousada Mirante Das Águas POUSADA **$**
(3255-2610; www.mirantedasaguas.com.br; Delmiro Gouveia 711, Coroa do Meio; d R$150;) Two blocks from the waterfront, the Pousada Mirante das Águas has standard rooms and family-friendly amenities, including a games room. The location in Coroa do Meio is about midway between downtown and the Passarela do Caranguejo; access either by a long walk or short bus or taxi ride.

Hotel Jangadeiro HOTEL **$**
(3211-1350; www.jangadeirose.com.br; Santa Luzia 269, Centro; s/d from R$145/175;) Located a few blocks south of the historic center's main plaza, this business-style hotel is dated but serviceable, good for a quick overnight stay in Aracaju. In-room perks include new bed linens, fluffy pillows and flat-screen TVs.

Pousada Olá POUSADA **$$**
(3243-7045; www.pousadaola.com.br; Niceu Dantas 618, Atalaia; d from R$136;) This simple, efficiently run guesthouse is one of several located near the Passarela do Caranguejo, offering easy access to the beach and some of Aracaju's best dining and drinking options. Note that this popular area is about as far away as you can get from the center of Aracaju, which usually means expensive taxi rides to and from the bus station or airport.

Pousada do Sol POUSADA **$$**
(2104-7338; www.hotelpousadadosol.com.br; Eng Francisco Manoel de Costa 43, Atalaia; s/d from R$160/200;) This well-located guesthouse, a stone's throw from many of Atalaia's waterfront attractions, is a travelers' favorite. Expect simple, spotless and bright guest rooms, a pleasant swimming pool and terrace, and a children's play area.

Mercure Aracaju del Mar HOTEL **$$**
(2106-9100; www.delmarhotel.com.br; Santos Dumont 1500, Atalaia; d from R$195;) This contemporary high-rise, featuring minimalist interior design, several bars and restaurants, and a large swimming pool complete with waterfalls and a bar, is a slick addition to Atalaia's waterfront; it's usually occupied by business travelers, but it's also family friendly.

Eating & Drinking

Although Aracaju is hardly a culinary capital, it does offer one particularly succulent dish: fresh, savory crabs. Just south of Atalaia, you'll find the popular Passarela do Caranguejo (Crab Lane), a row of open-sided restaurants facing the waterfront that serve the respected local dish; the locals' favorite restaurant is Cariri.

Restaurants and drinking spots stretch out along the waterfront in Atalaia. It's a good spot to stroll at night, when sidewalk stands sell crepes, coconuts and tapioca sweets. During the day, you'll find simple sandwich shops and per-kilo lunch spots on the blocks around downtown's main square. But the center empties out at night and is potentially unsafe for wandering.

★ **Cariri** SEAFOOD **$$**
(3243-1379; www.cariri-se.com.br; Santos Dumont 530, Atalaia; mains R$18-38; 8pm-late) If you have only one night in Aracaju, Cariri is the place to be for a taste of local culture.

VELHO CHICO: THE RIVER OF NATIONAL UNITY

For the *nordestino* (Northeasterner), it's impossible to speak about the Rio São Francisco without a swelling of pride. There is no river like the São Francisco, which is Brazil's third-most-important river, after the Amazon and the Paraguai. Those who live along its banks speak of it as a friend – hence the affectionate nickname Velho Chico or Chicão (Chico is a diminutive for Francisco).

The location of the São Francisco gave it great prominence during the colonial history of Brazil. With its headwaters in the Serra da Canastra, 1500m high in Minas Gerais, the Rio São Francisco flows north across the greater part of the Northeast *sertãos* (backlands) and completes its 3160km journey at the Atlantic Ocean after slicing through the states of Minas Gerais and Bahia, and delineating the Bahia–Pernambuco and Sergipe–Alagoas state borders.

For three centuries the São Francisco, also referred to as the 'river of national unity', represented the only connection between the small towns at the extremes of the *sertão* and the coast. 'Discovered' in the 17th century, the river was the best of the few routes available to penetrate the semiarid Northeastern interior. Thus, the frontier grew along the margins of the river. The economy of these settlements was based on cattle, which provided desperately needed food for the gold miners in Minas Gerais in the 18th century and later fed workers in the cacao (cocoa) plantations throughout southern Bahia.

The history of this area is legendary in Brazil: the tough *vaqueiros* (cowboys) who drove the cattle; the commerce in salt (to fatten the cows); the cultivation of rice; the rise in banditry; the battles between the big landowners; and the odd developments, like Canudos, with its strange religious fanaticism (and later its horrific destruction).

The slow waters of the São Francisco have been so vital to Brazil because, in a region with devastating periodic droughts, the river provides one of the only guaranteed water sources. Today the river valley is irrigated to produce a huge amount of produce for local consumption and export.

Owing to its life-sustaining importance, the São Francisco has been the source of much myth-making and storytelling. The *bicho da água* (water beast), for example, is part animal and part human. It walks on the bottom of the river and snores. The crews on the riverboats placate the *bicho da água* by throwing handfuls of tobacco into the water. *Nordestinos* also believe that São Francisco is a gift from God to the people of the *sertão* as recompense for all their suffering in the drought-plagued land.

This famed Northeastern restaurant on the Passarela do Caranguejo features live *forró* music in the traditional style of *pé de serra* (Luis Gonzaga's signature 'foothills' *forró*).

Club Paulista PIZZERIA $

(Av Santos Dumont 340; mains R$18-30; ⏲2-11:30pm Tue-Thu, 10am-11:30pm Fri-Sun) Extremely popular with locals, this easygoing pizzeria is just across the street from the beach in Atalaia. The menu features a large selection of calzones and pizzas, plus well-priced beef, fish, and chicken dishes (R$15 to R$45) at lunchtime.

Bada Grill BRAZILIAN $$

(☎3223-3664; Santos Dumont 526, Atalaia; mains R$25-45; ⏲11:30am-midnight Tue-Thu, to 2am Fri & Sat, to 6pm Sun) Located just north of the Passarela do Caranguejo and across the street from the beach, this casually elegant eatery has a breezy open terrace that's inviting for happy hour drinks and *petiscos* (snacks) such as the popular *lambretas gratinadas* (clams baked in cheese).

New Hakata JAPANESE $$

(☎3213-1202; www.newhakata.com.br; Beira Mar, Anexo ao Iate Clube, 13 de Julho; mains R$28-65; ⏲11am-late Mon-Sat, to 5pm Sun) This popular Japanese restaurant draws crowds with fresh seafood dishes, all-you-can-eat sushi and live jazz nights. It's next to the Yacht Club.

Point do Coelho BAR

(☎9854-9728; Praca Olimpio Campos; ⏲noon-9pm Mon-Fri) If you're in the historic center, this casual outdoor bar and eatery on the main square is your best bet for a cold beer with views of the cathedral. In fact, it's one of the only places that stays open after the downtown business crowd clears out after 5pm.

Orientation

Aracaju's Centro sits on the Rio Sergipe, guarded from the ocean by a sandy barrier island, the Ilha de Santa Luzia. To the south, past the river mouth, are the city beach neighborhoods of Coroa do Meio, Jardim Atlantico (Praia dos Artistas) and Atalaia, collectively referred to as the *orla* (waterfront). Most of the action and nightlife is concentrated in these suburban neighborhoods.

Information

ATMs are plentiful in Aracaju. You'll find internet cafes downtown, but out at the beaches, you'll probably have to use wi-fi or internet at your accommodations.

Emsetur (☎ 3214-8848; www.emsetur.se.gov.br; Rua Propriá s/n; ⏲10am-5pm Mon-Fri) The helpful main office of the state tourism authority distributes free maps of Aracaju. It also has an office in the new bus station (Rodoviária Nova).

Getting There & Away

AIR

Gol (☎ 0800-280 0465; www.voegol.com.br) and **TAM** (☎ 3212-8567; www.tam.com.br) can fly or connect you to other Brazilian cities from Aracaju's **airport** (AJU; ☎ 3212-8500), 11km south of the center.

BUS

Most long-distance buses leave from the **Rodoviária Nova** (New Bus Station; ☎ 3259-2848), 6km east of the center.

Aguia Branca (www.aguiabranca.com.br) and **Rota** (www.rotatransportes.com.br) each offer five daily departures to Salvador (R$58 to R$80, four to six hours). Rota buses also go to Maceió (R$52, four to five hours, four daily), as does **Real Alagoas** (☎ 3259-2832; www.realalagoas.com.br; three departures daily.) Aguia Branca goes to Penedo (R$16, three hours, one daily).

For further access to Penedo, catch a pricier but quicker and more direct Kombi van (approximately R$30, four daily); ask around to find out where the vans are currently departing from.

Getting Around

BUS & TAXI

There are two main bus stations: Rodoviária Nova, where buses come and go from other cities, and Rodoviária Velha, located downtown, where you can catch buses and minibuses to smaller towns and destinations near Aracaju.

From Rodoviária Nova, catch a bus into the city from a large shelter with a series of triangular roofs beside the station. Buses marked 'Centro' take you downtown. Alternatively, catch a taxi to downtown for around R$20, or to the beaches for around R$30 to R$40.

From Centro or downtown, several buses (R$2.75) run to and from the beach: bus 51, marked 'Atalaia/Centro' and bus 8, marked 'Santa Tereza/ Bairro Industrial'. Taxi fares between the bus station or the center and the beaches run around R$30 to R$40.

A taxi to the airport from the center costs around R$40, more if you're coming from the beaches. To get to the airport from downtown's Rodoviária Velha, take the Aeroporto city bus.

CAR

Find a range of car-rental agencies along Atalaia's waterfront. These agencies do steady business, as many destinations in the region are much easier to visit with your own car than by public transportation.

MIRACLE MAKERS

In many shrines and churches in the Northeast, visitors come face-to-face with carved wooden heads, arms, feet and other body parts, hung from ceilings or piled in baskets in a special room. A unique mixture of faith and folk art, these ex-votos are called *milagres* (miracles) and are left by supplicants seeking a cure for a specific ailment such as an injured limb or a congenital deformity. In exchange, the petitioner makes a vow (usually to a particular saint) promising to give up their wicked ways or perhaps make a long pilgrimage – which may even be performed on the knees.

The makers of these ex-votos are often self-taught artisans and their work has a primitive, almost cubist, quality. If the artisans are particularly skilled they may model their work – made of either wood or clay – on the sufferer. No one knows exactly how this custom originated, but the *milagre* probably has links to old Iberian traditions, mingled with African and indigenous customs. In some communities, there is an element of mysticism to these carved objects, as if they could absorb the ills of the sufferer.

Many churches and shrines in the *sertão* (backlands) have a *casa dos milagres* (miracle house) where such objects are displayed. During religious festivals, *milagre* artisans make the rounds, offering their services for a small fee.

Laranjeiras

0XX79 / POP 29,000

Positioned between three grassy, church-topped hills, Laranjeiras is the colonial gem of Sergipe and, together with São Cristóvão, it makes a short and sweet side trip from Aracaju for travelers interested in Sergipe's history. It's short on significant tourist attractions but long on visual interest – ideal for travelers interested in photography.

With a quiet grandeur, Laranjeiras has picturesque cobblestone roads, colonial buildings with intricate wood-carved doorways and terracotta roofs. From the higher points in town, there are lovely views over the meandering Rio Cotinguiba. The whole town seems unblemished by modern development; the surrounding countryside hides crumbling ruins of old sugar mills and estates.

First settled in 1605, Laranjeiras became the commercial center for its surrounding verdant sugar and cotton fields during the 18th and 19th centuries. At one point there were more than 60 sugar mills in and around Laranjeiras sending sugar down the Rio Cotinguiba to Aracaju for export to Europe.

Sights

Facing the bus station, the **Trapiche** is an imposing 19th-century structure that historically held cargo waiting to be shipped downriver. At the top of Alto do Bonfim (Bonfim Heights) is the picturesque 19th-century **Igreja NS do Bonfim**. Although the church is often closed, the fine views make it worth the climb. Reach it by following the street to the left of Nice's Restaurant.

Upriver 4km from town is the baroque **Igreja de Comandaroba**, constructed by Jesuits in 1734. Unfortunately, the church hasn't been well-maintained, and you're unlikely to see inside. A 1km tunnel leads from the church to the **Gruta da Pedra Furada**, a large cave built by the Jesuits to escape their persecutors.

Museu de Arte Sacra MUSEUM
(Museum of Sacred Art; 3281-2486; Praça Dr Heráclito Diniz Gonçalves 39; admission R$2; 10am-2pm Tue-Fri) Built in 1897, this colonial house still has its original wood floors and walls bordered with hand-painted flowers. One room contains life-sized wooden statues of saintly figures, including several used in the town's religious processions. Christ beneath the cross and NS das Dores have real human hair – donated by the faithful for prayers answered.

Museu Afro-Brasileiro MUSEUM
(3281-2418; José do Prado Franco 19; admission R$2; 10am-5pm Tue-Fri, 1-5pm Sat & Sun) Laranjeiras is considered to be the stronghold of Afro-Brazilian culture in Sergipe. This museum offers displays on sugar production, slave torture methods, Afro-Brazilian religions and Laranjeiras' cultural traditions.

Festivals & Events

During the last week of January, Laranjeiras hosts the **Festa de Reis** (also called Encontro Cultural), a religious and folklore festival of traditional music and dance. More folklore revelry occurs during **Semana Folclórico** (Folklore Week), usually the second week of August. You can also catch colorful religious processions during **Semana Santa** (Holy Week; the week preceding Easter).

Eating

Nice's Restaurant BRAZILIAN $
(Praça Dr Heráclito Diniz Gonçalves 4; mains R$12-25; 11:30am-10pm Mon-Sat) Though Laranjeiras doesn't have much in the way of tourist services, this casual eatery on the main square is a casual classic, serving up excellent grilled meats and seafood. Grab a table on the patio.

Getting There & Away

Both Coopertalse and São Pedro buses make the 21km trip between Laranjeiras and Aracaju's Rodoviária Velha (R$2.80, 25 minutes, half-hourly) from 6am to 9:30pm. Unofficial *colectivo* taxis run the same route at the same price.

São Cristóvão

0XX79 / POP 75,000

Atop a steep hill with expansive views over the countryside, the historic center of São Cristóvão houses a sleepy concentration of 17th- and 18th-century colonial buildings along narrow stone roads and a few wide plazas. Founded in 1590, São Cristóvão was the capital of Sergipe until 1855.

Of particular distinction is **Igreja de Senhor dos Passos** (Praça NS dos Passos; admission by donation), with a ceiling painted by José Teófilo de Jesus. The **Museu Histórico**

Sergipe (☎3261-1435; www.museuhsergipe.blogspot.com.ar; Praça São Francisco; admission R$2; ⊙10am-4pm Tue-Sun) is housed in the former Palácio do Governo and features paintings from Carybé and other Northeastern artists, a room for aficionados of the outlaw Lampião, and antique furniture and other relics recalling bygone days.

While in town, stop at one of a few casual bakeries to try *queijadas*, traditional Portuguese cheese pastries considered a local specialty.

Frequent buses make the 28km trip between São Cristóvão and Aracaju's Rodoviária Velha (R$2.80, 45 minutes). The town is 8km off Hwy BR-101.

ALAGOAS

Maceió

☎0XX82 / POP 932,000

Maceió is a modern city set on some truly beautiful beachfront. Though not well-known to international tourists (at least not yet), Brazilians have rediscovered Maceió as a vacation getaway, and the past few years have seen a boom in domestic tourism. The city has a small but buzzing dining and drinking scene, a new bike-share system, and friendly, laid-back streets that close to traffic for street parties on Sundays; it's also the gateway to wonderfully idyllic shorelines to the north and south. On the city's beaches, vivid, emerald-hued water laps the powdery sands that are lined with palms and brightly painted *jangadas* (traditional sailboats). By night, locals follow the meandering beachfront path as it weaves past thatched-roof restaurants and palm-shaded football pitches. Maceió's sights are relatively few, leaving you plenty of time to catch some rays and soak up the relaxed atmosphere.

Beaches

Protected by an offshore coral reef, Maceió's ocean waters are calm and a deep emerald color. City beaches include the popular **Praia de Ponta Verde**, **Praia de Pajuçara**, **Praia dos Sete Coqueiros** and **Jatiúca**; a pair of lounge chairs and a rental umbrella will run you about R$8 to R$15 for the afternoon. Be forewarned that Praia do Sobral and Praia da Avenida, closer to the city center, are polluted.

The nicest beaches north of the city are thought to be **Garça Torta** (14km) and **Pratagi** (17km), but **Jacarecica** (9km), **Guaxuma** (12km) and **Riacho Doce** (17km) are also tropical paradises. The Riacho Doce bus, which can be picked up in several spots along the coastal road, runs up the coast to these northern beaches.

Activities

Pedala Maceió BICYCLE RENTAL
(☎9183-9882; www.pedalamaceio.com.br; cnr Dr Antonio Gouveia & JP Filho; per hour R$14; ⊙6am-11pm) Grab a bicycle or a three-wheeler to explore Maceió's 20km-long waterfront bike path. This outfit operates four rental locations along the beaches.

Tours

From Praia de Pajuçara, **jangadas** (R$25) travel 2km offshore at low tide to natural pools formed by the reef. After a short journey aboard one of the delightfully old-fashioned, colorfully painted *jangadas*, you're free to float in the clear water; snorkel-mask rental (R$10) is optional. On weekends, floating bars serve beer and *agua de coco* (coconut water), making the whole experience more festive. You can arrange trips with any boat captain; stop in early to find out when the boats are sailing or just stroll down the beach and wait for someone to approach you first. The whole trip lasts about two hours.

A plethora of organized day trips are possible from Maceió, including a **beach tour** (R$25, taking in Praia do Francês, Barra de São Miguel and Praia do Gunga), an excursion to **Foz do São Francisco** (R$90), a trip to Porto de Galinahs (R$55) and a trip to the **natural pools** (R$90, including boat transport) off the coast of Maragogi. Another popular excursion is the **Nove Ilhas** (Nine Islands) tour (R$60); in addition to cruising the Lagoa Mundaú, you'll stop at the outlet of the lake into the ocean.

Such excursions are extremely easy to plan for much of the year: a large number of travel agencies' representatives camp out around Pajuçara's artisan market, advertising their services to passersby. In low season consider planning further ahead, contacting a few travel agencies through their web forms – a minimum number of passengers is required for most tours. Try contacting **Marcão Turismo** (☎9981-7896; www.turismomaceio.com.br; Quebrangulo 68, Cruz das Alamas) or **Edvantur Turismo** (☎9117-5657; www.edvanqueeuvoualagoas.com.br).

MACEIÓ IN CONTEXT

Unlike many other cities and towns in this part of Brazil, Maceió feels modern: you won't see any charming colonial architecture unless you leave the beaches and venture into downtown, which few visitors find reason to do. But Maceió has an interesting backstory. A small settlement here was officially established as a village in 1815. By 1839, Maceió was the capital of the state of Alagoas, and the city has remained an important sugar port for Northeast Brazil.

Thanks, in part, to its geographic position and industry, Maceió is prosperous, especially compared to the poor communities located in the interior of Alagoas. But the city is surrounded by favelas (slums) and, away from the beaches, plagued with crime. Due to the high murder rate, Maceió made headlines in 2010 as the so-called 'most violent city in Brazil.' Most travelers are blissfully unaware of this fact when they're snorkeling around the coral reef or relaxing on the beach, but it's smart to keep the context in mind – and consider the sharp divide between the tourist experience and the extreme poverty plaguing many of the city's residents – when traveling through.

Festivals & Events

Carnaval CARNAVAL

(mid-February) Maceió hosts a small but lively Carnaval with all of the usual trappings: music, food, dancing. The bigger parties happen at beaches outside the city, especially Barra de São Miguel.

Festa Junina RELIGIOUS

(2nd half of June) Fifteen days of folk dancing, fireworks, street food, bonfires, costumed revelry and free-flowing beer take over Maceió during Brazil's winter solstice; it's a Portuguese tradition beginning on St Anthony's day in mid-June and lasting through St Peter's day at the end of the month.

Sleeping

Several high-rise chain hotels have opened along the waterfront in recent years. In general, Maceió's lodging options are on the pricey side, especially considering that few pousadas offer much in the way of style or character – luckily, you're not going to spend much time in your room in this lively coastal city.

Gogó da Ema POUSADA $

(3327-0329; www.hotelgogodaema.com.br; Francisco Laranjeiras 97, Ponta Verde; s/d/tr from R$100/120/150;) On a quiet street near two lovely beaches, reliable budget pick Gogó da Ema (named for a famous old palm tree that fell in the city in 1955 and has come to symbolize Maceió itself) is a five-story guesthouse with a tropical theme. The 24-hour front desk is particularly helpful if you're arriving late or catching an early plane.

Pousada Aquarela do Brasil POUSADA $

(3231-0113; www.pousadaaquareladobrasil.com; Guimarães 367, Pajuçara; s/d from R$130/155;) Just off the waterfront, this pretty guesthouse offers simple but (relatively) sophisticated rooms with flat-screen TVs and modern artwork. Ground-level rooms have tiny private patios.

Pousada Hotel Maceio POUSADA $

(3316-8645; www.pousadahotelmaceio.com.br; Pompeu Sarmento 455; s/d from R$90/130;) This simple eight-room guesthouse is nothing fancy, but the place is clean, well-managed and conveniently located a half block from the beach action, making it one of the better-value sleeping options in the area.

Maceió Hostel e Pousada HOSTEL $

(3231-7762; www.maceiohostel.com.br; Jangadeiros Alagoanos 1528; dm/d from R$50/120;) A budget option a few blocks from the beach, this HI hostel is small – shared quads don't leave much room for your backpack – but are friendly and efficiently run. Doubles are basic and spotless, with good showers and large lockers.

Hotel Praia Bonita HOTEL $$

(2121-3700; www.praiabonita.com.br; Dr Antônio Gouveia 943, Pajuçara; s/d from R$133/169;) This small and friendly waterfront hotel, dwarfed by the high-rise buildings around it, has an attractive, modern design and a breakfast room that faces the *jangada* launch across the street. It's next door to several business hotels, so getting a taxi outside is a snap.

Maceió

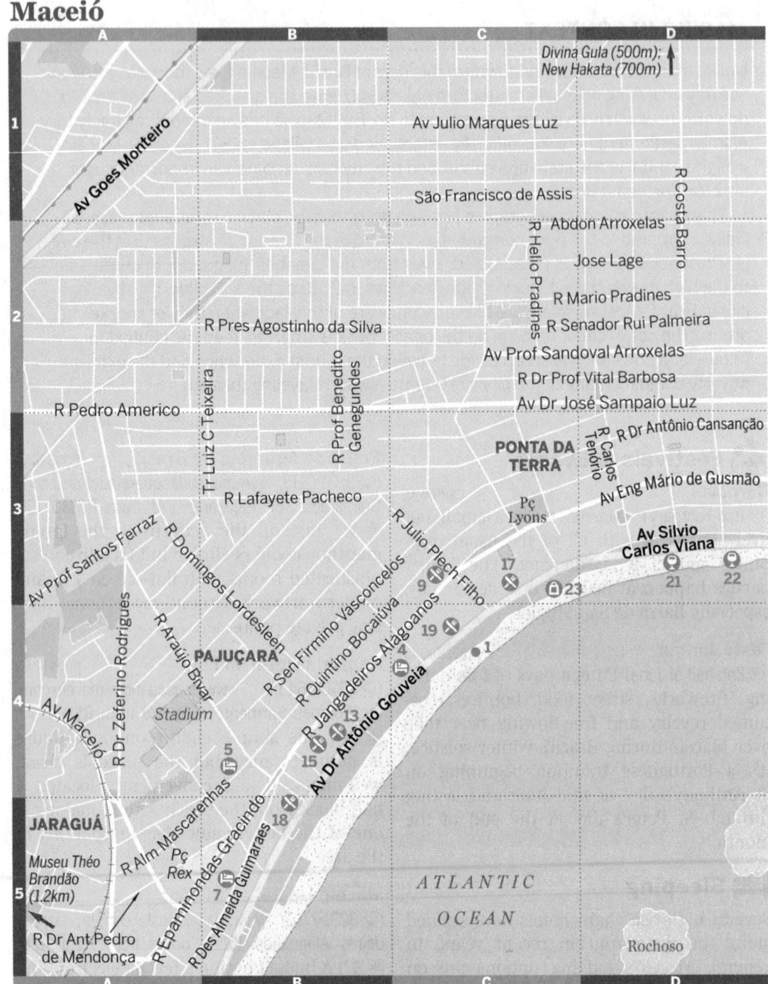

★ **Maceió Mar Hotel** HOTEL $$
(2122-8000; www.maceiomarhotel.com.br; Álvaro Otacílio 2991, Ponta Verde; d/tr from R$315/379;) This high-rise, beachfront hotel has spacious, brightly lit rooms with floor-to-ceiling windows, all with sea views. Recently renovated, with upscale amenities and a swimming pool, it's suited to both business travelers and families.

Eating

There's a wide selection of casual open-air eateries along the beachfront promenades of Pajuçara and Ponta Verde, if not a wide selection of menu options: most offer the same seafood dishes, or simple pizzas and sandwiches. Takeout stands along the shoreline also serve up açaí (berrylike fruit) and the Northeastern specialty *beiju de tapioca* (savory or sweet fillings folded up, taco-style, in fried manioc flour). On weekend evenings and more frequently in high season, look for food trucks at the bend on the promenade where Ponta Verde turns into Pajuçara: you'll find gourmet burgers, craft beer, even Greek food.

If you're more interested in memorable cuisine than beachfront ambience, head to the neighborhood of Jatiúca, where many

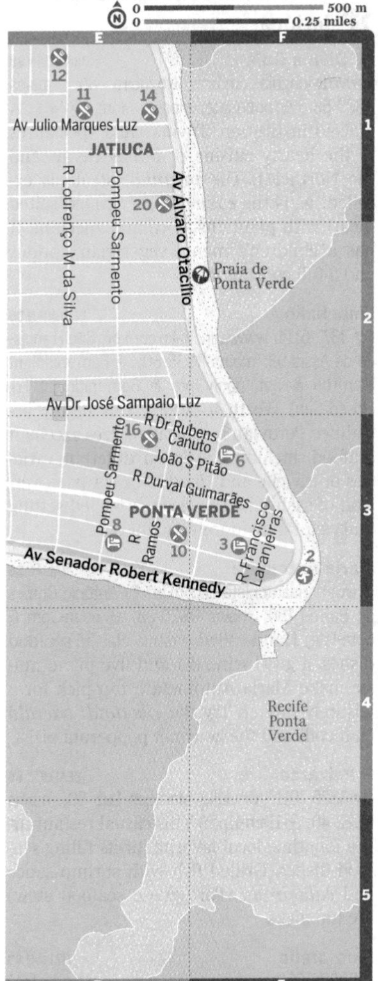

Maceió

Activities, Courses & Tours

1 Jangadas ... C4
2 Pedala Maceió ... F3

Sleeping

3 Gogó da Ema ... F3
4 Hotel Praia Bonita ... C4
5 Maceió Hostel e Pousada ... B4
6 Maceió Mar Hotel ... F3
7 Pousada Aquarela do Brasil ... B5
8 Pousada Hotel Maceio ... E3

Eating

9 Bom Preço ... C3
10 Le Corbu ... E3
11 Maria Antoineta ... E1
12 Massarella ... E1
13 Nakaffa ... B4
14 O Peixarão ... E1
15 Panificação Alteza ... B4
16 Panificação Alteza ... E3
17 Parmegianno ... C3
Restaurante Gogó da Ema ... (see 3)
18 Sorveteria Bali ... B5
19 Sueca Comedoria ... C4
20 Wanchako ... E1

Drinking & Nightlife

21 Kanoa Beach Bar ... D3
22 Lopana ... D3

Shopping

23 Mercado Praia de Pajuçara ... C3

of the locals' favorites are clustered. Local specialties to look for include *sururu* (small mussels) and *maçunim* (shellfish) cooked in coconut sauce, served as main courses or in a *caldo* (soup). Other seafood treats include *peixe agulha* (needlefish) and *siri na casca com coral* (crab in its shell with roe).

Pajuçara & Ponta Verde

★ Panificação Alteza BAKERY $

(3231-0447; João Pitão 1181, Ponta Verde; prepared foods per kilo R$20-26; 6am-8pm Mon-Sat) This gourmet minimarket, complete with a coffee bar and bakery, is the perfect place to get your caffeine fix while stocking up on fresh bread, tropical fruits, cold cuts, Argentinian wine and chocolate cake for your picnic or hotel room. There's now a **second outlet** (Jangadeiros Alagoanos 732, Pajuçara).

Sueca Comedoria BUFFET $

(3327-0359; www.suecacomedoria.com.br; Dr Antônio Gouveia 1103, Pajuçara; per kilo R$35; 11:30am-4pm Mon-Fri) Despite the name, this sleek eatery across from the beach doesn't serve Swedish food; it's a family-run self-serve spot offering fresh seafood and regional cuisine, ideal for a quick lunch when you need a break from the sun.

Nakaffa CAFE $

(3235-6459; www.nakaffa.com.br; Dr Antônio Gouveia 729, Pajuçara; mains R$12-25; noon-11pm) This cool, contemporary cafe specializes in frothy cappuccinos, light salads, gourmet sandwiches and decadent chocolate desserts. It's your best bet for a beachside cup of coffee after breakfast hours.

SAILING INTO THE PAST

Maceió's colorful wooden *jangadas* (sailboats) – lined up on the beach of Pajuçara, waiting to carry passengers to the natural pools around the coral reef offshore – are products of a long tradition in Northeast Brazil. *Jangadas* are made of native wood. No nails or other metal elements are used in their construction: the logs are held together with ropes, the slightly curved mast mounted with a simple triangular sail. Though the origins of the *jangada* aren't entirely known, historians believe that this style of sailboat has its roots in India and Mozambique – influences that would have made their way to the shipping capitals of Northeast Brazil after the arrival of Portuguese explorers.

Restaurante Gogó da Ema BRAZILIAN $
(www.hotelgogodaema.com.br; Laranjeiras 97; mains R$13-32; 11am-4pm & 6-11pm) A friendly, down-to-earth restaurant located at the pousada of the same name, Gogó da Ema does traditional Northeastern dishes, plus sandwiches, steaks and grilled fish. It's a good-value option for lunch or dinner any day of the week.

Sorveteria Bali ICE CREAM $
(3231-8833; www.sorvetesbali.com.br; Dr Antônio Gouveia 451, Pajuçara; scoops R$5; 10am-late) Grab an outdoor table and enjoy Maceió's best ice cream. Favorite flavors include walnut, guava and tapioca.

Le Corbu FRENCH $$
(Guimarães 877; mains R$28-45; noon-3pm & 7-10pm Wed-Fri, 7-10pm Sat, noon-3pm Sun) A step up, style-wise, from many of the restaurants near the beach, Le Corbu specializes in French cuisine. Come for the elegant set lunch Wednesdays and Thursdays (R$50), or in the evening to peruse the wine list.

Parmegianno BRAZILIAN $$
(3313-9555; Dr Antônio Gouveia 1259; mains for 2 R$32-45; 11am-late) Brazilian families flock to this popular chain restaurant, just across from the beach, for gourmet pizzas and hearty portions of shrimp, steak, fish, and chicken – accompanied with beans, rice and salad.

Jatiúca

★Divina Gula BRAZILIAN $$
(www.divinagula.com.br; Nogueira 85; mains R$29-58; noon-late, closed Mon;) A Maceió institution, Divina Gula specializes in the hearty cuisine of Minas Gerais and the Northeast. The *picanha* (steak) is excellent as is the *carne de sol* (grilled salted meat) with plantains, corn and zucchini. It has a children's menu, vegetarian options and a full cocktail list.

Wanchako PERUVIAN $$
(3377-6114; www.wanchako.com.br; São Francisco de Assis 93; mains R$35-60; 6pm-midnight Mon-Thu & Sat, noon-3pm & 6pm-midnight Fri, closed Sun) Worth a detour, this highly acclaimed Peruvian restaurant serves excellent seafood, including a dozen different varieties of ceviche and *tiradito* (a Peruvian version of sashimi). The sleek, art-filled setting makes for a memorable night out.

Maria Antoineta ITALIAN $$
(www.mariaantonieta-al.com.br; Dr Antônio Gomes de Barros 150; mains R$20-38; noon-3pm & 6pm-late) Hand-rolled pastas, classic seafood dishes, a good wine list and live piano music make Maria Antoineta a top pick for a leisurely dinner. Try the *risotto di baccalá* (salt cod) and the gourmet pepperoni pizza.

O Peixarão SEAFOOD $$
(3325-7011; Dr Júlio Marques Luz 50; mains R$22-40; 11am-11pm) This casual restaurant is a longtime local favorite for its filling seafood dishes. Grilled fish with shrimp sauce and *caldeirada* (Portuguese seafood stew) are top picks.

Massarella ITALIAN $$
(3325-6000; www.massarella.com.br; José Pontes Magalhães 271, Jatiúca; mains R$18-35; noon-late Tue-Sun;) This festive cantina is the place for homemade pastas and brick-oven pizzas; Italian pastas are traditionally prepared, and each plate is big enough for two to share. It's especially popular in summer.

Drinking & Entertainment

For a laid-back caipirinha (cocktail) with an ocean view, just pick any place along the waterfront in Ponta Verde or Pajuçara.

★Lopana BAR
(www.lopana.com.br; Viana 27; 11am-late) Maceió's best beachfront bar is always buzzing:

when an acoustic guitarist is playing and a good-looking crowd is drinking beer and caipirinhas under the sky-high palm trees, the place looks straight out of a movie.

Kanoa Beach Bar BAR
(Dr Antônio Gouveia 25; ⏲9am-midnight) This busy beach bar offers live music and free-flowing cocktails in a prime location on the oceanfront promenade.

Shopping

The busy **Mercado Praia de Pajuçara** (Pajuçara waterfront; ⏲10am-10pm) craft market sells lacework, hammocks, baskets and ceramics. Serious shoppers will prefer the deals and selection at the **Mercado do Artesanato** (Levada; ⏲7am-6pm Mon-Sat, to noon Sun) downtown.

Orientation

Maceió sits on a jagged peninsula between the Lagoa Mundaú and the ocean. The peninsula features two main headlands: one is the site of the city's port, and the other divides Praia de Pajuçara and Praia dos Sete Coqueiros from the more northern Praia de Ponta Verde and the long Praia de Jatiúca. The Centro is located near the oceanfront, 2km from Pajuçara and 4km from Ponta Verde.

Information

ATMs can be found in commercial areas along the beach, and at the **Bom Preço** grocery store in Pajuçara. Most travelers will access the internet from their accommodations, though a few internet cafes are also scattered around town.

Police (☎190)

Pronto Socorro (ambulance/first aid; ☎3221-5939)

Getting There & Away

AIR

Gol (☎3214-4078; www.voegol.com.br) and **TAM** (☎3214-4048; www.tam.com.br) can fly you or connect you to anywhere in Brazil from **Aeroporto Zumbi dos Palmares** (MCZ; ☎3036-5200).

BUS

The **bus station** (☎3221-4615; Av Leste Oeste s/n, Feitosa) is 4km north of the city center.

Real Alagoas (www.realalagoas.com.br) and **Rota** (www.rotatransportes.com.br) buses go to Aracaju (R$52, four to five hours, seven daily). Real Alagoas also goes north to Recife (R$38 to R$68, five to six hours, 10 daily.) Rota buses go to Salvador (R$117 to R$145, 11 hours, four daily).

The quickest way to get to Penedo is on one of the *colectivos* that depart from the Posto Sobral gas station in the city center. The ride lasts about 2½ hours and costs R$20; the same route provides access to Coruripe (R$12) and Praia do Gunga (R$10) as well as several small towns along the way. Ask your taxi driver to take you to the departure spot for *colectivos* to Penedo (Rua Zacarias de Azevedo 572, Centro). From Maceió's bus station, the fare is R$20 to R$25.

DEF runs meandering buses up the coast to Maragogi and Porto de Pedras, stopping at many of the beach villages along the way. Fares range

TAKING THE SCENIC ROUTE

When traveling from Penedo to Maceió, throw in an extra two hours and opt for the *pinga litoral* (coastal drip) bus. If constant stops and deviations off the main road don't drive you crazy, you'll get a refreshing glimpse into rural life, passing tiny churches, dusty roads leading off into jungle, and rustic fishing huts, with children waving as the bus rolls by.

From Penedo, the bus travels along the river toward the coast, passing the scattered fishing community in Piaçabuçu, then swings in from the river and north to Pontal do Peba, where it does a U-turn on the beach. From there it passes through Feliz Deserto, which has lots of cowboys and coconuts, one pousada (guesthouse) and plenty of seafood. The bus turns off Hwy AL-101 a bit further north at Miaí de Cima, where there are no pousadas, but many locals on the beach on weekends. The next time the bus turns off the main road is into Barreiras and pretty Coruripe before continuing to Pontal de Coruripe.

Next stop is Lagoa do Pau, with shrimp cultivation, weekend homes and a couple of pousadas. Then it's on to Poxim, past sugarcane fields and coconut palms. Approaching Maceió, it stops at the turnoffs for Barra de São Miguel and Praia do Francês. Passing the huge estuaries of the Mundaú and Manguaba lagoons, it's not long before the bus reaches the capital. If you plan to stay at Pajuçara or beaches further north, get off the bus as soon as it turns off the coast road and before it continues into the center of Maceió.

OFF THE BEATEN TRACK

PONTAL DE CORURIPE

A traditional fishing village that sees few visitors, Pontal de Coruripe lies in an area of verdant coconut plantations, on the edge of a long, deserted beach with beautiful emerald waters. On the peaceful streets of town, women sit in front of their homes gossiping and weaving palm baskets, placemats and handbags, while out at the cove just opposite the lighthouse, fishermen guide their boats across the sunlit sea. Watch the scenery while dining on fresh seafood at **Peixada da Madalena** (☎3273-7234; Ladeira do Farol 248; mains R$15-30; ⏲10am-6:30pm), one of a few restaurants clustered around the lighthouse.

Transportation to and from Pontal de Coruripe is frequent but fairly informal. The slow coastal bus heading for Maceió (R$10, two hours) passes through Pontal de Coruripe at least twice daily, with more limited service on Sundays.

from R$2.50 (to nearby Paripuera, one hour) to R$12.50 (to Maragogi, 3½ hours). There are four daily departures to Maragogi, and four making the return trip; six daily buses go to and from Porto de Pedras.

The quickest way to get to Maragogi is a *colectivo* (R$30, two hours). These depart from a gas station north of Maceió – again, you'll have to communicate with your taxi driver to get there, asking for '*colectivos* a Maragogi.' These shared taxis require four passengers to depart; they're quicker and cooler than the official bus lines.

Getting Around

TO/FROM THE AIRPORT

Maceió's airport is 20km north of the center. To reach the center, hop in one of the spiffy taxis operated by the local taxi collective (R$60); you pay inside the airport and take your ticket to a driver waiting curbside. It's a 30-minute drive to the city if there's no traffic. Buses also run between Ponta Verde and the airport (labeled Aeroporto–Ponta Verde) every 45 minutes or so (R$2.75). The same bus can be picked up in Pajuçara heading north along Rua Jangadeiros Alagoanos (there are several stops along this stretch) look for a bus with 'Aeroporto' on the front.

TO/FROM THE BUS STATION

To reach the center, take the Ouro Prêto bus; for the beaches, catch the Circular 1. A taxi to the center costs R$12 to R$15, and around R$20 to the beaches.

South of Maceió

This stretch of coast is characterized by small, quaint coastal villages – some with amazing beaches – surrounded by wide stretches of coconut plantations. The tourism hot spots on Alagoas' south coast are Praia do Francês and Barra de São Miguel.

Praia do Francês

☎0XX82

Francês is a surfer's paradise. Given its proximity to Maceió (22km), Praia do Francês has long functioned as a day-trip destination: cars and buses roll in on weekend days and clear out by sunset. But this is changing quickly as more travelers fall in love with the beach town, and pousadas have popped up left and right to accommodate the influx of visitors.

The action is concentrated on one end of Francês' fine, white sands, where just-offshore reefs create calm green waters, and a string of restaurants serve beer and fried shrimp. Alagoas' best waves are at the southern end – don't despair if you're not traveling with your own equipment, both bodyboards and longboards are available for rent right on the sand. Swimmers opt for the protected reef at the beach's northern end. Walk a few minutes in either direction to escape the crowds.

Sleeping & Eating

There's not much of a gourmet dining scene in this laid-back beach town, but there are several sandwich stands on the sand, and standard pizzerias and self-serve buffets in town and along the beach.

★**Pousada Ricardinho do Frances** POUSADA $
(☎3260-1488; www.pousadaricardinhodofrances.com.br; Arrecifes 10; d/tr from R$120/180) An ideal location close to the beach, plus fantastic breakfasts and tidy guest rooms with private balconies and hammocks, make this guesthouse one of the current favorites in town.

Pousada Aconchego POUSADA $$
(☎3260-1193; www.pousadaaconchego.com.br; Carapeba 159; d from R$155; ❄ ≋) Aconchego has pleasant rooms set around a lush garden. Hammocks, a pool and friendly service add to the charm.

Pousada Ecos do Mar POUSADA $$
(☎3260-1191; www.pousadaecosdomar.com.br; Carapeba 160; d from R$140; ❄ 📶) At this popular pousada, colorfully painted guest rooms have flat-screen TVs and minifridges, plus access to a swimming pool and a standout breakfast buffet.

ℹ Getting There & Away

From the bus station in Maceió, **Real Alagoas** (☎3336-6816) runs regular buses (R$4, 35 minutes) to and from Praia do Francês. Look for the bus marked 'Marechal-Francês'. A taxi from Maceió's airport to Praia do Francês costs around R$80.

Barra de São Miguel

☎0XX82 / POP 8200

The center of this small village sits on the riverbank, facing **Praia do Gunga**, an idyllic, white-sand beach that curves to a point at the meeting of the Rio São Miguel and the sea. Indeed, Barra isn't much of a destination in itself: it's better known as the gateway to Praia do Gunga, where the local beaches are protected by a huge offshore reef, leaving the waters calm for bathing or kayaking. During high season on Praia do Gunga, **dune buggies** take tourists on an hour-long adventure: you'll speed along the sands, stop to photograph the rocky dune-lined landscape, and go for a dip in a natural pool.

There are several popular pousadas in the area, including the lovely **Brisamar Pousada** (www.brisamarpousada.com.br; Margarida Oiticica Lima 38; d from R$185; ❄ 📶). Several open-air restaurants line the harbor, catering to the tourists coming and going from the beach.

Note that in Praia do Gunga, dining options are infamously overpriced: be aware that most of the *barracas* (food stalls) insist on a minimum consumption of upwards of R$50 per person. Many beachgoers prefer to bring their own picnic from Maceió, or buy simple snacks and sandwiches from the stands set up around the gigantic parking lot.

ℹ Getting There & Away

Barra de São Miguel is located 35km from Maceió. Brazilian tourists usually arrive in their own cars, while most foreign tourists visit Praia do Gunga on a day trip with a travel agency in Maceió (the standard 'beach tour' visits Praia do Francês, Barra de São Miguel and Praia do Gunga).

To arrive independently from Maceió, ask your taxi driver to take you to the Texaco petrol station in the southwest of Maceió where the *colectivos* (vans or buses) depart for Barra de São Miguel. Once in Barra, you can catch a *colectivo* taxi to and from Praia do Francês (R$5 to R$10, 20 minutes).

Marechal Deodoro

☎0XX82 / POP 51,000

On the banks of the tranquil Lagoa Manguaba, Marechal Deodoro is a small, peaceful town with pretty churches and a few streets of colonial architecture dating back to early settlement days. Marechal served as capital of Alagoas between 1823 and 1839, and although there's not a lot to see, it's an easy jaunt from Maceió – and if you're heading to the beaches south of Maceió on public transportation, you'll probably pass through anyway. If you have a few minutes, check out the pretty white-and-yellow facade of the **Igreja de NS da Conceição**, located on top of the hill above the lagoon. If you're around on a weekend, the **Saturday market**, held until noon along the waterfront, is particularly lively. Arrive early in the morning to see fishers working their nets out along the water.

Real Alagoas (www.realalagoas.com.br) buses marked 'Marechal-Francês' leave Maceió's bus station (R$4, 35 minutes) on a regular basis, as do minibuses headed to Marechal Deodoro via Praia do Francês. These depart frequently from a stop behind the Texaco petrol station (Rua Dias Cabral and Zacarias de Azevedo) southwest of Maceió's center. Buses, Kombi vans and *colectivo* taxis leave from Marechal's plaza for Praia do Francês (R$3, 15 minutes) and for Maceió.

Penedo

☎0XX82 / POP 60,400

Note the elegant sculpture of Christ, standing tall in a riverboat, at the entrance to town: it's a hint at the significance of Penedo's position on the Rio São Francisco. The city is the colonial masterpiece of the state, known for its many baroque churches and decorative architecture. It's not much to look at from the dusty (or muddy) riverfront square – to experience Penedo's charms, you'll have to wander up into the hilly cobblestoned streets. It's busy by day, when Penedo's downtown bustles with a daily market as people from surrounding villages pour in to do their shopping, and quiet at night. Apart from a few hotels and organized excursions on the river, Penedo is almost unaltered by tourism.

History

Since its founding, Penedo has been a commercial center, owing to its prime position on the Rio São Francisco. The town was founded sometime between 1535 and 1560 by Duarte Coelho Pereira, who descended the Rio São Francisco in pursuit of the indigenous Caetes who were responsible for killing a bishop. Penedo is claimed to be the river's first colonial settlement. It was also the scene of a fierce 17th-century battle between the Dutch and the Portuguese for control of the Northeast. In the 19th century, Penedo was one of the focal points of the abolitionist movement in Alagoas. In the 20th century, the city lost its prominence as a commercial center, which probably saved its colonial buildings from destruction.

Sights

Penedo has a rich collection of 17th- and 18th-century colonial buildings, including many churches. Unfortunately, regardless of the posted opening hours, these churches are not reliably open to visitors – your best bet is to walk around and see what's open.

Convento de São Francisco e Igreja NS dos Anjos CHURCH
(Praça Rui Barbosa; admission R$2) The Convento de São Francisco e Igreja NS dos Anjos was under construction for nearly 100 years before its completion in 1759, and is considered the finest church in the state. Even Dom Pedro II (Brazil's second and last emperor) paid a visit. Of particular note are the richly colored ceiling, the gold rococo altar and the statue of St Francis to the left of it that was carved by Aleijadinho.

Igreja de NS da Corrente CHURCH
(Praça 12 de Abril) The Igreja de NS da Corrente, completed in 1765, has some fine Portuguese azulejos (tiles), painted in green, purple and gold – colors rarely seen in Brazil, or Portugal for that matter. The Lemos family were big benefactors of the church (their family seal is marked on the floor) and abolitionists; slaves fled to the church for protection – some were even hidden behind panels of the church walls.

igreja de São Gonçalo Garcia CHURCH
(Floriano Peixoto) The Igreja de São Gonçalo Garcia was built at the end of the 18th century. The small oratório (Praça Barão de Penedo) is where the condemned spent their last night praying before being hanged.

Igreja NS do Rosário dos Pretos CHURCH
(Catedral do Penedo; Praça Marechal Deodoro) The Igreja NS do Rosário dos Pretos was built by slaves.

Museu do Paço Imperial MUSEUM
(Praça 12 de Abril 9; admission R$4; 11am-5pm Tue-Sat, 8am-noon Sun) Occupying the top floor of the house Dom Pedro II once slept in, the Museu do Paço Imperial displays lamps, portraits, furniture and elegant finery from the imperial period (17th and 18th centuries); it's tiny but nicely presented.

Activities

Regular ferries (R$2) depart from the center for **Neópolis**, a hilltop colonial town with historic buildings and fine crafts for sale. During high season, it may be possible to get in on an organized tour to the **Foz do São Francisco** (R$50 per person, four-person minimum for departure), where the river meets the sea at a beach with dunes and natural pools. The most frequent departures for this excursion leave 28km downriver in Piaçabuçu, easily accessible by collective van or bus from Penedo. Try **Farol da Foz Ecoturismo** (3552-1298; www.faroldafozecoturismo.com) for these and other trips in the area.

Festivals & Events

Festa do Senhor Bom Jesus dos Navegantes RELIGIOUS
(from 2nd Sun of Jan) This festival is held over four days, and features an elaborate procession of boats and a sailboat race.

Sleeping

If you're booking a hotel room online, be sure that you're searching for results in Penedo, Alagoas – otherwise you'll probably be looking at hotels in a Brazilian town in the state of Rio de Janeiro that's also named Penedo.

NORTH OF MACEIÓ: BEACH TOWNS

Many travelers zip up the coastline from Maceió with one destination in mind: Maragogi, and its spectacular offshore coral reef and snorkeling site. But if you have more than a day or two, it's worthwhile to slow down and explore some of the rustic beach villages along this stretch of Alagoas' northernmost shoreline with its fluffy white sands, green waters and tall coconut palms. These easygoing towns barely have the basics to support tourism – save for a few luxury pousadas (guesthouses) – but they offer an authentic look at the local lifestyle, and a chance to truly unplug. Wherever you go, it's advisable to get cash before heading out, as you won't find a bank until you reach Maragogi.

Heading north from Maceió, the first town you'll pass through is **Barra de Santo Antônio**, a mellow fishing village built along the mouth of the Rio Jirituba. Just south of the village is Praia Tabuba, a pretty, tranquil bay with a few bars and a couple of pousadas. There are reef tidal pools off the beach; ask at the bars about a ride there by *jangada* (sailboat). Next is **Barra do Camaragibe**, an idyllic fishing village on the edge of a small, reef-laden bay. *Jangadas* make trips south to Praia do Morro, a deserted beach with cliffs and clear waters.

The stretch from Barra do Camaragibe to Porto de Pedras, along the so-called Rota Ecológica (Ecological Route), is a lovely place to treat yourself. **São Miguel dos Milagres** has fine beaches with warm, shallow seas protected by offshore reefs. Splurge on a night or two in a stylish, environmentally conscious bungalow at **Pousada da Amendoeira** (☎082-3295-1213; www.amendoeira.com.br; Praia do Toque 7; d incl half-board from R$780;) , which also has an excellent restaurant specializing in gourmet seafood and organic regional dishes. If you're sticking around for a few days, eco-minded tour outfitter **Gato do Mato** (☎082- 3033-1040; www.gatodomato.com) runs highly recommended half-day excursions, ranging from river kayaking to snorkeling to oyster collecting; contact the agency ahead of time, as a minimum number of participants is required for most trips.

Porto de Pedras is a sweet little fishing town and, as it is the most established on this stretch of road, it boasts a few shops, bars and restaurants, plus a hilltop lighthouse offering great views. Further north, in **Japaratinga**, shallow waters are protected by coral reefs, and the beaches are backed by coconut trees and fishing huts. Under the moonlight, you can walk a couple of kilometers into the sea. Kombi vans regularly make the 10km trip north to Maragogi (R$7-10).

There are a variety of transport options to reach northern destinations. Real Alagoas (www.realalagoas.com.br) runs buses to Porto de Pedras (R$24, 3½ hours, five daily) via Barra do Camaragibe, São Miguel dos Milagres and Porto da Rua from the bus station in Maceió. Similar services by bus line DEF, as well as minibuses, *besta* (Kombi) vans and *colectivo* taxis traveling the same route, can be caught at the *posto* (post) Mar Azul at the northern edge of Maceió (ask your taxi driver to take you). Travel between these little towns is fairly easy up until about 7pm.

Pousada Colonial POUSADA $

(☎3551-2355; Praça 12 de Abril 21; d/tr/q R$120/160/200;) To fully soak up the colonial charms of Penedo, book a room at this charming historic house on the waterfront. Dating from 1734, the building has stained wood floors, dramatic high ceilings, antique furniture and old-fashioned wooden shutters, some of which open to fabulous views over the river. It could use some updates, but the place is memorable.

Hotel São Francisco HOTEL $$

(☎3551-2273; www.hotelsaofrancisco.tur.br; Floriano Peixoto 237; s/d from R$145/185;) Don't let the boxy exterior fool you: this 1960s-style hotel (considered an eyesore by some) has some of the nicest rooms around, with smooth parquet floors, large glass-encased showers, flat-screen TVs, minibars and private balconies. Thanks to its slight elevation over the river, most rooms also have lovely water views.

Eating & Drinking

Several supermarkets, sandwich kiosks and self-service eateries are on the main waterfront plaza; it's also a good place for a cold beer at night, when bars set up plastic tables on the cobblestones.

Oratório BRAZILIAN $$
(Beira Rio 301; mains R$12-28; ⌚10am-late) This casually elegant riverfront spot is popular throughout the day: come for a breakfast of coffee and fruit, lunch, or a dinner of grilled fish and marinated shrimp.

Forte da Rocheira BRAZILIAN $$
(☎3551-3273; Rocheira 2; mains R$22-48; ⌚11am-4pm daily, 6-10:30pm Fri & Sat) This former Dutch fortification has a splendid view out over the water. The location is slightly out of the way – just follow the signs, as the restaurant is well-advertised in town, and try to time your visit with sunset. Come for drinks and a simple seafood dinner.

Information

You'll find a **Bradesco bank** (Av Duque de Caixas 71) with an ATM on the riverfront. Other ATMs are located nearby, around the central square.

Getting There & Away

For transportation to Maceió and Aracaju, head to Penedo's small bus station, located a few blocks away along the river, behind the large supermarket.

For Maceió, bus options are the *expresso* (direct; R$22, 2½ hours, two daily) and the slower *pinga* (R$20, four hours, two daily), which stops at a number of small towns along the coast. Vans/minibuses also offer frequent service to Maceió (R$20). The same route provides access to Coruripe and Praia do Gunga.

Aguia Branca (www.aguiabranca.com.br) runs one daily bus to Salvador (R$85, ten hours). The company also runs a daily bus to Aracaju (R$16, three hours, one daily). Several informal Kombi vans and minibuses also make the trip each day: head to the bus station or Penedo's waterfront dock and bus stop to catch one.

Maragogi

☎0XX82 / POP 32,000

Maragogi is a small beach town with a cluster of pousadas and restaurants along its waterfront, old-fashioned sailboats bobbing in the sea, and wide, flat beaches where local kids play soccer every evening at sunset. Though these beaches aren't anything special, Maragogi is one of the most visited destinations in the state, thanks to its major draw: the sandbars and reefs that make up the **Galés marine reserve**, 6km offshore, where the underwater scene is rich with colorful sea life.

Activities

Many visitors visit the reserve on day trips from Maceió, but Maragogi is also a friendly destination to spend a night or two. Trips to the reserve (R$65) at low tide are easily organized through beachfront restaurants or hotels – the excursion is heavily advertised left and right. The helpful travel agency **Costazul** (☎3296-2125; www.costazulturismo.com.br; Francisco Holanda Cavalcante 6) can arrange this and other excursions, including day trips to Porto de Galinhas and Recife.

Sleeping & Eating

On the waterfront, smart-looking **Pousada Olho D'água** (☎3296-1263; www.pousadaolhodagua.com; Senador Rui Palmeira 94; d from R$300) offers a terrace overlooking the ocean, comfortable rooms with private balconies (some have views) and a lovely swimming pool. Another good-value option on the waterfront, **Pousada Mariluz** (☎3296-1511; www.pousadamariluz.com.br; Rua Sen Rui Palmeira 885; d from R$220; ❄) has small but cheerfully painted rooms, some with verandas facing the ocean. Note that you'll get a considerably lower price when traveling during the week or outside the high season.

Several seafood restaurants on the waterfront offer Bahian food, pizza, fresh juices and cocktails, plus relaxed outdoor seating on the beach. **Restaurante Frutas do Mar** (☎3296-1403; Senador Rui Palmeira 876; mains R$20-35; ⌚8am-10pm) is a locals' classic.

Information

Maragogi has a Banco do Brasil with an ATM. For more eating and sleeping options and additional tourist information (including a section in English), log onto www.maragogionline.com.br.

Getting There & Away

The quickest way to get to Maceió from Maragogi is by taxi *colectivo* (R$30, two hours). Go to Maragogi's main square and look for the taxi stand. Each taxi transports up to four passengers, so there's often a short delay while the driver waits for other travelers to show up. The trip takes just over two hours, thanks to the race-car-style drivers who weave in and out of traffic along the coastal roads.

DEF has four daily departures from the main square to Maceió (R$12.50, 3½ hours) and the beach villages south of Maragogi.

Travel agencies also provide private transfer, but as prices are generally exorbitant, consider it a last resort.

Pernambuco, Paraíba & Rio Grande do Norte

Includes ➡

Best Places to Eat

- ➡ Mesa da Ana (p511)
- ➡ Cruzeiro do Pescador (p528)
- ➡ Oficina do Sabor (p502)
- ➡ Camarões Potiguar (p521)
- ➡ Patuá (p502)

Best Places to Stay

- ➡ Toca da Coruja (p527)
- ➡ Pousada Ilha do Vento (p530)
- ➡ Spa da Alma (p527)
- ➡ Pousada Casa de Taipa (p530)
- ➡ Cama e Cafe Olinda (p499)

Why Go?

The nearly 1000km-long coastline edging the three states at Brazil's northeastern corner consists of one sandy, sunburnt beach after another, backed by dunes, palms or cliffs. It's dotted with villages and small towns that are just perfect for tasty meals, sunset drinks and chilling out in a homey pousada (guesthouse) – that's when you're not dipping, snorkeling, surfing, kitesurfing, windsurfing or diving in the delicious tropical waters. Or racing around the beaches and dunes with the wind in your hair on a beach-buggy ride.

The coast is home to four very different cities: gutsy, historic, cultural Recife; cute, artsy Olinda; appealingly revived João Pessoa; and the holiday playground of Natal. You'll never lack for urban vibes to spice up your beach idylls. What is arguably the continent's greatest aquatic treasure also lies 350km offshore: Fernando de Noronha, a tropical-island getaway unrivaled in South America for its world-class beaches, diving and scenery.

When to Go

Recife

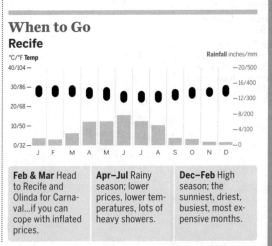

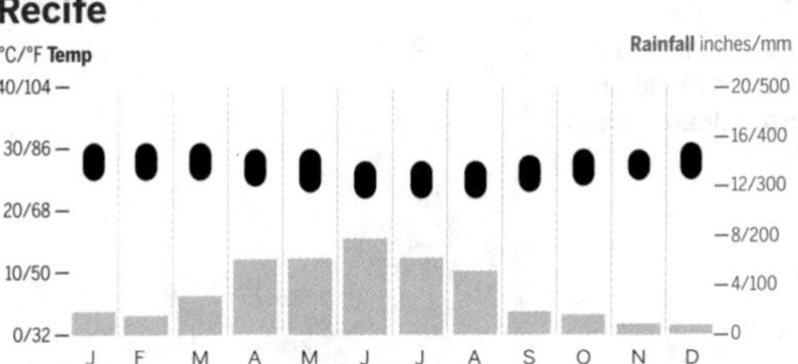

Feb & Mar Head to Recife and Olinda for Carnaval...if you can cope with inflated prices.

Apr–Jul Rainy season; lower prices, lower temperatures, lots of heavy showers.

Dec–Feb High season; the sunniest, driest, busiest, most expensive months.

Pernambuco, Paraíba & Rio Grande do Norte Highlights

1. Being stunned by the world-class beaches, scenery, diving and snorkeling at crowd-free **Fernando de Noronha** (p503).
2. Dancing in the streets and experiencing the unique culture of artsy **Olinda** (p498) during euphoric Carnaval.
3. Enjoying the stylish but unpretentious international beach scene of beautiful **Praia da Pipa** (p525).
4. Immersing yourself in the cultural, culinary and historical attractions of the region's best city, **Recife** (p487).
5. Digging your toes into sands less traveled at **São Miguel do Gostoso** (p529).
6. Feeling the wind in your hair on a beach-buggy ride from São Miguel do Gostoso to remote **Galinhos** (p530).
7. Taking in a stunning sunset to a saxophone rendition of *Bolero* in **João Pessoa** (p518).

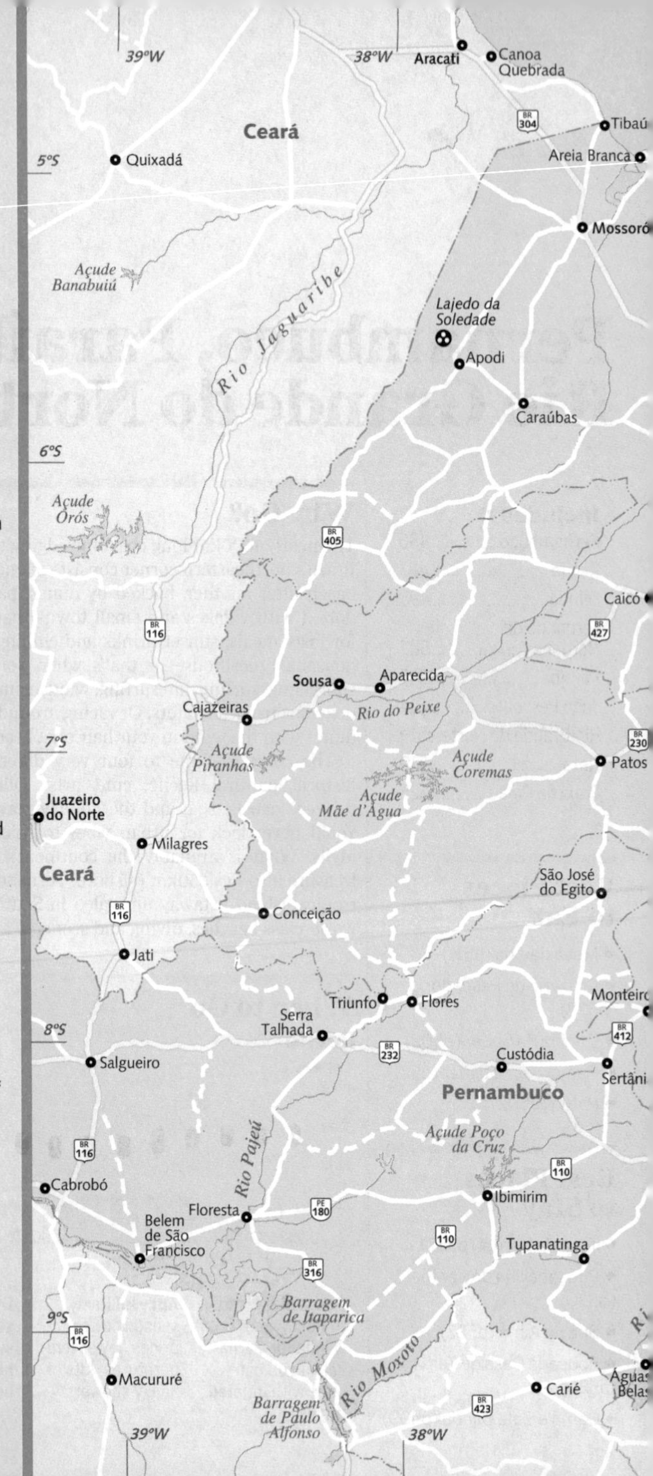

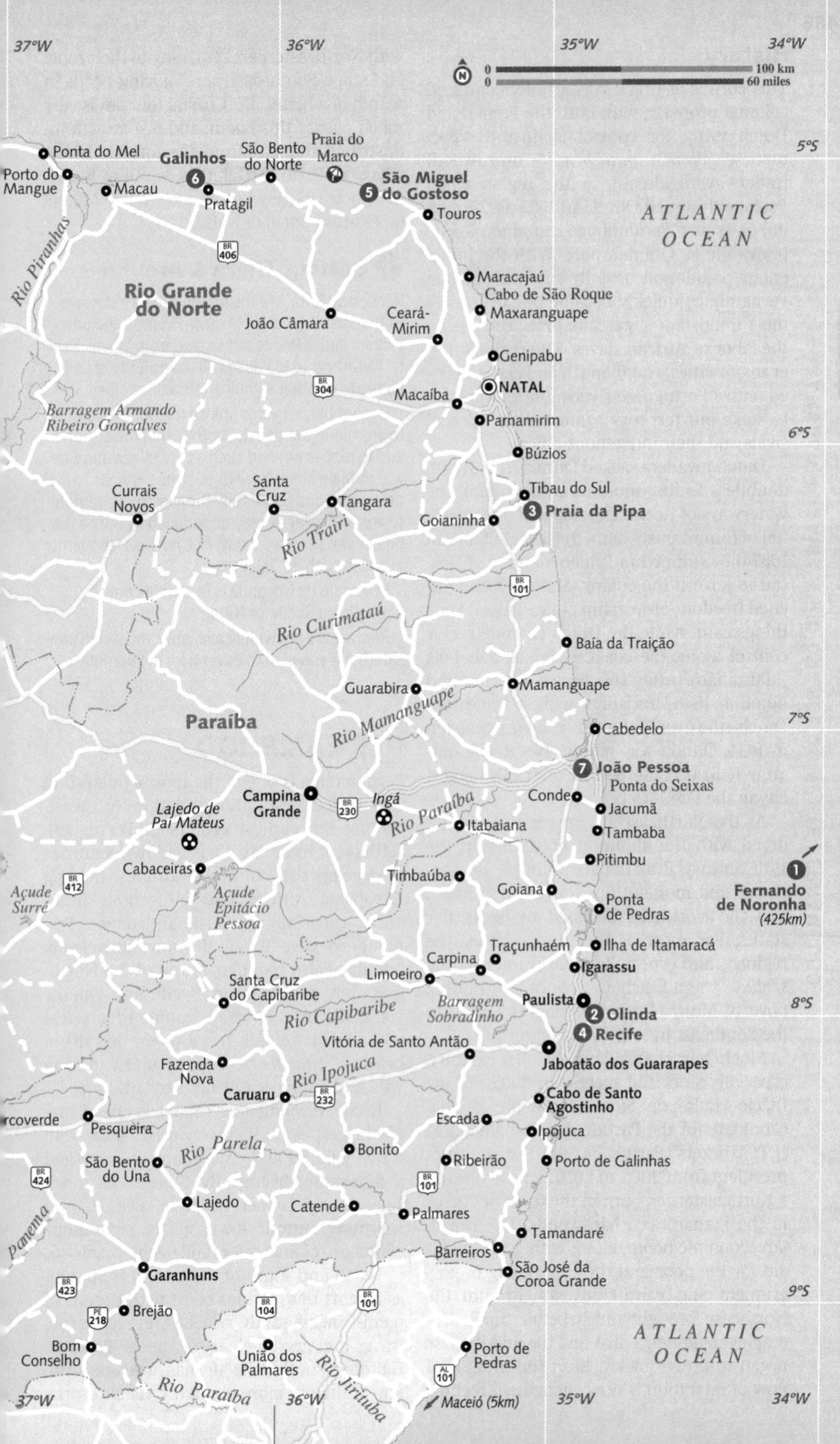

37°W
36°W
35°W
34°W
0 100 km
0 60 miles
5°S
6°S
7°S
8°S
9°S
ATLANTIC OCEAN
Ponta do Mel
Porto do Mangue
Macau
Galinhos
6
Pratagil
São Bento do Norte
Praia do Marco
5
São Miguel do Gostoso
Touros
Rio Piranhas
BR 406
Rio Grande do Norte
Maracajaú
Cabo de São Roque
Maxaranguape
João Câmara
Ceará-Mirim
Genipabu
BR 304
NATAL
Macaíba
Parnamirim
Barragem Armando Ribeiro Gonçalves
Búzios
Tibau do Sul
3
Praia da Pipa
Currais Novos
Santa Cruz
Tangara
Goianinha
Rio Trairi
BR 101
Rio Curimataú
Baía da Traição
Guarabira
Mamanguape
Rio Mamanguape
Paraíba
Cabedelo
7
João Pessoa
Ponta do Seixas
Conde
Jacumã
Campina Grande
BR 230
Ingá
Rio Paraíba
Itabaiana
Lajedo de Pai Mateus
Tambaba
Pitimbu
1
Fernando de Noronha
(425km)
Cabaceiras
BR 412
Açude Surré
Açude Epitácio Pessoa
Timbaúba
Goiana
Ponta de Pedras
Traçunhaém
Ilha de Itamaracá
Carpina
Igarassu
Limoeiro
Santa Cruz do Capibaribe
Barragem Sobradinho
Paulista
2
Olinda
Rio Capibaribe
4
Recife
Vitória de Santo Antão
Jaboatão dos Guararapes
Fazenda Nova
Rio Ipojuca
Caruaru
BR 232
Cabo de Santo Agostinho
rcoverde
Pesqueira
Escada
Ipojuca
Rio Parela
Bonito
São Bento do Una
Ribeirão
Porto de Galinhas
BR 424
BR 101
Lajedo
Catende
Palmares
panema
Tamandaré
Barreiros
Garanhuns
São José da Coroa Grande
BR 423
BR 101
PE 218
Brejão
BR 104
ATLANTIC OCEAN
Bom Conselho
União dos Palmares
Porto de Pedras
Rio Jiritubа
AL 101
Rio Paraíba
Maceió (5km)

History

This corner of Brazil was a hotly contested colonial property, with both the French and Dutch vying for control against the Portuguese. French *pau brazil* (brazilwood) traders were already in the region when Portugal founded Olinda in 1535 as the capital of its new Pernambuco captaincy. Recife began life as Olinda's port. With the indigenous population brutally subdued, coastal Pernambuco quickly became one of Brazil's most important sugarcane producers, using the labor of African slaves. The region's other major cities, Natal and João Pessoa, started out as Portuguese river-mouth forts built to stake out territory against their colonial rivals and their indigenous allies.

Dutch invaders sacked Olinda in 1631 but, doubtless feeling more at home among the waterways of Recife, developed it as the capital of (ambitiously named) New Holland. In 1637 they shipped in Prince Maurice of Nassau to govern the colony. Maurice's enlightened freedom-of-worship policy helped keep things calm while the Dutch extended their control along the coast as far as São Luís (Maranhão). After the prince was ordered home in 1644, uprisings against Protestant Dutch rule eventually led to their expulsion in 1654. Olinda was rebuilt, but Recife outgrew it to become South America's biggest city in the late 17th century.

As the Northeast's sugar economy floundered with the abolition of slavery in the 19th century, Brazil's balance of population, power and money tipped to the Southeast, and the Northeast declined to backwater status. For most of the 20th century the region – and especially its arid interior, the *sertão* – was a Brazilian byword for grinding poverty. Many Northeasterners migrated to the Southeast in search of a better life.

Much has changed in the 21st century, especially since the success in 2002 of Luíz Inácio (Lula) da Silva as the presidential candidate for the Partido dos Trabalhadores (PT; Workers' Party); he was the country's president from 2003 to 2010. Lula is himself a Northeasterner, born in the town of Caetés in the Pernambuco backwoods. The Brazilian economic boom, along with government aid for the poor and the channeling of government and private investment into the Northeast, brought much better times. Unemployment took a dive, and the middle class began to grow quickly. Even the traditional flow of migration is now changing direction, with Northeasterners returning to their roots and some Southeasterners moving north in search of a better life. Coastal tourism is very much part of this boom, and is a growth industry all the way from the former fishing village of Porto de Galinhas, south of Recife, to remote (for now) spots such as São Miguel do Gostoso north of Natal.

ℹ Getting There & Around

Recife and Natal are the region's main gateways. Both receive direct flights from Europe, including Lisbon, and in Recife's case also from Miami. Recife, Natal and João Pessoa all have plenty of daily flights from other significant Brazilian cities.

Decent bus services link all major cities and towns along the coasts, both within the region and to places beyond such as Fortaleza and Salvador. Main cities have direct bus services to Rio de Janeiro and São Paulo. Smaller, more remote towns and villages may be reached by only a few bus or van services a day, or even less frequently in cases such as Galinhos.

Fernando de Noronha is reachable only by flights from Recife or Natal.

Rental cars are widely available and worth considering if you plan to cover a lot of kilometers.

PERNAMBUCO

Pernambuco is one of the most exhilarating and varied destinations in the Northeast. Among the earliest centers of Portuguese settlement in Brazil, it has had five centuries to develop rich cultural traditions melding European, African and indigenous influences, especially in music and dance. Pernambuco gave Brazil the now universally popular *forró* (popular music of the Northeast) but, especially in Recife and Olinda, you'll discover a whole gamut of musical styles from frenetic *frevo* to the big drum beats of *maracatu* – particularly during wild and euphoric Carnaval celebrations.

Recife, Pernambuco's capital, is one of Brazil's biggest cities; it's a very urban place with a rich cultural and entertainment scene and a fascinating history. By contrast its much smaller and calmer neighbor, Olinda, is a charming, historic town, full of picturesque churches, colonial colors and talented artisans.

North and south of these centers stretches a short but glorious coast with dozens of palm-fringed sandy beaches, great surfing waves and crystal-clear reef pools. Porto de Galinhas, south of Recife, has developed into one of Brazil's more popular coastal resorts;

nearby Tamandaré is a mellower spot for a more relaxed beach stay.

But Pernambuco's most glittering gem sits more than 500km out into the Atlantic. The archipelago of Fernando de Noronha is a tropical-island getaway to dream about, a fervently protected aquatic Eden with near-empty, postcard-perfect beaches, surrounded by warm, brilliantly clear waters with world-class diving. It is probably Brazil's most awed destination.

Recife

☎081 / POP 1.5 MILLION (METROPOLITAN AREA 3.7 MILLION)

Recife (heh-*see*-fee), capital of Pernambuco, is one of the Northeast's most exciting cities. It has a vibrant cultural, entertainment and restaurant scene, an intriguing historic center (Recife Antigo), an impressive coastal setting and a fabulous Carnaval. It's a sprawling, urban place of glassy high-rises, crowded commercial areas, thundering traffic and extensive suburbs; if you like your cities gutsy, gritty and proud, Recife is for you. It takes its name from the offshore *recifes* (reefs) that calm the waters of its ports and shoreline.

The charming and far more tranquil historic town of Olinda lies on Recife's northern edge, just 6km from the city center, and many visitors opt to stay in Olinda and visit Recife during the day, or venture into Recife for its animated nightlife.

Sights

Recife Antigo

The narrow streets of Recife Antigo (also called the Bairro do Recife), where the city began, have been revitalized in recent years and the area is well worth a slice of your time.

★Paço do Frevo ARTS CENTER
(Map p488; www.pacodofrevo.org.br; Praça do Arsenal; admission R$6; ⏲9am-6pm Tue, Wed & Fri, to 7pm Thu, noon-7pm Sat & Sun) This new, strikingly red museum is a small and modern house of worship for *frevo,* the quintessential dance of the Recife Carnaval. It hosts exhibits, performances and classes of *frevo,* and highlights include a permanent top-floor exhibit that features giant Carnaval insignias from Recife's famous *blocos* (drumming and dancing processions), encased in glass on the floor. Signage is bilingual.

Museu Cais do Sertão MUSEUM
(Map p488; www.facebook.com/caisdosertao; Av Alfredo Lisboa; admission R$10; ⏲11am-5pm Tue-Sun) Inaugurated in 2014, this bold new museum highlights the culture of the *sertão* (the interior of Pernambuco state), especially as it relates to the godfather of *forró* music, Luiz Gonzaga (p503), who was a major player not only in bringing the music of the region to national prominence but the culture as well.

The museum is divided into seven spaces (Live, Occupy, Migrate, Believe, Sing, Create and Work) and includes re-creations of a typical home; interactive, digital and audiovisual exhibits; a karaoke and mixing room; and, most popular, an instrument room, where you can try your hand at a unwieldy accordion.

Sinagoga Kahal Zur Israel CULTURAL CENTER
(Map p488; www.kahalzurisrael.com; Rua do Bom Jesus 197; admission R$10; ⏲9am-4:30pm Tue-Fri, 2-5:30pm Sun) The oldest synagogue in the Americas, Sinagoga Kahal Zur Israel is now a Jewish cultural center and has interesting murals (in Portuguese and English) depicting the role of Jews in Recife's development.

Embaixada dos Bonecos Gigantes MUSEUM
(Map p488; ☎3441-5102; www.bonecosgigantesdeolinda.com.br; Rua do Bom Jesus 183; admission R$10; ⏲8am-6pm) Displays some of the giant puppets that feature in the Olinda Carnaval.

Marco Zero PLAZA
(Map p488; Praça Rio Branco) The Marco Zero, a small 'Km 0' marker in the middle of the broad waterside Praça Rio Branco, marks the place where the Portuguese founded Recife in 1537. It has given its name, unofficially, to the square and its immediate surrounds.

Santo Antônio

This district encompasses both the formal **Praça da República** (Map p488), surrounded by imposing 19th-century governmental buildings, at its northern end and a bustling commercial area further south, where the streets are lined with shops, stalls, fine facades and colonial churches in assorted states of preservation.

Capela Dourada CHAPEL
(Golden Chapel; Map p488; www.capeladourada.com.br; Rua do Imperador s/n; admission R$3; ⏲8-11:30am & 2-5pm Mon-Fri, 8-11:30am Sat) Built between 1696 and 1724, this gem of Brazilian baroque, part of the Convento de Santo Antônio, owes its name to the huge

Central Recife

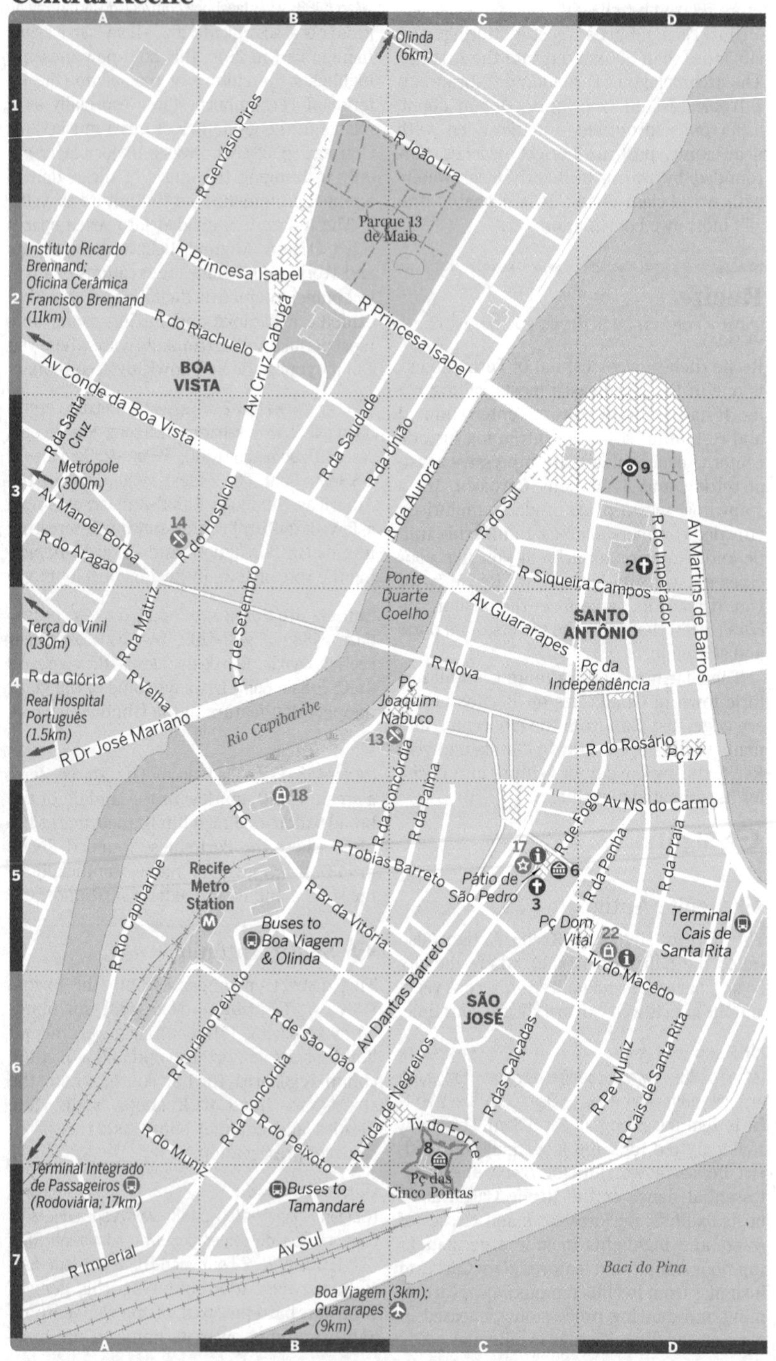

Central Recife

Top Sights

1 Paço do Frevo.......F3

Sights

2 Capela Dourada.......D3
3 Concatedral de São Pedro dos Clérigos.......C5
4 Embaixada dos Bonecos Gigantes.......F3
5 Marco Zero.......F4
6 Memorial Chico Science.......C5
7 Museu Cais do Sertão.......F3
8 Museu da Cidade do Recife.......C6
Pátio de São Pedro.......(see 6)
9 Praça da República.......D3
10 Sinagoga Kahal Zur Israel.......F3

Sleeping

11 Azul Fusca Hostel.......E4

Eating

12 Bistrô & Boteco.......F3
13 Restaurante Leite.......C4
14 Salada Mista.......A3

Drinking & Nightlife

15 Armazéns do Porto.......F4
16 Burburinho.......E4

Entertainment

17 Terça Negra.......C5

Shopping

18 Casa da Cultura.......B5
19 Centro de Artesanato de Pernambuco.......F3
20 Feirinha do Recife Antigo.......F3
21 Livraria Cultura.......E4
22 Mercado de São José.......D5

quantities of gold covering its elaborately sculpted walls, altars and ceiling.

Pátio de São Pedro SQUARE

(Map p488) This traffic-free square, lined with bars, restaurants and colorful 19th-century houses, is one of Santo Antônio's more peaceful spots and a good place to stop for a drink.

The 18th-century baroque **Concatedral de São Pedro dos Clérigos** (Map p488; Pátio de São Pedro; 8am-noon & 2-5pm Mon-Fri) – closed for long-term restoration on our visit – contains incredibly fine wood carvings, while the **Memorial Chico Science** (Map p488; 3355-3158; www.recife.pe.gov.br/chicoscience; Pátio de São Pedro 21; 9am-5pm Mon-Fri) FREE highlights the revered founder of the *mangue beat* musical movement, who died tragically in a Recife car accident in 1997.

Museu da Cidade do Recife MUSEUM, FORT
(Map p488; www.recife.pe.gov.br/cultura/museucidade.php; Praça das Cinco Pontas; ⌚9am-5pm Tue-Sat) FREE Recife's City Museum is housed in the Forte das Cinco Pontas (Five-Pointed Fort), built by the Dutch in 1630. It exhibits old maps and historic photos, but could be so much more interesting given Recife's fascinating history.

Brennand Workshop & Institute

The ceramics 'workshop' of Francisco Brennand and the art institute of his cousin Ricardo constitute a regional highlight; it's well worth setting aside half a day for the trip out to Várzea, on Recife's western edge, to see them. The only times both places are open simultaneously are Tuesday to Sunday afternoons.

They're best reached by taxi from Boa Viagem (R$200 or so). An economic route to the museums is to catch a CDU/Caxangá bus (R$2.45) from Boa Viagem to the end of its route on Rua Acadêmico Hélio Ramos, then a taxi round-trip from the bus stop to both Oficina Cerâmica Francisco Brennand and Instituto Ricardo Brennand (around 10km in total) for around R$80 to R$100.

★Oficina Cerâmica Francisco Brennand MUSEUM
(☎3271-2466; www.brennand.com.br; Várzea; admission R$10; ⌚8am-5pm Mon-Thu, to 4pm Fri, 10am-4pm Sat & Sun) Francisco Brennand, born in 1927 into an Irish immigrant family and now considered Brazil's greatest ceramicist, revitalized his family's abandoned tile factory to create his own line of decorative ceramic tiles. The expansive indoor and outdoor space in Várzea, 11km west of central Recife, is now mostly dedicated to his enormous and fascinating oeuvre, which ranges across painting, tile work and hundreds of highly original sculptures.

The grounds, set amid thick Atlantic rainforest, include a couple of temples, Moorish arches and all sorts of surreal sculptures, including rows of contorted busts and a garden of bizarre sexualized earthworms.

Instituto Ricardo Brennand MUSEUM
(☎2121-0352; www.institutoricardobrennand.org.br; Alameda Antônio Brennand, Várzea; adult/child R$20/10; ⌚1-5pm Tue-Sun) The scenic Instituto, located in Várzea, 11km west of central Recife, contains a massive collection of European and Brazilian art, swords, armor and historical artifacts, all set in a fake medieval castle on lovely grounds. It's best reached by taxi from Boa Viagem (R$200 or so) in combination with a visit to Oficina Cerâmica Francisco Brennand (p490).

An economic route to the museum is to catch a CDU/Caxangá bus (R$2.45) from Boa Viagem to the end of its route on Rua Acadêmico Hélio Ramos, then a taxi round-trip from the bus stop to both here and Oficina Cerâmica Francisco Brennand (around 10km in total) for around R$80 to R$100.

Festivals & Events

The Recife **Carnaval** (www.carnavalrecife.com) is a hard-to-believe explosion of color, costume, crowds, alcohol, fabulous music and dancing, and infectious happiness that adds up to one of Brazil's most euphoric and folkloric festivals. It has its claims to being the best Carnaval in the country, despite attracting far fewer tourists than Salvador's or Rio's. While there are many hundreds of music and dance events held on stages around the city, Carnaval is essentially a participatory event: people don't just sit and watch; they don elaborate costumes and dance for days to Brazilian rhythms, and especially to Recife's very own, frenetic *frevo*.

Galo da Madrugada (Cock of the Morning), which is claimed, probably correctly, to be the largest Carnaval *bloco* in the world, erects a giant cock on the Ponte Duarte Coelho and pulls more than a million people into central Recife for its parade on Carnaval Saturday morning, starting around 8am. Carnaval activity focuses around a number of *polos* (poles) dotted about the city. Recife Antigo (especially Marco Zero, Praça do Arsenal and the Paço Alfândega) and the Pátio de São Pedro are among the best areas to head for.

Carnaval in Olinda is so close that you could participate in both on the same day, and there is a lot of crossover in the events. Accommodations in both cities hike prices mercilessly and may demand three- to five-night minimum stays; some get booked up months, even a year, in advance.

Sleeping

Travelers have traditionally gravitated toward the high-rise, middle-class, beach suburb of Boa Viagem, which has the best range of accommodations and restaurants. It begins 3km south of the center and extends about 5km along the coast. The city center has limited and poor options, but at least one new hostel is making that choice more interesting these days.

Recife Antigo

Azul Fusca Hostel HOSTEL $
(Map p488; ☎3023-5007; www.azulfuscahostel.com; Mariz e Barros 328; dm weekend/weekday R$50/45;) The 'Blue Beetle' (as in Volkswagen Beetle) is an intriguing new hostel mere steps from Marco Zero. All spartan chic and minimalist steel, it offers two sparse 12-bed dorms and a design-forward common area full of mid-century modern furniture and top-end kitchen appliances. If you have just one day to take in Recife Antigo's cultural attractions, stay here.

Boa Viagem

Albergue Piratas da Praia HOSTEL $
(Map p492; ☎3326-1281; www.piratasdapraia.com; Av Conselheiro Aguiar 2034; dm with air-con R$53-59, r R$149;) You'd never know it was here, but this friendly, highly colorful hostel occupies the 3rd floor of a building named Edifício Barão de Camaçari (and is entered from Rua Osias Ribeiro). It's a bit like staying in a friend's apartment, as it has a good clean kitchen and wonderfully colorful common areas. The lone private room nets a hammock as well.

Cosmopolitan Hostel HOSTEL $
(Map p492; ☎3204-0321; www.cosmopolitanhostel.com; Paulo Setúbal 53; dm/s/d/tr from R$43/130/140/180;) This bright, welcoming hostel in a converted family home on a quiet residential street is the best budget bet for ambience, space and location. Private rooms and six- or seven-bed dorms (one is women-only) are set around a courtyard with mango and *acerola* (acidic, cherry-flavored fruit) trees. Amiable bilingual owner Filipe is a fount of local information, and a small family of fluffy rabbits adds to the homey feel.

★ **Pousada Casuarinas** POUSADA $$
(Map p492; ☎3325-4708; www.pousadacasuarinas.com.br; Antônio Pedro Figueiredo 151; s/d/tr R$140/160/190, with veranda R$150/170/200;) A tranquil former family home run by two sisters (who speak English, Italian and German), Casuarinas is a marvelous retreat from the heat and bustle outside. Spotless rooms are set around a shady courtyard, where regional folk art and knickknacks spice up the decor. Recife's best-value stay, bar none!

Pousada Vitória POUSADA $$
(☎3462-6446; www.pousadavitoriarecife.com.br; Capitão Zuzinha 234; s/d/tr R$150/170/235;) Aside from having more color and character than any other place in this price range, this cute 30-room pousada is a mere 1.5km from the airport, perfectly located for those just passing through. If available, staff will pick you up for free if you land between 6am and 6pm.

Vivaz Boutique Hotel BOUTIQUE HOTEL $$
(☎3097-7332; www.vivazboutiquehotel.com.br; Capitão Rebelinho 374, Pina; s/d from R$155/160;) On a restaurant-heavy street one block from the beach in Pina, Recife's first boutique hotel (call it economic-boutique, anyway) offers a marriage of whitewashed halls, vaguely Victorian-chic design motifs and low-lit charm at night. It's worth upgrading to the R$175 rooms for considerably more space. Some of the themed rooms look onto small urban gardens.

Cult Hotel/Hostel Design HOTEL $$
(☎2123-2777; www.culthostel.com.br; Av Conselheiro Aguiar 755; dm/s/d R$55/165/189;) Rooms are functional, clean and comfy; the staff is helpful; and the breakfast is ample at this dual hotel/hostel. But what's special here is the art and displays on Pernambuco culture and history that adorn the entire hotel. The hostel side offers the city's best dorm infrastructure, though clocking in at 12-, 18-, and 22-bed configurations, expect a crowd.

Eating

Recife has great places to eat, ranging from cheerful and bustling to refined establishments comparable with the country's finest.

Armazéns do Porto (Map p488; www.facebook.com/armazensdoporto; Av Alfredo Lisboa, Recife Antigo; ⏰10am-late) is a new drinking and dining complex next to Marco Zero; it's part of a larger, ongoing port revival complex, housing several bars and restaurants that come alive at night. Don't miss the nightly Northeastern food and artisan fair at Praça de Boa Viagem.

Central Recife

Salada Mista BUFFET $
(Map p488; Rua do Hospício 59, Boa Vista; per kg R$31.99; ⏰10:30am-8pm Mon-Fri, to 4pm Sat) One of the best of many *por kilo* (per

Boa Viagem

Boa Viagem

Sleeping

Eating

Drinking & Nightlife

kilogram) eateries in the center, Salada Mista has a big range of salad options in a clean and comfortable setting.

Bistrô & Boteco BRAZILIAN **$$**
(Map p488; www.facebook.com/bistroboteco recifeantigo; Av Alfredo Lisboa s/n, Recife Antigo; mains R$26-48, buffet lunch R$42, per kg R$59; ⏲11:30am-1am, to 6pm Sun) Bistrô & Boteco's grills, shrimp and salads are enhanced by its superb harbor views. The *prime rib de leitão* (suckling pig ribs) comes with a *rodízio* (smorgasbord) of vegetable accompaniments offered by waiters circulating from table to table. During the week, there's an expansive *por kilo* buffet, which turns all-you-can-eat on weekends.

Restaurante Leite BRAZILIAN **$$$**
(Map p488; ☎3224-7977; www.restauranteleite.com.br; Praça Joaquim Nabuco 147, Santo Antônio; mains R$53-96; ⏲11am-4pm Mon-Fri; 📶) One of the oldest restaurants in Brazil, this traditional lunch place was opened in 1882. Though modernized these days and void of much historical air, it remains a power-lunch favorite of politicos and businesspeople. If you're feeling spendy, this is old-school refined dining at its most classic: tables and waiters draped in white, accompanied by piano music. Reservations? Probably.

Boa Viagem

Bercy Village CREPERIE **$**
(Map p492; www.bercyvillage.com.br; Rui Batista 120; crepes R$19-29; ⏲6pm-midnight Mon-Thu, to 12:30am Fri & Sat, 5:30-11:30pm Sun; 📶🍷) Atmospheric Bercy Village serves up good-value savory and sweet crepes, and fab salads and sandwiches in a cool, semi-outdoor ambience that's pretty classy for a creperie. Perpignan (with filet mignon, gorgonzola

and raisins) and Champagne (with shrimp and Gruyère cheese) are big hits.

Mooo BURGERS $

(Av Domingoes Ferreira 4236, Loja B; burgers R$26-29; 6pm-midnight;) Brazil's gourmet burger revolution has spread countrywide and this is Recife's trendy entry into the fray. The burgers are great – try the Sertão option with *carne de sol* (a tasty, salted meat) and *coalho* cheese if you want to go local – but the onion rings may just outshine them. There are several options of fries (including poutine) and decent imported beers too.

Bring your vegetarian friends; there's a whole separate menu for them, including veggie, shitake and falafel burgers etc).

★Chica Pitanga BUFFET $$

(www.chicapitanga.com.br; Petrolina 19; per kg lunch weekday/weekend R$65.70/72.30, dinner R$57.80; 11:30am-3:30pm & 6-10pm Mon-Fri, 11:30am-4pm & 6-10pm Sat & Sun;) As near as *por kilos* restaurants can get to a gourmet experience, Chica Pitanga offers a changing array of diverse dishes every day. The dozen or so salad options might, for example, include tabbouleh or mango salad, while duck rice or shrimp in spinach sauce might appear among the hot dishes. Most dangerous pay-by-weight restaurant in Brazil!

Lighter regional dishes are served in the evenings. Cash and Visa only.

★Camarada Camarão SEAFOOD $$

(Map p492; 3325-1786; www.ocamarada.com.br; Baltazar Pereira 130; mains for 2 people R$73-180; noon-11pm Mon-Thu, to midnight Fri & Sat, to 10pm Sun;) Airy, bustling Camarada does shrimp in endlessly creative ways – think shimp fondue, salads, marinated in beer and served in *moquecas* (stews) – but it's also wildly popular for happy hour, when patrons flood the front deck with ice-cold draft beers in hand. The shrimp and lobster *moqueca* and *bobó de camarão* (shrimp in manioc sauce) are extraordinary.

If your appetite and budget are on the smaller side, try the delicious antipasto Camarada (R$35); otherwise prepare to go to war for a one-person portion of most dishes.

Parraxaxá BUFFET $$

(www.parraxaxa.com.br; Av Fernando Simões Barbosa 1200; per kg lunch weekday/weekend R$55.69/66.09, dinner R$55.09; 11:30am-11pm;) Festive decor and staff dressed in police and outlaw outfits spice up your meal at this fun Northeast-themed restaurant. The self-serve food is a cornucopia of tasty Northeastern dishes: *carne de sol, macaxeira* (cassava root), *baião de dois* (a spicy rice, beans and cheese dish) and grilled meats. There are good salads too.

Drinking & Nightlife

Recife is justly proud of its nightlife and the variety of music that can be found in the city. You can discover somewhere exciting to go every night of the week. Many venues are in Boa Viagem, but the streets behind Recife Antigo's Paço Alfândega also have lively bars. Tourist offices hand out useful entertainment guides, and several websites provide good listings, including Acontece no Recife (www.acontecenorecife.com.br/interna.asp?secao=2; in English, Spanish and Portuguese).

Recife has the largest gay scene in the Northeast, especially concentrated in the city-center neighborhoods of Boa Vista and Boa Viagem (on Praia de Boa Viagem in front of Edificio Portugal and Edificio Acaiaca). Track down a bilingual Guia Gay Recife (www.guiagayrecife.com.br) for GLS (Gays, Lesbians e Simpatizantes) listings.

Central Recife

Burburinho BOTECO

(Map p488; www.facebook.com/barburburinho; Tomazina 106, Recife Antigo; 11:30am-midnight Mon & Wed, to 6pm Tue, to 1am Thu, to 3am Fri, 6pm-4am Sat) Frequented by students, journalists and a generally bohemian crowd, Burburinho is nicer inside than it appears and usually has live music at least three times weekly – recently, blues/jazz and soul sessions on Thursdays and rock on Fridays and Saturdays. DJs spin eclectic vinyl on Monday nights.

It's a good spot for cheap daily lunch specials (from R$15 to R$20) of regional dishes; try the Northeastern version of *caçulé* (cassoulet) on Thursdays.

Metrópole GAY

(3423-0123; www.clubemetropole.com.br; Rua das Nínfas 125, Boa Vista; 10pm-6am Fri & Sat) Recife's best gay (and GLS) club has multiple spaces, from its main DJ-ruled 'NY Street' dance area to an outdoor area with a swimming pool. There are frequent theme parties and live shows by big-name artists.

Boa Viagem

Companhia do Chope BOTECO

(Map p492; www.chopperiacompanhia.com.br; Av Conselheiro Aguiar 2775; bar food R$33.50-84.50, chope R$5.35-9.30; 5pm-midnight Mon-Thu, 10am-12:30am Fri & Sat, 10am-midnight Sun;) Swarming with interesting people since 1984, this rambunctious *boteco* (small open-air bar) fills a breezy open-air shopping plaza in Boa Viagem. Some of Recife's best shared bar food (just try to resist those *coxinhas* – cornmeal balls filled with chicken – and *empadas* – little meat-filled pies) and coldest *chope* (draft beer) is delivered by nimble waiters as the easy-on-the-eyes crowd flirts its way through the evening.

Haus Lajetop & Beergarden BAR

(www.facebook.com/haaaaausbar; Av Herculano Bandeira 513, Galeria Joana D'Arc, Pina; cocktails R$10-22; 6pm-midnight Sun-Wed, to 2am Thu-Sat;) Tucked away in the back of the artsy Galeria Joana D'Arc, this boxy new bar and beer garden gets the balance right: a smart, industrial-chic atmosphere marrying unfinished concrete walls with reclaimed wooden doors and shutters on the ceiling; cool tunes; and an extensive cocktail, beer and wine list that is perfect for washing down the worldly bar eats. It's just north of and walkable from Boa Viagem.

Guaiamum Gigante BAR

(Map p492; www.grupoguaiamumgigante.com.br; Av Boa Viagem, 2A Jardim, Boa Viagem; 11:30am-midnight Mon-Wed, to 2am Thu-Sat, to 11pm Sun) An upscale, beach-facing *boteco* that is packed every night. The breezy outdoor patio serves as a decadent drinking den, and you can also sample tasty seafood (dishes for two cost from R$65 to R$110).

UK Pub LOUNGE

(Map p492; 3465-1088; www.ukpub.com.br; Francisco da Cunha 165, Boa Viagem; admission R$40-50; 11pm-6am Fri-Sun) UK Pub is a sophisticated lounge that draws a sexy Anglophile crowd for proper pints (Guinness, Old Speckled Hen and Newcastle are around R$35 a pint) plus varied live bands and DJs. Take your passport for ID.

Entertainment

Terça do Vinil LIVE MUSIC

(Largo do Santa Cruz, Boa Vista; 7pm-midnight) DJ's spin Música Popular Brasileira (MPB) on vinyl at this popular outdoor concert held every Tuesday night at Largo do Santa Cruz.

Terça Negra LIVE MUSIC

(Black Tuesday; Map p488; www.facebook.com/tercanegrarecife; Pátio de São Pedro; 8pm-1am Tue) This great free night of Afro-Brazilian rhythms takes place in the picturesque Pátio de São Pedro two Tuesdays a month. Check with the C.A.T (p496) info centre on the square or the Terça Negra Facebook page for scheduling.

Arena Pernambuco FOOTBALL

(3319-1919; www.itaipavaarenapernambuco.com.br; Av Deus É Fiel; tours R$20) Recifenses (residents of Recife) are passionate about their football, even though the most successful teams, Sport and Náutico, both have a history of yo-yoing between the national Série A and Série B. Náutico plays at the 46,000-seat Arena Pernambuco, a stadium built for the 2014 World Cup, 20km west of the city center in São Lourenço da Mata. Bilingual tours run hourly from 10am to 4pm.

Shopping

Centro de Artesanato de Pernambuco HANDICRAFTS

(Map p488; www.artesanatodepernambuco.pe.gov.br; Praça Rio Branco; 8am-6pm Mon-Sat, 9am-5pm Sun) Displays and sells the best of Pernambuco crafts in wood, ceramics, lace, lithographs and other media.

Mercado de São José MARKET

(Map p488; Praça Dom Vital, São José; 6am-5pm Mon-Sat, to noon Sun) As well as traditional Pernambuco handicrafts, such as lace and leather goods, palm baskets and clay figurines, this bustling city-center market sells all manner of food, and stocks shelves of medicinal herbs.

Casa da Cultura HANDICRAFTS

(Map p488; Floriano Peixoto, Santo Antônio; 9am-6pm Mon-Fri, to 5pm Sat, to 2pm Sun) An excellent source of Pernambuco crafts, and stocks a lot of T-shirts. The Casa da Cultura occupies a creepy colonial-era prison where prisoners languished until 1973.

Feirinha do Recife Antigo ARTS, CRAFTS

(Map p488; Rua do Bom Jesus; 2-10pm Sun) This interesting street market specializing in high-class artisanry, such as dresses, jewelry and ceramics, brings Recife Antigo to life on Sunday afternoons. Nearby bars open and there's often live music. On the last Sunday of the month, there are extras such as performances and kids activities.

MUSIC OF RECIFE & OLINDA

In Recife and Olinda you'll hear plenty of that very popular, typically Northeastern country music known as *forró*. You'll also come across music from further south in Brazil, such as samba, *pagode* and *choro*. But Pernambuco state, and these two cities in particular, is an exciting music-and-dance world of its own; it's home to some wonderful original genres, mostly bound up with Carnaval, featuring fabulously exotic costumes and fast-paced, mostly percussion-heavy music.

Top of the list has to be *frevo*, a feverishly fast brass-and-percussion music that inspires feverishly energetic dancing. Dancers sport supercolorful shiny costumes and twirl equally colorful mini-umbrellas. The origins of *frevo* are thought to lie in the marching-band music of Carnaval in 19th-century Recife and the capoeira movements of those who cleared the way for the bands. The umbrellas are today's equivalent of the capoeiristas' sticks or knives.

Maracatu nação (also called *maracatu de baque virado*) involves large African-style drum ensembles with dancers dressed as baroque-era Portuguese courtiers – an odd juxtaposition that derives from investiture ceremonies for leaders of the African slave community. *Maracatu rural* (or *maracatu de baque solto*) is rooted in similarly heavy drum rhythms, with dancers representing a melange of characters from animals to *baianas* (women dressed as Bahian 'aunts' in full skirts and turbans) and spectacular *caboclos de lança* (spear-carrying guards with enormous beehivelike headdresses of brilliantly colored tassles).

Then there's *caboclinho*, which has roots in the rituals of Brazil's indigenous groups. A set of characters, from kings and queens to witch doctors and the *caboclinhos* themselves (*índio*–Euro mixed-race characters wearing fantastic feathered headdresses), dance energetically to the *pífano* flute, maracas and big drums.

Pernambuco is also one of the homes of *afoxé*, an Afro-Brazilian music-and-dance genre based on the rhythms and spirit of Candomblé.

A more recent Recife contribution to Brazilian music is *mangue beat*, which emerged in the 1990s among young bands who combined traditional forms such as *maracatu* with electrified instruments and rhythms of rap, hip-hop and electronica. They did a lot to connect the younger generation with the traditions of their ancestors. Leader of the genre was singer Chico Science and his group Nação Zumbi, whose iconic 1996 album *Afrociberdelia* summed up the *mangue* movement as neatly as one word can. Science died in a car crash in 1997 and is still much mourned: Nação Zumbi plays on.

Livraria Cultura BOOKS, MUSIC
(Map p488; www.livrariacultura.com.br; Rua da Alfândega; 10am-10pm Mon-Sat, noon-9pm Sun) Probably the best bookstore north of Salvador, with a big English-language selection, including Lonely Planet guides, plus music and movies.

Information

DANGERS & ANNOYANCES

Surfing is prohibited at Praia Boa Viagem due to the danger of shark attacks. Swimmers there are advised to stay out of the water at high tide and not to go beyond the reef at any time. Since 1990 at least 31 shark attacks have been recorded along Recife's shores, most of them at Boa Viagem or the next beach south, Piedade.

Although crime levels have fallen significantly in recent years, Recife still has one of Brazil's highest murder rates. Tourists are more at risk from pickpockets and bag snatchers: stay alert to your surroundings and the people around you, and don't walk down unlit streets at night. Boa Viagem is arguably safer than the city center, though crime is an issue there, too.

EMERGENCY

Delegacia do Turista (Tourist Police; 3322-4867; www.policiacivil.pe.gov.br; Guararapes International Airport, Arrivals Hall; 24hr) Recife's tourist police is (perhaps unhelpfully) located in the airport only, down a hallway to the left of Luck Receptivo.

MEDICAL SERVICES

Real Hospital Português (3416-1122; www.rhp.com.br; Av Agamenon Magalhães 4760; 24hr) Modern 24-hour private hospital; its smaller clinic (3416-1800; www.rhp.com.br; Av Conselheiro Aguiar 2502, Boa Viagem) in Boa Viagem also offers 24-hour emergency service.

MONEY

Banco do Brasil (Av Dantas Barreto 541, Santo Antônio; ⏲ branch 10am-4pm Mon-Fri, ATMs 6am-10pm daily) Visa/Mastercard ATM in Santo Antônio.

Bradesco (Av Conselheiro Aguíar 3256, Boa Viagem) Visa/Mastercard ATM in Boa Viagem.

Bradesco (Av Marquês de Olinda 136, Recife Antigo) Visa/Mastercard ATM in Recife Antigo.

POST

Correios (Map p492; www2.correios.com.br; Hipermercado Extra, Av Domingos Ferreira 1818, Boa Viagem; ⏲ 8:30am-6pm Mon-Fri, 8am-noon Sat) Postal services.

TOURIST INFORMATION

Most Recife tourist offices, known as Centro de Atendimento ao Turista (C.A.T), have helpful, professional English-speaking staff and can provide good city maps.

C.A.T (Centro de Atendimento ao Turista; www.turismonorecife.com.br) Branches at the bus station (☎3182-8298; Rodoviária; ⏲7am-7pm), Guararapes International Airport (☎3182-8299; Arrivals Hall; ⏲24hr), Mercado de São José (Map p488; ☎3355-3022; ⏲6am-5pm Mon-Fri, to noon Sun), Patio de São Pedro (Map p488; ☎3355-3311; Santo Antônio; ⏲9am-6pm Mon-Fri), Praça da Boa Viagem (☎3182-8297; ⏲8am-8pm), and Praça do Arsenal (Map p488; ☎3355-3402; Rua da Guia s/n; ⏲8am-8pm). Do not confuse the airport C.A.T location with the smaller Jaboatão dos Guararapes, a separate municipality, whose tourist information booth is likely the first you'll see in the arrivals hall.

Getting There & Away

AIR

Recife's **Guararapes International Airport** (REC; ☎3322-4353) is at the south end of Boa Viagem, 2km inland, and offers direct flights to/from some 20 Brazilian cities. International destinations served include Buenos Aires, Lisbon, Frankfurt, Miami, Panama City and Praia (Cabo Verde).

BEACHES SOUTH OF RECIFE

Twenty years ago **Porto de Galinhas**, 70km south of Recife, was just another fishing village at the end of a dirt road, with a palm-fringed beach and a few holiday homes belonging to recifenses (people from Recife). Today it's one of Brazil's booming beach destinations; it has several large resort hotels strung along Praia Muro Alto and Praia do Cupe, north of the center, and dense festive crowds flock here at holiday times. Pedestrianization of the few streets that make up the town center, where the odd restaurant opens right onto the beach, has preserved some village ambience. Beautiful white-sand beaches stretch several kilometers in both directions from the town.

Porto de Galinhas gets its name (meaning 'Port of Chickens') from the period between 1853 and 1888, when the slave trade, but not slavery itself, was illegal in Brazil; ships would land here loaded with crates of *galinhas* (chickens) as cover for their human cargo. Today, sculptures of brainless-looking chickens dotted round town are a tasteless reminder of the past.

Bus 195 (R$12, two hours) leaves central Recife's **Terminal Cais de Santa Rita** (p498) hourly from 5:10am to 8:30pm, heading to Porto de Galinhas via Boa Viagem (Av Domingos Ferreira) and Recife Guararapes International Airport (outside the arrivals hall).

Further south, the **Tamandaré** area is much less frenetic and caters far more to the getaway ethos of independently minded travelers. Located 30km south of Porto de Galinhas (57km by road), it's a small, far less hyper beach town boasting a big stretch of coastline – 16km of lovely palm-fringed beaches.

Tamandaré itself has plenty of places to stay. Our favorite, **Pousada Recanto dos Corais** (☎3676-2115; www.pousadarecantodoscorais.com.br; Hermes Samico 317; r/tr R$140/180; ❄📶), is run by a doting, German-speaking southern Brazilian couple and has comfy, spotless little rooms, a good breakfast and sits just 300m from the beach. There's a two-night minimum stay at weekends. **Tapera do Sabor** (www.taperadosabor.com.br; São Jose 450; mains for 2 people R$72-98; ⏲9am-9pm Mon-Thu, to 10pm Fri-Sun; 📶) is a great seafood eatery at the end of the beach; it's a little more upscale than the plethora of beach-lined kiosks in town, and one of the few doing quality dishes in individual portions. Italian-owned **Pizzaria do Farol** (☎081-3676-2676; Av Dr Leopoldo Lins; pizzas R$12-33; ⏲7-11pm) serves thin and authentic brick-oven pizza.

BUS

Recife's bus station is the large **Terminal Integrado de Passageiros** (TIP; ☎3452-1088), generally known as the Rodoviária, 17km west of the center. TIP handles all interstate buses and many destinations within Pernambuco. You can purchase bus tickets in advance by calling **Disk Rodoviária** (☎3452-1211, Whatsapp 98867-7454; www.diskrodoviaria.com.br), a bus-ticket delivery service.

CAR & MOTORCYCLE

Recommended car-rental agencies with airport offices include **Avis** (☎0800-725-2847, 3322-4016; www.avis.com.br; Guararapes International Airport) and **Localiza** (☎3471-7016; www.localiza.com; Guararapes International Airport; ⏰24hr), but **Foco** (☎3031-3883; www.aluguefoco.com.br; Barão de Souza Leão 1672, Boa Viagem; ⏰24hr), just outside near the metro station, is local and cheaper. The latter coordinates with airport agency Pontual and can pick you up via shuttle.

Getting Around

Recife is spread out and some of the buses (R$2.45; R$1.20 on Sundays) take circuitous, confusing routes. Taxis will save you time and stress. Bus routes and schedules are online at www.granderecife.pe.gov.br (click Serviços then Atendimento ao Usuário then Itinerário). It is also served by a two-line metro (R$1.60) that is handy for the bus station, airport and football matches at Arena Pernambuco.

TO/FROM THE AIRPORT

Coopseta (☎3322-4153; Baggage Claim, Guararapes International Airport) prepaid taxis from the airport cost between R$20 and R$33 to Boa Viagem, and R$73 to Olinda or the bus station. During high traffic times prepaid taxis can be a better-value option then metered taxis; at other times it's cheaper to go with metered rivals **Coopstar** (☎3072-4433; Baggage Claim, Guararapes International Airport). Booths for both taxi companies are located inside the baggage-claim area. Prices are higher between 10pm and 6am.

Air-conditioned bus 042 leaves from outside the arrivals hall and heads to Boa Viagem and

The majority of tourists, especially those without cars, visit Tamandaré on a day trip from Porto de Galinhas. Traveling independently, you need to take a bus from Galinhas to Ipojuca, and another from there to Tamandaré. Approaching Tamandaré, most buses pass the turnings to the accommodations and restaurants along Praia dos Carneiros, 500m to 1km off the road. Some are signposted. **Viacão Cruzeiro** (☎081-2101-9000) runs buses to Tamandaré (R$15.50, three hours) from southern Av Dantas Barreto in central Recife at 7am, 10am, 2pm and 5:40pm Monday to Saturday, and 7:30am Sunday.

Seven kilometers north up the beach from Tamandaré, fashionable and ultrarelaxed **Praia dos Carneiros**, the belle of the bunch, is one of Northeast Brazil's loveliest strands. Never very crowded, it has wonderful calm, clear, shallow waters, fine sand shaded by coconut palms, and tidal pools formed by a rocky bar stretching across the wide mouth of the Rio Formoso. The beach is lined with private coconut groves, and a few fairly expensive beach lodgings and restaurants control the majority of beach access (though there is a public entrance). Any of the restaurants will make a fine base for a day of swimming, snorkeling, snoozing and strolling. (Unfortunately, our least favorite option hogs the best real estate.) **Sítio da Prainha** (☎081-3676-1498; www.sitiodaprainha.com.br; chalets incl dinner $450-550; ❄@📶🏊), offering chalet accommodations at the far northern end, sits where the Rio Ariquindá spills into the Formoso. It works in partnership with a good restaurant and bar, as well as a day-pass scheme that ranges from R$12 to R$90 per person, with food and activities ramping up as the price gets higher. The two-story chalets of **Pontal dos Carneiros** (☎081-3465-0055; www.pontaldoscarneiros.com.br; Sitio dos Manguinhos; 2-person bungalows R$690-990, 6-person R$890-1490; ❄📶🏊) offer a superluxury accommodation option, and the area's best restaurant, **Beijupirá** (www.beijupira.com.br; mains R$42-135; ⏰9am-5pm Sun-Thu, 9am-5pm & 6-9pm Fri & Sat), is right next door. Between Sítio da Prainha and Pontal dos Carneiros, **Bangalôs do Gameleiro** (☎081-3676-1421; www.praiadoscarneiros.com.br; apt R$350, bungalows R$450-600; ❄📶) is Carneiros' best deal: 12 cozy brick-and-tile cottages (and four apartments) spaced among the palms.

Moto-taxis cost R$7 and taxis R$20 between Tamandaré and Praia dos Carneiros.

the city center (R$3) but takes a convoluted route, which slows it considerably. At busy times, a better option for Boa Viagem is to walk to the right outside the arrivals hall and catch bus 040 CDU/Boa Viagem/Caxangá (which initially heads south) from the stop on busy Av Mascarenhas de Morais opposite a Mercedes Benz dealership.

Going to the airport from Boa Viagem, catch any Aeroporto bus on Av Domingos Ferreira; from the center, take a 033 Aeroporto bus from Terminal Cais de Santa Rita.

TO/FROM THE BUS STATION

To get to Boa Viagem from the Terminal Integrado de Passageiros (TIP; p497), take the metro to Joana Bezerra station, then follow the signs to 'SEI – Integraçao' for Boa Viagem–bound bus 080 (it leaves from embarkation point 2). The R$1.60 metro ticket from the Rodoviária metro station in the TIP covers both rides.

From Boa Viagem to the TIP, take a Joana Bezerra bus from Av Conselheiro Aguiar to Joana Bezerra metro station, then a Camaragibe-bound metro train to the Rodoviária.

If you arrive outside metro hours (5am to 11pm), taxis run R$66 to Boa Viagem and R$65 to Olinda.

TO/FROM BOA VIAGEM

In Boa Viagem southbound buses run along Av Domingos Ferreira; northbound buses run along Av Conselheiro Aguiar. The 032 Setúbal/Conde da Boa Vista bus runs north to Recife Antigo, Av Guararapes and Av Conde da Boa Vista (westbound) in the center, and back to Boa Viagem. Buses 031 Shopping Center and 033 Aeroporto run north from Boa Viagem to **Terminal Cais de Santa Rita** (Map p488) and back.

From the center to Boa Viagem, you can also take a Setúbal/Príncipe bus outside Recife metro station.

A taxi between central Recife and Boa Viagem costs around R$20 to R$30.

Olinda

081 / POP 368,000

Picturesque Olinda, set around a tree-covered hill 6km north of Recife, is the artsy, colonial counterpart to the big city's hubbub. It's an artist colony full of creative types and brimming with galleries, artisans' workshops, museums, lovely colonial churches and music in the streets. With twisting streets of colorful old houses and gorgeous vistas over treetops, church towers and red-tile roofs, this is one of the best-preserved and prettiest colonial towns in Brazil. The historic center has some lovely pousadas and good restaurants and bars, and makes a much more tranquil base than its bigger neighbor that stands towering in the distance.

Olinda was the original capital of Pernambuco, founded in 1535. Sacked and burnt, including all its Catholic churches, by the Calvinist Dutch in 1631, it was rebuilt; but it finally lost its ascendancy when Recife's merchants eclipsed Olinda's sugar barons in a bloody 18th-century feud called the Guerra dos Mascates. Although many Olinda buildings were originally constructed in the 16th century, most of what you see today dates from the 18th century and after. The whole picturesque historic center was declared a Unesco World Heritage site in 1982.

Sights

Olinda's sights are easy and enjoyable to visit on foot, although highly random opening hours make it impossible to look in on everything in one day. There are *a lot* of churches! A good place to start is Praça do Carmo, where most buses arrive. The square is overlooked by the recently restored **Igreja NS do Carmo** (Praça do Carmo; suggested dona-

BUSES FROM RECIFE

DESTINATION	COST FROM (R$)	TIME (HR)	COMPANY
Fortaleza	87	13	Expresso Guanabara (www.expressoguanabara.com.br)
João Pessoa	23	2	Progresso (www.progressoonline.com.br)
Maceió	38	4-5	Real Alagoas (www.realalagoas.com.br)
Natal	50	4½	Progresso (www.progressoonline.com.br)
Porto de Galinhas	12	2	Viação Cruzeiro (081-2101-9000)
Rio de Janeiro	432	38	Gontijo (www.gontijo.com.br), Itapemirim (www.itapemirim.com.br)
Salvador	167	18	Catedral Turismo (www.catedralturismo.com.br), Penha (http://vendas.nspenha.com.br)

tion R$2; 9am-noon & 2-5pm Tue-Sun), built in 1580. Climb up to Alto da Sé, which affords superb views of both Olinda and Recife. The area is peppered with food, drink and craft stalls.

Igreja da Sé CATHEDRAL
(9am-5pm) The imposing Igreja da Sé was originally built in 1537. Burnt in 1631, it has been reconstructed four times since, most recently from 1974 to 1984 in a mannerist style that attempts to re-create the original 16th-century look. Check the touching inscription in simple Portuguese on the wooden door to the left inside the entrance. It is located atop Alto da Sé (Cathedral Heights).

Convento de São Francisco MONASTERY
(Rua de São Francisco 280; admission R$3; 9am-12:30pm & 2-5:30pm Mon-Sat) This is a large structure containing the 16th-century Igreja NS das Neves and two later chapels, with rich baroque detailing and lovely azulejos (Portuguese ceramic tiles).

Mosteiro de São Bento MONASTERY
(Rua São Bento; 8-11:30am & 2:15-5:30pm Mon-Sat, 8-9:30am & 2:30-5pm Sun) The huge Mosteiro de São Bento, originally built in 1582, has some exceptional woodcarving in its church. Sunday-morning Mass (10am) is celebrated complete with Gregorian chants.

Museu do Mamulengo MUSEUM
(Rua São Bento 344; admission R$4; 10am-5pm Tue-Sat) The Museu do Mamulengo has a unique and surprisingly interesting collection of more than 1000 pieces devoted to the traveling puppet shows called Mamulengos, an authentic popular tradition of the Northeast.

Museu de Arte Contemporânea MUSEUM
(MAC; www.cultura.pe.gov.br/espacosculturais; Rua 13 de Maio 149; 9am-5pm Mon-Fri) FREE Housed in an 18th-century Inquisition jail, MAC is recommended for both its permanent and temporary exhibits.

Courses

Angola Mãe COURSE
(9251-1728, 3429-9503; www.capoeiraangolamae.de; Ilma Cunha 243; per 1½hr class R$20; classes 9am & 7:30pm Mon, Wed & Fri, roda 6:30pm Sun) If you'd like to check out a capoeira school, Angola Mãe teaches the slower and more traditional Angola style. The *roda* (open to the public) is the circular formation within which capoeira is performed.

Tours

Associação dos Condutores Nativos de Olinda GUIDED TOUR
(ACNO; 3053-5150; www.acno.com.br; Av da Liberdade 68) While in Olinda you'll no doubt hear the offer *'Guia!'* ('Guide!'). The best guides are those accredited by this local guides association. They wear red shirts with their names visible, and an ACNO tag, though the colors change every two years to reflect who remains credentialed with dues paid. The official charge for a two-hour tour is R$80 for two to three people.

Festivals & Events

Olinda's **Carnaval** (www.carnaval.olinda.pe.gov.br) celebrations last a full 11 days and have a spontaneity, inclusiveness and great irreverence that you don't get in big-city Carnavals. 'Pre-Carnaval' events get going the Sunday before Carnaval weekend, with the parade of the Virgens do Bairro Novo, a *bloco* of more than 400 'virgins' (men in drag) who are joined by up to 900,000 revelers. They start out at noon from Praça 12 de Março.

There are organized Carnaval events, including balls and gatherings of *maracatu* (Afro-Brazilian music with a slow, heavy beat) and *afoxé* (based on the rhythms and spirit of Candomblé) dance and music groups, but everything else happens in impromptu fashion on the streets, where endless groups of fabulously costumed musicians and dancers work their way through packed throngs of revelers, who often dance along to the rhythms of *frevo,* samba, *maracatu, caboclinho* or *afoxé*. The euphoric atmosphere and the sheer fun have to be experienced to be believed. Another famous feature of Olinda's Carnaval is the *bonecos gigantes,* huge puppets representing historical, cultural and other figures. A Carnaval high point is the parade of the top-hatted Homem da Meia-Noite (Man of Midnight) *boneco,* who emerges on Largo do Bonsucesso at midnight on Carnaval Saturday night.

Sleeping

Book several months ahead for accommodations during Carnaval and be prepared for massive price hikes.

★ **Cama e Cafe Olinda** B&B $
(8822-9083; www.camaecafeolinda.com; Rua da Bertioga 93; r R$165;) Austrian Sebastian and his Brazilian wife, Yolanda, are the hospitality gatekeepers at this signless B&B

Olinda

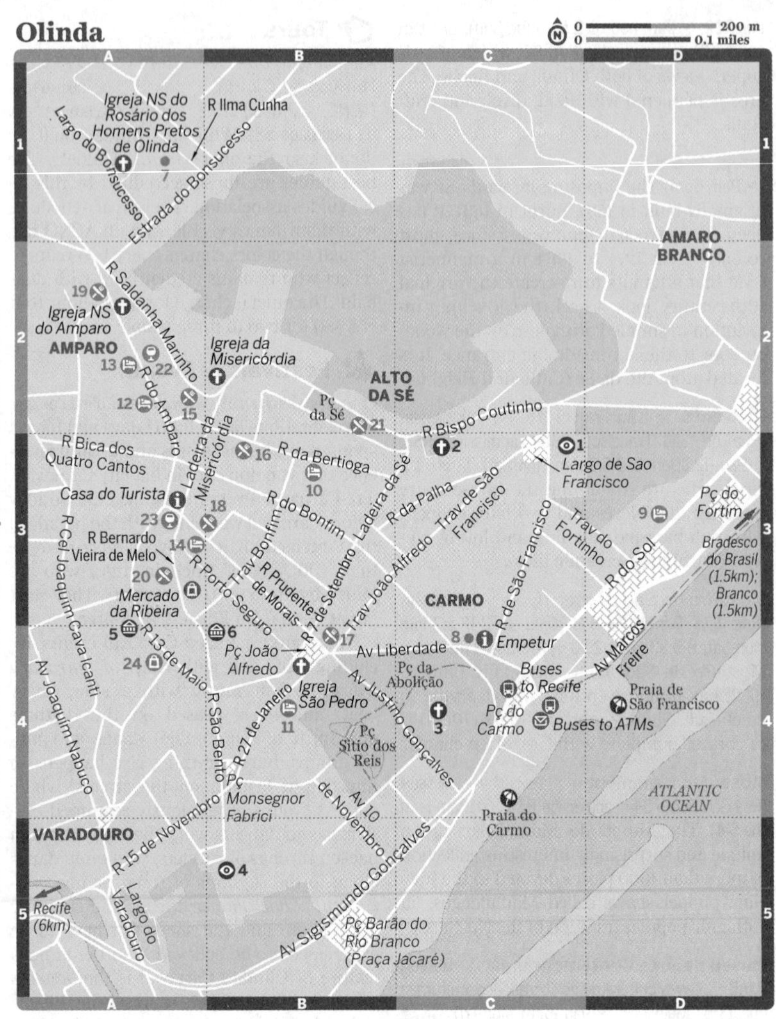

with just two rooms. It's chock-full of local art, lazy-day hammocks and views of both the sea and Recife. You'll encounter extraordinary care and character here; breakfast on the terrace (fruits and juices plucked straight from the property) is just one of many highlights. English, German and French spoken.

Albergue de Olinda HOSTEL $
(☎3429-1592; www.alberguedeolinda.com.br; Rua do Sol 233; dm/s/d/tr R$50/120/130/180; ❄📶🏊) Olinda's excellent HI hostel isn't on a colorful street, but offers modern amenities; spotless no-frills rooms; sex-seperate dorms; and a sizable garden with a lovely pool, loungers, outdoor kitchen, barbecue and plenty of hammocks.

Pousada do Carmo POUSADA $
(☎9501-7956; Rua do Amparo 215; d/tr R$130/165; ❄📶🏊) Having changed from German to Brazilian hands at the time of writing (and with its website still in the pipeline), the jury is out on the former Pousada Bela Vista, a longstanding budget staple. However, its large colorful lobby-lounge that leads through to three lower floors with 12 rooms and a pool, a breakfast area and terraces with views all the way to Recife remain.

Olinda

Stone walls lend the place a vaguely castlelike atmosphere, and the new owner has added a pleasant terrace bar and live music from Thursday to Saturday. Rooms are decked in bright primary colors and all have air-con, but some are small, windowless and claustrophobic.

Pousada de São Pedro POUSADA $$
(☎3439-9546; www.pousadapedro.com; Rua 27 de Janeiro 95; s/d/tr from R$170/200/240; ❄ 📶 🏊) The charming São Pedro occupies a 19th-century house full of art, crafts and antiques, and it has a lovely pool in the leafy, shady garden, plus a pretty special breakfast. But it also has its share of complaints about upkeep and cleanliness, so pick your druthers.

During our stay, it was oddly locked up and we were left to own our devices. Yet, you cannot discount its character. For a treat, request the top-floor *apartamento* (R$260), which has picture windows, a terrace with gorgeous views and a Jacuzzi bath. English, French and German are spoken.

Pousada do Amparo POUSADA $$
(☎3439-1749; www.pousadadoamparo.com.br; Rua do Amparo 199; s/d from R$258/315; ❄ 📶 🏊) The refined 17-room Amparo occupies two 18th-century houses with lovely gardens and views back toward Recife. It's full of character, very comfortable and is one of the loveliest spots to rest your weary head in the Northeast. English is spoken.

Flor de Coco, the pousada's French restaurant, is a good option for Sunday-night dinner when most top-end spots are closed. Creative seafood restaurant Beijupirá (p502) also shares this space.

Pousada dos Quatro Cantos POUSADA $$
(☎3429-0220; www.pousada4cantos.com.br; Prudente de Morais 441; s/d from R$244/280; ❄ 📶 🏊) High ceilings, tall windows, hardwood floors, lots of attractive art and a nice pool make this 19th-century house a delightful place to stay. While the cheapest (standard) rooms are quite acceptable, an extra R$101 will get you a much brighter, more characterful *luxo* abode. Rooms 119 and 115 frame Olinda's postcard-perfect view. English spoken.

Eating

A variety of good restaurants are tucked away among the old town's cobblestone streets. A great way to start an evening is with a tasty tapioca snack and a beer or caipirinha from the myriad **tapioca stands** (Praça da Sé; snacks R$3-11; ⏲approx 6-11pm) and food stalls overlooking Recife from Alto da Sé.

Estação Café CAFE $
(Prudente de Morais 440; items R$3.50-35; ⏲11:30am-8:30pm Tue-Thu, 12:30-11pm Fri & Sat, noon-8:30pm Sun; 📶) This artsy cafe is a perfect little pit stop for cappuccino, macchiato and light bites such as quiche, salad and crepes. There's free bossa nova and *chorinho* (samba-related instrumental music) at 8pm on Fridays and Saturdays, respectively.

Casa de Noca BRAZILIAN $
(www.casadenoca.com; Rua da Bertioga 243; meals for 2/3/5 people R$60/80/100; ⏲11am-11pm) For simple Northeastern food at its best, you can't beat this backyard restaurant that offers just one dish: large chunks of grilled *queijo coalho* (a salty white cheese that's grillable)

and slabs of surprisingly tender *carne de sol* atop a mountain of steamed *macaxeira.*

Creperia CREPERIE $

(www.facebook.com/creperiaolinda; Praça João Alfredo 168; crepes R$8.50-37, pizzas R$25-39; 11am-11pm;) A nice spot for crepes, pizza and salads, which you can enjoy on a pleasant outdoor patio under tall bamboo trees.

★**Patuá** BRAZILIAN $$

(3055-0833; www.restaurantepatua.com.br; Rua da Ribeira 79; mains R$35-85, seafood for 2 people R$89-171; 11am-3pm Tue, 11am-3pm & 6-10pm Wed-Sat, 11am-4pm Sun;) Humble, local and a kitchen magician, Chef Alcindo Queiroz serves regional *moquecas* and seafood that are an unexpected joy at this Olinda sleeper. Start with the Taperoá appetizer – flambéed shrimp over a fried banana drizzled with a pink peppercorn and star-anise sauce – then savor an excellent Pernambucana-style seafood stew. Douse it all in the vinegary housemade pepper sauce!

★**Oficina do Sabor** BRAZILIAN $$$

(3429-3331; www.oficinadosabor.com; Rua do Amparo 335; mains for 2 people R$48-142; noon-4pm & 6pm-midnight Tue-Sat, noon-5pm Sun;) With a specialty in baked pumpkin stuffed with assorted fillings – the shrimp, lobster and passion-fruit sauce variety is fantastic – this is one of the Northeast's best restaurants, and worth every centavo. It's also great on seafood in general (go for the crab in coconut and parsley appetizer), and offers an extensive Brazilian wine list, if you're curious.

Beijupirá SEAFOOD $$$

(3439-6691; www.beijupiraolinda.com.br; Saldanha Marinho s/n; mains R$52.60-105; noon-midnight Mon & Wed-Sat, to 5pm Sun) This romantic spot with views over Olinda's roofs is one of the region's best places for creative seafood. Try the shrimp in whisky and béchamel sauce with pineapple chunks, or the *beijucastanha* – a filet of the eponymous fish (cobia in English) in a chopped-cashew crust, served with spinach rice.

Drinking & Nightlife

Alto da Sé gets busy in the evenings as locals and visitors buy drinks and snacks from the street vendors, watch capoeira and savor the view and the breeze. There's usually live samba, *chorinho* or other Brazilian rhythms somewhere in Olinda Wednesday to Saturday nights and Sunday afternoons; tourist offices have information. On Friday nights from 9pm strolling musicians make a circuit through town, joined in song by onlookers, in what's known as the *serenata* or *seresta.*

★**Bodega de Véio** BAR

(www.facebook.com/bodegadoveio; Rua do Amparo 212; 10am-11:30pm Mon-Sat) Also a small and very eclectic general store, this wonderful little bar serves ice-cold bottled beer, shots of *cachaça* (potent sugarcane liquor) and great charcuterie plates (R$8 per 100g), while doing its best to manage the crowds of locals and tourists congregating on the street and small terrace at the side.

A party atmosphere develops most nights, and if you're running short of dental floss, spaghetti, mousetraps or violins, you can do your shopping right here.

Esquina do Peneira BAR

(Prudente de Morais 167; 10am-midnight) There's nothing remarkable about it other than its simplicity, but this corner hot spot across from the tourist office draws locals in droves day and night on weekends.

Shopping

Olinda is full of small shops and galleries selling a plethora of art and artisanry such as ceramics, textiles, and wood and stone carvings. Much of the work is incredibly colorful, and browsing these places is one of Olinda's great pleasures. The hub of the creative scene is Rua do Amparo, where many of the best artists and artisans have their homes, workshops and galleries.

A Casa do Cachorro Preto ARTS, CRAFTS

(13 de Maio 99; 4-9pm Thu-Sat) A cool gallery hosting monthly changing regional and national art – some of it for sale – with a backyard bar to boot. It doesn't yet have a live-music license, but Sunday is bring-your-own-vinyl night.

Information

DANGERS & ANNOYANCES

Crime (mostly petty) exists, especially during Carnaval. Don't walk alone along deserted streets at night.

EMERGENCY

Ciatur (Companhia de Apoio ao Turista) has branches at Av Justino Gonçalves (3181-3703; 24hr), and Rua do Ribeira (Rua do Ribeiro s/n). Very helpful and present around town, though English is only spoken at the airport tourist police.

FORRÓ FOR ALL

Wherever you go in Northeast Brazil you'll hear the strains of *forró* (fo-*hoh*), a simple country dance music that began life perhaps two centuries ago, and ended up taking the country by storm in the 1990s. Originally played by just three musicians with an accordion, triangle and *zabumba* (a handheld African drum), *forró* started out as music for popular dances in the Northeast, with simple lyrics speaking of the hard life of the countryside, the tribulations of love and the beauty of dance. The term *forró* actually encompasses several different musical styles and the dances that go with them, including the fast-paced *baião,* the even faster *arrasta-pé* and the slower *xote*.

Forró is danced in close couples with the man leading. At its simplest it's just two steps to the left and two to the right, but there are many variations and it's a good idea to take a class or two if you want to enjoy dancing *forró*.

The first icon of *forró* was Luiz Gonzaga (1912–89), who came from the small Pernambuco town of Exu. Known as O Rei do Baião (King of Baião), he was responsible for taking the sound of Pernambuco to the rest of the country, later influencing some internationally renowned Brazilian musicians. Despite his personal popularity, *forró* continued to be looked down on by the middle classes of São Paulo, Rio de Janeiro and other southern cities, as being backwoods Northeastern music. That was until the 1990s when some *forró* musicians modernized their sound, adding electric guitars, keyboards and drum sets. *Forró* then became a national craze, filling a void for an upbeat music that's easily danced with a partner. Meanwhile, the original accordion, triangle and *zabumba* style of *forró* has now also enjoyed a comeback and goes by the name *forró pé-de-serra* (foot-of-the-hills *forró*).

MONEY

The only ATM in the historical center is a Banco-24Horas inside **Padaria Largo do Amparo** (Rua do Amparo 395; ⏲8am-9pm). The nearest ATMs otherwise are Banco do Brasil and Bradesco, both close to each other on Av Getúlio Vargas about 2km north, reachable on any of several north-bound buses (1983, 1973, 910, 881) from the post office (p503), opposite Praça do Carmo.

POST

Correios (www.correios.com.br; Rua do Farol; ⏲9am-5pm Mon-Fri) Postal services.

TOURIST INFORMATION

Casa do Turista (☎3305-1060; www.olindaturismo.com.br; Prudente de Morais 472; ⏲8am-6pm Mon-Fri, from 9am Sat & Sun) The municipal tourist-information office has helpful staff, but little English. Its comprehensive website, however, is in English and Portuguese.

Empetur (Empresa de Turismo de Pernambuco; ☎3182-8294; www.pe.gov.br/orgaos/empetur-empresa-de-turismo-de-pernambuco; Av da Liberdade s/n; ⏲8am-6pm) The state tourist-info office has lovely English-speaking staff.

ℹ Getting There & Away

Bus 910 Piedade/Rio Doce runs about every half-hour from Boa Viagem (any stop on Av Conselheiro Aguiar) in Recife to Olinda and back. The 1983 Rio Doce/Princesa Isabel and 1992 Pau Amarelo buses run from **Terminal Cais de Santa Rita** (p498) in central Recife to Olinda and back. All cost R$3.35. Olinda's main bus stop is on Praça do Carmo.

From Recife airport, you can take bus 042 from outside Arrivals to Terminal Cais de Santa Rita, then the 1983 or 1992 from there to Olinda. Usually the quicker option, however, is to make the five-minute walk to Aeroporto metro station on Rua 10 de Julho, taking a 20-minute metro ride to the central Recife station (also called Estação Central; R$1.60), and then a 1992 Pau Amarelo bus to Olinda, departing about every 15 minutes from Rua Floriano Peixoto outside the station.

From Recife bus station (Terminal Integrado de Passageiros) to Olinda, take the metro to the central Recife station and then a 1992 Pau Amarelo bus.

Taxis to Olinda cost around R$45 from Boa Viagem, R$65 from Recife bus station and R$73 from the airport.

Fernando de Noronha

☎081 / POP 2630

While religion, science and philosophy continue to battle out what happens when we die, in Brazil there is little discourse on the subject: heaven plays second fiddle to the 21-island Fernando de Noronha archipelago. Located in the Atlantic, 525km from Recife and 350km from Natal, Noronha's natural beauty holds its own against any tropical locale in the world.

With crystal-clear waters, rich marine life – including the highest known concentration of resident dolphins in the world – and spectacular tropical landscapes, it's in a Brazilian class all of its own. The country's 'Beach bible,' *Guia Quatro Rodas Praias,* awards five stars to just five beaches in the whole country – and three are right here.

Give yourself plenty of time because Noronha is addictive. It's a wonderful place for doing things both on water (diving, surfing and snorkeling) and on land (hiking and touring), and the average stay is four or five nights. Thanks in large part to the **Parque Nacional Marinho de Fernando de Noronha** (Fernando de Noronha National Marine Park; www.parnanoronha.com.br; admission Brazilian/foreigner R$89/178) and conservation projects based here, the marine and coastal environment is tightly regulated: locals joke that it's the island of 'No' – no, you can't do this; no, you can't do that, etc.

With only between 270 and 400 plane seats normally available per day to Noronha, tourism doesn't overwhelm the islands, and it's rarely a problem to find an isolated patch of sand on a dreamy beach, even in high season. However, it's advisable to reserve accommodations and flights well ahead for December, January, February, July and August. The week or so either side of New Year can get booked up six months or more in advance.

Paradise comes at a premium: due to the cost of transporting goods from the mainland, prices are surreal and rooms cost about double what you'd pay on the mainland. But as a guaranteed highlight of any trip to South America, Fernando de Noronha is well worth the expense.

The largest and only inhabited island, Ilha de Fernando de Noronha is 10km long, with its population concentrated in the village of **Vila dos Remédios** and the adjoining, spread-out neighborhoods of **Vila do Trinta**, **Floresta Velha** and **Floresta Nova**. A single paved road, the BR-363, runs 7km from the port near the island's northeast tip, through the populated area, to the airport and down to Baía do Sueste on the south coast. Unpaved side roads lead to several other beaches. The spectacular extinct volcanic cone **Morro do Pico** is the highest point, 323m above sea level – and more than 4300m above the ocean floor. No, you cannot climb it.

The showery season is from February to June and the islands are blessed by fresh breezes year-round. The time zone here is one hour ahead of Brasília time.

History

A Portuguese aristocrat, Fernão de Loronha, was awarded the islands by his friend King Dom Manoel in 1504. He never set foot on the islands, though, and forgot about them. They were occupied intermittently by the English, the French (twice) and the Dutch (twice) before Portugal definitively retook them in 1737 and built 10 defensive forts.

THE PRICE OF PARADISE

Visitors to Fernando de Noronha have to pay two special charges. The state government environmental preservation tax, known as the TPA, is R$51.40 per day for the first four days, then progressively discounts per day for days five to 10 and then increases progressively by varying amounts for each extra day after that: a one-week/two-week/four-week stay costs, in total, R$318.68/848.10/3636.55, at 2015 rates. You pay by cash or credit card on arrival at the airport (the site is *still* not set up to receive payments from foreigners in advance). If you decide to stay longer than planned, go to the airport between 11am and 5pm at least one day before your original departure date and pay for your extra days – otherwise you'll pay double.

The second charge is the national park entry fee (and you're almost certain to enter the national park while here). The fee for anything up to 10 days is R$89 for Brazilians and R$178 for foreigners; you get a plastic card with your name on it to prove you've paid. It can be paid in cash (R$, US$ or euros) or by credit card at a **kiosk** (Bosque Flamboyant, Vila dos Remédios; 8am-10pm) in Vila dos Remédios, at the **Centro de Visitantes** (p512) at Vila do Boldró, or at two Postos de Informações e Controle (PICs) at park entrances: **PIC Golfinho-Sancho** (p512) and **PIC Sueste** (p512). Take your passport when you go to pay. A third PIC has been in the works at Praia do Leão for ages, though it remains stuck in bureaucratic limbo. It is also usually possible to buy the card with cash reais at the port from about 7am to 9am, if you are going diving or on a boat tour.

Since then, Noronha has been used as a penal colony, a military base (including for US troops in WWII), a US missile-tracking station and, now, a world-class tourist destination. A struggle between developers and environmentalists was resolved in 1988 when about 75% of the archipelago, including much of the main island and its surrounding waters, was declared a marine national park. It was included on the Unesco World Heritage list in 2002.

Sights

The Centro de Visitantes (p512) at Vila do Boldró includes a small open-air **turtle museum** (Alameda do Boldró s/n, Vila do Boldró; 24hr) FREE with displays on sea turtles by the Tamar Project (www.tamar.org.br), a not-for-profit organization working to protect endangered sea turtles, plus a Tamar information desk and shop.

Forte dos Remédios FORT
(24hr) FREE Easily the best preserved of the island's Portuguese forts, Forte dos Remédios is well worth a visit and has great views from its hilltop above Vila dos Remédios.

Beaches

There are 16 or 17 beaches on Noronha (depending on who you ask); all are clean, postcard-ready and almost deserted. The 'five-star' **Baía do Sancho**, **Praia do Leão** and **Baía dos Porcos** are all impossibly gorgeous, but there is a lot of competition. Note Porcos is accessible on foot only from neighboring Praia da Cacimba do Padre. The sandy beaches facing the Mar de Dentro (Inner Sea) on the northwest side of the island – **Cachorro** (at Vila dos Remédios), **Conceição**, **Boldró**, **Americano**, **Quixaba** and **Cacimba do Padre** – are also good for surfing.

Access to beaches in the national park is closed off from 6:30pm to 8am. On the opposite side of the island, **Praia do Atalaia**, which has shallow tide pools great for snorkeling, can only be accessed with reservations.

Baía dos Golfinhos is strictly off-limits to swimmers and all watercraft.

Activities

Boat Tours

A number of boats make enjoyable daily three-hour tours from the Porto, along the main island's northwest coast and back. Spinner dolphins like to swim and perform acrobatics near the boats, and a 40-minute snorkeling stop at Baía do Sancho is normally part of the trip. Prices include pickup and drop-off at your accommodation.

Trovão dos Mares II BOAT TOUR
(3619-1228; www.trovaodosmares.com.br) Recommended trips of about four hours with planasub (snorkeling while being slowly towed along by the boat) and lunch both included (R$230).

Naonda BOAT TOUR
(3619-1307; www.barconaonda.com) A recommended boat tour, and one of the least expensive at R$110 per person; for R$30 more you can add 30 minutes' planasub or lunch; or combine the two for R$210.

Diving

With 30m to 40m of visibility (at its very best in October), beautifully warm seas, a well-preserved underwater environment and abundant marine life – from iridescent fish to spinner dolphins and giant sea turtles – diving around Noronha is world class. There are 230 fish species, 15 coral varieties and five types of (harmless) shark. For certified divers, a two-tank dive including transfers and all equipment normally costs around R$475/501 with cash/credit card. Open Water courses cost around R$2600/2740 and *batismo* (baptism) dives for first-timers are around R$433/455.

★**Atlantis Divers** DIVING
(3206-8840; www.atlantisdivers.com.br; Praça dos Remedios, Vila dos Remédios; 9am-8pm) French-run, highly professional and a committed member of Abeta, Brazil's only ecotourism and adventure-tourism standards association.

Águas Claras DIVING
(3619-1225; www.aguasclaras-fn.com.br; Alameda do Boldró, Vila do Boldró; 9am-9pm) Friendly PADI National Geographic Dive Center, based near the Centro de Visitantes (p512).

Snorkeling

There are simply hundreds of good places to snorkel on the islands: the rocks in Baía do Sancho, where harmless lemon sharks are often present; the tranquil tide pools of Atalaia; or Baía do Sueste, where you can swim with turtles at high tide (local guides accompany you for R$50). Snorkel gear can be rented for R$15 to R$25 per day in Vila dos Remédios, at the harbor and at Baía do

I LOVE NATURE! - I LOVE BRAZIL! / GETTY IMAGES ©

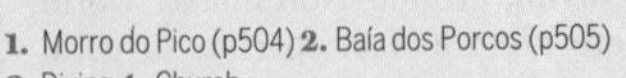

1. Morro do Pico (p504) **2.** Baía dos Porcos (p505)
3. Diving **4.** Church

2
MAURICIO M FAVERO / GETTY IMAGES ©

4

Fernando de Noronha

For many Brazilians a trip to the archipelago of Fernando de Noronha, 350km out into the Atlantic from Natal, is the holiday of a lifetime. What is it that makes this former penal colony and military base, comprising one medium-sized and 20 small islands, so magnetic?

The Beauty

Small-scale but majestic, the combination of long sandy strands, lush vegetation, towering rock pinnacles and ocean rollers breaking on dramatic rocky cliffs and islets has few parallels on the planet.

The Conservation

Much of the archipelago's land and sea areas are a strictly regulated national park, so fauna, flora, landscape and the marine environment are protected from the effects of overdevelopment. Visitor numbers are restricted so there is always plenty of space, and active conservation organizations zealously protect its dolphin and turtle populations.

The Beaches

The main island's 17 or so sandy bays are some of Brazil's most beautiful, mostly backed by thickly vegetated slopes or cliffs, and all fronted by wonderfully warm, clear waters. Some are protected by promontories or picturesque offshore islands and ideal for swimming and snorkeling; others have sets of ocean breakers rolling in and are a dream for surfers.

The Diving & Snorkeling

With 30m-plus visibility, beautifully warm seas and abundant marine life including big creatures such as turtles, dolphins and (harmless) sharks, the diving around Noronha is Brazil's best. For the same reasons, snorkeling is fantastic too.

Fernando de Noronha

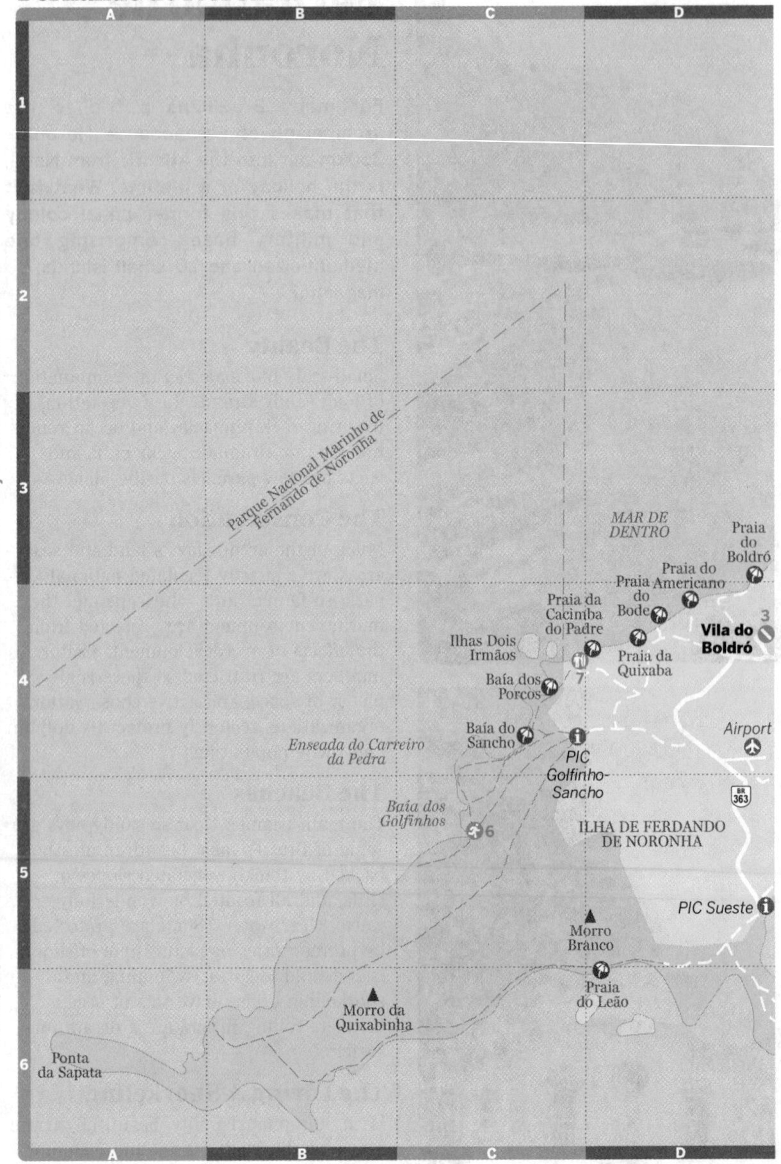

Sueste. Life jackets are required, rentable for R$10.

Snorkeling at Morro de São José requires advance reservations. These are accepted up to 10 days in advance at the Centro de Visitantes (p512) between 8:30am and noon and from 2pm to 6pm Monday to Friday, and from 3pm to 6pm Saturdays/holidays.

Dolphin-Watching

From the cliff-top lookout **Mirante dos Golfinhos** you can watch an average of more than 300 spinner dolphins cavorting

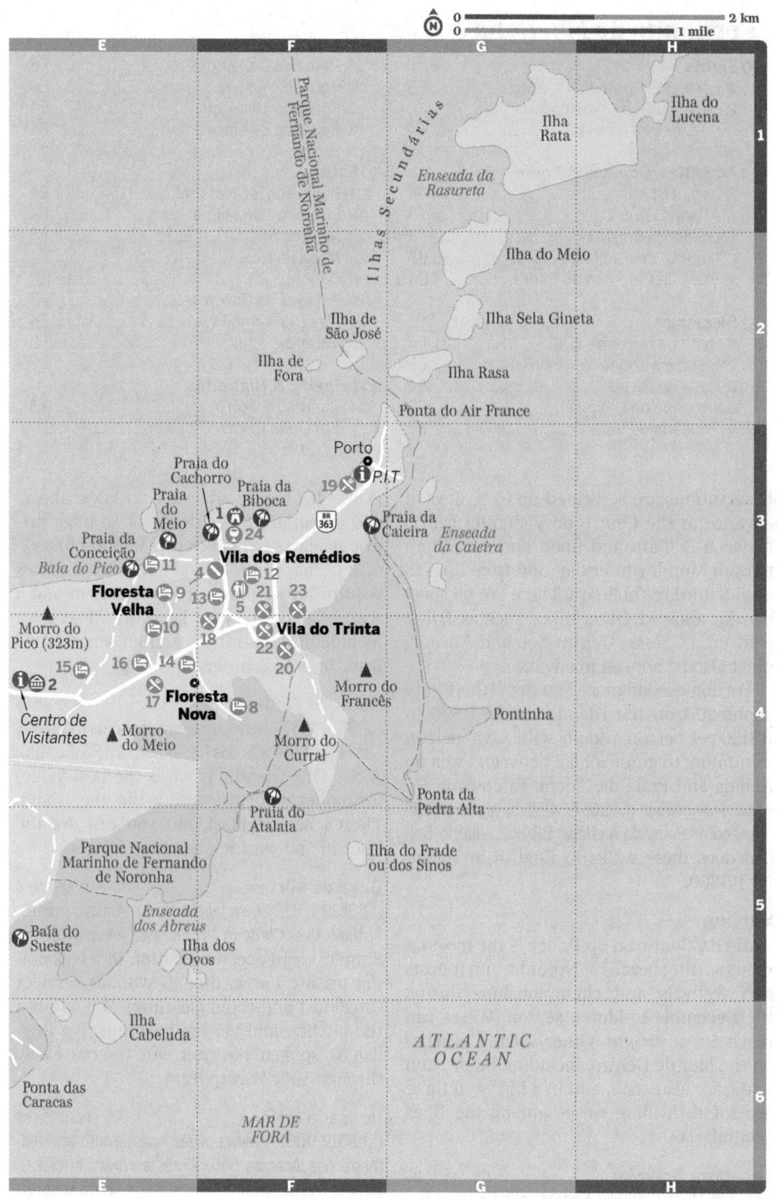

in Baía dos Golfinhos from 6:30am. Trainee biologists provide Portuguese commentary from Monday to Saturday.

Hiking

A few trails within the national park can only be walked with a local guide or with prior reservations. A great trail runs from **Vila do Trinta** to **Praia do Atalaia**, where there's good snorkeling in tidal pools (no flippers or sunscreen allowed), and then on to **Praia da Caieira**, where there are more tidal pools and the last 2km is on tough volcanic rock. It's about three to four hours return.

Fernando de Noronha

Sights

1 Forte dos Remédios ... F3
2 Museu a Céu Aberto da Tartaruga Marinha ... E4

Activities, Courses & Tours

3 Águas Claras ... D4
4 Atlantis Divers ... F3
5 Locadora SolyMar ... F3
6 Mirante dos Golfinhos ... C5
7 Praia da Cacimba do Padre ... C4

Sleeping

8 Beco de Noronha ... F4
9 Beijupirá Lodge Noronha ... E3
10 Casa de Mirtes ... E4
11 Pousada da Praia ... E3
12 Pousada do Vale ... F3
13 Pousada Golfinho ... F3
14 Pousada Naiepe ... E4
15 Pousada Teju-Açu ... E4
16 Pousada Zé Maria ... E4

Eating

17 Açaí e Raízes Noronha ... E4
18 Empório São Miguel ... F4
19 Mergulhão ... F3
20 Mesa da Ana ... F4
O Pico ... (see 16)
21 Palhoça da Colina ... F3
22 Pizzaria Namoita ... F4
23 Varanda ... F3

Drinking & Nightlife

24 Bar do Cachorro ... F3
Bar Duda Rei ... (see 11)

Reservations are acccepted up to 10 days in advance at the Centro de Visitantes (p512) between 8:30am and noon and from 2pm to 6pm Monday to Friday, and from 3pm to 6pm Saturdays/holidays. There are 96 spots per day allowed. Other hikes, such as **Trilha Pontinha Caiera**, **Capim Açu** and **Abreus**, must also be booked in advance.

Portuguese-language guides (there are about 200 on the island) charge R$90 to R$120 per person, usually with a two-person minimum, to guide a hike between Praia do Atalaia and Praia da Caiera. Fábio from **Pirata Passeios** (☎9657-6427; piratanoronha@gmail.com; Pousada Aleffawi, BR-363, Vila do Boldró) does these walks in English or Italian for R$200.

Surfing

Praia da Cacimba do Padre is the most famous surfing beach on Noronha and it hosts surf festivals and championships during the December-to-March season. Waves can reach 5m in height. Other surfing beaches on the Mar de Dentro, including Boldró and Bode, are also good, and in a big swell there are some thrilling waves among the Ilhas Secundárias.

Locadora SolyMar SURFING
(Rua São Miguel, Vila dos Remédios; boards per day R$50; ⏲7am-9pm) Rents surfboards.

Sleeping

Noronha has around 150 pousadas, ranging from very basic to luxurious. Most are in the area of Vila do Remédios, Vila do Trinta and Floresta Velha and only a handful have sea views. It's highly advisable to book ahead, and essential for the dozen or so most luxurious places (which charge R$500-plus) except perhaps in May and June. Some places require 100% credit-card prepayment and a scan or photo of your passport. Most rates include airport transfers. High season runs from June to February.

Pousada Golfinho POUSADA $
(☎3619-1837; www.pousadagolfinhofn.jimdo.com; São Miguel 144, Vila dos Remédios; s/d R$160/190; ❄📶) This friendly place is the best value-for-money budget pousada on the island. There's no breakfast, but you can use the kitchen and washing machine for free.

Casa de Mirtes HOMESTAY $
(☎3619-1792; www.facebook.com/casa.demirtes; Antônio Alves Cordeiro 457, Floresta Velha; d R$200) Simple, clean accommodation in a welcoming private home, though without services (breakfast and room cleaning). You can use the kitchen and garden barbecue. No English is spoken but you can reserve easily through Your Way (p512).

Pousada Naiepe POUSADA $$
(☎3619-0001; www.pousadanaiepe.com.br; Alameda das Acácias 555, Floresta Nova; r R$550; ❄📶) With just four solidly constructed rooms on the corner of the main road, this cute midrange pousada wins over travelers with its value for money and attention to detail. It features a gorgeous, hammock-strung patio and garden. When they're in, Duda, who speaks English, and Edilene are pillars of hospitality.

Pousada Teju-Açu POUSADA $$$
(☎3040-0299; www.pousadateju.com.br; Estrada da Alamoa, Boldró; s R$1654-1902, d R$1840-2115;) Located almost underneath Morro do Pico, Pousada Teju-Açu is a well-managed, quirkily designed pousada with a good restaurant. Rooms are spacious and quite stylish, with tiny bathrooms but huge beds, and there's a pleasant wood-decked pool area.

Beijupirá Lodge Noronha POUSADA $$$
(☎3619-1250; www.beijupiralodgenoronha.com.br; Amaro Preto, Floresta Velha; r R$900-1200;) Seven-room Beijupirá has an intimate, comfortable, cottagey feel with all sorts of tasteful art and knickknacks dotted about. Meals are from the same recipe book as the owners' fine seafood restaurants in Olinda and Porto de Galinhas, and there's a lovely big garden with great Morro do Pico views.

Beco de Noronha POUSADA $$$
(☎3619-1568; www.becodenoronha.com.br; Alameda das Acácias 3, Floresta Nova; s/d from R$513-653;) With quaint eco-artisanal touches (such as short pathways made of upturned bottles) and charmingly helpful staff, wood-built Beco is a good choice for a comfortable stay in a central location on the island. Bonus: there's a Japanese Ofuro bath in the garden!

Pousada do Vale POUSADA $$$
(☎3619-1293; www.pousadadovale.com; Pescador Sérgio Lino 18, Vila dos Remédios; s R$700-1050, d R$850-1150;) Intimate Vale is one of the friendliest and most service-oriented pousadas on the island. Rooms aren't as high-end as the prices suggest, but are bright and well appointed with design-forward touches including *mantas nordestinas* (colorful throws).

Pousada Zé Maria POUSADA $$$
(☎3619-1258; www.pousadazemaria.com.br; Nice Cordeiro 1, Floresta Velha; s R$817-2486, d R$1037-3106;) Luxurious Zé Maria boasts a stunning view of the Morro do Pico from its pool and is famed Brazil-wide for its over-the-top, all-you-can-eat R$149 seafood-buffet spectacle on Wednesday and Saturday evenings (reservations highly advisable). Owner Zé Maria catches about half the fish himself.

Pousada da Praia HOMESTAY $$$
(☎3619-1267; Praia da Conceição; d R$600-800;) The pousada formerly known as Casa do Joab was revamped and repackaged in 2015 under new ownership into a rustic-luxury homestay right on the sands of Praia da Conceicão, one of the only such options in Noronha. Historical protections prevent the alteration of some unfortunately small or odd window details, but otherwise you'll find sandside comfort previously unseen on the island. Contact Your Way (p512) for bookings.

Eating

Açaí e Raízes Noronha CAFE $
(BR-363, Floresta Nova; items R$13-40; 9am-11:30pm;) Locals and tourists alike people-watch from the veranda of this store that's good for *açaí* (berrylike fruit), tapioca and fresh sandwiches. It's one of the best spots to pick up the island's free wi-fi signal (and it has its own wi-fi, too).

Empório São Miguel BUFFET $
(Bosque Flamboyant, Vila dos Remédios; per kg R$52.80, mains R$38-98; 10am-11:30pm) The best of a few *por kilo* lunch places in Remédios. It also has some good à la carte fare at night and has undergone a pleasant makeover by new management.

O Pico FUSION $$
(www.facebook.com/opiconoronha; BR-363, Floresta Velha; dishes R$65-84; noon-11pm Wed-Mon;) O Pico serves excellent seafood rices, *moquecas,* pastas and specialty coffees from São Paulo, Minas Gerais and Espírito Santo, but it's the fresh and fabulous array of seviches (from R$45 to R$52) that, though not traditional, will soon have you forgetting about the Peruvian version; try the classic with *biquinho* peppers.

On Sunday evenings, the script is flipped and it becomes the island's most sought-after live-music venue. It's also an art and crafts shop that sells original Northeastern wares, most notably, gorgeous single-leaf woodcuts from famed Northeastern artist J Borges.

Pizzaria Namoita PIZZERIA $$
(BR-363, Vila do Trinta; pizza R$51-79; 7-11pm Fri-Wed, closed last Wed of month) São Paulo emigré Mauricio Vilela does his best to re-create *pizza paulistana* (p243), and does a fine job considering Noronha logistics. Favorites such as *cearense* (spicy ground sausage with chilies and mozzarella) are served in an atmospheric setting under a giant cashew tree in his front yard.

★**Mesa da Ana** BRAZILIAN $$$
(☎3619-0178; Estrada do Atalaia 230, Vila do Trinta; dinner per person R$150; seating 8:30pm)

Husband-and-wife team Ana (a Cordon Bleu grad) and Rock (pronounced 'hockey;' Noronha's resident artist eccentric) serve only eight to 10 people per night at this rustic island gem. The four-course fish-heavy meals are served in a wonderful island setting.

There's no advance menu: Ana goes with what the local catch dictates, and you'll find out what that is once you sit down at the long communal table! Delicious.

Mergulhão MEDITERRANEAN **$$$**
(☎3619-0215; www.mergulhaonoronha.com.br; Av Joaquim Ferreira Gomes 40, Porto; mains R$70-110; ⏲noon-10pm Mon-Sat; 🍷) Mergulhão makes full use of its breezy site offering stupendous views over the port, while its Mediterranean menu with a Brazilian twist is one of Noronha's most innovative. Try the signature *peixe crocante* (crispy fish stuffed with shrimp, cheese and palm hearts) or the *arroz do amado* (grilled octopus rice with *coalho* cheese, cashews and fresh tomatoes).

Varanda BRAZILIAN **$$$**
(☎3619-1546; www.restaurantevarandanoronha.com.br; Major Costa 130, Vila do Trinta; mains for 2 people R$89-222; 📶) One of the best-value upscale choices, within walking distance of most pousadas and run by a local professional chef. The *moqueca* and shrimp with okra and tumeric are outstanding.

Palhoça da Colina SEAFOOD **$$$**
(☎3619-1473; www.palhocadacolina.com; Estrada da Colina, Vila do Trinta; dinner per person R$150; ⏲from 8:30pm) A feast under an atmospheric *palapa* hut with tatami mats and pillows, in the yard of a local home. All-you-can-eat grilled catch of the day (barracuda, tuna or mackerel) is served on banana leaves, with great side dishes such as arugula and mango salad, and banana *farofa* (sautéed manioc flour).

There's a maximum of 20 people seated per night; reservations are required with a 50% deposit.

Drinking & Nightlife

Bar do Cachorro BAR
(Vila dos Remédios; ⏲noon-midnight) The famous open-air Dog Bar is the hub – in fact the only locale – of Noronha nightlife. It's busy every night but really packed from Thursdays through Sundays. There's music to dance to from around 10:30pm, including live *forró* on Fridays and a *chorinho feijoada* on Saturdays, and a saxophonist at sunset during the week.

Bar Duda Rei BAR
(Praia da Conceição; ⏲10am-sunset) Noronha's only real beach bar has a fabulous setting beneath a couple of palms, with Morro do Pico towering behind. It serves good food, too.

Information

INTERNET ACCESS

Noronha has free islandwide wi-fi, but signals vary greatly depending on location, and speeds are painfully slow. Fortunately most pousadas have their own better setups.

Cia da Lua (Bosque Flamboyant, Vila dos Remédios; wi-fi per 24hr R$30; ⏲10am-11pm Mon-Sat, from 5pm Sun) A decent signal (when it's not on the fritz!) from a private provider.

MEDICAL SERVICES

Hospital São Lucas (☎3619-1377; Bosque Flamboyant, Vila dos Remédios; ⏲24hr) Basic medical clinic.

MONEY

The ATMs at the airport and the Bradesco bank branch at Vila do Trinta, across from Poty Supermarket, accept international cards, but they can run out of cash at weekends, so do bring some with you.

TOURIST INFORMATION

National park information is available from the **Centro de Visitantes** (Vila do Boldró; ⏲8am-10pm), **PIC Golfinho-Sancho** (⏲8am-6:30pm) and **PIC Sueste** (⏲8am-6:30pm).

P.I.T (Posto Informações Turísticas; Porto; ⏲8am-6pm) Pick up a map at this tourist info booth above the port.

TRAVEL AGENCIES

Your Way (☎9949-1087; www.yourway.com.br) An indispensable contact on the island, this veteran ecotourism specialist is perfect for independent travelers of all budgets and is deeply engaged in improving the local community (eg with pet neutering and sustainable development). Fluent English-speaker Adriana offers unbiased tips and bookings for accommodations, restaurants and activities and insider tips of sea-turtle events – at no additional cost.

Adriana is also a director for Abeta, Brazil's national ecotourism association.

USEFUL WEBSITES

The island government site Fernando de Noronha (www.noronha.pe.gov.br) has every detail imaginable.

Getting There & Away

The **airport** (FEN; ☎3619-0950) sits in the middle of the main island. **Azul** (www.voeazul.com.br) and **Gol** (www.voegol.com.br) both fly

WORTH A TRIP

JACUMÃ & AROUND

The string of good beaches and small, spread-out villages from Jacumã to Tambaba, south of João Pessoa, make a relaxed and inexpensive stop on the way to or from Recife, or a day out from João Pessoa.

Jacumã, the biggest of the villages, has *forró* (popular music of the Northeast) bars by night and a thin 3km-long beach featuring colored sandbars, natural pools and pink cliffs (although other beaches in the area are more enticing). **Praia de Carapibus**, divided from Praia de Jacumã by a small bush-covered headland, is just 500m long, with low cliffs and pools, and merges into the broader **Praia da Tabatinga**, which curves nearly 2km south. The most beautiful beach is **Praia dos Coqueirinhos**, round the headland at the south end of Praia Tabatinga; it has coconut palms, high red cliffs, freshwater springs and a dozen *barracas* (stalls), but it can get overly crowded on weekends. **Praia de Tambaba**, 4km further south, is famed as the only official nudist beach in the region. Men may only enter the nude section if they are gay couples or accompanied by a woman. The clothing-optional part of Tambaba is also stunning, with a broad swath of petrified sandstone forming natural tidal pools along the shoreline. Tambaba hosts the one-of-a-kind **Open de Surf Naturista** (Nude Surfing Festival) in August.

Unless the tide is very high, it's possible to walk this entire coast along the beach.

Buses run about every 40 minutes to Jacumã (R$6, 45 minutes to 1½ hours) from 5am to 10pm. They depart from the third of the four bus stops along Rua Cícero Meireles, after leaving **João Pessoa bus station** (p518). The 5:30am departure (only) continues to Tambaba, and there's one daily bus back from Tambaba, leaving at 5:30pm from Pousada Arca do Bilu. Shared taxis (Map p515) also run between João Pessoa and Jacumã, charging R$6 per person (or R$24 for the whole car); in João Pessoa you can find them near the Lagoa and near the bus station: ask for 'Jacumã' outside the Terminal de Integração or in Rua Cícero Meireles. Regular taxis charge around R$80 to R$100 to Jacumã. **Slow Hostel** (p515), in partnership with the Universidade Federal da Paraiba (UFPB), offers a shared shuttle service twice a week (Tuesdays and Thursdays at 8:30am, returning at 5:30pm) for R$45.

Coming from the south on Hwy BR-101, ask to be dropped off at the turnoff for Conde and Jacumã, and from there catch a local bus, van or shared taxi.

Recife–Noronha–Recife daily; Azul also flies Natal–Noronha–Natal daily. Round-trip fares from either city normally range from R$700 to R$1200. Buy your ticket as early as you can. Your Way (p512) can usually find you the best deal.

GOL seats are available to Brazil, South America and Northeast Brazil airpass holders, but availablity is scarce.

Getting Around

A good bus service (R$3) runs the length of the BR-363 between the port, Vila dos Remédios, the airport and Baía do Sueste, about every 30 to 40 minutes from 7am to 11pm. You'll see bus-stop signs along the road. Hitchhiking, though we don't generally recommend it, is safe here and commonplace.

Taxis (some of which are buggies) have fixed rates from R$20 to R$45 depending on distance. The trip from the airport to Vila dos Remédios costs R$26.

A popular way to get around is to rent your own buggy. Rates for reliable vehicles range from R$150 to R$400 (on holidays) per 24 hours, plus fuel. (Be aware: vehicle owners on the island do not have insurance so you'll be expected to pay for any accidental damage.) Pousadas will usually organize a buggy for you, and all renters will deliver it to you. You can also rent motorcycles, if you are licensed for one back home.

BikeNoronha is a new Itaú-sponsored bike-hire scheme launched in late 2015. It has two stations of 10 bikes each at Bosque Flamboyant and the Visitors Center at Vila do Boldró. Plans are to have 100 bikes by the time you read this, spread throughout the main road from the port to Sueste Bay. The best part? They're free!

PARAÍBA

Sandwiched between Pernambuco and Rio Grande do Norte, the small, sunny state of Paraíba contains the easternmost point of the continent, Ponta do Seixas, where you are closer to Senegal than to southern Brazil. The tranquil, reasonably well developed coast is the state's most important economic region, fueled by the farming of sugarcane and pineapples, and some tourism. Cattle-ranching dominates the drought-affected interior, which also harbors some intriguing archaeological sites.

João Pessoa

☎083 / POP 721,000

The coastal city of João Pessoa – known as Jampa, a play on São Paulo's nickname of Sampa – is the capital of Paraíba and the third-oldest city in Brazil. It claims to have more trees than any other capital city, including an Atlantic rainforest preserve, and has a reputation for being friendly and safe. It's an increasingly popular holiday destination for Brazilian families. The 20km-long beachfront is agreeably clean, low-key and low-rise (no buildings above four stories allowed), with the central beach neighborhoods of Tambaú, Manaíra and Cabo Branco being the best areas to base yourself. The historic center, 7km inland, is steadily being spruced up after attaining National Heritage site status in 2007, and makes for an interesting wander. All in all, João Pessoa (or John Person), is a very nice spot to break up a journey.

History

Founded in 1585, the city was formerly known as Vila de Felipéia de NS das Neves. It was renamed in the 20th century for João Pessoa, a governor of Paraíba who formed an alliance with Getúlio Vargas to run for the Brazilian presidency in 1930. When courted by opposing political parties, João Pessoa uttered a pithy '*nego*' (I refuse), which is now given prominence in all Brazilian history books and emblazoned in bold letters on the Paraíba state flag. The Vargas–Pessoa ticket lost the election, and Pessoa was assassinated a few months later – an event which, ironically, sparked a revolutionary backlash that swept Vargas to power later in 1930.

Sights & Activities

Tambaú & the Coast

Estação Cabo Branco ARTS CENTER

(☎3214-8303; http://joaopessoa.pb.gov.br/estacaocb; Av João Cirilo Silva s/n; 9am-9pm Tue-Fri, 10am-9pm Sat & Sun) FREE Inaugurated in 2008, this cultural center 5km southeast of Tambaú was designed by famed Brazilian architect Oscar Niemeyer and is more interesting for its space-age architecture than for its exhibits, which are often underwhelming. An exception is Abelardo da Hora's female-form sculptures that are dotted around the grounds. The hexagonal glass main building provides great views from its top-floor terrace.

Bus 507 runs here from Av Epitacio Pessoa in Tambaú. If you walk left out of the parking lot at the south end of the complex and down to the beach (two minutes) through the Parque Municipal do Cabo Branco, then head 600m south along the beach, you'll be at **Ponta do Seixas**, the easternmost point of the Americas.

Praia de Tambaú BEACH

(Map p516) Praia de Tambaú, 7km east of the center, is an urban beach but nevertheless an enjoyable area to spend time. Bars, restaurants, coconut palms, fig trees and a broad promenade are strung along the seafront. Southward, **Praia Cabo Branco**, a beautiful stretch of sand, cliffs and palms, curves 5km round to Cabo Branco and Ponta do Seixas.

Ilha de Areia Vermelha BEACH

Ilha de Areia Vermelha is an island of red sand that emerges off the northern beaches at low tide for roughly half the days in each month. Boats park around the island and the party lasts until the tide comes in. You can catch a boat out there for R$20 to R$35 from Praia de Camboinha, 15km north of Tambaú.

Centro Histórico

Under the guidance of Iphan (Brazil's national cultural heritage institute), many parts of João Pessoa's historic center have been attractively renovated, with architectural styles ranging from baroque to art deco. The area makes for an enjoyable wander. Tourist offices have a useful walking-tour map available, and there are many important churches dotted around town.

★ **Centro Cultural São Francisco** MONASTERY

(Map p515; ☎3218-4505; www.igrejadesaofranciscopb.org; Praça São Francisco; admission with guided tour R$5; 8:30am-5pm Mon-Fri, 9am-2pm Sat & Sun) This is one of Brazil's most beautiful monasteries. São Francisco's construction was interrupted by battles with the Dutch and French, resulting in a beautiful but architecturally confused complex built over two

Central João Pessoa

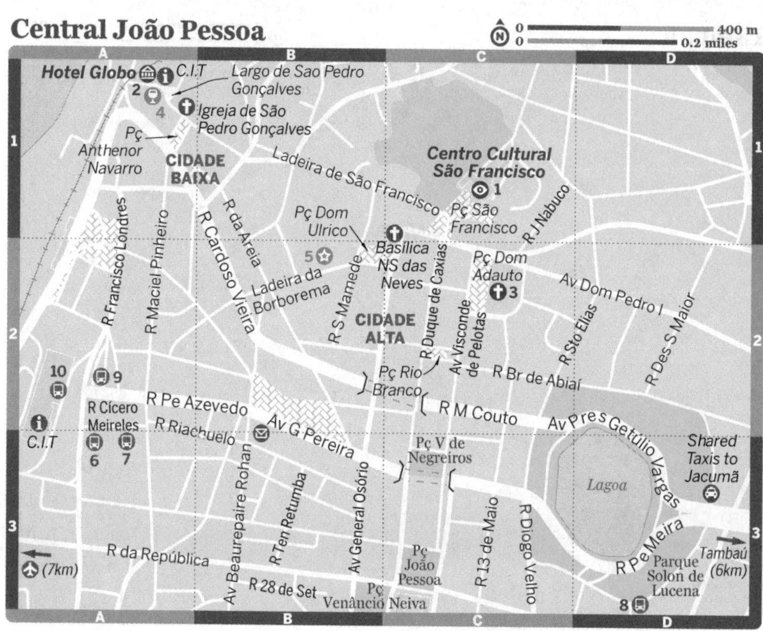

centuries (1589–1779). The facade, the church towers and the adjoining Santo Antônio monastery display a hodgepodge of styles.

Its highlight, especially for the quantity of gold adorning its altars, is the chapel, Capela de la Ordem Terceira de São Francisco. Portuguese-tile walls lead up to the church's carved jacaranda doors.

★**Hotel Globo** MUSEUM
(Map p515; Largo de São Pedro Gonçalves 7; 9am-5pm Mon-Fri, to 4pm Sat) Built in 1928 the old Hotel Globo houses a small museum and has a lovely rear terrace with views over tile roofs to the river. It was under a R$785-million restoration when we visited, scheduled to reopen by the time you read this.

Igreja NS do Carmo CHURCH
(Map p515; Praça Dom Adauto; 9:30-11am Mon-Fri) The 16th-century Igreja NS do Carmo stands at the center of an impressive complex of church buildings on Praça Dom Adauto, and faces the beautifully blue-tiled Casarão dos Azulejos.

Festivals & Events

João Pessoa cuts loose in the **Folia da Rua** (Party in the Streets), held the week before Carnaval proper (Friday to Friday); *blocos* (music and dancing groups) parade through parts of the city, some attracting up to a million revelers.

Central João Pessoa

Top Sights
1 Centro Cultural São Francisco............C1
2 Hotel Globo............A1

Sights
3 Igreja NS do Carmo............C2

Drinking & Nightlife
4 Vila do Porto............A1

Entertainment
5 Ateliê Multicultural Elioenai Gomes............B2

Transport
6 Buses to Airport............A3
7 Buses to Jacumã............A3
8 Buses to Tambaú & Manaíra............D3
9 Terminal de Integração............A2
10 Terminal Rodoviário Severino Camelo – Varadouro............A2

Sleeping & Eating

★**Slow Hostel** HOSTEL $
(Map p516; 3021-7218; www.facebook.com/slowhostel; Av Cajazeiras 108, Manaíra; dm with/without air-con R$55/45, s/d from R$80/110;

Tambaú

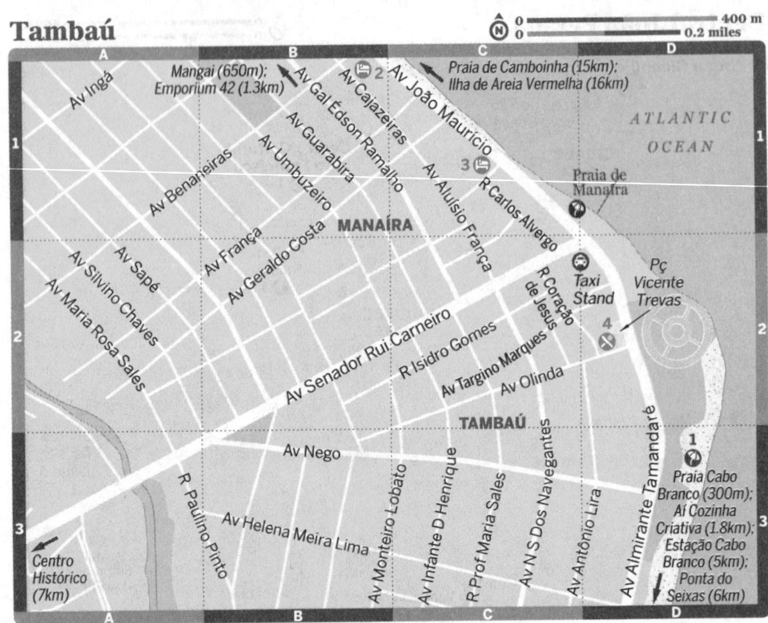

Tambaú

Sights

1 Praia de Tambaú ... D3

Sleeping

2 Slow Hostel ... B1
3 Verdegreen Hotel ... C1

Eating

4 Empório Café ... D2

) This excellent hostel has a friendly atmosphere and is set in a spacious house one short block from the beach. It's run by the charmingly helpful Marina and her family. Most of the rooms (single-sex and mixed dorms and one extreme-value private) have private bathrooms; common areas are spacious; and there are bicycles to rent.

Marina adores her city and knows everything you could possibly want to know. The adorable Northeastern touches from the hands of Marina's sweet mother at breakfast are a tasty treat!

Verdegreen Hotel HOTEL $$$

(Map p516; 3044-0000; www.verdegreen.com.br; Av João Maurício 255, Manaíra; s/d R$384/427;) Verdegreen is the eco-conscious choice, with solar-heated showers, reforested wood, half-flush toilets, and LED TVs and lighting throughout. It's all very hip and stylish, too, decked out in soothing greens and beiges with tasteful art and objets d'art scattered around. The staff is sweet and helpful, the hotel is fully nonsmoking and there are free bicycles for guests.

Empório Café CAFE $

(Map p516; www.facebook.com/emporiocafe; Coração de Jesus 145, Tambaú; mains R$17-39, cocktails R$8-20; 4pm-1am Mon, to 2am Tue-Thu, to 4am Fri & Sat, to midnight Sun;) This alternative-indie cafe-bar dishes up great-value salads, sandwiches, quiches, hummus and cheese-and-meat platters to a beautiful crowd. As the evening wears on, Empório packs in more trend and beauty for cocktails and indie tunes and is the town's GLS (Gays, Lesbians e Simpatizantes) gathering point.

Pão com Gergelim BURGERS $

(www.facebook.com/paocgergelim; Artur Enedino dos Anjos 78, Altiplano; burgers R$14-26; 6-11pm Tue-Sun;) Don't mind the mushroom-cloud bun; these rock-star-themed gourmet burgers are worth the 3km haul up to Altiplano, where the owners' oddly secured former home has been transformed into a trendy gathering point for beautiful carnivores.

Hand-cut fries and local craft beers round out this hidden residential hot spot. It's a R$15 taxi from Tambaú.

★ Mangai BUFFET **$$**

(www.mangai.com.br; Av General Édson Ramalho 696, Manaíra; per kg R$56.90; ⏲11am-10pm; 📶📝) Mangai's spectacular regional buffet is available in other cities, but it hails from João Pessoa. Most items are labeled in English, and there's plenty for vegetarians, as well as great meat and seafood dishes. Save room for some of the decadent desserts!

Aí Cozinha Criativa BUFFET **$$**

(☎3022-2222; www.facebook.com/aicozinha; Av Cabo Branco 2420, Hotel Ondas do Atlântico, Cabo Branco; mains R$38-87; ⏲3-11pm Mon-Thu, 4pm-midnight Fri & Sat; 📶) This fascinating Slow Food restaurant showcases the abundant ingredients of the *sertão* (the backlands or interior of the Northeast) in wonderfully gourmet ways. Special themed menus (Tuesday and Thursday; R$39 to R$48), for example, might feature fresh market *caju* (cashew fruit) that becomes carpaccio and the base for a *moqueca*. Don't dare skip the churros dunked in *doce de leite* (creamy milk-and-sugar concoction) for dessert!

Drinking & Entertainment

The historic center has a lively nocturnal scene with some good bars and music venues attracting students, their teachers and an informal, arty crowd. Saturday is the big party day, kicking off with an open-air *chorinho* music session in Praça Rio Branco from around noon to 3pm. As evening arrives, a samba session normally runs from about 7pm to 11pm every second Saturday at the **Ateliê Multicultural Elioenai Gomes** (Map p515; www.ateliemulticultural.com.br; Ladeira da Borborema 101).

It's safe to travel to the historic center by bus till late afternoon (or later if you're in a group), but best to take a taxi back later.

Nightlife in Tambaú is centered on and around Rua Coração de Jesus and in the well-done seafront kiosks, some of which offer live music.

OFF THE BEATEN TRACK

THE TIMELESS SERTÃO

The interior of the Northeast, known as the *sertão*, is not all drought-stricken countryside and dirt-poor towns, as its stereotype might have us believe. The sertanejos (residents of the *sertão*) are a proud people with a rich popular culture evident in their music, festivals and artisanship. There is also amazing natural beauty out there in the rocky backlands, and fascinating evidence of a history stretching right back to the dinosaurs. The towns of the *sertão* are equipped with adequate hotels and pousadas (guesthouses) and are served well enough by buses. The ideal (greenest and coolest) months to venture there are June and July. Natal-based Cariri Ecotours (p523) specializes in tours to these areas. These are a few highlight destinations to launch your explorations:

Ingá, Paraíba The **Pedra do Ingá** (http://pedradoinga.blogspot.com) is a single rock 23m long and nearly 4m high in the middle of the Rio Ingá. It's covered in beautiful carvings that are possibly up to 5000 years old. It's 95km west of João Pessoa and 46km short of Campina Grande, a city famed for its huge **Festa Junina**, a party lasting all June.

Lajedo de Soledade, Rio Grande do Norte Rock paintings up to 10,000 years old (including the world's oldest macaw pictures), ancient ceremonial sites and ice-age animal fossils are all found here. Guided visits are run from the **Museu do Lajedo** (☎3333-1017; www.lajedodesoledade.org.br; R$5; ⏲8am-5pm Tue-Sun), 75km southwest of Mossoró, near Apodi.

Lajedo da Pai Mateus, Cariri, Paraíba A bizarre, otherworldly, rocky landscape of round boulders, granite blocks, caves and ancient petroglyphs, some 70km west of Campina Grande; several recent Brazilian films were shot here. Excellent accommodations are available at **Fazenda Pai Mateus** (☎3356-1250; www.paimateus.com.br; s/d R$220/275; ❄📶🏊).

Serra da Capivara, Piauí The earliest evidence of humanity in the Americas and a vast 30,000 rock paintings can be found in a dramatic rocky landscape near São Raimundo Nonato.

Emporium 42 BAR

(Av Guarabira 1246, Manaíra; ⏲4pm-midnight Tue-Thu, to 2am Fri & Sat) Part store, part bar, this small craft beer emporium is the spot to come in Jampa. More than 200 artisanal beers come by the bottle (50 or so Brazilian), plus a few select on draft. There's a pleasant patio and a savory menu of *bolinhos* and *pastéis* (deep-fried dough filled with meat, cheese or seafood; R$13 to R$16) to soak up all the hops. It's an easy walk from most accommodations in Manaíra.

Vila do Porto BAR

(Map p515; www.facebook.com/restaurantevilado porto; Largo de São Pedro Gonçalves 8; ⏲11:30am-8pm Tue-Thu, to 10pm Fri & Sat) Join the sunset parties at Vila do Porto, a restaurant-bar and courtyard overlooking the river. There's samba here every Monday and the first and second Saturday of the month from 8pm.

★**Bolero at Sunset** LIVE MUSIC

(Praia do Jacaré; ⏲sunset) Almost every Brazilian tourist in João Pessoa heads to the north of the city to Cabodelo (10km from Tambaú) for sunset to see saxophonist Jurandy play Ravel's *Bolero* while being paddled up and down the Rio Paraíba in a small canoe. The daily event is a supremely kitschy, classically Brazilian phenomenon; some people come from Natal and Recife just for this. Don't linger afterwards – the area can get dicey once the crowds clear out.

Formerly, four overwater bars played host, charging covers of R$5 to R$8, but city licensing laws caught up with them in 2015 and some were torn down. But the show must go on! You can now buy a ticket to watch from the water on a catamaran (R$35), or watch for free from the riverside or at one of the remaining bars, which still charge the covers even though it's not technically legal to do so. Taxis from Tambaú are about R$30 each way; or ride bus 513 from Tambaú to the end of the line and transfer free to a Jacaré bus.

ℹ Information

Banco do Brasil (Av Senador Rui Carneiro 166, Tambaú) Visa/Mastercard ATM.

C.I.T (Centro de Informações Turísticas; www.destinoparaiba.pb.gov.br) has branches at the Airport (☎98828-9769; ⏲10am-4pm & 10pm-4am Mar-Sep, 9am-3pm and 9pm-3am Oct-Feb), bus station (Map p515; ☎3218-6655; Rua Francisco Londres, bus station; ⏲8am-6pm) Centro Histórico (Map p515; Hotel Globo, Largo de São Pedro Gonçalves 7; ⏲9am-5pm Mon-Fri, to 4pm Sat) Tambaú (☎3214-8185; Av Almirante Tamandaré 100; ⏲8am-7pm) The Paraíba tourism department (PBTUR) runs helpful, well-informed information offices.

ℹ Getting There & Away

Presidente Castro Pinto Airport (☎3041-4200), 8km west of the center, has flights to Rio, São Paulo, Brasília and the major cities of the Northeast.

João Pessoa's **bus station** (Map p515; ☎3221-9611; Rua Francisco Londres), Terminal Rodoviário Severino Camelo – Varadouro, is located 8km west of Tambaú in central João Pessoa.

ℹ Getting Around

A taxi from the airport to Tambaú costs around R$85. Airport buses (R$2.15) from central João Pessoa leave from the first of the four bus stops along Rua Cícero Meireles, coming from the bus station nearby.

A taxi from the bus station to Tambaú is around R$30.

Local buses run from the **Terminal de Integração** (Map p515; Padre Azevedo), across the street from the bus station. Buses 510 and 513 run frequently to Tambaú (R$2.70, 25 minutes) via Parque Solon de Lucena. Returning from Tambaú, catch them southbound on Av General Édson Ramalho or Rua Maria Sales.

BUSES FROM JOÃO PESSOA

DESTINATION	COST FROM (R$)	TIME (HR)	COMPANY
Fortaleza	100	10	Viação Nordeste (www.viacaonordeste.com.br)
Maceió	65	7½	Catedral Turismo (www.catedralturismo.com.br), São Geraldo (www.saogeraldo.com.br)
Natal	34	3	Viação Nordeste (www.viacaonordeste.com.br)
Recife	29	2	Progresso (www.progressoonline.com.br)
Salvador	130	16	Catedral Turismo (www.catedralturismo.com.br), Rota Transportes (www.rotatransportes.com.br)

RIO GRANDE DO NORTE

Pure air, sun, fine beaches and sand dunes symbolize this small state in Brazil's northeast corner. Rio Grande do Norte has one of the country's most spectacular coastlines, some 500km of beautiful beach after beautiful beach, many of them fronted by reefs with natural pools and backed by tall dunes or cliffs. The locals, known as Potiguares, are generally friendly and welcoming.

Natal

084 / POP 804,000

Rio Grande do Norte's capital is a clean, bright and rather bland city that has swelled as a hub for coastal package tourism, much of it catering to Brazilian families. Its main attractions are touristic beaches, buggy rides and other organized excursions, restaurants and nightlife – it won't appeal too much if you seek museums, theater or wild empty strands.

Most visitors stay in the beach neighborhood of Ponta Negra; it's a striking location, overlooked by fantastic dunes, with steady surf and some lively nightlife. The older part of Natal, including the unexciting city center, Cidade Alta, about 12km northwest of Ponta Negra, is on a peninsula flanked to the west by the Rio Potengi and to the east by Atlantic beaches and reefs.

History

An early Portuguese attempt to settle the Natal area in 1535 failed due to the hostility of the indigenous Potiguar people and French brazilwood traders. The Portuguese didn't return until December 25, 1597, when a fleet arrived at the mouth of the Rio Potengi with orders to build a fort to keep the French and Potiguares at bay; the name Natal is Portuguese for Christmas. On January 6, 1598, the day of the Reis Magos (Three Wise Men), the Portuguese began building their fortress, the Forte dos Reis Magos.

Apart from a period of Dutch occupation (1630–54), Natal remained under Portuguese control thereafter. During WWII its strategic location close to Brazil's northeastern tip prompted Presidents Getúlio Vargas and Franklin D Roosevelt to turn the sleepy city into a supply base for Allied operations in North Africa. Thousands of US military were stationed here and the city became known as the 'Trampoline to Victory.' These days, it's marketed as the Cidade do Sol (Sun City), and with good reason.

Sights & Activities

Forte dos Reis Magos FORT

(admission R$3; 8am-4pm) The fort that got Natal started in 1598 still stands in its original five-pointed-star shape on the reef at the tip of the peninsula at the north end of town. The views of the city, the Ponte Nova and the dunes across the Rio Potengi are fantastic.

The fort contains a chapel, a well, cannons and soldiers' quarters. It also boasts the Marco de Touros, a marker stone placed by the Portuguese in 1501 at Praia do Marco, near São Miguel do Gostoso, which is considered Brazil's oldest historical document. A taxi to the fort from Praia da Areia Preta (reached by bus 56 from Ponta Negra) costs around R$15.

Dunas de Genipabu ADVENTURE TOUR

Try a popular and exciting outing to the spectacularly high and steep dunes about 10km north of the city near Genipabu, where you can be driven up and down the sand mountains for an hour or so in a beach buggy. A number of operators are recommended: **Natal Vans** (Map p522; 3642-1883; www.natalvans.com.br; Duna Barcane Mall, Av Engenheiro Roberto Freire 3112, Ponta Negra; 7am-10pm Mon-Fri, to 9pm Sun) and **Marazul** (Map p522; 3219-6480; www.marazulreceptivo.com.br; Rua Vereador Manoel Sátiro 75, Ponta Negra; 8am-10pm) offer several fairly standardized out-of-town trips, easily booked through your accommodations.

You'll be asked if you want the trip *com ou sem emoção* (with or without excitement), and if you choose *com*, you'll be treated to thrills such as the Wall of Death and the Vertical Descent.

Operators generally include Genipabu as part of longer day trips (R$400 per buggy depending on season, plus R$40 to enter the dunes) that may involve a 15km beach drive north from Genipabu to Jacumã (with a river crossing by raft), and several other stops for zip-lining, dune surfing into lakes and other thrills. Buggies hold up to four passengers: operators can usually put separate individuals together to share the total cost.

Beaches

Natal's northern city beaches, **Praia do Meio** (Map p521), **Praia dos Artistas** (Map p521) and **Praia da Areia Preta**, stretching 5km south from the Forte dos Reis Magos to Farol de Mãe Luiza lighthouse, are lackluster urban beaches that get crowded at weekends and holidays. South of the lighthouse, the coast road Via Costeira continues 8km south to Ponta Negra, passing the calm **Praia da Barreira d'Água** and its resort hotels.

Praia de Ponta Negra BEACH

Praia de Ponta Negra, at the far south end of the city, is the nicest beach in Natal; it's 3km long and full of surfers, sailing boats and beach bars, with the city's best selection of hotels, pousadas and restaurants in the streets behind. The surf here is consistent, if small: you can rent boards from a few places for around R$10 per hour.

Morro da Careca DUNE

At the south end of Praia de Ponta Negra is the Morro da Careca, a spectacularly high sand dune with a steep face dropping straight into the sea. Access to the dune has been closed off to prevent further erosion and damage to the primary Atlantic rainforest that covers it.

Festivals & Events

Carnatal PARADE, MUSIC

(www.carnatal.com.br; Dec) Natal's out-of-season Carnaval, Carnatal, takes to the streets of the Lagoa Nova district over four days in early December, with Salvador-style *trios elétricos* (bands playing atop huge trucks) and *blocos* sporting names such as Burro Elétrico (Electric Donkey) and Cerveja & Coco (Beer & Coconut). It's the wildest out-of-season Carnaval in Brazil.

It's a great substitute for anyone who can't make it to the real deal.

Sleeping

Options for all budgets abound in Ponta Negra.

Republika Hostel HOSTEL $

(Map p522; 3236-2782; www.republikahostel.com.br; Porto das Oficinas 8944, Ponta Negra; dm R$45, s/d with fan R$80/100, with air-con R$100/120;) Republika's low-lit bar, comfy hammock and TV areas, and big, clean kitchen and eating area create a cozy atmosphere for mingling with fellow travelers. It's housed in a converted family home that evokes Santorini and is run by local hipster chef Anderson, who lived many years in England and Portugal. It's well located near some of Ponta Negra's best eats.

Albergue da Costa HOSTEL $

(Map p522; 3219-0095; www.alberguedacosta.com.br; Av Praia de Ponta Negra 8932, Ponta Negra; dm/d R$55/110;) This super-friendly HI hostel has comfortable dorms, good breakfasts, ample common spaces and laid-back management. Other attractions include free use of skateboards, bike and surfboard rental, and regular social activities such as live music and barbecues etc. English, Italian and Spanish are spoken.

Che Lagarto HOSTEL $

(Map p522; 3219-2227; www.chelagarto.com; Poeta Jorge Fernandes 45, Alto de Ponta Negra; dm R$30-42, r R$130;) Owner Chara spent eight years honing hospitality skills at a luxury pousada in Fernando de Noronha before opening the Natal edition of this South American chain of hip hostels. The all air-con facilities are good but could use some upkeep. The real coup is the atmospheric *caju* tree that spreads its massive limbs about the front patio lounge, which has an outdoor shower!

Casa Grande Apart-Hotel HOTEL $

(Map p522; 3236-3401; www.aparthotelcasagrande.com; Pedro da Fonseca Filho 3050, Alto de Ponta Negra; r R$130, with kitchen R$220-240;) Casa Grande offers exceptional rates (especially in low season, when they nearly halve) for spacious rooms three blocks from the beach. Most have hammock-strung balconies and some have sea views.

Pousada Castanheira POUSADA $$

(3236-2918; www.pousadacastanheira.com.br; Av Engenheiro Roberto Freire 5620, Alto de Ponta Negra; r from R$349;) It's quite a surprise to find such a secluded and leafy retreat just one short block up from Praia de Ponta Negra. Tile-floored rooms are cool and have bamboo furnishings; three of the 10 have sea views. There's a good pool area with a bar, plus a nice small front garden. One of the owners speaks English.

Pousada Manga Rosa POUSADA $$

(3219-0508; www.mangarosanatal.com.br; Erivan França 240, Ponta Negra; r R$230-250;) Manga Rosa sits right across from the tree-lined southern end of Praia Ponta Negra; it's as close as you can get to the sea without sleeping on the beach. It has a refreshingly rustic style, with a stone-faced

Central Natal

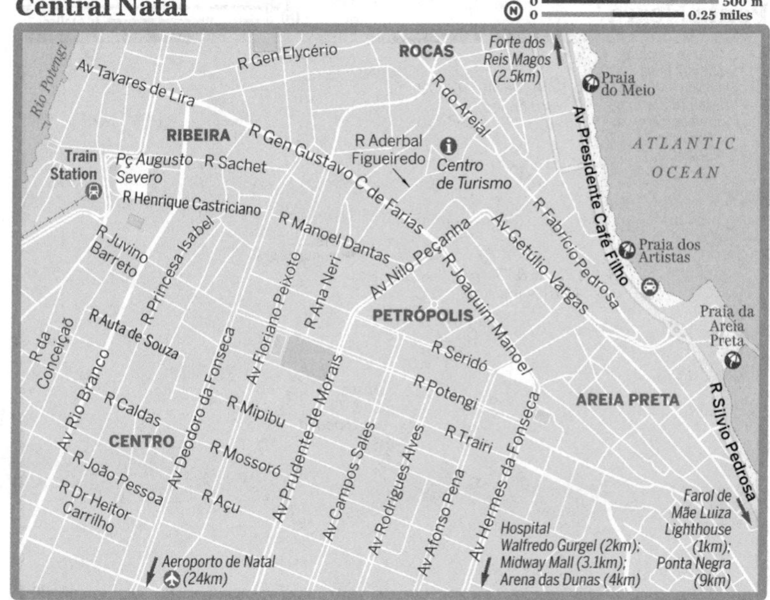

frontage and wooden stairways and balconies, but doesn't cheat on comfort.

The 15 rooms are moderately sized but bright and attractive, with wood furnishings, paintings and colorful bedspreads. Six have sea views.

★ Manary Praia Hotel BOUTIQUE HOTEL **$$$**
(Map p522; ☎3204-2900; www.manary.com.br; Francisco Gurgel 9067, Ponta Negra; s/d from R$450/496; ❄@📶🏊) One of the Northeast's most charming places to stay, the 23-room Manary is bedecked with beautiful nature photos by its late owner and creator, Eduardo Bagnoli, and tasteful artisanal artifacts from around the world. The detail is stunning: more thought was put into the one-room spa than nearly all the other spas in Brazil combined. To top it off, the poolside restaurant, Manary Gastronomia & Arte (Map p522; ☎3204-2900; www.manary.com.br; Francisco Gurgel 9067; mains R$45-82; ⏲noon-4pm & 7-11pm), which serves creative salads and superb seafood, is one of Natal's very best.

✕ Eating

★ Casa de Taipa BRAZILIAN **$**
(www.facebook.com/casadetaipatapiocariaecuscuzeria; Av Praia de Ponte Negra 8868, Ponta Negra; dishes R$12-36; ⏲5pm-midnight; 📶✎) What is probably Brazil's most famous *tapiocaria* flips the script on a traditionally R$4 street food and turns it into a gourmet treat fit for foodies. Droves of visitors and locals alike swarm this colorful and festive place for lightly pan-grilled tapioca 'pancakes' stuffed with sweet and savory goodies (vegetables, cheeses, grilled salted meats, prawns – even a *moqueca* version).

Save room for the ridiculous Mil Folhas, a stacked-high tapioca layer cake of *doce de leite*, caramelized bananas, grated coconut and crushed cashews. Get there early to avoid long waitlists.

★ Camarões Potiguar SEAFOOD **$$**
(Map p522; www.camaroes.com.br; Pedro da Fonseca Filho 8887, Ponta Negra; mains for 2 people R$66-119; ⏲11:30am-3:30pm & 6:30pm-midnight, to 11pm Sun) This bright, stylish and creative homage to the shrimp is arguably Natal's best dining experience, and it's permanently packed. Start with a tradtional shrimp and Catupiry *pastel* (thin square of dough stuffed with shrimp and cheese then fried) then follow up with anything from shrimp in a pumpkin to our fave: the Bonfim (sauteed with cashews, *coalho* cheese and fragrant *biquinho* peppers with *vatapá* –a seafood dish of African origins with a thick sauce of manioc paste, coconut and palm oil – risotto).

Ponta Negra

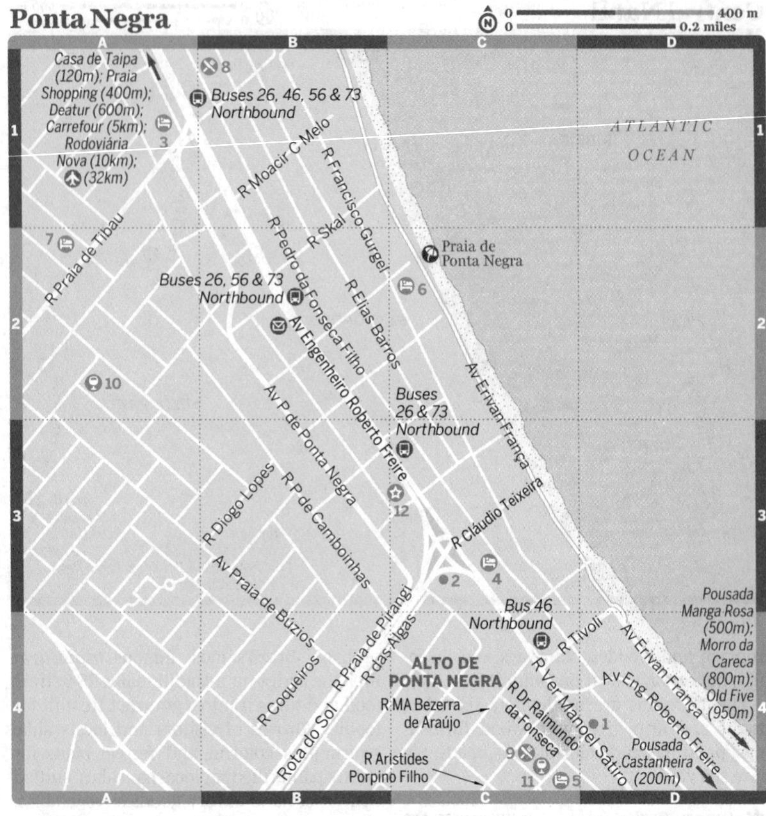

Ponta Negra

Activities, Courses & Tours

1 Marazul D4
2 Natal Vans C3

Sleeping

3 Albergue da Costa A1
4 Casa Grande Apart-Hotel C3
5 Che Lagarto C4
6 Manary Praia Hotel C2
7 Republika Hostel A2

Eating

8 Camarões Potiguar B1
9 Cipó Brasil C4
Manary Gastronomia & Arte ..... (see 6)

Drinking & Nightlife

10 Bar 54 ..... A2
11 Estacão do Malte C4

Entertainment

12 Decky C3

Everything is wonderful – including the service – and there are plenty of meat and fish dishes as well.

Old Five SEAFOOD $$

(☎3025-7005; www.natalinvesting.com/oldfive; Av Erivan França 230, Ponta Negra; mains R$25-85; 9am-midnight, to 10pm Sun;) Voted Natal's best beach bar, this American-owned Ponta Negra hot spot completely transformed the forgotten far end of the beach. During the day, dig your toes in the sand with a cocktail in hand and order from all manner of fresh seafood dishes (whole fish, risottos and pasta rife with fresh catches). At night, candles and lamps move the atmosphere into more romantic territory.

There's live music (MPB and reggae) from Thursday to Sunday, and you'll need to make a reservation at night.

Cipó Brasil PIZZERIA $$
(Map p522; www.cipobrasil.com.br; Aristides Porpino Filho 3111, Alto de Ponta Negra; pizzas R$21.50-83.50; 6pm-midnight;) A unanimous favorite, this fun jungle-themed place is great for sesame-crusted pizza (more than 30 types, from shrimp and four cheese to banana and chocolate) and both savory and sweet crepes. It's a starting point for evenings out. Get there early to avoid waiting.

Drinking & Nightlife

The Alto de Ponta Negra neighborhood in the upper part of Ponta Negra, around Rua MA Bezerra de Araújo and Rua Aristides Porpino Filho, is dense with a variety of bars, and packed from Wednesday to Saturday nights. Sex tourism is an unfortunate part of this scene. Petrópolis, in the city center, is the best neighborhood for hip local bars and *botecos*.

Estacão do Malte BAR
(Map p522; www.estacaodomalte.com; Poeta Jorge Fernandes 146, Alto de Ponta Negra; 6pm-midnight Tue-Sat) Though Brazil's excellent craft beer scene is criminally underrepresented at this bar for beer hounds, there are three local Natal beers on draft and a few others in the foreign-dominated list of 70 or so bottles.

Bar 54 BAR
(Map p522; www.facebook.com/54bar; Pôrto Mirim 8995, Ponta Negra; 6pm-2am Wed-Sat;) One of Ponta Negra's best bars, especially if you want to mingle with the cool kids away from the rowdier, tourist-geared bars. A breezy patio flush with vintage furniture and tables of reclaimed wooden cable spools set the vibe.

Entertainment

Decky LIVE MUSIC
(Map p522; www.facebook.com/deckybaroficial; Av Engenheiro Roberto Freire 9100, Ponta Negra; 6pm-5am Tue-Sat) One of the most popular spots in Ponta Negra, catering across several age brackets, Decky provides live rock, blues, jazz or MPB every night from 8:30pm. Plop down on the massive, breezy patio or inside the spacious main room with air-con. Expect a cover charge.

Arena das Dunas FOOTBALL
(3673-6800; www.arenadunas.com.br; Av Prudente de Morais 5121; tours R$30; 9am-4pm Tue-Sat) Natal gained the futuristic and intimate 31,375-seat Arena das Dunas, located about halfway between the city center and Ponta Negra, for its four group-stage matches in the 2014 World Cup. Today it's the main home of the city's two best teams, ABC and América (both usually found in national Série B).

Information

There is an intermittently staffed tourist-information desk at the bus station.

Banco do Brasil (www.bb.com.br; Dr Hernani Hugo Gomes 2700) Visa/Mastercard ATM.

Cariri Ecotours (9993-0027; www.caririecotours.com.br; Travessa Joaquim Fagundes 719, Tirol) A very experienced agency, recommended for adventurous coastal and inland tours from Natal. It can, for example, take you to Fortaleza along the beach, or to inland destinations such as Lajedo de Pai Mateus.

Centro de Turismo (Map p521; 3211-6149; www.turismo.natal.rn.gov.br; Aderbal Figueiredo 980, Petrópolis; 8am-7pm) This former jail near the city center now houses a lot of craft and souvenir stalls, and a minimally open tourist information desk. If you get here, treat yourself to a couple of scrumptious *bolinhos de macaxeira* (cassava patties with shrimp or meat) at the Marenosso Restaurante on-site.

Correios (Map p522; www.correios.com.br; Av Engenheiro Roberto Freire 1850, Ponta Negra; 8am-5pm Mon-Fri, to noon Sat) Postal services.

Deatur (Delegacia Especializada Assistência Ao Turista; 3232-7404; Praia Shopping, Av Engenheiro Roberto Freire 8790, Ponta Negra; 8am-6pm Mon-Fri) Natal's tourist police are helpful and may speak English, but are most unhelpfully closed on weekends.

Hospital Walfredo Gurgel (3232-7500; www.walfredogurgel.rn.gov.br; Av Salgado Filho, Tirol) The main public hospital, with emergency service.

Getting There & Away

AIR

Natal's new **Aeroporto de Natal** (Aeroporto Internacional Governador Aluízio Alves; 3343-6060; www.natal.aero; Av Ruy Pereira dos Santos 3100, São Gonçalo do Amarante) is in São Gonçalo do Amarante, around 35km west of Ponta Negra. It has scheduled flights from Lisbon, Buenos Aires, Milan and Cabo Verde in addition to many Brazilian cities.

OFF THE BEATEN TRACK

GALOS & GALINHOS

On a narrow sandbar between a lagoon and the ocean, 160km northwest of Natal, these two isolated fishing villages are still only emerging as beach destinations. Galinhos, with its sandy streets, warm, gentle waters, and the majority of the few accommodations, is a great place to unwind. Pristine beaches and dunes stretch 2km west to the lagoon mouth, and endlessly along the coast to the east. In Galos, 3.5km east up the lagoon, a mere 400 or so people live in even more peaceful surroundings.

The breezes here can be good for kitesurfing, and boat, buggy, horseback and horse-cart excursions are easily arranged. Especially recommended is the *'passeio ecológico'* (R$200 per person), a four- or five-hour boat excursion on the lagoon in which you catch and eat your own crab or fish lunch. There are numerous accommodations in Galinhos; in Galos there's just one – the wonderful **Pousada Peixe-Galo** (3552-2001; www.pousadapeixegalo.com.br; Rua da Candelária 30, Galos; r R$265;).

Access to Galos and Galinhos is not particularly easy, which is part of their charm. The most exciting approach is by beach buggy (R$300) from São Miguel do Gostoso (p530). A more conventional option, Expresso Cabral (www.expressocabral.com.br) runs buses from Natal's Rodoviária Nova at 6am on Monday, Friday and Sunday, returning at 5:15pm from Pratagil (R$25.70, three hours), which lies across the lagoon from Galinhos. From Pratagil, boats ferry passengers to Galinhos (per person R$5, 10 minutes) and Galos (15 minutes) from approximately 8am to 5pm. Accommodations can arrange private boats 24/7 for R$20 (Galos) or R$50 (Galinhos). Buses to Natal return from Pratagil at 5:15pm on Monday, Friday and Sunday.

Alternatively, take a Macau-bound Cabral bus (departing Natal every three hours from 6am to 6pm) as far as the Galinhos turnoff *('trevo de Galinhos')* on Hwy BR-406 (R$23.40, 2½ hours), and then taxi to Pratagil (R$50; organize through your accommodations in Galinhos or Galos).

Another option for returning from Galinhos to Natal is a shared van (R$30) leaving at 6am daily.

If you have your own vehicle you can leave it safely parked at Pratagil for free.

A taxi between Natal's airport to Pratagil should cost R$300. To Fortaleza it's around R$1000 (so probably not a good idea!).

BUS

Long-distance buses go from the **Rodoviária Nova** (3205-2931; Av Capitão Mor Gouveia 1237), northwest of Ponta Negra, which received a face-lift for the 2014 World Cup.

CAR & MOTORCYCLE

Recommended car-rental companies with airport desks include **Avis** (3343-6277; www.avis.com.br; Aeroporto de Natal; 6am-midnight) and **Localiza** (3343-6395; www.localiza.com; Aeroporto de Natal; 24hr). Located outside of Natal's airport, **Foco** (97400-1036; www.aluguefoco.com.br; Rua Nazireu Samuel 100, São Gonçalo do Amarante) offers slightly better rates than the in-airport competition. It liaises with airport agency P&P Turismo and picks you up via shuttle.

Getting Around

TO/FROM THE AIRPORT

Natal's new airport at São Gonçalo do Amarante is quite a haul, 35km west of Ponta Negra. **Trampolím da Vitória** (3343-5151; www.trampolimdavitoria.com) runs a public bus that's hardly worth the hassle from Ponta Negra. You need to catch bus 46, 54 or 73 along Av Engenheiro Roberto Freire to **Midway Mall** (www.midwaymall.com.br; Av Bernardo Vieira 3775, Tirol; R$2.65, 45 minutes), then switch for the 'R' bus, which hems and haws its way to the airport (R$2.80, 1½ hours, every 30 to 45 minutes from 5:10am to 11:30pm), passing the bus stop directly in front of the bus-station exit along the way. From the airport, catch the 'R' just outside Arrivals. Most travelers opt for the far more convenient shared van services such as **Natal Transfer** (3343-6272; www.nataltransfer.com.br) and **Van Service** (4141-2848; www.vanservice.com.br), which run shared vans to Natal ($40) and Praia da Pipa (R$95) leaving after each flight; to the airport, make a reservation in advance for pickup three hours before departure.

A taxi from the airport costs about R$100 to R$120 to Ponta Negra and R$228 or so to Praia da Pipa.

TO/FROM THE BUS STATION

For Ponta Negra (Av Engenheiro Roberto Freire), catch bus 66 (R$2.65) from the stop opposite the Petrobras gas station next to the Rodoviária Nova; a taxi costs R$30 to R$50 depending on time of day and location in Ponta Negra.

BUS

From stops north of Rota do Sol on Av Engenheiro Roberto Freire in Ponta Negra, buses 26, 46 and 73 run north to the Praia Shopping and Via Direta malls; 56 goes along the Via Costeira to Areia Preta then heads inland towards the city center.

City bus fares are R$2.65.

Praia da Pipa

084 / POP 6500

Pipa is one of Brazil's magical destinations: pristine beaches backed by tall cliffs, dreamy lagoons, decent surfing, dolphin- and turtle-filled waters, a great selection of pousadas, hostels, global restaurants and good nightlife. It was just another small, roadless fishing village when discovered by surfers in the 1970s; today Pipa rivals Jericoacoara (Ceará) as the Northeast's hippest beach town, and attracts partiers from Natal, João Pessoa, Recife and beyond at holidays and weekends, and a slew of international travelers year-round. Its laid-back, ecological and independent-traveler vibe still reigns and, with luck, Pipa may be just too small for that to change, despite the ranks of umbrella'ed tables along the main beaches catering to van loads of day-trippers from Natal.

Sights & Activities

The main beach, **Praia da Pipa** (Praia do Centro), about 1.5km long, has fishing boats, numerous bars and restaurants, and rock pools at low tide.

Praia do Madeiro curves northward from the headland at the far end of Baía dos Golfinhos and has a few upmarket hotels dotted along its length. It's good for beginner surfers (group/individual classes cost R$60/80).

Praia do Amor, the advanced surf beach, is accessed off the eastern part of Av Baía dos Golfinhos. You can rent surfboards here and in town for around R$20 per hour (or R$50 for the day); swimming can be dangerous.

Lagoa de Guaraíras, behind the river mouth at Tibau do Sul, 8km northwest of Pipa, is one of the area's most stunning landscapes, a massive, dune- and mangrove-bound lagoon, particularly spectacular at sunset. The dockside **Creperia Marinas** (www.hotelmarinas.com.br; Av Governador Aluizio Alves 301; crepes R$16-40; 11am-8pm) is a brilliant sunset-viewing spot.

Santuário Ecológico de Pipa NATURE RESERVE
(99982-8044; admission R$10; 7am-5pm) This small, privately owned reserve, 2km west along the main road from the town center, does a valuable job of protecting at least some of the Pipa coast from development. Well-marked trails lead through secondary forest to impressive lookouts over Baía dos Golfinhos and Praia do Madeiro, from which you can often see large green turtles at high tide.

BUSES FROM NATAL

DESTINATION	COST FROM (R$)	TIME (HR)	COMPANY
Aracati (Canoa Quebrada)	74	6	Expresso Guanabara (www.expressoguanabara.com.br), Viação Nordeste (www.viacaonordeste.com.br)
Belém	375	36	Expresso Guanabara (www.expressoguanabara.com.br)
Fortaleza	85	8	Viação Nordeste (www.viacaonordeste.com.br)
João Pessoa	34	3	Viação Nordeste (www.viacaonordeste.com.br)
Recife	50	4½	Autoviação Progresso (www.progressoonline.com.br)
Salvador	212	21	Gontijo (www.gontijo.com.br), São Geraldo (www.saogeraldo.com.br)
São Miguel de Gostoso	17.50	2½	Expresso Cabral (www.expressocabral.com.br)

BEACH-BUGGY PARADISE

With broad, sandy beaches that stretch along much of the 1800km-long coastline from Tamandaré (Pernambuco) to São Luís (Maranhão), the Northeast is Brazil's true beach-buggy paradise. These four-wheel, five-seat contraptions – usually built on a VW Beetle chassis – roar along beaches and up and down dunes the length of the region, with cargoes of happy tourists enjoying off-road trips amid fabulous scenery with the ocean wind in their hair.

If you can cope with the fact that buggies guzzle a liter of gasoline every 5km or 6km, and make an unholy racket, a buggy trip is invariably a lot of fun. One passenger sits in front with the driver; up to three sit in the back. Trips can be as short or long as you like, and you can stop wherever you please. The **Dunas de Genipabu** (p519) make a fun half-day outing from Natal, while the 180km round-trip from **São Miguel do Gostoso** (p530) to **Galinhos** and back is a fabulous day trip.

Even longer trips such as Natal to **Fortaleza** (in Ceará; 700km), Fortaleza to **Jericoacoara** (nearly 300km), or Jericoacoara to the **Lençóis Maranhenses** (in Maranhão; 300km) are quite feasible. The Natal to Fortaleza stretch is one of the most beautiful and least-developed coastlines in Brazil, strung with colored cliffs, rolling dunes, salt flats, reefs, palm-lined beaches, freshwater lagoons, tiny traditional fishing villages and some larger settlements popular with local weekenders. The trip takes four to five days and passes approximately 92 beaches; the cost ranges from R$1000 per Jeep per day, including transport, guide, meals and accommodations (up to three people) on the economical end, and up to R$6400 (based on double occupancy) for more comfortable pousadas, transport (by Land Rover) and an English-speaking guide. Make sure you go with an authorized driver, such as through **Natal Vans** (p519) and **Marazul** (p519). It's also possible to do the trip more comfortably in Jeeps, with agencies such as Natal's **Cariri Ecotours** (p523) or **Top Buggy** (☎99996-8184; www.topbuggy.com.br; Av Moema Tinoco 1559), or Jericoacoara's **Jeri Off Road** (p549).

For a slightly shorter trip, start from São Miguel do Gostoso, where a buggy, Jeep or 4WD pickup to Fortaleza costs around R$1200.

For good environmental reasons and/or consideration for other beach users, local regulations prohibit vehicle traffic on certain beaches and dunes on some or all days, and sometimes you have to duck inland around river mouths, mangrove areas and so on, but there is still plenty of beach to roar along.

Bicho do Mangue KAYAKING
(☎9928-1087; www.bichodomangue.blogspot.com.br; per person R$30) Does excellent three-hour guided kayak excursions starting about an hour before high tide. You can book through accommodations in Pipa.

Tours

★ **Mandacaru Expedições** TRAVEL AGENCY
(☎9988-5892; www.mandacaruexpedicoes.com.br) This excellent small Pipa-based agency can arrange any Brazilian travel experience or itinerary without extra agent's fees, based on its widely traveled owner's personal knowledge. There's an emphasis on high ecotouristic and safety standards. Highlights include buggy tours both north and south, tips for dolphin sightings and excursions further afield.

Roberta also has a great-value home for rent as well, just a 12-minute walk from the center.

Sleeping

Pipa has dozens of pousadas, hostels and hotels, ranging from dumpy to five-star gorgeous. Many accommodations offer good discounts in low season.

Hostel do Céu HOSTEL $
(☎3246-2235; www.hosteldoceu.jimdo.com; Rua do Céu 153; dm/d with fan R$50/150; @ 📶 ❄) It's no party hostel, but this Argentine family-run spot offers the best budget infrastructure in Pipa, with top-notch separate and mixed dorms and, if you can manage to snag it, the best-value private room in town: a colorful top-floor space complete with large, breeze-blown windows, and both sea *and* sunset views!

Pousada Xamã POUSADA $

(☎3246-2267; www.pousadaxama.com.br; Cajueiro 12; s/d/tr R$90/150/180; ❄@📶🏊) Hidden up a side street near Pipa's southeastern edge is one of the Northeast's best budget pousadas. Ultrahospitable owner Neuza presides over great-value, pleasantly decorated rooms, most of which open onto a leafy, flower-fringed pool and garden area, with hammocks and hummingbirds. The breakfast is good, and the pousada offers Natal airport pickups for R$180 to R$200 (up to four people).

Media Veronica Hostel HOSTEL $

(☎3246-2607; www.mediaveronicahostel.com.br; Albacora 267; dm/r R$45/120, all excl breakfast; ❄📶) In new, bigger digs just 100m from its old location, this hostel is a labor of love for Argentine Juan Pablo, who impresses with reasonable prices and an emphasis on cleanliness, security and information for guests. Dorms come in four-, six- and 10-bed configurations (the latter is cramped) and a few privates have sea and floral garden views.

Breakfast isn't provided, but guests get special breakfast deals (R$6 to R$15) at two nearby eateries.

★Spa da Alma POUSADA $$

(☎3246-2357; www.spadaalma.tur.br; Rua do Spa 9; s/d from R$300/330; ❄@📶🏊) 🍃 On lush, sprawling hilltop grounds, 1.5km beyond the southeast edge of town, this great-value place boasts luxury at midrange prices. The scattered bungalows offer wide bay windows and verandas with incredible views toward the beaches below; there's a gorgeous pool overrun with peacocks beside the restaurant, and a lovely multiservice garden spa down below. It's stunning, very private and the price is right.

Pousada Alto da Pipa POUSADA $$

(☎3246-2281; www.pousadaaltodapipa.com.br; Gameleira 555; r R$220; ❄@📶🏊) This cute and colorful pousada uphill from the main street has small, clean and pretty pastel-hued rooms, but it's the setting along a lush courtyard-garden, with palm trees and small footbridges over tiny ponds, that makes it a special find. There's a 20% discount for cash payments.

Pousada Tamanduá POUSADA $$

(☎3246-2734; www.pousadatamanduapipa.com.br; Tamanduá 3; r R$180-200; ❄📶🏊) A cute and intimate 10-room place, with pretty rooms adorned with framed Peruvian patchwork cushion covers, and appealing stone-and-wood stairs and walkways, run by an amiable young couple.

Morada dos Ventos POUSADA $$

(☎3246-2284; www.moradadosventos.com; Rua dos Colibris 3; 1-/2-bedroom apt R$300/500; ❄📶🏊) Large one- and two-bedroom hexagonal apartments in a breezy location; a good restaurant with a well-stocked bar; and a large garden and pool make this welcoming Brazilian-Scottish operation a dependable choice.

Paraíso das Tartarugas POUSADA $$

(☎99482-3806; www.paraisodastartarugas.net; Praia do Amor; s/d R$120/180, with sea views R$120/200; 📶) If you've dreamt of staying in a wooden shack inches from the ocean, 'Turtle Paradise' is your place. The seven rooms and apartments are rustic but clean and pleasant, and four have decks almost on top of the waves. Amiable owner Bruno is away in Argentina, so service and friendliness have suffered, but it remains pretty idyllic.

The pousada is 200m along the shore from the east end of the main beach; take care when the tide's up.

★Toca da Coruja POUSADA $$$

(☎3246-2226; www.tocadacoruja.com.br; Av Baía dos Golfinhos; r R$772-1245; ❄@📶🏊) 🍃 One of Brazil's most charming luxury pousadas, Toca da Coruja is an eco- and community-conscious place wrapped in sprawling tropical gardens with sagui monkeys, birds and two gorgeous pools. All rooms are huge, but the deluxe bungalows are gigantic, with breezy wraparound verandas in the style of old Northeast ranch houses.

DOLPHIN-VIEWING IN PIPA

Baía dos Golfinhos, to the west of Praia da Pipa, is where you can get up close and personal with dolphins within about 2½ hours either side of low tide. The area is backed by cliffs and accessible on foot only from the main beach – during which time you can get cold beer, coconuts and caipirinhas from enterprising locals. Try to avoid viewing dolphins from the boat tours; they do not have a reputation for properly respecting the marine life or the environmental rules in place.

The pousada is built with some recycled materials and rescued 19th-century farmhouse furniture, and has copper-ionization treatment for the pools. Bossa nova is quietly pumped through the jungly gardens. Most of the 100 staff are locals. The superb facilities include a top-class restaurant and a nice garden bar. Children under 10 not permitted.

Eating

Pipa is a wonderful place to eat out, but finding quality is more challenging than finding something cheap.

Gelateria Preciosa ICE CREAM $

(Av Bais dos Golfinhos 1074; scoops R$9-16; noon-midnight;) Beat the heat at this Italian-owned *gelateria*. The 16 flavors change daily, but stalwarts include the namesake Presciosa (with Belgian chocolate) and Variegato Amarena (cream-based with Italian cherries).

Dona Branca BUFFET $

(Av Baia dos Golfinhos; meals from R$15; 11am-9pm) Places like this are a dying breed in popular beach towns like Pipa. Take your pick of any two meat items from the grill, then fill your plate with rice, beans, salad and other goodies from the buffet. It's R$2 extra with fish or shrimp, and there's a R$3 fine if you don't finish your plate!

Oba JAPANESE $

(www.facebook.com/obayakisoba; cnr Albacora & Rua da Arara; mains R$22-33; 6-11pm, closed Wed) It's not often you'll find genuine Japazilian *yakisoba* from São Paulo at these prices, but this place is the real deal. Heaped plates of noodles with veggies, shrimp, chicken, steak etc are the highlight, and the lychee *sakerinhas* (using sake instead of *cachaça*) ratchet up the fun.

★ Cruzeiro do Pescador SEAFOOD $$

(3246-2026; www.cruzeirodopescador.com.br; cnr Av Baía dos Golfinhos & Concris; mains R$55-65, for 2 people R$105-150; 1-4pm & 7-10:30pm;) On the southeast edge of town, about 1.5km from the center, what looks like a typical mess of a house hides a don't-miss culinary experience. Chef Daniel does everything with homemade and homegrown finesse, from the poetically handwritten menus and the romantic candlelit setting to the products from his own garden. The flavors of his cooking – some pinched from India and Bahia – are delicious.

The smoked or grilled seafood is great, but call ahead as some dishes take two hours to prepare, such as the Seleção do Mar (R$200), a slow-grilled seafood feast of biblical proportions.

★ Tapas FUSION $$

(99465-4468; Bem-Te-Vis 8; dishes R$12.50-39; 6:30-11pm Tue-Sat, closed May & Jun;) Tapas is a culinary godsend, a labor of love of a well-traveled paulista couple who dish out large Brazilian tapas peppered with Thai, Indian, French and Italian influences in a casual and artsy space. Sesame-crusted fresh tuna is one specialty, but it's all tasty, including the shrimp with honey and ginger, and the arugula, lettuce, mango and Gorgonzola salad.

Pan'e Vino ITALIAN $$

(www.pipa.com.br/panevino; Albacora; mains R$18-42; 6:30-10:30pm Tue-Sun) Real Italian food from well-traveled Roman-born chef Michele, whose passion for fresh ingredients can be seen in his ever-changing menus: lamb with rosemary; Messina-style fish with capers, olives and white wine; plus homemade pasta, risottos and pots of real Italian basil (seeds smuggled direct from Italy!).

Aprecíe INTERNATIONAL $$

(99194-9771; www.facebook.com/aprecie restaurante; Bem-Te-Vis 34; mains R$35-52; 6:30-11:30pm, closed Wed) One of Pipa's few Potiguar chefs runs this notable and intimate newcomer of just seven tables. A small but well-rounded menu awaits; whichever of the substantially portioned highlights you choose – the sesame-crusted tuna, the fish in vermouth sauce or the pepper steak – you'll find yourself with order envy when you see the other two go by!

Garagem SEAFOOD $$

(Praia do Centro; mains R$18-38; 10:30am-sunset;) With superb views of Pipa's cliffs and dunes, Garagem got its start as a famous bar, and is still good for sundowners; but it's also the best spot in Pipa proper for a beach lunch (such as excellent Argentine *picanha* – rump steak – plus fresh fish, sandwiches and salads) and a Bohemia to wash it down. It's the westernmost bar on the main beach.

Drinking & Nightlife

Nativos Bar BAR

(Av Baía dos Golfinhos 748; cocktails R$10-22; 6pm-1am) The classiest and certainly the most beautiful along a bar-heavy stretch of

Av Baía dos Golfinhos that includes Oz and Tribus, Pipa's drinking trifecta.

Boate dos Calangos CLUB
(☎3246-2429; www.facebook.com/calangos; Av Baía dos Golfinhos; ⏲from 1am Fri-Sun) A big dance hall at the far end of Av Baía dos Golfinhos that fills for live *forró* on Sunday and Euro-style DJs the other nights.

Shopping

Bookshop BOOKS
(☎8882-7172; Gameleira; ⏲6-11pm Thu-Sat) A good selection of books in 18 languages, for rent or trade, and a chill spot for a beer or coffee.

Orientation

Pipa is small but it can be a little hard to get your bearings on arrival. The main, central beach faces north. At its east end the coastline curves southeast to Praia do Amor. To its west, Baía dos Golfinhos and then Praia do Madeiro curve northwest. The narrow main street, Av Baía dos Golfinhos, runs about 2km through town parallel to the main beach and Praia do Amor, with small streets and lanes running off it down to the beach or uphill inland. The inland streets in central Pipa are, from west to east, Céu, Bem-Te-Vis, Gameleira, Mata and Albacora (with Arara branching off Albacora). Full-size public buses and tour vans stop at the west end of Av Baía dos Golfinhos; public minibuses and microbuses terminate on Av Baía dos Golfinhos near the southeast edge of town.

Information

Pipa is extraordinarily well endowed with helpful, informative websites. Take your pick from www.pipa.com.br or www.mapaguiapipa.com.br.

Cash is king in Pipa – many places do not accept credit cards. At the time of writing, options for foreign cards included a **Bradesco ATM** at Praça dos Pescadores; and **Banco do Brasil** at the west end of town, which was scheduled to be moved to an as-yet-undecided location. Both are frequently out of money or on the fritz.

Crime does occur in Pipa, doubtless exacerbated by the crack habits of some people here. Don't leave belongings unattended on beaches and don't leave valuables lying around in your room.

Correios (www.correios.com.br; Rua dos Bem-Te-Vis 71; ⏲8am-noon & 1:30-4pm Mon-Fri) Postal services.

Pipatour (☎3246-2234; www.pipatour.com; Av Baía dos Golfinhos 767; ⏲3-8pm) Helpful agency for flight, bus and tour bookings; ask English-speaking Marisa about her budget sea-view pousada out the back.

Getting There & Around

TO/FROM THE AIRPORT

A private taxi between **Aeroporto de Natal** (p523) and Pipa should cost R$170 to R$200. **Pipa Aventura** (☎3246-2024; www.pipaaventura.com.br; Av Baía dos Golfinhos 654; R$80-90; ⏲24hr) offers airport transfers by reservation for R$80 per person (minimum two people) between 7am and 11pm, and R$90 between 11pm and 7am.

BUS

Oceano (☎3311-3333; www.expresso-oceano.com.br) runs 12 daily buses (six on Sundays) from Natal's **Rodoviária Nova** (p524) to Pipa (R$13.50, 1½ hours) and back. Last departure from Natal is at 6pm, and from Pipa at 6:10pm. Going to Pipa from Natal, you can also catch the bus at the stop on Av Salgado Filho in front of Carrefour in Lagoa Nova (reached from Ponta Negra by bus 26, 46 or 73), about 10 minutes after they leave the Rodoviária Nova. **Alternativo Vans** (☎99973-0353) runs microbuses from Natal's Rodoviária Nova to Pipa at 5:50am, 10am and 2:30pm, returning from Pipa to Natal at 8am, 12:30pm and 4:40pm (R$12, 2½ hours).

Schedules on all these services change frequently, so check in advance.

If you're coming by bus from the south, get out at Goianinha (1½ hours from João Pessoa), where minibuses – nicknamed 'Dolphin van' – run every 10 to 15 minutes to Pipa (R$3.75, 50 minutes, from 5am to 11:30pm) from behind the faded pale-blue church, 250m off the main road.

Pipatour (p529) can reserve bus seats from Goianinha to Recife or Salvador for a R$15 fee.

North of Natal

The nearly 400km of coastline between Natal and the Ceará state border (along which the coast veers from east facing to north facing) is a growing playground for weekenders and day-trippers from Natal, but there are still dozens of lovely beaches to enjoy. The further from Natal you go, the more isolated and empty the beaches become.

São Miguel do Gostoso

☎084 / POP 4100

'Gostoso,' 110km from Natal, is an increasingly popular weekend and holiday getaway, with excellent pousadas, restaurants and bars, and also has several gorgeous beaches nearby that are mostly near empty. If you want to go somewhere still undiscovered by package tourism and still be awed by the scenery, go here, now.

Sights & Activities

The main beaches in town – **Praia do Maceió**, **Praia da Xêpa** and **Praia do Cardeiro** – make up a wide, continuous 2km stretch of relaxing sands; but the true gem is **Praia de Tourinhos**, 8km west at the end of a gravel road. It's a beautiful semicircular bay with just a few kiosks, and nothing more. During the week you won't share it with more than a few others. You can walk there along the coast, or take a round-trip by moto-taxi (ride on the back of a motorcycle; R$25 per person) or buggy (R$120 for up to four).

★Buggy Trips to Galinhos ADVENTURE TOUR
(one way/round-trip for up to 4 people R$300/450) About three hours each way, this sand-traversing adventure from São Miguel do Gostoso to Galinhos is an unforgettable wind-blown expedition along a spectacular 90km sequence of long, empty beaches, dunes and lagoons. Organize through your accommodations.

Clube Kauli Seadi KITESURFING, WINDSURFING
(☎9197-1297; www.clubekauliseadi.com; Praia do Cardeiro; ⏲9am-5:20pm) Ponta do Santo Cristo, at the far east end of Praia do Cardeiro, catches the wind and is a very popular wind- and kitesurfing spot: Clube Kauli Seadi takes classes (R$780) and rents equipment (per day R$186).

Sleeping & Eating

★Pousada Ilha do Vento POUSADA, HOSTEL $
(☎3263-4048; www.ilhadovento.com.br; Caraúnas 70; dm/s/d R$50/140/170; ❄📶🏊) A superb option on a sizable garden property at the east end of town. Dorms and private rooms are spotless, comfy, well designed and pleasingly decorated; there's a great breakfast; and the well-traveled Italo-Brazilian owners are superhelpful and welcoming.

★Pousada Casa de Taipa POUSADA $$
(☎3263-4227; www.pousadacasadetaipa.com.br; Bagre Caia Coco 99; d R$230; ❄📶🏊) The owners of this spot, 300m from the beach, are English-speaking and lovely to the core. The property has a Northeastern culturural theme and is especially memorable for the artsy endeavors of one of the owners, who has fashioned tables from egg and coconut shells, and painted beautiful matching murals in each room, on each room door and on each keychain.

It's all set round a nice garden with a pool and a restaurant.

★Genesis Resto Bar BRAZILIAN $$
(Praia da Xêpa 86; mains R$28-39; ⏲6-10:30pm) What comes off as a tad ramshackle at first glance reveals itself as Gostoso's most adorable bistro, serving up a choice few gussied-up dishes – curried shrimp fettuccine, sesame-crusted tuna, a gourmet burger – in a whimsical space donned with rustic furniture and Frida Kahlo kitsch. It's run by a chef-sommelier couple, so there's excellent wine and an impressive 'secret' craft beer list, too.

Bar do Tico SEAFOOD $$
(Praia do Cardeiro; mains R$19-62; ⏲10am-8:30pm; 📶) Just across from wide Praia do Cardeiro, this simple beach bar does simple fare very well: the *filete de cavala* (mackerel), served with salad, fried potato or *macaxeira* chips and *farofa*, is a treat along with a couple of beers.

Information

There's a Bradesco ATM on the main street that accepts foreign cards, but it can be temperamental.

Getting There & Away

Expresso Cabral (☎3205-4572; www.expressocabral.com.br) runs four daily buses from Monday to Saturday from Natal's **Rodoviária Nova** (p524) to Gostoso (R$17.50, three hours, 6:15am, 9:45am, 3:30pm and 5pm) and back; on Sundays, departures from Natal are at 7:15am and 2:30pm.

Taxis from **Aeroporto de Natal** (p523) should cost R$270, while a buggy along the beach costs R$700. Returning to Natal, you may be able to find a shared taxi for R$25 per person. Westbound public transportation is nonexistent.

Ceará, Piauí & Maranhão

Includes ➡

Best Places to Eat

- Peixe Brasileiro (p553)
- Restaurante do Antônio (p567)
- Coco Bambu (p540)
- Restaurante Senac (p562)
- Pimenta Verde (p553)

Best Places to Stay

- Casa Zulu (p547)
- Casa Lavinia (p561)
- La Ferme de Georges (p567)
- Vila Kalango (p552)
- Villa Chic (p552)

Why Go?

These three Northeastern states stretch along Brazil's only north-facing coast and back deep into the arid interior. The main draw for visitors are the beaches of Ceará, arrayed for hundreds of glorious kilometers either side of Fortaleza, the state's fun-loving biggest city. These are some of the very best beaches in Brazil, some supporting growing resort towns, others at most a small, traditional fishing village. The hip travelers' hangout Jericoacoara, uniquely located inside a dune-swept national park, is the jewel in Ceará's gorgeous coastline.

An adventurous coastal route leads west from Jericoacoara to the scenic, wildlife-rich Delta do Parnaíba and the vast expanse of high dunes and clear lagoons known as the Lençóis Maranhenses, one of Brazil's highlights. The beauty of the Lençóis will floor you. Further west still lie two of Brazil's most picturesque, intriguing colonial gems: half-decayed, half-restored São Luís, with its markedly Afro-Brazilian culture, and its perfect sleepy neighbor Alcântara.

When to Go

Fortaleza

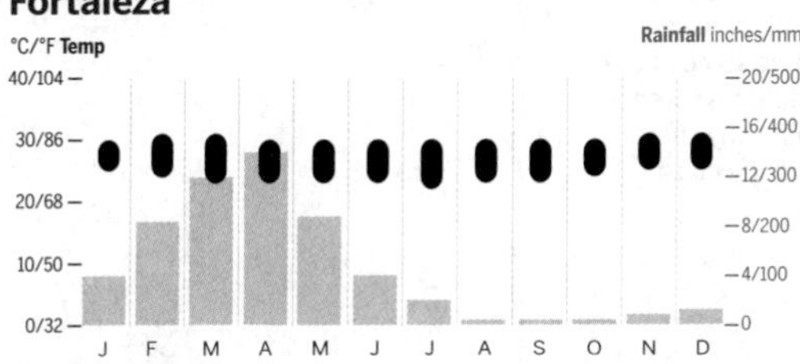

Jun São Luís erupts with color, music and dance in its Bumba Meu Boi festival.

Jul & Aug The Lençóis Maranhenses are at their most spectacular.

Jul–Jan Constant strong breezes make the coast one of the world's premier kitesurfing destinations.

Ceará, Piauí & Maranhão Highlights

1. Surfing, chilling, partying and staring at spectacular sunsets in the magical and cinematic village of **Jericoacoara** (p547).
2. Dipping into pristine lagoons between endless dunes in Maranhão's surreal **Parque Nacional dos Lençóis Maranhenses** (p565).
3. Enjoying the quirky combo of colonial heritage and Afro-Brazilian culture in **São Luís** (p557).
4. Stepping back in time at the charmingly crumbling colonial town of **Alcântara** (p563).
5. Having a long, palm-lined curve of beach almost to yourself at **Icaraí de Amontada** (p546).
6. Discovering the restaurants, nightlife and beach scene of **Fortaleza** (p534).
7. **Kitesurfing** (p548) or windsurfing some of the world's best breezes almost anywhere along the coast.

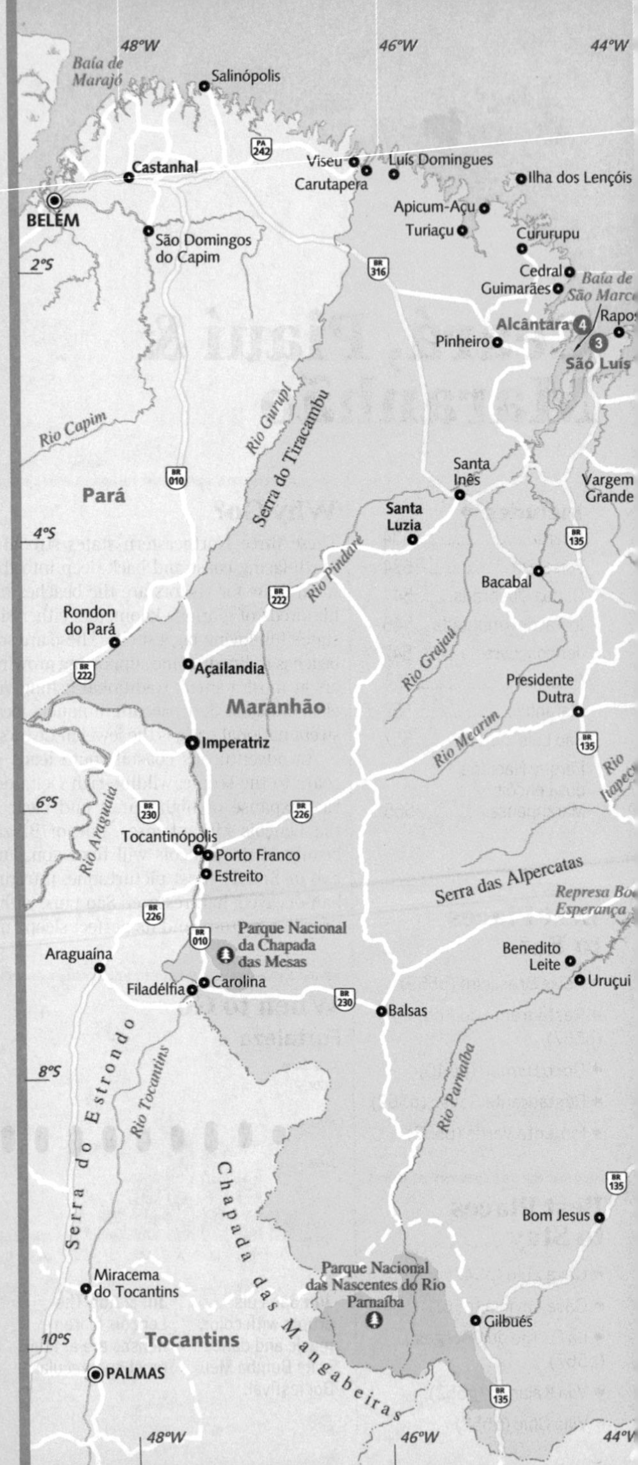

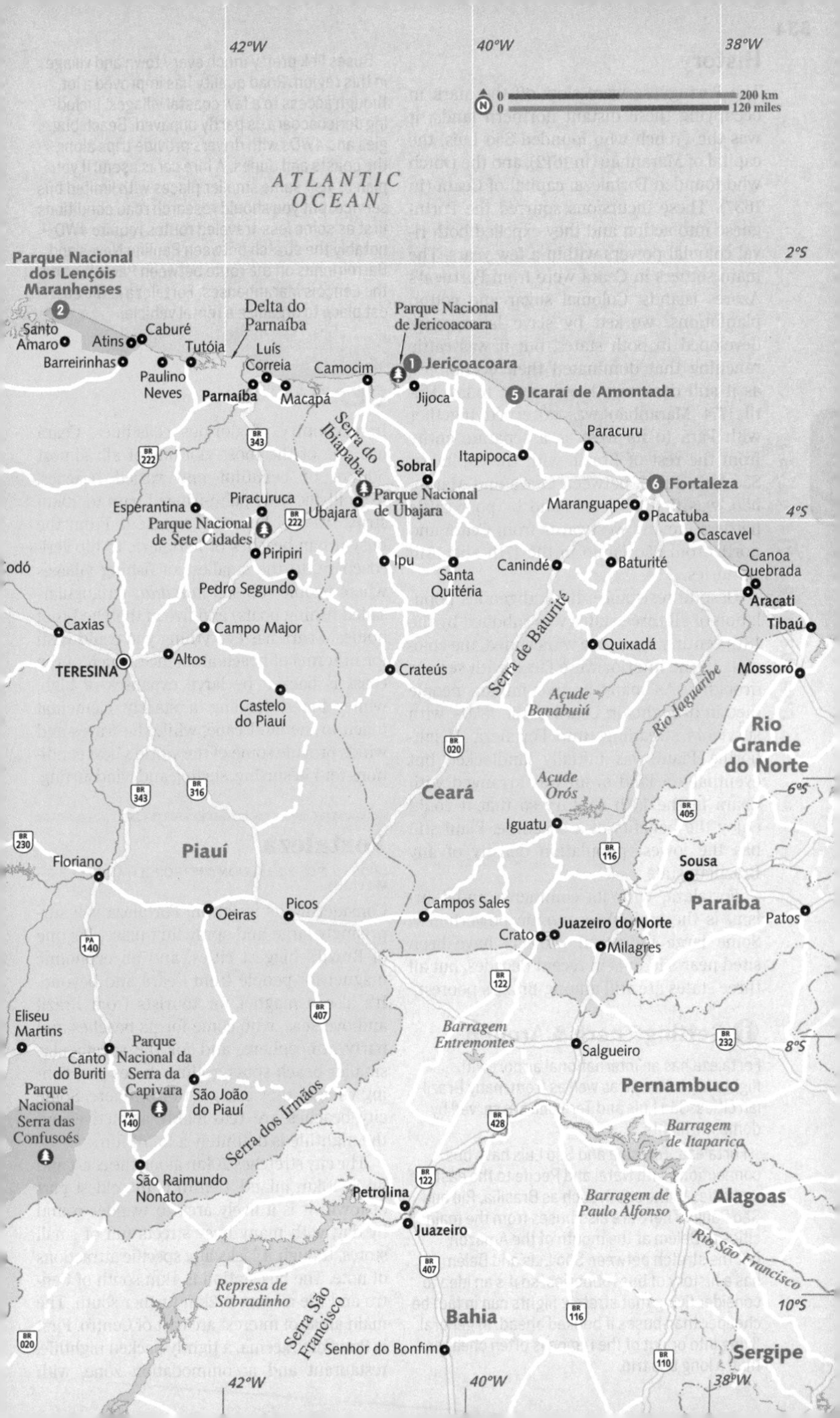
42°W
40°W
38°W
0
200 km
0
120 miles
ATLANTIC OCEAN
2°S
4°S
6°S
8°S
10°S
Parque Nacional dos Lençóis Maranhenses
2
Santo Amaro
Atins
Caburé
Barreirinhas
Paulino Neves
Tutóia
Delta do Parnaíba
Luís Correia
Parnaíba
Macapá
Camocim
Parque Nacional de Jericoacoara
1 Jericoacoara
Jijoca
5 Icaraí de Amontada
Paracuru
Itapipoca
Serra do Ibiapaba
Sobral
Parque Nacional de Ubajara
Ubajara
6 Fortaleza
Maranguape
Pacatuba
Cascavel
Canoa Quebrada
Aracati
Esperantina
Piracuruca
Parque Nacional de Sete Cidades
Piripiri
Pedro Segundo
Ipu
Santa Quitéria
Canindé
Baturité
Codó
Caxias
TERESINA
Altos
Campo Major
Crateús
Castelo do Piauí
Serra de Baturité
Quixadá
Tibaú
Mossoró
Açude Banabuiú
Rio Jaguaribe
Rio Grande do Norte
Ceará
Açude Orós
Iguatu
Piauí
Floriano
Sousa
Paraíba
Patos
Oeiras
Picos
Campos Sales
Crato
Juazeiro do Norte
Milagres
Barragem Entremontes
Salgueiro
Eliseu Martins
Canto do Buriti
Parque Nacional da Serra da Capivara
São João do Piauí
Parque Nacional Serra das Confusoés
Serra dos Irmãos
Pernambuco
Barragem de Itaparica
São Raimundo Nonato
Petrolina
Juazeiro
Barragem de Paulo Alfonso
Alagoas
Rio São Francisco
Represa de Sobradinho
Serra São Francisco
Bahia
Senhor do Bonfim
Sergipe
BR 343
BR 222
BR 020
BR 316
BR 230
BR 405
BR 116
PA 140
BR 407
BR 122
BR 232
BR 428
BR 110

History

The Portuguese were slow off the mark in occupying these distant northern lands; it was the French who founded São Luís, the capital of Maranhão (in 1612), and the Dutch who founded Fortaleza, capital of Ceará (in 1637). These incursions spurred the Portuguese into action and they expelled both rival colonial powers within a few years. The main settlers in Ceará were from Portugal's Azores islands. Colonial sugar and cotton plantations, worked by slave labor, were developed in both states, but it was cattle ranching that dominated their economies, as it still does to a large extent today. Until 1774 Maranhão was governed together with Pará to its west as a separate entity from the rest of Brazil, with the capital at São Luís. Piauí, between Ceará and Maranhão, was first settled inland by poor cattle herders moving westwards from Ceará and north from São Paulo in the 17th and 18th centuries.

Despite resistance, the indigenous population of all three states was subdued by the 18th century. Once the wars ended, the colonists in the interior were faced with serious droughts. As many as two million people died in droughts in Ceará in the 1870s, with survivors streaming into Fortaleza. Neighboring Piauí was initially landlocked but eventually a land swap was arranged with Ceará in the 19th century so that it could enjoy the benefits of a coastline. Piauí still has the lowest population density of any Brazilian state.

Fortaleza, with its commerce and tourism, is the region's economic powerhouse. Some large industrial projects have been sited near São Luís in recent decades, but all three states are still among Brazil's poorest.

Getting There & Around

Fortaleza has an international airport with flights from Europe as well as from many Brazilian cities. São Luís and Teresina are served by domestic flights.

Fortaleza, Teresina and São Luís have bus connections with Natal and Recife to the east, and cities to the south such as Brasília, Rio and São Paulo. There are also buses from the main cities to Belém at the mouth of the Amazon, but the stretch between São Luís and Belém has a history of bus robberies, so it's an idea to consider flying that stretch; flights can in fact be cheaper than buses if booked ahead. In general, flying into or out of the region is often cheaper than a long bus trip.

Buses link pretty much every town and village in this region. Road quality has improved a lot, though access to a few coastal villages, including Jericoacoara, is partly unpaved. Beach buggies and 4WDs with drivers provide trips along the coasts and dunes. A hire car is useful if you plan to visit some smaller places with limited bus service, but you should research road conditions first as some less-traveled routes require 4WD – notably the stretch between Paulino Neves and Barreirinhas on the route between Parnaíba and the Lençóis Maranhenses. Fortaleza is the easiest place to organise a rental vehicle.

CEARÁ

In a country of glorious coastlines, Ceará has one of the most glorious of all: almost 600km of beautiful and varied beaches, from idyllic little palm-fringed bays to 20km strips washed by ocean breakers. From the busy urban beaches of Fortaleza, to hip Jericoacoara, to the smallest of fishing villages where people still sail *jangadas* (triangular-sailed fishing boats) and live in thatched-roof homes, Ceará has everything you could wish for in terms of beach ambience. Much of the coast is backed by large expanses of high, white dunes, lending a starkly elemental touch to the landscape, while the waves and winds provide some of the world's best conditions for kitesurfing, surfing and windsurfing.

Fortaleza

☎085 / POP 2.5 MILLION (METROPOLITAN AREA 3.6 MILLION)

Considering its isolation, Fortaleza is a surprisingly large and sprawling place. It's one of Brazil's biggest cities, and an economic magnet for people from Ceará and beyond. It's also a magnet for tourists from Brazil and overseas, who come for its beaches and party atmosphere, and for the spectacular smaller beach spots, rolling dunes and fishing villages they can get to from here. Some city beaches are reasonably attractive and the nightlife is definitely a lot of fun.

The city stretches 20km along the coast and up to 10km inland. Centro is the oldest part of town; it is a lively area to wander round by day, with many busy streets full of small stores, though it lacks any specific attractions of note. The bus station is 4km south of Centro and the airport is 2km further south. The main areas of interest are east of Centro. First is Praia de Iracema, a tightly packed nightlife, restaurant and accommodation zone, with

Ceará Coast

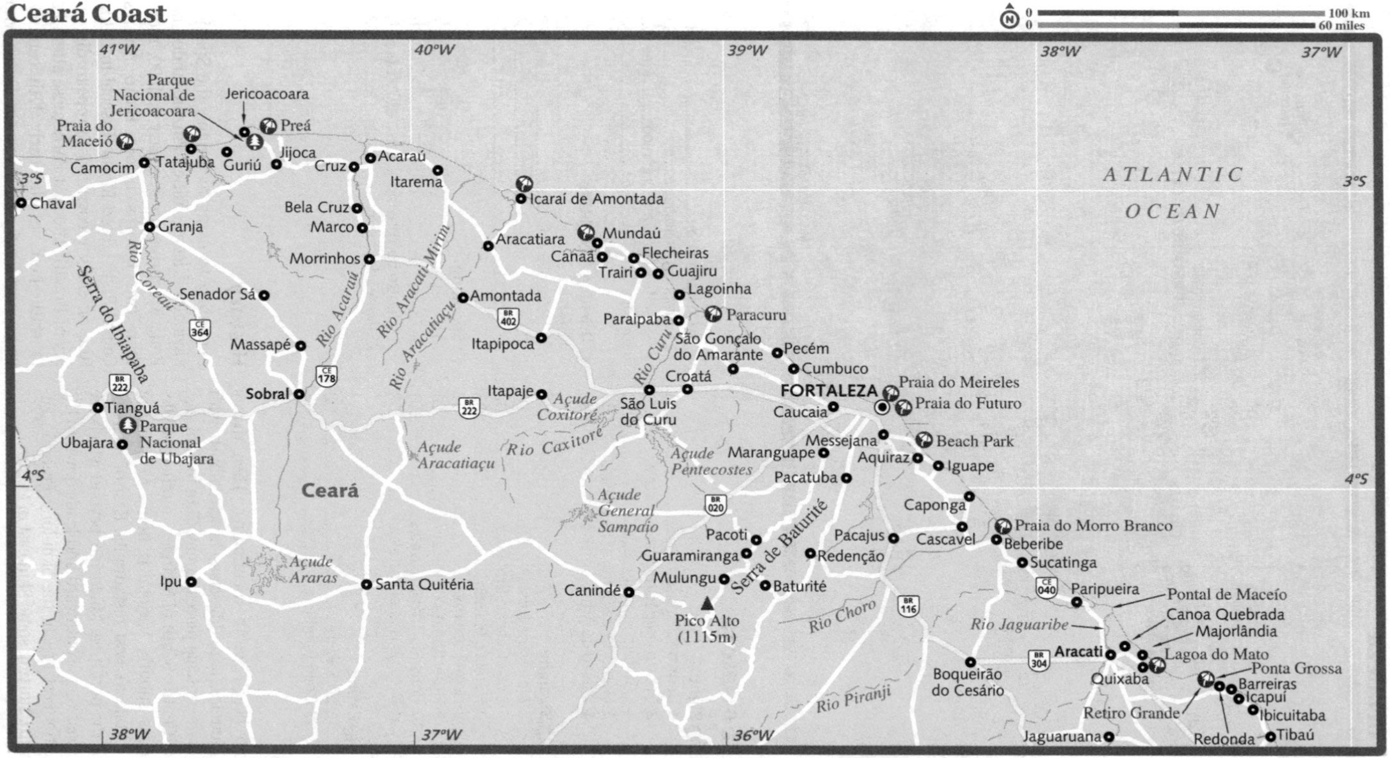
0 100 km
0 60 miles
41°W
40°W
39°W
38°W
37°W
3°S
4°S
ATLANTIC
OCEAN
Parque
Nacional de
Jericoacoara
Jericoacoara
Preá
Praia do
Maceió
Camocim
Tatajuba
Guriú
Jijoca
Cruz
Acaraú
Itarema
Chaval
Granja
Bela Cruz
Marco
Morrinhos
Icaraí de Amontada
Aracatiara
Mundaú
Canaã
Flecheiras
Trairi
Guajiru
Lagoinha
Paraipaba
Paracuru
São Gonçalo
do Amarante
Pecém
Cumbuco
Croatá
FORTALEZA
Praia do Meireles
Praia do Futuro
Caucaia
São Luis
do Curu
Messejana
Beach Park
Maranguape
Aquiraz
Iguape
Pacatuba
Caponga
Praia do Morro Branco
Beberibe
Cascavel
Pacajus
Redenção
Sucatinga
Paripueira
Pontal de Maceío
Canoa Quebrada
Majorlândia
Lagoa do Mato
Aracati
Quixaba
Ponta Grossa
Barreiras
Icapuí
Ibicuitaba
Retiro Grande
Redonda
Tibaú
Jaguaruana
Boqueirão
do Cesário
Rio Jaguaribe
Rio Choro
Rio Piranji
Serra do Ibiapaba
Rio Coreaú
Senador Sá
Massapé
Rio Acaraú
Rio Aracati-Mirim
Rio Aracatiaçu
Amontada
Itapipoca
Sobral
Tianguá
Parque
Nacional
de Ubajara
Ubajara
Itapaje
Açude
Coxitoré
Rio Caxitoré
Rio Curu
Açude
Aracatiaçu
Açude
Pentecostes
Ceará
Açude
General
Sampaio
Pacoti
Guaramiranga
Serra de Baturité
Mulungu
Baturité
Canindé
Pico Alto
(1115m)
Açude
Araras
Ipu
Santa Quitéria
CE 364
CE 178
BR 222
BR 402
BR 020
BR 116
BR 304
CE 040
38°W
37°W
36°W

Fortaleza

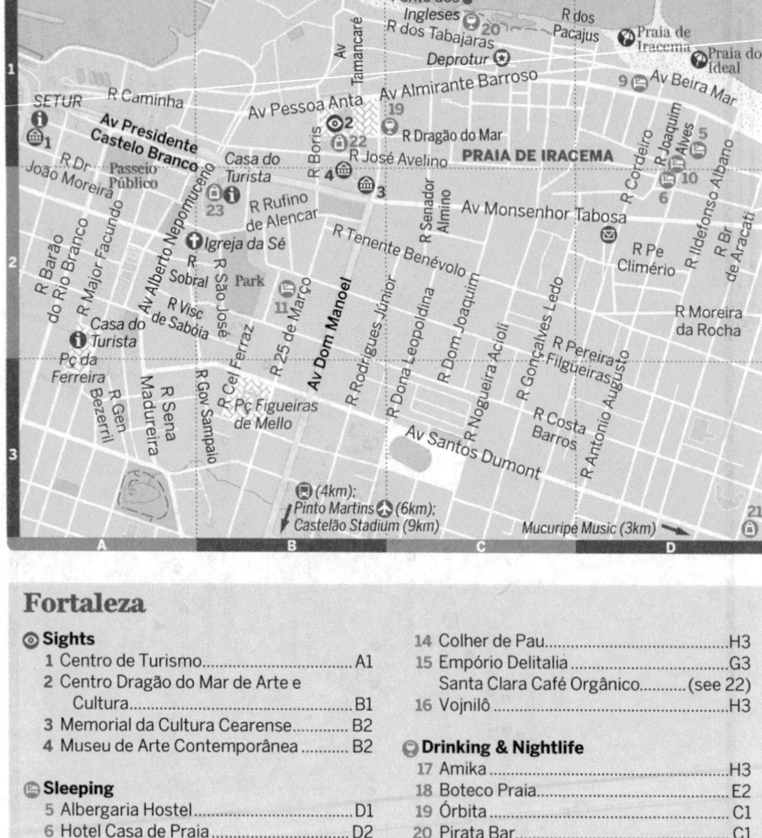

Fortaleza

Sights

1 Centro de Turismo............A1
2 Centro Dragão do Mar de Arte e Cultura............B1
3 Memorial da Cultura Cearense............B2
4 Museu de Arte Contemporânea............B2

Sleeping

5 Albergaria Hostel............D1
6 Hotel Casa de Praia............D2
7 Hotel La Maison............G3
8 Hotel Luzeiros............G2
9 Hotel Sonata de Iracema............D1
10 Pousada Três Caravelas............D1
11 Refugio Hostel Fortaleza............B2

Eating

12 50 Sabores............G2
13 Coco Bambu............H3
14 Colher de Pau............H3
15 Empório Delitalia............G3
Santa Clara Café Orgânico............(see 22)
16 Vojnilô............H3

Drinking & Nightlife

17 Amika............H3
18 Boteco Praia............E2
19 Órbita............C1
20 Pirata Bar............C1

Shopping

21 Ceart............D3
22 Ceart............B1
Centro de Turismo............(see 1)
23 Mercado Central............B2

no beach worth mentioning. Then there's Meireles, a middle-class beach suburb with many upscale places to stay, 2km to 4km east of Centro. South of Meireles, another middle-class suburb, Varjota, is home to many of Fortaleza's best restaurants. East of Meireles is the port area, Mucuripe, beyond which the coast veers southward and leads down to the city's best beach, the 5km-long Praia do Futuro, starting some 8km east of Centro.

History

According to many historians, the Spanish navigator Vicente Yáñez Pinzón landed on Praia Mucuripe on February 2, 1500, more than two months before Pedro Álvares Cabral first sighted Monte Pascoal in Bahia (the officially recognized European discovery of Brazil). The first Portuguese attempts to settle here, in the early 17th century, were short-lived, and it was the Dutch who

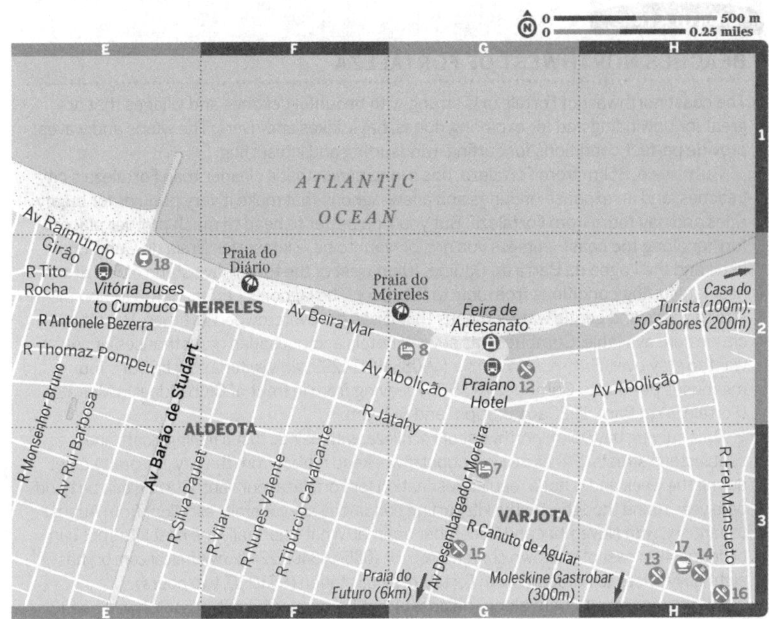

built Fort Schoonenborch in 1637. When the Dutch abandoned their Brazilian possessions in 1654, the Portuguese renamed this fort the Fortaleza de NS da Assunção (Fortress of Our Lady of the Assumption). Around it grew a village, then a town, then a city that came to be called Fortaleza.

Indigenous resistance slowed Portuguese colonization of interior Ceará until the 18th century, but cattle ranchers, and later cotton growers, occupied land. It was cotton exports in the 19th century that made Fortaleza an important town (it had previously played second fiddle to Aracati). Growing commerce and industry in Fortaleza, and droughts in the interior, have since pulled ever more migrants to the city. Since the early 1990s tourism has joined textiles and food among its leading industries.

Sights

Centro Dragão do Mar de Arte e Cultura ARTS CENTER

(☎3488-8600; www.dragaodomar.org.br; Dragão do Mar 81; ⊙8am-10pm Mon-Thu, to 11pm Sat & Sun) This excellent, extensive complex includes cinemas, performance spaces, a good cafe, a planetarium and two good museums: the **Museu de Arte Contemporânea** (MAC; www.dragaodomar.org.br; Centro Cultural Dragão do Mar, Dragão do Mar 81; ⊙9am-7pm Tue-Fri, 2-9pm Sat & Sun) FREE, and the **Memorial da Cultura Cearense** (MCC; www.dragaodomar.org.br; Centro Cultural Dragão do Mar, Dragão do Mar 81; ⊙9am-7pm Tue-Fri, 2-9pm Sat & Sun) FREE, which shows exhibits on Ceará's traditional way of life and culture. Elevated walkways join blocks on different streets and it all blends well with the surrounding older buildings, many of which have been restored to house bars, restaurants and artisans' workshops. It's a successful social focus for the city, and is very popular with locals.

Centro de Turismo MUSEUM

(☎3101-5508; Senador Pompeu 350; ⊙8am-6pm Mon-Fri, to 4pm Sat & Sun) The Centro de Turismo, a converted 19th-century jail, houses a lot of craft stalls and, upstairs from the tourist information office, the Museu de Arte e Cultura Popular, which has an impressive collection of Ceará crafts.

Beaches

For most tourists, Fortaleza's greatest attractions are its beaches. Fortaleza's north-facing beach, nearer the areas you're likely to be staying in, is lined by a broad and hugely popular pedestrian promenade running 4km from the Ponte dos Ingleses pier to Praia do Mucuripe. The nicest part is the central **Praia do Meireles**, which, with all its

WORTH A TRIP

BEACHES NORTHWEST OF FORTALEZA

The coast northwest of Fortaleza is strung with beautiful beaches and villages that are great for unwinding and for exploring dunes, bays, lakes and rivers. The winds and waves provide perfect conditions for surfing, windsurfing and kitesurfing.

Cumbuco, 35km from Fortaleza, has a long beach that's cleaner than Fortaleza's city beaches, and an expanse of dunes and a few lagoons that make it very popular for buggy rides and day tours from Fortaleza. But you'll do better to head to much prettier places further along the coast – unless you are, or want to be, a kitesurfer. Praia de Cumbuco itself and the Lagoa da Barra do Cauipe, 10km west of the town, have some of Brazil's best kitesurfing conditions from July to February. The lagoon's perfect combination of strong winds and gentle waters means that it can get overcrowded at times. Rental and classes are available. Cumbuco has several hotels and pousadas (guesthouses) if you want to stay over. **Empresa Vitória** (☎085-4011-1299; www.evitoria.com.br) runs four minibuses per day to Cumbuco (R$5.75), leaving from in front of Clube Ideal in Meireles (Fortaleza) at 9am, 11:20am, 3:50pm and 6:20pm.

On a curving bay 95km northwest of Fortaleza, with palms, rustic fishing boats and cobblestone streets, **Paracuru** is a popular weekend retreat from the city. It's pretty quiet during the week and is not a regular destination for Fortaleza tour vans. Surfing can be good here year-round though, and the kitesurfing conditions are generally excellent from August to January, with November and December optimal. What's normally the best kite spot can be found 4km east of the town center. **Fretcar** (085-☎3402-2244; www.fretcar.com.br) has eight daily buses to Paracuru from Fortaleza's bus station (R$10.10, two hours).

Lagoinha, about 20km along the coast from Paracuru (45km by road), has a beautiful, long beach – with coconut palms and *jangadas* (triangular-sailed fishing boats) – that extends 15km to the northwest and is one of the prettiest stretches of sand in Ceará. It's not yet heavily developed (though large constructions have broken ground and Fortaleza tour vans roll in daily) and is a good choice for a short visit from Fortaleza. There are 12 to 14 daily Fretcar buses from Fortaleza's bus station to Paraipaba (R$13.50, two hours), from where you need to catch a *lotacão* (shared taxi; R$6) from the main square for the final 20km to Lagoinha.

The end-of-the-road settlements of **Flecheiras** (136km from Fortaleza and 11km north of the town of Trairi) and **Mundaú** (142km from Fortaleza and 17km northwest of Trairi) are traditional fishing areas with long, wide stretches of beautiful sand, offshore reefs and dunes. They are still relatively undeveloped and make fine places for doing nothing much in a postcard-like setting. Little Flecheiras, a favored weekend retreat of well-heeled Fortaleza folk, is a good kitesurfing spot (best from August to November) and has several pousadas. In larger Mundaú, tourism still takes second place to fishing. The river trip along the Rio Mundaú is a lovely 1½-hour outing, especially the afternoon outing, which stops for sunset-viewing from high dunes.

Six Fretcar buses leave Fortaleza bus station daily for Flecheiras (R$21.20, three hours) and three for Mundaú (R$21.60, 3¾ hours, departing 6:30am, 12:30pm and 5:30pm).

high-rise hotels, resembles a northeastern Copacabana but also has numerous beach bars, beneath leafy trees, which are popular places to hang out by day or evening. The water here is less clean than at Praia do Futuro, although that doesn't deter surfers.

Praia do Futuro BEACH

A clean length of sand stretching 5km along Fortaleza's east-facing coast, this is easily the best city beach, although it's far from most accommodations. It's lined by open restaurants known as *barracas,* which serve seafood, beer and cocktails at tables on the sand, and attracts enormous crowds at weekends; fortunately the beach is long enough to accommodate everyone without being overcrowded.

The nicest part starts a couple of kilometers down from the industrial port at the north end. Unless you are a strong swimmer, beware of rough waves. You can reach Praia do Futuro on the 49 Caça e Pesca bus running east on Av Monsenhor Tabosa, Av Historiador Raimundo Girão and Av Beira Mar. Or get a bus to Terminal Papicu then a Papicu/Praia do Futuro or Papicu/Caça e Pesca bus from there.

Tours

Day trips from Fortaleza to beaches along the coast to the east and west (p538) are very popular. Dozens of travel agencies, hotels and pousadas will arrange these for you. Operators will normally come and pick you up from your accommodations. The main destinations (with transport-only prices per person) are Brazil's best water park, Beach Park (R$30); Cumbuco (R$30); Canoa Quebrada (R$45); Lagoinha (R$40); and Mundaú (R$45). The tours are easier than taking public buses, and you can take them just one way if you want to stay over.

Some agencies also offer longer-distance 4WD or beach-buggy tours, along Ceará's glorious beaches wherever possible, as far afield as Jericoacoara or even the Lençóis Maranhenses or Natal. With accommodations included, a three-day return trip to Jericoacoara costs from R$1540 per person. Try Jericoacoara-based Jeri Off Road (p549) to do it a bit more comfortably.

Festivals & Events

Réveillon (New Year's) sees a huge fiesta with live bands at Praia de Iracema. Carnaval is also at its liveliest in the Praia de Iracema district, which additionally sees four Saturdays of pre-Carnaval revelry in preceding weeks.

Parada pela Diversidade Sexual PARADE
(Jun) Fortaleza's Parada pela Diversidade Sexual (Sexual Diversity Parade) takes place on Av Beira Mar on the last Sunday of June; it's one of Brazil's biggest gay pride events.

Fortal PARADE, MUSIC
(www.fortal.com.br; Jul) Fortaleza's lively out-of-season Carnaval is held for four days over the last weekend of July and is attended by half a million people.

Sleeping

Competition between the many hotels means there are some excellent deals to be had, including some midrange-quality hotels at budget prices.

★ **Refugio Hostel Fortaleza** HOSTEL $
(3393-4349; www.refugiohostelfortaleza.com; Deputado João Lopes 31, Centro; dm with/without bathroom from R$50/40, r with fan R$120;) Easily Fortaleza's best hostel. German owner Karl has whipped an old mansion into shape, following an eco-ethos with breezy natural ventilation and solar-heated showers. The bathrooms and kitchen are astonishing for a hostel, while other design-forward common spaces of note include a sunny patio/BBQ area and various terraces. Dorms feature colorful lockers and original tiling and hardwood floors.

Best of all? The staff has hospitality down. And that Nespresso machine...

Albergaria Hostel HOSTEL $
(3032-9005; www.albergariahostel.com.br; Antônio Augo 111, Praia de Iracema; dm with fan/air-con R$40/45, d/tr R$128/148;) This cheerful, well-located, well-run hostel has very good facilities, including a restaurant-bar (with a trained chef) and a backyard with a pool, plus a sociable atmosphere helped along by the friendly English-speaking owner. There are separate-sex and mixed four-bed dorms (with privacy curtains and lockers with electrical outlets) and four good private rooms with bathroom. Breakfast is plentiful. Reservations only. Ask about its new hotel in Flecheiras.

Hotel La Maison HOTEL $
(3048-4200; www.hotellamaison.com.br; Av Desembargador Moreira 201, Meireles; r R$150;) This excellent-value place in Meireles is just a couple of blocks from the beach, and has 25 spotless rooms (those upstairs are generally brighter than downstairs) and bright, colorful common areas. The French owner knows the city very well, speaks English, and can point you in the right direction – whatever your needs. The fruit-heavy breakfast is substantial, but where's the Brie?

Pousada Três Caravelas POUSADA $$
(3453-2250; www.trescaravelas.com; Antônio Augo 182, Praia de Iracema; s/d/tr R$180/210/269;) A little more personalized than a hotel, this pousada in Iracema is run by friendly English-speaking owner Vera and offers the right amount of cozy for the price. Rooms are clean and simple, with colorful local art, and there's a restaurant on the premises.

Hotel Casa de Praia HOTEL $$
(3219-1022; www.hotelcasadepraia.com.br; Joaquim Alves 169, Praia de Iracema; s/d/tr R$150/180/210;) For its modest price, this friendly 40-room hotel offers many pluses: clean, neat medium-sized rooms with ocean views from some (best from the 3rd floor); efficient and helpful staff; a shallow rooftop pool; a good breakfast in a bright dining room; and an easy two-block walk to the seafront. It gets heavily booked, so it's essential to reserve.

Hotel Sonata de Iracema HOTEL $$$
(☎4006-1600; www.sonatadeiracema.com.br; Av Beira Mar 848, Praia de Iracema; s/d R$369/420;) The cute two-story street frontage is slightly misleading, as most of the hotel is contained in the 13-story block behind, but that means all the tasteful, bright and modern rooms have sea views. One of Fortaleza's nicest larger hotels, it has an outdoor pool deck too, and a very pleasant staff.

Hotel Luzeiros HOTEL $$$
(☎4006-8585; www.luzeirosfortaleza.com.br; Av Beira Mar 2600, Meireles; s R$326-374, d R$407-470;) The designer of Fortaleza's first design hotel could have been a little more daring, but the clean-lined, modern spaces and rooms, plus what is probably the best breakfast in Ceará, make it a sleek mainstay with a high-end clientele.

Eating

★ **50 Sabores** ICE CREAM $
(☎3023-0050; www.50sabores.com.br; Av Beira Mar 2982, Meirelles; 1/2 scoops R$11/15; ⏲10am-11:45pm;) One of Brazil's most famous ice cream shops, though with a terribly misleading name: there are actually 150 flavors here, including caipirinha (made with *cachaça* sugarcane liquor – you must be 18 to purchase!) and beer, among loads of Brazilian fruits and more classic options. Don't let anyone tell you one scoop of tapioca, one scoop *açaí* (berrylike fruit) isn't the perfect combination! There's a branch in **Mucuripe** (www.50sabores.com.br; Av Beira Mar 3958, Mucuripe; ⏲7am-midnight).

Empório Delitalia CAFE, PIZZERIA $
(www.delitalia.com.br; Av Desembargador Moreira 533; breakfast items R$5.30-16.50, pizzas R$26.50-60; ⏲6:30am-10pm Mon-Sat, 7:30am-10pm Sun;) Early risers could consider forgoing breakfast at their accommodations for the great juices, coffees, waffles, hot filled croissants, omelets and tapiocas at this classy, uncharacteristically early-opening cafe-emporium. Come anyway for Fortaleza's best deli and bakery (adjoining) and one of its better pizzerias (upstairs).

Santa Clara Café Orgânico CAFE $
(Centro Dragão do Mar, Praia de Iracema; items R$5-16; ⏲3-10pm Tue-Sun;) Santa Clara is one of the city's hot *pontos de encontros*, which loosely translated means 'where hot people go to mingle' (and cool down in the icy air-con). It's a wonderful little cafe on an upper level of Dragão do Mar, and serves organic coffee, sandwiches, crepes, omelets, waffles, tapiocas and a plethora of fancier coffee drinks.

★ **Coco Bambu** BRAZILIAN $$
(www.restaurantecocobambu.com.br; Canuto de Aguiar 1317, Varjota; mains for 2 people R$60-195; ⏲11am-midnight Sun-Thu, to 2am Fri & Sat;) This huge, festive eatery does a whole lot of everything – and it's all excellent, including the tropical-garden setting. The 16-page menu covers pizza, tapiocas, crêpes, pasta and regional mains (seafood is the specialty). All dishes are designed for two people.

★ **Colher de Pau** BRAZILIAN $$
(☎3267-6680; www.colherdepaufortaleza.com.br; Ana Bilhar 1178, Varjota; mains for 2 people R$30-153; ⏲11am-midnight, closed Mon;) The large, mostly open-air 'Wooden Spoon' is one of the best places in a neighborhood thronged with popular midrange restaurants. It's great for seafood, including a superb chunky *peixada* (fish, vegetables and herbs in coconut sauce) and is consistently voted among the best in town for regional Northeastern cuisine. It's also got atmosphere, and there's live *sertanejo*, samba and *forró* (the Northeast's quintessential popular country dance music) from 5pm Wednesday to Sunday.

Crocobeach SEAFOOD $$
(☎3521-9600; www.crocobeach.com.br; Av Clóvis Arrais Maia 3125, Praia do Futuro; buffet per kg R$64; ⏲8am-6pm Sun-Wed & Fri, to 2am Thu, to 7pm Sat;) For the full Praia do Futuro experience, head to *megabarraca* (mega-stall) Crocobeach, which has swimming pools, and live music on Saturdays and Sundays. It's a hypercomplex of fun and sun, and the buffet is excellent.

Moleskine Gastrobar BRAZILIAN $$
(www.moleskinegastrobar.com.br; Professor Dias da Rocha 578, Meireles; mains R$39-69; ⏲noon-2am Tue-Sat, to midnight Sun & Mon;) Fortaleza's *bola da vez* (current hot spot), this trendy gastrobar draws the young, hot and restless as much for its striking design – patchwork-denim-covered banquets, rope-hung lighting wrapped around suspended rail beams – as for it's grill-heavy menu. Start with the *bobó de camarão* (shrimp with manioc) croquettes before choosing a slab of *carne* (meat) from the impressive barbecue.

It's all set to a loungy soundtrack and abrupt visuals such as televised rapid-reel subway and beach scenes. Best beer list (good cocktails too!) and open-air terrace in town.

Vojnilô SEAFOOD $$$

(☎3267-3081; www.vojnilo.com; Frederico Borges 409, Varjota; mains R$52-75; ⏱7-11pm Mon, 1-3pm & 7-11:30pm Tue-Sat, noon-5pm Sun; 📶) This stone-walled, subtly maritime-themed restaurant with a confusing Macedonian name regularly wins top seafood accolades in the city. The seafood spaghetti, topped with two whole *lagostas* (small lobsters), and the house whole fish in caper sauce are both phenomenal. The fish is market-fresh and there's a seven-country wine list, too.

Drinking & Nightlife

Fortaleza is famed for its nightlife. The Dragão do Mar area is one of the best places to go out.

Boteco Praia BAR

(☎3248-4773; www.botecofortaleza.com.br; Av Beira Mar 1680, Meireles; ⏱5pm-3am Mon-Fri, noon-3am Sat & Sun; 📶) The number-one spot for evening drinks and conversation, Boteco Praia attracts all ages to its long, arcaded hall and its terrace facing the seafront promenade. You do pay for the privilege, though: R$7 per *chope* (draft beer), and R$9 to R$54 for tempting portions such as *picanha* steak, grilled octopus and spicy sausage offered by the attentive waiters. Live music nightly.

Órbita BAR

(www.orbitabar.com.br; Dragão do Mar 207, Praia de Iracema; admission R$30; ⏱9pm-4am Thu-Sun; 📶) Reminiscent of a college-town rock club (but with way better-looking people than your college most likely, or ours), this large, black-and-purple Dragão do Mar bar hosts live rock, surf and pop amid snooker tables and a legion of flirtatious upper-class clientele.

Mucuripe Music CLUB

(www.mucuripe.com.br; cnr Santo Dumont & Engenheiro Santana Júnior, Papicu; cover around R$25; ⏱10pm-5am Fri) In addition to being the best and most stylish disco in the Northeast, Mucuripe Music's new space is a huge, modern, local venue holding 1500 people and featuring VIP suites near the stage, which skirts between DJs and live *forró*, *sertaneja* (Northeastern country pop), *axé* (Afro-Brazilian pop), rock and more. If you lose a friend in here, they'll see you tomorrow.

Pirata Bar CLUB

(www.pirata.com.br; Tabajaras 325; admission R$40-50; ⏱8pm-3am) The bar and club scene around the Praia de Iracema waterfront area is rather touristy, but the 'Segunda-feira Mais Louca do Mundo' (Craziest Monday in the World) at Pirata is still legendary. Live bands play *forró* and other Brazilian dance rhythms to packed crowds right through the night.

Amika CAFE

(www.facebook.com/amikacoffeehouse; Ana Bilhar 1136B, Varjota; coffee R$4.25-9; ⏱1-8pm Tue-Sun; 📶) When you tire of sickly presweetened bus-station coffee, head to this trendy coffeehouse, where its business is to know beans. Three weekly-changing espressos from single-origin Minas Gerais plantations are available daily, as are the usual caffeine-junkie methods (Aeropress, Chemex etc). Serves light bites as well.

☆ Entertainment

Arena Castelão FOOTBALL

(☎3304-4501; www.arenacastelao.com; Av Alberto Craveiro 2901) Fortaleza's Castelão stadium, 9km south of the center, was completely renovated to seat 67,000 fans for the 2014 World Cup. The city's two top clubs, Ceará (www.cearasc.com) and Fortaleza (www.fortalezaec.net), play many of their games at the Castelão.

Shopping

You can find handicrafts from all around Ceará in Fortaleza. Some of the finest work is in delicate lace, a tradition that came with the Portuguese. Artisans also work with *carnaúba*-palm fronds, bamboo, vines and leather.

Ceart HANDICRAFTS

(www.fortaleza.ce.gov.br/turismo/produtos-artesanais; Centro Dragão do Mar; ⏱9am-9pm Tue-Fri, 3-9pm Sat & Sun) This beautiful state-run craft store sells lace, ceramics, wood carvings, baskets and bags of sisal and *carnaúba* palm, and textiles. There's a branch in **Aldeota** (www.fortaleza.ce.gov.br/turismo/produtos-artesanais; Av Santos Dumont 1589, Aldeota; ⏱9am-9pm Mon-Sat, 2:30-8:30pm Sun).

Mercado Central MARKET

(www.mercadocentraldefortaleza.com.br; Av Alberto Nepomuceno 199; ⏱8am-6pm Mon-Fri, to 4pm Sat, to 1pm Sun) Mainly geared to a tourist clientele, the three-story central market has good prices at more than 500 stalls that sell everything from leather bags and colorful palm baskets to excellent local cashews and a huge variety of *cachaça* – some bottles have fruit salad or crabs pickled inside. You might well find a desirable curio.

WORTH A TRIP

PARQUE NACIONAL DE UBAJARA

The entrance to **Parque Nacional de Ubajara** (admission with guide R$4; 9am-2:30pm Tue-Sun), Brazil's smallest national park, is 3km east from the center of the small town of Ubajara, 325km west of Fortaleza. The main attractions are giant caves, the cable car ride down to them, and walks in the surrounding forest. Atop a thickly forested escarpment 850m above sea level, Ubajara offers some spectacular vistas over the *sertão* (interior or backlands of the Northeast) below, and relatively cool temperatures that provide a welcome respite from the *sertão's* searing heat. Portal Ubajara (www.portalubajara.com.br) is a useful website.

Nine chambers with strange limestone formations extend more than 500m into the side of a mountain. The main formations seen inside the **caves** (guide R$5) are Pedra do Sino (Bell Stone), Salas da Rosa (Rose Rooms), Sala do Cavalo (Horse Room) and Sala dos Retratos (Portrait Room). A **cable car** (per person return R$8; 9am-2:30pm Tue-Sun) makes the descent from the park entrance to the caves quick and easy. Last entry to the cave is at 2pm, and the last cable car to head back up leaves when the last group exits the caves, around 3pm. If you fancy a beautiful hike instead, take the 7km trail down to the caves via two waterfalls and a lookout point. Hikers must be accompanied by a park guide, who leave from the entrance at 8am, 9am and 10am. Wear sturdy footwear and take enough to drink. You can catch the cable car back up.

Guanabara (3233-6759; www.expressoguanabara.com.br) buses leave Ubajara for Fortaleza (from R$48, seven hours, six daily).

Centro de Turismo HANDICRAFTS
(Senador Pompeu 350; 8am-6pm Mon-Fri, to 4pm Sat & Sun) The many stalls here focus on lace and embroidery and you can usually see lace-makers at work.

Information

DANGERS & ANNOYANCES

Beware of pickpocketing in the city center and petty theft on the beaches; gaggles of adolescents specialize in snatch and grab robbery along Av Beira-Mar (watch your necklaces and purses). Tourists waiting at bus stops to return from Praia do Futuro have been targeted. Empty streets in Centro and Praia de Iracema after dark are best avoided. Lodgings have upped security measures after a string of robberies in late 2014.

EMERGENCY

Deprotur (Delegacia de Proteção ao Turista; 3101-2488; www.policiacivil.ce.gov.br; Costa Barros 1971, Aldeota; 8am-6pm Mon-Fri) Tourist police in Fortaleza. Note the tourist police section is closed on weekends, but this is a 24-hour police station as well.

MEDICAL SERVICES

SAT (4009-0909; www.gruposat.com.br) The area's best travel-medicine specialist, with a multilingual 24-hour house-call service.

MONEY

Banco do Brasil (www.bb.com.br; Av Monsenhor Tabosa 634, Praia de Iracema) Visa/Mastercard ATM.

Bradesco (www.bradesco.com.br; Av da Abolição 1810, Meireles) Visa/Mastercard ATM.

Bradesco (www.bradesco.com.br; Av Pessoa Anta 274) Visa/Mastercard ATM.

TOURIST INFORMATION

Casa do Turista (Setfor; 3105-2670; www.fortaleza.ce.gov.br/turismo; Av Beira Mar, Mucuripe; 9am-9pm) The city tourism department operates this information booth on Meireles beach; staff may or may not speak English. You'll find good English map-guides and there are additional branches around the city, including Centro (3105-1444; Praça da Ferreira, Centro; 9am-5pm Mon-Fri, 8am-noon Sat) and Mercado Central (3105-1475; Basement level, Mercado Central, Av Nepomuceno 199; 9am-5pm Mon-Fri, 9am-noon Sat).

Setur (3101-5508; www.ceara.gov.br; Senador Pompeu 350, Centro de Turismo; 8am-6pm Mon-Fri) The Ceará tourism organization has useful information offices, with English-speaking attendants usually available. Also at the airport (3392-1667; Av Carlos Jereissati 3000, Aeroporto Pinto Martins; 6am-midnight).

Getting There & Away

AIR

Aeropuerto Pinto Martins (3392-1200; Av Carlos Jereissati 3000) has daily flights to/from Buenos Aires, Cabo Verde, Frankfurt, Lisbon, Miami and Milan as well as domestic flights through Brazil. It was undergoing a R$350-million expansion at the time of writing – an expansion that failed to be delivered by the 2014 World Cup and is now expected to be ready by 2020.

BUS

Fortaleza's **bus station** (☎3256-2200; Borges de Melo 1630) is 5.5km south of Meireles. Somewhat oddly for Brazil, you enter Fortaleza's buses from the back.

To Jericoacoara, several companies, such as **Enseada** (☎3091-2762; www.enseada.tur.br; Av Monsenhor Tabosa 1001, Loja 10) and **Vitorino** (☎3047-1047; www.vitorinotur.com.br; Av Monsenhor Tabosa 1067), offer direct door-to-door van transfers from Fortaleza hotels (R$75, six hours); most accommodations can book these for you. Another option is **Fretcar** (☎3402-2244; www.fretcar.com.br), which runs up to five buses daily to Jericoacoara (from R$55, six to seven hours) departing 7:30am, 7:50am, 2:45pm, 4pm and 4:30pm from Fortaleza's bus station. The 7:30am departure (year-round) and usually one afternoon bus (3pm, depending on season) also pick up at the airport about 15 minutes after leaving the bus station, and then at the **Praiano Hotel** (www.praiano.com.br; Av Beira Mar 2800) on Praia do Meireles about 30 minutes after that. The last part of the Fretcar trip is a one-hour ride in a *jardineira* (open-sided 4WD truck) along sandy tracks and the beach and through dunes from Jijoca to Jericoacoara. You can check Fretcar schedules and buy tickets (advisably a day ahead) at **Beach Point** (☎3086-7055; www.beachpointceara.tur.br; cnr Av Beira Mar & Oswaldo Cruz, No 1 Beira-Mar Trade Center; ⏲9am-noon & 1-8pm). The most exciting way of reaching Jericoacoara is by 4WD along the coast, an option offered by agencies such as Jeri Off Road (p549), which charges R$750 for up to four people.

CAR & MOTORCYCLE

Half-a-dozen rental agencies have airport desks, including the recommended **Avis** (☎3392-1369; www.avis.com.br; Aeroporto Pinto Martins; ⏲24hr), **Hertz** (☎3392-1465; www.hertz.com; Aeroporto Pinto Martins; ⏲24hr) and **Localiza** (☎3308-8350; www.localiza.com; Aeroporto Pinto Martins; ⏲24hr). There's a slew of local rental firms on Av Monsenhor Tabosa in Praia de Iracema, including **Maresia** (☎3219-8000; www.maresiarentacar.com.br; Av Monsenhor Tabosa 1001; ⏲8am-6:30pm), where the owner speaks some English.

Getting Around

TO/FROM THE AIRPORT

A **Coopaero** (☎3105-1136; www.coopaero.com.br) fixed-rate taxi from the airport to Meireles or Praia de Iracema costs R$42. Metered **Coopertaxi** (☎3477-5599) common taxis run R$37 or so to Meireles or Praia de Iracema, and R$20 to R$25 to the bus station.

Buses 027 Siqueira/Papicu/Aeroporto, 087 Expresso Siqueira/Papicu and 066 Parangaba/Papicu/Aeroporto all run to Terminal Papicu in the east of the city, where you can change to the 051 Grande Circular 1 for Meireles and Praia de Iracema. Alternatively, take an 066 to Terminal Parangaba, and change there to the 077 Parangaba/Mucuripe bus, which runs to the Centro Dragão do Mar, Praia de Iracema and Meireles; or take a 404 Aeroporto Benfica Rodoviária bus to the bus station *(rodoviária)* and then bus 013 Aguanambi I to Av Dom Manuel and the Centro Dragão do Mar.

TO/FROM THE BUS STATION

Bus 013 Aguanambi I leaves from outside the bus station and runs north up Av Dom Manoel to the Centro Dragão do Mar. For Praia de Iracema and Meireles, walk left outside the bus station, turn right at the traffic signal along Av Borges de Melo and walk to a bus stop about 200m along

BUSES FROM FORTALEZA

DESTINATION	COST FROM (R$)	TIME (HR)	COMPANY
Belém	194.60	24	Guanabara (www.expressoguanabara.com.br), Itapemirim (www.itapemirim.com.br)
Natal	85.33	9	Viação Nordeste (www.viacaonordeste.com.br)
Parnaíba	45.45	9	Guanabara (www.expressoguanabara.com.br)
Piripiri	49	8	Guanabara (www.expressoguanabara.com.br)
Recife	92	14	Guanabara (www.expressoguanabara.com.br)
Rio de Janeiro	473	48	Itapemirim (www.itapemirim.com.br)
São Luís	132	19	Guanabara (www.expressoguanabara.com.br)
Teresina	66	10	Guanabara (www.expressoguanabara.com.br)
Ubajara	45	7	Guanabara (www.expressoguanabara.com.br)

on the far (south) side of the street. From here buses 073 Siqueira/Praia de Iracema and 078 Siqueira/Mucuripe will take you up Av Dom Manuel to the Centro Dragão do Mar, then to Praia de Iracema and (the 078 only) Meireles.

A taxi from the bus station to Praia de Iracema costs around R$22.

BUS

Fortaleza has a very extensive city bus system with good frequency on most routes. Fares are mostly R$2.40 (R$1.80 on Sundays and holidays) and if you have to transfer at a Terminal de Integração (Integration Terminal), such as Papicu or Parangaba, you don't have to pay a second fare.

BICYCLE

Bicicletar (☎4003-9594; www.bicicletar.com.br; per day R$5), Fortaleza's city bike-share scheme, is free for the first hour from Monday to Friday (and for 90 minutes on Sundays). After that, it's R$5 per day. There are stations throughout the city. You'll need to register on the website or with the app. There are a few choice locations along the beach.

TAXI

Taxis are metered. A 4km trip across town from the Centro Dragão do Mar to Varjota, for example, costs about R$17.

Canoa Quebrada

☎088 / POP 4000

The coast southeast of Fortaleza has many fine beaches, many of them backed by dunes, but it is developed and built up. It's not until you reach the red-hued windswept wonderland of Canoa Quebrada, 140km from Fortaleza, that the coast starts to regain its natural majesty. Once a tiny village cut off from the world by its huge pink sand dunes and beloved of early hippie travelers, Canoa Quebrada today has shifted toward a more family-oriented beach spot, and it's a favorite destination of daily van tours from Fortaleza. But the craggy, eroding sand cliffs and the large dune expanses still lend Canoa that elemental, otherworldly feel for which it's famous. With numerous good pousadas and restaurants, and varied outdoor activities easily available, it's an enjoyable spot to relax for a few days.

The main street, Rua Dragão do Mar (Rua Principal), runs west to east along the ridge of the hill from which Canoa slopes down to the beach. The eastern, pedestrianized half of the street, which has most of the restaurants and bars, is nicknamed Broadway.

Activities

Southeast of Canoa a 30km stretch of beautiful uninterrupted beach, backed by colorful cliffs, sweeps round to the red-rock headland of **Ponta Grossa**. It's a great **beach-buggy trip** (R$350 for three or four hours round-trip, up to four people) and you can stop for a good-value lobster lunch when the seafood is in season (from July to December). North of Canoa a large area of high dunes stretches 12km to the mouth of the Rio Jaguaribe: a one-hour buggy trip with some exciting steep descents costs around R$300 for up to four people. Pousadas can recommend and organize authorized buggy drivers.

Kitesurfing is best around the mouth of the Rio Jaguaribe, 12km northwest, where there is reliable wind and calm waters; the season runs from July to December. It's reachable only by buggy.

Vôo Duplo Jerônimo PARAGLIDING
(☎98806-6570; 10-20min flight R$100) Tandem paragliding is hugely popular and huge fun if you have a head for heights. You'll ride the breezes above Canoa's beaches from the takeoff point at the east end of Broadway.

Brasil Kite Flat Water KITESURFING
(☎3421-7403; www.brasilkiteflatwater.com; Pousada Colibri, Rua do Toquinho) Italian transplant Daniel is an IKO Level II–certified kitesurfing instructor and offers a three-day (nine hours) beginner's course for R$900. He also rents equipment (R$150 per day including transport) but will size up your abilities before doing so.

Extreme KiteSchool Canoa Quebrada KITESURFING
(☎99781-9119, 99960-6070; www.kitesurfcanoa.com) A recommended kitesurfing outfitter.

Sleeping

Hostel Pousada Ibiza HOSTEL $
(☎3421-7262; www.hostelpousadaibiza.com; Dragão do Mar 360; dm R$48-55, d R$140-160; ❄📶) Dorms and rooms are smallish but brightened by colorful throws and flags, and each comes equipped with its own bathroom. But what's best about this hostel is the long, airy, balcony-lounge-bar overlooking the heart of the Broadway action. It shares premises with a pizzeria (downstairs) and has a small guest kitchen.

English and Spanish spoken. There's lots of smoking.

Pousada California POUSADA $$

(☎3421-7039; www.californiacanoa.com; Nascer do Sol 135; r R$200-300; ❄📶🏊) This popular 33-room pousada has a variety of neat, comfortable rooms on two sides of the street, and an attractive courtyard with a sociable bar and pool. Free fruit and coffee are available all day in the breakfast-room-cum-TV-lounge, a chill hang spot; there's a new gym and many bathrooms have been recently done up. English owned and Dutch managed.

Pousada Dolce Vita POUSADA $$

(☎3421-7213; www.canoa-quebrada.it; Descida da Praia s/n; r R$290-350; ❄📶🏊) The Dolce Vita is friendly and relaxed. Bungalows are arranged round a garden of palms, flowers and lawns with a beautiful pool at its center. Rooms are spotlessly clean and have more character than your average pousada; each is named for a Fellini film and decorated with movie memorabilia.

Il Nuraghe POUSADA $$

(☎3421-7418; www.nuraghe-canoa.com; Descida da Praia s/n; r R$275-375; ❄📶🏊) Located at the entrance to town, Il Nuraghe is arguably Canoa's nicest digs, with 26 stylish yet minimalist rooms, colored with fresh local art; the nicest of the rooms looks out onto the extraordinary pool (about 25m long). Features such as a small spa with a welcoming sauna and bathrobes show the Italian owners are trying a bit harder, and the overall vibe here drips chic romance.

Vila Canoa POUSADA $$

(☎3421-7183; www.vilacanoa.com; Av Beira Mar 35; r R$275-300; ❄📶🏊) Canoa's only beachfront pousada is welcoming and Dutch run, and an excellent choice. Cool, tasteful rooms are dotted around a garden of grass and flagstone pathways that slopes down to the pool, a great sunbathing deck and the pousada's own *barraca* (beach bar-restaurant), which has cozy beach cushions for guests (R$10 for nonguests)

Eating

La Torinese BAKERY $

(Dragão do Mar s/n; items R$3-15; ⏲7am-noon & 4-9pm; 📶) Near the beginning of Broadway, this new Italian bakery serves Canoa's best espresso, does a perfect little variety of early-rise, baked-in-house breakfast pastries (guava croissants!), along with decadent, profiterole-heavy sweets throughout the day. It's also a pleasant spot for a predinner Aperol spritz (an Italian aperitif made with prosecco, aperol and soda water).

★ **Lazy Days** SEAFOOD, INTERNATIONAL $$

(www.facebook.com/barraca.days; Praia; mains R$28-40; ⏲9am-5pm) At the eastern end of the beach, Lazy Days is the best of the beach *barracas* that rub up against Canoa's picturesque red cliffs. The excellent barbecue fish, simply but perfectly garnished with salt, lime and *chimichurri* (an Argentinian green sauce), is marvelous, or you can up the ante with the *trio mar* (fish, shrimp and lobster), all grilled on the Argentine-run *parilla* (grill; R$150).

It also does steaks and curries and a bang-up barbecue on weekends, with live music or DJs. And if you want to sleep as close to the ocean as you possibly can, it also has a couple of rustic upstairs rooms (R$120).

El Argentino ARGENTINE $$

(☎3421-7123; Dragão do Mar 15; steak R$34-60; ⏲11:30am-11:30pm; 📶) At the east end of Broadway with picture windows looking down to the beach, Argentino is the best spot for grilled meats and does an all-you-can-eat *rodízio* (smorgasbord) for R$90. The grillman here claimed this was 'the best steak in Ceará!' Carnivores commence!

Tapas SPANISH $$

(☎99965-9227; Nascer do Sol 138; mains R$28-58; ⏲5pm-midnight Tue-Sun; 📶) Tucked down an alley along Broadway, this cozy, Brazilian-run restaurant opens up to a far more pleasant open-air atmosphere where barefoot waitstaff move nimbly across the sand flooring. It serves great larger-portioned tapas, heavy on calamari, shrimp and other seafood. Some consider it the best food in town.

Cabana BRAZILIAN $$

(☎3421-7018; www.facebook.com/restaurantecabana.canoaquebrada; Dragão do Mar s/n; mains for 2 people R$38-98; ⏲4:30pm-midnight Tue-Fri, noon-midnight Sat & Sun Feb-Apr, Jun & Aug-Dec, 4:30pm-midnight Mon, noon-midnight Tue-Sun Jul & Jan, closed May) If you're uninterested in the plethora of foreign-owned restaurants in town, give your money to this Brazilian spot, a solid bet for local food such as *peixadas* and *caldeiradas* (both are types of local seafood stews), and a long list of shrimp, fish and filet mignon dishes. Food is consistent and good.

Bar Evolução PIZZERIA $$

(Eliziário 1060; pizzas R$27.50-35; ⏲7-11pm Thu-Tue) Great little Italian-run place serving up thin-crust, wood-oven pizzas with farm-fresh mozzarella in an atmospheric open-air eatery.

OFF THE BEATEN TRACK

REDONDA

The fishing village of Redonda, 35km southeast of Canoa Quebrada, beyond the headland of Ponta Grossa, is reminiscent of Canoa Quebrada 30 or 40 years ago – a fine place to forget the wider world for a few days. It's also a good spot to eat locally caught lobster at lower-than-usual prices (around R$70 to R$100 for a two-person serve). **Pousada O Pescador** (088-3432-3018; Rua Praia 496; r R$120-150), right on the beach, has simple but good rooms. Slightly fancier but still with a rustic ambience are the brick chalets of **Oh! Linda Pousada** (088-99307-3771; www.ohlindapousada.com.br; Rua da Serra 100; s/d/tr R$130/190/240;) up on the cliff top. You can get to Redonda from Fortaleza by taking a bus to Aracati (R$13.50, three hours, 10 daily), then a van from Aracati's Igreja Matriz to Redonda.

Vai da Certo ITALIAN $$
(Broadway 554; pizzas R$28-59, pastas R$26-51; 4:40pm-midnight Thu-Mon;) It's a tall order around these parts to procure most of your ingredients from Italy, but that's what the Italian chef at this Canoa newcomer is claiming to do. Many Italians in town consider this the best pizza, and some house-made pasta dishes, such as those with tagliatelle, are tasty as well.

Drinking & Nightlife

There's no need to structure your evening; just walk along Broadway and you'll find what's going on. On weekends, the vibe is electric, fueled by live music nearly every 10m. Reggae parties take place at **Freedom Bar** (6pm-midnight Fri & Sun) on the beach.

Regart Bar BAR
(Dragão do Mar s/n; cover R$3; 3pm-3am) Located at the entrance to Broadway, Regart is our favorite bar for its pleasant sidewalk seating and live music on weekends.

Information

The post office and Banco do Brasil and Bradesco ATMs are all in a small shopping plaza near the west end of Rua Dragão do Mar; the military police are across the street.

Getting There & Away

Commercial flights were approved in 2015 for the new airport at Aracati, but at time of writing its runways remained unused.

São Benedito (www.gruposaobenedito.com.br) runs five daily buses to/from Fortaleza bus station (R$24.50, 3¼ hours), departing 6am, 8:30am, 11am, 1:30pm, 4:40pm and 5:30pm. In Canoa you can buy tickets in advance at **Evânia** (3421-7046; Dradão do Mar s/n; 8am-8pm), the agency in town representing São Benedito. Alternatively, you can travel by tour van (R$45, 2½ hours) with companies such as **Oceanview** (3219-1300; www.oceanviewturismo.com.br). The tour vans pick up and drop off at accommodations in Fortaleza, departing around 8am and returning from the west end of Rua Dragão do Mar around 3:45pm.

Coming from Rio Grande do Norte, get off the bus at Aracati, 13km southwest of Canoa. From there with any luck you can catch São Benedito's Fortaleza–Canoa bus (R$1.10), departing 8:50am, 11:30am, 1:50pm, 4:20pm and 8:20pm. Otherwise, minibuses known colloquially as *topícs* (R$2.50, about every half-hour) depart 6am to 8pm from the Igreja Matriz in Aracati's center, about 1km from the bus station. Taxis charge R$25 to R$30 for the quick Aracati–Canoa run.

Icaraí de Amontada

088

Icaraizinho, as it's affectionately known, is the loveliest of the small beach spots between Fortaleza and Jericoacoara. Its wide beach of fine sand sits on a beautiful, palm-lined curve of bay, with a few fishing boats on the water, high dunes rising to the west, and rarely more than a handful of people in sight. It's reminiscent, some say, of Jericoacoara as it was 25 years ago. Icaraí is 190km from Fortaleza (beyond the reach of day-tour buses), has no ATM, and the 24km road linking it to Hwy CE-085 was only paved a few years ago. Icaraí has a selection of excellent pousadas and some good restaurants, and is a top windsurfing and kitesurfing spot (best from July to December).

Club Ventos WINDSURFING, KITESURFING
(3636-3006; www.clubventos.com) At the east end of the beach, Club Ventos takes windsurfing and kitesurfing classes and rents quality equipment; also rents kayaks and stand-up paddle (SUP) boards.

Sleeping & Eating

★Casa Zulu POUSADA $$
(☎3636-3016; www.casazulu.com; Francisco Gonçalves de Sousa 194; r/bungalows from R$250/300; ❄📶≋) A young French windsurfer built his dream pousada where once nothing but coconut palms stood, nailing the perfect marriage of rustic vibe and stylish comfort along the way. Colorful rooms (two bungalows, four apartments) are dripping with understated charm and artistic touches such as traditional straw hats and ornaments. It's all set around gorgeous leafy gardens with direct beach access.

There's a patio that's great for breakfast and drinks, a pool area, a slew of friendly dogs and cats, and windsurfing and kitesurfing lessons for guests. Pretty perfect.

Pousada Les Alizés POUSADA $$
(☎3636-3006; www.lesalizes.com.br; d/tr R$165/195; ❄📶≋) At the eastern end of the bay, Les Alizés has nine air-conditioned bungalows (that could use a touch-up) in its large beachside gardens. The excellent breakfast that's served in a breezy pavilion gazing out at the beach is a true delight.

Truth be told, it's a very nice location, but draconian measures for foreigners to secure reservations has spoiled the fun here a bit. Also, mind those sneaky toilet frogs!

Villa Mango CHALET $$$
(☎3636-3089; www.villamango.com.br; apt R$500, bungalows from R$490, with ocean views R$550; ❄📶≋) 🍃 Nine rustic but luxurious wooden stilt chalets (some two-level) stand in a garden that slopes down to the west end of the beach. You have a choice of natural wind ventilation or air-con. Villa Mango also offers a good restaurant, a bar, a pool and its own kitesurf club; and it does its best with sustainable initiatives, such as ecological drains and solar heating.

It's all set on idyllic, well-manicured grounds on a fairly isolated end of the beach.

Espaço Gourmet JAPANESE, BRAZILIAN $
(☎99473-5318; Noe Praciano Sampaio 194; R$15-40; ⏲6:30-11pm Mon-Sat) Who needs a menu? An honest-to-goodness Japazilian chef from São Paulo has slapped down less than five tables and cooks up what's fresh. That means anything from an insanely portioned chicken *yakisoba* (feeds three for R$15!) or cashew-nut pesto tagliatelle to fresh-caught tuna sushi and sashimi, which comes in twice a week. Options are limited; reservations prudent.

Eating here is about the pleasant vibe the chef cultivates, but the food is excellent, too.

Café Zapata BRAZILIAN $
(www.cafezapata.com; Joaquim Alves Parente 94; mains R$23-42; ⏲6:30-11pm Tue-Sun; 📶) This pretty garden restaurant on a narrow street leading towards the far east end of the beach focuses on interesting pastas such as seafood puttanesca, and fish and lobster lasagna. It's all pretty good, and so are the prices.

Getting There & Away

A daily Fretcar (p543) bus leaves Fortaleza bus station for Icaraí de Amontada (R$29.60, five hours) at 2:30pm (3pm on Sundays), returning at 5:50am (1:20pm Sundays). You do not need to backtrack to Fortaleza to continue on to Jericoacoara from here; you can catch a Fretcar bus (R$6, one hour) at 5:30am (1:30pm on Sunday) or **Cooperita** (☎3631-1432) minivan (*topique*) to Amontada (R$7, one hour) at 5:30am, 7am, 10:30am or 1pm Monday to Saturday, from where there are five Fretcar buses a day to Jijoca (R$13 to R$19, 2½ hours) departing 9:50am, 10:50am, 1:20pm, 6:20pm and 8:50pm. You can also take a 4WD along the coast (R$400).

Jericoacoara

☎088 / POP 3000

Jericoacoara, known to its many friends simply as 'Jeri,' is one of Brazil's most cinematic destinations. It magnetizes travelers with its perfect combination of hard-to-reach location (access is only by unpaved tracks through the dunes), stunning coastal scenery, exciting activities, excellent pousadas and restaurants, and fun nightlife. During the day, its beaches, dunes and lagoons are as postcardworthy as any destination in South America; at night, illuminated by moonlight and by the lights of inviting boutiques and restaurants, its enchantment cannot be overstated. In a word: magical.

The village's sandy streets are wedged between a broad beach, a series of grassy hills and the majestic Pôr do Sol (Sunset) dune, a towering mountain of sand that affords one of South America's most stunning sunsets. It is here each evening that Jeri's allure climaxes: a crowd swells – drinks in hand from an enterprising local with a cocktail cart – at what is allegedly one of the earth's few locations where you can see the rare phenomenon known as the 'Emerald Sunset,' which is when the tip of the setting sun turns bright green for the final instant before it slides below the horizon. Bring your camera. You'll need it regardless!

Jericoacoara's isolated position, inside a far-flung national park at the top edge of the country, is unique. We hope when the new Jericoacoara airport (30km away in Cruz municipality) opens in the near future, it will not lead to a transformation that shatters Jeri's otherwordly allure. The airport is at least well outside the national park.

Jeri itself is closed to unauthorized vehicles, though there is still more traffic than there should be. The main streets (of sand) run parallel to each other, westward towards the beach. In the middle is Rua Principal. To the north are Rua do Forró (where buses arrive) and then Rua da Igreja (also called Rua da Matriz); to the south (the dune side) are Rua São Francisco and Rua das Dunas.

Activities

The steady winds between late June and February make Jericoacoara a top destination for kitesurfing and windsurfing. There are also decent waves for surfing. Capoeira classes take place nightly on the beach. If

KITESURFING JERI & THE NORTHEAST

Steady, strong trade winds blowing across the Atlantic from Africa during the second half of the year place Brazil's northeast coast among the world's very best kitesurfing zones. Lovers of this exciting, physically demanding sport fly in from around the world and have spawned a whole infrastructure of kite schools, kite pousadas (guesthouses) and kite safaris. There is a full range of conditions from flat water to waves, and the steady easterly breeze blowing along the whole coast makes for some epic downwinder voyages.

Equipment rentals are widely available, but with rates of around R$280 per day it makes more sense for experienced surfers to bring their own. A rental car is a huge help both for transporting your gear and for reaching the best spots. Beginners can learn the art at almost any kitesurfing destination on the coast: a course of nine or 10 hours, usually spread over three days, costs around R$1350 with IKO-certified instructors. For proper safety standards and quality teaching, head to a school with instructors certified by the **International Kiteboarding Organization** (IKO; www.ikointl.com).

Jericoacoara is one of the most popular kitesurfing locations, thanks to its combination of traveler facilities and winds that blow at an average 23 to 30 knots for eight months of the year. From late June to February the breeze springs up midmorning and blows till sunset; it's strongest in September and October. The best spot for beginners is Preá (13km east of Jeri), at low tide, where there's idyllic side-on-shore wind conditions. Other good spots are the rivermouth waters at Guriú, 12km west of Jeri (though it's becoming more crowded), and along the shore for several kilometers back toward Jeri; and Tatajuba, 12km beyond Guriú, where there's a flat-water lagoon. For experienced kitesurfers, the 25km of downwind conditions from the Pôr do Sol (Sunset) dune all the way to Tatajuba is a coveted route. It's also possible to kitesurf the entire journey from Fortaleza to Jericoacoara.

Jeri has numerous kite schools. Freelance teachers may charge less, but it's better to use a school with IKO instructors such as **MH Kiteschool** (☎3669-2268; www.mhkiteschool.com; Pousada Bella Jeri, Travessa da Rua do Forró), with senior level instructor; **Kiteiscool** (☎99670-2330; www.kiteiscool.com; Praça Principal; ⏲8:30am-noon & 4:30-11pm); or Preá-based **Rancho do Kite** (☎3669-2080; www.ranchodokite.com.br; Principal, Preá; ⏲shop 10am-1pm & 3:30-11pm).

The whole coast around Jeri – from Barrinha, 6km east of Preá, to Camocim, 20km west of Tatajuba – is great for downwinders. It's easy to find a buggy for transport; it's R$140 for four or five people from Jeri to Guriú, for an example price. Much longer downwinders are equally possible, on any stretch of the coast, and can be organized through local pousadas, agencies and kite schools. Jeri Off Road (p549), for example, offers 'kitesurfaris' of several days with 4WD from Canoa Quebrada to Fortaleza (140km), Fortaleza to Jeri (300km), or Jeri to Barra Grande (100km), running around R$850 per day per vehicle.

Other Northeast kitesurfing locations include Natal, São Miguel do Gostoso, Galinhos, Canoa Quebrada, Fortaleza, Cumbuco, Flecheiras and Icaraí de Amontada.

you are of a calmer demeanor, you can visit the dunes and lakes outside town by buggy, take yoga classes or stroll along the beach to **Pedra Furada**, an arched rock 3km east of town. The most popular day trips head east (to Preá, Pedro Furada, Lago Azul and, the belle of the ball, Lago Paraíso) for R$50; or west (to Guriú and Tatajuba, with an option to see seahorses) for R$60. Both trips can also be done by all-terrain vehicle (ATV) for R$250 and R$300, respectively.

Buggy Rides

It's an excellent five-hour outing to fishing village Tatajuba, 24km west, where there's a beach at the mouth of a tidal river, and a large lagoon among the dunes behind the village. There are *barracas* beside the lagoon. One of the dunes actually overtook the old Tatajuba, which had to be moved to its present site – brick by brick. You can still see evidence of where the church used to be.

Jeri Off Road DRIVING TOUR
(☎3669-2268; www.jeri.tur.br; Pousada Bella Jeri, Travessa da Rua do Forró) This is a helpful and environmentally conscious agency that also organizes buggy adventures near and far.

Associação dos Bugueiros DRIVING TOUR
(Buggy Drivers' Association; ☎99687-8866; Principal) Organizes buggy rides from a storefront on Rua Principal across from the central square. Trips take up to four passengers and prices are for the vehicle (with driver), so if you join with others it's cheaper.

Capoeira

Classes (R$30, 1½ hours) are held at 7am or 8am and 4pm every day on the beach, followed daily (except Sunday) by a sunset *roda de capoeira* (open capoeira performance), which always attracts a crowd.

Dance

Academia Samba Jeri DANCE
(☎99678-3665; www.sambajericoacoara.moonfruit.com; Principal, above Padaria Central; 2/4 classes R$25/35) To get the most out of *forró* it helps to learn the dance – especially for men, who must lead. Head to teacher Mel at Academia Samba Jeri on Rua Principal for tuition in *forró,* samba or other Brazilian dances.

Massage

Ashti Ma Parithosh MASSAGE
(☎99681-0262; www.ashti.com.br; Rua da Forró; 75min massage R$130; ⏲10am-7:30pm) Massage is big business in Jeri; various masseuses round town have a chalkboard sign-up scheme outside their doors. We prefer the pricier and more professional services of English-speaking Asti, who trained in Brazil and Italy. Her 75-minute massage will deal with what ails you. Her space is on Rua da Forró, 50m from the beach.

Surfing

There are good waves for surfing (best from about March to May) right out in front of Praia de Jericoacoara. Neighboring Praia Malhada, round the bend to the east, has bigger waves for more advanced surfers. Board rental costs R$25 or so per hour, or around R$50 to R$60 per day.

Windsurfing

The same winds that make Jeri a kitesurfing mecca work for windsurfing too. July to January are the best months, with fine conditions for experienced riders right in front of Jeri beach.

Ticowind WINDSURFING
(☎9662-9291; www.ticowindjeri.com; Vila Kalango, Rua das Dunas 30) Ticowind is highly popular for its good quality/price combination (and it's thus sometimes necessary to book ahead for its services): it rents windsurfers for €49/249/407 per day/week/two weeks, and charges R$300 for a three-hour beginners course.

It also runs an SUP excursion to the mangroves (R$150 per person), and rent surfboards (R$25 per hour) and SUP equipment (R$50 to R$80 per hour).

Club Ventos WINDSURFING
(☎3669-2288; www.clubventos.com; Praia de Jericoacoara; ⏲9:30am-5:30pm) Just east of the foot of Rua do Forró, this outfit is professional and well equipped, though more expensive than some other similar outfits. It also rents kayaks, surfboards and SUP boards.

Tours

In addition to buggy day trips you can also take buggy or 4WD trips as far west as Parnaíba, the Lençóis Maranhenses and São Luís, a route known as the Rota das Emoções (Route of the Emotions). A tour is a lot easier, though more expensive, than taking public transportation: a four-day (and more!) 4WD expedition to São Luís, including accommodations, transportation, a Delta do Parnaíba boat trip and a Lençóis Maranhenses tour, costs R$3340/4440 for two/four people with Jeri Off Road.

Life's a Beach

In a country famed for its fabulous beaches, the shoreline of Ceará, Piauí and Maranhão has both hands on the supreme crown. The 1000km from Ceara's southeastern limits to São Luís is a rarely interrupted succession of long, sweeping, dune-backed strands and smaller palm-lined bays with a few fishing boats riding at anchor.

Jericoacoara

Set inside a national park with no paved roads (only sandy tracks), this hip, ultra-laid-back travelers' hangout (p547) just about has it all. Majestic dunescapes, world-class winds for kite- and windsurfers, a nightly party scene on the beach and in the music joints, good restaurants and dozens of good-value pousadas (guesthouses).

Atins

For that true end-of-the-road feeling, head down the jungle-clad Rio Preguiças to tiny Atins (p567), with a scattering of pousadas along its sandy streets, and the incredible expanse of high dunes and freshwater lagoons that is the Lençóis Maranhenses beginning a short walk away.

Icaraí de Amontada

Little Icaraí (p546), just far enough from Fortaleza to preserve its tranquillity, spreads round a gorgeous curve of palm-lined sand with a few fishing boats bobbing in the surf and rarely more than a handful of people in sight. A few surprisingly good pousadas and restaurants cater to those in the know.

Canoa Quebrada

A budget backpackers' destination that is transitioning into a more family-friendly spot, Canoa (p544) sits on an endless beach lined by pink cliffs on one side and high dunes on the other, and is full of fun things to do, from tandem paragliding to beach reggae parties.

1. Windsurfing, Jericoacoara **2.** Paragliding, Canoa Quebrada **3.** Ponta Grossa, Canoa Quebrada

2

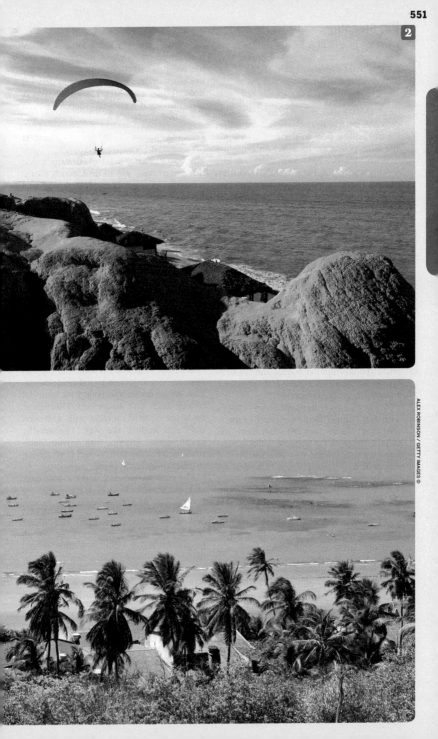

ALEX ROBINSON / GETTY IMAGES ©

Sleeping

There are dozens of pousadas and small hotels in Jericoacoara. Some close during May, the low point of Jeri's season. The high seasons are July and January.

Jeri Central HOSTEL $
(☎99747-8070; www.jericentral.com.br; São Francisco 222; dm R$60) The new, all-dorm Jeri Central adds a pool to the Jeri hostel mix and wins points for its as-yet-unblemished facilities. It's the next-door neighbor and sister property of longer-established Jericoacora Hostel; guests intermingle between properties as reception and breakfast for both are located here.

Jericoacoara Hostel HOSTEL $
(☎99747-8070; www.jericoacoarahostel.com.br; São Francisco 202; camping per person R$25, dm with fan/air-con R$50/60, d with fan/air-con R$160/195;) You won't be Instagramming its rather basic dorms and private rooms, but this hostel wins huge points for its welcoming atmosphere. The large patio and hammock space with well-stocked 'honor fridge' promote easy socializing, and trilingual manager Gaúcho is constantly assisting guests with travel advice, well-organized information boards and reasonably priced laundry service – and keeps on a watchful, anti-shenanigan patrol.

It shares a reception and some facilities with Jeri Central, its newer sister property next door. Guests take breakfast there and can use the pool, for example. Folks around town know this option as 'Pousada Tirol' if you need directions. Perhaps best of all it's directly across the street from Fretcar.

★ **Villa Chic** HOSTEL $$
(☎4062-9624; www.villachicjeri.com; Principal; dm/r R$65/220;) If you've outgrown the hostel party scene, the excellent dorms here are Jeri's best, but exist within the environment of a boutique pousada. Each eight-bed dorm (one mixed, one male, one female) boasts one and a half bathrooms (the 'half' has no shower), which are some of the most fashionable you'll come across at these prices.

The exposed stone walls are original, remnants of the traditional fisherfolk architecture of Jeri's past. Flashpacker's paradise!

Bella Jeri POUSADA $$
(☎3669-2268; www.bellajeri.com.br; Travessa da Rua do Forró; s/d R$200/250;) Bella Jeri has seven cute, tasteful rooms with brick walls, solid wood furniture and hammocks, plus a pleasant garden, pool and breezy roof terrace with views to the dune and the ocean. The breakfast is great, and the English-speaking owners also run Jeri Off Road (p549) and MH Kiteschool (p548), which makes it a one-stop shop for all you desire in Jeri.

Pousada Papaya POUSADA $$
(☎3669-2219; www.jeripapaya.com.br; Dunas 74; r from R$300;) Tucked away inside this walled oasis are 10 neat, comfy rooms with colorful check bedspreads, a pool in a flowery front garden, and attractive common areas inside and out. These features and a great breakfast make the Papaya a deservedly popular little choice.

Pousada Surfing Jeri POUSADA $$
(☎3669-2260; www.surfingjeri.com.br; São Francisco 150; d R$300-330;) Twenty-five solidly constructed rooms and apartments, with wood floors and ceilings, are set along a green, shady garden with a pool. It all adds up to a solidly sensible choice.

★ **Vila Kalango** POUSADA, CHALET $$$
(☎3669-2290; www.vilakalango.com.br; Dunas 30; r R$625-870;) A longtime top-end favorite, Vila Kalango's round brick bungalows are serene escape pods with beautiful canopy beds and native wood furniture. Some are elevated on stilts, with driftwood staircases leading the way. The smaller *apartamentos* (rooms with private bathroom) are equally tasteful and have air-con to offset their lack of breeze.

The staff is charming, and the pool deck and restaurant look out onto the beach.

Casa Fufi POUSADA $$$
(www.casafufi.com.br; Rua do Ibama; r R$390-510;) This newish, intimate top-ender offers just five rooms within its white stone and brick, thatched-roof construction, flanked by a healthy patch of grass (a rarity in Jeri) and a stylish pool deck. Breakfast is served privately on the expansive verandas, where there are hammocks and ample table space; and the spacious rooms all come with modern kitchens. Top honors for privacy and price.

Pousada Jeribá POUSADA $$$
(☎4062-9191; www.jeriba.com.br; Rua do Ibama; r R$630-1085;) Spacious rooms with gorgeous hardwood verandas and hammock chairs are set in tasteful, exposed-brick bungalows, amid colorful grounds draped

in lush tropical plants. Rooms 5 and 8 have the most panoramic views. The oceanfront patio and lounge is a near-perfect chill-out pad, with views over Jeri's dunes and prime windsurfing waters, and the classy restaurant is right next to it.

Eating

Jeri offers a great variety of excellent food for such a small place. Deciding on which charming spot to eat at can be painful.

Gelato & Grano ICE CREAM $
(Praça Principal 1; 1/2/3 scoops R$8/10/14; noon-midnight) If there's one thing you'll eventually pine for in this heat, it's ice cream. This wildly popular, farmhouse-chic gelato shop on the main square serves up 20 flavors and is constantly swarmed by sweet-toothed vacationers and locals alike. Brownie, Belgian chocolate and pistachio are the most popular, but Brazilian staples such as *açaí* and tapioca are here as well.

There's a second, smaller location closer to the beach on Rua Principal.

Club Ventos BUFFET $
(3669-2288; www.clubventos.com; Praia de Jericoacoara; per kg R$60; noon-5pm;) Soak up the spectacular views from the cashew-tree-shaded oceanfront terrace at Jericoacoara's best *por kilo* eatery, then settle into a lounge chair and catch some rays for the rest of the afternoon. An excellent selection of salads and vegetable options compensate for the limited – but tasty – array of main dishes.

Jeri Jú BRAZILIAN $
(Forró; meals R415-26; 7:30-11:30am & 12:30-8pm) This neat, family-run lunch spot is the best of the local economical eats specializing in *pratos feitos* (daily meal specials).

Padaria Santo Antônio BAKERY $
(São Francisco; 2am-9am) A Jericoacoara classic, this bakery opens in the wee hours of the morning to provide coffee and freshly baked goods to partygoers on their way home.

★ **Peixe Brasileiro** SEAFOOD $$
(cnr São Francisco & Beco do Guaxêlo; fish/shrimp/lobster per kg R$45/90/130; 7-11:30pm) Just a few tables in the sand alley where local fishers grill their fresh catch nightly. Pick your dinner by size from the family's *peixaria* (fish restaurant) next door: *pargo* (red snapper), *garoupa* (grouper), *robalo* (sea bass), shrimp and/or *langosta*. Weigh it, sit back and wait while they fire it up on the barbecue, garnished with nothing but lime and salt.

Unfortunately the fishmongers sometimes assume you have a bigger appetite than you do. Keep them honest: about 500g is a good fish portion per person. The entire experience is one to remember.

Pimenta Verde INTERNATIONAL, BRAZILIAN $$
(São Francisco; mains for 2 people R$82.50-102; noon-10:45pm, closed 2 Sun per month;) This delightful little corner restaurant, with only a few tables, pumps out memorable cuisine, from octopus Provençal (best dish in Jeri?) to a divine green-peppercorn filet and perfectly creamy seafood risotto. Cute artistic touches round out the culinary happiness.

Tamarindo BRAZILIAN $$
(99937-9057; www.tamarindojeri.com.br; Farmacia; medium pizza R$25-55, mains R$33-79.50; 6-11pm) The most creative dining experience in Jeri is romantically lit under the shadow of a giant tamarind tree. Nearly everything is cooked in the brick oven, which is the norm for pizza, but not for exquisite gems such as the Brazil-nut-crusted filet mignon. From the cocktails (frozen *tangeroskas* with ginger) to the staff and service, it's a class act. Expect the place to be swarming.

Bistro Caiçara BRAZILIAN $$
(99916-0072; Principal 16; mains R$30-85; 4pm-12:30am Mon-Sat;) This main-street newcomer has been a real crowd-pleaser for Chef Apolinário's more-creative-than-most seafood: *robalo* in soy, ginger and honey; passion-fruit or cashew-fruit sauces; sweet and spicy octopus etc. Service is top-notch and it all goes down very romantically on a candlelit 2nd-floor open-air patio overlooking Rua Principal.

Kaze JAPANESE $$
(99961-5791; Forró; rolls R$14-34, platters R$13/30/44 pieces R$24/54/84; 6pm-midnight) This is Jeri's go-to sushi spot, serving up mostly tuna, salmon, white fish, octopus, shrimp and sea bass, which is a few more varieties than you usually see outside São Paulo. It will fulfill your craving at any rate, and it's a classy spot in a breezy open-air 2nd-floor atmosphere.

Pizzaria Araxá PIZZERIA $$
(www.araxapousada.com; Dunas 2; pizzas R$27-45; 6:30-10:30pm) This intimate Italian-owned pizzeria inside a well-to-do pousada

LAYOVER: PIAUÍ

Piauí, one of the largest states in the Northeast, sits between Ceará and Maranhão and boasts several fantastic natural attractions, including the Delta do Parnaíba, the Parque Nacional de Sete Cidades and the Parque Nacional da Serra da Capivara (one of the top prehistoric sites in South America). Colonial settlement in Piauí began in the arid southern *sertão* (interior or backlands of the Northeast) and gradually moved north toward the coast, creating an oddly shaped territory with underdeveloped infrastructure. Today, Piauí is Brazil's poorest state. Parnaíba-based **Eco Adventure Tour** (3323-9595; www.ecoadventure.tur.br; Av Presidente Vargas 26) is an excellent sustainably minded ecotourism agency for all adventures in Piauí.

Parque Nacional de Sete Cidades

Sete Cidades is a small 62-sq-km **national park** (3343-1342; admission Brazilian/foreigner R$7.50/R$15; 8am-5pm) with bizarre rock formations that some have claimed are *sete cidades* (seven cities) left behind by some mysterious long-departed culture (aliens, Vikings etc). The place doesn't need such fantasies to make it worth visiting. The rock formations are indeed fantastic – some look like giant turtle shells, others resemble a castle, an elephant, a map of Brazil or the head of emperor Dom Pedro II – and there are also superb vistas over a landscape that combines caatinga (semi-arid land) and cerrado (savanna) vegetation. There are some 1500 intriguing rock paintings of between 3000 and 5000 years old; wildlife that includes marmosets, small rodents called *mocós* (cavies) that like to pose for photos, tarantulas and (we're told) rattlesnakes; and two delectable natural bathing pools.

The park entrance is 190km northeast of Teresina, 24km northeast of the small town of Piripiri and 8km north by paved road off Hwy BR-222. Expresso Guanabara runs 10 daily buses from Teresina to Piripiri (from R$30, three hours).

Delta do Parnaíba

Sometimes called the Delta das Américas, Delta do Parnaíba is a 2700-sq-km expanse of islands, beaches, lagoons, channels, high sand dunes and dense mangrove forest full of wildlife. Around 65% of its area is in the state of Maranhão, but the easiest access is from Parnaíba in Piauí. Agencies around Parnaíba's Porto das Barcas offer several half-day and day tours into the delta in fast motor launches or big party boats, starting from Porto dos Tatus, 14km north of Parnaíba. A better option if you're interested in peace, quiet and nature is to go with boatman **José Ribamar** (083-99924-5598; Rua da Gloria 900, Centro Ilha

produces Jeri's best pie. All the classics are represented (margherita, marinara etc) as well as white pizzas and, perhaps disappointingly, a few Brazilianized versions to appease the locals (chicken with Catupiry cheese etc). There are just a few tables, divided loft-style between those overlooking the pool and those in the sand below. Wi-fi is for pousada clients only.

Drinking & Entertainment

Everything starts at the cocktail *barracas* on the beach at the foot of Rua Principal. From early evening all manner of caipirinhas and *caipifrutas* are irresistibly mixed up with all manner of exotic fruit. Cocktails run R$7 to R$16 or so. We like Barraca da Socorro for its flashy lights, soundtrack and manual blender. From here partiers move on to other entertainments around the village.

Places and events change frequently, so ask around. For live-music nights, expect covers between R$15 and R$20.

Samba Rock Cafe BAR

(www.sambarockcafe.com; Principal; cocktails R$10-20; 9:45am-1:30am) Sitting on prime corner real estate across from the main square, this is easily Jeri's most atmospheric drinking spot. Rustic wood furniture seating is arranged under a massive, illuminated acacia tree. DJs spin electronica during happy hour from Thursday to Sunday (6pm to 8pm), and there's live Música Popular Brasileira (MPB; Monday, Wednesday and Saturday), samba (Tuesday and Friday), reggae (Thursday) and Latin (Sunday).

Grande) , who uses traditional and quiet wooden boats and can pick you up in Parnaíba. José speaks only Portuguese, but a multilingual guide is available, and you can make arrangements through José's German business partner **Anne Knapp** (49-176-344-59-816; www.deltaparnaiba.com). One of their day trips, known as Micro-Macro (R$420 for up to five people), will take you to the Morro Branco dunes; Pontal, where you can swim at a meeting point of freshwater and ocean; a fishing village; and then carry you by motorized canoe into mangrove channels, where you can hope to see plenty of wildlife such as howler and capuchin monkeys, caimans, iguanas, snakes and birds. Other options include a six- to seven-hour one-way tour through the delta to Tutoia (R$550 for up to eight people), and overnight trips.

Parnaíba is serviced by Expresso Guanabara (www.expressoguanabara.com.br) buses from Fortaleza (from R$50, 7½ to 11 hours, five daily), Camocim (R$22, 2½ hours, departing 4:08pm), São Luís (from R$87, eight to nine hours, two daily) and Teresina (from R$68, five to seven hours, nine daily).

Parque Nacional da Serra da Capivara

In the south of Piauí, the dramatic rocky landscape of the 1300-sq-km **Parque Nacional da Serra da Capivara** (Brazilian/foreigner R$11.50/25; 6am-6pm) , a Unesco World Heritage site, contains 40,000 prehistoric rock paintings – claimed to be the greatest concentration on the planet. Entered 35km north of the small town of São Raimundo Nonato, the park has 800 archaeological sites and has yielded what's considered to be the oldest evidence of human presence in the Americas, at least 50,000 years ago, predating previous 'earliest' finds by about 30,000 years. The rock art is mostly 6000 to 12,000 years old and includes depictions of deer and caimans, and people dancing, hunting and having sex.

More than R$50 million has been spent on developing the park's facilities and a museum in São Raimundo. The park has wooden walkways, disabled access to many sites, good vehicle tracks, walking trails, a visitors center, lookout points and helpful bilingual signs. Another attraction of the area is the appealing ceramics decorated with designs from Capivara rock art, produced by the villagers of Barreirinho just outside the park.

Princesa do Sul/Viação Transpiaui (3218-1761) makes the 500km odyssey from Teresina to São Raimundo Nonato four times daily (R$93, eight hours), departing 10am, 2:45pm, 8:15pm and 8:30pm, and return. Another approach is via Petrolina in Pernambuco, 280km east, to which you can fly from Recife, Salvador or São Paulo. A Gontijo (www.gontijo.com.br) bus leaves Petrolina for São Raimundo (R$59, six hours) at 2:10pm.

Cachaçaria Gourmet BAR
(www.facebook.com/cachacariagourmetjeri; Travessa Ismael; cachaça R$8-20; 6pm-midnight) If you'd like a stiff drink without a soundtrack, this cute and tiny bar specializes in Brazil's national firewater, *cachaça*. There are 90 or so labels, many of which come from Minas Gerais (as does the owner); around 30 labels are available at any given time, and the liquor is even mixed into frozen caipirinhas (a rarity, despite the obviousness of the idea!).

Restaurante Dona Amélia LIVE MUSIC
(www.facebook.com/donaamelia.restaurante; Forró; 11pm-4.30am Wed & Sat) Live band *forró* nights here are thronged with swaying couples on the dance floor from around 2:30am till closing.

Pousada Solar de Malhada LIVE MUSIC
(www.solardamalhada.com; Rua da Matriz) Hosts Jeri's best samba night from 10pm on Fridays.

Maloca LIVE MUSIC
(Igreja) At the top end of Rua Igreja, Maloca hosts Jeri's best *forró* night, from 10pm on Thursdays.

Information

Jeri's isolated position is both a blessing and a curse: use common sense from a security standpoint – do not walk on the dunes alone in the wee hours or leave valuables unattended in restaurants or on the beach. In high season, when crowds swell, crime rates inevitably rise.

With the exception of the beach, do not go barefoot in Jeri: wear flip-flops in town and on the Pôr do Sol (Sunset) dune to avoid *bicho-de-pê* (chigoe flea), a parasite that can embed in your foot and reproduce, which is – trust us – not fun.

Many pousadas and restaurants will accept Visa or Mastercard, but Jeri has no international-friendly ATM. Stock up with cash before arriving, at **Banco do Brasil** (Av Manoel Teixeira 139, Jijoca; ⌚ branch 9am-2pm Mon-Fri, ATMs 7am-6pm daily) in Jijoca, 23km southeast.

Tem de Tudo (Principal; ⌚7am-midnight) supermarket can usually give cash back, with a 10% charge for debit cards and 15% for credit cards, up to a R$500 limit. Jericoacoara Hostel/ Jeri Central (p552) offers the same service with no limit (in English).

BPTur (Batalhão de Policiamento Turístico do Ceará; ☎99682-7500; www.facebook.com/bpturce; Principal; ⌚24hr) Jeri's tourist police, located near Jeri Pousada.

Correios (www.correios.com.br; Forró 7; ⌚9am-noon & 1:30-4pm Mon-Fri) Postal services.

Global Connection (☎99900-2109; Forró; ⌚9am-10pm) Sells bus tickets for Jeri to Fortaleza and many other regional routes, organizes trips from Jericoacoara to Lençóis Maranhenses, plus sells air tickets.

Rota das Emoções (www.rotadasemocoes.com.br) has good info on the route from Jericoacoara to Parnaíba and Lençóis Maranhenses.

ℹ Getting There & Away

AIR

Construction of Jericoacoara airport, some 30km southeast of town, has been an on-off affair, but it may soon be possible to fly there from Brazilian cities and even other countries.

BUS

Fretcar (☎99700-7373; www.fretcar.com.br; São Francisco; ⌚6-6:15am, 8-11am, noon-5pm & 6-10:30pm) runs a service to Fortaleza (R$80 to R$101.50, six to seven hours), leaving at 6:15am, 3:15pm and, the most comfortable, at 10:30pm. You travel by *jardineira* (open-sided 4WD truck) as far as Jijoca, then by bus. The trip begins at Fretcar's office on Rua São Francisco, across from Jericoacoara Hostel. Buy tickets at least one day in advance.

You can also travel to Fortaleza in the tour vans of companies such as **Enseada** (p543), which drop off at Fortaleza hotels (R$75, six hours). Most accommodations can book these for you. The vans usually leave about 9am and some stop 2½ hours at Lagoa Paraíso, near Jijoca, en route.

CAMIONETES & BUGGY

The most frequent transportation between Jeri and Jijoca is by *camionetes* (4WD passenger trucks; R$15 one way), known as D-20, which leave whenever they fill with passengers – about every 30 minutes, and most frequently between about 6am and 10pm. In Jeri the departure point is in front of Padaria Jeripan on Rua São Francisco. In Jijoca *camionetes* meet your bus before scooping up more passengers around town. Alternatively, a buggy costs around R$80 for up to four people. From Jijoca there are up to nine Fretcar buses to Fortaleza (R$30 to R$44, five to six hours) and up to four to Camocim (R$12.15, 1½ to 2¼ hours).

CAR

If traveling to Jeri by car, it's best to leave your vehicle in Jijoca, where there are safe parking lots for R$10 per day; it's easy to damage vehicles on the trip to Jeri, and rental insurance is void in the sand). From Jijoca, get a *camionete* or buggy on to Jeri.

TO/FROM THE LENÇÓIS MARANHENSES

Moving on westward toward the Lençóis Maranhenses, the direct coastal route includes a 40km 4WD-only stretch from Paulino Neves to Caburé, so travelers by regular bus have to go almost to São Luís before heading 200km back east to Barreirinhas. There are several ways and routes and combinations of various types of vehicles for making the trip. We include of a few of the easier and better organized options.

The fastest and costliest option is a straight one-day transfer from Jeri. Jeri Off Road (p549), for example, can get you there in about nine hours for around R$1300 (up to four people). The trip heads to Paulino Neves by car (6½ hours), then on to Caburé along the coast by 4WD (40 minutes), then a scenic boat ride to Barreirinhas (must be reserved in advance). It's also possible to take in the Delta do Parnaíba (p554) en route.

The best combination of speed and economy is on public transport and can be organized by **Global Connection**. You'll catch a 6pm D-20 to Jijoca (R$15, 40 minutes), where you'll transfer to the 7pm (5pm on Sunday) **2M** (☎3322-8596) bus to Paulino Neves (R$58, 6½ hours), arriving around 2am. You can sleep overnight in Paulino Neves or continue on with a 4am public Toyota *jardineira* departure (or at 6am if arranged by Global Connection) on to Barreirinhas (R$30, two hours).

If you're not hell-bent on speed, there are also options using regular Fretcar (www.fretcar.com.br) buses from Jijoca to Camocim (R$12.15, 1½ to 2¼ hours) and a daily 4:08pm Expresso Guanabara (www.expressoguanabara.com.br) bus from Camocim to Parnaíba (R$22, 2½ hours), plus different possibilities from Parnaíba.

Heading to Jeri from the Lençóis, transportation schedules along the coastal route are less convenient, so a direct 4WD transfer is worth considering.

MARANHÃO

The atmosphere-laden colonial city of São Luís, its tranquil but gorgeous neighbor Alcântara, and the wild natural beauty of the Parque Nacional dos Lençóis Maranhenses have put the Northeast's furthest-flung state firmly on the travel map. The coastal route from Jericoacoara (Ceará) to the Lençóis Maranhenses is an adventure in itself.

Southern and eastern Maranhão are characterized by vast expanses of *babaçu* (palms) and typical *sertão* (backlands of the Northeast) landscapes, but the state's western and northwestern regions merge into humid Amazon rainforests.

São Luís

098 / POP 956,000

The World Heritage–listed historic center of São Luís is an enchanting neighborhood of steamy cobbled streets and pastel-colored colonial mansions, some handsomely restored, many still deep in tropical decay. It's a charming area with a unique atmosphere and one of the best concentrations of museums, galleries and craft stores in the Northeast; but unfortunately, a general sketchiness pervades some of its streets after dark. The city as a whole has a markedly Afro-Brazilian tinge to its culture, from its lively reggae scene to its highly colorful and unusual Bumba Meu Boi festivities. The trip across Baía de São Marcos to Alcântara, an impressive historic town slumbering in regal decay, is an added reason to put São Luís on your itinerary.

São Luís sits at the northwest corner of the 50km-long Ilha de São Luís, which is separated from the mainland only by narrow channels. The city itself is divided by the Rio Anil. South of the Anil, the street grid of the *centro histórico* (historic center) rambles up and down over hilly terrain, with its heart in the lower area known as Praia Grande. North of the Anil are modern suburbs, as well as the city's beaches that stretch along the island's north coast. The bus station is 9km southeast of the center and the airport 3km further southeast.

The widely available *Roteiro e Mapa Turístico São Luís* is an excellent map and information guide to the historic center, but be forewarned: many street names will not match the (rare) street signs – it seems each new mayor likes to rename the streets to their liking.

History

São Luís is the only city in Brazil that was founded by the French. In 1612 three French

BUMBA MEU BOI

São Luís is famous for its Bumba Meu Boi, a fascinating, wild, folkloric festival. Derived from African, indigenous and Portuguese influences that mingled in colonial times, it's a rich mixture of music, dance and theater, with fantastic and colorful costumes and masks. In a Carnavalesque atmosphere, participants dance, sing, act and tell the story of the death and resurrection of the bull – with plenty of room for improvisation. The festivities take place all over Maranhão, and in São Luís alone some 400 groups take to the streets every June. New songs, dances, costumes and poetry are created every year.

The story and its portrayal differ throughout the Northeast, but the general plot is as follows: Catrina, goddaughter of the local farm owner, is pregnant and feels a craving to eat the tongue of the best *boi* (bull) on the farm. She cajoles her husband, Chico, into killing the beast. When the dead bull is discovered, several characters (caricatures drawn from all levels of society) track down the perpetrator of the crime. Chico is brought to trial, but the bull is resuscitated by magic incantations and tunes. A pardon is granted, and the story reaches its happy ending when Chico is reunited with Catrina.

Groups traditionally start rehearsing on Easter Saturday in preparation for the 'baptism' of their *boi* on June 13, the feast of Santo Antônio, or June 23, the feast of São João. Many rehearsals are open to the public, and some groups begin months before Easter; check with tourist offices or your accommodations for schedules. During the festival, several groups perform in different places in the city every night from June 13 to 30. The more commercial performances may last only one hour, while local community celebrations can go on all night. Things get especially lively on the nights of June 23 to 24 and 29 to 30.

The Bumba Meu Boi period is also a good time to catch other Afro-Brazilian cultural manifestations, such as the Tambor de Crioula dance performed by women.

São Luís

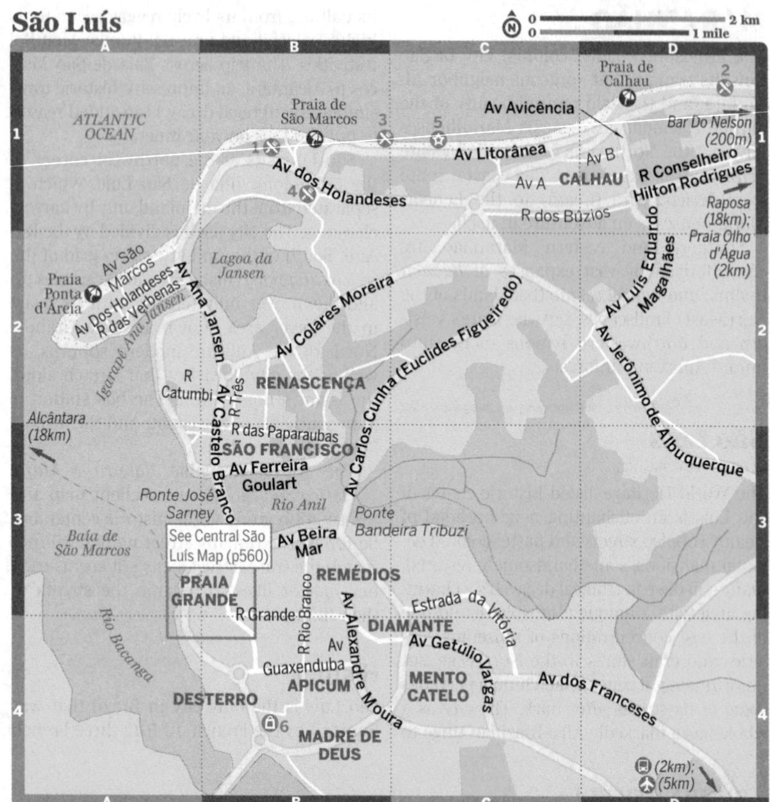

São Luís

Eating

1 Cabana do Sol B1
2 Cabana do Sol D1
3 L'Apero B1
4 Maracangalha B1

Entertainment

5 Casa das Dunas C1

Shopping

6 Ceprama B4

ships sailed for Maranhão to try to commandeer a piece of South America. Once established at São Luís the French used the local indigenous population, the Tupinambá, to assail tribes around the mouth of the Amazon in an effort to expand their foothold in the region. But when the inevitable Portuguese attack came in 1614, the French fled within a year and before long the Portuguese had 'pacified' the Tupinambá.

After a brief Dutch occupation between 1641 and 1644, São Luís developed gradually as a port for exporting sugar, and later cotton. The plantation owners prospered, and by the early 19th century São Luís was one of the wealthiest cities in Brazil, on the back of the labor of African slaves. Today the city has the third-highest Afro-Brazilian population in the country (after Rio and Salvador).

When demand for São Luís' crops slackened later in the 19th century, the city went into a long decline, but the economy has been stimulated by several megaprojects in recent decades. In the 1980s a big port complex was constructed at Itaqui, just west of São Luís, to export the mineral riches of the Carajás in neighboring Pará state, and Alcoa built an enormous aluminum-processing plant on the highway south of the city; both constructions remain key to the city's economy today. Thanks to the restoration of many of São Luís' beautiful old buildings, tourism is now also important, and bigger changes are afoot: Maranhão's governor, Flávio Dino, is seen by many as the Great New Hope after unseating one of Brazil's last political dynasties, the Sarney family, in 2014. After half a decade of mismanagement by the Sarneys, who have been widely accused of corruption, nepotism and general self-promotion (various hospitals, libraries and roads all bear the Sarney name), the Palácio dos Leões (the state governor's palace) was seized by former lawyer and federal judge Dino in 2015. He is charged with an uphill economic battle (Maranhão's GDP ranks 16th of Brazil's 26 states) that no politician would envy.

Sights

The center of São Luís has the best-preserved colonial neighborhood in the Northeast; it's full of 18th- and 19th-century mansions covered in colorful 19th-century European azulejos (decorative ceramic tiles; often blue, or blue and white). The tiles provided a durable means of protecting walls from São Luís' ever-present humidity and heat. The historic center has been under piecemeal restoration under Projeto Reviver (Project Revival) since the late 1980s, after many decades of neglect and decay. Many of the restored buildings house interesting museums, galleries, craft shops and restaurants. Much is still stalled or still needs to be restored, but their state of interrupted repair is also part of the city's charm.

Casa de Nhôzinho — MUSEUM

(Map p560; Portugal 185; 9am-6pm Tue-Sun) FREE At the eclectic and fascinating Casa do Nhôzinho, you can see a collection of ingenious fish traps, rooms of Maranhão indigenous artisanry, and hosts of colorful, delicate Bumba Meu Boi figurines made by the 20th-century master artisan Mestre Nhôzinho.

Centro de Cultura Popular Domingos Vieira Filho — MUSEUM

(Map p560; Rua do Giz 221; 9am-6pm Tue-Sun) FREE An impressive 19th-century mansion houses three fascinating floors of exhibits on São Luís' festivals – Carnaval, Bumba Meu Boi and Divino Espírito Santo – and its Afro-Brazilian cults such as Umbanda and Tambor de Mina. Staff will show you round and explain, but speakers of English or other non-Portuguese languages may or may not be available.

Museu Histórico e Artístico do Estado de Maranhão — MUSEUM

(Map p560; www.cultura.ma.gov.br/portal/mham; Rua do Sol 302; admission R$5; 9am-5:30pm Tue-Sun) In a restored 1836 mansion, the Museu Histórico e Artístico is set out as it might have been in days of yore, displaying all the furnishings, valuables and everyday belongings of an upper-class 19th-century family – including a private theater. It's very well done.

Casa das Tulhas — MARKET

(Map p560; Largo do Comércio; 7am-8pm) This 19th-century market building now trades in an interesting variety of typical Maranhão crafts and foods, from dried prawns and Brazil nuts to an artificially colored purple cassava liquor called *tiquira* and Maranhão's most regaled regional soda, Guaraná Jesus. It also has a couple of bars that get animated in late afternoon.

Museu de Artes Visuais — MUSEUM

(Map p560; Portugal 273; admission R$2; 9am-6pm Tue-Fri, to 4pm Sat & Sun) There's a fine collection of old azulejos, engravings, sculptures and paintings at the Visual Arts Museum, which has been under renovation but should have reopened by the time you read this.

Cafua das Mercês — MUSEUM

(Map p560; Jacinto Maia 43; admission R$2; 9am-5pm Mon-Fri) In a building that was once a holding facility for slaves newly arrived from Africa, this museum has a small but interesting exhibition on slavery, the slave trade and Afro-Brazilian culture. Exhibits include a replica whipping post, and a striking collection of modern wood carvings and statuettes from the parts of West Africa where the origins of many of São Luís' Afro-Brazilian population lie.

It's in a sketchy part of the historic center, so ask advice before going there. Be especially alert when walking in this area: the abandoned building directly to the left of Cafua's entrance is a crack den and robberies are not infrequent.

Centro de Pesquisa de História Natural e Arqueologia do Maranhão — MUSEUM

(Map p560; www.cultura.ma.gov.br/portal/cphna; Rua do Giz 59; 8am-noon & 2-6pm Mon-Fri) FREE Contains interesting exhibits of artifacts from Maranhão's indigenous cultures past and present, from contemporary feather adornments to ancient ax heads, plus models of megafauna that roamed Maranhão 95 million years ago.

Central São Luís

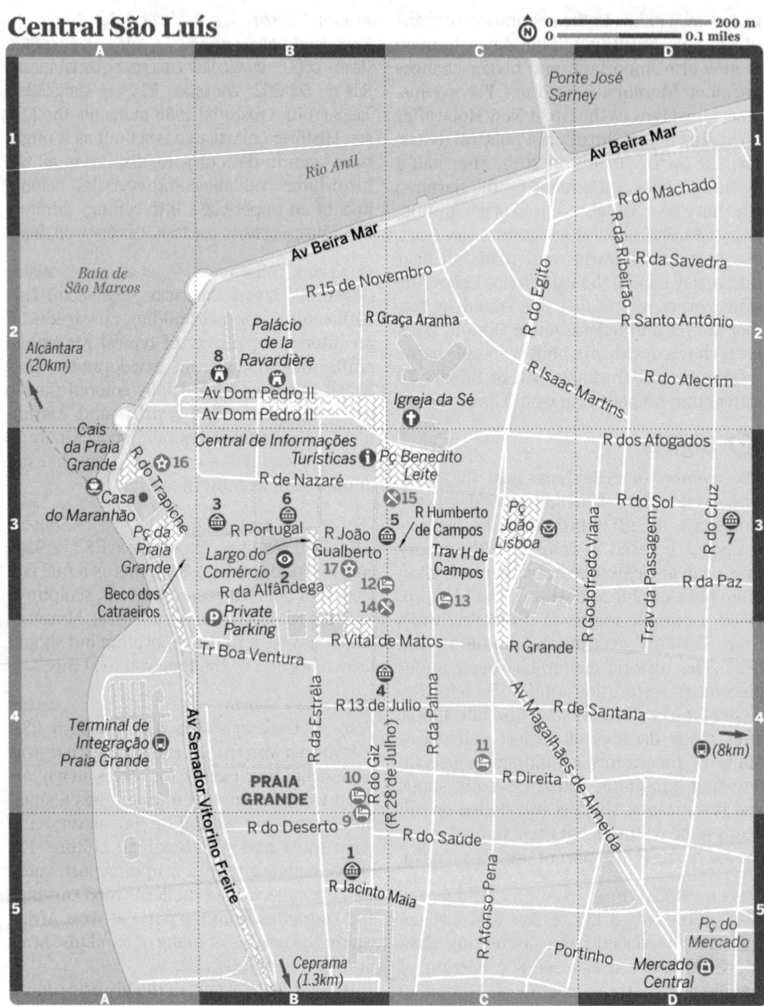

Central São Luís

Sights
1 Cafua das Mercês......B5
2 Casa das Tulhas......B3
3 Casa de Nhôzinho......B3
4 Centro de Cultura Popular Domingos Vieira Filho......B4
5 Centro de Pesquisa de História Natural e Arqueologia do Maranhão......C3
6 Museu de Artes Visuais......B3
7 Museu Histórico e Artístico do Estado de Maranhão......D3
8 Palácio dos Leões......B2

Sleeping
9 Casa Frankie......B5
10 Casa Lavinia......B4
11 Pousada Colonial......C4
12 Pousada Portas da Amazônia......B3
13 Solar das Pedras......C3

Eating
14 Dom Francisco......B3
15 Restaurante Senac......C3

Entertainment
16 Bar do Nelson......A3
17 Cafofinho da Tia Dica......B3

Palácio dos Leões PALACE

(Map p560; Av Dom Pedro II; ⌚8am-noon & 2-5:30pm Thu & Fri, 3-5:30pm Sat & Sun) FREE The Palácio dos Leões is the state governor's palace, built in the 18th century on the site of the original French fort. It contains a wealth of valuable antique furnishings and art, mostly French from the 18th and 19th centuries.

Beaches

The city's beaches are along the north-facing ocean coast, beginning about 4km north of the historic center. They can be busy and fun, but are far from Brazil's finest, and a distinct smell pervades most of the city's water. Beware of rough surf, tides and pollution.

Praia Ponta d'Areia is the closest beach to the center, and the busiest, with bars and restaurants for beach food. It can be polluted. Two kilometers further along, **Praia de São Marcos** is frequented by younger groups and surfers. The best local beach, **Praia de Calhau** is broad and attractive, with hard-packed sand perfect for football games. It is 9km from the center and popular on weekends. The large *barracas* lining the beach cater to late-night partiers throughout the week.

You can reach Ponta d'Areia, São Marcos and Calhau on bus 403 Calhau/Litorânea (R$2.60) from the **Terminal de Integração Praia Grande** (Av Senador Vitorino Freire).

Festivals & Events

São Luís has one of Brazil's richest folkloric traditions, evident in its many festivals, including Carnaval. For two to three weeks between early May and early June the city celebrates the **Festa do Divino Espírito Santo**, which has a uniquely strong Afro-Brazilian influence. São Luís' famous festival **Bumba Meu Boi** (p557) lasts through the second half of June. The **Tambor de Mina** festivals, in July, are important events for followers of the Afro-Brazilian religions.

Sleeping

★**Casa Frankie** POUSADA $

(Map p560; ☎3222-8198; www.casafrankie.com; Rua do Giz 394; s/d/tr R$80/100/120; ❄@📶🏊) The historic center's best deal is overseen by a low-key Dane, who has restored this colonial mansion – a former brothel – into simple but superb budget sleeps. Rooms are huge but it is the common spaces, including a breezy veranda with stunning original shutters, a lovely pool and a patio that wraps around a very giving mango tree, that set it apart.

Pousada Colonial POUSADA $

(Map p560; ☎3232-2834; www.hotelpousadacolonial.com.br; Afonso Pena 112; s/d/tr R$126/156/186; ❄@📶) A certain colonial charm pervades this refurbished old-town mansion, which featuresa an interior patio and unique raised azulejos inside and out. The rooms don't quite live up to the ambience, some having no natural light, but offer new mattresses with crisp sheets, split-system air-con and, in a few cases, views over the old town rooftops.

Solar das Pedras HOSTEL $

(Map p560; ☎3232-6694; www.ajsolardaspedras.com.br; Rua da Palma 127; dm/d R$40/90; 📶) This HI hostel in a restored 19th-century home has acceptable and clean facilities, including a sizable sitting area, though the rooms are rather dark and poorly ventilated, and the kitchen is small. Overall, it's the best backpacker option, but the architecture is the best thing it's got going for it. Discounts for HI members.

★**Casa Lavinia** B&B $$

(Map p560; ☎98103-1842; www.casalavinia.com; Rua do Giz 380; r R$250; ❄📶) The Italian owners have achieved a truly gorgeous conversion of this 19th-century mansion. The four big and beautiful rooms boast four-poster beds, polished-wood floors, and stylish, uncluttered decor and furnishings from Africa, Italy, Brazil and elsewhere. In the Padronal suite the bathroom alone is as big as three rooms in your average pousada. An excellent breakfast is served in a cool courtyard dining area. It's highly recommended to reserve ahead by email.

Pousada Portas da Amazônia POUSADA $$

(Map p560; ☎3182-8787; www.portasdaamazonia.com.br; Rua do Giz 129; s/d/tr R$120/160/210; ❄📶) Rambling and creaky old corridors in this restored mansion lead around two patio-gardens to simple but attractive, spacious and comfortable rooms, with excellent mattresses and modern air-con. There's an aged, colonial air about the place that is more attractive than the service. You can take the good buffet breakfast in one of the courtyards.

The attached pizzeria (pizzas R$29 to R$49) is decent and open on Sundays, but the wi-fi is atrocious.

Eating

Maranhense cuisine mixes Portuguese, African and indigenous influences, and much of the best of it comes from the sea. Regional specialties include *casquinha de caranguejo* (stuffed crab), *caldeirada de camarão* (shrimp stew) and the city's specialty, *arroz de cuxá* (rice with shrimp, toasted sesame and the slightly bitter herb *vinagreira*). Unfortunately the culinary scene in the historic center is rather sparse (and almost nonexistent on Sundays), and foodies must head out to the northern beaches for most of the best options.

★ Restaurante Senac BUFFET $$

(Map p560; Rua de Nazaré 242; lunch buffet R$38, dinner mains for 2 people R$40-83; ⊙noon-3pm Mon-Sat, 7-11pm Fri; 📶) Showpiece for the São Luis branch of Brazil's best-known cooking school, this place gets packed at lunchtimes for its superb all-you-can-eat buffet, which includes a big salad bar and eight or 10 hot meat and seafood dishes, plus rice, vegetables, yummy desserts – and a piano man. Dinner is Friday nights only; there's a good regional à la carte menu.

L'Apero FRENCH, BRAZILIAN $$

(Map p558; ☎3727-8121; Av Litoranêa, Modulo 4A; mains R$35-44; ⊙11am-1am Tue-Sat, 10am-10pm Sun; 📶) This French-run hyperkiosk on São Marcos' sands is a great bet for good food, good music and good times, especially on Sundays, when everyone in São Luís knows it's the only gig in town! There's live music or DJs most nights of the week.

Menu highlights include inventive *pasteís* (stuffed fried pastries) with Gorgonzola and sun-dried tomato, great fish with passion-fruit sauce and decent filet

Dom Francisco BRAZILIAN $$

(Map p560; Rua do Giz 155; lunch per kg R$34.90, mains R$25-35; ⊙11am-3:30pm & 6-11pm Mon-Sat) An excellent buffet that doesn't try to do every dish ever known to Maranhão, but rather a select repertoire of meals that are all wonderful. It's open at night for à la carte dining.

Maracangalha BRAZILIAN $$$

(Map p558; ☎3235-9305; www.facebook.com/maracangalha; Rua dos Gavioes 10; mains for 2 people R$42-128; ⊙noon-midnight Mon-Sat, 11:30am-5pm Sun; 📶) The creative seafood and meat dishes match the artsy atmosphere in both flair and presentation at this great top-end seafooder. The *caldeirada maranhense* – a seafood stew – is excellent. It's one of the city's best dining experiences and now in new digs closer to the *centro historíco*. The staff is impeccably on point.

The one flaw – and it's a major one – is their steadfast refusal to do dishes for just one person.

Cabana do Sol BRAZILIAN $$$

(Map p558; ☎3233-6628; www.cabanadosol.com.br; Av Litorânea 10, Calhau; mains for 2 people R$99-153; ⊙11am-midnight) This huge two-storey, picture-windowed 'cabin' is a memorable spot for *maranhense* cuisine. It's pricey, but the enormous portions for two can serve four with gusto. The specialty is *carne de sol* (tastily grilled salted meat) – the *picanha* (steak) version is superb – but there's a wealth of chicken and seafood dishes, too, including a memorable shrimp brochette (R$119).

The older, more traditional location is slightly closer town at **Praia de São Marcos** (Map p558; ☎3235-2585; www.cabanadosol.com.br; João Damasceno 24A, Praia de São Marcos; mains for 2 people R$99-153; ⊙11am-midnight; 📶).

Drinking & Entertainment

The *barracas* along Ponta d'Areia, São Marcos and Calhau beaches are popular drinking spots, with the added attraction of a sea breeze and, in the evenings, especially at Calhau, live music.

In the historic center things get lively in the evenings around Largo do Comércio, especially in front of **Cafofinho da Tia Dica** (Map p560; Beco da Alfândega; ⊙11am-midnight), and along Rua da Trapiche near the water.

São Luís is the reggae capital of Brazil, and many bars and clubs have regular reggae nights, sometimes live, sometimes just DJs and vast banks of speakers. Locals like to dance reggae in couples.

It's worth asking locals or tourist offices about what's currently hot; also check www.kamaleao.com/saoluis. There is a vibrant GLS (Gays, Lesbians e Simpatizanes) scene here.

Bar do Nelson LIVE MUSIC

(Map p560; ☎98840-3196; www.facebook.com/bardonelsonreggaeroots; Av Litorânea 135, Calhau; admission R$5-20; ⊙9pm-3am Thu-Sat) With its shanty clubhouse feel, Bar do Nelson is the most famous reggae spot in town, and it's good for live music and dancing. A second location has opened among the lively bars of **Rua da Trapiche** (Rua da Trapiche 39) in the historic center.

WORTH A TRIP

ALL HAIL ALCÂNTARA!

Across the Baía de São Marcos from São Luís is the colonial town of Alcântara. Built using slave labor between the 17th and 19th centuries, Alcântara was once the preferred residence of Maranhão's rich plantation owners. In decline since the latter half of the 19th century, Alcântara today is an atmospheric amalgam of ruined, maintained and restored mansions, houses and churches set along streets of artistic crisscrossed cobblestones. With a population no bigger today than 150 years ago, it is one of the country's most tranquil, authentic and stunningly beautiful historic sites. Keep an eye out for *guarás*, beautiful red ibises that are unusually plentiful around here and add yet another wonderful element to an Alcântara trip.

Since 1990 the Centro de Lançamento de Alcântara (CLA), the rocket-launching facility for the Brazilian space program, has operated nearby. It is an odd juxtaposition: rockets alongside a slumbering colonial town.

Don't miss the broad, hilltop **Praça da Matriz**, where the best-preserved *pelourinho* (whipping post) in Brazil stands beside the shell of the 17th-century **Igreja de São Matias**. Two 18th-century mansions on the square's west side have been turned into museums – **Museu Histórico de Alcântara** and the **Casa Histórica** – exhibiting the lifestyle of Alcântara's privileged families of yore, including a wealth of period furnishings and memorabilia. Visits are guided in Portuguese, and if you can manage to visit only one of the two, go for the Museu Histórico, which has more impressive collections.

Moving north along Rua Grande, with its beautiful row of two-story houses, you can look round the intriguing **Casa do Divino**, the main center of activities during Alcântara's famous Festa do Divino in May/June, before reaching the pretty, two-towered **Igreja de NS do Carmo**. Built in 1665 it was recently restored, and there's a ruined convent beside it. In front of and opposite the church stand the ruined 1° and 2° Palácios do Imperador (First and Second Palaces of the Emperor), built for a visit by the 19th-century emperor Dom Pedro II that never actually happened.

Alcântara is a straightforward day trip from São Luís, but an overnight stay here is enjoyable and allows more time for exploring and for excursions to colonies of red ibis.

Four boats/catamarans to Alcântara (R$15, 1¼ hours) leave daily from the **Cais da Praia Grande** (☎3232-0692; Av Senador Vitorino Freire) in São Luís. Times vary with tides but there are usually two departures between 7am and 9am. It's a good idea to check times and buy your ticket the day before, either by heading to Cais da Praia Grande or by calling the boat companies. The boats return from Alcântara at 5am and between 2pm and 3pm. Seasickness sufferers will be happier on the larger boats **Barraqueiro** (☎99119-5288; Cais de Praia Grande) and **Lusitania** (☎98869-1062; Cais de Praia Grande) than the catamarans **Lua Nova** (☎99111-2657; Cais de Praia Grande) and **Sabor de Mel** (☎99102-6902; Cais de Praia Grande).

Casa das Dunas LIVE MUSIC
(Map p558; ☎3227-8695; www.casadasdunasma.com.br; Av Litorânea s/n; ⏲4pm-2am Tue-Sun) The biggest thing to happen in São Luís since sliced *picanha:* this massive, architecturally stunning entertainment complex opened in 2015. Overlooking Praia do Calhau, it's equal parts bar and live-music venue, and a good bet for DJs, MPB and *forró*. Attracts national acts as well.

Shopping

São Luís is the place to find Maranhão handicrafts such as painted tiles, woodcarving, basketry, lace, ceramics and leatherwork. There are plenty of shops around Rua Portugal and Rua da Estrela in the historic center.

Ceprama HANDICRAFTS
(Map p558; Centro de Producão de Artesanato do Maranhão; Rua de São Pantaleão 1232, Madre de Deus; ⏲9am-6pm Mon-Sat) The large Ceprama, 2km southeast of the center, functions as an exhibition hall and major sales outlet.

Information

EMERGENCY

CPTur (Companhia de Polícia Militar de Turismo; Largo do Comércio; ⏲24hr) The tourist police force in charge of patrolling the streets. There is usually an English speaker here.

Detur (Delegacia Especial de Turismo; ☎3214-8682; Rua da Estrela 427; ⏲8am-6pm Mon-Fri) São Luís' tourist police station for reporting crime and obtaining police reports. Unbelievably, English is not spoken.

MEDICAL SERVICES

UDI Hospital (☎3216-7979; Av Carlos Cunha 2000, Jacaraty; ⏲24hr) Private hospital with emergency service.

MONEY

Banco do Brasil (www.bb.com.br; Av Dom Pedro II 78) Visa/Mastercard ATM.

Banco do Brasil (www.bb.com.br; Av Gomes de Castro 46) This is the only Banco do Brasil branch offering currency exchange.

Banco do Brasil (www.bb.com.br; Travessa Boa Ventura) Visa/Mastercard ATM.

POST

Correios (www.correios.com.br; ⏲8am-5pm Mon-Fri) Postal services.

TOURIST INFORMATION

The São Luís Convention & Visitors Bureau website (www.visitesaoluis.com) has some interesting material.

Central de Informações Turísticas (Setur; ☎3212-6210; www.saoluis.ma.gov.br/setur; Praça Benedito Leite; ⏲8am-6pm Mon-Fri, to noon Sat & Sun) The main information office of Setur, the city tourism department, and also the most helpful; English and French were spoken when we visited.

Maranhão Tourist Information (☎3256-2585; www.turismo.ma.gov.br; São Luís airport; ⏲24hr) Maranhão's official state tourist-information office, located in the Arrivals hall of the airport. English isn't a strong point, but the bilingual tourism site has helpful descriptions.

TRAVEL AGENCIES

Terra Nordeste (☎3221-1188; www.terra-nordeste.com; Rua do Giz 380; ⏲9am-6pm Mon-Fri) This excellent ecotourism-focused Northeast Brazil specialist is friendly, French owned and multilingual. It can organize any trip for any budget, from two days to a month or more, including treks across the Lençóis Maranhenses.

Getting There & Away

AIR

From **Aeroporto Internacional de São Luís – Marechal Cunha Machado** (☎3217-6100; Av dos Libaneses, Tirirical), there are direct flights to main destinations in the Amazon and Northeast, as well as Rio de Janeiro and São Paulo.

BUS

The **bus station** (☎3243-1305; www.rodoviariasaoluis.com.br; Av dos Franceses 300, Santo Antônio), Terminal Rodoviário de São Luis, is located 8km southeast of the historic center and has departures to many destinations. Night buses to Belém have a history of being robbed, so consider flying, which can be cheaper in any case.

Getting Around

Coopertaxi (☎3245-4404; São Luís airport) operates taxis from the airport. Drivers are not likely to use a meter (or even to have one) but official prices are posted in the arrivals hall dispatch booth. A ride to the *centro histórico* costs R$48 from the airport.

From the bus station, taxis run between R$30 and R$37. Traffic on the main roads in and out of São Luís is so heavy that this takes between one and two hours.

Bus 901 'São Cristóvão Aeroporto' runs between the airport – just outside the terminal and to the left – and Praça Deodoro, which is about 1km east of the most of the *centro histórico* accommodations; but note this is not a safe option at night. Between the bus station and the Terminal Praia Grande, the most direct bus is the Vila Sarney/Africanos bus. Bus fares are R$2.60.

BUSES FROM SÃO LUÍS

DESTINATION	COST FROM (R$)	TIME (HR)	COMPANY
Barreirinhas	46.50	4	Cisne Branco (www.cisnebrancoturismo.com.br)
Belém	143	13	Boa Esperança (www.viajeboaesperanca.com.br), Transbrasiliana (www.transbrasiliana.com.br)
Brasília	270	33	Transbrasiliana (www.transbrasiliana.com.br)
Fortaleza	132	17	Expresso Guanabara (www.expressoguanabara.com.br)
Parnaíba	87	10	Expresso Guanabara (www.expressoguanabara.com.br)
Teresina	74	7	Expresso Guanabara (www.expressoguanabara.com.br)

Parque Nacional dos Lençóis Maranhenses

098

The name of this 1550-sq-km **national park** FREE refers to its immense expanses of dunes, which look like *lençóis* (bed sheets) strewn across the landscape and stretch 70km along the coast and up to 50km inland. Located halfway between São Luís and the Piauí border, it is a spectacularly unique place, especially from about May to September when rain that has filtered through the sand forms thousands of crystal-clear pools and lakes between the dunes. The lagoons are at their best in June, July and August. The park also includes beaches, mangroves, lagoons and some interesting fauna, especially turtles and migratory birds.

The main base for visiting the park is the not-particularly-charming town of **Barreirinhas** on the picturesque Rio Preguiças near the park's southeast corner, 260km from São Luís. Other access points – well worth the effort of getting to if you have at least two nights to spend in the area – are the remote villages of **Atins**, where the Preguiças meets the ocean; and **Santo Amaro** on the park's western border, where the dunes come right to the edge of the village and where there are sandy river beaches in which you can bathe, even when the lagoons among the dunes are dry. Both are far more charming than Barreirinhas.

Activities

Several agencies in Barreirinhas offer half-day trips daily to **Lagoa Azul** (R$60 per person) and **Lagoa Bonita** (R$70), two of the park's biggest lagoons, northwest of town, in open-sided 4WD buses. You can also take a wonderful seven-hour **boat tour** (R$70) down the Rio Preguiças, between jungle, mangroves and dunes, to Mandacuru lighthouse (for great panoramas), the ocean beach at Caburé (where there are restaurants for lunch) and Atins at the river mouth. Both excursions are don't-misses if you are using Barreirinhas as your base. Recommended Barreirinhas agencies follow strict safety and environmental standards; agencies pool together, so it often won't matter which you choose.

From Atins, trips to lagoons such as **Lagoa Guajiru**, **Lagoa Sete Mulheres** or **Lagoa Tropical** cost R$70 per person each (guides decide which lagoon is optimal to visit depending on season).

From Santo Amaro, through a combination of 4WDing and walking, you can reach the little-visited **Lagoa Gaivota** and **Lagoa Betánia**.

A wonderful way to experience the Lençóis is to trek across them. It takes three or four days to cross from west to east or vice versa, sleeping in hammocks or fishers' huts in the few tiny, poor villages along the way. A locally arranged guide should cost around R$290 per day in Portuguese (R$350 in English). If you go east to west, you'll have the prevailing wind behind you. The most magical way of all is to trek by night under the full moon.

São Luís–based Terra Nordeste (p564) arranges well-organized trans-Lençóis hikes: a four-day return trip from São Luís with three days of trekking costs R$3000 to R$4000 for two people including transfers, meals, nights and guide (English, Spanish, French, Italian and German are available).

Keep in mind: quad bikes are completely forbidden inside the dunes, but that won't stop unscrupulous guides from trying to sell you trips on them. Just say no.

Caetés Turismo ADVENTURE TOUR
(3349-0528; www.caetesturismo.com.br; Av Brasília 40B, Barreirinhas; 8am-6pm) Run by local Roberdan Caldas, Caetés is a member of Abeta, Brazil's strict ecotourism organization, and can handle excursions both far and wide through Maranhão and Ceará.

São Paulo Ecoturismo TOUR
(3349-0079; www.saopauloecoturismo.com.br; Av Brasília 108, Barreirinhas; 7am-8pm) A recommended agency in Barreirinhas for organized tours in and around Parque Nacional dos Lençóis Maranhenses.

Sandwalkers WALKING
(98864-0526; sandwalkers.ma@gmail.com; Atins) Bernard de Laroche of Sandwalkers is one of the Lençóis' most experienced, knowledgeable and multilingual guides; you can ask for him at Chico Jacinto Bar on Boa Esperança near Pousada Flamboyant. In July and August, advance reservations are a must.

Sleeping & Eating

Barreirinhas & Around

Barreirinhas has plenty of accommodations. The Rio Preguiças meanders elaborately round the west, north and east of town, giving the place at least four separate riverfronts. A few steps from the main street of Av Joaquim Soeiro de Carvalho, the most important riverfront is pedestrianized Av Beira Rio, which has several restaurants – most French owned – and is the main boat-departure point. High season is July and August, but many places charge the same rates year-round, outside of holidays.

Casa do Professor Hostel HOSTEL **$**
(98808-2546; Projectada 305, Barreirinhas; campsites/hammocks/dm R$15/25/35;) The street doesn't lend itself to high hopes, but this family-run affair, overseen by an English professor, is simply and quite surprisingly well done. Hammocks are inside the dorms, and there's an artsy sand-floored backyard lounge space that's a great spot to swap travel tales over beers and barbecue.

The family is extra respectful, even going as far as to whisper to us on our visit so as to not wake sleeping guests – at 2pm!

Encantes do Nordeste CHALET **$$**
(3349-0288; www.encantesdonordeste.com.br; Rua Boa Vista s/n, Barreirinhas; s/d from R$245/329;) This ecofriendly pousada is a little gem of comfort 3.5km east of Barreirinhas' center. The sloping plot leads down past cozy chalets to a beautiful garden with a pool, from which it's just 200m to its lovely riverside restaurant, Bambaê. There's also a Zen lounge, which makes use of reclaimed woods and has Asian touches, and a massage area.

The pousada's own travel agency can arrange all Parque Nacional dos Lençóis Maranhenses excursions.

Pousada Sossego do Cantinho POUSADA **$$**
(3349-0753; www.sossegodocantinho.com.br; Rua Principal 2, Povoado Cantinho; r R$285;) On the riverbank 1.5km north of town, Swiss-owned Sossego is a perfect haven for resting for a couple of days, or as a relaxed base for excursions. The four large bungalows have big beds with lots of pillows, and there's a white-sand river beach at the foot of the gardens. Call to organize a boat pickup from Barreirinhas.

Pousada d'Areia POUSADA **$$**
(3349-0550; www.pousadadareia.com.br; Av Joaquim Soeiro de Carvalho 888, Barreirinhas; s/d/tr R$120/192/284;) Friendly staff, a good breakfast and a convenient location (the south end of the main street) make the Areia a solid choice – if you opt for the more expensive rooms at the rear, which are bright and new, with hammock-strung verandas. The cheaper rooms are smaller and much more enclosed.

Pousada do Porto POUSADA **$$**
(3349-0654; Anacleto de Carvalho 20, Barreirinhas; s/d/tr R$120/180/250;) Just upriver from the Cisne Branco bus stop, Pousada do Porto's best-value rooms are its upstairs units with river views; and there are real showers, a rarity in this price range.

A Canoa BRAZIILAN, PIZZERIA **$$**
(Av Beira Rio 300, Barreirinhas; mains R$22-39; 11:30am-11:30pm;) For grilled fish, wood-fired pizza, river breezes and live music nightly, head to this spot on the pedestrianized riverside strip.

O Jacaré INTERNATIONAL **$$**
(Av Beira Mar 109, Barreirinhas; mains R$25-47; 11am-2am;) The French owners of this riverfront pub-restaurant are trying to raise the bar in Barreirinhas. Several pages of the menu are devoted to cocktails and craft beer (Devassa on draft, Eisenbahn and Baden Baden in bottles – impressive for these parts!) and there's a variety previously unseen.

Order from fresh-cut fries, Thai-spun shrimp dishes, creative regional dishes such as *carne do sol* with white wine and Catupiry cheese, homemade burgers, pizza, pasta and good salads.

Caburé

This handful of rustic pousadas and restaurants sits on a beautiful, isolated sand peninsula between the lower Rio Preguiças and the Atlantic. It exists solely to serve tourists (mostly those on day trips from Barreirinhas), and while it's a nice enough place for lunch, you're much better off sleeping in funkier Atins, a 15-minute boat ride away at the mouth of the river. If you do choose to sleep here, you'll have it all to yourself after lunch.

Porto Caburé CHALET **$$**
(99909-1340; Caburé; r R$170;) These cute and colorful chalets are the nicest option in Caburé. Don't expect much, but there is a rustic appeal here, and you are surrounded by wild sands in all directions. You can easily laze away a day or two on the wraparound porches or in the thatch-roofed hammock area.

Cabana do Peixe SEAFOOD $$
(☎98732-2213; Caburé; mains for 2 people R$69-85; ⊙noon-4pm) The best and most atmospheric of the restaurants serving fresh fish and seafood stews to incoming day-trippers. We especially like the individual thatch-roofed tables that sit in the sands in front of the main dining area.

Atins & Around

Atins is a small but expanding village of sandy streets amid dune vegetation at the mouth of the Rio Preguiças. It has an ocean beach, a sizable foreign population and a surprising number of pousadas scattered among its dwellings. Some are tagging it the next Jericoacoara, as pousadas are popping up at an alarming rate these days. It's a far cry yet from that though; there are still more donkeys lying in the sand here than there are cars. It's a good base for visiting some of the more isolated parts of Parque Nacional dos Lençóis Maranhenses – you can have many gorgeous dunes and lagoons all to yourself.

Pousada Irmão Atins POUSADA $
(☎98864-4288; www.pousadairmaoatins.blogspot.com.br; Rua Principal, Atins; s/d with fan R$80/160, with air-con R$130/190; ❄@) This attractive, locally owned place offers clean and colorful rooms sporting verandas strung with hammocks, and bathrooms walled with hundreds of seashells, set along a strip of grassy garden. Good fish, chicken and shrimp dishes (R$28 to R$45) are served in the shell-floored dining area under a big *palapa* palm roof. Top budget honors.

Pousada da Rita POUSADA $
(☎99993-7537; Rua Principal, Atins; s/d R$60/120) Simple and clean rooms in a spick-and-span family home.

Rancho do Buna POUSADA $$
(Rancho Pousada; ☎9616-9646; www.ranchodobuna.com; Atins; s/d/tr/q with fan R$190/220/260/290, s/d with air-con R$150/190; ❄) This is easily one of the best pousadas, despite the large property's chickens, guinea fowl, peacocks, ducks, dogs and cats wailing a dawn chorus from 5am. The comfortable brick chalets (built using many recycled materials), the fascinating common area and the expansive grounds (with a pool and a duck pond), are all big on charm, though service has slipped a bit under new management.

Fan-cooled rooms are pricier due to size and greater privacy. There's well-prepared food (mains for two R$52 to R$70) including great breakfast tapiocas. It offers wonderful excursions to the dunes and lakes of Parque Nacional dos Lençóis Maranhenses, and can arrange transportation by boat or 4WD. English is sometimes spoken.

★**La Ferme de Georges** POUSADA $$$
(☎99172-2935, 98725-1389; www.georges.life; Atins; r with fan R$850-1300;) This boutique pousada is what people mean when they say, 'Atins is changing,' but this French–Belgian–English affair is a change for the better, for those with the dosh. The six triumphant chalets, all bastions of style and comfort (including European art, 600-thread count sheets, Thai mosquito nets) are richly constructed in quality *ipê* and *tatajuba* hardwoods and feature solar-powered showers.

The food is an obvious focus: breakfast is above and beyond (*açaí,* scrambled eggs with tarragon, fruits from the farm); gourmet dinners for guests run R$80 per person. The grassy lawn is a nice escape from all that sand, and the pousada has the best manager this side of Jericoacoara. Welcome to paradise.

★**Restaurante do Antônio** SEAFOOD $$
(Restaurante Canto dos Lençóis; ☎98881-3138; Canto de Atins; mains for 2 people R$60-80; ⊙7am-10pm) Get yourself here by foot, horseback, car, boat, on a tour, or any way you can to experience the wonderful grilled shrimp at this rustic culinary destination 7km west of Atins. The location, isolated between the dunes (600m away) and the sea (1.5km at low tide), is travel-memory fodder at its finest.

Pousadas can bring you here from Atins for around R$220 (for up to 10 people); you can make a half-day trip of it by visiting some lagoons before lunch here; or you can walk here after breakfast (it takes about two hours), enjoy a leisurely lunch, and walk back late afternoon.

Santo Amaro

Ciamat Camp CHALET $$
(☎99604-5824; www.ciamatcamp.com; Santo Amaro; s/d R$220/235) This Brazilian-Italian operation has just four comfortable wooden chalets scattered around its lovely and luxuriant riverside garden, across the Rio Alegre from the village. The operators will ferry you back and forth. Meals available.

Information

You'll find both **Banco do Brasil** (Av Joaquim Soeiro de Carvalho, Barreirinhas; ATMs 6am-10pm) and **Bradesco** (www.bradesco.com.br; Colonel Godinho, Barreirinhas) ATMs in Barreirinhas.

Getting There & Around

TO/FROM SÃO LUÍS

A good paved road, Hwy MA-402, runs east to Barreirinhas from Hwy BR-135 south of São Luís. **Cisne Branco** (3243-2847; www.cisnebrancoturismo.com.br; Anacleto de Carvalho 623, Barreirinhas) runs four daily buses from São Luís to Barreirinhas (R$46.50, 4½ hours), departing 6am, 8:45am, 2pm and 7:30pm), and returning 6am, 9am, 2pm & 6:45pm. Buses start and finish at São Luís' bus station, though, which is way out of the city center; you can be dropped at the São Luís airport turnoff, 800m from the terminals, if you are heading straight there. More convenient are the door-to-door 'vans' (minibuses) of **BRTur** (98896-6610; www.brtur.net.br; R$60); these take 4½ hours and will pick you up from your accommodations in São Luís around 7am, and start back from Barreirinhas at 5pm. **Coopcart** (3349-1511; Av Joaquim Soeiro de Carvalho, Barreirinhas; R$70) is the only door-to-door transfer service with morning departure from Barreirinhas, at 5am. Accommodations in São Luís and Barreirinhas will book these for you.

TO/FROM ATINS

To get to Atins from Barreirinhas, you can either take a Rio Preguiças **boat tour** (p565) (R$70), stopping for lunch in Caburé and disembarking at Atins about 2pm; hire a boat in Barreirinhas for a direct transfer (R$450 for up to four people, 1½ hours). Or take a Toyota 4WD (R$25, two hours), leaving around 10am from Rua Monsenhor Gentil (opposite Lojas Vitória) or in front of Farmácia Santa Rita de Cássia on Av Joaquim Soeiro de Carvalho. The Toyotas head back from Atins to Barreirinhas at 6am.

TO/FROM SANTO AMARO

For Santo Amaro, get a Cisne Branco bus or BRTur van as far as Sangue on Hwy MA-402 (R$40), then a prearranged 4WD along the 36km sandy track north to Santo Amaro (R$300). Either BRTur or your accommodations in Santo Amaro can organize the 4WD connection. Public transportation is considerably cheaper though (R$20), leaving at 6am and 3pm.

TO PARNAÍBA AND JERICOACOARA

Heading east from Barreirinhas, towards Parnaíba and Jericoacoara, the easiest way on public transportation is by taking one of the 4WD trucks leaving for Paulino Neves (R$20, 2½ hours) between 8am and 9am daily, from opposite Banco do Brasil on Av Joaquim Soeiro de Carvalho. Overnight in Paulino Neves and catch the 2M (p556) bus (R$58, 6½ hours, 7am) to Jijoca the next morning and a D-20 (R$15, 40 minutes) on to Jericoacoara.

From Paulino Neves to Tutoia, take a taxi (R$45 to R$75) or a *jardineira* (R$15 per person). From Tutoia there a few daily buses, including at 7am and 2pm, to Parnaíba (R$20, 2½ hours).

A 4WD from Parnaíba to Jericoacoara costs around R$600; ask at the travel agencies in Parnaíba bus station. Alternatively there's a daily 7:15am Guanabara (www.expressoguanabara.com.br) bus from Parnaíba to Camocim (R$22, 2½ hours). In Camocim you can catch 4WD trucks to Jericoacoara from the Mercado Central Monday through Saturday (R$45, 1½ to three hours), usually from 11am to noon, or take a buggy (an exciting ride costing around R$350 for up to four people). There are also four daily Fretcar buses (including one at 11:30am) from Camocim to Jijoca (R$12 to R$15, 1½ hours), from where D-20 trucks head to Jeri for R$15.

A direct 4WD transfer from Barreirinhas costs around R$800 for up to five people to Parnaíba, or R$1250 all the way to Jericoacoara.

TO CABURÉ

To reach Caburé from the east without going via Barreirinhas, you need 4WD transport that can make it along the beach for the final stretch from Paulino Neves.

The Amazon

POP 16 MILLION

Includes ➡

Best Nature Reserves

- ➡ Desenvolvimento Sustentável Mamirauá (p632)
- ➡ Xixuaú-Xipariná (p622)
- ➡ Floresta Nacional do Tapajós (p595)
- ➡ Parque Nacional do Jaú (p622)
- ➡ Parque Estadual do Jalapão (p605)

Best Places to Stay

- ➡ Pousada Jamaraquá (p596)
- ➡ Juma Lodge (p618)
- ➡ Pousada Bela Vista (p619)

Why Go?

Named after female warriors of Greek mythology, the Amazon is itself a place of nearly mythical status. What traveler hasn't imagined a trip to the Amazon, not only to admire the towering trees and awesome river, but to enter, in a real sense, the very life spring of the planet, the source of so much of the air we breath, the water we drink and the weather we rely on? To be sure, expecting a Discovery Channel–like experience (jaguars in every tree, spear-toting *índios* around every bend) is a recipe for disappointment. In fact, the Amazon's quintessential experiences are more sublime than superlative: canoeing through a flooded forest, dozing in a hammock on a boat chugging upriver, waking to the otherworldly cry of howler monkeys. On a river whose size is legendary, it's actually the little things that make it special. Give it some time, forget your expectations, and the Amazon cannot fail to impress.

When to Go

Manaus

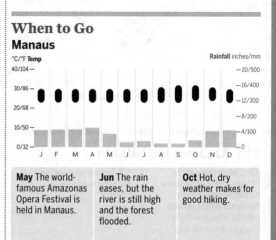

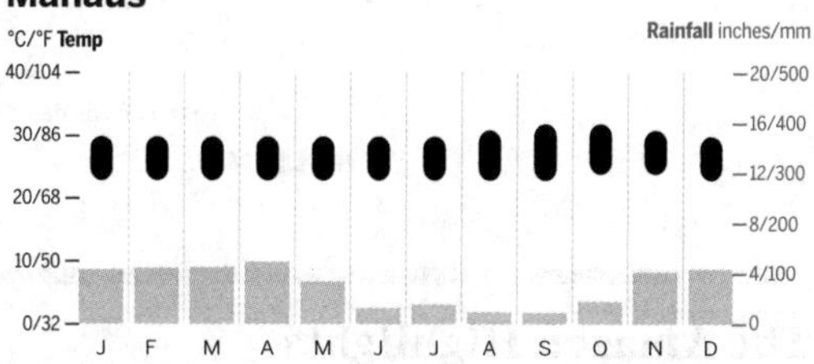

May The world-famous Amazonas Opera Festival is held in Manaus.

Jun The rain eases, but the river is still high and the forest flooded.

Oct Hot, dry weather makes for good hiking.

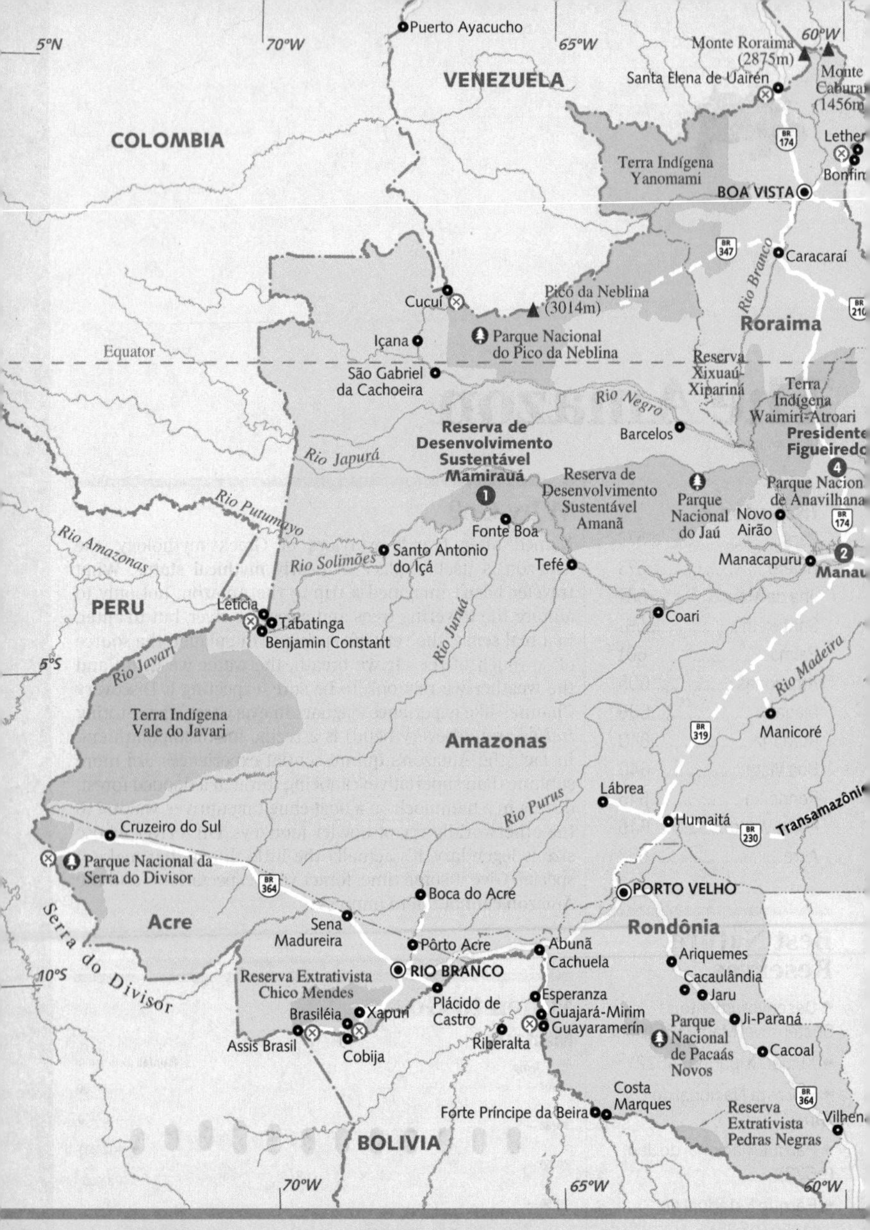

The Amazon Highlights

1. Gliding through the flooded forest at **Reserva de Desenvolvimento Sustentável Mamirauá** (p632), in search of the shaggy uacari monkey.

2. Testing your mettle on a **survival tour** (p617) outside Manaus.

3. Roughing it with rubber-tappers in **Floresta Nacional do Tapajós** (p595), outside Alter do Chão.

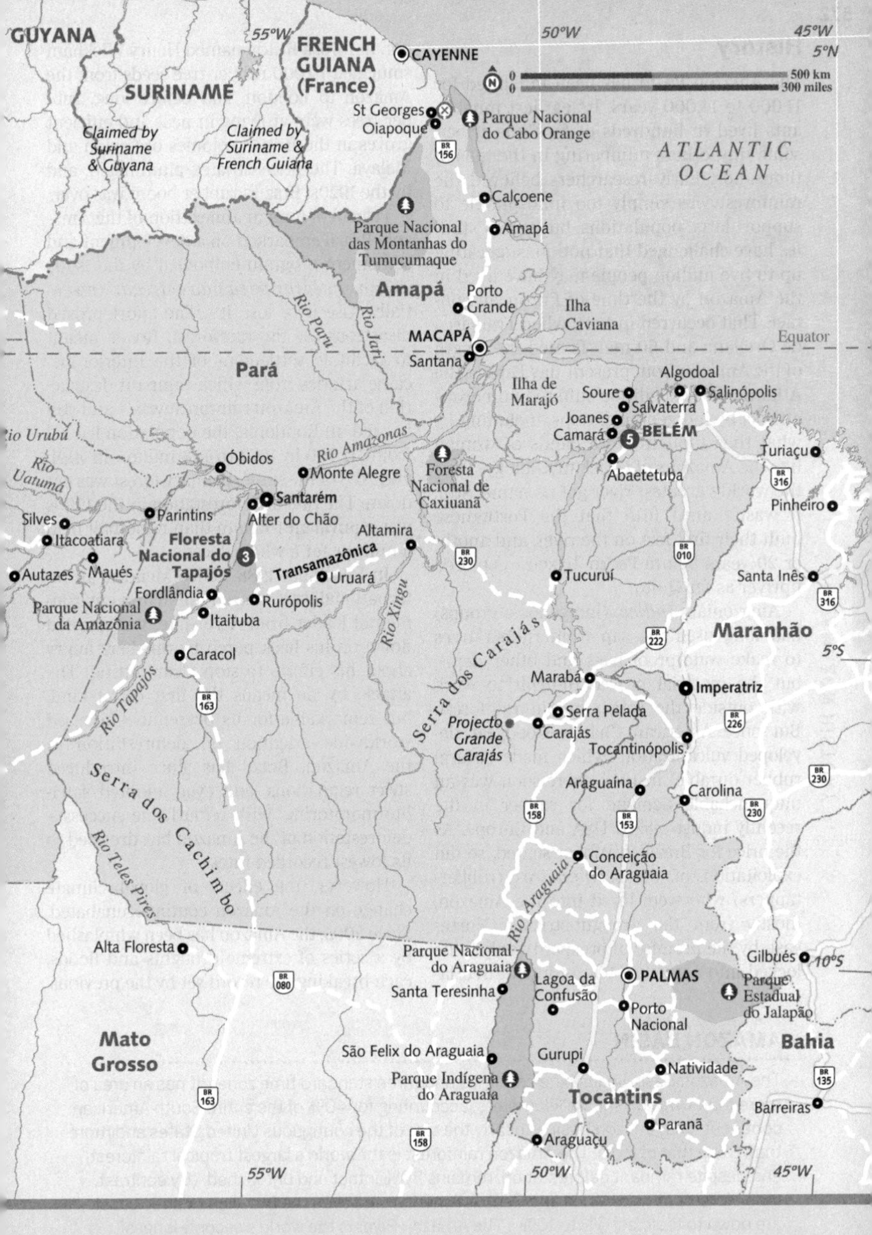

4 Climbing a tree – a really really big tree – in **Presidente Figueiredo** (p617).

5 Relaxing with regular folks (and practising your Portuguese) on an **overnight riverboat trip** (p573) between cities.

History

The Amazon Basin has been inhabited for 11,000 to 14,000 years. Its earliest inhabitants lived in hundreds of far-flung tribes, some tiny, others numbering in the tens of thousands. Early researchers believed the rainforest was simply too inhospitable to support large populations, but recent studies have challenged that notion, suggesting up to five million people may have lived in the Amazon by the time of European contact. That occurred in 1541, when Francisco de Orellana and 60 men floated the length of the Amazon from present-day Peru to the Atlantic. The expedition suffered numerous attacks by indigenous groups, including by what they thought were bands of women like the Amazons of Greek mythology. Thus the world's greatest river got its name. Still, it wasn't until 1616 that the Portuguese built their first fort on the river, and another 20 years before Pedro Teixeira explored upriver as far Quito.

Amazonian *índios* (indigenous groups) had long used the sap from rubber trees to make waterproof bags and other items, but the material proved difficult to work with outside the warm humid rainforest. But once American Charles Goodyear developed vulcanization (which made natural rubber durable) in 1842, there soon was an unquenchable demand for rubber in the recently industrialized USA and Europe. As the price for Brazilian rubber soared, so did exploitation of the *seringueiros* (rubber-tappers) who were lured into the Amazon, mostly from the drought-stricken Northeast, by the promise of prosperity only to be locked into a cruel system of indentured labor. In 1876, a Briton named Henry Wickham smuggled 70,000 rubber-tree seeds from the Amazon to London, and before long, rubber trees were growing in neat and efficient groves in the British colonies of Ceylon and Malaya. The price of latex plummeted, and by the 1920s, Brazil's rubber boom was over.

Fearful of foreign annexation of the Amazon, Brazil embarked on a development and settlement program embodied by the 1970s slogan, '*Integrar para não entregar*' (essentially, 'Use it or lose it'). The effort proved disastrous for the rainforest. Roads meant to facilitate settlement of the interior became arteries from which rampant destruction of the Amazon rainforest was – and still is – fed. In Rondônia, the population leaped from 111,000 in 1970 to 1.13 million in 1991, and 20% of the state's primary forest was cut down. The rate of deforestation in the 1980s was equivalent to more than a football field a minute, for a whole decade.

In December 1988, Chico Mendes, an internationally recognized union and environmental leader from Acre state, was gunned down on his back porch by ranchers angry about his efforts to stop clear-cutting. The attack, by no means the first of its kind, but remarkable for its brazenness, focused worldwide attention on deforestation in the Amazon. Brazil has since introduced strict regulations, and even adopted satellite monitoring, with remarkable success – deforestation of the Amazon has dropped to its lowest recorded rates.

However, the effects of global climate change on the Amazon continue unabated, Since 2005, the Amazon has been whiplashed by a series of extreme droughts and floods, each breaking the record set by the previous.

AMAZON BASIN

The Amazon Basin spans nine countries and three standard time zones. It has an area of more than 7 million square kilometers, accounting for 40% of the entire South American continent. The Amazon Basin is nearly the size of the contiguous United States and more than twice that of India. The Amazon rainforest is the world's largest tropical rainforest, and despite rampant deforestation, remains 80% intact and untouched. (By contrast, many forests in Asia, Africa and Central America, and even the Brazilian Atlantic coast, are down to their last 5% to 10%.) The Amazon River is the world's second-longest river – the Nile beats it by a hair – but the biggest in volume by far: when it's at its fullest, the river dumps 300 million liters of water into the ocean every second, sending a plume of fresh water more than a hundred miles out to sea. The Amazon discharges more water than the next seven biggest rivers combined, and two of the Amazon's tributaries, the Rio Negro and Rio Madeira, are themselves among the 10 largest rivers in the world. There are places, when the water is high, where the Amazon River stretches fully 50km across – a massive moving sea of creamy brown water too wide to see across.

There were severe droughts in 2010 and 2013, and record-breaking floods in 2012 and 2015, with water levels rising nearly 30m, more than double the 'normal' seasonal rise.

Depopulation of the forest – or 'rural abandonment' – has emerged as another worrying trend. Steady jobs are one reason, another is the lack of schools beyond the primary grades. You might think fewer people would be a benefit to the environment, but the opposite is true: stable forest communities actually help deter illegal fishing and clear-cutting, with minimal ecological impact of their own. The trend is also being felt by tour operators who say it's harder and harder to find skilled guides, especially among the younger generation.

Getting There & Away

Manaus and Belém are the major transportation hubs of the Amazon. Most travelers arrive by air – Manaus receives the bulk of international flights, including direct flights from Miami and Buenos Aires, while both cities have frequent domestic air service. Manaus has limited bus service, while Belém has buses arriving and departing from all over Brazil. Some travelers enter the Brazilian Amazon by boat from Peru or Colombia, crossing at what is known as the Triple Frontier; others arrive overland from Venezuela or Guyana, which have bus services to Manaus, or from Bolivia, at the border towns of Guajará-Mirim or Brasiléia. Those coming from the interior of Brazil, including Brasília or the Pantanal, can enter the Amazon via Porto Velho, where they catch a plane or riverboat to Manaus, or via Palmas in the state of Tocantins, connecting by bus or plane to Belém.

Getting Around

Virtually every major town along the Amazon and its largest tributaries has both a port and an airstrip – but no roads in or out. Choosing between flying and boating is really a matter of time, budget and preference; most travelers do a bit of both. Boat travel is a unique and memorable experience; it's a great way to connect with ordinary Brazilians, and travelers on months-long trips often appreciate a few days of forced downtime. That said, the distances are enormous and the boats very slow, especially going upstream. (At least going upstream you'll be closer to shore.) Flying is easy, safe, and fast – a three-day trip by boat takes an hour in the air – and gives you more time and energy to do fun stuff in your destination. You can browse and book flights online, and you may be surprised how comparable boat and plane fares can be.

Bus services are available in states along the edges of the rainforest, such as Pará, Tocantins and Rondônia. Highway conditions are improving, and there are more deluxe and direct options available, which help make the invariably long bus routes a bit less taxing.

PARÁ

Pará doesn't have the name 'Amazonas' like the state next door, so it might be easy to think it's not part of 'the Amazon' either. In fact, Pará has some terrific Amazonian destinations. The national forest along the Rio Tapajós has monster trees and a fascinating living history of rubber boom and bust, and is reachable via the laid-back beach town of Alter do Chão. The capital city, Belém, is lively and pleasant, and you can wander deserted beaches on the islands of Algodoal and Marajó.

Belém

☎ 0XX91 / POP 1.4 MILLION

Belém is a surprisingly rewarding city, with streets and parks shaded by mango trees, and a number of fascinating museums and heady restaurant-bars. From Belém, you can take overnight trips to Algodoal and Ilha de Marajó, both appealing coastal destinations, or cut southward to Tocantins state. And of course, it's a logical launchpad for journeys further up the Amazon River.

History

Belém was one of the first Portuguese settlements on the Amazon River. Founded in 1616, it prospered for more than two centuries, relying on enslaved *índios* (and later enslaved Africans) for finding and harvesting Amazonian treasures such as cacao, indigo and animal skins, all for export to Europe. But it was a fragile success, and an economic downturn in the early 19th century helped spark a popular uprising and bloody civil war.

The rubber boom at the turn of the century sent Belém's population rocketing, from 40,000 in 1875 to more than 100,000 in 1900. The city suddenly had electricity, telephones, streetcars and a distinctly European feel. Officials erected a few grand monuments such as the Teatro da Paz, earning the city the nickname 'the tropical Paris'.

Rubber eventually crashed, but the ports built during the boom have remained active. Today more than a million tons of cargo pass

Belém

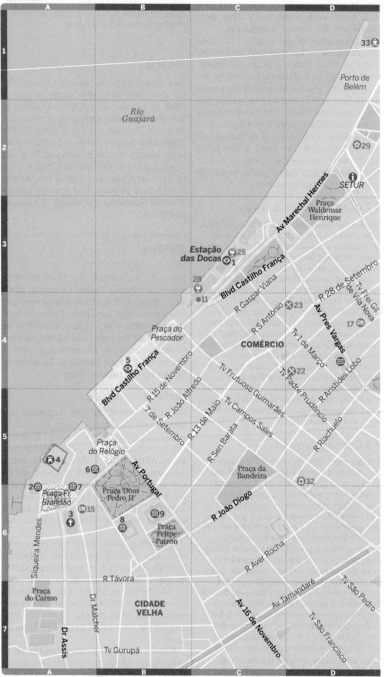

A
B
C
D
1
2
3
4
5
6
7
33
Porto de Belém
Rio Guajará
29
SETUR
Av Marechal Hermes
Praça Waldemar Henrique
Estação das Docas
25
1
Blvd Castilho França
28
11
R Gaspar Viana
R 28 de Setembro
Tv Frei Gil de Vila Nova
R S Antônio
23
Av Pres Vargas
17
Praça do Pescador
COMÉRCIO
Tv 1 de Março
5
Blvd Castilho França
R 15 de Novembro
22
R Aristides Lobo
R João Alfredo
Tv Frutuoso Guimarães
Tv Padre Prudêncio
7 de Setembro
R 13 de Maio
Tv Campos Sales
R Riachuelo
R Sen Barata
Praça do Relógio
4
6
Av Portugal
Praça da Bandeira
32
2
7
Praça Fr Brandão
Praça Dom Pedro II
R João Diogo
15
3
8
9
Praça Felipe Patron
Siqueira Mendes
R Aver Rocha
R Távora
Tv São Pedro
Av Tamandaré
Praça do Carmo
Dr Malcher
CIDADE VELHA
Av 16 de Novembro
Tv São Francisco
Dr Assis
Tv Gurupá

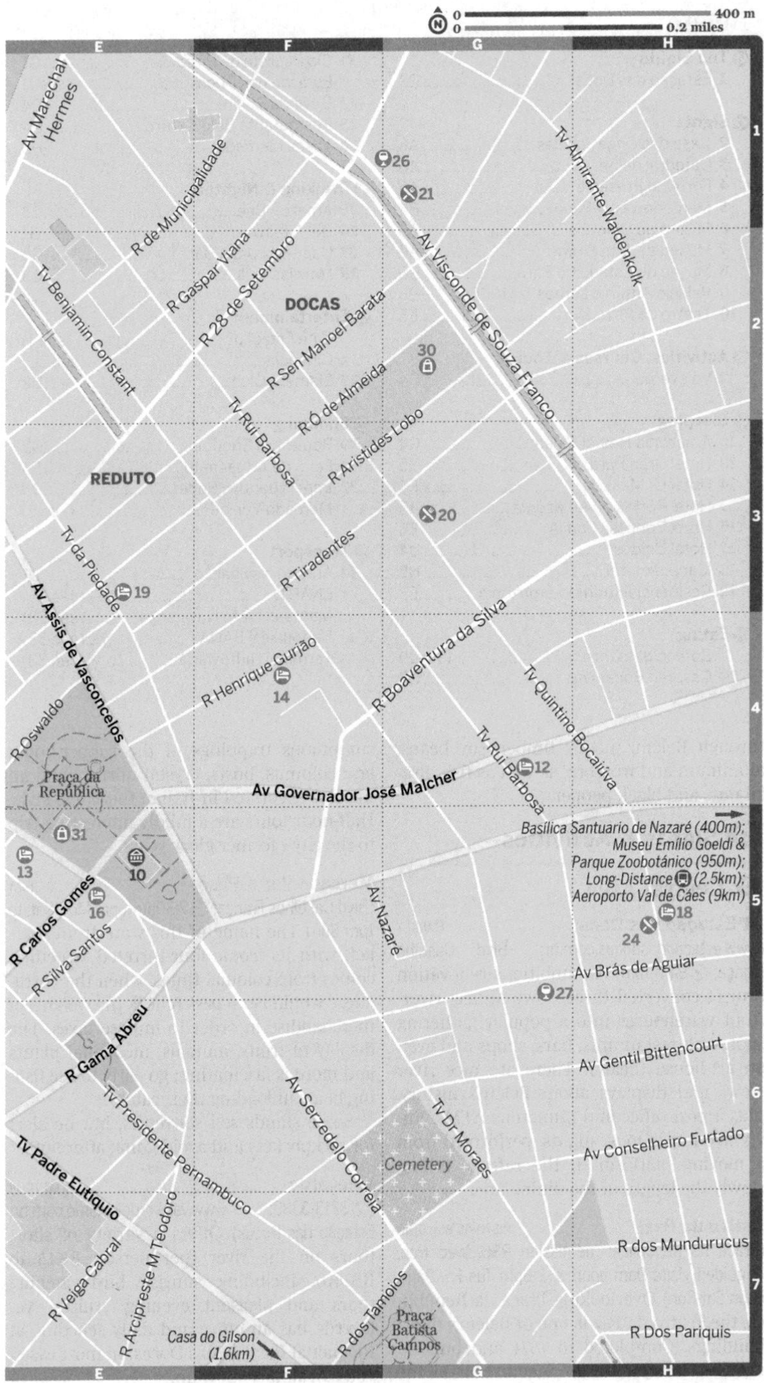
0 400 m
0 0.2 miles
Av Marechal Hermes
R de Municipalidade
R Gaspar Viana
R 28 de Setembro
Tv Benjamin Constant
DOCAS
R Sen Manoel Barata
R Ó de Almeida
R Aristides Lobo
Av Visconde de Souza Franco
Tv Almirante Waldenkolk
Tv Rui Barbosa
REDUTO
R Tiradentes
Tv da Piedade
Av Assis de Vasconcelos
R Henrique Gurjão
R Boaventura da Silva
Tv Quintino Bocaiúva
R Oswaldo
Praça da República
Av Governador José Malcher
Basílica Santuario de Nazaré (400m); Museu Emílio Goeldi & Parque Zoobotánico (950m); Long-Distance (2.5km); Aeroporto Val de Cáes (9km)
R Carlos Gomes
Av Nazaré
R Silva Santos
Av Brás de Aguiar
R Gama Abreu
Av Gentil Bittencourt
Tv Presidente Pernambuco
Av Serzedelo Correia
Tv Dr Moraes
Cemetery
Av Conselheiro Furtado
Tv Padre Eutíquio
R dos Mundurucus
R Veiga Cabral
R Arcipreste M Teodoro
R dos Tamoios
Praça Batista Campos
Casa do Gilson (1.6km)
R Dos Pariquis
26
21
30
20
19
14
12
31
13
10
16
18
24
27

Belém

Top Sights
1 Estação das Docas ... C3

Sights
2 Casa das Onze Janelas ... A6
3 Catedral da Sé ... A6
4 Forte do Presépio ... A5
5 Mercado Ver-o-Peso ... B4
6 Museo do Círio ... A5
7 Museu de Arte Sacra ... A6
8 Museu do Estado do Pará ... B6
9 Palácio Antonio Lemos & MABE ... B6
10 Teatro da Paz ... E5

Activities, Courses & Tours
11 Valeverde ... C4

Sleeping
12 Amazônia Hostel Belém ... G4
13 Hotel Grão Pará ... E5
14 Hotel Le Massilia ... F4
15 Hotel Portas da Amazônia ... A6
16 Hotel Princesa Louçã ... E5
17 Hotel Unidos ... D4
18 Manacá Hotel ... H5
19 Residencia Karimbo Amazônia ... E3

Eating
Boteco das Onze ... (see 2)
20 Casarão Bocaiúvas ... G3
21 Cia Paulista de Pizza ... G1
Estação das Docas ... (see 1)
22 Govinda Belem ... D4
23 Restaurante Belo Centro ... D4
24 Tasca Mercado ... H5

Drinking & Nightlife
25 Amazon Beer ... C3
26 Bar Fiteiro ... G1
27 Capital Lounge Bar ... G5
28 Marujos Grill ... C3

Entertainment
Cine Estação ... (see 1)
Cinépolis ... (see 30)
29 Element Club ... D2

Shopping
30 Boulevard Shopping ... G2
31 Feira de Artesanato ... E5
32 Imperador das Redes ... D5
Mercado Ver-o-Peso ... (see 5)

Transport
33 Arapari Navigação ... D1
ENART ... (see 33)
Marques Pinto Navigação ... (see 33)
Rodofluvial BANAV ... (see 33)
Terminal Hidroviária ... (see 33)

through Belém, mostly timber, soy beans, aluminum and iron ore, as well as fish, Brazil nuts and black pepper.

Sights & Activities

Central Area

★Estação das Docas MARKET
(www.estacaodasdocas.com.br; Blvd Castilho França; ⏲9am-1am) An ambitious renovation project converted three down-at-heel riverfront warehouses into a popular gathering spot, with restaurants, bars, shops and even an art-house theater. There are nice river views and displays about Belém's history, plus a post office and numerous ATMs. Enjoy live music most nights, performed from a moving platform in the rafters, rolling slowly the length of the dining area.

Teatro da Paz HISTORIC BUILDING
(Praça da República; admission R$6, Wed free; ⏲guided visits 9am-noon & 2-6pm Tue-Fri, 9am-noon Sat-Sun) Overlooking Praça da República, the Teatro da Paz is one of Belém's finest buildings. Completed in 1874 and built in neoclassical style, the architecture has all the sumptuous trappings of the rubber-boom era: columns, busts, crystal mirrors and an interior decorated in Italian theatrical style. Half-hour tours are a mildly interesting trip to the city's former glory years.

Mercado Ver-o-Peso MARKET
(Blvd Castilhos França; ⏲7:30am-6pm Mon-Sat, to 1pm Sun) The name of this waterfront market, with its iconic four-turreted structure, comes from colonial times, when the Portuguese would *ver o peso* (check the weight) of merchandise in order to impose taxes. The display of fruits, animals, medicinal plants and more is fascinating; go early to see fishing boats unloading their catch.

Some stands sell souvenirs, but be alert for pickpockets and avoid going after 5pm.

Valeverde BOAT TOUR
(☎3213-3388; www.valeverdeturismo.com.br; Estação das Docas) Offers a variety of short tours on the river (per person R$45 to R$160), including sunrise bird-watching tours and pleasant evening cruises. Valeverde has an office and daily schedule at the pier at Estação das Docas; in most cases, you can simply show up.

Cidade Velha

The 'Old City' has most of Belém's museums and galleries, fronting the river and four nearly adjoining plazas. The area is safe during the day, with plenty of people about, but is tucked below the Comercio neighborhood, which gets seedy at night. Take a taxi if you're there late.

Forte do Presépio FORTRESS

(Praça Fr Brandão; admission R$4, Tue free; ⏲10am-6pm Tue-Fri, to 2pm Sat & Sun) The city of Belém was founded in 1616 with the construction of this imposing fort, which was intended to protect Portuguese interests upriver against incursions by the French and Dutch. Today, it houses a small but excellent museum, primarily about Pará's indigenous communities (displays in Portuguese only), and has great river and city views from atop its thick stone walls.

Palácio Antonio Lemos & MABE MUSEUM, HISTORICAL BUILDING

(MABE; ☎3283-4665; Praça Dom Pedro II; ⏲10am-8pm Tue-Fri, 9am-1pm Sat & Sun) FREE This rubber-boom palace served as city hall in the late 1800s, and its 2nd floor now houses the Museu de Arte de Belém. The museum has gorgeous wood floors – cloth slippers are provided – and a fine collection of statuettes, antiques and Brazilian 20th-century paintings, such as Theodoro Braga's 1908 oil *Fundação da Cidade de Belém*. Two 1st-floor galleries hold rotating exhibits.

Museu do Estado do Pará MUSEUM

(Pará State Museum; ☎3225-2414; Praça Dom Pedro II; admission R$4, Tue free; ⏲10am-6pm Tue-Fri, to 1pm Sat & Sun) The State Museum of Pará is housed in the grand Palácio Lauro Sodré, originally the residence of Portugal's royal representatives in Belém and later home to various state governors. One such governor, Ernesto Lobo, was killed on the staircase during the Cabanagem Rebellion in 1835. The museum today is rather less thrilling, with a mildly interesting collection on the founding and growth of Belém and Pará.

Casa das Onze Janelas MUSEUM

(Praça Frei Brandão; admission R$3; ⏲10am-6pm Tue-Fri, 9am-1pm Sat & Sun) Once the home of a sugar baron, then a military hospital, the Casa das Onze Janelas now houses an excellent art gallery and one of Belém's finest restaurants, Boteco das Onze. Galleries on the 1st and 2nd floor contain a mix of classical and modern paintings and drawings, and a smattering of sculpture and photography. The cafe in back has a view of the Rio Guamá.

Museu de Arte Sacra MUSEUM

(Praça Frei Brandão; admission R$6, Tue free; ⏲10am-6pm Tue-Fri, 9am-1pm Sat & Sun) This museum has two parts: the impressive Igreja do Santo Alexandre and the adjoining Palâcio Episcopal (Bishop's Palace). Santo Alexandre was Belém's first church, founded by Jesuits in the early 17th century, and contains incredible cedar and plaster detailing. The rambling Bishop's Palace has a decent collection of modern art, though is frequently closed for events or maintenance.

Museo do Círio MUSEUM

(Jóao Alfredo; adult/student R$4/2, Tue free; ⏲10am-6pm Tue-Fri, 9am-1pm Sat & Sun) The many idiosyncrasies of Belém's famous religious festival, the Círio de Nazaré, are explained in this handsome museum, from the discovery of a tiny statue of Mary in a riverbank in 1700, to the story behind the 400m, 450kg rope that's now such an integral part of the procession, the faithful masses jostling for a chance to touch or pull it. Explanations in Portuguese only.

Catedral da Sé CHURCH

(Praça Frei Brandão; ⏲7am-noon & 2-7:30pm) FREE After years of slow, sad decline, Belém's historic cathedral now radiates, thanks to a major renovation. The exterior gleams a brilliant white, while the soaring interior has polished marble floors and intricate geometric designs on the walls and ceiling, and oversized paintings of the Virgin Mary and other saints in ornate gold-encrusted frames.

East of the Center

Basílica Santuario de Nazaré CHURCH

(Praça Justo Chermont; ⏲5:30am-8pm) FREE Rather humdrum from the outside, the Basílica Santuario de Nazaré has a truly spectacular interior. Sink into a cushioned pew and admire the soaring marble columns, brilliant stained-glass windows and ornate wood and tile work in every direction, even the ceiling. The basilica is the focal point of Brazil's largest religious festival, Círio de Nazaré, which draws more than a million worshippers to Belém every October.

Museu Emílio Goeldi & Parque Zoobotánico ZOO

(☎3219-3300; www.museu-goeldi.br; Av Governador Magalhães Barata 376; park, aquarium & permanent exhibit each R$2; ⏲9am-5pm Tue-Sun) This excellent museum and zoo contains many Amazonian animal species, from manatees and anacondas to jaguars and giant otters, plus an aviary, aquarium and a permanent exhibit of artifacts from ancient Amazonian peoples. It's popular with families on Sundays.

Bosque Rodrigues Alves ZOO
(☎3277-1112; Av Almirante Barroso 2305; admission R$2; ⏲9am-5pm Tue-Sun) Bosque Rodrigues Alves' aging but well-maintained animal enclosures and wide, tree-shaded paths are especially nice for families, with huge, curious structures including a castle and replica grotto. From the center, take any 'Alm. Borroso' bus, and get off when you see the park's long yellow exterior wall.

Festivals & Events

Every year on the morning of the second Sunday of October, Belém explodes with the sounds of hymns, bells and fireworks. Started in 1793, the **Círio de Nazaré** is Brazil's biggest religious festival. People from all over the country flock to Belém, and even camp in the streets, to participate in the grand event.

The diminutive image of NS de Nazaré (Our Lady of Nazareth) is believed to have been sculpted in Nazareth (Galilee) and to have performed miracles in medieval Portugal before getting lost in Brazil. It was rediscovered in 1700 by a humble cattleman on the site of the basilica, to which it later returned of its own accord after being moved away several times.

The day before the main annual event, the little statue, having previously been taken 23km north to Icoaraci, is carried in a river procession back to the cathedral in Belém. On the Sunday itself, well over a million people fill the streets to accompany the image from the Catedral da Sé to the Basílica Santuario de Nazaré. The image is placed on a flower-bedecked carriage, and thousands squirm and grope in an emotional frenzy to get a hand on the 400m rope pulling the carriage. Five hours and just 3.5km from the cathedral, the Virgin reaches the basilica, where she remains for the duration of the festivities.

Sleeping

Hotel Unidos HOTEL $
(☎3224-0660; www.hotelunidos.com.br; Ó de Almeida 545; s/d/tr R$100/120/150; ❄@📶) Unidos has large spotless rooms and competent, welcoming staff. The decor is admittedly plain with only small windows, but the rates are lower than comparably equipped alternatives, and there's an additional 15% discount for paying in cash. Easy walking distance to many restaurants and sights, and close to the bus stops for everything else.

Amazônia Hostel Belém HOSTEL $
(☎3278-4355; www.amazoniahostel.com.br; Av Governador José Malcher 592; dm R$54, s/d R$81/111, s/d without bathroom R$71/103; ❄@📶)

SURF THE POROROCA!

Every month or so, when alignment of the sun and moon makes tides their strongest, powerful waves can form at the mouth of certain rivers and barrel upstream with tremendous force. The phenomenon – which occurs when the tide briefly overpowers the force of the river – is technically a 'tidal bore' but in Brazil is better known as the *pororoca*, an indigenous word for 'mighty noise.' And no wonder: the waves can reach heights of 4m and speeds of 30km/h, and can rip full-sized trees off the bank with their force.

All of which is music to the ears of extreme surfers (and wave-surfing kayakers) in search of the mythic 'endless wave.' The record for the longest ride is 37 minutes, covering nearly 13km. Surfers generally report the *pororoca* to be stronger than a like-sized ocean wave, and it constantly changes size and speed according to the river's contours. What's more, the water is loaded with debris that's been swept off the shore and river bottom, including tree trunks and abandoned canoes. (At least the caimans tend to stay away.)

The National Pororoca Surfing Championship has been held at the town of São Domingos do Capim, 120km east of Belém on the Rio Guamá, since 1999. (A related competition is held on the Rio Araguari in Amapá.) The event usually takes place in March, on the full moon nearest the spring equinox, when the *pororoca* is strongest. The bash draws top-ranked surfers and includes street fairs, cultural performances, even a Miss Pororoca competition. A paved road makes getting there easier, though there still is no direct service; from Belém, go to Castanhal and transfer. Alternatively, Amazon Star Turismo, a travel agency in Belém, organizes *pororoca* packages.

A century-old rubber-baron mansion in a safe area is the perfect home for Belém's longest-running youth hostel. Smallish dorms have solid bunks and large lockers, plus 4m ceilings and gorgeous wood floors. Internet, kitchen and laundry are welcome features. Prices are high for a hostel, and management is oddly stingy with breakfast and linens, but it's still a nice spot. HI discount available.

Hotel Grão Pará HOTEL **$**
(☎3221-2121; www.hotelgraopara.com.br; Av Presidente Vargas 718; s/d R$120/140; ❄📶) A reliable if rather charmless high-rise hotel, with midsized rooms and updates including glass showers and marble counters. Street-facing rooms have views of Praça da República, but can be noisy – ask for a high floor. Service is friendly if somewhat uneven, but you can definitely count on a hearty breakfast and strong wi-fi signal.

★**Manacá Hotel** HOTEL **$$**
(☎3222-9224; www.manacahotel.com.br; Travessa Quintino Bocaiúva 1645; s/d/tr R$155/180/210; ❄📶🏊) Rooms in this boutique hotel are cozy and up to date (though a bit dark), while the common areas have beautiful wood and stone floors, and creative artwork on the walls. The neighborhood is equally appealing, with stylish shops and restaurants. Small swimming pool.

Hotel Le Massilia HOTEL **$$**
(☎3222-2834; www.massilia.com.br; Henrique Gurjão 236; s R$192-222, d R$228-246, tr & q R$246-288; ❄📶🏊) This French-run hotel near Praça da República has a guesthouse atmosphere, small swimming pool and recommended French restaurant. Rooms open onto a long leafy garden and have homey details such as wood paneling and decorative rugs; superiors have lofts and can sleep up to four, albeit somewhat cozily. A dip in the pool is a nice way to end the day.

Residencia Karimbo Amazônia GUESTHOUSE **$$**
(☎3298-1373; www.rkamazoniabrasil.sitew.com; Travessa Piedade 391; d/tr R$145/185) A true guesthouse, the owners, a friendly French-Brazilian family, live in the front part of the house while guests stay in five comfortable rooms, with bright artful decor, new bedding and well-appointed bathrooms. A 'VIP' room (first come, first served) has a private balcony overlooking the hotel's garden area, with a small pool and attractive wood patio.

Hotel Portas da Amazônia HOTEL **$$**
(☎3222-9952; www.portasdaamazoniabelempara.com.br; Dr Malcher 14; s R$109-139, d R$149-179; ❄📶) A former mansion with a gorgeous tile facade, this attractive boutique-ish hotel has just nine rooms and a recommended pizzeria. Huge front rooms have large windows overlooking Praça Brandão, but also frequent gonging of the nearby cathedral bells. Rear rooms have less light, but high ceilings and exposed brick. The surrounding area can get a bit dodgy late at night.

Hotel Princesa Louçã HOTEL **$$$**
(☎4006-7000; www.princesabelem.com.br; Av Presidente Vargas 882; s R$268-475, d R$299-525; ❄@📶🏊) Formerly the Hilton Belém, the Princesa Louçã continues as one of Belém's largest downtown hotels, centrally located opposite Praça da República, offering business-class comfort with a moderate price tag. Amenities include a business center, exercise room, lobby bar and swimming pool. Rooms are spacious and reasonably modern; those on the top floors have views of the river. Friendly service.

Eating

Center

Restaurante Belo Centro CAFETERIA **$**
(☎3241-8677; 2nd fl, Santo Antônio 264; per kg R$35; ⏲lunch Mon-Fri) This friendly, airy restaurant cooks up tasty self-serve, with plenty of options for vegetarians and carnivores. It's located on the 2nd floor in the middle of a busy commercial zone; look for the large vinyl sign hanging from the balcony and narrow carpeted stairs leading up from the street.

Govinda Belem INDIAN **$**
(☎3222-2272; www.restaurantegovindabelem.blogspot.com.br; Travessa Padre Prudencio 166; R$20; ⏲11:30-3pm Mon-Fri, noon-2:30 Sat; 🥬) Dishes here are Indian-ish (samosas, dahl etc) with tell-tale signs you're still in Brazil (*farofa, jambú*) but perfectly tasty and fully vegetarian – a welcome change from typical Brazilian fare and drawing a diverse clientele. Select three or four dishes from a menu divided by the day; Saturdays are the most inventive. Warmly decorated; fast, friendly service.

★**Estação das Docas** RESTAURANTS **$$**
(www.estacaodasdocas.com.br; Blvd Castilho França; ⏲10am-midnight Sun-Wed, to 3am Thu-Sat) One of the best places in Belém to eat no matter what you're hungry for. The bustling complex has

AMAZON FAST FACTS

➡ The Amazon River used to flow east to west.

➡ After leaving the Andes, the Amazon riverbed descends just 1.5cm per kilometer.

➡ Pink river dolphins (botos) can bend their necks and shrug their shoulders.

➡ Up to 30% of the animal biomass in the Amazon is ants.

➡ Half the rainfall in the Amazon never reaches the ground.

almost a dozen restaurants, most with indoor and outdoor seating and open for lunch, dinner and late-night feasting. Favorites include Lá em Casa, serving pricey but outstanding regional food, and Amazon Beer, with tasty pub grub to accompany its artisanal beer.

Outside the Center

★Tasca Mercado SANDWICHES $
(Travessa Quintino Bocaiúva 1696; sandwiches & salads R$16-45; ⏲8am-11pm) Fresh-baked baguettes, focaccia and other breads, plus flavorful additions such as garlic eggplant, caramelized onions and smoked salmon, are the raw materials for a variety of tasty sandwiches at this trendy high-ceilinged cafe. Salads, quiches, and chicken and fish dishes round out the menu. An attached natural-foods grocery is a good place to snag artisanal cheeses, yogurts and other snacks.

Casarão Bocaiúvas SEAFOOD $$
(☎8112-6300; Travessa Quintino Bocaiúva 945; R$25-45; ⏲11:30am-3:30pm & 6:30-11:45pm Thu & Sun, 11:30am-2:30am Fri & Sat) If you've visited a Pará beach town, you'll recognize some of the dishes at this popular restaurant. *Caranguejo* (crab feast) is an Algodoal staple and a crowd favorite here, served with a hammer for cracking the shells. And there's a taste of Ilha Marajó when you order the buffalo fillet.

Cia Paulista de Pizza PIZZA $$
(☎3212-2200; Av Visconde de Souza Franco 559; dishes R$18-35; ⏲10am-1am Sun-Thu, 10am-4am Fri & Sat) You wouldn't know from the dining room that this is actually a chain restaurant, as the wineglasses, tablecloths, attentive waiters and recorded jazz create a unique and classy ambience. Prices are quite affordable, and the pizza and pasta excellent.

Boteco das Onze BRAZILIAN $$
(Praça Frei Brandão; mains R$21-63; ⏲noon-midnight Tue-Sun, 5pm-midnight Mon) Part of Casa das Onze Janelas gallery, this is one of the city's best restaurant-bars. It has an indoor dining room with modern art on the walls and a breezy back patio overlooking the river. Meals include *moqueca de filhote,* a tasty stew prepared with catfish, shrimp and lobster. Live music most nights.

Drinking & Nightlife

Av Visconde de Souza Franco has several bars and clubs, where you can simply follow the music to find the current hot spot.

Amazon Beer BEER HALL
(www.amazonbeer.com.br; Av Marechal Hermes, Estação das Docas; ⏲5pm-1am) As much as Brazilians love beer, it's can be surprisingly tough to find anything heftier than a pilsner. This award-winning brewery is an exception, with an amber ale, a Dutch *witbier* (wheat beer), an IPA, even a unique açaí stout, all brewed on-site. Indoor and outdoor seating, a full menu, even souvenir beer glasses for sale. Often very busy.

Marujos Grill BAR
(☎3242-4809; www.marujos.com.br; Av Marechal Heremes, Estação das Docas; R$13-85; ⏲11am-1am) Outdoor tables have nice river views at this lively but low-key bar-restaurant. There's the Torre de Chopp (Tower of Beer), a 2.5L silo of suds for just R$49; otherwise there's a long list of beers and cocktails of the non-gargantuan variety. Occasional musical performances, for which a cover of R$6 may be added to your bill.

Bar Fiteiro BAR
(☎3224-0075; www.fiteirobar.com.br; Av Visconde de Souza Franco 555 at Senador Lemos; ⏲5pm-1am, from noon Sat) This spacious colorful bar has a fun irreverent air and a commitment to not let its customers go hungry – in fact, the bar's tagline is 'We Have Food'. There's live music most nights, often paired with special dish or drink special, like 'Feijoada com Samba' on Saturday afternoons.

Capital Lounge Bar BAR
(www.capitalbarlounge.com; Av Brás de Aguiar 420; ⏲7pm-3am Wed-Sat) A huge Union Jack and other flags from around the world suggest an old-school English pub, but the sleek booths, creative cocktails and pulsing DJ-mixed music give this much more of a club vibe. There's restaurant service but the

real action gets started long after dinner time. Popular with Belém's jet set.

Entertainment

Teatro da Paz holds a variety of theatrical events, from plays to symphonies to international dance performances. Most events have same-day tickets available.

Casa do Gilson LIVE MUSIC
(☎3272-7306; Travessa Padre Eutíquio 3172; ⊙8pm-3am Fri, noon-3am Sat & Sun) Come here for Belém's best live music. Opened in 1987, Gilson's draws intellectuals and hipsters alike with first-rate samba, *choro* (improvised samba-like music) and other music, and terrific food and atmosphere to boot. It's between ruas Nova and Tambés.

Element Club DANCE
(☎98137-3737; www.elementclub.com.br; Av Marechal Hermes & Travessa da Piedade; cover R$20-40; ⊙3pm-3am Fri-Sun) Throbbing music, flowing drink and a young nattily dressed crowd keep this club hopping into the wee hours. Mostly popular dance music, with occasional theme nights, such as Hawaiian or Samba.

Cine Estação CINEMA
(☎3212-5615; www.estacaodasdocas.com.br; Estação das Docas; admission R$10) Cine Estação has month-long runs of Brazilian and international art films, typically with screenings twice-nightly on three or four days per week.

Cinépolis CINEMA
(Av Visconde de Souza Franco, Boulevard Shopping) Cinépolis is a megatheater located in a megamall, with seven screens, including one for 3D films, and supercomfy stadium seating. Weekends can be extremely crowded.

Shopping

Feira de Artesanato MARKET
(Praça da República; ⊙7am-3pm Fri-Sun) A large crafts fair that has the city's biggest range of attractive artwork, and a lot of it is homemade. It's especially busy on Sundays.

Mercado Ver-o-Peso MARKET
(Av Castilho França; ⊙5am-6pm) This is Belém's most interesting place to browse and shop, whether for long pants, lacquered piranha or anything in between. Pará has gained national attention with *technobrega* music, a defiantly from-the-streets genre whose best collections aren't sold in stores but on amateur CDs in Ver-o-Peso (and on YouTube). Be wary of pickpockets in the early and late hours.

Boulevard Shopping MALL
(Av Visconde de Souza Franco 776) Belém's latest, biggest mall is a modern cement, steel and glass structure, brilliantly lit at night, and boasting top-tier clothing, electronics and department stores as well as a cinema complex.

Imperador das Redes OUTDOOR EQUIPMENT
(Padre Eutício at Riachuelo; ⊙7:30am-5pm Mon-Fri, to 2pm Sat) Large hammock store, with everything from light, simple hammocks to deluxe matrimonial ones with lace fringe and more (R$40 to $120).

Orientation

Belém's central park is called Praça da República, and several major avenues converge there. West of the plaza, and closer to the water, is Comércio, a busy commercial district whose narrow streets have a gritty vitality during the day, but turn lonely and dodgy at night. Further south is Cidade Velha (Old City), where Belém's best museums are located. East of the center is an upscale neighborhood called Nazaré, with cafés, a few hotels, and sights including the zoo and the basilica.

Information

DANGERS & ANNOYANCES

Pickpocketing is a problem in Mercado Ver-o-Peso and the Comercio districts; take care during the day and avoid at night. Take a cab if you're returning late from bars or the movies.

EMERGENCY

Police (☎190)

Tourist Police (CIPTUR; ☎3222-2602; Rua 28 de Setembro, Central station)

Tourist Police (CIPTUR; ☎3212-0948; Praça Waldemar Henrique s/n, Paratur Office)

INTERNET ACCESS

Equilibrium (Ó de Almeida; per hr R$4; ⊙8am-5:30pm Mon-Fri)

LAUNDRY

Laundromat (☎3224-0529; Av Serzadelo Correia at Av Bittencourt; per basket R$25; ⊙8am-8pm Mon-Fri, to 6pm Sat) Next-day service only.

Lav & Lev (☎3223-7247; Travessa Dr Moraes 576 at Av Conselheiro Furtado; ⊙8am-6pm Mon-Sat) Drop-off service costs R$13 per wash cycle (7kg maximum), R$13 per dry cycle (some loads may require more than one) and R$13 service charge. For R$20 more, they'll pick up and drop off your duds at your hotel.

MEDICAL SERVICES

Hospital Adventista de Belém (☎3084-8686; www.hab.org.br; Av Almirante Barroso 1758) One of the better private hospitals.

Around Belém

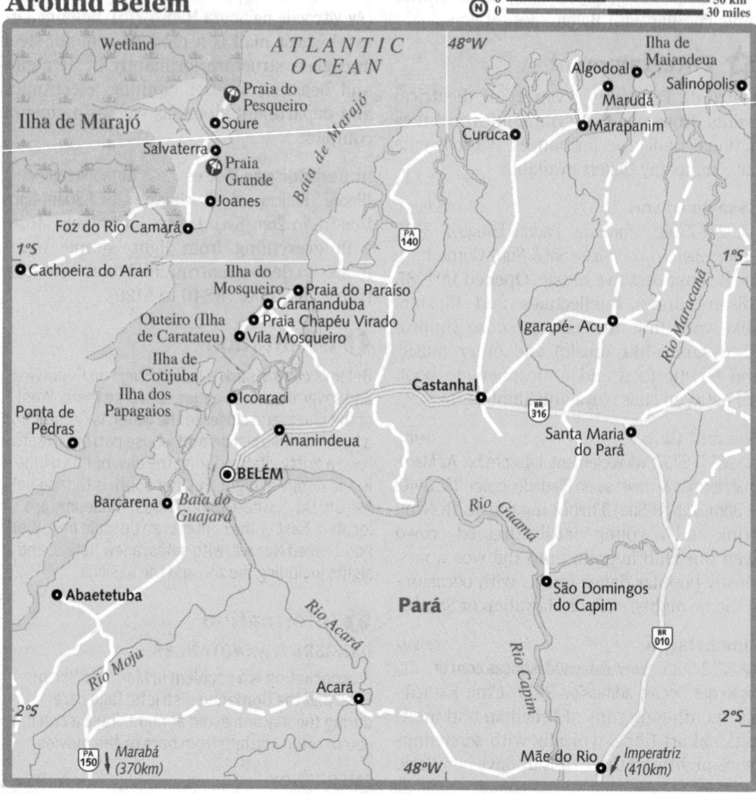

MONEY

Bradesco (Av Presidente Vargas 988 at Rua Silva Santos; ⊙10am-1pm & 2-4pm Mon-Fri)

Estação das Docas (Blvd Castilhos França) Numerous ATMs in a secure setting.

Turvicam (☎3201-5465; www.turvicam.com.br; Av Presidente Vargas 636; ⊙8am-6:30pm Mon-Fri, to 1pm Sat) Busy travel agency has currency exchange in rear.

POST

Main Post Office (☎3211-3147; Av Presidente Vargas 498; ⊙9am-5pm Mon-Fri)

TOURIST INFORMATION

SETUR (☎3212-0575; www.paraturismo.pa.gov.br; Praça Waldemar Henrique; ⊙8am-2pm Mon-Fri) A reasonably helpful branch office of the state tourism department.

TRAVEL AGENCIES

Amazon Star Turismo (☎3212-6244; www.amazonstar.com.br; Henrique Gurjão 210; ⊙8am-6pm Mon-Fri, to noon Sat) Offers free booking service for long-distance boat and plane tickets to and from Belém – easier and more reliable than booking directly. Also offers day trips around Belém, including bird-watching, nature walks and city tours (per person R$150 to R$300), plus overnight tours combining the above options, and multiday packages to Ilha de Marajó. Skilled, multilingual service.

Turvicam (☎3201-5465; www.turvicam.com.br; Av Presidente Vargas 636; ⊙8am-6:30pm Mon-Fri, to 1pm Sat) Sells plane tickets.

ℹ Getting There & Away

AIR

Belém's **Aeroporto Internacional Val-de-Cans** (☎3210-6000) is a hub for international, domestic and regional flights.

Azul (☎0800-887-1118, 4003-1118; www.voeazul.com.br)

Gol (☎0800-704-0465, 3210-6312; www.voegol.com.br)

MAP (☎in Manaus 092-2125-5000; www.voemap.com.br)

SETE (☎ 0800-605-7000; www.voesete.com.br)

Surinam Airways (☎ 3222-4831, 3210-6432; www.slm.firm.sr)

TAM (☎ 4002-5700, 3212-2166; www.tam.com.br)

TAP (☎ 0800-727-2347; www.flytap.com)

BOAT

All long-distance boats leave Belém from the handsomely renovated **Terminal Hidroviária** (Av Marechal Hermes). You can purchase tickets from the booths inside the terminal, but an easier and more reliable option is to contact **Amazon Star Turismo**, whose multilingual staff can book boat tickets, including over the phone or internet, for trips to or from Belém, for no extra cost.

Marques Pinto Navigação (☎ 3272-3847) and **ENART** (☎ 3224-1225) offer boat service to and from Manaus, and most points along the way. At last check, boats to Manaus left Wednesday and Friday, plus every other Tuesday, at 6pm with stops at Monte Alegre (hammock/hammock with air-con/cabin R$200/230/750, two to three days), Santarém (R$230/270/800, three to four days), Parintins (R$330/370/950, five days), and Manaus (R$370/400/1200, five to six days); cabins rates are for two people. Meals are not included, but you can purchase food onboard.

Arapari Navigação (☎ 3241-4977) and **Rodofluvial BANAV** (☎ 3269-4494, 8047-2440) alternate service to Ilha de Marajó, with daily ferries from Belém to Camará, (R$20 standard, R$35 'VIP' with air-con and airplane-style seating, three hours) at 6:30am and 2:30pm Monday to Saturday, and 10am on Sunday.

BUS

Belém's long-distance bus station is 3km east of the town center. Major destinations may be served by several lines, while *leito* and *semi-leito* (overnight sleeper) seats are available on some longer routes.

Itaperim (☎ 3226-3382; www.itaperim.com.br) Serves Fortaleza (R$266, 24 hours, once daily), Salvador (R$360, 33 hours, three departures weekly) and Rio de Janeiro (R$550, 53 hours, four departures weekly).

Rápido Excelsior (☎ 3249-6365) Daily services to Marudá (R$21.50, four hours, 6am, 9am, 12:30pm, 2:30pm and 4pm).

Sinprovan (☎ 3226-5879) Frequent service to Marudá (R$31, 3½ hours) in air-conditioned minibuses.

Transbrasilia (☎ 0800-726-7001, 3226-1942; www.transbrasiliana.com.br) Serves dozens of cities, near and far, including São Luis (R$131, 10 hours, one departure daily), Rio de Janeiro (R$425, 50 hours, four departures weekly) and Paraíso do Tocantins (R$145, 17 hours, three times daily).

ℹ Getting Around

Aeroporto Val de Cães is 8km north of the center on Av Júlio César. The 'Pratinha – Pres Vargas' bus (638) runs between the airport and Av Presidente Vargas (R$2.50, 40 minutes); the 'E Marex' bus also goes there, but you may have to change buses at the depot (no charge). Arriving by plane, turn left as you leave the terminal; buses stop at the traffic circle about 50m past the end of the terminal. A taxi between the airport and center is a fixed R$50 when booked inside the terminal; you may be able to catch one for less at the bus stop, though they pass somewhat infrequently.

The long-distance bus station is on the corner of Av Almirante Barroso and Av Governador José Malcher, 3km east of the city center. To get there from the center, take any 'Guama – P Vargas' bus (316) from Av Presidente Vargas. To get from the station into town, turn right out of the terminal and cross to the diagonally opposite corner; buses line up on Av Borroso in order to turn right onto Av Governador José Malcher, toward Praça de República. A taxi from the bus terminal costs R$20 to R$22.

AMAZON READING

Countless books have been written about the Amazon. Notable ones available in English include the following:

- *Atlas of the Amazon* by Michael Goulding
- *The Burning Season: The Murder of Chico Mendes and the Fight for the Amazon Rain Forest* by Andrew Revkin
- *The Thief at the End of the World: Rubber, Power, and the Seeds of Empire* by Joe Jackson
- *Fordlandia: The Rise and Fall of Henry Ford's Forgotten Jungle City* by Greg Grandin
- *The Lost City of Z: A Tale of Deadly Obsession in the Amazon* by David Grann
- *The Last of the Tribe: The Epic Quest to Save a Lone Man in the Amazon* by Monte Reel
- *The River of Doubt: Theodore Roosevelt's Darkest Journey* by Candice Millard

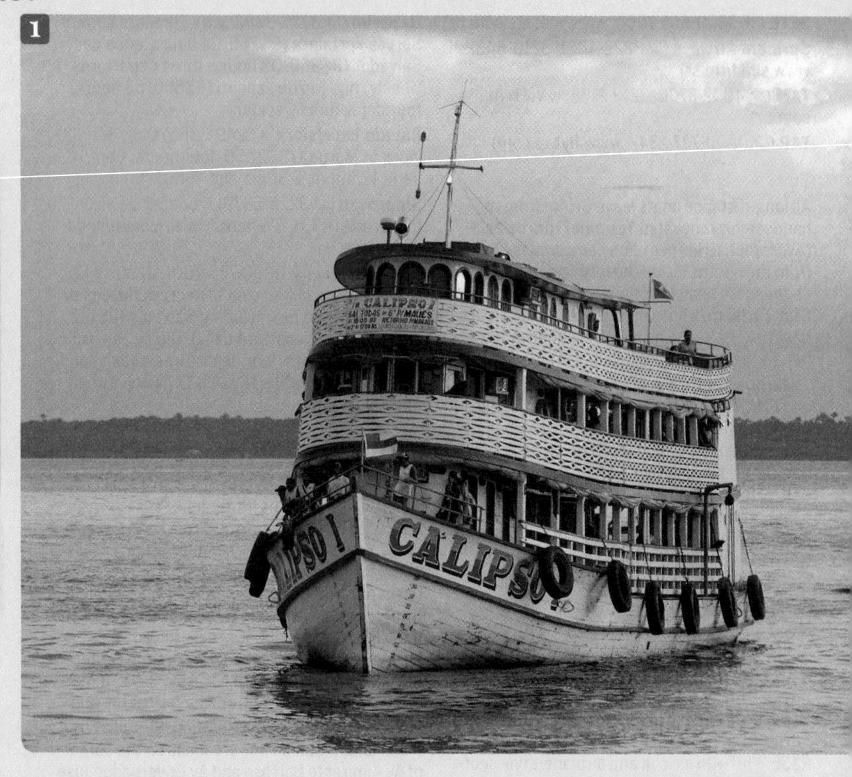

Riverboat Travel

Rivers are roads in the Amazon and riverboat trips are a uniquely Amazonian experience. Trips are long and languid, measured in days instead of hours. Much of the time is spent on the boat's upper deck, watching the scenery glide by, knocking back beers, talking and laughing over the ever-blasting music. The middle deck is where hammocks are slung, a place to read, nap or practice Portuguese with your neighbor. Night falls quickly and decisively, and night skies on the river can be spectacular.

For most people, a two- to three-day trip is plenty. For all its romantic appeal, riverboat travel can get rather tedious, especially with the constant pounding of the music and engine. There's virtually no chance of seeing wildlife and a boat typically travels far from shore. Consider taking a boat for one leg, and flying the others; air and boat fares can be surprisingly comparable, and you'll have more time for tours and other activities.

The two-day boat trip between Belém and Santarém is an interesting one, passing through the tidal zone around Belém, the narrows of Breves, the high bluffs around Monte Alegre and finally the main channel near Santarém. (The Santarém–Manaus leg, by contrast, follows the main channel only.) The Rio Negro, especially the upper regions, has little boat traffic and winds through massive archipelagos. Porto Velho to Manaus, along the Rio Madeira, is

ALEX ROBINSON / GETTY IMAGES ©

RICARDO SIQUEIRA/BRAZIL PHOTOS/LIGHTROCKET / GETTY IMAGES ©

RICARDO SIQUEIRA/BRAZIL PHOTOS/LIGHTROCKET/GETTY IMAGES ©

1. Amazon boat travel
2. Communal table, surrounded by hammocks
3. Passing time in hammocks

another good choice, a scenic backdoor route to the Amazon.

➡ You'll need a hammock and rope, and a light sheet in case the temperature drops. Most boats have a few private cabins with bunks, private bathrooms and air-conditioning, though for the price you may as well fly.

➡ Get to the boat early to secure a good hammock spot. Away from the restrooms is best.

➡ Bring water, dry snacks and extra toilet paper.

➡ Theft isn't rampant, but foreigners make tempting targets. Be especially alert when the boat stops in port, which can be in the middle of the night.

➡ Never leave cameras, cell phones or other valuables unattended in your hammock, and keep your backpack zipped and locked.

➡ Buffet-style meals are sold (or included) on all boats, but are notoriously unsanitary. Instead, stick with made-to-order burgers and sandwiches sold from the boat's grill.

➡ Make friends with the passengers around you, as they can keep an eye on your gear.

➡ Bring a thin cable and lock to secure your bag to one of the boat's center poles. Some thieves will snatch a promising piece of luggage and jump overboard; an accomplice waiting in a motorboat fishes thief and bag from the river and zips away to salvage whatever's not waterlogged. Victims can't jump in after them and captains will not stop or turn around.

Algodoal

0XX91 / POP 1400

The small fishing village of Algodoal on Ilha de Maiandeua, 180km northeast of Belém, has no cars or paved roads, and boasts expansive views over firm windswept beaches and a sometimes turbulent sea. A popular getaway for young Belenenses, Algodoal is jam-packed during a few frenetic months in the summer and over certain holidays, and quiet and virtually abandoned during down periods.

Sights

Praia da Caixa d'Água is the long beach in front of town. Across a tidal canal is **Praia do Farol**, a broad attractive beach that's good (and convenient) for swimming and sunbathing. Further on, past a rocky outcrop, is **Praia da Princesa** with a cluster of beach restaurants followed by 7km of lovely white sand. Across an even stronger canal is **Praia do Mupéua**, extending another 7km to Fortalezinha village.

Activities

Algodoal has various options for guided and do-it-yourself excursions. You can **canoe** (R$2) up the canal at Praia do Farol to spot birds and sometimes monkeys (best at sunset); visit Lago de Princesa (best April to June), walk or boat to the village of Fortalezinha, or even walk around the island.

Sunset is the best time to spot birds and wildlife, including the timid but radiant *guará* (scarlet ibis). However, high tide is when the canals are deepest and canoes can penetrate the furthest. Ideally, you'll be visiting when sunset and high tide happen to coincide! At high tide, you can canoe clear to Praia do Mupéua on the other side of the island (and from there walk back to town, about 7km) or else return along another canal to Porto do Mamede, Algodoal's main dock.

Partway up the canal from Praia do Farol, a path cuts through the forest and low sand dunes to Lago da Princesa and onward to Praia da Princesa (2km to 3km total). Boatmen can drop you at the path, and you can visit the lake, then return by foot along the beach (4km). The lake is just a small lagoon, and worth visiting only when full (April to June).

Another option is visiting **Fortalezinha**, a small village on the other side of the island, where you can walk the beach and grab lunch at one of several small restaurants. The **boat ride** from Algodoal to Fortalezinha is scenic but pricey (R$100); alternatively, you can catch a **canoe** (R$3 per person) from Porto do Mamede to the nearby community of Camboinha and follow well-marked paths from there.

From Fortalezinha it's possible to walk counter-clockwise back to Algodoal. (The reverse is much less pleasant, as you'll be walking against the wind.) It's a long (14km) but **scenic walk**. However, there's a powerful *furo* (tidal inlet) about halfway around that should never be crossed on foot. Wait for a fisherman to ferry you across or else turn back.

On any trip, be sure to bring mosquito repellent, water and sun protection.

Guided trips range from R$50 to R$180 per person, depending on what you do. For simple trips, boatmen can be hired at the mouth of the canal at Praia do Farol. Many hotels can recommend guides; Pousada Marhesias has the most in-depth information, including simple maps of the island.

Sleeping

Algodoal is awash with pousadas (guesthouses) of all shapes and sizes full to capacity during high season and holidays, but virtually empty (or simply closed) otherwise.

★ **Pousada Marhesias** POUSADA $

(3854-1129, 9112-3461; www.marhesias-algodoal.com; Bertoldo Costa 47; s R$120-135 d R$155-165;) This friendly well-run hotel has comfortable artful guest rooms facing a leafy garden. All have air-con and TV; suites are larger with private verandas. A large common deck has nice views of the sea and beach. Excellent restaurant and bar; wi-fi in the common areas; available tour information. Located on the far end of town, closest to the Praia do Farol.

Pousada Ponta do Boiador HOTEL $

(99215-9939; www.boiador.com; Bertoldo Costa; d standard/suite R$150/180;) Suites are newer, larger, better appointed and have breezy patios with hammocks. Standards are simpler and quite small, though their all-wood construction lends a clean, dry air. All have air-conditioning, hot showers and nice sea views. Best of all, the Boiador has direct beach access and a large waterfront deck with meal service, chilly beers and occasional live music.

Hotel Bela Mar POUSADA $
(☎3854-1128; http://belamarhotel.blogspot.com.br; Magalhães Barata; s/d with fan R$60/80, with air-con & minibar R$70/100; ❄) A clean, reliable choice, this is the first hotel you reach from the boat drop-off. A dozen tidy rooms are arranged around a pretty central garden, all with high ceilings and attractive decor. An ample breakfast spread is served in the hotel's spacious restaurant.

Eating

Some hotel restaurants serve only their own guests, for some or all meals, especially in low season. Just ask the waiter when you walk in.

Restaurante La Izla BRAZILIAN $$
(Bertolda Costa; mains R$15-30; ⏰11am-11pm) Friendly family-run eatery with a few tables on a sunny patio and a few more inside the owners' clapboard home. The menu is painted on the wall and consists of the Brazilian basics: choice of fried fish, chicken or beef, plus rice, *feijão* (beans) and *farofa* (manioc flour sautéed with butter).

Pousada Marhesias BRAZILIAN, ITALIAN $$
(Bertoldo Costa 47; mains R$15-55; ⏰7pm-10:30pm) Serving a little of everything, from fish and seafood to pasta and pizza, all freshly made and served in a large 2nd-floor dining area with a high peaked ceiling and tasteful decor. You can count on hearing some great jazz over your meal – it's almost all they play. Open for lunch for hotel guests only.

Orientation

Algodoal village is on the island's west coast. The streets are unpaved and unsigned. A tidal canal marks the northern end of town; across it are Praia do Farol and, beyond that, Praia da Princesa. Around the island are three more small communities: Fortalezinha, Mocoóca and Camboinha.

Information

There is no ATM on the island or even in Marudá, and not all hotels accept credit cards. Best to bring cash from Belém. Many hotels have wi-fi and there's free community wi-fi, though finding a strong signal can be tough. **Farmacias Kadosh** (⏰7:30am-8pm Mon-Sat, 7:30am-7pm Sun) is a small pharmacy selling sunscreen, bug spray, condoms, medicines etc.

DANGERS & ANNOYANCES

The island has several tidal channels, known as *furos* (meaning 'punctures' in Portuguese) that connect inland lagoons to the ocean. They rise and fall, and even change directions, according to the tide. The one between Praia do Farol and Praia da Princesa (known as Furo Velho) is especially treacherous and should never be crossed on foot. Fishermen are usually around and can ferry you across.

Getting There & Around

Access to Algodoal is via the mainland village of Marudá. Boats leave there for Algodoal (R$7, 40 minutes) at 9am, 11am, 1:30pm, 3:30pm and 5pm daily, plus 8:30pm Friday. Buses from Belém drop off (and pick up) passengers at the port, but vans only go as far as the bus station, which is five long blocks away, or R$10 in a taxi.

Arriving at Algodoal, a slew of donkey-cart drivers will vie for the chance to take you to your hotel (per person R$10). Some drivers will try to convince you to go to certain hotels where they earn a commission; always insist on going to the one of your choosing.

Boats return to the mainland at 6am, 8am, 10:30am and 1:30pm daily, plus 3pm Friday, and 3pm and 5pm Saturday and Sunday. Buses for Belém wait for passengers from the boat to leave, though you may need to make your way quickly to the Marudá's bus station to catch them.

Ilha de Marajó

☎0XX91 / POP 45,500

The 50,000-sq-km Ilha de Marajó, slightly larger than Switzerland, lies at the mouth of the Amazon river and is generally considered to be the largest river island in the world. (Some argue Marajó doesn't qualify because part of the island faces the open ocean.) It was the ancient home of the Marajoaras indigenous culture, notable for their large ceramic burial urns. Marajó remains a world apart, where bicycles outnumber cars and water buffalo graze around town. Legend has it the buffalo are descended from animals that swam ashore from a French ship that sank while en route from India to French Guiana. The island is well known for its buffalo cheese, buffalo steaks and buffalo-mounted police force.

Only the island's eastern shore is easily accessible to tourists. It has three small sleepy towns: Joanes (the smallest), Salvaterra (with the best beach but not much else) and Soure (the laid-back 'capital' of Marajó). Much of the island's interior is wetland, and is home to tens of thousands of birds, including the graceful *guará* (scarlet ibis). Be aware that Marajó is very wet from January to June, with almost daily rain.

Getting There & Away

Arapari Navigação (p583) and **Rodofluvial BANAV** (p583) (standard R$20, 'VIP' service, with air-con and airplane-style seating R$35, three hours) leave Belém's main boat terminal at 6:30am and 2:30pm Monday to Saturday and 10am on Sunday, arriving at a port south of Joanes called Foz do Rio Camará, or Camará for short. They return from the same port at 6:30am and 3pm Monday to Saturday, and 3pm Sunday.

Getting Around

Buses and minivans meet ferries arriving from Belém and at Camará, Marajó island's main port. Each has a sign to its destination; simply look for the place you're going to and get on. It's R$7 to Joanes, Salvaterra or the ferry port, and R$10 to R$15 to Soure, including the barge across the river and drop-off at your hotel. (The full-sized buses don't do hotel drop-offs, however.)

Moto-taxis are common in all three towns, and cost R$5 around town, R$5 to R$15 to outlying beaches, and R$30 between Joanes and Salvaterra.

Salvaterra and Soare are separated by the wide mouth of the Rio Paracauari. In Salvaterra, boats leave from a pier at the end of Salvaterra's main road; in Soure, they leave from a pier at the end of Travessa 14 (R$2, 15 minutes, 7am to 6pm); you can bring bicycles onboard. Boats also go from Soare to the car-ferry pier (8km from Salvaterra, R$1) or you can hop on the ferry itself for free.

Joanes

Head to sleepy Joanes for total isolation. It's got an appealing hotel and beach, the remains of a 17th-century Jesuit church, and hardly a soul in sight. There are no services, and the one hotel does not accept credit or debit cards.

Shuttles to and from the ferry at Camará cost R$7 (20 to 30 minutes). There are two morning shuttles from Joanes to Salvaterra and the boat pier (R$10, 7am and 9:30am) but no return service. Taxis charge R$60 to R$70 for the same trip, while moto-taxis cost R$30 (but carry only one person, of course). Biking is possible, but can be a long hot haul.

Pousada Ventania do Rio-Mar POUSADA $
(☎3646-2067; www.pousadaventania.com; Quarta Rua; s/d R$125/155) Atop a breezy headland overlooking the shore. Large rooms have whimsical decor, oversized paintings, and bathrooms (but no TV or air-con), and open onto a large patio. The beach is just steps away, and the staff can arrange a variety of excursions, including canoeing and fishing with local guides. Cash only.

Jacaré SEAFOOD $
(mains R$12-25; ⏲7am-10pm) One of a handful of beach restaurants serving the Marajoana favorites of grilled fish and buffalo steaks.

PREHISTORIC AMAZONIA

Most researchers agree that human occupation of the Amazon Basin began around 11,000 to 14,000 years ago, based on studies of ancient cave paintings near Monte Alegre, in Pará state. Around 6000 years ago, the Tapajoara people, living near present-day Santarém, started creating simple clay urns, the oldest known pottery in the Americas, and other indigenous Amazonians began mastering rudimentary agriculture.

By the last few centuries of the pre-Christian era, the Amazon was home to numerous cohesive communities, numbering in the thousands and led by chiefs. They produced good-quality pottery and cultivated maize and manioc intensively. It was in this time that the techniques of itinerate agriculture still used today were first developed, including selective burning, crop rotation and allowing the land periodic 'rest periods' to regenerate.

The Marajoara were among the most sophisticated pre-colonial Christian-era Amazonians, flourishing between AD 400 and 1350 on the wetlands of present-day Ilha de Marajó. They built massive earth platforms called *aterros* – the largest were 6m high and 250m long – to escape the annual floods. They buried their dead in elaborate urns, considered to be the most sophisticated ceramics produced in pre-colonial Brazil.

Interestingly, early human occupation of the Amazon has emerged as a proxy for today's environmental debates. Conservationists have long argued that large-scale occupation and development is incompatible with a healthy rainforest. However, recent research suggesting the early Amazon may have been far more populated than previously thought has been used by some to argue that greater exploitation of the rainforest is not only harmless, but has been part of its history for millennia.

Salvaterra

POP 20,500

Eighteen kilometers north from Joanes, Salvaterra has the island's best and longest beach, the aptly named Praia Grande, a short walk outside town. Salvaterra isn't as big as Soure, but is more compact, so it can feel busier.

Sights

Praia Grande is, as the name suggests, a big beach, a long wide swath of golden-brown sand about 500m south of Salvaterra proper. A slew of beach restaurants perched on stilts overlook the first section of the beach, but the far end is virtually deserted, save one large resort. Stingrays may be present but are easily scared off if you shuffle your feet as you enter and leave the water.

Sleeping & Eating

There are beach restaurants on Praia Grande, where you can fill up for R$15 to R$45.

Hotel Beira-Mar HOTEL $
(3765-1400; Rua 5, at Travessa 2; r with fan/air-con R$50/70;) A short walk from the center and Praia Grande; rooms here are of the large and plain variety, with graying tile floors, TV, and thin mattresses and linens. Wi-fi signal is spotty.

Pousada Bosque dos Aruãs POUSADA $
(3765-1115; Segunda Rua; s/d R$85/100, suite s/d R$155/175;) On an oceanfront lot shaded by mango trees, long wood cabins have two guest rooms apiece, each with small private patio, bright interior paint, TV and air-con. Two stand-alone suites are larger with slightly nicer amenities, like glass showers and veranda, and are nearer the water. Somewhat shabby overall, but very peaceful. Praia Grande is a 10-minute walk away. The hotel's **restaurant** (mains R$24-55; noon-3pm & 6-10pm) is one of Salvaterra's best.

Restaurante Umuarama SEAFOOD, PIZZA $
(cnr Travessa 2 & Rua 6; mains R$10-25; 11am-3pm, 7-10:30pm) Serves up shrimp, fish and buffalo dishes during the daytime, and pizza at night, in a low-key, open-air dining area. Located a short walk from Praia Grande, this is a popular and less expensive alternative to restaurants right on the beach.

Orientation

The main street through town is Av Victor Engelhard, which ends at the town pier. The cross streets are numbered starting at the pier – 1a Rua, 2a Rua etc – though few people refer to them as such. Praia Grande is about 500m south of town.

Information

The **post office** (8am-noon & 2-5pm Mon-Fri) is along the main drag. **BANAV** (3269-4494; 8-11am) sells ferry tickets from its office on the same street; otherwise, buy tickets on the shuttle or at the port.

Soure

POP 24,000

The 'Capital of Marajó', Soure is located on the far side of the Rio Paracauari. Although it's the biggest town on the island, Soure has a very laid-back vibe, with horses and water buffalo grazing on the soccer fields and double-wide streets, many of them dirt or grass with just a bike track weaving down the middle.

A bicycle is a great way to get around Soure. A guy named **Bimba** (Rua 4 btwn Travessas 18 & 19; per hr/day R$2/15) rents bikes from his house; it's the one with a stone facade, next to a hardware shop. Near Pousada O Canto do Francês, a local family also has **bikes for rent** (Travessa 8 btwn Ruas 6 & 7; per hr/day R$3/24; 8am-8pm).

Beaches

The beaches near Soure, which have a mix of salt- and freshwater, are often covered with fantastic seeds washed down from the Amazonian forests. If you enter the water, shuffle your feet to scare away stingrays.

Praia do Pesqueiro is Soure's most popular beach, a broad swath of soft beige sand, backed by thatch-roofed restaurants with tables set up in the sand. Pesqueiro is further from town (about 12km) than the other beaches, but along the way you can spot buffalo wallowing in marshes and catch a glimpse of Marajó's lush interior. A moto-taxi runs R$15 each way, while cabs charge R$40 for up to four people.

Praia Barra Velha and **Praia de Araruna** are narrow beaches edged by thick mangrove stands and separated from each other by a wide tidal channel. Barra Velho has several small restaurants, while Praia de Araruna is virtually deserted. High tide can reduce both shorelines to a thin strip of sand, but otherwise they're pleasant, and easy to reach by foot, bike or taxi. To get there, follow Travessa 14 out of town for about 4.5km to a fork in the road; to the right is a walkway leading to Praia Barra Velha, while to the left and a short distance further is a footbridge across the channel to Praia de Araruna.

Praia Garrote is a completely undeveloped beach at the mouth of the Rio Paracauari. To get there, follow Travessa 9 east out of town; the road makes a sharp right-hand turn and continues to a tidal inlet; fishermen there can ferry you across, and the beach is a short distance further.

Tours

Three nearby *fazendas* (ranches) make for interesting half-day trips. **Fazenda Bom Jesus**, **Fazenda São Jerônimo** and **Fazenda Araruna** offer the same basic activities, including riding water buffaloes, visiting mangroves and beaches, and spotting birds, monkeys and other animals. Bom Jesus is the most adventurous of the three – the grounds look more like a nature preserve than a ranch – though at São Jerônimo you can ride your buffalo in the surf.

Morning boat rides up Rio Paracauari can also be arranged, including passing through a mangrove 'tunnel' and a chance to see birds and pink dolphins. There are also city tours, with visits to local artisans, and beach-hopping tours. Prices start at R$70 to R$100 per person.

Hotels such as Pousada O Canto do Francês and Hotel Casarão da Amazônia can provide additional details and make reservations. The latter also offers multiday all-inclusive *fazenda* packages starting at R$1578 per person; check its website for details

Festivals & Events

On the second Sunday in November, Soure has its own **Círio de Nazaré** with a beautiful procession. Hotels can be booked up at this time.

Sleeping & Eating

Hotel Araruna HOTEL $

(☎8793-2481; nelsonmarajo@hotmail.com; Travessa 14 btwn Ruas 7 & 8; s/d R$75/99) Large simple rooms open onto breezy corridors. The rooms show their age, but are reasonably clean and certainly affordable. Quiet and convenient location, next to the tall Cosampa water towers, on the same road that leads to Praia de Araruna and Praia Barra Velha.

Pousada Restaurante Ilha Bela POUSADA $

(☎3741-1313; www.pousadailhabelasoure.com.br; Rua 1 at Travessa 13; s/d/q R$100/150/220; ❄📶) A short distance from Soare's ferry dock, this reliable guesthouse and restaurant has spotless rooms with updated amenities and a tasty breakfast served in the airy ground-level eatery. Quads have patios with views of the river. Festivals and other events are sometimes held in the plaza directly in front, and could make sleeping tough if you happen to visit then.

The hotel's **restaurant** (R$20-30; ⏰7am-3pm & 6-11:30pm, closed Tue) serves typical, fresh Marajoara fare.

Pousada O Canto do Francês POUSADA $

(☎3741-1298; http://ocantodofrances.blogspot.com.br; cnr Rua 6 & Travessa 8; s/d R$120/15; ❄📶) Nine spacious attractive suites have whitewashed walls, fine woodwork and comfortable beds. Breakfast is included and lunch and dinner can be ordered, though service is slow. Meals are served in the hotel's shady patio, and are a nice way to meet fellow guests. Quite removed from the center, but a nearby family rents bikes.

★ **Hotel Casarão da Amazônia** HOTEL $$

(☎3741-1988; www.casaraoamazonia.com.br; cnr Rua 4 & Travessa 9; s R$260-299, d R$299-329; ❄📶🏊) Occupying a beautifully restored 19th-century *casarão* (mansion), rooms here have high ceilings, flat-screen TVs and small but stylish bathrooms; some units are oddly narrow, but still comfortable. A newer garden annex has slightly larger rooms, with patios and hammocks. The hotel's large pool is heaven on a hot day, and the restaurant is one of the island's best.

Restaurante Patú Anu BRAZILIAN $

(☎3741-1359; cnr Rua 2 & Travessa 14; mains R$20-35; ⏰7:30am-10pm Mon-Sat, to 3pm Sun) A simple, reliable menu and a convenient location make this a popular eatery among locals, first-timers and repeat visitors alike. Large servings of chicken, beef, fish or shrimp, plus rice and beans.

Café Soare BRAZILIAN, FRENCH $$

(Rua 3 btwn Travessas 14 & 15; mains R$15-45; ⏰6:30pm-10pm Mon-Sat) Run by an earnest French expat, this small but excellent restaurant has just a few tables in its attractive dining area and a few more on the sidewalk. The buffalo steak with Gorgonzola cream sauce is a favorite, plus tasty crepes and mixed salads.

Hotel Casarão da Amazônia INTERNATIONAL $$

(Rua 4 & Travessa 9; R$25-50; ⏰11am-3pm & 7-10pm) It's no surprise that the island's nicest hotel also has its most sophisticated restaurant. It's not easy to attract experienced staff to this culinary hinterland, but the Italian owner's efforts have paid off. The kitchen produces unique dishes, from local specialties to international staples. Excellent service; seating is on a covered terrace.

Shopping

Cerâmica Mbara-yo CERAMICS
(Travessa 20 btwn Ruas 3 & 4) This is the modest shop of ceramicist Carlos Amaral, who combines traditional Aruã and Marajoara ceramic traditions with award-winning results. You can have a short tour of the workshop to see how the pieces are made. Numerous small, affordable pieces are for sale, and each has a particular tale or significance behind it.

Orientation

The streets running parallel to the river are Ruas (with Rua 1 closest to the Rio Paracauari). The perpendicular streets are Travessas, with Travessa 1 closest to the seashore. The main bus and passenger ferry deposits near the corner of Travessa 11 and Rua 1. Motorized canoes shuttle to downtown Salvaterra (R$3) and to the passenger ferry dock (R$2), leaving Soare from a long pier at Travessa 14 and Rua 1.

Information

Banco do Brasil (Rua 3 btwn Travessas 17 & 18; 10am-3pm Mon-Fri) Bank.

Bradesco (Rua 2 btwn Travessas 15 & 16; 10am-3pm Mon-Fri) Bank.

Cyber Gigabyte (Travessa 15 at Rua 2; per hr R$2.50; 8:30am-noon & 3:30-7:30pm Mon-Sat) Wi-fi connection available for the same rate.

Drogaria Big Farm (Rua 4 at Travessa 16; 7am-9pm Mon-Sat, 8am-noon Sun) Pharmacy and mini-mart.

Post Office (Rua 2 btwn Travessas 13 & 14; 9am-noon & 2-5pm Mon-Fri)

Getting There & Away

Edgar Transporte (3741-1763, 9634-0722; edgar-transporte@hotmail.com; Travessa 15 No 935 btwn Ruas 6 & 7; per person R$12) For transport between Camará and Soare, this professionally run shuttle service has modern, air-conditioned shuttles and confirmed reservations for just slightly more than standard service. Boat tickets, including VIP, can be purchased on the shuttle. Reserve one to three days in advance, especially in high season.

Santarém

0XX93 / POP 290,000

Santarém is a very worthwhile stop-off between Manaus and Belém. Although a bit gritty, it has a great tour operator and the waterfront promenade, breezy parks, and several good restaurants and sights. And just a short bus ride away is Alter do Chão, a cool little town with white-sand river beaches and a laid-back backpacker vibe. Both Santarém and Alter do Chão provide easy access to the Floresta Nacional (FLONA) do Tapajós and other jungle and river areas, with great hiking, canoing, wildlife spotting and visits to local communities. And this area is steeped in history, from ancient petroglyphs in nearby Monte Alegre to the boom and bust of Amazonian rubber.

History

The Santarém region has been a hub of human settlement for many thousands of years; some of the oldest remains of human settlement were discovered in Monte Alegre a short distance downstream. A Jesuit mission was established at the meeting of the Tapajós and Amazon rivers in 1661, and officially named Santarém in 1758.

The later history of Santarém was marked by the rubber boom and bust, and a series of gold rushes that started in the 1950s. The economy today is based mainly on soy and hardwoods and, increasingly, on gold and bauxite mining, whose severe environmental impact make them controversial.

Sights

ZooFIT ZOO
(3523-1989; http://zoofit.fit.br; Rua Moema, s/n; adult/child under 10 R$3/free; 8:30am-5pm Tue-Sun) Enclosures are rather desultory at this animal rehabilitation center, but creatures are not intended to stay for long. Friendly guides lead interesting tours (one to two hours), with up-close viewing of pumas, manatees, macaws and more, and occasionally a chance to hold or feed them. Fun for kids, especially. Reachable by taxi or bus.

Museu de Santarém MUSEUM
(Rua do Imperador, Praça Barão de Santarém; admission by donation; 8am-5pm Mon-Fri, 8am-1pm Sat) Housed in a large yellow waterfront mansion, this museum is also known as the Centro Cultural João Fona, after the Pará artist who painted the frescoes on its interior walls.

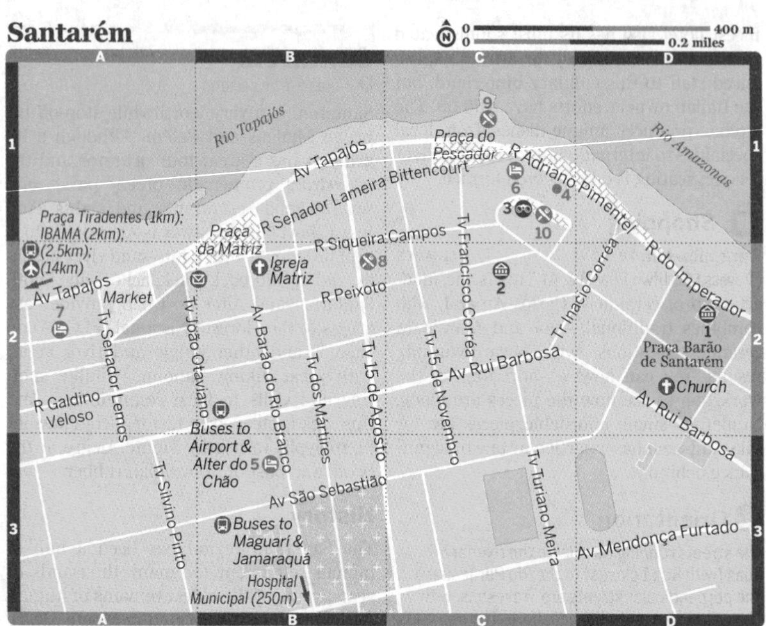

Santarém

Sights

1 Museu de Santarém D2
2 Museu Dica Frazão C2
3 Praça Mirante do Tapajós C1

Activities, Courses & Tours

4 Gil Serique C1

Sleeping

5 Barão Center Hotel B3
6 Brisa Hotel C1
7 Hotel Encontro das Águas A2

Eating

8 Delicias Caseiras B2
9 Massabor C1
10 Mirante Tapiocaria & Crepiocaria C1

It features, among other things, an excellent collection of stone and clay artifacts from the Tapajoara culture that flourished in this area more than 6000 years ago. Major renovation was underway when we passed through.

Museu Dica Frazão MUSEUM

(Peixoto 281; admission by donation; 8am-6pm Mon-Sat) Dona Dica Frazão has spent three-quarters of a century making clothing and fabrics from natural fibers, including grasses and wood pulp. Approaching 100 years old and lately confined to a wheelchair, she's still at it, making artwork and guiding guests through the display room of her creations, including a dress made for a Belgian queen, a tablecloth for a Pope and costumes for the Boi-Bumbá festival.

Praça Mirante do Tapajós VIEWPOINT

This pleasant oval-shaped plaza and vista point has two open-air eateries and nice river views. An observation tower affords an even better view, including of Santarém's own 'meeting of the waters'. Look for a set of stairs just east of Brisa Hotel.

Belterra HISTORIC SITE

(Hwy 163) Henry Ford briefly moved his Fordlândia (p598) operations here in the 1940s and this site, 40km from Santarém, makes for an easy day trip. There's a small museum of Ford-era photos and artifacts, a small grove of rubber trees and several green and white buildings, built for Ford managers; behind one (the Secretária de Educação) is a cement platform with river views. There's a water tower on the main drag, with a still-working industrial whistle that used to summon the workers.

Buses ($2.50, one hour) come and go every 30 to 60 minutes, until 9pm. Some guides, including Gil Serique and Big Tree Adventure Tours, may include a stop here.

Activities

Big Tree Adventure Tours ECOTOUR
(☎9195-3160; www.bigtreeadventuretours.com; per person per day US$110-390) Unique tours combine the natural, historical and commercial aspects of the Amazon. The agency's private 8-sq-km rainforest plot has good hiking and swimming; getting there, you'll drive past vast soy plantations – a macabre yet arresting sight. Multiday tours continue to Fordlândia, with visits to waterfalls and animal-rich floodplains. Led by the agency's engaging, knowledgeable and multilingual manager.

Big Tree is a branch of Zero Impact Brazil, an American-owned company that gathers the leftover parts of trees cut down by developers and re-sells them for specialty use, from pool cues to high-end guitars. Ask about visiting ZIB's sawmill in Santarém, with its incredible array of Amazonian wood such as 'tiger wood' and 'purpleheart'.

Festivals

The patron saint of fisherfolk, São Pedro, is honored on June 29, when boats decorated with flags and flowers sail in procession before the city.

Sleeping

Hotel Encontro das Águas HOTEL $
(☎3522-1287; encontrodasaguashotel@hotmail.com; 24 de Octubro 808; s R$95, d $R115-130; ❄📶) Large clean rooms have OK beds, fairly modern bathrooms and an affordable price, making them popular with tourists, families and traveling businesspeople alike. Friendly attentive service, and a convenient location just west of the market. Some rooms have large windows with river views and nice natural light.

Brisa Hotel HOTEL $
(☎3522-1018; brisahotel@hotmail.com; Bittencourt 5; s/d R$80/100; ❄📶) Rooms here are simple, clean and good value – and so, unfortunately, often full. The narrow hallway and cramped quarters are a bit claustrophobic, but the location is ideal, with restaurants and the waterfront promenade right in front, and Praça Mirante behind

★ **Tapajós Center Hotel** HOTEL $$
(☎3522-5353; www.tapajoscenterhotel.com.br; Avenida Tapajós 1827; s/d/tr R$120/170/200, superior R$170/220/250; P❄📶) Spacious rooms have warm accents, firm beds, modern TVs and air-conditioning, spotless bathrooms and (best of all) large verandas with bracing views of the river. The hotel's main drawback is that it's a good mile (1.5km) from the center of town; the waterfront can be a pleasant (albeit hot) walk and taxis are plentiful when you feel like a ride.

Barão Center Hotel HOTEL $$
(☎3064-9950; www.baraocenterhotel.com; Av Barão do Rio Branco; r R$245-275; ❄@📶) This upscale hotel appeals to business people connected to the massive ports just outside town. The rooms are comfortable and well equipped (flat-screen TV, air-con, key-card entry), though curiously lacking in windows. Fortunately, you can always escape to the rooftop restaurant, which has a terrific view of the city and river. Discount for paying in cash.

Eating

★ **Restaurante Piracema** BRAZILIAN $
(☎3522-7461; www.restaurantepiracema.com.br; Av Mendonca Furtado 73; R$20-45; ⏲11am-11:30pm Tues-Sat, until 3pm Sun) Considered by many to be the best restaurant in town, Piracema uses regional ingredients and flavors but serves dishes you'll find nowhere else. The signature dish is the *peixe á Piracema*, a spherical construction of layered smoked pirarucú (a freshwater fish), banana and cheese – strange but delicious, and large enough for two.

Massabor PIZZA $
(☎3522-0509; Av Tapajós; pizza & pasta R$7-30; ⏲5-11pm) Occupying a raised pier perched high over the water, this popular open-air restaurant opposite Praça do Pescador has nice breezes and views of the river, where you can often spot dolphins. The menu has mostly pizza and pasta.

Delicias Caseiras CAFETERIA $
(Travessa 15 de Agosto; dishes R$10; ⏲lunch Mon-Sat) Budget travelers rejoice: for just R$13 you can pile as much grub on your plate as humanly possible. Alas, main dishes are doled out by hairnetted ladies behind the warming trays, but portions are still generous and they often include some less-common options such as tongue and chicken patties.

Mirante Tapiocaria & Crepiocaria BRAZILIAN
(Praça Mirante do Tapajós; ⏲6-10:30pm) You've seen tapioca at your hotel breakfast – those spongy white crepes served with butter – but never like the creations served at this popular outdoor kiosk. Run by the same family as Restaurante Piracema (one of Santarém's best), tapiocas here come in all shapes and

flavors, from sweet to savory, served at tables set up on the plaza with nice river views.

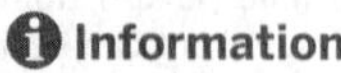

Information

EMERGENCY

Ambulance (☎192)

Police (☎190)

INTERNET ACCESS

Amazon's Star Cyber (Av Tapajós; per hr R$4; ⏰8am-7pm Mon-Fri, 8am-4pm Sat)

LAUNDRY

Lavandería Estoril (☎3523-1329; Travessa Turiano Meira 167; wash & dry per kg R$18, plus iron per kg $23; ⏰8am-6pm Mon-Sat) Same-day service if you drop off clothes in the morning.

MEDICAL SERVICES

Hospital Municipal (cnr Av Presidente Vargas & Av Barão do Rio Branco) Has an emergency room.

MONEY

Bradesco (Av Rui Barbosa; ⏰9am-3pm Mon-Fri)

POST

Main Post Office (Siqueira Campos; ⏰9am-5pm Mon-Fri)

TRAVEL AGENCIES

Santarém Tur (☎3522-4847; www.santarem tur.com.br; Adriano Pimentel 44; ⏰8am-6pm Mon-Fri, to noon Sat) Plane tickets and tour packages, including city tours, day trips to Alter do Chão by boat or car, and overnight riverboat tours to FLONA. Friendly and helpful staff.

Getting There & Away

AIR

All flights from Santarém go through Manaus or Belém.

Azul (☎3523-3287, 4003-1118; www.voeazul.com.br)

GOL (☎3522-3386, 0800-704-0465; www.voegol.com.br)

MAP (☎3529-0308, in Manaus 092-2125-5000; www.voemap.com.br)

TAM (☎3523-9744, 4002-5700; www.tam.com.br)

BOAT

There are two official ports for passenger boats, though an explosion of river traffic means virtually the entire waterfront can be crowded with boats. Look for large signs or banners indicating each boat's destination and departure times. Be aware that times listed here are subject to change.

The main port, Docas do Pará, is located 2.5km west of the center. There you can catch a slow boat to Belém (hammock R$180, double cabin R$800, 48 hours) at 11am Friday to Monday, which stops at Monte Alegre (hammock R$40, five to seven hours) along the way; to Manaus (hammock R$150, double cabin R$600, 40 to 48 hours) at noon Monday to Saturday, with a stop at Parantins (hammock R$70, 20 hours); or to Fordlândia (R$45; 12 to 15 hours) at 4pm Monday to Saturday and 2pm Sunday – take the Itaituba boat. Meals are not included, but can be purchased onboard. Buy your ticket in advance, especially in high season, to be sure you get a spot. Be aware you can only board during designated time slots: 6am to 7am, 10am to 10:30am, noon to 12:15pm, and 1pm to 2pm.

Another port, Praça Tiradentes, is located 1km west of the center on Av Tapajós and is used for boats to less-common destinations, including Macapá (hammock R$140 including meals, 36 hours, 6pm daily), Monte Alegre (hammock R$40, five to seven hours; take the 6pm Macapá boat), and Alenquer (hammock R$30, seven hours, 8pm Sunday to Friday, noon Saturday).

For Fordlândia and Monte Alegre, consider taking *a lancha rápida* (speedboat) offering comfortable airplane-style seating and half the travel time for just a few dollars more. Various independently owned boats use three nearly side-by-side piers just east of Praça Tiradentes; signs indicate which boat leaves on a given day. Altogether, there are daily departures for Fordlândia (R$54, 5 hours, 1pm) and Monte Alegre (R$50, 3 hours, 4pm, plus 9am Tuesday and Saturday).

BUS

The **bus station** (☎3523-4940) is 2.5km west of town. **Transbrasiliana** (☎3522-1342) has daily services to Rurópolis, Itaituba, Cuiabá and Belém, but the roads are extremely unreliable in the rainy season.

Buses to Alter do Chão (R$2.50, 60 minutes) stop on Av Rui Barbosa near Av Barão do Rio Branco roughly every hour between 5am and 10:30pm (until 6:30pm on Sundays).

Getting Around

The airport is 14km west of the city center. Buses (R$2.25, 30 minutes) run to the city every half-hour or so between 6:15am and 6:45pm on weekdays. Services are much reduced on weekends; ask at the airport info kiosk for the next departure time. The bus stop is to the right leaving the terminal doors. Taxis into town officially cost R$60, but you can sometimes get a better price by walking to the bus stop and waiting for an empty cab to pass. Going to the airport, catch the 'Aeroporto' (but not 'Aeroporto Velho') on Av Rui Barbosa near Av Barão do Rio Branco, between 5:25am and 6:15pm Monday to Friday, and 6:40am and 5:45pm on Saturday. There are no direct buses from the airport to Alter do Chão; a taxi there costs R$100.

If arriving by boat, 'Orla Fluvial' minibuses (R$2.25) shuttle between the city center and Docas do Pará every 20 to 30 minutes until 7pm. A taxi makes the same trip for R$15, and moto-taxis for R$4. It's possible to catch the bus to Alter do Chão by walking or cabbing three long blocks straight up from Docas do Pará to Av São Sebastião. (Look for a Banco do Brasil on the opposite corner; consider taking out cash there as the ATMs are unreliable in Alter do Chão.) Be aware the bus is often full by the time it reaches that stop, so you may have to stand.

Moto-taxis are the best way, beyond walking, to get around town. Most trips cost R$4.

Floresta Nacional (FLONA) do Tapajós

Behemoth samaúma trees, with trunks too big for even 20 people to stretch their arms around, are a highlight of this 5440-sq-km reserve on the east side of the Rio Tapajós. Within the reserve, numerous small communities live primarily by rubber tapping, fishing and gathering Brazil nuts. Several also have modest ecotourism initiatives, and a trip here is a unique way to experience not just the forest, but also village life within it.

Around Santarém

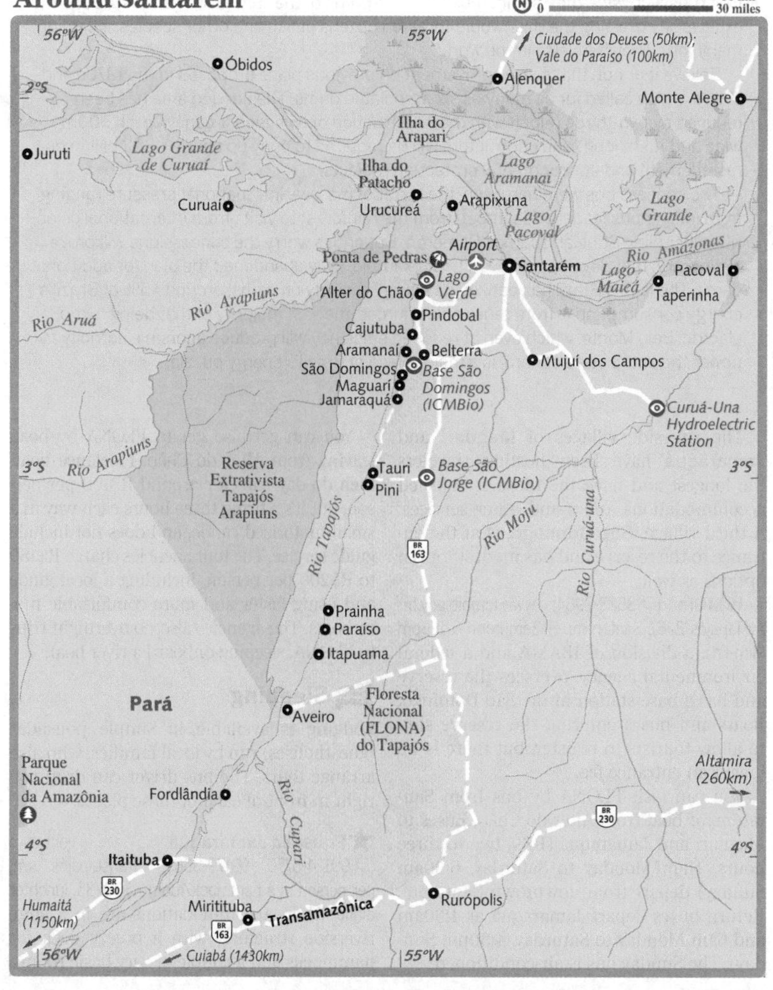

THE BELO MONTE DAM

Construction officially began in 2011 on the Belo Monte Dam on the Rio Xingu in southern Pará, and is scheduled to be completed in 2019. The fight over the controversial project was bitter and protracted, and, this being Brazil, there's always the chance for disruption and delay. If and when completed, the dam (actually a trio of dams) would be the world's third-largest hydroelectric complex, reportedly capable of generating 11,000 megawatts, or enough to power 23 million homes. But critics point out that fluctuations in river flow mean the dam is unlikely to average more than 40% capacity, and could drop to under 10%. Subtracting from that the energy lost in the thousands of kilometers of transmission lines, and the fact that dams in the Amazon are notorious for actually emitting methane (due to decomposition of flooded rainforest) and Belo Monte could well rank as the world's most inefficient power-generating dam.

Then there's the impact on the forest, the river and the people living there: at least 450 sq km of forest would be flooded, forcing the relocation of around 12,000 people. A 100km stretch of the mighty Xingu River would essentially dry up, including the part that runs alongside the Paquiçamba territory, home of the Juruna indigenous group. And experts say draining the river would threaten dozens of fish and other species, including many found nowhere else in the world.

Believe it or not, that's an improvement on previous plans proposed in the 1970s and 1990s, which called for as many as six associated dams. The flooded area has been reduced by two-thirds (albeit with the construction of twin feeder canals, each 500m wide and 12km long) and contractors will be required to pony up nearly US$2 billion on resettlement and environmental protection projects.

The concessions were hard won, the result of massive international pressure ranging from indigenous leaders decamped from the rainforest to visits from international celebrities including Sting and James Cameron. But critics worry the concessions will prove temporary; that developers haven't, for example, truly abandoned the plan for additional dams. The fact is Brazil has banked its energy security on dams; around 45% of Brazil's energy consumption is from renewable sources, the vast majority of that being hydroelectric. Belo Monte, which even at reduced efficiency will produce enough electricity to power the entire state of Pará, is a major piece of Brazil's energy puzzle.

The riverside villages of **Maguarí** and **Jamaraquá** have been hosting travelers the longest and have the most established accommodations, tours and other services. A third village, **São Domingo**, is at the entrance to the reserve and has modest tourist options as well.

ICMBio (☎3523-2964; www.icmbio.gov.br; Av Tapajós 2267, Santarém; ⏲8am-noon & 2-6pm Mon-Fri), a division of IBAMA and a federal environmental agency, oversees the reserve and has a base station in the São Domingo. Boats and buses entering the reserve stop to allow tourists to register, but there is no longer an entrance fee.

You can visit FLONA by bus from Santarém, or boat from Alter do Chão. Buses to Maguarí and Jamaraquá (R$9, two to three hours, 11am Monday to Saturday, 6:30am Sunday) depart from downtown Santarém. Return buses depart Jamaraquá at 4:30am and 6am Monday to Saturday, 4:30pm Sunday). The Sunday bus is air-conditioned.

You can get also get to FLONA by boat, leaving from Alter do Chão. Freelance boatmen do day trips for around R$100 per person, but it's a tiring three hours each way in a small motorized canoe, and does not include guide service. The tour agencies charge R$180 to R$200 per person, including a local guide and using faster and more comfortable motorboats. The agencies also do overnight trips to FLONA, sleeping onboard a river boat.

Sleeping

Lodging is available in simple pousadas (guesthouses) run by local families, who also arrange tours. The bus driver can drop you right in front of each of these places.

★ **Pousada Jamaraquá** POUSADA $
(☎99124-5750, 99179-9569; Transtapajós s/n; per person in a hammock/room R$30/35, lunch or dinner R$25) Accommodations are in a large riverside structure, with a breezy deck for hammocks and a couple of very basic rooms.

There's a nice sandy beach when the water's low, and you can swim from the deck when it's high. On the downside, the bathrooms are located back at the main house, about 100m away. Friendly service; the bus stops in front.

Pousada Floresta do Tapajós POUSADA **$**
(☎99113-8458; Transtapajós s/n; per person R$45) Better known as 'Pousada de Bata', for its austere and highly knowledgeable owner and main tour guide, this guesthouse has an airy new hammock area, decent bathrooms and a friendly family atmosphere. Located in a quiet leafy plot about 500m past the main village center; if arriving by bus, ask the driver to drop you here.

Pousada Maguary POUSADA **$**
(☎99115-9540; Transtapajós s/n; incl breakfast & lunch R$50) You feel like part of the family here, and no wonder: the warm elderly owners were among the first in FLONA to open their home to community tourism. Unfortunately, the dim low-ceiling hammock area and run-down toilets make this a less appealing option for many visitors.

Alter do Chão

☎0XX93 / POP 7800

Alter do Chão, 33km west of Santarém, is best known for its Ilha do Amor (Island of Love), a picturesque island ringed by a white sand beach directly in front of town. The island is especially striking when the water is low (August to December) and beach restaurants and cool calm water make it a great place to chill out. In high water, the island is much smaller and sometimes completely submerged.

But Alter do Chão is much more than a beach town. The lagoon it fronts (Lago Verde) is home to myriad animals and can be explored by canoe or stand-up paddle. It's also the departure point for terrific boat tours to nearby forest reserves and isolated communities, and boasts one of the best indigenous art stores in the Amazon region.

Sights & Activities

Lago Verde

This huge three-fingered lake is surrounded by forest, and has places to swim, snorkel with ornamental fish, and spot birds and animals (including a resident family of monkeys). Tour agencies do good **boat tours** (per person R$50 to R$75, two to three hours, two to six people) or you can hire one of the yellow-shirted freelance boatmen on the waterfront; the latter are cheaper, but may not have the same service or equipment that agencies do.

Ponta de Cururú

Most afternoons, large numbers of pink and grey dolphins congregate just offshore from this sandy point near the mouth of the Rio Tapajós for an evening snack. It's a great place to go for sunsets and dolphin-spotting, and many guides combine tours of Lago Verde or Canal do Jarí with a stop here.

Adventure Sports

Adventure sports are a natural fit for many visitors here, and Alter do Chão offers plenty of options, including stand-up paddleboarding (SUP), windsurfing, kayaking, mountain biking and tree climbing (*arbolismo* in Portugese). Ask at Mãe Natureza (p599), **Espaço Alter do Chão** (☎9122-9643; ⏱vary) or Gil Serique (p599) for prices and availability.

Beaches

When the water is low, you can wade from the waterfront to **Ilha do Amor**. Otherwise, rowboats will take you across for R$4 per person. A bevy of shacks serve food and drinks year-round, and have chairs set up along the water's edge. Walk a few blocks west on the waterfront promenade to reach **Praia do Cajueiro**, another nice beach, wrapping clear around to the Tapajós river. Beaches further afield are best reached in a car or on a beach-hopping tour, including **Pindobal** (8km), **Cajutuba** (16km), **Aramanai** (26km) and **Ponta de Pedras** (28km). These beaches are quite built up with waterfront restaurants; if you're looking for an isolated beach experience, talk to a tour agency.

Tours

Besides short trips around Alter do Chão (Lago Verde, Ponta do Cururú,

> **WATCH YOUR STEP**
>
> Stingrays are a concern around Ilha do Amor, Lago Verde and Tapajós river, especially in the afternoon and evening. Fortunately they're very skittish, so it's safe to swim and wade where other people are doing the same. It's also a good idea to shuffle your feet whenever entering and exiting the water (here or anywhere in the Amazon); this kicks up a cloud of sand in front of you and scares rays away.

WORTH A TRIP

FORDLÂNDIA

History buffs will enjoy a trip to Fordlândia, where you can explore the remains of Henry Ford's ill-fated Amazonian enterprise. You can wander cavernous factories, climb the town's iconic 36-meter-high water tower, and more. That said, it's a long way to go (and come back) for just a half-day of sights – travelers short on time or lacking a burning interest in early-20th-century industrial history may consider giving it a pass.

Rubber was (and is) absolutely essential to the manufacture of automobiles – used in everything from gaskets to tires. In the early 1900s, Britain had a near monopoly on the world's rubber supply, having smuggled rubber-tree seeds out of the Amazon and grown them, with great success, in plantations in Asia. Fordlândia, founded in 1928, was Henry Ford's attempt to establish his own source of rubber. But in typical Ford fashion, the project was as much sociological as it was economic or horticultural. Ford forbade workers from drinking, smoking or using prostitutes (which they circumvented by paddling out to barges moored offshore). He insisted American-style homes and dormitories be built, but their thick walls and asbestos roofs turned them into ovens. Worst of all, virtually no one sent from company headquarters in Dearborn, Michigan, had experience with the Amazon or its trees; tens of thousands of rubber trees were planted only to die from blight because they'd been planted too close together. (In the wild, rubber trees are always widely spaced.) Operations were moved briefly to Belterra (which can be visited as a day trip from Santarém) but in 1945, with synthetic rubber rapidly supplanting the natural product, the company sold Fordlândia back to Brazil for a loss, in today's dollars, of over $200 million. Ford himself never visited.

Today, Fordlândia is a rather downbeat town, and surprisingly little has been done to preserve or promote the town's unique history. Two of the main sights are visible right from the pier: the *caixa de água* (water tower), which you can climb via a narrow ladder, and two huge factories, known locally as *casonas* (big houses) filled with abandoned machinery, vehicles and random parts, many stamped 'Michigan'. Further afield are Fordlândia's cemetery, the collapsed remains of the town's once-grand hospital, and 'Vila Americana' a row of American-style houses, some of which can be visited.

The boat schedules are such that you'll need to stay at least a night. **Pousada Americana** (☎3505-3073; www.pousada-americana.blogspot.com; Av Boa Vista 31; s/d R$100/120) has spacious rooms, sparkling bathrooms, and air-con in most units. A newly built annex has a large patio with hammocks, and the property's fruit trees are home to numerous birds, including several talkative parrots. From the ferry, bear left 500m.The owners also happen to be Fordlândia's go-to tour guides. A four-hour tour, including vehicle, is R$60 to R$100 per group.

From Santarém, there are daily departures for Fordlândia by speedboat (R$54, five hours, 1pm) and slow boat (R$45, 12 to 15 hours, 4pm Monday to Saturday, 2pm Sunday; take the Itaituba boat). Returning, the speedboat passes by at 2pm to 3pm, and the slow boat around 8pm to 10pm (earlier on Sundays). You'll enjoy nice views of the verdant forest, especially going upriver when the boat hugs the shore.

beach-hopping) there are some great options for longer multiday tours. These include canoeing the animal-rich **Canal do Jarí**, hiking and visiting villages in **Floresta Nacional (FLONA) do Tapajós** and the **Reserva Extrativista (RESEX) Tapajós-Arapiuns**, river trips up the **Rio Arapiuns** and adventure routes into the **Parque Nacional da Amazônia**. Discuss details with tour agencies in town; prices range from R$180 to $300 per person per day, all-inclusive.

Areia Branca Ecotour ECOTOUR
(☎99121-5646, 3527-1386; www.areiabrancaecotour.com.br; Orla Fluvial; ⏲8am-noon & 2-7pm Mon-Fri, to 1pm Sat & Sun) Located on the waterfront a short distance from the plaza, this small competent agency is run by friendly multilingual siblings from Alter do Chão. Tours are available to all the standard destinations, but the specialty here are multiday packages to less-visited communities such as Santi in RESEX Tapajós-Arapiuns and Marituba and Bregança in FLONA Tapajós. Dry-season tours are especially rewarding.

Mãe Natureza ECOTOUR

(☎99131-9870, 3527-1264; www.maenatureza ecoturismo.com.br; Praça 7 de Setembro; ⏲8:30am-1pm & 4-11pm) A reliable and experienced agency run by genial Argentinean expats. Be sure to ask about weeklong adventure tours to remote indigenous areas and the Brinco das Moças waterfall, deep in RESEX Tapajós-Arapiuns. Day trips including tree-climbing, kite-surfing, or stand-up paddleboarding can also be arranged.

Gil Serique ECOTOUR

(☎9115-8111; www.gilserique.com; Av Copacabana 45 at PA-457; per person per day from R$100) Gil is a lithe and groovy guy, a teller of tales, and one of the area's top naturalists. Born and raised nearby, Gil's tours are part history, ecology and family lore, related with infectious enthusiasm and near-perfect English. Visits to Lago Maicá, a gorgeous floodplain teeming with birds and other wildlife, are especially memorable. Pricier than others, but worth it.

From the bus drop-off, walk down to the plaza and bear right along the waterfront. It's the house at the end, painted with travel-related logos. Gil can often offer discount lodging, airport pickup and other help to clients; inquire in advance.

Festivals

The **Festa do Çairé** in the second week of September is the major folkloric event in western Pará. The Çairé is a standard held aloft to lead a flower-bedecked procession; its origins may go back to symbols used by early missionaries to help convert *índios* (indigenous groups).

Sleeping

★ **Pousada do Tapajós Hostel** HOSTEL, INN $

(☎99210-2166; pousadatapajos.com.br; Rua Lauro Sodré 100; dm R$50, d/tr/q R$140/165/195; ❄📶) Five blocks west of the center, dorms here are clean and comfortable, though a bit cramped, with sturdy bunks and large lockers. Private rooms are sparkling, modern and well removed from the dorms. Ample breakfast, open kitchen, large backyard with hammocks. Guests (and even some non-guests) often get together over breakfast to book excursions. Spotty wi-fi.

Albergue da Floresta HOSTEL, POUSADA $

(☎99209-5656; www.alberguedafloresta-alterdo chao.blogspot.com; Travessa Antônio Pedrosa s/n; hammock R$30, dm $50, cabin s R$120, d R$170-200) This relaxed backpacker favorite has a spacious hammock area, dorms and colorful wood cabins with fans and private bathrooms; breakfast available for R$20 and there's an outdoor kitchen. Nestled in the trees east of the center; follow the signs past Espaço Alter do Chão up a leafy dirt road. Angolan capoeira classes, bike and kayak rental.

Pousada do Mingote HOTEL $

(☎3527-1158; www.pousadadomingote.com.br; Travessa Antônio A Lobato s/n; s R$100-120, d R$160-180; ❄) Standard rooms at this longtime hotel are plain and rather dark, some still sporting old-school air-conditioners. Newer superior rooms have air-con, basin sinks and generally more space and light. Either way, the location can't be beat, just a half-block down from the bus stop, and a half-block up from the plaza.

Pousada Vila Da Praia HOTEL $$

(☎9197-7214, 3529-1909; http://viladapraiapou sada.blogspot.com; PA-457 at Av Copacabana; s/d R$130/170; ❄) Friendly service, simple but comfortable rooms, and a great location make this a recommendable option. Rooms vary considerably; some are oddly small, others sleep up to six; all come with TVs, air-conditioning and a substantial breakfast, served in an open-air dining area. Just a block from the waterfront.

Eating

Tribal BRAZILIAN $

(Travessa Antônio Lobato; dishes R$10-36; ⏲11am-11pm) *Churrasco* plates come with a spear of steak, sausage, chicken and tongue, while well-prepared fish dishes serve two easily, with potato salad to spare. This spacious two-floor open-air dining area is located a block and a half up from the plaza, on the opposite side of Rua Dom Macedo.

Siria VEGETARIAN $

(Travessa Agostinho Lobato s/n; dish R$20; ⏲lunch & dinner; 🖉) The lovely chef-owner prepares just one vegan dish per sitting, served as a *prato feito* (plate of the day) and announced on a sandwich board in front. From chickpea omelets to vegetable tarts, count on it being outstanding, served with brown rice, fresh salad and creative drinks, like hibiscus and *maracujá* (passion fruit) iced tea, plus dessert. Colorful outdoor dining area, occasional live music and movies.

Arco-Iris da Amazônia BRAZILIAN $$

(☎3527-1182; arcoirisdaamazonia@bol.com.br; Praça 7 de Setembro; R$18-45; ⏲6-11pm, closed

WORTH A TRIP

MONTE ALEGRE

The hot sandstone hills behind Monte Alegre (population 56,500), about 120km downstream from Santarém, are dotted with caves and bizarre rock outcroppings. They, in turn, are adorned with dozens of rock paintings from ancient Amazonians. The paintings are red, yellow and brown, and depict human and animal figures, handprints and geometric designs. Studies conducted in the 1990s by pioneering archaeologist Anna Roosevelt, a great-granddaughter of Theodore Roosevelt, suggest the caves at Monte Alegre were occupied from 10,900 to as much as 13,150 years ago – thousands of years earlier than previously thought. (Artifacts in Chile and central Brazil have returned similar dates.) This caused quite a ruckus and forced archaeologists to rethink when and how ancient people first arrived in South America. Most still believe the first migrants arrived from Asia across the Bering Strait, but rather than spreading gradually southward from there, it appears at least some Paleoindian groups made their way to Central and South America fairly quickly, probably using boats and hugging the coastline, reaching as far south as Patagonia in just a few thousand years (or less), instead of several thousand. From those southbound groups, splinter parties must have cut eastward and inland (or even turned the corner at Tierra del Fuego), eventually populating the Amazon and the rest of the interior.

Monte Alegre's cave paintings are quite accessible from Santarém. The best-known site is Serra do Paituna, with the stunning Pedra Pintada cavern, where Roosevelt's primary excavations took place, and a distintive ridgetop rock formation called Pedra do Pilão. Two other sites, Serra do Ererê and Serra de Itauajuri, are harder to reach (especially in rainy season) but have excellent paintings as well. All three require a vehicle and guide (the area was recently designated a state park), and include moderately strenuous hiking. Bring sturdy shoes and plenty of water.

Nelsí Sadeck (☎3533-1430, 9653-4785; nelsi.sadeck@gmail.com; Rua do Jaquara 320) is an amiable former teacher who assisted Roosevelt's excavations, and is Monte Alegre's go-to guide. Tours are R$150 to R$200 per day (up to four people) and use of a truck to runs R$300 per day. There's a daily speedboat and slow boat service from Santarém, but the schedule is such you'll need to stay two or more nights to have sufficient time; **Hotel Shekinah** (☎3533-1489; www.hotelshekinah.com.br; Rua 7 de Setembro 74; s/d R$70/100; P ❄ 📶 🏊) is a reliable option.

Tue) Art and jewelry store by day, fine restaurant by night. One of three side-by-side restaurants serving dinner and drinks right on the plaza, the Arco-Iris' dishes are expertly prepared with fresh sophisticated flavors, from lamb to crepes to hamburgers. Portions are on the small side, but there's definitely a quality over quantity argument to be made here. Prompt, friendly service.

Farol da Ilha BRAZILIAN **$$**
(Orla Fluvial s/n; dishes R$17-30; ⏰11am-5pm Mon, to 10pm Thu-Sun, closed Tue & Wed) Travelers tend to miss this low-key waterfront restaurant, despite it having first-rate fish meals and outstanding river and island vistas from its 2nd-floor dining area. Most dishes serve two people, and are priced accordingly. Solo diners can order cheaper chicken dishes or just come for drinks and the view.

☆ Entertainment

★**Epaço Alter do Chão** LIVE MUSIC
(☎9122-9643; www.espacoalter.com.br; end of PA-457; cover from R$14; ⏰8am-1am Tue-Sat; 📶) There's always something worth seeing at this cool music-culture-restaurant space at the east end of the waterfront promenade. There's live *carimbó* most Saturday nights, and guest bands play rock, *forró*, samba, reggae and more; check Facebook or the chalk board out front for the latest. Meals and drinks are tasty, too, though service can be slow. Free wi-fi.

Shopping

★**Araribá Cultura Indígena** HANDICRAFTS
(☎3527-1324; www.araribah.com.br; Travessa Antônio Lobato; ⏰9am-9pm) Arguably the best indigenous art store in the Amazon, with items ranging from inexpensive necklaces to museum-quality masks and ceremonial costumes, and representing communities

throughout the Amazon basin. Shipping available; credit cards accepted.

Orientation

The highway to Alter do Chão is PA-457; the bus from Santarém stops on the corner of Rua Dom Macedo Costa and Travessa Antônio A Lobato, kitty-corner from Araribá Cultura Indígena store. It's a good place to get off – pretty much everyone does – just a block from Praça 7 de Setembro, the main square, and within walking distance of most lodging options.

Information

Accessing money and the internet can be a real headache in Alter do Chão. There were no ATMs that accepted foreign cards when we last visited – better to bring cash from Santarém – and wi-fi connections at hotels were frustratingly poor. There's a small cyber cafe at **Cuicera Ecotour** (Rua Dom Macedo s/n; per hr R$4; 8am-8:30 Mon-Fri, to 6pm Sat) just across PA-457, the main road into town. The **post office** (PA-457 at Rua Dom Macedo Costa; 9am-noon, 2-5pm Mon-Fri) and **pharmacy** (3527-1105; PA-457; 9am-8pm) are a few blocks up from the waterfront. Most hotels accept credit cards, but not all.

Getting There & Away

Buses from Alter do Chão to Santarém (R$2.50, one hour) depart hourly from 5:30am to 10pm, except on Sunday, when services end around 6pm. Catch the bus a block up from Praça 7 de Setembro, at the corner of Rua Dom Macedo Costa and Travessa Antônio A Lobato. There is no bus to the airport from Alter do Chão, unfortunately. It's possible to take the bus as far as the airport turnoff, and wait for the airport bus from Santarém to pass, usually within 30 to 60 minutes. Otherwise, a taxi to the airport (or to Santarém or the riverboat ports) costs a painful R$90.

TOCANTINS

The state of Tocantins was created in 1989 from what was previously the northern half of Goiás. It's in a transition zone between the Amazon rainforest to the north and the cerrado (savanna) in the southeast. This makes for plenty of outdoor opportunities, and the state is making a concerted effort to portray itself as Brazil's next ecotourism hot spot. It certainly has the potential, from easy-to-reach hiking and waterfalls around Taquarussú to vast protected areas like Parque Estadual do Jalapão and Ilha do Bananal, a Pantanal-like wetland.

Palmas

0XX63 / POP 231,000

Thirty years ago, the broad valley bisected by the Rio Tocantins held just a scattering of rural *fazendas* (ranches). Starting in 1989, a new state capital was built from scratch, and construction, state government and economic incentives brought thousands of Brazilians to this unlikely landscape, 1000km north of Brasília and 1600km south of Belém. The city itself is sure to strike most first-timers as sterile and shadeless, but it has a way of growing on you, with a number of good outdoorsy options nearby.

Sights & Activities

Most of the sights of interest are in **Praça Girossóis**, purportedly the second-largest municipal square in the world after the Red Square in Moscow.

Palacio Araguaia PALACE

(3218-1000; 8am-6pm) FREE Built on the only hill in town, the Palacio Araguaia, the state capitol building, looks over the plaza and Palmas itself. The lobby has huge colorful mosaics and, in one corner, an impressive scale model of Praça Girossóis. No shorts or tank tops; 2nd floor closed on weekends.

Memorial Coluna Prestes MEMORIAL

(Praça Girossóis; 8am-6pm Tue-Sun) FREE Housed in a curious white, tubular structure near Palacio Araguaia, the Memorial Coluna Prestes tells the life story of Captain Luis Carlos Prestes, who led 1500 rebel soldiers against the military dictatorship in 1924. The march lasted three years and covered 25,000km, and is credited with helping bring democracy to Brazil, especially its long-isolated interior.

Tours

Jalapão Extremo ECOTOUR

(99968-1166, 3322-7990; www.jalapaoextremo.com.br; Jalapao Eco Tour, 409 Norte, AL 29, Lote 13, Plano Diretor Norte) This youthful and adventurous agency offers tours of Jalapão State Park, Taquarussu and around, from one to seven days (R$150 to R$3000 per person), including visiting remote waterfalls and touring Jalapão's famous sand dunes. Travel by 4WD vans; lodging includes camping and modest hotels. Excellent guides, mostly Brazilian clientele. The extreme heat and strenuous excursions may prove challenging for some. A sister agency, Jalapão Eco Tour, which also has an office in Palmas, may handle some logistics.

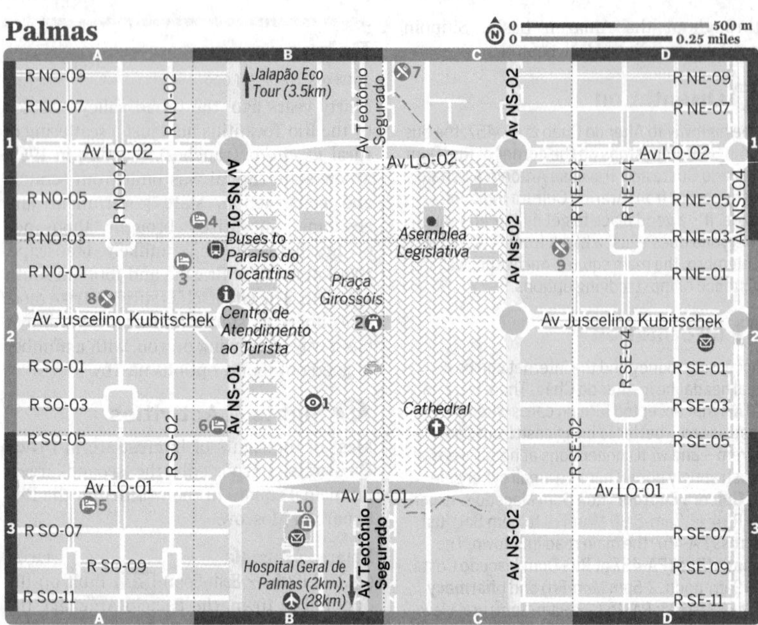

Palmas

Sights

1 Memorial Coluna Prestes B2
2 Palacio Araguaia B2

Sleeping

3 Eduardu's Hotel A2
4 Hotel Serra Azul B1
5 Pousada das Artes Hotel A3
6 Pousada dos Girassóis B2

Eating

7 Churrascaría Portal do Sul C1
8 Don Vergilio A2
9 Restaurante Seara C2

Shopping

10 Palmas Shopping B3

Sleeping

Hotel Serra Azul HOTEL $

(3215-1505; Rua NO-03; s/d R$110/130;) Clean rooms, affordable prices and convenient location make this Palmas' best budget option. Rooms are small with few frills, but face onto a sunny courtyard with a quaint dining room where breakfast is served. Close to the bus stop for those who don't have a car, and offering secure parking for those who do.

Eduardu's Hotel HOTEL $$

(3215-9300; http://hoteleduardus.com.br; cnr Ruas NO-01 & NO-02; s/d standard R$149/195, deluxe R$210/265;) Whatever you do, don't miss the rooftop pool and patio, which have a terrific view of the city and lake. Large rooms have fresh paint and modern appointments; deluxe rooms are larger, but standards have balconies. Street parking only.

Pousada dos Girassóis HOTEL $$

(3219-4500; www.pousadadosgirassois.com.br; Av NS-01; weekdays d R$291, weekends R$175-246;) Rooms at this longtime favorite have details such as modern paintings, glass showers and a writing desk with a leather chair. Large windows and private verandas make some units feel more spacious. The pool area is oddly small and uninviting. Up to 30% discount on weekends.

Pousada das Artes Hotel HOTEL $$

(3219-1500; http://arteshotel.com.br; 103 Sul Av, LO-01 78; s/d R$256/274;) This well-located upscale hotel lives up to its name with artful rooms and unique architecture. Both are the handiwork of architect and artist Graça Arnús, who designed the building and painted the intriguing artworks in the guest rooms and common areas. Accommodations are comfortable and modern, and the small pool a welcome bonus. The hotel hosts occasional art expositions.

Eating

Don Vergilio PIZZA $
(☎3212-1400; www.domvergilio.com.br; Av Juscelino Kubitscheck 159; mains R$18-45, per kg R$50-52; ⏱11am-2:30pm & 6pm-midnight Mon-Sat, 6pm-midnight Sun) Popular pizzeria and per-kilo spot, open late for those nighttime munchies. Pizzas have thick roped crusts and come in varieties both usual (Margherita) and not-so-usual (strogonoff; banana). There also are calzones, salads and an ample lunchtime buffet, including homemade pastas.

Restaurante Seara BUFFET $
(Rua NE-03 btwn Av NS-02 and Rua NE-02; per kg R$32; ⏱11am-3pm Mon-Sat) Large bustling per-kilo place that's popular with workers at nearby government offices. Friendly service and well-prepared food, but best of all it's open until 3pm, when it seems every other self-service restaurant is dead and gone by 2pm.

Churrascaría Portal do Sul BRAZILIAN $$
(☎3225-8744; 102 Norte, Conj. 01, Lote 04; rodízio R$55.50) Get nice and hungry and treat yourself to the all-you-can-eat *rodízio* (a buffet of fresh meats) at this large eatery north of the plaza. The dining area won't win any awards for decor; then again, the only looking around you'll be doing is to see what aromatic skewer is coming next.

Orientation

Palmas' layout is highly logical, but still confuses most first-time visitors. All *quadras* (blocks) are numbered, and the main avenues are named for their direction: 'NS' for *norte–sul* (north–south) and 'LO' for *leste–oeste* (east–west). Smaller *ruas* (roads), are named according to their quadrant – like 'NO' for the northwest or 'SE' for southeast – in relation to Praça Girossóis, the center of the city. Only Palmas' two main thoroughfares have regular names: Av Juscelino Kubitschek (known as Av JK) and Av Teotônio Segurado.

Information

EMERGENCY

Ambulance (☎192)

Police (☎190)

INTERNET ACCESS

MSD Inform@tica (☎3215-8562; Quadra 103 Nte, Rua NO-03; per hr R$3; ⏱9am-10pm Mon-Sat, noon-10pm Sun) Fast, inexpensive internet service.

LAUNDRY

Quality Lavandería (☎3215-5060; cnr Av NS-01 & Av LO-01; wash/dry per kg R$10, plus ironing per kg R$15; ⏱8am-6:30pm Mon-Fri, 9am-1pm Sat) Can do your laundry the same day if you drop it off early, and will deliver loads of 2kg or more to your hotel.

MEDICAL

Droganita (☎3228-5804; ⏱24hr) One of several pharmacies in Galeria Bela Palma.

Hospital Geral de Palmas (☎3218-7802; Quadra 201 Sul, Av LO-5) Between Av Teotônio Segurado and Av NS-01, this is the city's main public hospital; 24-hour emergency room.

Hospital Oswaldo Cruz (☎3219-9000; Quadra 501 Sul, Av NS-01) Between Av LO-09 and Av LO-11, this private hospital is in Palmas' medical district; 24-hour emergency room.

MONEY

There are ATMs located at **Palmas Shopping**, a small busy mall on the south side of Praça Girossóis.

Banco do Brasil (Quadra 103-Sul, cnr Av Juscelino Kubitschek & Av NS-01)

Bradesco (Quadra 104 Nte, cnr Av Juscelino Kubitschek & Av NS-02)

POST OFFICE

Post Office (Palmas Shopping; ⏱10am-9pm Mon-Fri, 10am-1pm Sat)

Post Office (Av JK btwn Rua SE-04 & Av NS-04)

TOURIST INFORMATION

Centro de Atendimento ao Turista (CATUR; ☎2111-2771; www.palmas.tur.gov.br; Quadra 103, Av NS-01 at Av Juscelino Kubitschek; ⏱8am-4pm Mon-Fri)

Getting There & Around

AIR

The airport is located 26km south of the city center. A taxi from the airport to the hotel area costs R$75 to R$80, and the same to return. Alternatively, catch the red bus 75 at the airport curb (hourly from 7am to 7pm) to the 'Terminal', where you can switch to bus 20 (hourly from 7:35am to 7:35pm), which passes **Galeria Bela Palma** in the center. Do the reverse to get back. In either direction, the first leg is R$3; the second leg is free.

Azul (☎4003-1118, 3219-3872; www.voeazul.com.br)

GOL (☎0800-704-0465, 3219-3794; www.voegol.com.br)

Passaredo (☎0800-770-3757, 3219-3840; www.voepassaredo.com.br)

SETE (☎0800-605-7000, 3219-3854; www.voesete.com.br)

TAM (☎4002-5700, 3219-3784; www.tam.com.br)

Around Palmas

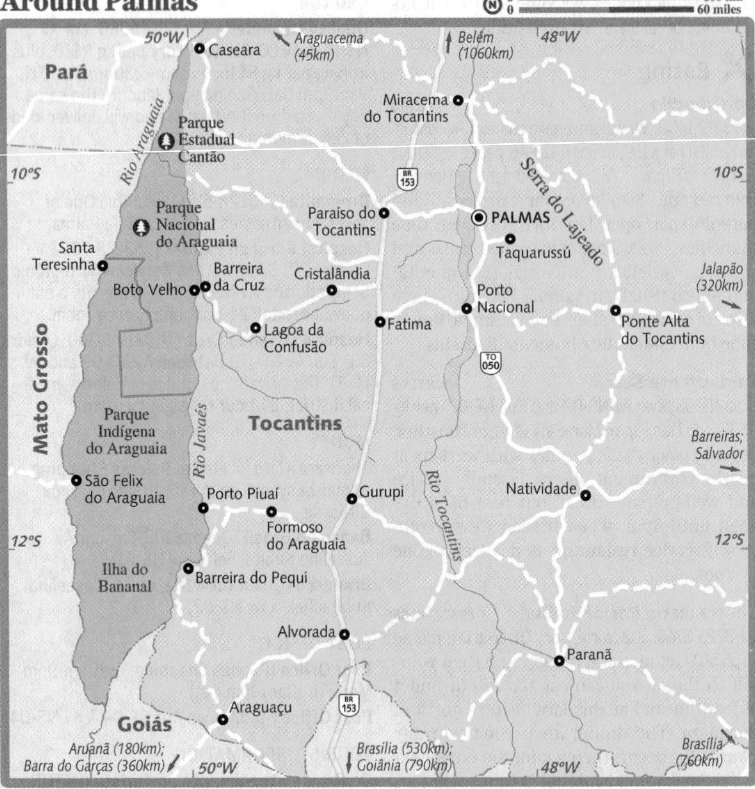

BUS

Most long-distance buses do not enter Palmas, stopping instead in the highway-side town of Paraíso do Tocantins, 15km west of Palmas; note that departures listed here are from Paraíso. To get between Paraíso and Palmas, minibuses operated by **Tocantinsense** (☎3214-4194; www.tocantinense.com.br) loop around every 30 to 60 minutes (R$10, 45 minutes) from roughly 6:30am to 10pm, with reduced services on weekends. Catch inbound shuttles at the Paraíso bus station, outbound ones at the bus stop in front of Galeria Bela in Palmas. **Transbrasiliana** (☎0800-726-7001; www.transbrasiliana.com.br) has services to Belém (R$175, 18 hours), Brasília (R$120, 13 hours) and São Paulo (R$255).

For Taquarussú, take any bus (including bus 01 or 90 in front of Galeria Bela, R$3) to the *terminal urbano*, where you can transfer to Bus 45.

CAR

Car-rental agencies include **Avis** (☎3215-3336, airport 3219-3802; cnr Rua SO-03 & Rua SO-04), **Hertz** (☎3219-3859; airport) and **Localiza** (☎0800-979-2020).

Taquarussú

☎0XX63 / POP 5000

This cozy town is nestled in the green Serra do Carmo hills, 30km southeast of Palmas, in an area studded with waterfalls and blanketed in forest. The state and local tourism boards have dedicated themselves to making Taquarussú an ecotourism mecca, with modest success. Guides are needed for most outings, and it's helpful to have a rental car of your own from Palmas.

Information

The **Centro de Atendimento ao Turista** (CATUR; ☎3554-1515; Rua 20-A; ⌚8am-noon & 2-6pm Mon-Fri, to 4pm Sat & Sun), near the plaza, is the best place for information about the area, and to hire a guide to visit the falls. There's a Banco do Brasil ATM next to CATUR, and a small **clinic** (⌚24hr) on the road toward Fazenda Encantada.

Activities

There are 80 identified waterfalls, caves and pools in the area, of which 10 to 15 are open and accessible to the public during most of the year. The tourist office encourages visitors to use guides for all the sites, though several of the most popular ones are easy to visit on your own. **Cachoeira de Roncadeira** is the tallest waterfall in the area (70m), and **Cachoeira Escorrega Macaco**, just 100m away, is nearly as tall (60m). Both tumble picturesquely down sheer rust-brown cliffs, fringed by green vegetation, into small pools good for wading and swimming. The falls are located 1.5km down a well-marked trail; follow signs toward Hotel Fazenda Encantada and look for a large turnoff and parking area as the road ascends just out of town. **Cachoeira Taquaruçú** is a beefy cascade with a choppy swimming hole that can get crowded on hot summer weekends. Look for the large roadside parking area along the highway from Palmas, about 4.5km before reaching Taquarussú; the falls are a 150m walk from there. A R$4 per person trail fee applies if you come without a guide.

Other popular spots that are best visited with a guide include the **Cachoeira do Rappel**, on the Fazenda Encantada grounds and used for rappelling (naturally), and **Vale do Vai-Quem-Quer**, a broad valley with a series of falls and good swimming spots. Before setting out, discuss with your guide what type of falls you'd like to see, how much hiking and driving you want, and whether the car you have is adequate for all sites (some require 4WD, especially in the rainy season).

Sleeping & Eating

Pousada Lokau POUSADA $
(☎3554-1238; 3a Av; r per person R$40) Part art gallery, part guesthouse, the Lokau has five clean, comfortable rooms opening onto a pleasant garden. They can be a bit musty at first, but high ceilings and stand-up fans help. To get here, turn left after the plaza, right just before Restaurante Mandala, left at the roundabout and it's at the next corner on your left.

Restaurante Mandala BRAZILIAN $
(Av Belo Horizonte; R$12-20; ⊙lunch daily, dinner Wed-Sun) Right around the corner from the plaza, on the road toward Fazenda Encantada. The fixed-plate lunch comes with pasta, rice, beans, salad, *farofa* (manioc flour sautéed with butter) and a choice of meat, all for R$13.

Getting There & Away

From Palmas by car, take Hwy TO-010 past the bus station and follow the signs, passing first through the town of Taquaralto.

From Palmas, take any bus (including bus 01 or 90 in front of Galeria Bela, R$3) to the *terminal urbano*, where you can transfer to bus 45 for Taquarussú.

Parque Estadual do Jalapão

Jalapão State Park is a unique 34,000-sq-km area in far eastern Tocantins, combining cerrado vegetation, hills, caves, crystalline rivers and springs, 40m-high sand dunes, waterfalls, freshwater bathing spots, odd rock formations, quite a range of wildlife – including anteaters, armadillos, macaws and rheas – and very few people. Jalapão Extremo (p601) arranges multiday tours of the park, including transport, hotels, food and guide services. The best season to explore Jalapão is the dry season from May to September.

AMAZONAS

Amazonas is Brazil's largest state, spanning almost 1.6 million sq km. You could fit four Germanys within its borders with room left over for, say, Greece. It is here that the massive Solimões, Negro and Madeira rivers converge to form the Rio Amazonas, the granddaddy of them all. Manaus is the state capital and, with nearly three million people in and around the city, the largest metro area in the Amazon region. Manaus is a logical base for coming and going, and offers some genuinely rewarding tours, sights and urban amenities. But don't forget that Amazonas – not to mention Amazônia as a whole – is an incredibly big chunk of earth, and there are many places other than Manaus offering outstanding tours (and most with far fewer people). That includes Tefé and the excellent Mamirauá Reserve; the nearby town of Novo Airão, gateway to Jaú, Anavilhanas, and Baixo Rio Branco-Jauaperi (Xixiau-Xiparina) reserves; and Rio Negro gems Barcelos and São Gabriel da Cachoeira; and more.

Manaus

☎0XX92 / POP 2.1 MILLION

Manaus is the Amazon's largest city, an incongruous pocket of urbanity in the middle of the jungle, a major port for ocean vessels that's 1500km from the ocean. The Amazonian rainforest has a population density half that of Mongolia's, but the journey there invariably begins in (or passes through) this gritty bustling metropolis. Don't be surprised if you feel a little out of whack.

Manaus is no colonial gem, but does have some genuinely rewarding sights, including a leafy zoo with as many animals out of the cages as in them, and a beach-and-museum combo that gets you out of the city center. It's a place to stock up on anything you forgot to pack, or to refill your tank with beer and internet after a week in the forest.

You can book jungle tours from Manaus, mostly three to six day excursions, ranging from budget to upscale. Plenty are run by honest professionals, but the city is also full of slippery touts whose tours are not only miserable and a waste of money, but often dangerous – see our tips for avoiding scams (p610).

Another bit of advice: don't get stuck in Manaus! It's strangely easy to forget that a city of three million people is not, in fact, a very logical place to experience a natural wonder like the Amazon. Remember there are many places, both upriver and down, that are fairly easy to reach and may offer something closer to the Amazonian adventure you've been imagining.

Sights

City Center

★Teatro Amazonas THEATER

(☎3232-1768; Praça São Sebastião; guided tour R$20; ⊙9:15am-5pm, tours every 30min until 4pm) This gorgeous theater was built at the height of the rubber boom, using European designers, decorators and even raw materials. The original driveway was Brazilian, though, made of Amazonian rubber to soften the clatter of late-arriving carriages. The theater's performance schedule includes an excellent opera festival in April and May. Guided tours offer an up-close look at the theater's opulent construction.

Centro Cultural Usina Chaminé MUSEUM

(☎3633-3026; Av Beira Rio at José Paranaguá; ⊙10am-4pm Tue-Fri, 5-8pm Sun) FREE Also known as the Museu dos Cinco Sentidos (Museum of the Five Senses), this innovative museum uses the five senses to evoke and illustrate indigenous and Caboclos life and culture. You can hear recordings of native languages, smell Amazonian spices, admire indigenous folk art, and more, as you pass from room to room.

Museu Amazônico MUSEUM

(☎3234-3242; www.museuamazonico.ufam.edu.br; Ramos Ferreira; ⊙8am-noon & 2-5pm Mon-Fri) FREE Housed in a converted mansion, the Museu Amazônico has a small but excellent collection of indigenous items and artifacts from around the Amazon, many from archaeological studies in Amazonas state.

Palacete Provincial MUSEUM

(Praça da Polícia; ⊙9am-5pm Tue & Wed, 9am-7pm Thu-Sat, 4-8pm Sun) FREE The 'Image and Sound' center at this handsome cultural complex has a huge collection of films, including century-old documentaries by Portuguese filmmaker Silvino Santos, some of the earliest recordings of Amazonian native people. The art gallery is decent, too, but the police and archaeology displays are snoozers. Young eager guides are available for tours.

Porto Flutuante FERRY TERMINAL

(Estação Hidroviária de Manaus) FREE Inaugurated in 1902, Manaus' 'floating port' was a technical marvel of its day, able to adjust 15m or more to seasonal water levels. (Look for high water marks on a wall facing the river.) Closed for renovation at last check, it will certainly reopen with improved shopping and eating areas, and great river views.

Outside the City Center

Centro Cultural dos Povos da Amazônia MUSEUM

(☎2123-5301; www.povosdamazonia.am.gov.br; Praça Francisco Pereira da Silva s/n; ⊙9am-4pm Mon-Fri) FREE At the heart of this massive cultural complex is the excellent Museu do Homem do Norte (Museum of Northern Man), which contains an incredible array of artifacts and multimedia exhibits on Amazonian indigenous groups. From the center, buses 625, 711 and 705 all pass by, or ask a taxi to take you to the 'Bola da Suframa'.

Bosque da Ciência (INPA) ZOO

(Forest of Science; http://bosque.inpa.gov.br/principal.htm; Av Cabral; admission R$5; ⊙9am-noon & 2-5pm Tue-Fri, 9am-4pm Sat & Sun) Occupying a lush forest plot within the city, Bosque da

JUNGLE TRIPPING

The top priority for most foreign visitors to Manaus is a jungle trip. While anything's possible, the most common trip is three to five days based at a jungle lodge or on a riverboat, with day trips for hiking, canoeing, fishing for piranha, spotting caiman at night and visiting local villages. Sleeping in hammocks in the forest for a night or two is usually possible, but not required. Many operators also offer so-called survival tours, which are spent mostly or entirely in forest camps.

Thinking carefully about what sort of trip you want can help determine which operator is best for you. How much do you want to rough it? Do you want a bed or a hammock? What about sleeping aboard a boat? Private bathroom, shared or pit toilet? Do you want to spend a night or two in the forest or do day trips from the lodge? How much do mosquitoes bother you? Do you prefer hiking or canoeing? There is no shame in choosing more or less comfort – you are there to enjoy yourself, after all.

There are also a few questions to ask the tour operator: does the guide speak English (or a language you understand)? How long will you spend getting there? What is the trip itinerary? How much hiking and/or canoeing will you do? How large are the groups? Ask to see recent pictures of the accommodations and activities, and a guest comment book.

And talk to other travelers! Virtually every foreigner you see in Manaus is planning a trip or returning from one, and they are the best source of honest, up-to-date info.

The Amazon is teeming with animals, but seeing them can be quite hard. (It's a much better place to be wowed by the flora and the river itself, rather than wildlife.) On a typical trip, you are very likely to see pink and gray dolphins and a slew of birds, including herons, parrots and possibly macaws. Monkeys, sloths and caimans are relatively common, but seeing them is no sure thing. River otters and tapirs are even more elusive, and you're almost sure *not* to see jaguars, manatees or anacondas – they are extremely hard to spot. White-water areas tend to have more animals, but they also have more mosquitoes and thicker vegetation. State and national reserves have more (and less skittish) wildlife. The biggest factor in seeing animals is luck, followed by the quality of the forest and the diligence of your guide. Refrain from chatting unnecessarily.

Bring closed shoes or boots for hiking, sandals for around the lodge, long-sleeved shirt and pants, mosquito repellent, a hat and sunscreen, rain gear, flashlight, roll of toilet paper, daypack and a water bottle. And bring binoculars! Even a small pair makes a big difference, yet few operators have extra pairs. Plastic bags, including a heavy-duty one large enough for your entire pack, are useful for rainstorms and leaky boats. Leave whatever you don't need at your hotel in Manaus – virtually all offer free, secure luggage storage.

Ciência (aka INPA, for the research institution that runs it) has enclosures for rescued manatees, giant otters and more, and many smaller animals simply roaming around, such as squirrel monkeys, sloths and anteaters.

To get there from Praça da Matriz, the 810 'Especial' minibus (R$3) stops right outside the gates, while bus 519 (R$2.50) stops a half-block away. A taxi costs R$35.

★ **Jardim Botânico Adolpho Ducke** PARK
(☎3582-3188; http://jardimbotanicodemanaus.org; Av Margarita s/n; admission R$8-10, Tue free; with tower R$24-$30, Tue R$16; ⏲9am-5pm Tue-Sun (last entry 4pm)) **FREE** Spanning more than 100 sq km, this 'garden' is actually the world's largest urban forest. There's a network of five short trails (guides and closed shoes required, two to three hours, free with admission) and an open-air **museum** (MUSA; Museu da Amazônia) which includes rotating exhibits on Amazonian flora and fauna and a spectacular 42m observation tower. Busier on weekends.

Comfortable shuttles (R$30 round trip, 45 minutes) leave from outside the tourist office (CAT) at 9am and 4pm. Otherwise, catch bus 676 (R$2.50, one hour) from Praça da Matriz.

Museu do Seringal Vila Paraíso MUSEUM
(Rubber Museum; ☎3631-3632; admission R$5; ⏲8am-4pm Tue-Fri, 9am-1pm Sat & Sun) Located on the grounds of a former rubber-baron estate, this unique museum includes tours of the grand historic townhouse, a replica rubber-tapper shack and smokehouse, and a leafy trail showing how rubber trees are

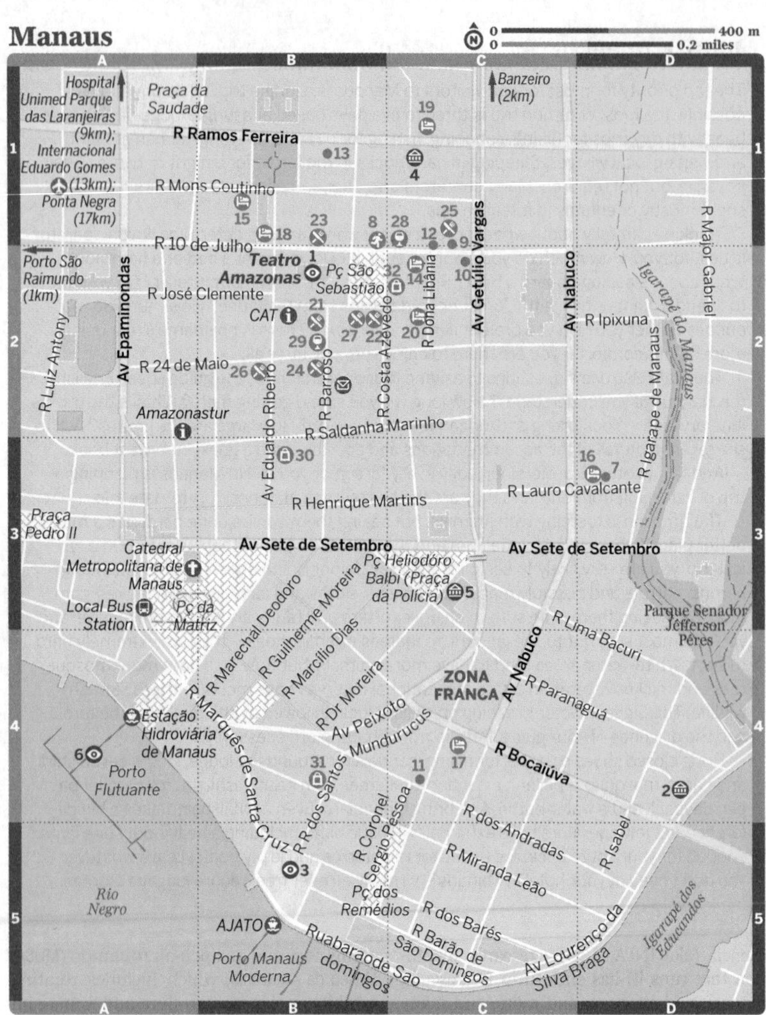

tapped. Sounds gimmicky, but is intriguing. Consider combining it with a stop at Praia da Lua, Manaus' best beach.

Boats to the museum (R$10, 25 minutes, via Praia da Lua) leave frequently from Marina Davi, just past the Hotel Tropical in Ponta Negra. From the center, take bus 120 or 121 (R$3, 20 minutes) to the end of the line, then walk or catch a free 'Especial' bus to the marina.

Praia da Lua — BEACH

Manaus' best beach has fine white sand and tea-colored water, and can be coupled with a visit to the Museu do Seringal for a nice city escape. Like all river beaches, Lua is biggest when the water is low (September to December). Beach shacks serve fish and beer at tables set up along the water.

Catch a boat to Praia da Lua (R$5, 10 minutes) from Marina Davi, just past Ponta Negra. Take bus 120 or 121 (R$3, 20 minutes) to the turnaround, and then walk or wait for the free 'Especial' bus to the marina.

Encontro das Águas — RIVER

Just beyond Manaus, the warm dark Rio Negro pours into the cool creamy Rio Solimões, but because of differences in temperature, speed and density, their waters don't mix,

Manaus

Top Sights
1 Teatro Amazonas B2

Sights
2 Centro Cultural Usina Chaminé D4
3 Mercado Municipal Adolfo Lisboa B5
4 Museu Amazônico C1
5 Palacete Provincial C3
6 Porto Flutuante A4

Activities, Courses & Tours
7 Amazon Antonio Jungle Tours D3
8 Amazon Eco Adventures B1
9 Amazon Gero Tours C1
10 Amazon Green Tours C2
11 Amazonas Indian Turismo C4
12 Iguana Turismo C1
13 Swallows & Amazons B1

Sleeping
14 Boutique Hotel Casa Teatro C2
15 Go Inn Manaus B1
16 Hostel Manaus D3
17 Hotel Colonial Manaus C4
18 Hotel Manaós B1
19 Hotel Saint Paul C1
20 Local Hostel C2

Eating
21 Casa da Pamonha B2
22 Casa do Pensador B2
23 Delícias Caseiras B1
24 Restaurante Castelinho B2
25 Scarola Pizzaria C1
26 Skina dos Sucos B2
27 Tambaqui De Banda B2

Drinking & Nightlife
28 Bar do Armando C1
29 Mao Bar B2

Entertainment
Teatro Amazonas .... (see 1)

Shopping
30 Carrefour B3
31 Comercial São Bento B4
32 Galeria Amazônica C2

instead flowing side by side for several kilometers. The bi-color phenomenon occurs throughout the Amazon, but nowhere as dramatically as here.

Day trips always include a stop here, and many tour operators at least pass by en route to their lodges.

Activities

Day trips on the river have always been a popular activity in Manaus, but the number of guides and boats has exploded recently (leftovers from World Cup 2014). Quality varies, and paying more doesn't necessarily guarantee a good trip. Most trips include a visit to the Meeting of the Water and Parque Ecológico Janauari, and possibly swimming with dolphins. The vast majority of trips sold on the street, and even at reputable tour agencies, are consolidated onto huge cattle boats; bargain hard for these because there's really not much bang for your buck.

Amazon Eco Adventures (p615) is a notable exception, offering tours with small groups, comfortable speedboats, and excellent guides. You'll go swimming at the meeting of the waters rather than just bobbing by, and activities like visiting indigenous villages and swimming with dolphins don't have that icky theme-park feel. Their trips to Presidente Figueiredo are equally rewarding, forgoing the touristy waterfalls for stunning caves and wispy falls instead, where few visitors go. Pricier than others, but well worth it.

Tropical Tree Climbing (p615) and Amazon Tree Climbing (p617) also offer great day trips, scaling massive tropical trees with ropes and elbow grease, and there are fine day-trips to be had in nearby Novo Airão (p618).

Festivals & Events

Inaugurated in 1997, the annual **Manaus Opera Festival** brings high-quality opera deep into the rainforest at the Teatro Amazonas (p606). The three-week gala usually takes place in late April and early May, and audience apparel ranges from tuxedos and ballroom gowns to jeans and T-shirts that have obviously done duty in the jungle (they do draw the line at shorts, tank tops and flip-flops). Tickets (R$5 to R$60) are available at the Teatro Amazonas several weeks before the festival opens.

In November, the ever-more-popular **Amazon Film Festival** screens dozens of films related in some way to the Amazon, from rare Brazilian features filmed in Manaus to foreign documentaries about destruction of the rainforest. Headliners are shown in Teatro Amazonas, but you can see films every

JUNGLE TRIP SCAMS

Manaus is teeming with scammers and touts. Most peddle cut-rate tours that turn out to be woefully uninspired: awful accommodations, surly guides, and sad, damaged forest with no wildlife. Tourists have been seriously injured, and even a few killed, on tours with unscrupulous or inexperienced guides. Mainly, though, they get duped: swindled out of their time, money and a chance to really enjoy the Amazon. Here are some tips and pointers to avoid getting scammed.

Don't be naive. The smooth-talking guy who approaches you on the street, or snags you at the door of your hostel, with promises of an epic adventure at a rock-bottom price is scamming you. Period.

Do not tell touts what hotel or tour agency you're considering. They're trying to squeeze a commission out of the hotel or operator. The magic words are 'I already have a reservation', whether it's true or not. Touts only get paid for bringing people without reservations or prior bookings.

No legitimate tour agency 'fishes' for clients at the airport. Those that do are cut-rate operators trying to snag unsuspecting tourists. Some touts shamelessly lie about who they work for, claiming to have been sent there to pick you up. Many legit agencies do offer airport pickups, but they send someone with your name on a sign.

Never pay for a tour anywhere except at the agency's main office. Touts often pretend they are with a legitimate agency but steer you to a cafe or airport bench to make the deal. They even make phony phone calls to convince you the main office is closed, or that you must commit right away to get the best price or the 'last seat on the boat'. These are all scams.

Confirm the agency is registered with the state tourism authority. Go to www.visitamazonas.am.gov.br, select the Portuguese version (it's more up-to-date than the English one), then *Agências de Turismo*.

Above all, don't risk your life to save a little time or money. In the end, it's tourists who keep scammers in business by booking with them. There are legitimate established agencies for all budgets and tastes; take the time to find one that works for you.

night of the week for free at a large outdoor screen set up right in the Praça São Sebastião.

The June Festival Folclórico do Amazonas features a wide variety of regional folklore performances, including rehearsals of the Parintins Boi-Bumbá teams. The festival culminates on June 29 with the Procissão Fluvial de São Pedro (St Peter River Procession), when hundreds of riverboats parade on the Rio Negro before Manaus to honor the patron saint of fishers.

Sleeping

★Hostel Manaus HOSTEL $
(☎3233-4545; www.hostelmanaus.com; Cavalcante 231; dm with fan/air-con R$45/50, s without bathroom R$80, d with/without bathroom R$140/125; ❄@📶) Manaus' first hostel is still its best, though competition is getting stiff. Spacious, warmly decorated common areas and a rooftop dining area set it apart from other hostels, and there's a highly recommended tour operator on-site. On the downside, it's several long blocks from the center. Large basic dorms and tidy private rooms are adequate. Kitchen access, self-service laundry, friendly staff.

Local Hostel HOSTEL $
(☎3213-6079; http://localhostel.com.br; Rua Marçal 72; dm R$45-49, d R$130-143, tr R$183; ❄) A great hostel in almost every way: a block from the Opera House, friendly youthful staff and clientele, and clean comfortable dorms with privacy curtains, reading lights and individual power outlets. Spiffy private rooms are a worthwhile splurge. The main drawback is the limited common space, which makes meeting fellow travelers (or just relaxing with a book) somewhat tougher.

Hotel Colonial Manaus HOTEL $
(☎3233-3216; www.hotelcolonialmanaus.com; Quintino Bocaiúva 462; s/d/tr $70/90/130; 📶) One of the better non-hostel options in this price range, though not perfect. Occupying a renovated colonial home, front rooms have

high ceilings and rich wood floors, but noise from the front desk can be annoying. Rear rooms (especially those with windows) are better. Breakfast is in a tiny dining room below reception. Gritty area, especially at night.

Hotel Manaós HOTEL $$
(☎3633-5744; www.hotelmanaos.com.br; Av Eduardo Ribeiro 881; s/d R$139/159; ❄📶) One of Manaus' oldest hotels, though you'd never know from large modern rooms and updated amenities. Newer bedding, bathrooms, air-conditioning and televisions lend creature comforts, while the creaky old elevator and the '70s-style lobby are lingering reminders of the hotel's former self. The location is ideal: kitty-corner from Praça Sebastião, with many rooms overlooking the Opera House. Ample breakfast.

Boutique Hotel Casa Teatro HOTEL $$
(☎3633-8381; www.casateatro.com.br; Rua 10 de Julho 632; s/d R$185/210, without bathroom R$140/160; ❄📶) Rooms are modern and cute, but *really* small – basically, boutique walk-in closets. Standards have bunks and shared bathrooms, while en-suite rooms at least have double beds, though not much floor space. Common areas are truly lovely, including cozy sitting rooms and a rooftop patio with views of the opera house. Great location and service, but brace yourself for the sardine treatment.

Hotel Saint Paul HOTEL $$
(www.hotelsaintpaul.tur.br; Rua Ramos Ferreira 1115; s R$150-189, d R$189-216 ; ❄📶🏊) This hotel offers business-class comfort and service on a quiet street near the city center. Rooms are moderately sized (some oddly narrow) with first-rate amenities and attractive decor; suites include a large sitting area, while some upper-floor rooms have views of the Opera House. There's an enticing circular swimming pool in back, plus fitness room and generous breakfast spread.

Go Inn Manaus HOTEL $$
(☎3306-2600; www.atlanticahotels.com.br/hotel/manaus/go-inn-manaus; Monsenhor Coutinho 560; s/d R$181/204; ❄📶) A bit plastic, perhaps, but still a welcome oasis of business-class comfort amid Manaus' mostly gritty downtown options. Rooms are smallish but very comfortable and clean, with modern bathrooms and technology. There's an extra large restaurant and well-stocked convenience store, plus a lobby business area, a small fitness room, and a kids' playroom. No swimming pool, alas.

Chez les Rois POUSADA $$
(☎3584-5130; www.chezlesrois.com.br; Rua Pérola Negra Q/G 01, Conj. Manauense, Barrio Vieiralves; s/d/tr R$138/165/205; ❄@📶🏊) Occupying an attractive colonial home in a swanky neighborhood, Chez les Rois has handsome woodwork and great common areas, with little nooks where you can read or soak up the sun, plus a welcoming pool. Guest rooms are smallish, and you'll probably need a taxi to get around, but the overall ambience is worth a few bumped elbows and extra reais.

Eating

Skina dos Sucos JUICE BAR $
(cnr Av Eduardo Ribeiro & Rua 24 de Maio; juices R$4-8, snacks R$4-12; ⏰7am-8pm Mon-Sat) Stake out some counter space at this busy eatery, where you can order filling snacks and sandwiches to go along with large *sucos* (fresh juices) made from Amazonian fruits, including guaraná (a tropical berry thought to have numerous medicinal properties), *cupuaçú* (sweet cousin of the cacao fruit) and *graviola* (custard apple).

★**Casa do Pensador** PIZZERIA, BRAZILIAN $
(Praça São Sebastião; mains R$13-28; ⏰4-11pm) Simple wood tables set up on the plaza facing Teatro Amazonas make this an easy low-key place for dinner and a beer. The menu is equally low-key, mostly pizza (including a couple of veggie options) and standard rice-beans-meat dishes.

Tambaqui De Banda BRAZILIAN
(☎3622-8162; www.tambaquidebanda.com.br; Praça São Sebastião; mains for 2 people R$55-75; ⏰11am-11pm) The look here is plastic, the location is ideal and the food surprisingly good. Nearly all dishes are for two or more people – bring some friends – and the group-friendly menu makes for a boisterous ambience, at outdoor tables facing the opera house, and a large air-cooled indoor area. The specialty is huge grilled boneless tambaqui (fish) fillets, served with all the fixin's.

Delícias Caseiras BRAZILIAN, SELF-SERVICE $
(Rua 10 de Julho; lunch per kg R$30, mains R$20-45; ⏰11am-3pm) The tables are crammed together and the fans are blowing full blast to accommodate the scads of loyal clients at this great hole-in-the-wall eatery just off Praça São Sebastião. Lunch self-serve is outstanding, especially for the price, but it's also open for dinner, serving home-style classics.

Casa da Pamonha VEGETARIAN $
(Barroso 375; per kg R$34; 7am-7pm Mon-Fri, to 2pm Sat) Cool, friendly and artsy, this vegetarian place has soy burgers, Spanish tortillas, fresh juices, tasty cakes and more during its popular lunchtime buffet, and light snacks in the morning and evening.

Scarola Pizzaria PIZZERIA, BRAZILIAN $
(3234-8542; Rua 10 de Julho 739; mains R$18-45, per kg R$33-38; 10am-11pm) Good food, good service and good *chope* (draft beer) make for a varied clientele, from backpackers back from jungle trips to professionals pontificating on the latest opera performance. The affordable lunch spread has all the standards, including fresh grilled meats, while pizza is the dinner of choice. One of the few places around that's open late, even on Sunday.

Restaurante Castelinho BUFFET $$
(3633-3111; www.restaurantecastelinho.com.br; Barroso 317; per kg R$41; 11am-3pm Mon-Fri) The food and service at this popular per-kilo place are perfectly good, but the highlight has to be the building itself: a beautiful, high-ceilinged rubber-era mansion that served as a private residence, doctor's office and foreign consulate before being converted into a restaurant.

Banzeiro BRAZILIAN $$$
(3234-1621; www.restaurantebanzeiro.com.br; Rua Libertador 102, Nossa Sra. Das Gracas; dishes R$90-145; 11:30am-3pm & 7-11pm, closes 10pm Sun) One of Manaus' top gourmet restaurants, especially for fish. River fish such as pirarucú and tambaqui and other Amazonian specialties are served in various preparations, from cheese and banana, to parsley and *formigas* (ants). Pricey but truly one-of-a-kind. Online reservations recommended.

Drinking & Entertainment

Bar do Armando BAR
(Rua 10 de Julho 593; 5pm-1am) Near the opera house, this is a traditional rendezvous place for Manaus' intellectual and bohemian types, but all sorts of people crowd around the outdoor tables for beers and conversation.

Mao Bar BAR
(3345-4550; www.maohostel.com; Rua Barroso; 5pm-late Tue-Sat) The hostel here is so-so, but the bar is super cool – a moodily lit, semi-subterranean spot on the basement level with great music and drinks and a laid-back backpacker vibe. Occasional live music and movie screenings.

★ **Porão do Alemão** LIVE MUSIC
(www.poraodoalemao.com.br; Estrada da Ponta Negra 1986; entry R$25; 10:30pm-late Wed-Sat) Located on Estrada de Ponta Negra, this longtime bar-club features Brazilian and international rock and pop, and has a safe lively scene popular with tourists and locals alike. VIP area upstairs (R$40).

Teatro Amazonas MUSIC
(Praça São Sebastião; 8pm, except Mon) Performances at Manaus' iconic theater range from professional opera and jazz to student guitar and dance. Quality varies: some are terrific, others barely tolerable, most are free. A line for tickets starts forming at 7pm, but you can usually arrive right before the show starts to snag a balcony or rear seat (which afford an easy escape, if needed).

Copacabana Chopperia BAR, DANCING
(3584-4569; Estrada do Turismo, Tarumã; 7pm-3am Thu-Sun) Rio-style bar and dance club, with a semi-open-air bar, performance stage and dance floor, with room for seven *thousand* revelers. DJs spin everything from samba and MPB to electronica and funk. Check out the club's Facebook page for details and deals. Located on Estrada do Turismo, a long avenue near Ponta Negra with numerous bars and restaurants.

Shopping

Galeria Amazônica HANDICRAFTS
(3233-4521; www.galeriamazonica.org.br; Costa Azevedo 272; 8am-8pm Mon-Sat) Right on Praça São Sebastião, this is Manaus' top shop for genuine-article Amazonian handiwork, including gorgeous basketwork, pottery and folk art. Prices are on the high side, but so is the quality.

Mercado Municipal Adolfo Lisboa MARKET
(3232-9210; Rua dos Barés 46; 6am-5pm Mon-Sat, until 7pm Fri, 6am-noon Sun) Manaus' historic city market was inaugurated in 1882, a downscaled replica of Paris's famed Les Halles market. Safe and bustling, the central building has mostly handicraft shops, wares ranging from predictible kitsch to high quality. A side building houses a working-fish-market visit early in morning to see the vast array of Amazonian fish on display. Great little eateries throughout.

Comercial São Bento OUTDOOR GEAR
(Miranda Leão 133; 8am-5:30pm Mon-Fri, to 4pm Sat) One of several *casas de redes* (hammock shops) clustered on and around this

corner; this one has a monster selection and friendly service. For riverboat trips, suitable cloth hammocks start at R$30, while larger, prettier, more durable ones go for R$60 to R$190. If you'll be sleeping in the jungle, consider getting a mosquito net (R$14 to R$30) as well.

Carrefour DEPARTMENT STORE
(Av Eduardo Ribeiro; ⏲7am-9pm Mon-Sat, to 4pm Sun) This large downtown supermarket is a good place to buy batteries, rain ponchos, toiletries etc.

Information

EMERGENCY

Ambulance (☎192)

State Police (☎190) A police station is located across from the bus station on Praça da Matriz.

Tourist Police (☎3231-1998; Av Eduardo Ribeiro) At the Centro de Atendimento ao Turista.

INTERNET ACCESS

Juliana Cyber Café (Nabuco at Bocaiúva; per hr R$2.50; ⏲8am-10pm Mon-Sat, 2-10pm Sun)

Selva Net (Joaquim Sarmento 306 at 24 de Maio; per hr R$4; ⏲7am-7pm Mon-Fri, to 6pm Sat)

LAUNDRY

Lavandería Central (☎3631-1322; Rua Quintino Bocaiúva 607; per piece R$2; ⏲8am-noon & 2-5pm Mon-Fri, 8am-1pm Sat) Located a block east of Av Nabuco. Add R$1 per piece for ironing. Quick service.

LEFT LUGGAGE

Most hotels store bags for free while you're on a jungle trip. The airport and long-distance bus station have luggage storage for a small fee.

MEDICAL SERVICES

Fundação de Medicina Tropical (Tropical Medicine Foundation; ☎2127-3555; Av Pedro Teixeira 25) Also known as Hospital de Doenças Tropicais, this well-regarded hospital specializes in tropical diseases. Free yellow-fever vaccines available.

Hospital Unimed Parque das Laranjeiras (☎3633-4431; Av Japurá 241) One of the best private hospitals in the city.

MONEY

Banco do Brasil (Guilherme Moreira 315; ⏲9am-3pm Mon-Fri)

Bradesco (Av Eduardo Ribeiro 475 at Rua Saldanha Marinho)

POST

Post Office (Barroso 220; ⏲8am-4pm Mon-Fri, 8am-noon Sat)

TOURIST INFORMATION

CAT (☎3182-6250; www.visitamazonas.am.gov.br; Av Eduardo Ribeiro 666 ; ⏲8am-5pm Mon-Fri, 8am-noon Sat & Sun) Friendly and helpful branch of the state tourism agency, located on the southwest corner of Praça São Sebastião.

TRAVEL AGENCIES

Paradise Turismo (☎3633-8301; Av Eduardo Ribeiro 656; ⏲8am-6pm Mon-Fri, 8:30am-noon Sat)

Getting There & Away

AIR

Manaus' main airport, **Aeroporto Internacional Eduardo Gomes** (☎3652-1210; Av Santos Dumont 1350), is located 13km north of the city center. Modern, spiffy and cavernous – thank you World Cup 2014! – it has info kiosks, ATMs, luggage lockers, restaurants, shopping and wi-fi. Charter planes and smaller regional airlines may use a separate terminal (known as 'Eduardinho'), about 600m east of the main one.

American Airlines (☎0300-789-7778, 3652-1911; www.aa.com)

Azul (☎3652-1830, 4003-1118; www.voeazul.com.br)

Copa Air (☎3652-1442, 0800-771-2672; www.copaair.com)

Gol (☎0800-704-0465, 3652-1593; www.voegol.com.br)

MAP (☎3652-1931, 2125-5000; www.voemap.com.br)

TAM (☎3652-1211, 4002-5700; www.tam.com.br)

TAP (☎3652-1973, 0800-727-2347; www.flytap.com)

BOAT

Large passenger boats plying the Rio Solimões use Manaus' main passenger port, **Estação Hidroviária de Manaus** (www.portodemanaus.com.br; Porto Flutuante). Speedboats to Tefé, Tabatinga and Parintins use the smaller Porto Manaus Moderna (behind Mercado Municipal Adolfo Lisboa), while fast and slow boats headed up the Rio Negro generally dock at Porto São Raimundo, a seedy port about 1.5km northwest of the center. Passenger boats going downstream to Belém usually make stops in Itacoatiara, Parintins, Santarém and Monte Alegre. Headed up the Rio Solimões, boats call at Tefé, Benjamin Constant and Tabatinga. Boats to Porto Velho take the Rio Madeira, of course, making stops at Manicoré and Humaitá.

The main port's **ticket office** (☎3233-7061, 3088-5764; Marquês de Santa Cruz; ⏲6:15am-5:45pm) sells passage for most long-distance riverboats. It has been housed in a small office facing the plaza while the terminal undergoes a major renovation; once completed, expect the office to move inside to a more user-friendly location. It is not recommended to buy tickets from the men with desks along the sidewalk in front of the boat terminal; although they're slightly cheaper, you're the first to be bumped if the boat is full.

AJATO (☎3622-6047; www.terminalajato.com.br; Porto Manaus Moderna; ⊙8am-5pm Mon-Fri, 8am-noon Sat) operates comfortable speedboats upstream to Tefé (R$240, 13 hours, 6am, 7am Tuesday) and Tabatinga (R$550, 36 hours, 6am Tuesday, Thursday, Friday and Sunday) and downstream to Parantins (R$160, eight hours, 7am Monday, 6am Tuesday and Friday). There's also service up the Rio Madeira as far as Manicoré (R$210, 14 hours, 6am Monday, Tuesday, Thursday, Friday and Saturday).

Slow boats going up the Rio Negro use Porto São Raimundo. Departures for Barcelos (hammock R$120, double cabin R$300, 25 to 30 hours) are on Tuesday, Wednesday and Friday at 6pm and for São Gabriel (hammock R$340, 72 hours) at 5pm and 6pm Friday. Boat companies serving those towns include **Azevedo** (☎9143-1223, 3625-6984; Porto São Raimundo), **Vencedor** (☎9202-1028, 9117-8757; Porto São Raimundo), **Natal** (☎9381-2926, 9122-8553; Porto São Raimundo), **Gênesis** (☎8171-4442, 9152-3444) and **Tanaka** (☎9239-8024, in São Gabriel ca Cachoeira 097-3471-1730; Porto São Raimundo).

Speedboats serve the same stops in about half the time, operated by Tanaka and Taylor, departing Porto São Raimundo for Barcelos (R$150, 12 hours) and São Gabriel (R$400, 24 hours) every Tuesday and Friday at 3pm. Bring a camping pad if you've got one: many passengers lie in the aisle to get some sleep.

Slow boats along the Rio Solimões do not include meals, but those along the Rio Negro often do. Speedboats always include meals.

BUS

Manaus' small **long-distance bus station** (Rua Recife 2784) is 6km north of town, in the same direction as the airport.

Eucatur (☎3301-5800; www.eucatur.com.br) has services to Boa Vista (R$120, 11 to 12 hours, 10am, 6pm, 7pm, 8pm and 11pm). If you plan to continue directly to Venezuela, take the 6pm or 7pm buses from Manaus in order to have the best chance of catching the one and only bus to the border, which leaves Boa Vista at 7am.

Asatur (☎in Boa Vista 3224-2630; www.asaturturismo.com.br) also serves Boa Vista (R$75 to R$106, 7pm and 8pm); the 8pm departure is 'VIP' with nearly fully reclining seats and onboard wi-fi.

Aruanã (☎3615-2450) has a bus service to Presidente Figueiredo (R$25, two hours, 6am, 10am, 12:30pm, 6pm and 11pm) and to Itacoatiara (R$43, four hours, 6am, 7am, 10:30am, 1pm, 2pm and 7pm).

CAR

Rental agencies at the airport include **Localiza** (☎3652-1176), **Unidas** (☎3652-1327), **Avis** (☎3652-1579) and **Hertz** (☎3652-1421).

Getting Around

Bus fare is R$2.50 on most routes. Taxis are plentiful, but rather expensive – from R$15 within the center, more for destinations beyond that or if you get mired in traffic.

TO/FROM THE AIRPORT

Buses 306 'Aeroporto' (R$2.50) and 813 'Aeroporto-Ejecutivo' (R$5) run about every half-hour between the airport and Praça da Matriz in the center of town; the latter is air-conditioned, less crowded and definitely worth the extra reais. At the airport, turn right out of the main doors and walk to the bus stop at the end of the terminal. In town, the most convenient stops are Praça da Matriz and on Av Getúlio Vargas near Rua José Clemente.

Taxis at the airport charge a fixed R$75 for the 20-minute ride into town, while the return trip costs around R$65. In either case, be sure to agree on a price before setting off.

TO/FROM THE BUS STATION

Buses 306 and 813 (the same ones you take to the airport) also pass the bus station; get on either at Praça da Matriz or on Av Gétulio Vargas. The bus station is small and easy to miss, so be sure to keep your eyes peeled.

You can catch the same buses back into town. Leaving the bus station, use the pedestrian bridge to cross Rua Recife and turn left along the busy street on the far side of the gas station there. The bus stop is 100m further along, on the far side of the street.

A taxi between the bus station and the center costs R$35 to R$40.

RIVERBOATS FROM MANAUS' MAIN PORT (ESTAÇÃO HIDROVIÁRIA)

DESTINATION	DEPARTURE	TIME	UPPER DECK (R$)	2-PERSON CABIN (R$)
Belém	Wed & Fri; 11am	4 days	300-325	1000-1200
Porto Velho	Tue; 6pm	4 days	200	600
Santarém	Mon-Sat; 11am	36 hours	160	750-1000
Tabatinga	Wed, Fri & Sat; noon	7 days	350	1500
Tefé	Tue-Thu, Sat & Sun; 5-6am	36 hours	150	590

Around Manaus

Jungle Trips

Most agencies have a small lodge or jungle camp where guests stay, from which activities such as canoeing, hiking and fishing are launched. Many have amenities such as electricity and flush toilets, but not all. Prices usually include meals, lodging, transport and guides, and range between R$150 to R$350 per person per day; this normally includes time spent traveling to and from the lodge, not just the time you're actually there. Prices vary primarily by the type of accommodations: hammocks with shared toilets are the cheapest option, followed by dorms and private rooms, then riverboats and specialized tours.

★**Tropical Tree Climbing** ECOTOUR
(www.tropicaltreeclimbing.com; BR-178 Km 144, Presidente Figueiredo) Tours with this warm French-Venezuelan outfit include garden-fresh meals, hiking through verdant forest and, of course, climbing a tree (or two) – usually a huge *angelim* or *samaúma*. The owner-guide (photographer Leo Principe) is patient and knowledgeable, and uses a unique rope system that makes the 50m climb reasonably easy. Overnight in comfy new guest rooms or even up in a tree!

Tours of one to seven days are available, including dedicated photo safaris. Longer trips include visits to waterfalls and other area sights. Advance reservations essential.

Amazon Antonio Jungle Tours ECOTOUR
(☎3234-1294, 9961-8314; www.antonio-jungletours.com; Hostel Manaus, Rua Lauro Cavalcante 231) On the scenic (and mosquito-free) Rio Urubú, Amazon Antonio's lodge has dorms, private rooms, chalets, even a two-bedroom cabin, all impeccably maintained, warmly decorated, and eco-oriented. Overnight hikes journey deep into primary forest, and you're free to stay after your package is over, relaxing, canoeing and soaking up views from the lodge's observation tower. Slightly pricier, but worth it.

Amazon Eco Adventures ECOTOUR
(http://amazonecoadventures.com; Rua 10 de Julho at Rua Tapajós; ⏲8am-6pm) This newer floating lodge has just five rooms, each with bathroom and fan, and a large patio with hammocks for relaxing and swimming. It's parked on a huge lake where the black water (i.e. mosquito-free) Rio Urubú meets the white water (i.e. animal-rich) Amazon – the best of both worlds. Tours ply the floodplains alongside the Amazon, loaded with birds and monkeys.

Amazon Gero Tours ECOTOUR
(☎99198-0111, 99983-6273; www.amazongero.com; Rua 10 de Julho 695) Gero Mesquita, an effusive and all-round good guy, runs a popular lodge in the Juma-Mamori area with comfortable dorms and private rooms, and a cadre of skilled guides (several former guides have opened agencies of their own). Besides standard tours, Gero arranges multiday treks into untouched forest and offers 'social sustainability' programs where travelers work on needed community projects.

Malocas Jungle Lodge ECOTOUR
(☎3648-0119, 99128-4741; www.malocas.com) Tranquility prevails at this simple place, located on a quiet bend of the Rio Preto da Eva and run completely on solar power. Rooms occupy a large circular *maloca* (traditional wood and thatch-roof structure) and are somewhat downtrodden, but the overall vibe is great. Small group tours (six or less) include hiking, canoeing and swimming in the area's many waterfalls. Operated by a friendly French-Brazilian couple.

Dolphin Lodge ECOTOUR
(☎3663-0392, 8806-4777; www.dolphinlodge.tur.br) Once the preferred lodge of an agency selling upscale group packages, Dolphin Lodge operates independently now, with comfortable rooms and unblemished views

WORTH A TRIP

PARINTINS

Tens of thousands of people descend on Parantins on the last weekend of June for the **Boi-Bumbá festival**, an Amazonian version of the Northeast's Bumba Meu Boi, and one of the Amazon's largest parties. The festival centers on a rivalry between two 'clans', the Caprichoso, who dress all in blue, and Garantido, who dress in red. Parintins' hotels are booked months in advance, but travelers can usually score hammock space on one of the hundreds of riverboats that head there from Manaus and elsewhere. A five-night boat trip east from Manaus including transportation to and from Parantins and lodging aboard the boat (but no meals) costs around R$700.

Around Manaus

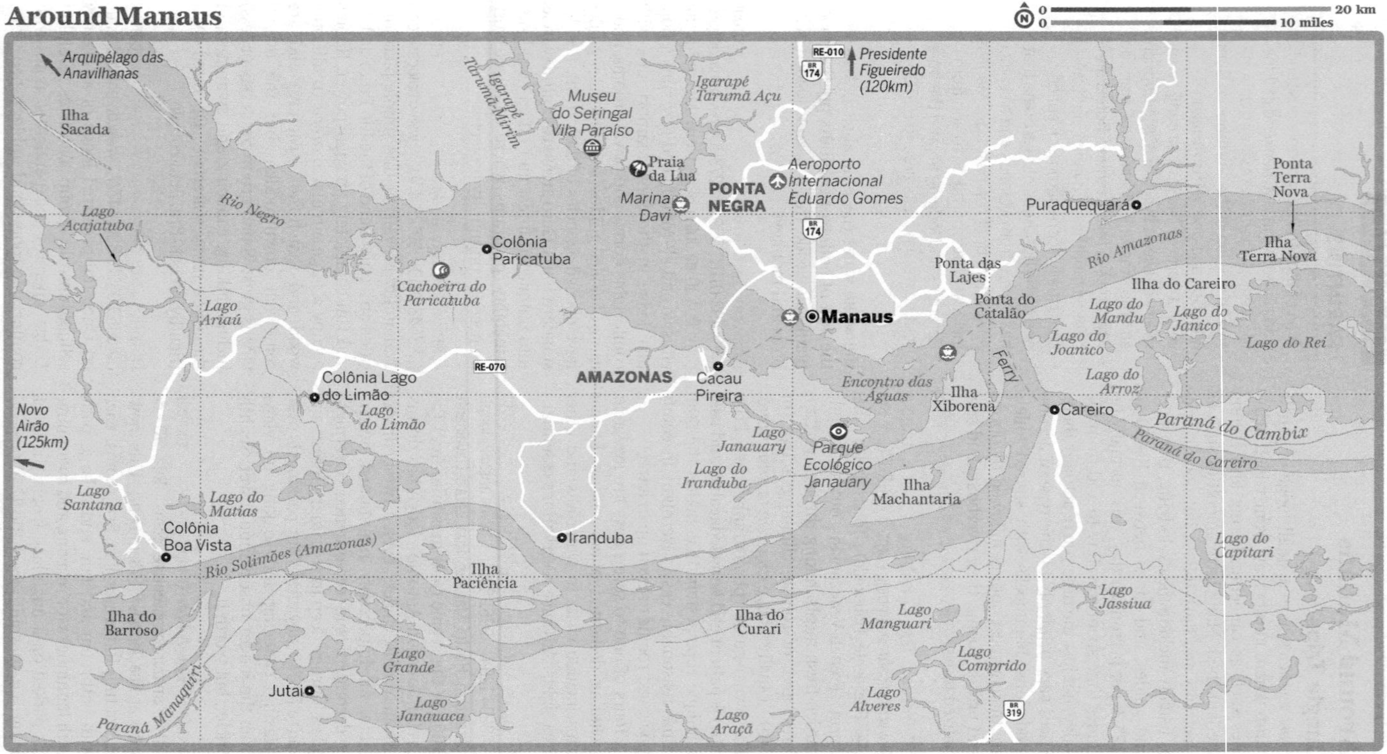

0 — 20 km
0 — 10 miles

Arquipélago das Anavilhanas
Ilha Sacada
Lago Acajatuba
Rio Negro
Igarapé Tarumã-Mirim
Museu do Seringal Vila Paraíso
Praia da Lua
Marina Davi
PONTA NEGRA
Igarapé Tarumã Açu
Aeroporto Internacional Eduardo Gomes
RE-010
BR 174
Presidente Figueiredo (120km)
Puraquequara
Ponta Terra Nova
Ilha Terra Nova
Rio Amazonas
Ponta das Lajes
Ponta do Catalão
Ilha do Careiro
Lago do Mandu
Lago do Janico
Lago do Rei
Lago do Joanico
Lago do Arroz
Manaus
Colônia Paricatuba
Cachoeira do Paricatuba
Lago Ariaú
RE-070
Colônia Lago do Limão
Lago do Limão
AMAZONAS
Cacau Pireira
Encontro das Águas
Ilha Xiborena
Ferry
Careiro
Paraná do Cambix
Paraná do Careiro
Novo Airão (125km)
Lago Janauary
Parque Ecológico Janauary
Lago do Iranduba
Ilha Machantaria
Lago Santana
Lago do Matias
Colônia Boa Vista
Iranduba
Rio Solimões (Amazonas)
Ilha Paciência
Lago do Capitari
Lago Jassiua
Ilha do Barroso
Ilha do Curari
Lago Manguari
Lago Grande
Lago Comprido
Jutaí
Lago Janauaca
Lago Alveres
BR 319
Paraná Manaquiri
Lago Araçá

from its perch atop a high riverbank in the Mamori-Juma area. The friendly owner ably runs the lodge and tours, while the online booking system is steadily improving.

Amazonas Indian Turismo ECOTOUR
(☎99240-5888; amazonasindian@hotmail.com; Andradas 311) This longtime budget agency has a rustic camp on the Rio Urubú, with latrine toilets and no electricity. You won't spend much time there, though, as the operator specializes in multiday hikes through the forest, sleeping in makeshift camps, hammocks slung between two trees. Notable for being indigenous-owned and operated; most guides are Wapixano, and all speak English.

Amazon Green Tours ECOTOUR
(☎99625-2843, 99106-5650; www.amazongreentour.com; Rua 10 de Julho 775) A husband and wife, both jungle born, are the heart of this small, highly professional agency. Survival tours are a specialty, but even day hikes are imbued with interesting info and demonstrations. A spacious new lodge has comfortable air-conditioned rooms, plus chalets and a hammock area. The owners run workshops to help locals learn English and other skills; ask about participating.

Iguana Turismo ECOTOUR
(☎3633-6507; www.amazonbrasil.com.br; Hotel Dez de Julho, Rua 10 de Julho 679) This well-oiled operator has comfortable dorms and cabins, a youthful vibe and accessible rates. Large groups can lend a cattle-herd feel (and there's an actual cattle herd in the pasture across the river) but you can't expect true isolation at these rates. Tours are decent, guides get high marks, and there's good swimming, canoeing and dolphin-spotting from the lodge's pier.

Lo Peix ECOTOUR
(☎98182-4793; www.lopeix.com; per person tour 3-12 days R$435-1680) The Spanish-Brazilian owners spent years exploring the Amazon in a riverboat before starting a tour company offering the same thing. Tours hit places like Anavilhanas archipelago, Jaú National Park, prehistoric sites near Airão Velho and more, with frequent stops for canoeing, hiking, snorkeling and visiting local communities. The custom-built boat has small comfortable berths, solar power, and up-to-date safety equipment.

Swallows & Amazons ECOTOUR
(www.swallowsandamazonstours.com; Ramos Ferreira 922) This long-established South African–Brazilian agency specializes in riverboat tours, with different boats available for different levels of comfort, from open-air hammocks to air-conditioned cabins. Tours mostly go up the Rio Negro, including Anavilhanas archipelago and Jaú National Park, exploring smaller tributaries along the way, with plenty of hiking, canoeing and fishing. Online booking recommended.

WORTH A TRIP

PRESIDENTE FIGUEIREDO

Self-named the 'Terra de Cachoeiras' (Land of Waterfalls), this dusty little town is surrounded by dozens of waterfalls and caves. Among the most impressive are Iracema, Cachoeira da Onza, Caverna do Maroaga, Gruta Judéia, Santuario, Asaframa and Pedra Furada (the most distant of the falls, 60km from town). You need a vehicle to visit the waterfalls here; you can rent a car from Manaus (125km south), or take the bus and hire a guide in Presidente Figueiredo; there's a tourist kiosk a short distance from the bus station. Several agencies in Manaus offer tours in this area, too, notably **Amazon Eco Adventures** (p615) and **Tropical Tree Climbing** (p615). Be aware that this is the only leisure spot easily accessible by road from Manaus, and so it gets obscenely packed most weekends.

Amazon Tree Climbing ECOTOUR
(☎8195-8585; www.amazontreeclimbing.com) Yellow-shirted guides lend a youthful vibe to this outfit, whose tours range from half-day trips near Manaus with views of the Meeting of the Waters to all-day excursions that may also include visiting an indigenous village or swimming with pink dolphins. Getting to the top of the massive trees can be quite challenging physically, but the experience is unforgettable.

Manati Lodge ECOTOUR
(☎99134-9360; http://manatilodge.com) There's no mistaking this small friendly lodge, with its structures built of stilts and super-bright red, green and yellow colors (among others). Located along the Rio Negro just upstream from Manaus, tours here include hiking and canoeing, as well as visits to tourist sights like swimming with pink dolphins and

feeding pirarucú (freshwater fish). English, French, Spanish and Portuguese spoken.

Jungle Lodges

Jungle lodges cater to an upscale client base; the activities are usually the same as those offered by operators in Manaus, but the lodging, food and service tend to be somewhat more refined (and the prices substantially higher).

Amazon Lodge LODGE $$$
(☎93308-1181; www.amazonlodgeamazonas.com.br; per person per night US$250-600) A homey floating lodge in a secluded corner of the long Juma lake. Standard rooms are small but comfortable, while larger suites have private outdoor showers; none have private toilets, however.

★ **Juma Lodge** LODGE $$$
(☎3232-2707; www.jumalodge.com; per person per night R$700-1500) The deluxe lakefront cabins here stand dramatically on 15m stilts, connected by wood walkways, with huge screened windows and private patios. West-facing units can get hot in the late afternoon, but that's when you might be sipping a caipirinha in the lodge's shady deck or spacious communal dining area. Tours make use of comfortable motorized canoes, though groups can be large.

Rio Negro Basin

The Upper Rio Negro is one of the most beautiful and unusual regions of Brazilian Amazonia. Novo Airão is a sleepy but up-and-coming town about 180km upriver from Manaus; it's easy to reach and serves as gateway to three major destinations: Jaú National Park, Anavilhanes Archepelago, and the remote Reserva Xixuaú-Xipariná. Further upriver is Barcelos, a well-known fishing destination but still fairly off the beaten path for independent travelers. Barcelos is adjacent to Mariuá Archipelago, the largest fluvial archipelago in the world (Anavilhanes is second) with over 750 islands and excellent beaches, canoeing and camping. Further still, and seeing even fewer travelers, is São Gabriel da Cachoeira, a pleasant town surrounded by rich forest and beckoning peaks. São Gabriel has some nascent ecotourism options, and is a backdoor adventure route to Colombia or Venezuela, via the triple-frontier town of Cucuí.

Novo Airão

☎0XX92 / POP 20,000

The 2011 opening of the Ponte Rio Negro (Rio Negro Bridge) was a game changer for communities on the other side of the Rio Negro from Manaus, especially dusty little Novo Airão. With traffic freed from slow lumbering barges, Novo Airão has become a popular getaway for weekend warriors from Manaus and, increasingly, a departure point for ecotours on the Rio Negro and its tributaries. Not exactly charming, but working hard to become so, Novo Airão can be a welcome alternative to Manaus, with a handful of good lodging and eating options, and easy access to excursions of all lengths.

Sights & Activities

Ama Boto WILDLIFE WATCHING
(☎99337-6510; www.amaboto.com.br; Av Getulio Vargas s/n; adult/child R$15/7.50; ⏲8am-5pm) This is the original 'swimming with pink dolphins' operation and helped put Novo Airão on the map. Visits begin on the hour (except 1pm) with a 15-minute presentation on pink dolphins (in Portuguese) followed by a 20- to 30-minute in-the-water experience. Guests stand on a platform that's a meter underwater, and can watch, touch and pet the dolphins as the presenter feeds them. You can swim, but only if certain individuals (known for biting) are not present; life jackets required.

Located 500m upriver from Pousada Bela Vista, just past the marina.

Visit Amazônia ECOTOUR
(☎99472-7335; www.visitamazonia.org; Rua Ademar de Barros 14B; ⏲9am-noon & 2-5pm Mon-Fri) This agency's owner, a no-nonsense Scotsman, has spent decades helping to protect and establish responsible ecotourism in a gorgeous animal-rich area known as Xixuaú-Xipariná. He still specializes in trips there – very highly recommended – but now also offers tours from Novo Airão to Anavilhanes archipelago, Jaú National Park, and elsewhere.

Em Cantos da Amazônia ECOTOUR
(☎99200-0351, 3365-1405; www.emcantosdaamazonia.com; Pousada Bela Vista, Av Getulio Vargas 47 at Av Ajuricaba; ⏲8am-6pm) Day trips with this friendly operator explore the islands and waterways of the Anavilhanes archipelago, while longer trips, including overnight, go as far as Airão Velho and Jaú National Park.

BLACK & WHITE

There are three types of rivers in the Amazon Basin: *branco* (white), *negro* (black) and *claro* (clear). White rivers (actually more a creamy beige) come from the Andes and get their color from sediment eroded from those 'young' mountains. White water rivers – including the Solimões and Madeira – are loaded with nutrients, supporting abundant plants and wildlife along their paths.

Black rivers, such as the Rio Negro and Rio Urubú, originate in northern Amazonia and flow over much older land, with far less sediment to wash downstream. Black rivers are slower and warmer than white rivers, allowing the vegetation in them time to rot and to release organic acids. Those acids turn the water 'black', actually a tealike color. The same acids kill mosquito larvae, meaning black-water areas have amazingly few mosquitoes and a low incidence of malaria and other diseases.

Clear rivers mostly originate in southern and central Brazil, and have neither the sediment nor the organic acids that would make them white or black. The Tapajós and Xingu rivers are clear, and small tributaries in predominantly white- or black-water areas can be clear if their course happens to allow it.

Both white- and black-water rivers flood seasonally, but the result is not the same, at least in name. Forest flooded with black water is referred to as *igapó*, while forest flooded with white water is called *várzea*.

Sleeping & Eating

Pousada Lanna POUSADA $

(3365-1765; Avenida Ajuricaba 8; d/tr/q R$40/50/60;) Rooms at this basic hotel are small and boxy, arranged along a narrow hallway, but do have televisions, wi-fi, air-conditioning and even a fresh coat of paint. Alas, the showers are cold and breakfast is not included. Close to the river and bus station.

★ **Pousada Bela Vista** POUSADA $$

(3365-1023; www.pousada-belavista.com; Av Getulio Vargas 47 at Av Ajuricaba; s/d R$150/210;) Novo Airão's best overall guesthouse is run by a friendly German-Brazilian couple and features comfortable rooms, swimming pool and outstanding views of the Rio Negro. It's right at the end of the main drag and has great meal and bar service, too. Gets very busy on weekends with Brazilians, but mostly quiet midweek. An in-house tour operator offers recommended excursions.

Anavilhanas Jungle Lodge LODGE $$$

(3622-8996; www.anavilhanaslodge.com; per person 2 nights, 3 days all-inclusive from R$2100;) This well-run and well-liked lodge is located on a secluded spot just downriver from town. Comfortable modern cabins have electric lighting, private bathrooms, even air-conditioning, yet the rich forest and winding waterways of the namesake Anavilhanas archipelago are directly across the water from the lodge. Tours include canoeing, hiking and interacting with dolphins at Ama Boto. Popular with families.

Restaurante Florestas BRAZILIAN $

(3365-1614; Av Ajuricaba & Rua Barbosa; 2-11pm Mon-Fri, 11am-10pm Sat & Sun) The friendly owner is as skilled in the kitchen as she is welcoming to guests. Fish, meat and vegetarian dishes are prepared with the freshest of ingredients, including herbs and veggies from the restaurant's own garden. Even the pizza at night is outstanding, with homemade sauce and perfectly cooked crust.

Flor do Luar BRAZILIAN $$$

(99418-0865; Rua Presidente Getulio Vargas s/n; R$70-120; Fri-Sun) Owned by a developer known for ultra-upscale properties in the Amazon and elsewhere, this is not your ordinary floating restaurant. Dishes are creative variations on regional favorites and service is impeccable. Prices are high but not outrageous. There's an interesting art gallery attached, and you can even swim from the waterfront patio.

Getting There & Away

Collective taxi services (referred to locally as *taxi lotação*) are quick and plentiful, zipping between Manaus and Novo Airão ($50, 2½ hours) many times per day. The taxi stop in Manaus is on the westbound side of AM-070, about 700m before the bridge; taxis depart as soon as there are four passengers, from roughly 6am to 5pm, and will drop you at your hotel. Leaving Novo Airão, the stop is on the main drag opposite the bus stop, and hotel drop-off in Manaus costs an extra R$10 to R$20. Alternately, Master/Arauná buses leave Manaus' bus station at 11:30am and 4pm, and leave Novo Airão at 5:30am and 4pm (R$40, 4 hours).

Barcelos

☎0XX92 / POP 27,500

Barcelos is no secret to fishermen, foreign and Brazilian alike, who flock to the small town for *tucanaré* (peacock bass) package tours. Fleets of yachts and riverboats serve eager khaki-clad anglers, and locals earn good money as guides and boat crew. Non-fishing tourism, however, is relatively rare, though not for lack of potential. Barcelos provides access to the world's largest river archipelago and Brazil's highest waterfall, and holds a lively ornamental fish festival each January.

Sights & Activities

Praia Grande BEACH

This is Barcelos' biggest and most accessible beach. It's on an island directly opposite town, and is a short boat ride (R$3) from the main dock. Shacks serve hot meals and cold drinks, especially on summer weekends. There are many smaller, more secluded beaches a bit further away, where boatmen can drop you off for a few hours.

Arquipélago Mariuá NATURE RESERVE

(per person per day R$150) Hostel Manaus arranges engaging tours of various lengths to this massive collection of islands, the largest river archipelago in the world. You'll ply the winding waterways, visit island communities, sleeping on the beach or in local homes, and look out for otters, macaws and other wildlife.

Serra do Aracá State Park WATERFALL, PARK

Although this state park was established in 1990 to preserve the unique canyons carved out by the Rio Aracá, it wasn't until recently that the massive waterfall at its heart was officially measured and certified. Turns out, Cachoeira do El Dorado is Brazil's highest waterfall, plunging 353m over a sandstone cliff into a mist-swept pool below.

Adventure tours to the waterfall are a minimum of 10 days and cost around R$200 to R$250 per person per day. Ask at Hostel Barcelos about arranging a trip; at least one month advance planning required.

Sleeping & Eating

Hostel Barcelos HOSTEL $

(http://hostelbarcelos.com; Anauali 46; hammock R$15, dm with fan $30, s/d with air-con R$40/80; wi-fi) Comfortable rooms, a swimming pool, a laid-back vibe, and a friendly Luxembourger owner who serves a mean fruit juice cocktail all make this the go-to spot for independent travelers arriving in Barcelos. Guests can make use of bicycles, kayaks, wi-fi and a collection of international movies. Located near the airport; reservations essential.

The owner has info on a variety of guided and DIY excursions, including visiting an observation tower, ornamental fish farms, turtle breeding grounds and fruit farms (with great bird-watching).

Hotel Rio Negro HOTEL $

(☎3321-1260; hotelrionegrobarcelos@hotmail.com; s/d R$75/105; air-con) An attractive reliable choice that has large clean rooms with TV and air-conditioning; rear units have views of the river. The hotel also has its own pier and can arrange short fishing trips for people not interested in the big multiday packages.

Camaleón Beach Grill BRAZILIAN $

(mains R$10-45) A wooden stairway leads from the plaza down to platforms where umbrella-shaded tables have views overlooking the river and Praia Grande beyond. Grilled fish and meats are served with standard sides.

Information

Bradesco (Av Mariuá s/n) Bank.

Banco do Brasil (Av Mariuá s/n) Bank.

Megastar (Av Mariuá s/n; per hr R$3; ⏲8am-midnight Mon-Sat) Internet access.

Tourist Office (Av Mariuá s/n)

Getting There & Away

Various companies provide slow-boat and speed-boat services between São Raimundo port in Manaus and Barcelos, including Tanaka/Diamantina (p614), Gênesis (p614), **Expresso Gênesis** (☎in Barcelos 99152-3444, in Manaus 092-99202-1028; Porto São Raimundo), Natal (p614), Vencedor (p614), and Almirante Azevêdo (p614); be sure you're buying tickets from the correct operator for the day and time you want! Slow boats leave Manaus for Barcelos (hammock R$120, 24 hours) on Tuesday, Wednesday and Friday at around 6pm, returning to Manaus on Monday, Wednedsay, Thursday and Friday (various departure times). Speedboats with airplane-style seating make the same trip in about 12 hours, departing Manaus on Tuesday and Friday at 3pm (R$150) and leaving Barcelos the same days at 7pm.

MAP (p613) has flights to and from Manaus and Barcelos on Tuesday and Friday. The Tuesday flight to Barcelos, and the Friday departure from Barcelos go via São Gabriel da Cachoiera.

São Gabriel da Cachoeira

☎0XX97 / POP 44,000

São Gabriel da Cachoeira is the Upper Rio Negro's largest city, and the nearest to the Colombian and Venezuelan borders, but you'd never guess either from the town's pleasant laid-back vibe. (The large army base is a clue, however.) The town sits on a lovely bend of the Rio Negro, with a long series of rapids tumbling picturesquely by, and sandy beaches lapped by the Negro's blood-orange water. Outside town, several buttes jut up from the rainforest, including a three-peaked mountain known as Bela Adormecida (Sleeping Beauty). São Gabriel has long been the jumping-off point for 10-day journeys up Brazil's highest peak, Pico da Neblina (2994m), a rocky wedge awhirl in freezing fog, though the beaurocratic challenges of getting a permit to do so deter all but a few mountaineers.

A word of caution: most of the forest around São Gabriel is Yanomami indigenous land and makes for great hiking and boating, but official permission is required to enter. Guides in São Gabriel were having considerable difficulty getting permissions at the time of research; Yanomami leaders reportedly want tourists to use only indigenous guides, at an added cost. Some freelance guides will enter without permission, but you run a serious risk of being detained and possibly fined. Alternatively, there are a handful of places that do not require permission but still offer rewarding hiking, canoeing and wildlife-spotting. In any case, advance inquiries are strongly suggested.

Sights & Activities

Climbing **Bela Adormecida** (per person per day R$250, 2-person minimum) is the most popular excursion, and includes motoring up the ink-black Rio Curicuriari, with its picturesque rapids and rock formations, visiting Yanomami villages and hiking through towering rainforest to reach the thousand-meter peaks. The trip takes four to five days.

If permission to enter Yanomami territory is not forthcoming, **camping trips** (per person per day R$250) can be arranged in non-indigenous areas, including hiking through animal-rich forest and swimming in low chunky waterfalls.

Ilha do Sol is a long sandy island in the middle of the river opposite Barrio Praias. Boats ferry beach-goers from the shore to the island (R$3, five minutes), where you'll find a small restaurant and great swimming. Sundays are especially busy.

Pousada Pico da Neblina is a good place to inquire about excursions of all kinds.

Sleeping & Eating

★**Pousada Pico da Neblina** POUSADA $
(☎99511-1456; www.pousadapicodaneblina.com; Rua Capitão Euclides, Barrio da Praia; s/d R$35/55; ❄📶) Occupying a grand old mansion with views of São Gabriel's best beach, Pico da Neblina is used mostly for long-term rentals but reserves one room for travelers, with air-conditioning and wi-fi. Breakfast isn't included, but there are several eateries nearby. The breezy exterior passageways are nice for hanging up a hammock, and the Australian owner arranges excellent tours.

Hotel Deus Me Deu HOTEL $
(☎3471-1395; Av Presidente Castelo Branco 313; s/d R$55/100) The 2nd-floor reception area has a sunny patio with tables and chairs, overlooking the street. Rooms in the rear are clean, basic and perfectly acceptable; some with air-conditioning. No wi-fi, but there's an internet cafe directly below, and most other services are within a couple of blocks. Run by a friendly family that lives on-site.

La Cave Du Conde BRAZILIAN
(☎3471-1738; Rua Brig. Eduardo Gomes 444; mains R$15-45; ⏰7-10:30pm Tue-Sat) The refined menu, bar service and warm rustic ambience make this a pleasant surprise in the middle of the Amazon, but the main reason to come is to sample authentic regional and indigenous dishes, including São Gabriel's famous ant soup, made from fish, veggies, spices and a handful of bugs.

Restaurante Dina BUFFET $
(☎3471-1552; 31 de Março s/n; per kg $30; ⏰7am-3pm, closed Mon) Popular friendly self-service spot located two long blocks from the soccer field.

Information

Amazon Cyber (Av Presidente Castelo Branco s/n; per hr R$3; ⏰9am-9pm Mon-Fri) Located below the Hotel Deus Me Deu.

Banco do Brasil (Av Presidente Castelo Branco s/n; ⏰8am-1pm Mon-Fri) Bank.

Bradesco (Av Presidente Castelo Branco s/n; ⏰8am-1pm Mon-Fri) Bank.

Post Office (Rua 31 de Março; ⏰7:30am-noon & 1:30-4pm Mon-Fri)

Getting There & Away

Slow boats leave the São Raimundo port in Manaus for São Gabriel (hammock R$340, 60 to 70 hours) on Fridays only; Gênesis (p614) leaves at 6pm and Tanaka (p614) at 7pm. Tanaka also has speedboats, leaving from the same port on Tuesday and Friday at 3pm (R$400, 24 hours).

The return is slightly quicker, with slow boats departing São Gabriel Fridays at 8am (Tanaka) and at 9am on Tuesdays (Gênesis), and speedboats departing Tuesday and Friday at 9am (Tanaka).

MAP (3471-2244, in Manaus 092-2125-5000; www.voemap.com) has flights to and from Manaus and São Gabriel da Cachoiera on Tuesday and Friday. The Friday flight to São Gabriel, and the Tuesday departure from São Gabriel, make stops in Barcelos.

Reserva Xixuaú-Xipariná

Five hundred kilometers north of Manaus, Reserva Xixuaú-Xipariná is a massive swath of protected rainforest that's one of the best places in the Amazon to see the giant river otters, as well as monkeys, dolphins, wild boars and caimans. The area has been granted status as an 'extractive reserve' (*reserva extratavista*, or RESEX); when all is said and done, the reserve will span a whopping 6340 sq km. Although technically in southern Roraima state, the reserve is accessible via Novo Airão and the upper Rio Negro. And while pricey and sometimes beset by logistical snafus, this is still one of the best overall ecotourism destinations in the Amazon.

A large traditional-style lodge overlooking the river greets visitors to the reserve, and serves as the central gathering area, with a breezy dining area (where fresh meals are served family-style) and chairs and hammocks for relaxing between tours. Accommodations are in a small private cabins, each with double beds, bathroom and verandas. The nearby community has a public telephone and even satellite internet.

Tours are led by local guides, most of whom speak Portuguese only. The forest here is immaculate, and teeming with birds and animals. Hiking and canoeing are both possible year-round, though you'll spend more time doing one or the other depending on the water level. A week is the recommended minimum stay, but it's possible to visit for a shorter time if you come and go by speedboat. Visits start at €140 per person per day, and vary depending on length of stay, size of your group and mode of transport.

Although the reserve is managed by a local cooperative, most tours there are handled by Visit Amazonia (p618), based in Novo Airão. The agency is run by a Scottish expat who lived and worked in the region for decades, and was instrumental in establishing its protected status and initiating ecotourism there.

Parque Nacional do Jaú

Spanning nearly 23,000 sq km, Jaú is Brazil's second-biggest national park, and one of the largest tracts of protected tropical rainforest in the world. It stretches west from the Rio Negro along the Jaú and Carabinani rivers, and is rich in flora and fauna. The park was designated a Unesco World Heritage listing in 2000.

There are no lodges in the park, so it's best to visit with a tour outfit that specializes in riverboat tours, such as Swallows & Amazons (p617) or Lo Peix (p617) in Manaus, or Visit Amazônia (p618) or Em Cantos da Amazônia (p618) in Novo Airão. Advance booking is essential, as the operator must obtain special permission to enter the park.

Tefé

0XX97 / POP 61,000

A gritty bustling city overlooking a massive lake, Tefé is best known as the jumping-off point to Reserva de Desenvolvimento Sustentável Mamirauá (Mamirauá Reserve), one of the best overall eco-destinations in the Amazon. But city leaders are working hard to convince Mamirauá-bound tourists to spend time in and around town, with options for hiking, boating and visiting local villages, including in the newly established Floresta Nacional de Tefé (FLONA Tefé). A visit to Mamirauá is still the best reason to visit Tefé, but travelers with an extra day or two will find some worthwhile ways to spend them here.

Sights & Activities

Tefé has various historical, cultural and ecological attractions in addition to Mamirauá, and the hardworking **Secretária de Turismo** (99151-9049; http://secretariadeturismot.wix.com/visitetefe) has collobarated with city leaders, ICMBio and local communities to make them accessible to travelers.

(Continued on page 631)

BERNDT FISCHER / GETTY IMAGES ©

Amazon Wildlife

A huge variety of animals call the Amazon home: piranha and pink dolphins ply the waters, macaws fill the air in squawking flight, squirrel monkeys dart through the trees, and tarantulas and poison dart frogs lurk in the underbrush. The lush rainforest and murky water can make spotting animals quite hard, but all the more rewarding when you do.

Contents

Above Black howler monkey

TOM BRAKEFIELD / GETTY IMAGES ©

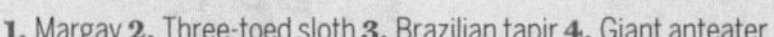

1. Margay **2.** Three-toed sloth **3.** Brazilian tapir **4.** Giant anteater

M AVILA / GETTY IMAGES ©

Land Mammals

Jaguar Jaguars are the Americas' largest cat, though Amazonian jaguars are smaller than those elsewhere. During flooding season, they can live for months entirely in the tree tops, munching mainly on sloths. Where to see: Mamirauá, FLONA Tapajós, Upper Rio Negro

Margay Small cat that's a master climber with paws that can rotate 180 degrees. Where to see: Mamirauá, Upper Rio Negro

Three-toed sloth A fairly common sight, sloths (or *preguiça* in Portuguese) are a favorite prey of jaguars and harpy eagles. Where to see: everywhere

Squirrel monkey Aptly named, squirrel monkeys are tiny and agile, living in clans numbering into the hundreds. Where to see: everywhere

Capuchin monkey Early explorers thought this small monkey's brown fur looked like the hooded cape of Capuchin friars. Where to see: everywhere

Howler monkey The male howler monkey's deathly cry can be heard for miles, though spotting the brown or black tree-dwellers can be tough. Where to see: Mamirauá, around Manaus

Coati Related to raccoons and similarly clever, coati have long tails and long sensitive noses, which they use to forage for insects, lizards and other small prey. Where to see: everywhere

Giant anteater Distantly related to sloths, Amazonian giant anteaters are skilled climbers, useful for feeding on insect nests built in tree trunks. Where to see: everywhere, but difficult to spot

Brazilian tapir Up to 3ft tall and weighing more than 440lb, tapirs are a prized but challenging prey for jaguars, caiman, even anaconda, and of course humans. Where to see: everywhere, but difficult to spot

Spider monkey The largest and most intelligent of Amazon monkeys, spider monkeys are also among the most sensitive to human intrusion. Where to see: primary forest areas

Birds

Toucan Its long colorful beak allows the toucan to crack hard nuts, but makes long flight difficult. Its distinctive whistle lets you know one's near. Where to see: everywhere

Ibis With long curved beaks, the brilliant scarlet ibis, or *guará*, prefers mangroves and estuaries, while the larger green ibis is common further inland. Where to see: Algodoal, Ilha Marajó, around Manaus, Mamirauá

Macaw Known as *araras*, Amazonian macaws can be scarlet, green or blue. Macaws mate for life, and pairs can be seen (and heard) in long squawking flights in the morning and evening. Where to see: everywhere

Amazon parrot Catch-all name for various closely-related species of parrots, mostly green with splashes of red, yellow or blue, and highly adept at mimicking human speech. Where to see: everywhere

Harpy eagle More than 3ft tall, harpy eagles are the Americas' largest raptors, known to snatch monkeys and sloths right out of trees. Where to see: everywhere, but difficult to spot

Hoatzin This pheasant-like bird may be a living link between dinosaurs and modern birds, with its reptilian appearance, poor flying, and claws on its chicks' wings. Where to see: FLONA do Tapajós, around Manaus, Upper Rio Negro, Mamirauá

Yellow-rumped cacique This talkative yellow-and-black bird is one of the most commonly seen birds in the Amazon, known for building its dangling bag-like nests near active wasps nests. Where to see: everywhere

Wattled jacana A common bird with a loud urgent call, found in wetlands throughout the Amazon. Male jacanas incubate the eggs, while females may maintain up to four active partners. Where to see: everywhere

1

3

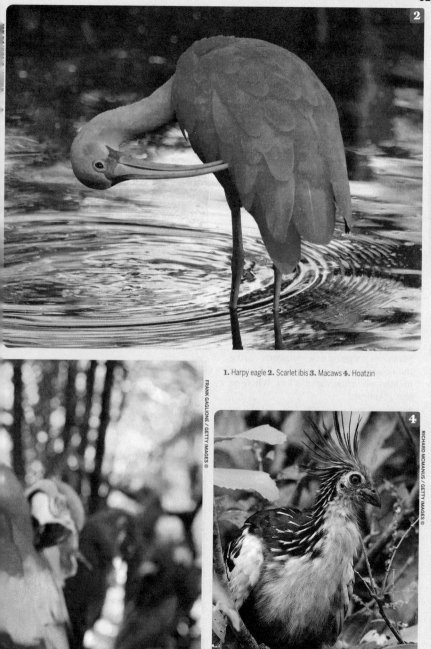

1. Harpy eagle **2.** Scarlet ibis **3.** Macaws **4.** Hoatzin

FRANK GAGLIONE / GETTY IMAGES ©

RICHARD MCMANUS / GETTY IMAGES ©

Aquatic Animals

Giant otter Up to 6ft long, giant otters are playful and social, though hunting and trapping (for their soft, extremely dense pelt) has reduced their numbers to critical levels. Where to see: Baixo Rio Branco-Jauaperi Reserve, Upper Rio Negro

Boto The Amazon's famous pink dolphins are easy to spot, living in large numbers throughout the river system. Unlike other dolphins, botos can bend their necks and paddle backward, adaptions that help them navigate the flooded forest without getting stuck. Where to see: everywhere

Tucuxi The Amazon's 'other' dolphin looks and behaves much like a bottlenose dolphin, but growing to just 5ft. Unlike botos, tucuxi do not venture into the flooded forest to feed. Where to see: everywhere

Amazon manatee Although they grow to nearly 10ft and up to 1000lb, manatees are extremely difficult to spot in the wild and their precise numbers are unknown. Manatees gorge on aquatic plants during the flood season, and may fast for several months when the water is low. Where to see: Mamirauá

Pirarucú The world's largest scaled fish, pirarucú (also known as arapaima, outside the Amazon) can grow to 10ft and 480lb and breathe air from the surface. Where to see: around Manaus, Mamirauá

Stingray Most Amazonian rays have distinctive spots and a nasty sting if you step on them. They are more closely related to Pacific rays than Atlantic ones, one of the clues that the Amazon originally flowed east to west. Where to see: everywhere

Piranha The Amazon's most famous fish is found through the river system, and ranges from 5.5in to 10in. There are at least 30 species of piranha, including the small but aggressive red-bellied piranha. Contrary to myth, piranha rarely bite humans. Where to see: everywhere

1. Giant otter **2.** Boto **3.** Amazon manatee

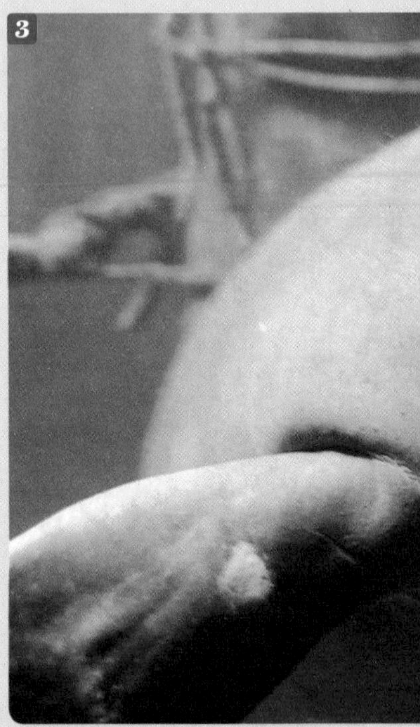

2

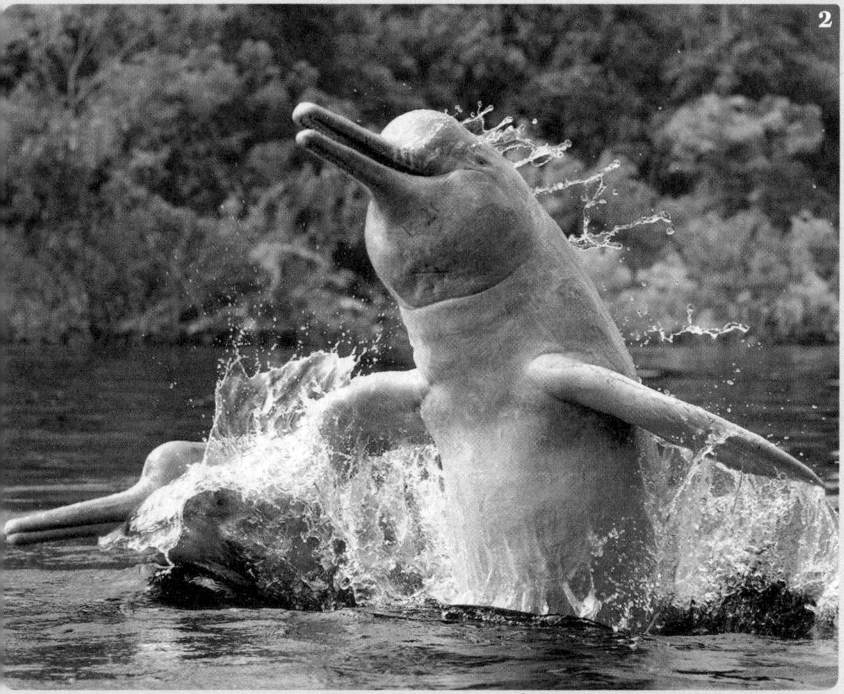

LUIZ FERNANDO SOUZA FERNANDES / GETTY IMAGES ©

Poison dart frog

Reptiles, Insects & Amphibians

Caiman Caiman are related to alligators and live throughout the Amazon. The largest, black caiman, can grow to 20ft, but most are 7ft or less. Where to see: everywhere

Anaconda The world's largest snake is known to grow up to 37ft and weigh more than 500lb, though stories of much larger ones abound. They live mostly in swamps and river channels, and eat fish, turtles, and occasionally caiman or land animals such as deer and rodents. Where to see: around Manaus, Mamirauá, but difficult to spot

Tarantula The Amazon has several species of huge hairy arachnids, including one with a leg span of more than 13in. Most tarantulas live in burrows, and hunt insects, frogs, even small birds. Where to see: everywhere

Morpho butterfly The brilliant metallic blue wings of the morpho butterfly have a way of brightening up any forest path. They can grow up to 8in across, though most are somewhat smaller. Where to see: everywhere

Ants A single acre of Amazonian rainforest can have more than 3.5 million ants, and collectively ants make up 10% to 30% of the Amazon's total animal biomass. There are dozens of species, including leaf-cutter ants and aggressive bullet ants. Where to see: everywhere

Poison dart frog Most poison dart frogs are tiny (around half an inch) and brightly colored. Some secrete a powerful toxin, which indigenous Amazonians used to make their blow darts even more potent. Where to see: everywhere, but difficult to spot

(Continued from page 622)

Spanning over a 10,000 sq km, **Floresta Nacional de Tefé (FLONA Tefé)** can be visited through various community-based tours. Most begin with a long boat ride across Tefé lake to small riverside communities within the reserve. Depending on the season, you'll have a chance to see and learn about essential activities such as farinha production, açaí processing, Brazil nut collection and bee keeping. Hiking through the forest includes encountering huge tropical trees and hopefully some monkeys and other wildlife. Meals are prepared in the communities, and overnight trips can be arranged. Prices for the tour are a bit steep (per person per day R$300 to R$600, less per person for groups of four or more) but it's clear the communities are trying hard to make this ecotourism thing work.

Nearer to Tefé, **As Misões** (The Missions) was founded in 1897 and boasts a huge church and a cemetery full of former missionaries. It has also served as a vocational training center, and many of Tefé's masons, metalworkers and other tradesmen got their start there.

In town, **Seminario San José** (The Seminary) is a striking structure that occupies the entire northern side of Praça Tulio Avevêdo. It was once a seminary and is now used for cultural and educational events.

Tefé has a small **Encontro das Aguas** (Meeting of the Waters), where an offshoot of the creamy brown Solimões merges with the red-black water pouring out of Lago de Tefé. It's an excellent place to spot pink dolphins.

Sleeping

★ Pousada Multicultura POUSADA $
(☎ 3343-5837; www.pousadamulticultura.com; Rua 15 de Junho 136; s/d/tr R$90/130/170, with lake view R$130/170/210; ❄ 📶) The UK-Brazilian couple who took over management of this popular guesthouse are maintaining all its best features – large comfortable rooms, tourist info for visitors – while making some unique additions, including new tours and a restaurant-bar with views of Tefé lake.

Stylo's Hall Hotel HOTEL $
(☎ 3343-2337; hotelstyloshall@hotmail.com; Rua Duque de Caxias 10; s R$80-120, d R$120-150) Wow! Every room here is beautifully and uniquely decorated in the theme of a different country or world city: Paris, Hollywood, Israel etc. Rooms are huge, with firm new beds and spotless bathrooms, and have gorgeous views of the river. Located within steps of the speedboat pier, on the top floor of a shopping center (oddly enough).

Egas Hotel HOTEL $
(☎ 3343-6299; egashotel@hotmail.com; cnr Ruas Getúlio Vargas & Daniel Servalho; s R$100, d R$150-180; ❄ 📶) Large clean rooms, most opening onto breezy corridors, and a convenient location near both parks and opposite a bank and internet cafe. Friendly service.

Aracati Hotel HOTEL $
(☎ 3343-3888; Rua Olavo Bilac 342; s/d/tr R$50/80/120; ❄ 📶) Small boxy rooms are brightly painted, reasonably clean and cheap. Located on a busy commercial road a short distance from Praça Tulio Azevêdo, units facing the street can get very loud.

Eating & Drinking

Restaurante Grãu de Mostardo BRAZILIAN $
(Rua Hermes Tupinambá; per kg R$34, mains R$15-30; ⏲ 11am-midnight, closed Wed) Terrific per kilo restaurant, with a breezy open-air dining room on the 2nd floor, and an air-conditioned area above that. High-quality food and friendly service make it popular with locals and visitors alike. Serves mostly pizza at night.

Restaurant Ki-Papo BUFFET, BRAZILIAN $
(Rua Juruá; per kg R$27; ⏲ 11am-3pm) Friendly low-key per-kilo place with good food and an amazing panoramic view of Lago de Tefé. A short walk east of the center, but well worth it.

Restaurante Stylo BRAZILIAN $
(Floriano Peixoto 190; mains R$18-45; ⏲ 10am-11pm Mon-Sat) The most reliable eatery in the center, with hefty, well-prepared dishes served at outdoor tables right on the street corner. The menu includes all the standard fish, meat and chicken dishes, plus a few less-common ones, such as *lingua na brasa* (grilled tongue).

Pizzaria Varandas PIZZERIA $
(pizza R$20-40; ⏲ 3-11pm Tue-Sun) Bright welcoming pizzeria, with classic checkered table settings, both inside and along the sidewalk. You can order up to three different topping combinations on a single pizza, including dessert toppings such as banana with condensed milk.

Banzerê BAR
(☎ 3343-4448; Duque de Caixias 35; ⏲ 3pm-3am Wed-Sun) One of several small roadside

restaurant-bars in a mango-tree-shaded spot known as Muralha, located just off Tefé's main drag, with open-air tables and nice river views. Food and drink service.

Orientation

Most of the main hotels, restaurants and services are within a block or two of Tefé's two central plazas. The main plaza – not because it's larger, but because it has the church – is Praça Santa Tereza, a long tapered wedge running roughly east–west, with the church on the western end. A block north is Praça Tulio Azevêdo, a more traditional square with trees, benches and newsstands. Beyond that is the municipal market and the waterfront. Both plazas are bordered by busy streets, down which flows a constant stream of scooters and moto-taxis.

Information

EMERGENCY

Ambulance (☎192)

Hospital São Miguel (☎3343-2469; Rua Marechal Deodoro 66)

Police (☎190)

INTERNET ACCESS

There's free and reasonably reliable wi-fi signal in Praça Tulio Azevêdo, across from Banco do Brasil.

Eganet (Rua Gétulio Vargas; per hr R$5; ⏲8am-10pm Mon-Fri, to 8pm Sat) Opposite Egas Hotel.

LAUNDRY

Lavandería do Paulo (Daniel Servalho 345; per item R$0.50-2; ⏲7am-7pm Mon-Sat) Located down a long narrow passageway between houses. Drop off your clothes by 10am for same-day service.

MONEY

Banco do Brasil (Rua Olavo Bilac at Praça Tulio Azevêdo; ⏲9am-2pm Mon-Fri)

Bradesco (cnr Ruas Getúlio Vargas & Daniel Servalho)

POST

Post Office (Estrada Aeroporto; ⏲8am-4pm Mon-Fri)

TRAVEL AGENCIES

Pousada Multicultura (☎3343-5837; www.pousadamulticultura.com; Rua 15 de Junho 136) The multilingual owners can purchase boat and plane tickets to and from Tefé for a 15% service fee, and have information about Mamirauá Reserve and other area tours and sights.

Getting There & Away

AIR

Azul (☎4003-1118, 3343-9580; www.voeazul.com.br) currently operates one daily flight to and from Manaus five or six days per week. The airport was undergoing a major expansion at the time of research, so check for additional flights or airlines.

BOAT

Slow boats between Manaus and Tefé (hammock R$155, double cabin R$600, 36 hours) depart in both directions six to seven days per week. Boats to and from Tabatinga (R$165, 40 to 48 hours) don't dock in Tefé proper; instead, take a boat to the village of Nogueira and taxi from there to Alvarães. Do the reverse if arriving from Tabatinga, but be aware that taxis and boats are available only during the daytime.

AJATO (☎3343-5306, in Manaus 092-3622-6047; ajatonavegacao@r7.com) has comfortable speedboat service to and from Manaus (R$230, 13 hours), with departures six to seven days per week at around 6am, and to and from Tabatinga ($400, 23 to 24 hours), with four departures weekly.

Advance reservations are recommended, especially for speedboats.

Reserva de Desenvolvimento Sustentável Mamirauá

The remarkable **Mamirauá Sustainable Development Reserve** offers visitors pristine rainforest, abundant animal life and fairly easy access, located just 1½ hours by boat from Tefé, with its reliable air and boat service. The primary lodge in the reserve offers outstanding tours and comfortable accommodations – one of the Amazon's best ecotourism operations, though the price can be prohibitive. A second, newly opened lodge is simpler, but has fewer visitors and a more accessible price.

Nearly enclosed by the Solimões and Japurá rivers, Mamirauá is Brazil's largest area of intact *várzea*, a unique forest ecosystem defined by seasonal flooding by sediment-rich 'white water' rivers. When the water is high (May to July), there is literally no exposed ground in the 11,400-sq-km reserve. As the water recedes, it can leave behind (or strip away) a meter or more of soil. Huge islands form and disappear seasonally, and a house that's built on 2.5m stilts may be at ground level in just a few years. Trees and plants are adapted to live for several months underwater, while normally ground-dwelling animals (from insects to jaguars) spend the same period exclusively in the treetops.

Mamirauá abuts two extractive reserves to the north and west, and the massive Amanã Reserve to the east, which in turn borders Jaú National Park. Altogether, they span around 67,000 sq km – nearly the size of Ireland – and form the second-largest block of protected tropical rainforest in the world. (The largest is also in the Amazon, along the Guyana Shield.)

Mamirauá was Brazil's first 'sustainable development reserve' (there are now more than 20) and is ably managed by the **Instituto Mamirauá** (☎3343-4160; www.mamiraua.org.br; Rua Daniel Servalho at Rua Monterio de Souza; ⏰8am-noon & 2-6pm Mon-Fri, 8am-noon Sat) in Tefé. Sustainable reserves are designed to ensure conservation and scientific research, while promoting sustainable practices and employment for the local population, including ecotourism. There are numerous small communities within the Mamirauá Reserve whose residents work part-time as tour guides, cooks, boat drivers, research assistants and nature wardens without abandoning traditional work such as fishing, planting and hunting. Management of the reserve and its primary lodge is due to revert to local control in 2022.

Mamirauá's wildlife is more abundant and less skittish than that in other places. The reserve's signature creature is the uacari (wah-*car*-ee) monkey, endemic to Mamirauá and notable for its crimson face, shaggy white coat and spectacular leaps between trees. Uacaris are highly elusive, though, and spotting one is far from guaranteed. You're much more likely to see howler, capuchin and squirrel monkeys, plus sloths, caimans, dolphins and dozens of bird species, such as macaws, toucans and hoatsin. Manatees and jaguars live in the reserve, too, but are rarely spotted.

High water here is May to July, when the forest is completely flooded and you glide through the water in canoes. (This is not to be confused with rainy season, which runs from December to April.) This is when monkeys and sloths are most visible, and tends to be the busiest time. During low water, roughly September to November, hiking is possible and aquatic animals, especially fish and caimans, are more concentrated.

Tours

Untamed Angling FISHING

(www.untamedangling.com) An upscale fishing operator that recently partnered with Pousada Uacari to host exclusive fly-fishing tours from September to November. Anglers stay at Uacari, but have their own guides and excursions, primarily targeting pirarucú (arapaima), the world's largest scaled fish, growing up to 3m and 220kg. Book directly with the agency.

Sleeping & Activities

Pousada Uacari LODGE **$$$**

(www.pousadauacari.com.br; per person for 3/4/7 nights from R$1840/2120/2930) Mamirauá Reserve's primary ecolodge is built entirely on floating logs and parked on a lovely river bend well into the reserve. Spacious bungalows have hot-water bathrooms, fans and a small patio with hammock; generous and delicious meals are served in a large common area. Guided excursions include paddling through the forest, sunset and dolphin-spotting trips, and visiting a local community, while researchers give interesting nighttime lectures.

An English-speaking naturalist is at the main lodge at all times (and accompanies some excursions), but most guides speak Portuguese only. There are special packages for jaguar-spotting, bird-watching, and photography that include a private guide and a superior room.

Pousada Casa do Caboclo LODGE

(☎98804-4669; http://www.pousadacasadocaboclo.com; Boca de Mamirauá; per person per day R$300) The first and only authorized alternative to Pousada Uacari for travelers visiting the reserve. Simple rooms, shared toilets and not-so-comfy boats don't compete with Pousada Uacari for comfort or polish (especially during the midday heat), but it's a great option for budget travelers or those looking for a less-touristed spot.

It's located in Boca de Mamirauá, an aptly named community at the mouth of the reserve, and all tours are within the protected area. That means you'll see the same animals and vegetation, sometimes even more as the area gets fewer visitors. Guests can also climb three observation towers left behind by a Japanese film crew – a unique bonus.

Run by a friendly local couple who spent years working as staff and guides at Uacari.

The Triple Frontier

The Brazilian town of Tabatinga and the Colombian town of Leticia lie side by side on the eastern bank of the Amazon River, about 1100km west of Manaus, while the far bank belongs to Peru. A logical travel hub, the 'triple frontier' also happens to be a good area for taking jungle trips, particularly to remote areas up the Rio Javari (the Brazil–Peru border) and further up the Amazon in Colombia.

Most travelers stay in Leticia, which is more pleasant and better equipped than Tabatinga or the small villages on the Peruvian side. Remember that Tabatinga is an hour ahead of Leticia.

Tabatinga

☎0XX97 / POP 53,150

Tabatinga is most notable as the place where the Amazon River enters Brazil.

Sleeping & Eating

Hotel Restaurant Te Contei? HOTEL $
(☎3412-2377; Av da Amizade 1813; s/d R$55/75; ❄) Large rooms with air-conditioning off a breezy upstairs patio and corridor. The back rooms have less street noise, and there's a popular self-serve restaurant (per kg $32) on the ground floor.

Hotel Takana HOTEL $
(☎3412-3557; Oswaldo Cruz 970; s/d R$95/125, s/d ste R$150/170; ❄📶) Tabatinga's best hotel has reasonably modern rooms, with hot water, air-conditioning, TV and minibar, plus a lush central courtyard. A bit removed from the main drag, but that's not necessarily a bad thing. Suites are larger and have king-size beds.

Restaurante Tres Fronteiras do Amazonas BRAZILIAN $
(☎3412-2341; Rua Rui Barbosa 353; mains R$20-45; ⏰7am-9pm) This attractive palm-thatched open-air restaurant offers a wide choice of fish and meat dishes, plus a selection of drinks, including cheap caipirinhas (cocktails). The food is an odd Brazilian-Colombian-Peruvian hodgepodge and the menu is in Portuñol. Located 200m west of Av da Amizade.

★ **São Jorge** PERUVIAN $$
(Av da Amizade 1941; mains R$20-40; ⏰9am-9:30pm Mon-Sat, to 6pm Sun) Locals on both sides of the border rave about the authentic ceviche at this simple Peruvian-run spot: the mountainous pile of excellent citrus-cooked fish and onions served on a bed of sweet potatoes and chunky corn serve two. It seems strange to walk from Colombia to Brazil for Peruvian ceviche, but that's the beauty of the tri-border!

Orientation

Tabatinga's main artery is Av da Amizade (aka Av Principal), which runs parallel to the river for 3km from Tabatinga's airport to Leticia and the international border. The most useful cross streets include Rua Marechal Rondon (250m south of the border), Rua Rui Barbosa (650m), Av Marechal Mallet (900m), Rua Santos Dumont (1.2km) and Rua Duarte Coelho (1.7km). Rua Santos Dumont leads to Porto da Feira, Tabatinga's small-boat port; you can also get there by going down Av Marechal Mallet, turning left at the end and passing the market. Porto Fluvial, where boats for Manaus dock, is at the end of Rua Duarte Coelho.

Information

CONSULATES

Colombian Consulate (☎3412-2104; http://tabatinga.consulado.gov.co; Sampaio 623)

UP RIVER, DOWN RIVER

From the time South America and Africa went their separate ways, and for 150 million years after that, the Amazon River actually flowed east to west, the opposite direction to which it flows today. That's why Amazonian stingrays are most closely related to Pacific species, and how tell-tale sediment from eastern South America ended up in the middle of the rainforest. It was only 15 to 20 million years ago that the Andes shot up and blocked the river's westward exit. Around the same time, a smaller ridge of land, now called the Purus Arch, rose like a spine in the middle of the continent.

East of the Purus Arch, the river started draining into the Atlantic Ocean, but west of there, the water was trapped and a huge inland sea formed. (Sediment deposited during that period form the sandy soil typical of the Amazon today.) Eventually the water poured over the Purus Arch, gouging a deep channel near present-day Óbidos – still the narrowest and deepest part of the river – and the Amazon returned to being a river, but now flowing west to east.

EMERGENCY

Hospital de Guarnição de Tabatinga (☎3412-2403, 192; Rua Duarte Coelho, at Av da Amizade)

Police (☎190)

IMMIGRATION OFFICE

Polícia Federal (☎3412-2180; Av da Amizade 26; ⏲8am-6pm) One hundred meters south of Rua Duarte Coelho.

INFORMATION

Tourist Information Center (Centro de Informação Turística; Av da Amizade s/n; ⏲8am-6pm Mon-Fri, to noon Sun)

INTERNET ACCESS

Digitalnet (☎3412-3505; Pedro Teixera 397; per hr R$3; ⏲8am-noon & 2-10pm Mon-Sat) On the street parallel to Av Marechal Mallet, one block south.

MONEY

Bradesco (Av da Amizade, at Av Marechal Mallet)

POST

Post Office (☎3412-2442; Av da Amizade 1087; ⏲8am-5pm Mon-Fri)

TRAVEL AGENCIES

CNN Câmbio e Turismo (☎3412-2600; Av da Amizade 2017) Also exchanges money.

Getting There & Away

AIR

The airport is 4km south of Tabatinga; coming from Leticia, catch one of the *coletivos* marked 'Comara.'

Azul (☎3412-1124, reservations 0800-887-1118; www.voeazul.com.br) is the only airline operating here, with one flight per day to and from Manaus.

BOAT

Slow boats to Manaus (hammock R$350, seven days) leave from the Porto Fluvial every Wednesday and Saturday, plus some Tuesdays, between 8am and 2pm. Arrive early to stake out good hammock space, as boats can be quite crowded.

Speedboats operated by **AJATO** (☎3412-2227, in Manaus 092-3622-6047; ⏲8am-5pm Mon-Fri, 8am-noon Sat) leave Tabatinga for Manaus (R$550, 35 hours) on Tuesday, Thursday, Saturday, and Sunday mornings.

To get to Tefé, the Sunday and Thursday speedboats to Manaus now make a stop in Tefé proper (R$400, 20 to 22 hours). Otherwise, take a Manaus-bound slow boat as far as the town of Alvarães (R$140, 44 to 48 hours) where you can catch a shared taxi to the village Nogueira (R$10, 20 minutes) and then a motorboat (R$10, 20 minutes) into Tefé; note that taxis and local boats only operate during the daytime.

The Triple Frontier

Bear in mind that departure days and times change regularly; always check in advance.

TO/FROM COLOMBIA

The international border is marked by nothing more than a few moneychangers on the Brazilian side and a Colombian police officer directing traffic on the other side. You are free to move between Tabatinga and Leticia as much as you like, but if you plan to travel onward, even to Amacayacu National Park, you should clear immigration for both countries before leaving town. There's a Colombian consulate in Tabatinga.

TO/FROM PERU

High-speed passenger boats between Tabatinga and Iquitos (Peru) are operated by **Transtur** (☎3412-2945, in Iquitos 51-65-29-1324; http://www.transtursa.com; Rua Marechal Mallet 248) and **Transportes Golfinho** (☎3412-3186, in Iquitos 51-65-225-118; www.transportegolfinho.com; Rua Marechal Mallet 306, Tabatinga). Boats depart Tabatinga's Porto da Feira daily around 5am, Brazilian time (boarding begins an hour earlier), arriving in Iquitos about 10 hours later; fares are US$70 each way. Be sure to get a Brazilian exit stamp the day before; you'll stop first at the island community of Santa Rosa, where the Policía Internacional Peruviano (PIP) handles Peruvian border control. If you're staying in Leticia, be aware that nighttime taxi rates are triple the daytime rate. Be warned, too, that there are slower, cheaper boats to Iquitos, but they are not comfortable and barely seaworthy.

If you just want to get to Santa Rosa, small motorboats go back and forth frequently from Porto da Feria (R$3, five minutes) from around 6am to 6pm.

There's a Peruvian consulate in Leticia, Colombia.

Getting Around

For a *coletivo* (minibus) from the airport to town (R$2), walk to the left outside the airport terminal and down the approach road to the corner of the main road. Some continue into Leticia. Taxis and moto-taxis are ubiquitous and inexpensive.

A taxi from the airport costs R$20 to hotels in Tabatinga and R$30 to those in Leticia. Mototaxis are ubiquitous and cheap (R$4 to R$10) but most cannot cross the international border.

Leticia (Colombia)

0XX8 / POP 39,667

Leticia is a remarkably spruce little town, with brightly painted houses, pleasant outdoor eateries and well-maintained parks and streets. For travelers, it's got hotels in all price categories, regularly scheduled flights to and from Bogota, and a long-standing military presence that keeps the city and surrounding region safe. It's also the starting point for trips to Colombia's Parque Nacional Natural Amacayacu, and up the Rio Javari into Peru.

There are no border checkpoints between Tabatinga and Leticia, and you're free to pass back and forth provided you stay within either town. However, do clear immigration if you plan to go any further into Colombia or Peru, even on short-term jungle trips.

Sights

Museo Etnográfico Amazónico MUSEUM
(592 7729; Carrera 11 No 9-43; 8:30-11:30am & 1:30-5pm Mon-Fri, 9am-1pm Sat) This small museum located inside the dolphin-pink-colored Biblioteca del Banco de la República building has a small collection of indigenous artifacts including musical instruments, textiles, tools, pottery and weapons, and lots of ceremonial masks. It's all signed in English, and makes a good introduction to the indigenous cultures of the region.

Reserva Tanimboca OUTDOORS
(592 7679, 310 791 7470; www.tanimboca.com; Km11, Via Tarapacá; full-day pass COP$120,000, ziplining COP$65,000, kayaking COP$40,000; 8am-4pm;) Visitors can monkey around atop 35m-high trees, then slide 80m along ziplines from one tree to another through the beautiful forest canopy. There's also kayaking, or splurge for an overnight stay in one of two treehouses (per person including breakfast COP$110,000), which includes a nocturnal jungle hike. There is also the possibility of sleeping in hammocks or beds in a dorm (per person hammock/bed COP$25,000/30,000). The reserve also arranges multiday jungle trips from its office in Leticia.

Sleeping

Unlike in Brazil, hotels do not commonly offer free breakfast.

Mahatu Jungle Hostel HOSTEL $
(311 539 1265; www.mahatu.org; Calle 7 No 1-40; dm COP$25,000, s/d COP$60,000/70,000;) You can begin your jungle exploration in Leticia at this beautiful hostel, which sits on 5 hectares, complete with duck- and geese-filled ponds, throngs of *pericos* and loads of exotic fruit trees – cashew, *asaí, cananguche* and *copasú* among them. Rooms are very simple and fan-cooled with shared bath, but you're paying for the lush environs.

Hospedaje Los Delfines GUESTHOUSE $
(592 7488; losdelfinesleticia@hotmail.com; Carrera 11 No 12-85; s/d/tr COP$40,000/70,000/90,000;) Doña Betty extends a genial welcome to her guests at this budget 10-room place. With potable water treated on-site, a lovely garden full of fruit and flowers, and friendly owners who are usually ready to do deals on room prices, this place is good value, although the fan-cooled rooms themselves are rather dark and pretty basic.

Hotel Yurupary HOTEL $$
(592 6529, 311 505 6875; www.hotelyurupary.com; Calle 8 No 7-26; r incl breakfast COP$98,000-165,000;) The enormous tribal woodwork key-rings may be a little out of step with the gleamingly modern lobby, but this midrange place has some lovely traditional handicrafts in it too, and rooms are bright and comfortable. The outside courtyard features a great swimming pool, garden, bar and restaurant.

Eating

Food in Leticia is generally good and reasonably priced. The local specialty is fish, including gamitana and pirarucú.

Leticia (Colombia)

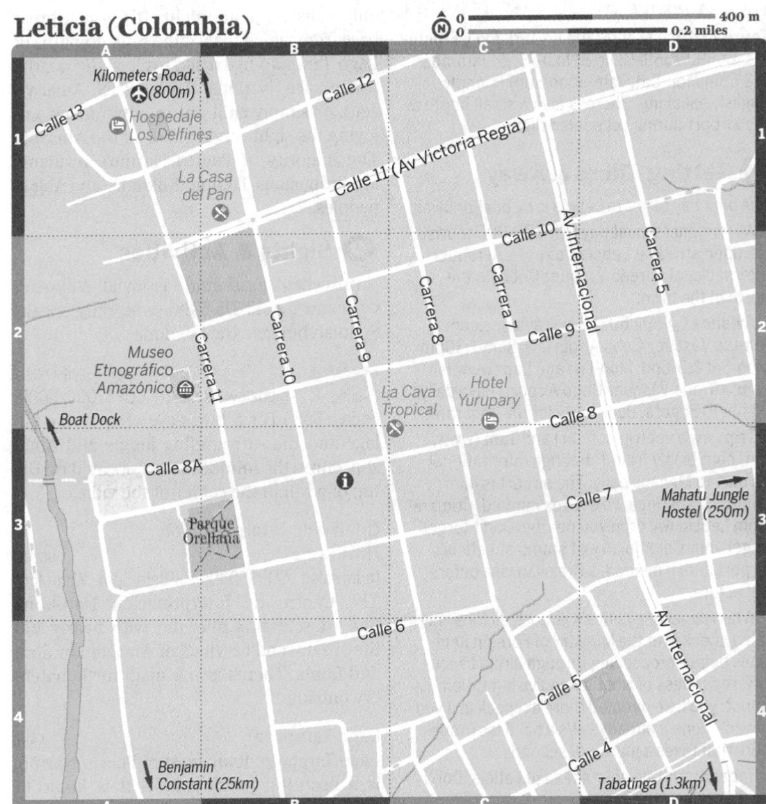

La Cava Tropical COLOMBIAN $
(Carrera 9 No 8-22; set meals COP$7000; ⏲10am-6pm; ❄) This open-air restaurant is the locals' lunchtime favorite. The set meals include a soup (often a tasty *sancocho*), small salad, a meat dish with a side of beans or veggies, and bottomless fresh juice at a very reasonable price. It can get quite crowded during the weekday lunch rush and there's an air-con section!

La Casa del Pan BAKERY $
(Calle 11 No 10-20; breakfast COP$5000-10,000; ⏲7am-noon & 1-8pm) Facing Parque Santander, this friendly spot for a basic but filling breakfast of eggs, bread and coffee is a favorite with budget travelers.

ℹ Information

CONSULATES

Brazilian Consulate (☎8 592 7530; Calle 9 No 9-73) Citizens of some countries, including the USA, Canada, Australia and New Zealand, need a visa to enter Brazil and it may be costly, especially for US citizens. Bring a passport photo and yellow-fever vaccination certificate to the Brazilian consulate.

Peruvian Consulate (☎8 592 7755; Calle 11 No 5-32) If you're coming from or going to Iquitos, get your entry or exit stamp at the Peruvian consulate.

EMERGENCY

San Rafael de Leticia Hospital (☎592 7826; Carrera 10 No 13-78) The only hospital in town.

MONEY

Most businesses in Leticia accept Brazilian reais as well as Colombian pesos. Always check online for the current exchange rate. Banks have ATMs.

Banco de Bogotá (cnr Carrera 10 & Calle 7) ATM.

Banco BBVA (cnr Carrera 10 & Calle 7) ATM.

Cambios El Opita (cnr Carrera 11 & Calle 8; ⏲9am-5pm Mon-Sat) Currency exchange.

TOURIST INFORMATION

Tourist Office (Secretaría de Turismo y Fronteras; ☎592 7569; Calle 8 No 9-75; ⏰7am-noon & 2-5pm Mon-Sat, 7am-noon Sun) Friendly, English-speaking. There is also a small booth at the airport during scheduled flights.

Getting There & Away

The only way to get to Leticia is by boat or by air.

All foreigners must pay COP$20,000 tourist tax upon arrival at Leticia's airport, Aeropuerto Internacional Alfredo Vásquez Cobo, to the north of the town.

Avianca (☎592 6021; www.avianca.com; Alfredo Vásquez Cobo Airport; ⏰8am-1:30pm Mon-Sat & 3-6pm Mon-Fri) and **Lan** (www.lan.com; Alfredo Vásquez Cobo Airport) have daily flights to Bogotá. Book early for the best rates.

Trip (www.voetrip.com.br) and **Tam** (www.tam.com.br) fly from Tabatinga International Airport to Manaus daily. The airport is 4km south of Tabatinga; *colectivos* marked 'Comara' from Leticia will drop you nearby. Don't forget to get your Colombian exit stamp at Leticia's airport and, if needed, a Brazilian visa before departure.

When departing Letica's airport, all foreigners must check in at the Ministry of Foreign Relations before proceeding through airport security, regardless of whether you've left Colombia or not; you'll be directed there at check in if you haven't done it already – it's a painless procedure that takes a matter of seconds.

Tabatinga is one hour ahead of Leticia. Don't miss your boat!

Getting Around

The main mode of public transportation is by moto-taxi, the folks on motorcycles that zip around town with an extra helmet. The base rate is COP$2000. Frequent *colectivos* (COP$2000 to COP$6000) link Leticia with Tabatinga and the 'Kilometer' villages north of Leticia's airport. Standard taxis are pricier than in the rest of Colombia; a short ride from the airport to town runs COP$8000, to Tabatinga's airport COP$15,000 and to the Porto Bras in Tabatinga COP$10,000.

Puerto Nariño (Colombia)

☎0XX8 / POP 6000

The tiny Amazonian village of Puerto Nariño, 75km upriver from Leticia, has taken the concept of green living and turned it into an art form. Motorized vehicles are banned. Rainwater is collected in cisterns for washing and gardening. Electricity comes from the town's energy-efficient generator, but only runs until midnight. It's also a great base from which to visit the pink dolphins of Lago Tarapoto by kayak, explore the nearby Amacayacu National Park (PNN Amacayacu), or simply chill out in a hammock, enjoying the sights and sounds of the Amazon. The majority of Puerto Nariño's residents are indigenous Tikuna, Kokoma, and Yagua peoples.

Sights & Activities

An excellent local guide is jovial **Willinton Carvajal** (☎313 375 5788), who only speaks Spanish but gets the job done.

Mirador VIEWPOINT

(Calle 4; high/low season COP$7000/5000; ⏰6am-5pm) For a bird's-eye view of the village and the surrounding jungle and Amazon, climb the mirador tower, located on the top of a hill in the center of the village.

Centro de Interpretación Natütama MUSEUM

(admission COP$5000; ⏰9am-5pm Wed-Mon) The Centro de Interpretación Natütama has a fascinating museum with nearly 100 life-sized wood carvings of Amazonian flora and fauna. There's also a small turtle hatchery outside.

Lago Tarapoto LAKE

Lago Tarapoto, 10km west of Puerto Nariño, is a beautiful jungle lake that is home to pink and gray dolphins, manatees and massive Victoria Regia waterlilies. A half-day trip to the lake in a *peque-peque* can be organized from Puerto Nariño (COP$50,000 for up to four people), and is the main draw for visitors.

Sleeping & Eating

Malokas Napü GUESTHOUSE $

(☎314 235 3782; www.maiocanapo.com; Calle 4 No 5-72; r per person with/without balcony COP$30,000/25,000; @) Our favorite hotel has the look and feel of a treehouse fort, surrounded as it is by a thickly forested garden. The rooms are simple but comfortable, with basic furnishings, fans and shared baths with super-refreshing rain-style showers, and everyone who works here is above and beyond friendly.

Cabañas del Friar CABAÑAS $

(☎311 502 8592; altodelaguila@hotmail.com; r per person COP$20,000) About 15 minutes west of town, famous friar Hector José Rivera and his crazy monkeys run this hilltop jungle oasis overlooking the Amazon. The complex includes several extremely simple huts, shared facilities and a lookout tower. The true joy of staying here is the playful interaction between the monkeys, dogs and macaws, and the utter isolation.

To get here, take the main street (parallel to the Amazon, two blocks back) west out of town across the big bridge to the well-maintained sidewalk; keep left at the cemetery and walk through the high-school campus (fascinating in itself), then turn right immediately after passing the school football pitch.

Hotel Lomas del Paiyü HOTEL $
(☎313 268 4400, 313 268 4400, 313 871 1743, 313 871 1743; hotellomasdelpaiyu@yahoo.com; Calle 7 No 2-26; s/d COP$25,000-35,000/50,000-80,00) This tin-roofed 22-room hotel is a reliable choice and has quite a bit of rough charm. Some bathrooms are almost as big as the rooms and while the cheaper rooms come in the form of rustic cabañas with communal hammocks, the very nicest double has a gorgeous balcony with town views.

Hotel Casa Selva HOTEL $$
(www.casaselvahotel.com; Carrera 2 No 6-72; s/d/t/q incl breakfast COP$130,000/155,000/205,000/254,000) Easily the grandest place in town, the Casa Selva allows you to do the jungle in some comfort, with 12 spacious and comfortable rooms, lots of dark wood and a prime position in the center of the village.

Information

There are no banks or ATMs in Puerto Nariño, and credit cards are not accepted anywhere, so bring plenty of cash from Leticia.

Getting There & Away

High-speed boats to Puerto Nariño depart from Leticia's dock at 8am, 10am and 2pm daily (COP$29,000, two hours); round-trip boats to Leticia depart at 7:30am, 11am and 4pm.

UNCONTACTED

The fact that there are uncontacted indigenous groups living deep in the rainforest can be hard to fathom, and many have believed it to be a myth. But a recent short film depicting such groups (filmed in Brazil using a small plane and long range lenses, and showing some *índios* shooting arrows at the circling plane) has shown such groups are not so illusory – or rare – as once thought. Anthropologists believe there are around 100 uncontacted indigenous groups worldwide (defined as a group with no peaceful contact with mainstream society) of which nearly two thirds live in the Brazilian and Peruvian Amazon.

Arriving at those numbers and estimating how many people belong to each group is difficult but not impossible. Contacted tribes often tell of uncontacted families living in remote areas of their territories. Occasionally members of an uncontacted group will emerge from the jungle, having left or been expelled from their land. Experts believe most uncontacted groups have seen or even encountered non-*índios* – and have probably seen and heard airplanes. Funai, Brazil's federal indigenous affairs agancy, employs researchers who study footprints, abandoned huts and other clues to track uncontacted groups and produce a rough census.

Several uncontacted groups are believed to live in Rondônia, including at least three in the Uru-eu-Wau-Wau indigenous reserve, in the center of the state. The reserve suffers rampant illegal mining and logging, and uncontacted groups have retreated ever deeper into the forest. Rondônia also is home to an indigenous man believed to be the last member of an unknown tribe. He has refused all contact, despite being surrounded by pastures and plantations. He is called the 'man in the hole' because he has a hole in his hut, protected by sharp spikes, where he hides when outsiders approach. After gunmen attempted to kill him in 2009 (presumeably ranchers or their henchmen), Funai alloted the man a 30-sq-km territory and restricted all future contact. For the complete account, pick up a copy of Monte Reel's excellent book *The Last of the Tribe* (2010).

For information on uncontacted groups generally, contact **Survival** (www.survivalinternational.org), the NGO that produced the film using aerial footage, and visit its fascinating page, **Uncontacted Tribes** (www.uncontacted.org).

You can purchase tickets at **Transportes Fluviales** (☎592 6752; Calle 8 No 11) near the riverfront in Leticia. Boats can get very full, so buy your tickets early or the day before.

Rio Javari

The meandering Rio Javari provides Brazil and Peru with a border, and travelers with excellent opportunities to see the Amazon rainforest up close and undisturbed. A handful of jungle lodges offer accommodations and activities similar to those found elsewhere in the Amazon Basin; prices range from around US$75 to US$125 per day per person.

Zacambú Lodge is on Lake Zacambú in a beautiful lake region on the Peruvian side of the Javari river. Operated by Leticia-based **Amazon Jungle Trips** (☎in Leticia 57-8-592-7377; www.amazonjungletrips.com.co; Av Internacional No 6-25), it's the closest of the lodges to the triple frontier – about 70km from Tabatinga, or three hours by motorboat. Accommodations are simple but comfortable, in hammocks or small rooms, with shared toilets. Most excursions are made by motorboat or canoe, for obvious reasons – the bird-watching is particularly good.

Reserva Natural Heliconia (☎in Leticia 57-311-508 5666; www.amazonheliconia.com) has simple but cozy thatch-covered cabins with private bathroom, and hiking and boating tours of the forest and waterways. There are also organized visits to indigenous villages and special tours devoted to bird-watching. Parent agency is based in Leticia.

RORAIMA

The tropical rainforest that blankets Roraima's southern half (bisected by the equator) gives way to broad savanna in the middle of the state, and remote and beautiful mountains in the north. It includes most of the Brazilian territories of the Yanomami, one of the country's largest surviving indigenous peoples. The state capital, Boa Vista, still doesn't make the itinerary of most travelers, but has better and better tour options every year. Roraima is home to Monte Roraima (2875m), but this intriguing flat-topped mountain sits right on the Brazil-Venezuela-Guyana border, and the best way up is from the Venezuelan side.

Boa Vista

☎0XX95 / POP 297,000

For travelers, Boa Vista serves mostly as a transfer point for those to Guyana or to Venezuela's beautiful high plains.

Sights & Activities

Praia Grande BEACH

A tawny sandbar beach emerges on the far bank of the Rio Branco, opposite Boa Vista, during low water, roughly December to April. Known as Praia Grande, it is indeed big and beachy, and makes for a pleasant afternoon visit. Its transitory existence means there is no shade – bring an umbrella or consider waiting until the afternoon. Porto do Babazinho offers ferry service for R$4 round trip, and can provide food and drinks. Be alert for stingrays.

Porto do Babazinho ADVENTURE TOUR

(☎9111-3511; babazinhorr@yahoo.com; Av Major Williams 1) Porto do Babazinho is home-base for longtime local guide Sebastião de Souza e Silva (aka Babazinho), who leads and arranges a variety of adventuresome outings, from windsurfing lessons and rentals to daylong and multiday hiking, canoeing and animal-spotting excursions, all at reasonable rates.

Roraima Adventures TOUR

(☎3624-9611; www.roraima-brasil.com.br; Coronel Pinto 97; ⏲8am-noon & 2-6pm Mon-Fri, 8am-noon Sat) Offers professional multiday camping tours all over Roraima, including Serra do Tepequém and Mt Roraima in Venezuela, and even into the Yanomami Reserve (provided the proper permissions can be secured).

Sleeping & Eating

Hotel Euzébio's HOTEL $

(☎2121-0300; www.hoteleuzebios.com.br; Cecília Brasil 160; s/d standard R$92/126, superior R$138/172; ❄📶🏊) Standard rooms are clean but small; superiors are bigger, more cheerful and come with hot water and minibar. All rooms have air-con and TV, and the swimming pool is a treat. A bit removed from the center, but closer to the appealing walkways and nighttime restaurants in the center of Av Capitan Ene Garcez. There's a 10% to 15% discount for paying in cash.

Boa Vista

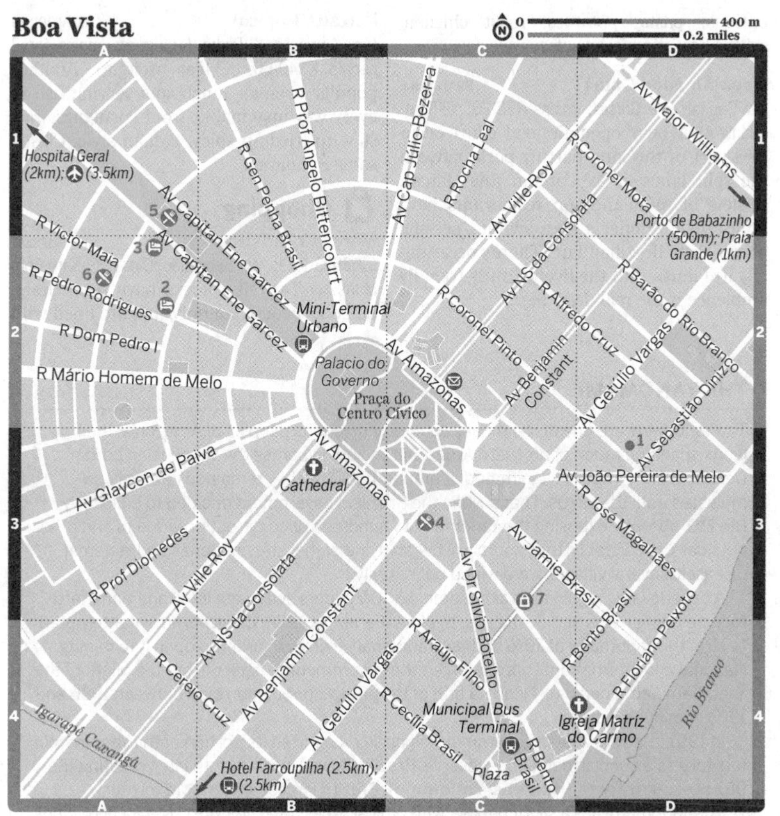

Boa Vista

Activities, Courses & Tours

1 Roraima Adventures D3

Sleeping

2 Hotel Euzébio's A2
3 Uiramutam Palace A2

Eating

4 La Gondola C3
5 Open-Air Food Court A1
6 Peixada Tropical A2

Shopping

7 Mercado Turístico C3

Uiramutam Palace HOTEL $
(☎3198-0000; www.uiramutam.com.br; Av Capitan Ene Garcez 427; s/d/tr standard R$80/110/130, deluxe R$135/175/195; ❄📶🏊) Standard rooms are awfully plain for the price, but the deluxe units are larger and cheerier, with spiffy bathrooms (porcelain sinks, glass showers), flat-screen TVs and a 20% cash discount to boot. The pool is a welcome mid-afternoon diversion, notwithstanding the huge satellite dish peering up from one corner of the pool area.

Hotel Farroupilha HOTEL $
(☎3624-4226; Av das Guianas 1400; s/d R$70/90; ❄📶) Basic hotel located opposite the bus terminal; a reliable option if you're just passing through, less so if you're planning to stay a while. Rooms are clean and reasonably comfortable, with air-conditioning but no hot water. Breakfast is decent but ends oddly early (at 8:30am) and is not served at all on Sunday. Wi-fi is spotty.

★ **La Gondola** BUFFET $
(☎3224-9547; Av Benjamin Constant 35 W; per kg R$25; ⏲11am-3pm) Facing the plaza across a busy intersection, this small per-kilo place offers outdoor, fan-cooled or air-con dining areas, in addition to the typical per-kilo

options: pasta, potatoes, roast chicken, grilled beef, rice, beans etc.

Open-Air Food Court BRAZILIAN $
(Av Capitan Ene Garcez; mains R$5-20; ⏲5pm-midnight) A busy open-air food court occupies part of the long narrow park between the split lanes of Av Capitan Ene Garcez. A slew of mom-and-pop restaurants have tables set up under a high awning, serving cheap, tasty Brazilian fare. There's occasionally live music, but the lively, family-friendly ambience is the real draw here.

Peixada Tropical SEAFOOD $$
(cnr Ajuricaba & Pedro Rodrigues; mains for 2 people R$40-60; ⏲10am-midnight) Another popular open-air lunch spot serving fish in every way imaginable, from Portuguese fish stew to fried-up spicy, Bahian style. Closed some Sundays.

Shopping

Mercado Turístico MARKET
(☎3623-1615; Av Sebastião Diniz; ⏲8am-6pm Mon-Sat) Two city blocks have been designated as pedestrian-only, and are lined with

THE YANOMAMI

The Yanomami are one of the most populous indigenous peoples of Amazonia, their lands spanning much of northern Amazônia, including across the Venezuelan border. Despite their numbers – estimated at around 15,000 – they remained relatively unmolested until the 1970s. That's when the Brazilian government decided to build Hwy BR-210, abruptly exposing the Yanomami to hundreds of construction workers and other outsiders. Predictably, the Yanomami began dying of measles, influenza and venereal diseases; several villages were wiped out entirely.

A decade later, a gold rush sent some 40,000 miners swarming into Yanomami territory, polluting rivers and destroying the forest anew. In 1988, the government attempted to strip the Yanomami of 70% of their traditional territory in order to open it to mining. National and international uproar forced the government to back off, but the plight of the Yanomami remained dire. Nearly a fifth of the group's population died between 1986 and 1993, mostly of disease.

In 1991, the Venezuelan government officially recognized its portion of the Yanomami territory as a special indigenous reserve. Brazil followed suit a month later, creating the 96,650-sq-km **Terra Indígena Yanomami**, Brazil's largest single *índio* territory.

The Yanomami are a slight people, with typical Amerindian features. The focal point of each community is the *yano*, a large round timber-and-thatch structure where each family has its own section facing onto an open central area used for communal dance and ceremony. Each family arranges its own area by slinging hammocks around a constantly burning fire that forms the center of family life.

Their traditional diet includes monkey, tapir, wild pig and a variety of insects, plus fruits, yams, bananas and manioc. The Yanomami hold elaborate ceremonies and rituals and place great emphasis on inter-tribal alliances, primarily to minimize feuds. When nearby soil and hunting grounds are exhausted, the *yano* is dismantled and the village moves to a new site.

Disease is cured with shaman dances, healing hands and various herbs, including *yakoana* (a hallucinogenic herbal powder). When a tribe member dies, the body is hung from a tree until dry, then burned to ashes. The ashes are mixed with bananas, which are then eaten by friends and family of the deceased to incorporate and preserve the spirit.

Anthropologist Napoleon Chagnon lived with the Yanomami off and on for three decades and described them in his best-selling book *The Fierce People* as aggressive and living in a state of 'chronic warfare'. He received acclaim when the book was published in 1968, but his methods and findings have come under increased scrutiny over the years, including accusations that he knowingly exacerbated a measles outbreak and that he greatly exaggerated the degree of violence within the community. The controversy highlighted the ethical dilemmas inherent in studying isolated indigenous groups and the importance, above all, of emphasizing nuance over grand (and usually Western-centric) proclamations.

stalls selling everything from handicrafts to cashew nuts.

Information

CONSULATES

Venezuelan Consulate (☎0xx95-3623-6612; Av Benjamin Constant 968; ⏰8am-noon Mon-Fri) Travelers of many nations need to obtain a Venezuelan tourist card before entering Venezuela by land. The process can be completed in Boa Vista and usually takes about 30 minutes.

EMERGENCY

Hospital Geral has a 24-hour emergency room.

Ambulance (☎192)

Police (☎190)

INTERNET ACCESS

Red Zone (cnr Araújo Filho & Av Benjamin Constant; per hr R$2; ⏰9am-midnight)

MEDICAL SERVICES

Hospital Geral (☎2121-0620; Av Brg. Eduaro Gomes 1364) Main public hospital, located 2km from the center of town toward the airport.

MONEY

Banco do Brasil (Av Glaycon de Paiva 56; ⏰8am-2pm Mon-Fri) Changes euros and US dollars.

Bradesco (cnr Av Sebastão Diniz & Inácio Magalhães) Reliable ATMs.

POST

Main Post Office (☎3621-3535; cnr Av Amazonas & Av NS da Consolata; ⏰8am-4:30pm Mon-Fri, 8am-noon Sat)

TRAVEL AGENCIES

Timbó Turismo (☎3224-4077; timbotur@osite.com.br; Av Benjamin Constant at Rua Araújo Filho; ⏰8am-noon & 2-6pm Mon-Fri, 8am-noon Sat) Sells plane and bus tickets.

Getting There & Away

AIR

Frequent promotions mean flying is often only slightly more expensive than the bus. There was not direct air service from Boa Vista to Guyana or Suriname at the time of research; connect through Belém instead.

Azul (☎4003-1118, 3198-0171; www.voeazul.com.br)

GOL (☎0800-704-0465, 3198-0135; www.voegol.com.br)

TAM (☎4002-5700, 3198-0140; www.tam.com.br)

BUS

Eucatur (☎0800-455-050, 3623-1318; www.eucatur.com.br) has five daily buses to Manaus (R$119, 10 to 12 hours, 9am, 6pm, 7pm, 8pm and 9pm); the 7pm and 9pm are direct.

Amatur (☎3224-0004) operates daily buses to Bonfim on the Guyana border (R$18, 1½ hours, 7am, 10am, 2pm and 4:30pm). From there, you cross the border to Lethem and catch a bus to Georgetown (R$95 from Boa Vista, 15 to 16 hours, Monday, Tuesday, Thursday, Friday and Sunday).

To enter Venezuela, you need to get to the Brazilian border town of Pacaraíma; from the bus station, there's one daily bus (R$21, 3½ hours, 7am) and numerous collective taxis (R$35, 2½ hours).

Getting Around

Around town, taxis marked 'Lotação' operate like buses, following fixed routes and carrying up to four passengers (R$4).

The airport is 3.5km northwest of the city center. To get there, you can take 'Carana-Aeroporto' bus 206 (R$3, 6am to 11:15pm) from the bus terminal on Av Dr Silvio Botelho. Taxis between the airport and center charge R$30.

The **bus station** (Av das Guianas, Bairro São Vicente) is 2.5km southwest of the center. Several buses go there, including '214-Jockei Clube' and '215-Nova Ciudad' (all R$3, every 20 to 30 minutes, 5:30am to midnight). A taxi from the center to the bus station costs about R$15; a *lotação* cab is R$4.

Santa Elena de Uairén (Venezuela)

☎0XX289 / POP 30,000

Santa Elena de Uairén (Santa Elena) is a dusty town located a few kilometers north of the only land-border crossing between Brazil and Venezuela. The town is higher and cooler than Boa Vista, and provides access to Venezuela's vast and beautiful Gran Sabana. The region is dotted with waterfalls and curious flat-topped mountains called *tepuis*; the largest and most famous *tepui* is Mt Roraima, a spectacular natural monument and the spot where Brazil, Venezuela and Guyana meet.

Brazilian and Venezuelan immigration procedures are all dealt with at the border, locally known as La Línea, 15km south of Santa Elena (and about 1km apart from each other). US and Israeli citizens require visas to visit Venezuela. These must be obtained in advance and in person from a

Venezuelan consulate abroad, and are a headache. While they only cost US$30, they can take several weeks to issue, so plan well in advance. Citizens of most other countries can travel visa-free. Yellow fever cards are not required for re-entry to Brazil, but the vaccination is highly recommended.

Sights & Activities

Gran Sabana OUTDOORS

Santa Elena is at the southern tip of the massive Parque Nacional Canaima (30,000 sq km). At its heart is the Gran Sabana, a high savanna dotted with *tepuis* and crisscrossed by rivers. Trips here include great vista points, swimming in natural pools and visiting spectacular waterfalls, including the 100m **Salto Aponwao**. Other options include rafting and visiting the town/region of **El Paují**, a combination of natural attractions and counterculture community.

Mt Roraima HIKING

The largest and highest of the *tepuis* is 2810m Mt Roraima, and climbing it is the reason most people come to Santa Elena. The standard trip is six days, including three spent exploring the wild 60-sq-km moonscape on top. Highlights up there include **La Ventana** with terrific views; **El Foso**, a round, deep sinkhole with interior arches; and a series of freezing quartz-lined ponds called the **Jacuzzis**. If a tour doesn't appeal, you can hire a guide and porters in the towns of San Francisco de Yuruaní (66km north of Santa Elena) or Paraitepui (26km east). Reaching the top requires no technical climbing, but you definitely should be in good shape. Mt Roraima straddles Venezuela, Brazil and Guyana, but this is the only non-vertical route to the top.

Tours

All Santa Elena tour agencies run one-, two- or three-day jeep tours around the Gran Sabana, with visits to the most interesting sights, mostly waterfalls. Budget between US$70 and US$100 per person per day, depending on group size and whether the tour includes just guide and transportation, or food and accommodations as well.

For most visitors, the main attraction is a Roraima tour, generally offered as an all-inclusive six-day package for US$300 to US$400 per person (you get what you pay for). If you have your own gear and food and don't need a porter, most agencies will organize a guide and transportation to Paraitepui, the starting point for the Roraima trek, for US$150. Check on specifics, including group size, hiker-to-guide ratio and equipment quality before signing up for any Roraima tour.

Most agencies also sell Salto Ángel and Orinoco Delta tours.

Backpacker Tours ADVENTURE TOUR

(☎0414-886-7227, 995-1430; www.backpacker-tours.com; Urdaneta s/n) The local powerhouse, it has the most organized and expensive, and best-equipped of Roraima and the region. Also rents mountain bikes.

Kamadac ADVENTURE TOUR

(☎0414-094-4341, 995-1408; www.kamadac.de; Urdaneta s/n) A German- and Venezuelan-owned agency, Kamadac offers staples (Gran Sabana, six-day Roraima climbs) as well as some more adventurous tours (Auyantepui, Akopán Tepui).

Ruta Salvaje ADVENTURE SPORTS

(☎0414-889-4164, 995-1134; www.rutasalvaje.com; Av Mariscal Sucre s/n) Ruta Salvaje offers Roraima and Gran Sabana tours, plus rafting trips, paragliding and day trips to various sights around the region.

Mystic Tours TOUR

(☎0424-912-3741, 416-1081; www.mystictours.com.ve; Urdaneta s/n) Operating for more than 20 years, Mystic Tours offers some of the least expensive tours to Roraima, as well as other local tours with a New Age bent.

Sleeping

Posada Michelle GUESTHOUSE $

(☎995-2017; hotelmichelle@cantv.net; Urdaneta s/n; s/d/tr US$5/6/7;) The undisputed backpacker headquarters and the best place to find companions to form a tour group. The 23 rooms have private bathrooms, hot water and fans to cool you down. There's also a basic kitchen. Recently returned Roraima hikers can take advantage of half-day rest and shower (US$2 per room) or shower only (US$0.50) rates before taking the night bus out.

Posada Backpacker Tours GUESTHOUSE $

(☎995-1415; www.backpacker-tours.com; Urdaneta s/n; dm/s/d/tr US$4/6/7/8;) This simple but friendly 12-room *posada* in the center of Santa Elena has brightly painted rooms with private bathrooms and hot water. It's run by Backpacker Tours, who tend to lodge travelers booked on Roraima treks here.

Posada Los Pinos GUESTHOUSE $
(☎0289-995-1524, 0414-886-7227; www.backpacker-tours.com; Los Pinos s/n; s/d/tr US$8/10/12; @ 🛜 ❄) You'll receive a warm welcome at this excellent, super-comfortable option a short walk from the center. Los Pinos has colorful en-suite rooms with fridge and TV, all set in a large garden with a small pool. Mountain bikes can also be hired.

Eating

ServeKilo Nova Opção BRAZILIAN, BUFFET $
(Av Perimetral s/n; buffet per kg US$0.50; ⏲11am-3pm; 🌿) For almost two decades, this Brazilian eatery has replenished famished hikers with its scrumptious buffet. Vegetarian options are available.

Tumá Serö VENEZUELAN, INTERNATIONAL $
(off Calle Bolívar; menú US$1.50; ⏲7am-8pm) For a cheap meal in a fun atmosphere head to this 'boulevard of food' with dozens of different outlets serving everything from *arepas* to noodles.

ℹ Information

MEDICAL SERVICES

Hospital Rosario Vera Zurita (☎995-1155; Icabarú) The main hospital in Santa Elena is very basic. If you have a serious complaint, cross the border into Brazil or head for Ciudad Guayana.

MONEY

Moneychangers (for US dollars and euros) work the corner of Bolívar and Urdaneta, popularly known as Cuatro Esquinas. Here you'll find some of the best rates in the country – though like anywhere, it's technically illegal. It's safer to ask your *posada* or travel agency to arrange currency exchange.

If you've run out of money and don't want to take a hit by withdrawing money at the official exchange rate in Venezuela, there's a bank with an ATM across the Brazilian border before the bus station. You don't need to have your passport stamped if you're not going past the border town of Pacaraima, and you can then change Brazilian reals to Venezuelan bolívares on the black market in Santa Elena.

ℹ Getting There & Away

AIR

Santa Elena's tiny airport is 7km southwest of town, off the road to the Brazilian border. At present there are no scheduled flights here, and even the irregular Cessna service from Canaima, a godsend for travelers not wanting to do the punishingly long overland journey via Ciudad Guyana, is no longer running. Only chartered planes currently land here, so if you're in a group it's worth investigating prices.

BORDER CROSSINGS

Both Venezuelan and Brazilian passport formalities are done at the border itself, locally known as La Línea, 15km south of Santa Elena de Uairén. *Por puestos* from Icabarú travel to the bus station in the Brazilian border town of Pacaraima, but you have to commandeer the whole taxi or they won't wait for you while you have your passport stamped at the Venezuelan and Brazilian immigration offices at La Línea. There's no departure tax here, though you need a yellow-fever card to enter Brazil.

BUS & JEEP

The bus terminal is on the Ciudad Guayana Hwy, about 2km east of the town's center. There is no public transport here – catch a taxi (US$0.50). Ten buses depart daily to Ciudad Bolívar (US$4, 10 to 12 hours), all stopping at Ciudad Guayana. Some continue to Caracas (US$7, 20 hours).

ℹ CROSSING THE BORDER TO GUYANA

A Brazilian-built bridge – with a cool lane-crossing system that switches from Brazil's right-hand driving to Guyana's left-hand driving – straddles the Takutu River from Bonfim on Brazil's side to Lethem, Guyana. Stamp out of customs and immigration at the bridge on the Brazil side and stamp into the corresponding office on the Guyana end. Travelers from the USA, Canada, EU countries, Australia, New Zealand, Japan, the UK and most Caribbean countries do not need a visa; confirm with the nearest embassy or consulate. If you do need a visa, file your application at least six weeks before you leave your home country. As well as a passport, carry an international yellow-fever vaccination certificate with you (although you probably won't be asked for this), and keep other immunizations up-to-date. Moneychangers abound – you can't miss 'em.

RONDÔNIA

In 1943, President Getúlio Vargas created the Territory of Guaporé from chunks of Amazonas and Mato Grosso. In 1981, it became the state of Rondônia, named for Marechal Cândido Rondon, the enlightened and humane soldier who 'tamed' this region in the 1920s when he constructed a telegraph line linking it to the rest of Brazil. He exhorted his agents to '*Morrer, se preciso for, matar nunca!*' ('Die, if necessary, but never kill!').

More recently, Rondônia was the epicenter of the notorious clear-cutting of the rainforest in the 1980s, equivalent to more than a football field a minute, for a whole decade. Fortunately, deforestation in Rondônia has dropped considerably from those highs, now accounting for less than 10% of overall cutting in the Amazon.

Porto Velho

0XX69 / POP 455,000

Porto Velho is a vital link in Brazil's agricultural economy, as soybeans and other products are shipped on huge barges from here up the Rio Madeira and transferred directly to ocean liners headed abroad. That same ride – albeit on a boat not a barge – draws some travelers up from Cuiabá and the Pantanal on the slow route to Manaus and the Amazon. The city itself has a few bright spots, but mostly serves as a transfer point.

Sights

Estrada de Ferro Madeira–Mamoré HISTORIC SITE

(Madeira-Mamoré Railway Museum; cnr Avs Sete de Setembro & Farqhuar) Right on prime waterfront, the massive warehouses and rusting trains at this historic railyard would make an ideal home for hip bars and eateries, museums and galleries, and shady walkways, not unlike Belém's excellent Estação das Docas. That's long been the plan, but there's little to show for a decade-plus of planning and promises. For now, visitors can wander the hot hulking grounds, browse souvenir stands and book a river tour, imagining what was – and what could be.

Activities

The broad Rio Madeira forms the western boundary of Porto Velho. Formed in the Bolivian Andes, it's 3200km long and has a peak average flow of 1.4 billion liters a minute – the sixth-largest river in the world. It enters the Amazon River 150km downstream from Manaus.

At 5:30pm on weekdays, and hourly from 8am to 6pm on weekends, **riverboats** make 50-minute cruises along the Rio Madeira from the dock in front of the Madeira–Mamoré train station (R$15 per person). While not exactly thrilling, this is a reasonable way to idle away an hour or so – with luck you'll see a few pink dolphins. You can buy snacks and drinks onboard.

Sleeping

Vitória Palace Hotel HOTEL $

(3221-9232; Duque de Caxias 745; s/d R$50/60;) Rooms here are simple and reasonably tidy, though showing their age. Too much furniture makes them feel smaller than they are, but high ceilings help. Consider asking for a back room, as the front ones open right onto the dining area. Breakfast is skimpy.

Hotel Marrocos HOTEL $

(3224-4444; reservas@hotelmarrocos.com; Rua Joaquim Nabuco 2471; s/d R$95/129;) Occupying a converted retail center, the guest rooms here are in former storefronts, their large display windows blacked out and draped with curtains. Nevertheless, the beds are comfortable, the bathrooms spotless and the service friendly.

Larison Hotéis HOTEL $$

(3229-0509; www.larisonhoteis.com.br; Av Carlos Gomes 756; s/d $160/203;) Large spotless rooms with firm beds, luxurious linens, modern bathrooms and reliable air-con and internet make this a gem in Porto Velho's otherwise dreary hotel selection. The hotel caters to business travelers, so weekend rates are a serious steal – nearly 40% off. Friendly service.

Hotel Vila Rica HOTEL $$$

(3224-3433; www.hotelvilarica.com.br; Av Carlos Gomes 1616; s/d R$195/245;) Porto Velho's original luxury hotel is showing its age, but still boasts comfortable rooms with excellent views from the top floors. A swimming pool sets it apart from the rest, and on Saturdays the hotel hosts a popular lunch buffet, *Feijoada do Vila* (per plate R$48).

Eating

Caffé Restaurante BUFFET $

(3224-3176; Av Carlos Gomes 1097; per kg R$32-35; 11am-3pm Mon-Sat) The excellent

Porto Velho

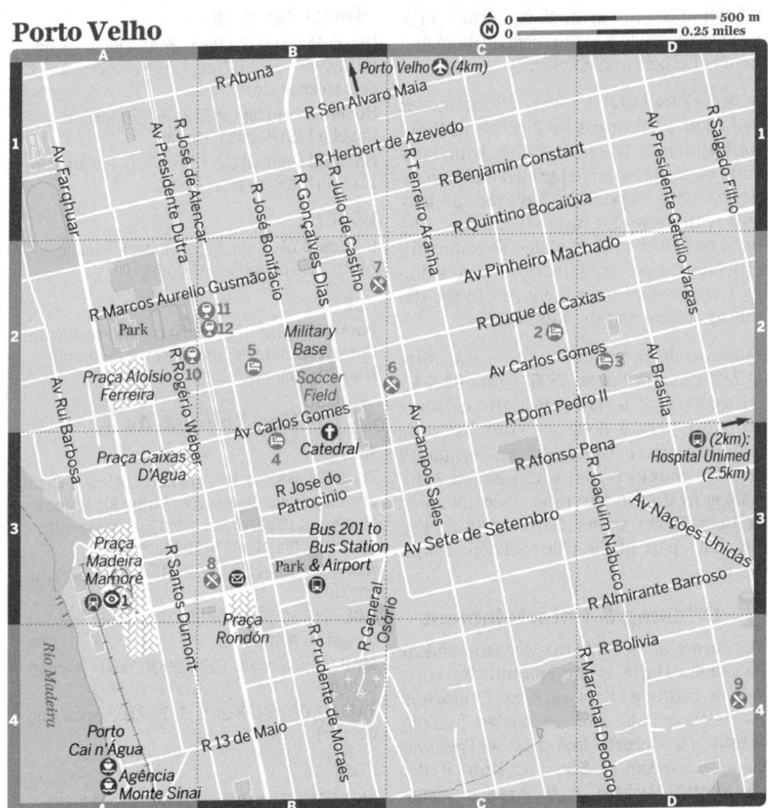

buffet includes a wide selection of mains – from shepherds pie to fried fish – and a slew of sides and a refrigerated case full of succulent desserts, all served in a nice and cool dining area. Popular with professionals, but still reasonably priced.

Fiorela PIZZA $

(Pinheiro Machado at Campos Sales; dishes R$22; 6pm-midnight, closed Mon) Waiters at this loud, glaring, family-favorite eatery rotate around with platters of pasta and pizza, including chocolate and banana varieties for dessert.

O Rei do Peixe SEAFOOD $

(Rua Rogério Weber at Sete de Setembro; mains R$10-35; 11am-11pm) One of several open-air restaurants across from the plaza that are popular with local workers and families. For R$12 you can pile up your plate with a wide selection of mains and sides; add a pitcher

Porto Velho

Sights

1 Estrada de Ferro Madeira-Mamoré A3

Sleeping

2 Hotel Marrocos C2
3 Hotel Vila Rica D2
4 Larison Hotéis B3
5 Vitória Palace Hotel B2

Eating

6 Caffé Restaurante C2
7 Fiorela B2
8 O Rei do Peixe B3
9 Remanso do Tucunaré D4

Drinking & Nightlife

10 Dom Pedro A2
11 Emporium B2
12 Studio B2

of fresh juice for a great cheap meal. As the name suggests, fish is the specialty here, but there's also beef and chicken.

Casa do Tambaqui BRAZILIAN **$$**
(Av Farquar 1008; mains for 2 people R$45-60) Tambaqui is a huge river fish with tasty white meat, often served grilled and *sem espinhas* (without bones). That's the specialty here, with dishes for two to five people. The menu has no individual plates, so come with a friend (or else very hungry). The tidy dining room looks across the street to the old railway station and the Rio Madeira.

Remanso do Tucunaré BRAZILIAN **$$**
(3221-2353; Av Brasília 1506; dishes R$21-45; 11am-10pm) The good fish dishes serve two easily; try a delicious *caldeirada de tucunaré* (river-fish stew) or *tambaquí* (big fish chunks boiled with onion and tomatoes in a soup-like sauce, accompanied by rice). Decor is decidedly downmarket, but that's part of the charm. Popular with locals.

Drinking & Entertainment

The corner of Av Pinheiro Machado and Av Presidente Dutra is the epicenter of Porto Velho's nightlife. Bars such as **Emporium** (Av Presidente Dutra 3366; 5pm-1am Tue-Sun), **Studio** (Av Pinheiro Machado at Av Presidente Dutra; 5pm-1am Tue-Sun) and **Dom Pedro** (Av Pinheiro Machado at Av Presidente Dutra; 6pm-1am Tue-Sun) – all clustered within a half-block – serve up beer, mixed drinks and a cool, bohemian-ish atmosphere that draws a mixed-age crowd. Weekends are busiest and occasionally feature live music.

Information

EMERGENCY

Ambulance (192)

Emergency Room (3224-5225; Julio de Castiho 149, Hospital Central)

Police (190)

INTERNET ACCESS

PortoNet (per hr R$2.50; 8am-10:30pm Mon-Sat, 5-10:30pm Sun)

LAUNDRY

Lavandería Mamoré (3221-3266; Av Pinheiro Machado 1455 at Rua Deodoro; per piece R$1.50-8; 8am-6pm Mon-Sat) Quick and professional, but prices are ridiculously high. You can save a bit by forgoing ironing.

MEDICAL SERVICES

Drogaria Natal (Av Pinheiro Machado, at Julio de Castiho; 7am-1am) Large pharmacy and convenience store.

Hospital Central (3224-5225; Julio de Castiho 149) Public hospital.

Hospital Unimed (3216-6800; Rio Madeira 1618) Private hospital.

MONEY

Bradesco (Av Sete de Setembro) Reliable ATMs. Also on Av Carlos Gomes.

POST

Post Office (3217-3667; cnr Av Presidente Dutra & Av Sete de Setembro; 8am-5pm Mon-Fri, 9am-noon Sat)

Getting There & Away

AIR

Porto Velho airport is 7km north of town. There are daily direct flights to and from Rio Branco, Manaus, Cuiabá, Brasília and São Paulo with onward connections from there.

Azul (4003-1118, 3219-7454; www.voeazul.com.br)

GOL (0800-704-0465, 3219-7498; www.voegol.com.br)

MAP (in Manaus 2125-5000; www.voemap.com.br)

TAM (0800-123-200, 3219-7502; www.tam.com.br)

BOAT

Slow boats down the Rio Madeira to Manaus (R$250 hammock, double cabin with fan/air-con R$700/900, 2½ days) leave Tuesdays, Wednesdays and Saturdays at 2pm from Porto Cai n'Água at the end of Rua 13 de Maio. You'll need your own hammock, and meals are available for purchase. Buy tickets from one of the four authorized brokers at the port, including **Agência Monte Sinai** (99346-7101, 3223-1987; transportesmontesinai@hotmail.com; 8am-6pm Mon-Sat). You can claim a spot and sleep on board for two to three days before departure.

BUS

The **bus station** (cnr Av Jorge Teixeira & Av Carlos Gomes) is 2km east of the center.

Eucatur (3222-2233; www.eucatur.com.br) runs daily buses to Rio Branco (R$75, eight to nine hours, 11am, 10pm, 10:05pm and midnight) and Cuiabá (R$170 to R$270, 25 hours, 2:30am, 5am, 6am, 9am, noon, 1:30pm and 8pm), with connection to Brasilia and beyond.

Real Norte (3225-2891) serves Rio Branco (R$75, nine to 10hours) as well, with departures at 7am, noon, 9pm, 11pm and 11:55pm; service tends to be slower and the buses are older than Eucatur's. Real Norte also has services to Guajará-Mirim (R$63, six hours) at 6:30am, 10am, 2pm, 3pm, 6pm, 11:30pm and 1am.

Collective taxis serve Guajará-Mirim (per person R$100) and are much faster, usually around four hours. The price is based on a minimum of four passengers, so you may have to wait for the car to fill up.

Getting Around

Buses with signs reading 'Almirante' or 'Hospital de Base via Aeroporto' run between the city center and the bus station and the airport, passing each every 30 minutes (every hour on weekends). Pick it up at the bus station or airport terminal (in both cases, the stop is to your right as you leave the main doorway), or along Av Sete de Setembro. A taxi between the bus station and town costs R$15; to or from the airport is R$40.

Guajará-Mirim

0XX69 / POP 42,200

This low-key town on the Rio Mamoré came into existence as the southern terminus of the Madeira-Mamoré railway. Both Guajará-Mirim and Bolivian Guayaramerín across the river are free-trade zones with a steady stream of shopping tourists. For travelers, it's mainly a border-crossing point.

Sights

Museu Histórico Municipal MUSEUM

(cnr Avs Constituição & 15 de Novembro) FREE This sad little museum includes stuffed and pickled animals, random photographs and a handful of indigenous artifacts. Too bad they don't focus on the one thing that's actually historic here: the Madeira-Mamoré railroad, which used this very building as a station during its short existence.

Sleeping & Eating

Hotel Mine-Estrela HOTEL $

(3541-1206; Av 15 de Novembro 460; s/d R$50/80;) Offers large basic rooms with cable TV, internet, and a location that's convenient to restaurants and passing taxis for getting to the port or bus station. Maintenance seems to have suffered in recent years – hopefully a temporary issue – but it remains a reliable budget choice if you're just passing through.

Pousada Costa POUSADA

(3541-6516; Avenida Tiradentes 236; s/d R$60/90;) Colorful decor and warm service from the live-in owners make this an agreeable choice. Rooms are smallish, but have hot water and air-conditioning. It's a bit removed from the port and center, but the owners are happy to call for a moto-taxi or cab (or you can walk a block to the main drag).

Hotel Jamaica HOTEL $

(3541-3722; Av Leopoldo de Matos 755; s/d R$80/140;) Near the cathedral, the Jamaica has excellent service and large comfortable rooms arranged along an internal corridor and lobby. Rooms vary in size; those in front are larger, but the rear units get less hallway traffic. All have a flat-screen TVs and include a well-supplied breakfast.

Lanchonete e Pizzaria Pit Stop PIZZERIA $

(3541-4213; Av 15 de Novembro 620; dishes US$4-6; 5-10pm) A popular if somewhat sterile eatery serving decent pizzas. It has a huge wide-screen TV, so you're sure not to miss a moment of the latest *novela* (soap) or soccer game.

Restaurante Oásis SELF-SERVICE $

(3541-1621; Av 15 de Novembro 460; per kg R$34; 11am-3pm, closed Tue) This longtime favorite in Guajará-Mirim can be counted on for a tasty, well-prepared lunch buffet, including fresh grilled meats. The airy dining area gets some street noise, but is still a pleasant and convenient place for a midday break.

Information

EMERGENCY

Police (190)

INTERNET ACCESS

TriboNet (Av 15 de Novembro; per hr R$1.75; 8am-midnight Mon-Fri, 1-11pm Sat & Sun) Fast connection.

MEDICAL SERVICES

Hospital Regional (3541-7129, 192; cnr Marechal Deodoro & Av Costa Marques) You may have to wait a long time for service at this crowded public hospital. Offers yellow-fever vaccinations, free of charge from 8am to 1pm Monday to Friday.

MONEY

There are numerous moneychangers at the port in Guayaramerín, on the Bolivian side.

Banco do Brasil (Av Mendonça Lima 388; 9am-2pm Mon-Fri) Exchanges US cash but not traveler's checks.

Bradesco (Av Costa Marques 430) Reliable ATMs.

Guajará-Mirim

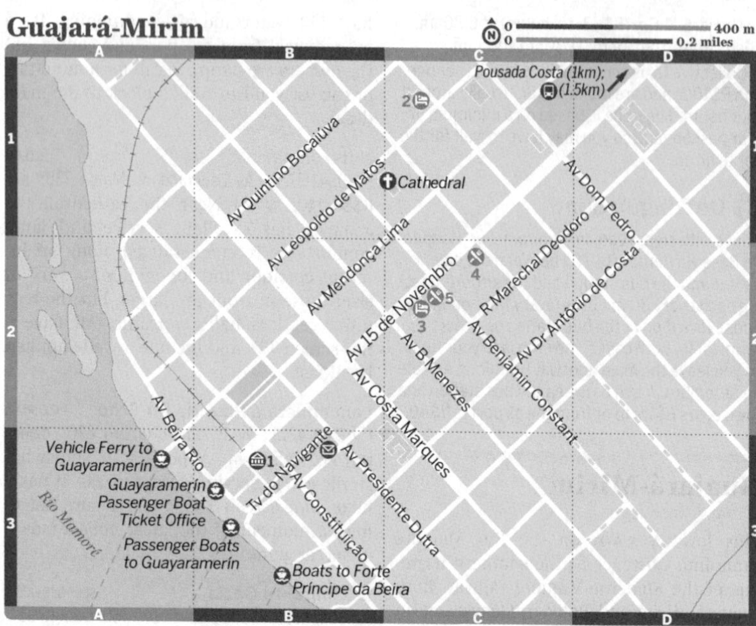

Guajará-Mirim

Sights

1 Museu Histórico Municipal........B3

Sleeping

2 Hotel Jamaica........C1
3 Hotel Mine-Estrela........C2

Eating

4 Lanchonete e Pizzaria Pit Stop........C2
5 Restaurante Oásis........C2

POST

Post Office (☎3541-2777; cnr Av Presidente Dutra & Marechal Deodoro; ⏲8am-4pm Mon-Fri, from 9am Tue)

Getting There & Around

The **bus station** (Av 15 de Novembro) is 2km east of the center; taxis from there into town cost R$20 to R$30, moto-taxis are R$12. **Viação Rondônia** (☎in Porto Velho 3225-2891) runs seven daily buses to Porto Velho (R$62.50, six to seven hours) at 1am, 6:30am, 10am, 1pm, 2pm, 6pm and 11:55pm; the 1pm and 11:55pm departures are direct and about an hour quicker.

TO/FROM BOLIVIA

Motorboats ferry passengers across the Rio Mamoré between Guajará-Mirim and Guayaramerín, Bolivia (R$7, 10 minutes). A minimum of 10 passengers is usually required, but it's rare to wait more than 30 minutes. The port and **ticket office** (☎3541-7221; ⏲24hr) in Guajará-Mirim are on Av Beira Rio.

Bolivian Consulate (☎0xx69-3541-8622; Rua 15 de Novembro 255; ⏲8am-noon & 2-6pm Mon-Fri) Visas can normally be issued on the same day; for US citizens, the fee is a whopping US$160.

Polícia Federal (☎3541-0200; cnr Avs Presidente Dutra & Bocaiúva; ⏲7am-9pm) The immigration office is an unmarked door on Av Presidente Dutra, but you can use the main entrance on Av Quintino Bocaiúva after hours and on weekends.

Guayaramerín (Bolivia)

☎0XX3 / POP 40,450

Knocking on Brazil's back door, Guayaramerín is twinned with the Brazilian town of Guajará-Mirim on the other side of the Río Mamoré. This lively town thrives on all kinds of trade (legal and illegal) with Brazil, and its streets are full of dusty motorcycle tracks and markets heaving with synthetic garments. It is now the northern terminus for river transportation along the Río Mamoré.

Sleeping & Eating

Hotel Santa Ana HOTEL $

(☎855-3900; 25 de Mayo 611; s/d with fan B$70/140) The best of the cluster of hotels on this corner, with spacious rooms, all equipped with fans. Reasonable value, though be sure to avoid the windowless rooms.

Hotel Balneario San Carlos HOTEL $$

(☎855-3555; San Carlos, near 6 de Agosto; s/d/tr B$250/350/450; ❄ 🏊) The choice for anyone here on business, this hotel has a restaurant, redundant sauna, pool room and 24-hour hot water.

Snack Bar Antonella FAST FOOD $

(Main Plaza; mains B$15-30) Pleasant place for a beer and a snack as you watch the world go round the plaza.

Information

There is a slow internet connection at **Masas** (per hr B$5) just off the plaza.

A block east of the plaza, the relatively efficient **Brazilian consulate** (☎855-3766; cnr Avs Beni & 24 de Septiembre; ⊙9am-5pm Mon-Sat) issues visas in three days. Moneychangers hanging around the port area deal in US dollars, Brazilian reais and bolivianos. **Prodem** on the corner of the plaza can give you cash advances on Visa and MasterCard.

Getting There & Away

AIR

The airport is on the edge of town and the airline offices are on the nearby 16 de Julio, around the corner of 25 de Mayo. **TAM** (☎855-3924; Av 16 de Julio) flies to Riberalta on Sunday mornings (B$130, 20 minutes) and has a daily flight to Trinidad (B$523, 50 minutes), except Tuesday and Thursday. **EcoJet** (☎901-105055, 465-2617; www.ecojet.bo; cnr Av 6 de Agosto & Santa Cruz) has daily flights to Trinidad, which connect to La Paz, Cochabamba or Santa Cruz, and a Sunday flight to Sucre and Tarija. Flights to Cobija via Riberalta (per person B$600) are by private rental *avionetta* (light aircraft) and must be full (five people) to depart. Call **Avioneta Ariel** (☎852-3774) or **El Capitán** (☎7686-2742) at least a day in advance.

BOAT

Cargo boats up the Río Mamoré to Trinidad (around B$250/350 without/with food) leave very irregularly and take six days. Ask at the port captain's office opposite the immigration office for information.

BUS, CAMIÓN & TAXI

The bus terminal is on the south end of town, beyond the market. Buses run to Riberalta (B$25, 2½ hours) several times daily. Foolhardy **Vaca Diez** departs daily in the morning for Rurrenabaque (B$120, 18 hours to three days) and La Paz (B$170, 30 to 60 hours) via Santa Rosa and Reyes. Do not contemplate either journey if there is even a hint of rain or else be prepared to help pull the bus out of muddy holes every couple of hours. There are daily buses to Cobija (B$70, 16 hours) and Trinidad (B$240, 22 to 35 hours). Be aware that if enough tickets aren't sold, any of these runs may be summarily canceled. Flying to either destination is your best option and you will not regret the extra expense. Shared taxis to Riberalta (B$50 per person, two hours) leave from the terminal when they have four passengers.

TO/FROM BRAZIL

Crossing to Brazil from the northern Bolivian towns of Cobija and Guayaramerín involves crossings of the Ríos Acre and Mamoré respectively.

Guayaramerín to Guajará-Mirim

Popping into the Brazilian town of Guajará-Mirim for the day from Bolivian Guayaramerín is really easy. Day visits are encouraged, and you don't even need a visa. *Lanchas* (small boats; B$10) across the river leave from the port every half an hour from 6am to 6pm, and sporadically through the night. To travel further into Brazil or to enter Bolivia, you'll have to complete border formalities. The immigration offices in **Guajará-Mirim** (Av Quintina Bocaiúva, Guajará-Mirim; ⊙8am-noon & 2-6pm Mon-Fri) and **Guayaramerín** (☎855-4413, after hours 7395-2902; cnr Av Costañera & Santa Cruz; ⊙7:30am-7:30pm) are in the respective port areas.

Cobija to Brasiléia

It's a long, hot slog across the bridge from Cobija to Brasiléia. Entry/exit stamps are available at **immigration in Cobija** (p657) at the Bolivian end of the bridge and from **Brasiléia's Polícia Federal** (Av Prefeito Moreira; ⊙8am-noon & 2-5pm). With some negotiation, taxis will take you to the Polícia Federal in Brasiléia, wait while you clear immigration, then take you on to the center or to the bus terminal. Alternatively, take the *lancha* (B$5) across the Río Acre; from there it's another 1.5km to the Polícia Federal. If you need a visa, get one at the **Brazilian consulate in Cobija** (p657).

Although officials don't always check, technically everyone needs to have a yellow-fever vaccination certificate to enter Brazil. If you don't have one, head for the convenient and relatively sanitary clinic at the port at Brasiléia on the Brazilian side.

ACRE

Present-day Acre was originally part of Bolivia, but by the end of the 19th century it was mostly populated by Brazilian *seringueiros* (rubber-tappers), spreading south from the Amazonas. In August 1902, Bolivia sent its army to assert control and was met by fierce resistance from the *seringueiros* in what is known here, a bit melodramatically, as the 'Acrean Revolution.' Bolivia eventually ceded the territory to Brazil in exchange for two million British pounds and a promise to build a railroad from the border to Porto Velho to facilitate Bolivian exports. (The railroad was never completed and some in Bolivia say the money was never paid.) The Brazilian government, however, had never really supported the upstart Acreans and refused to name Acre a state, designating it the nation's first 'federal territory' instead. Thus the 'autonomist' movement was born, a sometimes-armed conflict that culminated, 60 years later, in Acre winning full statehood.

Acre is the home state of martyred union and environmental leader Chico Mendes, and was a key battleground for the conflict over deforestation. Hundreds of union leaders, activists and ordinary workers died in the conflicts, including Mendes, who was assassinated in 1988. But thanks to those struggles, today a full third of the state is under environmental protection or designated as indigenous lands.

Remember that Acre is in a different time zone (one hour earlier) from Porto Velho and Manaus.

Rio Branco

☎0XX68 / POP 365,000

Rio Branco, the capital of Acre, was founded in 1882 by rubber-tappers on the banks of the Rio Acre. Once a brash, uneasy town, Rio Branco has transformed itself into a genuinely pleasant place, with several excellent cultural outlets and easy access to some interesting sites, including Xapuri, the hometown of the environmentalist Chico Mendes.

Sights

Palacio Rio Branco HISTORIC BUILDING

(Praça Povos da Floresta; ⌚8am-6pm Tue-Fri, 4-6pm Sat & Sun) FREE Acre's first capital building, the imposing Palacio Rio Branco is now mostly a tourist attraction. A maze of interconnected rooms contain interesting and well-done displays on prehistoric artifacts, indigenous communities, Chico Mendes and the Acrean Revolution.

Memorial dos Autonomistas MEMORIAL

(Autonomists Memorial; ☎3224-2133; Praça Eurico Dutra; ⌚8am-6pm Tue-Fri, 4-8pm Sat & Sun) FREE In its spiffy home on the main plaza, the Memorial dos Autonomistas has a permanent display on Acre's battle for statehood, plus space for rotating art exhibits. It's also where José Guiomard dos Santos is buried; though not Acrean by birth, Guiomard served as federal administrator of the region and later, as senator, helped pass legislation giving Acre its statehood.

Museu da Borracha MUSEUM

(Rubber Museum; Av Ceará 1441; ⌚8am-6pm Tue-Fri) FREE The longtime Museum of Rubber was closed for renovation when we passed through, but is well worth a second look for its fascinating history of rubber-tapping in Acre. The museum's three rooms have displays ranging from how tappers learned to extract the milky sap without killing the tree (a tool called a *cabrita*, meaning 'little goat', was key) to the life and work of Chico Mendes and the Rural Workers Union. Portuguese only.

Mercado Velho MARKET

(Praça Bandeira) Not only a great place for a meal or that late-afternoon beer, Rio Branco's refurbished riverside Mercado Velho is a favorite spot for city-sponsored cultural events, including live music, dance performances, poetry readings and comedy troupes, usually held evenings and weekends.

Sleeping

Hotel do Papai HOTEL $

(☎3223-2044; Floriano Peixoto 849; s/d R$80/120; ❄📶) The Papai's huge reception area gives way to clean rooms with updated TVs and air-conditioning. Large colorful scenes of Amazônia are painted on the high walls of the rooms, making up somewhat for the oldish beds and bathrooms, and lack of natural light. The elderly and charmingly grumpy owner tends the desk.

Hotel Guapindaia Centro HOTEL $

(☎3223-5747; www.hoteisguapindaia.com.br; Floriano Peixoto 550; s/d R$90/130; P❄📶) Clean crisp rooms, albeit a bit small, have sage-colored walls, updated bathrooms and quiet air-con, and include a huge breakfast spread.

Rio Branco

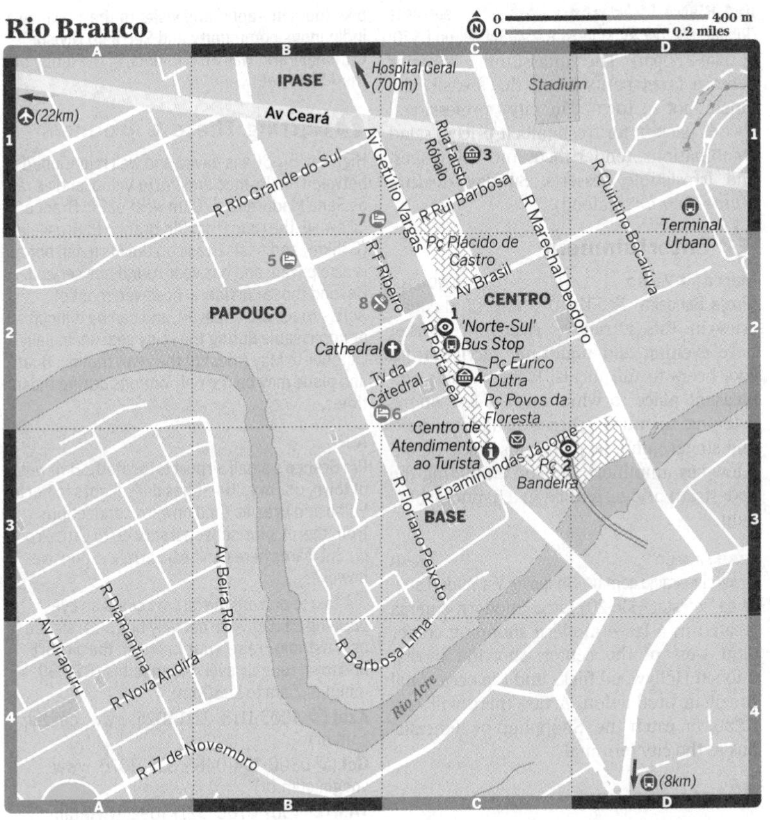

Rio Branco

Sights

1 Memorial dos Autonomistas C2
2 Mercado Velho C3
3 Museu da Borracha C1
4 Palacio Rio Branco C2

Sleeping

5 Hotel do Papai B2
6 Hotel Guapindaia Centro C2
7 Hotel Guapindaia Praça Business B1

Eating

8 AFA Bistrô D'Amazônia B2
Mercado Velho .... (see 2)

Entertainment

Mercado Velho .... (see 2)

Hotel Guapindaia Praça Business HOTEL $$
(3224-7677; www.hoteisguapinda.com.br; Rui Barbosa 354; s/d R$110/170;) Rooms are pretty tiny at this business-minded hotel, though you can't beat the location, a block from a leafy plaza and the city's narrow central park. The large air-conditioned lobby and professional service are a breath of fresh air, and guest rooms are spotless, if not spacious.

Eating

Mercado Velho MARKET $
(Praça Bandeira; dishes from R$6; 7am-10pm) Dubbed the 'Old Market', this is actually part of a highly successful urban-renewal effort of several years ago. An old port building was transformed into an attractive food market where you can order anything from grilled comfort foods to complete mains, served at indoor booths or at tables overlooking a tidy riverfront plaza. Especially popular in the evenings, when there's live music.

AFA Bistrô D'Amazônia BUFFET $$
(Ribeiro 99; per kg Mon-Fri R$54, Sat & Sun R$70; ⌚11am-2:30pm) The unassuming exterior belies a fancy-pants bistro that's easily the lunch spot in town. The city's professional classes pack in for fresh (albeit pricey) salad combinations, tender meat and fish dishes, and irresistible desserts. Sundays feature *frutas do mar* (seafood).

☆ Entertainment

Mercado Velho LIVE MUSIC
(Praça Bandeira; ⌚5-11pm) Many of the eateries in this attractive riverfront market have evening and nighttime service, from cool beers to full meals. It's a popular and pleasant place to while away a few hours, listening to music (there's usually at least one singer/guitarist plying his trade before a low-key amplifier) and contemplating the pedestrian bridge, bathed in a hypnotic blue light.

Cine Araujo CINEMA
(www.cinearaujo.com.br; Shopping Via Verde, Estrada da Floresta; R$16-20) Large modern cinema located in a large modern shopping center 6km west of the center, showing mostly dubbed Hollywood flicks and the occasional Brazilian production. A taxi there will cost R$30, or catch the 'Shopping' or 'Floresta' bus at the city terminal.

ℹ Information

EMERGENCY

Emergency Room (Hospital Geral; ☎192, 3223-3080; cnr Av Nações Unidos & Hugo Carneiro)

Police (☎190)

MONEY

Banco do Brasil (Rua Porta Leal 85)

Bradesco (Rua Porta Leal 83)

POST

Post Office (Epaminondas Jácome 447; ⌚7am-4pm Mon-Fri, 8am-noon Sat)

TOURIST INFORMATION

Centro de Atendimento ao Turista (Praça Povos da Floresta; ⌚8am-9pm Mon-Sat, 9-noon Sun) Not terribly helpful, but a good place to start.

TRAVEL AGENCIES

Discovery Viagens (☎9238-9495; www.discoveryviagens.com; AFA Hotel, Ribeiro 109; ⌚8am-5pm Mon-Fri) Local tour operator offering guided excursions of all sorts, including bike tours in Xapuri and visits to the Yawanawá indigenous community and Serra do Divisor National Park. Has an info desk in the lobby of the AFA Hotel.

ℹ Getting There & Around

Highway BR-364 is paved and well maintained between Rio Branco and Porto Velho, and as far as Sena Madureira, 170km west of Rio Branco. Likewise, the road from Rio Branco to Brasiléia (235km) and Assis Brasil on the Peruvian border is also paved, and has year-round bus service. Beyond those corridors, however, most of Acre's roads are unpaved, and can be difficult or impassable during the rainy season, usually October to May (most of the year, that is). Boat and plane may be the only options during those times.

AIR

Rio Branco's small airport is located 22km west of town, on Hwy 364. It has daily flights to Porto Velho and Brasília (and onward connections from there), plus seasonal service to Cruzeiro do Sul. Fares here can be bizarrely expensive, however.

A taxi to or from the airport costs an eye-popping R$100. Alternatively bus 304, signed as 'Custódio Freire' runs between the airport and town roughly every 45 minutes (R$2.90, 45 minutes, 5am to 11:30pm).

Azul (☎4003-1118, 3211-1025; www.voeazul.com.br)

Gol (☎0800-704-0465, 3211-1070; www.voegol.com.br)

TAM (☎4002-5700, 3211-1092; www.tam.com.br)

BOAT

The Rio Acre is navigable all the way to the Peruvian border at Assis Brasil but there's little river traffic (and none that follows a schedule). Heading in the other direction, it's possible to catch a boat down the Rio Purus from the town of Boca do Acre, north of Rio Branco, theoretically all the way to Manaus. That said, if Manaus is your destination, there's a much more frequent and reliable boat service on the Rio Madeiro, leaving from Porto Velho.

BUS

Long-distance buses leave from the **Rodoviária Internacional de Rio Branco** (☎3221-3693; www.rodoviariainternacional.com; Km 125, Hwy 364), a sleek new bus terminal located 8km southwest of town. **Petroacre** (☎3221-1452) has services to Xapuri (R$30, 3½ hours, 6am and 1:45pm), Brasiléia (R$36, four hours, 6am, noon and 2:45pm), Assis Brasil (R$47.50, six hours, 6am and noon) and Cruzeiro do Sol ($112, 12 to 14 hours, 7:15am and 7:30pm)

Eucatur (☎3233-3741; www.eucatur.com.br) and **Viação Rondônia** (☎3221-1349) have three to four departures daily to Porto Velho (R$80, eight to 10 hours) usually once in the morning and the rest nonstop overnighters.

At Rio Branco's bustling **terminal urbano** (city bus terminal; Rua Sergipe btwn Av Ceará & Rua Benjamin Constant) you pay your fare at a bank of turnstiles and buses come and go from clearly marked platforms. At least three different city buses run between the downtown terminal and the Rodoviária Internacional; they are marked either 'Norte-Sul,' 'Parque Industrial' or 'Jacarandá' (R$2.90, 20 to 30 minutes, every 15 minutes). A taxi to or from the city center costs R$30; a moto-taxi R$15.

Xapuri

☎0XX68 / POP 16,600

This tidy little town of neat wooden houses along broad streets was home to environmental and labor hero Chico Mendes. It lies about 12km northwest of Hwy BR-317, the main road between Rio Branco (241km away) and Brasiléia (74km away).

Sights & Activities

Casa Chico Mendes HISTORIC BUILDING

(www.chicomendes.org.br; Batista de Moraes 494; 8:30am-4:30pm Tue-Fri, 9am-1pm Sat) FREE This simple wood house is where Chico Mendes lived with his family until his murder on the back steps in 1988. Tours include a graphic description of the moment he was shot, with bloodstains still on the walls. Across the street, the Chico Mendes Foundation center has poster-sized photos of Mendes and a collection of personal items and international awards.

Closed for renovation at our last visit.

Museu do Xapuri MUSEUM

(Rua C Brandão; 8:30am-5:30pm Tue-Sat, 9am-1pm Sun) FREE This small but interesting museum tells how Xapuri, located at the confluence of two rivers, was once a major transport hub for rubber, nuts, wood and other products, and a favorite of Middle Eastern merchants peddling everything from shovels to perfume. Housed in an attractive mansion that served as the city hall from 1929 to 2000.

Pousada Ecológica Seringal Cachoeira ECOTOUR

(☎9947-8399; per person R$50-70) Various guided hikes are available at this comfortable lodge, 32km from Xapuri. One hike leaves at 4am for a fascinating real-life look at how workers collect latex and Brazil nuts, with good opportunities to spot wildlife too. There's also tree-climbing and a canopy tour, with 500m of rope bridges and ziplines. Open to guests and nonguests alike; reservations recommended.

Sleeping

Pousada das Chapurys POUSADA $

(☎3542-2253; pousada_chapurys@hotmail.com; Sadala Koury 1385; s/d/tr R$70/100/130;) A short walk from the bus terminal, this is the old standby of Xapuri's hotels, and still a pleasant and convenient place to stay. The friendly owners were close friends of Chico Mendes, and have photos and memorabilia in the hotel's dining area (as well as some fascinating stories). Rooms are large and comfortable, though showing their age.

★ **Pousada Ecológica Seringal Cachoeira** LODGE $

(☎9947-8399; dm R$60, d R$130, all incl breakfast;) Located 32km outside Xapuri where martyred union leader Chico Mendes first tapped rubber trees and collected Brazil nuts. It's still a working rubber forest, but an ecolodge offers visitors cozy accommodations plus guided hikes and activities. Lodging is in large dorms or comfortable stand-alone 'chalets', while meals (lunch and dinner R$30) are served in the spacious main building.

On Hwy BR-317, look for a turnoff 4km south of the Xapuri junction; from there it's another 16km by well-maintained dirt road to the lodge. A taxi from Xapuri costs R$100.

Eating & Drinking

Pizzaria Tribos PIZZERIA $

(☎3542-2531; Rua C Branbão; mains R$18-35; dinner) One of a handful of kiosks in a small park a block off the main plaza, Tribos serves up tasty pizzas at small outdoor tables and gets kudos for playing a nice mix of international rock.

Bebum Bar BAR

(Praça Getúlio Vargas) In a park off the main plaza, this kiosk is a popular watering hole for Xapuri's young and restless.

Information

Banco da Amazona (Rua C Bradão) Next to the gas station.

CHICO MENDES & HIS LEGACY

In the mid-1970s, an ambitious military-government plan to tame the Amazon attracted a flood of developers, ranchers, logging companies and settlers into Acre, who clear-cut rubber and Brazil trees to make room for ranches. Francisco Alves Mendes Filho, better known as Chico Mendes, was a 30-something rubber-tapper, but one of the few who could read and write, and had long taken an interest in improving the lives of fellow *seringueiros* (rubber-tappers). In 1977, he cofounded the Sindicato dos Trabalhadores Rurais de Xapuri (Xapuri Rural Workers' Union) to defy the violent intimidation and dispossession practiced by the newcomers.

Mendes organized *empates* (stoppages), nonviolent human blockades to stop the clear-cutting. But Mendes was not initially an environmentalist – his motivation was to help rubber-tappers, whose livelihood happened to depend on a healthy, intact forest. Likewise, the environmental movement (largely based in the USA at the time) was focused on preserving 'virgin' forest, which it assumed to be empty of humans save a few *índio* tribes.

The joining of those groups – rubber-tappers and US environmentalists – was one of Mendes' key accomplishments. He convinced rubber-tappers to see themselves as stewards of the forest and allies of indigenous peoples. And he helped conceive of 'extractive reserves', to this day an important means of protecting land and people there. He won numerous international awards in the process, including election to the UN Environment Organization's Global 500 Honor Roll in 1987.

Mendes' fame abroad made life increasingly dangerous at home. Killings of rural workers and activists, including priests and lawyers, jumped from single digits in the 1960s, to over a hundred in 1980, to nearly 500 between 1985 and 1987, according to Amnesty International.

In December 1988, he moved to establish his birthplace, Seringal Cachoeira, as an extractive reserve, defying a local rancher and strongman, Darly Alves da Silva, who claimed the land. Mendes had already denounced Silva to the police for threatening his life and for the murder of a union representative earlier that year. Mendes received numerable death threats, but resisted the urging of colleagues to flee Acre state. On December 22, 1988, Mendes stepped onto the back porch of his home in Xapuri and was shot at close range by men hiding in the bushes. He staggered into the house, where his wife and children were watching TV, and bled to death.

Mendes' murder was the first of hundreds to be thoroughly investigated and prosecuted, owing to the massive international reaction to his killing. Darly Alves da Silva and his son Darci Pereira da Silva were sentenced to 19 years in prison for ordering and committing the crime. Both da Silvas escaped from jail in 1993, apparently just walking free, suggesting complicity among the guards, but were recaptured in 1996, after another outcry, and returned to jail. The men completed their sentences in 2009; Darci reportedly lives in the Pantanal area, but Darly has remained in the area, and can be seen around Xapuri to this day.

Mendes' life and death brought unprecedented international attention to the environmental crisis in the Amazon. But activism on behalf of the forest and people who live there remains a dangerous undertaking. On February 12, 2005, a US-born nun named Dorothy Stang was gunned down in the small town of Anapú, in the soy and cattle country of Pará state, by two men reportedly acting on the orders of rancher Vitalmiro Bastos de Moura, whom Stang had accused of illegally clearing land. The gunmen were quickly caught and convicted, but holding Bastos de Moura accountable has proved difficult. He was sentenced to 30 years in prison three times, and all three times his conviction was overturned and he was released. A second rancher was convicted of the crime in 2010, but released in 2012. Bastos de Moura was re-tried and re-convicted in 2013, and is in prison again – for now. The prospects of finding justice for scores of other murder victims, whose deaths will never attract the international attention that Mendes' and Stang's did, are decidedly bleak.

Tourist Information Kiosk (7am-noon & 2-5pm Mon-Fri) Opposite the bus station, this place has more handicrafts than tourist information, but does have friendly attendants and a handy brochure about Xapuri.

Getting There & Away

Petroacre (p654) has a bus service from Xapuri to Rio Branco (R$30, 3½ hours, 6am and 3:20pm daily). There's only one bus from Xapuri to Brasiléia (R$10, two hours) departing at 10am. Alternatively, you can catch a cab to the *trocamento* (junction) on Hwy BR-317 (R$15) and catch a passing Rio Branco or Brasiléia bus there.

Cobija (Bolivia)

Capital of the Pando and Bolivia's wettest (1770mm of precipitation annually) and most humid spot, Cobija sits on a sharp bend of the Río Acre. Cobija means 'covering' and, with a climate that makes you feel as though you're being smothered with a soggy blanket, it certainly lives up to its name.

Cobija was founded in 1906 under the name 'Bahía,' and in the 1940s it boomed as a rubber-producing center. The town's fortunes dwindled with the shriveling of that industry and it has been reduced to little more than a forgotten village, albeit with a Japanese-funded hospital and a high-tech Brazil-nut processing plant.

Sleeping & Eating

It is not customary in Bolivia to include free breakfast in room rates.

Hotel Nanijo's HOTEL **$$**
(842-2230; 6 de Agosto 147; s/d B$200/350;) A large, modern hotel, with the best facilities in town. All rooms have tiled floors and cable TV and the courtyard splash pool is very welcome in the sticky climate.

Esquina de la Abuela INTERNATIONAL **$$$**
(Molina, near Sucre; mains B$40-65) This is Cobija's nicest eatery with alfresco tables and fresh, well-cooked chicken and meat dishes served under a gigantic *palapa* (palm) wigwam.

Information

There are many ATMs around the plaza. The post office is also on the plaza and a number of telephone places are nearby. Internet use is expensive (B$8 per hour) and to connect you'll need to head to Calle Mercado, predictably located next to the market.

Bolivian Immigration (3546-5760; Av Internacional, Modulo Fronterizo 567; 9am-noon & 2-5pm Mon-Fri) Bolivian immigration is in the Prefectural building on the main plaza, with another branch at the airport.

Brazilian Consulate (842-2110; Av René Barrientos; 8:30am-12:30pm Mon-Fri) The Brazilian consulate is a half-block from the main plaza, next to the Banco Mercantil de Bolivia. It grants visas.

Prodem (Plaza Principal 186) In addition to giving cash advances on Visa and MasterCard and changing US dollars, Prodem has an ATM.

Getting There & Away

AIR

Flights arrive and depart from Aeropuerto Anibal Arab, 5km from the center at the top end of Av 9 de Febrero. **TAM** (842-4145; Av 9 de Febrero 59) flies daily to La Paz (B$746, two hours), except Sunday. Flights to Guayaramerín via Riberalta are in *avionetas*; ask at the airport or call (7621-0035). It pays to book your flights well in advance.

BUS & CAMÍON

There is no bus terminal in Cobija, but buses pull into their respective offices on Av 9 de Febrero out towards the airport. Services to Riberalta and Guayaramerín (B$70, 16 hours) depart daily between 5am and 8am. There is one tortuous service to La Paz via Rurrenabaque run by La Yungueña (B$280, 35 to 60 hours), but if you are really smart, you'll take a flight.

Getting Around

Moto-taxis charge a set B$4 to anywhere in town, B$10 to the airport. Taxis charge B$20 to the international airport. A cheaper option is to hop on *micro A* (B$2.50), which shuttles between the airport and the market.

Brasiléia

0XX68 / POP 22,300

The border town of Brasiléia is separated from Cobija, Bolivia, by the meandering Rio Acre and Igarapé Bahia. There's precious little to do here, unless you're in the market for a computer or DVD player – for that, you can join the crowds crossing into Cobija to take advantage of the lower prices and a duty-free border.

Sleeping & Eating

Pousada Las Palmeras POUSADA **$**
(3546-3284; Rua Odilon Pratagi 125 at Geny Assis; s/d R$60/80;) Brasiléia's most appealing

hotel also has to be its unluckiest – it's been flooded several times when the Rio Acre tops its banks, including in March 2015. The hardworking owner has rebuilt each time, and so Las Palmeras is open once again, with narrow singles and spacious doubles, all with air-con, TV, minibar and hot water. Breakfast is excellent.

Saborella BRAZILIAN $
(Rua Odilon Pratagi s/n; mains R$15-37; ⏲11am-3pm daily, 5-10pm Tue-Sun) Daily specials make ordering easy at this small restaurant, one of few genuinely agreeable places in town. Located a half-block from the bus station.

Orientation

Hwy BR-317 from Rio Branco approaches Brasiléia from the southeast, through the adjacent but independent town of Epitáciolândia. The Brasiléia bus station is just across a small bridge; from there it's a 300m walk (or R$8 taxi ride) to the center of town. If you do walk, bear right out of the bus terminal, and follow Rua Odilon Pratagi to Av Prefeito R Moreira, where most of the action is located.

A bridge over the Igarapé Bahia connects Epitáciolândia to Cobija, and is the official border crossing, with immigration offices for both countries nearby. A smaller, more convenient bridge spans the Rio Acre, making it possible to walk from one downtown to the other in just a few minutes. The smaller bridge – which is dedicated to Wilson Pinheiro, a rubber-tapper union president and friend of Chico Mendes who was assassinated in July 1980 – is at the end of Av Prefeito R Moriera; there is a customs post there, but no immigration officers.

Information

Banco do Brasil (Av Prefeito R Moreira No 470)

Police (☎3546-3207, 190; Av Prefeito R Moreira No 456; ⏲24hr)

Post Office (Av Prefeito R Moreira btwn Banco das Amazonas & tourist information kiosk; ⏲8am-noon & 2-5pm Mon-Fri)

Getting There & Away

BUS

The bus station is 500m from most of the hotels and the main commercial strip; a taxi in either direction costs R$7. PetroAcre (p654) has daily departures to Rio Branco (R$30, four hours) plus services to Xapuri (R$12, two hours) and Assis Brasil (R$12, two hours). You can usually catch a collective taxi to any of the above as well, which are pricier but much quicker.

TO/FROM PERU

Access to Peru is through the village of Assis Brasil, 110km west of Brasiléia. Once an adventure route, the road is now paved and has daily bus services. Complete Brazilian immigration procedures in Brasiléia, and Peruvian immigration at the border town of Iñapari.

Real Norte has bus services between Assis Brasil and Rio Branco and Brasiléia.

TO/FROM COBIJA (BOLIVIA)

You are free to cross back and forth between Cobija and Brasiléia without passing immigration, provided you're going for a short period. If you plan to continue inland, or stay longer than a couple of days, you ought to clear immigration officially.

Bolivian immigration (p657) faces Cobija's main plaza. There's also a checkpoint on the main international bridge, which is open round the clock. In Brazil, the **Polícia Federal** (☎3546-3204; ⏲8am-7pm) handle immigration procedures; the office is in Epitáciolândia, just across the main international bridge. In Cobija, the **Brazilian consulate** (p657) is a half-block from the main plaza, on Av General Rene Barrientos, next to the Banco Mercantil de Bolivia.

Understand Brazil

Brazil Today

It's a challenging moment in Brazil. The largest corruption scandal in the nation's history has battered an economy already in recession and incited widespread protests. With unemployment on the rise, Brazil's currency in free-fall and surging crime in the cities, Brazilians are not surprisingly pessimistic about the future. There is hope, however, that the 2016 Olympic Games will bring a boost to the economy – and to the nation's spirits.

Best on Film

Tropa de Elite (Elite Squad, 2007) An action film of crime and corruption as an elite police squad and drug lords clash. Don't miss the sequel (*The Enemy Within*).

Central do Brasil (Central Station, 1998) Walter Salles' moving tale of a homeless boy and an older woman on a road trip across Brazil.

Reaching for the Moon (2013) Tragic love story between an American poet and Brazilian architect, set in 1950s Petrópolis.

Bel Borba Aqui (2012) Colorful documentary of an artist who uses Salvador as his canvas.

Ao Som As Redor (Neighboring Sounds, 2012) Critically acclaimed film dealing with the wealthy and the underclass in Recife.

Best in Print

Brazil on the Rise (Larry Rohter, 2010) Insightful portrait of the politics, culture and challenges of the South American nation.

The Lost City of Z (David Grann, 2009) Gripping journey into the Amazon to retrace the steps of lost explorer Colonel Fawcett.

Death in Brazil (Peter Robb, 2005) Well-written travelogue that delves into history, culture and corruption.

A Scandal of Epic Proportions

Brazil has long grappled with corruption. Embezzlement, bribes and money laundering occur with dispiriting frequency in a country ranked 69th in the world for its perceived level of public corruption. Yet even a people accustomed to this pervasive problem were shocked at the vast size of the scandal that recently came to light. In 2014, an undercover investigation by Brazilian police unearthed a colossal kickback scheme tied to Petrobras, Brazil's massive state-run oil company.

Prosecutors allege that top officials from Petrobras colluded with a cartel of companies to overcharge on contracts, with jaw-dropping sums of money being funneled to the governing Workers' Party. The kickbacks, which allegedly began in 2004 when former president Lula was in office, total a whopping US$3 billion. The reach of the scheme boggles the imagination, and involved phantom corporations, Rolex watches, yachts, prostitutes and helicopters, with one elderly man flying huge bricks of cash around the world (sometimes as much as €500,000 at a time).

Protests

The scandal has already brought down major titans of industry and high-ranking government officials. By late 2015, some 117 indictments had been issued, five politicians arrested and criminal cases brought against more than a dozen companies. The fallout is damning for the ruling Workers' Party, which no one expects to survive the next major election. Many Brazilians believe that President Dilma Rousseff was also involved. She chaired the board of Petrobras for seven years, during the period when many of the bribes are believed to have occurred. Although she was quickly cleared of any involvement in the scheme, Brazilians have taken to the streets in massive protests calling for her impeachment. By late 2015,

Dilma's approval rating had fallen to 8%, a historic low. In the turmoil, even once-close allies are abandoning her (including the vice president), and with impeachment a very credible threat, Dilma's days in office may be numbered.

Economic Woes

Enormous repercussions from the scandal have sent shockwaves far and wide. It has affected the GDP, unemployment and inflation, not to mention foreign investment. One study released in 2015 estimated the price tag of the corruption scandal at R$87 billion – about 1% of Brazil's GDP – owing to reductions in investments and layoffs in construction (two construction companies that colluded with Petrobras filed for bankruptcy). In September, Standard & Poor's downgraded Brazil's sovereign credit rating to junk status. Meanwhile Brazil's currency, the real, remains on a downward spiral, falling (40% in 2015) to its lowest point in two decades. In other discouraging news, by late 2015, Brazil's stock market was down 20%, unemployment had reached a five-year high and the overall economy was on track to shrink by more than 2.5% by the year's end.

The Olympic Makeover

One glimmer of hope is the Summer Olympic Games of 2016, being held in Rio de Janeiro. Eduardo Paes, Rio's mayor, is betting big. His wager: that a wealth of private and public investment showered on the city will pay off, much as it did for Barcelona after its Olympic games. Since 2009, Rio has been hard at work revitalizing formerly derelict parts of town. The epicenter of Rio's rebirth is the Porto Maravilha (Marvelous Port), an astounding 5 million square meters of waterfront near downtown that now boasts new museums, green spaces and live-work spaces.

After more than US$1.7 billion of investment and seven years of construction, the project is nearing completion. The unsightly elevated highway that once marred the skyline has been torn down and replaced by tunnels, with new parks laid over the top. A new high-tech light rail will travel along 26km of rails through downtown, looping past the striking Praça Mauá, with its two new grand museums. Picturesque colonial buildings, forgotten beneath years of grime, have been restored, while new bike lanes and waterfront walking paths connect the district with other parts of downtown.

Even more impressive is the Herculean R$8 billion expansion of Rio's metro system: a 17km extension running from Ipanema to Barra that will carry an estimated 300,000 passengers a day. Engineers and laborers have been working around the clock to meet the 2016 deadline.

POPULATION: **205 MILLION**

GDP: **US$3.3 TRILLION**

INFLATION: **9.6%**

MONTHLY MINIMUM WAGE: **R$788**

INFANT MORTALITY PER 1000 LIVE BIRTHS: **19 (USA: 6)**

UNEMPLOYMENT: **7.5% (USA: 5.1%)**

if Brazil were 100 people

54 would be white
38 would be mulatto (mixed white and black)
6 would be black
2 would be other

belief system

(% of population)

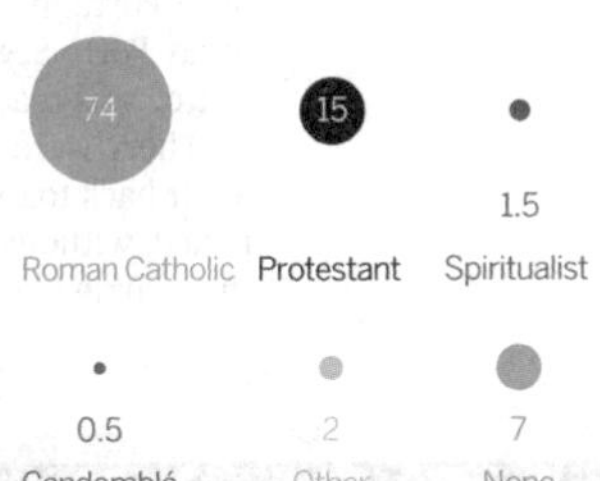

population per sq km

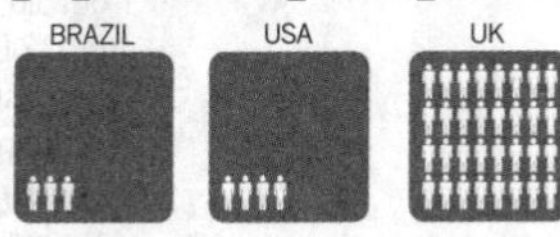

History

Brazil's population, the fifth biggest in the world, reached its lands from Africa, Asia, Europe and other parts of the Americas – diverse origins that have created one of the planet's most racially mixed societies. How they came, intermingled and developed the unique Brazilian identity that charms visitors today is a rough-and-tumble story of courage, greed, endurance and cruelty, eventually yielding a fitful progress toward the democracy the country now enjoys.

French philosopher Jean-Jacques Rousseau based his optimistic view of human nature (the noble savage) in part on early Portuguese descriptions of indigenous people who were 'innocent, mild and peace-loving'.

Before the Portuguese

It's generally believed that the early inhabitants of the Americas arrived from Siberia in waves between about 12,000 and 8000 BC, crossing land now submerged beneath the Bering Strait, then gradually spreading southward over many millennia. Some scholars, however, believe that humans arrived much earlier (25,000 to 35,000 BC) in groups that traveled by boat across the Pacific.

Researchers in the remote Serra da Capivara in the Northeastern state of Piauí have found some of Brazil's earliest evidence of human presence. The oldest traces of human life in the Amazon region can be seen on a detour from a river trip between Santarém and Belém: a series of rock paintings estimated to be 12,000 years old near Monte Alegre.

By the time the Portuguese arrived, there were probably between two and four million people in what's now Brazil.

Cabral & Chums

The course of Brazilian history was changed forever in 1500, when a fleet of 12 Portuguese ships carrying nearly 1200 men rolled up near what is today Porto Seguro. When they arrived, their indigenous reception committee was ready and waiting.

'There were 18 or 20 men,' marveled scribe Pero Vaz de Caminha in a letter back to the Portuguese king. 'They were brown-skinned, all of them naked, without anything at all to cover their private parts. In their hands they carried bows and arrows.'

TIMELINE

c 12,000 BC

Early inhabitants of the Americas arrive from Siberia in waves from 12,000 to 8000 BC, crossing land now submerged beneath the Bering Strait, then gradually spreading southward over many millennia.

1500

Portuguese explorer Pedro Álvares Cabral makes landfall around present-day Porto Seguro and claims possession of the land – believed at first to be an island – for the Portuguese crown.

1549

Tomé de Sousa is named Brazil's first governor. He centralizes authority and founds the city of Salvador, which will remain Brazil's capital for more than two centuries.

The festivities didn't last long. Having erected a cross and held Mass in the land they baptized Terra da Vera Cruz (Land of the True Cross), the Portuguese took to the waves once again. With lucrative spice, ivory and diamond markets in Asia and Africa to exploit, Portugal had bigger fish to fry elsewhere. It wasn't till 1531 that the first Portuguese settlers arrived in Brazil.

Brazil's Indigenous People

For Brazil's *índios* (indigenous people), April 22, 1500, marked the first chapter in their gradual extermination. Sixteenth-century European explorers along the Amazon encountered large, widespread populations; some were practicing agriculture while others were nomadic hunter-gatherers. Coastal peoples fell into three main groups: the Guarani (south of São Paulo and in the Paraguai and Paraná basins inland), the Tupi or Tupinambá (along most of the rest of the coast) and the Tapuia (peoples inhabiting shorter stretches of coast in among the Tupi and Guarani). The Tupi and Guarani had much in common in language and culture. A European adaptation of the Tupi-Guarani language later spread throughout colonial Brazil and is still spoken by some people in Amazonia.

Over the following centuries a four-front war was waged on the indigenous way of life. It was a cultural war, as well as a physical, territorial and biological one. Many *índios* fell victim to the *bandeirantes* – groups of roaming adventurers who spent the 17th and 18th centuries exploring Brazil's interior, pillaging *índio* settlements as they went. Those who escaped such a fate were struck down by the illnesses shipped in from Europe, to which they had no natural resistance. Others were worked to death on sugar plantations.

Quilombo (directed by Cacá Diegues) is an epic history flick in which the vast Palmares *quilombo* – a community of runaway slaves led by the legendary Zumbi – is reconstructed in Rio's Baixada Fluminense.

Sugar & Slavery

Brazil didn't boast the ivory and spices of Africa and the East Indies, and the only thing that had interested the Portuguese in the early years after they had found it was a rock-hard tree known as *pau brazil* (brazilwood), which yielded a valuable red dye. Merchants began sending a few ships each year to harvest brazilwood and take it back to Europe, and the colony changed its name to Brazil in tribute to the tree. Alas, the most accessible trees were rapidly depleted, and the *índios* soon stopped volunteering their labor. But after colonization in 1531, the settlers soon worked out that Brazil was a place where sugarcane grew well. Sugar came to Brazil in 1532 and hasn't left since. It was coveted by a hungry European market, which used it for medicinal purposes, to flavor foods and even in wine.

Perhaps envisaging Brazil's sugarcoated future, the colonists turned to this new industry. They lacked just one thing: a workforce.

One of Brazil's great folk heroes is Chico Rei, an African king enslaved and brought to work in the mines, but who managed to buy his freedom and later the freedom of his tribe.

1550

Facing a shortage of labor (as *índios* die from introduced European diseases), Portugal turns to the African slave trade; open-air slave markets flourish in the slowly growing colony.

1621

The Dutch West India Company sets up shop in Northeastern Brazil, heralding the beginning of the Dutch presence in Brazil. Its goal: to wrest control of the colony from Portugal.

1644–54

Over a decade, the Portuguese wage war against Holland's presence in Brazil, pushing the Dutch back to Recife; the Dutch surrender in 1654, ending Holland's presence in Brazil.

1650s

Communities of runaway slaves, called *quilombos*, flourish, eventually becoming targets of *bandeirantes*. Hundreds of these communities will become towns following abolition in the late 1800s.

The Slave Trade

African slaves started to pour into Brazil's slave markets from about 1550. They were torn from a variety of tribes in Angola, Mozambique and Guinea, as well as the Sudan and Congo. Whatever their origins and cultures, their destinations were identical: slave markets such as Salvador's Pelourinho or Belém's Mercado Ver-o-Peso. By the time slavery was abolished in Brazil in 1888, around 3.6 million Africans had been shipped to Brazil – nearly 40% of the total that came to the New World.

Africans were seen as better workers and less susceptible to the European diseases that had proved the undoing of so many *índios*. In short, they were a better investment. Yet the Portuguese didn't go out of their

BRAZIL'S ÍNDIOS TODAY

When the Portuguese arrived in 1500, there were, by the most common estimates, between two and four million *índios* (indigenous people) already living in Brazil, in over 1000 different tribes. Five centuries later there are an estimated 700,000 *índios* left, living in a little over 200 tribes. Slavery, diseases, armed conflict and loss of territory all took a savage toll on Brazil's native peoples, to the point where in the 1980s *índio* numbers were under 300,000 and it was feared they might die out completely. Since then there has been a marked recovery in the indigenous population, partly thanks to international concern about groups such as the Yanomami, who were threatened with extermination by disease and violence from an influx of gold prospectors into their lands. Government policy has become more benign and huge areas of Brazil are now Terra Indígena (Indigenous Land). Just over 1 million sq km – more than 12% of the whole country – is now either officially registered as Indigenous Land or in the process of registration

There are those who think that 12% of national territory reserved for 0.25% of the national population is too much and fail to respect *índio* rights to these lands. Disputes between indigenous groups and loggers, miners, homesteaders, hunters, road builders and reservoir constructors are still common, and sometimes violent.

It's thought there may still be more than 60 uncontacted tribes, mostly small groups in the Amazon forests – home to about 60% of Brazil's *índios* (and almost all of the existing Indigenous Lands).

Most of Brazil's *índios* still live traditional lifestyles, hunting (some still with blowpipes and poisoned arrows) and gathering and growing plants for food, medicine and utensils. Their homes are usually made of natural materials such as wood or grass. Ritual activity is strong, body- and face-painting is prevalent, and most indigenous people are skilled in making pottery, basketry, masks, headdresses, musical instruments and other artisanry with their hands. None of those known to the outside world are truly nomadic. Indigenous Lands generally have an exemplary record of environmental conservation because their inhabitants continue to live sustainable lifestyles.

1695

Palmares, the largest *quilombo* in Brazil's Northeast – and home to more than 20,000 inhabitants – is finally destroyed following decades of attacks by Portuguese troops.

1696

News of the discovery of gold in Brazil reaches Lisbon. In ensuing years, tens of thousands of migrants stream into present-day Minas Gerais, Mato Grosso, Goiás and southern Bahia.

1750

The Spanish concede to the Portuguese the Treaty of Madrid, which hands over 6 million sq km to the Portuguese and puts Brazil's western borders largely where they are today.

1750s

Gold (and later diamonds) begin to define the colonial economy. In Minas Gerais the population explodes from 30,000 in 1710 to 500,000 by the end of the century.

way to protect this investment. Slaves were brought to Brazil in subhuman conditions: taken from their families and packed into squalid ships for the monthlong journey to Brazil.

Masters & Slaves

For those who survived such ordeals, arrival in Brazil meant only continued suffering. A slave's existence was one of brutality and humiliation. Kind masters were the exception, not the rule, and labor on the plantations was relentless. Slaves were required to work as many as 17 hours each day, before retiring to the squalid *senzala* (slave quarters), and with as many as 200 slaves packed into each dwelling, hygiene was a concept as remote as the distant coasts of Africa. Dysentery, typhus, yellow fever, malaria, tuberculosis and scurvy were rife; malnutrition a fact of life. Syphilis also plagued a slave population sexually exploited by its masters.

Sexual relations between masters and slaves were so common that a large mixed-race population soon emerged. Off the plantations there was a shortage of white women, so many poorer white settlers lived with black or indigenous women. Brazil was already famous for its sexual permissiveness by the beginning of the 18th century.

A book about the relationship between slaves and masters on Pernambuco's sugar plantations, Gilberto Freyre's *The Masters and the Slaves* (1933), revolutionized Brazilian thinking about the African contribution to Brazilian society.

Resistance & the Quilombos

Resistance to slavery took many forms. Documents of the period refer to the desperation of the slaves who starved themselves to death, killed their babies or fled. Sabotage and theft were frequent, as were work slowdowns, stoppages and revolts.

Other slaves sought solace in African religion and culture. The mix of Catholicism (made compulsory by slave masters) and African traditions spawned a syncretic religion on the sugar plantations, known today as Candomblé. The slaves masked illegal customs with a facade of Catholic saints and rituals. The martial art capoeira grew out of these communities.

Many slaves escaped from their masters to form *quilombos,* communities of runaway slaves that quickly spread across the countryside. The most famous, the Republic of Palmares, which survived through much of the 17th century, was home to some 20,000 people before it was destroyed by federal troops.

As abolitionist sentiment grew in the 19th century, many (unsuccessful) slave rebellions were staged, the *quilombos* received more support and ever-greater numbers of slaves fled the plantations. Only abolition itself, in 1888, stopped the growth of *quilombos.*

The Bandeirantes & the Gold Rush

The *bandeirantes,* too, were keen to make inroads into Brazil. These bands of explorers roamed Brazil's interior in search of indigenous

1763

With gold flowing from Minas Gerais through Rio de Janeiro, the city grows in wealth and population; the Portuguese court transfers the capital of Brazil from Salvador to Rio.

1789

The first organized movement toward independence springs to life. Tiradentes and 11 other conspirators organize the Inconfidência Mineira to overthrow the Portuguese. The plot fails, however, and Tiradentes is executed.

1807

Napoleon invades Portugal and the Portuguese prince regent (later known as Dom João VI) and his entire court of 15,000 flee for Brazil. The royal coffers shower wealth upon Rio.

1815

Dom João VI declares Rio the capital of the United Kingdom of Portugal and Brazil. The same year, a mounting financial crisis forces the king to return to Portugal.

slaves, mapping out undiscovered territory and bumping off the odd indigenous community along the way.

The *bandeirantes* took their name from the trademark flag-bearer who would front their expeditions. During the 17th and 18th centuries, group after group of *bandeirantes* set out from São Paulo. The majority were bilingual in Portuguese and Tupi-Guarani, born of Portuguese fathers and indigenous mothers. They benefited from both indigenous survival techniques and European weaponry.

By the mid-17th century they had journeyed as far as the peaks of the Peruvian Andes and the Amazon lowlands. It was the exploits of these discoverers that stretched Brazil's borders to their current extent. In 1750, after four years of negotiations with the Spanish, their conquests were secured. The Treaty of Madrid handed more than 6 million sq km to the Portuguese and put Brazil's western borders more or less where they are today.

History Books

Brazil: Five Centuries of Change (Thomas E Skidmore)

The History of Brazil (Robert Levine)

A Concise History of Brazil (Boris Fausto)

The *bandeirantes* were known for more than just their colorful flags. Protected from *índio* arrows by heavily padded cotton jackets, they waged an all-out war on Brazil's indigenous people, despite the fact that many of them had indigenous mothers. Huge numbers of *índios* fled inland, searching for shelter in the Jesuit missions. But there were few hiding places – it is thought the *bandeirantes* killed or enslaved well in excess of 500,000 *índios*.

Gold

'As yet we have no way of knowing whether there might be gold, or silver or any kind of metal or iron [here],' reported Pero Vaz de Caminha to his king in 1500.

Though it wasn't discovered until nearly two centuries later, there certainly was gold in Brazil. Unsurprisingly, it was the *bandeirantes* who, in between decapitating *índios*, discovered it in the Serra do Espinhaço in Minas Gerais.

For part of the 18th century Brazil became the world's greatest gold 'producer,' unearthing wealth that helped build many of Minas Gerais' historic cities. The full title of Ouro Prêto, one of the principal beneficiaries of the gold boom, is actually Vila Rica de Ouro Prêto (Rich Town of Black Gold).

Other wild boom towns such as Sabará, Mariana and São João del Rei sprang up in the mountain valleys. Wealthy merchants built opulent mansions and bankrolled stunning baroque churches, many of which remain to this day.

Gold produced a major shift in Brazil's population from the Northeast to the Southeast. When gold was first discovered, there were no white settlers in the territory of Minas Gerais. By 1710 the population had reached 30,000, and by the end of the 18th century it was 500,000.

1822

Left in charge of Brazil after his father Dom João VI returns to Portugal, the prince regent Dom Pedro I declares independence from Portugal and crowns himself 'emperor' of Brazil.

1831

Brazil's first homegrown monarch, Dom Pedro, proves incompetent and abdicates the throne. His son Pedro II takes power in 1840 and ushers in a long period of growth and stability.

mid-1830s

The coffee bush, which flourishes in Rio de Janeiro province, plays a major role in the colony's economy. *Fazendas* (ranches) spring up as Brazil becomes a major coffee exporter.

1835

Inspired by the successful Haitian Revolution some years earlier, Brazilian slaves in Salvador stage an uprising – Brazil's last big slave revolt – which narrowly fails.

An estimated one-third of the two million slaves brought to Brazil in the 18th century were sent to the goldfields, where their lives were often worse than in the sugar fields.

But the gold boom didn't last. By 1750 the mining regions were in decline and coastal Brazil was returning to center stage. Many of the gold hunters ended up in Rio de Janeiro, which grew rapidly.

Dom João Vi

Brazil became a temporary sanctuary to the Portuguese royal family in 1807. Running scared from Napoleon, whose army was at that moment advancing on Lisbon, some 15,000 court members fled to Rio de Janeiro, led by the prince regent, Dom João.

Like so many *estrangeiros* (foreigners) arriving in Brazil, the regent fell in love with the place and granted himself the privilege of becoming the country's ruler. He opened Rio's Jardim Botânico (Botanical Gardens) to the public in 1822, and they remain there to this day in the upmarket Jardim Botânico neighborhood.

Even after Napoleon's defeat at Waterloo in 1815, Dom João showed no sign of abandoning Brazil. When his mother, Dona Maria I, died the following year, he became king and declared Rio the capital of the United Kingdom of Portugal and Brazil. Brazil became the only New World colony ever to have a European monarch ruling on its soil.

'Order and Progress,' the slogan on Brazil's flag, comes from French philosopher Auguste de Comte (1797–1857), whose elevation of reason and scientific knowledge over traditional religious beliefs influenced the young Brazilian republic.

Independence

Independence eventually came in 1822, 30 years after the Inconfidência Mineira (an uprising against Portuguese colonization). Legend has it that on the banks of São Paulo's Ipiranga river, Brazil's then regent, Dom João's son Pedro, pulled out his sword, bellowing, *'Independência ou morte!'* (Independence or death!). With the same breath he declared himself Emperor Dom Pedro I.

The Portuguese quickly gave in to the idea of a Brazilian empire. Without a single shot being fired, Dom Pedro I became the first emperor of an independent Brazil. The *povo brasileiro* (Brazilian people), however, were not as keen on Pedro as he was about their newly born nation. From all accounts he was a blundering incompetent, whose sexual exploits (and resulting string of children) horrified even the most permissive of Brazilians. After nine years of womanizing he was forced to abdicate, leaving his five-year-old son, Dom Pedro II, to take over.

A period of crisis followed: the heir to the throne was, after all, just a child. Between 1831 and 1840 Brazil was governed by so-called *regências* (regencies), a time of political turmoil and widespread rebellions. The only solution was the return of the monarchy and a law was passed to declare Dom Pedro II an adult, well before his 18th birthday.

1865

Brazil, allied with Uruguay and Argentina, wages the 'War of the Triple Alliance' on Paraguay. South America's bloodiest conflict leaves untold thousands dead, and wipes out half of Paraguay's population.

1888

Slavery is abolished in Brazil, the last country in the New World to do so. The law is signed by Princesa Isabel, admired by many blacks as their benefactress.

1889

A military coup, supported by Brazil's wealthy coffee farmers, overthrows Pedro II. The monarchy is abolished and the Brazilian Republic is born. Pedro II goes into exile in Paris.

1890

Demand for rubber skyrockets with the start of the US automobile industry. This fuels boom times in Brazil, the world's only natural exporter until 1910, in Amazonian cities such as Belém and Manaus.

Aged just 15, Dom Pedro II received the title of Emperor and Perpetual Defender of Brazil, precipitating one of the most prosperous spells in the country's history, barring the war with Paraguay in 1865. Invaded by its neighbor, Brazil teamed up with Argentina and Uruguay and thrashed the Paraguayans back across the border.

Paraguay was left crippled – its population slashed to just 200,000, of whom around 180,000 were women. Brazil, too, suffered heavily: around 100,000 men died, many of them slaves sent to war in the place of wealthier Brazilians.

Abolition & the Republic

Since the 16th century, slavery had formed the backbone of a brutally unequal society in Brazil. 'Every dimension of our social existence is contaminated,' lamented abolitionist Joaquim Nabuco in 1880.

A masterpiece of Brazilian literature, *Rebellion in the Backlands* vividly describes the Canudos massacre. Author Euclides de Cunha witnessed the end of Canudos as a correspondent for a São Paulo newspaper.

To undo something so deeply ingrained into the Brazilian way of life was never likely to be easy. Brazil prevaricated for nearly 60 years before any sort of resolution was reached. The 19th century was punctuated by a series of halfhearted legislative attempts to lay the slave industry to rest. Repeatedly, such laws failed.

Slave trafficking to Brazil was banned in 1850, but continued clandestinely. Another law, in 1885, freed all slaves over the age of 65. The lawmakers had obviously forgotten that the average life expectancy for a slave at this time was 45. Not until May 13, 1888 – 80 years after Britain had freed its slaves – was slavery itself officially banned in Brazil. Unsurprisingly, this didn't make a huge immediate difference to the welfare of the 800,000 freed slaves, who were largely illiterate and unskilled. Thousands were cast onto the streets without any kind of infrastructure to support them. Many died, while others flooded to Brazil's urban centers, adding to the cities' first slums. Still today, blacks overall remain among the poorest and worst-educated groups in the country.

Not far out of the door behind slavery was the Império Brasileiro. In 1889 a military coup, supported by Brazil's wealthy coffee farmers, decapitated the old Brazilian empire and the republic was born. The emperor went into exile in Paris, where he died a couple of years later.

A military clique ruled Brazil for the next four years until elections were held, but because of ignorance, corruption, and land and literacy requirements, only about 2% of the adult population voted. Little changed, except that the power of the military and the now-influential coffee growers increased, while it diminished for the sugar barons.

Open Borders

In the final decade of the 19th century, Brazil opened its borders. Millions of immigrants – from Italy, Japan, Spain, Germany, Portugal and elsewhere –

1890s
With slavery abolished, Brazil opens its borders to meet its labor needs. Over the next four decades, millions arrive from Italy, Portugal, Spain, Germany and later Japan and other countries.

1920
The rubber boom goes bust as the Dutch and English plant their own rubber trees in the East Indies. Brazil's monopoly on the world rubber market deflates.

1930
Getúlio Vargas comes into power. Inspired by European fascists, President Vargas presides over an authoritarian state, playing a major role in Brazilian politics until his fall from power in 1951.

1937
Getúlio Vargas announces a new constitution for what he calls the 'Estado Novo' (New State); he passes minimum wage laws in 1938, expands the military and centralizes power.

PRINCESA ISABEL: LIBERATOR OF SLAVES

Princesa Isabel's parents didn't leave much space on their daughter's birth certificate. Born at the Palácio de São Cristóvão to Pedro II and Teresina Cristina on July 29, 1846, she found herself the proud owner of no less than 10 names. Isabel Cristina Leopoldina Augusta Micaela Gabriela Rafaela Gonzaga de Bragança e Bourbon. She's better known today, however, by this memorable title: the liberator of slaves.

For over 300 years Brazilian society had been defined by the slave trade. Keen to cover their tracks, slave traders destroyed many documents relating to their line of work. But it is believed that around 3.6 mllion slaves were shipped from Africa to Brazil between 1550 and 1888, used as free labor for the sugar (and later coffee) plantations.

The first real steps toward abolition came in 1826 when the English, having themselves banned slavery in 1807, forced Brazil to outlaw slave-trafficking. Yet over the following decades the numbers of slaves entering Brazil only rose. A series of equally ineffective laws proceeded, of which – as is often the case in Brazil – not a single one '*pegou*' (caught on).

On May 13, 1888, after nearly 80 years of prevarication and crossed words with the pro-abolition English, Isabel put pen to paper on the document that would define her life – the Lei Aurea. The document contained less than 200 words but its implications were huge. 'Slavery,' it pointed out, 'is now extinct in Brazil.'

Increasingly, however, historians look at her actions with cynicism. Abolition eradicated an unquestionable evil from Brazilian society, yet in many ways it posed more questions than it answered. What, for example, would Brazil's 800,000 freed slaves, largely illiterate, unskilled and unemployed, now do to support themselves?

Isabel seems not to have anticipated this particular question. Thousands of ex-slaves were cast out onto the streets without any kind of infrastructure to support them. Many died, while others flooded to Brazil's urban centers, adding to the city's first favelas (slums).

Rio's world-famous Mangueira samba school marked the centenary year of the Lei Aurea with a scathing critique of the law, entitled '100 years of freedom, reality or illusion?' 'Could it be that the Lei Aurea so dreamt about, signed so long ago, was not the end of slavery?' it asked.

A visit to the impoverished Mangueira favela in Rio's North Zone, in which many of the inhabitants are paid miserable wages to work as porters and maids for the city's better off, shows the answer is a resounding yes. As the samba points out, Princesa Isabel freed Brazil's Blacks from 'the whips of the senzala' but left them stranded 'in the misery of the favela'.

streamed into Brazil to work on the coffee *fazendas* (ranches), and to make new lives in the rapidly growing cities, especially Rio and São Paulo, adding further textures to Brazil's ethnic mixture and confirming the shift of Brazil's economic center of gravity from the Northeast to the Southeast.

1942

Initially maintaining neutrality, Brazil enters WWII on the side of the Allies, providing raw materials, plus 25,000 troops (the only Latin American nation to do so).

1950

Newly constructed Maracanã Stadium in Rio plays center stage in the FIFA World Cup. Brazil dominates until the final, when, before 200,000 fans, it suffers a stunning loss to Uruguay.

1954

Following an explosive political scandal, the military calls for the resignation of President Getúlio Vargas. He pens a melodramatic letter then shoots himself through the heart at his Rio palace.

1956

Juscelino Kubitschek de Oliveira (better known as JK), is elected president, and builds a new capital – Brasília. JK had to borrow heavily to finance the project, leading to inflation that will dog the economy for decades.

Over the next century, immigrants continued to flood into Brazil. The country became a haven for Jews fleeing persecution at the hands of the Nazis, as well as Nazis looking to avoid being put on trial for war crimes. Arabs, universally known as *turcos* by the Brazilians, also joined the influx of newcomers. Many of the traders you'll meet at Rio de Janeiro's Rua Uruguaiana flea market hail from the Middle East.

Set during the military dictatorship, Bruno Barreto's film *Four Days in September* (1998) is based on the 1969 kidnapping of the US ambassador to Brazil by leftist guerrillas.

Getúlio Vargas, Populist Dictator

The Vargas era began in 1930 when members of the newly formed Liberal Alliance party decided to fight back after the defeat of their candidate, Getúlio Vargas, in the presidential elections. The revolution kicked off on October 3 in Rio Grande do Sul and spread rapidly through other states. Twenty-one days later President Júlio Prestes was deposed and on November 3 Vargas became Brazil's new 'provisional' president.

The formation of the Estado Novo (New State) in November 1937 made Vargas the first Brazilian president to wield absolute power. Inspired by the fascist governments of Salazar in Portugal and Mussolini in Italy, Vargas banned political parties, imprisoned political opponents and censored artists and the press.

Despite this, many liked Vargas. The 'father' of Brazil's workers, he introduced new labor laws and remained popular throughout his tenure. In 1951 he was elected president, this time democratically. But Vargas' new administration was plagued by the hallmark of Brazilian politics – corruption. Amid calls from the military for his resignation, Vargas responded dramatically. He penned a note saying, 'I leave this life to enter into history,' and on the following morning, August 24, 1954, fired a single bullet through his own heart.

The Generals Take Over

Brazil is the only country in the New World that was both the seat of an empire (when the Portuguese king came here) and an independent monarchy (when Dom Pedro I declared independence).

In 1964 the left-leaning president João Goulart was overthrown in a so-called *revolução* (revolution) – really a military coup, which many Brazilians believed was backed by the US government. President Lyndon Johnson did nothing to dampen such theories when he immediately cabled his warmest wishes to the new Brazilian administration.

Brazil's military regime was not as brutal as those of Chile or Argentina – a reality that led to the somewhat unkind saying, 'Brazil couldn't even organize a dictatorship properly.' Yet for the best part of 20 years, freedom of speech was an unknown concept and political parties were banned.

The Brazilian economy flourished. Year after year in the late 1960s and early 1970s, the economy grew by over 10% as Brazil's rulers borrowed heavily from international banks. But in the absence of rural land reform, millions moved to the cities, where favelas filled up the open spaces.

1958

Brazil wins its first football World Cup. The team catapults to victory over Sweden, largely on the skills of a precocious 17-year-old unknown by the name of Pelé.

1960

The capital is officially moved from Rio de Janeiro to Brasília. Architects Oscar Niemeyer and Lúcio Costa play a starring role in building hypermodern Brasília from scratch in just 41 months.

1964

President Goulart is overthrown by a military coup – with strong evidence of US involvement. So begins the era of dictatorship, with generals running the show for the next 20 years.

1968

The government passes the repressive Ato Institutional 5 law, which purges opposition legislators, judges and mayors from public office; most political parties are banned. Protests erupt nationwide.

THE ORIGINS OF THE FAVELA

In the 1870s and '80s, terrible droughts coupled with the decline of the sugar industry brought economic devastation. Offering a vision of hope, messianic movements became popular among Brazil's poor. The most famous was that of Canudos, led by an itinerant preacher Antônio Conselheiro (Antônio the Counselor), who wandered for years through the backlands preaching and prophesying the appearance of the Antichrist and the end of the world. He railed against the new republican government and in 1893 eventually settled with his followers at Canudos, in the interior of northern Bahia. Within 1½ years Canudos had grown to a city of 35,000.

The republican government sensed plots in Canudos to return Brazil to the monarchy. It took them several attempts, however, before a federal force of 8000 well-supplied soldiers – many of whom hailed from Rio – took Canudos after vicious, hand-to-hand, house-to-house fighting. It was a war of extermination that nearly wiped out every man, woman and child from Canudos; the settlement was then burned to the ground to erase it from the nation's memory.

The surviving soldiers and their wives returned to Rio, where they were promised land in exchange for their victory. The government, however, reneged on the promise, and the soldiers occupied the nearby hillside of Morro da Providência. Oddly enough, as the first tenants put up makeshift shelter and settled in, they came across the same hardy shrub they found in the arid lands surrounding Canudos. Called *favela*, this plant caused skin irritations to all who came in contact with it – according to some accounts, the protective shrub even helped repel the army's initial invasions. Hillside residents began calling their new home the Morro da Favela, and the name caught on. Soon the word 'favela' was used to describe the ever-increasing number of informal communities appearing around Rio, which quickly gathered a mix of former slaves and poverty-stricken inhabitants from the interior, who came to the city seeking a better life.

During this time, Brazil's obsession with 'megaprojects' was born. Under the quick-spending regime, construction began on numerous colossal (and mostly ill-fated) plans, including the Transamazônica highway, the Rio-Niterói Bridge and the Ilha do Fundão, which was to house Rio's Federal University.

The Workers Organize

By the late 1970s, the economic boom was dying and opposition to the regime began to spread from the educated middle class to the working class. A series of strikes in the São Paulo car industry signaled the intent of the militant new workers' movement. At the helm was Luíz Inácio 'Lula' da Silva, who famously lost one *dedo* (finger) in a factory accident but made up in charisma what he lacked in the finger department.

1968

The Brazilian economy booms, averaging an incredible 10% growth for the next six years. Rapid income growth continues into the 1970s.

1972

The era of megaprojects and skyrocketing deficits begins, with the opening of the 5300km Transamazônica highway. It cost nearly US$1 billion, but never achieved its goal of colonizing the Amazon.

1979–80

The consistent decline of workers' wages leads to strikes across the country. Unions call for justice and young workers join with intellectuals and activists to form Brazil's Workers' Party (PT).

1984

The Movimento Sem Terra (MST; Landless Workers' Movement) – an organization calling for land reform – is founded. The fringe organization of 6000 families grows to more than 1.5 million today.

The Partido dos Trabalhadores (PT; Workers' Party), Brazil's first-ever mass political party to speak for the poor, grew out of these strikes, and helped pave the way toward *abertura* (opening), a cautious return to civilian rule between 1979 and 1985. With popular opposition gathering force, the military announced gradual moves toward a democratic Brazil.

Democracy & Debt

In 1985 a presidential election took place, though the only voters were members of the national congress. Unexpectedly, Tancredo Neves, opposing the military candidate, came out on top, and millions of Brazilians took to the streets to celebrate the end of military rule.

From 1980 to 1994, Brazilians suffered devastating hyperinflation, which peaked above 2000% for several years. At this rate, rent doubled every 10 weeks, food and clothes went up 40% a month and credit cards charged 25% a month interest.

Immediately a spanner was thrown in the works: Neves died from heart failure before he could assume the presidency. His vice-presidential candidate, the whiskered José Sarney, took over. Sarney – who had supported the military until 1984 – held office until 1989, a period in which runaway inflation helped Brazil rack up a gargantuan foreign debt.

In the 1989 direct presidential election, the first ever that could be called democratic, it was a Northeastern political climber by the name of Collor who was victorious, beating Lula, the PT's candidate, by the smallest of margins.

A Troubled Administration

Fernando Collor de Mello, former governor of the small state of Alagoas, revolutionized consumer laws. Sell-by dates, however, couldn't save him from disgrace. An ever-lengthening list of scandals involving Collor and his intimate associate PC Farias – alleged corruption on a vast scale, alleged drug deals, family feuds – led to a congressional inquiry, huge student protests and eventually the president's impeachment.

Though out of office, 'Fernandinho' managed to avoid a prison sentence, receiving little more than an eight-year ban from politics. Found not guilty of 'passive corruption' by the Supreme Court in 1994, he moved to Miami, where he remained for five years. In 1998 Collor returned to Brazil, and after several unsuccessful attempts to re-enter Brazilian politics was elected to congress as a senator for Alagoas. In August 2015 he was charged for corruption linked to the Petrobras scandal, and is currently under investigation.

Brazil's Boom Days

Following Collor's impeachment, Vice President Itamar Franco found himself in the hot seat. Despite his reputation as an eccentric, his administration was credited with competence and integrity. Franco's greatest achievement was to stabilize Brazil's violently erratic economy, introducing a new currency, the real. Pegged to the US dollar, the real caused

1988

Amazonia rubber-tappers' leader and environmentalist Chico Mendes is murdered by a local rancher and his son. The public outcry following Mendes' death forces the government to create extractive reserves.

1994

Following the impeachment of President Collor, Vice President Itamar Franco takes power. He introduces a new currency, the real, which stabilizes the economy and ushers in an economic boom.

2002

After four unsuccessful attempts, Luíz Inácio 'Lula' da Silva is elected president. The former union leader serves a moderate first term, despite upper-class fears of radical agendas.

2003

President Lula launches Bolsa Família, a program of cash payments to Brazil's 11 million poorest families. The social program is credited with reducing poverty by 27% during Lula's first term.

inflation to plummet from a rate of over 5000% in late 1993 to under 10% in 1994.

The Plano Real sparked an economic boom that lasted two decades, though it was his successor, former finance minister Fernando Henrique Cardoso, who presided through the mid-1990s over a growing economy and record foreign investment. He is often credited with laying the groundwork that put Brazil's hyperinflation to bed, though often at the neglect of social problems.

Come the 2002 election, Lula, at the fourth time of asking, toned down his socialist rhetoric, and promised to repay Brazil's international debts. This propelled Lula to a convincing victory over the center-right candidate Jose Serra. For the first time ever, Brazil had a government on the left of the political spectrum and a president who really knew what poverty was like. One of 22 children born to a dirt-poor illiterate farmworker from Brazil's stricken Northeast, Lula had worked as a shoeshine boy, then a mechanic, then a trade-union leader.

His accession initially alarmed investors, who had envisioned a left-leaning renegade running the economy amok. In fact, he surprised friends and foes alike with one of the most financially prudent administrations in years, while still addressing Brazil's egregious social problems.

When Lula left office in 2010, Brazil's economic prosperity was clear. Brazil became a net foreign creditor for the first time in 2008 and the country weathered the economic recession at the end of the decade better than any other developing country. He also helped achieved notable success in antipoverty measures, and helped millions enter the middle class – all of which helps explain why Lula was rated Brazil's most popular president in history; in his final months in office his approval rating was above 80%.

The first favela (slum) appeared on Rio's landscape in 1897, but it wasn't until 1994 that the communities (which today number over 600) were included on maps.

Trouble Ahead

Riding Lula's coattails, fellow party member Dilma Rousseff was elected Brazil's first ever female president in 2010. A former Marxist guerilla, Dilma came down on hard on corruption – at least initially. During her first year in office, six of her government ministers lost their positions due to their involvement in corruption scandals. Her second term, however, imploded when high-ranking members of her own party were linked to a massive corruption scandal. Yet even before this came to light, Rousseff's popularity was tanking, owing in part to anger over the obscene amount of money being spent on the 2014 World Cup – money that protestors said would be better spent on health, education and poverty reduction. To make matters worse, the burgeoning Brazilian economy had stalled, with GDP growth averaging a mere 2% per year during her first term, and outright shrinking one year into her second term in 2015.

The Accidental President of Brazil, by Fernando Henrique Cardoso, is an elucidating memoir by one of Brazil's most popular presidents, a former sociology professor vaulted into power.

2011
Dilma Rousseff is sworn in as president of Brazil, becoming the first woman ever to hold the office. As Lula's handpicked successor, she largely continues the policies of her predecessor.

2014
Brazil hosts the 2014 FIFA World Cup, spending around US$12 billion in preparation for the event, which is staged at 12 different cities across the country.

2014
News emerges of Brazil's largest corruption scandal in history. High-ranking politicians and oil-company executives are linked to a US$4-billion scheme that shakes the country to its core.

2015
In the run-up to the Summer Olympics, Rio spends R$37 billion on stadiums, infrastructure and civic beautification, adding a new metro line, a downtown light rail and new museums.

Life in Brazil

Brazil is a nation of astounding diversity, forged from African, European and indigenous influences, along with the influences of tens of millions of immigrants who flooded into the country in the late 19th and early 20th centuries. Brazilians of today represent a complicated portrait of colors and creeds and hail from a wide range of socioeconomic backgrounds. The lifestyle is no less diverse – not surprising for a country that's home to both age-old indigenous cultures and modern metropolises.

Japanese immigration began in 1908, and today São Paulo has the world's largest Japanese community outside of Japan.

Multiculturalism

Brazilian identity has been shaped not only by the Portuguese, who provided its language and main religion, but also by native *índios*, Africans and the many immigrants over the years from Europe, the Middle East and Asia.

Indigenous culture, though often ignored or denigrated by urban Brazilians, has helped shape modern Brazil and its legends, dance and music. Many indigenous foods and beverages, such as tapioca, manioc (cassava), potatoes, *erva maté* (tea-like beverage made from the leaves of the erva maté tree) and guaraná (a berry that is a stimulant; also a popular soft drink) have become staples.

The influence of African culture is also evident, especially in the Northeast. The slaves imported by the Portuguese brought with them their religion, music and cuisine, all of which have become a part of Brazilian identity.

Brazil had several waves of voluntary immigration. After the end of slavery in 1888, millions of Europeans were recruited to work in the coffee fields. The largest contingent was from Italy (some one million arrived between 1890 and 1920), but there were also many Portuguese and Spaniards, and smaller groups of Germans and Russians.

Immigration is only part of the picture when considering Brazil's diversity. Brazilians are just as likely to mention regional types, often accompanied by their own colorful stereotypes. Caboclos, who are descendents of the *índio,* live along the rivers in the Amazon region and keep alive the traditions and stories of their ancestors. *Gaúchos* populate Rio Grande do Sul, speak a Spanish-inflected Portuguese and can't quite shake the reputation for being rough-edged cowboys. By contrast, *baianos,* descendants of the first Africans in Brazil, are stereotyped for being the most extroverted and celebratory of Brazilians. *Mineiros* (residents of Minas Gerais state) are considered more serious and reserved than Brazil's coastal dwellers, while *sertanejos* (residents of the backlands – called *sertão* – of the Northeast) are dubbed tough-skinned individuals with strong folk traditions. *Cariocas* (residents of Rio city) are superficial beach bums according to *paulistanos* (residents of São Paulo city), who are often denigrated as being workaholics with no zeal for life – a rivalry that anyone who's lived in LA or New York can understand.

Dozens of uncontacted indigenous groups still live in the Amazon. In 2007, 89 Metyktire suddenly emerged in a village in Pará, the first time this particular group (feared dead) had been encountered since 1950.

Today there are dozens of terms to describe Brazilians' various racial compositions, and it is not uncommon for apparently white Brazilians to have a mix of European, African and indigenous ancestors. Yet, despite appearances of integration and racial harmony, underneath is a brutal reality. Although blacks and mulattoes account for 45% of the population, they are sorely underrepresented in government and business, and often see little hope of rising out of poverty. The indigenous are even more openly discriminated against, continuing a cycle that began with the genocidal policies of the first Europeans.

Population

Brazil is the world's fifth-most-populous country, but it also has one of the smallest population densities, with around 24 people per sq km. Most of Brazil's population lives along the coast, particularly in the South and Southeast, home to 75% of the country's inhabitants. Until the mid-20th century, Brazil was largely a rural country – today, its population is more than 80% urban. The population in cities has exploded in the last half-century, though growth is slowing.

The Northeast has the highest concentration of Afro-Brazilians, with Salvador as its cultural capital. In the Amazon live Caboclos (literally 'copper-colored'; the mixed descendants of indigenous peoples and the Portuguese). In the South is the most European of the Brazilian population, descendants of Italian and German immigrants.

While there is much more mixing between races, Brazil is a long way from being a color-blind society. Afro-Brazilians make up the bulk of low-paid workers, and are far more likely to live in favelas (slums) than in middle-class neighborhoods. More than 40% of Afro-Brazilians live in poverty (twice the rate of whites). Afro-Brazilians die younger than whites, earn less and have a greater risk of going to prison. Barely 2% of Afro-Brazilians attend university, though a new quota system (approved by the supreme court in 2012) aims to address the longstanding racial imbalance. Black political representatives and even high-ranking black employees are rarities – clear examples of the lack of opportunities for blacks in Brazil.

The indigenous population today numbers more than 700,000, comprising 200 tribes. Although this is a fraction of the estimated two million or more in Brazil at the time of European arrival, the indigenous population has shown a remarkable resurgence in recent years: the population has tripled since 1970. Customs and beliefs vary widely from tribe to tribe – as do the strengths of these traditions in the face of expulsion from traditional lands, declining numbers, missionary activity and other influences.

After centuries of genocidal attacks, slavery, dispossession and death from imported diseases, Brazil's indigenous population is growing again but still faces a host of problems. Most of them live in the Amazon rainforest, and therefore the threats that the rainforest faces – logging, mining, ranching, farming, roads, settlements, dams, hydroelectric schemes – also threaten the indigenous whose way of life depends on it.

Lifestyles

Constructing a portrait of the typical Brazilian is a complicated task, given the wide mix of social, cultural and economic factors in play. One thing that everyone agrees on is the huge chasm separating rich from poor.

The country's middle and upper class live in comfortable apartments or houses, with all the trappings of the first world, including good health care in private clinics, cars, vacation homes and easy access to the latest gadgets and trends (though prices for luxury goods are much higher here, eg an iPhone 6 without a plan costs R$3200). The wealthiest send their children to private schools and abroad to university. Maids are common – even among middle-class Brazilians – and some families have chauffeurs and cooks. Depending on where one lives in the country,

Domesticas (Maids), the first film by Fernando Meirelles, delves into the lives of five women who work as *domesticas*, creating a compelling portrait of Brazil's often overlooked underclass.

How to Be a Carioca, by Priscilla Ann Goslin, is a humorous portrait of the Rio dweller, with tongue-in-cheek riffs on beach-going, driving, soap operas, football and *carioca* slang.

Benedita da Silva: An Afro-Brazilian Woman's Story of Politics and Love is the memoir of Brazil's first Afro-Brazilian female senator, detailing her rise from the favelas to becoming an important political voice.

WOMEN IN BRAZIL

Brazil had one of the earliest feminist movements in Latin America, and women were among the first in the region to gain the right to vote, in 1932. Today there is a growing number of feminist NGOs, dedicated to educating women about their legal rights and family planning, while also training police how to handle cases of domestic violence. In Brasília there's even a feminist lobby. More importantly, Brazil's head of state is a woman. Dilma Rousseff, who became Brazil's first female president in 2011, serves as a major icon for breaking down barriers for women.

In spite of advances, many *machista* (chauvinist) stereotypes persist, and women are still sorely underrepresented in positions of power. Women occupy only about 10% of seats in the National Congress, which is one of the lowest figures in Latin America (where women on average make up around 20% of the legislature).

In other spheres, women represent 45% of the workforce – a huge leap from decades past but still below the average in Latin America (where women comprise 53% of the workforce). Unfortunately, the wage gap remains high, with men earning 30% more than women of the same age and income level.

Instances of domestic abuse are frighteningly common (one report stated that every 24 seconds a woman is beaten in Brazil, and that 10 women a day die from domestic violence). In response, the first women's police station opened in 1990 specifically to handle violence against women. Today there are more than 300 women's police stations, largely staffed by female police officers.

Women receive 120 days of paid maternity leave (men receive five days of paternity leave). Abortions are still illegal in Brazil (except in cases of rape and maternal health risks), and an estimated one million are performed each year, often with substantial health risks. More than 200,000 women each year are hospitalized from clandestine abortions.

crime is likely to be of high concern. Those who can take extra precautions, opting for high-security buildings or even hiring bodyguards.

Somewhere below the elite are working-class folks struggling to put food on the table and pay the rent; the children tend to live at home until they are married. Couples tend to marry younger.

At the bottom of the socioeconomic ladder are *favelados* (slum dwellers), who live in self-constructed housing (usually boxy concrete or brick dwellings) in crowded makeshift communities. Ranging in size from a few thousand inhabitants to over 70,000, favelas are found in nearly every urban area in Brazil. Most residents have electricity and running water, though open sewers run through many favelas. Access to education, adequate health care, transportation and other essential infrastructure can often be limited, though this is slowly changing under government-funded favela improvement schemes.

The Ukrainian community in Brazil numbers 550,000, the majority of whom live in the South. Prudentopolis is a city of Orthodox churches and Slavic features, with 75% of the population of Ukrainian descent.

In the countryside, conditions for the poor can be even worse. Unequal land distribution dating back to the colonial era means that thousands of homeless rural families are left to squat on vacant land or work long hours as itinerant laborers for low wages.

Regardless of socioeconomic background, most Brazilians have a healthy appreciation for a good party (Carnaval is but one manifestation). This joie de vivre can be seen in football matches, on the beaches, in the samba clubs and on the streets. The flip side of this trait is *saudade*, that woeful manifestation of longing or deep regret, given much play on old bossa nova records.

Brazilian Rhythms

Shaped by the mixing of varied influences from three continents, Brazilian popular music has always been characterized by great diversity. The *samba canção* (samba song), for example, is a mixture of Spanish bolero with the cadences and rhythms of African music. Bossa nova was influenced by samba and North American music, particularly jazz. *Tropicália* mixed influences ranging from bossa nova and Italian ballads to blues and North American rock. Brazil is still creating new and original musical forms today.

Samba & Choro

The birth of modern Brazilian music essentially began with the birth of samba, first heard in the early 20th century in a Rio neighborhood near present-day Praça Onze. Here, Bahian immigrants formed a tightly knit community in which traditional African customs thrived – music, dance and the Candomblé religion. Such an atmosphere nurtured the likes of Pixinguinha, one of samba's founding fathers, as well as Donga, one of the composers of 'Pelo Telefone,' the first recorded samba song (in 1917) and an enormous success at the then-fledgling Carnaval.

The Brazilian Sound, by Chris McGowan and Ricardo Pessanha, is a well-illustrated, readable introduction to Brazilian music, with insight into regional styles and musicians (famous and obscure). Useful discography included.

Samba continued to evolve in the homes and *botequims* (bars with table service) around Rio. The 1930s are known as the golden age of samba. Sophisticated lyricists such as Dorival Caymmi, Ary Barroso and Noel Rosa popularized *samba canção*, melody-driven samba laid over African percussion. Songs in this style featured sentimental lyrics and an emphasis on melody (rather than rhythm), foreshadowing the later advent of cool bossa nova.

The 1930s was also the golden age of samba songwriting for Carnaval. *Escolas de samba* (samba schools or clubs), which first emerged in 1928, soon became a vehicle for samba songwriting, and by the 1930s samba and Carnaval would be forever linked.

Great *sambistas* (samba singers) continued to emerge in Brazil over the next few decades, although other emerging musical styles diluted their popularity. Artists such as Cartola, Nelson Cavaquinho and Clementina de Jesus made substantial contributions to both samba and styles of music that followed from samba.

Traditional samba went through a rebirth a little over a decade ago with the opening of old-style *gafieiras* (dance halls) in Lapa. Today, Rio is once again awash with great *sambistas*. Classic *sambistas* such as Alcione and Beth Carvalho still perform, while rising stars such as Teresa Christina and Grupo Semente are intimately linked to Lapa's rebirth. Other talents include Diogo Nogueira, the deep-voiced samba son of legendary singer João Nogueira, and Mart'nália, daughter of samba icon Martinho da Vila.

Another popular artist still active in Rio is Maria Rita, the talented singer and songwriter whose voice is remarkably similar to that of her late mother, Elis Regina – one of Brazil's all-time greats. Rita's album *Samba Meu Samba Meu* is still one of her best.

Choro is a relative of samba. Characterized by its jazzy sound, melodic leaps and sometimes rapid-fire tempo, *choro* is mostly instrumental music and highly improvisational. It's played on the *cavaquinho* or guitar alongside a recorder or flute. The flutist Pixinguinha (1898–1973) is one of the great legends of *choro*.

Bossa Nova

In the 1950s came bossa nova (literally, new wave), sparking a new era of Brazilian music. Bossa nova's founders – songwriter and composer Antônio Carlos (Tom) Jobim and guitarist João Gilberto, in association with the lyricist-poet Vinícius de Moraes – slowed down and altered the basic samba rhythm to create a more intimate, harmonic style. This initiated a new style of playing instruments and of singing.

Bossa Nova: The Story of the Brazilian Music that Seduced the World, by Ruy Castro, is an excellent book that captures the vibrant music and its backdrop of 1950s Rio.

Bossa nova's seductive melodies were very much linked to Rio's Zona Sul, where most bossa musicians lived. Songs such as Jobim's 'Corcovado' and Roberto Menescal's 'Rio' evoked an almost nostalgic portrait of the city with their quiet lyricism. Bossa nova was also associated with the new class of university-educated Brazilians, and its lyrics reflected the optimistic mood of the middle class in the 1950s.

By the 1960s, bossa nova had become a huge international success. Bossa nova classics were adopted, adapted and recorded by such musical luminaries as Frank Sinatra, Ella Fitzgerald and Stan Getz, among others.

In addition to the founding members, other great Brazilian bossa nova musicians include Marcos Valle, Luiz Bonfá and Baden Powell. Bands from the 1960s such as Sergio Mendes & Brasil '66 were also quite influenced by bossa nova, as were other artists who fled the repressive military dictatorship to live and play abroad. More recent interpreters of the seductive bossa sound include the Bahian-born Rosa Passos and *carioca* Paula Morelenbaum.

Tropicália

One of Brazil's unique artistic movements, emerging in the late 1960s, *tropicália* was a direct response to the dictatorship that held power from 1964 to 1984. Leading the movement were Caetano Veloso and Gilberto Gil, making waves with songs of protest against the national regime. In addition to penning defiant lyrics, *tropicalistas* introduced the public to electric instruments, fragmentary melodies and wildly divergent musical styles.

Tropical Truth: A Story of Music and Revolution in Brazil, by Caetano Veloso, describes the great artistic experiment of *tropicália* in 1960s Brazil. Although digressive at times, Veloso captures the era's music and politics.

Important figures linked to *tropicália* include Gal Costa, Jorge Ben Jor, Maria Bethânia, Os Mutantes and Tom Zé. Although *tropicália* wasn't initially embraced by the public, who objected to the electric and rock elements (in fact, Veloso was booed off the stage on several occasions), by the 1970s its radical ideas had been absorbed and accepted, and lyrics of protest were ubiquitous in songwriting of the time.

While 'pure' *tropicália* bands aren't around any more, the influence can still be heard in the music of groups such as AfroReggae, one of Rio's leading funk bands.

Música Popular Brasileira (MPB)

Música Popular Brasileira (MPB) is a catchphrase to describe all popular Brazilian music after bossa nova. It includes *tropicália, pagode,* and Brazilian pop and rock. All Brazilian music has roots in samba; even in Brazilian rock, heavy metal, disco or pop, the samba sound is often present.

MPB first emerged in the 1970s along with talented musicians such as Edu Lobo, Milton Nascimento, Elis Regina, Djavan and dozens of others, many of whom wrote protest songs not unlike the *tropicalistas*. Chico Buarque is one of the first big names from this epoch, and is one of Brazil's best songwriters. His music career began in 1968 and spanned a time during which many of his songs were banned by the military dictatorship – in fact, his music became a symbol of protest during that era.

Jorge Ben Jor is another singer whose career, which began in the 1960s, has survived up to the present day. Highly addictive rhythms are omnipresent in Ben Jor's songs, as he incorporates African beats and elements of funk, samba and blues in his eclectic repertoire. The celebratory album *África Brasil* and his debut album, *Samba Esquema Novo* (with recognizable hits such as 'Mas, Que Nada!'), are among his best.

Carlinhos Brown continues to make immeasurable contributions to Brazilian music, particularly in the realm of Afro-Brazilian rhythms. Born in Bahia, Brown has influences that range from merengue (fast-paced dance-hall music originating in the Dominican Republic) to Candomblé music to straight-up funk in the style of James Brown (the US artist from whom Carlinhos took his stage name). In addition to creating the popular percussion ensemble Timbalada, he has a number of excellent albums of his own (notably *Alfagamabetizado*). Involved in many diverse projects, Brown was even nominated for an Oscar in 2012 for best original song ('Real in Rio' for the film *Rio*), which he and Sergio Mendes composed.

Raul Seixas (1945–89) is often called 'the father of Brazilian rock'. Many of his wild rock anthems are well known, and it's not uncommon to hear shouts of 'toca Raul!' (play Raul!) at concerts. Curiously, Paulo Coelho (the future bestselling New Age author) co-wrote many of his songs.

Brazilian Rock, Pop & Hip-Hop

MPB tends to bleed into other genres, particularly into rock and pop. One artist who moves comfortably between genres is Bebel Gilberto (the daughter of João Gilberto), who blends bossa nova with modern beats on jazz-inflected bilingual albums such as *All in One* (2009). Another heiress of Brazilian traditions is the Rio-born Marisa Monte, popular at home and abroad for her fine singing and songwriting. Mixing samba, *forró* (traditional, fast-paced music from the Northeast), pop and rock, Marisa has created a number of fine solo albums (*Barulinho Bom – A Great Noise* in English – is one of her best) and has performed on many others. Her brief collaboration with Arnaldo Antunes and Carlinhos Brown resulted in the fine album *Tribalistas* (2003). Other notable young singers who hail from a bossa line include Roberta Sá, whose most recent album, *Segunda Pele* (2012), features elements of bossa, jazz and even reggae; and Fernanda Porto, whose music is often described as drum 'n' bossa, a blend of electronica and bossa grooves – check out her 2009 album *Auto-Retrato*.

The expat singer-songwriter and performance artist Cibelle incorporates a mix of pop, folk and Brazilian sounds in her lush (mainly English-language) recordings, such as those on *The Shine of Dried Electric*

CANNIBALISM, BRAZILIAN-STYLE

The eating of human flesh, as practiced by at least a few pre-Columbian tribes, contributed to some notion of Brazilian identity. In the 1920s, the intellectual movement of anthropophagy (a fancy word for cannibalism) came to denote Brazil's lust for new ideas and culture from abroad that would be consumed, digested and then transformed into something uniquely Brazilian.

In music, bossa nova incorporated (ingested) American jazz, blues and classical music, but created something entirely new. A few years later, along came the *tropicalistas*, who were open admirers of Oswald de Andrade's 1928 *Manifesto Antropofágico* (Cannibalistic Manifesto). *Tropicália* devoured elements of American rock and roll, blues, jazz and British psychedelic styles, as well as samba and even bossa nova, and produced a powerful new sound entirely Brazilian in its construction.

This notion of cultural cannibalism has been used to explain the prodigious output of Brazil not only in music, but also in fiction, painting and even filmmaking. As Caetano Veloso described, 'Antropofagia is a Brazilian state of being.'

Leaves (2006). She came to prominence as the main vocalist on Suba's noteworthy album *São Paulo Confessions* (1999). With a host of Grammy nominations to her name, Céu has many fans both at home and abroad. She has recorded three albums over the last seven years, creating dreamlike melodies with elements of *tropicália*, samba, reggae and jazz. Her latest, *Caravana Sereia Bloom* (2012), is a colorful work with songs inspired by a road trip across Brazil.

Brazilian hip-hop emerged from the favelas of Rio sometime in the 1980s, and has been steadily attracting followers ever since. Big names such as Racionais MCs first emerged out of São Paulo, but Rio has its share of more recent success stories. One of the best on the scene is Marcelo D2 (formerly of Planet Hemp), earning accolades for albums like *A Procura da Batida Perfeita* (2003) and *A Arte do Barulho* (2008).

Better known to international audiences is Seu Jorge, who starred in the film *Cidade de Deus* and performed brilliant Portuguese versions of Bowie songs on Wes Anderson's film *The Life Aquatic*. His best solo work is *Cru* (2005), an inventive hybrid of hip-hop and ballads, with politically charged beats.

Most of today's hip-hop artists hail from São Paulo. A few names to look out for include Emicida, a youthful rapper admired for his cutting improvisational rhymes. Check out his funk-laden single 'Triunfo,' one of his early breakthrough hits. Rael de Rima is a fast-rapping lyricist with a strong sense of musicality, often performing with guitar and a full back-up band (a rarity for many hip-hop artists). MC Criolo, whose

THE IPOD 20: SOUNDS FROM BRAZIL

One of the world's great music cultures, Brazil has an astounding array of talented musicians. A list of our favorite songs could fill a small book, but we've limited our highly subjective pick to 20 songs from 20 different artists.

- 'Sampa' – Caetano Veloso
- 'Alvorado' – Cartola
- 'Calice' – Chico Buarque & Milton Nascimento
- 'Aguas de Março' – Elis Regina (written by Tom Jobim)
- 'Hoje é Dia da Festa' – Elza Soares
- 'Namorinho de Portão' – Gal Costa
- 'Quilombo, o El Dorado Negro' – Gilberto Gil
- 'Desafinado' – João Gilberto
- 'Mas Que Nada' – Jorge Ben Jor
- 'A Procura da Batida Perfeita' – Marcelo D2
- 'Novo Amor' – Maria Rita
- 'Carinhoso' – Marisa Monte (written by Pixinguinha)
- 'Besta é Tu' – Novos Baianos
- 'Panis et Circenses' – Os Mutantes
- 'Beira Mar' – Raimundo Fagner and Zeca Baleiro
- 'Funk Baby' – Seu Jorge
- 'Acenda o Farol' – Tim Maia
- 'Garota de Ipanema' – Tom Jobim
- 'Não me deixe só' – Vanessa da Mata
- 'Felicidade' – Vinícius de Moraes

songs tackle urban violence, police brutality and racism, has become a huge hit in the favelas.

Brazil gets its share of mega-rockers on world tours. It also has a few homegrown talents. The group Legião Urbana from Brasília remains one of the all-time greats among rock lovers. The band (which folded shortly after the death of lead singer Renato Russo in 1996) enjoyed enormous success in the 1980s and early 1990s, and has sold more than 15 million records. Raul Seixas, Skank, O Rappa, Paralamas Sucesso and the Rio-based Barão Vermelho are other essential names. The versatile and original Ed Motta, from Rio, injects soul, jazz and traditional Brazilian music into rock.

In other genres, indie-rock favorites Los Hermanos was a top band that created catchy albums before breaking up in 2007. Check out *Ventura* (2003) or *Bloco do Eu Souzinho* (2001), one of the seminal pop-rock albums of its time. Vanguart, fitting somewhere in the folk-rock genre, is also a group to watch. The band's self-titled debut album (2007) channels samba, blues and classic rock. Other breakout successes include the saucy girl-band Cansei de Ser Sexy (Tired of Being Sexy), who blend '80s new wave and electro-pop with irreverent lyrics (sung in English) and up-tempo beats.

Regional Music

The Northeast has perhaps the most regional musical and dance styles. The most important is *forró,* a lively, syncopated music centered on the accordion and the *zabumba* (an African drum). Although a few artists, such as Luiz Gonzaga and Jackson do Pandeiro, have achieved national status, *forró* was long dismissed by urbanites as unsophisticated. The film *Eu, Tu, Eles* (Me, You, Them) brought down-home *forró* to center stage, aided in part by Gilberto Gil singing the hit *Esperando na Janela.*

The *trio elétrico,* also called *frevo baiano,* began more as a result of a change in technology rather than in music. It started as a joke when, during Carnaval in Salvador in the 1950s, a group of musicians spearheaded by innovative musical talents Dodo and Osmar (aka Adolfo Nascimento and Osmar Alvares Macedo) got on top of a truck and played *frevo* with electric guitars. The *trio elétrico* is not necessarily a trio, but it's still the backbone of Salvador's Carnaval, when trucks piled high with speakers – with musicians perched on top – drive through the city surrounded by dancing mobs. Another important element of Carnaval on the streets of Salvador is the *bloco afro* (Afro-Brazilian percussion group). Filhos de Gandhi and Grupo Olodum are the most famous of these – Filhos has deep African roots and is strongly influenced by Candomblé; Olodum invented samba-reggae.

Mangue beat (also known as *mangue bit*), from Recife, combines folkloric and regional styles with international influences as diverse as hip-hop, neo-psychedelic and *tejano* (instrumental folk music with roots in northern Mexico and southern Texas). The early leaders of the genre were Chico Science and Nação Zumbi – the title of whose 1996 masterpiece, *Afrociberdelia,* kind of summed up what its music was about.

Axé is a label for the profuse samba-pop-rock-reggae-funk-Caribbean fusion music that emerged from Salvador in the 1990s. Taking its cue from Salvador's older Carnaval forms, *axé* was popularized by the powerful, flamboyant Daniela Mercury. Other exponents include the groups Ara Ketu and Chiclete com Banana. At its best it's great, super-energetic music – hear Daniela sing 'Toda Menina Baiana' (Every Bahian Girl) – but some bands overcommercialized it at the end of the '90s.

The influence of Brazilian indigenous music was absorbed and diluted, as was so much that derived from Brazil's indigenous cultures. The *carimbó* music of the Amazon region (where the majority of *índios* live today) is influenced primarily by the blacks of the coastal zones.

Top Music Sites & Blogs

The Saudade Project (http://sites.google.com/sitethesaudadeproject)

Slipcue (www.slipcue.com/music/brazil/brazillist.html)

Brazilian Music Day (http://brazilianmusicday.org)

The Brazilian Sound (http://thebraziliansound.blogspot.com)

The Beautiful Game

Brazilians, quite simply, are football mad. No one goes to work on big international game days, with everyone packing into neighborhood bars or on the sidewalks out front to watch the game. After a big win, the whole country erupts with a rowdy night of partying. And should the team lose, the sadness in the air is palpable. Everyone cheers for the national team, but for most of the year, the local club team is the one that matters most.

Futebol, by Alex Bellos (2002), is a fascinating and humorous look at the culture behind Brazil's nationwide obsession, with stories of the legendary players and the way that football has shaped Brazilian society.

The Game, the Fans

Most of the world generally acknowledges that Brazilians play the world's most creative, artistic and thrilling style of football. They are also generally known as lousy defenders, but no one seems to mind since they make the attack so exciting. The fans, too, are no less fun to watch. Skillful moves and adroit dribbling past an opponent receive a Spanish bullfight-style 'olé!' while fans do their best to rev up the action by pounding drums (or the backs of the chairs), waving huge flags, setting off fireworks and smoke bombs or sometimes launching nefarious liquids over the grandstands of opposing fans.

Legends of the Sport

Brazil has raised many world-famous players through its ranks, from the Afro-Brazilian player Leonidas da Silva – who helped break down racial barriers (and scored the only bicycle kick goal ever in World Cup history in 1938) – to Romario, a powerful striker who scored more than 900 goals during his career. The greatest of all though is Pelé, sometimes referred to simply as 'O Rei' (the king). Throughout a 22-year career, the teams he played on won 53 titles, including three World Cups (the first, in Sweden in 1958, when he was just 17 years old). By the time he retired in the 1970s, he had played in 1366 games and scored more than 1200 goals, making him one of the world's greatest all-time goal scorers.

European Vacation

Until recently, most of the best players left Brazil for more lucrative contracts with European clubs. Over the last decade, however, many Brazilian stars have returned home to play for more adoring fans and not insubstantial contracts. The strengthening of the real against the euro, along with Brazil's economic boom, have allowed top Brazilian clubs to offer salaries near to the wages Brazilian players earn in Europe. TV rights and corporate sponsorship have also helped deepen the pockets of Brazilian clubs. The return of more players to Brazil, coupled with the ongoing growth of new talent in the big clubs could help transform Brazil into one of the world's footballing giants – on the club level as well as the international level.

The Clubs

Brazil has a staggering number of league teams – more than 400 according to the Brazilian Football Confederation (CBF) – with 20 top-level pro teams (part of the so-called Campeonato Brasileiro Série A). Apart from a couple of short breaks for the Christmas–New Year holiday and Carnaval, professional club competitions go on all year. There are a bewildering number of competitions throughout the year, with hotly contested state championships – particularly in Rio (the Campeonata Carioca) and São Paulo (the Campeonata Paulista). Expect intense and bitter matches, especially when historic hometown rivals match-up such as Flamengo versus Fluminense in Rio; Palmeiras versus Corinthians in São Paulo; Atlético Mineiro versus Cruzeiro in Belo Horizonte; and Grêmio (Gisele Bündchen's favorite team) versus Internacional in Porto Alegre. Here's a quick rundown of the top four club teams in Brazil:

For insight into what's happening in the Brazilian football scene – from player news to upcoming matches – visit www.sambafoot.com.

Flamengo

The most successful among Rio's big four, Flamengo has an enormous fan base both in Rio and around the world – an estimated 36 million followers, which makes them the most popular football club in Brazil. Flamengo certainly does not lack for cash flow, with annual revenue of over R$200 million. Famous players who have donned the iconic red-and-black jerseys include Zico, often hailed as the best player never to win a World Cup; Leonidas, leading scorer at the 1938 World Cup; Bebeto, Mario Zagallo and Romario.

Fluminense

Founded by sons of the elite in Rio back in 1902, Fluminense has contributed a number of top players to the national team. It has also been hailed as the 'champion of the century', for winning the largest number of Campeonato Carioca titles in the 20th century (28 in all). Current stars include Fred (aka Frederico Chaves Guedes), who scored the fastest goal in Brazilian history (finding the net 3.17 seconds after the game's start). Like Flamengo, Fluminense plays its home games in the newly upgraded Maracanã stadium.

Santos

This port city 80km southeast of São Paulo has a legendary footballing reputation. Santos has won eight national championships and has nur-

BRAZILIAN FOOTBALL: THE CLUBS

If you get a chance, see a game live; there's no experience quite like it. Many stadiums went through upgrades in preparation for the World Cup. Here's a short list of top teams to catch.

CLUB	CITY	STADIUM (CAPACITY)	JERSEYS
Bahia	Salvador	Fonte Nova (57,000)	white
Botafogo	Rio de Janeiro	João Havelange (47,000)	black & white stripes
Corinthians	São Paulo	Arena Corinthians (68,000)	white; black collar
Cruzeiro	Belo Horizonte	Mineirão (65,000)	blue
Flamengo	Rio de Janeiro	Maracanã (80,000)	red; black hoops
Fluminense	Rio de Janeiro	Maracanã (80,000)	red, green & white stripes
Grêmio	Porto Alegre	Arena do Grêmio (61,000)	blue, black & white stripes
Internacional	Porto Alegre	Beira-Rio (60,000)	red
Náutico Capibaribe	Recife	Arena Pernambuco (46,000)	red & white stripes
Palmeiras	São Paulo	Arena Palestra Itália (60,000)	green
Santos	Santos	Vila Belmiro (26,000)	white
São Paulo	São Paulo	Morumbi (67,000)	white; red & black hoops
Vasco da Gama	Rio de Janeiro	São Januário (35,000)	white; black slash

tured the talents of some of Brazil's all-time greats, including Pelé, who played on the team from 1957 to 1974. On the World Cup teams of 1962 and 1970, eight of the 11 starting players came from Santos. Its most recent star was Neymar, whose youth (he scored his 100th goal as a professional in 2012 at age 20) and skill earned him comparisons to Lionel Messi and Pelé. In both 2011 and 2012, Neymar won the South American Footballer of the Year award. Unable to resist bigger fame (and income) abroad, Neymar signed a five-year contract with FC Barcelona in 2013.

Corinthians

The most popular of São Paulo's three big teams, Corinthians is also Brazil's most valuable club team with an estimated worth of over US$350 million. The team vaulted to fame in 2012, winning both the Copa Libertadores and the FIFA Club World Cup (defeating English superpower Chelsea 1-0 in the final). Their archrivals are Palmeiras, a team they face (and often defeat) in the legendary Derby Paulista. Fans are noted for their die-hard loyalty. Over 30,000 supporters made the trip to Japan in the 2012 Club World Cup final.

The first time Brazil hosted the World Cup, in 1950, the national team lost in a dramatic final against Uruguay before some 200,000 fans in Rio's Maracanã stadium. The unforgettable day of infamy was later called '*maracanaço*' and is still in common parlance.

The World Cup

Brazil, the most successful football nation in the history of the game (with five World Cup victories), became the fifth country to host the World Cup twice. Aside from Rio, where the final took place, 11 other cities across the country staged games. Brazil spent around R$26 billion in preparation for the 2014 event, including stadium construction, upgrades to airports, roads and other infrastructure. Unfortunately, dreams for a grand victory celebration were crushed when Brazil suffered an embarrassing 7-1 loss to a far-superior Germany team in the semifinals. The game was held in Estádio Mineirão in Belo Horizonte, and the scandalous defeat (in the first half Germany scored four goals in six minutes) was later dubbed mineiraço. Many Brazilians were so disappointed that they even booed their own players as they left the field.

Cinema & Literature

Brazil has a flourishing film industry, though many productions don't see screen time beyond the country's borders. Key periods in Brazilian cinema include the avant-garde Cinema Novo movement of the 1960s and the hard-hitting socially conscious films of the last decade, with a new crop of talented directors emerging on the scene. In the realm of literature, Brazil has produced a handful of great writers, including the Bahian legend Jorge Amado and the brilliant modernist Clarice Lispector.

Cinema

In the 1960s the Cinema Novo movement emerged in Brazil, focusing on the country's bleak social problems. Young filmmakers, influenced by Italian neorealism and the French new wave, set about making a series of experimental films embracing the avant-garde filming techniques of the time. One of the great films made during this epoch was Anselmo Duarte's 1962 *O Pagador de Promessas* (The Payer of Vows), a poetic story about a man who keeps his promise to carry a cross after the healing of his donkey. It won the Palme d'Or at the Cannes film festival. Another great pioneer of Cinema Novo is the director Glauber Rocha. In *Deus é o Diabo na Terra do Sol* (Black God, White Devil; 1963), Rocha explored the struggle, fanaticism and poverty of Northeastern Brazil. It's one of the great films of the period.

Brazilian Cinema, edited by Randal Johnson and Robert Stam, provides a fascinating overview of the great movements that have shaped the industry, exploring Cinema Novo, tropicalism and other important influences.

The 1964 military coup stymied much creative expression in the country, and Cinema Novo died out just as its filmmakers were entering their prime. The first significant film to be made after the 1960s was Carlos Diegues' *Bye Bye Brasil* (1980). It chronicles the adventures of a theater troupe as it tours the country, witnessing the profound changes in Brazilian society in the second half of the 20th century.

In the 1980s Hector Babenco emerged as one of Brazil's rising stars. In *Pixote* (1981), Babenco brought to life the yawning chasm between haves and have-nots in a story about a homeless child who gets swept from innocent waif to criminal by the currents of the underworld. Two decades later, his film *Carandiru* (2003) offered an inside look at São Paulo's hellish state penitentiary of the same name.

Fernando Meirelles earned his credibility with *Cidade de Deus,* the 2002 film based on a true story by Paolo Lins. The film, which showed brutality and hope coexisting in a Rio favela (slum), earned four Oscar nominations. More importantly, it brought much attention to the urban poor in Brazil.

Set in 1970 during the height of the military dictatorship, *O Ano em Que Meus Pais Saíram de Férias* (The Year My Parents Went on Vacation; 2006), directed by Cao Hamburger, is a poignant coming-of-age story. Brazil's official Oscar entry for best foreign film in 2007 tackles complex issues with sensitivity in the story of one young boy left adrift in a working-class neighborhood of São Paulo. Political repression, the World Cup of 1970 and Jewish culture all form the backdrop of Hamburger's remarkably well-made film.

One of the most talked-about films of recent years is the 2007 *Tropa de Elite* (Elite Squad), which depicts police brutality in the favelas; it also makes a very clear link between middle-class college kids who buy drugs

TOP FILMS

- *O Som ao Redor* (Neighboring Sounds, 2012) by Kleber Mendonça Filho
- *Tropa de Elite* (Elite Squad, 2007) by José Padilha
- *Casa de Areia* (House of Sand, 2005) by Andrucha Waddington
- *Carandiru* (2003) by Hector Babenco
- *Cidade de Deus* (City of God, 2002) by Fernando Meirelles
- *Madame Satã* (2002) by Karim Aïnouz
- *Central do Brasil* (Central Station, 1998) by Walter Salles
- *O Que é Isso Companheiro* (Four Days in September, 1998) by Bruno Barreto
- *Pixote* (1981) by Hector Babenco
- *Bye Bye Brasil* (1980) by Carlos Diegues
- *O Pagador de Promessas* (The Payer of Vows, 1962) by Glauber Rocha.
- *Orfeu Negro* (Black Orpheus, 1959) by Marcel Camus

and the deaths of young children in the favelas who are recruited by drug lords to help meet the demand for cocaine and other substances. It was made by José Padilha, the acclaimed director of the disturbing documentary *Bus 174* (2002), which depicts a high-profile bus hijacking that took place in Rio de Janeiro in 2000.

Walter Salles is Brazil's best-known director, whose Academy Award–winning *Central do Brasil* (Central Station; 1998) should be in every serious Brazilianist's film library. The central character is an elderly woman who works in the main train station in Rio, writing letters for illiterates with families far away. A chance encounter with a young homeless boy leads her to accompany him into the real, unglamorized Brazil on a search for his father. Salles' film *Diarios de Motocicleta* (The Motorcycle Diaries; 2004) chronicles the historic journey of Che Guevara and Alberto Granada across South America, while *On the Road* (2012) is a colorful adaptation of the Jack Kerouac classic. Some of Salles' best works came earlier. His first feature film, *Terra Estrangeiro* (Foreign Land; 1995), holds an important place in the renaissance of Brazilian cinema.

An Anthology of Twentieth-Century Brazilian Poetry (1972) is a fine introduction to Brazilian poets. It's edited by American poet Elizabeth Bishop, who planned a short trip to Santos and ended up staying 15 years.

Literature

Brazil's most famous writer is Jorge Amado, who died in August 2001. Born near Ilhéus in 1912, and a longtime resident of Salvador, Amado wrote colorful romances about Bahia's people and places. His early work was strongly influenced by communism. His later books are lighter in subject, but more picturesque and intimate in style. The two most acclaimed are *Gabriela, Cravo e Canela* (Gabriela, Clove and Cinnamon), which is set in Ilhéus, and *Dona Flor e Seus Dois Maridos* (Dona Flor and Her Two Husbands), set in Salvador. *Tenda dos Milagres* (Tent of Miracles) explores race relations in Brazil, and *Farda Fardão Camisola de Dormir* (Pen, Sword and Camisole) laughs its way through the petty worlds of military and academic politics. *Terras do Sem Fim* (The Violent Land) is an early Amado classic.

Clarice Lispector (1920–77), one of Latin America's great 20th-century novelists, is surprisingly little known outside the country. Her existentialism-influenced writings focus on human isolation, alienation and moral doubt, and convey a deep understanding of women's feelings. The short-story collections *Laços de Família* (Family Ties) and *Soulstorm* are among her best works.

All of these works are available in English translations.

Flavors of Brazil

Brazilian cuisine is as syncretic as the country itself. The most basic 'Brazilian' meal can include Portuguese olive oil, native manioc, Japanese sushi, African okra, Italian pasta, German sausage and Lebanese tabbouleh. Regional flavors add to the culinary variety, with seafood and coconut *moqueca* (fish stew), sun-dried beef, and pork-and-black bean *feijoada* (stew) among the classics. Sizzling steaks, tender Amazonian fish, fresh tropical juices, decadent snacks, refreshing cocktails and heavenly desserts are also key elements of the Brazilian dining experience.

Staples & Regional Specialties

Brazilian cuisine varies from region to region, but there are a few dishes you'll find across the country. *Arroz e feijão* (rice and beans) is a staple of the Brazilian diet. On top of the beans, Brazilians often sprinkle *farofa* – manioc flour sautéed in butter, perhaps with bits of egg or bacon.

Above: Chicken and shrimp dish with caipirinha (p689)

Grilled meats, known as *churrasco* or *grelhadas,* are the meal's crowning glory: chicken, beef or pork is dredged in salt and grilled over an open fire. A green salad or sautéed or steamed vegetables round out the main course.

Bahia & the Northeast

Eat Smart in Brazil, by Joan and David Peterson, provides an excellent introduction to Brazil's culinary history, some classic recipes and an extensive and very useful glossary.

Bahian cuisine, developed in the kitchens of the region's slave-based sugar plantations, reveals its African origins in dishes such as *moqueca,* a delicious seafood stew with coconut milk; spicy *malagueta* peppers; and *dendê* (palm) oil. On the streets of Bahia you can't escape the smell of *acarajé* – fritters made with brown beans and shrimp fried in *dendê* oil.

By contrast, drier inland areas of the Northeast known as the *sertão* produce *carne seca* or *carne de sol,* beef that has been salted and dried. Squash is also very popular.

The Amazon

Amazonian cuisine is strongly influenced by the region's native Tupi people, who live largely on manioc, freshwater fish, yams and beans, and exotic fruit. *Caldeirada* is a popular fish stew not unlike bouillabaisse, and *pato no tucupí* is a regional favorite made with duck, garlic, lip-tingling *jambú* leaves and the juice of both lemons and manioc roots. Fish like *tambaquí* and *pirarucú* are technically protected species, but those you see on menus come from fish farms – so you can safely order them without worry of contributing to their decline.

The Central West

The indigenous Maué so revere guaraná – an Amazonian fruit with a caffeine-packed seed that resembles the human eye – that its plant is said to have given birth to the tribe's founder.

Occupying the prairie-like cerrado, the Central West is dominated by sprawling *fazendas* (ranches) that produce pork and beef, as well as staples such as corn, rice, kale and manioc. The region's rivers offer up the meaty dourado fish, the pintado (a type of catfish) and the infamous piranha. The Pantanal is also a goldmine for fish lovers with outstanding pintado and pacú.

Rio, São Paulo & the Southeast

In the mountainous state of Minas Gerais, pork is popular, as is the kale-like *couve,* which is sautéed in oil with garlic and onions. *Frango ao molho pardo* (chicken stewed in its own blood with vegetables) sounds gruesome but tastes delicious.

São Paulo, the gastronomic capital of Brazil, has both five-star dining rooms and humble ethnic restaurants that reflect the city's many immigrant communities. You'll find outstanding Japanese, Lebanese and Italian food, and the wood-oven–baked pizza is world-class.

Rio offers excellent food from every region. *Feijoada,* a bean-and-meat stew served with rice, *farofa,* kale and sliced orange, is the city's contribution to the national cuisine. It is traditionally served on Saturday.

The South

Maria-Brazil.org (www.maria-brazil.org) has a very good section on Brazilian food, including easy-to-follow recipes and a guide to shopping in the country's supermarkets and street fairs.

Italian and German food rules the day in the South. Expect to see lots of sausage and sauerkraut in the German enclaves of Joinville and Blumenau. Brazilian wine, the quality of which improves year by year, comes from grapes lovingly imported from Italy and planted in the accommodating soil of Rio Grande do Sul. The far south is *gaúcho* (Brazilian cowboy) country, and grilled beef restaurants are excellent here. The region preserves another cowboy tradition – *erva maté* tea.

Pan-Brazilian Fusion

Like much of the world, Brazil has undergone a kind of culinary renaissance in the last decade. One result has been a new, high-end, pan-

Moqueca (seafood stew)

Brazilian fusion cuisine, which showcases native ingredients, from the Amazonian fruits of the north to the grass-fed beef of the south. In major cities, you can find unique combinations that fuse Brazilian elements with Asian, French, Italian and other Latin American recipes.

Drinks

Juices

Brazilian *sucos* (juices) are divine. Staples include known quantities such as mango, orange, papaya, banana, passion fruit, watermelon and avocado. Then there are the Amazonian fruits like *açaí* (a berrylike fruit), *graviola* (custard apple), *cupuaçu* (pearlike fruit) and *fruta do conde* (sugar-apple fruit). Fresh *agua de côco* (coconut juice) is available across the country and is highly recommended.

Cookbooks

The Brazilian Table (Yara Roberts)

The Brazilian Kitchen (Leticia Moreinos Schwartz)

The Food and Cooking of Brazil (Fernando Farah)

Beer

Brazilians enjoy their beer served *bem gelada* (icy cold). Bohemia and Original are among the best national brands, though there are a growing number of (better) microbrews, including Devassa from Rio, Colorado from São Paulo and Eisenbahn from Santa Catarina. *Chope* (*sho*-pee) is a pale-blond pilsner draft that's lighter and generally superior to canned or bottled beer.

Caipirinhas

The caipirinha is the unofficial Brazilian national drink. Ingredients are simple – *cachaça* (a high-proof sugarcane alcohol) with crushed lime, sugar and ice – but the results are sublime. You can replace the *cachaça* with vodka (to make a *caipirosca*) or sake (to create *caipisakes or sakerinhas*) and the lime with a variety of fruit, including passion fruit, pineapple, mango, kiwi or the cherrylike *pitanga*.

Where to Eat & Drink

Eating out in Brazil can mean fried treats at the corner *lanchonete* (snack bar or greasy spoon); a lunchtime *prato feito* (ready-to-eat hot meal including rice, beans, a meat dish and salad) at a *bar* (pub) or *botequim* (working man's restaurant); a gorge session at a sit-down *rodízio* (all-you-can-eat) restaurant; or à la carte dining on white linen.

To eat quickly and well, head to a *por-kilo* restaurant, which serves food by weight, and costs from R$35 to R$60 per kilogram. Offerings generally include fresh salads and veggies, rice, beans, grilled meat and fish, plus regional specialties.

Churrascarias are generally *rodízio*-style and include a salad bar, plus meat that's brought from the grill to your table and carved for you. Prices vary wildly, from R$35 to R$100 for the all-the-meat-you-can-eat experience. *Rodízio* restaurants serving pizza and *massa* (pasta) are also popular and cost between R$18 and R$30.

Food Glossary

MAIN DISHES		
barreado	(ba·rre·*a*·do)	a mixture of meats and spices cooked in a sealed clay pot for 24 hours and served with banana and *farofa* (garnish of manioc flour sautéed with butter); the state dish of Paraná
bobó de camarão	(bo·*bo* de ka·ma·*rowng*)	manioc paste flavored with dried shrimp, coconut milk and cashew nuts
carne de sol	(*kar*·ne de sol)	tasty, salted meat, grilled and served with beans, rice and vegetables
casquinha de siri	(kas·*kee*·nya de see·*ree*)	stuffed crab
cozido	(ko·*zee*·do)	a meat stew heavy on vegetables
feijoada	(fay·zho·*a*·da)	bean-and-meat stew served with rice and orange slices, traditionally eaten for Saturday lunch
feijão tropeiro	(fay·*zowng* troh·*peh*·ro)	beans mixed with toasted manioc flour, crunchy pork rind, sausage, eggs, kale, garlic and onions
moqueca	(mo·*ke*·ka)	Bahian fish stew cooked in a clay pot with *dendê* (palm) oil, coconut milk and spicy peppers
pato no tucupí	(*pa*·to no too·koo·*pee*)	roast duck flavored with garlic, juice of the manioc plant and tongue-tingling *jambú* leaves; a favorite in Pará
picanha	(pee·*kah*·nya)	Brazil's favorite cut of beef comes from the cow's rump
pirarucu ao forno	(pee·ra·oo·*koo* ow *forr*·no)	delicious Amazonian fish, oven cooked with lemon and other seasonings
tutu á mineira	(too·*too* a mee·*nay*·ra)	savory black-bean mash typical of Minas Gerais
vatapá	(va·ta·*pa* a)	seafood dish of African origins with a thick sauce of manioc paste, coconut and *dendê* oil

SNACKS		
acarajé	(a·ka·ra·*zhe*)	Bahian fritters made of brown beans and dried shrimp fried in *dendê* oil
empadão	(eng·pa·*downg*)	a tasty pie, typical of Goiás, made from meat, vegetables, olives and eggs
quibe	(*kee*·be)	cracked wheat stuffed with spiced meat then deep-fried
pão de queijo	(powng de *kay*·zho)	balls of cheese-stuffed tapioca bread
pastel	(pas·*tel*)	thin square of dough stuffed with meat, cheese or fish, then fried

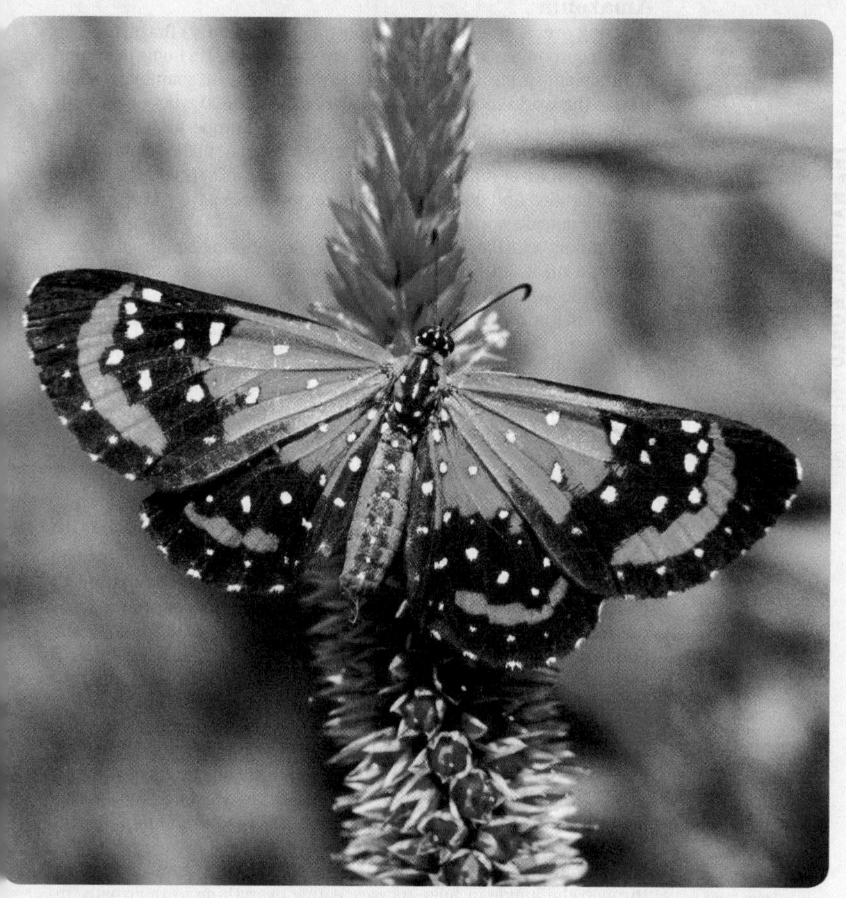

The Natural World

Home to the world's largest rainforest, as well as some of the greatest wetlands, Brazil boasts some of the most astounding plant and animal life on earth. More known species of plants, freshwater fish, amphibians and mammals are found in Brazil than in any other country in the world. Unfortunately, Brazil is also renowned for the destruction of its natural environment. Conservation remains a hot topic, and protecting Brazil's natural wonders is increasingly seen as pivotal for Brazil's future.

The Land

Brazil is the world's fifth-largest country (after Russia, China, Canada and the USA). Its 8.5 million sq km occupy almost half of South America. Brazil has five principal biomes (major regional plant and animal groupings): Amazonia, Atlantic rainforest, caatinga (semiarid land), cerrado (the central savanna) and the wetlands of the Pantanal.

Above Butterfly on flower

Iguaçu Falls, along with other scenic Brazilian locations, featured in the James Bond movie *Moonraker* (1979) and the Oscar-winning *The Mission* (1986) with Robert de Niro and Jeremy Irons.

Amazonia

Covering over 4 million sq km (almost half the country) Brazilian Amazonia incorporates 30% of the world's tropical forest. It's home to around 45,000 plant species (some 20% of the world total), 311 mammals (about 10% of the world total), 1000 bird species (15%), 1800 types of butterfly and around 2000 species of fish (in contrast, Europe has about 200). The forest still keeps many of its secrets: to this day, major tributaries of the Amazon River remain unexplored, thousands of species have not yet been classified and dozens of human communities have eluded contact with the outside world.

Including a further 2 million sq km in neighboring countries, the entire Amazon Basin holds 20% of the world's freshwater and produces 20% of the world's oxygen.

Seasonal rainfall patterns mean that the water levels of the Amazon River and its tributaries rise and fall at different times of the year. This produces dramatic alterations in the region's geography. Water levels routinely vary by 10m to 15m between low and high marks; during high-water periods, areas totaling at least 150,000 sq km (about the size of England and Wales together) are flooded.

The Amazon on Film

Amazon: Land of the Flooded Forest(National Geographic)

Amazon – River of the Future (Jacques Cousteau)

Amazon – Journey to a Thousand Rivers (Jacques Cousteau)

The Burning Season: The Chico Mendes Story (John Frankenheimer)

Forest Layers

The rainforest is stratified into layers of plant and animal life. Most of the animal activity takes place in the canopy layer, 20m to 30m above ground, where trees compete for sunshine, and butterflies, sloths and the majority of birds and monkeys live. Here hummingbirds hover for pollen, and macaws and parrots seek out nuts and tender shoots. A few tall trees reaching up to 40m, even 50m, poke above the canopy and dominate the forest skyline. These 'emergent trees' are inhabited by birds such as the harpy eagle and toucan and, unlike most other rainforest plants, disperse their seeds by wind.

The dense foliage of the canopy layer blots out sunlight at lower levels. Below the canopy is the understory. Epiphytes (air plants) hang at midlevels, and below them are bushes, saplings and shrubs growing up to 5m in height. Last is a ground cover of ferns, seedlings and herbs – plants adapted to very little light. Down here live ants and termites, the so-called social insects. The *saubas* (leaf-cutter ants) use leaves to build underground nests for raising fungus gardens, while army ants swarm through the jungle in huge masses, eating everything in their path. Insects, fungi and roots fight for access to nutrients, keeping the forest floor quite tidy.

The forest's soils are typically shallow. Many trees have buttress roots that spread over wide patches of ground to gather more nutrients.

Atlantic Rainforest

The pirarucu has gills, but they are basically useless. It breathes with lungs instead and has to surface for air about every 10 minutes or it will drown.

Brazil's 'other' tropical rainforest, the Mata Atlântica (Atlantic rainforest), is actually older than the Amazon forest and evolved independently. It once extended along the country's southeast-facing coast, from Rio Grande do Norte to Rio Grande do Sul. Today, three-quarters of Brazil's population and all its main industrial cities are located in what used to be the Mata Atlântica, and only 7% of the original forest remains.

Along the coast, there are still long stretches of this luxuriant forest. Some areas boast what may be the highest biodiversity levels on earth. The Atlantic rainforest also contains many unique species. You'll find 26 primate species (21 of which are found only here), 2000 butterfly species (including 900 found nowhere else) and some 600-plus bird species, with may endemics among them. Unsurprisingly, many of these species are endangered, including the four types of lion tamarin

Hummingbird

and the two woolly spider monkeys (the largest primates in the Americas).

Pantanal

The Pantanal is a vast swampy wetland in the center of South America, about half the size of France – some 210,000 sq km spread across Brazil, Bolivia and Paraguay. It's the largest inland wetland on earth, and 140,000 sq km of it lies in Brazil, in the states of Mato Grosso and Mato Grosso do Sul.

During the wet season, from October to March, the waters from the higher surrounding lands run into the Pantanal, inundating as much as two-thirds of it for half the year. The Pantanal, though 2000km upstream from the Atlantic Ocean, is only 100m to 200m above sea level and drains very slowly.

This seasonal flooding has made systematic farming impossible, severely limiting human impact on the area, and it creates an enormously rich feeding ground for wildlife. It is the best area to head for in all Brazil if you want to see wildlife, boasting greater visible numbers of animals and at least as much variety of creatures as Amazonia, with which it shares many species. The Pantanal supports numerous species, including iconic creatures like the giant anaconda, the jaguar, the puma, the giant anteater, the hyacinth macaw, the giant otter, and the black howler and brown capuchin monkeys – and millions of caimans. The most visible mammal is the capybara, the world's largest rodent, which is often seen in family groups or even large herds.

Amazon Books

- *Tree of Rivers (John Hemming)*
- *The Smithsonian Atlas of the Amazon (Michael Goulding)*
- *The Last Forest (Mark London and Brian Kelly)*
- *One River (Wade Davis)*
- *The Lost Amazon (Isabel Kuhl)*

Wildlife

Brazil's teeming flora and fauna make it one of the planet's best destinations for nature-lovers.

Giant anteater at back

Mammals

Anteaters & Sloths

The giant anteater (up to 2m long) lives off termites and ants. Its meat is prized in some areas of Brazil, and it's a threatened species. The collared or lesser anteater, up to 1.4m long, is yellow and black, mainly nocturnal, and often climbs trees.

The giant ground sloth, which grew to the size of an elephant, once inhabited much of Brazil. It was easy prey for prehistoric hunters and was presumably hunted to extinction 10,000 years ago.

Sloths have strong arms and legs, and spend most of their time hidden (and sleeping) in trees. You have a good chance of seeing some if you get a bit off the beaten track in Amazonia: from a moderate distance they look like clumps of vegetation high in trees. The species you're most likely to see is the brown-throated three-toed sloth.

Dolphins, Manatees & Whales

On many rivers in the Amazon Basin you should catch glimpses of the pink dolphin. It's most often seen where tributaries meet larger rivers, and is most active in the early morning and late afternoon. Sightings are tantalizing – and getting good photos virtually impossible – as the dolphin surfaces unpredictably, for just a second or so at a time, to breathe. Often it won't even lift its head above the surface. The pink dolphin has a lumpy forehead, a long beak and no dorsal fin (just a ridge). Adults are 1.8m to 2.5m long, weighing 85kg to 160kg.

Amazonian rivers are also home to the gray dolphin, a bit smaller than the pink and often found together with it. Unlike the pink dolphin, the gray also inhabits the sea, in coastal waters from Florianópolis to Panama. When it surfaces it usually lifts its head and part of its body out of the water.

Larger than the dolphin is the Amazon manatee, a slow-moving vegetarian that is illegally hunted for its meat and in danger of extinction. Prospects are even poorer for the marine West Indian manatee, of which there are just 500 left in coastal waters from the state of Alagoas northward.

Seven whale species occur off Brazil's coasts, with good sightings off Praia do Rosa between June and October. The rare humpback whale breeds in the same months in the Parque Nacional Marinho de Abrolhos, off the coast of southern Bahia.

Hummingbirds beat their wings up to 80 times a second, allowing them to hover while extracting pollen from flowers and making a light humming noise as they do so.

Felines

Many visitors dream of sighting a wild jaguar, but few have the luck of seeing one in the wild. The elusive and splendid jaguar is widely but thinly distributed in Brazil, occurring in Amazonia and the Pantanal among other regions. Jaguars hunt at night, covering large distances. They prey on a wide variety of animals, in trees, in water and on the ground, including sloths, monkeys, fish, deer, tapirs, capybaras and agoutis – but rarely people.

The puma, almost as big as the jaguar and similarly elusive, is the same beast as North America's cougar or mountain lion. As well as preying on deer, it sometimes attacks herds of domestic animals, such as sheep or goats.

Monkeys

About 80 of the world's approximately 300 primate species (which also include marmosets and tamarins) are found in Brazil, many of them unique to the country. Southeast Brazil's two species of woolly spider monkey, the southern *muriqui* and northern *muriqui*, with their thick brown fur, are the largest primates in the Americas and both are endangered, the northern species critically so and down to a population of under 300.

Howler monkeys are known for their distinctive roar. They live in groups of up to 20 that are led by a single male. In Amazonia you're most likely to encounter the red howler monkey. Further south, including in the Pantanal, the black howler monkey is the local species. The brown howler monkey inhabits the small remaining areas of the Mata Atlântica.

The two types of uakari monkey, the black-headed and the bald, inhabit Amazonian flooded forest. The bald uakari has a red or pink bald head and thick, shaggy body fur ranging from chestnut-red to white (giving rise to the popular names red uakari and white uakari).

Birds

With its diverse habitats and extraordinary number of species, Brazil is a major hot spot for bird-watchers.

MAN BITES PIRANHA

Why are people scared of piranhas? Humans eat piranhas a billion times more often than piranhas eat people. They're reasonably tasty, if a bit small and bony. A standard activity on an Amazon jungle trip is catching your own piranha lunch.

A piranha is not just a piranha, of course. It could be any of about 40 species of the *Serrasalmo* genus. Piranhas are found in the basins of the Amazon, Orinoco, Paraguay and São Francisco Rivers and in the rivers of the Guianas. Some live on seeds and fruits, some on other fish, and only a handful of species are potentially a risk to larger creatures. These types are most dangerous when stuck in tributaries, meanders or lakes that get cut off from main rivers in the dry season. When they have eaten all the other fish, the piranhas will attack more or less anything, including wounded mammals entering their waters. The scent of blood or bodily fluids in the water can whip a shoal into a feeding frenzy. Confirmed accounts of human fatalities caused by piranhas are extremely few, but plenty of Amazonian river folks have scars or missing fingers to testify just how sharp and vicious those little triangular teeth can be.

BERNDT FISCHER / GETTY IMAGES ©

Top Toucan
Bottom Caracara

Macaw

Birds of Prey

Much like great cats, birds of prey command respect and are always an object of fascination. Brazil has around 40 species of eagle, hawk, falcon, kite, caracara and kestrel, some quite common, and they're not very easy to tell apart.

The largest bird of prey in the Americas is the ferocious harpy eagle, with claws bigger than human hands. It eats sizable mammals (including monkeys) and nests at least 25m above the ground in large jungle trees. Although a few harpies still inhabit Mata Atlântica, the bird is found chiefly in Amazonia.

Field Guides

Birds of Brazil (Ber van Perlo)

Medicinal and Useful Plants of the Upper Amazon (James L Castner)

Neotropical Rainforest Mammals (Louise Emmons)

A Neotropical Companion (John Kricher)

Brazil: Amazon and Pantanal (David L Pearson and Les Beletsky)

Parrots

These are the kinds of bird that have come to symbolize tropical rainforests, and people travel from all over the world to see some of Brazil's dozens of species.

The name scarlet macaw is given to two large, gloriously colored species: *Ara chloroptera,* also called the red-and-green macaw, which grows up to 95cm long, with blue-and-green wings and a red-striped face; and *Ara macao,* which is a bit smaller (about 85cm long) with blue-and-yellow wings (yellow underneath, blue on top). The latter bird is restricted to Amazonia, but the red-and-green macaw also inhabits the Pantanal, cerrado and even caatinga.

Toucans

Among the most colorful groups of Latin American birds are toucans, which despite their large beaks are able to fly with a surprising agility. Toucans live at forest treetop level and are often best seen from boats.

Waterfall, Parque Nacional da Chapada dos Guimarães (p370)

Brazil's biggest is the toco toucan, whose habitat ranges from Amazonia to the cerrado to the Pantanal. Around 55cm long, including its bright orange beak, the plumage is black except for a white neck area. In Amazonia you may see the white-throated toucan or the yellow-ridged toucan. Both are fairly large birds, with black beaks.

Waterfowl

Highly visible birds in the Pantanal and Amazonia include herons, egrets, storks, ibises, spoonbills and their relatives. The tiger heron, with its brown and black stripes, is particularly distinctive. The sight of hundreds of snowy egrets gathering in a waterside rookery looks like a sudden blooming of white flowers in the treetops.

For 15 years Mark Plotkin devotedly tracked down Amazonian shamans to understand some of their encyclopedic knowledge of medicinal plants. His *Tales of a Shaman's Apprentice* is both a travelogue and adventure story.

Of the storks, one of the most striking is the tall, black-headed and scarlet-necked jabiru found in the Pantanal and Amazonia. In the Pantanal, also look for the similarly sized maguari stork, which is mainly white with a pinkish face, and the smaller wood stork, with its black head and beak with a curved end. The beautiful pink roseate spoonbill is another Pantanal resident. The spectacular scarlet ibis lives in flocks along the Northeast coast.

Plants

The last ice age did not reach Brazil and the rainforests have never suffered long droughts, so the area has had an unusually long period of time to develop plant species that are found nowhere else in the world.

Though estimates run at around 45,000, it would be impossible to determine an exact number of plant species in the Amazon, let alone in the whole of Brazil, as new plants are being discovered all the time and, unfortunately, others are disappearing with frightening frequency. The great majority of the plants in Brazil's rainforests are trees – estimated at some 70% of the total vegetation. Many rainforest trees look similar even though they are of different species, but a trained eye can distinguish more than 400 species of tree per hectare in some areas.

National Parks & Protected Areas

Much of Brazil is, officially at least, under environmental protection. Over 1000 areas, covering some 1.3 million sq km (around 15% of the whole country), are protected. Some of these are run by the federal government, some by state governments and some by private individuals or nongovernmental organizations (NGOs).

Terras Indígena (Indigenous Lands) occupy about 12% of Brazilian territory, nearly all in the Amazon. Though they are not explicitly dedicated to nature conservation, their inhabitants tend to use them with minimal environmental impact.

Environmental Issues

Sadly, Brazil is as renowned for its forests as it is for destroying them. At last count more than one-fifth of the Brazilian Amazon rainforest had been completely destroyed. Cutting down forests for cattle ranches and to grow crops (namely soybeans) and illegal logging are among the chief threats to the Amazon. The good news is that the rate of

TOP RESERVES & NATIONAL PARKS

Fernando de Noronha archipelago (p504) Fabulous marine park of islands, 350km from Natal.

Floresta Nacional do Tapajós (FLONA; p595) Lush Amazonian rainforest preserve.

Ilha de Marajó (p587) Huge river island in the mouth of the Amazon.

Ilha Grande (p121) Hilly island covered by virgin Atlantic rainforest, a few hours from Rio.

Mamirauá Reserve (p632) Amazonian floodplain reserve teeming with wildlife; excellent ecotourism program.

Pantanal (p373) Vast wetlands that are one of Brazil's best places to see wildlife.

Parque Estadual da Pedra Azul (p216) Dramatic 1822m blue-tinged rock formation with natural pools and forest.

Parque Estadual de Itaúnas (p211) Sand dunes, beaches and a sea-turtle preserve.

Parque Nacional da Chapada Diamantina (p462) Large mountainous park in Bahia with stunning scenery, waterfalls and rivers.

Parque Nacional da Chapada dos Guimarães (p370) Waterfalls, canyons and bizarre rock formations.

Parque Nacional da Chapada dos Veadeiros (p357) High-altitude cerrado (savanna) with picturesque landscapes near Brasília.

Parque Nacional da Serra da Capivara (p555) Park in southern Piauí with thousands of prehistoric paintings and unique rock formations.

Parque Nacional do Itatiaia (p136) Ruggedly beautiful mountainous park, 150km from Rio.

Parque Nacional do Iguaçu (p285) Brazilian side of the spectacular waterfalls.

Parque Nacional dos Lençóis Maranhenses (p565) Enormous expanse of sand dunes and clear rain pools.

Praia do Rosa (p312) Beach town in Santa Catarina that's a famed whale sanctuary.

Pantanal wetlands (p373)

deforestation has slowed in recent years, falling year-on-year from nearly 13,000 sq km in 2008 to under 5000 sq km in 2012. Though there was some concern in 2015 that deforestation rates are once again on the rise.

The greatest number of different tree species ever found in 1 hectare (10,000 sq meters) was 476, recorded in an area of Atlantic rainforest in the hills of Espírito Santo state.

Big development projects are also affecting the Amazon. The government has some 30 large hydroelectric dams in the works for the Amazon region. The biggest is the massive Belo Monte dam on the Rio Xingu in Pará, which will flood at least 450 sq km of rainforest, and displace some 12,000 people, including thousands of indigenous people who have resided along the river for centuries. As of the time of writing, construction was 50% complete, with the dam expected to be fully operation by 2019.

The Pantanal wetlands also face serious threats, including the rapid spread of intensive soy, cotton and sugarcane farming on Brazil's central plains, which are the source of most of the Pantanal's water. The sugarcane is the raw material of ethanol motor fuel, the international growth of which has led to the creation of dozens of new ethanol distilleries in Mato Grosso do Sul. Herbicides, fertilizers and other chemicals from the plantations drizzle their way into Pantanal waters, and forest clearance on the plains leads to erosion and consequent silting of Pantanal rivers. The growing cities around the Pantanal (many of which lack adequate waste-treatment plants) and ongoing industrial development also pose serious risks to this region.

On Brazil's coasts, growth of cities and burgeoning tourism developments threaten many delicate coastal marine ecosystems, despite the creation of protected areas on extensive tracts of land and sea.

Survival Guide

Directory A–Z

Accommodations

Brazilian accommodations range from battered, windowless cells to sumptuous seaside guesthouses, with many possibilities in between. Nearly every pousada (guesthouse), hostel and hotel serves some form of *café da manha* (breakfast). Private rooms with communal bathrooms are called *quartos*. Rooms with a private bathroom are *apartamentos*.

At the bottom end of the price scale, you'll find cheap hotel rooms outside of major cities and resort areas. Expect a bare room with nothing but a bed and maybe a fan.

Midrange listings are usually comfortable but not stylish, with decent beds, air-conditioning, hot-water bathrooms and cable TV. The top end offers more spacious digs, with maybe a veranda, a pool and other amenities. Many midrange and top-end hotels have safes in the rooms for storing valuables.

Reservations

In tourist centers, especially Rio, it's wise to make reservations during July (school holidays), and from Christmas to Carnaval. The same holds for any vacation mecca (eg Búzios, Ilha Bela, Morro de São Paulo) on weekends, and anywhere during major festivals. For prime peak times (eg Carnaval), make contact months ahead.

Hostels

Youth hostels in Brazil are called *albergues da juventude*. The HI-affiliated Federação Brasileira de Albergues da Juventude (www.hostel.org.br) has more than 90 hostels in the country, most with links on the website. There are also scores of private hostels. Rio is by far the country's hostel capital, with over 130 at last count. Quality varies considerably, but they're generally good places to meet Brazilian and foreign travelers.

A dorm bed in a hostel costs between R$40 and R$75.

Hotels

Brazil's hotels range from the good, modern and luxurious to shabby and moldy. At the more expensive places, taxes of 15% are often added to the price. Prices typically rise by about 30% during the high season, and room rates double or even triple during Carnaval and around New Year's Eve. Hotels in business-oriented cities such as São Paulo, Curitiba, Porto Alegre and Brasília usually give discounts for stays on weekends.

Jungle Lodges

One popular type of remote-area accommodations is the jungle lodge, which caters to tourists in or on the edge of the forest. Though they are sometimes pricey, you're paying for the experience of lodging in the rainforest, rather than amenities – which are midrange at best. The largest number of jungle lodges are found outside of Manaus.

Pousadas

A pousada typically means a small, family-owned guesthouse, though some hotels call themselves 'pousadas' to improve their charm quotient. Pousadas can cost as little as R$140 for a rustic double and as much as R$500 for a lavish option.

SLEEPING PRICE RANGES

The following price ranges refer to a double room with bathroom in high season (December to March).

$ less than R$160
$$ R$160–R$350
$$$ more than R$350

The price range for Rio, São Paulo and Brasília is higher:

$ less than R$200
$$ R$200–R$500
$$$ more than R$500

Rental Accommodations

It's possible to rent holiday, short- or long-term apartments through a local holiday-rental agencies. AirBnB (www.airbnb.com) has thousands of listings across Brazil for finding rooms or apartment rentals.

Customs Regulations

Travelers entering Brazil can bring in 2L of alcohol, 400 cigarettes, and one personal computer, video camera and still camera. Newly purchased goods worth up to US$500 are permitted duty-free. Meat and cheese products are not allowed.

Electricity

Introduced by law in 2011, Brazil's new universal standard sockets (pictured below) are incompatible with many plugs from abroad. Most (but not all) will, however, take the standard European two-pronged plug (pictured right). Older hybrid sockets accept both the European two-pronged plug and the American two-pronged plug.

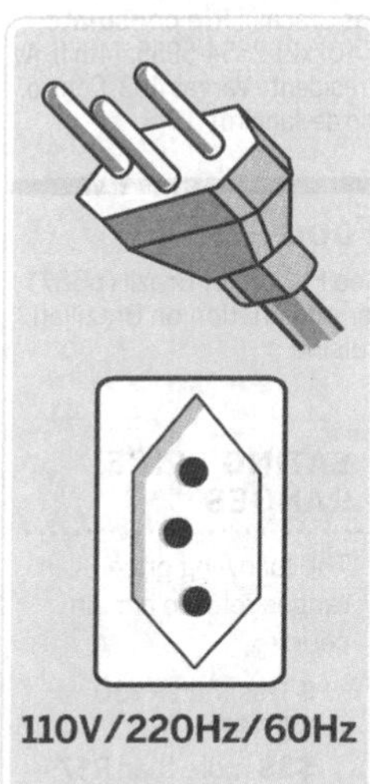

110V/220Hz/60Hz

BOOK YOUR STAY ONLINE

For more accommodations reviews by Lonely Planet authors, check out lonelyplanet.com/brazil/hotels/. You'll find independent reviews, as well as recommendations on the best places to stay. Best of all, you can book online.

110V/220Hz/60Hz

Embassies & Consulates

The embassies are all in Brasília, but many countries have consulates in Rio and São Paulo, and often other cities as well. For addresses in Brasília, SES stands for Setor de Embaixadas Sul.

➡ **Argentine Embassy** (☎0xx61-3212-7600; www.cpabl.mrecic.gov.ar; SES Quadra 803, Lote 12, Brasília); **Foz do Iguaçu consulate** (☎0xx45-3574-2969; www.cpabl.mrecic.gov.ar; Travessia Bianchi 26; ⏰10am-3pm Mon-Fri); **Porto Alegre consulate** (☎0xx51-3321-1360; Rua Coronel Bordini 1033); **Rio consulate** (☎0xx21-2553-1646; Praia de Botafogo 228, Room 201, Botafogo); **São Paulo consulate** (☎0xx11-3897-9522; www.cpabl.mrecic.gov.ar; Av Paulista 2313, Bela Vista)

➡ **Australian Embassy** (☎0xx61-3226-3111; www.brazil.embassy.gov.au; Av das Nações, SES, Q 801, Conj K, Lota 7, Brasília); **Rio consulate** (☎0xx21-3824-4624; www.dfat.gov.au/missions/countries/brri.html; 23rd fl, Av Presidente Wilson 231)

➡ **Bolivian Consulate** (☎0xx61-3366-3136; www.embolivia.org.br; SES Av das Nações 06, Quadra 809, Lote 34); **Brasiléia consulate** (☎0xx68-3546-5760; Julio Matiolli Nro. 84, Centro Municipio de Epitaciolandia Acre, Brasil; ⏰8am-noon & 2-4pm Mon-Fri); **Corumbá consulate** (☎067-3231-5605; consuladoboliviacorumba@gmail.com; cnr Porto Carrero & Firmo de Matos; ⏰8am-12:30pm & 2-5:30pm Mon-Fri); **Guajará-Mirim consulate** (☎0xx69-3541-8622; Rua 15 de Novembro 255; ⏰8am-noon & 2-6pm Mon-Fri); **Rio consulate** (☎0xx21-2552-5490; www.consuladodeboliviaenrio.org.br; No 101, Av Rui Barbosa 664)

➡ **Canadian Embassy** (☎0xx61-3424 5400; www.brazil.gc.ca; Av das Nações, SES, Q 803, Lote 16, Brasília); **Rio consulate** (☎0xx21-2543-3004; www.brasil.gc.ca; 13th fl, Av Atlântica 1130, Copacabana); **São Paulo consulate** (☎0xx11-5509-4321; www.canadainternational.gc.ca; 16th fl, Torre Norte, Av das Nações Unidas 12901)

➡ **Colombian Embassy** (☎0xx61-3214-8900; http://brasil.embajada.gov.co; Av das Nações, SES, Q 803, Lote 10, Brasília); **Tabatinga consulate** (☎097-3412-2104; http://tabatinga.consulado.gov.co; Sampaio 623)

PRACTICALITIES

- The biggest Portuguese-language daily newspapers are *Jornal do Brasil* (www.jbonline.com.br) and *O Globo* (www.globo.com.br), both from Rio, and *O Estado de São Paulo* and *Folha de São Paulo,* out of São Paulo. The weekly *Veja* is a current-affairs magazine, and in Rio and São Paulo it comes with a good pullout guide to what's happening locally. For English-language news in Rio, check out the *Rio Times* (www.riotimesonline.com).
- TV programming revolves around sports, comedy shows and the nightly *telenovelas* (soap operas). *O Globo* is the largest nationwide TV network.
- Brazil uses the PAL system for video/DVD.
- The electrical current is not standardized in Brazil and can be almost anywhere between 110V and 220V. The most common power points have two sockets, and most will take both round and flat prongs. Carry a converter and use a surge protector with electrical equipment.
- Brazilians use the metric system for weights and measures.

- **Dutch Embassy** (0xx61-3961-3200; http://brazilie.nlambassade.org; Av das Nações, SES, Quadra 801, Lote 05, Brasília); **Rio consulate** (0xx21-2157-5400; riodejaneiro.nlconsulado.org; 6th fl, Ataulfo de Paiva)
- **French Embassy** (0xx61-3222-3999; www.ambafrance-br.org; Av das Nações, SES, Q 801, Lote 04, Brasília); **Rio consulate** (0xx21-3974-6699; http://riodejaneiro.ambafrance-br.org; Av Presidente Antônio Carlos 58, Centro)
- **German Embassy** (0xx61-3442-7000; www.brasilia.diplo.de; Av das Nações, SES, Q 807, Lote 25, Brasília); **Rio consulate** (0xx21-2554-0004; www.rio-de-janeiro.diplo.de; Carlos de Campos 417)
- **Guyanese Embassy** (0xx61-3248-0874; Casa 24, SHIS Quadra 5, Conj 19, Brasília)
- **Irish Embassy** (0xx61-3248-8800; SHIS QL 12 Conjunto 5, Casa 9, Brasília)
- **Israeli Embassy** (0xx61-2105-0500; embassies.gov.il; Av das Nações, SES, Q 809, Lote 38, Brasília)
- **New Zealand Embassy** (0xx-3248-9900; www.nzembassy.com/brazil; SHIS QI 09, Conjunto 16, Casa 1, Brasília); **New Zealand Consulate** (0xx11-3898-7400; www.nzembassy.com/brazil; Paulista 2421, 12th Fl, Bela Vista, São Paulo)
- **Paraguayan Embassy** (0xx-61-3242-3968; Av das Nações, SES, Quadra 811, Lote 42, Brasília); **Foz do Iguaçu consulate** (0xx45-3523-2898; fozconsulpar@mre.gov.py; R Marechal Deodoro da Fonseca 901; 9am-1pm Mon-Fri)
- **Peruvian Embassy** (0xx61-3242-9933; www.embperu.org.br; Av das Nações, SES, Quadra 811, Lote 43, Brasília); **Rio consulate** (0xx21-2551-9596; www.consuladoperurio.com.br; 2nd fl, Av Rui Barbosa 314, Flamengo)
- **UK Embassy** (0xx61-3329-2300; www.reinounido.org.br; Av das Nações, SES, Quadra 801, Conj K, Lote 08, Brasília); **Rio consulate** (0xx21-2555-9600; www.reinounido.org.br; 2nd fl, Praia do Flamengo 284, Flamengo); **São Paulo consulate** (0xx11-3094-2700; www.ukinbrazil.fco.gov.uk; Fereira de Arauja 741, 2nd fl, Pinheiros, São Paulo)
- **Uruguayan Embassy** (0xx61-3322-6534; www.emburuguai.org.br; Av das Nações, SES, Quadra 803, Lote 14, Brasília); **Porto Alegre consulate** (0xx51-3325-6200; Av 24 de Outubro 850); **Rio consulate** (0xx21-2553-6030; www.emburuguai.org.br; 6th fl, Praia de Botafogo 210)
- **US Embassy** (0xx61-3312-7000; brazil.usembassy.gov; Av das Nações, SES, Quadra 801, Lote 3, Brasília); **Rio consulate** (0xx21-3823-2000; brazil.usembassy.gov; Av Presidente Wilson 147, Centro); **Salvador consulate** (0xx71-3113-2090; Room 1401, Salvador Trade Center, Torre Sul, Av Tancredo Neves 1632); **São Paulo consulate** (0xx11-3250-5000; http://saopaulo.usconsulate.gov; Henri Dunant 500, Chácara Santo Antônio)
- **Venezuelan Embassy** (0xx61-2101-1010; http://brasil.embajada.gob.ve; Av das Nações, SES, Quadra 803, Lote 13, Brasília); **Boa Vista consulate** (0xx95-3623-6612; Av Benjamin Constant 968; 8am-noon Mon-Fri); **Manaus consulate** (0xx92-3584-3813; Río Jamary 10, Conj Vieiralves, Nossa Senhora das Graças); **Rio consulate** (0xx21-2554-5955; 14th fl, Av Presidente Vargas 463, Centro, Rio de Janeiro)

Food

See Flavors of Brazil (p687) for information on Brazilian cuisine.

EATING PRICE RANGES

The following price ranges refer to a main course.

$ less than R$30
$$ R$30–75
$$$ more than R$75

Gay & Lesbian Travelers

Brazilians are pretty laid-back when it comes to most sexual issues, and homosexuality is more accepted here than in any other part of Latin America. That said, the degree to which you can be out in Brazil varies greatly by region, and in some smaller towns discrimination is prevalent.

Rio is the gay capital of Latin America, though São Paulo and, to a lesser extent, Salvador also have lively scenes. Gay bars in Brazil are all-welcome affairs attended by Gays, Lesbians e Simpatizantes (GLS), a mixed heterosexual and homosexual crowd far more concerned with dancing and having a good time than anything else.

There is no law against homosexuality in Brazil, and the age of consent is 18, the same as for heterosexuals.

Health

For an ambulance in Brazil, call ☎192, or an emergency number.

Good medical care is available in the larger cities but may be difficult to find in rural areas. Medical care in Brazil may be extremely expensive.

Each Brazilian pharmacy has a licensed pharmacist. Most are well supplied.

Infectious Diseases

The diseases of most concern are mosquito-borne infections, including malaria, yellow fever and dengue fever, which are not a significant concern in temperate regions.

DENGUE

Found throughout Brazil, dengue is transmitted by Aedes mosquitoes, which bite preferentially during the daytime and are more common in densely populated, urban environments.

Dengue usually causes flu-like symptoms, including fever, muscle aches, headaches, nausea and vomiting, often followed by a rash. There is no vaccine or treatment for dengue fever except to take analgesics such as acetaminophen/paracetamol and to drink plenty of fluids.

MALARIA

Malaria is transmitted by mosquito bites, usually between dusk and dawn. The main symptoms are high spiking fevers, which may be accompanied by chills, sweats, headache, body aches, weakness, vomiting or diarrhea. Severe cases may involve the central nervous system and lead to seizures, confusion, coma and death.

Taking prophylaxis (malaria pills) is strongly recommended for forested areas within the nine states of the Amazonia region.

If you develop a fever after returning home, see a physician, as malaria symptoms may not occur for months.

TYPHOID

Typhoid fever is caused by ingestion of food or water contaminated by a species of salmonella known as *Salmonella typhi*. Fever occurs in virtually all cases. Other symptoms may include headache, malaise, muscle aches, dizziness, loss of appetite, nausea and abdominal pain. Either diarrhea or constipation may occur.

Unless you expect to take all your meals in major hotels and restaurants, typhoid vaccine is a good idea.

YELLOW FEVER

Yellow fever is a life-threatening viral infection transmitted by mosquitoes in forested areas. The illness begins with flu-like symptoms, which may include fever, chills, headache, muscle aches, backache, loss of appetite, nausea and vomiting. These symptoms usually subside in a few days, but one person in six enters a second, toxic phase characterized by recurrent fever, vomiting, listlessness, jaundice, kidney failure and hemorrhage, leading to death in up to half of the cases. There is no treatment.

The yellow-fever vaccine is strongly recommended for all travelers to Brazil, except those visiting only Rio de Janeiro, São Paulo and the coastal areas south of São Luís. Proof of vaccination is no longer required from travelers arriving from a yellow-fever-infected country in Africa or the Americas.

Water Quality

Tap water in Brazilian cities such as Rio and São Paulo is generally safe to drink, but it tastes awful. In remote areas, tap water may be suspect. Many hotels and guesthouses filter their water – be sure to inquire about the status where you're staying.

ZIKA VIRUS: WARNING FOR PREGNANT TRAVELERS

Brazil has experienced an outbreak of Zika virus infections since 2015. Transmitted by mosquitoes, Zika rarely causes illness – only one in five infected people will experience the flu-like symptoms. The virus, however, has been linked to microcephaly (abnormally small head size with possible brain damage) in babies born to women who were infected while pregnant. The US Center for Disease Control (CDC) recommends pregnant women consider postponing travel to Brazil (and other countries where virus transmission is ongoing).

Vigorous boiling for one minute is the most effective means of water purification, though you can also use a water filter, ultraviolet light (such as a steripen) or iodine pills.

Insurance

A travel-insurance policy to cover theft, loss and medical problems is a good idea. The policies handled by STA Travel and other student-travel organizations are usually good value. Some policies offer lower and higher medical-expense options; the higher ones are chiefly for countries such as the USA that have extremely high medical costs. There is a wide variety of policies available, so check the fine print.

Some policies specifically exclude 'dangerous activities,' which can include scuba diving, motorcycling and even hiking.

You may prefer a policy that pays doctors or hospitals directly rather than you having to pay on the spot and claim later. If you have to claim later, make sure you keep all documentation.

Check that the policy covers ambulances or an emergency flight home.

Worldwide travel insurance is available at www.lonelyplanet.com/bookings. You can buy, extend and claim online any time – even if you're already on the road.

Internet Access

Many hostels and hotels, as well as some cafes and restaurants, provide wi-fi access (indicated in this book with the icon 📶). It's usually free, although pricier hotels sometimes charge for it.

Internet cafes are slowly disappearing, though you can usually find at least one in most destinations. Most places charge between R$5 and R$10 an hour.

Legal Matters

If something is stolen from you, report it to the police. No big investigation is going to occur, but you will get a police report to give to your insurance company.

In recent years Brazil has gotten quite strict about drink-driving. Police checkpoints stop cars at random.

The penalties for drug possession are harsh, and you don't want to end up in a Brazilian prison. Some police checkpoints are set up outside nightclubs to stop taxis and give the full pat down to club-goers on their way home (hint, don't carry anything!). Police along the coastal drive from Rio to Búzios and Rio to São Paulo are notorious for hassling young people and foreigners. Border areas are also a danger, particularly around the Bolivian border.

If you are arrested, know that you have the right to remain silent, and that you are innocent until proven guilty. You also have a right to be visited by your lawyer or a family member.

A large amount of cocaine is smuggled out of Bolivia and Peru through Brazil. Be very careful with drugs. If you're going to buy, don't buy from strangers and don't carry anything around with you.

Marijuana is plentiful in Brazil and very illegal. Nevertheless, it's widely used, and, like many other things in Brazil, everyone except the military and the police has a rather tolerant attitude towards it. Bahia seems to have the most open climate.

If you're coming from one of the Andean countries and have been chewing coca leaves, be especially careful to clean out your pack before arriving in Brazil. Sentences are stiff even for possession of coca leaves.

Because of the harsh penalties involved with possession or apparent possession, it's wise to stay away from drugs in any form.

Maps

The best maps in Brazil are the Quatro Rodas series. These good regional maps (Norte, Nordeste etc) are available throughout Brazil. Quatro Rodas also publishes the *Atlas Rodoviário* road atlas, useful if you're driving, as well as excellent street atlases for the main cities.

Money

Brazil's currency is the real (hay-*ow;* often written R$); the plural is reais (hay-*ice*). One real is made up of 100 centavos.

ATMs

ATMs are the easiest way of getting cash in big cities and are common. In many smaller towns, ATMs exist but don't always work for non-Brazilian cards. Make sure you have a four-digit PIN (longer PINs may not work). In general, Citibank, Banco do Brasil and Bradesco are the best ATMs to try.

Bargaining

A little bargaining for hotel rooms should become second nature. Before you agree to take a room, ask for a better price. '*Tem desconto?*' (Is there a discount?) and '*Pode fazer um melhor preço?*' (Can you give a better price?) are the phrases to use. There's sometimes a discount for paying *à vista* (cash).

You should also bargain when shopping in markets, and if you're about to ride in unmetered taxis, arrange the price before departing.

Cash

It might be handy to keep cash in reserve, though you'll want to be exceptionally cautious when traveling with it. Cash should be in US dollars or euros.

FRAUD WARNING

Credit-card and ATM fraud is widespread in Brazil, especially in the Northeast. Card cloning (*Clonagem* in Portuguese) is the preferred method: an entrepreneurial opportunist sticks a false card reader into an ATM that copies your card and steals the PIN when you come along and withdraw money. Shazam! A few hours later, $1500 disappears from your account in Recife while you and your card are safe and sound sipping caipirinhas on the beach in Natal!

To combat fraud, restaurants will bring the credit-card machine to your table or ask you to accompany them to the cashier to run a credit-card transaction. Never let someone walk off with your card. Other tips:

- Use high-traffic ATMs inside banks during banking hours only.
- Always cover the ATM keypad when entering personal codes.
- Avoid self-standing ATMs whenever possible and never use an ATM that looks tampered with.

Credit Cards

You can use credit cards for many purchases and to make cash withdrawals from ATMs and banks. Visa is the most widely accepted card, followed by MasterCard. Amex and Diners Club cards are less useful. Visa cash advances are widely available, even in small towns with no other currency-exchange facilities; you'll need your passport, and the process can be time-consuming, especially at the ubiquitous but bureaucratic Banco do Brasil.

Tipping

In restaurants the 10% service charge will usually be included in the bill.

On jungle trips, it's customary to tip your guide at the end, and certainly appreciated if you can give a little to the assistant or boat operator(s).

Tipping is also optional for low-wage earners such as hotel housekeepers, juice-bar baristas, beach vendors, hair stylists and shoe shiners.

Parking assistants receive no wages and are dependent on tips, usually R$2 or more.

Most people round up taxi fares to the nearest real, but tipping is not expected.

Opening Hours

Banks 9am–3pm Monday to Friday

Bars 7pm–2am

Juice bars & cafes 8am–10pm

Malls 10am–9pm Monday to Saturday, 3pm–10pm Sunday

Restaurants noon–2:30pm and 6pm–10pm

Shops 9am–6pm Monday to Friday and 9am–1pm Saturday

Public Holidays

April 19, the Dia do Índio (Indigenous Day), is not a national holiday but is nevertheless marked by festivities in indigenous villages around the country.

New Year's Day January 1

Carnaval February/March (the two days before Ash Wednesday)

Good Friday & Easter Sunday March/April

Tiradentes Day April 21

May Day/Labor Day May 1

Corpus Christi Late May/June (60 days after Easter Sunday)

Independence Day September 7

Day of NS de Aparecida October 12

All Souls' Day November 2

Proclamation of the Republic November 15

Christmas Day December 25

Safe Travel

Brazil receives a lot of bad press about its violence and high crime rate. Use common sense and take general precautions applicable throughout South America:

- Carry only the minimum cash needed plus a fat-looking wad to hand over to would-be thieves.
- Dress down, leave the jewelry at home and don't walk around flashing iPhones, iPads and other expensive electronics.
- Be alert and walk purposefully. Criminals home in on dopey, hesitant, disoriented-looking individuals.
- Use ATMs inside buildings. Before doing so, be very aware of your surroundings. Thieves case ATMs and exchange bureaus.
- Check the windows and doors of your room for security, and don't leave anything valuable lying around.
- Don't take anything unnecessary to city beaches (bathing suit, towel, small amount of cash – nothing else!).
- After dark, don't ever walk along empty streets, in deserted parks or on urban beaches.

Scams & Robbery Techniques

Distraction is a common tactic employed by street thieves. The aim is to throw potential victims off guard so that they're easier prey. It may be something as simple as asking you for a cigarette or a light so that you slow down and take your attention off other people around you.

There have also been reports of druggings, including spiked drinks. While you're temporarily unconscious or semiconscious as a result of some noxious substance being slipped into your beverage, you're powerless to resist thieves. If you start to feel unaccountably dizzy, disoriented, fatigued or just mentally vacant not long after imbibing, your drink may have been spiked. If you suspect this to be the case, call for help, quickly extricate yourself from the situation and try to get to a safe place – your hotel room.

Exercise *extreme* caution when someone you don't know and trust offers you a drink of *any* kind or even cigarettes, sweets etc. If the circumstances make you suspicious, the offer can be tactfully refused by claiming stomach or other medical problems.

Cut-Rate Tour Operators & Touts

In Manaus, Cuiabá and other parts of the Amazon and the Pantanal, there's a major problem with freelancers and shady operators selling cut-rate tours that turn out to be ecologically unsound, awful and/or unsafe. As a rule, never book a tour (or even accept help) from someone who approaches you unsolicited at the airport or on the street. Go directly to the offices in town, or book on websites ahead of time.

Shopping

Handicrafts, artwork and CDs all make fine souvenirs. Try to buy arts and crafts directly from the artist or artisan.

For genuine indigenous arts and crafts, have a look in the Artíndia stores of Funai (the government indigenous agency) and museum gift shops.

Artisans in the Northeast produce a rich assortment of artistic items. Salvador and nearby Cachoeira are most notable for their rough-hewn wood sculptures. Ceará specializes in fine lace. The interior of Pernambuco, in particular Caruaru, is famous for wildly imaginative ceramic figurines.

Candomblé stores are a good source of curios, ranging from magical incense guaranteed to increase sexual allure, wisdom and health, to amulets and ceramic figurines of Afro-Brazilian gods.

Telephone

Domestic Calls

You can make domestic calls – intercity or local – from normal card pay phones on the street and in telephone offices. The phone cards you need are sold in denominations of 20 to 100 units (costing between R$5 and R$20) by vendors and at newsstands and anywhere you see advertising *cartões telefônicos*.

For calls within the city you're in, just slide the card into the phone, then check the readout to see if it's given you proper credit, and dial the eight-digit number. Local fixed-line phone calls cost only a few units.

For calls to other cities, you need to precede the number with 0, then the code of your selected carrier, then the two or three digits representing the city area code. City codes are therefore usually given in the format 0xx-digit-digit, with the 'xx' representing the carrier code. A long-distance call usually eats up between five and 10 phonecard units per minute.

You need to include the city code (0xx-digit-digit) when calling to another city, even if that city has the same city code as the one you're calling from.

To make a *chamada a cobrar* (intercity collect) call, stick a 9 in front of the 0xx. To make a local collect call, dial ☎9090 and then the number. A recorded message in Portuguese will ask you to say your name and the name of the state where you're calling from, after the beep.

International Calls

Brazil's country code is 55. When calling internationally to Brazil, omit the initial 0xx of the area code.

For international *a cobrar* (collect) calls, secure a Brazilian international operator by dialing ☎0800-703-2111 (Embratel).

GOVERNMENT TRAVEL ADVICE

The following government websites offer travel advisories and information on the security situation in Brazil and elsewhere.

Australian Department of Foreign Affairs & Trade (☎1300 139 281; www.smarttraveller.gov.au)

British Foreign Office (☎0845-850-2829; www.gov.uk/foreign-travel-advice)

Canadian Department of Foreign Affairs (☎1-800-267 6788; http://travel.gc.ca/travelling/advisories)

US State Department (☎1-888-407-4747; http://travel.state.gov)

Cell (Mobile) Phones

Brazil uses the GSM 850/900/1800/1900 network, which is compatible with North America, Europe and Australia, but the country's 4G LTE network runs on 2500/2690 (for now), which is not compatible with many North American and European smartphones, including initial releases of the iPhone 5. *Celular* (cell) phones have eight-digit numbers (nine-digit numbers in São Paulo) starting with 6, 7, 8 or 9. Calls to mobiles are more expensive than calls to landlines. Mobiles have city codes, just like landlines, and if you're calling from another city, you have to use them.

Tim (www.tim.com.br), Claro (www.claro.com.br), Oi (www.oi.com.br) and Vivo (www.vivo.com.br) are the major operators. Foreigners can purchase a local SIM with a passport instead of needing a Brazilian CPF (tax ID number) – a major bureaucratic roadblock dismantled.

BRAZILIAN CITY CODES & CARRIERS

Brazil has several rival long-distance telephone carriers. When making a long-distance call (either between cities or internationally), you have to select a carrier and include its two-digit *código de prestadora* (code) in the number you dial. Brazilian city codes are commonly quoted with an xx representing the carrier code, eg ☎0xx21 for Rio de Janeiro or ☎0xx71 for Salvador.

This construction may look complicated, but in practice it's straightforward. For one thing, you can use the main carriers, Embratel (☎21) or Oi Telemar (☎31) for any call; for another, other major carriers usually have their names and codes widely displayed in their localities, particularly on public phones.

For example, to call from Rio de Janeiro to Fortaleza (city code ☎0xx85), in the state of Ceará, you dial 0 followed by 21, 23, 31 or 85 (the codes of the four carriers that cover both Rio and Ceará), followed by 85 for Fortaleza, followed by the number.

For an international call, dial 00 followed by either 21, 23 or 31 (the international carriers), followed by the country code, city code and number.

Time

Brazil has four time zones:

Most of the country is GMT/UTC minus three hours. This includes Rio, São Paulo, the South, Northeast, Brasília and half of the Amazon.

Mato Grosso, Mato Grosso do Sul and most of the Amazon are one hour behind Brasília time (GMT/UTC minus four hours).

A tiny part of Amazonas state and all of Acre are two hours behind Brasília time (GMT/UTC minus five hours).

The Fernando de Noronha archipelago is one hour *ahead* of Brasília time (GMT/UTC minus two hours).

Brazilian daylight-saving time runs from mid-October to mid-February, during which period clocks are advanced one hour – but only in the Southeast, South and Central West.

Toilets

Public toilets are not common but can be found at every bus station and airport in most cities and towns; there's usually a charge of around R$0.50 to R$1. People will generally let you use the toilets in restaurants and bars. As in other Latin American countries, toilet paper isn't flushed. There's usually a basket next to the toilet to put paper in.

Tourist Information

Tourist offices in Brazil are a mixed bag. Some offices have dedicated, knowledgeable staff, and others have little interest in helping tourists.

Embratur (www.visitbrasil.com), the Brazilian tourism institute, provides limited online resources.

Travelers with Disabilities

Travelers in wheelchairs don't have an easy time in Brazil, but in the large cities there is a concerted effort to keep people mobile. Problems you'll encounter include immensely crowded public buses, and restaurants with entrance steps. It pays to plan your trip through contact with some of the relevant organizations.

Rio is probably the most accessible city in Brazil for disabled travelers to get around in, but that doesn't mean it's always easy. The metro system has electronic wheelchair lifts, but these aren't always operational. The streets and sidewalks along the main beaches have curb cuts and are wheelchair accessible, but most other areas do not have cuts. Many restaurants also have entrance steps. For transport around Rio, contact Coop Taxi (☎3295-9606).

Most of the newer hotels have wheelchair-accessible

rooms, and some cable TV is closed captioned.

Lonely Planet's free *Accessible Travel* guide can be downloaded here: http://lptravel.to/AccessibleTravel

Useful Organizations

The **Centro de Vida Independente** (☎021-2512-1088; www.cvi-rio.org.br; Rua Marquês de São Vicente 225, Gávea, Rio de Janeiro) can provide advice for those with disabilities about travel in Brazil.

Those in the USA may like to contact the **Society for Accessible Travel & Hospitality** (☎212-447 7284; www.sath.org); its website is a resource for travelers with disabilities. Another website to check out is www.access-able.com.

Visas

Citizens of the US and Australia need a visa. Citizens of the UK, France, Germany and New Zealand do not. Tourist visas are valid for arrival in Brazil within 90 days of issue and then for a 90-day stay. The fee and length depends on your nationality; it's usually between US$35 and US$65, though for US citizens it costs US$160 (but is valid for 10 years). Processing times vary from one to 10 business days, sometimes less depending on nationality and consulate efficiency. Brazilian consulates will never provide expedited visa services under any circumstances, so plan ahead. You'll generally need to present one passport photograph, proof of travel and a valid passport.

People under 18 years of age who wish to travel to Brazil without a parent or legal guardian must present a notarized Visa Consent Form from the nontraveling parent/guardian or from a court.

Visa Extensions

Brazil's Polícia Federal, who have offices in the state capitals and border towns, handle visa extensions for those nationalities allowed to extend (Schengen region passport holders, for example, must leave for 90 days before re-entering for a second 90-days – extending is not an option).

Entry/Exit Cards

On entering Brazil, all tourists must fill out a *cartão de entrada/saida* (entry/exit card); immigration officials will keep half, you keep the other. They will also stamp your passport and, if for some reason they are not granting you the usual 90-day stay in Brazil, the number of days you are allowed to stay will be written in your passport.

When you leave Brazil, the second half of the entry/exit card will be taken by immigration officials. Don't lose your card while in Brazil, as it could cause hassles and needless delays when you leave.

Passports

By law you must carry a passport with you at all times, but many travelers opt to carry a photocopy (preferably certified) when traveling about town and to leave their passport securely locked up at their hotel.

Volunteering

RíoVoluntário (☎0xx21-2262-1110; www.riovoluntario.org.br), headquartered in Rio de Janeiro, supports several hundred volunteer organizations involved in social work, the environment and health care.

Rio-based **Iko Poran** (☎0xx21-2252-8214; www.ikoporan.org; Pintora Djanira 58, Santa Teresa) links the diverse talents of volunteers with needy organizations. Iko Poran also provides housing for volunteers.

Elsewhere in Rio state, **Regua** (www.regua.co.uk; Reserva Ecológica de Guapi Assu) accepts volunteers from all over the world for reforestation and other conservation work.

The UK-based Task Brasil (www.taskbrasil.org.uk) is another organization that places volunteers in Rio.

Women Travelers

Depending on the region, women traveling alone will experience a range of responses. In São Paulo, for example, where there are many people of European ancestry, foreign women without traveling companions will scarcely be given a sideways glance. In the more traditional rural areas of the Northeast, where a large percentage of the population is of ethnically mixed origin, blonde-haired and light-skinned women, especially those without male escorts, will certainly arouse curiosity.

Flirtation – often exaggerated – is a prominent element in Brazilian male-female relations. It goes both ways and is nearly always regarded as amusingly innocent banter; no sense of insult, exploitation or serious intent should be assumed.

Transportation

GETTING THERE & AWAY

Most travelers start their Brazilian odyssey by flying into Rio, but the country has several other gateway airports, as well as land borders with every country in South America except Chile and Ecuador.

Flights and tours can be booked online at lonelyplanet .com/bookings.

Entering the Country

Immigration and customs formalities are fairly straightforward, though you'll want to be sure to have your visa in order if you're from a country that needs one, such as the USA, Canada or Australia.

Air

Airports & Airlines

The most popular international gateways are Aeroporto Galeão (GIG) in Rio de Janeiro and São Paulo's Aeroporto Guarulhos (GRU). From both, connecting flights leave regularly to airports throughout the country. Salvador (SSA) and Recife (REC) receive a few direct scheduled flights from Europe.

TAM is Brazil's main international carrier, with flights to New York (USA), Miami (USA), Paris (France), London (UK), Lisbon (Portugal) and seven South American cities. The US Federal Aviation Administration has assessed TAM as Category 1, which means it is in compliance with international aviation standards.

Tickets

For high-season travel, roughly between mid-December and the end of February, tickets to Brazil cost about US$300 more than they do during the rest of the year.

INTERNATIONAL AIR PASSES

If you're combining travel in Brazil with other countries in southern South America, air passes can be decent value if you're covering a lot of ground in 30 days and don't mind a fixed itinerary.

The Visit South America air pass offered by airlines of the **Oneworld Alliance** (www.oneworld.com) allows stops in more than 60 cities in 10 South American countries. Prices are calculated on a per-flight, per-distance basis. Sample fares include US$260 from Rio de Janeiro to Lima (Peru), US$220 from São Paulo to Buenos Aires

CLIMATE CHANGE & TRAVEL

Every form of transport that relies on carbon-based fuel generates CO_2, the main cause of human-induced climate change. Modern travel is dependent on airplanes, which might use less fuel per mile per person than most cars but travel much greater distances. The altitude at which aircraft emit gases (including CO_2) and particles also contributes to their climate change impact. Many websites offer 'carbon calculators' that allow people to estimate the carbon emissions generated by their journey and, for those who wish to do so, to offset the impact of the greenhouse gases emitted with contributions to portfolios of climate-friendly initiatives throughout the world. Lonely Planet offsets the carbon footprint of all staff and author travel.

(Argentina) and US$200 from Santiago (Chile) to Lima (Peru).

The Gol South America air pass is valid for travel on Gol's network, including routes between Brazil and Chile, Argentina, Paraguay, Uruguay, Peru and Bolivia. Fares are US$629 plus tax for four flights, US$822 for five flights; each additional flight is US$140.

Land

There's direct land access to Brazil from nine countries. Several border towns can also be reached by river from Bolivia or Peru. If arriving overland from Colombia or Venezuela, you'll need to have a certificate of a yellow-fever vaccine to enter Brazil (not to mention a visa!).

Border Crossings

ARGENTINA

The main border point used by travelers is Puerto Iguazú–Foz do Iguaçu, a 20-hour bus ride from Buenos Aires. Further south, you can cross from Paso de los Libres (Argentina) to Uruguaiana (Brazil), which is also served by buses from Buenos Aires.

Direct buses run between Buenos Aires and Porto Alegre (R$250, 18 hours) and Rio de Janeiro (R$450, 42 hours). Other destinations include Florianópolis (R$315, 25 hours), Curitiba (R$370, 34 hours) and São Paulo (R$375, 36 hours).

BOLIVIA

Brazil's longest border runs through remote wetlands and forests, and is much used by smugglers. The main crossings are at Corumbá, Cáceres, Guajará-Mirim and Brasiléia.

The busiest crossing is between Quijarro (Bolivia) and Corumbá (Brazil), which is a good access point for the Pantanal. Quijarro has a daily train link with Santa Cruz (Bolivia). Corumbá has bus connections with Bonito, Campo Grande, São Paulo, Rio de Janeiro and southern Brazil.

Cáceres, in Mato Grosso (Brazil), has a daily bus link with Santa Cruz (Bolivia) via the Bolivian border town of San Matías.

Guajará-Mirim (Brazil) is a short river crossing from Guayaramerín (Bolivia). Both towns have onward bus links into their respective countries (Guayaramerín also has flights), but from late December to late February heavy rains can make the northern Bolivian roads a very difficult proposition.

Brasiléia (Brazil), a 4½-hour bus ride from Rio Branco, stands opposite Cobija (Bolivia), which has bus and plane connections into Bolivia. Bolivian buses confront the same wet-season difficulties.

CHILE

Although there is no border with Chile, direct buses run via Argentina between Santiago and Brazilian cities such as Porto Alegre (R$415, 36 hours), São Paulo (R$446, 54 hours) and Rio de Janeiro (R$486, 62 hours).

COLOMBIA

Leticia, on the Rio Amazonas in far southeast Colombia, is contiguous with Tabatinga (Brazil). You can cross the border on foot or by Kombi van or taxi. From within Colombia, Leticia is only really accessible by air. Tabatinga is a quick flight (or a several-day Amazon boat ride) from Manaus or Tefé.

FRENCH GUIANA

The Brazilian town of Oiapoque, a rugged 560km bus ride from Macapá (R$120, 12 to 15 hours), stands across the Rio Oiapoque from St Georges (French Guiana). A road connects St Georges to the French Guiana capital, Cayenne, with minibuses shuttling between the two. (Get there early in the morning to catch one.)

GUYANA & SURINAME

From Boa Vista, there are daily buses to Bonfim, Roraima (R$26, 1½ hours), on the Guyanese border, a short motorized-canoe ride from Lethem (southwest Guyana; R$4).

Overland travel between Suriname and Brazil involves first passing through either French Guiana or Guyana.

PARAGUAY

The two major border crossings are Ciudad del Este (Paraguay)–Foz do Iguaçu (Brazil) and Pedro Juan Caballero (Paraguay)–Ponta Porã (Brazil). Direct buses run between Asunción and Brazilian cities such as Florianópolis (R$320, 20 hours), Curitiba (R$240, 14 hours), São Paulo (R$205, 20 hours) and Foz do Iguaçu (R$80, five hours).

PERU

There is at least one daily bus connecting Rio Branco (Brazil) to Puerto Maldona-

> **BOLIVIAN ENTRY REQUIREMENTS**
>
> Any US citizen entering Bolivia is required to have a visa, which costs US$135. Citizens from most other nations receive free 30-day entry. Although technically it's possible to obtain a visa at the border, it's wise to secure this beforehand – particularly if arriving overland, as long delays are likely. Bolivian Immigration has a whole host of other requirements, including a certificate of yellow-fever vaccine, proof of financial solvency, and more. Visit www.bolivia-usa.org for the latest.

do (Peru) via the border at Assis (Brazil)–Iñapari (Peru) on the new US$2.75-billion Interoceanic Hwy. You can also reach Assis on daily buses from Epitáciolândia (R$18, two hours) and cross the Rio Acre to Iñapari.

URUGUAY

The crossing most used by travelers is at Chuy (Uruguay)–Chuí (Brazil). This is actually one town, with the international border running down the middle of its main street. Other crossings are Río Branco (Uruguay)–Jaguarão (Brazil), Isidoro Noblia (Uruguay)–Aceguá (Brazil), Rivera (Uruguay)–Santana do Livramento (Brazil), Artigas (Uruguay)–Quaraí (Brazil) and Bella Unión (Uruguay)–Barra do Quaraí (Brazil). Buses run between Montevideo and Brazilian cities such as Porto Alegre (R$220, 12 hours), Florianópolis (R$290, 18 hours) and São Paulo (R$420, 32 hours).

VENEZUELA

From Manaus, five daily buses run to Boa Vista (R$120, 12 hours), from where you can connect to Puerto La Cruz (Venezuela; R$240, 20 hours) for access to Caracas or Isla Margarita.

Bus

International buses travel between Brazil and Argentina, Paraguay and Uruguay, along decent roads. Prices of bus tickets between countries are substantially more than you'd pay if you took a bus to the border, crossed on foot and caught another on the other side, but you'll lose a lot of time that way. If arriving by bus, make sure your papers are in order.

Car & Motorcycle

If you plan to take a vehicle into Brazil, be informed about essential documents, road rules, and info on fuel and spare parts. At the border you will be asked to sign a bond called a *termo de responsabilidade,* which lists the owner's identification details and home address, your destination, and a description of the vehicle (make, model, year, serial number, color and tag number). You will also be asked to pay a bank guarantee (the amount to be determined by customs) and sign a statement agreeing that if you stay for more than 90 days, you will contact customs in the area where the entry was registered to apply for an extension for the permit. This must be presented to customs at the time of departure. If your vehicle overstays its permitted time in Brazil, it is liable to be seized and the bank guarantee forfeited. It's illegal to sell the vehicle in Brazil.

River

Bolivia

From Trinidad in Bolivia you can reach Brazil by a boat trip of about five days down the Río Mamoré to Guayaramerín, opposite the Brazilian town of Guajará-Mirim.

Peru

Fast passenger boats make the 400km trip (around US$100, eight to 10 hours) along the Amazon River between Iquitos (Peru) and Tabatinga (Brazil). From Tabatinga you can continue 3000km down the river to its mouth.

GETTING AROUND

Air

Because of the great distances in Brazil, the occasional flight can be a necessity, and may not cost much more than a long-haul bus journey. If you intend to take more than just a couple of flights, a Brazil Airpass will probably save you money. Book ahead if traveling during busy times – from Christmas to Carnaval, around Easter, and July and August. Always reconfirm your flights, as schedules frequently change.

Airlines in Brazil

Brazil has two major national carriers, Gol and LATAM (a merger between the Chilean LAN and Brazilian TAM airlines), and a handful of smaller regional airlines. Brazil's main carriers:

Avianca (☎0300-789-8160; www.avianca.com)

Azul (☎0800-887-1118; www.voeazul.com.br)

Gol (☎0300-115-2121; www.voegol.com.br)

LATAM (☎0800-570-5700; www.latam.com)

Air Passes

A Brazil Airpass is a good investment if you're planning on covering a lot of ground in 30 days or less. Gol offers an air pass involving four/five domestic flights anywhere on its extensive network for US$571/733, plus taxes; each additional flight costs US$162. TAM's air pass gives you four/five flights for US$582/772 (US$532/672 if you fly TAM to Brazil). Additional flights cost U$170 each (US$120 if you fly TAM to Brazil).

Either of these passes must be purchased before you get to Brazil, and you have to book your air-pass itinerary at the time you buy it – or possibly pay penalties for changing reservations. Many travel agents sell the air pass, as does the Brazilian travel specialist **Brol** (www.brol.com).

If for any reason you do not fly on an air-pass flight you have reserved, you should reconfirm all your other flights. Travelers have sometimes found that all their air-pass reservations had been scrubbed from the computer after they missed, or were bumped from, one flight.

Bicycle

You don't see many long-distance cyclists in Brazil. Among the hazards are crazy drivers, roads without shoulder roomand the threat of theft.

If you're determined to tackle Brazil by bike, go over your bike with a fine-tooth comb before leaving home and fill your repair kit with every imaginable spare part. There are several decent bike shops in Rio for buying equipment and gear as well as renting bikes (which average R$60 per day).

Boat

The Amazon region is one of the last great bastions of passenger river travel in the world. Rivers still perform the function of highways throughout much of Amazonia, with vessels of many shapes and sizes putt-putting up and down every river and creek that has anyone living near it.

Bus

Bus services in Brazil are generally excellent. Departure times are usually strictly adhered to, and most of the buses are clean, comfortable and well-serviced Mercedes, Volvo and Scania vehicles.

All major cities are linked by frequent buses – one leaves every 15 minutes from Rio to São Paulo during peak hours – and there is a surprising number of long-distance buses. Every big city, and most small ones, has at least one main long-distance bus station, known as a *rodoviária* (ho-do-vi-*ah*-ree-ya).

Brazil has numerous bus companies and the larger cities have several dozen rival agencies. The easiest resource to search national bus routes is **Busca Ônibus** (www.buscaonibus.com.br).

Classes

There are three main classes of long-distance bus. The ordinary *convencional* or *comum* is indeed the most common. It's fairly comfortable and usually has a toilet onboard. An *executivo* or *semi-leito* is more comfortable (with reclining seats), costs about 25% more and stops less often. A *leito* (overnight sleeper) can cost twice as much as a *comum* and has fully reclining seats with blankets and pillows, air-con and sometimes an attendant serving sandwiches, coffee, soda and *água mineral* (mineral water).

With or without toilets, buses generally make pit stops for food and bathroom breaks every three or four hours.

Air-con on buses is sometimes strong; carry a light sweater or jacket to keep warm.

Costs

Bus travel throughout Brazil can be expensive; *convencional* fares average around R$12 to R$15 per hour. Sample fares from Rio:

Belém *convencional/executivo/leito* R$533/615/700, 52 hours

Florianópolis *convencional* R$236, 18 hours

Foz do Iguaçu *convencional/executivo* R$215/240, 22 hours

Salvador *convencional* R$280/300, 25 hours

São Paulo *convencional/executivo/leito* R$92/115/172, six hours

Buying Tickets

Usually you can go down to the bus station and buy a ticket for the next departing bus. In general, though, it's a good idea to buy the day before departure. On weekends, holidays and from December to February, advance purchase is always a good idea. If you have a PayPal account, you can buy tickets online at www.clickbus.com.br.

Car & Motorcycle

Bringing Your Own Vehicle

All vehicles in Brazil must carry the registration document and proof of insurance. To take a vehicle into or out of Brazil, you might be asked for a *carnet de passage en douane*, which is a kind of vehicle passport, or a *libreta de pasos por aduana*, which is a booklet of customs passes. Contact your local automobile association for details about all documentation.

Driver's License

Your home-country driver's license is valid in Brazil, but because local authorities probably won't be familiar with it, it's a good idea to carry an International Driving Permit (IDP) as well. This gives police less scope for claiming that you are not driving with a legal license. IDPs are issued by your national motoring association and usually cost the equivalent of about US$15. It is illegal for foreigners to drive motorbikes in Brazil unless they have a Brazilian license.

Fuel & Spare Parts

Ordinary gasoline (called *combustível* or *gasolina*) costs around R$3.40 per liter. Travelers taking their own vehicles need to check in advance what spare parts and gasoline are likely to be available.

Hire

A small four-door car with insurance and unlimited kilometers costs around R$100 a day (R$130 with air-con). You can sometimes get discounts for longer rentals.

To rent a car you must be 25 years old (21 with some rental firms, including Avis), have a credit card in your name and a valid driver's license from your home country (not just an IDP).

Minimum insurance coverage is always tacked onto the

Domestic Air Routes

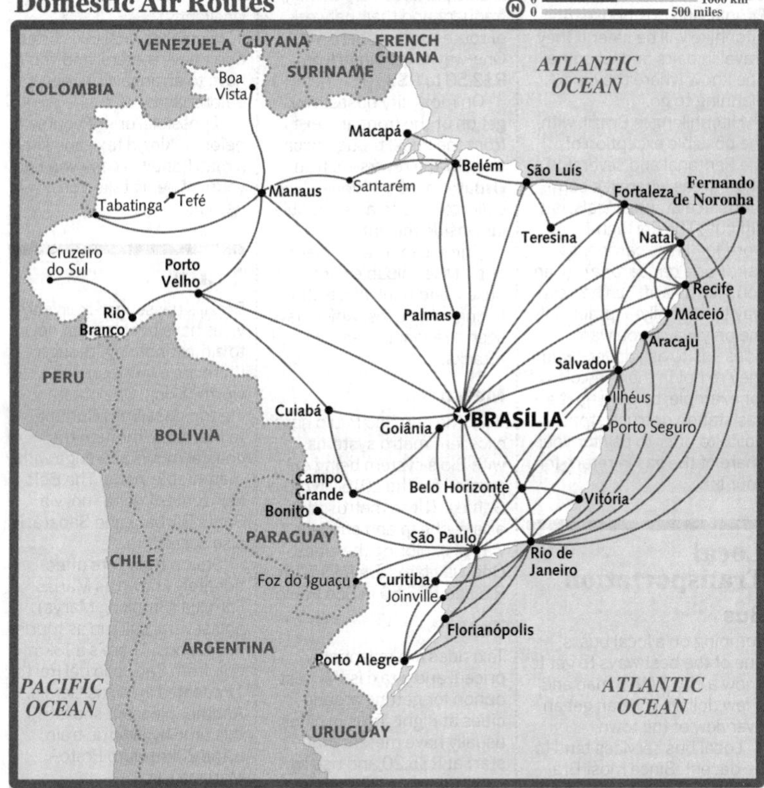

cost of renting, though you can get extra protection (a wise idea) for another R$20 to R$40 per day.

In Brazil, 4WD vehicles are hard to come by and can be expensive (more than R$200 per day). Motorbike rental is even harder to find. Riders planning a long trip might have better luck purchasing a bike in Brazil and reselling it at the end of the trip.

Road Rules & Hazards

Brazil is a dangerous place to drive, with more than 40,000 people killed in automobile accidents each year. Some roads are especially hazardous, such as the busy highways between Rio and São Paulo. The cult of speed is insatiable.

Owing to the danger of robbery, at night many motorists don't stop at red lights but merely slow down. This is particularly common in São Paulo. In big cities, keep your windows closed and doors locked when stationary.

Driving at night is particularly hazardous; other drivers are more likely to be drunk and, at least in the Northeast and the interior, the roads are often poor and unreliable. Poorly banked turns are the norm. To save a bit of fuel, some motorists drive at night with their headlights turned to low beam or turned off completely.

Brazilian speed bumps are quite prevalent. Always slow down as you enter a town.

Further headaches for drivers in Brazil are posed by poor signposting, impossible one-way systems, tropical rainstorms, drivers overtaking on blind corners, flat tires – common, but there are *borracheiros* (tire repairers) stationed at frequent intervals along the roads – and, of course, the police pulling you over for bogus moving violations.

For security, choose hotels with off-street parking; most midrange and top-end places offer this option.

Hitchhiking

Hitchhiking is never entirely safe in any country, and is not recommended. Travelers who decide to hitchhike should understand that they are taking a small but potentially serious risk. People who do choose to hitchhike will be safer if they travel in pairs and let someone know where they are planning to go.

Hitchhiking in Brazil, with the possible exception of the Pantanal and several other areas where it's commonplace among locals, is difficult. The Portuguese word for 'lift' is *carona*, so ask, '*Pode dar carona?*' (Can you give us a lift?). The best way to hitchhike – practically the only way if you want rides – is to ask drivers when they're not in their vehicles; for example, by waiting at a gas station or truck stop. It's polite to offer to pay for your share of the gas in return for your lift.

Local Transportation

Bus

Jumping on a local bus is one of the best ways to get to know a city. With a map and a few dollars you can get an overview of the town.

Local bus services tend to be decent. Since most Brazilians take the bus to work, municipal buses are usually frequent and their network of routes comprehensive. One-way fares range from R$2.50 to R$3.70.

On most city buses, you get on at the front and exit from the back, though occasionally the reverse is true. Usually there's a money collector sitting at a turnstile just inside the entrance.

Crime can be a problem: don't take valuables onto the buses, and think twice about taking minibuses, which have seen a recent increase in attacks.

Metro

Both Rio and São Paulo have excellent metro systems, with Rio's system being expanded for the 2016 Olympic Games. These metros are a safe, cheap and efficient way of exploring the cities. One-way fares are R$3.70 in Rio and R$3.50 in São Paulo.

Taxi

Taxi rides are reasonably priced, and a taxi is the best option for getting around cities at night. Taxis in cities usually have meters that start at R$5.20 and rise by something like R$2 per kilometer (more at night and on weekends).

In small towns, taxis often don't have meters, and you'll have to arrange a price – beforehand.

If possible, orient yourself before taking a taxi, and keep a map handy in case you find yourself being taken on a wild detour.

Train

Brazil's passenger-train services have been scaled down to almost nothing, though there are a few journeys well worth taking. One outstanding trip goes from Curitiba to Morretes, through the coastal mountain range with memorable views. The Belo Horizonte–Vitória run, via Santa Bárbara and Sabará, is also scenic.

Steam trains are affectionately known as Marias Fumaça (Smoking Marys), and several still run as tourist attractions. There's a 13km ride from São João del Rei to Tiradentes in Minas Gerais. Another pleasant short trip, this time by electric train, is the 22km Ouro Preto–Mariana run.

Language

Portuguese is spoken by around 190 million people worldwide, 90% of whom live in Brazil. Brazilian Portuguese today differs from European Portuguese in approximately the same way that British English differs from American English. European and Brazilian Portuguese show some differences in spelling, pronunciation and, to some extent, vocabulary. For example, in Portugal, the word for 'train' is *comboio* and in Brazil you'd say *trem*.

Most sounds in Portuguese are also found in English. The exceptions are the nasal vowels (represented in our colored pronunciation guides by ng after the vowel), which are pronounced as if you're trying to make the sound through your nose; and the strongly rolled *r* (represented by rr in our pronunciation guides). Also note that the zh sounds like the 's' in 'pleasure'. The stressed syllables (generally the second-last syllable of a word) are indicated with italics. If you keep these few points in mind and read our pronunciation guides as if they were English, you'll have no problems being understood.

BASICS

Hello.	*Olá.*	o·*laa*
Goodbye.	*Tchau.*	tee·*show*
How are you?	*Como vai?*	*ko*·mo vai
Fine, and you?	*Bem, e você?*	beng e vo·*se*
Excuse me.	*Com licença.*	kong lee·*seng*·saa
Sorry.	*Desculpa.*	des·*kool*·paa

WANT MORE?

For in-depth language information and handy phrases, check out Lonely Planet's *Brazilian Portuguese Phrasebook*. You'll find it at **shop.lonelyplanet.com**, or you can buy Lonely Planet's iPhone phrasebooks at the Apple App Store.

Please.	*Por favor.*	por faa·*vorr*
Thank you.	*Obrigado.* *Obrigada.*	o·bree·*gaa*·do (m) o·bree·*gaa*·daa (f)
You're welcome.	*De nada.*	de *naa*·daa
Yes.	*Sim.*	seeng
No.	*Não.*	nowng

What's your name?
Qual é o seu nome? kwow e o se·oo *no*·me

My name is ...
Meu nome é ... *me*·oo *no*·me e ...

Do you speak English?
Você fala inglês? vo·*se faa*·laa eeng·*gles*

I don't understand.
Não entendo. nowng eng·*teng*·do

ACCOMMODATIONS

Do you have a ... room?	*Tem um quarto de ...?*	teng oom *kwaarr*·to de ...
double	*casal*	kaa·*zow*
single	*solteiro*	sol·*tay*·ro
twin	*duplo*	*doo*·plo

How much is it per night/person?
Quanto custa por noite/pessoa? *kwang*·to *koos*·taa porr *noy*·te/pe·*so*·aa

Can I see it?
Posso ver? *po*·so verr

campsite	*local para acampamento*	lo·*kow paa*·raa aa·kang·paa·*meng*·to
guesthouse	*hospedaria*	os·pe·daa·*ree*·a
hotel	*hotel*	o·*tel*
youth hostel	*albergue da juventude*	ow·*berr*·ge daa zhoo·veng·*too*·de

DIRECTIONS

Where is ...?
Onde fica ...? ong·de *fee*·kaa ...

What's the address?
Qual é o endereço? kwow e o eng·de·*re*·so

Could you please write it down?
Você poderia escrever num papel, por favor? vo·se po·de·*ree*·aa es·kre·*verr* noom paa·*pel* porr faa·*vorr*

Can you show me (on the map)?
Você poderia me mostrar (no mapa)? vo·se po·de·*ree*·aa me mos·*traarr* (no *maa*·paa)

at the corner	*na esquina*	na es·*kee*·naa
at the traffic lights	*no sinal de trânsito*	no see·*now* de *trang*·zee·to
behind ...	*atrás ...*	aa·*traaz* ...
in front of ...	*na frente de ...*	naa *freng*·te de ...
left	*esquerda*	es·*kerr*·daa
next to ...	*ao lado de ...*	ow *laa*·do de ...
opposite	*do lado oposto ...*	do *laa*·do o·*pos*·to ...
right	*direita*	dee·*ray*·taa
straight ahead	*em frente*	eng *freng*·te

EATING & DRINKING

What would you recommend?
O que você recomenda? oo ke vo·se he·ko·*meng*·daa

What's in that dish?
O que tem neste prato? o ke teng *nes*·te *praa*·to

I don't eat ...
Eu não como ... e·oo nowng *ko*·mo ...

Cheers!
Saúde! sa·oo·de

That was delicious.
Estava delicioso. es·*taa*·vaa de·lee·see·*o*·zo

Bring the bill/check, please.
Por favor traga a conta. porr faa·*vorr traa*·gaa aa *kong*·taa

I'd like to reserve a table for ...	*Eu gostaria de reservar uma mesa para ...*	e·oo gos·taa·*ree*·aa de he·zer·*vaarr* oo·maa *me*·zaa *paa*·raa ...
(eight) o'clock	*(às oito) horas*	(aas *oy*·to) *aw*·raas
(two) people	*(duas) pessoas*	(*doo*·aas) pe·*so*·aas

Key Words

bottle	*garrafa*	gaa·*haa*·faa
breakfast	*café da manha*	ka·fe daa ma·*nyang*
cold	*frio*	*free*·o
cup	*xícara*	*shee*·kaa·raa
dessert	*sobremesa*	so·bre·*me*·zaa
dinner	*jantar*	zhang·*taarr*
drink	*bebida*	be·*bee*·daa
entree	*entrada*	eng·*traa*·daa
fork	*garfo*	*gaarr*·fo
glass	*copo*	*ko*·po
hot (warm)	*quente*	*keng*·te
knife	*faca*	*faa*·kaa
lunch	*almoço*	ow·*mo*·so
market	*mercado*	merr·*kaa*·do
menu	*cardápio*	kaar·*da*·pyo
plate	*prato*	*praa*·to
restaurant	*restaurante*	hes·tow·*rang*·te
spicy	*apimentado*	aa·pee·meng·*taa*·do
spoon	*colher*	ko·*lyerr*

KEY PATTERNS

To get by in Portuguese, mix and match these simple patterns with words of your choice:

When's (the next flight)?
Quando é (o próximo vôo)? *kwaang*·do e (o *pro*·see·mo *vo*·o)

Where's the (tourist office)?
Onde fica (a secretaria de turismo)? ong·de *fee*·kaa (aa se·kre·taa·*ree*·aa de too·*rees*·mo)

I'm looking for (a hotel).
Estou procurando (um hotel). es·to pro·koorr·*ang*·do (oom o·*tel*)

Do you have (a map)?
Você tem (um mapa)? vo·se teng (oom *maa*·paa)

Is there (a toilet)?
Tem (banheiro)? teng (ba·*nyay*·ro)

I'd like (a coffee).
Eu gostaria de (um café). e·oo gos·taa·*ree*·aa de (oom *kaa*·fe)

I'd like to (hire a car).
Eu gostaria de (alugar um carro). e·oo gos·taa·*ree*·aa de (aa·loo·*gaarr* oom *kaa*·ho)

Can I (enter)?
Posso (entrar)? *po*·so (eng·*traarr*)

Could you please (help me)?
Você poderia me (ajudar), por favor? vo·se po·de·*ree*·aa me (aa·zhoo·*daarr*) por faa·*vorr*

Do I have to (get a visa)?
Necessito (obter visto)? ne·se·*see*·to (o·bee·*terr vees*·to)

Useful Telephone Phrases

I'd like to make an international call to...
Quero fazer uma ligação internacional para... ke·ro faa·zerr oo·maa lee·gaa·*sowng* eeng·terr·naa·syo·*now* paa·raa ...

I'd like to reverse the charges.
Quero fazê-la a cobrar. ke·ro faa·ze·la aa ko·*braarr*

I'm calling from a public/private phone in ...
Estou falando dum telefone público/particular no ... es·*to* faa·*laan*·do doom te·le·fo·ne *poo*·blee·ko/paarr·tee·koo·*laarr* no ...

The area code/number is...
O código/número é... o *ko*·dee·go/*noo*·me·ro e ...

Meat & Fish

beef	*carne de vaca*	*kaar*·ne de *vaa*·kaa
chicken	*frango*	*frang*·go
crab	*siri*	see·*ree*
fish	*peixe*	*pay*·she
lamb	*carneiro*	karr·*nay*·ro
meat	*carne*	*kaar*·ne
oyster	*ostra*	*os*·traa
pork	*porco*	*porr*·ko
seafood	*frutos do mar*	*froo*·tos do maarr
shrimp	*camarão*	ka·ma·*rowng*
tuna	*atum*	aa·*toong*
veal	*bezerro*	be·ze·ho

Fruit & Vegetables

apple	*maçã*	maa·*sang*
apricot	*damasco*	daa·*maas*·ko
avocado	*abacate*	aa·baa·*kaa*·te
cabbage	*repolho*	he·*po*·lyo
capsicum	*pimentão*	pee·meng·*towng*
carrot	*cenoura*	se·*no*·raa
cherry	*cereja*	se·*re*·zhaa
corn	*milho*	*mee*·lyo
cucumber	*pepino*	pe·*pee*·no
grapes	*uvas*	*oo*·vaas
lemon	*limão*	lee·*mowng*
lettuce	*alface*	ow·*faa*·se
mushroom	*cogumelo*	ko·goo·*me*·lo
onion	*cebola*	se·*bo*·laa
orange	*laranja*	laa·*rang*·zhaa
peach	*pêssego*	*pe*·se·go
pineapple	*abacaxí*	aa·baa·kaa·*shee*
potato	*batata*	baa·*taa*·taa
spinach	*espinafre*	es·pee·*naa*·fre
strawberry	*morango*	mo·*rang*·go
tomato	*tomate*	to·*maa*·te
watermelon	*melancia*	me·lang·*see*·aa

Other

bread	*pão*	powng
cake	*bolo*	*bo*·lo
cheese	*queijo*	*kay*·zho
chilli	*pimenta*	pee·*meng*·taa
eggs	*ovos*	o·vos
honey	*mel*	mel
ice cream	*sorvete*	sorr·*ve*·te
jam	*geléia*	zhe·*le*·yaa
lentil	*lentilha*	leng·*tee*·lyaa
olive oil	*azeite*	a·*zay*·te
pepper	*pimenta*	pee·*meng*·taa

Drinks

rice	*arroz*	a·*hoz*
salt	*sal*	sow
sauce	*molho*	*mo*·lyo
sugar	*açúcar*	aa·*soo*·kaarr
beer	*cerveja*	serr·*ve*·zhaa

CARIOCA SLANG

Cariocas (inhabitants of Rio de Janeiro) pepper their language with lots of interesting oaths and expressions.

Oi!	Hello!
Tudo bem?	Everything OK?
Tudo bom.	Everything's OK.
Chocante!	That's great!/Cool!
Merda!	That's bad!/Shit!
Ta ótimo!/Ta legal!	Great!/Cool!/OK!
Meu deus!	My God!
Ta louco!	It's/You're crazy!
Nossa!	Gosh! (lit: Our Lady)
Opa!	Whoops!
Oba!	Wow!
Falou!	You said it!
Eu estou chateado com ...	I'm mad at ...
Tem jeito?	Is there a way?
Sempre tem jeito.	There's always a way.

Signs

Banheiro	Toilet
Entrada	Entrance
Não Tem Vaga	No Vacancy
Pronto Socorro	Emergency Department
Saída	Exit
Tem Vaga	Vacancy

coffee	*café*	kaa·*fe*
fruit juice	*suco de frutas*	*soo*·ko de *froo*·taas
milk	*leite*	*lay*·te
red wine	*vinho tinto*	*vee*·nyo *teeng*·to
soft drink	*refrigerante*	he·free·zhe·*rang*·te
tea	*chá*	shaa
(mineral) water	*água (mineral)*	*aa*·gwaa (mee·ne·*row*)
white wine	*vinho branco*	*vee*·nyo *brang*·ko

EMERGENCIES

Help!	*Socorro!*	so·*ko*·ho
Leave me alone!	*Me deixe em paz!*	me *day*·she eng paas
Call ...!	*Chame ...!*	*sha*·me ...
a doctor	*um médico*	oom *me*·dee·ko
the police	*a polícia*	aa po·*lee*·syaa

It's an emergency.
É uma emergência. e oo·maa e·merr·*zheng*·see·aa

I'm lost.
Estou perdido. es·*to* perr·*dee*·do (m)
Estou perdida. es·*to* perr·*dee*·daa (f)

I'm ill.
Estou doente. es·*to* do·*eng*·te

It hurts here.
Aqui dói. a·*kee* doy

I'm allergic to (antibiotics).
Tenho alergia à (antibióticos). te·nyo aa·lerr·*zhee*·aa aa (ang·tee·bee·o·tee·kos)

Where are the toilets?
Onde tem um banheiro? on·de teng oom ba·*nyay*·ro

SHOPPING & SERVICES

I'd like to buy ...
Gostaria de comprar ... gos·taa·*ree*·aa de kong·*praarr* ...

I'm just looking.
Estou só olhando. es·*to* so o·*lyang*·do

Can I look at it?
Posso ver? *po*·so verr

How much is it?
Quanto custa? *kwang*·to *koos*·taa

It's too expensive.
Está muito caro. es·*taa mweeng*·to *kaa*·ro

Can you lower the price?
Pode baixar o preço? *po*·de bai·*shaarr* o *pre*·so

There's a mistake in the bill.
Houve um erro na conta. o·ve oom e·ho naa *kong*·taa

ATM	*caixa automático*	*kai*·shaa ow·too·*maa*·tee·ko
credit card	*cartão de crédito*	kaarr·*towng* de *kre*·dee·to
post office	*correio*	ko·*hay*·o
tourist office	*escritório de turismo*	es·kree·*to*·ryo de too·*rees*·mo

TIME & DATES

What time is it?
Que horas são? kee *aw*·raas sowng

It's (10) o'clock.
São (dez) horas. sowng (des) *aw*·raas

Half past (10).
(Dez) e meia. (des) e *may*·aa

morning	*manhã*	ma·*nyang*
afternoon	*tarde*	*taar*·de
evening	*noite*	*noy*·te
yesterday	*ontem*	*ong*·teng
today	*hoje*	*o*·zhe
tomorrow	*amanhã*	aa·ma·*nyang*
Monday	*segunda-feira*	se·*goong*·daa·*fay*·ra
Tuesday	*terça-feira*	*terr*·saa·*fay*·raa
Wednesday	*quarta-feira*	*kwaarr*·taa·*fay*·raa
Thursday	*quinta-feira*	*keeng*·taa·*fay*·raa
Friday	*sexta-feira*	*ses*·taa·*fay*·raa
Saturday	*sábado*	*saa*·baa·do
Sunday	*domingo*	do·*meeng*·go

Question Words

How?	*Como é que?*	*ko*·mo e ke
What?	*Que?*	ke
When?	*Quando?*	*kwang*·do
Where?	*Onde?*	*ong*·de
Which?	*Qual?/Quais?* (sg/pl)	kwow/kais
Who?	*Quem?*	keng
Why?	*Por que?*	porr ke

January	*janeiro*	zha·*nay*·ro
February	*fevereiro*	fe·ve·*ray*·ro
March	*março*	*marr*·so
April	*abril*	aa·*bree*·oo
May	*maio*	*maa*·yo
June	*junho*	*zhoo*·nyo
July	*julho*	*zhoo*·lyo
August	*agosto*	aa·*gos*·to
September	*setembro*	se·*teng*·bro
October	*outubro*	o·*too*·bro
November	*novembro*	no·*veng*·bro
December	*dezembro*	de·*zeng*·bro

TRANSPORT

Public Transport

boat	*barco*	*baarr*·ko
bus	*ônibus*	*o*·nee·boos
plane	*avião*	aa·vee·*owng*
train	*trem*	treng

When's the ... (bus)?	*Quando sai o ... (ônibus)?*	*kwang*·do sai o ... (*o*·nee·boos)
first	*primeiro*	pree·*may*·ro
last	*último*	*ool*·tee·mo
next	*próximo*	*pro*·see·mo

a ... ticket	*uma passagem de ...*	*oo*·maa paa·*sa*·zheng de ...
1st-class	*primeira classe*	pree·*may*·raa *klaa*·se
2nd-class	*segunda classe*	se·*goom*·daa *klaa*·se
one-way	*ida*	*ee*·daa
return	*ida e volta*	*ee*·daa e *vol*·taa

What time does it leave/arrive?
A que horas sai/chega? aa ke *aw*·raas sai/*she*·gaa

Does it stop at ...?
Ele para em ...? *e*·le *paa*·raa eng ...

Please stop here.
Por favor pare aqui. poor faa·*vorr* *paa*·re aa·*kee*

bus stop	*ponto de ônibus*	*pong*·to de *o*·nee·boos
ticket office	*bilheteria*	bee·lye·te·*ree*·aa
timetable	*horário*	o·*raa*·ryo
train station	*estação de trem*	es·*taa*·sowng de treng

Numbers

1	*um*	oom
2	*dois*	doys
3	*três*	tres
4	*quatro*	*kwaa*·tro
5	*cinco*	*seeng*·ko
6	*seis*	says
7	*sete*	*se*·te
8	*oito*	*oy*·to
9	*nove*	*naw*·ve
10	*dez*	dez
20	*vinte*	*veeng*·te
30	*trinta*	*treeng*·taa
40	*quarenta*	kwaa·*reng*·taa
50	*cinquenta*	seen·*kweng*·taa
60	*sessenta*	se·*seng*·taa
70	*setenta*	se·*teng*·taa
80	*oitenta*	oy·*teng*·taa
90	*noventa*	no·*veng*·taa
100	*cem*	seng
1000	*mil*	*mee*·oo

Driving & Cycling

I'd like to hire a ...	*Gostaria de alugar ...*	gos·taa·*ree*·aa de aa·loo·*gaarr* ...
bicycle	*uma bicicleta*	*oo*·maa bee·see·*kle*·taa
car	*um carro*	oom *kaa*·ho
motorcycle	*uma motocicleta*	*oo*·maa mo·to·see·*kle*·ta

bicycle pump	*bomba de bicicleta*	*bong*·baa de bee·see·*kle*·taa
helmet	*capacete*	kaa·paa·*se*·te
mechanic	*mecânico*	me·*ka*·nee·ko
petrol/gas	*gasolina*	gaa·zo·*lee*·naa
service station	*posto de gasolina*	*pos*·to de gaa·zo·*lee*·naa

Is this the road to ...?
Esta é a estrada para ...? es·taa e aa es·*traa*·daa *paa*·raa ...

(How long) Can I park here?
(Quanto tempo) Posso estacionar aqui? (*kwang*·to *teng*·po) *po*·so es·taa·syo·*naarr* aa·*kee*

I have a flat tyre.
Meu pneu furou. *me*·oo pee·*ne*·oo foo·*ro*

I've run out of petrol.
Estou sem gasolina. es·*to* seng ga·zoo·*lee*·naa

GLOSSARY

afoxé – music of Bahia, which has strong African rhythms and close ties to Candomblé

albergue – lodging house or hostel

albergue da juventude – youth hostel

aldeia – originally a village built by Jesuits to convert *índios* to Christianity; now the term for any small, usually indigenous, village

apartamento – hotel room with a private bathroom

arara – macaw

artesanato – handcrafted workmanship

azulejos – Portuguese ceramic tiles with a distinctive blue glaze, often seen in churches

babaçu – versatile palm tree that is the basis of the rural economy in Maranhão

bairro – district

bandeirantes – bands of 17th- and 18th-century roaming adventurers who explored the vast Brazilian interior while searching for gold and *índios* to enslave; typically born of an *índio* mother and a Portuguese father

barraca – any stall or hut, including food and drink stands common at beaches, parks etc

beija-flor – literally 'flower kisser'; hummingbird; also the name of Rio's most famous samba school

berimbau – musical instrument that accompanies capoeira

bilheteria – ticket office

bloco – large group, usually numbering in the hundreds, of singing or drumming Carnaval revelers in costume, organized around a neighborhood or theme

boate – nightclub with a dance floor, sometimes featuring strippers; also boîte

bonde – cable car, tram or trolley

bossa nova – music that mixes North American jazz with Brazilian influences

boteco – small, open-air bar

boto – freshwater dolphin of the Amazon

Bumba Meu Boi – the most important festival in Maranhão, a rich folkloric event that revolves around a Carnavalesque dance/procession

caatinga – scrub vegetation of the *sertão*

Caboclo – literally 'copper-colored'; person of mixed Caucasian and *índio* ancestry

cachoeira – waterfall

Candomblé – Afro-Brazilian religion of Bahia

capivara – capybara; the world's largest rodent, which looks like a large guinea pig and lives in the Pantanal

capixaba – resident of Espírito Santo state

capoeira – martial art/dance developed by the slaves of Bahia

carioca – resident of Rio de Janeiro

casa grande – big house or plantation owner's mansion

casal – married couple; double bed

chapada – tableland or plateau that divides a river basin

churrascaria – restaurant featuring barbecued meat

cidades históricas – historic colonial towns

Círio de Nazaré – Brazil's largest religious festival, which takes place in Belém

coronel – literally 'colonel'; rural landowner who typically controlled the local political, judicial and police systems; any powerful person

correio – post office

delegacia de polícia – police station

Embratur – Brazilian Tourist Board

engenho – sugar mill or sugar plantation

escolas de samba – large samba clubs that compete in the annual Carnaval parade

estalagem – inn

estrangeiro – foreigner

fantasia – Carnavalesque costume

favela – slum, shantytown

favelado – resident of a favela

fazenda – ranch or farm, usually a large landholding; also cloth, fabric

fazendeiro – estate owner

feira – produce market

ferroviária – train station

festa – party

Filhos de Gandhi – Bahia's most famous Carnaval bloco

fio dental – literally 'dental floss'; Brazil's famous skimpy bikini

Flamengo – Rio's most popular football team; also one of Rio's most populated areas

Fluminense – native of Rio state; also the football team that is Flamengo's main rival

forró – popular music of the Northeast, recently enjoying a wave of nationwide popularity

frevo – fast-paced, popular music from Pernambuco

frigobar – minibar

Funai – Fundação Nacional do Indio; government *índio* agency

Fusca – Volkswagen Beetle, Brazil's most popular car

futebol – football

futevôlei – volleyball played without hands

gafieira – dance hall

garimpeiro – prospector or miner; originally an illegal diamond prospector

garimpo – mining camp

gaúcho – cowboy of southern Brazil

gringo – foreigner or person with light hair and complexion; can even refer to light-skinned Brazilians

gruta – grotto or cavern

hidrovia – aquatic freeway

hidroviária – boat terminal

hospedagem – cheap boardinghouse used by locals

Iemanjá – Afro-Brazilian goddess of the sea

igapó – flooded Amazon forest

igarapé – creek or small river in Amazonia

igreja – church

ilha – island

índio – indigenous person; translates as 'Indian'

jacaré – caiman

jangada – beautiful sailboat of the Northeast

jangadeiros – crews who use *jangadas*

jeito/jeitinho – possibly the most Brazilian expression, both a feeling and a form of action; from *dar um jeito*, meaning 'to find a way to get something done,' no matter how seemingly impossible, even if the solution may not be completely orthodox or legal

leito – sleeping berth

literatura de cordel – literally 'string literature'; popular literature of the Northeast

litoral – coastal region

machista – male chauvinist

mãe de santo – female Afro-Brazilian spiritual leader

malandro do morro – vagabond; scoundrel from the hills; a popular figure in Rio's mythology

maloca – *índio* dwelling

Maracanã – soccer stadium in Rio

mercado – market

mestiço – a person of mixed *índio* and European parentage

mineiro – resident of Minas Gerais

moço/a – waiter or other service industry worker

morro – hill; a person or culture of the favelas

mulato/a – person of mixed black and white parentage

novela – soap opera; Brazil's most popular TV shows

NS – Nosso Senhor (Our Lord) or Nossa Senhora (Our Lady)

orixá – deity of the Afro-Brazilian religions

pagode – popular samba music

pai de santo – male spiritual leader in Afro-Brazilian religions

palácio – palace or large government building

palafita – stilt or a house built on stilts

pampas – grassy plains of the interior of southern Brazil

parque nacional – national park

pau brasil – now-scarce brazilwood tree; a red dye made from the tree that was the colony's first commodity

paulista – resident of São Paulo state

paulistano – resident of São Paulo city

PCB – Communist Party of Brazil

pensão – guesthouse

posta restante – poste restante

posto – post; lifeguard posts along Rio de Janeiro's beaches, used as names for different sections of beach

posto de gasolina – a gas (petrol) station

posto telefônico – telephone office

pousada – guesthouse

praça – plaza or town square

praia – beach

PT – Partido dos Trabalhadores (Worker's Party); Brazil's newest and most radical political party

quarto – hotel room without a bathroom

quente – hot

quilombo – community of runaway slaves

Quimbanda – black magic

rápido – fast

real – Brazil's unit of currency since 1994; plural reais

rio – river

rodoferroviária – bus and train station

rodoviária – bus station

s/n – abbreviation for *sem número* (without number), used in some street addresses

sambista – samba composer or dancer

sambódromo – street with tiers of seating built for samba parades

senzala – slave quarters

serra – mountain range

sertanejo – resident of the *sertão*

sertão – the drought-prone backlands of the Northeast

telefonista internacional – international telephone operator

Terra da Vera Cruz – Land of the True Cross; the original Portuguese name for Brazil

terreiro – Afro-Brazilian house of worship

travessa – lane

travesti – transvestite; a popular figure throughout Brazil, considered by some to be the national symbol

trem – train

trio elétrico – three-pronged electrical outlet; electrically amplified bands that play atop trucks

tropicália – important cultural movement centered in Bahia in the late 1960s

Tupi – indigenous people and language that predominated along the coast at the time of the European invasion

Umbanda – white magic, a mixture of Candomblé and spiritism

vaqueiro – cowboy of the Northeast

várzea – Amazonian floodplain

zona da mata – bushland just inside the litoral in the Northeastern states

Behind the Scenes

SEND US YOUR FEEDBACK

We love to hear from travelers – your comments keep us on our toes and help make our books better. Our well-traveled team reads every word on what you loved or loathed about this book. Although we cannot reply individually to your submissions, we always guarantee that your feedback goes straight to the appropriate authors, in time for the next edition. Each person who sends us information is thanked in the next edition – the most useful submissions are rewarded with a selection of digital PDF chapters.

Visit **lonelyplanet.com/contact** to submit your updates and suggestions or to ask for help. Our award-winning website also features inspirational travel stories, news and discussions.

Note: We may edit, reproduce and incorporate your comments in Lonely Planet products such as guidebooks, websites and digital products, so let us know if you don't want your comments reproduced or your name acknowledged. For a copy of our privacy policy visit lonelyplanet.com/privacy.

OUR READERS

Many thanks to the travelers who used the last edition and wrote to us with helpful hints, useful advice and interesting anecdotes:

A Zoe Abrams **B** Carolina Barros, Annelies Bossaerts **C** Diana Caplinska, Emily Chiswick-Patterson **D** Hector Del Olmo **L** Igor Livshits **M** Shaila Mahomed, Helena Marambio, Juan Miguel Mariatti, Claudio Milletti **N** Gragnon Nathalie, Riccardo Negri, Kris Nicolai **R** Elisa Renzi, Jenny Robb, Johanna Rydelius **S** Rafael Santos, Matan Shacham, Cynthia Smith, Paul Sorensen, Liam Spencer, Howard Spodek, Bridget Stap, Paul Steele, Torje Sunde **T** Yury Tulchinsky **W** Tim Wardle, Frans Wildenborg, Ronald Wolff, Julie Woods

AUTHOR THANKS

Regis St Louis

Many thanks to new and old friends who helped with tips and advice. In particular I'd like to thank Cristiano Nogueira, Jakki Saysell, Alberto Armendáriz, Marcelo Esteves, Marcio Zaidan, Vitor Souza, Philip de Wit, Bindu Mathur, Thiago Mourão, Ian Papareskos, Eduardo Cruxen, and Kevin Raub. *Beijos* to Cassandra, Magdalena and Genevieve for joining me on the road.

Gary Chandler

Thank you to Bettine Robers in Tefé, Fernanda Sá Vieira at Mamirauá, Pedro Neto in Manaus, Karim Abu Bakr in Santarém, Gil Serique in Alter do Chão, Chris Clark and Claus Pfeiffer in Novo Airão, and Regis St. Louis and MaSovaida Morgan at LP. Thank you to my family and in-laws for help on the home front, and to Eva and Leo—kids extraordinaire. And to Liza, who I love and admire more than I can say—thank you for everything.

Gregor Clark

Muito obrigado to the countless Brazilians who generously shared their smiles, thumbs-up and local knowledge of Brazil—from Maira, Alex and family in Minas to Angela and Margarida in Rio state, and others too numerous to name. Back in Vermont, big muriqui-style *abraços* to Meigan and Chloe for keeping me happy, helping me research and embracing life on the road with me, and to Gaen, who always makes coming home the best part of the trip.

Bridget Gleeson

Thank you to the tourism board in Lençóis for their ongoing assistance with maps and information about Parque Nacional Chapada Diamantina, to the posada staff who made my birthday on Morro de São Paulo special, and to all of the friendly Brazilian people who always along my way when I'm traveling alone in the Northeast.

Anna Kaminski

I would like to thank MaSovaida for entrusting me with this chapter, my fellow scribes Kevin, Paul and Regis for advice while on the road and everyone who's helped me along the way. In particular, Joel for his wonderful hospitality and assistance in Cuiaba, Gil and Luis for all their hard work and help in Campo Grande, Corumbá and Bonito, Bonifacio for guiding me on the Transpantaneira, Maria and Vinicius in Bonito and Douglas and Vitoria at the Cristalino Jungle Lodge.

Kevin Raub

Thanks to my wife, Adriana Schmidt Raub, who sure does do her best to teach me the Brazilian dance when I run into roadblocks on the road (even though I don't dance)! MasoVaida Morgan; and all my partners-in-crime. On the road, Malu Sabatino, Daniella Barbosa, Helena Costa, Rodrigo Angel, Ion David, Kely Zimath, Thiago Luiz, Marcia Gazola, Edu Passarelli, Vanessa Carvalho, Mario Saraiva, Craig Smit, Lucas Mello, Filipe Correia, Joana Pires, Ana Muller, Roberta Rodrigues, Raissa Monteiro, Shannon Sims, Sebastian Koch, Marina Prado, Ana Muller. Marcio & Paula Hernandez and Julien Leroy.

ACKNOWLEDGEMENTS

Climate map data adapted from Peel MC, Finlayson BL & McMahon TA (2007) 'Updated World Map of the Köppen-Geiger Climate Classification', *Hydrology and Earth System Sciences*, 11, pp1633–44.

Cover photograph: Corcovado, Rio de Janeiro, Antonino Bartuccio/4Corners

THIS BOOK

This 10th edition of Lonely Planet's *Brazil* guidebook was researched and written by Regis St Louis, Gary Chandler, Gregor Clark, Bridget Gleeson, Anna Kaminski and Kevin Raub. Regis, Gary, Gregor, Bridget, and Kevin also worked on the previous edition along with John Noble and Paul Smith. This guidebook was produced by the following:

Destination Editor MaSovaida Morgan

Product Editors Kate Chapman, Martine Power

Senior Cartographer Mark Griffiths

Book Designer Virginia Moreno

Assisting Editors Carolyn Bain, Judith Bamber, Carly Hall, Victoria Harrison, Elizabeth Jones, Helen Koehne, Katie O'Connell, Charlotte Orr, Susan Paterson, Christopher Pitts

Cartographer Julie Dodkins

Cover Researcher Naomi Parker

Thanks to Anita Banh, Barbara Di Castro, Ryan Evans, Kate Mathews, Catherine Naghten, Mazzy Prinsep, Vicky Smith, Tony Wheeler, Amanda Williamson

Index

Map Pages **000**
Photo Pages **000**

Map Pages **000**
Photo Pages **000**

Map Pages **000**
Photo Pages **000**

N

O

P

Q

R

Map Pages **000**
Photo Pages **000**

Map Legend

Sights
- Beach
- Bird Sanctuary
- Buddhist
- Castle/Palace
- Christian
- Confucian
- Hindu
- Islamic
- Jain
- Jewish
- Monument
- Museum/Gallery/Historic Building
- Ruin
- Shinto
- Sikh
- Taoist
- Winery/Vineyard
- Zoo/Wildlife Sanctuary
- Other Sight

Activities, Courses & Tours
- Bodysurfing
- Diving
- Canoeing/Kayaking
- Course/Tour
- Sento Hot Baths/Onsen
- Skiing
- Snorkeling
- Surfing
- Swimming/Pool
- Walking
- Windsurfing
- Other Activity

Sleeping
- Sleeping
- Camping

Eating
- Eating

Drinking & Nightlife
- Drinking & Nightlife
- Cafe

Entertainment
- Entertainment

Shopping
- Shopping

Information
- Bank
- Embassy/Consulate
- Hospital/Medical
- Internet
- Police
- Post Office
- Telephone
- Toilet
- Tourist Information
- Other Information

Geographic
- Beach
- Gate
- Hut/Shelter
- Lighthouse
- Lookout
- Mountain/Volcano
- Oasis
- Park
- Pass
- Picnic Area
- Waterfall

Population
- Capital (National)
- Capital (State/Province)
- City/Large Town
- Town/Village

Transport
- Airport
- Border crossing
- Bus
- Cable car/Funicular
- Cycling
- Ferry
- Metro station
- Monorail
- Parking
- Petrol station
- Subway/Subte station
- Taxi
- Train station/Railway
- Tram
- Underground station
- Other Transport

Note: Not all symbols displayed above appear on the maps in this book

Routes
- Tollway
- Freeway
- Primary
- Secondary
- Tertiary
- Lane
- Unsealed road
- Road under construction
- Plaza/Mall
- Steps
- Tunnel
- Pedestrian overpass
- Walking Tour
- Walking Tour detour
- Path/Walking Trail

Boundaries
- International
- State/Province
- Disputed
- Regional/Suburb
- Marine Park
- Cliff
- Wall

Hydrography
- River, Creek
- Intermittent River
- Canal
- Water
- Dry/Salt/Intermittent Lake
- Reef

Areas
- Airport/Runway
- Beach/Desert
- Cemetery (Christian)
- Cemetery (Other)
- Glacier
- Mudflat
- Park/Forest
- Sight (Building)
- Sportsground
- Swamp/Mangrove

Anna Kaminski

Mato Grosso & Mato Grosso do Sul Anna has been traveling extensively around Latin America for the last 15 years, ever since she'd begun majoring in the turbulent history of the continent at university, and in Brazil for over a decade, drawn by the sheer diversity of the country, the lust for life of its people and the *rodizios* at their *churrascaria* restaurants. Having previously gone in search of big cats in various parts of the Amazon, she finds that the Pantanal trumps the lot: on this visit alone she had three jaguar sightings. Anna tweets at @ ACKaminski.

Kevin Raub

São Paulo State, Paraná, Santa Catarina, Rio Grande do Sul, Brasília & Goiás, Pernambuco, Paraíba & Rio Grande do Norte, Ceará, Piauí & Maranhão Kevin grew up in Atlanta and started his career as a music journalist in New York, working for *Men's Journal* and *Rolling Stone* magazines. He ditched the rock 'n' roll lifestyle for travel writing and moved to Brazil, where he has now traversed 21 of 26 Brazilian states in pursuit of *caipirinha* bliss. He was also LP's man on the ground for the 2014 FIFA World Cup in Brazil. This is Kevin's 35th Lonely Planet guide. Follow him on Twitter (@RaubOnTheRoad).

OUR STORY

A beat-up old car, a few dollars in the pocket and a sense of adventure. In 1972 that's all Tony and Maureen Wheeler needed for the trip of a lifetime – across Europe and Asia overland to Australia. It took several months, and at the end – broke but inspired – they sat at their kitchen table writing and stapling together their first travel guide, *Across Asia on the Cheap*. Within a week they'd sold 1500 copies. Lonely Planet was born.

Today, Lonely Planet has offices in Franklin, London, Melbourne, Oakland, Beijing and Delhi, with more than 600 staff and writers. We share Tony's belief that 'a great guidebook should do three things: inform, educate and amuse'.

OUR WRITERS

Regis St Louis

Rio de Janeiro City Regis first visited Brazil back in 2003, and he fell hard for Rio de Janeiro: its stunning landscapes, dynamic music scene, and the open and celebratory spirit of the *cariocas*. Since then he's traveled all across the country, celebrating Carnaval in Bahia, Ouro Preto and Rio, watching wildlife in the Pantanal, hunting for the perfect beach in Santa Catarina and traveling the length of the Brazilian Amazon. His writing has appeared in the *Chicago Tribune*, the *Telegraph*, on BBC.com and elsewhere. He is also the coordinating author of Lonely Planet's *Rio de Janeiro* guide and *South America on a Shoestring*. He splits his time between New Orleans and the tropics. Regis also wrote the Plan Your Trip, Understand and Survival chapters.

Gary Chandler

The Amazon Gary has traveled and written about Latin America for two decades. He has contributed to over twenty guidebooks to the region, including El Salvador, Honduras, Mexico, and Guatemala. He first covered the Amazon for Lonely Planet in 2004—this assignment marks his fifth time back. Gary was raised in a small California ski town, attended UC Berkeley and Columbia University, and now lives with his wife and fellow travel writer, Liza Prado, and their two children in Denver, Colorado.

Gregor Clark

Rio de Janeiro State, Minas Gerais & Espírito Santo Gregor's love of all things Brazilian began with his first Portuguese class at age 19. In a quarter century of Brazilian travel, he's visited virtually every state from the Amazon to the Uruguayan border. Highlights of this research trip include spotting wolves and monkeys with his two teenage daughters, climbing Papagaio and Mamanguá peaks, and writing by firelight on chilly Visconde de Mauá evenings. Gregor contributes regularly to Lonely Planet's European and Latin American titles. He lives in Vermont (USA).

Bridget Gleeson

Bahia, Sergipe & Alagoas Based in Buenos Aires, Bridget is a travel writer and occasional photographer. She's traveled all over South America for work and for pleasure, but Bahia is still one of her favorite places on the continent. This was her third time covering the region for Lonely Planet.

OVER PAGE MORE WRITERS

Published by Lonely Planet Publications Pty Ltd
ABN 36 005 607 983
10th edition – June 2016
ISBN 978 1 74321 770 2
© Lonely Planet 2016 Photographs © as indicated 2016
10 9 8 7 6 5 4 3 2 1
Printed in China

Although the authors and Lonely Planet have taken all reasonable care in preparing this book, we make no warranty about the accuracy or completeness of its content and, to the maximum extent permitted, disclaim all liability arising from its use.

All rights reserved. No part of this publication may be copied, stored in a retrieval system, or transmitted in any form by any means, electronic, mechanical, recording or otherwise, except brief extracts for the purpose of review, and no part of this publication may be sold or hired, without the written permission of the publisher. Lonely Planet and the Lonely Planet logo are trademarks of Lonely Planet and are registered in the US Patent and Trademark Office and in other countries. Lonely Planet does not allow its name or logo to be appropriated by commercial establishments, such as retailers, restaurants or hotels. Please let us know of any misuses: lonelyplanet.com/ip.